GLOBAL BUSINESS ENVIRONMENT

GLOBAL BUSINESS ENVIRONMENT

Compiled from:

Understanding the Business Environment: Inside and Outside the Organisation
Third Edition
Claire Capon

Economics for Business
Sixth Edition
John Sloman, Kevin Hinde and Dean Garratt

International Business: Environments and Operations
Fifteenth Edition
John D. Daniels, Lee H. Radebaugh and Daniel P. Sullivan

International Business
Sixth Edition
Alan M. Rugman and Simon Collinson

International Business: A Managerial Perspective
Eighth Edition
Ricky W. Griffin and Michael W. Pustay

International Business: The New Realities
Third Edition
S. Tamer Cavusgil, Gary Knight and John R. Riesenberger

Corporate Responsibility: Governance, compliance and ethics in a sustainable environment
Second Edition
Tom Cannon

PEARSON

Harlow, England • London • New York • Boston • San Francisco • Toronto • Sydney • Auckland • Singapore • Hong Kong
Tokyo • Seoul • Taipei • New Delhi • Cape Town • Sao Paulo • Mexico City • Madrid • Amsterdam • Munich • Paris • Milan

Pearson Education Limited
Edinburgh Gate
Harlow
Essex CM20 2JE

And associated companies throughout the world

Visit us on the World Wide Web at:
www.pearson.com/uk

Compiled from:

Understanding the Business Environment: Inside and Outside the Organisation
Third Edition
Claire Capon
ISBN 978-0-273-70814-8

Economics for Business
Sixth Edition
John Sloman, Kevin Hinde and Dean Garratt
ISBN 978-0-273-79246-8

International Business: Environments and Operations
Fifteenth Edition
John D. Daniels, Lee H. Radebaugh and Daniel P. Sullivan
ISBN 978-1-292-01679-5

International Business
Sixth Edition
Alan M. Rugman and Simon Collinson
ISBN 978-0-273-76097-9

International Business: A Managerial Perspective
Eighth Edition
Ricky W. Griffin and Michael W. Pustay
ISBN 978-1-292-01821-8

International Business: The New Realities
Third Edition
S. Tamer Cavusgil, Gary Knight and John R. Riesenberger
ISBN 978-0-273-78706-8

Corporate Responsibility: Governance, compliance and ethics in a sustainable environment
Second Edition
Tom Cannon
ISBN 978-0-273-73873-2

ISBN 978-1-78448-643-3

Printed and bound in Great Britain by CPI Group.

CONTENTS

GLOBAL BUSINESS ENVIRONMENT

CHAPTER 1

The external environment

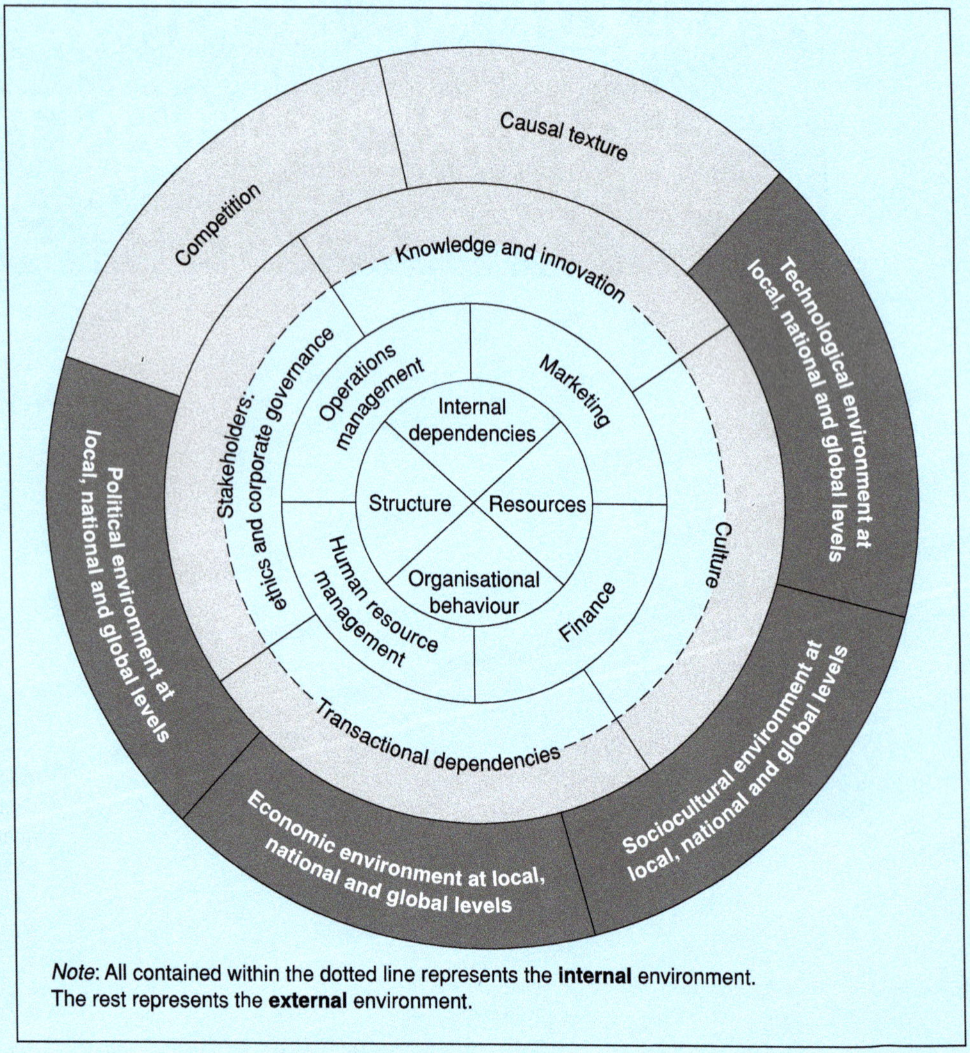

Figure 1.1 Business environment model

Chapter objectives

This chapter aims to provide an introduction to the business environment and its analysis. The idea of both PEST analysis and LoNGPEST analysis are introduced, information sources for such analyses and the process for performing analyses of the external environment are also discussed.

Therefore, when you have read this chapter and worked through the associated activities you should be able to achieve the objectives specified below.

1. **Define PEST and LoNGPEST analysis.**
2. **Identify and discuss relevant sources of information that assist in environmental analysis.**
3. **Explain the process for carrying out a PEST or LoNGPEST analysis.**
4. **Perform PEST and LoNGPEST analyses.**

This case study shows how the economic downturn has had an impact in China as new car sales have declined in the West, Japan and China.

ENTRY CASE STUDY 1.1

Toyota trims output in China as market slows

FT

by Jonathan Soble in Tokyo

A weakening Chinese car market has forced Toyota to curb production in the country and threatened the Japanese carmaker's ambitious sales targets. Toyota and other global carmakers have been counting on a boom in car ownership in China – the world's second-biggest market by volume – to help offset plunging sales in the US.

Demand in western Europe and Japan has also been in decline and Toyota's move will confirm suggestions that the slowdown has now spread to China. Toyota said it had slowed the production line at its Camry plant in Guangzhou, which it operates with local joint venture partner Guangzhou Automotive. 'The market overall is not expanding as quickly as we thought initially. We're making adjustments,' Toyota said, without giving more details.

After growing at a double-digit pace through the first half of the year, overall passenger-car sales in China fell for the first month in more than two years in August, shrinking by 6.2 per cent, according to the national industry association. Analysts on Monday attributed part of the decline in sales to the Beijing Olympics, which forced cars off the road in the Chinese capital and may have kept potential buyers elsewhere at home in front of their televisions. But Toyota's production cut suggests the Japanese carmaker is bracing for a more protracted slowdown in car sales. China's state-subsidised petrol refineries have been allowed to pass some price rises on to drivers while the stock market, a source of much new middle-class wealth, has gone into retreat.

The Japanese carmaker made 450,000 cars in China last year, accounting for most of the cars it sold in the country and making it one of the three largest sellers in China. Toyota's official sales forecasts call for a 40 per cent increase in Chinese sales this year to 700,000 cars. The company left that projection figure unchanged in July when it cut its global sales projection by 3.5 per cent. Toyota's first-quarter net profit fell 28 per cent after a decline in US sales of trucks and sport-utility vehicles. It has cut production in the US and is now retooling plants there to focus on small cars.

Separately, shares in Isuzu Motors, the Japanese light-truck maker, fell to their lowest level in more than three years on Monday after Goldman Sachs cut its rating on the company from 'buy' to 'neutral'. Sales in the US tumbled more than 20 per cent in the first eight months of the year while domestic sales dropped 14 per cent. Isuzu's stock fell 10 per cent to close at ¥291 on Monday.

Source: from 'Toyota trims output in China as market slows', *The Financial Times*, 29 September 2008 (Soble, J.).

Introduction

This chapter introduces the idea of organisations analysing their external environment in order to make sense of the volatile world in which they operate, such that appropriate management and business decisions can be taken. In contemplating the complex and dynamic world in which they operate, organisations have to consider many influences and issues. The entry case study on Toyota illustrates the impact of an economic downturn on a company's operations.

Analysis of the external environment can be done at a broad general level by use of PEST and **LoNGPEST** analyses, which are covered in this chapter and Chapter 2. Further examination of other components of the external environment needs to occur for a full understanding of the external environment to be possible. These other components include competition, competitors, customers and other external stakeholders.

To be able to compete effectively, organisations need to understand who their competitors are and the best way to compete with them. For example the airline Lufthansa has sought to compete with both low-cost carriers in Europe and on longer-haul routes, by understanding very clearly the relationship between costs, price and profits and improving their fleet. Improvements in the cost, price, profit relationship may be achieved by employing cost-cutting strategies and for airlines this can mean ensuring planes are full and being more stringent about charging for excess baggage and even charging for issuing a paper ticket. These approaches are used by airlines to survive in a complex and turbulent environment, caused by a rapidly changing environment, including an economic downturn, increasing fuel prices and changing consumer behaviour which follows several years in which war, terrorism and bankruptcy have impacted on the aviation industry.

Organisations may choose to compete by offering low-priced, good-value products and services, such as Hyundai cars, or by offering a better or luxury product or service at a higher price, such Audi or BMW. We look at the issues of competition in Chapter 3. Equally, the understanding of competitors and their behaviour ties in directly with the need to understand the marketplace, who your customers are, where they are located, and how they can be persuaded to buy the products and services offered by your company rather than those of one of your competitors. This is explored in Chapter 8. For airlines the access customers now have to information on flights and fares via the internet has resulted in airlines having to work harder to compete and make their offering attractive and appealing to customers.

The tool of **PEST analysis** is examined and developed for the purpose of analysing the external environment or outside world. Analysis of the external environment is an ongoing process for organisations that takes the dynamic and changing nature of the external environment seriously.

Hence, in summary, this chapter examines:

- the elements and levels of the external environment faced by organisations;
- the benefits of external environmental analysis;
- the guidelines for undertaking LoNGPEST analysis;
- in brief, the part that competition plays in the organisation's external environment.

The elements and levels of the external environment

The **external environment** is literally the big wide world in which organisations operate. Whatever the nature of their business, organisations do not and cannot exist in splendid isolation from the other organisations or individuals around them, be they customers, employees or suppliers. It is therefore clear that the external environment of any organisation is a large and complex place.

The term 'environment' in this case refers to much more than the ecological 'green' issues that the word commonly evokes. 'Environment' here is more appropriately interpreted as the external context in which organisations find themselves undertaking their activities. Each organisation has a unique external environment that has unique impacts on the organisation, due to the fact that organisations are located in different places and are involved in different business activities, with different products, services, customers and so on. In addition to this unique context, individual organisations will all have their own distinctive view of the world surrounding them, leading them to interpret what is happening in the external environment correctly or incorrectly, depending on their ability to understand the external forces affecting them. This suggests it is crucial for organisations to undertake external environmental analysis and to aim to get it right.

Careful and accurate analysis of the external environment benefits organisations by providing overall greater understanding and an appreciation of the context in which the organisation operates. The key benefits of external environmental analysis are best realised if it is undertaken on a long-term, ongoing basis. These benefits can be summarised as follows:

- managers in the organisation achieve a greater understanding and appreciation of the external environment, leading to improvement in long-term and strategic planning;
- highlighting of the principal external environmental influences generating change;
- anticipation of threats and opportunities within a timescale of long enough duration to allow responses to be considered.[1]

Check your understanding

Do you understand what is meant by the term 'external environment'?

Check your understanding by explaining what the external environment of an organisation is.

External environments can be defined and analysed using PEST analysis, examining political, economic, sociocultural and technological categories into which external influences on the organisation can be placed.

- *Political* influences on organisations encompass both those with a big and small letter 'p', i.e. politics in the conventional sense, with the rules and regulations imposed by government, as well as the **political influences** on organisations of various trade associations, trade unions and chambers of commerce.
- *Economic* influences on organisations include the impact of banks, stock markets, the world money markets, and trading blocs such as the European Union.
- *Sociocultural* influences on organisations include changes in the age and structure of populations, the manner in which populations behave, and the way in which the culture of a population or country changes and develops.
- *Technological* developments influence the magnitude and rate of change that organisations face, and how this affects their capacity to meet their customers' demands. Technological developments have included the development of increasingly sophisticated computer hardware and software. The development of media and communications technology covers electronics and telecommunications, including use of the internet. The ongoing development of the internet as a way of doing business and accessing information has meant a whole new 'media' which needs to be understood in terms of its potential use and reliability.

Basic analysis of an organisation's external environment can be done by breaking down the external influences on the organisation into the PEST categories and assessing the impact of the individual elements identified in each category.

However, there exists a second dimension to the external environment of organisations. This is the level at which the influences occur. There are three levels that will be considered alongside the PEST categories. The levels are local, national and global (LoNG).

- The *local* level can be said to be the immediate town, city or region in which the organisation operates.
- The *national* level is then the home country in which an organisation identifies its headquarters.
- The *global* level then becomes anything outside the local and national levels.

A company operating in and being influenced by the **global level** of the external environment will be trading in a foreign country, be it right next door or on the other side of the world. A company in this situation is subject not only to the laws and culture of its local and national environments but also to the laws and culture of the foreign country in which it is trading. In addition to national rules and regulations, there are the laws and procedures of both home and host countries specifically governing importing/exporting and foreign direct investment activity to consider.

The literature of international business clearly differentiates the terms 'international' and 'global'. Some of the issues considered here are 'international'; i.e. they are issues that occur between nations. However, the third level will be described as 'global', i.e. affecting all parts of the world in similar and simultaneous ways. This is because many of the issues of globalisation in the twenty-first century increasingly affect the local and national levels of organisations' external environments.

The traditional PEST analysis, then, is a short, one-dimensional view of the external environment. The two-dimensional analysis will be referred to in this text as a LoNG (local, national and global) PEST analysis. A generic LoNGPEST analysis could look like the grid shown in Table 1.1.

The grid represents the view that these external influential elements, whether political, economic, sociocultural or technological, all exist at local, national and global levels. The political, economic and **sociocultural influences** are easily identified at the three different levels. However, it could be argued that all types of technology affect and influence organisations at all levels of the environment.

Table 1.1 Generic LoNGPEST grid

<table>
<tr><th></th><th>Political</th><th>Economic</th><th>Sociocultural</th><th>Technological</th></tr>
<tr><td>Local</td><td>• Local government
• Local offices of national government
• Local associations
– Chambers of commerce
– Business Link</td><td>• Local bank branches
• Local economy</td><td>• Local community
• Social capital</td><td rowspan="3">• Communications technology
– Mobile phones and faxes
– Video conferencing
– Internet and world wide web
• Organisations and the application of technology
– The personal computer
– The banking and financial services industry</td></tr>
<tr><td>National</td><td>• National government
• Devolution for Scotland and Wales
• National bodies
– Employers' bodies
– Employees' bodies</td><td>• Central bank
– Bank of England
• Stock market
– London</td><td>• Demographic change
• Social change</td></tr>
<tr><td>Global</td><td>• Alliances and agreements
– UK and USA
– UK and China
– EU
– Cold War
– CIS
– CBSS
– Eastern Europe
• International bodies
– The Commonwealth
– NATO</td><td>• Trading blocs and bodies
– EU
– EFTA
– OECD
– NAFTA
– ASEAN
• World money markets
• WTO</td><td>• Global demographics
• Cross-cultural issues
– Language
– Behaviour
– Culture shock</td></tr>
</table>

It should be noted that not every organisation will identify strongly influential elements in all four PEST categories at all three levels all the time. However, the possibility should be considered for any organisation when carrying out a LoNGPEST analysis because elements have to be identified before they can be evaluated and discounted.

The next section of this chapter offers some guidelines for use when carrying out external environmental analysis. The grid in Table 1.1 shows the possible different external environmental influences on an organisation. These external environmental influences are discussed in more detail in Chapter 2.

Check your understanding

Do you understand what is meant by LoNGPEST?

Check your understanding by naming one influence from each of the following categories: technology; local/political; national/economic; global/sociocultural.

Performing external environmental analysis

As has been stated previously, the external environment is an immensely complex and dynamic place. Therefore, performing an analysis of the external environment of an organisation requires access to a wide range of information. This information may already exist within the organisation or it may have to be sought, collected and collated from other sources. Sources of information within an organisation will encompass information from the four key functional areas of marketing, production, finance and human resource management. This will include sales reports, customer/client survey results, reports on staff skills and availability, and budgets and cashflow statements detailing the amount and availability of cash. In addition, information should be available on the systems in place in the organisation, including that on their capability and capacity, and efficiency and effectiveness. This type of information provided by internal sources, if it is up to date, will provide details of the resources available to deal with current influences in the external environment and indicate the level of resources needed to respond to possible future influences from the external environment.

External information sources are compiled by organisations other than that undertaking analysis of its external environment. The external information sources most widely available and accessible to everyone are the press, television and radio. In the UK the most familiar press includes the daily and Sunday broadsheet newspapers, which all contain business pages or sections in addition to reporting the general political and economic news. These are The *Independent*, the *Daily Telegraph*, *The Times*, The *Guardian*, the *Financial Times*, the *Sunday Times*, the *Sunday Telegraph*, The *Observer*, and the *Independent on Sunday*. Publications such as *The Economist* and *Management Today* supply more extensive coverage of the economy and the latest developments in the world of trade and commerce than that provided by the daily and Sunday press.

The annual report and accounts of a company also provide a summary of recent activities and may offer clues to or an indication of future activities. The annual report and accounts of publicly quoted companies are readily available from the companies themselves or via their website, so are easily obtainable by competitor companies. Specific information concerning an industry will be available from industry- or trade-specific publications.

Current affairs programmes on radio and television cover economic and political news as well as reporting company and industry news and events. For example, Radio 4's *Today* programme comprises items of economic, political and business news and is broadcast at breakfast time on weekday mornings. In addition, economic, political and business news is reported on television news programmes, for example on ITV and BBC1 at teatime and in the late evening. Daily news broadcasts, such as *Newsnight* on BBC2 and Channel 4 News, are longer news programmes than the broadcasts on BBC1 and ITV and consequently devote more time to economic, political and business news stories.

The internet and electronic information are other sources of information which are widely available in organisations. An immense and extensive amount of information can be found on the internet, although one must be aware of who or which organisation originated the information, as this will affect its reliability and accuracy. Much printed and broadcast material can now be accessed via the internet, and many organisations have their own website.

The other method of accessing information electronically is via the use of subscription databases such as Lexis/Nexis, which gives access to the world's

Table 1.2 Blank grid for LoNGPEST analysis

	Political	Economic	Sociocultural	Technological
Local				
National				
Global				

press. Other subscription databases which can be found in libraries include MINTEL, FAME and journal databases.

There is likely to be an increase in the number of websites available on a subscription-only basis. For example the FT internet archive is now subscription only.

The use of the LoNGPEST framework and information will allow analysis of the external environment of an organisation to be completed. The following guidelines will help in applying the LoNGPEST framework. It is suggested that a blank grid like the one in Table 1.2 is used when carrying out external environmental analysis.

Guidelines for external environmental analysis

1 Identify the influences affecting the organisation.

2 Categorise the influences by using the LoNGPEST grid.
   (a) First, decide whether the influence is political, economic, sociocultural or technological.
   (b) Second, decide whether the influence is local, national or global.

3 Make sure you can explain how and why a particular influence is affecting an organisation. Remember, elements in the external environment do not exist in isolation at any level and can impinge on and influence one another.

4 Select and judge which categories are most important to the company, for example **technological influences** at the global level or **economic influences** at the **national level**.

5 Select key individual influences from the important categories. For example, the important category economic influences at the national level may contain the crucial influence of falling interest rates.

6 Consider the important categories and influences you have identified. Do any of these pose threats or opportunities to which the company must react immediately or in the longer term, when anticipating and planning the future?

7 How should the organisation react to and deal with the opportunities and threats? Do short-term opportunities take priority over long-term threats or vice versa?

Check your understanding

Do you understand the importance of information gathering and its reliability in undertaking external environmental analysis?

Check your understanding by stating where you would search for information on the following types of influence: political, economic, sociocultural and technological.

Summary

This chapter examined the external environment influences (PEST) which impact on organisations and how those factors could also be assessed at the local, national and global levels of the external environment. The following summary covers all aspects of this chapter.

1 Organisations analyse their external environment in an effort to understand what it is that impacts on them. In broad general terms, factors impacting on organisations arise from the PEST factors (political, economic, sociocultural and technological), competition and the marketplace.

2 Undertaking external environmental analysis allows managers to better understand the external environment and hence have an improved idea of how to respond to threats and opportunities in the external environment.

3 Political influences on organisations include legislation and industry regulations. Economic influences include the impact of banks, stock markets and trading blocs. Sociocultural influences cover age, structure and behaviour of populations. The impact of technology is wide-reaching and includes computer hardware, computer software, communications technology and electronic media.

4 The second dimension to PEST analysis is that provided by consideration of the PEST categories at local, national and global levels, giving rise to LoNGPEST. The local level is the immediate town, city or region in which the company operates. The national level is the home country with which the organisation identifies. Hence the global level is anything beyond the local and national levels.

5 Information for performing a PEST or LoNGPEST analysis exists both inside and outside the organisation and takes the form of sales reports, budgets, press articles and TV programmes.

6 The guidelines for performing a LoNGPEST analysis cover identification of factors impacting on the organisation, their categorisation and an assessment of their impact on the organisation and its decision making.

Chapter objectives and the exit case study

While reading this chapter and engaging in the activities, you should have learned how to apply theory and models and analyse situations. The exit case study and the questions which follow will provide an opportunity to assess how well you have met the relevant chapter objectives relating to specific material covered in the chapter.

Chapter objective	Check you have achieved this by
4 Perform PEST and LoNGPEST analyses.	answering case study questions 1 and 2.

EXIT CASE STUDY 1.2

Cadbury to cut further 580 jobs

FT

by Maggie Urry

Cadbury on Tuesday announced a further 580 job cuts as part of a cost saving plan announced last year. The 'vision into action' plan envisaged reducing the group's 50,000 headcount by 7,500. The confectioner said the cuts would generate 'significant' savings in 2009 and the group had announced measures that would capture 60 per cent of the savings it had planned. Todd Stitzer, chief executive, said the other 40 per cent had been identified and would be revealed after consultations with employees. The group was on track to make a mid-teen margin by 2011. Cadbury shares rose 3.6 per cent in opening trading up 17¾ at 516½p.

Mr Stitzer said 'affordable treats' such as chocolate, candy and gum, made it resilient if not immune to the worsening economic conditions. 'We operate in a resilient category with a strong business model,' he said, 'our revenue performance remains robust despite the weaker economic background.' Mr Stitzer reconfirmed guidance given with the group's interim profits in July that sales growth would be at the top end of a 4 to 6 per cent range and that margins would rise by 120 basis points, after announcing third quarter revenues up 6 per cent on a like-for-like basis. For the first nine months, revenues were up 7 per cent.

Ken Hanna, finance director who is to leave the group next spring, said that while most of the revenue increase reflected higher prices needed to offset rises in raw material costs, volumes were still expected to be positive for the year. Cocoa prices had risen particularly sharply and the outlook for 2009 was for further increases. The group expected its input prices to rise by 6 to 8 per cent in 2009, with higher cocoa costs the primary cause, up from 5 to 6 per cent in 2008.

Of the job losses, 250 would be achieved by removing a layer of regional management between the seven business units and the head office in the UK. In future the seven units would report directly to Mr Stitzer. Many of these job losses would be senior managers. The other 330 jobs were to go in Australia and New Zealand where the confectionery business would be streamlined, with fewer lines and a plant optimization programme. Mr Stitzer said Cadbury was still reviewing the future of the Australian beverage business where sales fell by 5 per cent in the quarter. He said it was a competitive market but he expected that business to have a reasonable year. The group demerged its American beverages activities in May having previously sold its European drinks business.

Revenues in the UK rose 11 per cent, with the relaunched Wispa bar a particular success. Strong increases were also achieved in South Africa, up 22 per cent, and in Asian emerging markets, up 19 per cent. However, in mainland Europe revenues increased by 4 per cent with weaker performances in France, Spain and northern Europe. In the Americas, revenues were up 7 per cent, but the US gum market slowed while Canada was weak.

Cadbury expects the fall in the pound to increase its revenues for 2008 by 7 per cent and its underlying profits by 12 per cent because of the translation of international results into sterling.

Source: from 'Cadbury to cut further 580 jobs', *The Financial Times*, 14 October 2008 (Urry, M.).

Exit case study questions

1 Using the guidelines for external environmental analysis in this chapter, the information in the Cadbury case study and your own general knowledge, perform a PEST analysis of the external environment faced by Cadbury.

2 Consider your analysis for question 1 and comment on how Cadbury could respond to its external environment.

Short-answer questions

1 Define the term 'external environment'.
2 Explain the term 'LoNGPEST'.
3 Explain the difference between 'international' and 'global'.
4 Name three economic factors which could impact on organisations.
5 Name three political factors which could impact on organisations.
6 Name three sociocultural factors which could impact on organisations.
7 Name three technological factors which could impact on organisations.
8 Name three trading blocs.
9 Where can organisations find the information which will allow them to analyse their external environment?
10 Write down the three key benefits to organisations of undertaking external environmental analysis.

Chapter objectives and assignment questions

While reading this chapter and engaging in the activities, you should have learned how to apply theory and models and analyse situations. This means you should be able to meet the chapter objectives outlined at the beginning of the chapter. The table below shows which chapter objectives can be tested by the different questions.

Chapter objective	Check you have achieved this by
1 Define PEST and LoNGPEST analysis.	answering assignment question 2.
2 Identify and discuss relevant sources of information that assist in environmental analysis.	answering assignment questions 1a, 1b, 2 and 3.
3 Explain the process for carrying out a PEST or LoNGPEST analysis.	answering assignment questions 2 and 3.
4 Perform PEST and LoNGPEST analysis.	answering assignment questions 1a and 1b.

Assignment questions

1 (a) Refer to the section 'Performing external environmental analysis' in this chapter. Identify and collect appropriate information to perform a LoNGPEST analysis of your own college, university or organisation. Your LoNGPEST analysis should contain a completed grid and relevant discussion and explanation.

or

(b) Refer to the section 'Performing external environmental analysis' in this chapter. Identify and collect appropriate information on a public- or private-sector organisation of your choice. Perform a LoNGPEST analysis on your chosen organisation. Your LoNGPEST analysis should contain a completed grid and relevant discussion and explanation.

2 External environmental analysis is an ongoing process for any organisation. Advise an organisation wishing to undertake external environmental analysis for the first time and seeking to set up a system to allow external environmental analysis to take place on an ongoing basis in the future. Present your advice in the form of a 2000-word report.

3 Identify and collect appropriate information from a variety of media sources that show how a particular organisation is evolving. Evaluate and analyse the general usefulness and reliability of the information sources you identify as currently available. Comment on the usefulness of the information to managers within the organisation that is being affected by changes in the external environment. Your answer should take the form of a 2000-word essay.

WEBLINKS available at www.pearsoned.co.uk/capon

The websites for this chapter are for some of the key bodies in the UK impacting on organisations. There are more websites, including those for international and global bodies, at the end of Chapter 2.

- The following website is for British Chambers of Commerce: **http://www.chamberonline.co.uk**
- The following website is for the House of Commons: **http://www.parliament.uk/about_commons/about_commons.cfm**
- The following website is for the Bank of England: **http://www.bankofengland.co.uk**
- The following website is for the London Stock Exchange: **http://www.londonstockexchange.com/Default.asp**
- The following website is for the European Union: **http://www.europa.eu.int**

FURTHER READING

The following book chapters all look at the external environment.

- Johnson, G, Scholes, K and Whittington, R (2008) *Exploring Corporate Strategy*, 8th edn, Chapter 2, Harlow: Financial Times Prentice Hall.
- Lynch, R (2006) *Corporate Strategy*, 4th edn, Chapter 3, Harlow: Financial Times Prentice Hall.
- Palmer, A and Hartley, B (2006) *The Business Environment*, 5th edn, Chapter 1, Maidenhead: McGraw Hill.
- Thompson, J L and Martin, F (2005) *Strategic Management: Awareness, Analysis and Change*, 5th edn, Chapter 4, London: Thomson Learning.
- Worthington, I and Brittion, C (2006) *The Business Environment*, 5th edn, Chapter 1, Harlow: Financial Times Prentice Hall.

REFERENCE

1 Duncan, Peter M and Ginter, W Jack (1990) 'Macro-environmental analysis for strategic management', *Long Range Planning*, 23(6), December.

CHAPTER 2

The composition of the external environment

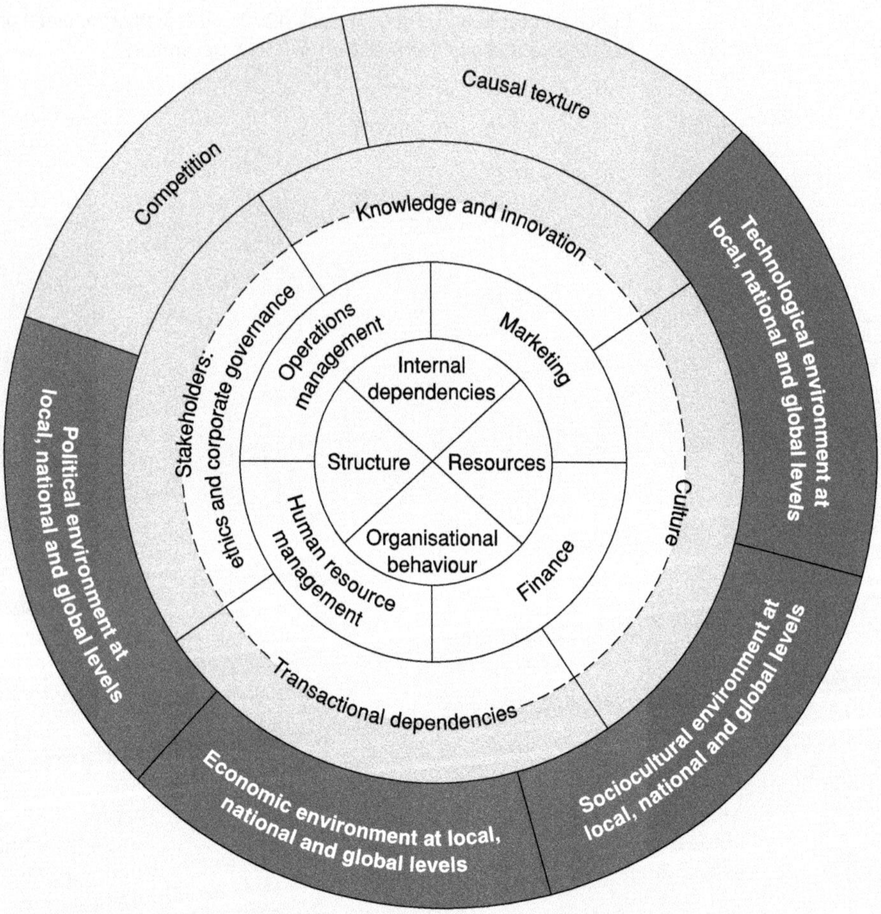

Figure 2.1 Business environment model

Chapter objectives

This chapter aims to define in detail many of the bodies which shape the external environment for organisations at the local, national and global levels. This should allow both PEST analysis and LoNGPEST analysis, which were introduced in Chapter 1, to be performed by thinking more widely and in more detail. Therefore, when you have read this chapter and worked through the associated activities you should be able to achieve the objectives specified below.

1. **Analyse the external environment of an organisation by using PEST and LoNGPEST, drawing conclusions from the analysis.**
2. **Select the most appropriate data and information sources for undertaking analysis of an organisation's external environment.**
3. **Discuss the links between economic and political factors and how this shapes external environments.**

ENTRY CASE STUDY 2.1

Nafta drives car production

FT

by Richard Lapper

At the Volkswagen car plant near the Mexican city of Puebla, the arms of bright orange robots trace precise arcs through the air and gently stamp grey metal car doors into shape. Next door, amid posters urging them to 'take pride in your work', men and women fix dashboards into car bodies that move slowly down an assembly line. The products of these efforts – elegant red, white and lemon-yellow Beetles – stand in formation a few hundred yards away on Avenue B, in another spotlessly clean factory hall. This is the face of Mexico's car industry: efficient, technologically advanced and increasingly oriented to export. Thomas Karig, a vice president at Volkswagen in Mexico, says the decision in 1997 to base world-wide production of the New Beetle at the plant has borne fruit. 'Sales of the model have exceeded forecasts. Mexico is very competitive.'

Volkswagen's success mirrors broader trends. Over the past 20 years, output of new cars has increased four-fold, reaching 1,416,665 units in 2007. Investment has flooded into the sector. Since 2002 more than $10bn has been ploughed into car plants, with a further $6bn–$7bn injected into the booming components business, according to industry figures. The industry as a whole accounts for 13.4 per cent of all manufacturing jobs and, in the component sector alone, employment has more than doubled from 200,000 to 470,000 in the last 10 years. Exports have surged, with 80 per cent of new cars sold abroad, compared with 41 per cent in 1988. Overall, the sector generated $43bn in 2007, an amount that makes it the biggest single earner of foreign exchange.

Carmakers are sourcing more and more of their components from Mexican suppliers, with the industry increasingly concentrated in clusters of manufacturers based in northern and central cities. Nissan, which manufacturers in Aguascalientes and Cuernavaca, now brings in between 60 and 70 per cent of its components from local suppliers, compared with less than half a decade ago. 'We are increasing locally procured parts,' says Shoichi Miyatani, president of the company's Mexican operation. He adds that only the very most advanced state-of-the-art components are brought in from outside. The big driver of all this growth has been the gradual migration of chunks of the once mighty US motor industry south of the Rio Grande in the wake of the North American Free Trade Agreement (Nafta) in 1994. The deal attracted US manufacturers to locate new capacity in Mexico, mainly because wage rates are less than a sixth of their levels north of the border.

The US industry is far from dead. Two years ago Toyota, for example, chose to base a new north American plant in Texas. But all three US majors – General Motors, Chrysler and Ford – have significant operations in Mexico. Nafta helped make the Mexican industry more internationally focused. As Eduardo Solís, president of the Mexican Association of Motor Manufacturers, puts it:

→

'You must manufacture in the dollar zone what you sell in the dollar zone.'

But two other developments have given extra momentum to exports. First, over the past decade Mexico has entered into a string of free-trade agreements with other trading blocs, most notably the European Union, Japan and Mercosur, the South American customs union linking Argentina and Brazil. Second, the decline of the dollar against the euro and yen has helped to boost competitiveness significantly. The peso has appreciated against the greenback, but only marginally, and certainly to a much lesser extent than the currencies of rival production centres such as Brazil. As a result, Mexican carmakers are selling greater volumes to Europe and Asia. Volkswagen sold more than 60 per cent of its output outside the Nafta area. Nissan began exporting its new Tiida model to Europe in 2007 for the first time. 'We exported more than we planned to Europe,' says Mr Miyatani at Nissan.

Export success masks deepening problems in the domestic market. Here, the problem is the scale of imports of second-hand vehicles from the US, sales of which are undercutting domestic demand for new cars. Mexico is obliged by its membership of Nafta to open up to imports of cars made since 1994, with a final deadline due next year. New rules allowing the import of used cars were introduced three years ago and led to a rapid rise in imports, with more than 1m vehicles brought in annually during 2006 and 2007. At the same time, sales of new cars in Mexico itself have gradually fallen, sinking to 288,833 in 2007, the lowest figure since 1998. Smaller, so-called subcompact cars – popular among lower-income families – have been particularly depressed, with that niche seeing a fall of between 15 and 20 per cent. Mr Solís says it is particularly difficult to monitor the safety and emissions standards of these second-hand vehicles. 'In the US, a 10-year-old car is virtually scrap,' he says. 'These cars come in and we don't know where they are.'

Source: from 'Nafta drives car production', *The Financial Times*, 16 June 2008 (Lapper, R.).

Introduction

This chapter follows on directly from Chapter 1 and seeks to examine in much greater detail the generic LoNGPEST model – *see* Table 2.1. The constituent elements of the external environment and their influence on organisations are discussed here. The chapter examines the nature and influence on organisation of politics, economics, society and culture and technology, all at the local, national and global levels.

The political elements of the external environment

The political external environment comprises local and national government, local associations, trade unions and employers' bodies. All of these are likely to hold a political viewpoint. Countries and organisations that are the result of political agreement and cooperation are also considered in this section. Because national and global economies are largely organised and run by governments, there are many areas of overlap between the political and economic environments. In this chapter the use of separate sections attempts to clarify and analyse political and economic environments individually. There are many political elements in the external environment, so analysing political elements of the external environment is sometimes confusing. This section principally examines the effects that external environmental elements have on

Table 2.1 Generic LoNGPEST grid

	Political	Economic	Sociocultural	Technological
Local	• Local government • Local offices of national government • Local associations – Chambers of commerce – Business Link	• Local bank branches • Local economy	• Local community and social capital	• Mobile phones and faxes • Video conferencing • Internet and world wide web • Manufacturing technology
National	• National government • Devolution for Scotland and Wales • National bodies – Employers' bodies – Employees' bodies	• Central bank – Bank of England • Stock market – London	• Demographic change • Social change – inequality of income – family and household structure	
Global	• Alliances and agreements – UK and US – UK and China – EU – Cold War – CIS – CBSS – Eastern Europe • International bodies – The Commonwealth – NATO	• Trading blocs and bodies – EU – EFTA – OECD – NAFTA – ASEAN • World money markets • WTO	• Global demographics – Europe – Asia – Africa • Cross-cultural issues – Language – Behaviour – Culture shock	

organisations, but inevitably it will become clear that organisations also affect the external environment around them. This is perhaps especially so for employers' organisations, as will be seen later.

The local political environment

At the **local level**, the political elements of the external environment are local government, local offices of national government and local associations – *see* Table 2.2.

Local government

Local government has a significant impact on the businesses within its boundaries. It has responsibilities for regulating private-sector business activity and for directly providing a wide range of services. Some of these responsibilities have a very direct effect on businesses and others a more minimal influence. Local authorities have a statutory responsibility, i.e. they are bound by law to uphold trading standards and environmental health. As such, they hold great powers over all organisations within their area, and have the authority to close them down if severe breaches of law are discovered.

Table 2.2 The local political environment

	Political	Economic	Sociocultural	Technological
Local	• Local government • Local offices of national government • Local associations – Chambers of commerce – Business Link			
National				
Global				

The services provided by the local authority include social services such as care of the elderly, education and services used by private householders and organisations alike, such as refuse collection, street cleaning, transport and planning permission for new buildings or extensions to existing premises. Clearly, a local authority's policies on trade refuse collection, street cleaning and transport to and from the city centre are all going to affect local businesses and shops in the city centre. A congestion charge, such as that introduced in London by Ken Livingstone in early 2003, will be aimed at reducing the amount of traffic in a particular area and is likely to have a detrimental effect on the amount of passing trade for shops in the area. The provision and promotion of effective and cheap public transport, however, ought to go some way to counterbalancing these detrimental effects.

Local government is also responsible for setting and collecting council tax from residents and business rates from commercial organisations. The money raised via council tax and business rates will partially fund the services that local authorities provide, although the main source of funding for local government is money provided by national government. For the purpose of environmental analysis, this illustrates neatly that the levels of the external environment are as interdependent as organisations and their external environments.

It is also important to remember that a local authority is a large public-sector organisation operating in its own external environment. In many UK regions, cities, towns and villages, the local authority is the biggest local employer and the largest organisation. It too has customers and suppliers, and with the introduction of Compulsory Competitive Tendering (CCT) by the Conservative governments of the 1980s, local authorities now also have competitors for the provision of services in the locality where previously they had the monopoly. Here we begin to observe one of the complexities of environmental analysis.

Clearly demonstrated here are the interdependencies between different elements of the environment: one organisation has a complex external environment consisting of other organisations and individuals; it in turn is an element in each of these organisations' individual external environments.

Local offices of national government

As national government has responsibility for the direct provision of many welfare services, the local offices of national government departments play a key role in the lives of local organisations and the local people. There is a local interface between the Department for Work and Pensions, the local offices of the Inland Revenue, and the Department for Education and Skills local Jobcentre Plus service. The current Labour government introduced a review of welfare provision geared towards removing the disincentives to finding work that the welfare system can engender, and towards promoting the opportunities that unemployed people can offer organisations. The 1998 Green Paper 'A New Contract for Welfare' laid out proposals to introduce the first wholescale reform of the welfare state since its introduction in 1945. This has affected organisations in the local environment by providing funding for training and employment of those who are workless through various initiatives under what is called the 'New Deal'.

Local associations

For private-sector organisations in the model, local associations are defined as trade and business associations operating in the geographic vicinity.

Chambers of Commerce

The British Chambers of Commerce are a network of quality accredited chambers of commerce, which are independent, non-profit-making and non-political organisations which are funded via membership subscriptions. British Chambers of Commerce offer business training, and information on a range of issues, such as exporting, suppliers and saving on overheads. At local, regional and national levels the British Chambers of Commerce act to put forward views and opinions on matters affecting their member businesses with a view to influencing local and national government and other decision-making bodies. Chambers of Commerce also offer a powerful voice in terms of comment in the media concerning businesses at the local, regional and national level.

Business Link

Business Links are privately led partnerships between Training and Enterprise Councils, Chambers of Commerce, Enterprise Agencies, local authorities and government. Business Link partnerships are involved in providing advice via a one-stop shop for small and medium-sized businesses. Business Link partnerships operate very much on a regional and local level; for example, in

South Yorkshire, Business Link services are available for Barnsley, Doncaster, Rotherham and Sheffield.

Business Link partnerships generally provide advice and expertise in the areas of raising finance, entering export markets, employee training and managing change. A Business Link partnership aims to provide advice and expertise at a price that small and medium-sized businesses can afford. The partnerships are funded by the Department of Trade and Industry, with the condition that by the fifth year of existence the partnership must be at least 25 per cent self-funding.[1]

The national political environment

The national government and national bodies constitute the national political environment – *see* Table 2.3.

National government

The ways in which the national government manages the economic environment are dealt with under the relevant section below. As a result of the UK's membership of the **European Union (EU)**, the distinction of a national political environment is becoming blurred. Acts that appear on the surface to have been the British Parliament making laws governing British businesses turn out to have originated in Brussels and required all member countries to implement them. Examples of European decisions enacted by the national British government are the fitting of seatbelts to coaches, vans and lorries, adding costs to transport companies; the export ban on British beef in the wake of the BSE

Table 2.3 The national political environment

	Political	Economic	Sociocultural	Technological
Local				
National	• National government • Devolution for Scotland and Wales • National bodies – Employers' bodies – Employees' bodies			
Global				

crisis in the 1990s and its impact on British beef farmers; and the abolition of duty-free goods within the European Union, meaning that tax-free shopping has come to an end except for intercontinental flights.

Examples of the purely national political environment affecting organisational activity are therefore increasingly hard to find, but focus largely on the legislation passed regarding permissible commercial activity, production and service functions and human resource strategies. This latter example is dealt with in Chapter 7, but to give one example, the 1995 Disability Discrimination Act (DDA) made it illegal for organisations not to provide access for disabled workers or customers on their premises. The direct effect of this legislation, which was stronger than anything preceding it, caused many organisations to commission alterations to their existing facilities in order to comply with the new law. The DDA covers equal access to goods, facilities and services, and employment and education.

Although its effects could be said to be largely economic, the national government's political decision making affects most citizens directly through its annual budget. Government has to raise money to provide for its services. It does this via taxation revenue that it uses to pay for publicly funded services such as education, the National Health Service, public transport subsidies, and social and welfare services such as the state pension for those too old to be economically active. Some of the money raised by taxation is distributed via local government and some is distributed and spent directly by national government. This is covered in more detail under the national economic environment, later in this chapter.

Decisions with an economic effect on business may be classified as political when taken by government. One such decision was made in November 1992 by Norman Lamont, then Chancellor of the Exchequer (Finance Minister) in the Conservative government. The pound sterling had been entered into the Exchange Rate Mechanism (ERM), the European Union's mechanism for preparing its member nations' currencies for European Monetary Union (EMU) and eventual merger into a single European Currency Unit (ECU), now better known as the euro. The ERM was designed to bring all its currencies to a level value by setting a range of exchange rate limits beyond which a currency should not be allowed to rise or fall. Norman Lamont took the decision to withdraw the pound from the ERM and hence effectively took Britain out of the first group of countries to enter EMU. The pound was removed from the ERM because its value fell outside the exchange rate range within which it was supposed to remain. However, the decision was also taken for political reasons, as the Conservative party was showing early signs of the internal divisions over European policy that partially led to its defeat in the 1997 elections.

The withdrawal of the pound from the ERM resulted in what the City referred to subsequently as 'Black Wednesday', when there was an immediate 10–15 per cent devaluation of the pound in relation to other currencies. Consequently, businesses in Britain trading with overseas companies were affected. Companies importing goods, components or raw materials into the UK from overseas had to pay more for them. In 1992 the UK economy was depressed and importing companies faced the dilemma of whether to pass the increased costs on to consumers or to absorb the increased cost in whole or in part, via reduced profit margins. On the day the pound was removed from the ERM, Yorkshire Television news reported on a company based in Hull that was facing exactly this dilemma. The company imported high-quality, up-market German kitchens and kitchen appliances, manufactured by companies such as AEG, Siemens and Bosch. In contrast, companies exporting UK manufactured goods found it easier as the lower cost of production made UK goods more price competitive abroad. This partly contributed to the growth of the UK economy in 1993.

From this it can be seen that the link between the national political and economic environments is clear. Politicians are elected by the people and run the economy. In doing so, they decide the economic policy that affects both individuals and organisations operating at the national level of the environment.

Devolution in Scotland and Wales

The Labour government elected on 1 May 1997 had promised in its election manifesto to hold referendums on devolution in both Scotland and Wales. This was duly implemented. In Wales the referendum was held on 18 September 1997 and 50.1 per cent of the electorate turned out to vote, with 50.3 per cent voting for a Welsh Assembly and 49.7 per cent voting against. In Scotland the referendum on 11 September had a turnout of 60.4 per cent, with 74.3 per cent of those who voted supporting the creation of a Scottish Parliament and 63.5 per cent voting to give the Scottish Parliament limited tax-varying powers.[2]

The Scottish Parliament consists of a total of 129 seats, of which 73 are directly elected and 56 allocated to additional members. Directly elected members were elected by a constituency to represent them. The additional members were elected by the electorate voting for a party and the additional seats given to members of the party voted for. The allocation of additional seats is complex but is representative of the voting pattern in the electorate as a whole.[3]

The Scottish Parliament appointed a First Minister, Donald Dewar, who in turn appointed members to and headed the Scottish Executive. The First Minister and Scottish Executive are drawn from the party or group commanding the majority in the Scottish Parliament. The Scottish Parliament is able to pass laws in a number of areas for Scotland, including health, education, local government, housing, economic development, trade, transport, criminal and civil law, courts, prison, police and fire services, animals, the environment, agriculture, food standards, forestry, fisheries, sport and the arts. The Scottish Parliament also has powers to repeal legislation passed at Westminster as far as Scotland is affected.[4]

The Welsh Assembly contains 60 directly elected seats and 40 additional seats. In contrast to the Scottish Parliament, the Welsh Assembly does not have the same powers governing the establishment of legislation and the repeal of Westminster legislation. The areas of responsibility devolved to the Welsh Assembly include economic development, agriculture and food, industry and training, education, local government, health and personal social services, housing, environment, planning, transport and roads, arts and culture, the built heritage and sport and recreation. The Secretary of State for Wales has the power to make secondary legislation in these areas. For example, the Secretary of State for Wales is able to decide the school curriculum in Wales.[5]

National bodies

National bodies represent businesses and employees and present views on employment and trade issues to one another, and to the government and opposition parties. Both employer and employee organisations try to shape and influence events in the external environment for the benefit of their members. Employer and employee national bodies are often closely aligned with the government or a particular political party. Employers' organisations traditionally support the Conservative Party, while the Labour Party is linked financially and in terms of membership to the trade unions. For the Labour Party to achieve victory at the 1997 general election, it was thus crucial for it to have gained support from both sides of the negotiation table.

Employers' bodies

Examples of national employers' bodies include employers' organisations such as the Institute of Directors (IOD) and the Confederation of British Industry (CBI). The IOD was formed in 1903 and its members are individual company directors from large FTSE 100 companies through to smaller entrepreneurial start-up businesses. The IOD provides members with information, advice, training, conferences and publications. In addition the IOD seeks to be an influential organisation in representing the concerns of its members to government and does this via lobbying and the media. The CBI was founded in 1965, bringing together several other industry bodies. Members of the CBI are companies, including both multinationals and small and medium-sized enterprises as well as trade associations and employers' organisations. The CBI seeks to provide UK industry with a forum for developing and influencing policy on a host of areas which impact on business organisations, such as the economy, legislation and technology. Additionally the CBI seeks to encourage efficiency and competitiveness in UK industry and in doing so develop the contribution of UK industry to the economy.

These organisations provide a forum for employers or owners of businesses to put forward their views and be represented on issues affecting businesses, such as the national minimum wage, the euro and the 2008 financial crisis. Both the IOD and CBI frequently use the printed and broadcast media to do this. At the time of the election of the Labour government, in 1997, the CBI was contributing to the minimum wage debate via the media. Labour had made the introduction of a minimum wage in the UK a manifesto pledge, and the CBI was suggesting a minimum wage of £3.50 per hour as an acceptable amount. It pitched this figure between the £4.29 per hour favoured by the Trades Union Congress and the £3.00 per hour suggested by 'certain employers'.[6] The rate at which the minimum wage was initially set was £3.60 for workers aged over 21, and by October 2008 this had risen to £5.73 per hour.

Employees' bodies

In contrast, trade unions are national bodies representing employees. Examples of trade unions are UCU, representing teachers in further and higher education, USDAW, representing shop and distribution workers, and UNISON, representing public-sector employees. Trade unions represent their members in negotiations with employers on issues concerning pay and conditions, whether in the private or public sector. They are linked to the Labour Party, although reforms made to party membership after Labour's 1992 election defeat attempted to reduce the unions' impact and promote the concept of 'one member, one vote'. Most trade unions are affiliated to the Trades Union Congress, which is the largest voluntary organisation and the largest pressure group in the UK. The TUC operates to represent its member unions collectively at a national level.

There has been a steady decline in trade union membership since 1979 and the reasons for this decline include a reduction in the number of jobs in manufacturing industries, which typically had high levels of union membership among employees. This fall in union membership has been consolidated by an increase in the percentage of people working for small companies where it is often more difficult for unions to organise themselves. Additionally, larger numbers of unemployed people or people not working have helped to reduce the level of trade union membership. Finally, under the Conservative administrations led by Margaret Thatcher in the 1980s, trade union membership and the power of the unions were drastically curbed. This occurred as the view taken by the Thatcher governments was that Britain's industrial unrest of the 1970s and the cause of its industrial decline was due to the unions' rise to political power. In contrast, the Employment Relations Act 1999 established a new statutory procedure for recognition of independent trade unions in the workplace, although it did not include the adoption of European-style workers' councils. Union influence, however, is unlikely to rise to previous post-war levels.

The global political environment

Alliances and agreements

The global political environment (*see* Table 2.4) encompasses alliances and agreements between countries that have an effect on the international activities

Table 2.4 The global political environment

	Political	Economic	Sociocultural	Technological
Local				
National				
Global	• Alliances and agreements – UK and USA – UK and China – EU – Cold War – CIS – CBSS – Eastern Europe • International bodies – The Commonwealth – NATO			

that each country's citizens may undertake. Two or more countries may come together to establish independent or semi-independent global bodies to oversee or regulate the conduct of international trade and commerce, as well as to work towards the improvement of social issues, such as health, poverty or human rights.

Alliances and agreements occur between two or more countries for mutual benefit. The countries involved concur to support each other in global politics or in bilateral or multilateral economic activity. In extreme cases, consent may be given to the merger of countries into a single entity, or one country may consent to divide into separate countries to fulfil ideals of cultural identity, national integrity or economic benefit; for example, Czechoslovakia separated in 1993 to become the Czech Republic and Slovakia.

The UK and the US

A good example of an alliance in which two countries concur to support each other is the close and special relationship between the UK and the US. Although there are few formal bilateral treaties, a special relationship exists as a result of the two countries' historical and linguistic ties. In the 1980s the relationship between the UK and the US was personified by the close friendship and mutual support of Conservative Prime Minister Margaret Thatcher and US Republican President Ronald Reagan. Both headed conservative governments in their respective countries and combined radical free-market agendas with strong global politics. This caused some difficulty for President Reagan during the UK–Argentine Falklands War in 1982, as his special relationship with the UK required support of Britain's efforts, while US links with the rest of the American continent precluded actual aggression against Argentina. On a separate occasion in 1986, Margaret Thatcher approved the use of US airbases in the UK to launch bomb attacks against Libya.

The special relationship continues between the UK Prime Minister and the US President. In the 2003 Gulf War to liberate Iraq there was close agreement between the UK and the US, while France and Germany were in less agreement over the decision to go to war without a UN mandate. There had been greater global consensus over the 1991 Gulf War, where international forces, the UK and US among them, liberated Kuwait from Iraqi invasion.

The UK and China

China is extremely important on the global political stage because of its sheer size, geographically, politically and economically. The Chinese market is an important part of Britain's overseas trade, with the UK exporting to China and importing Chinese goods. The return of Hong Kong to China is an example of an agreement at the global level of the external environment, which was designed to promote business stability and minimise political and economic risk for British business in China. On 1 July 1997, the British colony of Hong Kong was handed back to China after 99 years of British rule under the terms of a lease forced from the Chinese at the height of Britain's imperial activity. This was unlike the fate of any of the UK's other colonial possessions, which all left the Empire to become independent countries in the Commonwealth – *see* Table 2.9 in this chapter. Hong Kong, however, had not been independent before the colony was established but had always been part of China, so had to be returned to it at the end of the lease.

The negotiations governing the return of Hong Kong to China were started in the early 1980s by Margaret Thatcher and Deng Xiaoping, China's then paramount leader. In the late 1970s Deng Xiaoping engineered economic reforms in China and allowed the slow development of a more market-based economy, while retaining strict political control over personal liberty. He died on 19 February 1997 prior to the deadline for Hong Kong's return to China, which duly went ahead. China described itself as 'one country – two systems', referring to the promise to continue unchanged for a minimum of 50 years Hong Kong's capitalist free-market economy under Chinese communist rule. This free-market economy has long been the gateway to the Chinese market for foreign businesses and for Chinese exports to the world and so it is greatly in China's interest to maintain the status quo.

China's lack of a democratic political system should not have been a cause for concern, as the British colony had been ruled without recourse to democracy. Nevertheless, following Britain's long-held policy of establishing democratic systems before withdrawing from colonial possessions, the last Governor of Hong Kong, former Conservative politician Chris Patten, attempted to introduce some last-minute democracy to the colony. In the 1990s Hong Kong people were allowed to vote for the first time for a minority of members of Hong Kong's governing body, the Legislative Council (Legco). However, the return of Hong Kong to China in 1997 saw the dismantling of the Legco and the appointment by Beijing of a replacement administration and a new Chief Executive of the Hong Kong Special Administrative Region, Tung Chee-hwa, a wealthy local businessman who had previously been ennobled by the Queen.

The European Union

In 1957 the European Economic Community was established by the Treaty of Rome. There were six founding countries, with a further twenty-one countries joining the European Union by 2007 (*see* Table 2.5). In 2008 the EU describes its aims as being 'peace, prosperity and freedom for its 495 million citizens – in a fairer, safer world'.[7]

The 1997 Treaty of Amsterdam covered new rights for EU subjects concerning issues such as freedom of movement and employment. The Agenda 2000 blueprint presented to the European Parliament in July 1997 allowed the EU to expand eastwards and for former Communist countries of Eastern Europe (*see* Table 2.5) to become members. Enlargement of the EU is viewed as an opportunity to unite Europe and extend and consolidate political stability and economic prosperity more widely. The criteria laid down by the European Council in Copenhagen in 1993 required potential member states to demonstrate democracy, human rights, a functioning market economy, and a commitment to the EU's aims covering political, economic and monetary union. The political and economic conditions of applicant countries have to be judged satisfactory by the EU before it allows their admittance. Negotiations to admit

Table 2.5 European Union member countries

Year of entry	European Union member countries		
1957	• Belgium • Italy	• France • Luxembourg	• Germany • Netherlands
1973	• UK	• Denmark	• Ireland
1981	• Greece		
1986	• Spain	• Portugal	
1995	• Austria	• Finland	• Sweden
2004	• Cyprus • Hungary • Malta • Slovenia	• Czech Republic • Latvia • Poland	• Estonia • Lithuania • Slovakia
2007	• Bulgaria	• Romania	

Source: http://www.europa.eu.int/

Table 2.6 **European Union candidate countries**

• Croatia	• Macedonia	• Turkey

Source: http://www.europa.eu.int/

new members are complex and examine how the significant differences in economic and social development between member and potential members states can be tackled.[8]

In 2007 there were three countries awaiting admittance to the EU (*see* Table 2.6). Croatia is expected to join by 2012 and Macedonia's negotiations will be lengthy, particularly since the country's elections in the summer of 2008 were not conducted in a sufficiently open and safe manner and violence erupted on the streets. Turkey has now met conditions to be considered as a candidate country, although negotiations will be lengthy and there is no expected date for Turkey's accession to the EU.

The Cold War

World political events result in alliances being created and demolished, hence altering the political map of the world. In order to understand events in the late 1990s, it is essential to consider some political background. After the Second World War (1939–45), the world was plunged into the Cold War, an ideological battle between democratic and Communist political systems backed up by the technology of nuclear warfare, bringing for the first time in history the constant threat of a Third World War that would annihilate millions of civilians and destroy entire countries. The two sides of the Cold War, put simplistically, consisted of the US and Western Europe – with its institutions such as NATO, EFTA and the EU – and the then Soviet Union (USSR or Union of Soviet Socialist Republics) and Eastern Europe, with its equivalent institutions: the Warsaw Pact was the mutual defence treaty signed by Communist countries in the USSR sphere of influence, and Comecon was the alliance of planned economies.

The division of East and West was never more starkly evident than in the division of Germany on its defeat by the victorious Allies into two states: the western, democratic, free-market Federal Republic of Germany (FRG), and the eastern, Communist, **planned economy** of the German Democratic Republic (GDR). The former capital of Berlin, geographically inside the GDR, was itself split into two halves and a wall built down the centre between East and West. The Berlin Wall came to symbolise the Cold War.

The Cold War split was mirrored in the Far East during the Korean War (1950–53), where US forces supported the democratic South Korea against the Chinese-backed Communist north. The country remains divided into two administrations and a state of civil war still exists officially. Similarly, the People's Republic of China (PRC) and the Republic of China on Taiwan both claim to be the legitimate government of China, after a similar civil war whose hostilities ended in 1949, but peace has never been negotiated. The US originally backed the Republic of China, and did not switch allegiances until president Nixon visited the PRC in 1973. In Vietnam, the American-backed south eventually fell to the Communist north after many years of bloody war, uniting the country under a Communist government in the early 1970s.

In Europe in the late 1980s and early 1990s, the geopolitical map altered considerably and unexpectedly as a result of the collapse of strict controls over personal liberty in many Communist-controlled countries. This had begun with the last ever President of the USSR, Mikhail Gorbachev, who introduced policies of *glasnost* (openness) and *perestroika* (economic restructuring) during his term in office. These alterations to the political map provided unprecedented opportunities for trade and commerce and began in the GDR, when the Communist regime lost control over the population and the Berlin Wall was suddenly dismantled in a popular uprising that was not opposed by the police or military forces. By 3 October 1990 East and West Germany had officially reunified under the former FRG's government. As a result of reunification, the German government moved its parliament from Bonn, capital of the FRG, back to Berlin.

Commonwealth of Independent States

The ending of the Cold War resulted in other changes to the geopolitical map of Eastern Europe. During the years 1989–91 the USSR collapsed as the Soviet government in Moscow went the way of the GDR government, and the Soviet Union dissolved the federation into its component independent states, which then came together under the auspices of a looser association called the Commonwealth of Independent States (CIS) – *see* Table 2.7.

Council of Baltic Sea States

The Council of Baltic Sea States (CBSS) was established in March 1992, when the foreign ministers of the member states met in Copenhagen at the invitation of the Danish and German foreign ministers – *see* Table 2.8. The foreign ministers were seeking to strengthen cooperation and coordination between Baltic sea states and viewed the creation of the CBSS as helping to achieve this aim, along with the promotion of democratic and economic development in the region.[9]

Table 2.7 Members of the Commonwealth of Independent States (CIS)

• Armenia	• Azerbaijan	• Belarus
• Georgia	• Kazakhstan	• Kyrgyzstan
• Moldova	• Russia	• Tajikistan
• Turkmenistan	• Ukraine	• Uzbekistan

Source: http://www.cisstat.com

Table 2.8 Members of the Council of Baltic Sea States (CBSS)

• Denmark	• Estonia	• Finland
• Germany	• Iceland	• Latvia
• Lithuania	• Norway	• Poland
• Russia	• Sweden	• European Commission

Source: http://www.battinfo.org/CBSS.htm, 28 April 2000.

Eastern Europe

Countries such as Poland, Hungary, Czechoslovakia, Romania and Yugoslavia all experienced cataclysmic change after the dissolution of the USSR. In geographic terms Poland, Hungary and Romania remained unchanged, in contrast to Czechoslovakia and Yugoslavia, which altered significantly. Czechoslovakia, for reasons of national and economic identity, split into two countries, the Czech Republic and Slovakia. In the 1990s civil war split Yugoslavia into several independent countries: Croatia, Bosnia Herzegovina, the former Yugoslav Republic of Macedonia and Slovenia, with Montenegro and Serbia remaining as a rump Yugoslavian Federation. A multinational peacekeeping force administered Kosovo: geographically a small country between Serbia, Montenegro, Albania and Macedonia.

However, in February 2008 Kosovo's parliament declared independence from Serbia. Russia had backed Serbia and opposed this move by Kosovo. However, countries including Germany, Italy, France, the UK, USA, Turkey and Albania recognised Kosovo as an independent state, while Russia, Cyprus, Romania and Slovakia refused to do likewise. Following Kosovo's declaration of independence the EU took over the administrative roles undertaken by the UN, and NATO continued to provide security in Kosovo.[10,11,12]

In January 2001 Zoran Djindijic was democratically elected as Prime Minister of Serbia, three months after toppling Slobodan Milosevic. Zoran Djindijic pushed for economic reform in Serbia and helped engineer the arrest and extradition of Slobodan Milosevic to the United Nations court in The Hague. Milosevic was tried for war crimes committed during the Balkan wars of the 1990s, dying of a heart attack in 2006, before the end of his trial. However, in March 2003 Zoran Djindijic was assassinated and there followed uncertainty for Serbia. In July 2008, Radovan Karadzic who was practising as an alternative therapist in Belgrade, was captured and taken to the International Court at The Hague to be put on trial for war crimes. Serbia's admission as an EU candidate country will only begin to be considered once headway has been made in capturing Ratko Mladic who is also wanted for war crimes and is thought to be hiding in Serbia.

All these former Eastern bloc countries have seen major changes to their political and economic systems, with elections taking place in many countries and greater opportunities for international trade and commerce becoming available. Some of these opportunities allow Western companies to invest and manufacture in countries such as Poland, Hungary, Slovakia and the Czech Republic; for example, Volkswagen bought Skoda in the Czech Republic and now manufactures Skoda cars which sell successfully all over Europe.

International bodies

The international bodies discussed here are bodies that have a global political influence on the world political order. This is important, as peace and political stability are key elements in allowing a country to have an active economy and stable trade with other countries.

The Commonwealth

The Commonwealth derives from Britain's imperial past and comprises countries from all regions of the world, including Europe, the Pacific, Asia, Africa and the Caribbean. The countries belonging to the Commonwealth are shown in Table 2.9 and range from India, with a population of over 900 million people, to Naura in the Pacific, with 8000 people. The Commonwealth consists of 53 countries, 52 of which are former colonies or protectorates of the UK, the exception being Mozambique, a former Portuguese colony. Mozambique was admitted as a member in November 1995 due to its close association with the Commonwealth in opposing apartheid in South Africa and because it wanted to reap the benefits of membership. Apartheid was the official system of keeping the white minority population in South Africa in a position of power and wealth, while the black and coloured populations had no access to money or political decision making. South Africa withdrew from the Commonwealth in 1961 following pressure from other member countries over apartheid. It was readmitted only in 1994 after the development of a new, democratic and multiracial constitution, with Nelson Mandela, a leading dissident of the old regime, released from imprisonment and elected president in the country's first ever democratic elections.

In contrast, Nigeria was suspended from the Commonwealth in November 1995 after its most recent military coup. The deteriorating relationship between Nigeria and the Commonwealth was caused by the Nigerian military cancelling the presidential elections in 1993 and in November 1995 executing nine minority rights leaders, including the author Ken Saro-Wiwa. The Commonwealth held a summit meeting in November 1995 in New Zealand and acted quickly and forcibly by suspending Nigeria from the Commonwealth.[13,14] Nigeria's suspension from the Commonwealth was finally lifted in April 1999, following the election of a civilian government led by President Olusegun Obasanjo.[15]

In 2002 the Commonwealth was discussing the suspension of Zimbabwe, due to President Mugabe's tyrannical regime, which has devastated its agriculture and economy. However, a few short months later in 2003 Robert Mugabe withdrew Zimbabwe from the Commonwealth.

The examples discussed above illustrate that the Commonwealth is an international body that can, along with other international bodies, affect and

Table 2.9 Members of the Commonwealth

Year of entry	Countries			
1931	• Australia	• Canada	• New Zealand	
1947	• India			
1948	• Sri Lanka			
1957	• Malaysia	• Ghana		
1960	• Nigeria[1]			
1961	• Sierra Leone	• Cyprus	• Tanzania	
1962	• Uganda	• Jamaica	• Trinidad and Tobago	
1963	• Kenya			
1964	• Malawi	• Zambia	• Malta	
1965	• Singapore	• Gambia		
1966	• Lesotho	• Botswana	• Barbados	• Guyana
1968	• Nauru	• Mauritius	• Swaziland	
1970	• Tonga	• Western Samoa		
1972	• Bangladesh			
1973	• The Bahamas			
1974	• Grenada			
1975	• Papua New Guinea			
1976	• Seychelles			
1978	• Solomon Islands	• Tuvalu	• Dominica	
1979	• St Vincent and the Grenadines	• St Lucia	• Kiribati	
1980	• Zimbabwe[2]	Vanuatu		
1981	• Antigua and Barbuda	• Belize		
1982	• Maldives			
1983	• St Kitts and Nevis			
1984	• Brunei			
1989	• Pakistan[3]			
1990	• Namibia			
1994	• South Africa[4]			
1995	• Cameroon	• Mozambique		

Notes:
1 Suspended 1995, rejoined in 1999.
2 Zimbabwe was withdrawn from the Commonwealth by Robert Mugabe in 2003.
3 Rejoined, had withdrawn in 1972.
4 Rejoined, had withdrawn in 1961.

Source: http://www.thecommonwealth.org/about/general/general/1.html

Table 2.10 Members of NATO

Year of entry	Countries		
1949	• Belgium	• Canada	• Denmark
	• France	• Iceland	• Italy
	• Luxembourg	• Netherlands	• Norway
	• Portugal	• UK	• USA
1952	• Turkey	• Greece	
1955	• Germany		
1982	• Spain		
1999	• Czech Republic	• Poland	• Hungary
2004	• Bulgaria	• Estonia	• Latvia
	• Lithuania	• Romania	• Slovakia
	• Slovenia		

Source: http://www.nato.int/welcome/home.htm

influence the status of a country with regard to participating in trade and commerce on a global level. Accordingly, the role of the Commonwealth is to further economic and social development, democracy and human rights in its member countries.[16]

The North Atlantic Treaty Organisation

The North Atlantic Treaty Organisation (NATO) was formed in April 1949 and consisted of 12 members, with a further 14 countries joining between 1952 and 2004 – *see* Table 2.10. NATO's primary role is to ensure the security of its member countries and in the first instance this largely involved countering the threat created by the Cold War until that came to an end in 1990/1. Since then NATO has reorganised and restructured to develop security arrangements for the whole of Europe and to allow 'peacekeeping and crisis management tasks undertaken in co-operation with countries which are not members of the Alliance and with other international organisations'.[17] The ending of the Cold War created an opportunity for the expansion of NATO and in July 1997 agreement was reached between member countries to allow the Czech Republic, Poland and Hungary to become members in 1999. This was followed by a second wave of former Eastern bloc countries joining NATO in 2004, including the Baltic States of Estonia, Latvia and Lithuania (*see* Table 2.10).

Check your understanding

Do you understand the impact that political factors in the external environment can have on an organisation like Volkswagen?

Check your understanding by referring to the entry case study, identifying and explaining the political factors which have made it possible for Volkswagen to manufacture in Mexico.

Political and economic links

The alliances and agreements between countries described in the previous section altered the political map and political systems for the countries involved. Alterations to their economic systems also occurred alongside the political changes. In terms of international business, the assessment of political and economic risks is a major factor when deciding which target market and mode of entry would be appropriate in various countries. Comparative analysis of various countries' political and economic stability, potential and future trends enables companies to take a judgement about whether or not to invest in or export to that destination.

Democracy

Democracy is the system of government most recognisable to those born and brought up in the West. Democracy comes from the Greek *demos*, 'the people', and *kratis*, 'power', and describes those systems where the people are able to choose, through a system of voting, those who represent them in the corridors of power and decision making. As it is impossible for every individual in society to be completely free and unfettered by the rules of the state, democratic systems are the mutual agreements under which people are able to live together collectively and yet express a collective opinion on periodic change via fair and proper elections. It would be understandable to think of all Western governments as being equally democratic, yet not each country has the same system. Democratic systems divide broadly into those that have evolved and those that are the product of a sudden and cataclysmic change, e.g. popular revolution. The latter are those that have perhaps the greatest spread of democracy in their institutions.

For example, the UK is called a constitutional monarchy and has a parliamentary system. Despite a 40-year interruption under Oliver Cromwell, the UK's monarchy can be traced back a thousand years. The current system has evolved through a system of concessionary changes to the point where its system of hereditary figurehead monarch, popularly elected House of Commons and mix of hereditary and appointed second chamber, the House of Lords. The House of Lords is used as a blueprint of democratic government and has around 750 peers of which 92 hereditary peers are elected by their colleagues. Countries such as the US, France and Germany, in contrast, have all had occasion to invent their political systems from scratch after revolution or war. These systems are based on written constitutions and codes of conduct, and feature elected government at all levels, including both chambers and head of state (president).

Autocracy

The exact opposite of democracy, autocratic systems are those where one person retains all power in his or her hands. The historical embodiment of autocracy was the absolute monarchy, where the king held all political and economic power. During the Cold War, this lack of democratic process was most keenly observed under Communism, where the people were unable to choose the political party to represent them and had little or no personal liberty (these systems are more appropriately called oligarchies, since they are dominated by a powerful elite).

The free market

Providing in-depth knowledge of economics is not the purpose of this text, but to be able to discuss a variety of political and economic contexts, it is necessary to define different economic systems. The **free market** is that situation in which there is little or no regulation of commercial activity on the part of political entities. In a free market, the market forces of demand and supply will lead to perfect competition, providing all that the people need or want at a price they can afford. If there is no demand for a product or service in a free market, that product will not sell, no matter how cheaply it is priced.

The planned economy

In Communist countries, attempts were made to eradicate the free market and its differences between rich and poor, by planning and orchestrating all economic activity from central government. Thus people were not free to seek whatever job they wished, and organisations could not recruit whoever they wanted. All jobs, housing, production, services and food were organised by the state via its work units, or state-owned organisations. Market forces were denied, as consumers were able to purchase products or services only from the state-owned factories and companies, whether they were good or bad. No decision was left to the individual, no matter how small. Thus individuals' every need was catered for in a basic way, but individualism, innovation and creativity were stifled.

The mixed economy

Most Western economies are a mixture of free and planned economic activity. Where there is no regulation on business, employees and consumers alike are at risk. Regulation in the UK protects employees at work through health and safety and employment protection legislation, while the consumer is protected by the Sale of Goods and Trades Descriptions Acts.

Links between countries' political and economic systems

When considering the global political environment (*see* Table 2.4) or the global economic environment (*see* Table 2.14), it is essential first to know something about the political and economic systems of various countries and regions in the world. Figure 2.2 is a matrix that plots various countries (*see*

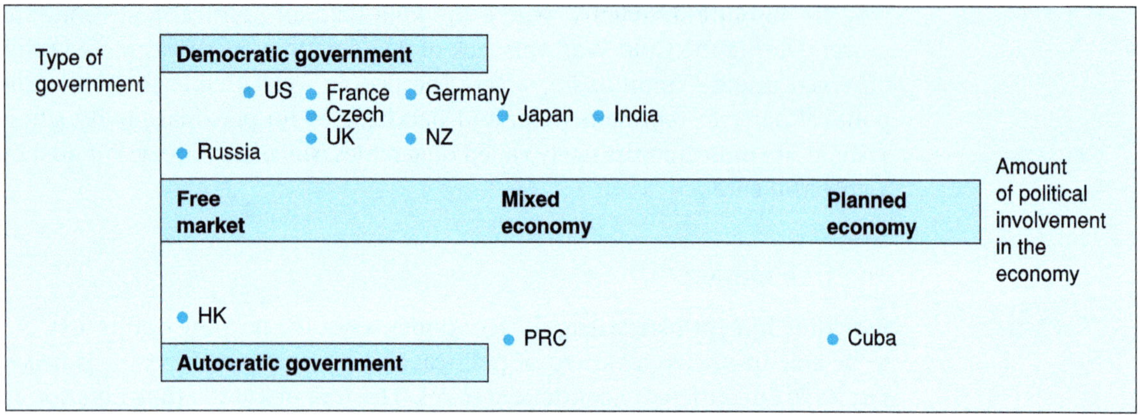

Figure 2.2 Government type and political involvement in the economy

Table 2.11) in relation to one another based on their level of democracy and the level of political interference in the economy. For the sake of this text, this matrix has been completed in a highly subjective and unsubstantiated manner, and indeed countries' positions will alter over time subject to political and economic change. In terms of assessing political and economic risk before entering new markets, organisations should invest in more objective forms of analysis, either done in-company or by external experts. The countries are plotted according to the background information given in Table 2.11.

Check your understanding

Do you understand how the political and economic systems of countries in the former Eastern bloc, like Slovakia, have changed?

Check your understanding by placing Slovakia on the grid in Figure 2.2, both today and before the end of the Cold War.

The economic elements of the external environment

As has been stated, the economic environment faced by organisations is shaped and influenced by the political environment as well as by the economic bodies that are constituents of the external environment. The previous section examined the political elements of the external environment. In this section the role of economic bodies such as banks, stock markets, world money markets, **trading blocs** and bodies is considered.

The local economic environment

Local bank branches

Banks are a key local economic environmental player for companies, as the relationship between a company, big or small, and its bank is a local one

Table 2.11 Country summaries

Cuba	After a Communist revolution over 30 years ago, dictator Fidel Castro has presided over a decaying planned economy. Following the dissolution of the USSR, Cuba's main source of political and economic support, Cuba has found it increasingly difficult to survive under the US trade embargo.
Germany	A federal republic, united finally in 1991, its mixed economy is one of the post-war European success stories, despite the costs of integrating the former Communist East.
Japan	Since the Second World War Japan has been a constitutional monarchy. However, the Liberal Democrats have been elected for most of those 50 years. The original successful Asian tiger economy, its success is also often attributed to the high levels of government intervention in the economy.
India	The largest democracy in the world.
Hong Kong	Directly ruled from London for 99 years, Hong Kong reverted to the sovereignty of the People's Republic of China in 1997. A radical free market, it remains to be seen how this will continue under the 'one country, two systems' plan.
New Zealand	A Westminster system in the Commonwealth, it has seen a Labour government heavily interested in privatisation.
Russia	Since the collapse of the Soviet Union, the Russians have elected their leader for the first time in their history. The emergence of a mafia indicates a lack of regulation in the economy.
People's Republic of China	Controlled by the Chinese Communist Party following 'liberation' in 1949, China has liberalised its economy radically since the late 1980s without relinquishing any political power.
United Kingdom of Great Britain and Northern Ireland	Often called the 'Mother of Parliaments', the UK is a constitutional monarchy without a constitution, and only directly electing one of its two Houses of Parliament. There has been widescale privatisation since the early 1980s.
United States of America	With a written constitution, the Americans directly elect both Houses and their President. The federal system essentially allows for a variety in levels of free-market approach.

between the two organisations. The relationship between a company and its bank is not normally one of national or global importance or influence. Hence a company's relationship with the bank with which it holds a business account will tend to be governed by issues concerning the amount of money in the account, overdraft and loan facilities. *See* Table 2.12.

The local economy

The general state of the local economy also exerts a direct influence on organisations. If the local economy is buoyant, the customer base for products and

Table 2.12 The local economic environment

	Political	Economic	Sociocultural	Technological
Local		• Local bank branches • Local economy		
National				
Global				

service will be wide and profitable. However, wages will be high and employees in short supply from among the local population. In areas with a depressed local economy, there will be little opportunity for selling products or services to people with little disposable income, but the workforce should be cheap and plentiful.

The national economic environment

The main influences on businesses at a national level come from the actions of the country's national bank and stock market (*see* Table 2.13). These two organisations together influence the value of investments held by businesses and individuals and hence affect the amount of cash available in the economy.

Government actions in relation to the economy also obviously have a great influence. The most common forms of taxation are income tax, corporation tax, value added tax (VAT) and duty on imports/exports. VAT is payable on many goods and services and at the time of writing stands at 15 per cent for most goods in the UK. The Conservative government increased the rate of VAT across the board from 8 to 17.5 per cent and also increased the number of items on which VAT is charged. The most opposed introduction of VAT was on domestic fuel, which had been zero rated and was to be charged at 8 per cent. This was not abolished but was reduced to 5 per cent by the Labour government in 1997. Basic food items and children's clothes are zero rated, i.e. VAT is chargeable but it stands at 0 per cent. Food items considered to be luxury items are subject to VAT at the standard rate.

The rate of taxation affects businesses as higher income tax lessens the amount of disposable income that people have available to spend on goods

Table 2.13 The national economic environment

	Political	Economic	Sociocultural	Technological
Local				
National		• Central bank – Bank of England • Stock market – London		
Global				

and services, and VAT makes goods and services more expensive to the consumer than the price set by the manufacturer or service deliverer. Therefore, it is crucial to the standard of living of the individual citizen, to the profitability of private-sector organisations, and to the standard of public services that a balance is achieved between taxation and public spending.

Businesses are effected by corporation tax as the higher the rate, the greater the amount of tax due on any profits made and hence the lower the amount of money available to pay dividends to shareholders and spend on activities such as marketing, product development, pay increases and updating equipment and facilities used to run the business.

Although much of the above is concerned with affecting the economic environment of the country, the decision making behind the management of the economy is essentially political, as it can be political parties' economic strategies that voters find key at the ballot box. Additionally, budgets from opposing political parties often show different approaches towards solving the same problems. Details of the latest budget can be found at the Treasury website – see the weblinks section at the end of this chapter.

The central bank – Bank of England

In the UK the central bank is the Bank of England. In May 1997 the new Labour Chancellor of the Exchequer, Gordon Brown, gave independence in the setting of the base rate of interest to the Bank of England and its Governor Eddie George. This separated out the economic and political decision-making processes concerning interest rates for the first time in the UK's history. Under the previous system, the Chancellor of the Exchequer and the Governor of the Bank of England would meet regularly and jointly agree changes to the base rate of interest. The base rate directly influences businesses and individuals as repayment of overdrafts, loans or mortgages will increase with higher interest rates, hence reducing the amount of activity in the economy. For example, when interest rates are high, businesses spend less on new equipment, advertising and product development and individuals spend less on the goods and services produced by businesses.

The effects of the government handing over decision making on base interest rates to the central bank should be that the influence of short-term political need on economic management is removed. Interest rates, a key economic management tool, should be decided from a purely economic perspective. When a government minister is deciding interest rates, they can be manipulated for political advantage before an election, as Nigel Lawson did when Chancellor of the Exchequer before the 1987 election. The so-called 'Lawson Boom' that he engendered led directly to the recession of the early 1990s. The Bank of England, in contrast, should take only rational, objective decisions about long-term economic strategy. This is in line with other European countries' practice and further prepares the UK for the possibility of entry to the euro at some date in the future.

The London Stock Market

The stock market is where shares of publicly quoted companies are traded. London is an international financial centre.

Company names and share prices are published in all the daily broadsheet newspapers and on the internet. The shares of a company will trade on the stock market at a market price and the price will go up or down depending on the performance of the company and how it is viewed by the City. For example, a company that announces good profits is likely to see a rise in its share price and vice versa. However, good performance can be measured by factors other than profit. Manchester United, a profitable company, had a share price of £1.64 in February 1998; after being beaten 3–2 by Barnsley and knocked out of the FA cup on 25 February 1998, Manchester United shares fell 25p to £1.39. Continued good profits and better performance by the team on the pitch saw the share price climb steadily to £1.52 in June 1998, and to £3.00 in May 2005 at the time of the takeover of the club by Malcolm Glazer.

The value of shares will also be altered by overall movements in the stock market. If the economy is in recession and stagnating, then it is also likely that the stock market has fallen. In November 2008 the FTSE was around 4000; about 12 months previously it had been approaching 7000. Hence share prices were low and in November 2008 the high street retailers were expecting a poor Christmas and started sales at the end of November. The Bank of England sought to stimulate the economy by cutting interest rates to 3 per cent and the Chancellor of the Exchequer cut VAT by 2.5 per cent, but also increased the top rate of income tax to 45 per cent for people earning over £150,000 per annum.

The global economic environment

The global economic environment is shaped by how countries decide to behave economically in relation to each other; for example, countries may decide to group together on a regional basis and confer trade benefits and support on each other. The other economic influence at a global level is the effect of the world money markets. *See* Table 2.14.

Trading blocs and bodies

These are geographic blocs made up of a number of countries that agree to act together in some way with regard to trade and commerce. The countries may, for example, agree to allow special concessions on the taxing and movement of goods within the trading bloc or merely support each other with regard to economic issues.

The European Union

Because of the close association between politics and the economy, it is necessary to mention the European Union again under trading blocs and bodies. The EU's Single European Market came into operation in 1993 and allows free movement of goods between member states. However, the issue of differing rates of taxation in different member states has yet to be dealt with fully. For example, the tax on wine, beer and cigarettes is much lower in France than in

Table 2.14 The global economic environment

	Political	Economic	Sociocultural	Technological
Local				
National				
Global		• Trading blocs and bodies – EU – EFTA – OECD – NAFTA – ASEAN • World money markets • WTO		

the UK and this is clearly shown by the popularity of day trips to France to stock up on cheap drink and cigarettes. The sale of drinks from pubs and retail outlets in the UK has been badly hit, particularly in the south-east of England, with the closest and best access to France. However, day trips to France to stock up on cheaper goods will remain popular until duty rates throughout the EU are harmonised.

The 1991 **Maastricht Treaty on European Union** covers the issues of currency, **immigration** controls and defence policy. It set the timetable for the first round of European monetary union (EMU) that occurred in 1999. The deadline for meeting the necessary economic targets to join the first wave of European monetary union was the end of 1997. The key economic target that countries had to meet was the deficit:GDP (gross domestic product) ratio, which had to be 3 per cent or less. All member states except Greece met this target. However, along with Greece, Denmark, the UK and Sweden did not join the single European currency in the first wave.[18] The expectation is that the euro will generate an area of economic stability with low inflation and low interest rates.

European Free Trade Area

The European Free Trade Area (EFTA) was established in 1960 by the Stockholm Convention. Initially EFTA had seven member states: Austria, Denmark, Norway, Portugal, Sweden, Switzerland and the UK. Eventually some states left EFTA to join the European Union and new states joined EFTA. EFTA currently has four member states – Iceland, Liechtenstein, Norway and Switzerland[19] – and seeks to promote free trade and economic integration by managing the EFTA free trade area, participating in the European Economic Area (EEA), and developing a network of free trade agreements. The European Economic Area was created on 1 January 1994 when the three EFTA states, Iceland, Liechtenstein and Norway, and all EU states combined to create a large free-trade area. The EEA agreement allows free movement of people, goods and capital between participating nations.

Since the end of the Cold War, EFTA has sought to develop relationships with Central and Eastern European countries. This has led to the establishment of free-trade agreements with countries such as the Czech Republic, Poland, Latvia, Lithuania, Estonia, Bulgaria, Romania, Slovakia and Hungary. Currently EFTA is focusing on developing links with other countries, for example Peru, Columbia and Argentina and the South African Customs Union (SACU).[20]

Organisation for Economic Cooperation and Development

The Organisation for Economic Cooperation and Development (OECD) was established in 1961 and is based in Paris (*see* Table 2.15). On 5 June 1947 a speech by George C Marshall, US Secretary of State, gave rise to the post-war European Aid Program, commonly known as the Marshall plan. The view of the US government was that there had to be agreement among some or preferably all European countries as to the aid required and its use to reconstruct Western Europe. Therefore, European and North American countries came

Table 2.15 Members of the OECD

Year of joining	Countries		
1961	• Austria • Denmark • Greece • Italy • Norway • Sweden • UK	• Belgium • France • Iceland • Luxembourg • Portugal • Switzerland • USA	• Canada • Germany • Ireland • Netherlands • Spain • Turkey
1964	• Japan		
1969	• Finland		
1971	• Australia		
1973	• New Zealand		
1994	• Mexico		
1995	• Czech Republic		
1996	• Hungary, Korea, Poland		
2000	• Slovakia		

Source: http://www.oecd.org/pages/0,3417,en_36734052_36761800_1_1_1_1_1,00.html

together to establish the Organisation for European Economic Cooperation (OEEC). Its chief role was to facilitate the planning, allocation and implementation of post-war aid to Western Europe. However, in 1961 the OEEC decided that the reconstruction of post-war Western Europe was complete and sought to convert the OEEC into the OECD. The OECD did not focus on the giving and use of aid but on making the economies of the member countries involved prosper. To this end the policies of the OECD seek to:

- support sustainable economic growth;
- boost employment;
- raise living standards;
- maintain financial stability;
- assist other countries' economic development;
- contribute to growth in world trade.[21]

North American Free Trade Agreement

In 1994 the **North American Free Trade Agreement** (NAFTA) between the governments of Canada, the US and Mexico was established. The principal strands of NAFTA relate to:

- encouraging goodwill and collaboration between NAFTA countries;
- establishment of a larger and more secure market for goods and services produced in NAFTA countries;
- strengthening and sharpening the competitiveness of companies from NAFTA countries in global markets;

- the generation of additional employment opportunities in NAFTA countries;
- the improvement of working conditions and living standards in NAFTA countries;
- the protection and implementation of workers' basic rights.[22]

Trade and the movement of jobs and goods between NAFTA countries are key issues for the countries involved. Many car companies such as Volkswagen and US companies General Motors, Chrysler and Ford all have technological advanced manufacturing facilities in Mexico. These were often set up because wage rates in Mexico are much lower at about 15 per cent of those in the US (*see* entry case study). This has meant there has been growing export sales, and Volkswagen centres worldwide production of the Beetle in Mexico (*see* entry case study). However, in recent years there has been a decline in the sale of small cars, like the Beetle in Mexico, as NAFTA rules mean Mexico has to allow the import of older second-hand US-manufactured cars, which are cheaper and therefore appealing to the Mexican market. However, Mexico is one of the world's larger economies and is also a large exporter, and has established free-trade agreements with the EU, Japan and Mercosur, the South American trade bloc (*see* entry case study).

The Association of South East Asian Nations

The **Association of South East Asian Nations** (ASEAN) was formed in 1967 in Bangkok with five founding members and a further four members joining between 1984 and 1997 (*see* Table 2.16). In July 1997 Burma and Laos were admitted, but Cambodia's entry was postponed due to violence that threatened civil war.[23] Cambodia's entry finally occurred in 1999.

The three main objectives of ASEAN are:

- to promote the economic, social and cultural development of the region through cooperative programmes;
- to safeguard the political and economic stability of the region against big power rivalry;
- to serve as a forum for the resolution of intra-regional differences.[24]

Table 2.16 Members of ASEAN

Year of entry	Countries		
1967	• Indonesia • Singapore	• Malaysia • Thailand	• Philippines
1984	• Brunei		
1995	• Vietnam		
1997	• Laos	• Myanmar (Burma)	
1999	• Cambodia		

Source: http://www.aseansec.org/74.htm

The world money market

The world money market encompasses the world's stock markets and the exchange value of currencies against each other. The main stock markets that make up or have the biggest influence on the world money market are New York, London, Tokyo and Hong Kong. A collapse in one is quite likely to result in a drop in another, with the value of stocks falling and wiping value from the shares of companies.

This was clearly evident in the economic crises of 2008 that saw the major stock markets of London, New York and Tokyo plummet. This also meant that during 2008, currencies such as the pound, euro, yen and yuan all fell against the Americian dollar.

The World Trade Organisation

The **World Trade Organisation** (WTO) is located in Geneva, Switzerland, and officially came into existence on 1 January 1995, replacing its predecessor, the General Agreement on Tariffs and Trade (GATT). The WTO has 153 member countries and 30 observer governments, of which 21 have applied for membership. In administering the rules of trade and helping trade occur, the WTO monitors national policies, cooperates with other international bodies, handles trade disputes and helps provide training and technical assistance for developing economies.

The role of the WTO is summarised as:

- administering the rules of trade between nations;
- helping producers of goods and services, exporters and importers conduct their business.[25]

The biggest change in the WTO in recent years has been the conclusion of China's long-term efforts and negotiations to become a member. China took up its membership of the WTO on 1 January 2002, earning it most favoured nation (MFN) trading status on an immediate and permanent basis.[26] MFN status ensures China's exporters access to US markets. Prior to membership of the WTO, China's MFN status was reviewed annually by the American Congress.

China's drive to join the WTO was been long and slow since it first applied to join GATT in 1987. Consequently in 1997 the thawing of previously frosty political relations between China and the US provided an opportunity for progress on China's entry to the WTO and negotiations took place in Geneva. Final agreement on the terms of China's entry to the WTO was reached on 15 November 1999.

Admittance to the WTO is a significant step towards allowing China's fast-growing economy to face more international competition and allowing foreign exporters and investors access to the country. However, membership requires China to adopt a thorough approach to many complicated issues that establish barriers to trade and commerce. These include the dismantling of investment restrictions, quotas, subsidies and tariffs. China agreed to accept WTO rules, open its economy to the rest of the world and to continue to engage in market-based reforms.

Check your understanding

Do you understand the impact that economic factors in the external environment can have on an organisation like Volkswagen?

Check your understanding by referring to the entry case study, identifying and explaining the economic factors which have made it possible for Volkswagen to manufacture in Mexico.

The sociocultural elements of the external environment

The sociocultural elements of the external environment include the age and structure of a national population, the way a population or society behaves, and elements determining how the culture of a population develops. This section will look at some of these and how businesses and organisations are affected. Greater detail on culture and organisational behaviour can be found in Chapters 5 and 6 respectively.

The local sociocultural environment

Local community and social capital

The local community is part of an organisation's external environment (*see* Table 2.17). The local community may be passive as regards the organisation, or the local community and organisations can have an active influence on

Table 2.17 The local sociocultural environment

	Political	Economic	Sociocultural	Technological
Local			• Local community and social capital	
National				
Global				

each other. For example, a local transport company regularly burns old and broken wooden pallets in its yard and produces a dense black smoke, making the atmosphere unpleasant for people who live in nearby houses with gardens overlooking the firm's yard. This local company has a very direct influence on the quality of life in the local community. The local people may act either individually or collectively and complain to the local council department dealing with pollution. If appropriate action is taken to stop the pollution, this is a very good example of a local firm, its local community and local government affecting and being affected by each other's actions.

There may be other local community influences to which the organisation is subject. A school is a public-sector organisation that interacts significantly with its local community. The community is greatly dependent on how well the school performs due to the personal nature of the service that the school provides. This kind of interdependence is considered in Chapter 3.

Social capital is defined as community spirit and neighbourliness with which people identify. Social capital can take the form of trust which is felt by people living in a neighbourhood. Social capital held by individuals also arises from the number of groups people belong to, such as a local football team, Women's Institute, scouts, or yoga class, and the networks of family and friends with which people interact.[27] Hence people who experience a high level of social capital have good neighbours, see family and friends regularly and belong to social groups and clubs.

The national sociocultural external environment

Demographic change

Demographic change is change in the age and structure of a population. This section considers demographic changes in the population of the UK (*see* Table 2.18). There are three issues which are discussed, namely longevity, immigration and birth rates.

The population of the United Kingdom is currently around 60 million people and estimates are that it will be 75 million people by 2051.[28,29] Longevity, rising immigration and higher birth rates, mainly among migrants, will account for 69 per cent of the population growth.[30]

The number of older people in the United Kingdom has increased: in 1961 there were 16 million people aged over 50 in the UK and by 2021 there will be 22.5 million people, an increase of 40 per cent against an overall population increase of 15 per cent.[31] The 2001 census also highlighted this trend and for the first time, since the first census in 1801, there are now more people aged over 60 than under 16 in the UK's population. The 2001 census also showed there were 1 million people aged over 85 years, five times more than in 1951,[32] and is estimated to grow to around 3 million people by 2031.[33]

Immigration into the United Kingdom had increased largely due to the enlargement of the EU and this has led to an increase in the birth rate. Increasing

Table 2.18 The national sociocultural environment

	Political	Economic	Sociocultural	Technological
Local				
National			• Demographic change • Social change – inequality of income – family and household structure	
Global				

birth rates will clearly add to the population and at the moment the growth in birth rates is significant in the United Kingdom. In the United Kingdom in 2001 the birth rate for UK-born women was 1.5 children each and 2.3 children for non-UK-born women. In 2006 the figures had increased to 1.7 and 2.5 respectively, giving an overall birth rate of 1.8 children per woman.[34] The birth rate needs to be 2.1 children for a country to maintain its population.

Social change

Social change covers the changes and developments in the way societies behave. The changes in society examined in this section are the evolving family and household groups present in UK society and the inequality of income. The role and influence of government are also considered.

Family and household structure in UK society

The demographic changes discussed earlier in this chapter are reflected in changing household structures in the UK. The number of single person households is growing and changes in marriage, divorce and the role of women in the home and at work mean different family structures.

In 2008 the proportion of single person households in the United Kingdom was 28 per cent of all households. Single person households are a diverse group and there are three main types of single person household: single young professional people with very good incomes, divorcees and elderly people.

The greater number of older people in the population and the higher life expectancy of both men and women now results in a growing number of older people living in single person households. This increase is also due to people having always lived in a single person household or the death of a partner or spouse. The average lifetime is 81 years for a woman and 77 years for a man in the UK.

There are various reasons for the growth in the number of single person households and these are discussed below. Traditionally 30 or 40 years ago a young person would have anticipated being single for a short time and remaining in the parental home, before marrying in their mid-twenties and settling down to a lifelong marriage, raising the average 2.4 children and being part of a traditional family unit. Society viewed being single as something undesirable that occurred as a result of misfortune and not an alternative that people chose. Being single was the result of being widowed or divorced because of an unfaithful spouse; indeed, both of these still occur today.

However, today in the twenty-first century there are two general trends regarding young adults and their housing. The first trend is that young adults will get a job and leave home permanently after school or university and will be living independently by their mid-twenties. A proportion of these single young people will be well-off professional people with successful careers and good incomes. Approximately two-thirds of single women and over half of single men are in the ABC1 economic group, with three-quarters of single men and two-thirds of single women in full-time employment.

The other emerging trend is that of so called 'boomerang kids', i.e. children who leave the parental home, often to go to university, only to return and live at home until their late twenties or early thirties, as they are unable to afford to rent or buy their own home. Therefore, the number of adult children living at home has increased significantly since 1993, when 60 per cent of men and 40 per cent of women in their twenties were living at home. In 2008, 80 per cent of men and 50 per cent of women in their twenties were still living at home. Additionally, over the same time period the median age for a first marriage had increased from 26 to 30 years for a man and from 24 to 28 years for a woman.[35]

The number of single person households is increased by marriage and divorce rates and the UK has the highest divorce rate in the EU, with around 35 per cent of marriages ending in divorce, compared with a rate of around 10 per cent in the mid-1970s. This is a consequence of divorce being less shameful and more frequent than 30 or 40 years ago. Between 1970 and 1997 the increased divorce rate, coupled with a 50 per cent fall in the number of first-time marriages, added to the number of single person households. However, in 2006 the divorce rate in the UK had fallen to its lowest level for 22 years and marriage rates were at their lowest level since records began in 1862.[36]

The increase in the single person household in the UK has led to businesses considering their market segments. For example, supermarkets need to cater for single person households, who do not want to buy large packs that contain portions that are unwanted. This is an expensive way to shop, particularly as a pensioner on a budget. There is also an increasing demand for single person household packs of healthy food to be widely available.[37] The young professionals will be big investors in technology, including online, computer and entertainment equipment for the home as well as entertainment outside the home, such as cinemas and gyms.

Further social changes have occurred with regard to the family and the role of women. In 1971 married couples with children comprised 52 per cent of families and 12 per cent of children were born outside marriage. In contrast, by 2007 the figure was 37 per cent of families were married couples with children and 44 per cent of children were born outside marriage.[38] Further social changes in the family include alterations in the role of parents. In 1985 both parents worked in half of all two-parent families with children; the figure was 62 per cent a decade later.

Today fewer people believe that it is a wife and mother's job to look after the home than did so in 1986. However, mothers still spend four times longer than fathers on cooking and housework.[39] The growth in the number of women in the workplace and the resulting greater financial independence of women are due to several factors. First, women are no longer expected to marry and be totally financially dependent on a husband. Since the 1960s there has been improved and increased access to higher and further education, which has meant greater access to better jobs and careers for women. This, coupled with the introduction of legislation in the 1970s covering equality of women in the workplace in terms of equal opportunities and equal pay, has contributed to women's greater role in the workplace.

There are some mixed messages to be observed in the political reactions to social change. In contrast to the moral rhetoric of family values that it espoused at the hustings, the Conservative government in the late 1980s introduced independent taxation for married women for the first time, thereby recognising both the earning potential and the legal status of married women. Nevertheless, in an effort to promote the responsibility of fathers in providing for their children beyond separation and divorce, it also established the Child Support Agency, whose job was to track down and make the errant fathers pay for their children living in one-parent families with their mothers.

Inequality of income in UK society

UK society is one of widening inequality: the well-off have got richer and the less well-off have become poorer. Income inequality has grown rapidly since 1977, fuelled to a large extent by the Conservative governments in power from 1979 to 1997. These governments introduced policies that led to large pay packets and rewards for successful people, in contrast to fewer and increasingly meagre social security benefits for the less well-off, which overall have increased more slowly than wages. Additionally, the wage differences between skilled and unskilled workers has increased, as skilled workers have benefited from technological change and unskilled workers have suffered as a result of the decline in the trade unions.[40] Hence the income distribution gap in the UK is one of the greatest among the industrialised countries of the world.

There are many ways in which government is reacting, as any organisation should, to these changes in the external environment. In terms of the ageing population, government takes the view that more of the burden of social security, healthcare and pensions needs to be provided for privately since the workforce cannot keep up the level of provision traditionally offered by the welfare state when it was introduced. The Blair government was concerned about the widening gap in UK society, and established a Social Exclusion Unit to bring into the mainstream of opportunity and care those who had been excluded for social or systematic reasons, with a view to including more disadvantaged groups in mainstream provision.

This widening inequality is apparent when looking at different areas of the country. In England the problems of poverty, ill health and unemployment are mainly concentrated in cities in the south and the depressed industrial north, with pockets of rural poverty in Cornwall, Kent, Cumbria and Northumbria. London has the highest level of low incomes, about 25 per cent of people, and the south-east the lowest number of people on low incomes at about 18 per cent. In the south, outside of poor inner-city areas, there is generally a higher standard of living, with the problems of unemployment, poverty and ill health occurring less frequently than in impoverished areas. However, the stress of modern living is felt in both the city and the countryside, with fewer people working longer hours. This is illustrated by city workers attending working breakfasts and evening meetings and people in the countryside working longer hours on the land or in the holiday industry for minimal pay.[41]

The global sociocultural environment

Changes in populations at a global level impact on the opportunity for trade and economic development, hence some of the global demographic trends are examined in this section (*see* Table 2.19). In addition, some of the sociocultural issues that affect organisations once they leave their home environment and operate overseas are also considered. Definitions of culture and how it affects individuals and national society are covered in detail in Chapter 5.

Global demographics

There are differing trends in the development of populations in a variety of countries and continents. At a global level these demographic changes will impact on the economic development of different countries and regions in the world.

Europe

The European Union's economic growth rate will potentially shrink to 1.25 per cent a year, due to its ageing population and therefore less productive

Table 2.19 The global sociocultural environment

	Political	Economic	Sociocultural	Technological
Local				
National				
Global			• Global demographics – Europe – Asia – Africa • Cross-cultural issues – Language – Behaviour – Culture shock	

population. This is half the US growth rate of 2.5 per cent per year. One view on tackling the issue of the decline of Europe's economy is to raise the retirement age by five years, significantly increasing pension funding and also increasing productivity, while reducing unemployment.[42] The alternative view to tackling this problem is for Europe to re-examine its current approach to immigration.

It is estimated that without significant policy changes in the EU, Europe's share of world output may decrease from its current 18 per cent to 10 per cent by 2050.[43] This trend is mirrored in Japan, whose share of world output could fall from 8 per cent to 4 per cent. This is in stark contrast to the USA where it is estimated its share of world output could rise from 23 per cent to 26 per cent over the same period.[44] This is attributed to the greater levels of immigration in the US, which brings more workers and increasing fertility rates, as immigrants tend to be young and of childbearing age.[45] This argument that Europe's demographic problem may be helped by immigration is also echoed by the British Venture Capitalist Association (BVCA) which sees at least part of the solution to Europe's demographic problems lying in an enlightened approach to economic migration. The BVCA also points to the 'influx of South American economic migrants' into the US, who will contribute to the expected buoyancy in the US economy.[46]

Asia

Changes in populations at a global level impact on companies and the opportunity for doing business in different countries and regions around the world. For example, significant reductions in fertility rates in Asia during the 1980s resulted in a sizeable reduction in levels of absolute poverty, which is defined as the percentage of a population surviving on less than a dollar a day.[47] The impact of lower fertility rates and the resultant slower population growth is that there is faster economic expansion along with a reduction in poverty.[48] Faster and improved economic expansion is logically due to smaller families having fewer expenses and being able to earn more, which in turn improves the opportunities people have to spend and save.[49] However, it is estimated that around 50 per cent of improvement in economic growth in developing countries arises from a one-off 'demographic window' which occurs when large numbers of working adults support fewer children and older people.[50] Hence, Asian countries will experience population downturns and South Korea, Taiwan and Japan are all experiencing a population downturn and an increasing number of older people in the population.

In Japan the population trend has moved to one of a shrinking population with the birth rate falling to 1.26 children per woman in 2005.[51] However, Japanese people have traditionally experienced longevity, in part due to their traditional diet which is low in saturated fat and high in fish. Therefore, by 2006 life expectancy in Japan was 82 years and 20 per cent of the population were aged over 65, but by 2050 this will have doubled to 40 per cent of the population. China's experience will be similar: today older people represent 7.5 per cent of the population and by 2050 this will have increased to 25 per cent of China's population.[52,53]

Africa

In Africa HIV and AIDS are having an impact on the population and life expectancy and this in turn impacts on economic development. HIV and Aids are forecast to make the populations of the 53 most affected countries 480 million fewer than expected by 2050. The total population of these countries is over 4 billion and the percentage reduction will be 8 per cent by 2050.[54] The impact of HIV and Aids is greatest in Africa, with the population of the 38 most affected countries being 16 million lower in 2000 than otherwise expected. This figure is expected to reach 320 million by 2050, which is 19 per cent or almost one-fifth reduction in the population.[55] In most of these countries high fertility rates will likely result in growing populations; however, Botswana, Lesotho, South Africa and Swaziland are forecast to have lower populations in 2050 than today.[56] This is supported by the projected life expectancy in these countries: in Botswana life expectancy in 2003 was 40 years, against the predicted 68 years without the impact of HIV and Aids; in South Africa, life expectancy was 48 years against the expected 67 years. In 2050, life expectancy in these countries is forecast to be only 56 years.[57]

In conclusion, overall during the next 50 years the world's population is expected to age faster than ever before (*see* Table 2.20, which shows median ages, i.e. the age that divides a population into two halves). During in the same period of time the world's population will grow at an annual rate of 1.2 per cent, giving a net increase of 77 million people every year, with 50 per cent of

Table 2.20 Median ages

	2000 – median age	2050 – median age
Least developed countries	18.1 years	27.1 years
Developing countries	24.1 years	35.7 years
Developed countries	37.3 years	42.5 years
Overall	26.4 years	36.8 years

Source: from UN Population Division Data from 'People, plagues and prosperity', *The Financial Times*, 27 February 2003 (Wolf, M.).

the increase arising from just six countries: India, 21 per cent; China, 12 per cent; Pakistan, 5 per cent; Bangladesh, Nigeria and the USA, 4 per cent each.[58]

Cross-cultural issues

Organisations have to consider political and economic circumstances in other countries when contemplating international business operations. Culture plays an important part in determining how international business is undertaken in different countries and regions of the world. The cross-cultural issues which commonly have to be understood and dealt with when doing business and working abroad are language, behaviour and culture shock.

Language

The most obvious illustration of culture is language. Investing in accurate language assistance when operating in another cultural context is a vital but largely underestimated consideration for organisations assessing the potential costs of international operations. The cost of getting it wrong is often much greater, but is often ignored in short-term decision making. It is only necessary to consider how many misunderstandings occur between native speakers of English who originate from the UK, the USA and Australia to begin to appreciate the difficulties of translating and interpreting other languages. For example, the British lecturer will invigilate an exam, while an American will proctor the exam. While British tourists on holiday in Australia will want to buy flip-flops to wear on the beach, they will be confused when the shop assistant offers a pair of 'thongs' instead.

The back catalogue of language mistranslations and the choice of unfortunate words for products is huge. Volkswagen's multi-passenger vehicle (MPV) suffered when it was introduced to the UK from being called Sharon, a name not associated with the profile of customer to whom it was expected to be sold. Proton, Malaysia's national car manufacturer, did its market research and decided not to introduce its basic model to the UK under its Malaysian name, as 'Saga' is the brand name of products targeted at senior citizens, to whom Proton did not wish to limit sales. The Vauxhall Nova, General Motors' 1980s mini hatchback, was branded Opel Corsa in the rest of Europe because 'Nova', which was meant to have connotations of new, actually translates as 'does not go' in many European languages. The Rolls-Royce Silver Mist had to be renamed for the German-speaking market because *Mist* in German is a colloquial word for excrement.

However, translation or the choice of words meaning other things in different languages is not the only skill required overseas. Interpreting – which is not translating the words, but rather saying the right thing in the target language – is a crucial skill. At a business meeting between British and Chinese businesspeople, when the British host says, 'We hope you have enjoyed your stay in the UK', a direct translation will sound arrogant and rude. Therefore, a skilled interpreter will replace this phrase with the customary 'We are sorry we did not look after you properly', and the courtesy requirements of both sides are fulfilled.

Behaviour

Other types of cross-cultural issues would relate to the consumption of alcohol in Muslim states and of beef in India, where the cow is sacred to Hindus (McDonald's had to substitute a Hindu-friendly version of the burger). How much physical contact or personal space people are customarily allowed is also problematic, as some cultures remain physically very distant from each other, while in others regular touching is commonplace. Again, whether or not physical contact is permissible between the sexes or between people of the same sex is an issue. For example, in many Middle and Far Eastern cultures, any touching between the sexes is unacceptable, while man-to-man handholding and bodily contact are quite normal. This understandably becomes a minefield to the foreign executive. In Japan, blowing one's nose in public is quite taboo, while in China the public expectoration of waste is unsurprising.

Therefore, the behaviour of foreign executives, the design of products and services, and the labelling, packaging and advertising of goods and services must all be subject to intense scrutiny.

Culture shock

The greater the distance between home and host culture, the more likely it is that the host culture will provide elements of everyday life that shock the individual travelling there. From language to food, from individual behaviour to collective customs, culture shock is a real and debilitating influence on the individual businessperson abroad. As it is based in experience, it is difficult to know how culture shock can be dealt with until it has been experienced, since there is still a huge difference between knowing something is going to happen and actually experiencing it. Nevertheless, organisations can invest in pre-departure orientation programmes, training people for overseas postings through visits, access to expatriates who have already lived in that culture and indigenous members of the population. It is essential to consider not only the expatriate executive, but also the relocation and comfort of family members as well.

Check your understanding

Do you understand the sociocultural factors that could impact on an international company like Coca-Cola?

Check your understanding by identifying and explaining sociocultural factors that could impact on Coca-Cola.

The technological elements of the external environment

Technology has an influence on all aspects of business from the very general to the very specific and as such is not split into the local, national and global levels (*see* Table 2.21). To provide a flavour of the impact of technology this section identifies and discusses the impact of technology on business.

The advent of technology has made it easier for people to communicate with each other, whether they operate in the political, economic, social or general business arena. Communications technology takes the form of mobile phones, fax machines, video conferencing, the internet and the world wide web and the key benefit is that staff are contactable all the time while at work and should be able to contact customers and clients without having to return to an office.

Video conferencing is becoming increasingly popular among businesses. Large companies such as British Petroleum (BP) have been using video conferencing since 1983 and have in-house studios in global locations. The greatest benefits of video conferencing are conferred when people in two or more places in different parts of the world use it. SmithKline Beecham has over 30 video conferencing studios worldwide and is able to carry out video conference meetings (see Table 2.22). It is likely that the increased threat of international

Table 2.21 The technological external environment: communications technology

	Political	Economic	Sociocultural	Technological
Local				• mobile phones and faxes • video conferencing • internet and world wide web • manufacturing technology
National				
Global				

Table 2.22 Benefits of video conferencing

• Less time spent travelling to and from meetings, therefore reducing the cost and stress of travelling.
• More people can attend meetings and be called into the meeting at relatively short notice if their knowledge and expertise are required.
• Eye contact and body language can be observed, a clear advantage over phone conferencing.
• Enhancement of teamworking and communication among teams whose work is spread out across the globe.

terrorism and the spread of illnesses such as Avian flu will result in an increased use of video conferencing by organisations seeking to reduce the risks to which their workforce may be exposed.

The internet is an array of interconnected networks to which millions of computers around the world are attached. There are a large number of internet sites that hold information: for example, company sites or the *Financial Times* site. The world wide web (WWW) allows linking of internet sites and research and retrieval tools, hence the WWW and the internet are often seen as one and the same. Search engines such as Google allow searches to be carried out very easily and it is equally easy to repeat and refine any searches that have previously been carried out.[59]

Companies can take up a presence on the internet by setting up a website. This will give a company 24 hours a day, 365 days a year, worldwide exposure on the internet. Companies are able to use their internet presence to advertise their products and services and collect addresses and details from potential customers who visit the site, with a view to e-mailing or posting further information. The internet is equally accessible by both large and small companies, although large companies may have more money to spend on designing a site.

A company that has set up an internet site also has to consider how it is going to persuade people to visit the site. Many companies advertise in the more traditional media, such as the television and press, and include their internet address in the advertisement. An additional method is to be included on search engines so that when users type in a keyword such as books or beer the relevant internet sites are listed. Companies are also able to advertise on search engines by paying to have their logo appear, although costs are high.[60]

Banking and financial services is a good example of an industry where service delivery has been continually altered and modernised since the late 1970s. In banking the most obvious application of technology has occurred in the development of the cashpoint machine. The other main technological development has been in the use of central computer-based systems to hold customer details and account records. These applications of computer technology allow any customer with a passbook or cashpoint card to withdraw money from their bank or building society account anywhere in the country and even overseas. This greater reliance on technology to perform at least some routine tasks has been part of the reason that both banks and building societies have been able to use and train their staff to sell a much wider range of financial services. The development of new ways of delivering banking and financial services has continued to develop and today internet banking is common.

Check your understanding

Do you understand the technological factors that could impact on vacuum manufacturer Dyson, which has moved production from the UK to the Far East?

Check your understanding by identifying and explaining technological factors that could impact on Dyson.

Summary

This chapter examined the composition of the external environment at the local, national and global levels. The following summary covers all aspects of this chapter.

1 The local political environment includes local government and national government operating at a local level and local business associations such as Chambers of Commerce. Local government is responsible for regulating private-sector business, for example via trading standards, and for providing a range of public services, e.g. refuse collection and schools. Chambers of Commerce offer their business members access to training and business information on, for example, exporting goods.

2 The national political environment includes national government for the whole UK, Scotland and Wales and national bodies such as the CBI and trade unions. National governments pass legislation, which may impact on business, e.g. health and safety legislation. National governments are responsible for collecting taxation and deciding how it is to be allocated and spent to provide public-sector services such as healthcare and education. Employers' bodies like the CBI and employee organisations such as trade unions (e.g. UNISON) seek to get the best deal for their members in the workplace environment and this may involve lobbying government to pass particular legislation or make a particular decision.

3 The global political environment includes alliances and agreements, such as the special relationship between the UK and the US. Other global factors include international bodies such as the Commonwealth and NATO, which, respectively, play a role in the world economy and the establishment of peace, which is needed to allow economies to flourish.

4 The local economic environment of an organisation will be shaped by its relationship with its bank, which is usually of local significance. The state of the local economy in which a business is located will influence the ease with which labour can be recruited and retained.

5 The national economic environment includes the Bank of England and the stock market. The Bank of England sets the base interest rate, which in turn determines the level of interest businesses and individuals pay on loans, which impacts on the amount of money consumers and industry have to spend, which clearly determines the level of economic activity experienced.

6 The global economic environment includes trading blocs such as the EU and NAFTA, world money markets and the WTO. Trading blocs confer free movement of goods between member states and significant tax concessions on goods imported from member states. For example, goods move freely between EU countries such as France, Germany and the UK. The WTO handles trade negotiations between countries, monitors trade policies and deals with trade disputes.

7 The local sociocultural environment includes the local community and social capital. An organisation's interactions with its local community may impact on the organisation's level of work, particularly if the organisation is, for example, a school. Social capital is defined as community spirit and neighbourliness, and this can either draw communities together or drive them apart.

8 The national sociocultural external environment includes demographic change and social change. Demographic changes are changes in the age and structure of a population. In the UK the key changes centre on longevity, immigration and birth rates. Social change includes development and alterations in the way society behaves. This can include changes to income levels, family and **household structure**.

9 The global sociocultural external environment encompasses change in populations and their impact at a global level on the opportunities for trade and economic development. Such impacts include fertility rates, HIV/Aids, and age of populations, which is higher in the developed world than in the developing world. Also at a global level, the impact of cross-cultural issues, such as language, behaviour and culture shock, can be significant for companies.

10 The impact of technology on organisations occurs at all levels. Improved communications technology allows easier and faster communication between organisations, their employees, customers and potential customers. The use of the internet and the world wide web can allow customers access to an organisation and the products and services it offers, all day, every day.

Chapter objectives and the exit case study

While reading this chapter and engaging in the activities, you should have learned how to apply theory and models and analyse situations. The exit case study and the questions which follow will provide an opportunity to assess how well you have met the relevant chapter objectives relating to specific material covered in the chapter.

Chapter objective	Check you have achieved this by
1 Analyse the external environment of an organisation by using PEST and LoNGPEST, drawing conclusions from the analysis.	answering case study questions 1, 2 and 4.
2 Select the most appropriate data and information sources for undertaking analysis of an organisation's external environment.	answering case study questions 3 and 4.

EXIT CASE STUDY 2.2

Tui slashes number of holiday packages

FT

by Pan Kwan Yuk

Tui Travel has slashed the number of holidays it is offering next summer by 16 per cent as Britons, who have so far been reluctant to forgo their break in the sun, put their suitcases into storage. The group, formed last year from the merger of Germany's Tui and the UK's First Choice, said it was reducing its capacity by 16 per cent from an earlier plan of 9 per cent after booking volumes fell 17 per cent behind the level seen this time last year. The capacity reduction mirrors cuts at rival Thomas Cook, which at the end of September said it would reduce the number of summer holidays for 2009 by 6 per cent after bookings fell by 4 per cent. Peter Long, Tui chief executive, said a worsening economic outlook, further rises in UK unemployment and sustained weakness in the pound against the euro had all contributed to the weaker booking volume.

However, he was careful to stress that the reduction in capacity has helped mitigate this and average selling prices are up 10 per cent on the previous year. 'Unlike retailers, we can constantly tune the level of stock and adapt the number of holidays on sale [to maintain revenue and profit margins],' he said. The company also said it had seen a 'marginal' rise in the cancellations rate, from 6.6 per cent last year to 7.7 per cent. 'The increase is hardly surprising . . . but it is not an alarming figure . . . it is not an area of concern,' he said. Instead, Mr Long believes the collapse of small rival XL in September and the recent wave of consolidation in the sector has left the business well-placed to weather the downturn.

'I can't stand up and say we are just ignoring what is going on in the world, but we have the capability to adapt and trade through,' he said. 'What our customers are saying to us is that their annual summer holiday is important. With everything that is going on it is perhaps even more important that they take that break.' He added that the demise of XL, which left many passengers stranded in their holiday destinations, should lead to a resurgence in package holiday bookings. 'People don't want to take a risk when it comes to their holidays,' he said.

Mr Long's comments came as Tui reported a 43 per cent rise in underlying annual profits and increased its synergy targets as it made better-than-expected progress on integration. The group said it was now targeting annual merger synergy targets of £175m by 2010, an increase of £25m on its previous target. Of that, £15m will come from UK integration and £10m from the overseas businesses.

For the 12 months to September 30, the group swung from a pre-tax profit of £18.4m to a loss of £266.6m, largely as a result of costs related to the merger with First Choice. Stripping out the one-off costs, pre-tax profit rose from £222.8m to £319.7m. Total revenue increased by 9 per cent to £13.9bn and the group is paying a year-end dividend of 6.9p a share, making a total payment for the year of 9.7p, up 16 per cent. This is in contrast to Holidaybreak, the specialist travel company, which on Thursday said it was sharply cutting its final dividend in light of uncertain market conditions. Shares in Holidaybreak fell 4p, or 2.4 per cent, to 163p in afternoon trading, while Tui shares gained 2½p, or 1.25 per cent, to 202½p.

Source: from 'Tui shashes number of holiday packages', *The Financial Times*, 27 November 2008 (Yuk, P.K.).

Exit case study questions

1 Perform a LoNGPEST analysis of the external environment faced by the holiday industry.

2 Consider your answer to question 1 and comment on how the following types of holidays are affected by the external environment: domestic holidays in the UK; European holidays; or long-haul destinations.

3 Identify further sources of information which would enhance and improve your analysis in question 1.

4 Discuss the advantages and disadvantages of undertaking analysis of the external environment of an organisation or industry.

Short-answer questions

1 Name three influences from the political external environment, one each from the local, national and global levels.

2 Name three influences from the economic external environment, one each from the local, national and global levels.

3 Name three influences from the sociocultural external environment, one each from the local, national and global levels.

4 Explain why the influence of technology on an organisation is considered differently from the influence of economic, political and sociocultural factors.

5 Define autocracy.

6 Describe a democracy.

7 List the characteristics of a free market.

8 List the characteristics of a planned economy.

9 List the characteristics of a mixed economy.

10 Explain the function of Chambers of Commerce in the business community.

11 Summarise the role of the IOD and CBI in business.

12 Explain the role of trade unions.

13 Explain the role of NATO in the external environment.

14 Describe the role of the Commonwealth in the external environment.

15 Illustrate the role of the Bank of England in the economy of the UK.

16 Explain the role of the London stock market in the economy of the UK.

17 Indicate the role of the WTO in global trade.

18 Explain the role of NAFTA in North American trade.

19 Explain the role of ASEAN.

20 Explain the role of EFTA and how it differs from the EU.

21 Indicate by example what you understand alliances and agreements to be.

22 Define 'social capital'.

23 What is the main difference in public spending on pensions in the UK and other European countries?

24 Name the six countries with the fastest growing population over the next 50 years.

25 Why, by 2003, had life expectancy fallen in South Africa and Botswana to just 48 years and 40 years respectively?

Chapter objectives and assignment questions

While reading this chapter and engaging in the activities, you should have learned how to apply theory and models and analyse situations. This means you should be able to meet the chapter objectives outlined at the beginning of the chapter. The table below shows which chapter objectives can be tested by the different questions.

Chapter objective	Check you have achieved this by
1 Analyse the external environment of an organisation by using PEST and LoNGPEST, drawing conclusions from the analysis.	answering assignment questions 1 and 3.
2 Select the most appropriate data and information sources for undertaking analysis of an organisation's external environment.	answering assignment questions 1, 2 and 3.
3 Discuss the links between economic and political factors and how this shapes external environments.	answering assignment questions 1 and 3.

Assignment questions

1 Choose *one* of the following organisations: Institute of Directors (IOD), Confederation of British Industry (CBI) or Trades Union Congress (TUC). Identify and collect appropriate information and write an essay of 2000 words that demonstrates and evaluates the influence of your chosen organisation on the individual employee, the workplace and the economy. Comment on the sources of information used.

2 Select two organisations from different industries or sectors and collect relevant and appropriate information. Compare and contrast the impact of technology on your chosen organisations over the past three years and present your findings in a 2000-word report. Comment on the sources of information used.

3 Identify and collect appropriate information and write an essay of 2000 words comparing and contrasting the roles of ASEAN and NAFTA in their home geographic regions. Comment on the sources of information used.

WEBLINKS available at www.pearsoned.co.uk/capon

The websites listed here are for international bodies that impact on the external environment of organisations. Websites for UK-based bodies are listed at the end of Chapter 1.

- The following website is for the European Union:
  http://www.europa.eu.int/
- The website for the European Free Trade Area is shown below:
  http://www.efta.int/

- The website of the European Bank for Reconstruction and Development is shown below: **http://www.ebrd.org/**
- The following website is for the Council of Baltic Sea States: **http://www.cbss.st**
- The following website is for the North America Free Trade Association: **http://www.nafta-sec-alena.org/**
- The following website is for the Association of South East Asian Nations: **http://www.asean.org**
- The website for the Commonwealth is shown below: **http://www.thecommonwealth.org/**
- The website for NATO is shown below: **http://www.nato.int/**
- The website of the World Trade Organisation is shown below: **http://www.wto.org/**
- The website of the World Bank Group is shown below: **http://www.worldbank.org/**
- The following website is for the International Monetary Fund: **http://www.imf.org/**
- The website of the Organisation for Economic Cooperation and Development is shown below: **http://www.oecd.org/**
- The Treasury website is shown below: **http://www.hm-treasury.gov.uk**

FURTHER READING

These book chapters all look at the external environments faced by organisations.

- Johnson, G, Scholes, K and Whittington, R (2008) *Exploring Corporate Strategy*, 8th edn, Chapter 2, Harlow: Financial Times Prentice Hall.
- Lynch, R (2006) *Corporate Strategy*, 4th edn, Chapter 3, Harlow: Financial Times Prentice Hall.
- Palmer, A and Hartley, B (2006) *The Business Environment*, 5th edn, Chapters 2, 3, 4 and 5, Maidenhead: McGraw Hill.
- Thompson, J L and Martin, F (2005) *Strategic Management: Awareness, Analysis and Change*, 5th edn, Chapter 4, London: Thomson Learning.
- Worthington, I and Brittion, C (2006) *The Business Environment*, 5th edn, Chapters 3, 4, 5 and 16, Harlow: Financial Times Prentice Hall.

REFERENCES

1 http://www.businesslink.org
2 http://www.bbc.co.uk/politics97/analysis/rozenberg2.shtml
3 Ibid.
4 Ibid.
5 Ibid.
6 Manning, A (1997) 'If it's good enough for everyone else, it's good enough for us', *Independent on Sunday*, 11 May.

7 http://europa.eu/abc/panorama/index_en.htm
8 Barber, L (1997) 'No turning back from brave new Europe', *Financial Times*, 17 July.
9 http://www.cbss.st/history/
10 BBC News (2008) 'Kosovo MPs proclaim independence', 17 February.
11 BBC News (2008) 'Bush salutes Kosovo's independence', 19 February.
12 BBC News (2008) 'UN to transfer powers in Kosovo', 12 June.
13 Ejime, P (1996) Panafrican News Agency (PANA), 'Reconciling Nigeria with the Commonwealth', 23 June.
14 Ejime, P (1997) Panafrican News Agency (PANA), 'Nigeria reassessing Commonwealth membership', 21 August.
15 http://www.thecommonwealth.org/Templates/YearbookHomeInternal.asp?NodeID=138917
16 http://www.thecommonwealth.org/
17 http://www.nato.int/welcome/home.htm
18 *Daily Telegraph*, 28 February 1998.
19 http://www.efta.int/content/about-efta/member-states
20 http://www.efta.int/content/free-trade/fta-countries
21 http://www.oecd.org/pages/0,3417,en_36734052_36734103_1_1_1_1_1,00.html
22 http://www.nafta-sec-alena.org/DefaultSite/index_e.aspx?ArticleID=282
23 Bardacke, T (1997) 'Cambodia rebuffed by Asean', *Financial Times*, 11 July.
24 http://www.aseansec.org/64.htm
25 http://www.wto.org/english/thewto_e/whatis_e/whatis_e.htm
26 Jonquieres, G de and Walker, T (1997) 'New dawn in the east', *Financial Times*, 3 March.
27 http://www.statistics.gov.uk/CCI/nugget.asp?ID=314
28 BBC News (2007) 'Population at least 75m by 2051', 10 October.
29 BBC News (2007) 'Mothers in 30s boost population', 11 December.
30 Ibid.
31 BBC News (2008) 'Minorities set to be US majority', 14 August.
32 Brown, K (2002) 'A lost generation leaves Britain older and calmer', *Financial Times*, 5 October.
33 BBC News 11 December 2007, op. cit.
34 BBC News 11 December 2007, op. cit.
35 Frean, A (2008) 'Return home of the "boomerang kids" stretches parents to limit', *The Times*, 7 February.
36 Batty, D (2007) 'Divorce total lowest for 29 years', *Guardian*, 30 August.
37 http://www.euromonitor.com/One_person_households_Opportunities_for_consumer_goods_companies
38 BBC News (2008) 'One parent families on the rise', 11 April.
39 Jury, L (1998) 'Britions remain true to family values', *Independent*, 7 August.
40 http://www.statistics.gov.uk/cci/nugget.asp?id=332
41 http://www.poverty.org.uk/02/index.shtml
42 Parker, G (2002) 'Brussels warns of ageing population crisis', *Financial Times*, 11 December.
43 Ibid.
44 Ibid.
45 Ibid.
46 Gimbel, F (2003) 'BVCA to call for immigration increase', *Financial Times*, 23 March.
47 Williams, F (2002) 'UN finds link between fertility rate and wealth', *Financial Times*, 3 December.
48 Ibid.
49 Ibid.
50 Ibid.
51 BBC News (2007) 'Japan eyes demographic time bomb', 19 November.
52 BBC News (2007) 'Ageing threatens China's economy', 18 December.
53 BBC News (2006) 'China braced for pensioner boom', 16 October.

54 Wolf, M (2003) 'People, plagues and prosperity', *Financial Times*, 26 February.
55 Ibid.
56 Ibid.
57 Ibid.
58 Ibid.
59 Shankar, B and Sharda, R (1997) 'Obtaining business intelligence on the Internet', *Long Range Planning*, 30(1), February.
60 Bird, J (1996) 'Untangling the web', *Management Today*, March.

The working of competitive markets

Business issues covered in this chapter

- How do markets operate?
- How are market prices determined and when are they likely to rise or fall?
- Under what circumstances do firms have to accept a price given by the market rather than being able to set the price themselves?
- What are the influences on consumer demand?
- What factors determine the amount of supply coming on to the market?
- How do markets respond to changes in demand or supply?

4.1 BUSINESS IN A COMPETITIVE MARKET

If a firm wants to increase its profits, should it raise its prices, or should it lower them? Should it increase its output, or should it reduce it? Should it modify its product, or should it keep the product unchanged? The answer to these and many other questions is that it depends on the market in which the firm operates. If the market is buoyant, it may well be a good idea for the firm to increase its output in anticipation of greater sales. It may also be a good idea to raise the price of its product in the belief that consumers will be willing to pay more. If, however, the market is declining, the firm may well decide to reduce output, or cut prices, or diversify across into an alternative product.

The firm is thus greatly affected by its market environment, an environment that is often outside the firm's control and subject to frequent changes. For many firms, prices are determined not by them, but by the market. Even where they do have some influence over prices, the influence is only slight. They may be able to put prices up a small amount, but if they raise them too much, they will find that they lose sales to their rivals.

The market dominates a firm's activities. The more competitive the market, the greater this domination becomes. In the extreme case, the firm may have no power at all to change its price: it is what we call a ***price taker***. It has to accept the market price as given. If the firm attempts to raise the price above the market price, it will simply be unable to sell its product: it will lose all its sales to its competitors. Take the case of farmers selling wheat. They have to accept the price as dictated by the market. If individually they try to sell above the market price, no one will buy.

In competitive markets, consumers too are price takers. When we go into shops we have no control over prices. We have to accept the price as given. For example, when you get to the supermarket checkout, you cannot start haggling with the checkout operator over the price of a can of beans or a tub of margarine.

So how does a competitive market work? For simplicity we will examine the case of a ***perfectly competitive market***. This is where both producers and consumers are too numerous to have any control over prices whatsoever: a situation where everyone is a price taker.

Clearly, in other markets, firms will have some discretion over the prices they charge. For example, a manufacturing company such as Ford will have some discretion over the prices it charges for its Fiestas or Mondeos. In such cases the firm has some 'market power'. (We will examine different degrees of market power in Chapters 11 and 12.)

The price mechanism

In a ***free market*** individuals are free to make their own economic decisions. Consumers are free to decide what to buy with their incomes: free to make demand decisions. Firms are free to choose what to sell and what production methods to use: free to make supply decisions. The resulting demand and supply decisions of consumers and firms are transmitted to each other through their effect on *prices*: through the ***price mechanism***.

The price mechanism works as follows. Prices respond to *shortages* and *surpluses*. Shortages cause prices to rise. Surpluses cause prices to fall.

If consumers decide they want more of a good (or if producers decide to cut back supply), demand will exceed supply. The resulting *shortage* will cause *the price of the good to rise*. This will act as an incentive to producers to supply more, since production will now be more profitable. At the same time, it will discourage consumers from buying so much. *The price will continue rising until the shortage has thereby been eliminated.*

If, on the other hand, consumers decide they want less of a good (or if producers decide to produce more), supply will exceed demand. The resulting *surplus* will cause *the price of the good to fall*. This will act as a disincentive to producers, who will supply less, since production will now be less profitable. It will encourage consumers to buy more. *The price will continue falling until the surplus has thereby been eliminated.*

This price, where demand equals supply, is called the ***equilibrium price***. By ***equilibrium*** we mean a point of balance or a point of rest: in other words, a point towards which there is a tendency to move.

The same analysis can be applied to labour markets (and those for other factors of production), except that here the demand and supply roles are reversed. Firms are the demanders of labour. Households are the suppliers. If the demand for a particular type of labour exceeded its supply, the resulting shortage would drive up the wage rate (i.e. the price of labour), thus reducing firms' demand for that type of labour and encouraging more workers to take up that type of job. Wages would continue rising until demand equalled supply: until the shortage was eliminated.

Likewise if there were a surplus of a particular type of labour, the wage would fall until demand equalled supply. As with price, the wage rate where the demand for labour equals the supply is known as the *equilibrium* wage rate.

The response of demand and supply to changes in price illustrates a very important feature of how economies work.

KEY IDEA 9

People respond to incentives. **It is important, therefore, that incentives are appropriate and have the desired effect.**

The effect of changes in demand and supply

How will the price mechanism respond to changes in consumer demand or producer supply? After all, the pattern of consumer demand changes over time. For example, people may decide they want more downloadable music and fewer CDs. Likewise the pattern of supply also changes. For example, changes in technology may allow the mass production of microchips at lower cost, while the production of hand-built furniture becomes relatively expensive.

In all cases of changes in demand and supply, the resulting changes in *price* act as both *signals* and *incentives*.

Definitions

Price taker A person or firm with no power to be able to influence the market price.

Perfectly competitive market (preliminary definition) A market in which all producers and consumers of the product are price takers. There are other features of a perfectly competitive market; these are examined in Chapter 11.

Free market One in which there is an absence of government intervention. Individual producers and consumers are free to make their own economic decisions.

The price mechanism The system in a market economy whereby changes in price in response to changes in demand and supply have the effect of making demand equal to supply.

Equilibrium price The price where the quantity demanded equals the quantity supplied: the price where there is no shortage or surplus.

Equilibrium A position of balance. A position from which there is no inherent tendency to move away from current prices and quantities.

A change in demand

KI 9 p47

A rise in demand is signalled by a rise in price. This then acts as an incentive for firms to produce more of the good: the quantity supplied rises. Firms divert resources from goods with lower prices relative to costs (and hence lower profits) to those goods that are more profitable.

A fall in demand is signalled by a fall in price. This then acts as an incentive for firms to produce less: such goods are now less profitable to produce.

A change in supply

A rise in supply is signalled by a fall in price. This then acts as an incentive for consumers to buy more: the quantity demanded rises. A fall in supply is signalled by a rise in price. This then acts as an incentive for consumers to buy less: the quantity demanded falls.

> **KEY IDEA 10**
> ***Changes in demand or supply cause markets to adjust.*** **Whenever such changes occur, the resulting 'disequilibrium' will bring an automatic change in prices, thereby restoring equilibrium (i.e. a balance of demand and supply).**

The interdependence of markets

The interdependence of goods and factor markets

KI 9 p47

A rise in demand for a good will raise its price and profitability. Firms will respond by supplying more. But to do this they will require more inputs. Thus the demand for the inputs will rise, which, in turn, will raise the price of the inputs. The suppliers of inputs will respond to this incentive by supplying more. This can be summarised as follows:

Goods market

- Demand for the good rises.
- This creates a shortage.
- This causes the price of the good to rise.
- This eliminates the shortage by choking off some of the demand and encouraging firms to produce more.

Factor market

- The increased supply of the good causes an increase in the demand for factors of production (i.e. inputs) used in making it.
- This causes a shortage of those inputs.
- This causes their prices to rise.
- This eliminates their shortage by choking off some of the demand and encouraging the suppliers of inputs to supply more.

Goods markets thus affect factor markets. Figure 4.1 summarises this sequence of events. (It is common in economics to summarise an argument like this by using symbols.)

KI 10 p48

Interdependence exists in the other direction too: factor markets affect goods markets. For example, the discovery of raw materials will lower their price. This will lower the costs of production of firms using these raw materials and increase the supply of the finished goods. The resulting surplus will lower the price of the good, which, in turn, will encourage consumers to buy more.

The interdependence of different goods markets

KI 10 p48

A rise in the price of one good will encourage consumers to buy alternatives. This will drive up the price of alternatives. This in turn will encourage producers to supply more of the alternatives.

Let us now turn to examine each side of the market – demand and supply – in more detail.

Figure 4.1 The price mechanism: the effect of a rise in demand

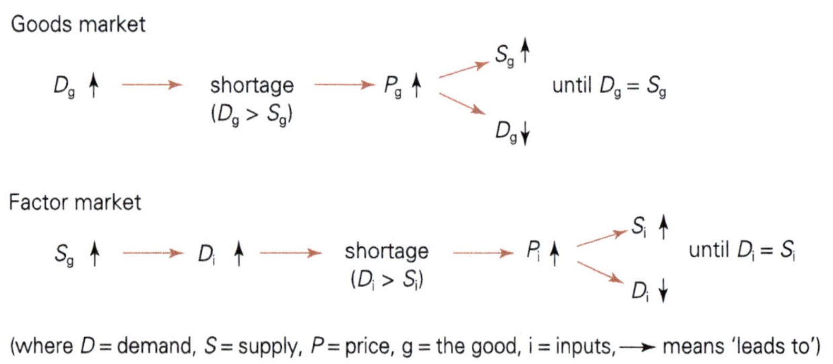

4.2 DEMAND

The relationship between demand and price

The headlines announce, 'Major crop failures in Brazil and East Africa: coffee prices soar.' Shortly afterwards you find that coffee prices have doubled in the shops. What do you do? Presumably you will cut back on the amount of coffee you drink. Perhaps you will reduce it from, say, six cups per day to two. Perhaps you will give up drinking coffee altogether.

This is simply an illustration of the general relationship between price and consumption: *when the price of a good rises, the quantity demanded will fall*. This relationship is known as the ***law of demand***. There are two reasons for this law:

- People will feel poorer. They will not be able to afford to buy so much of the good with their money. The purchasing power of their income (their *real income*) has fallen. This is called the ***income effect*** of a price rise.
- The good will now be dearer relative to other goods. People will thus switch to alternative or 'substitute' goods. This is called the ***substitution effect*** of a price rise.

Similarly, when the price of a good falls, the quantity demanded will rise. People can afford to buy more (the income effect), and they will switch away from consuming alternative goods (the substitution effect).

Therefore, returning to our example of the increase in the price of coffee, we will not be able to afford to buy as much as before, and we will probably drink more tea, cocoa, fruit juices or even water instead.

A word of warning: be careful about the meaning of the words ***quantity demanded***. They refer to the amount consumers are willing and able to purchase at a given price over a given time period (for example, a week, or a month, or a year). They do *not* refer to what people would simply *like* to consume. You might like to own a luxury yacht, but your demand for luxury yachts will almost certainly be zero.

The demand curve

Consider the hypothetical data in Table 4.1. The table shows how many kilos of potatoes per month would be purchased at various prices.

Columns (2) and (3) show the ***demand schedules*** for two individuals, Tracey and Darren. Column (4), by contrast, shows the total ***market demand schedule***. This is the total demand by all consumers. To obtain the market demand schedule for potatoes, we simply add up the quantities demanded at each price by *all* consumers: i.e. Tracey, Darren and everyone else who demands potatoes. Notice that we are talking about demand *over a period of time* (not at a *point* in time). Thus we would talk about daily demand or weekly demand or annual demand or whatever.

Table 4.1 The demand for potatoes (monthly)

	Price (pence per kg) (1)	Tracey's demand (kg) (2)	Darren's demand (kg) (3)	Total market demand (tonnes: 000s) (4)
A	20	28	16	700
B	40	15	11	500
C	60	5	9	350
D	80	1	7	200
E	100	0	6	100

Definitions

The law of demand The quantity of a good demanded per period of time will fall as the price rises and rise as the price falls, other things being equal (*ceteris paribus*).

Income effect The effect of a change in price on quantity demanded arising from the consumer becoming better or worse off as a result of the price change.

Substitution effect The effect of a change in price on quantity demanded arising from the consumer switching to or from alternative (substitute) products.

Quantity demanded The amount of a good that a consumer is willing and able to buy at a given price over a given period of time.

Demand schedule for an individual A table showing the different quantities of a good that a person is willing and able to buy at various prices over a given period of time.

Market demand schedule A table showing the different total quantities of a good that consumers are willing and able to buy at various prices over a given period of time.

Figure 4.2 Market demand curve for potatoes (monthly)

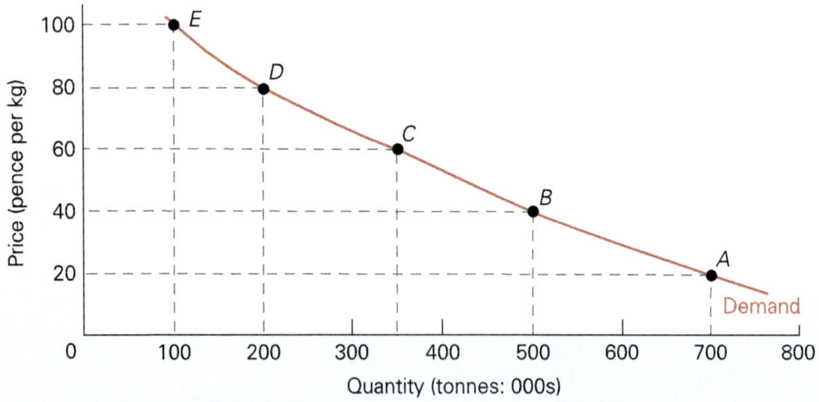

The demand schedule can be represented graphically as a ***demand curve***. Figure 4.2 shows the market demand curve for potatoes corresponding to the schedule in Table 4.1. The price of potatoes is plotted on the vertical axis. The quantity demanded is plotted on the horizontal axis.

Point *E* shows that at a price of 100p per kilo, 100 000 tonnes of potatoes are demanded each month. When the price falls to 80p we move down the curve to point *D*. This shows that the quantity demanded has now risen to 200 000 tonnes per month. Similarly, if the price falls to 60p, we move down the curve again to point *C*: 350 000 tonnes are now demanded. The five points on the graph (*A–E*) correspond to the figures in columns (1) and (4) of Table 4.1. The graph also enables us to read off the likely quantities demanded at prices other than those in the table.

A demand curve could also be drawn for an individual consumer. Like market demand curves, individuals' demand curves generally slope downward from left to right (they have negative slope): the lower the price of a product, the more is a person likely to buy.

Two points should be noted at this stage:

- In textbooks, demand curves (and other curves too) are only occasionally used to plot specific data. More frequently they are used to illustrate general theoretical arguments. In such cases the axes will simply be price and quantity, with the units unspecified.
- The term 'curve' is used even when the graph is a straight line! In fact, when using demand curves to illustrate arguments we frequently draw them as straight lines – it's easier.

Definition

Demand curve A graph showing the relationship between the price of a good and the quantity of the good demanded over a given time period. Price is measured on the vertical axis; quantity demanded is measured on the horizontal axis. A demand curve can be for an individual consumer or a group of consumers, or more usually for the whole market.

Other determinants of demand

Price is not the only factor that determines how much of a good people will buy. Demand is also affected by the following.

Tastes. The more desirable people find the good, the more they will demand. Tastes are affected by factor such as advertising, fashion, observations of other consumers, considerations of health and experiences from consuming the good on previous occasions.

The number and price of substitute goods (i.e. competitive goods). The higher the price of ***substitute goods***, the higher will be the demand for this good as people switch from the substitutes. For example, the demand for coffee will depend on the price of tea. If tea goes up in price, the demand for coffee will rise.

The number and price of complementary goods. ***Complementary goods*** are those that are consumed together: cars and petrol, shoes and polish, bread and butter. The higher the price of complementary goods, the fewer of them will be bought and hence the less the demand for this good. For example, the demand for compact discs will depend on the price of CD players. If the price of CD players goes up, so that fewer are bought, the demand for CDs will fall.

Income. As people's incomes rise, their demand for most goods will rise. Such goods are called ***normal goods***. There are exceptions to this general rule, however. As people get richer, they spend less on ***inferior goods***, such as cheap margarine, and switch to better-quality goods.

Distribution of income. If, for example, national income were redistributed from the poor to the rich, the demand for luxury goods would rise. At the same time, as the poor got poorer, they might have to turn to buying inferior goods, whose demand would thus rise too.

KI 13 p 71

Expectations of future price changes. If people think that prices are going to rise in the future, they are likely to buy more now before the price does go up.

Pause for thought

1. *By referring to each of these six determinants of demand, consider what factors would cause a rise in the demand for butter.*
2. *Do all these six determinants of demand affect both an individual's demand and the market demand for a product?*

Figure 4.3 An increase in demand

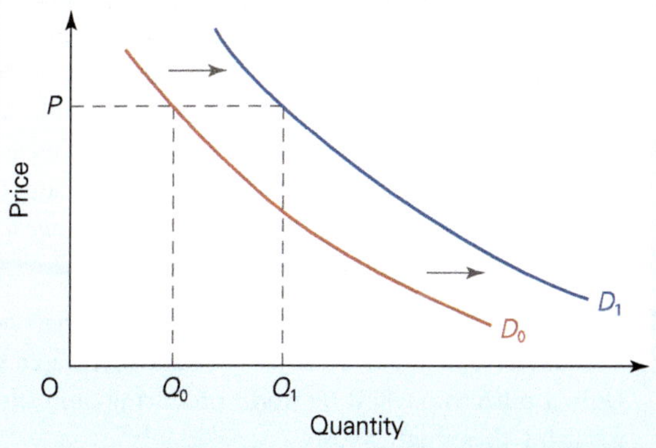

Movements along and shifts in the demand curve

A demand curve is constructed on the assumption that 'other things remain equal' (*ceteris paribus*). In other words, it is assumed that none of the determinants of demand, other than price, changes. The effect of a change in price is then simply illustrated by a movement along the demand curve: for example, from point *B* to point *D* in Figure 4.2 when price rises from 40p to 80p per kilo.

What happens, then, when one of these other determinants does change? The answer is that we have to construct a whole new demand curve: the curve shifts. If a change in one of the other determinants causes demand to rise – say, income rises – the whole curve will shift to the right. This shows that at each price more will be demanded than before. Thus in Figure 4.3 at a price of *P*, a quantity of Q_0 was originally demanded. But now, after the increase in demand, Q_1 is demanded. (Note that D_1 is not necessarily parallel to D_0.)

If a change in a determinant other than price causes demand to fall, the whole curve will shift to the left.

To distinguish between shifts in and movements along demand curves, it is usual to distinguish between a change in *demand* and a change in the *quantity demanded*. A shift in demand is referred to as a ***change in demand***, whereas a movement along the demand curve as a result of a change in price is referred to as a ***change in the quantity demanded***.

Pause for thought

By referring to the determinants of demand, consider what factors would cause a rightward shift in the demand for family cars.

Definitions

Substitute goods A pair of goods which are considered by consumers to be alternatives to each other. As the price of one goes up, the demand for the other rises.

Complementary goods A pair of goods consumed together. As the price of one goes up, the demand for both goods will fall.

Normal goods Goods whose demand rises as people's incomes rise.

Inferior goods Goods whose demand falls as people's incomes rise.

Change in demand The term used for a shift in the demand curve. It occurs when a determinant of demand *other* than price changes.

Change in the quantity demanded The term used for a movement along the demand curve to a new point. It occurs when there is a change in price.

4.3 SUPPLY

Supply and price

Imagine you are a farmer deciding what to do with your land. Part of your land is in a fertile valley. Part is on a hillside where the soil is poor. Perhaps, then, you will consider growing vegetables in the valley and keeping sheep on the hillside.

Your decision will depend to a large extent on the price that various vegetables will fetch in the market, and likewise the price you can expect to get from sheep and wool. As far as the valley is concerned, you will plant the vegetables that give the best return. If, for example, the price of potatoes is high, you will probably use a lot of the valley for growing potatoes. If the price gets higher, you may well use the whole of the valley, perhaps being prepared to run the risk of potato disease. If the price is very high indeed, you may even consider growing potatoes on the hillside, even though the yield per acre is much lower there. In other words, the higher the price of a particular crop, the more you are likely to grow in preference to other crops.

This illustrates the general relationship between supply and price: *when the price of a good rises, the quantity supplied will also rise*. There are three reasons for this:

- As firms supply more, they are likely to find that, beyond a certain level of output, costs rise more and more rapidly. Only if price rises will it be worth producing more and incurring these higher costs.

  In the case of the farm we have just considered, once potatoes have to be grown on the hillside, the costs of producing them will increase. Also if the land has to be used more intensively, say by the use of more and more fertilisers, again the cost of producing extra potatoes is likely to rise quite rapidly. It is the same for manufacturers. Beyond a certain level of output, costs are likely to rise rapidly as workers have to be paid overtime and as machines approach their full capacity. If higher output involves higher costs of production, producers will need to get a higher price if they are to be persuaded to produce extra output.
- The higher the price of the good, the more profitable it becomes to produce. Firms will thus be encouraged to produce more of it by switching from producing less profitable goods.
- Given time, if the price of a good remains high, new producers will be encouraged to set up in production. Total market supply thus rises.

The first two determinants affect supply in the short run. The third affects supply in the long run. (We distinguish between short-run and long-run supply later, in section 5.4.)

The supply curve

The amount that producers would like to supply at various prices can be shown in a ***supply schedule***. Table 4.2 shows a monthly supply schedule for potatoes, both for an individual farmer (farmer X) and for all farmers together (the whole market).

The supply schedule can be represented graphically as a ***supply curve***. A supply curve may be an individual firm's supply curve or a market supply curve (i.e. that of the whole industry).

Figure 4.4 shows the *market* supply curve of potatoes. As with demand curves, price is plotted on the vertical axis and quantity on the horizontal axis. Each of the points *a*–*e*

Definitions

Supply schedule A table showing the different quantities of a good that producers are willing and able to supply at various prices over a given time period. A supply schedule can be for an individual producer or group of producers, or for all producers (the market supply schedule).

Supply curve A graph showing the relationship between the price of a good and the quantity of the good supplied over a given period of time.

Table 4.2 The supply of potatoes (monthly)

	Price of potatoes (pence per kg)	Farmer X's supply (tonnes)	Total market supply (tonnes: 000s)
a	20	50	100
b	40	70	200
c	60	100	350
d	80	120	530
e	100	130	700

Figure 4.4 Market supply curve of potatoes (monthly)

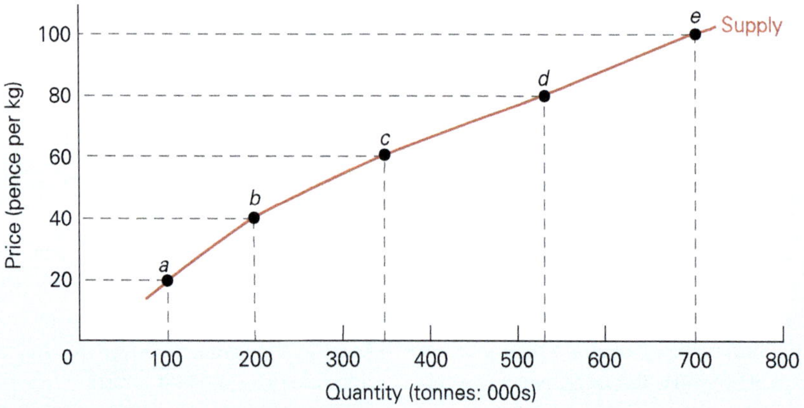

corresponds to a figure in Table 4.2. Thus for example, a price rise from 60p per kilogram to 80p per kilogram will cause a movement along the supply curve from point *c* to point *d*: total market supply will rise from 350 000 tonnes per month to 530 000 tonnes per month.

Not all supply curves will be upward sloping (positively sloped). Sometimes they will be vertical, or horizontal, or even downward sloping. This will depend largely on the time period over which firms' response to price changes is considered. This question is examined in Chapter 5 (pages 69–70).

Pause for thought

1. *How much would be supplied at a price of 70p per kilo?*
2. *Draw a supply curve for farmer X. Are the axes drawn to the same scale as in Figure 4.4?*

Other determinants of supply

Like demand, supply is not determined simply by price. The other determinants of supply are as follows.

KI 3 p 20

The costs of production. The higher the costs of production, the less profit will be made at any price. As costs rise, firms will cut back on production, probably switching to alternative products whose costs have not risen so much.

The main reasons for a change in costs are as follows:

- Change in input prices: costs of production will rise if wages, raw material prices, rents, interest rates or any other input prices rise.
- Change in technology: technological advances can fundamentally alter the costs of production. Consider, for example, how the microchip revolution has changed production methods and information handling in virtually every industry in the world.
- Organisational changes: various cost savings can be made in many firms by reorganising production.
- Government policy: costs will be lowered by government subsidies and raised by various taxes.

The profitability of alternative products (substitutes in supply). If some alternative product (a ***substitute in supply***) becomes more profitable to supply than before, producers are likely to switch from the first good to this alternative. Supply of the first good falls. Other goods are likely to become more profitable if their prices rise or their costs of production fall. For example, if the price of carrots goes up, or the cost of producing carrots comes down, farmers may decide to produce more carrots. The supply of potatoes is therefore likely to fall.

The profitability of goods in joint supply. Sometimes when one good is produced, another good is also produced at the same time. These are said to be ***goods in joint supply***. An example is the refining of crude oil to produce petrol. Other grade fuels will be produced as well, such as diesel and paraffin. If more petrol is produced, due to a rise in demand, then the supply of these other fuels will rise too.

Nature, 'random shocks' and other unpredictable events. In this category we would include the weather and diseases affecting farm output, wars affecting the supply of imported raw materials, the breakdown of machinery, industrial disputes, earthquakes, floods and fire, etc.

The aims of producers. A profit-maximising firm will supply a different quantity from a firm that has a different aim, such as maximising sales.

Pause for thought

By reference to each of the above determinants of supply, identify what would cause (a) the supply of potatoes to fall and (b) the supply of leather to rise.

Expectations of future price changes. If price is expected to rise, producers may temporarily reduce the amount they sell. Instead they are likely to build up their stocks and only release them on to the market when the price does rise. At the same time they may plan to produce more, by installing new machines, or taking on more labour, so that they can be ready to supply more when the price has risen. KI 13 p 71

The number of suppliers. If new firms enter the market, supply is likely to rise.

Movements along and shifts in the supply curve

The principle here is the same as with demand curves. The effect of a change in price is illustrated by a movement along the supply curve: for example, from point *d* to point *e* in Figure 4.4 when price rises from 80p to 100p. Quantity supplied rises from 530 000 to 700 000 tonnes.

If any other determinant of supply changes, the whole supply curve will shift. A rightward shift illustrates an increase in supply. A leftward shift illustrates a decrease

Definitions

Substitutes in supply These are two goods where an increased production of one means diverting resources away from producing the other.

Goods in joint supply These are two goods where the production of more of one leads to the production of more of the other.

in supply. Thus in Figure 4.5, if the original curve is S_0, the curve S_1 represents an increase in supply (more is supplied at each price), whereas the curve S_2 represents a decrease in supply (less is supplied at each price).

A movement along a supply curve is often referred to as a ***change in the quantity supplied***, whereas a shift in the supply curve is simply referred to as a ***change in supply***.

Figure 4.5 Shifts in the supply curve

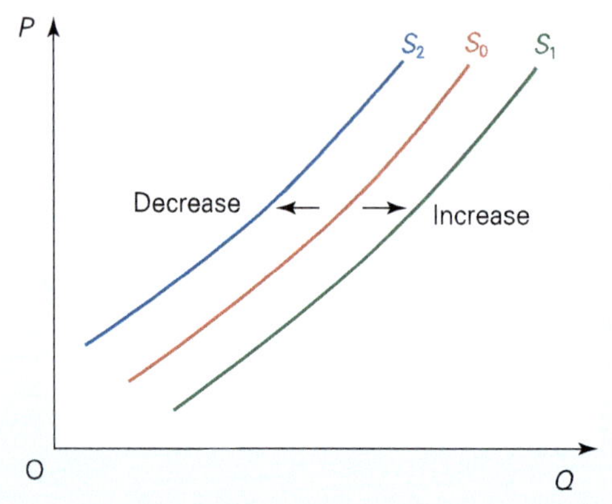

Pause for thought

By referring to the determinants of supply, consider what factors would cause a rightward shift in the supply of family cars.

4.4 PRICE AND OUTPUT DETERMINATION

Equilibrium price and output

We can now combine our analysis of demand and supply. This will show how the actual price of a product and the actual quantity bought and sold are determined in a free and competitive market.

Let us return to the example of the market demand and market supply of potatoes, and use the data from Tables 4.1 and 4.2. These figures are given again in Table 4.3.

What will be the price and output that actually prevail? If the price started at 20p per kilogram, demand would exceed supply by 600 000 tonnes (*A* – *a*). Consumers would be unable to obtain all they wanted and would thus be willing to pay a higher price. Producers, unable or unwilling to supply enough to meet the demand, will be only too happy to accept a higher price. The effect of the shortage, then, will be to drive up the price. The same would happen at a price of 40p per kilogram. There would still be a shortage; price would still rise. But as the price rises, the quantity demanded falls and the quantity supplied rises. The shortage is progressively eliminated.

What would happen if the price started at a much higher level: say, at 100p per kilogram? In this case supply would exceed demand by 600 000 tonnes (*e* – *E*). The effect of this surplus would be to drive the price down as farmers competed against each other to sell their excess supplies. The same would happen at a price of 80p per kilogram. There would still be a surplus; the price would still fall.

In fact, only one price is sustainable. This is the price where demand equals supply: namely 60p per kilogram, where both demand and supply are 350 000 tonnes. When supply matches demand the market is said to ***clear***. There is no shortage and no surplus.

The price, where demand equals supply, is called the *equilibrium price* (see page 47). In Table 4.3, if the price starts at any level other than 60p per kilogram, there will be a tendency for it to move towards 60p. The equilibrium price is the only price at which producers' and consumers' wishes are mutually reconciled: where the producers' plans to supply exactly match the consumers' plans to buy.

Table 4.3 The market demand and supply of potatoes (monthly)

Price of potatoes (pence per kg)	Total market demand (tonnes: 000s)	Total market supply (tonnes: 000s)
20	700 (*A*)	100 (*a*)
40	500 (*B*)	200 (*b*)
60	350 (*C*)	350 (*c*)
80	200 (*D*)	530 (*d*)
100	100 (*E*)	700 (*e*)

Definitions

Change in the quantity supplied The term used for a movement along the supply curve to a new point. It occurs when there is a change in price.

Change in supply The term used for a shift in the supply curve. It occurs when a determinant other than price changes.

Market clearing A market clears when supply matches demand, leaving no shortage or surplus.

Figure 4.6 The determination of market equilibrium (potatoes: monthly)

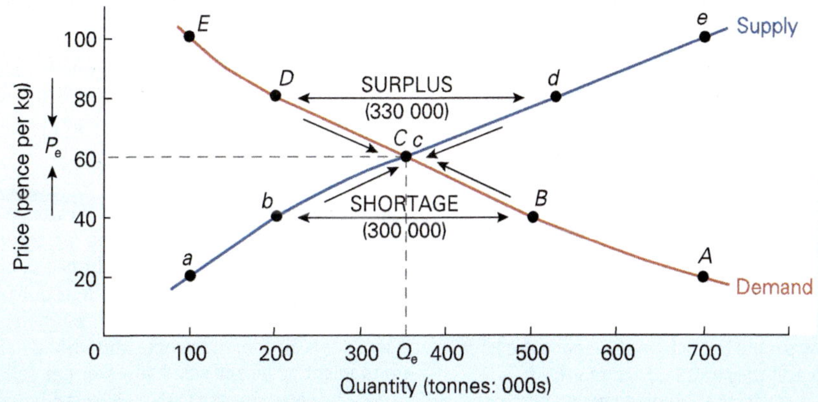

KEY IDEA 11

Equilibrium is the point where conflicting interests are balanced. **Only at this point is the amount that demanders are willing to purchase the same as the amount that suppliers are willing to supply. It is a point which will be automatically reached in a free market through the operation of the price mechanism.**

Demand and supply curves

The determination of equilibrium price and output can be shown using demand and supply curves. Equilibrium is where the two curves intersect.

Figure 4.6 shows the demand and supply curves of potatoes corresponding to the data in Table 4.3. Equilibrium price is P_e (60p) and equilibrium quantity is Q_e (350 000 tonnes).

At any price above 60p, there would be a surplus. Thus at 80p there is a surplus of 330 000 tonnes (*d* – *D*). More is supplied than consumers are willing and able to purchase at that price. Thus a price of 80p fails to clear the market. Price will fall to the equilibrium price of 60p. As it does so, there will be a movement along the demand curve from point *D* to point *C*, and a movement along the supply curve from point *d* to point *c*.

At any price below 60p, there would be a shortage. Thus at 40p there is a shortage of 300 000 tonnes (*B* – *b*). Price will rise to 60p. This will cause a movement along the supply curve from point *b* to point *c* and along the demand curve from point *B* to point *C*.

Point *Cc* is the equilibrium: where demand equals supply.

Movement to a new equilibrium

KI 11 p 55

The equilibrium price will remain unchanged only so long as the demand and supply curves remain unchanged. If either of the curves shifts, a new equilibrium will be formed.

A change in demand

KI 10 p 48

If one of the determinants of demand changes (other than price), the whole demand curve will shift. This will lead to a movement *along* the *supply* curve to the new intersection point.

For example, in Figure 4.7, if a rise in consumer incomes led to the demand curve shifting to D_2, there would be a shortage of $h - g$ at the original price P_{e_1}. This would cause price to rise to the new equilibrium P_{e_2}. As it did so there would be a movement along the supply curve from point *g* to point *i*, and along the new demand curve (D_2) from point *h* to point *i*. Equilibrium quantity would rise from Q_{e_1} to Q_{e_2}.

Pause for thought

What would happen to price and quantity if the demand curve shifted to the left? Draw a diagram to illustrate your answer.

The effect of the shift in demand, therefore, has been a movement *along* the supply curve from the old equilibrium to the new: from point *g* to point *i*.

Figure 4.7 The effect of a shift in the demand curve

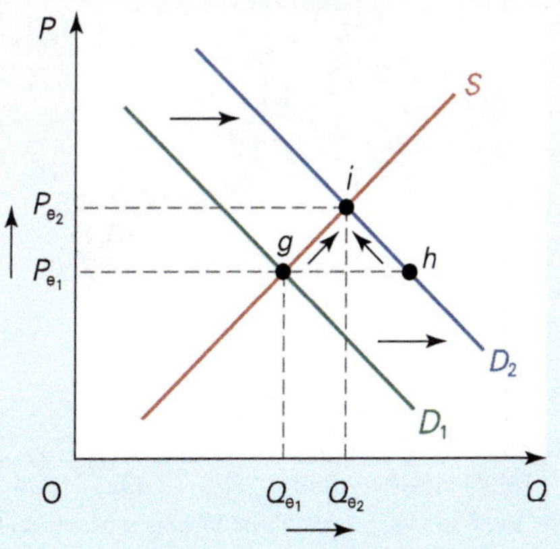

BOX 4.1 UK HOUSE PRICES

The ups and downs of the housing market

If you are thinking of buying a house sometime in the future, then you may well follow the fortunes of the housing market with some trepidation. In the late 1980s there was a housing price explosion in the UK: between 1984 and 1989 house prices doubled. After several years of falling or gently rising house prices in the early and mid-1990s, there was another boom from 1996 to 2007, with house prices tripling in value over that period. For those on low incomes, owning a home of their own was becoming increasingly difficult.

However, from 2008 to 2009 the return of falling house prices induced many people to postpone buying in the hope of paying lower prices if they waited. Further price falls in 2011 and 2012 led many to continuing deferring purchases as long as prices kept falling.

House prices since the early 1980s

The diagram shows what happened to house prices in the period 1983 to 2012. Initially, there was rapid house price inflation up to 1989, reaching a peak in 1988.

In their rush to buy a house before prices rose any further, many people in this period borrowed as much as they were able. Building societies and banks at that time had plenty of money to lend and were only too willing to do so. Many people, therefore, took out very large mortgages. In 1983 the average new mortgage was 2.08 times average annual earnings. By 1989 this figure had risen to 3.44.

After 1989 there followed a period of *falling* prices. From 1990 to 1995, house prices fell by 12.2 per cent. As a result of this, many people found themselves in a position of *negative equity*. This is the situation where the size of their mortgage is greater than the value of their house. In other words, if they sold their house, they would end up still owing money! For this reason many people found that they could not move house.

Then, in 1996, house prices began to recover and for the next three years rose moderately – by around 5 per cent per annum. But then they started rising rapidly again, and by 2003, house price inflation had returned to rates similar to those in the 1980s. Was this good news or bad news? For those trapped in negative equity, it was good news. It was good news also for old people who wished to move into a retirement home and who had a house to sell. It was bad news, however, for the first-time buyer! In the mid-1990s the gross house price to earnings ratio for first-time buyers was just over 2 but by 2007 the price of a house was over 5 times higher than a first-time buyer's earnings. It became increasingly difficult for younger people to get on to the housing ladder.

Since 2008 prices have fallen overall. While this appears to be good news for first-time buyers, many remain reluctant to buy for fear of future prices falls and hence a return to the negative equity problems of the early 1990s. As we shall see in many parts of this book, what is good news for one person is often bad news for another.

The determinants of house prices

House prices are determined by demand and supply. If demand rises (i.e. shifts to the right) or if supply falls (i.e. shifts to the left), the equilibrium price of houses will rise. Similarly, if demand falls or supply rises, the equilibrium price will fall.

UK house price inflation (annual %, adjusted quarterly)

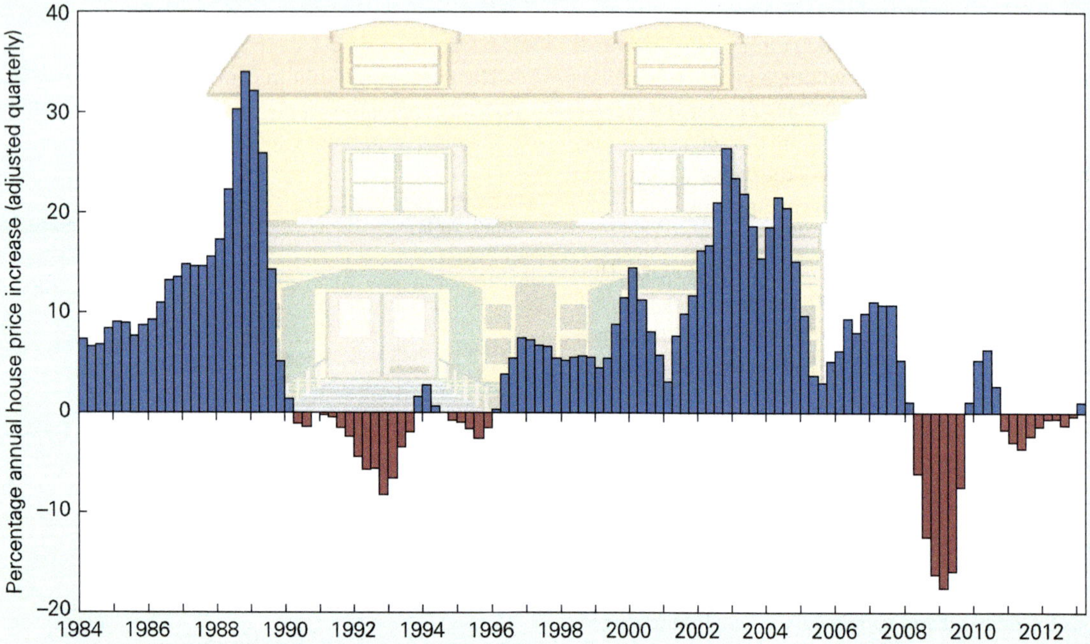

Source: Based on data in *Halifax House Price Index* (Lloyds Banking Group)

So why did UK house prices rise so rapidly in the 1980s, only to fall in the early 1990s and then rise rapidly again in the late 1990s through to 2007? The answer lies primarily in changes in the *demand* for housing. Let us examine the various factors that affected the demand for houses.

Incomes (actual and anticipated). The second half of the 1980s and from 1996 to 2007 were periods of rapidly rising incomes. The economy was experiencing economic 'boom' during these times. Many people wanted to spend their extra incomes on housing: either buying a house for the first time, or moving to a better one. What is more, many people thought that their incomes would continue to grow, and were thus prepared to stretch themselves financially in the short term by buying an expensive house, confident that their mortgage payments would become more and more affordable over time.

The early 1990s and from 2008 to 2012, by contrast, were periods of low or negative growth, with rising unemployment and falling incomes. People had much less confidence about their ability to afford large mortgages.

The desire for home ownership. The desire for home ownership has increased over the years. In recent times this has been fuelled by a host of television programmes focused on buying and selling property.

The cost of mortgages. During the second half of the 1980s, mortgage interest rates were generally falling. This meant that people could afford larger mortgages, and thus afford to buy more expensive houses. In 1989, however, this trend was reversed. Mortgage interest rates were now rising. Many people found it difficult to maintain existing payments, let alone to take on a larger mortgage. From 1996 to 2003 mortgage rates were generally reduced again, once more fuelling the demand for houses. From 2003 to 2007 interest rates rose again, but this was not enough to deter the demand for housing. From 2008 to 2012 interest rates remained low, although this did not cause an increase in housing demand due to the continued economic uncertainty created by the financial crisis and banks being cautious over their lending.

The availability of mortgages. In the late 1980s, mortgages were readily available. Banks and building societies were prepared to accept smaller deposits on houses, and to grant mortgages of 3½ times a person's annual income, compared with 2½ times in the early 1980s. In the early 1990s, however, banks and building societies were more cautious about granting mortgages. They were aware that, with falling house prices, rising unemployment and the growing problem of negative equity, there was a growing danger that borrowers would default on payments.

With the recovery of the economy in the mid-1990s, however, and with a growing number of mortgage lenders, mortgages became more readily available and for greater amounts relative to people's income. This pushed up prices. In 2001 the average house price was 3.4 times greater than a person's earnings, but this rose steadily to reach 5.74 times a person's earnings in 2007. From late 2007 to 2012, however, problems in acquiring loans from the banking sector, falling house prices and rising unemployment all signalled a repeat of the early 1990s.

Speculation. A belief that house prices will continue to move in a particular direction can exacerbate house price movements. In other words, speculation tends to increase house price volatility. In the 1980s and from the mid-1990s to 2007, people generally believed that house prices would continue rising. This encouraged people to buy as soon as possible, and to take out the biggest mortgage possible, before prices went up any further. There was also an effect on supply. Those with houses to sell held back until the last possible moment in the hope of getting a higher price. The net effect was for a rightward shift in the demand curve for houses and a leftward shift in the supply curve. The effect of this speculation, therefore, was to help bring about the very effect that people were predicting (see section 5.4).

In the early 1990s, and again from 2008, the opposite occurred. People thinking of buying houses held back, hoping to buy at a lower price. People with houses to sell tried to sell as quickly as possible before prices fell any further. Again the effect of this speculation was to aggravate the change in prices – this time a fall in prices.

A global dimension to falling house prices

The fall in UK house prices in 2008 had global origins. The dramatic growth in mortgage lending in the UK was also a feature of many other industrialised countries at this time, most notably the USA, where there had been similar dramatic rises in house prices.

Banks and other mortgage lenders bundled up these large mortgage debts into 'financial instruments' and sold them on to other global financial institutions so that they could meet their everyday liquidity requirements of paying bills and meeting customers' demands for cash. This worked well while there was economic prosperity and people could pay their mortgages. However, it became apparent in 2007 that many of the mortgages sold, notably in the USA, were to people who could not meet their repayments.

As the number of mortgage defaults increased, the value of the mortgage-laden financial instruments sold on to other financial institutions fell. As banks found it increasingly difficult to meet their liquidity requirements, they reduced the number of mortgages to potential home owners. By the beginning of 2013, UK prices had fallen by nearly 20 per cent since the peak in 2007. The uncertainty over how far house prices might fall was discouraging consumers from moving home and, as the financial crisis turned into economic recession, house building fell dramatically and construction firms were laying off workers.

?

1. *Draw supply and demand diagrams to illustrate what was happening to house prices (a) in the second half of the 1980s and from the late 1990s to 2007; (b) in the early 1990s and 2008–12.*
2. *Are there any factors on the supply side that contribute to changes in house prices? If so, what are they?*
3. *Find out what has happened to house prices over the past three years. Attempt an explanation of what has happened.*

BOX 4.2 STOCK MARKET PRICES

Demand and supply in action

Firms that are quoted on the stock market (see page 37 and section 19.5) can raise money by issuing shares. These are sold on the 'primary stock market'. People who own the shares receive a 'dividend' on them, normally paid six-monthly. This varies with the profitability of the company.

People or institutions that buy these shares, however, may not wish to hold on to them for ever. This is where the 'secondary stock market' comes in. It is where existing shares are bought and sold. There are stock markets, primary and secondary, in all the major countries of the world.

There are more than 2500 companies whose shares are listed on the London Stock Exchange and shares are traded each Monday to Friday (excluding bank holidays). The prices of shares depend on demand and supply. For example, if the demand for Tesco shares at any one time exceeds the supply on offer, the price will rise until demand and supply are equal. Share prices fluctuate throughout the trading day and sometimes price changes can be substantial.

To give an overall impression of share price movements, stock exchanges publish share price indices. The best known one in the UK is the FTSE 100, which stands for the 'Financial Times Stock Exchange' index of the 100 largest companies' shares. The index represents an average price of these 100 shares. The chart shows movements in the FTSE 100 from 1995 to 2012. The index was first calculated on 3 January 1984 with a base level of 1000 points. It reached a peak of 6930 points on 30 December 1999 and fell to 3287 on 12 March 2003; it then rose again, reaching a high of 6730 on 12 October 2007. In the midst of the financial crisis the index fell to a low of 3781 on 21 November 2008, but by early 2010 it partially recovered, passing 6000 for a brief period, before levelling out and fluctuating around an average of 5500 to mid-2012, only to rise above 6000 again at the start of 2013.

But what causes share prices to change? Why were they so high in 1999, but only just over half that value just three years later, and why has this trend repeated itself in the late 2000s? The answer lies in the determinants of the demand and supply of shares.

Demand

There are five main factors that affect the demand for shares.

The dividend yield. This is the dividend on a share as a percentage of its price. The higher the dividend yields on

Financial Times Stock Exchange Index (FTSE) (3/1/1984 = 1000)

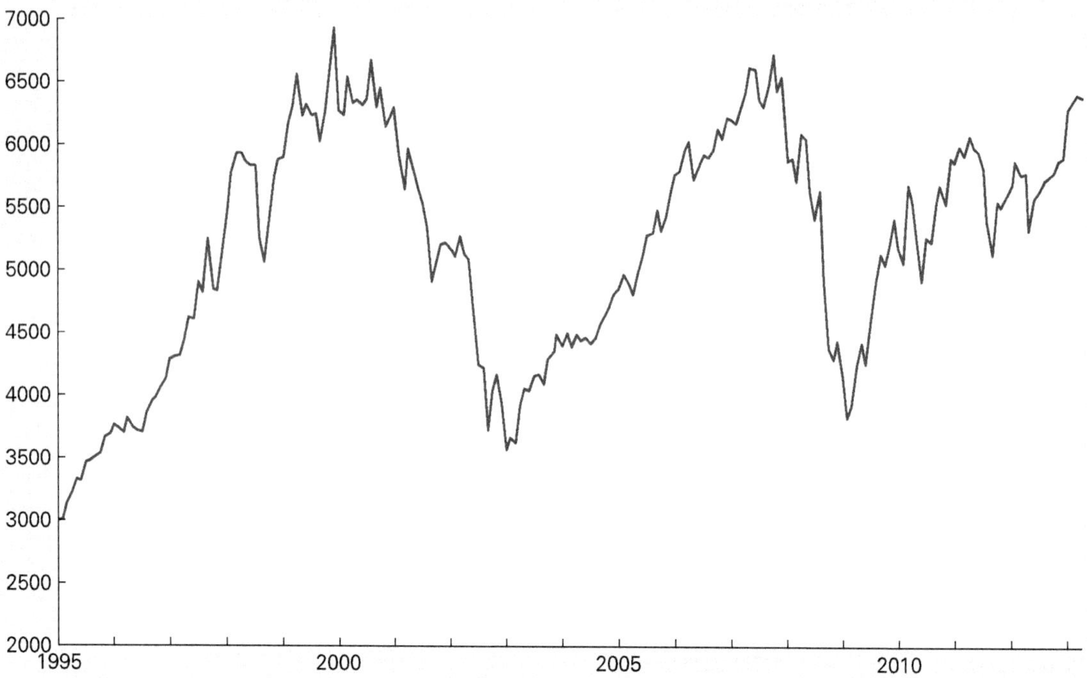

shares the more attractive they are as a form of saving. One of the main explanations of rising stock market prices from 2003 to 2007 was high profits and resulting high dividends. Similarly, the slowdown in the world economy after 2007 led to falling profits and falling dividends.

The price of and/or return on substitutes. The main substitutes for shares in specific companies are other shares. Thus if, in comparison with other shares, Tesco shares are expected to pay high dividends relative to the share price, people will buy Tesco shares. As far as shares in general are concerned, the main substitutes are other forms of saving. Thus if the interest rate on savings accounts in banks and building societies fell, people with such accounts would be tempted to take their money out and buy shares instead. Another major substitute is property. If house prices rise rapidly, as they did from the late 1990s to 2007, this will reduce the demand for shares as many people switch to buying property in anticipation of even higher prices. If house prices level off, this makes shares relatively more attractive as an investment and can boost the demand for them.

From late 2007, when house prices and share prices fell dramatically, investors looked towards other, safer, investments such as gold, government debt (Treasury bills and gilts) or even holding cash.

Incomes. If the economy is growing rapidly and people's incomes are thus rising rapidly, they are likely to buy more shares. Thus in the mid to late 1990s, when UK incomes were rising at an average annual rate of over 3 per cent, share prices rose rapidly (see chart). As growth rates fell in the early 2000s, so share prices fell. Similarly, when economic growth improved from 2003 to 2007 shares prices increased, but they fell back with the global financial crisis in 2007/8 and the onset of recession and declining real incomes from 2008.

Wealth. 'Wealth' is people's accumulated savings and property. Wealth rose in the 1990s and 2000s, and many people used their increased wealth to buy shares.

Expectations. From 2003 to 2007 people expected share prices to go on rising. They were optimistic about continued growth in the economy. But as people bought shares, this pushed their prices up even more, thereby fuelling further speculation that they would go on rising and encouraging further share buying. In recent years, by contrast, confidence has been shaken. A global banking crisis and fears of impending recession started a dramatic fall in share prices. Uncertainty over how and when the global economy will recover has caused share prices to be volatile in the past few years.

Supply

The factors affecting supply in the secondary market are largely the same as those affecting demand, but in the opposite direction.

If the return on alternative forms of saving falls, people with shares are likely to hold on to them, as they represent a better form of saving. The supply of shares to the market will fall. If incomes or wealth rise, people again are likely to want to hold on to their shares.

As far as expectations are concerned, if people believe that share prices will rise, they will hold on to the shares they have. Supply to the market will fall, thereby pushing up prices. If, however, they believe that prices will fall (as they did in 2008), they will sell their shares now before prices do fall. Supply will increase, driving down the price.

Share prices and business

Companies are crucially affected by their share price. If a company's share price falls, this is taken as a sign that 'the market' is losing confidence in the company. This will make it more difficult to raise finance, not only by issuing additional shares in the primary market, but also from banks.

It will also make the company more vulnerable to a takeover bid. This is where one company seeks to buy out another by offering to buy all its shares. A takeover will succeed if the owners of more than half of the company's shares vote to accept the offered price. Shareholders are more likely to agree to the takeover if the company's share price has not been performing very well.

Can you buck the market?

Many individuals like to play the market, thinking that they can make easy profits. However, beware! The 'efficient markets hypothesis' predicts that historical share price information, such as that shown in the chart or in the pages of today's financial press, provides no help whatsoever in determining future share prices. Why? Because the current share price *already* reflects what people anticipate will happen. Future share price movements will occur only as *new* (unanticipated) information arrives – and it's pure chance if you can predict the unanticipated! In this purist view, the market for shares is said to be a perfectly efficient market (see section 19.5 for further analysis).

If the rate of economic growth in the economy is 3 per cent in a particular year, why are share prices likely to rise by more than 3 per cent that year?

A change in supply

KI 10 p48

Likewise, if one of the determinants of supply changes (other than price), the whole supply curve will shift. This will lead to a movement *along* the *demand* curve to the new intersection point.

For example, in Figure 4.8, if costs of production rose, the supply curve would shift to the left: to S_2. There would be a shortage of $g - j$ at the old price of P_{e_1}. Price would rise from P_{e_1} to P_{e_3}. Quantity would fall from Q_{e_1} to Q_{e_3}. In other words, there would be a movement along the demand curve from point *g* to point *k*, and along the new supply curve (S_2) from point *j* to point *k*.

To summarise: a shift in one curve leads to a movement along the other curve to the new intersection point.

KI 11 p55

Sometimes a number of determinants might change. This may lead to a shift in *both* curves. When this happens, equilibrium simply moves from the point where the old curves intersected to the point where the new ones intersect.

Figure 4.8 The effect of a shift in the supply curve

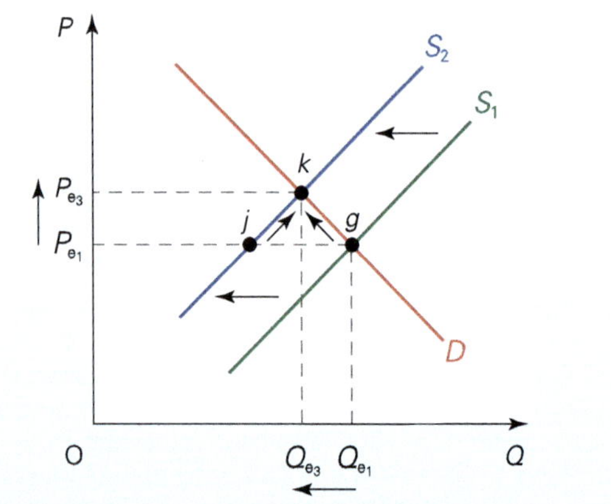

SUMMARY

1a A firm is greatly affected by its market environment. The more competitive the market, the less discretion the firm has in determining its price. In the extreme case of a perfect market, the price is entirely outside the firm's control. The price is determined by demand and supply in the market, and the firm has to accept this price: the firm is a price taker.

1b In a perfect market, price changes act as the mechanism whereby demand and supply are balanced. If there is a shortage, price will rise until the shortage is eliminated. If there is a surplus, price will fall until that is eliminated.

2a When the price of a good rises, the quantity demanded per period of time will fall. This is known as the 'law of demand'. It applies both to individuals' demand and to the whole market demand.

2b The law of demand is explained by the income and substitution effects of a price change.

2c The relationship between price and quantity demanded per period of time can be shown in a table (or 'schedule') or as a graph. On the graph, price is plotted on the vertical axis and quantity demanded per period of time on the horizontal axis. The resulting demand curve is downward sloping (negatively sloped).

2d Other determinants of demand include tastes, the number and price of substitute goods, the number and price of complementary goods, income, the distribution of income and expectations of future price changes.

2e If price changes, the effect is shown by a movement along the demand curve. We call this effect 'a change in the quantity demanded'.

2f If any other determinant of demand changes, the whole curve will shift. We call this effect 'a change in demand'. A rightward shift represents an increase in demand; a leftward shift represents a decrease in demand.

3a When the price of a good rises, the quantity supplied per period of time will usually also rise. This applies both to individual producers' supply and to the whole market supply.

3b There are two reasons in the short run why a higher price encourages producers to supply more: (a) they are now willing to incur higher costs per unit associated with producing more; (b) they will switch to producing this product and away from now less profitable ones. In the long run there is a third reason: new producers will be attracted into the market.

3c The relationship between price and quantity supplied per period of time can be shown in a table (or schedule) or as a graph. As with a demand curve, price is plotted on the vertical axis and quantity per period of time on the horizontal axis. The resulting supply curve is upward sloping (positively sloped).

3d Other determinants of supply include the costs of production, the profitability of alternative products, the profitability of goods in joint supply, random shocks and expectations of future price changes.

3e If price changes, the effect is shown by a movement along the supply curve. We call this effect 'a change in the quantity supplied'.

3f If any determinant *other* than price changes, the effect is shown by a shift in the whole supply curve. We call this effect 'a change in supply'. A rightward shift represents an increase in supply; a leftward shift represents a decrease in supply.

4a If the demand for a good exceeds the supply, there will be a shortage. This will lead to a rise in the price of the good.

4b If the supply of a good exceeds the demand, there will be a surplus. This will lead to a fall in the price.

4c Price will settle at the equilibrium. The equilibrium price is the one that clears the market: the price where demand equals supply. This is shown in a demand and supply diagram by the point where the two curves intersect.

4d If the demand or supply curve shifts, this will lead either to a shortage or to a surplus. Price will therefore either rise or fall until a new equilibrium is reached at the position where the supply and demand curves *now* intersect.

REVIEW QUESTIONS

1 Using a diagram like Figure 4.1, summarise the effect of (a) a reduction in the demand for a good; (b) a reduction in the costs of production of a good.

2 Referring to Table 4.1, assume that there are 200 consumers in the market. Of these, 100 have schedules like Tracey's and 100 have schedules like Darren's. What would be the total market demand schedule for potatoes now?

3 Again referring to Table 4.1, draw Tracey's and Darren's demand curves for potatoes on one diagram. (Note that you will use the same vertical scale as in Figure 4.2, but you will need a quite different horizontal scale.) At what price is their demand the same? What explanations could there be for the quite different shapes of their two demand curves? (This question is explored in Chapter 5.)

4 The price of pork rises and yet it is observed that the sales of pork increase. Does this mean that the demand curve for pork is upward sloping? Explain.

5 This question is concerned with the supply of oil for central heating. In each case consider whether there is a movement along the supply curve (and in which direction) or a shift in it (and whether left or right): (a) new oil fields start up in production; (b) the demand for central heating rises; (c) the price of gas falls; (d) oil companies anticipate an upsurge in the demand for central-heating oil; (e) the demand for petrol rises; (f) new technology decreases the costs of oil refining; (g) all oil products become more expensive.

6 For what reasons might the price of foreign holidays rise? In each case, identify whether these are reasons affecting demand or supply (or both).

7 The price of cod is much higher today than it was 20 years ago. Using demand and supply diagrams, explain why this should be so.

8 The number of owners of compact disc players has grown rapidly and hence the demand for compact discs has also grown rapidly. Yet the price of CDs has fallen. Why? Use a supply and demand diagram to illustrate your answer.

9 What will happen to the equilibrium price and quantity of butter in each of the following cases? You should state whether demand or supply or both have shifted and in which direction: (a) a rise in the price of margarine; (b) a rise in the demand for yoghurt; (c) a rise in the price of bread; (d) a rise in the demand for bread; (e) an expected increase in the price of butter in the near future; (f) a tax on butter production; (g) the invention of a new, but expensive, process of removing all cholesterol from butter, plus the passing of a law which states that butter producers must use this process. In each case, assume *ceteris paribus*.

10 If both demand and supply change, and if we know in which direction they have shifted but not by how much, why is it that we will be able to predict the direction in which *either* price or quantity will change, but not both? (Clue: consider the four possible combinations and sketch them if necessary: *D* left, *S* left; *D* right, *S* right; *D* left, *S* right; *D* right, *S* left.)

5 Chapter

Business in a market environment

Business issues covered in this chapter

- How responsive is consumer demand to changes in the market price? How responsive is it to changes in consumer incomes and to the prices of competitor products?
- How is a firm's sales revenue affected by a change in price?
- How responsive is business output to changes in price?
- How does the responsiveness (or 'elasticity') of demand and supply to changes in price affect the working of markets?
- Why are markets likely to be more responsive in the long run than in the short run to changes in demand or supply?
- What is meant by 'risk' and 'uncertainty' and what is their significance to business?
- How do firms deal with uncertainty about future market movements?

In Chapter 4 we examined how prices are determined in perfectly competitive markets: by the interaction of market demand and market supply. In such markets, although the *market* demand curve is downward sloping, the demand curve faced by the individual firm will be horizontal. This is illustrated in Figure 5.1.

The market price is P_m. The individual firm can sell as much as it likes at this market price: it is too small to have any influence on the market – it is a price taker. It will not force the price down by producing more because, in terms of the total market, this extra would be an infinitesimally small amount. If a farmer doubled the output of wheat sent to the market, it would be too small an increase to affect the world price of wheat!

In practice, however, many firms are not price takers; they have some discretion in choosing their price. Such firms will face a downward-sloping demand curve. If they raise their price, they will sell less; if they lower their price, they will sell more. But firms will want to know more than this. They will want to know just *how much* the quantity demanded will fall. In other words, they will want to know how *responsive* demand is to a rise in price. This responsiveness is measured using a concept called 'elasticity'.

Figure 5.1 Market demand curve for an individual firm under conditions of perfect competition

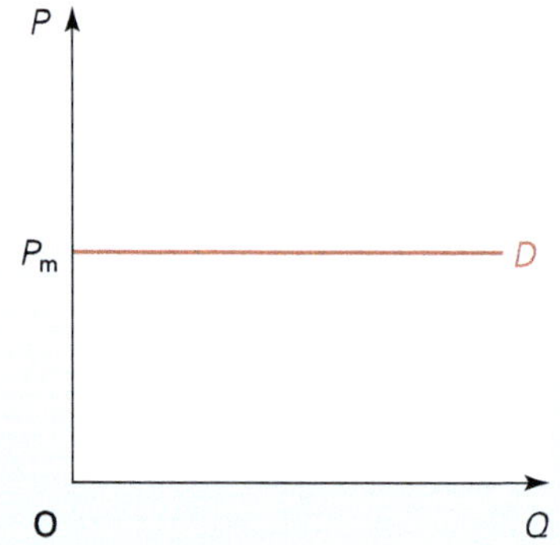

KEY IDEA 12

***Elasticity*. The responsiveness of one variable (e.g. demand) to a change in another (e.g. price). This concept is fundamental to understanding how markets work. The more elastic variables are, the more responsive is the market to changing circumstances.**

5.1 PRICE ELASTICITY OF DEMAND

The responsiveness of quantity demanded to a change in price

The demand for an individual firm

For any firm considering changing its price, it is vital to know the likely effect on the quantity demanded. Take the case of two firms facing very different demand curves. These are shown in Figure 5.2.

Firm A can raise its price quite substantially – from £6 to £10 – and yet its level of sales only falls by a relatively small amount – from 100 units to 90 units. This firm will probably be quite keen to raise its price. After all, it could make significantly more profit on each unit sold (assuming no rise in costs per unit), and yet sell only slightly fewer units.

Firm B, however, will think twice about raising its price. Even a relatively modest increase in price – from £6 to £7 – will lead to a substantial fall in sales from 100 units to 40 units. What is the point of making a bit more profit on those units it manages to sell, if in the process it ends up selling a lot fewer units? In such circumstances the firm may contemplate lowering its price.

The responsiveness of market demand

KI 10 p48

Economists too will want to know how responsive demand is to a change in price: except in this case it is the responsiveness of *market* demand that is being considered. This information is necessary to enable them to predict the effects of a shift in supply on the market price of a product.

Figure 5.3 shows the effect of a shift in supply with two quite different demand curves (D and D'). Assume that initially the supply curve is S_1, and that it intersects with both demand curves at point a, at a price of P_1 and a quantity of Q_1. Now supply shifts to S_2. What will happen to price and quantity? Economists will want to know! The answer is that it depends on the shape of the demand curve. In the case of demand curve D, there is a relatively large rise in price (to P_2) and a relatively small fall in quantity (to Q_2): equilibrium is at point b. In the case of demand curve D', however, there is only a relatively small rise in price (to P_3), but a relatively large fall in quantity (to Q_3): equilibrium is at point c.

Given the importance of knowing the responsiveness of demand to a change in price, we will need some way of measuring this responsiveness. *Elasticity* is the measure we use.

Figure 5.3 Market supply and demand

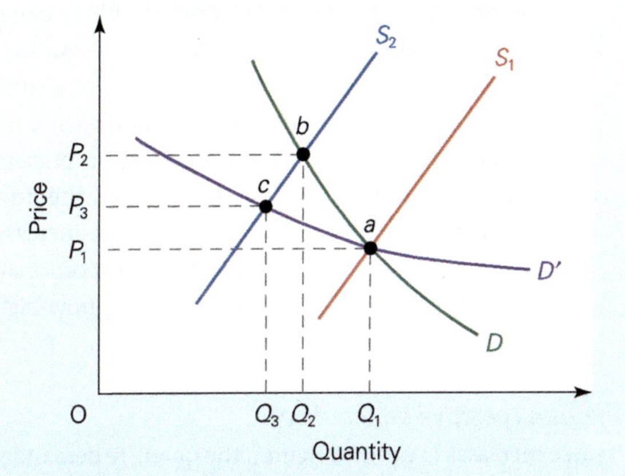

Figure 5.2 The demand for an individual firm's product

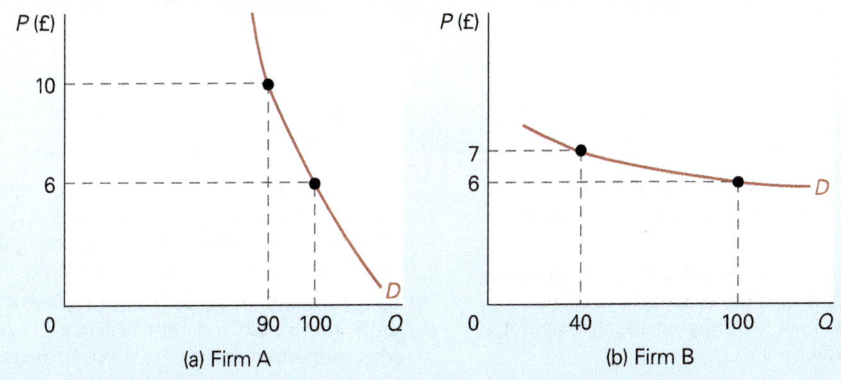

Defining price elasticity of demand

What we will want to compare is the size of the change in quantity demanded of a given product with the size of the change in price. ***Price elasticity of demand*** does just this. It is defined as follows:

$$P\varepsilon_D = \frac{\text{proportionate (or percentage) change in quantity demanded}}{\text{proportionate (or percentage) change in price}}$$

If, for example, a 20 per cent rise in the price of a product causes a 10 per cent fall in the quantity demanded, the price elasticity of demand will be:

$-10\%/20\% = -0.5$

Three things should be noted at this stage about the figure that is calculated for elasticity.

The use of proportionate or percentage measures

Elasticity is measured in proportionate or percentage terms for the following reasons:

- It allows comparison of changes in two qualitatively different things, which are thus measured in two different types of unit: i.e. it allows comparison of quantity changes (quantity demanded) with monetary changes (price).
- It is the only sensible way of deciding *how big* a change in price or quantity is. Take a simple example. An item goes up in price by £1. Is this a big increase or a small increase? We can answer this only if we know what the original price was. If a can of beans goes up in price by £1, that is a huge price increase. If, however, the price of a house goes up by £1, that is a tiny price increase. In other words, it is the percentage or proportionate increase in price that we look at in deciding how big a price rise it is.

The sign (positive or negative)

If price increases (a positive figure), the quantity demanded will fall (a negative figure). If price falls (a negative figure), the quantity demanded will rise (a positive figure). Thus price elasticity of demand will be negative: a positive figure is being divided by a negative figure (or vice versa).

The value (greater or less than 1)

If we now ignore the sign and just concentrate on the value of the figure, this tells us whether demand is ***elastic*** or ***inelastic***.

Elastic ($\varepsilon > 1$). This is where a change in price causes a proportionately larger change in the quantity demanded. In this case the price elasticity of demand will be greater than 1, since we are dividing a larger figure by a smaller figure.

Inelastic ($\varepsilon < 1$). This is where a change in price causes a proportionately smaller change in the quantity demanded. In this case the price elasticity of demand will be less than 1, since we are dividing a smaller figure by a larger figure.

Unit elastic ($\varepsilon = 1$). ***Unit elasticity*** is where the quantity demanded changes proportionately the same as price. This will give an elasticity equal to 1, since we are dividing a figure by itself.

The determinants of price elasticity of demand

The price elasticity of demand varies enormously from one product to another. But why do some products have a highly elastic demand, whereas others have a highly *in*elastic demand? What determines price elasticity of demand?

The number and closeness of substitute goods

This is the most important determinant. The more substitutes there are for a good, and the closer they are, the more will people switch to these alternatives when the price of the good rises: the greater, therefore, will be the price elasticity of demand.

For example, the price elasticity of demand for a particular brand of a product will probably be fairly high, especially if there are many other, similar brands. If its price goes up, people can simply switch to another brand: there is a large substitution effect. By contrast, the demand for a product in general will normally be pretty inelastic. If the price of food in general goes up, demand for food will fall only slightly. People will buy a little less, since they cannot now afford so much: this is the *income* effect of the price rise. But there is no alternative to food that can satisfy our hunger: there is therefore virtually no *substitution* effect.

Definitions

Price elasticity of demand A measure of the responsiveness of quantity demanded to a change in price.

Elastic If demand is (price) elastic, then any change in price will cause the quantity demanded to change proportionately more. (Ignoring the negative sign) it will have a value greater than 1.

Inelastic If demand is (price) inelastic, then any change will cause the quantity demanded to change by a proportionately smaller amount. (Ignoring the negative sign) it will have a value less than 1.

Unit elasticity When the price elasticity of demand is unity, this is where quantity demanded changes by the same proportion as the price. Price elasticity is equal to 1.

The proportion of income spent on the good

The higher the proportion of our income we spend on a good, the more we will be forced to cut consumption when its price rises: the bigger will be the income effect and the more elastic will be the demand.

Thus salt has a very low price elasticity of demand. This is because we spend such a tiny fraction of our income on salt that we would find little difficulty in paying a relatively large percentage increase in its price: the income effect of a price rise would be very small. By contrast, there will be a much bigger income effect when a major item of expenditure rises in price. For example, if mortgage interest rates rise (the 'price' of loans for house purchases), people may have to cut down substantially on their demand for housing – being forced to buy somewhere much smaller and cheaper, or to live in rented accommodation.

> **Pause for thought**
>
> *Think of two products and estimate which is likely to have the higher price elasticity of demand. Explain your answer.*

The time period

When price rises, people may take a time to adjust their consumption patterns and find alternatives. The longer the time period after a price change, then, the more elastic is the demand likely to be.

5.2 THE IMPORTANCE OF PRICE ELASTICITY OF DEMAND TO BUSINESS DECISION MAKING

A firm's sales revenue

One of the most important applications of price elasticity of demand concerns its relationship with a firm's sales revenue. The ***total sales revenue (TR)*** of a firm is simply price times quantity:

$$TR = P \times Q$$

For example, 3000 units (Q) sold at £2 per unit (P) will earn the firm £6000 (TR).

KI 12 p 63

Let us assume that a firm wants to increase its total revenue. What should it do? Should it raise its price or lower it? The answer depends on the price elasticity of demand.

Elastic demand and sales revenue

As price rises, so quantity demanded falls, and vice versa. When demand is elastic, quantity changes proportionately more than price. Thus the change in quantity has a bigger effect on total revenue than does the change in price. This can be summarised as follows:

P rises; *Q* falls proportionately more; therefore *TR* falls.
P falls; *Q* rises proportionately more; therefore *TR* rises.

In other words, total revenue changes in the same direction as *quantity*.

This is illustrated in Figure 5.4. The areas of the rectangles in the diagram represent total revenue. But why? The area of a rectangle is its height multiplied by its length. In this case, this is price multiplied by quantity purchased, which, as we have seen, gives total revenue.

Demand is elastic between points *a* and *b*. A rise in price from £4 to £5 causes a proportionately larger fall in quantity demanded: from 20 to 10. Total revenue *falls* from £80 (the striped area) to £50 (the shaded area).

When demand is elastic, then, a rise in price will cause a fall in total revenue. If a firm wants to increase its revenue, it should *lower* its price.

> **Pause for thought**
>
> *If a firm faces an elastic demand curve, why will it not necessarily be in the firm's interests to produce more? (Clue: you will need to distinguish between revenue and profit. We will explore this relationship in Chapter 6.)*

Figure 5.4 Elastic demand between two points

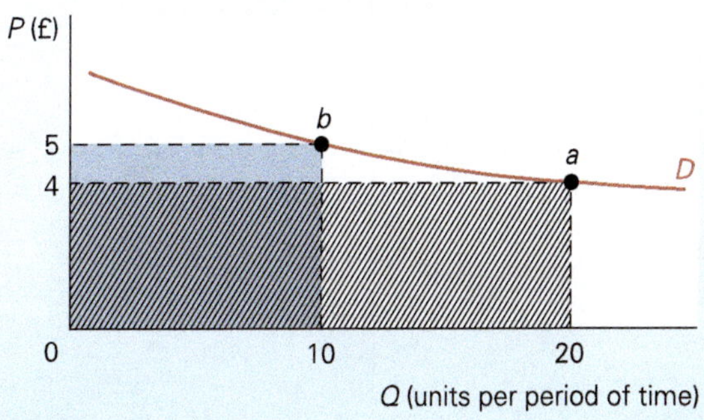

> **Definition**
>
> **Total (sales) revenue (TR)** The amount a firm earns from its sales of a product at a particular price. $TR = P \times Q$. Note that we are referring to *gross* revenue: that is, revenue before the deduction of taxes or any other costs.

Inelastic demand and sales revenue

When demand is inelastic, it is the other way around. Price changes proportionately more than quantity. Thus the change in price has a bigger effect on total revenue than does the change in quantity. To summarise the effects:

P rises; *Q* falls proportionately less; *TR* rises.
P falls; *Q* rises proportionately less; *TR* falls.

In other words, total revenue changes in the same direction as price.

This is illustrated in Figure 5.5. Demand is inelastic between points *a* and *c*. A rise in price from £4 to £8 causes a proportionately smaller fall in quantity demanded: from 20 to 15. Total revenue *rises* from £80 (the striped area) to £120 (the shaded area).

If a firm wants to increase its revenue in this case, therefore, it should *raise* its price.

Figure 5.5 Inelastic demand between two points

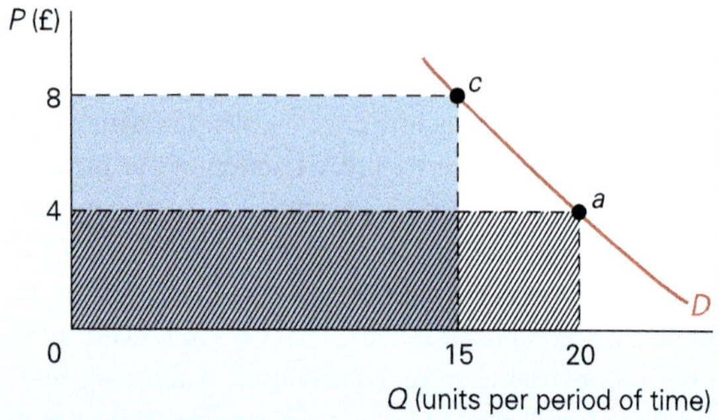

Special cases

Figure 5.6 shows three special cases: (a) a totally inelastic demand ($P\varepsilon_D = 0$), (b) an infinitely elastic demand ($P\varepsilon_D = 1$) and (c) a unit elastic demand ($P\varepsilon_D = -1$).

BOX 5.1 THE MEASUREMENT OF ELASTICITY

An optional technical box

We have defined price elasticity as the percentage or proportionate change in quantity demanded divided by the percentage or proportionate change in price. But how, in practice, do we measure these changes for a specific demand curve?

A common mistake that students make is to think that you can talk about the elasticity of a whole *curve*. The mistake here is that in most cases the elasticity will vary along the length of the curve.

Take the case of the demand curve illustrated in diagram (a). Between points *a* and *b*, total revenue rises ($P_2Q_2 > P_1Q_1$): demand is thus elastic between these two points. Between points *b* and *c*, however, total revenue falls ($P_3Q_3 < P_2Q_2$). Demand here is inelastic.

Normally, then, we can refer to the elasticity only of a *portion* of the demand curve, not of the *whole* curve.

There is, however, an exception to this rule. This is when the elasticity just so happens to be the same all the way along a curve, as in the three special cases illustrated in Figure 5.6.

Although we cannot normally talk about the elasticity of a whole curve, we can nevertheless talk about the elasticity between any two points on it. Remember the formula we used was:

$$\frac{\text{\% or proportionate } \Delta Q}{\text{\% or proportionate } \Delta P}$$

(where Δ means 'change in').

(a) Different elasticities along different portions of a demand curve

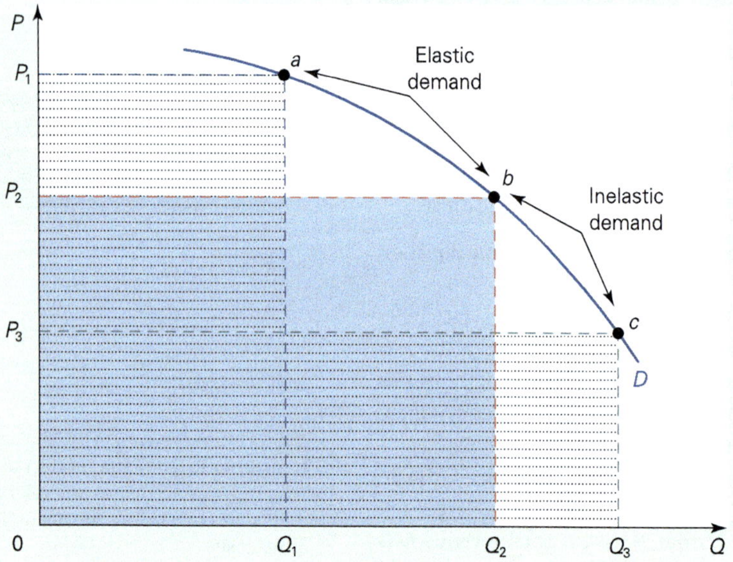

Figure 5.6 (a) Totally inelastic demand ($P\varepsilon_D = 0$); (b) Infinitely elastic demand ($P\varepsilon_D = \infty$); (c) Unit elastic demand ($P\varepsilon_D = -1$)

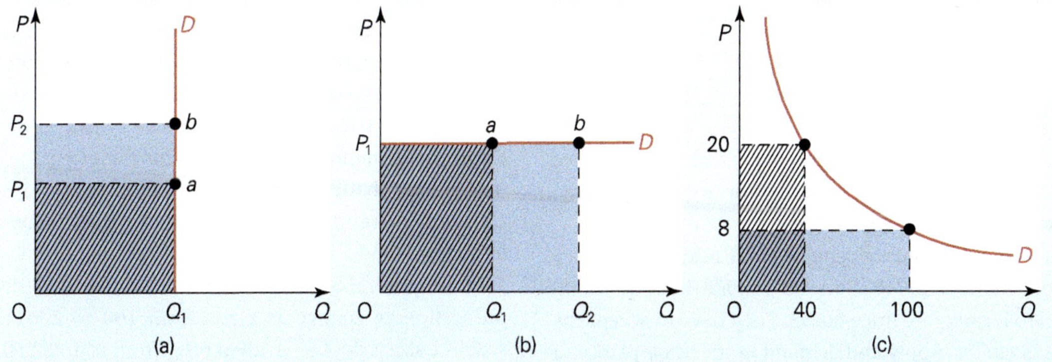

(b) Measuring elasticity using the arc method

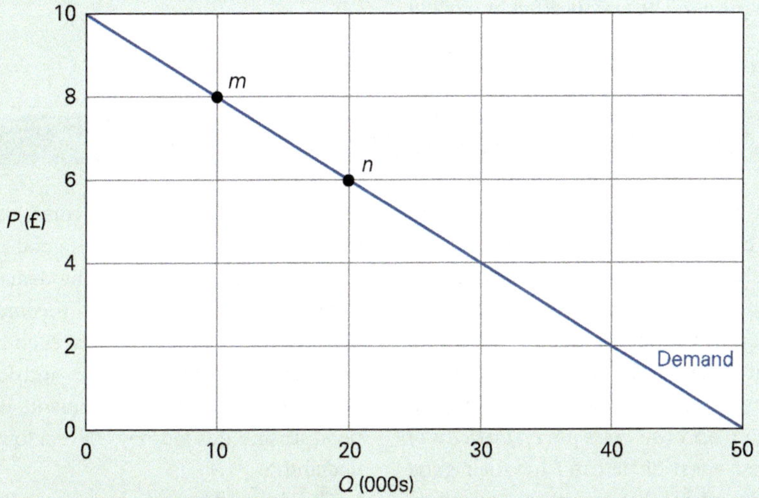

The way we measure a *proportionate* change in quantity is to divide that change by the level of Q: i.e. $\Delta Q/Q$. Similarly, we measure a proportionate change in price by dividing that change by the level of P: i.e. $\Delta P/Q$. Price elasticity of demand can thus now be rewritten as:

$$\frac{\Delta Q}{Q} \div \frac{\Delta P}{P}$$

But just what value do we give to P and Q? Consider the demand curve in diagram (b). What is the elasticity of demand between points m and n? Price has fallen by £2 (from £8 to £6), but what is the proportionate change? Is it −2/8 or −2/6? The convention is to express the change as a proportion of the average of the two prices, £8 and £6: in other words to take the mid-point price, £7. Thus the proportionate change is −2/7.

Similarly the proportionate change in quantity between points m and n is 10/15, since 15 is mid-way between 10 and 20.

Thus using the *average (or 'mid-point') formula*, elasticity between m and n is given by:

$$\frac{\Delta Q}{\text{average } Q} \div \frac{\Delta P}{\text{average } P} = \frac{10}{15} \div \frac{-2}{7} = -2.33$$

Since 2.33 is greater than 1, demand is elastic between m and n.

?

Referring again to diagram (b), what is the price elasticity of demand between a price of (a) £6 and £4; (b) £4 and £2? What do you conclude about the elasticity of a straight-line demand curve as you move down it?

Totally inelastic demand

This is shown by a vertical straight line. No matter what happens to price, quantity demanded remains the same. It is obvious that the more the price is raised, the bigger will be the revenue. Thus in Figure 5.6(a), P_2 will earn a bigger revenue than P_1.

Infinitely elastic demand

This is shown by a horizontal straight line. At any price above P_1 demand is zero. But at P_1 (or any price below) demand is 'infinitely' large.

This seemingly unlikely demand curve is in fact relatively common. Many firms that are very small (like the small-scale grain farmer) are price takers. They have to accept the price as given by supply and demand in the *whole market*. If individual farmers were to try to sell above this price, they would sell nothing at all. At this price, however, they can sell to the market all they produce. (Demand is not *literally* infinite, but as far as the farmer is concerned it is.) In this case, the more the individual farmer produces, the more revenue will be earned. In Figure 5.6(b), more revenue is earned at Q_2 than at Q_1.

Unit elastic demand

This is where price and quantity change in exactly the same proportion. Any rise in price will be exactly offset by a fall in quantity, leaving total revenue unchanged. In Figure 5.6(c), the striped area is exactly equal to the shaded area: in both cases total revenue is £800.

You might have thought that a demand curve with unit elasticity would be a straight line at 45° to the axes. Instead it is a curve called a *rectangular hyperbola*. The reason for its shape is that the proportionate *rise* in quantity must equal the proportionate *fall* in price (and vice versa). As we move down the demand curve, in order for the *proportionate* (or percentage) change in both price and quantity to remain constant, there must be a bigger and bigger *absolute* rise in quantity and a smaller and smaller absolute fall in price. For example, a rise in quantity from 200 to 400 is the same proportionate change as a rise from 100 to 200, but its absolute size is double. A fall in price from £5 to £2.50 is the same percentage as a fall from £10 to £5, but its absolute size is only half.

Pause for thought

Two customers go to the fish counter at a supermarket to buy some cod. Neither looks at the price. Customer A orders 1 kilo of cod. Customer B orders £3 worth of cod. What is the price elasticity of demand of each of the two customers?

5.3 OTHER ELASTICITIES

Firms are interested to know the responsiveness of demand not just to a change in price: they will also want to know the responsiveness of demand to changes in other determinants, such as consumers' incomes and the prices of goods that are substitute or complementary to theirs. They will want to know the ***income elasticity of demand*** – the responsiveness of demand to a change in consumers' incomes (Y); and the ***cross-price elasticity of demand*** – the responsiveness of demand for their good to a change in the price of another (whether a substitute or a complement).

Income elasticity of demand ($Y\varepsilon_D$)

We define the income elasticity of demand for a good as follows:

$$Y\varepsilon_D = \frac{\text{proportionate (or percentage) change in quantity demanded}}{\text{proportionate (or percentage) change in income}}$$

For example, if a 2 per cent rise in consumer incomes causes an 8 per cent rise in a product's demand, then its income elasticity of demand will be:

$8\%/2\% = 4$

The major determinant of income elasticity of demand is the degree of 'necessity' of the good.

In a developed country, the demand for luxury goods expands rapidly as people's incomes rise, whereas the demand for more basic goods, such as bread, rises only a little. Thus items such as cars and foreign holidays have a high income elasticity of demand, whereas items such as potatoes and bus journeys have a low income elasticity of demand.

The demand for some goods actually decreases as income rises. These are inferior goods such as cheap margarine. As people earn more, so they switch to butter or better-quality

Definitions

Income elasticity of demand The responsiveness of demand to a change in consumer incomes: the proportionate change in demand divided by the proportionate change in income.

Cross-price elasticity of demand The responsiveness of demand for one good to a change in the price of another: the proportionate change in demand for one good divided by the proportionate change in price of the other.

margarine. Unlike normal goods, which have a positive income elasticity of demand, inferior goods have a negative income elasticity of demand (a rise in income leads to a *fall* in demand).

Income elasticity of demand and the firm

Income elasticity of demand is an important concept to firms considering the future size of the market for their product. If the product has a high income elasticity of demand, sales are likely to expand rapidly as national income rises, but may also fall significantly if the economy moves into recession.

Firms may also find that some parts of their market have a higher income elasticity of demand than others, and may thus choose to target their marketing campaigns on this group. For example, middle-income groups may have a higher income elasticity of demand for certain high-tech products than lower-income groups (who are unlikely to be able to afford such products even if their incomes rise somewhat) or higher-income groups (who can probably afford them anyway, and thus would not buy much more if their incomes rose).

> **Pause for thought**
>
> *Assume that you decide to spend a quarter of your income on clothes. What is (a) your income elasticity of demand; (b) your price elasticity of demand?*

Cross-price elasticity of demand ($C\varepsilon_{D_{ab}}$)

This is often known by its less cumbersome title of 'cross elasticity of demand'. It is a measure of the responsiveness of demand for one product to a change in the price of another (either a substitute or a complement). It enables us to predict how much the demand curve for the first product will shift when the price of the second product changes. For example, knowledge of the cross elasticity of demand for Coca-Cola with respect to the price of Pepsi would allow Coca-Cola to predict the effect on its own sales if the price of Pepsi were to change.

We define cross-price elasticity as follows:

$$C\varepsilon_D = \frac{\text{proportionate (or percentage) change in demand for good a}}{\text{proportionate (or percentage) change in price of good b}}$$

If good b is a *substitute* for good a, a's demand will *rise* as b's price rises. For example, the demand for bicycles will rise as the price of public transport rises. In this case, cross elasticity will be a positive figure. If b is *complementary* to a, however, a's demand will *fall* as b's price rises and thus as the quantity of b demanded falls. For example, the demand for petrol falls as the price of cars rises. In this case, cross elasticity will be a negative figure.

Cross-price elasticity of demand and the firm

The major determinant of cross elasticity of demand is the closeness of the substitute or complement. The closer it is, the bigger will be the effect on the first good of a change in the price of the substitute or complement, and hence the greater will be the cross elasticity – either positive or negative.

Firms will wish to know the cross elasticity of demand for their product when considering the effect on the demand for their product of a change in the price of a rival's product (a substitute). If firm b cuts its price, will this make significant inroads into the sales of firm a? If so, firm a may feel forced to cut its prices too; if not, then firm a may keep its price unchanged. The cross-price elasticities of demand between a firm's product and those of each of its rivals are thus vital pieces of information for a firm when making its production, pricing and marketing plans. KI 1 p 7 KI 8 p 38

Similarly, a firm will wish to know the cross-price elasticity of demand for its product with any complementary good. Car producers will wish to know the effect of petrol price increases on the sales of their cars.

Price elasticity of supply ($P\varepsilon_S$)

Just as we can measure the responsiveness of demand to a change in one of the determinants of demand, so too we can measure the responsiveness of supply to a change in one of the determinants of supply. The ***price elasticity of supply*** refers to the responsiveness of supply to a change in price. We define it as follows:

$$P\varepsilon_S = \frac{\text{proportionate (or percentage) change in quantity supplied}}{\text{proportionate (or percentage) change in price}}$$

Thus if a 15 per cent rise in the price of a product causes a 30 per cent rise in the quantity supplied, the price elasticity of supply will be:

$30\%/15\% = 2$

In Figure 5.7, curve S_2 is more elastic between any two prices than curve S_1. Thus, when price rises from P_1 to P_2 there is a larger increase in quantity supplied with S_2 (namely, Q_1 to Q_3) than there is with S_1 (namely, Q_1 to Q_2).

Determinants of price elasticity of supply

The amount that costs rise as output rises. The less the additional costs of producing additional output, the more firms

> **Definition**
>
> **Price elasticity of supply** The responsiveness of quantity supplied to a change in price: the proportionate change in quantity supplied divided by the proportionate change in price.

Figure 5.7 Price elasticity of supply

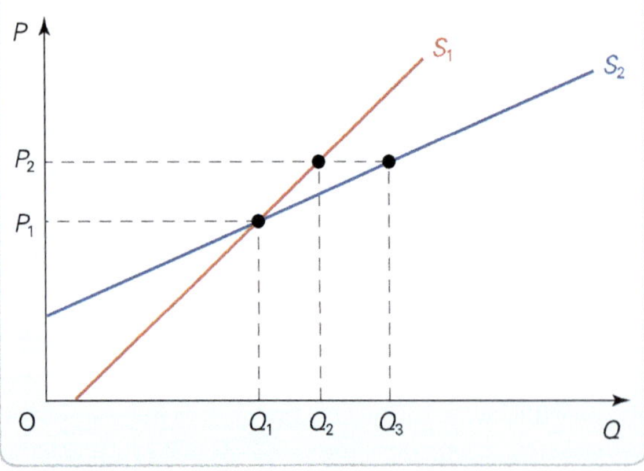

Figure 5.8 Supply in different time periods

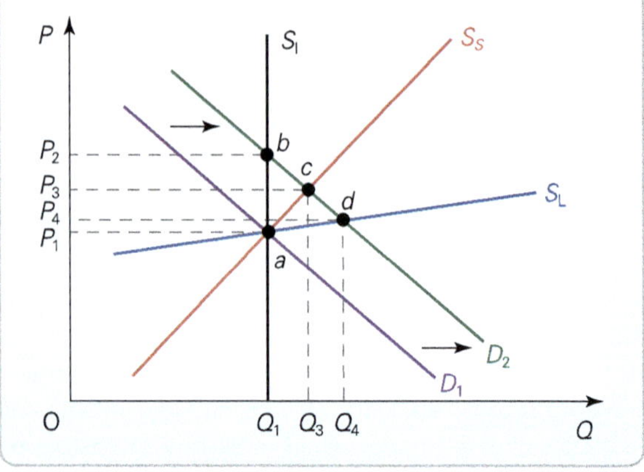

will be encouraged to produce for a given price rise: the more elastic will supply be.

Supply is thus likely to be elastic if firms have plenty of spare capacity, if they can readily get extra supplies of raw materials, if they can easily switch away from producing alternative products and if they can avoid having to introduce overtime working (at higher rates of pay). If all these conditions hold, costs will be little affected by a rise in output, and supply will be relatively elastic. The less these conditions apply, the less elastic will supply be.

Time period (see Figure 5.8)

- Immediate time period. Firms are unlikely to be able to increase supply by much immediately. Supply is virtually fixed, or can vary only according to available stocks. Hence, supply is highly inelastic. In the diagram S_I is drawn with $P\varepsilon_S = 0$. If demand increases to D_2, supply will not be able to respond. Price will rise to P_2. Quantity will remain at Q_1. Equilibrium will move to point *b*.
- Short run. If a slightly longer time period is allowed to elapse, some inputs can be increased (e.g. raw materials), while others will remain fixed (e.g. heavy machinery). Supply can increase somewhat. This is illustrated by S_S. Equilibrium will move to point *c* with price falling again, to P_3, and quantity rising to Q_3.
- Long run. In the long run, there will be sufficient time for all inputs to be increased and for new firms to enter the industry. Supply, therefore, is likely to be highly elastic. This is illustrated by curve S_L. Long-run equilibrium will be at point *d* with price falling back even further, to P_4, and quantity rising all the way to Q_4. In some circumstances the supply curve may even slope downward. (See the section on economies of scale in Chapter 9, pages 136–7.)

5.4 THE TIME DIMENSION OF MARKET ADJUSTMENT

KI 35 p 316

The full adjustment of price, demand and supply to a situation of disequilibrium will not be instantaneous. It is necessary, therefore, to analyse the time path which supply takes in responding to changes in demand, and which demand takes in responding to changes in supply.

Short-run and long-run adjustment

As we have already seen, elasticity varies with the time period under consideration. The reason is that producers and consumers take time to respond to a change in price. The longer the time period, the bigger the response, and thus the greater the elasticity of supply and demand.

This is illustrated in Figures 5.9 and 5.10. In both cases, as equilibrium moves from points *a* to *b* to *c*, there is a large short-run price change (P_1 to P_2) and a small short-run quantity change (Q_1 to Q_2), but a small long-run price change (P_1 to P_3) and a large long-run quantity change (Q_1 to Q_3).

Price expectations and speculation

In a world of shifting demand and supply curves, prices do not stay the same. Sometimes they go up; sometimes they come down. If prices are likely to change in the foreseeable future, this will affect the behaviour of buyers and sellers *now*. If, for example, it is now December and you are thinking of buying a new winter coat, you might decide to wait until the January sales, and in the meantime make do with your old coat. If, on the other hand, when January comes you see a new summer jacket in the sales, you might well buy it now and not wait until the summer, for fear

Figure 5.9 Response of supply to an increase in demand

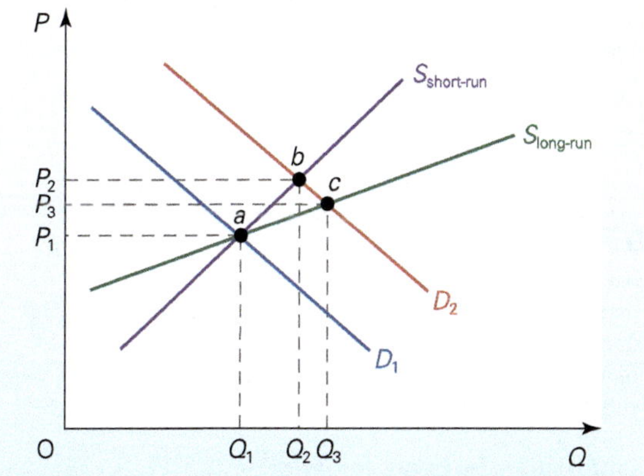

Figure 5.10 Response of demand to an increase in supply

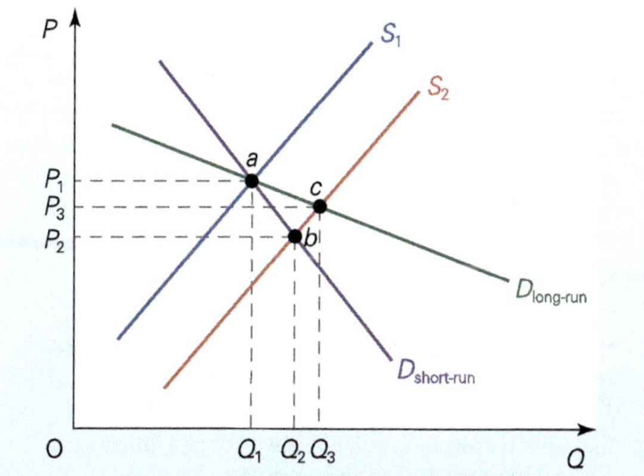

that the price will have gone up by then. Thus a belief that prices will go up will cause people to buy now; a belief that prices will come down will cause them to wait.

The reverse applies to sellers. If you are thinking of selling your house and prices are falling, you will want to sell it as quickly as possible. If, on the other hand, prices are rising sharply, you will wait as long as possible so as to get the highest price. Thus a belief that prices will come down will cause people to sell now; a belief that prices will go up will cause them to wait.

KEY IDEA 13

People's actions are influenced by their expectations. **People respond not just to what is happening now (such as a change in price), but to what they anticipate will happen in the future.**

This behaviour of looking into the future and making buying and selling decisions based on your predictions is called ***speculation***. Speculation is often partly based on current trends in price behaviour. If prices are currently rising, people may try to decide whether they are about to peak and go back down again, or whether they are likely to go on rising. Having made their prediction, they will then act on it. This speculation will thus affect demand and supply, which in turn will affect price. Speculation is commonplace in many markets: the stock exchange (see Box 4.2), the foreign exchange market and the housing market (see Box 4.1) are three examples. Large firms often employ specialist buyers who choose the right time to buy inputs, depending on what they anticipate will happen to their price.

Speculation tends to be ***self-fulfilling***. In other words, the actions of speculators tend to bring about the very effect on prices that speculators had anticipated. For example, if speculators believe that the price of BP shares is about to rise, they will buy more BP shares, shifting demand to the right. But by doing this they will ensure that the price *will* rise. The prophecy has become self-fulfilling.

Speculation can either help to reduce price fluctuations or aggravate them: it can be stabilising or destabilising.

Stabilising speculation

Speculation will tend to have a ***stabilising*** effect on price fluctuations when suppliers and/or demanders believe that a change in price is only *temporary*. KI 13 p 71

Assume, for example, that there has recently been a rise in price, caused, say, by an increase in demand. In Figure 5.11(a) demand has shifted from D_1 to D_2. Equilibrium has moved from point *a* to point *b*, and price has risen from P_1 to P_2. How do people react to this rise in price? KI 10 p 48

Given that they believe this rise in price to be only temporary, suppliers bring their goods to market now, before price falls again. Supply shifts from S_1 to S_2. Demanders, however, hold back until price does fall. Demand shifts from D_2 to D_3. The equilibrium moves to point *c*, with price falling back towards P_1.

A good example of stabilising speculation is that which occurs in agricultural commodity markets. Take the case of wheat. When it is harvested in the autumn there will be a plentiful supply. If all this wheat were to be put on the market, the price would fall to a very low level. Later in the year, when most of the wheat would have been sold, the price would then rise to a very high level. This is all easily predictable.

Definitions

Speculation This is where people make buying or selling decisions based on their anticipations of future prices.

Self-fulfilling speculation The actions of speculators tend to cause the very effect that they had anticipated.

Stabilising speculation This is where the actions of speculators tend to reduce price fluctuations.

BOX 5.2 ADJUSTING TO OIL PRICE SHOCKS

Short-run and long-run demand and supply responses

Between December 1973 and June 1974, the Organization of Petroleum Exporting Countries (OPEC) put up the price of oil from $3 to $12 per barrel. It was further raised to over $30 in 1979. In the 1980s the price fluctuated, but the trend was downward. Except for a sharp rise at the time of the Gulf War in 1990, the trend continued through most of the 1990s, at times falling as low as $11.

In the early 2000s, oil prices were generally higher, first fluctuating between $19 and $33 per barrel and then, from 2004 to 2006, steadily rising. The price then increased dramatically from January 2007, when it was just over $50 per barrel, to mid-2008 when it reached $147 per barrel. By late 2008 the price had fallen back sharply to under $50 per barrel as fears of a world recession cut the demand for oil. As the global economy began to recover, the oil price rose steadily, reaching $128 per barrel by early 2011. Since then prices have remained relatively stable and stood at around $100 in July 2012.

The price movements can be explained using simple demand and supply analysis.

The initial rise in price

In the 1970s OPEC raised the price from P_1 to P_2 (see diagram (a)). To prevent surplus at that price, OPEC members restricted their output by agreed amounts. This had the effect of shifting the supply curve to S_2, with Q_2 being produced. This reduction in output needed to be only relatively small because the short-run demand for oil was highly price inelastic: for most uses there are no substitutes in the short run.

Long-run effects on demand

The long-run demand for oil was more elastic (see diagram (b)). With high oil prices persisting, people tried to find ways of cutting back on consumption. People bought smaller cars. They converted to gas or solid-fuel central heating. Firms switched to other fuels. Less use was made of oil-fired power

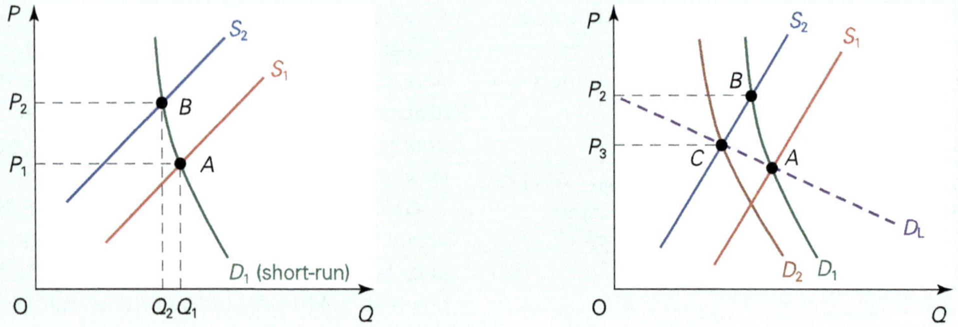

Figure 5.11 Speculation (initial rise in price)

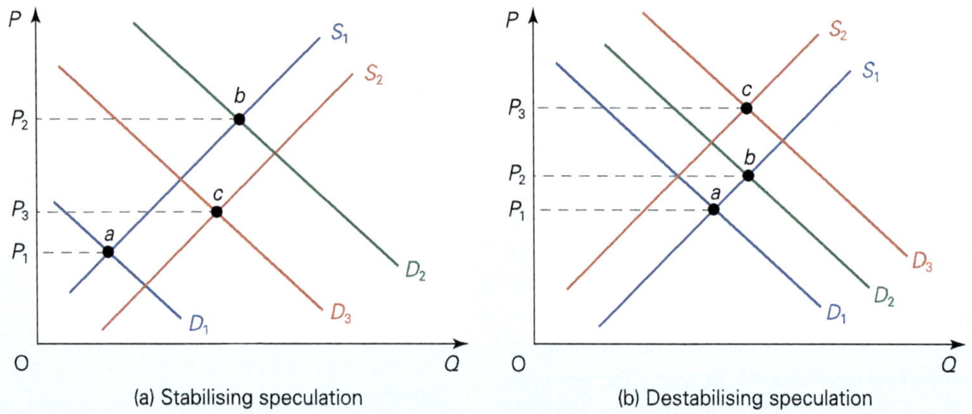

stations for electricity generation. Energy-saving schemes became widespread both in firms and in the home.

This had the effect of shifting the short-run demand curve from D_1 to D_2. Price fell back from P_2 to P_3. This gave a long-run demand curve of D_L: the curve that joins points *A* and *C*.

The fall in demand was made bigger by a world recession in the early 1980s.

Long-run effects on supply

With oil production so much more profitable, there was an incentive for non-OPEC oil producers to produce oil. Prospecting went on all over the world and large oil fields were discovered and opened up in the North Sea, Alaska, Mexico, China and elsewhere. In addition, OPEC members were tempted to break their 'quotas' (their allotted output) and sell more oil.

The net effect was an increase in world oil supplies. In terms of the diagrams, the supply curve of oil started to shift to the right from the mid-1980s onwards, causing oil prices to fall through most of the period up to 1998.

Back to square one?

By the late 1990s, with the oil price as low as $10 per barrel, OPEC once more cut back supply. The story had come full circle. This cut-back is once more illustrated in diagram (a).

The trouble this time was that worldwide economic growth was picking up. Demand was shifting to the right. The result was a rise in oil prices to around $33, which then fell back again in 2001 as the world slipped into recession and the demand curve shifted to the left.

There were then some very large price increases, first as a result of OPEC in late 2001 attempting once more to restrict supply (a leftward shift in supply), and then, before the Iraq war of 2003, because of worries about possible adverse effects on oil supplies (a rightward shift in demand as countries stocked up on oil). The worries about long-run security of supply continued after the invasion of Iraq and the continuing political uncertainty in the region.

The rises in the price of oil from 2004 through to mid-2008 were fuelled partly by rapidly expanding demand (a rightward shift in short-run demand), especially in countries such as China and India, and by speculation on the future price of oil. On the supply side, producers could not respond rapidly to meet this demand and there has been further disruption to supply in some oil-producing countries, including Nigeria and Algeria (a leftward shift in short-run supply). However, the dramatic rise in oil prices fuelled inflation across the world. Consumers and industry faced much higher costs and looked at methods to conserve fuel.

In late 2008, the global financial crisis was followed by recession. The price of oil began to fall back as the demand curve for oil shifted leftwards. It fell from a peak of $147 per barrel in July 2008 to a mere $34 per barrel by the end of the year. But then, as the world economy slowly recovered, and the demand for oil rose, so oil prices rose again. By early 2011, oil was trading at around $128 per barrel.

With both demand and supply being price *inelastic* in the short run, large fluctuations in price are only to be expected. And these are amplified by speculation.

The problem is made worse by an income elastic demand for oil. Demand can rise rapidly in times when the global economy is booming, only to fall back substantially in times of recession.

? ***Give some examples of things that could make the demand for oil more elastic. What specific policies could the government introduce to make demand more elastic?***

So what do farmers do? The answer is that they speculate. When the wheat is harvested they know its price will tend to fall, and so instead of bringing it all to market they put a lot of it into store. The more price falls, the more they will put into store *anticipating that the price will later rise*. But this holding back of supplies prevents prices from falling. In other words, it stabilises prices.

Later in the year, when the price begins to rise, they will gradually release grain on to the market from the stores. The more the price rises, the more will they release on to the market *anticipating that the price will fall again by the time of the next harvest*. But this releasing of supplies will again stabilise prices by preventing them rising so much.

Destabilising speculation

Speculation will tend to have a ***destabilising*** effect on price fluctuations when suppliers and/or buyers believe that a change in price heralds similar changes to come.

Assume again that there has recently been a rise in price, caused by an increase in demand. In Figure 5.11(b), demand has shifted from D_1 to D_2 and price has risen from P_1 to P_2. This time, however, believing that the rise in price heralds further rises to come, suppliers wait until the price rises further. Supply shifts from S_1 to S_2. Demanders buy now before any further rise in price. Demand shifts from D_2 to D_3. As a result the price continues to rise: to P_3.

Box 4.1 examined the housing market. In this market, speculation is frequently destabilising. Assume that people see house prices beginning to move upward. This might be the result of increased demand brought about by a cut in mortgage interest rates or by growth in the economy. People may well believe that the rise in house prices signals a boom in the housing market: that prices will go on rising. Potential buyers will thus try to buy as soon as possible

Definition

Destabilising speculation This is where the actions of speculators tend to make price movements larger.

before prices rise any further. This increased demand (as in Figure 5.11(b)) will thus lead to even bigger price rises. This is precisely what happened in the UK housing market in 1999–2007.

Pause for thought

Draw two diagrams like Figures 5.11(a) and (b), only this time assume an initial fall in demand and hence price. The first diagram should show the effects of stabilising speculation and the second the effect of destabilising speculation.

Conclusion

In some circumstances, then, the action of speculators can help keep price fluctuations to a minimum (stabilising speculation). This is most likely when markets are relatively stable in the first place, with only moderate underlying shifts in demand and supply.

Pause for thought

What are the advantages and disadvantages of speculation from the point of view of (a) the consumer; (b) firms?

In other circumstances, however, speculation can make price fluctuations much worse. This is most likely in times of uncertainty, when there are significant changes in the determinants of demand and supply. Given this uncertainty, people may see price changes as signifying some trend. They then 'jump on the bandwagon' and do what the rest are doing, further fuelling the rise or fall in price.

5.5 DEALING WITH UNCERTAINTY

Risk and uncertainty

KI 8 p 38

When price changes are likely to occur, buyers and sellers will try to anticipate them. Unfortunately, on many occasions no one can be certain just what these price changes will be. Take the case of stocks and shares. If you anticipate that the price of, say, BP shares is likely to go up substantially in the near future, you may well decide to buy some now and then sell them later after the price has risen. But you cannot be certain that they will go up in price: they may fall instead. If you buy the shares, therefore, you will be taking a gamble.

Now gambles can be of two types. The first is where you know the odds. Let us take the simplest case of a gamble on the toss of a coin. Heads you win; tails you lose. You know that the odds of winning are precisely 50 per cent. If you bet on the toss of a coin, you are said to be operating under conditions of ***risk***. *Risk is when the probability of an outcome is known.* Risk itself is a measure of the *variability* of an outcome. For example, if you bet £1 on the toss of a coin, such that heads you win £1 and tails you lose £1, then the variability is –£1 to +£1.

The second form of gamble is the more usual. This is where the odds are not known or are known only roughly. Gambling on the Stock Exchange is like this. You may have a good idea that a share will go up in price, but is it a 90 per cent chance, an 80 per cent chance or what? You are not certain. Gambling under these sorts of conditions is known as operating under ***uncertainty***. *This is when the probability of an outcome is not known.*

You may well disapprove of gambling and want to dismiss people who engage in it as foolish or morally wrong. But 'gambling' is not just confined to horses, cards, roulette and the like. Risk and uncertainty pervade the whole of economic life and decisions are constantly having to be made whose outcome cannot be known for certain. Even the most morally upright person will still have to decide which career to go into, whether and when to buy a house, or even something as trivial as whether or not to take an umbrella when going out. Each of these decisions and thousands of others are made under conditions of uncertainty (or occasionally risk).

KEY IDEA 14

People's actions are influenced by their attitudes towards risk. **Many decisions are taken under conditions of risk or uncertainty. Generally, the lower the probability of (or the more uncertain) the desired outcome of an action, the less likely will people be to undertake the action.**

We shall be examining how risk and uncertainty affect economic decisions at several points throughout the book. For example, in the next chapter we will see how it affects people's attitudes and actions as consumers, and how taking out insurance can help to reduce their uncertainty. At this point, however, let us focus on firms' attitudes when supplying goods.

Definitions

Risk This is when an outcome may or may not occur, but where its probability of occurring is known.

Uncertainty This is when an outcome may or may not occur and where its probability of occurring is not known.

Stock holding as a way of reducing the problem of uncertainty. A simple way that suppliers can reduce risks is by holding stocks. Take the case of the wheat farmers we saw in the previous section. At the time when they are planting the wheat in the spring, they are uncertain as to what the price of wheat will be when they bring it to market. If they keep no stores of wheat, they will just have to accept whatever the market price happens to be at harvest time. If, however, they have storage facilities, they can put the wheat into store if the price is low and then wait until it goes up. Alternatively, if the price of wheat is high at harvest time, they can sell it straight away. In other words, they can wait until the price is right.

Pause for thought

The demand for pears is more price elastic than the demand for bread and yet the price of pears fluctuates more than that of bread. Why should this be so? If pears could be stored as long and as cheaply as flour, would this affect the relative price fluctuations? If so, how?

Purchasing information. One way of reducing uncertainty is to buy information. A firm could commission various forms of market research or purchase the information from specialist organisations. It is similar for consumers. You might take advice on shares from a stockbroker, or buy a copy of a consumer magazine, such as *Which?*. The buying and selling of information in this way helps substantially to reduce uncertainty.

Better information can also, under certain circumstances, help to make any speculation more stabilising. With poor information, people are much more likely to be guided by rumour or fear, which could well make speculation destabilising as people 'jump on the bandwagon'. If people generally are better informed, however, this is likely to make prices go more directly to a long-run stable equilibrium.

Dealing in futures markets

Another way of reducing or even eliminating uncertainty is by dealing in ***futures*** or ***forward markets***. Let us examine the activities first of sellers and then of buyers.

Sellers

Suppose you are a farmer and want to store grain to sell some time in the future, expecting to get a better price then than now. The trouble is that there is a chance that the price will go down. Given this uncertainty, you may be unwilling to take a gamble.

An answer to your problem is provided by the *commodity futures market*. This is a market where prices are agreed between sellers and buyers *today* for delivery at some specified date in the *future*.

For example, if it is 20 October today, you could be quoted a price *today* for delivery in six months' time (i.e. on 20 April). This is known as the six-month ***future price***. Assume that the six-month future price for wheat is £60 per tonne. If you agree to this price and make a six-month forward contract, you are agreeing to sell a specified amount of wheat at £60 on 20 April. No matter what happens to the ***spot price*** (i.e. the current market price) in the meantime, your selling price has been agreed. The spot price could have fallen to £30 (or risen to £100) by April, but your selling price when 20 April arrives is fixed at £60. There is thus *no risk to you whatsoever of the price going down*. You will, of course, lose out if the spot price is *more* than £60 in April.

Buyers

Now suppose that you are a flour miller. In order to plan your expenditures, you would like to know the price you will have to pay for wheat, not just today, but also at various future dates. In other words, if you want to take delivery of wheat at some time in the future, you would like a price quoted *now*. You would like the risks removed of prices going *up*.

Let us assume that today (20 October) you want to *buy* the same amount of wheat on 20 April that a farmer wishes to sell on that same date. If you agree to the £60 future price, a future contract can be made with the farmer. You are then guaranteed that purchase price, no matter what happens to the spot price in the meantime. There is thus *no risk to you whatsoever of the price going up*. You will, of course, lose out if the spot price is *less* than £60 in April.

The determination of the future price

Prices in the futures market are determined in the same way as in other markets: by demand and supply. For example, the six-month wheat price or the three-month coffee price will be that which equates the demand for those futures with the supply. If the five-month sugar price is currently £200 per tonne and people expect by then, because of an anticipated good beet harvest, that the spot price for sugar will be £150 per tonne, there will be few who will want to buy the futures at £200 (and many who will want to sell). This excess of supply of futures over demand will push the price down.

Speculators

Many people operate in the futures market who never actually handle the commodities themselves. They are

Definitions

Futures or forward market A market in which contracts are made to buy or sell at some future date at a price agreed today.

Future price A price agreed today at which an item (e.g. commodities) will be exchanged at some set date in the future.

Spot price The current market price.

BOX 5.3 DON'T SHOOT THE SPECULATOR

Well not yet, anyway!

In February 2008 the United Nations Food and Agricultural Organisation stated that the price of cereals had risen 83 per cent over the previous 12 months, with dire consequences for developing nations in particular. In July 2008 the price of oil rose to the unprecedented high of $147 per barrel, with devastating consequences for the millions of users of oil and oil-based products. Between early September and late October 2008 the FTSE 100 fell by 35 per cent, from a high of 5646 to a low of 3665 (see Box 4.2), a fall that had not been seen since October 1987, offering misery to millions of ordinary investors and those with pensions.

Much of the blame for these dramatic changes is placed on speculators who are seen as exacerbating the problem. They are seen as greedy and acting immorally, and affecting the lives of millions of ordinary people through their actions. Thankfully, no one in power has yet adopted Vladimir Lenin's declaration to a meeting at the Petrograd Soviet in 1918 that 'Speculators who are caught and fully exposed as such shall be shot . . . on the spot.' However, religious leaders, politicians and regulators have been calling for, and getting, stricter controls over their operations.

This commonly held view of the speculator, however, is not held by everyone. Consider the following taken from *The Financial Times* in regard to the rapid rise in commodity prices in early 2011.

> . . . where are commodity prices headed next?
>
> There are many problems in understanding, let alone forecasting, the behaviour of commodity prices. In the long term, which means decades, the real price of commodities is determined by the supply side costs of extraction, . . . over shorter term horizons, these factors are incapable of explaining commodity price fluctuations, because they change so slowly. Prices, on the other hand, can change dramatically over short periods. Since demand and supply curves are both very steep (especially for oil), a very small shift in either curve can have very large effects on oil prices, making them very hard to predict.
>
> There are two possible explanations for the surge in commodity prices since last August. The first and 'fundamental' explanation is that the growth in global industrial production has been maintained at levels well above long term trends. . . .
>
> The second, and 'speculative' explanation is that the Fed's decision to expand liquidity has leaked into all risk assets, including commodities, via financial market demand for these assets. . . . Paul Krugman and others have argued that the 'speculative' explanation can be eliminated on a priori grounds, because financial operators never take delivery of physical commodities. Ultimately they do not increase the real demand for commodities, and therefore they can have no effect on the price. Financial demand can of course alter the prices for futures and options on commodities, but since the prices of these derivative contracts must eventually home in on the price for the physical, this will eventually be a zero sum game. On this argument, financial speculation is irrelevant.
>
> . . . but it seems to me that for short periods . . . rising futures prices could lead to the expectation of higher prices for physical commodities, in which case physical players might decide to 'hoard' stocks, and reduce the rate of extraction so that they can benefit from the subsequent rise in prices. By changing inventory levels and extraction rates, this type of real activity could tighten the physical market and, at least for a time, raise prices. . . .
>
> So which of these explanations best fits the evidence? . . . The calculations suggest that while a large part of the rise in oil and other commodity prices may have been caused by fundamentals, nevertheless commodity prices may have overshot their 'equilibrium' levels at times in recent months. . . .[1]

Are speculators largely adjusting their decisions in line with changing circumstances? In other words, are they being efficient? Or are they being inefficient and causing increased price volatility?

? ***How might it be beneficial for the economy if speculators were less efficient?***

[1] Gavyn Davies, 'Fundamentals and speculation in commodity markets' *The Financial Times* 16 May 2011.

neither producers nor users of the commodities. They merely speculate. Such speculators may be individuals, but they are more likely to be financial institutions.

Let us take a simple example. Suppose that the six-month (April) coffee price is £1000 per tonne and that you, as a speculator, believe that the spot price of coffee is likely to rise above that level between now (October) and six months' time. You thus decide to buy 20 tonnes of April coffee futures now.

But you have no intention of taking delivery. After four months, let us say, true to your prediction, the spot price (February) has risen and as a result the April price (and other future prices) have risen too. You thus decide to *sell* 20 tonnes of April (two-month) coffee futures, whose price, let us say, is £1200. You are now 'covered'.

When April comes, what happens? You have agreed to buy 20 tonnes of coffee at £1000 per tonne and to sell 20 tonnes of coffee at £1200 per tonne. All you do is hand the futures contract to buy to the person to whom you agreed to sell. They sort out delivery between them and you make £200 per tonne profit.

If, however, your prediction had been wrong and the price had *fallen*, you would have made a loss. You would have been forced to sell coffee contracts at a lower price than you had bought them.

Speculators in the futures market thus incur risks, unlike the sellers and buyers of the commodities, for whom the futures market eliminates risk. Financial institutions offering futures contracts will charge for the service: for taking on the risks.

SUMMARY

1a Price elasticity of demand measures the responsiveness of demand to a change in price. It is defined as the proportionate (or percentage) change in quantity demanded divided by the proportionate (or percentage) change in price.

1b If quantity demanded changes proportionately more than price, the figure for elasticity will be greater than 1 (ignoring the sign): it is elastic. If the quantity demanded changes proportionately less than price, the figure for elasticity will be less than 1: it is inelastic. If they change by the same proportion, the elasticity has a value of 1: it is unit elastic.

1c Given that demand curves are downward sloping, price elasticity of demand will have a negative value.

1d Demand will be more elastic the greater the number and closeness of substitute goods, the higher the proportion of income spent on the good and the longer the time period that elapses after the change in price.

1e Demand curves normally have different elasticities along their length. We can thus normally refer only to the specific value for elasticity between two points on the curve or at a single point.

2a It is important for firms to know the price elasticity of demand for their product whenever they are considering a price change. The reason is that the effect of the price change on the firm's sales revenue will depend on the product's price elasticity.

2b When the demand for a firm's product is price elastic, a rise in price will lead to a reduction in consumer expenditure on the good and hence to a reduction in the total revenue of the firm.

2c When demand is price inelastic, however, a rise in price will lead to an increase in total revenue for the firm.

3a Income elasticity of demand measures the responsiveness of demand to a change in income. For normal goods it has a positive value. Demand will be more income elastic the more luxurious the good and the less rapidly demand is satisfied as consumption increases.

3b Cross-price elasticity of demand measures the responsiveness of demand for one good to a change in the price of another. For substitute goods the value will be positive; for complements it will be negative. The cross-price elasticity will be greater the closer the two goods are as substitutes or complements.

3c Price elasticity of supply measures the responsiveness of supply to a change in price. It has a positive value. Supply will be more elastic the less costs per unit rise as output rises and the longer the time period.

4a A complete understanding of markets must take into account the time dimension.

4b Given that producers and consumers take a time to respond fully to price changes, we can identify different equilibria after the elapse of different lengths of time. Generally, short-run supply and demand tend to be less price elastic than long-run supply and demand. As a result any shifts in demand or supply curves tend to have a relatively bigger effect on price in the short run and a relatively bigger effect on quantity in the long run.

4c People often anticipate price changes and this will affect the amount they demand or supply. This speculation will tend to stabilise price fluctuations if people believe that the price changes are only temporary. However, speculation will tend to destabilise these fluctuations (i.e. make them more severe) if people believe that prices are likely to continue to move in the same direction as at present (at least for some time).

5a A lot of economic decision making is made under conditions of risk or uncertainty.

5b Risk is when the probability of an outcome occurring is known. Uncertainty is when the probability is not known.

5c One way of reducing risks is to hold stocks. If the price of a firm's product falls unexpectedly, it can build up stocks rather than releasing its product on to the market. If the price later rises, it can then release stocks on to the market. Similarly with inputs: if their price falls unexpectedly, firms can build up their stocks, only to draw on them later if input prices rise.

5d A way of eliminating risk and uncertainty is to deal in the futures markets. When firms are planning to buy or sell at some point in the future, there is the danger that price could rise or fall unexpectedly in the meantime. By agreeing to buy or sell at some particular point in the future at a price agreed today (a 'future' price), this danger can be eliminated. The bank or other institution offering the price (the 'speculator') is taking on the risk, and will charge for this service.

REVIEW QUESTIONS

1. Why does price elasticity of demand have a negative value, whereas price elasticity of supply has a positive value?
2. Rank the following in ascending order of elasticity: jeans, black Levi jeans, black jeans, black Levi 501 jeans, trousers, outer garments, clothes.
3. How might a firm set about making the demand for its brand less elastic?
4. Will a general item of expenditure like food or clothing have a price elastic or inelastic demand?
5. Assuming that a firm faces an inelastic demand and wants to increase its total revenue, how much should it raise its price? Is there any limit?
6. Can you think of any examples of goods which have a totally inelastic demand (a) at all prices; (b) over a particular price range?
7. Which of these two pairs are likely to have the highest cross-price elasticity of demand: two brands of coffee, or coffee and tea?
8. Why are both the price elasticity of demand and the price elasticity of supply likely to be greater in the long run?
9. Redraw Figure 5.11, only this time assume that it was an initial shift in supply that caused the price to change in the first place.
10. Give some examples of decisions you have taken recently that were made under conditions of uncertainty. With hindsight, do you think you made the right decisions? Explain.
11. What methods can a firm use to reduce risk and uncertainty?
12. If speculators believed that the price of cocoa in six months was going to be below the six-month future price quoted today, how would they act?

ADDITIONAL PART B CASE STUDIES IN THE *ECONOMICS FOR BUSINESS* MyEconLab (www.pearsoned.co.uk/sloman)

B.1 **The interdependence of markets.** A case study of the operation of markets, examining the effects on a local economy of the discovery of a large coal deposit.

B.2 **Adam Smith (1723–1790).** Smith, the founder of modern economics, argued that markets act like an 'invisible hand' guiding production and consumption.

B.3 **Shall we put up our price?** Some examples of firms charging high prices in markets where demand is relatively inelastic.

B.4 **Any more fares?** Pricing on the buses: an illustration of the relationship between price and total revenue.

B.5 **Elasticities of demand for various foodstuffs.** An examination of the evidence about price and income elasticities of demand for food in the UK.

B.6 **Adjusting to oil price shocks.** A case study showing how demand and supply analysis can be used to examine the price changes in the oil market since 1973.

B.7 **Income elasticity of demand and the balance of payments.** This examines how a low income elasticity of demand for the exports of many developing countries can help to explain their chronic balance of payments problems.

B.8 **The cobweb.** An outline of the theory that explains price fluctuations in terms of time lags in supply.

B.9 **The role of the speculator.** This assesses whether the activities of speculators are beneficial or harmful to the rest of society.

B.10 **Rationing.** A case study in the use of rationing as an alternative to the price mechanism. In particular, it looks at the use of rationing in the UK during the Second World War.

B.11 **Rent control.** This shows how setting (low) maximum rents is likely to lead to a shortage of rented accommodation.

B.12 **Agriculture and minimum prices.** This shows how setting (high) minimum prices is likely to lead to surpluses.

B.13 **The fallacy of composition.** An illustration from agricultural markets of the fallacy of composition: 'what applies in one case will not necessarily apply when repeated in all cases'.

B.14 **Coffee prices.** An examination of the coffee market and the implications of fluctuations in the coffee harvest for growers and coffee drinkers.

B.15 **Response to changes in petrol and ethanol prices in Brazil.** This case examines how drivers with 'flex-fuel' cars responded to changes in the relative prices of two fuels: petrol and ethanol (made from sugar cane).

WEBSITES RELEVANT TO PART B

Numbers and sections refer to websites listed in the Web appendix and hotlinked from this book's website at **www.pearsoned.co.uk/sloman**

- For news articles relevant to Part B, see the *Economics News Articles* link from the book's website.
- For general news on markets, see websites in section A, and particularly A2, 3, 4, 5, 8, 9, 18, 20–26, 35, 36. See also site A42 for links to economics news articles from newspapers worldwide.
- For links to sites on markets, see the relevant sections of I4, 7, 11, 17.
- For data on the housing market (Box 4.1), see sites B7, 8, 11.
- For student resources relevant to Part B, see sites C1–7, 9, 10, 19; D3.
- For sites favouring the free market, see C17 and E34.

Chapter 9

Costs of production

Business issues covered in this chapter

- What do profits consist of?
- How are costs of production measured?
- What is the relationship between inputs and outputs in both the short and long run?
- How do costs vary with output in both the short and long run?
- What are meant by 'economies of scale' and what are the reasons for such economies?
- How can a business combine its inputs in the most efficient way?

9.1 THE MEANING OF COSTS

Opportunity cost

KI 3 p 20

When measuring costs, economists always use the concept of ***opportunity cost***. Opportunity cost is the cost of any activity measured in terms of the sacrifice made in doing it: in other words, the cost measured in terms of the opportunities forgone (see Chapter 2). If a car manufacturer can produce 10 small saloon cars with the same amount of inputs as it takes to produce 6 large saloon cars, then the opportunity cost of producing 1 small car is 0.6 of a large car. If a taxi and car hire firm uses its cars as taxis, then the opportunity cost includes not only the cost of employing taxi drivers and buying fuel, but also the sacrifice of rental income from hiring its vehicles out.

Measuring a firm's opportunity costs

Just how do we measure a firm's opportunity cost? First we must discover what factors of production it has used. Then we must measure the sacrifice involved in using them. To do this it is necessary to put factors into two categories.

Factors not owned by the firm: explicit costs

The opportunity cost of those factors not already owned by the firm is simply the price that the firm has to pay for them. Thus if the firm uses £100 worth of electricity, the opportunity cost is £100. The firm has sacrificed £100 which could have been spent on something else.

These costs are called ***explicit costs*** because they involve direct payment of money by firms.

Definitions

Opportunity cost Cost measured in terms of the next best alternative forgone.

Explicit costs The payments to outside suppliers of inputs.

Factors already owned by the firm: implicit costs

When the firm already owns factors (e.g. machinery), it does not as a rule have to pay out money to use them. Their opportunity costs are thus ***implicit costs***. They are equal to what the factors *could* earn for the firm in some alternative use, either within the firm or hired out to some other firm.

Here are some examples of implicit costs:

- A firm owns some buildings. The opportunity cost of using them is the rent it could have received by letting them out to another firm.
- A firm draws £100 000 from the bank out of its savings in order to invest in new plant and equipment. The opportunity cost of this investment is not just the £100 000 (an explicit cost), but also the interest it thereby forgoes (an implicit cost).
- The owner of the firm could have earned £15 000 per annum by working for someone else. This £15 000 is the opportunity cost of the owner's time.

If there is no alternative use for a factor of production, as in the case of a machine designed to produce a specific product, and if it has no scrap value, the opportunity cost of using it is *zero*. In such a case, if the output from the machine is worth more than the cost of all the *other* inputs involved, the firm might as well use the machine rather than let it stand idle.

What the firm paid for the machine – its ***historic cost*** – is irrelevant. Not using the machine will not bring that money back. It has been spent. These are sometimes referred to as ***sunk costs***.

Pause for thought

Assume that a farmer decides to grow wheat on land that could be used for growing barley. Barley sells for £100 per tonne. Wheat sells for £150 per tonne. Seed, fertiliser, labour and other costs of growing crops are £80 per tonne for both wheat and barley. What are the farmer's costs and profit per tonne of growing wheat?

KEY IDEA 18

The 'bygones' principle **states that sunk (fixed) costs should be ignored when deciding whether to produce or sell more or less of a product. Only variable costs should be taken into account.**

Likewise, the ***replacement cost*** is irrelevant. That should be taken into account only when the firm is considering replacing the machine.

Definitions

Implicit costs Costs which do not involve a direct payment of money to a third party, but which nevertheless involve a sacrifice of some alternative.

Historic costs The original amount the firm paid for factors it now owns.

Sunk costs Costs that cannot be recouped (e.g. by transferring assets to other uses).

Replacement costs What the firm would have to pay to replace factors it currently owns.

BOX 9.1 THE FALLACY OF USING HISTORIC COSTS

Or there's no point crying over spilt milk

'What's done is done.'

'Write it off to experience.'

'You might as well make the best of a bad job.'

These familiar sayings are all everyday examples of a simple fact of life: once something has happened, you cannot change the past. You have to take things as they are *now*.

If you fall over and break your leg, there is little point in saying, 'If only I hadn't done that I could have gone on that skiing holiday; I could have taken part in that race; I could have done so many other things (sigh).' Wishing things were different won't change history. You have to manage as well as you can *with* your broken leg.

It is the same for a firm. Once it has purchased some inputs, it is no good then wishing it hadn't. It has to accept that it has now got them, and make the best decisions about what to do with them.

Take a simple example. The local convenience store in early December decides to buy 100 Christmas trees for £10 each. At the time of purchase this represents an opportunity cost of £10 each, since the £10 could have been spent on something else. The shopkeeper estimates that there is enough local demand to sell all 100 trees at £20 each, thereby making a reasonable profit (even after allowing for handling costs).

But the estimate turns out to be wrong. On 23 December there are still 50 trees unsold. What should be done? At this stage the £10 that was paid for the trees is irrelevant. It is a historic cost. It cannot be recouped: the trees cannot be sold back to the wholesaler!

In fact the opportunity cost is now zero. It might even be negative if the shopkeeper has to pay to dispose of any unsold trees. It might, therefore, be worth selling the trees at £10, £5 or even £1. Last thing on Christmas Eve it might even be worth giving away any unsold trees. KI 3 p 20

Why is the correct price to charge (for the unsold trees) the one at which the price elasticity of demand equals –1? (Assume no disposal costs.)

9.2 PRODUCTION IN THE SHORT RUN

The cost of producing any level of output will depend on the amount of inputs used and the price that the firm must pay for them. Let us first focus on the quantity of inputs used.

KEY IDEA 19

Output depends on the amount of resources and how they are used. **Different amounts and combinations of inputs will lead to different amounts of output. If output is to be produced efficiently, then inputs should be combined in the optimum proportions.**

Short-run and long-run changes in production

If a firm wants to increase production, it will take time to acquire a greater quantity of certain inputs. For example, a manufacturer can use more electricity by turning on switches, but it might take a long time to obtain and install more machines, and longer still to build a second or third factory.

If, then, the firm wants to increase output in a hurry, it will only be able to increase the quantity of certain inputs. It can use more raw materials, more fuel, more tools and possibly more labour (by hiring extra workers or offering overtime to its existing workforce). But it will have to make do with its existing buildings and most of its machinery.

The distinction we are making here is between ***fixed factors*** and ***variable factors***. A *fixed* factor is an input that cannot be increased within a given time period (e.g. buildings). A *variable* factor is one that can.

The distinction between fixed and variable factors allows us to distinguish between the ***short run*** and the ***long run***.

The short run is a time period during which at least one factor of production is fixed. In the short run, then, output can be increased only by using more variable factors. For example, if a shipping line wanted to carry more passengers in response to a rise in demand, it could accommodate more passengers on existing sailings if there was space. It could increase the number of sailings with its existing fleet, by hiring more crew and using more fuel. But in the short run it could not buy more ships: there would not be time for them to be built.

The long run is a time period long enough for all inputs to be varied. Given long enough, the shipping company can have a new ship built, making all factors of production variable.

The actual length of the short run will differ from firm to firm. It is not a fixed period of time. Thus if it takes a farmer a year to obtain new land, buildings and equipment, the short run is any time period up to a year and the long run is any time period longer than a year. But if it takes a shipping company three years to obtain an extra ship, the short run is any period up to three years and the long run is any period longer than three years.

For this and the next section we will concentrate on *short-run* production and costs. We will look at the long run in sections 9.4 and 9.5.

Pause for thought

How will the length of the short run for the shipping company depend on the state of the shipbuilding industry?

Production in the short run: the law of diminishing returns

Production in the short run is subject to *diminishing returns*. You may well have heard of 'the law of diminishing returns': it is one of the most famous of all 'laws' of economics. To illustrate how this law underlies short-run production, let us take the simplest possible case where there are just two factors: one fixed and one variable.

Take the case of a farm. Assume the fixed factor is land and the variable factor is labour. Since the land is fixed in supply, output per period of time can be increased only by increasing the number of workers employed. But imagine what would happen as more and more workers crowded on to a fixed area of land. The land cannot go on yielding more and more output indefinitely. After a point the additions to output from each extra worker will begin to diminish.

We can now state the ***law of diminishing (marginal) returns***.

KEY IDEA 20

The law of diminishing marginal returns. **When increasing amounts of a variable factor are used with a given amount of a fixed factor, there will come a point when each extra unit of the variable factor will produce less additional output than the previous unit.**

Definitions

Fixed factor An input that cannot be increased in supply within a given time period.

Variable factor An input that *can* be increased in supply within a given time period.

Short run The period of time over which at least one factor is fixed.

Long run The period of time long enough for *all* factors to be varied.

Law of diminishing (marginal) returns When one or more factors are held fixed, there will come a point beyond which the extra output from additional units of the variable factor will diminish.

A good example of the law of diminishing returns is given in Case D.3 in MyEconLab. The case looks at diminishing returns to the application of nitrogen fertiliser on farmland.

The short-run production function: total product

Let us now see how the law of diminishing returns affects total output or ***total physical product*** (*TPP*).

KI 19 p 130 The relationship between inputs and output is shown in a ***production function***. In the simple case of the farm with only two factors – namely, a fixed supply of land ($\bar{L}n$) and a variable supply of farm workers (*Lb*) – the production function would be:

$$TPP = f(\bar{L}n, Lb)$$

Definitions

Total physical product The total output of a product per period of time that is obtained from a given amount of inputs.

Production function The mathematical relationship between the output of a good and the inputs used to produce it. It shows how output will be affected by changes in the quantity of one or more of the inputs.

Table 9.1 Wheat production per year from a particular farm (tonnes)

	Number of workers (*Lb*)	*TPP*	*APP* (= *TPP*/*Lb*)	*MPP* (= Δ*TPP*/Δ*Lb*)
a	0	0	–	
				3
	1	3	3	
				7
	2	10	5	
b				14
	3	24	8	
				12
c	4	36	9	
				4
	5	40	8	
				2
	6	42	7	
d				0
	7	42	6	
				–2
	8	40	5	

This states that total physical product (i.e. the output of the farm) over a given period of time is a function of (i.e. depends on) the quantity of land and labour employed.

The production function can also be expressed in the form of a table or a graph. Table 9.1 and Figure 9.1 show a hypothetical production function for a farm producing wheat. The first two columns of Table 9.1 and the top diagram in Figure 9.1 show how wheat output per year varies as extra workers are employed on a fixed amount of land.

Figure 9.1 Wheat production per year (tonnes) from a particular farm

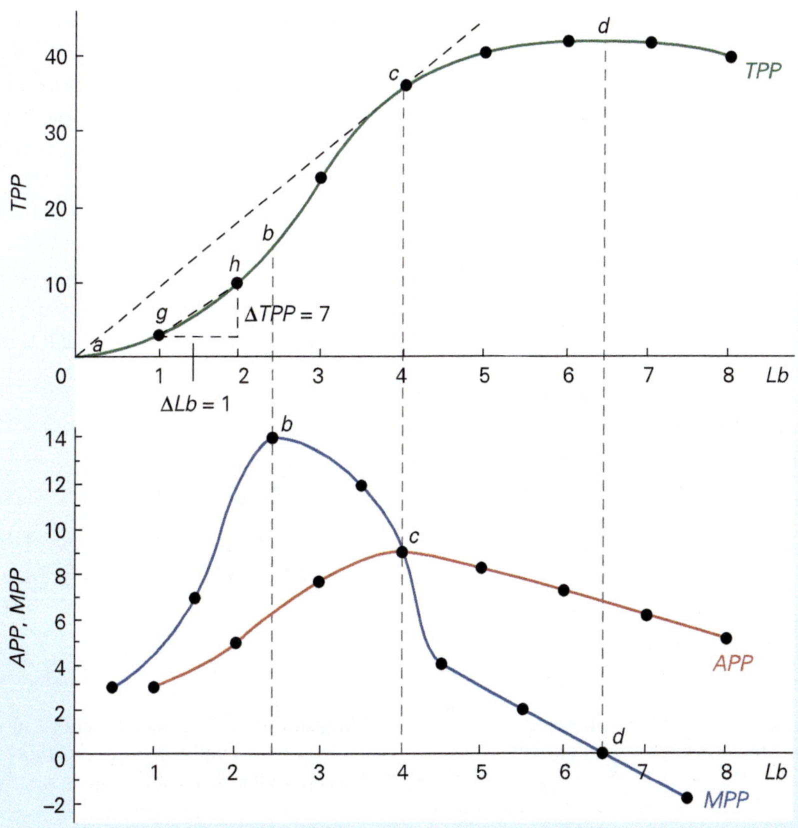

With nobody working on the land, output will be zero (point *a*). As the first farm workers are taken on, wheat output initially rises more and more rapidly. The assumption behind this is that with only one or two workers efficiency is low, since the workers are spread thinly across multiple tasks. With more workers, however, they can work as a team – each, perhaps, doing some specialist job – and thus they can use the land more efficiently. In the top diagram of Figure 9.1, output rises more and more rapidly up to the employment of the third worker (point *b*).

After point *b*, however, diminishing marginal returns set in: output rises less and less rapidly, and the *TPP* curve correspondingly becomes less steeply sloped.

When point *d* is reached, wheat output is at a maximum: the land is yielding as much as it can. Any more workers employed after that are likely to get in each other's way. Thus beyond point *d*, output is likely to fall again: eight workers produce less than seven workers.

The short-run production function: average and marginal product

In addition to total physical product, two other important concepts are illustrated by a production function: namely, ***average physical product (*****APP*****)*** and ***marginal physical product (*****MPP*****)***.

Average physical product

This is output (*TPP*) per unit of the variable factor (*Qv*). In the case of the farm, it is the output of wheat per worker.

$APP = TPP/Qv$

Thus in Table 9.1, the average physical product of labour when four workers are employed is 36/4 = 9 tonnes per year.

Marginal physical product

This is the *extra* output (ΔTPP) produced by employing *one more* unit of the variable factor, (where the symbol Δ denotes 'a change in').

Thus in Table 9.1 the marginal physical product of the fourth worker is 12 tonnes. The reason is that, by employing the fourth worker, wheat output has risen from 24 tonnes to 36 tonnes: a rise of 12 tonnes.

In symbols, marginal physical product is given by:

$MPP = \Delta TPP/\Delta Qv$

Thus in our example:

$MPP = 12/1 = 12$

The reason why we divide the increase in output (ΔTPP) by the increase in the quantity of the variable factor (ΔQv) is that some variable factors can be increased only in multiple units. For example, if we wanted to know the *MPP* of fertiliser and we found out how much extra wheat was produced by using an extra 20 kg bag, we would have to divide this output by 20 (ΔQv) to find the *MPP* of *one* more kilogram.

Note that in Table 9.1 the figures for *MPP* are entered in the spaces between the other figures. The reason is that *MPP* can be seen as the *difference* in output *between* one level of input and another. Thus in the table the difference in output between five and six workers is 2 tonnes.

The figures for *APP* and *MPP* are plotted in the lower diagram of Figure 9.1. We can draw a number of conclusions from these two diagrams.

- The *MPP* between two points is equal to the slope of the *TPP* curve between those two points. For example, when the number of workers increases from 1 to 2 ($\Delta Lb = 1$), *TPP* rises from 3 to 10 tonnes ($\Delta TPP = 7$). *MPP* is thus 7: the slope of the line between points *g* and *h*.
- *MPP* rises at first: the slope of the *TPP* curve gets steeper.
- *MPP* reaches a maximum at point *b*. At that point the slope of the *TPP* curve is at its steepest.
- After point *b*, diminishing returns set in. *MPP* falls. *TPP* becomes less steep. KI 20 p 130
- *APP* rises at first. It continues rising as long as the addition to output from the last worker (*MPP*) is greater than the average output (*APP*): the *MPP* pulls the *APP* up. This continues beyond point *b*. Even though *MPP* is now falling, the *APP* goes on rising as long as the *MPP* is still above the *APP*. Thus *APP* goes on rising to point *c*.
- Beyond point *c*, *MPP* is below *APP*. New workers add less to output than the average. This pulls the average down: *APP* falls.
- As long as *MPP* is greater than zero, *TPP* will go on rising: new workers add to total output.
- At point *d*, *TPP* is at a maximum (its slope is zero). An additional worker will add nothing to output: *MPP* is zero.
- Beyond point *d*, *TPP* falls. *MPP* is negative.

Pause for thought

What is the significance of the slope of the line ac in the top part of Figure 9.1?

Definitions

Average physical product (*APP*) Total output (*TPP*) per unit of the variable factor (*Qv*) in question: *APP* = *TPP*/*Qv*.

Marginal physical product (*MPP*) The extra output gained by the employment of one more unit of the variable factor: *MPP* = $\Delta TPP/\Delta Qv$.

9.3 COSTS IN THE SHORT RUN

Having looked at the background to costs in the short run, we now turn to examine short-run costs themselves. We will be examining how costs change as a firm changes the amount it produces. Obviously, if it is to decide how much to produce, it will need to know just what the level of costs will be at each level of output.

Costs and inputs

A firm's costs of production will depend on the factors of production it uses. The more factors it uses, the greater will its costs be. More precisely, this relationship depends on two elements.

KI 19 p 130

The productivity of the factors. The greater their physical productivity, the smaller will be the quantity of them that is needed to produce a given level of output, and hence the lower will be the cost of that output. In other words, there is a direct link between *TPP*, *APP* and *MPP* and the costs of production.

The price of the factors. The higher their price, the higher will be the costs of production. In the short run, some factors are fixed in supply. Their total costs, therefore, are fixed, in the sense that they do not vary with output. For example, rent on land is a ***fixed cost***. It is the same whether the firm produces a lot, a little or nothing.

The cost of variable factors, however, does vary with output. The cost of raw materials is a ***variable cost***. The more that is produced, the more raw materials are used and therefore the higher is their total cost.

Total cost

The ***total cost (TC)*** of production is the sum of the *total variable costs* (*TVC*) and the *total fixed costs* (*TFC*) of production.

$TC = TVC + TFC$

Consider Table 9.2 and Figure 9.2. They show the total costs for an imaginary firm for producing different levels

Table 9.2 Total costs for firm X

Output (*Q*)	*TFC* (£)	*TVC* (£)	*TC* (£)
0	12	0	12
1	12	10	22
2	12	16	28
3	12	21	33
4	12	28	40
5	12	40	52
6	12	60	72
7	12	91	103

Definitions

Fixed costs Total costs that do not vary with the amount of output produced.

Variable costs Total costs that do vary with the amount of output produced.

Total cost (*TC*) The sum of total fixed costs (*TFC*) and total variable costs (*TVC*): $TC = TFC + TVC$.

Figure 9.2 Total costs for firm X

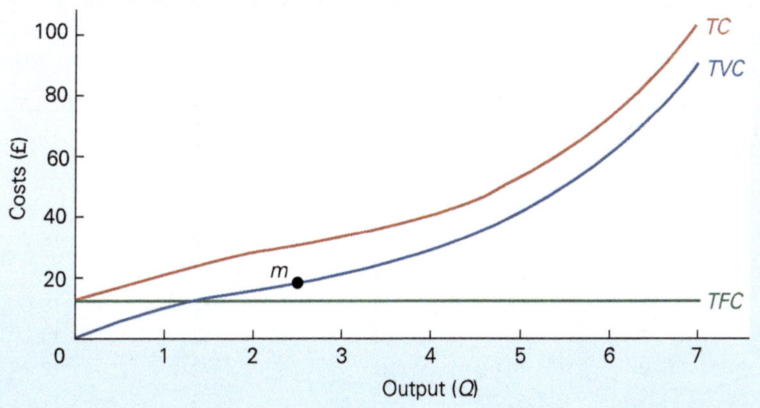

of output (Q). Let us examine each of the three cost curves in turn.

Total fixed cost (TFC)

In our example, total fixed cost is assumed to be £12. Since this does not vary with output, it is shown by a horizontal straight line.

Total variable cost (TVC)

With a zero output, no variable factors will be used. Thus *TVC* = 0. The *TVC* curve, therefore, starts from the origin.

KI 20 p 130

The shape of the *TVC* curve follows from the law of diminishing returns. Initially, *before* diminishing returns set in, *TVC* rises less and less rapidly as more variable factors are added. For example, in the case of a factory with a fixed supply of machinery, initially as more workers are taken on the workers can do increasingly specialist tasks and make a fuller use of the capital equipment. This corresponds to the portion of the *TPP* curve that rises more rapidly (up to point *b* in the top diagram of Figure 9.1).

As output is increased beyond point *m* in Figure 9.2, diminishing returns set in. Given that extra workers (the extra variable factors) are producing less and less extra output, the extra units of output they do produce will be costing more and more in terms of wage costs. Thus *TVC* rises more and more rapidly. The *TVC* curve gets steeper. This corresponds to the portion of the *TPP* curve that rises less rapidly (between points *b* and *d* in Figure 9.1).

Total cost (TC)

Since *TC* = *TVC* + *TFC*, the *TC* curve is simply the *TVC* curve shifted vertically upwards by £12.

Average and marginal cost

Average cost (*AC*) is cost per unit of production.

$$AC = TC/Q$$

Thus if it costs a firm £2000 to produce 100 units of a product, the average cost would be £20 for each unit (£2000/100).

Like total cost, average cost can be divided into the two components, fixed and variable. In other words, average cost equals ***average fixed cost*** (*AFC* = *TFC*/*Q*) plus ***average variable cost*** (*AVC* = *TVC*/*Q*).

$$AC = AFC + AVC$$

Marginal cost (*MC*) is the *extra* cost of producing *one more unit*: that is, the rise in total cost per one unit rise in output.

$$MC = \frac{\Delta TC}{\Delta Q}$$

where Δ means 'a change in'.

For example, assume that a firm is currently producing 1 000 000 boxes of matches a month. It now increases output by 1000 boxes (another batch): Δ*Q* = 1000. As a result its total costs rise by £30: Δ*TC* = £30. What is the cost of producing *one* more box of matches? It is:

$$MC = \frac{\Delta TC}{\Delta Q} = \frac{£30}{1000} = 3\text{p}$$

(Note that all marginal costs are variable, since, by definition, there can be no extra fixed costs as output rises.)

Given the *TFC*, *TVC* and *TC* for each output, it is possible to derive the *AFC*, *AVC*, *AC* and *MC* for each output using the above definitions. For example, using the data of Table 9.2, Table 9.3 can be constructed.

What will be the shapes of the *MC*, *AFC*, *AVC* and *AC* curves? These follow from the nature of the *MPP* and *APP* curves (which we looked at in section 9.2).

Definitions

Average (total) cost (*AC*) Total cost (fixed plus variable) per unit of output: *AC* = *TC*/*Q* = *AFC* + *AVC*.

Average fixed cost (*AFC*) Total fixed cost per unit of output: *AFC* = *TFC*/*Q*.

Average variable cost (*AVC*) Total variable cost per unit of output: *AVC* = *TVC*/*Q*.

Marginal cost (*MC*) The cost of producing one more unit of output: *MC* = Δ*TC*/Δ*Q*.

Table 9.3 Costs

Output (*Q*) (units)	*TFC* (£)	*AFC* (*TFC*/*Q*) (£)	*TVC* (£)	*AVC* (*TVC*/*Q*) (£)	*TC* (*TFC* + *TVC*) (£)	*AC* (*TC*/*Q*) (£)	*MC* (Δ*TC*/Δ*Q*) (£)
0	12	–	0	–	12	–	
1	12	12	10	10	22	22	10
2	12	6	16	8	28	14	6
3	12	4	21	7	33	11	5
4	12	3	28	7	40	10	7
5	12	2.4	40	8	52	10.4	12
6	12	2	60	10	72	12	20
7	12	1.7	91	13	103	14.7	31

Marginal cost (MC)

KI 20 p 130

The shape of the *MC* curve follows directly from the law of diminishing returns. Initially, in Figure 9.3, as more of the variable factor is used, extra units of output cost less than previous units. *MC* falls. This corresponds to the portion of the *TVC* curve in Figure 9.2 to the left of point *m*.

Beyond a certain level of output, diminishing returns set in. This is shown as point *x* in Figure 9.3 and corresponds to point *m* in Figure 9.2. Thereafter *MC* rises. Additional units of output cost more and more to produce, since they require ever-increasing amounts of the variable factor.

Average fixed cost (AFC)

This falls continuously as output rises, since *total* fixed costs are being spread over a greater and greater output.

Average variable cost (AVC)

The shape of the *AVC* curve depends on the shape of the *APP* curve. As the average product of workers rises, the average labour cost per unit of output (the *AVC*) falls: up to point *y* in Figure 9.3. Thereafter, as *APP* falls, *AVC* must rise.

Average (total) cost (AC)

This is simply the vertical sum of the *AFC* and *AVC* curves. Note that, as *AFC* gets less, the gap between *AVC* and *AC* narrows.

Figure 9.3 Average and marginal costs

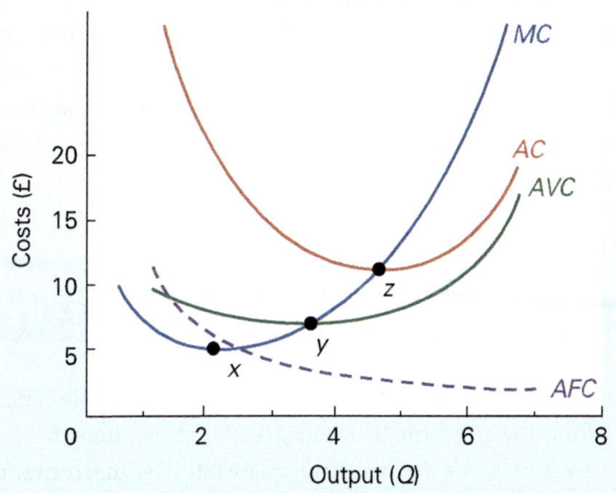

The relationship between average cost and marginal cost

This is simply another illustration of the relationship that applies between *all* averages and marginals.

BOX 9.2 **SHORT-RUN COST CURVES IN PRACTICE**

When fixed factors are divisible

Are short-run cost curves always the shape depicted in this chapter? The answer is no. Sometimes, rather than being U-shaped, the *AVC* and *MC* curves are flat bottomed, like the curves in the diagram. Indeed, they may be constant (and equal to each other) over a *substantial* range of output.

The reason for this is that sometimes fixed factors may not have to be in full use all the time. Take the case of a firm with 100 identical machines, each one requiring one person to operate it. Although the firm cannot use *more* than the 100 machines, it could use fewer: in other words, some of the machines could be left idle. Assume, for example, that instead of using 100 machines, the firm uses only 90. It would need only 90 operatives and 90 per cent of the raw materials. Similarly, if it used only 20 machines, its total variable costs (labour and raw materials) would be only 20 per cent of those incurred at full capacity. What we are saying here is that *average* variable cost remains constant – and over a very large range of output: using anything from 1 machine to 100 machines.

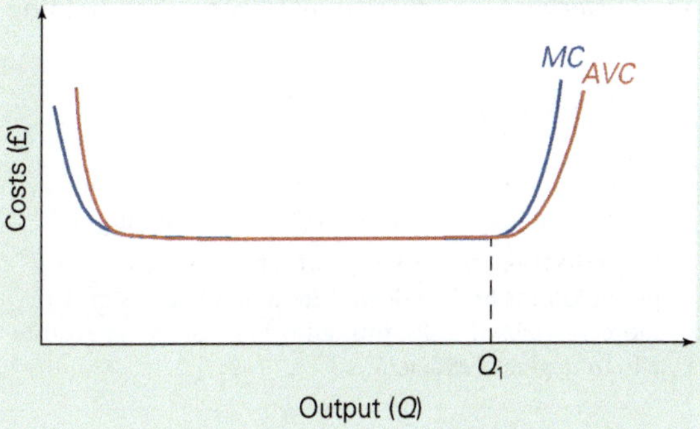

The reason for the constant *AVC* (and *MC*) is that by varying the amount of fixed capital used, the *proportions* used of capital, labour and raw materials can be kept the same and hence the average and marginal productivity of labour and raw materials will remain constant.

Only when all machines are in use (at Q_1) will *AVC* start to rise if output is further expanded. Machines may then have to work beyond their optimal speed, using more raw materials per unit of output (diminishing returns to raw materials), or workers may have to work longer shifts with higher (overtime) pay.

1. *Assume that a firm has 5 identical machines, each operating independently. Assume that with all 5 machines operating normally, 100 units of output are produced each day. Below what level of output will AVC and MC rise?*
2. *Manufacturing firms like the one we have been describing will have other fixed costs (such as rent and managerial overheads). Does the existence of these affect the argument that the AVC curve will be flat bottomed?*

As long as the cost of additional units of output is less than the average, their production must pull the average cost down. That is, if *MC* is less than *AC*, *AC* must be falling. Likewise, if additional units cost more than the average, their production must drive the average up. That is, if *MC* is greater than *AC*, *AC* must be rising. Therefore, the *MC* crosses the *AC* at its minimum point (point *z* in Figure 9.3).

Pause for thought

Before you read on, can you explain why the marginal cost curve will always cut the average cost curve at its lowest point?

Since all marginal costs are variable, the same relationship holds between *MC* and *AVC*.

9.4 PRODUCTION IN THE LONG RUN

In the long run *all* factors of production are variable. There is time for the firm to build a new factory (maybe in a different part of the country), to install new machines, to use different techniques of production, and in general to combine its inputs in whatever proportion and in whatever quantities it chooses.

When planning for the long run, then, a firm will have to make a number of decisions: about the scale of its operations, the location of its operations and the techniques of production it will use. These decisions will affect the costs of production. It is important, therefore, to get them right.

Table 9.4 Short-run and long-run increases in output

Short run			Long run		
Input 1	Input 2	Output	Input 1	Input 2	Output
3	1	25	1	1	15
3	2	45	2	2	35
3	3	60	3	3	60
3	4	70	4	4	90
3	5	75	5	5	125

The scale of production

If a firm were to double all of its inputs – something it could do in the long run – would it double its output? Or would output more than double or less than double? We can distinguish three possible situations.

- *Constant returns to scale*. This is where a given percentage increase in inputs will lead to the same percentage increase in output.
- *Increasing returns to scale*. This is where a given percentage increase in inputs will lead to a larger percentage increase in output.
- *Decreasing returns to scale*. This is where a given percentage increase in inputs will lead to a smaller percentage increase in output.

Notice the terminology here. The words 'to scale' mean that *all* inputs increase by the same proportion. Decreasing returns to *scale* are therefore quite different from *diminishing* marginal returns (where only the *variable* factor increases). The differences between marginal returns to a variable factor and returns to scale are illustrated in Table 9.4.

In the short run, input 1 is assumed to be fixed in supply (at 3 units). Output can be increased only by using more of the variable factor (input 2). In the long run, however, both input 1 and input 2 are variable.

In the short-run situation, diminishing returns can be seen from the fact that output increases at a decreasing rate (25 to 45 to 60 to 70 to 75) as input 2 is increased. In the long-run situation, the table illustrates increasing returns to scale. Output increases at an *increasing* rate (15 to 35 to 60 to 90 to 125) as both inputs are increased.

Economies of scale

The concept of increasing returns to scale is closely linked to that of ***economies of scale***. A firm experiences economies of scale if costs per unit of output fall as the scale of production increases. Clearly, if a firm is getting increasing returns to scale from its factors of production, then as it produces more, it will be using smaller and smaller amounts of factors per unit of output. Other things being equal, this means that it will be producing at a lower unit cost. KI 19 p 130

There are a number of reasons why firms are likely to experience economies of scale. Some are due to increasing returns to scale; some are not.

Specialisation and division of labour. In large-scale plants, workers can do more simple, repetitive jobs. With this ***specialisation and division of labour***, less training is

Definitions

Economies of scale When increasing the scale of production leads to a lower cost per unit of output.

Specialisation and division of labour Where production is broken down into a number of simpler, more specialised tasks, thus allowing workers to acquire a high degree of efficiency.

needed; workers can become highly efficient in their particular job, especially with long production runs; there is less time lost in workers switching from one operation to another; supervision is easier. Workers and managers who have specific skills in specific areas can be employed.

Indivisibilities. Some inputs are of a minimum size. They are indivisible. The most obvious example is machinery. Take the case of a combine harvester. A small-scale farmer could not make full use of one. They only become economical to use, therefore, on farms above a certain size. The problem of ***indivisibilities*** is made worse when different machines, each of which is part of the production process, are of a different size. For example, assume there are two types of machine, one producing a maximum of 6 units a day, the other packaging a maximum of 4 units a day. If all machines are to be fully utilised, a minimum of 12 units per day will have to be produced, involving two production machines and three packaging machines.

The 'container principle'. Any capital equipment that contains things (blast furnaces, oil tankers, pipes, vats, etc.) will tend to cost less per unit of output, the larger its size. The reason has to do with the relationship between a container's volume and its surface area. A container's cost will depend largely on the materials used to build it and hence roughly on its *surface area*. Its output will depend largely on its *volume*. Large containers have a bigger volume relative to surface area than do small containers. For example, a container with a bottom, top and four sides, with each side measuring 1 metre, has a volume of 1 cubic metre and a surface area of 6 square metres (6 surfaces of 1 square metre each). If each side were now to be doubled in length to 2 metres, the volume would be 8 cubic metres and the surface area 24 square metres (6 surfaces of 4 square metres each). Thus an eightfold increase in capacity has been gained at only a fourfold increase in the container's surface area, and hence an approximate fourfold increase in cost.

Greater efficiency of large machines. Large machines may be more efficient, in the sense that more output can be gained for a given amount of inputs. For example, only one worker may be required to operate a machine whether it be large or small. Also, a large machine may make more efficient use of raw materials.

By-products. With production on a large scale, there may be sufficient waste products to enable them to make some by-product. For example, a wood mill may produce sufficient saw dust to make products such as charcoal briquettes or paper.

Multistage production. A large factory may be able to take a product through several stages in its manufacture. This saves time and cost moving the semi-finished product from one firm or factory to another. For example, a large cardboard-manufacturing firm may be able to convert trees or waste paper into cardboard and then into cardboard boxes in a continuous sequence.

All the above are examples of ***plant economies of scale***. They are due to an individual factory or workplace or machine being large. There are other economies of scale that are associated with the firm being large – perhaps with many factories.

Organisational. With a large firm, individual plants can specialise in particular functions. There can also be centralised administration of the firms. Often, after a merger between two firms, savings can be made by ***rationalising*** their activities in this way.

Spreading overheads. Some expenditures are economic only when the *firm* is large, such as research and development: only a large firm can afford to set up a research laboratory. This is another example of indivisibilities, only this time at the level of the firm rather than the plant. The greater the firm's output, the more these ***overhead costs*** are spread.

Financial economies. Large firms may be able to obtain finance at lower interest rates than small firms, as they are perceived as having lower default risks. Additionally they may be able to obtain certain inputs cheaper by purchasing in bulk.

Economies of scope. Often a firm is large because it produces a range of products. This can result in each individual product being produced more cheaply than if it was produced in a single-product firm. The reason for these ***economies of scope*** is that various overhead costs and financial and organisational economies can be shared between the products. For example, a firm that produces a whole range of CD players, DVD players and recorders, games consoles, TVs and so on can benefit from shared marketing and distribution costs and the bulk purchase of electronic components.

Definitions

Indivisibilities The impossibility of dividing a factor of production into smaller units.

Plant economies of scale Economies of scale that arise because of the large size of the factory.

Rationalisation The reorganising of production (often after a merger) so as to cut out waste and duplication and generally to reduce costs.

Overheads Costs arising from the general running of an organisation, and only indirectly related to the level of output.

Economies of scope When increasing the range of products produced by a firm reduces the cost of producing each one.

Diseconomies of scale

When firms get beyond a certain size, costs per unit of output may start to increase. There are several reasons for such ***diseconomies of scale***:

- Management problems of coordination may increase as the firm becomes larger and more complex, and as lines of communication get longer. There may be a lack of personal involvement and oversight by management.
- Workers may feel 'alienated' if their jobs are boring and repetitive, and if they feel an insignificant, and under-valued, small part of a large organisation. Poor motivation may lead to shoddy work.
- Industrial relations may deteriorate as a result of these factors and also as a result of the more complex inter-relationships between different categories of worker.
- Production-line processes and the complex interdependencies of mass production can lead to great disruption if there are hold-ups in any one part of the firm.

Whether firms experience economies or diseconomies of scale will depend on the conditions applying in each individual firm.

Location

In the long run, a firm can move to a different location. The location will affect the cost of production, since locations differ in terms of the availability and cost of raw materials, suitable land and power supply, the qualifications, skills and experience of the labour force, wage rates, transport and communications networks, the cost of local services, and banking and financial facilities. In short, locations differ in terms of the availability, suitability and cost of the factors of production.

Transport costs will be an important influence on a firm's location. Ideally, a firm will wish to be as near as possible to both its raw materials and the market for its finished product. When market and raw materials are in different locations, the firm will minimise its transport costs by locating somewhere between the two. In general, if the raw materials are more expensive to transport than the finished product, the firm should locate as near as possible to the raw materials. This will normally apply to firms whose raw materials are heavier or more bulky than the finished product. Thus heavy industry, which uses large quantities of coal and various ores, tends to be concentrated near the coal fields or near the ports. If, on the other hand, the finished product is more expensive to transport (e.g. bread or beer), the firm will probably be located as near as possible to its market.

When raw materials or markets are in many different locations, transport costs will be minimised at the 'centre of gravity'. This location will be nearer to those raw materials and markets whose transport costs are greater per mile.

The size of the whole industry

As an *industry* grows in size, this can lead to ***external economies of scale*** for its member firms. This is where a firm, whatever its own individual size, benefits from the *whole industry* being large. For example, the firm may benefit from having access to specialist raw material or component suppliers, labour with specific skills, firms that specialise in marketing the finished product, and banks and other financial institutions with experience of the industry's requirements. What we are referring to here is the ***industry's infrastructure***: the facilities, support services, skills and experience that can be shared by its members.

The member firms of a particular industry might experience ***external diseconomies of scale***. For example, as an industry grows larger, this may create a growing shortage of specific raw materials or skilled labour. This will push up their prices, and hence the firms' costs.

> **Pause for thought**
>
> ***Would you expect external economies of scale to be associated with the concentration of an industry in a particular region? Explain.***

The optimum combination of factors

In the long run, all factors can be varied. The firm can thus choose what techniques of production to use: what design of factory to build, what types of machine to buy, how to organise the factory, and whether to use highly automated processes or more labour-intensive techniques. It must be very careful in making these decisions. Once it has built its factory and installed the machinery, these then become fixed factors of production, maybe for many years: the subsequent 'short-run' time period may in practice last a very long time!

For any given scale, how should the firm decide what technique to use? How should it decide the optimum 'mix' of factors of production?

> **Definitions**
>
> **Diseconomies of scale** Where costs per unit of output increase as the scale of production increases.
>
> **External economies of scale** Where a firm's costs per unit of output decrease as the size of the whole *industry* grows.
>
> **Industry's infrastructure** The network of supply agents, communications, skills, training facilities, distribution channels, specialised financial services, etc. that support a particular industry.
>
> **External diseconomies of scale** Where a firm's costs per unit of output increase as the size of the whole industry increases.

The profit-maximising firm will obviously want to use the least costly combination of factors to produce any given output. It will therefore substitute factors, one for another, if by so doing it can reduce the cost of a given output. What, then, is the optimum combination of factors?

The simple two-factor case

Take first the simplest case where a firm uses just two factors: labour (L) and capital (K). The least-cost combination of the two will be where:

$$\frac{MPP_L}{P_L} = \frac{MPP_K}{P_K}$$

In other words, it is where the extra product (MPP) from the last pound spent on each factor is equal. But why should this be so? The easiest way to answer this is to consider what would happen if they were not equal.

If they were not equal, it would be possible to reduce cost per unit of output, by using a different combination of labour and capital. For example, if:

$$\frac{MPP_L}{P_L} > \frac{MPP_K}{P_K}$$

KI 4 p 22

more labour should be used relative to capital, since the firm is getting a greater physical return for its money from extra workers than from extra capital. As more labour is used per unit of capital, however, diminishing returns to labour set in. Thus MPP_L will fall. Likewise, as less capital is used per unit of labour, the MPP_K will rise. This will continue until:

$$\frac{MPP_L}{P_L} = \frac{MPP_K}{P_K}$$

At this point, the firm will stop substituting labour for capital.

Since no further gain can be made by substituting one factor for another, this combination of factors or 'choice of techniques' can be said to be the most efficient. It is the least-cost way of combining factors for any given output. Efficiency in this sense of using the optimum factor proportions is known as ***technical or productive efficiency***.

The multifactor case

Where a firm uses many different factors, the least-cost combination of factors will be where:

$$\frac{MPP_a}{P_a} = \frac{MPP_b}{P_b} = \frac{MPP_c}{P_c} \ldots = \frac{MPP_n}{P_n}$$

where a . . . n are different factors of production.

The reasons are the same as in the two-factor case. If any inequality exists between the MPP/P ratios, a firm will be able to reduce its costs by using more of those factors with a high MPP/P ratio and less of those with a low MPP/P ratio until the ratios all become equal. A major problem for a firm in choosing the least-cost technique is in predicting future factor price changes.

If the price of a factor were to change, the MPP/P ratios would cease to be equal. The firm, to minimise costs, would then like to alter its factor combinations until the MPP/P ratios once more become equal. The trouble is that, once it has committed itself to a particular technique, it may be several years before it can switch to an alternative one. Thus if a firm invests in labour-intensive methods of production and is then faced with an unexpected wage rise, it may regret not having chosen a more capital-intensive technique.

Postscript: decision making in different time periods

We have distinguished between the short run and the long run. Let us introduce two more time periods to complete the picture. The complete list then reads as follows.

Very short run (immediate run). All factors are fixed. Output is fixed. The supply curve is vertical. On a day-to-day basis, a firm may not be able to vary output at all. For example, a flower seller, once the day's flowers have been purchased from the wholesaler, cannot alter the amount of flowers available for sale on that day. In the very short run, all that may remain for a producer to do is to sell an already-produced good.

Short run. At least one factor is fixed in supply. More can be produced, but the firm will come up against the law of diminishing returns as it tries to do so. KI 20 p 130

Long run. All factors are variable. The firm may experience constant, increasing or decreasing returns to scale. But although all factors can be increased or decreased, they are of a fixed *quality*.

Very long run. All factors are variable, *and* their quality and hence productivity can change. Labour productivity can increase as a result of education, training, experience and social factors. The productivity of capital can increase as a result of new inventions (new discoveries) and innovation (putting inventions into practice).

Improvements in factor quality will increase the output they produce: TPP, APP and MPP will rise. These curves will shift vertically upward.

Just how long the 'very long run' is will vary from firm to firm. It will depend on how long it takes to develop new techniques, new skills or new work practices.

It is important to realise that decisions *for* all four time periods can be made *at* the same time. Firms do not

Definition

Technical or productive efficiency The least-cost combination of factors for a given output.

BOX 9.3 UK COMPETITIVENESS: MOVING TO THE NEXT STAGE

The importance of location

In May 2003 Professor Michael Porter and Christian Ketels of Harvard Business School published a review of the UK's competitiveness on behalf of the UK government. The authors declared that since 1980 the UK had done remarkably well in halting its economic decline on world markets, and had in fact matched and even bettered its main rivals in many industrial sectors. However, they were quick to sound a note of caution.

> The UK currently faces a transition to a new phase of economic development. The old approach to economic development is reaching the limits of its effectiveness, and government, companies, and other institutions need to rethink their policy priorities. This rethinking is not a sign of the past strategy's failure; it is a necessary part of graduating to the new stage.[1]

Porter's view is that economic development is achieved through a series of stages. The factor-driven stage identifies factors of production as the basis of competitive advantage: you have an advantage in those industries where you have a plentiful supply of the relevant factors of production. The investment-driven stage of development focuses upon efficiency and productivity as the key to competitive success. The third stage, into which Porter believes the UK is shifting, is innovation-driven. Here competitive advantage is achieved through the production of innovative products and services.

The importance of industrial clusters

One of the key characteristics of a successful innovation-led development strategy is the existence of industrial clusters.

> Clusters are geographically proximate groups of interconnected companies, suppliers, service providers, and associated institutions in a particular field, linked by commonalties and complementarities.[2]

Porter suggests that clusters are vital for competitiveness in three crucial respects:

- Clusters improve productivity. The close proximity of suppliers and other service providers enhances flexibility.
- Clusters aid innovation. Interaction among businesses within a cluster stimulates new ideas and aids their dissemination.
- Clusters contribute to new business formation. Clusters are self-reinforcing, in so far as specialist factors such as dedicated venture capital, and labour skills, help reduce costs and lower the risks of new business start-up.

Given that national economies tend to specialise in certain industrial clusters, we can identify where clusters occur and their importance, by considering their share of national output and export earnings. Export earnings in particular are a good indicator of how globally competitive a cluster might be.

The UK's industrial clusters were seen by Porter as being relatively weak, and in fact many traditional clusters, such as steel and car manufacturing, had thinned to the point where they now lacked critical mass and failed to benefit from the clustering effect. Where the UK had strengths were in the areas of services, such as financial services and media, defence, products for personal use, health care and telecommunications.

Porter and Katels concluded that, to improve its competitiveness, the UK must not only support what clusters it has but 'mount a sustained programme of cluster development to create a more conducive environment for productivity growth and innovation through the collective action of companies and other institutions'.[3]

The UK government responded to this report and currently supports cluster development in a number of ways, including through the creation of Enterprise Zones. These zones include the Humber Estuary Renewable Energy Cluster and The Modern Manufacturing and Technology Growth area in Sheffield. Eligible companies within these zones receive benefits such as reductions in business rates and simplified planning regulations. Cluster development has become an integral part of the remit of other policy areas, including science and innovation, export and foreign investment promotion and small and medium-sized enterprise policies.

Recent evidence

The performance of UK clusters has not changed greatly since the earlier report by Porter and Katels, but more information is coming to light. The European Cluster Observatory, an EU project, has identified locations where employment is highly concentrated in particular industrial clusters across Europe.[4]

The table shows the UK position. Information from the Observatory also shows that the UK leads the rest of Europe in cluster developments in areas such as Education and

[1] M. E. Porter and C. H. M. Ketels, UK Competitiveness: moving to the next stage (DTI and ESRC, May 2003), p. 5.
[2] Ibid., p. 27.
[3] Ibid., p. 46.
[4] See www.clusterobservatory.eu

make short-run decisions *in* the short run and long-run decisions *in* the long run. They can make both short-run and long-run decisions today. For example, assume that a firm experiences an increase in consumer demand and anticipates that it will continue into the foreseeable future. It thus wants to increase output. Consequently, it makes the following four decisions *today*:

- *(Very short run)* It accepts that for a few days it will not be able to increase output. It informs its customers that they will have to wait. It may temporarily raise prices to choke off some of the demand.
- *(Short run)* It negotiates with labour to introduce overtime working as soon as possible, to tide it over the next few weeks. It orders extra raw materials from its suppliers. It launches a recruitment drive for new

The Top UK industry clusters ranked by employment, 2009

Region	Cluster category	Employees	Size (%)	Specialisation (quotient)	Focus (%)
Inner London	Financial services	233 734	4.25	3.04	9.82
Inner London	Business services	219 044	3.64	2.59	9.21
Outer London	Business services	122 757	2.04	2.07	7.33
Outer London	Transportation and logistics	100 707	2.02	2.04	6.02
Berks, Bucks and Oxon	Business services	95 295	1.58	2.44	8.66
Inner London	Education and knowledge creation	89 444	3.31	2.35	3.76
Surrey, E and W Sussex	Business services	81 724	1.36	2.02	7.18
Inner London	Media and publishing	76 111	3.92	2.80	3.20
Hants and Isle of Wight	Business services	62 199	1.03	2.10	7.47
Beds and Herts	Business services	60 947	1.01	2.31	8.20
E Scotland	Financial services	59 747	1.09	2.05	6.62
Berks, Bucks and Oxon	Education and knowledge creation	58 363	2.16	3.32	5.30
E Anglia	Education and knowledge creation	36 276	1.34	2.36	3.78
W Midlands	Automotive	35 419	1.62	2.30	2.97
E Scotland	Education and knowledge creation	34 416	1.27	2.39	3.81
W Yorks	Education and knowledge creation	31 638	1.17	2.01	3.21
Berks, Bucks and Oxon	IT	30 184	1.96	3.01	2.74
NE Scotland	Oil and gas	11 792	3.98	25.22	4.45

Source: Based on EU Cluster Observatory, www.clusterobservatory.eu

Notes:
The European Cluster Observatory uses three measures to define a cluster, all based on employment. The three measures are size, specialisation and focus. If, for each measure, a location meets a specific criterion it is awarded a star. Only industries that achieved three stars are included in the above table.

The criteria for awarding a star are as follows:
Size: This gives employment in the cluster as a percentage of European employment in that industry. If a cluster is in the top 10 per cent of similar clusters in Europe in terms of employees, it receives a star (Europe is defined as the EU-27, Iceland, Israel, Norway, Switzerland and Turkey)
Specialisation: If a specialisation quotient of 2 or more achieved, it is awarded a star. The specialisation quotient is given by

$$\frac{\text{UK employment in a region in a cluster category/total UK employment}}{\text{European employment in a cluster category/total European employment}}$$

Focus: This shows the extent to which the regional economy is focused upon the industries comprising the cluster category. This measure shows employment in the cluster as a percentage of total employment in the region. The top 10 per cent of clusters which account for the largest proportion of their region's total employment receive a star.

Knowledge Creation, Business Services, Finance and Transportation and Logistical Services, with most of these clusters occurring in London and the South East.

The UK has been very successful relative to the rest of Europe in developing clusters in the provision of Education and Knowledge Creation, notably in Oxford, Cambridge and East Scotland. Outside of these sectors the UK advantage relative to the rest of Europe is very limited, although there are pockets of success. For example, the UK has achieved some success in IT (around Oxford and the south coast of England), oil and gas (around Aberdeen in Scotland) and the automotive industry (in the West Midlands). These locations have achieved the size, specialisation and focus that have enabled them to develop positive spillovers and linkages which create local prosperity. Much more, though, has to be done.

? *What policies or initiatives might a 'programme of cluster development' involve? Distinguish between policies that government and business might initiate.*

labour so as to avoid paying overtime longer than is necessary.

- *(Long run)* It starts proceedings to build a new factory. The first step may be to discuss requirements with a firm of consultants.
- *(Very long run)* It institutes a programme of research and development and/or training in an attempt to increase productivity.

Pause for thought

1. *What will the long-run market supply curve for a product look like? How will the shape of the long-run curve depend on returns to scale?*
2. *Why would it be difficult to construct a very-long run supply curve?*

Although we distinguish these four time periods, it is the middle two we are primarily concerned with. The reason for this is that there is very little that the firm can do in the very short run. And in the very long run, although the firm will obviously want to increase the productivity of its inputs, it will not be in a position to make precise calculations of how to do it. It will not know precisely what inventions will be made, or just what will be the results of its own research and development.

9.5 COSTS IN THE LONG RUN

When it comes to making long-run production decisions, the firm has much more flexibility. It does not have to operate with plant and equipment of a fixed size. It can expand the whole scale of its operations. All its inputs are variable, and thus the law of diminishing returns does not apply. The firm may experience economies of scale or diseconomies of scale, or its average costs may stay constant as it expands the scale of its operations.

Since there are no fixed factors in the long run, there are no long-run fixed costs. For example, the firm may rent

BOX 9.4 MINIMUM EFFICIENT SCALE

The extent of economies of scale in practice

Two of the most important studies of economies of scale have been those made by C. F. Pratten[1] in the late 1980s and by a group advising the European Commission[2] in 1997. Both studies found strong evidence that many firms, especially in manufacturing, experienced substantial economies of scale.

In a few cases long-run average costs fell continuously as output increased. For most firms, however, they fell up to a certain level of output and then remained constant.

The extent of economies of scale can be measured by looking at a firm's *minimum efficient scale* (*MES*). The *MES* is the size beyond which no significant additional economies of scale can be achieved: in other words, the point where the *LRAC* curve flattens off. In Pratten's studies he defined this level as the minimum scale above which any possible doubling in scale would reduce average costs by less than 5 per cent (i.e. virtually the bottom of the *LRAC* curve). In the diagram *MES* is shown at point *a*.

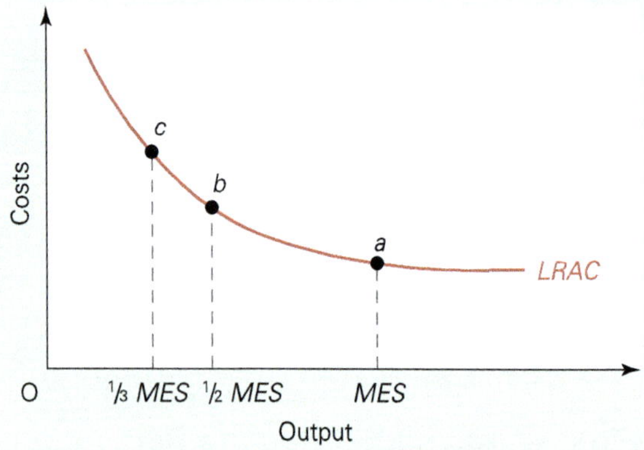

[1] C. F. Pratten, 'A survey of the economies of scale', in *Research on the 'Costs of Non-Europe'*, vol. 2 (Office for Official Publications of the European Communities, 1988).

[2] European Commission/Economists Advisory Group Ltd, 'Economies of scale', The Single Market Review, Subseries V, Volume 4 (Office for Official Publications of the European Communities, 1997).

Table (a)

Product	MES as % of production		% additional cost at ½ MES
	UK	EU	
Individual plants			
Cellulose fibres	125	16	3
Rolled aluminium semi-manufactures	114	15	15
Refrigerators	85	11	4
Steel	72	10	6
Electric motors	60	6	15
TV sets	40	9	9
Cigarettes	24	6	1.4
Ball-bearings	20	2	6
Beer	12	3	7
Nylon	4	1	12
Bricks	1	0.2	25
Tufted carpets	0.3	0.04	10
Shoes	0.3	0.03	1
Firms			
Cars	200	20	9
Lorries	104	21	7.5
Mainframe computers	>100	n.a.	5
Aircraft	100	n.a.	5
Tractors	98	19	6

Sources: Based on Pratten, F. and Emerson, M. (1988) *The Economics of 1992*, Oxford University Press, data from Tables on pp. 126–40, Section 6.1 'Size phenomena: economies of scale'

The *MES* can be expressed in terms either of an individual factory or of the whole firm. Where it refers to the minimum efficient scale of an individual factory, the *MES* is known as *the minimum efficient plant size* (*MEPS*).

more land in order to expand its operations. Its rent bill therefore goes up as it expands its output. All costs, then, in the long run are variable costs.

Long-run average costs

Although it is possible to draw long-run total, marginal and average cost curves, we will concentrate on ***long-run average cost*** (LRAC) ***curves***. These curves can take various shapes, but a typical one is shown in Figure 9.4.

It is often assumed that, as a firm expands, it will initially experience economies of scale and thus face a downward-sloping *LRAC* curve. After a point (Q_1 in Figure 9.4), however, all such economies will have been achieved and thus the curve will flatten out. Then, possibly after a period of constant *LRAC* (between Q_1 and Q_2), the firm will get so large that it will start experiencing diseconomies of scale and thus a rising *LRAC*. At this stage, production and financial economies begin to be offset by the managerial problems of running a giant organisation. The effect of this is to give an L-shaped or saucer-shaped curve.

Definition

Long-run average cost (*LRAC*) curve A curve that shows how average cost varies with output on the assumption that *all* factors are variable. (It is assumed that the least-cost method of production will be chosen for each output.)

Table (b)

Plants	MES as % of total EU production
Aerospace	12.19
Tractors and agricultural machinery	6.57
Electric lighting	3.76
Steel tubes	2.42
Shipbuilding	1.63
Rubber	1.06
Radio and TV	0.69
Footwear	0.08
Carpets	0.03

Source: see footnote 2

The *MES* can then be expressed as a percentage of the total size of the market or of total domestic production. Table (a), based on the Pratten study, shows *MES* for plants and firms in various industries. The first column shows *MES* as a percentage of total UK production. The second column shows *MES* as a percentage of total EU production. Table (b), based on the 1997 study, shows *MES* for various plants as a percentage of total EU production.

Expressing *MES* as a percentage of total output gives an indication of how competitive the industry could be. In some industries (such as footwear and carpets), economies of scale were exhausted (i.e. *MES* was reached) with plants or firms that were still small relative to total UK production and even smaller relative to total EU production. In such industries there would be room for many firms and thus scope for considerable competition.

In other industries, however, even if a single plant or firm were large enough to produce the whole output of the industry in the UK, it would still not be large enough to experience the full potential economies of scale: the *MES* is greater than 100 per cent. Examples from Table (a) include factories producing cellulose fibres, and car manufacturers. In such industries there is no possibility of competition. In fact, as long as the *MES* exceeds 50 per cent there will not be room for more than one firm large enough to gain full economies of scale. In this case the industry is said to be *a natural monopoly*. As we shall see in the next few chapters, when competition is lacking, consumers may suffer by firms charging prices considerably above costs.

A second way of measuring the extent of economies of scale is to see how much costs would increase if production were reduced to a certain fraction of *MES*. The normal fractions used are $^1/_2$ or $^1/_3$ *MES*. This is illustrated in the diagram. Point *b* corresponds to $^1/_2$ *MES*; point *c* to $^1/_3$ *MES*. The greater the percentage by which *LRAC* at point *b* or *c* is higher than at point *a*, the greater will be the economies of scale to be gained by producing at *MES* rather than at $^1/_2$ *MES* or $^1/_3$ *MES*. For example, in the table there are greater economies of scale to be gained from moving from $^1/_2$ *MES* to *MES* in the production of electric motors than in cigarettes.

The main purpose of the studies was to determine whether the single EU market is big enough to allow both economies of scale and competition. The tables suggest that in all cases, other things being equal, the EU market is large enough for firms to gain the full economies of scale *and* for there to be enough firms for the market to be competitive.

The second study also found that 47 of the 53 manufacturing sectors analysed had scope for further exploitation of economies of scale.

In the 2007–13 Research Framework, the European Commission agreed to fund a number of research projects. These will conduct further investigations of *MES* across different industries and consider the impact of the expansion of the EU.

?

1. *Why might a firm operating with one plant achieve* MEPS *and yet not be large enough to achieve* MES*? (Clue: are all economies of scale achieved at plant level?)*
2. *Why might a firm producing bricks have an* MES *which is only 0.2 per cent of total EU production and yet face little effective competition from other EU countries?*

Figure 9.4 A typical long-run average cost curve

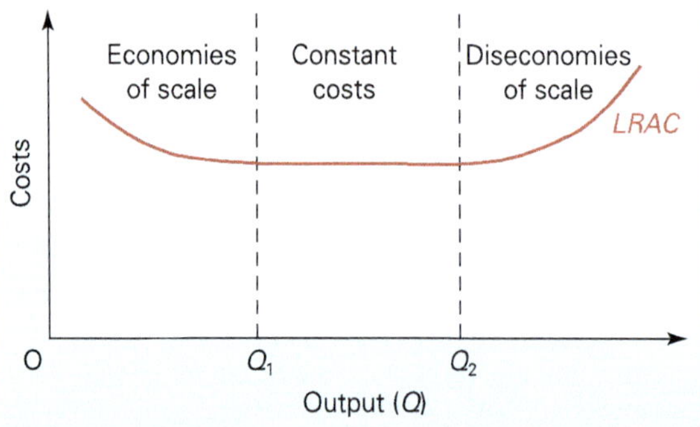

Figure 9.5 Constructing long-run average cost curves from short-run average cost curves

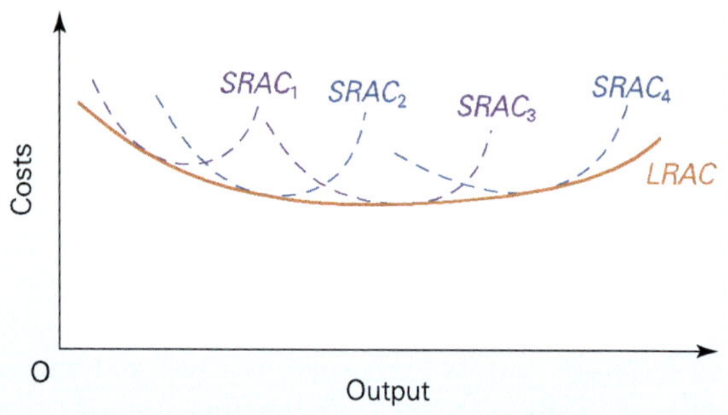

Firms do experience economies of scale. Some experience continuously falling *LRAC* curves. Others experience economies of scale up to a certain output and thereafter constant returns to scale. However, evidence is inconclusive on the question of diseconomies of scale. There is little evidence to suggest the existence of technical diseconomies, but the possibility of diseconomies due to managerial and industrial relations problems cannot be ruled out.

Assumptions behind the long-run average cost curve

We make three key assumptions when constructing long-run average cost curves.

Factor prices are given. At each level of output, a firm will be faced with a given set of factor prices. If factor prices *change*, therefore, both short- and long-run cost curves will shift. For example, an increase in wages would shift the curves vertically upwards.

However, factor prices might be different at *different* levels of output. For example, one of the economies of scale that many firms enjoy is the ability to obtain bulk discount on raw materials and other supplies. In such cases the curve does *not* shift. The different factor prices are merely experienced at different points along the curve, and are reflected in the shape of the curve. Factor prices are still given for any particular level of output.

The state of technology and factor quality are given. These are assumed to change only in the very long run. If a firm gains economies of scale, it is because it is being able to exploit *existing* technologies and make better use of the existing availability of factors of production. As technology improves the curves will shift downwards.

KI 4 p 22

Firms choose the least-cost combination of factors for each output. The assumption here is that firms operate efficiently: that they choose the cheapest possible way of producing any level of output. In other words, at every point along the *LRAC* curve the firm will adhere to the cost-minimising formula:

$$\frac{MPP_a}{P_a} = \frac{MPP_b}{P_b} = \frac{MPP_c}{P_c} \cdots = \frac{MPP_n}{P_n}$$

where a . . . n are the various factors that the firm uses.

If the firm did not choose the optimum factor combination, it would be producing at a point above the *LRAC* curve.

The relationship between long-run and short-run average cost curves

Take the case of a firm which has just one factory and faces a short-run average cost curve illustrated by $SRAC_1$ in Figure 9.5.

In the long run, it can build more factories or expand its existing facilities. If it thereby experiences economies of scale (due, say, to savings on administration), each successive factory will allow it to produce with a new lower *SRAC* curve. Thus with two factories it will face curve $SRAC_2$; with three factories curve $SRAC_3$, and so on. Each *SRAC* curve corresponds to a particular amount of the factor that is fixed in the short run: in this case, the factory. (There are many more *SRAC* curves that could be drawn between the ones shown, since factories of different sizes could be built or existing ones could be expanded.)

From this succession of short-run average cost curves we can construct a long-run average cost curve. This is shown in Figure 9.5 and is known as the ***envelope curve***, since it envelops the short-run curves.

Pause for thought

Will the envelope curve be tangential to the bottom of each of the short-run average cost curves? Explain why it should or should not be.

Definition

Envelope curve A long-run average cost curve drawn as the tangency points of a series of short-run average cost curves.

BOX 9.5 FASHION CYCLES

Costs and prices in the clothing industry

For many products, style is a key component of their success. A good example is clothing. If manufacturers can successfully predict or even drive a new fashion, then sales growth can be substantial.

With any new fashion, growth is likely to be slow at first. Then as the fashion 'catches on' and people want to be seen wearing this fashionable item, sales grow until a peak is eventually reached. In the case of clothing, if it is 'this year's fashion' then the peak will be reached within a couple of months. Then, as the market becomes saturated and people await the next season's fashions, so sales will fall.

This rise and fall is known as the 'fashion cycle' and is illustrated in the following diagram, which shows five stages: introduction of a style; growth in popularity; peak in popularity; decline in popularity; obsolescence.

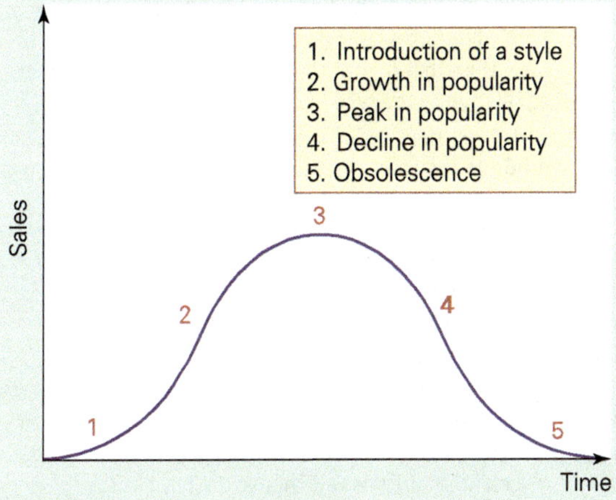

The variation of costs and prices over the fashion cycle

Costs and prices tend to vary with the stages of the fashion cycle. At the introductory stage, average costs are likely to be high. Within that stage, the fixed costs of design, setting up production lines, etc. are being spread over a relatively small output; average fixed costs are high. Also, there is a risk to producers that the fashion will not catch on and thus they are likely to factor in this risk when estimating costs. Finally, demand from those wishing to be ahead in fashion and wearing the very latest thing is likely to be relatively price inelastic; they will be willing to pay a high price to obtain such items. The result of all these factors is that price is likely to be high in the introductory stage.

Assuming the fashion catches on, average costs will begin to fall and the fashion is likely to be taken up by cheaper High Street chains. Prices will correspondingly fall.

Beyond the peak, costs are unlikely to fall much further, but intense competition between retailers is likely to continue driving prices down. The garments may end up on sales rails. (Note that with fashions that do not catch on, the price may fall rapidly quite early on as producers seek to cut their losses.)

Then, with the new season's fashions, the cycle begins again.

The greater the importance of fashion for a particular type of garment, the greater is likely to be the seasonable price variability. The taller the 'bell' in the diagram, i.e. the greater the rise and fall in sales, the greater is likely to be the difference in price between the different stages.

Technology and the fashion cycle

We have seen that costs are an important element in the fashion cycle and in prices and sales through the different phases of the cycle. Fixed costs are highly dependent on technology. Advances in the textile industry have included more easily adaptable machines which are relatively easily programmed and design software which allows designers to change fashion parameters on the screen rather than with physical materials. These advances have meant that the fixed costs of introducing new fashions have come down. With lower fixed costs, average costs will tend to decline less steeply as output rises.

?

1. *If consumers are aware that fashion clothing will fall in price as the season progresses, why do they buy when prices are set high at the start of the season? What does this tell us about the shape of the demand curve for a given fashion product (a) at the start, and (b) at the end of the season?*
2. *How might we account for the changing magnitudes of the fashion price cycles of clothing? What role do fixed costs play in the explanation?*
3. *Despite new technology in the car industry, changing the design and shape of cars has risen as a share of the total production costs. How is this likely to have affected the fashion cycle in the car industry?*

SUMMARY

1a When measuring costs of production, we should be careful to use the concept of opportunity cost.

1b In the case of factors not owned by the firm, the opportunity cost is simply the explicit cost of purchasing or hiring them. It is the price paid for them.

1c In the case of factors already owned by the firm, it is the implicit cost of what the factor could have earned for the firm in its next best alternative use.

2a A production function shows the relationship between the amount of inputs used and the amount of output produced from them (per period of time).

2b In the short run it is assumed that one or more factors (inputs) are fixed in supply. The actual length of the short run will vary from industry to industry.

2c Production in the short run is subject to diminishing returns. As greater quantities of the variable factor(s) are used, so each additional unit of the variable factor will add less to output than previous units: total physical product will rise less and less rapidly.

2d As long as marginal physical product is above average physical product, average physical product will rise. Once *MPP* has fallen below *APP*, however, *APP* will fall.

3a With some factors fixed in supply in the short run, their total costs will be fixed with respect to output. In the case of variable factors, their total cost will increase as more output is produced and hence as more of them are used.

3b Total cost can be divided into total fixed and total variable cost. Total variable cost will tend to increase less rapidly at first as more is produced, but then, when diminishing returns set in, it will increase more and more rapidly.

3c Marginal cost is the cost of producing one more unit of output. It will probably fall at first (corresponding to the part of the *TVC* curve where the slope is getting shallower), but will start to rise as soon as diminishing returns set in.

3d Average cost, like total cost, can be divided into fixed and variable costs. Average fixed cost will decline as more output is produced. The reason is that the total fixed cost is being spread over a greater and greater number of units of output. Average variable cost will tend to decline at first, but once the marginal cost has risen above it, it must then rise.

4a In the long run, a firm is able to vary the quantity it uses of all factors of production. There are no fixed factors.

4b If it increases all factors by the same proportion, it may experience constant, increasing or decreasing returns to scale.

4c Economies of scale occur when costs per unit of output fall as the scale of production increases. This can be due to a number of factors, some of which are directly caused by increasing (physical) returns to scale. These include the benefits of specialisation and division of labour, the use of larger and more efficient machines, and the ability to have a more integrated system of production. Other economies of scale arise from the financial and administrative benefits of large-scale organisations having a range of products (economies of scope).

4d Long-run costs are also influenced by a firm's location. The firm will have to balance the need to be as near as possible both to the supply of its raw materials and to its market. The optimum balance will depend on the relative costs of transporting the inputs and the finished product.

4e To minimise costs per unit of output, a firm should choose that combination of factors which gives an equal marginal product for each factor relative to its price: i.e. $MPP_a/P_a = MPP_b/P_b = MPP_c/P_c$, etc. (where a, b and c are different factors). If the *MPP/P* ratio for any factor is greater than that for another, more of the first should be used relative to the second.

4f Four distinct time periods can be distinguished. In addition to the short- and long-run periods, we can also distinguish the very-short- and very-long-run periods. The very short run is when all factors are fixed. The very long run is where not only the quantity of factors but also their quality is variable (as a result of changing technology, etc.).

5a In the long run, all factors are variable. There are thus no long-run fixed costs.

5b When constructing long-run cost curves, it is assumed that factor prices are given, that the state of technology is given and that firms will choose the least-cost combination of factors for each given output.

5c The *LRAC* curve can be downward sloping, upward sloping or horizontal, depending in turn on whether there are economies of scale, diseconomies of scale or neither. Typically, *LRAC* curves are drawn as saucer-shaped or L-shaped. As output expands, initially there are economies of scale. When these are exhausted, the curve will become flat. When the firm becomes very large, it may begin to experience diseconomies of scale. If this happens, the *LRAC* curve will begin to slope upward again.

5d An envelope curve can be drawn which shows the relationship between short-run and long-run average cost curves. The *LRAC* curve envelops the short-run *AC* curves: it is tangential to them.

REVIEW QUESTIONS

1 Are all explicit costs variable costs? Are all variable costs explicit costs?

2 Up to roughly how long is the short run in the following cases?

(a) A mobile disco firm.
(b) Electricity power generation.
(c) A small grocery retailing business.
(d) 'Superstore Hypermarkets plc'.

In each case, specify your assumptions.

3 Given that there is a fixed supply of land in the world, what implications can you draw from Figure 9.1 about the effects of an increase in world population for food output per head?

4 The following are some costs incurred by a shoe manufacturer. Decide whether each one is a fixed cost or a variable cost or has some element of both.

(a) The cost of leather.
(b) The fee paid to an advertising agency.
(c) Wear and tear on machinery.
(d) Business rates on the factory.
(e) Electricity for heating and lighting.
(f) Electricity for running the machines.
(g) Basic minimum wages agreed with the union.
(h) Overtime pay.
(i) Depreciation of machines as a result purely of their age (irrespective of their condition).

5 Assume that you are required to draw a *TVC* curve corresponding to Figure 9.1. What will happen to this *TVC* curve beyond point *d*?

6 Why is the minimum point of the *AVC* curve at a lower level of output than the minimum point of the *AC* curve?

7 Which economies of scale are due to increasing returns to scale and which are due to other factors?

8 What economies of scale is a large department store likely to experience?

9 Why are many firms likely to experience economies of scale up to a certain size and then diseconomies of scale after some point beyond that?

10 Why are bread and beer more expensive to transport per mile than the raw materials used in their manufacture?

11 Name some industries where external economies of scale are gained. What are the specific external economies in each case?

12 How is the opening up of trade and investment between eastern and western Europe likely to affect the location of industries within Europe that have (a) substantial economies of scale; (b) little or no economies of scale?

13 If factor X costs twice as much as factor Y ($P_X/P_Y = 2$), what can be said about the relationship between the *MPP*s of the two factors if the optimum combination of factors is used?

14 Could the long run and the very long run ever be the same length of time?

15 Examine Figure 9.4. What would (a) the firm's long-run total cost curve and (b) its long-run marginal cost curve look like?

16 Under what circumstances is a firm likely to experience a flat-bottomed *LRAC* curve?

Chapter 10

Revenue and profit

Business issues covered in this chapter

- How does a business's sales revenue vary with output?
- How does the relationship between output and sales revenue depend on the type of market in which a business is operating?
- How do we measure profits?
- At what output will a firm maximise its profits? How much profit will it make at this output?
- At what point should a business call it a day and shut down?

In this chapter we will identify the output and price at which a firm will maximise its profits, and how much profit will be made at that level. Remember that we defined a firm's total profit ($T\Pi$) as its total revenue minus its total costs of production.

$$T\Pi = TR - TC$$

In the previous chapter we have looked at costs in some detail. We must now turn to the revenue side of the equation. As with costs, we distinguish between three revenue concepts: total revenue (TR), average revenue (AR) and marginal revenue (MR).

10.1 REVENUE

Total, average and marginal revenue

Total revenue (TR)

Total revenue is the firm's total earnings per period of time from the sale of a particular amount of output (Q).

For example, if a firm sells 1000 units (Q) per month at a price of £5 each (P), then its monthly total revenue will be £5000: in other words, £5 × 1000 ($P \times Q$). Thus:

$$TR = P \times Q$$

Definition

Total revenue A firm's total earnings from a specified level of sales within a specified period: $TR = P \times Q$.

Figure 10.1 Deriving a firm's *AR* and *MR*: price-taking firm

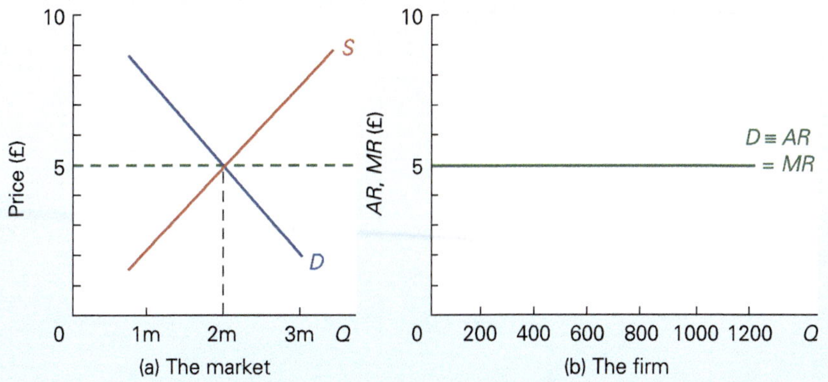

Average revenue (AR)

Average revenue is the average amount the firm earns per unit sold. Thus:

$$AR = TR/Q$$

So if the firm earns £5000 (*TR*) from selling 1000 units (*Q*), it will earn £5 per unit. But this is simply the price! Thus:

$$AR = P$$

The only exception to this is when the firm is selling its products at different prices to different consumers. In this case *AR* is simply the (weighted) average price.

Marginal revenue (MR)

Marginal revenue is the extra total revenue gained by selling one more unit, per time period. So if a firm sells an extra 20 units this month compared with what it expected to sell, and in the process earns an extra £100, then it is getting an extra £5 for each extra unit sold: $MR = £5$. Thus:

$$MR = \Delta TR/\Delta Q$$

We now need to see how each of these three revenue concepts (*TR*, *AR* and *MR*) varies with output. We can show this relationship graphically in the same way as we did with costs.

The relationship will depend on the market conditions under which a firm operates. A firm which is too small to be able to affect market price will have differently shaped revenue curves from a firm which is able to choose the price it charges. Let us examine each of these two situations in turn.

Revenue curves when price is not affected by the firm's output

Average revenue

If a firm is very small relative to the whole market, it is likely to be a ***price taker***. That is, it has to accept the price given by the intersection of demand and supply in the whole market. If the firm chose to charge a higher price it would lose all its sales to competitors. Charging a lower price would not be rational as the firm can sell as much as it is capable of producing at the prevailing price. This is illustrated in Figure 10.1.

Diagram (a) shows market demand and supply. Equilibrium price is £5. Diagram (b) looks at the demand for an individual firm which is tiny relative to the whole market. (Look at the difference in the scale of the horizontal axes in the two diagrams.)

Being so small, any change in the firm's output will be too insignificant to affect the market price. The firm thus faces a horizontal demand 'curve' at this price. It can sell 200 units, 600 units, 1200 units, or any other amount it is capable of producing, without affecting this £5 price.

Average revenue is thus constant at £5. The firm's average revenue curve must therefore lie along exactly the same line as its demand curve.

Marginal revenue

In the case of a horizontal demand curve, the marginal revenue curve will be the same as the average revenue curve, since selling one more unit at a constant price (*AR*) merely adds that amount to total revenue. If an extra unit is sold at a constant price of £5, an extra £5 is earned.

Definitions

Average revenue Total revenue per unit of output. When all output is sold at the same price, average revenue will be the same as price: $AR = TR/Q = P$.

Marginal revenue The extra revenue gained by selling one or more unit per time period: $MR = \Delta TR/\Delta Q$.

Price taker A firm that is too small to be able to influence the market price.

Table 10.1 Deriving total revenue

Quantity (units)	*Price* = *AR* = *MR* (£)	*TR* (£)
0	5	0
200	5	1000
400	5	2000
600	5	3000
800	5	4000
1000	5	5000
1200	5	6000
.	.	.

Table 10.2 Revenues for a firm facing a downward-sloping demand curve

Q (units)	*P* = *AR* (£)	*TR* (£)	*MR* (£)
1	8	8	
2	7	14	6
3	6	18	4
4	5	20	2
5	4	20	0
6	3	18	−2
7	2	14	−4
.	.	.	.

Figure 10.2 Total revenue curve for a price-taking firm

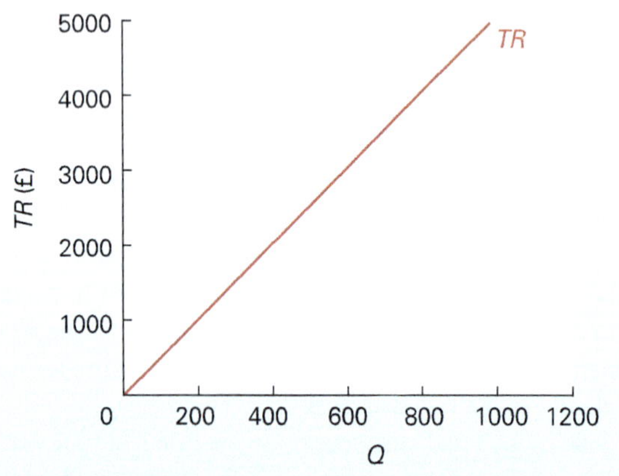

Total revenue

Table 10.1 shows the effect on total revenue of different levels of sales with a constant price of £5 per unit.

As price is constant, total revenue will rise at a constant rate as more is sold. The *TR* 'curve' will therefore be a straight line through the origin, as in Figure 10.2.

Pause for thought

What would happen to the TR curve if the market price rose to £10? Try drawing it.

Revenue curves when price varies with output

The three curves (*TR*, *AR* and *MR*) will look quite different when price does vary with the firm's output.

If a firm has a relatively large share of the market, it will face a downward-sloping demand curve. This means that if it is to sell more, it must lower the price. But it could also choose to raise its price. If it does so, however, it will have to accept a fall in sales. When a firm faces a downward-sloping demand curve it is referred to as a ***price maker*** (or ***price chooser***).

Average revenue

Remember that average revenue equals price. If, therefore, the price has to be reduced to sell more output, average revenue will fall as output increases.

Table 10.2 gives an example of a firm facing a downward-sloping demand curve. The demand curve (which shows how much is sold at each price) is given by the first two columns.

Note that, as in the case of a price-taking firm, the demand curve and the *AR* curve lie along exactly the same line. The reason for this is simple: *AR* = *P*, and thus the curve relating price to quantity (the demand curve) must be the same as that relating average revenue to quantity (the *AR* curve).

Pause for thought

Consider the items you have recently purchased. Classify them into products purchased from markets where sellers were price takers and those where the sellers were price makers.

Marginal revenue

When a firm faces a downward-sloping demand curve, marginal revenue will be less than average revenue, and may even be negative. But why?

If a firm is to sell more per time period, it must lower its price (assuming it does not advertise). This will mean

Definition

Price maker (Price chooser) A firm that has the ability to influence the price charged for its good or service.

lowering the price not just for the extra units it hopes to sell, but also for those units it would have sold had it not lowered the price.

Thus the marginal revenue is the price at which it sells the last unit, *minus* the loss in revenue it has incurred by reducing the price on those units it could otherwise have sold at the higher price. This can be illustrated with Table 10.2.

Assume that price is currently £7. Two units are thus sold. The firm now wishes to sell an extra unit. It lowers the price to £6. It thus gains £6 from the sale of the third unit, but loses £2 by having to reduce the price by £1 on the two units it could otherwise have sold at £7. Its net gain is therefore £6 – £2 = £4. This is the marginal revenue: it is the extra revenue gained by the firm from selling one more unit. Try using this method to check out the remaining figures for *MR* in Table 10.2. (Note that in the table the figures for *MR* are entered in the spaces between the figures for the other three columns.)

KI 12 p 63

There is a simple relationship between marginal revenue and *price elasticity of demand*. Remember from Chapter 5 (see pages 65–6) that if demand is price elastic, a *decrease* in price will lead to a proportionately larger increase in the quantity demanded and hence an *increase* in revenue. Marginal revenue will thus be positive. If, however, demand is inelastic, a decrease in price will lead to a proportionately smaller increase in sales. In this case the price reduction will more than offset the increase in sales and as a result revenue will fall. Marginal revenue will be negative.

If, then, marginal revenue is a positive figure (i.e. if sales per time period are 4 units or fewer in Figure 10.3), the demand curve will be elastic at that point, since a rise in quantity sold (as a result of a reduction in price) would lead to a rise in total revenue. If, on the other hand, marginal revenue is negative (i.e. at a level of sales of 5 or more units in Figure 10.3), the demand curve will be inelastic at that point, since a rise in quantity sold would lead to a *fall* in total revenue.

Figure 10.3 *AR* and *MR* curves for a firm facing a downward-sloping demand curve

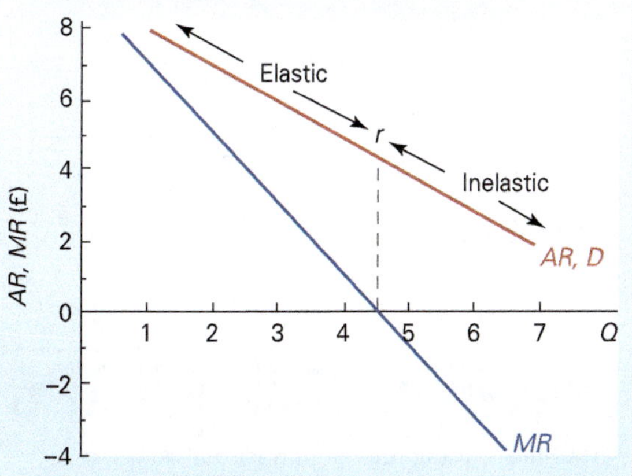

Figure 10.4 Total revenue for a firm facing a downward-sloping demand curve

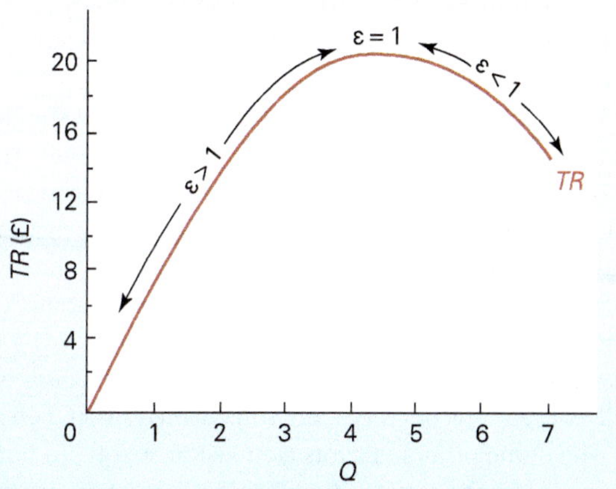

Thus the demand (*AR*) curve of Figure 10.3 is elastic to the left of point *r* and inelastic to the right.

Total revenue

Total revenue equals price times quantity. This is illustrated in Table 10.2. The *TR* column from Table 10.2 is plotted in Figure 10.4.

Unlike in the case of a price-taking firm, the *TR* curve is not a straight line. It is a curve that rises at first and then falls. But why? As long as marginal revenue is positive (and hence demand is price elastic), a rise in output will raise total revenue. However, once marginal revenue becomes negative (and hence demand is inelastic), total revenue will fall. The peak of the *TR* curve will be where *MR* = 0. At this point, the price elasticity of demand will be equal to –1.

Shifts in revenue curves

We saw (Chapter 4) that a change in *price* will cause a movement along a demand curve. It is similar with revenue curves, except that here the causal connection is in the other direction. Here we ask what happens to revenue when there is a change in the firm's *output*. Again the effect is shown by a movement along the curves.

A change in any *other* determinant of demand, such as tastes, income or the price of other goods, will shift the demand curve. By affecting the price at which each level of output can be sold, it will cause a shift in all three revenue curves. An increase in revenue is shown by a vertical shift upwards; a decrease by a shift downwards.

10.2 PROFIT MAXIMISATION

We are now in a position to put costs and revenue together to find the output at which profit is maximised, and also to find out how much that profit will be.

There are two ways of doing this. The first and simpler method is to use total cost and total revenue curves. The second method is to use marginal and average cost and marginal and average revenue curves. Although this method is a little more complicated, it makes things easier when we come to compare profit maximising under different market conditions (see Chapters 11 and 12).

We will look at each method in turn. In both cases we will concentrate on the short run: namely, that period in which one or more factors are fixed in supply. In both cases we take the case of a firm facing a downward-sloping demand curve: i.e. a price maker.

Figure 10.5 Finding maximum profit using totals curves

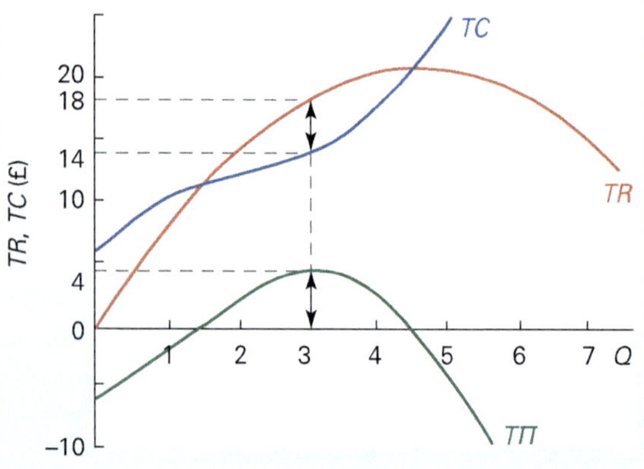

Short-run profit maximisation: using total curves

Table 10.3 shows the total revenue figures from Table 10.2. It also shows figures for total cost. These figures have been chosen so as to produce a *TC* curve of a typical shape.

Total profit (*TΠ*) is found by subtracting *TC* from *TR*. This can be seen in Table 10.3. Where (*TΠ*) is negative, the firm is making a loss. Total profit is maximised at an output of 3 units: namely, where there is the greatest gap between total revenue and total costs. At this output, total profit is £4 (£18 – £14).

The *TR*, *TC* and (*TΠ*) curves are plotted in Figure 10.5. The size of the maximum profit is shown by the arrows.

Short-run profit maximisation: using average and marginal curves

Finding the maximum profit that a firm can make is a two-stage process. The first stage is to find the profit-maximising output. To do this we use the *MC* and *MR* curves. The second stage is to find out just how much profit is at this output. To do this we use the *AR* and *AC* curves.

Table 10.3

Q (units)	*TR* (£)	*TC* (£)	*TΠ* (£)
0	0	6	−6
1	8	10	−2
2	14	12	2
3	18	14	4
4	20	18	2
5	20	25	−5
6	18	36	−18
7	14	56	−42
.	.	.	.

Stage 1: Using marginal curves to arrive at the profit-maximising output

There is a very simple ***profit-maximising rule***: if profits are to be maximised, *MR must equal MC*. From Table 10.4 it can be seen that *MR* = *MC* at an output of 3 (Table 10.4 is based on the figures in Table 10.3). This is shown as point *e* in Figure 10.6.

Figure 10.6 Finding the profit-maximising output using the marginal curves

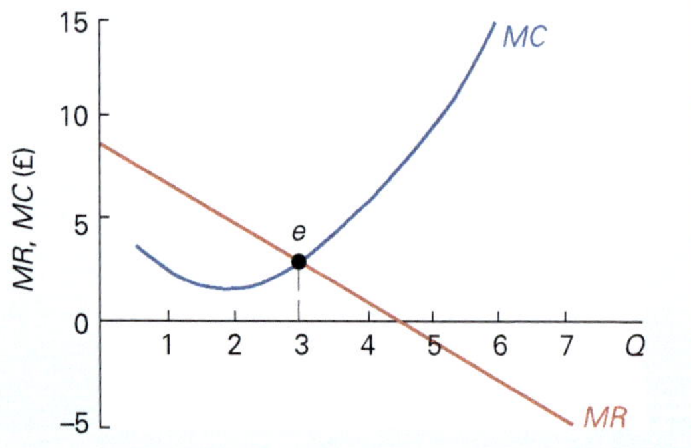

Definition

Profit-maximising rule Profit is maximised where marginal revenue equals marginal cost.

Table 10.4

Q (units)	$P = AR$ (£)	TR (£)	MR (£)	TC (£)	AC (£)	MC (£)	TR (£)	$A\Pi$ (£)
0	9	0		6	–		−6	–
			8			4		
1	8	8		10	10		−2	−2
			6			2		
2	7	14		12	6		2	1
			4			2		
3	6	18		14	$4^2/_3$		4	$-1^1/_3$
			2			4		
4	5	20		18	$4^1/_2$		2	$^1/_2$
			0			7		
5	4	20		25	5		−5	−1
			−2			11		
6	3	18		36	6		−18	−3
			−4			20		
7	2	14		56	8		−42	−6
.	.	.	.	.	.	.	.	.

Pause for thought

Why are the figures for MR and MC entered in the spaces between the lines in Table 10.4?

KI 4 p 22

But why are profits maximised when $MR = MC$? The simplest way of answering this is to see what the position would be if MR did not equal MC.

Referring to Figure 10.6, at a level of output below 3, MR exceeds MC. This means that by producing more units there will be a bigger addition to revenue (MR) than to cost (MC). Total profit will *increase*. *As long as* MR *exceeds* MC*, profit can be increased by increasing production.*

At a level of output above 3, MC exceeds MR. All levels of output above 3 thus add more to cost than to revenue and hence *reduce* profit. *As long as* MC *exceeds* MR*, profit can be increased by cutting back on production.*

Profits are thus maximised where $MC = MR$: at an output of 3. This can be confirmed by examining the $T\Pi$ column in Table 10.4.

Students worry sometimes about the argument that profits are maximised when $MR = MC$. Surely, they say, if the last unit is making no profit, how can profit be at a *maximum*? The answer is very simple. If you cannot *add* anything more to a total, the total must be at the maximum. Take the simple analogy of going up a hill. When you cannot go any higher, you must be at the top.

Stage 2: Using average curves to measure the size of the profit

Once the profit-maximising output has been discovered, we now use the average curves to measure the *amount* of profit at the maximum. Both marginal and average curves corresponding to the data in Table 10.4 are plotted in Figure 10.7.

First, average profit ($A\Pi$) is found. This is simply $AR - AC$. At the profit-maximising output of 3, this gives a figure for $A\Pi$ of £6 − £$4^2/_2$ = £$1^1/_3$. Then total profit is obtained by multiplying average profit by output:

$$T\Pi = A\Pi \times Q$$

This is shown as the shaded area. It equals £$1^1/_3 \times 3$ = £4. This can again be confirmed by reference to the $T\Pi$ column in Table 10.4.

Pause for thought

What will be the effect on a firm's profit-maximising output of a rise in fixed costs?

Some qualifications

Long-run profit maximisation

Assuming that the AR and MR curves are the same in the long run as in the short run, long-run profits will be maximised at the output where MR equals the *long-run MC*. The reasoning is the same as with the short-run case.

Figure 10.7 Measuring the maximum profit using average curves

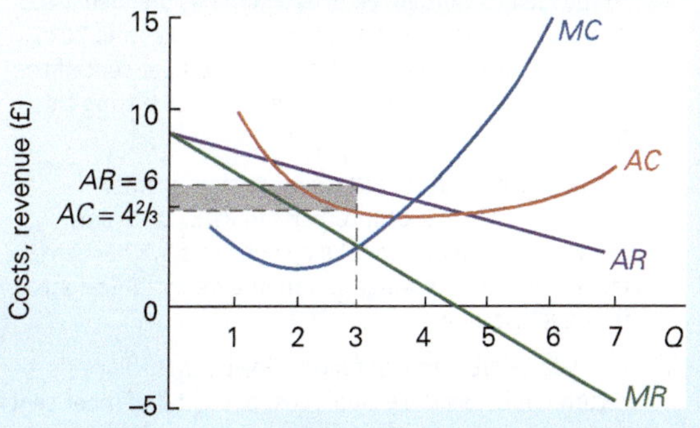

The meaning of 'profit'

KI 3 p 20

One element of cost is the opportunity cost to the owners of the firm incurred by being in business. This is the minimum return that the owners must make on their capital in order to prevent them from eventually deciding to close down and perhaps move into some alternative business. It is a *cost* since, just as with wages, rent, etc., it has to be covered if the firm is to continue poducing. This opportunity cost to the owners is sometimes known as ***normal profit***, and *is included in the cost curves*.

What determines this normal rate of profit? It has two components. First, someone setting up in business invests capital in it. There is thus an opportunity cost of capital. This is the interest that could have been earned by lending it in some riskless form (e.g. by putting it in a savings account in a bank). Nobody would set up a business unless they expected to earn at least this rate of profit. Running a business is far from riskless, however, and hence a second element is a return to compensate for risk. Thus:

normal profit (%) = rate of interest on a riskless loan + a risk premium

The risk premium varies according to the line of business. In those with fairly predictable patterns, such as food retailing, it is relatively low. Where outcomes are very uncertain, such as mineral exploration or the manufacture of fashion garments, it is relatively high.

Thus if owners of a business earn normal profit, they will (just) be content to remain in that industry. If they earn more than normal profit, they will also (obviously) prefer to stay in this business. If they earn less than normal profit, then after a time they will consider leaving and using their capital for some other purpose.

Given that normal profits are included in costs, any profit that is shown diagrammatically (e.g. the shaded area in Figure 10.7) must therefore be over and above normal profit. It is known by several alternative names: ***supernormal profit***, ***pure profit***, ***economic profit***, ***abnormal profit*** or sometimes simply ***profit***. They all mean the same thing: the excess of profit over normal profit.

Loss minimising

It may be that there is no output at which the firm can make a profit. Such a situation is illustrated in Figure 10.8: the *AC* curve is above the *AR* curve at all levels of output.

Definitions

Normal profit The opportunity cost of being in business. It consists of the interest that could be earned on a riskless asset, plus a return for risk-taking in this particular industry. It is counted as a cost of production.

Supernormal profit (also known as **pure profit**, **economic profit**, **abnormal profit** or simply **profit**) The excess of total profit above normal profit.

BOX 10.1 OPPORTUNITY COST OF CAPITAL IN PRACTICE

Opportunity costs of capital and company structures

Opportunity costs of capital play an important role in determining the structure of large corporations. The RWE Group is one of Europe's largest electricity and gas companies. Its core operations are in Germany, the Netherlands and the UK. In the UK it operates through its NPower subsidiary, which it purchased in 2002.

By 2011 Jürgen Grossmann, RWE's chief executive, was considering if NPower should remain part of the RWE portfolio. According to the *Financial Times*:

> RWE has been reviewing its strategic options, advised by Goldman Sachs, as it grapples with net debt of €27.5bn (£24.7bn).
>
> To reduce this burden, Mr Grossmann has pledged asset disposals of up to €8bn a year between 2011 and 2013. Selling NPower, which generates about 9 per cent of the UK's electricity, will go a long way towards hitting this target. . . .
>
> Analysts point out that NPower has significantly underperformed its counterparts in RWE. Last year, NPower's return on capital employed was 5.3 per cent, making Britain the worst performing geographical area in the RWE group.
>
> Last year, RWE's annual report showed that NPower's return fell below the group's cost of capital of 9 per cent before tax, ... [However] NPower remains a cash-generating business, achieving an operating profit of €277m last year.[1]

When making his decision Mr Grossmann will not look at past performance alone. He will also assess NPower's prospects for the future. On the demand side, there is a consumer perception that gas and electricity companies are charging 'unfair' prices. This is making producers reluctant to raise prices, fearing the effects of negative publicity. On the supply side, distribution costs are rising and from 2013 more powerful emissions regulations will exert additional upward pressure on costs.

Finally, the decision must also take into account the prospects for the rest of the RWE Group. Are the prospects of the other constituent parts better or worse than NPower's?

?

1. *Explain why, even though NPower generated €277 million in profit in 2010, it may make sense for RWE to sell the company.*
2. *Under what circumstances would another company consider buying NPower?*

[1] David Blair, Gerrit Wiesmann and Ausha Sakoui, RWE considers pulling plug on NPower (*The Financial Times*, 5 July 2011). © The Financial Times Limited. All Rights Reserved.

Figure 10.8 Loss-minimising output

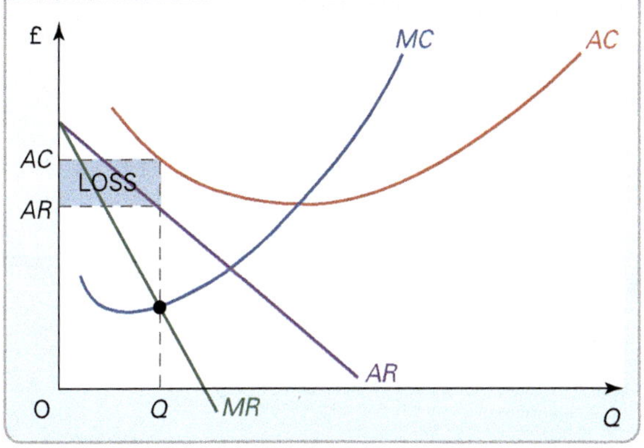

Figure 10.9 The short-run shut-down point

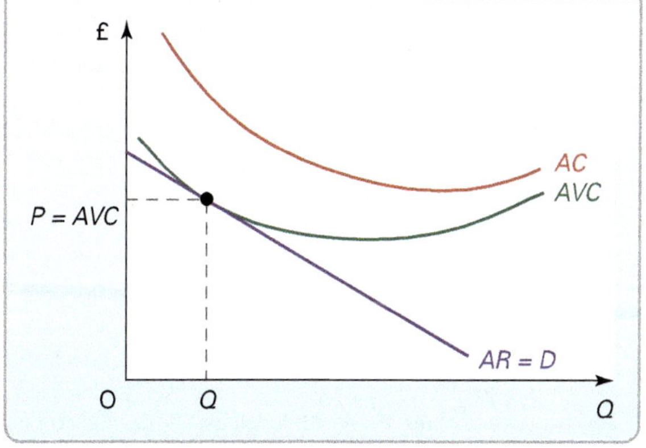

In this case, the output where *MR* = *MC* will be the loss-minimising output. The amount of loss at the point where *MR* = *MC* is shown by the shaded area in Figure 10.8.

Whether or not to produce at all

KI 18 p 129

The short run. Fixed costs have to be paid even if the firm is producing nothing at all. Rent has to be paid, business rates have to be paid, etc. Providing, therefore, that the firm is more than covering its *variable* costs, it can go some way to paying off these fixed costs and therefore will continue to produce.

It will shut down if it cannot cover its variable costs: that is, if the *AVC* curve is above, or the *AR* curve is below, that illustrated in Figure 10.9. This situation is known as the ***short-run shut-down point***.

The long run. All costs are variable in the long run. If, therefore, the firm cannot cover its long-run average costs (which include normal profit), it will close down. The ***long-run shut-down point*** will be where the *AR* curve is tangential to the *LRAC* curve.

Pause for thought

Why might it make sense for a firm which cannot sell its output at a profit to continue in production for the time being?

Definitions

Short-run shut-down point This is where the *AR* curve is tangential to the *AVC* curve. The firm can only just cover its variable costs. Any fall in revenue below this level will cause a profit-maximising firm to shut down immediately.

Long-run shut-down point This is where the *AR* curve is tangential to the *LRAC* curve. The firm can just make normal profits. Any fall in revenue below this level will cause a profit-maximising firm to shut down once all costs have become variable.

BOX 10.2 **SELLING ICE CREAM WHEN I WAS A STUDENT**

John's experience of competition

When I was a student, my parents lived in Exeter in Devon, and at that time, the city's bypass became completely jammed on a summer Saturday as holidaymakers made their way to the coast. Traffic queues were several miles long.

For a summer job, I drove a small ice-cream van. Early on, I had the idea of selling ice cream from a tray to the people queuing in their cars. I made more money on a Saturday than the rest of the week put together. I thought I was on to a good thing.

But news of this lucrative market soon spread, and each week new ice-cream sellers appeared – each one reducing my earnings! By the middle of August there were over 30 ice-cream sellers from five different ice-cream companies. Most tried to get to the beginning of the queue, to get ahead of their rivals.

Imagine the scene. A family driving to the coast rounds a bend and is suddenly met by a traffic jam and several ice-cream sellers all jostling to sell them an ice cream. It was quite surreal. Not surprisingly, many of the potential customers refused to buy, feeling somewhat intimidated by the spectacle. It was not long before most of us realised that it was best to disperse and find a section of the road where there were no other sellers.

But with so many ice-cream sellers, no one made much money. My supernormal earnings had been reduced to a normal level. I made about the same on Saturday selling to people stuck in queues as I would have done if I had driven my van around the streets.

?

Imagine that you live in a popular and sunny seaside town and that the local council awarded you the only licence to sell ice cream in the town. Would you be earning normal or supernormal profit? Explain your answer.

SUMMARY

1a Just as we could identify total, average and marginal costs, so too we can identify total, average and marginal revenue.

1b Total revenue (*TR*) is the total amount a firm earns from its sales in a given time period. It is simply price times quantity: $TR = P \times Q$.

1c Average revenue (*AR*) is total revenue per unit: $AR = TR/Q$. In other words, $AR = P$.

1d Marginal revenue is the extra revenue earned from the sale of one more unit per time period.

1e The *AR* curve will be the same as the demand curve for the firm's product. In the case of a price taker, the demand curve and hence the *AR* curve will be a horizontal straight line and will also be the same as the *MR* curve. The *TR* curve is an upward-sloping straight line from the origin.

1f A firm that faces a downward-sloping demand curve must obviously also face the same downward-sloping *AR* curve. The *MR* curve will also slope downwards, but will be below the *AR* curve and steeper than it. The *TR* curve will be an arch shape starting from the origin.

1g When demand is price elastic, marginal revenue will be positive and the *TR* curve will be upward sloping. When demand is price inelastic, marginal revenue will be negative and the *TR* curve will be downward sloping.

1h A change in output is represented by a movement along the revenue curves. A change in any other determinant of revenue will shift the curves up or down.

2a Total profit equals total revenue minus total cost. By definition, then, a firm's profits will be maximised at the point where there is the greatest gap between total revenue and total cost.

2b Another way of finding the maximum-profit point is to find the output where marginal revenue equals marginal cost. Having found this output, the level of maximum profit can be found by finding the average profit ($AR - AC$) and then multiplying it by the level of output.

2c Normal profit is the minimum profit that must be made to persuade a firm to stay in business in the long run. It is counted as part of the firm's cost. Supernormal profit is any profit over and above normal profit.

2d For a firm that cannot make a profit at any level of output, the point where $MR = MC$ represents the loss-minimising output.

2e In the short run, a firm will close down if it cannot cover its variable costs. In the long run, it will close down if it cannot make normal profits.

REVIEW QUESTIONS

1 Draw a downward-sloping demand curve. Now put in scales of your own choosing for both axes. Read off various points on the demand curve and use them to construct a table showing price and quantity. Use this table to work out the figures for a marginal revenue column. Now use these figures to draw an *MR* curve.

2 Copy Figures 10.3 and 10.4 (which are based on Table 10.2). Now assume that incomes have risen and that, as a result, two more units per time period can be sold at each price. Draw a new table and plot the resulting new *AR*, *MR* and *TR* curves on your diagrams. Are the new curves parallel to the old ones? Explain.

3 What can we say about the slope of the *TR* and *TC* curves at the maximum-profit point? What does this tell us about marginal revenue and marginal cost?

4 Using the following information, construct a table like Table 10.3.

Q	0	1	2	3	4	5	6	7
P	12	11	10	9	8	7	6	5
TC	2	6	9	12	16	21	28	38

Use your table to draw diagrams like Figures 10.5 and 10.7. Use these two diagrams to show the profit-maximising output and the level of maximum profit. Confirm your findings by reference to the table you have constructed.

5 The following table shows the average cost and average revenue (price) for a firm at each level of output.

(a) Construct a table to show *TC*, *MC*, *TR* and *MR* at each level of output (put the figures for *MC* and *MR* midway between the output figures).
(b) Using *MC* and *MR* figures, find the profit-maximising output.
(c) Using *TC* and *TR* figures, check your answer to (b).
(d) Plot the *AC*, *MC*, *AR* and *MR* figures on a graph.
(e) Mark the profit-maximising output and the *AR* and *AC* at this output.
(f) Shade in an area to represent the level of profits at this output.

Output	1	2	3	4	5	6	7	8	9	10
AC (£)	7.00	5.00	4.00	3.30	3.00	3.10	3.50	4.20	5.00	6.00
AR (£)	10.00	9.50	9.00	8.50	8.00	7.50	7.00	6.50	6.00	5.50

6 Normal profits are regarded as a cost (and are included in the cost curves). Explain why.

7 What determines the size of normal profit? Will it vary with the general state of the economy?

8 A firm will continue producing in the short run even if it is making a loss, providing it can cover its variable costs. Explain why. Just how long will it be willing to continue making such a loss?

9 Would there ever be a point in a firm attempting to continue in production if it could not cover its *long-run* average (total) costs?

10 The price of pocket calculators and digital watches fell significantly in the years after they were first introduced and at the same time demand for them increased substantially. Use cost and revenue diagrams to illustrate these events. Explain the reasoning behind the diagram(s) you have drawn.

11 In February 2000, Unilever, the giant consumer products company, announced that it was to cut 25 000 jobs, close 100 plants and rely more on the Internet to purchase its supplies. It would use part of the money saved to increase promotion of its leading brands, such as Dove skincare products, Lipton tea, Omo detergents and Calvin Klein cosmetics. The hope was to boost sales and increase profits. If it meets these targets, what is likely to have happened to its total costs, total revenue, average costs and average revenue? Give reasons for your answer.

ADDITIONAL PART D CASE STUDIES IN THE *ECONOMICS FOR BUSINESS* MyEconLab (www.pearsoned.co.uk/sloman)

D.1 **Malthus and the dismal science of economics.** A gloomy warning, made over 200 years ago by Robert Malthus, that diminishing returns to labour would lead to famine for much of the world's population.

D.2 **Division of labour in a pin factory.** This is the famous example of division of labour given by Adam Smith in his *Wealth of Nations* (1776).

D.3 **Diminishing returns to nitrogen fertiliser.** This case study provides a good illustration of diminishing returns in practice by showing the effects on grass yields of the application of increasing amounts of nitrogen fertiliser.

D.4 **Diminishing returns in the bread shop.** An illustration of the law of diminishing returns.

D.5 **The relationship between averages and marginals.** An examination of the rules showing how an average curve relates to a marginal curve.

D.6 **Deriving cost curves from total physical product information.** This shows how total, average and marginal costs can be derived from a total product information and the price of inputs.

WEBSITES RELEVANT TO PART D

Numbers and sections refer to websites listed in the Web appendix and hotlinked from this book's website at **www.pearsoned.co.uk/sloman**

- For news articles relevant to Part D, see the Economics News Articles link from the book's website.
- For student resources relevant to Part D, see sites C1–7, 9, 10, 14, 19, 20.
- For a case study examining costs, see site D2.
- For sites that look at companies, their scale of operation and market share, see B2; E4, 10; G7, 8.
- For links to sites on various aspects of production and costs, see section Microeconomics > Production in site I7 and 11.

Products, marketing and advertising

Business issues covered in this chapter

- In what ways can firms differentiate their products from those of their rivals?
- What strategies can firms adopt for gaining market share, developing their products and marketing them?
- What elements are likely to be contained in a marketing strategy?
- How extensive is advertising in the UK and how does it vary from product to product?
- What are the effects of advertising and what makes a successful advertising campaign?

KI 1 p 7
For most firms, selling their product is not simply a question of estimating demand and then choosing an appropriate price and level of production. In other words, they do not simply take their market as given. Instead they will seek to *influence* demand. They will do this by developing their product and differentiating it from those of their rivals, and then marketing it by advertising and other forms of product promotion.

What firms are engaging in here is ***non-price competition***. In such situations the job of the manager can be quite complex. It is likely to involve making a series of strategic decisions, not just concerning price, but also concerning each product's design and quality, its marketing and advertising, and the provision of various forms of after-sales service.

Central to non-price competition is ***product differentiation***. Most firms' products differ in various ways from those of their rivals. Take the case of washing machines. Although all washing machines wash clothes, and as such are close substitutes for each other, there are many differences between brands. They differ not only in price, but also in their capacity, their styling, their range of programmes, their economy in the use of electricity, hot water and detergent, their reliability, their noise, their after-sales service, etc. Firms will attempt to design their product so that they can stress its advantages (real or imaginary) over the competitor brands. Just think of the specific features of particular models of car, hi-fi equipment or brands of cosmetic, and then consider the ways in which these features are stressed by advertisements. In fact, think of virtually any advertisement and consider how it stresses the features of that particular brand.

Definitions

Non-price competition Competition in terms of product promotion (advertising, packaging, etc.) or product development.

Product differentiation Where a firm's product is in some way distinct from its rivals' products.

8.1 PRODUCT DIFFERENTIATION

Features of a product

A product has many dimensions, and a strategy to differentiate a product may focus on one or more of these dimensions.

- *Technical standards*. These relate to the product's level of technical sophistication: how advanced it is in relation to the current state of technology. This would be a very important product dimension if, for example, you were purchasing a PC.
- *Quality standards*. These relate to aspects such as the quality of the materials used in the product's construction and the care taken in assembly. These will affect the product's durability and reliability. The purchase of consumer durables, such as televisions, hi-fi and toys, will be strongly influenced by quality standards.
- *Design characteristics*. These relate to the product's direct appeal to the consumer in terms of appearance or operating features. Examples of design characteristics are colour, style and even packaging. The demand for fashion products such as clothing will be strongly influenced by design characteristics.
- *Service characteristics*. This aspect is not directly concerned with the product itself, but with the support and back-up given to the customer after the product has been sold. Servicing, product maintenance and guarantees would be included under this heading. When purchasing a new car, the quality of after-sales service might strongly influence the choice you make.

Any given product will possess a 'bundle' of the above attributes. Within any product category, each brand is likely to have a different mix of technical and quality standards and design and service characteristics. Consumers will select the bundle of attributes or characteristics they most prefer (see section 6.3). The fact that these different dimensions exist means that producers can focus the marketing of their product on factors other than price – they can engage in non-price competition.

Vertical and horizontal product differentiation

When firms are seeking to differentiate their product from those of their rivals (product differentiation), one important distinction they must consider is that between *vertical* and *horizontal* differentiation.

Vertical product differentiation. This is where products differ in quality, with some being perceived as superior and others as inferior. In general, the better the quality, the more expensive will the product be. Take the case of a DVD recorder. The cheaper (inferior) models will just have basic functions. More expensive models will have more and better functions, such as picture zooming, editing facilities, Dolby 5.1 'surround sound' and thumbnail outlines of recorded films.

Vertical product differentiation will usually be in terms of the quantity and quality of functions and/or the durability of the product (often a reflection of the quality of the materials used and the care spent in making the product). Thus a garment will normally be regarded as superior if it is better made and uses high-quality cloth. In general, the vertical quality differences between products will tend to reflect differences in production costs.

Horizontal product differentiation. This refers to differences between products that are not generally regarded as superior or inferior, but merely reflections of the different tastes of different consumers. One person may prefer black shoes and another brown. One may prefer milk chocolate, another plain. Within any product range there may be varieties which differ in respect to style, design, flavour, colour, etc. Such attributes are neither better, nor worse, simply different.

Horizontal differences within a range do not significantly alter the costs of production, and it is common for the different varieties to have the same price. A pot of red paint is likely to be the same price as a pot of blue (of the same brand). The point is that the products, although horizontally different, are of comparable quality.

> **Pause for thought**
>
> ***Identify two other products that are vertically differentiated, two that are horizontally differentiated and two that are both.***

In practice, most product ranges will have a mixture of horizontal and vertical differentiation. For example, some of the differences between different makes and models of motor car will be vertical (e.g. luxury or basic internal fittings, acceleration and fuel consumption); some will be horizontal (e.g. hatchback or saloon, colour and style).

> **Definitions**
>
> **Vertical product differentiation** Where a firm's product differs from its rivals' products with respect to quality.
>
> **Horizontal product differentiation** Where a firm's product differs from its rivals' products, although the products are seen to be of a similar quality.

Market segmentation

Different features of a product will appeal to different consumers. This applies both to vertically differentiated features and to horizontally differentiated ones. Where features are quite distinct, and where particular features or groups of features can be seen to appeal to a particular category of consumers, it might be useful for producers to divide the market into segments. Taking the example of cars again, the market could be divided into luxury cars, large, medium and small family cars, sports cars, multi-terrain vehicles, six-seater people carriers, etc. Each type of car occupies a distinct market segment, and within each segment the individual models are likely to be both horizontally and vertically differentiated from competitor models.

When consumer tastes change over time, or where existing models do not cater for every taste, a firm may be

BOX 8.1 THE BATTLE OF THE BRANDS

The rise, fall and rise of own-label brands

From fairly humble beginnings, supermarket own-label brands really took off in the late 1980s and early 1990s. By 1995 they accounted for over half of supermarket sales in the UK.

However, by the mid-2000s own-label brands' share of supermarket sales had fallen to around one third. By the late 2000s, however, own-label supermarket brands had become popular once again. The market shares of own-label products varies from close to 100 per cent in categories where it is difficult to 'add value' such as fresh fruit to below 10 per cent for products such as energy drinks and chocolate.

So, how do own-label brands compete? Why have their fortunes fluctuated over time?

They don't have significant differences in costs of production . . .

Branded manufacturers were always thought to be able to take advantage of large economies of scale in sourcing and production. However, new technologies and close working relationships between retailers and suppliers have allowed supermarkets to provide own-label products in smaller batches but at lower costs, thus offsetting any advantage that brand manufacturers may have. Technology has also helped to improve the quality of products, making it possible for own-label producers to imitate the ideas of brand manufacturers and engage in their own innovations.

. . . but they do offer different product characteristics

Branded and own-label products are perceived by consumers as offering different product characteristics (table (a)). According to Mintel, branded goods are typically associated with positive associations, such as being trustworthy and authentic, when compared to own-label goods. Own label products, however, are much more likely to be seen as offering value for money and being family friendly, when compared to the branded alternatives.

(a) Perceived characteristics of branded and own-label products, 2011

	Percentage of respondents	
Characteristic	**Branded product**	**Own-label product**
Trustworthy	52	32
Traditional	51	22
Authentic	41	25
Family friendly	28	45
Healthy	19	17
Value for money	16	82
Bland	2	28

Source: Mintel 2011

The major supermarket chains such as Tesco, Asda, Sainsbury's and Morrisons have all developed their own premium brands, either to compete in particular segments, for example in healthy eating ranges, such as 'Be Good to Yourself' or 'Taste the Difference', or more generally, for example Tesco's 'Finest' range. Mintel states that these ranges are seen as having strong value-for-money credentials, suggesting that products within them are viewed as competitive by consumers. However, some of the 'value' own-label brands are not seen as offering superior value for money than the branded alternative. This suggests that, by 2011, although many customers see these products as low cost, the lower quality may not always justify the price! This weakens the ability of the supermarket to use these products as a competitive tool.

They take advantage of changing economic prosperity

The decline in market share of own-brands from the early 1990s to 2007 was partly due a period of prolonged economic growth. The rise in disposable income during this period led to increased conspicuous consumption, and many branded goods are associated with affluence and increased quality of lifestyle.

The recessions of the early 1990s and from 2008, by contrast, saw a growth in market share of own-label brands as consumers sought to economise. Supermarkets were able to tap into the price sensitivity of consumers with a range of good value-for-money own-label products; branded products failed to follow suit.

Nevertheless, customers still value brands. Brand manufacturers rely on consumers developing a loyal attachment to a product over a number of years. This is able to identify a new segment of the market – a ***market niche***. Having identified the appropriate market niche for its product, the marketing division within the firm will then set about targeting the relevant consumer group(s) and developing an appropriate strategy for promoting the product. (In the next section we will explore more closely those factors which are likely to influence a business's marketing strategy.)

Definition

Market niche A part of a market (or new market) that has not been filled by an existing brand or business.

strengthened by substantial investments in advertising and marketing. Branding is concerned with conveying an image and a style of living, as well as showing the product's function, its convenience and its value. All this takes time to develop, and successful brands, such as Kelloggs and Hovis, have been popular for over 100 years.

Brands dominate many market segments . . .

While the trend in recent times has been back towards own-label brands, it is important to recognise that there is still substantial variability in own-label penetration across products. As Table (b) illustrates, in some product segments, the penetration of supermarkets' own-brands is considerable (e.g. fruit, vegetables and nuts). In others, however, branded products dominate (e.g. cereal bars and confectionary).

Where products are viewed as fairly homogeneous, at least in the eyes of the consumer, or requiring limited technological input, product differentiation by brand is difficult to achieve. There are no real cost advantages and supermarket own-label brands can compete keenly on price.

On the other hand, where products are more differentiated, consumers may identify their particular product by branding. Examples include products targeted at a particular group (defined by gender, age or socioeconomic status), products that reflect a certain style of living (e.g. healthy eating), products that embody high quality or innovative characteristics, or have a long history. In these markets, own-label brands compete actively by differentiating their products. They do not have to compete strictly on price because sophisticated products command a greater premium.

The disadvantage for supermarkets is that their advertising expenditures are largely concerned with branding the store *as a whole*, rather than particular own-label lines. Their promotional expenditures are thus somewhat diluted. Brand manufacturers, on the other hand, are specialists in targeting their advertising and promotional expenditures towards particular markets. They achieve economies from marketing the brand, with the result that their sales per pound of promotional expenditure are higher. Economies of scale in marketing provide a powerful competitive advantage for brand manufacturers.

(b) Market penetration of own-label brands in selected UK markets, 2011

Market segment	Market share (%)
Fresh fruit and vegetables	96
Nuts	74
Dried fruits	67
Cakes and cake bars	50
Biscuits	22
Crisps and snacks	21
Yoghurt	19
Sugar confectionary	14
Cereal bars	8
Chocolate confectionary	8

Source: *Mintel* reports (2011)

. . . but brand manufacturers still have to be responsive to competitive pressures from low-cost own-label rivals

The leading supermarkets use own-label brands to promote their store name but they recognise how important brands are to customers. Likewise, the success of own-labels, particularly value lines, in times of recession, stimulates manufacturers of branded goods to compete fiercely. For example, Unilever recently announced, along with Procter and Gamble and L'Oréal, that they would extend their product ranges to include more 'value lines'. They have also restructured their businesses to reduce cost. Thus, own-label brands keep prices keen and quality high and that means consumers have more choice.

?

1. *How has the improvement in the quality of own-brands affected the price elasticity of demand for branded products? What implications does this have for the pricing strategy of brand manufacturers?*
2. *Why don't brand manufacturers readily engage in the production of supermarket own-label products?*
3. *How might brand manufacturers respond to the development of a new product line?*

8.2 MARKETING THE PRODUCT

What is marketing?

There is no single accepted definition of marketing. It is generally agreed, however, that marketing covers the following activities: establishing the strength of consumer demand in existing parts of the market, and potential demand in new niches; developing an attractive and distinct image for the product; informing potential consumers of various features of the product; fostering a desire by consumers for the product; and, in the light of all these, persuading consumers to buy the product.

Clearly, marketing must be seen within the overall goals of the firm. There would be little point in spending vast sums of money in promoting a product if it led to only a modest increase in sales and sales revenue.

Figure 8.1 Growth vector components

		Product: Current	Product: New
Market	*Current*	**A** Market penetration	**B** Product development
	New	**C** Market development	**D** Diversification

Source: I. Ansoff, *Corporate Strategy* (McGraw-Hill, 1965); 'Strategies for diversification', *Harvard Business Review* (September–October 1957)

Product/market strategy

Once the nature and strength of consumer demand (both current and potential) have been identified, the business will set about meeting and influencing this demand. In most cases it will be hoping to achieve a growth in sales. To do this, one of the first things the firm must decide is its *product/market strategy*. This will involve addressing two major questions:

KI 23 p 181

- Should it focus on promoting its existing product, or should it develop new products?
- Should it focus on gaining a bigger share of its existing market, or should it seek to break into new markets?

In 1957 Igor Ansoff illustrated these choices in what he called a ***growth vector matrix***. This is illustrated in Figure 8.1.

The four boxes show the possible combinations of answers to the above questions: Box A – *market penetration* (current product, current market); Box B – *product development* (new product, current market); Box C – *market development* (current product, new market); Box D – *diversification* (new product, new market).

- *Market penetration*. In the market penetration strategy, the business will seek not only to retain existing customers, but to expand its customer base with current products in current markets. Of the four strategies, this is generally the least risky: the business will be able to play to its product strengths and draw on its knowledge of the market. The business's marketing strategy will tend to focus upon aggressive product promotion and distribution. Such a strategy, however, is likely to lead to fierce competition from current business rivals, especially if the overall market is not expanding and if the firm can therefore gain an increase in sales only by taking market share from its rivals.
- *Product development*. Product development strategies will involve introducing new models and designs in current markets. This may involve either vertical differentiation (e.g. the introduction of an upgraded model) or horizontal differentiation (e.g. the introduction of a new style).
- *Market development*. With a market development strategy the business will seek increased sales of current products by expanding into new markets. These may be in a different geographical location (e.g. overseas), or new market segments. Alternatively, the strategy may involve finding new uses and applications for the product.
- *Diversification*. A diversification strategy will involve the business expanding into new markets with new products. Of all the strategies, this is the most risky given the unknown factors that the business is likely to face.

Once the product/market strategy has been decided upon, the business will then attempt to devise a suitable *marketing strategy*. This will involve looking at the marketing mix.

Definition

Growth vector matrix A means by which a business might assess its product/market strategy.

Pause for thought

What unknown factors is the business likely to face following a diversification strategy?

The marketing mix

In order to differentiate the firm's product from those of its rivals, there are four variables that can be adjusted. These are as follows:

- product;
- price;
- place (distribution);
- promotion.

The particular combination of these variables, known as 'the four Ps', represents the business's ***marketing mix***, and it is around a manipulation of them that the business will devise its marketing strategy.

Figure 8.2 illustrates the various considerations that might be taken into account when looking at product, price, place and promotion.

Definition

Marketing mix The mix of product, price, place (distribution) and promotion that will determine a business's marketing strategy.

- *Product considerations*. These involve issues such as quality and reliability, as well as branding, packaging and after-sales service.
- *Pricing considerations*. These involve not only the product's basic price in relation to those of competitors' products, but also opportunities for practising price discrimination (the practice of charging different prices in different parts of the market: see Chapter 17), offering discounts to particular customers, and adjusting the terms of payment for the product.
- *Place considerations*. These focus on the product's distribution network, and involve issues such as where the business's retail outlets should be located, what warehouse facilities the business might require, and how the product should be transported to the market.
- *Promotion considerations*. These focus primarily upon the amount and type of advertising the business should use. In addition, promotion issues might also include selling techniques, special offers, trial discounts and various other public relations 'gimmicks'.

Every product is likely to have a distinct marketing *mix* of these four variables. Thus we cannot talk about an ideal value for one (e.g. the best price), without considering the

Figure 8.2 Model of the customer market offering dimensions of the marketing mix

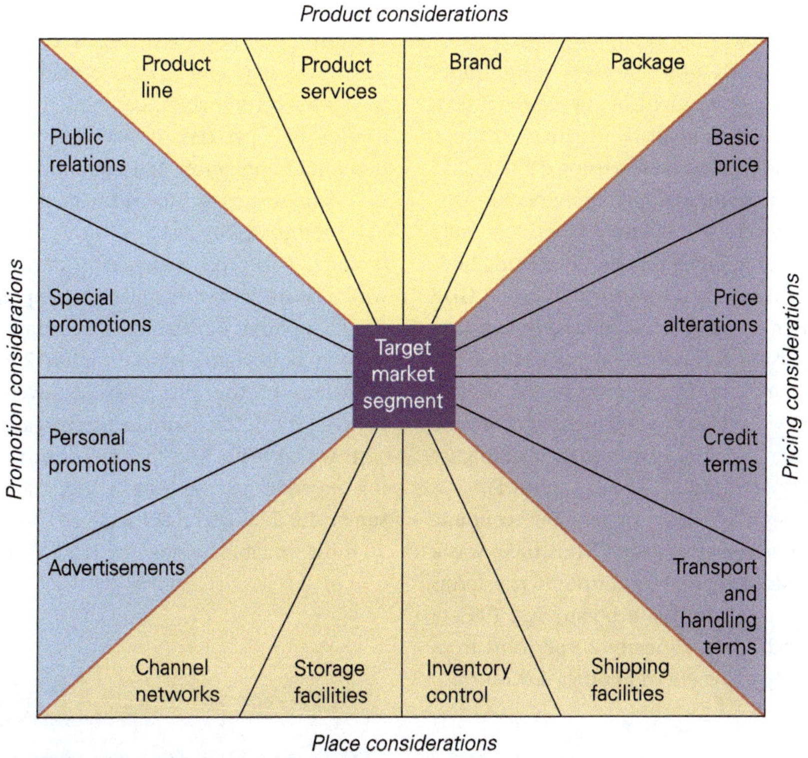

Source: based on H. A. Lipson and J. R. Darling, *Introduction to Marketing: an administrative approach* (John Wiley & Sons, Inc., 1971). Reproduced with permission

other three. What is more, the most appropriate mix will vary from product to product and from market to market. If you wanted to sell a Rolls-Royce, you would be unlikely to sell any more by offering free promotional gifts or expanding the number of retail outlets. You might sell more Rolls-Royces, however, if you were to improve their specifications or offer more favourable methods of payment.

What the firm must seek to do is to estimate how sensitive demand is to the various aspects of marketing. The greater the sensitivity (elasticity) in each case, the more the firms should focus on that particular aspect. It must be careful, however, that changing one aspect of marketing does not conflict with another. For example, there would be little point in improving the product's quality if, at the same time, the product was promoted by the use of marketing gimmicks that led consumers to believe they were buying an inferior, 'mass consumption' product.

Another consideration that must be taken into account is the stage in the product's life cycle (see section 17.6). The most appropriate marketing mix for a new and hence unfamiliar product, and one which may be facing little in the way of competition, may well be totally inappropriate for a product that is long established and may be struggling against competitors to maintain its market share.

8.3 ADVERTISING

One of the most important aspects of marketing is advertising. The major aim of advertising is to sell more products, and business spends a vast quantity of money on advertising to achieve this goal. By advertising, the business will not only be informing the consumer of the product's existence and availability, but also deliberately attempting to persuade and entice the consumer to purchase the good. In doing so, it will tend to stress the specific and unique qualities of this firm's product over those of its rivals. This will be discussed in more detail below.

Advertising facts and figures

Advertising and the state of the economy

Advertising expenditure, like other business expenditure, is subject to the cyclical movement of the national economy. Indeed, advertising is particularly sensitive to the ups and downs in the economy. In times of rising demand and growing profitability of business, expenditure on advertising tends to rise substantially. Conversely, when economic growth slows, and product demand falls, advertising budgets will be cut. Thus between 1984 and 1989, when GDP in real terms (i.e. after accounting for inflation) increased by 22 per cent, advertising expenditure increased by 48 per cent in real terms. Similarly, in the long period of economic growth from 1992 to 2000, advertising expenditure in real terms grew faster, accounting for a higher and higher proportion of household expenditure (see Table 8.1).

Conversely, in times of recession or very low economic growth, advertising budgets will be cut. Thus there was a 15 per cent fall in advertising expenditure in real terms between 1989 (the peak of the 1980s boom) and 1991 (a year of recession), and a fall of nearly 20 per cent from 2007–9 as the economy experienced another downturn.

Advertising media

When considering advertising expenditure by the main categories of media, there has been a long historical trend over which total press advertising has fallen from a high of 84.7 per cent in 1938 (although it reached a peak of nearly 90 per cent in 1953) to 27.4 per cent in 2010. By contrast, advertising on television (which only started in the UK in the mid-1950s) now accounts for some 26 per cent of total advertising expenditure and direct mail for about 11 per cent. Other types of advertising – posters, radio and cinema – account for less than 10 per cent between them. The most dramatic growth in advertising expenditure, however, is on the Internet, which increased from virtually nothing in 1998 to 26.1 per cent in 2012. Figure 8.3 compares the proportions in 2010 with 2005.

Product sectors

The distribution of advertising expenditure by product sectors shows that some 21 per cent of advertising expenditure is for consumables: i.e. food, drink, cosmetics, etc. A further 16.7 per cent is for consumer durables such as household appliances and equipment, and 14.2 per cent for retailers, such as supermarkets. Both these sectors tend to be dominated by just a few firms producing each type of product. This type of market is known as an 'oligopoly', which is Greek for 'few sellers'. Oligopolists often compete heavily in terms of product differentiation and advertising. (Oligopoly is examined in Chapter 12.)

Details of the allocation of advertising expenditure between the different product sectors are given in Table 8.2.

If we take the 20 companies with the highest advertising expenditure, most are within the consumables, consumer durables and retail sectors. The same applies to the 20 most valuable brands (see Table 8.3).

Pause for thought

Try to use the ideas of the growth vector matrix and marketing mix to explain the reasons for the high advertising expenditures of a few of the companies in Table 8.3.

Table 8.1 UK total advertising expenditure

	At current prices (£bn)	At constant (2008) prices (£bn)	As percentage of GDP	As percentage of household expenditure
1988	6.95	11.90	1.46	2.42
1990	8.17	12.40	1.43	2.38
1992	8.05	10.90	1.29	2.10
1994	9.21	11.92	1.33	2.16
1996	10.95	13.48	1.40	2.27
1998	13.10	15.60	1.49	2.40
2000	15.37	17.92	1.57	2.49
2002	15.24	17.32	1.42	2.24
2004	16.81	18.61	1.40	2.25
2006	16.33	17.32	1.22	1.99
2007	17.08	17.70	1.21	1.98
2008	16.59	16.59	1.15	1.89
2009	14.50	14.20	1.03	1.69
2010	15.68	14.86	1.07	1.73
2011	16.10	14.61	1.06	1.73
2012*	16.80	14.87	1.09	1.78

Note: * = forecast
Source: Based on data in *Advertising Statistics Yearbook 2009* (NTC Publications, 2009), *The Advertising Expenditure Report 2011* (Advertising Association), OFCOM site (2012). Advertising Association/WARC, reproduced with permission

Figure 8.3 Distribution of UK advertising expenditure by sector

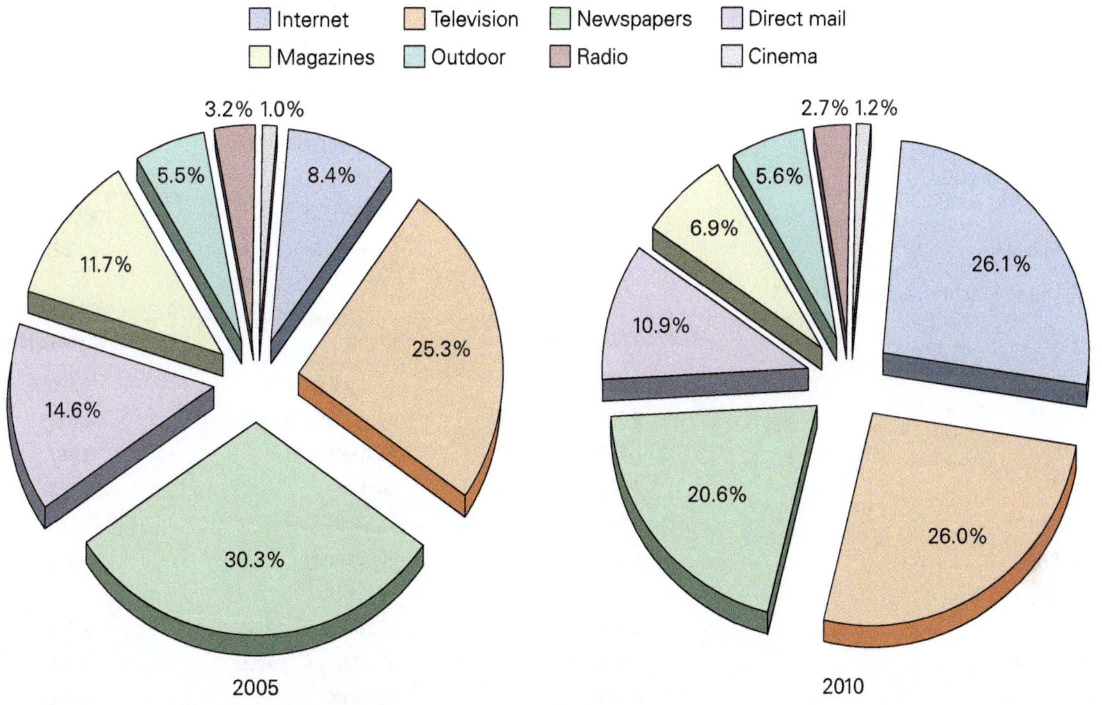

Source: Based on UK advertising expenditure, by sector (Ofcom, 2012)

Table 8.2 UK advertising expenditure by product sector (percentage of total advertising expenditure)

	1986	1990	1995	2000	2005	2008
Retail	13.8	12.4	17.9	13.5	14.5	14.2
Industrial	8.7	7.4	7.7	16.7	12.9	12.3
Financial	10.2	10.5	9.7	11.7	13.9	12.9
Government	3.3	3.2	2.5	2.4	5.4	6.4
Services	8.5	10.8	10.7	11.1	16.2	16.7
Durables	20.5	19.6	20.2	21.4	17.2	16.7
Consumables	35.0	36.1	31.2	23.5	19.9	20.8
Total	100.0	100.0	100.0	100.0	100.0	100.0

Source: Based on data in *Advertising Statistics Yearbook 2009* (NTC Publications, 2009). Advertising Association/WARC, reproduced with permission

The advertising/sales ratio

If we wished to consider the intensity of advertising within a given product sector, we could construct an ***advertising/sales ratio***. This relates the total expenditure on advertising for a particular product to the total value of product sales. A selection of products and their advertising/sales ratios in the USA can be seen in Table 8.4.

Transportation services have the highest advertising/sales ratio at 22.2 per cent. This tells us that 22.2 per cent of all earnings by firms supplying transportation services (rail, air, taxis, etc.) go on advertising their product. At the other extreme, companies producing and/or selling industrial organic chemicals spend only 0.1 per cent of their sales revenue on advertising their products.

The wide variation in advertising intensity can be put down to two factors: market structure and product characteristics. As mentioned above, oligopolistic markets are likely to see high advertising outlays. But what types of product will be the most heavily advertised? There are three main categories here.

Definition

Advertising/sales ratio A ratio that reflects the intensity of advertising within a market.

Table 8.3 The top advertisers and advertising brands in the UK (2011)

(a) The top 20 advertisers in the UK

Advertiser	Total spending on advertising (£m)	Advertiser	Total spending on advertising (£m)
1. Procter & Gamble	203.92	11. Morrisons	73.61
2. British Sky Broadcasting	145.14	12. L'Oréal	70.21
3. Unilever	125.53	13. Marks & Spencer	68.72
4. Tesco	114.65	14. Sainsbury's	68.21
5. Asda	113.36	15. Nestlé	67.41
6. COI (Central Office of Information)	105.41	16. Argos	67.32
7. DFS	94.37	17. GlaxoSmithKline	61.41
8. Reckitt Benckiser	80.98	18. B&Q	57.33
9. BT	79.43	19. 02	49.00
10. Kellogg's	76.99	20. McDonald's	48.82

(b) The top 20 brands in the UK

Brand	Market value ($m)	Brand	Market value ($m)
1. Vodafone	19 832	11. Kit Kat	2 180
2. Virgin	8 005	12. Aquafresh	2 013
3. 02	7 830	13. Lipton	1 787
4. BP	7 320	14. Fairy	1 628
5. Orange	6 518	15. Rolls-Royce	1 521
6. Tesco	4 370	16. Bentley	1 448
7. Sainsbury's	3 255	17. Skittles	1 393
8. HSBC	3 134	18. Innocent drinks	1 372
9. Reebok	2 820	19. Marks & Spencer	1 348
10. Barclays	2 769	20. Ariel	1 296

Source: Nielsen and MPP Consulting. Available from www.rankingthebrands.com, reproduced with permission

Table 8.4 US Advertising/sales ratio: 2010

Product category	Advertising/ sales ratio (%)	Product category	Advertising/ sales ratio (%)
Transportation services	22.2	Investment advice	2.5
Perfumes, Cosmetics, etc	20.1	Motor vehicles and Car bodies	2.3
Motion picture, Videotape production	19.4	Hotels and Motels	2.2
Food and kindred products	11.5	Household appliances	1.7
Educational services	9.8	Accident and health insurance	1.1
Soap, Detergent, Toilet preparations	9.2	Farm machinery and equipment	1.0
Fats and Oils	8.9	Management consulting services	1.0
Amusement parks	8.0	Computer and office equipment	0.7
Beverages	6.1	Personal credit institutions	0.7
Household furniture	6.0	Hospitals	0.6
Department stores	5.0	Ball and roller bearings	0.4
Sugar and Confectionery products	3.3	Computer storage devices	0.3
Paints, Varnishes, Lacquers	3.0	Aircraft	0.2
Dairy products	2.5	Industrial organic chemicals	0.1

Source: Nielsen and MPP Consulting. Available from http://www.rankingthebrands.com, reproduced with permission

The first category is goods that represent a large outlay for consumers (e.g. furniture, electrical goods and other consumer durables). Consumers will not want to make a wrong decision: it would be an expensive mistake. They will thus tend to be cautious in their purchasing decision and will be likely to search for information before selecting a particular product. Advertisers will seek to provide information (but, of course, only information relating to their particular product).

The second category is new products which producers are attempting to establish on the market. The third category is goods, such as educational services, which experience constant changes in their customer base.

Products with the lowest advertising/sales ratio will, by contrast, tend to be those goods whose specifications change very little, or where competition is minimal, or where they are selling to just a few large companies who will be familiar with the equipment or other inputs they are buying. For example, industrial organic chemicals have a ratio of just 0.1 per cent.

The intended effects of advertising

We have argued that the main aim of advertising is to sell more of the product. But when we are told that brand X will make us more beautiful, enrich our lives, wash our clothes whiter, give us get-up-and-go, give us a new taste sensation or make us the envy of our friends, just what are the advertisers up to? Are they merely trying to persuade consumers to buy more?

In fact, there is a bit more to it than this. Advertisers are trying to do two things:

- Shift the product's demand curve to the right.
- Make it less price elastic.

This is illustrated in Figure 8.4. D_1 shows the original demand curve with price at P_1 and sales at Q_1. D_2 shows the curve after an advertising campaign. The rightward shift allows an increased quantity (Q_2) to be sold at the original price. If, at the same time, the demand is made less elastic, the firm can also raise its price and still experience an increase in sales. Thus in the diagram, price can be raised to P_2 and sales will be Q_3 – still substantially above Q_1. The total gain in revenue is shown by the shaded area.

How can advertising bring about this new demand curve?

Figure 8.4 The effect of advertising on the demand curve

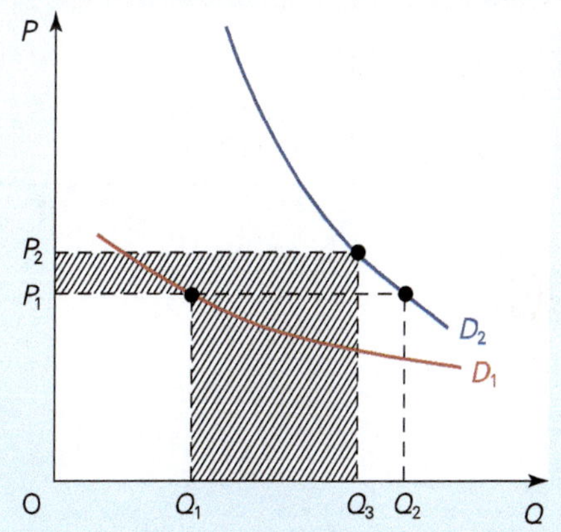

BOX 8.2 ADVERTISING AND THE LONG RUN

Promoting quality

It is relatively straightforward to measure the short-term impact of an advertising campaign; a simple before and after assessment of sales will normally give a good indication of the advertising's effectiveness. But what about the medium- and longer-term effects of an advertising campaign? How will sales and profits be affected over, say, a five-year period?

The typical impact of advertising on a product's sales is shown in Figure (a). Assume that there is an advertising campaign for the product between time T_1 and T_2. There is a direct effect on sales while the advertising lasts and shortly afterwards. Sales rise from S_1 to S_2. After a while (beyond time T_3), the direct effect of the advertising begins to wear off, and wears off completely by time T_4. This is illustrated by the dashed line. But the higher level of sales declines much more slowly, given that many of the new customers continue to buy the product out of habit. Sales will eventually level off (at point T_5). It is likely, however, that sales will not return to the original level of S_1; there will be some new customers who will stick with the product over the long term. This long-term effect is shown by the increase in sales from S_1 to S_3.

But just what is this long-term effect? One way to explore the impact of advertising over the long run is to evaluate how advertising and profitability in general are linked.

In Figure (b) the argument is made that advertising shapes the key element of profitability, namely relative customer value. Customer value is determined by the product's perceived quality (and hence utility) relative to price. The more that advertising can enhance the perceived quality of a product, the more it will increase the product's profitability.

How this benefits the business over the longer term is best seen through examples.

Purina Petcare is the world's leading pet care company. It produces a range of pet-food brands, including Felix, Winalot, Go Cat, Bonio and Bakers. Bakers is a success story of a long-term advertising campaign that began in 1994, when the dog-food market was dominated by tinned meat and Bakers was one of a small number of dry dog-food brands. Working with a small advertising agency, Purina developed an advertising campaign around the idea that 'dogs would choose Bakers'. This campaign was awarded a gold medal by the Institute of Practitioners in Advertising, the UK trade body and professional institute, which noted:

> 10 years on, this powerful campaign is still running. Bakers achieved both its short-term objective of becoming the market leader and long-term objective of increasing the size of the market. The length of the campaign is testament to the strong sales response, having so far delivered an estimated £58.3 million for the brand.[1]

[1] www.ipaeffectivenessawards.co.uk/pdfs/Embargoed_2005_winners_release.pdf

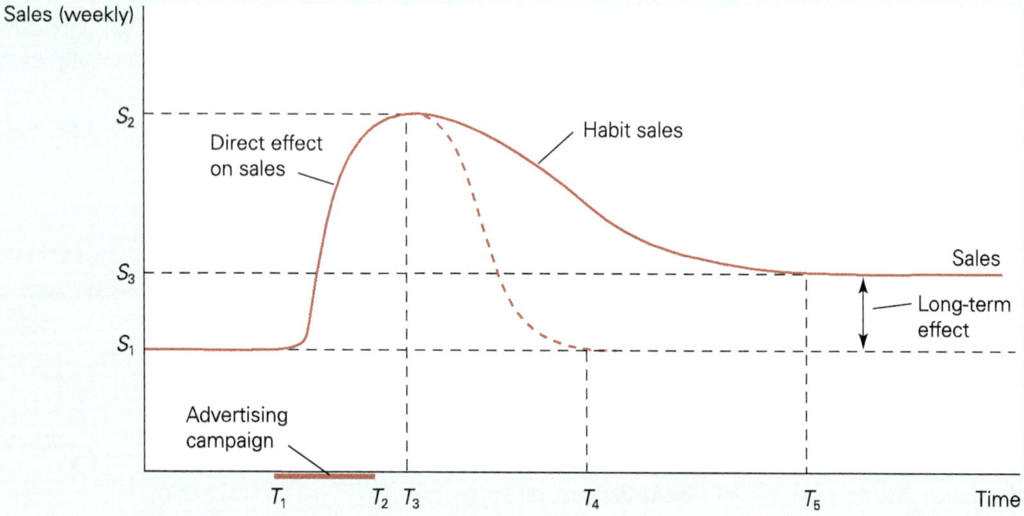

(a)

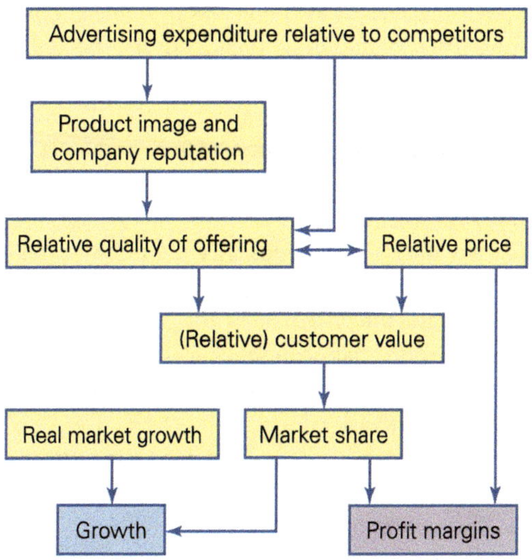

(b)

PG Tips, launched in 1930, is another brand that leads its respective market. The UK tea market has been dominated by PG Tips since 1958, when it became market leader, a position it still holds today, with some 27 per cent of the 'traditional' tea market in 2011. The 'chimp' adverts, then the Aardman T-Birds and more recently Johnny Vegas and Monkey, have established a clear brand image, enabling PG Tips to hold its ground in a highly competitive market and charge a price premium. (Blind tests have revealed that consumers cannot distinguish between any of the leading tea brands!) Market analysis shows that PG Tips has a price elasticity of demand of –0.4 compared with its nearest rival, Tetley, which has an elasticity of –1.4. It was estimated that between 1980 and 2000 advertising the PG Tips brand cost £100 million but generated in the region of £2 billion in extra sales.

Another example of a successful long-term campaign is Audi, which was one of the winners of the 2011 Institute of Practitioners in Advertising (IPA) Effectiveness Awards. Praising the advertising campaign's focus on design, performance and innovation, the IPA acknowledged that 'Audi went from being the understated alternative to Mercedes and BMW, to the fastest growing prestige car brand of the last eight years. In 1999, against ambitious growth targets, the communications strategy was overhauled to position Audi as the leader in the prestige sector. "Vorsprung durch Technik" – the relentless desire to challenge and evolve – became the focus of the campaign which generated an incremental 50 000 car sales and payback of £7.50 for every £1 spent.'[2] In 2000, Audi had a 1.5 per cent share of the UK market. By 2010, this had grown to 5.3 per cent.

An alternative way to illustrate the impact of advertising on longer-term profitability is to assess how companies approach advertising in a recession. What happens when advertising expenditure is cut, and how does profitability return once the recession is over and advertising expenditure once again begins to rise?

Recessions place many firms under significant pressures due to declining consumer demand. A study[3] published in 2011 examined the impact of marketing, in recessionary periods, upon long-term profitability. It reviewed 18 previous academic articles and reports. Firm-wide pressures to cut costs often result in large declines in advertising expenditure. However, the study finds that these cutbacks may be short-sighted. The long-term prospects of some firms can be improved during economic downturns. Firms that are able to engage in marketing activities during recessions are associated with superior shareholder value, customer loyalty and long-term profitability. Those which rein in expenditures put future profits, and perhaps ultimately their survival, at risk.

During the recent downturn many media-savvy companies have attempted to maintain advertising activity despite their declining budgets. Increasing use has been made of Internet-based advertising. Websites such as YouTube and Facebook have been used as platforms to support 'viral' or word-of-mouth campaigns. For example, the Cadbury's Dairy Milk chocolate brand was rejuvenated in 2008, following the re-launch of its long-standing 'glass and a half' adverts. The successful 'drumming gorilla' advert substantially increased sales. Although the campaign made use of traditional media, it was launched online. The advert has been viewed millions of times, on various websites, at no cost to the company.

The message is that advertising should seek to continually promote a product's quality. This is the key to long-term sales and profits. What is also apparent is that successful brands have advertising campaigns which have been consistent over time. A brand image of quality is not created overnight, and once it is established, it requires continued investment if it is to endure and yield profits over the longer term.

?

1. *How are long-run profits and advertising linked?*
2. *Why does quality 'win out' in the end?*

[2] www.ipaeffectivenessawards.co.uk/IPA-Brand-Films

[3] L. O'Malley, V. Story and V. O'Sullivan, 'Marketing in a recession: retrench or invest', *Journal of Strategic Marketing*, 19(3) (2011).

Shifting the demand curve to the right. This will occur if the advertising brings the product to more people's attention and if it increases people's desire for the product.

KI 12 p 63 *Making the demand curve less elastic*. This will occur if the advertising creates greater brand loyalty (i.e. lowering the product's cross-elasticity of demand). People must be led to believe (rightly or wrongly) that competitors' brands are inferior. This will allow the firm to raise its price above that of its rivals with no significant fall in sales. There will be only a small substitution effect of this price rise because consumers have been led to believe that there are no close substitutes.

The more successful an advertising campaign is, the more it will shift the demand curve to the right and the more it will reduce the price elasticity of demand.

Assessing the effects of advertising

The supporters of advertising claim that not only is it an important freedom for firms, but also it provides specific benefits for the consumer. By contrast, critics of advertising suggest that it can impose serious costs on the consumer and on society in general. In this section we will assess the basis of this difference.

Pause for thought

Before considering the points listed below, see if you can identify the main arguments both for and against the use of advertising.

The arguments put forward in favour of advertising include the following:

- KI 8 p 38 Advertising provides information to consumers on what products are available.
- Advertising may be necessary in order to introduce new products. Without it, firms would find it difficult to break into markets in which there were established brands. In other words, it is a means of breaking down barriers to the entry of new firms and products.
- It can aid product development by helping the firm emphasise the special features of its product.
- It may encourage price competition, if prices feature significantly in the advertisement.
- By increasing sales, it may allow the firm to gain economies of scale (see section 9.4), which in turn will help to keep prices down.

On the other side, the following arguments are put forward against advertising:

- Advertising is designed to persuade people to buy the product. Consumers do not have perfect information and may thus be misled into purchasing goods whose qualities may be inferior to those goods which are not advertised.
- Scarcity is defined as the excess of human wants over the means of fulfilling them. Advertising is used to *create* wants. It could thus be argued to increase scarcity. KI 2 p 16
- It increases materialism.
- Advertising costs money: it uses resources. These resources could be put to alternative uses in producing more goods.
- If there are no reductions in costs to be gained from producing on a larger scale, the costs of advertising will tend to raise the price paid by the consumer. Even if the firm has potential economies of scale, it may be prevented from expanding its sales by retaliatory advertising from its rivals.
- Advertising can create a barrier to the entry of new firms by promoting brand loyalty to *existing* firms' products. New firms may not be able to afford the large amount of advertising necessary to create a new brand image, whereas existing firms can spread the cost of their advertising over their already large number of sales. In other words, there are economies of scale in advertising which act as a barrier to entry (see page 167).

  This barrier is strengthened if existing firms sell many brands each (for example, in the washing powder industry many brands are produced by just two firms). This makes it even harder for new firms to introduce a new brand successfully, since the consumer already has so many to choose from.

  The fewer the competitors, the less elastic will be the demand for each individual firm, and the higher will be the profit-maximising price (see Chapter 12).
- People are constantly subjected to advertisements, whether on television, in magazines, on bill-boards, etc., and often find them annoying, tasteless or unsightly. Thus advertising imposes costs on society in general. These costs are external to the firm: that is, they do not cost the firm money, and hence are normally ignored by the firm.

The effects of advertising on competition, costs and prices are largely an empirical issue (an issue of *fact*), and clearly these effects will differ from one product to another. However, many of the arguments presented here involve judgements as to whether the effects are socially desirable or undesirable. Such judgements involve questions of taste and morality: things that are questions of opinion and cannot be resolved by a simple appeal to the facts. KI 1 p 7

SUMMARY

1a When firms seek to differentiate their product from those of their competitors, they can adjust one or more of four dimensions of the product: its technical standards, its quality, its design characteristics, and the level of customer service.

1b Products can be vertically and horizontally differentiated from one another. Vertical differentiation is where products are superior or inferior to others. Horizontal differentiation is where products differ, but are of a similar quality.

2a Marketing involves developing a product image and then persuading consumers to purchase it.

2b A business must choose an appropriate product/market strategy. Four such strategies can be identified: market penetration (focusing on current product and market); product development (new product in current market); market development (current product in new markets); diversification (new products in new markets).

2c The marketing strategy of a product involves the manipulation of four key variables: product, price, place and promotion. Every product has a distinct marketing mix. The marketing mix is likely to change over the product's life cycle.

3a Advertising expenditure is cyclical, expanding and contracting with the upswings and downswings of the economy.

3b Most advertising expenditure goes on consumables and durable goods.

3c The advertising intensity within a given product sector can be estimated by considering the advertising/sales ratio. The advertising/sales ratio is likely to be higher the more oligopolistic the market, the more expensive the product, the newer the product, and the more that the customer base for a product is subject to change.

3d The aims of advertising are to increase demand and make the product less price elastic.

3e Supporters of advertising claim that it: provides consumers with information; brings new products to consumers' attention; aids product development; encourages price competition; and generates economies of scale through increasing sales.

3f Critics of advertising claim that it: distorts consumption decisions; creates wants; pushes up prices; creates barriers to entry; and produces unwanted side-effects, such as being unsightly.

REVIEW QUESTIONS

1 How might we account for the growth in non-price competition within the modern developed economy?

2 Distinguish between vertical and horizontal product differentiation. Give examples of goods that fall into each category.

3 Consider how the selection of the product/market strategy (market penetration, market development, product development and diversification) will influence the business's marketing mix. Identify which elements in the marketing mix would be most significant in developing a successful marketing strategy.

4 Why might the advertising/sales ratio be a poor guide to the degree of exposure of the consumer to advertisements for a particular category of product?

5 Imagine that 'Sunshine' sunflower margarine, a well-known brand, is advertised with the slogan, 'It helps you live longer' (the implication being that butter and margarines high in saturates shorten your life). What do you think would happen to the demand curve for a supermarket's own brand of sunflower margarine? Consider both the direction of shift and the effect on elasticity. Will the elasticity differ markedly at different prices? How will this affect the pricing policy and sales of the super-market's own brand? Could the supermarket respond other than by adjusting the price of its margarine?

6 On balance, does advertising benefit (a) the consumer; (b) society in general?

ADDITIONAL PART C CASE STUDIES IN THE *ECONOMICS FOR BUSINESS* MyEconLab (www.pearsoned.co.uk/sloman)

C.1 **Bentham and the philosophy of utilitarianism.** This looks at the historical and philosophical underpinning of the ideas of utility maximisation.

C.2 **Choices within the household.** Is what is best for the individual best for the family?

C.3 **Taking account of time.** The importance of the time dimension in consumption decisions.

C.4 **The demand for butter.** An examination of a real-world demand function.

C.5 **What we pay to watch sport.** Consideration of the demand function for season tickets to watch spectator sports such as football.

WEBSITES RELEVANT TO PART C

Numbers and sections refer to websites listed in the Web appendix and hotlinked from this book's website at **www.pearsoned.co.uk/sloman**

- For news articles relevant to Part C, see the *Economics News Articles* link from the book's website.
- For general news on demand, consumers and marketing, see websites in section A, and particularly A2, 3, 4, 8, 9, 11, 12, 23, 25, 36. See also site A41 for links to economics news articles and to search particular topics (e.g. advertising).
- For data, information and sites on products and marketing, see sites B2, 10, 11, 13, 17.
- For student resources relevant to Part C, see sites C1–7, 19.
- For data on advertising, see site E37.
- For links to sites on various aspects of advertising and marketing, see section *Industry and Commerce > Consumer Protection > Advertising* in sites I7 and 11.

Profit maximisation under perfect competition and monopoly

Business issues covered in this chapter

- What determines the degree of market power of a firm?
- Why does operating under conditions of perfect competition make being in business a constant battle for survival?
- How do firms get to become monopolies and remain so?
- At what price and output will a monopolist maximise profits and how much profit will it make?
- How well or badly do monopolies serve the consumer compared with competitive firms?
- Why will the size of entry barriers to an industry (the degree of 'contestability' of a market) affect the amount of profit a monopolist can make?

11.1 ALTERNATIVE MARKET STRUCTURES

It is traditional to divide industries into categories according to the degree of competition that exists between the firms within the industry. There are four such categories.

At the most competitive extreme is a market structure referred to as ***perfect competition***. This is a situation where there are a large number of firms competing. Each firm is so small relative to the whole industry that it has no power to influence market price. It is a price taker. At the least competitive extreme is ***monopoly***, where there is just one firm in the industry, and hence no competition from *within* the industry. In the middle comes ***monopolistic competition***, which involves quite a lot of firms competing and where there is freedom for new firms to enter the industry, and ***oligopoly***, where there are only a few firms and where entry of new firms is difficult.

To distinguish more precisely between these four categories, the following must be considered:

Definitions

Perfect competition A market structure in which there are many firms; where there is freedom of entry to the industry; where all firms produce an identical product; and where all firms are price takers.

Monopoly A market structure where there is only one firm in the industry.

Monopolistic competition A market structure where, like perfect competition, there are many firms and freedom of entry into the industry, but where each firm produces a differentiated product and thus has some control over its price.

Oligopoly A market structure where there are few enough firms to enable barriers to be erected against the entry of new firms.

- How freely can firms enter the industry: is entry free or restricted? If it is restricted, just how great are the barriers to the entry of new firms?
- The nature of the product. Do all firms produce an identical product, or do firms produce their own particular brand or model or variety?
- The degree of control the firm has over price. Is the firm a price taker or can it choose its price, and if it can, how will changing its price affect its profits? What we are talking about here is the nature of the demand curve it faces. How elastic is it? If it puts up its price, will it lose (a) all its sales (a horizontal demand curve), or (b) a large proportion of its sales (a relatively elastic demand curve), or (c) just a small proportion of its sales (a relatively inelastic demand curve)?

KI 12 p 63

> KEY IDEA 21
>
> ***Market power benefits the powerful at the expense of others.*** **When firms have market power over prices, they can use this to raise prices and profits above the perfectly competitive level. Other things being equal, the firm will gain at the expense of the consumer. Similarly, if consumers or workers have market power, they can use this to their own benefit.**

Table 11.1 shows the differences between the four categories.

KI 1 p 7

The market structure under which a firm operates will determine its behaviour. Firms under perfect competition behave quite differently from firms that are monopolists, which behave differently again from firms under oligopoly or monopolistic competition.

This behaviour, or conduct, will in turn affect the firm's performance: its prices, profits, efficiency, etc. In many cases it will also affect other firms' performance: *their* prices, profits, efficiency, etc. The collective conduct of all the firms in the industry will affect the whole industry's performance.

Some economists thus see a causal chain running from market structure, through conduct, to the performance of that industry.

Structure → Conduct → Performance

This does not mean, however, that all firms operating in a particular market structure will behave in exactly the same way. For example, some firms under oligopoly may be highly competitive, whereas others may collude with each other to keep prices high. This conduct may then, in turn, influence the development of the market structure. For example, the interaction between firms may influence the development of new products or new production methods, and may encourage or discourage the entrance of new firms into the industry.

> **Pause for thought**
>
> *Give one more example in each of the four market categories in Table 11.1.*

It is for this reason that government policy towards firms – known as 'competition policy' – prefers to focus on the *conduct* of individual firms, rather than simply on the market structure within which they operate. Regulators focus on aspects of conduct such as price fixing and other forms of collusion. Indeed, competition policy in most countries accepts that market structures evolve naturally (e.g. because of economies of scale or changing consumer preferences) and do not necessarily give rise to competition problems.

Nevertheless, market structure still influences firms' behaviour and the performance of the industry, even though it does not, in the case of oligopoly and monopoly, rigidly determine it. We look at these influences in this chapter and the next. First, we look at the two extreme market structures: perfect competition and monopoly.

Table 11.1 Features of the four market structures

Type of market	Number of firms	Freedom of entry	Nature of product	Examples	Implication for demand curve for firm
Perfect competition	Very many	Unrestricted	Homogeneous (undifferentiated)	Cabbages, carrots (these approximate to perfect competition)	Horizontal. The firm is a price taker
Monopolistic competition	Many/several	Unrestricted	Differentiated	Builders, restaurants	Downward sloping, but relatively elastic. The firm has some control over price
Oligopoly	Few	Restricted	1. Undifferentiated or 2. Differentiated	1. Cement 2. Cars, electrical appliances	Downward sloping, relatively inelastic but depends on reactions of rivals to a price change
Monopoly	One	Restricted or completely blocked	Unique	Local water company, many prescription drugs	Downward sloping, more inelastic than oligopoly. Firm has considerable control over price

BOX 11.1 CONCENTRATION RATIOS

Measuring the degree of competition

We can get some indication of how competitive a market is by observing the number of firms: the more firms, the more competitive the market would seem to be. However, this does not tell us anything about how *concentrated* the market might be. There may be *many* firms (suggesting a situation of perfect competition or monopolistic competition), but the largest two firms might produce 95 per cent of total output. This would make these two firms more like oligopolists.

Thus even though a large number of producers may make the market *seem* highly competitive, this could be deceiving. Another approach, therefore, to measuring the degree of competition is to focus on the level of concentration of firms.

The simplest measure of industrial concentration involves adding together the market share of the largest so many firms: e.g. the largest three, five or fifteen. This would give what is known as the '3-firm', '5-firm' or '15-firm concentration ratio'. The resulting figures can be used to assess whether or not the largest firms in an industry dominate the market. There are different ways of estimating market share: by revenue, by output, by profit, etc.

The table shows the 5-firm concentration ratios of selected industries in the UK by output. As you can see, there is an enormous variation in the degree of concentration from one industry to another.

One of the main reasons for this is differences in the percentage of total industry output at which economies of scale are exhausted (see Box 9.4). If this occurs at a low level of output, there will be room for several firms in the industry which are all benefiting from the maximum economies of scale.

The degree of concentration will also depend on the barriers to entry of other firms into the industry (see pages 167–8) and on various factors such as transport costs and historical accident. It will also depend on how varied the products are within any one industrial category. For example, in categories as large as furniture and construction there is room for many firms, each producing a specialised range of products.

So is the degree of concentration a good guide to the degree of competitiveness of the industry? The answer is that it is *some* guide, but on its own it can be misleading. In particular, it ignores the degree of competition from abroad, and from other industries within the country.

?

1. *What are the advantages and disadvantages of using a 5-firm concentration ratio rather than a 10-firm, 3-firm or even a 1-firm ratio?*
2. *Why are some industries like bread baking and brewing relatively concentrated, in that a few firms produce a large proportion of total output (see case studies E8 and E9 in MyEconLab), and yet there are also many small producers?*

Concentration ratios for business by industry (2004)

Industry	5-firm ratio	15-firm ratio	Industry	5-firm ratio	15-firm ratio
Sugar	99	99	Alcoholic beverages	50	78
Tobacco products	99	99	Soap and toiletries	40	64
Oils and fats	88	95	Accountancy services	36	47
Confectionary	81	91	Motor vehicles	34	54
Gas distribution	82	87	Glass and glass products	26	49
Soft drinks, mineral water	75	93	Fishing	16	19
Postal/courier services	65	75	Advertising	10	20
Telecommunications	61	75	Wholesale distribution	6	11
Inorganic chemicals	57	80	Furniture	5	13

Source: based on data in Table 8.31 of *United Kingdom Input-Output Analyses* 2006 (National Statistics)

Then we turn to look at the two intermediate cases of monopolistic competition and oligopoly (Chapter 12).

These two intermediate cases are sometimes referred to collectively as ***imperfect competition***. The vast majority of firms in the real world operate under imperfect competition. It is still worth studying the two extreme cases, however, because they provide a framework within which to understand the real world. They provide important benchmarks for comparison. For example, regulators would find it difficult to identify anti-competitive behaviour if they could not show how outcomes would differ in a more competitive environment.

Some industries tend more to the competitive extreme, and thus their performance corresponds to some extent to perfect competition. Other industries tend more to the other extreme: for example, when there is one dominant firm and a few much smaller firms. In such cases, their performance corresponds more to monopoly.

Definition

Imperfect competition The collective name for monopolistic competition and oligopoly.

11.2 PERFECT COMPETITION

The theory of perfect competition illustrates an extreme form of capitalism. In it firms are entirely subject to market forces. They have no power whatsoever to affect the price of the product. The price they face is that determined by the interaction of demand and supply in the whole *market*.

Assumptions

The model of perfect competition is built on four assumptions:

1. Firms are *price takers*. There are so many firms in the industry that each one produces an insignificantly small proportion of total industry supply, and therefore has *no power whatsoever* to affect the price of the product. Hence it faces a horizontal (perfectly elastic) demand 'curve' at the market price: the price determined by the interaction of demand and supply in the whole market.
2. There is complete *freedom of entry* into the industry for new firms. Existing firms are unable to stop new firms setting up in business. Setting up a business takes time, however. Freedom of entry therefore applies in the long run.
3. All firms produce an *identical product*. The product is 'homogeneous' i.e. all products in the market are identical and are perfect substitutes for each other. There is therefore no branding or advertising.
4. Producers and consumers have *perfect knowledge* of the market. That is, producers are fully aware of prices, costs, technology and market opportunities. Consumers are fully aware of price, quality and availability of the product.

These assumptions are very strict. Few, if any, industries in the real world meet these conditions. Certain agricultural markets perhaps are closest to perfect competition. The market for fresh vegetables is an example.

Pause for thought

It is sometimes claimed that the market for various stocks and shares is perfectly competitive, or nearly so. Take the case of the market for shares in a large company, such as BP. Go through each of the four assumptions above and see if they apply in this case. (Don't be misled by the first assumption. The 'firm' in this case is not BP itself, but rather the owners of the shares.)

The short-run equilibrium of the firm

In the ***short run***, we assume that the number of firms in the industry cannot be increased; there is simply no time for new firms to enter the market.

Figure 11.1 shows a short-run equilibrium for both industry and a firm under perfect competition. Both parts of the diagram have the same scale for the vertical axis. The horizontal axes have totally different scales, however. For example, if the horizontal axis for the firm were measured in, say, thousands of units, the horizontal axis for the whole industry might be measured in millions or tens of millions of units, depending on the number of firms in the industry.

Let us examine the determination of price, output and profit in turn.

Definition

The short run under perfect competition The period during which there is too little time for new firms to enter the industry.

Figure 11.1 Short-run equilibrium of industry and firm under perfect competition

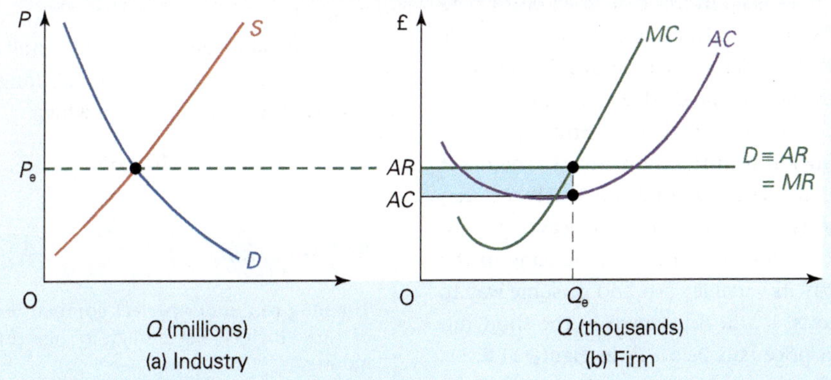

Figure 11.2 Loss minimising under perfect competition

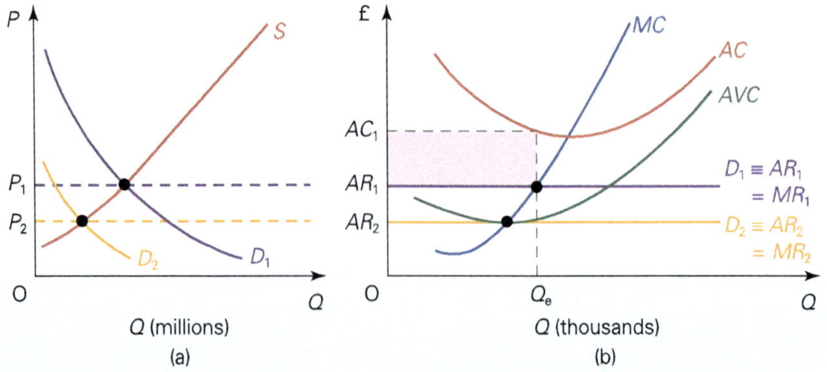

Price

The price is determined in the industry by the intersection of market demand and supply. The firm faces a horizontal demand (or average revenue) 'curve' at this price. It can sell all it can produce at the market price (P_e). It would sell nothing at a price above P_e, however, since competitors would be selling identical products at a lower price.

Output

KI 4 p 22

The firm will maximise profit where marginal cost equals marginal revenue ($MR = MC$), at an output of Q_e. Note that, since the price is not affected by the firm's output, marginal revenue will equal price (see page 149 and Figure 10.1). Thus the firm's *MR* 'curve' and *AR* 'curve' (= demand 'curve') are the same horizontal straight line.

Profit

If the average cost (*AC*) curve (which includes normal profit) dips below the average revenue (*AR*) 'curve', the firm will earn supernormal profit. Supernormal profit per unit at Q_e is the vertical difference between *AR* and *AC* at Q_e. Total supernormal profit is the shaded rectangle in Figure 11.1 (i.e. profit per unit times quantity sold).

What happens if the firm cannot make a profit at *any* level of output? This situation would occur if the *AC* curve were above the *AR* curve at all points. This is illustrated in Figure 11.2 where the market price is P_1. In this case, the point where $MC = MR$ represents the *loss-minimising* point (where loss is defined as anything less than normal profit). This amount of the loss is represented by the shaded rectangle.

KI 18 p 129

As we saw in Chapter 10, whether the firm is prepared to continue making a loss in the short run or whether it will close down immediately depends on whether it can cover its *variable* costs. Provided price is above average variable cost (*AVC*), the firm will continue producing in the short run: it can pay its variable costs and go some way to paying its fixed costs. It will shut down in the short run only if the market price falls below P_2 in Figure 11.2: i.e. when variable costs of production cannot be covered.

The long-run equilibrium of the firm

In the ***long run***, if typical firms are making supernormal profits, new firms will be attracted into the industry. Likewise, if existing firms can make supernormal profits by increasing the scale of their operations, they will do so, since all factors of production are variable in the long run.

The effect of the entry of new firms and/or the expansion of existing firms is to increase industry supply, meaning that at every price level the quantity produced would be higher. This is illustrated in Figure 11.3.

Pause for thought

Before you read on, can you explain why perfect competition and substantial economies of scale are likely to be incompatible?

The industry supply curve shifts to the right. This in turn leads to a fall in price. Supply will go on increasing, and price falling, until firms are making only normal profits. This will be when price has fallen to the point where the demand 'curve' for the firm just touches the bottom of its long-run average cost curve. Q_L is thus the long-run equilibrium output of the firm, with P_L the long-run equilibrium price.

KI 10 p 48

Since the *LRAC* curve is tangential to all possible short-run *AC* curves (see section 9.5), the full long-run equilibrium will be as shown in Figure 11.4 where:

KI 11 p 55

$$LRAC = AC = MC = MR = AR$$

Definitions

The long run under perfect competition The period of time which is long enough for new firms to enter the industry.

Figure 11.3 Long-run equilibrium under perfect competition

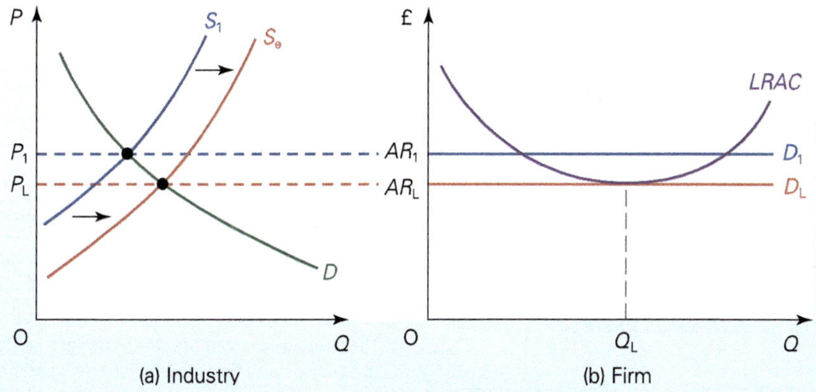

Figure 11.4 Long-run equilibrium of the firm under perfect competition

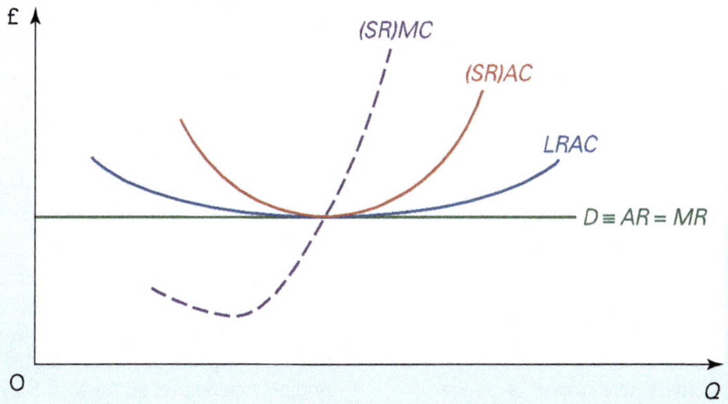

The incompatibility of perfect competition and substantial economies of scale

Why is perfect competition so rare in the real world – if it even exists at all? One important reason for this has to do with economies of scale.

In many industries, firms may have to be quite large if they are to experience the full potential economies of scale. But perfect competition requires there to be *many* firms. Firms must therefore be small under perfect competition: too small in most cases for them to achieve economies of scale.

Once a firm expands sufficiently to achieve economies of scale, it will usually gain market power. It will be able to undercut the prices of smaller firms, which will thus be driven out of business. Perfect competition is destroyed. Perfect competition could only exist in any industry, therefore, if there were no (or virtually no) economies of scale.

Does the firm benefit from operating under perfect competition?

Under perfect competition the firm faces a constant battle for survival. If it becomes less efficient than other firms, it will make less than normal profits and be driven out of business. If it becomes more efficient, it will earn supernormal profits. But these supernormal profits will not last for long. Soon other firms, in order to survive themselves, will be forced to copy the more efficient methods of the new firm. They are able to do this because the perfect knowledge assumption implies that new methods can be copied by all producers.

KEY IDEA 22

Economic efficiency **is achieved when each good is produced at the minimum cost and where consumers get maximum benefit from their income.**

BOX 11.2 E-COMMERCE

A modern form of perfect competition?

The relentless drive towards big business in recent decades has seen many markets become more concentrated and increasingly dominated by large producers. However, forces are at work that are undermining this dominance and bringing more competition to markets. One of these forces is *e-commerce*.

In this case study, we will consider just how far e-commerce is returning 'power to the people'.

Moving markets back towards perfect competition?

To see the extent to which e-commerce is making markets more competitive, let's look at the assumptions of perfect competition.

Large number of firms. The growth of e-commerce has led to many new firms starting up in business. It's not just large firms like Amazon.com that are providing increased competition for established firms, but the thousands of small online companies that are being established every year. Many of these firms are selling directly to us as consumers. This is known as 'B2C' (business-to-consumers) e-commerce. But many more are selling to other firms ('B2B'). More and more companies, from the biggest to the smallest, are transferring their purchasing to the Web and are keen to get value for money.

The reach of the Web is global. This means that firms, whether conventional or web-based, have to keep an eye on the prices and products of competitors in the rest of the world, not just in the local neighbourhood. Firms' demand curves are thus becoming more price elastic. This is especially so for goods that are cheap to transport, or for services such as insurance and banking where no transport is required.

Perfect knowledge. There are various ways in which e-commerce is adding to the consumer's knowledge. There is greater price transparency, with consumers able to compare prices on-line. Online shopping agents, such as Kelkoo, Shopzilla and Google Shopping, can quickly locate a list of alternative suppliers. There is greater information on product availability and quality and this information is available at very little cost to the consumer. Virtual shopping malls, full of e-retailers, place the high street retailer under intense competitive pressure.

The pressure is even greater in the market for intermediate products. Many firms are constantly searching for cheaper sources of supply, and the Internet provides a cheap and easy means of conducting such searches.

Freedom of entry. Internet companies often have lower start-up costs than their conventional rivals. Their premises are generally much smaller, with no 'shop-front' costs and lower levels of stockholding; in fact many of these businesses are initially operated from their owners' homes. Marketing costs can also be relatively low, especially given the ease with which companies can be located with search engines. Internet companies are often smaller and more specialist, relying on Internet 'outsourcing' (buying parts, equipment and other supplies through the Internet), rather than making everything themselves. They are also more likely to use delivery firms rather than having their own transport fleet. All this makes it relatively cheap for new firms to set up and begin trading over the Internet.

One consequence of e-commerce is that the distinction between firms and consumers is becoming increasingly blurred. With the rise of eBay, more and more people are finding going into business incredibly easy. Some people are finding a market for all the junk they've collected over the

It is the same with the development of new products. If a firm is able to produce a new product that is popular with consumers, it will be able to gain a temporary advantage over its rivals. But again, any supernormal profits will last only as long as it takes other firms to respond. Soon the increase in supply of the new product will drive the price down and eliminate these supernormal profits. Similarly, the firm must be quick to copy new products developed by its rivals. If it does not, it will soon make a loss and be driven out of the market.

Thus being in perfect competition is a constant battle for survival. It might benefit the consumer, due to the lower prices and higher quantities. However, most firms in such an environment would love to be able to gain some market power: power to be able to restrict competition and to retain supernormal profits into the long run.

The extreme case of market power is that of monopoly: a firm that faces no competition – at least not from *within* its industry. Monopoly is the subject of the next section.

11.3 MONOPOLY

What is a monopoly?

This may seem a strange question because the answer seems obvious. A monopoly exists when there is only one firm in the industry.

But whether an industry can be classed as a monopoly is not always clear. It depends how narrowly the industry is defined. For example, a textile company may have a monopoly on certain types of fabric, but it does not have a monopoly on fabrics in general. The consumer can buy years, while others are selling products they produce at home and yet others specialise in selling on products using the marketing power of eBay. As a consequence there are over 100 million active eBay users worldwide, and hundreds of thousands of people make a full-time living from buying and selling on eBay. In 2011 the total value of goods sold on eBay was $68.6 billion having grown over 600 per cent from a figure of $9.3 billion ten years earlier.

Not only do these factors make markets more price competitive, they also bring other benefits. Costs are driven down, as firms economise on stockholding, rely more on outsourcing and develop more efficient relationships with suppliers. 'Procurement hubs', online exchanges and trading communities are now well established in many industries. The competition also encourages innovation, which improves quality and the range of products.

What are the limits to e-commerce?

In 20 years, will we be doing all our shopping on the Internet? Will the only shopping malls be virtual ones? Although e-commerce is revolutionising some markets, it is unlikely that things will go anything like that far.

The benefits of 'shop shopping' are that you get to see the good, touch it and use it. You can buy the good there and then, and take instant possession of it: you don't have to wait. Shopping is also an enjoyable experience. Many people like wandering round the shops, meeting friends, seeing what takes their fancy, trying on clothes, browsing through DVDs, and so on. 'Retail therapy' for many is a leisure activity. Many consumers are willing to pay a 'premium' for these advantages.

Online shopping is limited by current technology and infrastructure. The quality of Internet access has improved significantly as broadband has become widely available. However, you still have to wait for goods to be delivered; and what if deliveries are late or fail completely? (See Box 6.2.) The busiest time for Internet shopping is in the run-up to Christmas. In 2011 Yodel, the UK's second largest household delivery company (after the Royal Mail), failed to deliver around 15 000 parcels per day as Christmas approached.[1] Their delivery infrastructure simply could not cope with the increase in demand. Additionally, online shopping requires access to a credit or debit card, which might not be available to everyone, particularly younger consumers and those on low incomes.

Also costs might not always be as low as expected. How efficient is it to have many small deliveries of goods? How significant are the lost cost savings from economies of scale that larger producers or retailers are likely to generate?

Nevertheless, e-commerce has made many markets, both retail and B2B, more competitive. This is especially so for services and for goods whose quality is easy to identify online. Many firms are being forced to face up to having their prices determined by the market.

?

1. *Why may the Internet work better for replacement buys than for new purchases?*
2. *Give three examples of products that are particularly suitable for selling over the Internet and three that are not. Explain your answer.*
3. *In 2008 eBay sellers called for a boycott of the site, following changes in the fees being charged and the removal of their ability to leave feedback on buyers. Explain how eBay can both increase competition across the economy and simultaneously acquire very substantial monopoly power.*

[1] Surge in online orders hits deliveries Financial Times, 23/12/11.

fabrics other than those supplied by the company. A rail company may have a monopoly over rail services between two cities, but it does not have a monopoly over public transport between these two cities. People can travel by coach or air. They could also use private transport.

To some extent, the boundaries of an industry are arbitrary. What is more important for a firm is the amount of monopoly *power* it has, and that depends on the closeness of substitutes produced by rival industries. The Post Office, before 2006, had a monopoly over the delivery of letters, but it faces competition in communications from telephone, faxes and e-mail.

Barriers to entry

For a firm to maintain its monopoly position, there must be barriers to the entry of new firms. Barriers also exist under oligopoly, but in the case of monopoly they must be high enough to block the entry of new firms. Barriers can take various forms.

Economies of scale. If the monopolist's average costs go on falling significantly up to the output that satisfies the whole market, the industry may not be able to support more than one producer. This case is known as ***natural monopoly***. This is more likely if the market is small. For example, two bus companies might find it unprofitable to serve the same routes, each running with perhaps only half-full buses, whereas one company with a monopoly of the routes could make a profit. Electricity transmission via a national grid is another example of a natural monopoly.

Even if a market could support more than one firm, a new entrant is unlikely to be able to start up on a very large scale. Thus the monopolist which is already experiencing

Definition

Natural monopoly A situation where long-run average costs would be lower if an industry were under monopoly than if it were shared between two or more competitors.

economies of scale can charge a price below the cost of the new entrant and drive it out of business. If, however, the new entrant is a firm already established in another industry, it may be able to survive this competition.

Economies of scope. A firm that produces a range of products is also likely to experience a lower average cost of production due to economies of scope. For example, a large pharmaceutical company producing a range of drugs and toiletries can use shared research, marketing, storage and transport facilities across its range of products. These lower costs make it difficult for a new single-product entrant to the market, since the large firm will be able to undercut its price and drive it out of the market.

Product differentiation and brand loyalty. If a firm produces a clearly differentiated product, where the consumer associates the product with the brand, it will be very difficult for a new firm to break into that market. Rank Xerox invented, and patented, the plain paper photocopier. After this legal monopoly (see below) ran out, people still associated photocopiers with Rank Xerox. It is still not unusual to hear someone say that they are going to 'Xerox the article' or, for that matter, 'Hoover their carpet'. Other examples of strong brand image include Guinness, Kelloggs Cornflakes, Coca-Cola, Nescafé and Sellotape.

Lower costs for an established firm. An established monopoly is likely to have developed specialised production and marketing skills. It is more likely to be aware of the most efficient techniques and the most reliable and/or cheapest suppliers. It is likely to have access to cheaper finance. It is thus operating on a lower average total cost curve. New firms would therefore find it hard to compete on price and would be likely to lose any price war.

Pause for thought

Illustrate the situation described above using AC curves for both a new entrant and an established firm.

Ownership of, or control over, key inputs or outlets. If a firm governs the supply of vital inputs (say, by owning the sole supplier of some component part), it can deny access to these inputs to potential rivals. On a world scale, the de Beers company has a monopoly in fine diamonds because all diamond producers market their diamonds through de Beers.

Similarly, if a firm controls the outlets through which the product must be sold, it can prevent potential rivals from gaining access to consumers. For example, Birds Eye Walls used to supply freezers free to shops on the condition that they stocked only Wall's ice cream in them.

Legal protection. The firm's monopoly position may be protected by patents on essential processes, by copyright, by various forms of licensing (allowing, say, only one firm to operate in a particular area) and by tariffs (i.e. customs duties) and other trade restrictions to keep out foreign competitors. Examples of monopolies, or near monopolies, protected by patents include most new medicines developed by pharmaceutical companies (e.g. anti-AIDS drugs), Microsoft's Windows operating systems and agro-chemical companies, such as Monsanto, with various genetically modified plant varieties and pesticides.

Mergers and takeovers. The monopolist can put in a takeover bid for any new entrant. The sheer threat of takeovers may discourage new entrants.

Aggressive tactics. An established monopolist can probably sustain losses for longer than a new entrant. Thus it could start a price war, mount massive advertising campaigns, offer attractive after-sales service, introduce new brands to compete with new entrants, and so on.

Equilibrium price and output

Since there is, by definition, only one firm in the industry, the firm's demand curve is also the industry demand curve.

Compared with other market structures, demand under monopoly will be relatively inelastic at each price. The monopolist can raise its price and consumers have no alternative firm to turn to within the industry. They either pay the higher price, or go without the good altogether. KI 12 p63

Unlike the firm under perfect competition, the monopoly firm is thus a 'price maker'. It can choose what price to charge. Nevertheless, it is still constrained by its demand curve. A rise in price will reduce the quantity demanded.

As with firms in other market structures, a monopolist will maximise profit where $MR = MC$. In Figure 11.5 profit is maximised by producing a quantity of Q_m. The supernormal profit obtained is shown by the shaded area. KI 4 p22

These profits will tend to be larger, the less elastic is the demand curve (and hence the steeper is the *MR* curve), and

Figure 11.5 Profit maximising under monopoly

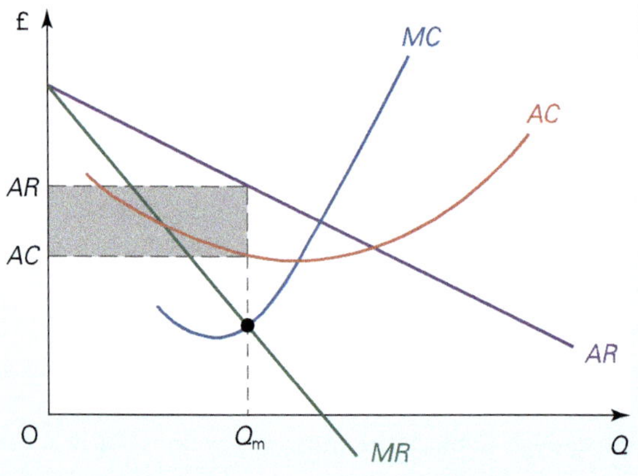

thus the bigger is the gap between *MR* and price (*AR*). The actual elasticity will depend on whether reasonably close substitutes are available in *other* industries. The demand for a rail service will be much less elastic (and the potential for profit greater) if there is no bus service between the same destinations.

KI 21 p 161 Since there are barriers to the entry of new firms, a monopolist's supernormal profits will not be competed away in the long run. The only difference, therefore, between short-run and long-run equilibrium is that in the long run the firm will produce where *MR* = *long-run MC*.

Comparing monopoly with perfect competition

Because it faces a different type of market environment, the monopolist will produce a quite different output and at a quite different price from a perfectly competitive industry. Let us compare the two.

KI 21 p 161 *The monopolist will produce a lower output at a higher price in the short run.* Figure 11.6 compares the profit-maximising position for an industry under monopoly with that under perfect competition. Note that we are comparing the monopoly with the whole *industry* under perfect competition. That way we can assume, for the sake of comparison, that they both face the same demand curve. We also assume for the moment that they both face the same cost curves.

The monopolist will produce Q_1 at a price of P_1. This is where *MC* = *MR*.

If the same industry were under perfect competition, however, it would produce at Q_2 and P_2 – a higher output and a lower price. But why? The reason for this is that for each of the firms in the industry – and it is at this level that the decisions are made – marginal revenue is the same as price. Remember that the *firm* under perfect competition faces a perfectly elastic demand (*AR*) curve, which also equals *MR* (see Figure 11.1). Thus producing where *MC* = *MR* also means producing where *MC* = *P*. When *all* firms under perfect competition do this, price and quantity in the *industry* will be given by P_2 and Q_2 in Figure 11.6.

Figure 11.6 Equilibrium of the industry under perfect competition and monopoly with the same *MC* curve

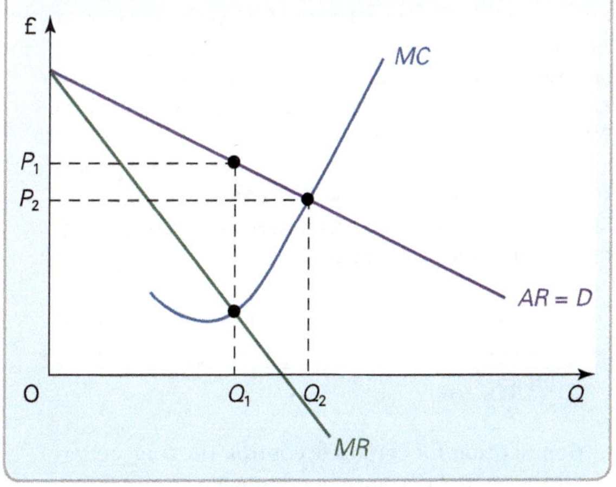

The monopolist may also produce a lower output at a higher price in the long run. Under perfect competition, freedom of entry eliminates supernormal profit and forces firms to produce at the bottom of their *LRAC* curve. The effect, therefore, is to keep long-run prices down. Under monopoly, however, barriers to entry allow profits to remain supernormal in the long run. The monopolist is not forced to operate at the bottom of the *AC* curve. Thus, other things being equal, long-run prices will tend to be higher, and hence output lower, under monopoly. (In section 20.2 we examine this in more detail by considering the impact of monopoly on consumer and producer surplus. You might wish to take a preliminary look at pages 314–5 now.)

> **Pause for thought**
>
> *If the shares in a monopoly (such as a water company) were very widely distributed among the population, would the shareholders necessarily want the firm to use its monopoly power to make larger profits?*

Costs under monopoly. The sheer survival of a firm in the long run under perfect competition requires that it uses the most efficient known technique, and develops new techniques wherever possible. The monopolist, however, sheltered by barriers to entry, can still make large profits even if it is not using the most efficient technique. It has less incentive, therefore, to be efficient.

On the other hand, the monopoly may be able to achieve substantial economies of scale due to larger plant, centralised administration and the avoidance of unnecessary duplication (e.g. a monopoly water company would eliminate the need for several sets of rival water mains under each street). If this results in an *MC* curve substantially below that of the same industry under perfect competition, the monopoly may even produce a *higher* output at a *lower* price.

Another reason why a monopolist may operate with lower costs is that it can use part of its supernormal profits for research and development and investment. It may not have the same *incentive* to become efficient as the perfectly competitive firm which is fighting for survival, but it may have a much greater *ability* to become efficient than has the small firm with limited funds.

Although a monopoly faces no competition in the goods market, it may face an alternative form of competition in

BOX 11.3 WINDOWS CLEANING

The Microsoft Monopoly under challenge?

In March 2004 the European Commission fined Microsoft €497 million for an Abuse of a Dominant Position in the operating system market. It found that Microsoft had harmed competition in the media player market by bundling *Windows Media Player* with its operating system. Further, Microsoft had refused to supply information about its secret software code to suppliers of alternative network software at reasonable rates. Such code was needed to allow non-Windows network software to be interoperable with ('talk' to) Windows network software. Without it, firms who had purchased *Windows Network* servers would be solely tied in to Microsoft server software. This, in turn, would discourage the development of application software products by Microsoft's rivals.

In April 2006, Microsoft launched an appeal against the judgment claiming that the EU's ruling violated international law by forcing the company to share information with rivals. However, the Court of First Instance found in the Commission's favour. Microsoft complied with the first ruling and unbundled *Windows Media Player* from its operating systems, much to the annoyance of computer suppliers who argued that their customers could easily upload alternative media players from the Web.

However, until October 2007 Microsoft continued to charge high royalty rates and fees for interoperability information that would allow competitors to access secret source code on the *Windows Network System*. As a result, in February 2008 the Commission penalised Microsoft a further €899 million for non-compliance with its 2004 decision and Microsoft became the first company in fifty years of EU competition policy to be fined for non-compliance with a Commission decision.[1] Microsoft took the Commission to court in an attempt to overturn the fine, losing its case in 2012.

This is not the end of Microsoft's dealings with the European Commission. In 2009 the Commission announced an investigation into the bundling of *Internet Explorer* with *Windows*. The bundling was thought to be restricting competition in the market for web browsers.[2] Microsoft took the Commission seriously and agreed to remove *Explorer* from the European versions of *Windows 7*. To promote competition they offered users an option of downloading one browser from a list of twelve. However, only three years later Microsoft may once again be engaging in anti-competitive behaviour. The Commission is examining the possibility that *Windows 8* will discourage, or even prevent, users from using other browsers. In July 2012 the Commission publicly threatened Microsoft with severe penalties if it breaks the 2009 bundling agreement with its *Windows 8* product.

Is Microsoft playing a 'game' with the competition authorities – maximising profits by pushing as hard as possible against the legal framework?

Earlier anti-monopoly rulings in other countries

Microsoft is no stranger to anti-monopoly lawsuits. In 2005 Microsoft was fined 33bn Won ($32 million; £18.4 million) by South Korea's Fair Trade Commission for breaches of anti-monopoly legislation that covered very similar issues to those in the EU investigation.

In August 2008, Microsoft was investigated by Taiwan's Fair Trade Commission because of its monopoly position in the operating system market.

Perhaps the most famous investigation began on 18 May 1998, when the US government accused Microsoft of abusing its market power and seeking to crush its rivals. The US Justice Department alleged that Microsoft had committed the following anti-competitive actions:

- In May 1995 Microsoft attempted to collude with Netscape Communications to divide the Internet browser market. Netscape Communications refused.
- Microsoft had forced personal computer manufacturers to install *Internet Explorer* in order to obtain a *Windows 95* operating licence.
- Microsoft insisted that PC manufacturers conformed to a Microsoft front screen for *Windows*. This included specified icons, one of which was Microsoft's *Internet Explorer*.
- It had set up reciprocal advertising arrangements with America's largest Internet service providers, such as America Online. Here Microsoft would promote America Online via *Windows*. In return, America Online would not promote Netscape's browsers.

One solution, posed by Federal Judge Thomas Penfield Jackson in 2000, was that Microsoft be split in two to prevent it operating as a monopoly. One company would produce and market the *Windows* operating system; the other would produce and market the applications software, such as *Microsoft Office* and the web browser, *Internet Explorer*.

This was overturned on appeal in June 2001 and Microsoft agreed to provide technical information about *Windows* to other companies so that potential rivals could write software that would compete with Microsoft's own software. Also Microsoft would not be allowed to retaliate against computer manufacturers that installed rival products or removed icons for Microsoft applications.

Microsoft and the public interest

These lawsuits raise an important issue: is Microsoft acting for or against the public interest?

[1] See Antitrust: Commission imposes €899 million penalty on Microsoft for non-compliance with March 2004 Decision, IP/08/318, 27 February 2008.

[2] See Antitrust: Commission confirms sending of a Statement of Objections to Microsoft on the tying of Internet Explorer to Windows Reference, MEMO/09/15, 17 Janurary 2009.

financial markets. A monopoly, with potentially low costs, which is currently run inefficiently, is likely to be subject to a takeover bid from another company. This ***competition for corporate control*** may thus force the monopoly to be efficient in order to prevent being taken over.

Definition

Competition for corporate control The competition for the control of companies through takeovers.

The classic case against monopoly suppliers is that they charge higher prices and offer lower quantities to consumers than would be the case under perfect competition. In addition, the supernormal profit that monopolies earn may be detrimental to society if it is used to continue to support the monopoly position, say by lobbying or bribing government officials. Further, if no competition prevails then monopoly suppliers may become more inefficient.

However, the competition authorities have never penalised Microsoft simply for possessing monopoly power. It has been fined when it has *abused* its market power. That is, it is not the monopoly market structure that matters per se to competition authorities; rather, it is the behaviour of the firm when it has monopoly power. Through its actions, Microsoft had raised barriers to entry by restricting the opportunities for potential rival firms to offer alternative products to customers. Choice was thereby restricted.

In its defence, Microsoft has argued that it has continually sought to reinvest its profits in new product development and offered a number of innovative solutions over the past 30 years for individuals and businesses alike. (Can you think of all the versions of *Windows* and the 'free updates' there have been?)

Further, in an environment where technology is changing rapidly, Microsoft's control over standards gives the user a measure of stability, knowing that any new products and applications will be compatible with existing ones. In other words, new software can be incorporated into existing systems. In this respect Microsoft can be viewed as operating in society's interest. Microsoft would argue that it has a right to protect its in-house software code from competitors and receive a fair price for it. Indeed, it is a natural response for a firm to protect its intellectual property rights. Failure to do so could lead to the firm's demise.

Network effects

Microsoft is a vertically integrated firm (see pages 227–9), with a dominant position in the operating system market (i.e. *Windows*) and in certain application software (*Office* and *Windows Media Player*) markets. It has built this position by creating networks of users. These networks bring both benefits and costs to society.

Network effects arise when consumers of a product benefit from it being used by *other* consumers. In the case of Microsoft's products, firms benefit from lower training costs because individuals who have learnt to use Microsoft products elsewhere can be readily absorbed into the firm. Individuals benefit too because they do not have to learn to use new software when they move to another organisation and the learning costs are fairly low as a new version of the software is introduced.

The negative aspect of developing strong networks is that users can get 'locked in' to using the software and they become reluctant to switch to alternative systems. Protecting the network is vital to Microsoft's competitive edge.

Challenges to Microsoft monopoly

Microsoft is facing increasing competitive pressure. The recent challenges from competition authorities (referred to above) have opened up the browser market, for example. Microsoft's *Internet Explorer* is no longer the dominant browser; since the mid-2000s its market share has fallen significantly as other browsers have become widely used. In July 2003, it had an 82.7 per cent share of the global browser market; by July 2012, this had fallen to 16.3 per cent – third behind Google's Chrome (42.9%) and Firefox (33.7%).[3]

There is also a growing challenge from new Internet firms, such as Google and Facebook. Both Google and Facebook have created enormous networks of users who are then targeted with tailored adverts paid for by firms who want to reach these vast audiences.

This is a very different business model from that of Microsoft and, as part of the desire to create large networks of users, free products are being released that will compete with that of Microsoft. For example, Google's *Google Docs* and Apache's *Open Office* compete with Microsoft's *Office*. These are becoming increasingly well known and have growing market shares.

Microsoft still dominates the operating system market. In July 2012, the various versions of *Windows* had a 69 per cent market share. Apple's *Mac* has been the only serious contender for standalone computers – its market share was 8 per cent. However, with the rise of tablet computers and smart phones, Linux's open-source operating system, *Android*, had gained a market share of nearly 7 per cent – a share likely to increase substantially in the future.[4]

You might want to follow subsequent events as the news unfolds (see section A of the Hotlinks section of this text's website for links to newspaper sites).

?

1. ***In what respects might Microsoft's behaviour be deemed to have been: (a) against the public interest; (b) in the public interest?***
2. ***Being locked in to a product or technology is only a problem if such a product can be clearly shown to be inferior to an alternative. What difficulties might there be in establishing such a case?***

[3] For figures on browser usage, see http://www.w3schools.com/browsers/browsers_stats.asp

[4] *Wikimedia Traffic Analysis Report – Operating Systems* (July 2012).

Innovation and new products. The promise of supernormal profits, protected perhaps by patents, may encourage the development of new (monopoly) industries producing new products. It is this chance of making monopoly profits that encourages many people to take the risks of going into business.

11.4 POTENTIAL COMPETITION OR POTENTIAL MONOPOLY? THE THEORY OF CONTESTABLE MARKETS

Potential competition

KI 23 p 181

In recent years, economists have developed the theory of contestable markets. This theory argues that what is crucial in determining price and output is not whether an industry is *actually* a monopoly or competitive, but whether there is the real *threat* of competition.

If a monopoly is protected by high barriers to entry – say that it owns all the raw materials – then it will be able to make supernormal profits with no fear of competition.

If, however, another firm *could* take over from it with little difficulty, it will behave much more like a competitive firm. The threat of competition has a similar effect to actual competition.

As an example, consider a catering company that is given permission by a factory to run its canteen. The catering company has a monopoly over the supply of food to

BOX 11.4 'IT COULD BE YOU'

Bidding for the UK National Lottery

Since its launch in November 1994, the UK National Lottery has struck at the heart of the British psyche because it offers the opportunity to win a fortune and support worthwhile ventures. By the middle of 2012 the lottery had created over 2900 millionaires. It had also generated over £28 billion for 'Good Causes' and contributed £2.2 billion to the 2012 London Olympic and Paralympic Games.

Around 70 per cent of UK adults play the lottery, spending on average about £3 per week. Around £41 billion had been paid out in prize money by March 2012. On average, for every pound spent on the lottery, 50p is paid in prizes, 28p goes to the National Lottery Distribution Fund, which is distributed to arts, sports and charities that bid for it, 12p goes to the government in the form of Lottery Tax, 5p goes to the retailer and 5p goes to Camelot, the operator, and its Canadian parent company, Ontario Teachers' Pension Plan.

Sales of lottery tickets grew dramatically in the early years of operation but waned around the turn of the century. In the past decade there has been a recovery following the launch of a second lottery in 2002. Sales have grown by 12 per cent in the five years to 2012 and continue to grow. Sales in the quarter-year to 30 June 2012 were £1.67 billion – a 9.5 per cent increase on the previous year.

The institutional framework

There are a number of institutions involved in providing the lottery. The Department of Culture, Media and Sport oversees the lottery as directed by the National Lottery Act and dictates its strategic direction. It appoints the National Lottery Commission (NLC), which ensures that bids for the lottery licence and the running of the lottery games maximise the returns for 'Good Causes'. There are also a number of distribution bodies that provide lottery funds to thousands of local projects.

The main point of contact for lottery buyers is Camelot, which runs the lotto and scratchcard games via retail outlets, mobile phones, digital television and the Internet. Camelot won the first, second and third licences for the right to run the UK National Lottery from 1994, 2002 and 2009 respectively. Camelot's extended third-term licence will expire in 2023.

The rationale for a monopoly supplier

Camelot is a monopoly supplier of the UK National Lottery, although it need not be so. The legislation currently allows for two licences, one to operate the infrastructure and another to run the games. It is possible for other companies to run games on the computer network owned by Camelot, much in the same way that Network Rail owns the railway tracks, tunnels, etc. and allows competition between firms on particular routes on the network. Indeed, this option was briefly undertaken by Camelot in 1998, when Vernons Pools sold its 'Easy Play' game using the National Lottery retailer network. Its sales, though, were poor and it was scrapped in May 1999.

However, the government has a strong preference for a single owner of the infrastructure and a single supplier of National Lottery games. The rationale for having a single owner of the infrastructure is fairly standard; this is a natural monopoly and it would be pointless having two lottery computer networks, just as it would be having two separately owned rail lines from Edinburgh to London. With one firm controlling the infrastructure, economies of scale can be reaped.

One of the arguments for having a single supplier of games is known, rather bizarrely, as 'peculiar economies of scale'.[1] This is a situation in which a company that offered a portfolio of innovative lottery games would be more likely to induce additional players to participate in games because they can raise the size of the prize to be won. In other words, good game design can lead to more and bigger jackpots and thus more people buying lottery tickets. This reduces the average costs of supplying tickets and raises the money for 'Good Causes'.

Arguably, more than one firm may be able to supply an innovative portfolio of games if the market is large enough. However, the government is concerned about the risks involved in regulating relationships between network owners and network users (a problem that has occurred in regulating

[1] See, for example, P. Daffern, 'Assessment of the effects of competition on the National Lottery', Technical Paper No. 6, Department of Culture, Media and Sport, 2006.

the workers in that factory. If, however, it starts charging high prices or providing a poor service, the factory could offer the running of the canteen to an alternative catering company. This threat may force the original catering company to charge 'reasonable' prices and offer a good service.

Perfectly contestable markets

A market is ***perfectly contestable*** when the costs of entry and exit by potential rivals are zero, and when such entry can be made very rapidly. In such cases, the moment the possibility of earning supernormal profits occurs, new firms will enter, thus driving profits down to a normal level. The sheer threat of this happening, so the theory goes, will ensure that the firm already in the market will (a) keep its prices down, so that it just makes normal profits, and (b) produce as efficiently as possible, taking advantage of any economies of scale and any new technology. If the existing firm did not do this, entry would take place and potential competition would become actual competition.

Definition

Perfectly contestable market A market where there is free and costless entry and exit.

the railways – see Box 22.3). For example, there might be a lengthy legal dispute if a supplier of games is accused of unacceptable performance but it, in turn, accuses the network owner of poor service. This would then have a detrimental effect on the money raised for 'Good Causes'. Thus the government has always preferred a single firm framework for running the National Lottery.

Bidding for the National Lottery monopoly

Unlike auctions to run national rail franchises or a local bus route, bidding for the lottery does not involve any payment on the part of the successful bidder. The bid is purely a detailed business plan outlining all aspects of running the lottery, but its main emphasis is on providing likely revenue scenarios from games that would maximise money for 'Good Causes' and safeguard players. It was the uncertainty over future revenue flows that led the government in 1994 to require a paper-based bidding scheme for the first lottery licence. This view did not change when subsequent licences came up for renewal.

The NLC is responsible for evaluating the bids and awarding the licence. There were seven bidders for the first licence but for the second licence there were only two tabled 'bids', one from Camelot and other from Sir Richard Branson's The People's Lottery (and initially the NLC rejected both before settling on the incumbent).

For the third licence, the NLC tried to encourage as many bids as possible to come forward. Only one other bidder, Sugal and Dumani UK Ltd, submitted a bid. Camelot won because the NLC believed that, at a similar level of sales, they would be slightly more generous to Good Causes and that 'there was a higher probability that they would achieve higher sales over the length of the licence'.[2]

Clearly, incumbent firms like Camelot have considerable advantages over potential rivals when contracts have to be renewed and thus the number of new bidders is likely to be low. Two problems, in particular, stand out for rivals.

The 'Winner's Curse'. If a potential entrant outbids the incumbent in an auction to run (say) a local bus service, then it could be that winner has paid too much. After all, the incumbent has more knowledge about running the bus service and the likely revenues that may prevail. This situation is known as the 'Winner's Curse' and a similar scenario may occur in respect of the lottery. Potential bidders may be put off from bidding because they don't have the same knowledge about the UK lottery market.

Arguably, the lottery market might be considered a mature market and more is now known about lottery sales and the gaming market in general. However, there are strong incentives for risk-averse regulators to continue with accepting bids from incumbent firms because they are known to provide a certain level of sales and service.

The handover problem. If Camelot were to lose the lottery licence, there would be some large risks in transferring to the new bidder. Arguably, Camelot could sell its infrastructure to the new lottery provider, but there is a valuation dilemma. In terms of opportunity cost, Camelot would value the infrastructure at scrap value (if it has no alternative use for it), whereas a winner with no alternative source for such infrastructure would value Camelot's assets at close to their replacement value. This could lead to some difficult negotiations.

Because of this difficulty, the NLC did require bidders for the third lottery licence to provide new infrastructure, but recognised that this would take time to have in place (imagine trying to replace 30 000 retail terminals as well as to make online, television and mobile games work well). Given this difficulty, it is not surprising that there was only one rival bidder to Camelot.

Camelot managed to achieve a first-mover advantage (see page 192) by winning the initial lottery licence in 1994. It is now to continue providing the UK National Lottery until 2023 and so will have been sole monopoly provider for 29 years. Removing Camelot after that date could prove to be difficult.

?

1. *If Camelot is maximising revenue, what is the price elasticity of demand for lottery tickets?*
2. *To what extent is the National Lottery market a contestable market?*

[2] NLC press release, 'Preferred bidder announced for the third National Lottery licence', 7/8/2007. Available at www.natlotcomm.gov.uk/CLIENT/news_item.ASP?NewsId=49

Contestable markets and natural monopolies

So why in such cases are the markets not *actually* perfectly competitive? Why do they remain monopolies?

The most likely reason has to do with economies of scale and the size of the market. To operate on a minimum efficient scale, the firm may have to be so large relative to the market that there is only room for one such firm in the industry. If a new firm does come into the market, then one or other of the two firms will not survive the competition. The market is simply not big enough for both of them.

If, however, there are no entry or exit costs, new firms will be perfectly willing to enter even though there is only room for one firm, provided they believe that they are more efficient than the existing firm. The existing firm, knowing this, will be forced to produce as efficiently as possible and with only normal profit.

The importance of costless exit

Setting up in a new business usually involves large expenditures on plant and machinery. Once this money has been spent, it becomes fixed costs. If these fixed costs are no higher than those of the existing firm, then the new firm could win the battle. But, of course, there is always the risk that it might lose.

KI 18 p 129

But does losing the battle really matter? Can the firm not simply move to another market?

It does matter if there are substantial costs of exit. This will be the case if the capital equipment cannot be transferred to other uses. In this case these fixed costs are known as ***sunk costs***. The losing firm is left with capital equipment it cannot use. The firm may therefore be put off entering in the first place. The market is not perfectly contestable, and the established firm can make supernormal profit.

If, however, the capital equipment can be transferred, the exit costs will be zero (or at least very low), and new firms will be more willing to take the risks of entry. For example, a rival coach company may open up a service on a route previously operated by only one company, and where there is still only room for one operator. If the new firm loses the resulting battle, it can still use the coaches it has purchased. It simply uses them for a different route or sells them for a fair price on the second-hand market. The cost of the coaches is not a sunk cost.

Costless exit, therefore, encourages firms to enter an industry, knowing that, if unsuccessful, they can always transfer their capital elsewhere.

The lower the exit costs, the more contestable the market. This implies that firms already established in other similar markets may provide more effective competition against monopolists, since they can simply transfer capital from one market to another. For example, studies of airlines in the USA show that entry to a particular route may be much easier for an established airline, which can simply transfer planes from one route to another.

Assessment of the theory

Simple monopoly theory merely focuses on the existing structure of the industry and makes no allowance for potential competition. The theory of contestable markets, however, goes much further and examines the *size* of entry barriers and exit costs. The bigger these are, the less contestable the market and therefore the greater the monopoly power of the existing firm. Various attempts have been made to measure monopoly power in this way.

One criticism of the theory, however, is that it does not take sufficient account of the possible reactions of the established firm. There may be no cost barriers to entry or exit (i.e. a perfectly contestable market), but the established firm may let it be known that any firm that dares to enter will face all-out war! This may act as a deterrent to entry. In the meantime, the established firm may charge high prices and make supernormal profits.

If a monopoly operates in a perfectly contestable market, it might bring the 'best of both worlds' for the consumer. Not only will it be able to achieve low costs through economies of scale, but also the potential competition will keep profits and hence prices down.

Definition

Sunk costs Costs that cannot be recouped (e.g. by transferring assets to other uses).

Pause for thought

Think of two examples of highly contestable monopolies (or oligopolies). How well is the consumer's interest served?

SUMMARY

1a There are four alternative market structures under which firms operate. In ascending order of firms' market power, they are: perfect competition, monopolistic competition, oligopoly and monopoly.

1b The market structure under which a firm operates will affect its conduct and its performance.

2a The assumptions of perfect competition are: a very large number of firms, complete freedom of entry, a homogeneous product and perfect knowledge of the good and its market by both producers and consumers.

2b In the short run, there is not time for new firms to enter the market, and thus supernormal profits can persist. In the long run, however, any supernormal profits will be competed away by the entry of new firms.

2c The short-run equilibrium for the firm will be where the price, as determined by demand and supply in the market, is equal to marginal cost. At this output the firm will be maximising profit.

2d The long-run equilibrium will be where the market price is just equal to firms' long-run average cost.

2e There are no substantial economies of scale to be gained in a perfectly competitive industry. If there were, the industry would cease to be perfectly competitive as the large, low-cost firms drove the small, high-cost ones out of business.

3a A monopoly is where there is only one firm in an industry. In practice, it is difficult to determine where a monopoly exists because it depends on how narrowly an industry is defined.

3b Barriers to the entry of new firms will normally be necessary to protect a monopoly from competition. Such barriers include economies of scale (making the firm a natural monopoly or at least giving it a cost advantage over new (small) competitors), control over supplies of inputs or over outlets, patents or copyright, and tactics to eliminate competition (such as takeovers or aggressive advertising).

3c Profits for the monopolist (as for other firms) will be maximised where $MC = MR$.

3d If demand and cost curves are the same in a monopoly and a perfectly competitive industry, the monopoly will produce a lower output and at a higher price than the perfectly competitive industry.

3e On the other hand, any economies of scale will in part be passed on to consumers in lower prices, and the monopolist's high profits may be used for research and development and investment, which in turn may lead to better products at possibly lower prices.

4a Potential competition may be as important as actual competition in determining a firm's price and output strategy.

4b The threat of this competition is greater, the lower are the entry and exit costs to and from the industry. If the entry and exit costs are zero, the market is said to be *perfectly* contestable. Under such circumstances, an existing monopolist will be forced to keep its profits down to the normal level if it is to resist entry of new firms. Exit costs will be lower, the lower are the sunk costs of the firm.

4c The theory of contestable markets provides a more realistic analysis of firms' behaviour than theories based simply on the *existing* number of firms in the industry.

REVIEW QUESTIONS

1. Why do economists treat normal profit as a cost of production? What determines (a) the level and (b) the rate of normal profit for a particular firm?
2. Why is perfect competition so rare?
3. Why does the market for fresh vegetables approximate to perfect competition, whereas that for frozen or tinned ones does not?
4. Illustrate on a diagram similar to Figure 11.3 what would happen in the long run if price were initially below P_L.
5. As an illustration of the difficulty in identifying monopolies, try to decide which of the following are monopolies: a train-operating company; your local evening newspaper; British Gas; the village post office; the Royal Mail; Interflora; the London Underground; ice creams in the cinema; Guinness; food on trains; TippEx; the board game 'Monopoly'.
6. Try this brain teaser. A monopoly would be expected to face an inelastic demand. After all, there are no direct substitutes. And yet, if it produces where $MR = MC$, MR must be positive, demand must therefore be elastic. Therefore the monopolist must face an elastic demand! Can you solve this conundrum?
7. For what reasons would you expect a monopoly to charge (a) a higher price and (b) a lower price than if the industry were operating under perfect competition?
8. In which of the following industries are exit costs likely to be low: (a) steel production; (b) market gardening; (c) nuclear power generation; (d) specialist financial advisory services; (e) production of fashion dolls; (f) production of a new drug; (g) contract catering; (h) mobile discos; (i) car ferry operators? Are these exit costs dependent on how narrowly the industry is defined?
9. Think of three examples of monopolies (local or national) and consider how contestable their markets are.

Chapter 12

Profit maximisation under imperfect competition

Business issues covered in this chapter

- How will firms behave under monopolistic competition (i.e. where there are many firms competing, but where they produce differentiated products)?
- Why will firms under monopolistic competition make only normal profits in the long run?
- How are firms likely to behave when there are just a few of them competing ('oligopolies')?
- What determines whether oligopolies will engage in all-out competition or instead collude with each other?
- What strategic games are oligopolists likely to play in their attempt to out-do their rivals?
- Why might such games lead to an outcome where all the players are worse off than if they had colluded?
- Does oligopoly serve the consumer's interests?

Very few markets in practice can be classified as perfectly competitive or as a pure monopoly. The vast majority of firms do compete with other firms, often quite aggressively, and yet they are not price takers: they do have some degree of market power. Most markets, therefore, lie between the two extremes of monopoly and perfect competition, in the realm of 'imperfect competition'. There are two types of imperfect competition: namely, monopolistic competition and oligopoly (see section 11.1).

12.1 MONOPOLISTIC COMPETITION

Monopolistic competition is nearer to the competitive end of the spectrum. It can best be understood as a situation where there are a lot of firms competing, but where each firm does nevertheless have some degree of market power (hence the term 'monopolistic' competition): each firm has some discretion as to what price to charge for its products.

Assumptions of monopolistic competition

- There is *quite a large number of firms*. As a result, each firm has only a small share of the market and, therefore, its actions are unlikely to affect its rivals to any great extent. What this means is that each firm in making its decisions does not have to worry about how its rivals will react. It assumes that what its rivals choose to do will not be influenced by what it does.

This is known as the assumption of ***independence***. (As we shall see later, this is not the case under oligopoly. There we assume that firms believe that their decisions do affect their rivals, and that their rivals' decisions will affect them. Under oligopoly we assume that firms are interdependent.)

Figure 12.1 Equilibrium of the firm under monopolistic competition (a) Short run (b) Long run

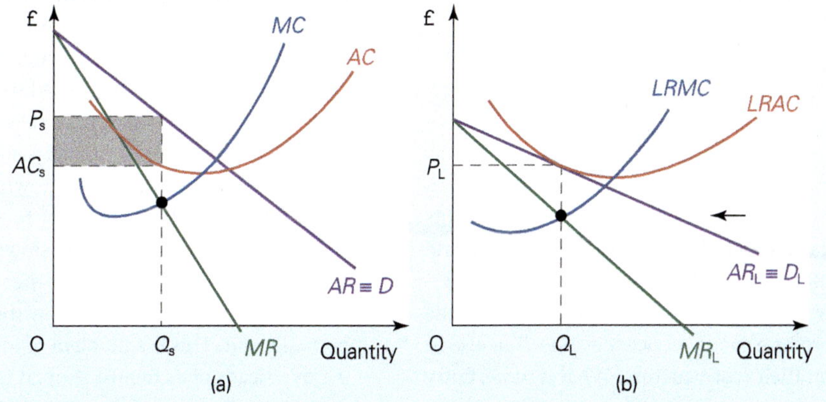

- There is freedom of entry of new firms into the industry. If any firm wants to set up in business in this market, it is free to do so.

In these two respects, therefore, monopolistic competition is like perfect competition.

- Unlike perfect competition, however, each firm produces a product or provides a service that is in some way different from its rivals. As a result, it can raise its price without losing all its customers. Thus its demand curve is downward sloping, albeit relatively elastic given the large number of competitors to whom customers can turn. This is known as the assumption of ***product differentiation***.

Petrol stations, restaurants, hairdressers and builders are all examples of monopolistic competition.

When considering monopolistic competition it is important to take account of the distance consumers are willing to travel to buy a product. In other words, the geographical size of the market matters. For example, McDonald's is a major global and national fast-food restaurant. However, in any one location it experiences intense competition in the 'informal eating-out' market from Indian, Chinese, Italian and other restaurants (see Box 12.1). So in any one local area, there is competition between firms each offering differentiated products.

Definitions

Independence (of firms in a market) When the decisions of one firm in a market will not have any significant effect on the demand curves of its rivals.

Product differentiation When one firm's product is sufficiently different from its rivals' to allow it to raise the price of the product without customers all switching to the rivals' products. A situation where a firm faces a downward-sloping demand curve.

Equilibrium of the firm

Short run

As with other market structures, profits are maximised at the output where $MC = MR$. The diagram will be the same as for the monopolist, except that the *AR* and *MR* curves will be more elastic. This is illustrated in Figure 12.1(a). As with perfect competition, it is possible for the monopolistically competitive firm to make supernormal profit in the short run. This is shown as the shaded area. KI 4 p 22

Just how much profit the firm will make in the short run depends on the strength of demand: the position and elasticity of the demand curve. The further to the right the demand curve is relative to the average cost curve, and the less elastic the demand curve is, the greater will be the firm's short-run profit. Thus a firm facing little competition and whose product is considerably differentiated from its rivals may be able to earn considerable short-run profits. KI 12 p 63

Pause for thought

Which of these two items is a petrol station more likely to sell at a discount: (a) engine oil; (b) sweets? Why?

Long run

If typical firms are earning supernormal profit, new firms will enter the industry in the long run. As new firms enter, they will take some of the customers away from established firms. The demand for the established firms' products will therefore fall. Their demand (*AR*) curve will shift to the left, and will continue doing so as long as supernormal profits remain and thus new firms continue entering. KI 10 p 48

Long-run equilibrium will be reached when only normal profits remain: when there is no further incentive for new firms to enter. This is illustrated in Figure 12.1(b). The firm's demand curve settles at D_L, where it is tangential to (i.e. just touches) the firm's *LRAC* curve. Output will be Q_L: where KI 11 p 55

$AR_L = LRAC$. (At any other output, $LRAC$ is greater than AR and thus less than normal profit would be made.)

Limitations of the model

There are various problems in applying the model of monopolistic competition to the real world:

- Information may be imperfect. Firms will not enter an industry if they are unaware of the supernormal profits currently being made, or if they underestimate the demand for the particular product they are considering selling.
- Firms are likely to differ from each other, not only in the product they produce or the service they offer, but also in their size and in their cost structure. What is more, entry may not be completely unrestricted. For example, two petrol stations could not set up in exactly the same place – on a busy crossroads, say – because of local authority planning controls. Thus although the typical or 'representative' firm may only earn normal profit in the long run, other firms may be able to earn long-run supernormal profit. They may have some cost advantage or produce a product that is impossible to duplicate perfectly.
- Existing firms may make supernormal profits, but if a new firm entered, this might reduce everyone's profits below the normal level. Thus a new firm will not enter and supernormal profits will persist into the long run. An example would be a small town with two chemist shops. They may both make more than enough profit to persuade them to stay in business. But if a third set up (say midway between the other two), there would not be enough total sales to allow them all to earn even normal profit. This is a problem of indivisibilities. Given the overheads of a chemist shop, it is not possible to set up one small enough to take away just enough customers to leave the other two with normal profits.
- One of the biggest problems with the simple model outlined above is that it concentrates on price and output

BOX 12.1 EATING OUT IN BRITAIN

A monopolistically competitive sector

The 'eating-out' sector (i.e. takeaways, cafés and restaurants) is a highly competitive market in the UK, with sales, in 2010, of some £72.1 billion, according to the Office for National Statistics.[1] The sector has grown less strongly in recent years than in the late 1990s. The value of its sales grew at an average rate of just 3.2 per cent per annum over the decade from 2000 – barely enough to cover the effects of inflation.

The sector exhibits many of the characteristics of a monopolistically competitive market.

- *Large number of local buyers*. According to a Mintel survey in 2008, around 93 per cent of UK adults had eaten out within the previous three months.
- *Large number of firms*. In 2011 there were nearly 121 000 hotel, restaurant, takeaway and pub enterprises in the UK. These firms employed 1 362 000 individuals. Although the sector has some large national and global chains, these are usually competing in local markets.
- *Competitive prices*. Margins are very tight because firms have to price very competitively to catch local custom. Only around 60 per cent of these businesses survive longer than three years.
- *Differentiated products*. To attract customers, suppliers must each differentiate their product in various ways, such as food type, ambience, comfort, service, quality, advertising and opening hours. Firms have to cater for the dynamic nature of consumer preferences and respond to the behaviour of competitors. They must constantly adapt or go under.

Lunchtime food

A significant growth area in the eating-out sector has been the sandwich and lunchtime food sector. Lunch is seen by many as a refuelling exercise rather than leisure activity. This means that consumers value convenience, fast service and value for money.

In recent years the sector has been ferociously competitive with the advent of meal deals and price promotions. Mintel[2] reports that the sector grew rapidly through the mid-2000s, but reached maturity by around 2009. Competition in the mature market has forced some high-profile closures (e.g. O'Brian's) and allowed others to expand (e.g. Subway).

Only around 40 per cent of consumers eat lunch at home every day. These tend to be those not working and the retired. Hence there is a large lunchtime food market for the remaining 60 per cent of people, about half of whom state that they always buy food (rather than bring food from home).

In 2011 the most popular lunchtime foods were sandwiches and wraps, fruit, soup and salads. Most of these lunches are not consumed at the place of purchase. Only 3 per cent of those consuming weekday lunches found the time to sit down in a restaurant, café or bar. Niche take-out markets are becoming increasingly popular, for example sushi and burritos, especially in areas with high populations, such as London. For more price-conscious consumers the recent downturn has triggered a growth in 'classic' sandwiches, since they often represent better value for money.

However, the consumer is still looking for the retailer to 'add value'. The 75 pence jam sandwich offered by Marks and Spencer's was a failure and quickly withdrawn from the market! Consumers who focus on value added are often willing to pay a premium to have sandwiches made in front of them, perceiving this as providing them with greater choice and a fresher final product.

[1] Input-Output Supply and Use Tables, ONS (2012).

[2] Sandwiches and Lunchtime Foods, Mintel (2011).

decisions. In practice, the profit-maximising firm under monopolistic competition will also need to decide the exact variety of product to produce, and how much to spend on advertising it. This will lead the firm to take part in non-price competition (which we examined in Chapter 8).

KI 12 p 63

Comparing monopolistic competition with perfect competition and monopoly

Comparison with perfect competition

It is often argued that monopolistic competition leads to a less efficient allocation of resources than perfect competition.

Figure 12.2 compares the long-run equilibrium positions for two firms. One firm is under perfect competition and thus faces a horizontal demand curve. It will produce an output of Q_1 at a price of P_1. The other is under monopolistic competition and thus faces a downward-sloping demand curve. It will produce the lower output of Q_2 at the higher price of P_2. A crucial assumption here is that a firm would have the *same* long-run average cost (*LRAC*) curve in both cases. Given this assumption, we can make the following two predictions about monopolistic competition:

Figure 12.2 Long-run equilibrium of the firm under perfect and monopolistic competition

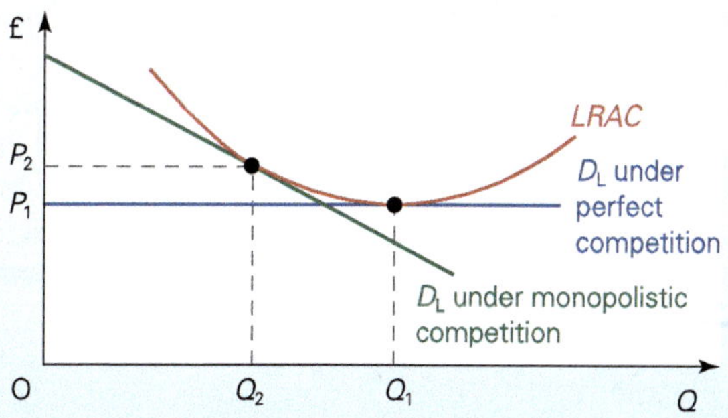

In addition to having to fight for customers, lunchtime food sellers are facing problems on the supply side. The sector has been hit by rising food costs. Smaller sellers are finding it hard to compete due, in part, to the sheer number of outlets of the largest players, including supermarkets and grocery stores, which dominate the 'channels to market'.

The Indian restaurant

The traditional Indian curry house – the institution that made curry the UK's favourite dish – accounted for 24 per cent of meals eaten out by UK adults in 2007. In recent times, however, Indian restaurants have suffered from changing British preferences and supply-side pressures. They are also facing direct competition from ready-to-eat curries sold in local supermarkets and the sale of curry in local pubs. For example, JD Wetherspoon's offers a one night a week 'curry club' menu at a price comfortably undercutting most curry houses.

Competition to attract the discerning local customer has been keen *within* the Indian restaurant trade. In the 1990s 'Curry Wars' developed around the country, with local Indian restaurants undercutting each other's prices. Profits tumbled. Eventually, strong cultural ties among the local Asian communities helped to avert such cut-throat competition. It was realised that, as prices in Indian restaurants were considerably less than in Italian and French ones, fixing minimum curry prices would raise incomes. In effect 'curry cartels' were being proposed.

Such activity – however well intentioned – is illegal in the UK. It is also unlikely to last for long as other segments of the market develop to undercut curry-house prices or attract consumers with a new culinary offering.

The Indian restaurant has had to relaunch its appeal. One reported method of attracting customers to Birmingham's 'Balti Belt' in the early 2000s was for rival Indian restaurants to have the most visible Las Vegas-style neon sign. This, however, has not been a common response and the lower end of the market is still stagnating. Many restaurants claimed to have received awards, often with an unclear provenance. These proclaimed the outstanding quality of the food or the chef's capabilities. However, consumers quickly cottoned on to this practice and such awards are slowly disappearing from many towns and cities.

In some parts of the UK Indian restaurants have recognised that only promoting themselves in a way that threatens rivals may not be the best option. Traders in some localities have chosen to act collectively, attempting to alter consumer tastes in their favour, aiming to increase the total market size. For example, Bradford's curry houses achieve significant publicity through an annual public vote for the best Asian restaurant. There are also equivalent national activities based around organisations such as the Federation of Specialist Restaurants.

Innovation is starting to develop in the premium end of the market where returns are greatest. Mintel reports, for example, that some of the high-end Indian restaurants in London have achieved Michelin stars. There is growth in this market segment but there is some debate about the sustainability of these high-end ventures, given the nature of international competition for high-quality chefs.

It will be interesting to see how the market develops over the next 10 years.

1. *What has happened to the price elasticity of demand for Indian restaurant curries over time? What can be said about cross-price elasticity of demand for pub meals?*
2. *Collusion between restaurants would suggest that they are operating under oligopoly, not monopolistic competition. Do you agree?*

- Less will be sold and at a higher price.
- Firms will not be producing at the least-cost point.

By producing more, firms would move to a lower point on their *LRAC* curve. Thus firms under monopolistic competition are said to have ***excess capacity***. In Figure 12.2 this excess capacity is shown as $Q_1 - Q_2$. In other words, monopolistic competition is typified by quite a large number of firms (e.g. petrol stations), all operating at less than optimum output, and thus being forced to charge a price above that which they could charge if they had a bigger turnover.

Pause for thought

Which would you rather have: five restaurants to choose from, each with very different menus and each having spare tables so that you could always guarantee getting one; or just two restaurants to choose from, charging a bit less but with less choice and making it necessary to book well in advance?

So how does this affect the consumer? Although the firm under monopolistic competition may charge a higher price than under perfect competition, the difference may be very small. Although the firm's demand curve is downward sloping, it is still likely to be highly elastic due to the large number of substitutes. Furthermore, the consumer may benefit from monopolistic competition by having a greater variety of products to choose from. Each firm may satisfy some particular requirement of particular consumers.

Comparison with monopoly

The arguments are very similar here to those when comparing perfect competition and monopoly.

On the one hand, freedom of entry for new firms and hence the lack of long-run supernormal profits under monopolistic competition are likely to help keep prices down for the consumer and encourage cost saving. On the other hand, monopolies are likely to achieve greater economies of scale and have more funds for investment and research and development.

12.2 OLIGOPOLY

Oligopoly occurs when just a few firms between them share a large proportion of the industry. Some of the best-known companies are oligopolists, including Ford, Coca-Cola, BP and Nintendo.

There are, however, significant differences in the structure of industries under oligopoly, and similarly significant differences in the behaviour of firms. The firms may produce a virtually identical product (e.g. metals, chemicals, sugar, petrol). Most oligopolists, however, produce differentiated products (e.g. cars, soap powder, soft drinks, electrical appliances). Much of the competition between such oligopolists is in terms of the marketing of their particular brand. Marketing practices may differ considerably from one industry to another.

The two key features of oligopoly

Despite the differences between oligopolies, there are two crucial features that distinguish oligopoly from other market structures.

Barriers to entry

Unlike firms under monopolistic competition, there are various barriers to the entry of new firms. These are similar to those under monopoly (see pages 167–8). The size of the barriers, however, will vary from industry to industry. In some cases entry is relatively easy, whereas in others it is virtually impossible, perhaps due to patent protection or prohibitive research and development costs.

Interdependence of the firms

Because there are only a few firms under oligopoly, each firm will take account of the behaviour of the others when making its own decisions. This means that they are mutually dependent: they are ***interdependent***. Each firm is affected by its rivals' actions. If a firm changes the price or specification of its product, for example, or the amount of its advertising, the sales of its rivals will be affected. The rivals may then respond by changing their price, specification or advertising. No firm can therefore afford to ignore the actions and reactions of other firms in the industry. KI 1 p 7

Definitions

Excess capacity (under monopolistic competition) In the long run, firms under monopolistic competition will produce at an output below that which minimises average cost per unit.

Interdependence (under oligopoly) Each firm will be affected by its rivals' decisions. Likewise its decisions will affect its rivals. Firms recognise the importance of this interdependence and it affects their decisions. It is one of the two key features of oligopoly.

KEY IDEA 23

People often think and behave strategically. **How you think others will respond to your actions is likely to influence your own behaviour. Firms, for example, when considering a price or product change will often take into account the likely reactions of their rivals.**

It is impossible, therefore, to predict the effect on a firm's sales of, say, a change in its price without first making some assumption about the reactions of other firms. Different assumptions will yield different predictions. For this reason there is no single, generally accepted theory of oligopoly. Firms may react differently and unpredictably.

Competition and collusion

Oligopolists are pulled in two different directions:

- The interdependence of firms may make them wish to *collude* with each other. If they can club together and act as if they were a monopoly, they could jointly maximise industry profits.
- On the other hand, they will be tempted to *compete* with their rivals to gain a bigger share of industry profits for themselves.

These two policies are incompatible. The more fiercely firms compete to gain a bigger share of industry profits, the smaller these industry profits will become! For example, price competition drives down the average industry price, while competition through advertising raises industry costs. Either way, industry profits fall.

Sometimes firms will collude. Sometimes they will not. The following sections examine first ***collusive oligopoly*** (both explicit and tacit), and then ***non-collusive oligopoly***.

Collusive oligopoly

KI 21 p 161

When firms under oligopoly engage in collusion, they may agree on prices, market share, advertising expenditure, etc. Such collusion reduces the uncertainty they face. It reduces the fear of engaging in competitive price cutting or retaliatory advertising, both of which could reduce total industry profits.

Cartels

A formal collusive agreement is called a ***cartel***. The cartel will maximise profits if it acts like a monopoly: if the members behave as if they were a single firm. This is illustrated in Figure 12.3.

KI 4 p 22

The total market demand curve is shown with the corresponding market *MR* curve. The cartel's *MC* curve is

Figure 12.3 Profit-maximising cartel

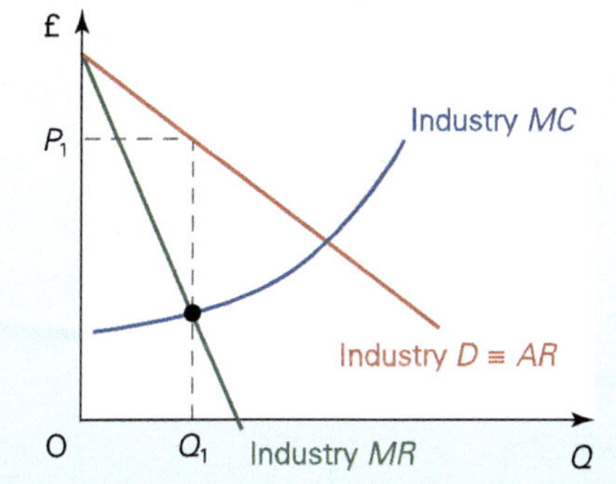

the *horizontal* sum of the *MC* curves of its members (since we are adding the *output* of each of the cartel members at each level of marginal cost). Profits are maximised at Q_1 where $MC = MR$. The cartel must therefore set a price of P_1 (at which Q_1 will be demanded).

Having agreed on the cartel price, the members may then compete against each other using *non-price competition*, to gain as big a share of resulting sales (Q_1) as they can.

Alternatively, the cartel members may somehow agree to divide the market between them. Each member would be given a ***quota***. The sum of all the quotas must add up to Q_1. If the quotas exceeded Q_1, either there would be output unsold if price remained fixed at P_1, or the price would fall to clear the market.

But if quotas are to be set by the cartel, how will it decide the level of each individual member's quota? The most likely method is for the cartel to divide the market between the members according to their current market share. That is the solution most likely to be accepted as 'fair'.

In many countries cartels are illegal, being seen by the government as a means of driving up prices and profits and thereby as being against the public interest. (Government policy towards cartels is examined in Chapter 21.)

Definitions

Collusive oligopoly When oligopolists agree, formally or informally, to limit competition between themselves. They may set output quotas, fix prices, limit product promotion or development, or agree not to 'poach' each other's markets.

Non-collusive oligopoly When oligopolists have no agreement between themselves – formal, informal or tacit.

Cartel A formal collusive agreement.

Quota (set by a cartel) The output that a given member of a cartel is allowed to produce (production quota) or sell (sales quota).

Where open collusion is illegal, firms may simply break the law, or get round it. Alternatively, firms may stay within the law, but still *tacitly* collude by watching each other's prices and keeping theirs similar. Firms may tacitly 'agree' to avoid price wars or aggressive advertising campaigns.

Pause for thought

If this 'fair' solution were adopted, what effect would it have on the industry MC curve in Figure 12.3?

Tacit collusion

One form of ***tacit collusion*** is where firms keep to the price that is set by an established leader. The leader may be the largest firm: the firm which dominates the industry. This is known as ***dominant firm price leadership***. Alternatively, the price leader may simply be the one that has proved to be the most reliable one to follow: the one that is the best barometer of market conditions. This is known as ***barometric firm price leadership***. Let us examine each of these two types of price leadership in turn.

Dominant firm price leadership. How does the leader set the price? This depends on the assumptions it makes about its rivals' reactions to its price changes. If it assumes that rivals will simply follow it by making exactly the same percentage price changes up or down, then a simple model can be constructed. This is illustrated in Figure 12.4. The leader assumes that it will maintain a constant market share (say 50 per cent).

The leader will maximise profits where its marginal revenue is equal to its marginal cost. It knows its current position on its demand curve (say, point *a*). It then estimates how responsive its demand will be to industry-wide price changes and thus constructs its demand and *MR* curves on that basis. It then chooses to produce Q_L at a price of P_L: at point *l* on its demand curve (where *MC* = *MR*). Other firms then follow that price. Total market demand will be Q_T, with followers supplying that portion of the market not supplied by the leader: namely, $Q_T - Q_L$.

There is one problem with this model. That is the assumption that the followers will want to maintain a constant market share. It is possible that, if the leader raises its price, the followers may want to supply more, given that the new price (= *MR* for a price-taking follower) may well be above their marginal cost. On the other hand, the followers may decide merely to maintain their market share for fear of invoking retaliation from the leader, in the form of price cuts or an aggressive advertising campaign.

Figure 12.4 A price leader aiming to maximise profits for a given market share

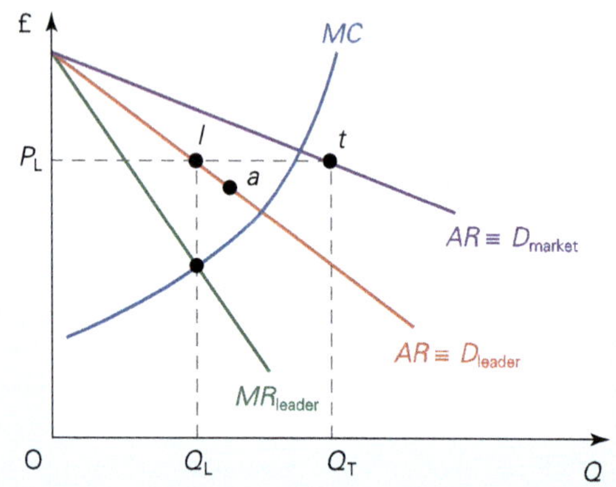

Barometric firm price leadership. A similar exercise can be conducted by a barometric firm. Although the firm is not dominating the industry, its price will be followed by the others. It merely tries to estimate its demand and *MR* curves – assuming, again, a constant market share – and then produces where *MR* = *MC* and sets price accordingly.

In practice, which firm is taken as the barometer may frequently change. Whether we are talking about oil companies, car producers or banks, any firm may take the initiative in raising prices. If the other firms are merely waiting for someone to take the lead – say, because costs have risen – they will all quickly follow suit. For example, if one of the bigger building societies or banks raises its mortgage rates by 1 per cent, this is likely to stimulate the others to follow suit.

Other forms of tacit collusion. An alternative to having an established leader is for there to be an established set of simple 'rules of thumb' that everyone follows.

One such example is ***average cost pricing***. Here producers, instead of equating *MC* and *MR*, simply add a certain percentage for profit on top of average costs. Thus, if average costs rise by 10 per cent, prices will automatically be raised by 10 per cent. This is a particularly useful rule of thumb in times of inflation, when all firms will be experiencing similar cost increases.

Another rule of thumb is to have certain ***price benchmarks***. Thus clothes may sell for £9.95, £24.95 or £39.95 (but not, say, £12.31 or £36.42). If costs rise, then firms simply raise their price to the next benchmark, knowing that other firms will do the same. (Average cost pricing and other pricing strategies are considered in more detail in Chapter 17.)

Definitions

Tacit collusion A situation where firms have an unspoken agreement to engage in a joint strategy. For example, oligopolists take care not to engage in price cutting, excessive advertising or other forms of competition. There may be unwritten 'rules' of collusive behaviour such as price leadership.

Dominant firm price leadership When firms (the followers) choose the same price as that set by a dominant firm in the industry (the leader).

Barometric firm price leadership Where the price leader is the one whose prices are believed to reflect market conditions in the most satisfactory way.

Rules of thumb can also be applied to advertising (e.g. you do not criticise other firms' products, only praise your own); or to the design of the product (e.g. lighting manufacturers tacitly agreeing not to bring out an everlasting light bulb).

Pause for thought

If a firm has a typical-shaped average cost curve and sets prices 10 per cent above average cost, what will its supply curve look like?

Factors favouring collusion

KI 1 p 7

Collusion between firms, whether formal or tacit, is more likely when firms can clearly identify with each other or some leader and when they trust each other not to break agreements. It will be easier for firms to collude if the following conditions apply:

- There are only very few firms, all well known to each other.
- They are open with each other about costs and production methods.
- They have similar production methods and average costs, and are thus likely to want to change prices at the same time and by the same percentage.
- They produce similar products and can thus more easily reach agreements on price.
- There is a dominant firm.
- There are significant barriers to entry and thus there is little fear of disruption by new firms.
- The market is stable. If industry demand or production costs fluctuate wildly, it will be difficult to make agreements, partly due to difficulties in predicting and partly because agreements may frequently have to be amended. There is a particular problem in a declining market where firms may be tempted to undercut each other's price in order to maintain their sales.
- There are no government measures to curb collusion.

Non-collusive oligopoly: the breakdown of collusion

In some oligopolies, there may be only a few (if any) factors favouring collusion. In such cases, the likelihood of price competition is greater.

Even if there is collusion, there will always be the temptation for individual oligopolists to 'cheat', by cutting prices or by selling more than their allotted quota. The danger, of course, is that this would invite retaliation from the other members of the cartel, with a resulting price war. Price would then fall and the cartel could well break up in disarray.

When considering whether to break a collusive agreement, even if only a tacit one, a firm will ask: (1) 'How much can we get away with without inviting retaliation?' and (2) 'If a price war does result, will we be the winners? Will we succeed in driving some or all of our rivals out of business and yet survive ourselves, and thereby gain greater market power?'

The position of rival firms, therefore, is rather like that of generals of opposing armies or the players in a game. It is a question of choosing the appropriate *strategy*: the strategy that will best succeed in outwitting your opponents. The strategy that a firm adopts will, of course, be concerned not just with price, but also with advertising and product development.

Non-collusive oligopoly: assumptions about rivals' behaviour

Even though oligopolists might not collude, they will still need to take account of rivals' likely behaviour when deciding their own strategy. In doing so they will probably look at rivals' past behaviour and make assumptions based on it. There are three well-known models, each based on a different set of assumptions.

Assumption that rivals produce a given quantity: the Cournot model

One assumption is that rivals will produce a particular *quantity*. This is most likely when the market is stable and the rivals have been producing a relatively constant quantity for some time. The task, then, for the individual oligopolist is to decide its own price and quantity given the presumed output of its competitors.

The earliest model based on this assumption was developed by the French economist Augustin Cournot in 1838. The ***Cournot model*** (which is developed in Web Appendix 4.2) takes the simple case of just two firms (a ***duopoly***) producing an identical product: for example, two electricity generating companies supplying the whole country.

Definitions

Average cost pricing Where a firm sets its price by adding a certain percentage for (average) profit on top of average cost.

Price benchmark This is a price which is typically used. Firms, when raising prices, will usually raise them from one benchmark to another.

Cournot model A model of duopoly where each firm makes its price and output decisions on the assumption that its rival will produce a particular quantity.

Duopoly An oligopoly where there are just two firms in the market.

Figure 12.5 The Cournot model of duopoly: Firm A's profit-maximising position

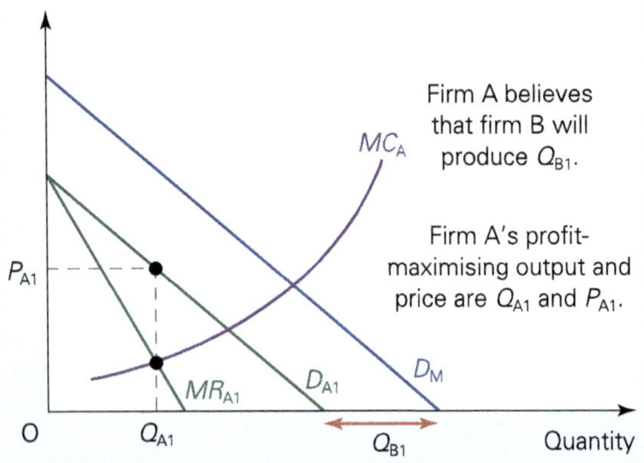

This is illustrated in Figure 12.5, which shows the profit-maximising price and output for firm A. The total market demand curve is shown as D_M. Assume that firm A believes that its rival, firm B, will produce Q_{B1} units. Thus firm A perceives its own demand curve (D_{A1}) to be Q_{B1} units less than total market demand. In other words, the horizontal gap between D_M and D_{A1} is Q_{B1} units. Given its perceived demand curve of D_{A1}, its marginal revenue curve will be MR_{A1} and the profit-maximising output will be Q_{A1}, where $MR_{A1} = MC_A$. The profit-maximising price will be P_{A1}.

If firm A believed that firm B would produce *more* than Q_{B1}, its perceived demand and *MR* curves would be further to the left and the profit-maximising quantity and price would both be lower.

Profits in the Cournot model. Industry profits will be *less* than under a monopoly or a cartel. The reason is that price will be lower than the monopoly price. This can be seen from Figure 12.5. If this were a monopoly, then to find the profit-maximising output, we would need to construct an *MR* curve corresponding to the market demand curve (D_M). This would intersect with the *MC* curve at a higher output than Q_{A1} and a *higher* price (given by D_M). Nevertheless, profits in the Cournot model will be higher than under perfect competition, since price is still above marginal cost.

Assumption that rivals set a particular price: the Bertrand model

An alternative assumption is that rival firms set a particular price and stick to it. This scenario is more realistic when firms do not want to upset customers by frequent price changes or want to produce catalogues which specify prices. The task, then, for a given oligopolist is to choose its own price and quantity in the light of the prices set by rivals.

The most famous model based on this assumption was developed by another French economist, Joseph Bertrand, in 1883. Bertrand again took the simple case of a duopoly, but its conclusions apply equally to oligopolies with three or more firms.

The outcome is one of price cutting until all supernormal profits are competed away. The reason is simple. If firm A assumes that its rival, firm B, will hold price constant, then firm A should undercut this price by a small amount and as a result gain a large share of the market. At this point, firm B will be forced to respond by cutting its price. What we end up with is a price war until price is forced down to the level of average cost, with only normal profits remaining.

Nash equilibrium. The equilibrium outcome in either the Cournot or Bertrand models is not in the *joint* interests of the firms. In each case, total profits are less than under a monopoly or cartel. But, in the absence of collusion, the outcome is the result of each firm doing the best it can, given its assumptions about what its rivals are doing. The resulting equilibrium is known as a ***Nash equilibrium***, after John Nash, a US mathematician (and subject of the film *A Beautiful Mind*) who introduced the concept in 1951.

In practice, when competition is intense, as in the Bertrand model, the firms may seek to collude long before profits have been reduced to a normal level. Alternatively, firms may put in a ***takeover bid*** for their rival(s).

The kinked demand-curve assumption

In 1939 a theory of non-collusive oligopoly was developed simultaneously on both sides of the Atlantic: in the USA by Paul Sweezy and in Britain by R. L. Hall and C. J. Hitch. This ***kinked demand theory*** has since become perhaps the most famous of all theories of oligopoly. The model seeks to explain how it is that, even when there is no collusion at all between oligopolists, prices can nevertheless remain stable.

The theory is based on two asymmetrical assumptions:

- If an oligopolist cuts its price, its rivals will feel forced to follow suit and cut theirs, to prevent losing customers to the first firm.
- If an oligopolist raises its price, its rivals will *not* follow suit since, by keeping their prices the same, they will thereby gain customers from the first firm.

Definitions

Nash equilibrium The position resulting from everyone making their optimal decision based on their assumptions about their rivals' decisions.

Takeover bid Where one firm attempts to purchase another by offering to buy the shares of that company from its shareholders.

Kinked demand theory The theory that oligopolists face a demand curve that is kinked at the current price: demand being significantly more elastic above the current price than below. The effect of this is to create a situation of price stability.

Figure 12.6 (a) Kinked demand for a firm under oligopoly (b) Stable price under conditions of a kinked demand curve

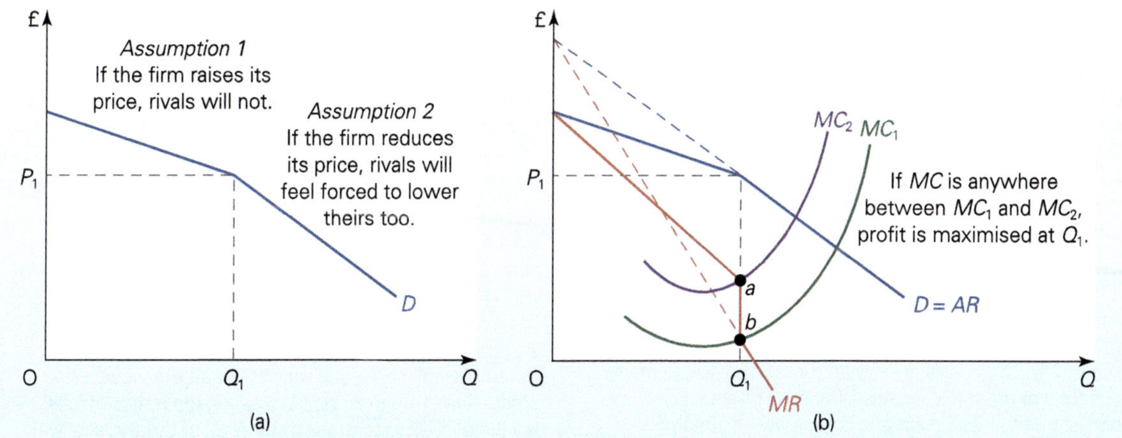

On these assumptions, each oligopolist will face a demand curve that is *kinked* at the current price and output (see Figure 12.6(a)). A rise in price will lead to a large fall in sales as customers switch to the now relatively lower-priced rivals. The firm will thus be reluctant to raise its price. Demand is relatively elastic above the kink. On the other hand, a fall in price will bring only a modest increase in sales, since rivals lower their prices too and therefore customers do not switch. The firm will thus also be reluctant to lower its price. Demand is relatively inelastic below the kink. Thus oligopolists will be reluctant to change prices at all.

This price stability can be shown formally by drawing in the firm's marginal revenue curve, as in Figure 12.6(b).

To see how this is done, imagine dividing the diagram into two parts either side of Q_1. At quantities less than Q_1 (the left-hand part of the diagram), the *MR* curve will correspond to the shallow part of the *AR* curve. At quantities greater than Q_1 (the right-hand part), the *MR* curve will correspond to the steep part of the *AR* curve. To see how this part of the *MR* curve is constructed, imagine extending the steep part of the *AR* curve back to the vertical axis. This and the corresponding *MR* curve are shown by the dotted lines in Figure 12.6(b).

As you can see, there will be a gap between points *a* and *b*. In other words, there is a vertical section of the *MR* curve between these two points.

Profits are maximised where $MC = MR$. Thus, if the *MC* curve lies anywhere between MC_1 and MC_2 (i.e. between points *a* and *b*), the profit-maximising price and output will be P_1 and Q_1. Thus prices will remain stable *even with a considerable change in costs.*

Oligopoly and the consumer

If oligopolists act collusively and jointly maximise industry profits, they will in effect be acting together as a monopoly. In such cases, prices may be very high. This is clearly not in the best interests of consumers.

Furthermore, in two respects, oligopoly may be more disadvantageous than monopoly:

- Depending on the size of the individual oligopolists, there may be less scope for economies of scale to lower costs and mitigate the effects of market power.
- Oligopolists are likely to engage in much more extensive advertising than a monopolist. This is likely to raise costs and prices.

These problems will be less severe, however, if oligopolists do not collude, if there is some degree of price competition and if barriers to entry are weak.

Moreover, the power of oligopolists in certain markets may to some extent be offset if they sell their product to other powerful firms. Thus oligopolistic producers of baked beans or soap powder sell a large proportion of their output to giant supermarket chains, which can use their market power to keep down the price at which they purchase these products. This phenomenon is known as ***countervailing power***.

In some respects, oligopoly may be more beneficial to the consumer than other market structures:

Pause for thought

Assume that two brewers announce that they are about to merge. What information would you need to help you decide whether the merger would be in the consumer's interests?

Definition

Countervailing power When the power of a monopolistic/oligopolistic seller is offset by powerful buyers who can prevent the price from being pushed up.

BOX 12.2 REINING IN BIG BUSINESS

Market power in oligopolistic industries

KI 21 p 161

In recent years the car industry, the large supermarket chains and BT in charging broadband suppliers for using its fibre optic cables have all been charged with 'ripping off' the consumer. Such has been the level of concern, that all three industries were referred to the UK Competition Commission (see section 20.1). In this box we consider developments in each sector in turn.

Car industry

The Competition Commission report, published in April 2000, found that car buyers in Britain were paying on average some 10 to 12 per cent more than those in France, Germany and Italy for the same models.[1] The price discrepancies between Britain and mainland Europe were maintained by car manufacturers blocking cheaper European cars coming into the UK. This was achieved by threatening mainland European car dealers with losing their dealership if they sold to British buyers, and delaying the delivery date of right-hand-drive models to European dealers in the hope that British buyers would change their minds and go back to a British dealership.

As the problem involved more than one EU country, the European Commission (EC) also examined the issue. It concluded that the motor vehicle manufacturers had agreements with distributors that were too restrictive. In 2002, the EC changed the 'Block Exemption' regulations governing the sector to allow distributors to set up in different countries and to sell multiple brands of car within their showrooms. Furthermore, distributors which are offered an exclusive 'sales territory' distribution agreement by car manufacturers are now allowed to resell cars to other distributors which are not part of the manufacturer's network. This has helped to develop other sales outlets such as car supermarkets and Internet retailers. In addition, the regulation has opened up the repair and spare parts sector to more firms.

Changes in the regulations, and the addition of ten new EU member states in 2004 and another two in 2007, have made the car market more competitive by increasing the sources of supply. Slowly, prices of new car prices have been converging across the EU towards the lower-price markets.[2]

With the recession of 2008/9, the demand for new cars plummeted. Competition became intense and new cars were heavily discounted. Some dealers went out of business and there were mergers of car manufacturers, such as Fiat and Chrysler. Many car factories went on to short-time working. In the first half of 2012, new car registrations were down in all major Continental European countries, with the exception of Germany where registrations remained stable.

But what about the UK? In the first half of 2012 the UK market for new cars was growing. New registrations were up around 3 per cent on the previous year. However, sales were still 15 per cent below levels achieved in 2007. This said, some car producers have done well during the downturn, especially UK-based manufacturers such as Jaguar Land Rover, Nissan and Toyota, which have all expanded production through 2011/12, creating thousands of jobs. It will be interesting to see whether all of these events will make the car market more, or less, competitive when the world economy expands again.

Supermarkets

Consumers, suppliers and regulators have commented upon the use (or abuse) of market power in the supermarket sector during recent times. Three major areas of concern have arisen.

Barriers to entry. The most important barrier to entry is the difficulty in getting planning permission to open a new supermarket, thus restricting consumer choice. Furthermore, supermarkets own covenants on land ('land banks') suitable for siting new stores and by not releasing them to competitors they thereby restrict competition.

Another barrier is the large economies of scale and the huge buying power of the established supermarkets, which make it virtually impossible for a new player or for the smaller convenience stores to match their low costs. Indeed, the big supermarkets have used their scale to enter the convenience sector with considerable effect. Thus brands like 'Tesco Metro' and 'Sainsbury's Local' have been successful in driving out many small stores from the market.

Relationships with suppliers. One of the most contentious issues concerns the major supermarket chains' huge buying power. They have been able to drive costs down by forcing suppliers to offer discounts. Many suppliers, such as growers, have found their profit margins cut to the bone. However, in many cases these cost savings to the supermarkets have not been passed on to shoppers.

Price competition. National advertising campaigns tell us that supermarkets are concerned about keeping prices lower than their competitors on a number of items. However, this can often mask certain pricing concerns. For some goods the supermarkets have, on occasion, adopted a system of 'shadow pricing', a form of tacit collusion whereby they all observe each other's prices and ensure that they remain at

---

[1] Competition Commission (2000), 'New cars: a report on the supply of new motor cars within the UK' (Cm 4660). Available at www.competition-commission.org.uk/rep_pub/reports/2000/439cars.htm

[2] http://ec.europa.eu/competition/sectors/motor_vehicles/prices/report.htmlx

similar levels – often similarly high levels rather than similarly low levels! This has limited the extent of true price competition, and the resulting high prices have seen profits grow as costs have been driven ever downwards. Somewhat perversely, this activity may be presented to consumers as competitive behaviour – 'we will not charge you more than our competitors'!

Moreover, the supermarkets have been observed charging high prices where there is little or no competition, notably in rural locations, and charging lower prices on some items, often below cost, where competition is more intense.

But intense price competition tends to be only over basic items, such as the own-brand 'value' products. To get to the basic items, you normally have to pass the more luxurious ones, which are much more highly priced. Supermarkets rely on shoppers making impulse buys of the more expensive lines: lines that have much higher profit margins.

In response to these claims, the Competition Commission reported in 2008 that it found little evidence of tacit collusion.[3] Further, the nature of below-cost selling on grocery items by the supermarkets did not mislead consumers in relation to the overall cost of shopping at a particular store. Indeed, temporary promotions on some products, including fuel, may represent effective competition between supermarkets and lower the average price of a basket of goods for customers.

However, the Commission did have some concerns in relation to the existence of a number of stores owned by the same supermarket chain in a particular location (e.g. Tesco Metro and Tesco Superstore) and the covenants on land owned by supermarkets that restrict entry by competitors. To this end it proposed a 'competition test' in planning decisions and action to prevent land agreements, both of which would lessen the market power of supermarkets in local areas. The Commission also found that the supermarkets had substantial buying power and that the drive to lower supply prices may have had an inhibiting effect on innovation.

The Commission proposed the creation of a new strengthened and extended Groceries Supply Code of Practice that would be enforced by an independent ombudsman and incorporated the bigger firms. Following failed attempts to create a voluntary code of practice between the supermarkets and government, consultation on the creation of an ombudsman occurred in 2010. Parliamentary time has been set aside with the hope of creating this statutory body by 2013. We await the outcome of this with interest.

Broadband

In 2011 Ofcom, the independent regulator and competition authority for the UK communications industries, decided that BT should cut the price of its wholesale broadband product. The wholesale broadband market allows competitors such as TalkTalk and SkyBroadband to use the BT network in certain parts of the UK. The ruling was expected to lead to cheaper Internet access, mainly for customers in rural areas, where there is little competition.

Granting competitors access to the BT network was allowed following a European Commission decision in 2008. At the time, BT was wary of this decision, pointing out that it would only invest in expanding the broadband network if it could achieve satisfactory returns. This would partly depend on the price it charged rivals for accessing its fibre optic networks.

BT was unhappy with the 2011 Ofcom ruling and asked the Competition Commission to review the decision. In June 2012 the Competition Commission ruled that Ofcom had reached the correct judgment.[4]

The ruling centred around the appropriateness of BT including 'deficit repair charges' in its wholesale broadband costs. The 'deficit repair charge' was to assist the filling of a £3 billion deficit in the BT pension scheme. By levying this charge on companies such as TalkTalk and SkyBroadband, BT was forcing them to assist in funding its pension liabilities. The regulator's decision came down to its judgment on the cause of BT's pension deficit. Was it due to poor management on the part of BT? Or, was it a legitimate business cost? If the deficit was a result of poor management then shareholders ought to bear the costs, not competitors.[5]

The Commission concluded that BT had managed its pension scheme poorly. Hence 'deficit repair charges' should not be part of wholesale broadband access fees. By including them, providers such as TalkTalk and SkyBroadband were not being charged in relation to the true cost of the fibre optic networks. The charges were anti-competitive. BT is currently 'considering its position'.

?

1. *Identify the main barriers to entry in each of the three sectors.*
2. *Update each of the cases and consider the economic implications for consumers.*

[3] Competition Commission (2008), 'Market investigation into the supply of groceries in the UK'. Available at www.competition-commission.org.uk/inquiries/ref2006/grocery/index.htm

[4] Competition Commission (2012) 'British Telecommunications plc v Ofcom telecommunications price control appeal: Wholesale broadband access charge control' (1187/3/3/11, June). Available at www.competition-commission.org.uk/

[5] BT rebuffed on pensions cost (*Financial Times* 24 June 2012).

- Oligopolists, like monopolists, can use part of their supernormal profit for research and development. Unlike monopolists, however, oligopolists will have a considerable *incentive* to do so. If the product design is improved, this may allow the firm to capture a larger share of the market, and it may be some time before rivals can respond with a similarly improved product. If, in addition, costs are reduced by technological improvement, the resulting higher profits will improve the firm's capacity to withstand a price war.
- Non-price competition through product differentiation may result in greater choice for the consumer. Take the case of stereo equipment. Non-price competition has led to a huge range of different products of many different specifications, each meeting the specific requirements of different consumers.

It is difficult to draw any general conclusions, since oligopolies differ so much in their performance.

Oligopoly and contestable markets

The theory of contestable markets has been applied to oligopoly as well as to monopoly, and similar conclusions are drawn.

The lower the entry and exit costs for new firms, the more difficult it will be for oligopolists to collude and make supernormal profits. If oligopolists do form a cartel (whether legal or illegal), this will be difficult to maintain if it very soon faces competition from new entrants. What a cartel has to do in such a situation is to erect entry barriers, thereby making the 'contest' more difficult. For example, the cartel could form a common research laboratory, denied to outsiders. It might attempt to control the distribution of the finished product by buying up wholesale or retail outlets. Or it might simply let it be known to potential entrants that they will face all-out price, advertising and product competition from all the members if they should dare to set up in competition.

The industry is thus likely to behave competitively if entry and exit costs are low, with all the benefits and costs to the consumer of such competition – even if the new firms do not actually enter. However, if entry and/or exit costs are high, the degree of competition will simply depend on the relations between existing members of the industry.

Pause for thought

Which of the following markets do you think are contestable: (a) credit cards; (b) brewing; (c) petrol retailing; (d) insurance services; (e) compact discs?

12.3 GAME THEORY

As we have seen, the behaviour of a firm under non-collusive oligopoly depends, in part, on how it thinks its rivals will react to its decisions. When considering whether to cut prices in order to gain a larger market share, a firm will ask itself two key questions: first, how much it can get away with, without inciting retaliation; second, if its rivals do retaliate and a price-war ensues, whether it will be able to 'see off' some or all of its rivals, while surviving itself.

Economists use ***game theory*** to examine the best strategy a firm can adopt for each assumption about its rivals' behaviour.

Single-move games

The simplest type of 'game' is a single-move or single-period game, sometimes known as a normal-form game. This involves just one 'move' by each firm in the game. For example, two or more firms are bidding for a contract which will be awarded to the lowest bidder. When the bids are all made, the contract will be awarded to the lowest bidder; the 'game' is over.

Definition

Game theory (or the theory of games) The study of alternative strategies that oligopolists may choose to adopt, depending on their assumptions about their rivals' behaviour.

Simple dominant strategy games

Many single-period games have predictable outcomes, no matter what assumptions each firm makes about its rivals' behaviour. Such games are known as dominant strategy games. The simplest case is where there are just two firms with identical costs, products and demand. They are both considering which of two alternative prices to charge. Table 12.1 shows typical profits they could each make.

Let us assume that at present both firms (X and Y) are charging a price of £2 and that they are each making a profit of £10 million, giving a total industry profit of £20 million. This is shown in the top left-hand cell (A).

Now assume they are both (independently) considering reducing their price to £1.80. In making this decision, they will need to take into account what their rival might do, and how this will affect them. Let us consider X's position. In our simple example there are just two things that its rival, firm Y, might do. Either Y could cut its price to £1.80, or it could leave its price at £2. What should X do?

Table 12.1 Profits for firms X and Y at different prices

		X's price £2	X's price £1.80
Y's price	£2	**A** £10 m each	**B** £5 m for Y, £12 m for X
Y's price	£1.80	**C** £12 m for Y, £5 m for X	**D** £8 m each

One alternative is to go for the *cautious* approach and think of the worst thing that its rival could do. If X kept its price at £2, the worst thing for X would be if its rival Y cut its price. This is shown by cell C: X's profit falls to £5 million. If, however, X cut its price to £1.80, the worst outcome would again be for Y to cut its price, but this time X's profit only falls to £8 million. In this case, then, if X is cautious, it will *cut its price to £1.80*. Note that Y will argue along similar lines, and if it is cautious, it too will cut its price to £1.80. This policy of adopting the safer approach is known as ***maximin***. Following a maximin approach, the firm will opt for the alternative that will *max*imise its *min*imum possible profit.

An alternative is to go for the *optimistic* approach and assume that your rivals react in the way most favourable to you. Here the firm will go for the strategy that yields the highest possible profit. In X's case this will be again to cut price, only this time on the optimistic assumption that firm Y will leave its price unchanged. If firm X is correct in its assumption, it will move to cell B and achieve the maximum possible profit of £12 million. This approach of going for the maximum possible profit is known as ***maximax***. Note that again the same argument applies to Y. Its maximax strategy will be to cut price and hopefully end up in cell C.

Given that in this 'game' *both* approaches, maximin and maximax, lead to the *same* strategy (namely, cutting price), this is known as a ***dominant strategy game***. The result is that the firms will end up in cell D, earning a lower profit (£8 million each) than if they had charged the higher price (£10 million each in cell A).

As we saw, the equilibrium outcome of a game where there is no collusion between the players is known as a *Nash equilibrium*. The Nash equilibrium in this game is cell D.

KEY IDEA 24

***Nash equilibrium*. The position resulting from everyone making their optimal decision based on their assumptions about their rivals' decisions. Without collusion, there is no incentive for any firm to move from this position.**

In our example, collusion rather than a price war would have benefited both firms. Yet, even if they did collude, both would be tempted to cheat, or renege, on the agreement and cut prices. This is known as the ***prisoners' dilemma*** (see Box 12.3).

More complex games with no dominant strategy

More complex 'games' can be devised with more than two firms, many alternative prices, differentiated products and various forms of non-price competition (e.g. advertising). In such cases, the cautious (maximin) strategy may suggest a different policy (e.g. do nothing) from the high-risk (maximax) strategy (e.g. cut prices substantially).

In many situations, firms will have a number of different options open to them and a number of possible reactions by rivals. In such cases, the choices facing firms may be many. They may opt for a compromise strategy between maximax and maximin. This could be a strategy that is more risky than the maximin one, but with the chance of a higher profit; but not as risky as the maximax one, but where the maximum profit possible is not so high.

Multiple-move games

In many situations, firms will *react* to what their rivals do; their rivals, in turn, will react to what they do. In other words, the game moves back and forth from one 'player' to the other like a game of chess or cards. Firms will still have to think strategically (as you do in chess), considering the likely responses of their rivals to their own actions. These multiple-move games are known as *repeated games* or *extensive-form games*.

One of the simplest repeated games is the ***tit-for-tat***. This is where a firm will cut prices, or make some other aggressive move, *only* if the rival does so first. To illustrate this in a multiple-move situation let us look again at the example

Definitions

Maximin The strategy of choosing the policy whose worst possible outcome is the least bad.

Maximax The strategy of choosing the policy which has the best possible outcome.

Dominant strategy game Where different assumptions about rivals' behaviour lead to the adoption of the same strategy.

Prisoners' dilemma Where two or more firms (or people), by attempting independently to choose the best strategy, based upon what other(s) are likely to do, end up in a worse position than if they had cooperated from the start.

Tit-for-tat Where a firm will cut prices, or make some other aggressive move, *only* if the rival does so first. If the rival knows this, it will be less likely to make an initial aggressive move.

we considered in Table 12.1, but this time we will extend it beyond one time period.

Assume that firm X is adopting the tit-for-tat strategy. If firm Y cuts its price from £2.00 to £1.80, then firm X will respond in round 2 by also cutting its price. The two firms will end up in cell D – worse off than if neither had cut their price. If, however, firm Y had left its price at £2.00 then firm X would respond by leaving its price unchanged too. Both firms would remain in cell A with a higher profit than cell D.

As long as firm Y knows that firm X will respond in this way, it has an incentive not to cut its price. Thus it is in X's interests to make sure that Y clearly 'understands' how X will react to any price cut. To do this X can make a threat.

The importance of threats and promises

In many situations, an oligopolist will make a threat or promise that it will act in a certain way. As long as the threat or promise is ***credible*** (i.e. its competitors believe it), the firm can gain and it will influence its rivals' behaviour.

Take the simple situation where a large oil company, such as Esso, states that it will match the price charged by

> **Definition**
>
> **Credible threat (or promise)** One that is believable to rivals because it is in the threatener's interests to carry it out.

BOX 12.3 THE PRISONERS' DILEMMA

Game theory is relevant not just to economics. A famous non-economic example is the prisoners' dilemma.

Nigel and Amanda have been arrested for a joint crime of serious fraud. They are both guilty. Each is interviewed separately and given the following alternatives:

- First, if they say nothing, the court has enough evidence to sentence both to a year's imprisonment.
- Second, if either Nigel or Amanda alone confesses, he or she is likely to get only a three-month sentence but the partner could get up to ten years.
- Third, if both confess, they are likely to get three years each.

What should Nigel and Amanda do?

Let us consider Nigel's dilemma. Should he confess in order to get the short sentence (the maximax strategy)? This is better than the year he would get for not confessing. There is, however, an even better reason for confessing. Suppose Nigel doesn't confess but, unknown to him, Amanda does confess. Then Nigel ends up with the long sentence. Better than this is to confess and to get no more than three years: this is the safest (maximin) strategy.

Amanda is in the same dilemma. The result is simple. When both prisoners act selfishly by confessing, they both end up in position D with relatively long prison terms. Only when they collude will they end up in position A with relatively short prison terms, the best combined solution.

		Amanda's alternatives: Not confess	Amanda's alternatives: Confess
Nigel's alternatives	Not confess	**A** Each gets 1 year	**B** Nigel gets 10 years Amanda gets 3 months
	Confess	**C** Nigel gets 3 months Amanda gets 10 years	**D** Each gets 3 years

Of course the police know this and will do their best to prevent any collusion. They will keep Nigel and Amanda in separate cells and try to persuade each of them that the other is bound to confess.

Thus the choice of strategy depends on:

- Nigel's and Amanda's risk attitudes: i.e. are they 'risk lovers' or 'risk averse'?
- Nigel's and Amanda's estimates of how likely the other is to own up.

?
1. *Why is this a dominant strategy game?*
2. *How would Nigel's choice of strategy be affected if he had instead been involved in a joint crime with Adam, Ashok, Diana and Rikki, and they had all been caught?*

Let us now look at two real-world examples of the prisoners' dilemma.

Standing at concerts

When people go to some public event, such as a concert or a match, they often stand in order to get a better view. But once people start standing, everyone is likely to do so: after all, if they stayed sitting, they would not see at all. In this Nash equilibrium, most people are worse off, since, except for tall people, their view is likely to be worse and they lose the comfort of sitting down.

Too much advertising

Why do firms spend so much on advertising? If they are aggressive, they do so to get ahead of their rivals (the maximax approach). If they are cautious, they do so in case their rivals increase their advertising (the maximin approach). Although in both cases it may be in the individual firm's best interests to increase advertising, the resulting Nash equilibrium is likely to be one of excessive advertising: the total spent on advertising (by all firms) is not recouped in additional sales.

?
Give one or two other examples (economic or non-economic) of the prisoners' dilemma.

Figure 12.7 A decision tree

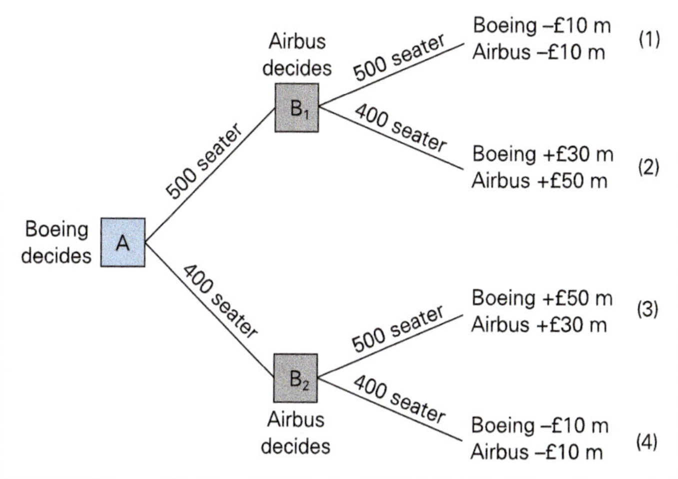

any competitor within a given radius. Assume that competitors believe this 'price promise' but also that Esso will not try to *undercut* their price. In the simple situation where there is only one other filling station in the area, what price should it charge? Clearly it should charge the price which would maximise its profits, assuming that Esso will charge the *same* price. In the absence of other filling stations in the area, this is likely to be a relatively high price.

Now assume that there are several filling stations in the area. What should the company do now? Its best choice is probably to charge the same price as Esso and hope that no other company charges a lower price and forces Esso to cut its price. Assuming that Esso's threat is credible, other companies are likely to reason in a similar way. Hence Esso's credible threat has the effect of keeping fuel prices high.

Pause for thought

Assume that there are two major oil companies operating filling stations in an area. The first promises to match the other's prices. The other promises to sell at 1p per litre cheaper than the first. Describe the likely sequence of events in this 'game' and the likely eventual outcome. Could the promise of the second company be seen as credible?

The importance of timing

Most decisions by oligopolists are made by one firm at a time rather than simultaneously by all firms. Sometimes a firm will take the initiative. At other times it will respond to decisions taken by other firms.

Take the case of a new generation of large passenger aircraft which can fly further without refuelling. Assume that there is a market for a 500-seater version of this type of aircraft and a 400-seater version, but that the individual markets for each aircraft are not big enough for the two manufacturers, Boeing and Airbus, to share them profitably. Let us also assume that the 400-seater market would give an annual profit of £50 million to a single manufacturer and the 500-seater would give an annual profit of £30 million, but that if both manufacturers produced the same version, they would each make an annual loss of £10 million.

Assume that Boeing announces that it is building the 400-seater plane. What should Airbus do? The choice is illustrated in Figure 12.7. This diagram is called a ***decision tree*** and shows the sequence of events. The small square at the left of the diagram is Boeing's decision point (point A). If it had decided to build the 500-seater plane, we would move up the top branch. Airbus would now have to make a decision (point B_1). If it too built the 500-seater plane, we would move to outcome 1: a loss of £10 million for both manufacturers. Clearly, with Boeing building a 500-seater plane, Airbus would choose the 400-seater plane: we would move to outcome 2, with Boeing making a profit of £30 million and Airbus a profit £50 million. Airbus would be very pleased!

Boeing's best strategy at point A, however, would be to build the 400-seater plane. We would then move to Airbus's decision point B_2. In this case, it is in Airbus's interests to build the 500-seater plane. Its profit would be only £30 million (outcome 3), but this is better than a £10 million loss if it too built the 400-seater plane (outcome 4). With Boeing deciding first, the Nash equilibrium will thus be outcome 3. KI 24 p 189

Definition

Decision tree (or game tree) A diagram showing the sequence of possible decisions by competitor firms and the outcome of each combination of decisions.

There is clearly a ***first-mover advantage*** here. Once Boeing has decided to build the more profitable version of the plane, Airbus is forced to build the less profitable one. Naturally, Airbus would like to build the more profitable one and be the first mover. Which company succeeds in going first depends on how advanced they are in their research and development and in their production capacity.

More complex decision trees. The aircraft example is the simplest version of a decision tree, with just two companies and each one making only one key decision. In many business situations, much more complex trees could be constructed. The 'game' would be more like one of chess, with many moves and several options on each move. If there were more than two companies, the decision tree would be more complex still.

Pause for thought

Give an example of decisions that two firms could make in sequence, each one affecting the other's next decision.

The usefulness of game theory

The advantage of the game-theory approach is that the firm does not need to know which response its rivals will make. It does, however, need to be able to measure the effect of each possible response. This will be virtually impossible to do when there are many firms competing and many different responses that could be made. The approach is only useful, therefore, in relatively simple cases, and even here the estimates of profit from each outcome may amount to no more than a rough guess.

It is thus difficult for an economist to predict with any accuracy what price, output and level of advertising the firm will choose. This problem is compounded by the difficulty of predicting the type of strategy – safe, high risk, compromise – that the firm will adopt.

In some cases, firms may compete hard for a time (in price or non-price terms) and then realise that maybe no one is winning. Firms may then jointly raise prices and reduce advertising. Later, after a period of tacit collusion, competition may break out again. This may be sparked off by the entry of a new firm, by the development of a new product design, by a change in market demand, or simply by one or more firms no longer being able to resist the temptation to 'cheat'. In short, the behaviour of particular oligopolists may change quite radically over time.

Definition

First-mover advantage When a firm gains from being the first one to take action.

SUMMARY

1a Monopolistic competition occurs where there is free entry to the industry and quite a large number of firms operating independently of each other, but where each firm has some market power as a result of producing differentiated products or services.

1b In the short run, firms can make supernormal profits. In the long run, however, freedom of entry will drive profits down to the normal level. The long-run equilibrium of the firm is where the (downward-sloping) demand curve is tangential to the long-run average cost curve.

1c The long-run equilibrium is one of excess capacity. Given that the demand curve is downward sloping, its tangency point with the *LRAC* curve will not be at the bottom of the *LRAC* curve. Increased production would thus be possible at *lower* average cost.

1d In practice, supernormal profits may persist into the long run: firms have imperfect information; entry may not be completely unrestricted; there may be a problem of indivisibilities; firms may use non-price competition to maintain an advantage over their rivals.

1e Monopolistically competitive firms, because of excess capacity, may have higher costs, and thus higher prices, than perfectly competitive firms, but consumers may gain from a greater diversity of products.

1f Monopolistically competitive firms may have less economies of scale than monopolies and conduct less research and development, but the competition may keep prices lower than under monopoly. Whether there will be more or less choice for the consumer is debatable.

2a An oligopoly is where there are just a few firms in the industry with barriers to the entry of new firms. Firms recognise their mutual dependence.

2b Oligopolists will want to maximise their joint profits. This will tend to make them collude to keep prices high. On the other hand, they will want the biggest share of industry profits for themselves. This will tend to make them compete.

2c They are more likely to collude: if there are few of them; if they are open with each other; if they have similar products and cost structures; if there is a dominant firm; if there are significant entry barriers; if the market is stable; and if there is no government legislation to prevent collusion.

2d Collusion can be open or tacit.

2e A formal collusive agreement is called a 'cartel'. A cartel aims to act as a monopoly. It can set the price and leave the members to compete for market share, or it can assign quotas. There is always a temptation for cartel members to 'cheat' by undercutting the cartel price if they think they can get away with it and not trigger a price war.

2f Tacit collusion can take the form of price leadership. This is where firms follow the price set by either a dominant firm in the industry or one seen as a reliable 'barometer' of market conditions. Alternatively, tacit collusion can simply involve following various rules of thumb such as average cost pricing and benchmark pricing.

2g Even when firms do not collude they will still have to take into account their rivals' behaviour. In the Cournot model, firms assume that their rivals' output is given and then choose the profit-maximising price and output in the light of this assumption. The resulting price and profit are lower than under monopoly, but still higher than under perfect competition. In the Bertrand model, firms assume that their rivals' price is given. This will result in prices being competed down until only normal profits remain.

2h In the kinked-demand curve model, firms are likely to keep their prices stable unless there is a large shift in costs or demand.

2i Non-collusive oligopolists will have to work out a price strategy. This will depend on their attitudes towards risk and on the assumptions they make about the behaviour of their rivals.

2j Whether consumers benefit from oligopoly depends on: the particular oligopoly and how competitive it is; whether there is any countervailing power; whether the firms engage in extensive advertising and of what type; whether product differentiation results in a wide range of choice for the consumer; how much of the profits are ploughed back into research and development; and how contestable the market is. Since these conditions vary substantially from oligopoly to oligopoly, it is impossible to state just how well or how badly oligopoly in general serves the consumer's interest.

3a Game theory is a way of modelling behaviour in strategic situations where the outcome for an individual or firm depends on the choices made by others. Thus game theory examines various strategies that firms can adopt when the outcome of each is not certain.

3b The simplest type of 'game' is a single-move or single-period game, sometimes known as a normal-form game. Many single-period games have predictable outcomes, no matter what assumptions each firm makes about its rivals' behaviour. Such games are known as dominant strategy games.

3c Non-collusive oligopolists will have to work out a price strategy. They can adopt a low-risk 'maximin' strategy of choosing the policy that has the least-bad worst outcome, or a high-risk 'maximax' strategy of choosing the policy with the best possible outcome, or some compromise. Either way, a 'Nash' equilibrium is likely to be reached which is not in the best interests of the firms collectively. It will entail a lower level of profit than if they had colluded.

3d In multiple-move games, play is passed from one 'player' to the other sequentially. Firms will respond not only to what firms do, but also to what they say they will do. To this end, a firm's threats or promises must be credible if they are to influence rivals' decisions.

3e A firm may gain a strategic advantage over its rivals by being the first one to take action (e.g. launch a new product). A decision tree can be constructed to show the possible sequence of moves in a multiple-move game.

REVIEW QUESTIONS

1. Think of ten different products or services and estimate roughly how many firms there are in the market. You will need to decide whether 'the market' is a local one, a national one or an international one. In what ways do the firms compete in each of the cases you have identified?
2. Imagine there are two types of potential customer for jam sold by a small food shop. One is the person who has just run out and wants some now. The other is the person who looks in the cupboard, sees that the pot of jam is less than half full and thinks, 'I will soon need some more.' How will the price elasticity of demand differ between these two customers?
3. Why may a food shop charge higher prices than supermarkets for 'essential items' and yet very similar prices for delicatessen items?
4. How will the position and shape of a firm's short-run demand curve depend on the prices that rivals charge?
5. Assuming that a firm under monopolistic competition can make supernormal profits in the short run, will there be any difference in the long-run and short-run elasticity of demand? Explain.
6. Firms under monopolistic competition generally have spare capacity. Does this imply that if, say, half of the petrol stations were closed down, the consumer would benefit? Explain.
7. Will competition between oligopolists always reduce total industry profits?
8. In which of the following industries is collusion likely to occur: bricks, beer, margarine, cement, crisps, washing powder, blank audio or video cassettes, carpets?
9. Draw a diagram like Figure 12.4. Illustrate what would happen if there were a rise in market demand.
10. Devise a box diagram like that in Table 12.1, only this time assume that there are three firms, each considering the two strategies of keeping price the same or reducing it by a set amount. Is the game still a 'dominant strategy game'?
11. What are the limitations of game theory in predicting oligopoly behaviour?
12. Which of the following are examples of effective countervailing power?
    (a) A power station buying coal from a large local coal mine.
    (b) A large factory hiring a photocopier from Rank Xerox.
    (c) Marks and Spencer buying clothes from a garment manufacturer.
    (d) A small village store (but the only one for miles around) buying food from a wholesaler.

    Is it the size of the purchasing firm that is important in determining its power to keep down the prices charged by its suppliers?

ADDITIONAL PART E CASE STUDIES IN THE *ECONOMICS FOR BUSINESS* MyEconLab (www.pearsoned.co.uk/sloman)

E.1 **Is perfect best?** An examination of the meaning of the word 'perfect' in perfect competition.

E.2 **B2B electronic marketplaces.** This case study examines the growth of firms trading with each other over the Internet (business to business or 'B2B') and considers the effects on competition.

E.3 **Measuring monopoly power.** An examination of how the degree of monopoly power possessed by a firm can be measured.

E.4 **X-inefficiency.** A type of inefficiency suffered by many large firms, resulting in a wasteful use of resources.

E.5 **Competition in the pipeline.** An examination of attempts to introduce competition into the gas industry in the UK.

E.6 **Airline deregulation in the USA and Europe.** Whether the deregulation of various routes has led to more competition and lower prices.

E.7 **The motor vehicle repair and servicing industry.** A case study of monopolistic competition.

E.8 **Bakeries: oligopoly or monopolistic competition.** A case study on the bread industry, showing that small-scale local bakeries can exist alongside giant national bakeries.

E.9 **Oligopoly in the brewing industry.** A case study showing how the UK brewing industry is becoming more concentrated.

E.10 **OPEC.** A case study examining OPEC's influence over oil prices from the early 1970s to the current day.

E.11 **Cut throat competition.** An examination of the barriers to entry to the UK razor market.

WEBSITES RELEVANT TO PART E

Numbers and sections refer to websites listed in the Web appendix and hotlinked from this book's website at **www.pearsoned.co.uk/sloman**

- For news articles relevant to Part E, see the Economics News Articles link from the book's website.
- For general news on companies and markets, see websites in section A, and particularly A1, 2, 3, 4, 5, 8, 9, 18, 23, 24, 25, 26, 35, 36. See also A38, 39 and 43 for links to newspapers worldwide; and A42 for links to economics news articles from newspapers worldwide.
- For sites that look at competition and market power, see B2; E4, 10, 18; G7, 8. See also links in I7, 11, 14 and 17. In particular see the following links in sites I7: Microeconomics > Competition and Monopoly.
- For a site on game theory, see A40 including its home page. See also D4; C20; I17 and 4 (in the EconDirectory section).

CHAPTER 1

Overview of International Business and Globalization

OBJECTIVES

After studying this chapter, you should be able to

1. Define *globalization* and *international business* and explain how they affect each other
2. Grasp why companies engage in international business and why its growth has accelerated
3. Discuss globalization's future and the major criticisms of it
4. Illustrate the different ways a company can accomplish its global objectives
5. Recognize the need to apply social science disciplines to understand how international and domestic business differ

© corocota - Fotolia.com

MyManagementLab®

Improve Your Grade!

When you see this icon, visit **www.mymanagementlab.com** for activities that are applied, personalized, and offer immediate feedback.

The world's a stage; each plays his part, and takes his share.

—Dutch proverb

CASE The Globalized Business of Sports

Sports may be the most globalized legitimate business in the world.[1] Historically, most players and teams in most sports have competed only on their own home turf; today, however, fans demand to see the best, and "best" has become a global standard. Satellite TV brings live events from just about anywhere in the world to fans just about anywhere else. This gives the key players in the sports-promotion business—team owners, league representatives, and sports associations—broadened audience exposure, expanded fan bases, and augmented revenues, especially through advertising that cuts across national borders.

Nevertheless, competition among teams sponsored by national sports federations goes back more than a century, most notably the World Cup in football (soccer) and the Olympics. More national organizations participate in these events than there are countries in the United Nations. And probably more people follow these competitions than follow most of the goings-on at the UN. In fact, you were likely part of the record global television audience for at least some of the 2010 World Cup in South Africa and the 2012 Summer Olympics games in London. (The chapter's opening photo shows Wenlock, the London games' mascot, dressed as a Queen's Guard. Hundreds of thousands of stuffed mascot toys were made in China and shipped to the games.)

How do these international competitions relate to business? Cities and countries compete to host the events in order to attract tourists and publicize to the world (especially potential investors) the opportunities that might exist for business. In turn, global companies pay for marketing rights as sponsors, such as the $957 million paid by eleven companies for the London Olympics. For instance, Coca-Cola's Facebook page enabled millions of Facebook visitors from dozens of countries to upload videos dealing with the games. Finally, individual athletes compete not only for medals, but also for lucrative contracts to endorse products. Michael Phelps' swimming successes have led to contracts with Visa, Omega, Hilton, Procter & Gamble, Under Armour, Subway, and HP.

While the participation in the Olympics and the World Cup has long been global, the location of competition has been less so, largely because of the cost of staging the events. This is now changing. The 2010 World Cup was the first in Africa. The first South American Olympics is scheduled for Brazil in 2016, and the first Middle East World Cup is slated for Qatar in 2022.

THE INTERNATIONAL JOB MARKET

Because more fans expect to see the world's best teams and players, the search for talent has become worldwide. You can now find U.S. and European professional basketball scouts in remote areas of Nigeria looking for tall high-potential youngsters. Baseball agents have opened live-in training camps for teenagers in the Dominican Republic in exchange for a percentage of any of their future professional signing bonuses. Keep in mind, though, that assembling talent is necessary but insufficient for making a sports business successful. Shrewd marketing and financial management are crucial too. For instance, the Barcelona football club, arguably the best professional soccer team in recent years, has turned to young business graduates to help turn around its financial problems.

Most of today's top-notch athletes are willing to follow the money wherever it may take them. For example, many of the best Brazilian soccer players are with European teams that offer much higher payrolls than their Brazilian counterparts. England's professional soccer league (Premiership) includes players from about 70 countries, which helps improve the caliber of play and increase the TV fan base outside England.

How the ATP Courts Worldwide Support

If you're a fan of individual sports, you've probably noticed that players are globe hoppers. Take tennis. No single country boasts enough interested fans to keep players at home for year-round competition, yet today's top-flight tennis pros come from every continent except Antarctica. For 2013, the Association of Tennis Professionals (ATP) sanctioned 64 tournaments in 31 countries. It also requires member pros to play in a certain number of events—and thus stop over in a number of countries—to maintain international rankings.

Because no tennis pro can possibly play in every tournament, organizers must attract enough top draws to fill stadium seats and land lucrative TV contracts. So tournaments compete for top-billed stars, not only with other tournaments but also with such regular international showcases as the Olympics and the Davis Cup. Prizes for two weeks' worth of expert serving and volleying can be extremely generous (about US $2.55 million for the 2013 singles champions of the Australian Open).

Remember, too, that tournaments earn money through ticket sales, corporate sponsorship agreements, television contracts, and leasing of advertising space. The more people in the stadium and TV audience, the more sponsors and

MAP 1.1 Examples of National Sports

Some 33 countries have either defined a national sport by law or de facto have a national sport. Some national sports are shared by more than one country, such as cricket by six former British colonies in the Caribbean. Some others have been established to protect an historical heritage, such as tejo in Colombia. Note also that Canada has two designations, one for winter and one for summer.

Source: The information on sports was taken from Wikipedia, http://en.wikipedia.org/wiki/National_sport (accessed January 30, 2013)

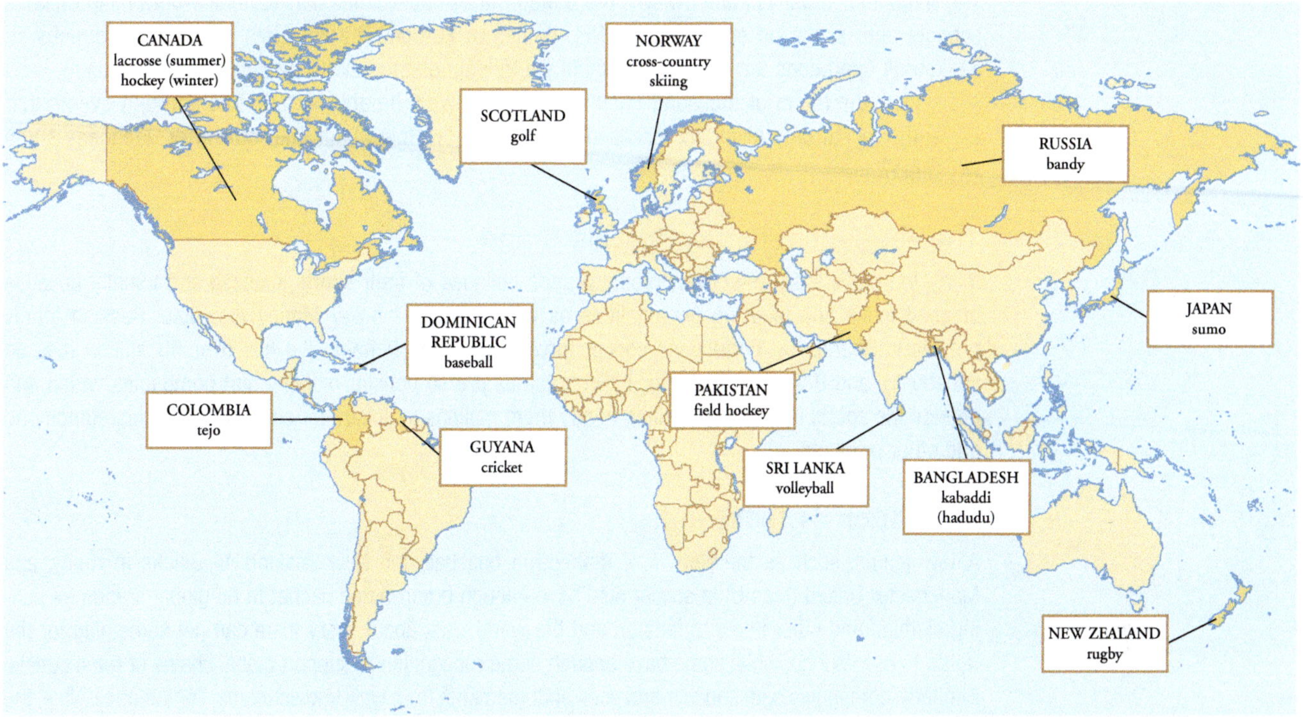

advertisers will pay to get their attention. Moreover, international broadcasts attract sponsorship from international companies. The partner and sponsor list for the 2013 Australian Open tennis tournament included a South Korean automaker (Kia), a Dutch brewer (Heineken), a Swiss watchmaker (Rolex), a French clothing company (Lacoste), and a U.S. sporting goods firm (Wilson). Such sponsorship of world-watched sporting events generally pays off in a higher market growth rate.

From National to International Sports Pastimes

Some countries have legally designated a national sport as a means of preserving traditions; others effectively have one. Map 1.1 shows a sample of these. However, other sports have sometimes replaced national sports in popularity, such as cricket replacing field hockey as India's most popular sport.

The International Baseball Federation now has over 100 member countries, even though baseball was popular only in its North American birthplace for most of its history. As TV revenues flattened in North America, Major League Baseball (MLB) began broadcasting games to international audiences. Increased exposure not only broadened the global fan base, it also showed youngsters all over the world how the game was played. As late as 1986, only 14 percent of MLB players were born outside the United States; by 2013, that number had climbed to over 28 percent. The average MLB clubhouse is now a bastion of multilingual camaraderie, with players and coaches talking baseball in Spanish, Japanese, Mandarin, and Korean as well as English.

THE WIDE WORLD OF TELEVISED SPORTS

Not surprisingly, other professional sports groups have expanded their global TV coverage (and marketing programs). Most viewers of Stanley Cup hockey watch from outside North America. Fans watch NASCAR races (National Association for Stock Car Auto Racing) in more than 120 countries and NBA games in about 200. If you lived in Tunisia and enjoyed simultaneous access to multiple TV channels, you could watch more hours of NBA action than there are hours in the year.

TV isn't the only means by which sports organizations are seeking foreign fan bases and players. The National Football League (NFL) of the United States underwrites flag-football programs in Chinese schools and is playing some regular NFL games in Europe. The NBA has appointed a director of basketball operations for India to help build youth leagues there. With the growth of broadband, we'll soon enter the realm of thousand-channel TV, where we'll be able to tune into sporting events that currently appeal only to highly localized niche markets. How about Thai boxing or Japanese sumo wrestling?

The Top-Notch Pro as Upscale Brand

Many top players are effectively global brands because of their sports success and usually because of good looks and pleasing personalities as well. Philippine boxer Manny Pacquiao, Russian tennis pro Maria Sharapova, Portuguese soccer forward Cristiano Ronaldo (he has over 50 million fans on Facebook), and U.S. basketball star LeBron James are so popular globally that companies within and outside the sports industry are willing to pay them millions of dollars for endorsing clothing, equipment, and other products.

Promotion as Teamwork

A few teams, such as the New York Yankees in baseball, the New Zealand All Blacks in rugby, and Manchester United (Man U) in soccer also have enough brand-name cachet to be global brands for selling clothing and other items to fans around the world. Just about every team can get something for the rights to use its logo, while some have enough name recognition to support global chains of retail outlets. Similarly, companies both sponsor and seek endorsements from well-known teams. For instance, Nike, the U.S. sports shoes and apparel giant, has fought hard to become the top sportswear and equipment supplier to European soccer teams. The success of this campaign has stimulated Nike's international sales to become greater than those in the United States.

Many nonsports companies, such as Canon (cameras, office equipment), Sharp (consumer electronics), and Carlsberg (beer), sponsor teams mainly to get corporate logos emblazoned on uniforms. Still others, such as United Airlines in Chicago, pay for the naming rights to arenas and other venues. Of course, teams themselves can be attractive international investments. For instance, the owners of the Boston Red Sox baseball team (U.S.A.) bought the Liverpool Football Club of the United Kingdom.

Sports and You

What does all this mean to you as a sports fan? Chances are you fantasized at one time about going pro in some sport, but you've probably given up that fantasy and settled into the role of spectator. Now that pro sports has become a global phenomenon (thanks to better communications), you can enjoy a greater variety—and a higher level of competition—than any generation before you.

That's the upside, but we must point out that people don't always take easily to another country's sport. Despite many efforts, cricket, although popular in countries that were British colonies for centuries, has never become popular elsewhere. (In post-colonial United States, it was popular, but it gradually gave way to baseball.) Nor has American football gained much popularity outside the United States. A former NFL lineman expressed a reason: that rules for cricket and American football are so complicated that one must learn them as children. However, basketball and soccer have traveled to new markets more readily because they are easier to understand and require no specialized equipment.

Further, there is disagreement about the economic effect of successfully winning a bid to host big international competitions such as the World Cup and Olympics. On the one hand, they help spur tourism, foreign investment, and infrastructure construction, and improvement of blighted areas that will speed future economic growth. (The cost of building facilities for the 2012 London Olympics was about $15 billion.) On the other hand, in light of threats from global terrorism the cost of security has skyrocketed, while hosts may have to spend on stadiums and facilities that have no use afterward. Many competitions have ended with substantially increased local and national debt.

Nor is everyone happy with the unbridled globalization of sports—or at least with some of the effects. Brazilian soccer fans lament the loss of their best players, and French fans protested the purchase of the Paris Saint-Germain (PSG) football club by the Qatar Investment Authority. ■

CRN
Case Review Note

QUESTIONS

1-1. Professional athlete A is a star, and professional athlete B is an average player. How has the globalization of professional sports affected each of these both positively and negatively?

1-2. As you read the chapter, identify and show an example of each international mode of operations that is illustrated in the globalization of professional sports.

INTRODUCTION

International business consists of all commercial transactions between two or more countries.

- The goal of private business is to make profits.
- Government business may or may not be motivated by profit.

Globalization refers to the widening set of interdependent relationships among people from different parts of a world that happens to be divided into nations. The term sometimes refers to the elimination of barriers to international movements of goods, services, capital, technology, and people that influence the integration of world economies.[2] Throughout history, wider human connections have expanded people's access to more varied resources, products, services, and markets. We've altered the way we want and expect to live, and we've become more deeply affected (positively and negatively) by conditions outside our immediate domains.

The opening case shows how far-flung global contact allows the world's best sports talent to compete, and their fans to watch them, just about anywhere. Likewise, managers in almost every industry consider ever more distant places as sources of supplies and markets. As consumers we know from "Made in" labels that we commonly buy products from all over the world, but these labels do not tell us everything. So many different components, ingredients, and specialized business activities from different countries go into products that it's often a challenge to say exactly where they were made. Belgium is renowned for its chocolate, but a Belgian Neuhaus bonbon includes ingredients from the Ivory Coast, Philippines, Ecuador, São Tomé, and Venezuela.[3] Because Apple ships its iPhones from China, they appear to be Chinese products, but less than 4 percent of their value is created in China.[4]

HOW DOES *INTERNATIONAL BUSINESS* FIT IN?

Studying international business is important because

- Most companies either are international or compete with international companies.
- Modes of operations may differ from those used domestically.
- The best way of conducting business may differ by country.
- An understanding helps you make better career decisions.
- An understanding helps you decide what governmental policies to support.

Globalization enables us to get more variety, better quality, or lower prices. Our daily meals contain spices that aren't grown domestically and fresh produce that's out of season in one local climate or another. Our cars cost less than they would if all the parts were made and the labor performed in one place. All of these connections between supplies and markets result from the activities of **international business,** defined as all commercial transactions, including sales, investments, and transportation, that take place between two or more countries. Private companies undertake such transactions for profit; governments may undertake them either for profit or for other reasons.

The Study of International Business Why should you study international business? Simply, it makes up a large and growing portion of the world's business. Global events and competition affect almost all companies, large and small, regardless of industry. They sell output and secure supplies and resources abroad, and they compete against products, services, and companies from foreign countries. Thus, most managers need to take into account

FIGURE 1.1 Factors in International Business Operations

The conduct of a company's international operations depends on two factors: its objectives and the means by which it intends to achieve them. Likewise, its operations affect, and are affected by, two sets of factors: physical/social and competitive.

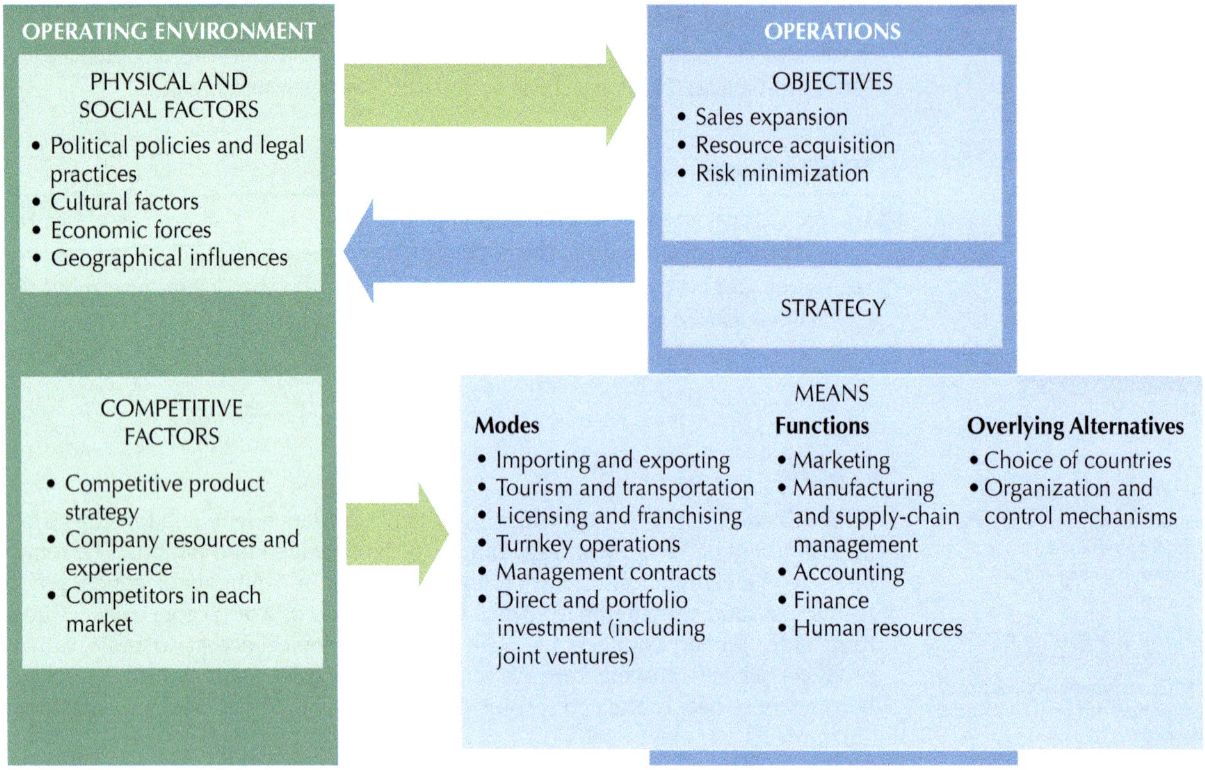

CRN Case Review Note

international business when setting their operating strategies and practices. Like the NBA teams in the opening case, which search globally for talent and additional markets, as a manager in almost any industry you'll need to consider (1) where you can obtain the best required inputs at the best possible price and (2) where you can best sell the product or service you've put together from those inputs.

Understanding the Environment/Operations Relationship The best way to do business abroad may not be the same as the best way at home. Why? First, when your company operates internationally, it will engage in *modes* of business, such as exporting and importing, which differ from those it uses domestically. Second, physical, social, and competitive conditions differ among countries and affect the optimum ways to conduct business. Thus, international companies have more diverse and complex operating environments than purely domestic ones. Figure 1.1 outlines the set of relationships between international environments and operations.

Even if you never have direct international business responsibilities, understanding some of the complexities may be useful to you. Companies' international operations and their governmental regulations affect overall national conditions—economic growth, employment, consumer prices, national security—as well as the success of individual industries and firms. A better understanding of international business will help you make more informed decisions, such as where you want to work and what governmental policies you want to support.

Globalization

- Has been growing.
- Is less pervasive than generally thought.
- Has economic and non-economic dimensions.
- Is stimulated by several factors.

THE FORCES DRIVING GLOBALIZATION

Measuring globalization is problematic, especially for historical comparisons. First, a country's interdependence must be measured indirectly.[5] Second, when national boundaries shift, such as in the breakup of the former Soviet Union or the reunification of East and West

Germany, domestic business transactions can become international ones and vice versa. Nevertheless, various reliable indicators assure us that economic interdependence has been increasing, at least since the mid-twentieth century. Currently, about 25 percent of world production is sold outside its country of origin, compared to about 7 percent in 1950. Restrictions on imports have generally been decreasing, and output from foreign-owned investments as a percentage of world production has increased. In periods of rapid economic growth, such as most years since World War II, world trade grows more rapidly than world production. However, in recessionary periods, such as that which began in 2008, global trade and investment shrink even more than the global economy. In fact, the world was less connected economically in 2012 than in 2007.[6]

At the same time, however, globalization is less pervasive than you might suppose. In fact, many Americans find it hard to believe that only about 15 percent of the value of goods and services bought in the United States comes from other countries. In much of the world (especially in poor rural areas), people lack the resources to connect much beyond their isolated domains. Such isolation is changing quickly, though; witness Africa, where telephone connectivity has increased markedly since the advent of mobile phones.[7] Only a few countries—mainly very small ones—either sell over half their production abroad or depend on foreign output for more than half their consumption. This means that most of the world's goods and services are still sold in the countries in which they're produced. Moreover, the principal source of capital in most countries is domestic rather than international.

Granted, these measurements address only *economic* aspects of global interdependence. Various studies have made more comprehensive comparisons by including, say, people-to-people contacts through travel and communications, technological interchanges, government-to-government relationships, and acceptance and adaptation of attributes from foreign cultures such as words from other languages.[8] Despite these ranking differences, the studies' results have several commonalities:

- *Size of countries*—Smaller countries tend to be more globalized than larger ones, mainly because their smaller land masses and populations permit a lower variety of production.
- *Income of the countries' populations*—Countries with higher-income populations tend to be more globalized than those with lower-income populations because their citizens can better afford foreign products, travel, and communications with people they have met abroad.
- *Variance among globalization aspects*—Although a country may rank as highly globalized on one dimension, it may be low on another, such as the United States being high on technological scales but low on economic ones.

FACTORS IN INCREASED GLOBALIZATION

What factors have contributed to the growth of globalization in recent decades? Most analysts cite the following seven factors:

1. Increase in and application of technology
2. Liberalization of cross-border trade and resource movements
3. Development of services that support international business
4. Growth of consumer pressures
5. Increase in global competition
6. Changes in political situations and government policies
7. Expansion of cross-national cooperation

Of course, these factors are interrelated, and each deserves a closer look.

Increase in and Application of Technology Many of the proverbial "modern marvels" and efficient means of production have come about from fairly recent technical advances. These include new products, such as hand-held mobile technology devices, as well as new applications of old products, such as guar beans from India now being used in oil and natural gas mining.[9] Thus, much of what we trade today either did not exist or was unimportant in trade a decade or two ago. Why have technical developments increased so much? More than half the scientists who have ever lived are alive today. One reason, of course, is population growth. But another is rising productivity—taking fewer hours to produce the same thing—which frees up more people to *develop* new products because fewer people can *produce* them. This rising productivity also means that on average people can buy more, including the new products, by working the same number of hours. The entry of new products into the market creates a need for other complementary products (such as cases and apps for smart phones), thus accelerating the need for scientists and engineers.

Many new products, as well as new ways to produce old ones, cannot easily take place in a single country. Much new technical innovation takes so many financial and intellectual resources that companies must cooperate to take on portions of development. These efforts may necessitate collaboration among and dependence on firms in different countries that have financial resources and specialized capabilities. A noteworthy example of interdependent technology, and one you may have watched on worldwide TV transmission, was the 2010 rescue of Chilean miners. Success would have been unlikely without the innovations and products from a variety of countries: the Center Rock drill bit from the United States, a high-strength cable from Germany, a super-flexible fiber optics communications cable from Japan, and a special cell phone from South Korea.[10]

Once new products are developed, the optimum scale size of production seldom corresponds with the market demand in a single country. Consequently, companies may need to sell both domestically and internationally in order to spread the fixed developmental and production costs over more units of production.

Advances in Communications and Transportation Strides in communications and transportation now allow us to discover and desire products and services developed in far parts of the world. Meanwhile, the costs of these improvements have risen more slowly in most years than costs in general. A three-minute phone call from New York to London that cost $10.80 in 1970 costs less than $0.20 today, while a call using Voice over Internet Protocol (VoIP) is virtually free.

Innovations in transportation mean that more countries can compete for sales to a given market. The sale of foreign-grown flowers in the United States used to be impractical; today, however, flowers from as far away as Ecuador, Israel, the Netherlands, and New Zealand compete with each other for the U.S. market because growers can ship them quickly and economically.

CRN
Case Review Note

Or recall the opening case. Innovations allow individual athletes and teams to go head to head at venues around the world and sports media to broadcast competitions to fans everywhere. If it weren't for modern means of transportation and communications, a tennis pro couldn't play in Morocco right after finishing a tournament in Miami, and advertising wouldn't generate enough prize money to induce the pro to do all that traveling.

Improved communications and transportation also enhance a manager's ability to oversee foreign operations, such as more easily visiting foreign facilities and communicating with managers therein. Thanks to the Internet, companies can immediately exchange pictures of samples. Even small companies can reach global customers and suppliers. However, you may ponder the following question: Has the Internet been a bigger force in globalization than the laying of the first trans-oceanic cable across the Atlantic in 1858 that reduced communication time from 10 days to a matter of a few minutes?

Liberalization of Cross-Border Trade and Resource Movements To protect its own industries, every country restricts the movement across its borders of not only goods and services but also the resources—workers, capital, tools, and so on—needed to produce them. Such restrictions, of course, set limits on international business activities and, because regulations can change at any time, contribute to a climate of uncertainty. Over time, however, most governments have reduced such restrictions, primarily for three reasons:

1. Their citizens want a greater variety of goods and services at lower prices.
2. Competition spurs domestic producers to become more efficient.
3. They hope to induce other countries to lower their barriers in turn.

Services that Support International Business Companies and governments have developed a variety of services that facilitate global commerce. Take sales in a foreign country and currency. Today, because of bank credit agreements—clearing arrangements that convert one currency into another and insurance that covers such risks as nonpayment and damage en route—most producers can be paid relatively easily for goods and services sold abroad. When Nike sells sportswear to a French soccer team, a bank in France collects payment in euros from the soccer team when the shipment arrives at French customs (probably from somewhere in Asia) and pays Nike in U.S. dollars through a U.S. bank.

Growth in Consumer Pressures More consumers know more today about products and services available in other countries, can afford to buy them, and want the greater variety in quality, price, and characteristics that access to them offers. However, because greater affluence is spread unevenly, both among and within countries as well as from year to year, consumers' ability to avail themselves of this variety differs substantially. As a result, more companies are now responding to those markets where incomes and consumption are growing most rapidly, such as China.

Greater affluence has also spurred companies to spend more on research and development (R&D) and to search worldwide—via the Internet, industry journals, trade fairs, and trips abroad—for innovations and products they can sell to ever-more-demanding consumers. By the same token, consumers are more proficient today at scouring the globe for better deals, such as searching the Internet for lower-priced prescription drugs abroad.

Increase in Global Competition The present and potential pressures of increased foreign competition can persuade companies to buy or sell abroad. For example, a firm might introduce products into markets where competitors are already gaining sales, or seek supplies where competitors are getting cheaper or more attractive products or the means to produce them.

In recent years, many companies have merged or acquired operations to gain the efficiencies to better compete, such as the publishing merger between the Random House division of the German firm Bertelsman with the Penguin division of the U.K. firm Pearson, or to become large enough to compete with or become global leaders, such as the merger between the Brazilian chilled and frozen food firms Perdigão and Sadia.[11]

So-called **born-global companies** start out with a global focus because of their founders' international experience[12] and because advances in communications give them a good idea of where global markets and supplies are. Take SoundCloud, a Swedish audio-sharing Web service. Of its two co-founders, one was born in England and the other in Sweden. The two moved to Germany within months after the firm's start-up and soon broke into the U.S. market, where they also secured $50 million in financing.[13] Many new companies locate in areas with numerous competitors and suppliers, a situation known as **clustering** or **agglomeration.** They quickly observe how their competitors benefit from foreign opportunities. And because suppliers and human talent gravitate to these areas, they gain easier access to the resources needed for international moves.[14]

CRN
Case Review Note

Regardless of industry, most firms and individuals have to become more global; in today's competitive business environment, failure to do so can be disastrous. Once a few companies have responded to foreign opportunities, others inevitably follow suit. And they learn from each other's foreign experiences. As the opening case suggests, for example, the early success of foreign-born baseball players in U.S. leagues undoubtedly spurred U.S. basketball and football organizations to look for and develop talent abroad.[15]

Changes in Political Situations and Government Policies For nearly half a century after World War II, business between Communist countries and the rest of the world was minimal. Today, only a few countries do business almost entirely within a political bloc. In fact, political changes sometimes open new frontiers for international business, such as Myanmar's cessation of military rule that has influenced international companies to seek footholds there. Nevertheless, governments still prefer international business with certain countries and even deny such business with others for political reasons, such as many countries' sanctions against doing business with Iran because of its efforts to develop nuclear capabilities.

Governments seem more willing to support programs, such as improving airport and seaport facilities to foster speed and cost efficiencies for delivering goods internationally. They also now provide an array of services to help domestic companies sell more abroad, such as collecting information about foreign markets, furnishing contacts with potential buyers, and offering insurance against nonpayment in the home-country currency.

Expansion of Cross-National Cooperation Governments have come to realize that their own interests can be addressed through international cooperation by means of treaties, agreements, and consultation. The willingness to pursue such policies is due largely to these three needs:

1. To gain reciprocal advantages
2. To attack problems jointly that one country acting alone cannot solve
3. To deal with areas of concern that lie outside the territory of any nation

Gain Reciprocal Advantages Essentially, companies don't want to be at a disadvantage when operating internationally, so they petition their governments to act on their behalf. Thus, governments join international organizations and sign treaties and agreements for a variety of commercial activities.

Some treaties and agreements allow countries' commercial ships and planes to use certain of each others' seaports and airports. Some cover commercial-aircraft safety standards and flyover rights; some protect property, such as foreign-owned investments, patents, trademarks, and copyrights. Countries also enact treaties for reciprocal reductions of import restrictions (remaining prepared, of course, to retaliate when another party interferes with trade flows by raising trade barriers or cutting diplomatic ties).

Multinational Problem Solving Governments often act to coordinate activities along their mutual borders by building highways, railroads, and hydroelectric dams that serve the interests of all parties. The adjacent photo shows a dam between Brazil and Paraguay. (However, there are still border inefficiencies. For instance, trains between Italy and Sweden must change locomotives three or four times because of different national systems.)[16] They also cooperate to solve problems that they either cannot or will not solve by themselves. First, the resources needed to solve a problem may be too great for one country to manage; sometimes no single country is willing to pay for a project that will also benefit another country, as witnessed by Japan and the United States sharing the costs of ballistic-missile defense technology. In any case, many problems are inherently global—think of global climate change or nuclear proliferation—and can't be easily addressed by a single country. That's why cooperative efforts have developed to fight the spread of diseases such as malaria, to set warning systems against such natural disasters as tsunamis, and to take action on environmental problems such as global warming.

Second, one country's policies may affect those of others. Higher real-interest rates in one country, for example, can attract funds very quickly from individuals and firms in countries with lower rates, thus creating a shortage of investment funds in the latter. Similarly, a country may manipulate the value of its currency so that companies abandon suppliers in one country for those in another, with an undervalued currency thus contributing to unemployment in the abandoned country. To coordinate economic policies in these and other areas, the

The Itaipu Dam is a joint project between the governments of Brazil and Paraguay and is on the Parana River separating the two countries. It is the largest hydroelectric generating facility in the world, and its height is equivalent to a 65-story building.
Source: Shutterstock

most economically important countries meet regularly to share information and pool ideas. The most notable coordination, known as the Group of Twenty or G20 countries, consists of 19 of the world's most important countries plus representation from the European Union of its members not included in the 19. These countries account for over 80 percent of the world's production and trade as well as about two-thirds of the world's population. The adjacent photo shows representatives at a 2012 meeting in Mexico.

Areas Outside National Territories Three global areas belong to no single country: the noncoastal areas of the oceans, outer space, and Antarctica. Until their commercial viability was demonstrated, they excited little interest for either exploitation or multinational

The G20 (Group of 20) countries meet to discuss global conditions. Shown here at a 2012 meeting in Los Cabos, Mexico are the heads of state from the 19 member countries plus the European Union.
Source: epa european pressphoto agency b.v./Alamy

cooperation. The oceans, however, contain food and mineral resources and constitute the surface over which much international commerce passes. Today, we need agreements to specify the amounts and methods of fishing to be allowed, to address questions of oceanic mineral rights (such as on oil resources below the Arctic Ocean), and to deal with piracy of ships.

Likewise, there is disagreement on the commercial benefits to be reaped from outer space. Commercial satellites, for example, pass over countries that receive no direct benefit from them but argue that they should. If that sounds a little far-fetched, remember that countries do charge foreign airlines for flying over their territories.[17]

Antarctica, with minerals and abundant sea life along its coast, attracts thousands of tourists each year, has a highway leading to the South Pole, and has thus been the subject of agreements to limit commercial exploitation. However, there is still disagreement about the continent's development—how much there should be and who does it.

Much of the cooperation we've described has been undertaken by international organizations, which we discuss in more detail in later chapters, especially in Chapter 7.

THE COSTS OF GLOBALIZATION

Although we've discussed interrelated reasons for the rise in international business and globalization, remember that the consequences of the rise remain controversial. To thwart the globalization process, *antiglobalization* forces regularly protest international conferences and governmental policies—sometimes violently and sometimes by using instruments of globalization to make the protest. Figure 1.2 shows such a use of globalization humorously. We focus here on three issues: *threats to national sovereignty, environmental stress,* and *growing income inequality and personal stress.* We revisit these and others in more depth later; watch for them also in several of our Point-Counterpoint features.

FIGURE 1.2 Social networks are global by nature and are used to reach an ever expanding audience. The cartoon implies using globalization to stem globalization.
Source: Len Hawkins/CartoonStock

THREATS TO NATIONAL SOVEREIGNTY

Critics of globalization claim

- Countries' sovereignty is diminished.
- The resultant growth hurts the environment.
- Some people lose both relatively and absolutely.
- Greater insecurity increases personal stress.

You've probably heard the slogan "Think globally, act locally." In essence, it means that local interests should be accommodated before global ones. Some observers worry that the proliferation of international agreements, particularly those that undermine local restrictions on how goods are produced and sold, will diminish a nation's **sovereignty**—its freedom to "act locally" and without externally imposed restrictions.

The Question of Local Objectives and Policies Countries seek to fulfill their citizens' economic, political, and social objectives by setting rules reflecting national priorities, such as those governing worker protection and environmental practices. However, some critics argue that individual countries' priorities are undermined by opening borders to trade. For example, if a country has stringent regulations on labor conditions and requires clean production methods, cheaper production may occur in countries with less rigorous rules. The result, by opening borders to trade, may be that the strict country must either forgo its labor and environmental priorities to be competitive or face the downside of fewer jobs and economic output.

The Question of Small Economies' Overdependence In addition, critics say that small economies depend so much on larger ones for supplies and sales that they are vulnerable to foreign mandates, including everything from defending certain positions at the United Nations to supporting a large economy's foreign military or economic actions. Nobel economist George Akerlof has noted that consequences of this dependence are intensified by poor countries' inadequate administrative capacity to deal with globalization.[18] These countries are also concerned that large international corporations are powerful enough to dictate their operating terms (say, by threatening to relocate), exploit legal loopholes to avoid political oversight and taxes, and counter the small economies' best interests by favoring their home countries' political and economic interests.

The Question of Cultural Homogeneity Finally, critics charge that globalization homogenizes products, companies' work methods, social structures, and even language, thus undermining the cultural foundation of sovereignty. In essence, they argue that countries have difficulty maintaining the traditional ways of life that unify and differentiate their cultures. Recall in our opening case that despite countries' designation of national sports to maintain tradition, some are losing out to imported sports anyway. Fundamentally, many critics feel helpless when it comes to stopping the incursion of foreign influences by such means as satellite television, print media, and Internet sites.[19]

CRN
Case Review Note

ENVIRONMENTAL STRESS

Much criticism of globalization revolves around the economic growth it brings. According to one argument, growth consumes more nonrenewable natural resources and increases environmental damage—despoliation through toxic runoffs into rivers and oceans, air pollution from factory and vehicle emissions, and deforestation that can affect weather and climate. In addition, globalization opponents contend that by buying from more distant locations, the added transportation increases the *carbon footprint*, which refers to the total set of greenhouse gases emitted. They point further to the more than 1000 container ships plying the seas, each of which pollutes as much as 50 million cars do because of reliance on heavy oil as a fuel.[20]

The Argument for Global Growth and Global Cooperation Not everyone agrees with such a conclusion. Others argue that globalization has positive results for both sustaining natural resources and maintaining an environmentally sound planet. Global cooperation, they say, fosters superior and uniform standards for combating environmental problems, while global competition encourages companies to seek resource-saving and eco-friendly technologies, such as automobiles that use less gas and emit fewer pollutants.

The positive effects of pursuing global interests, however, may conflict with what a country's citizens think is best for themselves. Consider the effect of global pressure on Brazil to help protect the world's climate by curtailing logging activity in the Amazon region. Unemployed Brazilian workers have felt that job creation in the logging industry is more important than climate protection outside Brazil.

GROWING INCOME INEQUALITY AND PERSONAL STRESS

In measuring economic well-being, we not only look at our absolute situations but also compare ourselves to others. We generally don't find our economic status satisfactory unless we're doing better *and* keeping up with others.

Income Inequality By various measurements, income inequality, with some notable exceptions, has been growing both among and within a number of countries. Critics claim that globalization has affected this disparity by helping to develop a global superstar system, creating access to a greater supply of low-cost labor, and developing competition that leads to winners and losers.

The superstar system is especially apparent in sports, where global stars earn far more than the average professional player or professionals in sports with a more limited worldwide following. It also carries over to other professions, such as business, where charismatic top people can command many times what others can.

Although globalization has brought unprecedented opportunities for firms to profit by gaining more sales and cheaper or better supplies, critics argue that profits have gone disproportionately to the top executives rather than to the rank and file. Nobel economist Robert Solow supports this criticism by arguing that greater access to low-cost labor in poor countries has reduced the real wage growth of labor in rich countries.[21] And even if overall worldwide gains from globalization are positive, there are bound to be some losers in either an absolute or relative sense (who will probably become critics of globalization). The speed with which technology and competition expand globally affects the number of winners and losers along with the relative positions of individuals, companies, and countries. As an example, relocation of U.S. manufacturing jobs to China and India has helped the latter grow more rapidly than the United States, thus lessening the U.S.'s *relative* economic leadership over those countries.[22] Likewise, some displaced workers have lost economic and social standing relative to workers whose jobs were not moved. The challenge, therefore, is to maximize the gains from globalization while simultaneously minimizing the costs borne by the losers.

Personal Stress Certain repercussions of globalization can't be measured in strictly economic terms. What about the stress imposed on the people whose relative economic and social status suffers, or those who fear the loss of their jobs?[23] There is some evidence that the growth in globalization goes hand in hand not only with increased insecurity about job and social status but also with costly social unrest.[24] Further, although few of the world's problems are brand new, we may worry about them more now because globalized communications bring exotic sagas of misery into living rooms everywhere.[25]

Point

Is Offshoring Good Strategy?

Point **Yes** **Offshoring** is the dependence on production in a foreign country, usually by shifting from a domestic source. *If offshoring succeeds in reducing costs, it's good.* This is happening with many companies. Most branded clothing companies locate offshore to have work done by cheaper sewing machine operators. Many investment companies, such as Fidelity in India, are hiring back-office workers in poor countries to cut the cost of industry research. What good are cost savings? It's basic. If you can cut your costs, you can cut your prices or improve your product. Thus, by offshoring work to India, Claimpower, a small U.S. medical-insurance billing company, cut costs, lowered the prices it charges doctors, quadrupled its business in two years, and hired more U.S. employees because of the growth.[26]

What's the main complaint about offshoring? Too many domestic jobs end up abroad. As we discuss this, keep in mind that employment results from offshoring are difficult to isolate from other employment changes. Sure, unemployment in most high-income countries has increased substantially since 2008, but this was probably due mainly to improvements in production technology and the global recession. Let's try to pinpoint direct results of offshoring.

IBM is a good example. More than 70 percent of its nearly 400,000 employees are based outside the United States. By shipping some of its programming work abroad, IBM saves a tidy $40 an hour per worker—which comes out to $168 million a year.[27] If IBM failed to enact such cost savings, analysts agree that its competitors in low-wage countries, such as Infosys from India, could underprice IBM with competitive products and services.[28] Moreover, when you become price-competitive, you sell more both at home and abroad. You may also increase sales abroad if you locate near foreign customers. As you *create* jobs in this process, you improve your chances of survival.[29] IBM, for instance, is actually saving jobs by offshoring. Again, it's basic business: Cost savings generate growth, and growth creates more jobs.[30]

Not just any jobs, either: This process lets companies create more *high-value* jobs at home—the ones performed by people like managers and researchers, who draw high salaries. When that happens, demand for qualified people goes up. In the United States, that process has already resulted in a higher percentage of white-collar and professional employees in the workforce. These are *high-income* people, and more of them are employed as a result of sending *low-income* jobs to countries with lower labor costs.[31]

Further, offshoring is a natural extension of *outsourcing,* the process of companies' contracting work to other companies so that they can concentrate on what they do best.[32] This contributes to making a company more efficient. What is the difference, then, of outsourcing to a domestic versus a foreign location?

Admittedly, workers do get displaced from offshoring, but *aggregate* employment figures show that these workers find other jobs, just like workers who get displaced for other reasons. In a dynamic economy, people are constantly shifting jobs, partly due to technology. The prevailing employment for U.S. women was once as telephone operators; direct dialing technology changed that. Passenger aircraft used to carry five cockpit crew members; technology eliminated the need for the navigator, flight engineer, and radio operator. On the near-future horizon, pilotless passenger aircraft and package-carrying drone helicopters will reduce the cockpit crew to one or even zero,[33] while driverless cars will reduce demand for traffic policemen, auto insurers, emergency room personnel, and makers of such products as road signals and guard rails.[34]

What all this means is that the shifting of jobs is commonplace, and shifting because of outsourcing is no different from doing so for any other reason. In any case, because there are bound to be upper limits on the amount of outsourcing work a country can do, the direst predictions about job loss are exaggerated: There simply aren't enough unemployed people abroad who have the needed skills *and* who will work at a sufficiently low cost. Further, as production increases in outsourced facilities abroad, wage rates go up there.

Offshoring isn't for all companies or all types of operations. Some firms are bringing many operations *back* from abroad, a situation known as **reshoring**, because of such factors as poor quality, consumer pressure, concerns about competitive security, and advantages of locating production near technical development. In fact, about a fifth of the companies that have gone to offshoring now say that the savings are less than they expected.[35] That brings us back to what we said explicitly at the outset: Offshoring works when you cut operating costs *effectively.*

Is Offshoring Good Strategy?

Counterpoint

No Some things are good for some of the people some of the time, and that's *almost* the case with offshoring. Unfortunately, it is good for only a *few* people but not for *most.* I keep hearing about the cost savings, but when I buy goods or services I rarely find anything that's cheaper than it used to be. Whether buying a Ralph Lauren shirt, getting medical services from a doctor who is saving money through Claimpower, or having Fidelity manage my assets, I have seen no lower prices for me. Instead, the lower production costs have resulted in higher compensation for already high-paid employees and for shareholders. Further, Claimpower's growth had to be at the expense of other companies in the business, not because of growth in the number of people getting medical services but because of its price decreases.

One study took a close look at 16 high-income countries and found that, in aggregate, the percentage of national income going to labor has gone down while the percentage of national income going to profits is up.[36]

Here's a key problem: When you replace jobs by offshoring, you're exchanging *good* jobs for *bad* ones. Most of the workers who wind up with the short end of the offshoring stick struggled for decades to get reasonable work hours and a few basic benefits, such as healthcare and retirement plans. More important, their incomes allowed them to send their kids to college, and the result was an upwardly mobile—and productive—generation.

Now many of these employees have worked long and loyally for their employers and have little to show for it in the offshoring era. Yes, I know governments give them unemployment benefits but these never equal what the employees had before, and they run out.[37] On top of everything else, they may have no other usable skills, and at their ages, who's going to foot the bill for retraining them? The increase in what you call "high-value jobs" doesn't do *them* any good. Further, when *reshoring* occurs (usually because managers didn't think through the offshoring decision adequately in the first place), you can bet they re-hire domestic workers at less cost than before they offshored those jobs.

Offshoring may lead to short-term cost savings, but many studies indicate that it merely diverts companies' attention from taking steps to find innovative means of more efficient production, such as better operating techniques and machinery.[38] Concentrating on these latter alternatives may cut costs, increase production, and maintain the jobs that are going abroad.

While we're on the subject of job "value," what kinds of jobs *are* we creating in poor countries? Because countries are competing with lower wages, it encourages them to keep wages from rising, a sort of race to the bottom. However, multinational enterprises (MNEs) no doubt pay workers in low-wage countries more than they could get otherwise, and I'll grant that some of these jobs—the white-collar and technical jobs—are pretty good. But for most people, the hours are long, the working conditions are barbaric, and the pay is barely enough to survive. When you use such suppliers, your reputation can suffer. Recently in Bangladesh, workers were killed when locked doors prevented their escape from a fire, and others were killed when their ramshackle workplace building collapsed. There is also little job security. As salaries creep up where companies are offshoring, the companies merely move to even cheaper places to get the job done. For instance, this is what happened to workers in the island country of Mauritius. As soon as Mauritians began to think they might expect a better way of life, MNEs found workers elsewhere to do their sewing.[39]

Admittedly, in a dynamic economy, people have to change jobs more often than they would in a stagnant economy—*but not to the extent caused by offshoring.* There's still some disagreement about the effects of offshoring on a country's employment rate. Researchers are looking into the issue, but what they're finding is that more of the so-called better jobs are also being outsourced. A study of 4,700 major U.S. and European organizations showed that 750,000 finance, IT, and other high-level jobs will be offshored between 2012 and 2016.[40] So are we really creating higher-level jobs at home? Here's the bottom line: In countries like the United States, workers simply aren't equipped to handle the pace of change when it means that jobs can be exported faster than the average worker can retrain for different skills.

WHY COMPANIES ENGAGE IN INTERNATIONAL BUSINESS

Let's now focus on some of the specific ways firms can create value by going global. Take another look at Figure 1.1, where you'll see three major operating objectives that underlie the reasons for engaging in international business:

- Expanding sales
- Acquiring resources
- Reducing risk

Normally, these three objectives guide all decisions about whether, where, and how to engage in international business. Let's examine each in more detail.

EXPANDING SALES

Pursuing international sales usually increases the potential market and potential profits.

CRN Case Review Note

A company's sales depend on the desire and ability of consumers to buy its goods or services. Obviously, there are more potential consumers in the world than found in any single country. Now, higher sales ordinarily create value, but only if the costs of making the additional sales don't increase disproportionately. Recall, for instance, the opening case. Televising sports competitions to multiple countries generates advertising revenue in excess of the increased transmission costs. In fact, additional sales from abroad may enable a company to reduce its per-unit costs by covering its fixed costs—say, up-front research costs—over a larger number of sales. Because of lower unit costs, it can boost sales even more.

So increased sales are a major motive for expanding into international markets, and many of the world's largest companies—such as Volkswagen (Germany), Ericsson (Sweden), IBM (United States), Michelin (France), Nestlé (Switzerland), and Sony (Japan)—derive more than half their sales outside their home countries. Bear in mind, though, that international business is not the purview only of large companies. In the United States, 97 percent of exporters are small and mid-sized firms (SMMs), which account for about a third of U.S. direct export value. Further, many sell products to large companies, which install them in finished products slated for sale abroad.[41]

ACQUIRING RESOURCES

Foreign sources may give companies

- Lower costs.
- New or better products.
- Additional operating knowledge.

Producers and distributors seek out products, services, resources, and components from foreign countries—sometimes because domestic supplies are inadequate (as with crude oil shipped to the United States). They're also looking for anything that will create a competitive advantage. This may mean acquiring a resource that cuts costs, such as Rawlings's reliance on labor in Costa Rica—a country that hardly plays baseball—to produce baseballs.

Sometimes firms gain competitive advantage by improving product quality or differentiating their products from those of competitors; in both cases, they're potentially increasing market share and profits. Most automobile manufacturers, for example, hire design companies in northern Italy to help with styling. Many companies establish foreign R&D facilities to tap additional scientific resources.[42] They also learn while operating abroad, and they acquire product knowledge for entering new markets at home, such as what PepsiCo is doing in order to enter the fast-growth U.S. yogurt market.[43] Further, the diversity of employees and operations bring companies new perspectives.

REDUCING RISK

International operations may reduce operating risk by

- Smoothing sales and profits.
- Preventing competitors from gaining advantages.

Operating in countries with different business cycles can minimize swings in sales and profits. The key is the fact that sales decrease or grow more slowly in a country that's in a recession and increase or grow more rapidly in one that's expanding economically. During 2011, for example, Gap's North American sales fell 5 percent, but this was mainly offset by its sales growth of 11 percent elsewhere.[44] Moreover, by obtaining supplies of products or components both domestically and internationally, companies may be able to soften the impact of price swings or shortages in any one country.

Finally, companies often go international for defensive reasons. Perhaps they want to counter competitors' advantages in foreign markets that might hurt them elsewhere. By operating in Japan, for instance, Procter & Gamble (P&G) delayed foreign expansion on the part of potential Japanese rivals by slowing their amassment of resources needed to enter into other international markets where P&G was active.

Similarly, British-based Natures Way Foods followed a customer, the grocery chain Tesco, into the U.S. market. This move expanded its sales and its relationship with Tesco. Moreover, it reduced the risk that Tesco would find an alternative supplier who might then threaten Natures Way's relationship with Tesco in the U.K. market.

MODES OF OPERATIONS IN INTERNATIONAL BUSINESS

When pursuing international business, an organization must decide on one of the suitable *modes of operations* included in Figure 1.1. In the following sections, we discuss each of these modes.

MERCHANDISE EXPORTS AND IMPORTS

Merchandise exports and imports are usually a country's most common international economic transactions.

Exporting and importing are the most popular modes of international business, especially among smaller companies. **Merchandise exports** are tangible products—goods—that are sent *out* of a country; **merchandise imports** are goods brought *into* a country. Because we can actually *see* these goods as they leave and enter the country, we sometimes call them *visible exports* and *imports*. The athletic shoes that an Indonesian plant sends to the United States are exports for Indonesia and imports for the United States. For most countries, the export and import of goods are the major sources of international revenues and expenditures.

SERVICE EXPORTS AND IMPORTS

Service exports and imports are international nonproduct sales and purchases.

- They include travel, transportation, banking, insurance, and the use of assets such as trademarks, patents, and copyrights.
- They are very important for some countries.
- They include many specialized international business operating modes.

The terms *export* and *import* often apply only to *merchandise*. For non-merchandise *international earnings*, we use the terms **service exports** and **service imports** and are referred to as *invisibles*. The provider and receiver of payment makes a *service export;* the recipient and payer makes a *service import*. Services constitute the fastest growth sector in international trade and take many forms. In this section we discuss the most important:

- Tourism and transportation
- Service performance
- Asset use

Tourism and Transportation Let's say that the Williams sisters, Venus and Serena, and some U.S. tennis fans take Air France from the United States to Paris for the French Open tennis tournament. Their tickets on Air France and travel expenses in France are service exports for France and service imports for the United States. Obviously, then, tourism and transportation are important sources of revenue for airlines, shipping companies, travel agencies, and hotels.

The economies of some countries depend heavily on revenue from these sectors. In Greece and Norway, for example, a significant amount of employment and foreign-exchange earnings comes from foreign cargo carried on their shipping lines. Tourism earnings are more important to the Bahamian economy than earnings from export of merchandise. (As we'll see in our closing case, regional legislation and diplomatic relations affect the work of Dubai Ports World.)

CRN
Case Review Note

Service Performance Some services, including banking, insurance, rental, engineering, and management services, net companies earnings in the form of *fees:* payments for the performance of those services. On an international level, for example, companies may pay fees for engineering services rendered as so-called **turnkey operations,** which are construction projects performed under contract and transferred to owners when they're operational. The U.S. company Bechtel currently has turnkey contracts in many countries, such as expanding a copper facility in Chile, building a commuter railway in England, and constructing public housing in Gabon. Companies also pay fees for **management contracts**—arrangements in which one company provides personnel to perform general or specialized management functions for another, such as Disney's management of theme parks in France and Japan.

Asset Use When one company allows another to use its assets—such as trademarks, patents, copyrights, or expertise—under contracts known as **licensing agreements**, they receive earnings called **royalties**. For example, Adidas pays a royalty for the use of the Real Madrid football team's logo on jackets it sells. Royalties also come from franchise contracts. **Franchising** is a mode of business in which one party (the *franchisor*) allows another (the *franchisee*) to use a trademark as an essential asset of the franchisee's business. As a rule, the franchisor (say, McDonald's) also assists continuously in the operation of the franchisee's business, perhaps by providing supplies, management services, or technology.

INVESTMENTS

Dividends and interest paid on foreign investments are also considered service exports and imports because they represent the use of assets (capital). The investments themselves, however, are treated in national statistics as separate forms of service exports and imports. Note that *foreign investment* means ownership of foreign property in exchange for a financial return, such as interest and dividends, and it may take two forms: *direct* and *portfolio.*

CRN
Case Review Note

Direct Investment In **foreign direct investment (FDI)**, sometimes referred to simply as *direct investment,* the investor takes a controlling interest in a foreign company. When, for example, U.S. investors bought the Liverpool Football Club, it became a U.S. FDI in the United Kingdom. Control need not be a 100 percent or even a 50 percent interest; if a foreign investor holds a minority stake and the remaining ownership is widely dispersed, no other owner may effectively counter the investor's decisions. When two or more companies share ownership of an FDI, the operation is a **joint venture**. (There are also non-equity joint ventures.)

Key components of portfolio investment are

- Noncontrolling interest of a foreign operation.
- Extension of loans.

Portfolio Investment A **portfolio investment** is a *noncontrolling* financial interest in another entity. It usually takes one of two forms: stock in a company or loans to a company (or country) in the form of bonds, bills, or notes purchased by the investor. They're important for most companies with extensive international operations, which routinely move funds from country to country for short-term financial gain.

TYPES OF INTERNATIONAL ORGANIZATIONS

Basically, an "international company" is any company that operates in more than one country, but we have a variety of terms to designate different types of operations. Highly committed international companies usually draw on multiple operating types. Companies work together—in *joint ventures, licensing agreements, management contracts, minority ownership,* and *long-term contractual arrangements*—all of which are known as **collaborative arrangements**. The term **strategic alliance** is sometimes used to mean the same, but it usually refers either to an agreement that is of critical importance to one or more partners or to an agreement that does not involve joint ownership.

An MNE (sometimes called MNC or TNC) is a company with foreign direct investments.

Multinational Enterprise A **multinational enterprise (MNE)** usually refers to any company with foreign direct investments. This is the definition we use in this text. However, some writers reason that a company must have direct investments in some minimum number of countries to be an MNE. The term **multinational corporation** or **multinational company (MNC)** is often used as a synonym for MNE, while the United Nations uses the term **transnational company (TNC)**.

Does Size Matter? Some definitions require a certain size—usually giant. However, a small company, usually described within the United States as having fewer than 500 employees, can have foreign direct investments and adopt any of the operating modes we've discussed.

Although most small companies remain small, some, if successful, become medium or large companies.[45] Vistaprint is a good example. Founded in 1995, its sales grew to $6.1 million in 2000 and to over $1 billion in 2012 with operations mainly in North America and Europe.

WHY INTERNATIONAL BUSINESS DIFFERS FROM DOMESTIC BUSINESS

Although foreign external environmental differences are problematic

- Some anecdotes of failures are merely myths.
- They must be weighed against domestic opportunities and risks.
- Understanding social science disciplines and how they affect all business functions helps assure success abroad.

Let's now turn to the conditions in a company's *external environment* that may affect its international operations. Earlier we indicated that the best way of doing business abroad may differ from that in a company's domestic environment. Although there are many anecdotes illustrating operational problems when companies have failed to consider foreign environmental differences, these differences are not so daunting that they prevent success. First, some of the anecdotes are merely myths that have been repeated so often their truths are seldom challenged. Second, gaining start-up success domestically is also problematic almost anywhere in the world; thus when companies look objectively at their domestic opportunities and risks, foreign entries may seem less formidable. Third, a good understanding of what one will encounter helps reduce operating risks, and smart companies don't form or develop the means to implement international strategies without examining the conditions abroad that are indicated in the left-hand side of Figure 1.1 and organized into the following categories:

- *Physical factors* (such as a country's geography or demography)
- *Social factors* (such as its politics, law, culture, and economy)
- *Competitive factors* (such as the number and strength of a company's suppliers, customers, and rival firms)

In examining these categories, we delve into the realm of the *social sciences,* which helps in explaining how external conditions affect patterns of behavior in different parts of the world.

PHYSICAL AND SOCIAL FACTORS

The physical and social factors we show above can affect how companies produce and market products, employ personnel, and even maintain accounts. Remember that any of these factors may require a company to alter its operation abroad (compared to domestically) for the sake of efficiency.

Natural conditions affect

- Where different goods and services can be best produced.
- Operating risks

Geographic Influences Managers who are knowledgeable about geography are in a position to determine the location, quantity, quality, and availability of the world's resources, as well as ways to exploit them. The uneven distribution of resources throughout the world helps explain why different products and services are produced in different places. Further, countries differ in size of landmass and population.

Again, take sports. Norway fares better in the Winter Olympics than in the Summer Olympics because of its climate, and except for the well-publicized Jamaican bobsled team (whose members actually lived in Canada), you seldom hear of tropical countries competing in the Winter Olympics. East Africans' domination in distance races is due in part to their ability to train at higher altitudes than most other runners.

Geographic barriers—mountains, deserts, jungles, and so forth—often affect communications and distribution channels. And the chance of natural disasters and adverse climatic conditions (hurricanes, floods, droughts, earthquakes, volcanic eruptions, tsunamis) can make business riskier in some areas than in others while affecting supplies, prices, and operating conditions in far-off countries. Keep in mind also that climatic conditions may have short- or long-term cycles. For instance, recent melting of Arctic ice floes along with new ship technologies have allowed more ships to use a Northwest Passage to cut transport costs by saving as much as 15 days at sea.[46]

Finally, population distribution and the impact of human activity on the environment may exert strong future influences on international business, particularly if ecological changes or regulations cause companies to move or alter operations.

Politics often determines where and how international business can take place.

Political Policies Not surprisingly, a nation's political policies influence how international business takes place within its borders (indeed, *whether* it will take place). For instance, Cuba once had a minor-league baseball franchise, which went the way of diplomatic relations between Cuba and the United States back in the 1960s. Several Cuban baseball players are now members of professional U.S. teams, although most of them had to defect from Cuba to play abroad. (Even more Cuban boxers than baseball players have defected.)

Obviously, political disputes—particularly military confrontations—can disrupt trade and investment. Even conflicts that directly affect only small areas can have far-reaching effects. The 2002 and 2009 terrorist hotel bombings in Indonesia resulted in a decrease in the country's international tourism revenue and investment capital because individuals and businesses abroad perceived it as too risky.

Each country has its own laws regulating business. Agreements among countries set international law.

Legal Policies Domestic and international laws play a big role in determining how a company can operate abroad. *Domestic law* includes both home- and host-country regulations on such matters as taxation, employment, and foreign-exchange transactions. British law, for example, determines how the U.S.-investor-owned Liverpool Football Club is taxed and which nationalities of people it employs in the U.K. Meanwhile, U.S. law determines how and when the earnings from the operation are taxed in the United States.

CRN
Case Review Note

International law—in the form of legal agreements between countries—determines how earnings are taxed by *all* jurisdictions. International law may also determine how (and whether) companies can operate in certain places. As we point out in our closing case, strong bilateral agreements and good legalese is an important part of the trade flow that allows unhindered movement of Dubai Ports World's ships across the seas. When transactions between countries involve disputes, such as whether a French football team must pay Nike for imported uniforms when it questions the quality, the contract usually specifies the country's law that will make the determination.

Finally, the ways in which laws are *enforced* also affect a firm's foreign operations. In the realm of trademarks, patented knowledge, and copyrights, most countries have joined in international treaties and enacted domestic laws dealing with violations. Many, however, do very little to enforce either the agreements or their own laws. This is why companies not only must understand agreements and laws but also must determine how fastidiously they're enforced in different countries.

Countries' behavioral norms influence how companies should operate there.

Behavioral Factors The related disciplines of anthropology, psychology, and sociology can help managers better understand different values, attitudes, and beliefs. In turn, such understanding can help managers make operational decisions abroad. Let's return once again to the opening case. Although professional sports are spreading internationally, the popularity of specific sports differs among countries, while rules and the customary way of play for the same sport sometimes differ as well. Because of tradition, tennis's grand slam tournaments are played on hard courts in Australia and the United States, on clay in France, and on grass in England. A baseball game in the United States continues until there is a winner, while Japanese games end with a tie if neither team is ahead after 12 innings. Presumably the reason for the baseball difference is that the culture of Japan values harmony more than U.S. culture does, whereas U.S. culture values competitiveness more than the Japanese do.

CRN
Case Review Note

Economics explains country differences in costs, currency values, and market size.

Economic Forces Economics explains why countries exchange goods and services, why capital and people travel among countries in the course of business, and why one country's currency has a certain value compared to another's. Recall from our opening case that the percentage of non-U.S.-born players on major-league rosters has been on the rise. Although players from the Dominican Republic form the largest share of non-U.S.-born players, the

CRN
Case Review Note

idea of putting a major-league baseball team there isn't feasible because too few Dominicans can afford the ticket prices necessary to support a team. Obviously, higher incomes in the United States and Canada enable major league teams to offer higher salaries that attract Dominican players.

Economics also helps explain why some countries can produce goods or services for less. And it provides the analytical tools to determine the impact of an international company's operations on the economies of both host and home countries, as well as the impact of the host country's economic environment on a foreign firm.

THE COMPETITIVE ENVIRONMENT

Companies' competitive situations may differ by

- Their rankings among countries.
- The competitors they face by country.
- The resources they can commit internationally.

In addition to its physical and social environments, every globally active company operates within a competitive environment. Figure 1.1 highlights the key competitive factors in the external environment of an international business: product strategy, resource base and experience, and competitor capability.

Competitive Strategy for Products Products compete by means of *cost* or *differentiation strategies*, the latter usually by:

- developing a favorable *brand image,* usually through advertising or from long-term consumer experience with the brand; or
- developing *unique characteristics,* such as through R&D efforts or different means of distribution.

Using either approach, a firm may mass-market a product or sell to a niche market (the latter approach is called a *focus strategy*). Different strategies can be used for different products or for different countries, but a firm's choice of strategy plays a big part in determining how and where it will operate. Take Fiat, an Italian automobile company that competes with its best-selling models by using a cost strategy aimed at mass-market sales. This strategy has influenced Fiat to shift some fabrication of engine plants to China, where production costs are low, and to sell in India and Argentina, which are cost-sensitive markets. At the same time, Fiat has centered its production of its Alfa Romeo, Ferrari, and Maserati vehicles in Italy because these compete with a high-priced focus strategy that requires access to both the expertise and image of high technical competence. Whereas the competitive U.S. market has not been conducive to a mass-market Fiat brand strategy, Fiat sells over a quarter of all its Ferraris in the United States and is selling its Fiat 500 (a sort of boutique car) in the United States with a focus strategy. Its U.S. strategy will widen if it merges with Chrysler.

Company Resources and Experience Other competitive factors are a company's size and resources compared to those of its competitors. A market leader, for example—say, Coca-Cola—has resources for much more ambitious international operations than a smaller competitor like Royal Crown. Royal Crown sells in about 60 countries, Coca-Cola in more than 200.

In large markets (such as the United States), companies have to invest much more to secure national distribution than in small markets (such as Ireland). Further, they'll probably face more competitors in large markets than in small ones. Conversely, national market share and brand recognition have a bearing on operating in a given country. A company with a long-standing dominant national market position uses operating tactics that are quite different from those employed by a newcomer. Such a company, for example, has much more clout with suppliers and distributors. Remember, too, that being a leader in one country doesn't guarantee being a leader anywhere else. For example, in terms of global market share, Toyota and General Motors see-saw in the number one and two positions, but in many countries they hold neither of these top two positions.

Competitors Faced in Each Market Finally, success in a market (whether domestic or foreign) often depends on whether the competition is also international or local. Large commercial aircraft makers Boeing and Airbus, for example, compete almost only with each other in every market they serve. What they learn about each other in one country is useful in predicting the other's strategies elsewhere. In contrast, the British grocery chain Tesco faces different competition in almost every foreign market it enters.

Looking to the Future

Three Ways of Looking at Globalization

At this juncture, there's a big difference of opinion on the future of international business and globalization. Basically, there are three major viewpoints:

- Further globalization is inevitable.
- International business will grow primarily along regional rather than global lines.
- Forces working against further globalization and international business will slow down the growth of both.

Globalization Is Inevitable

The view that globalization is inevitable reflects the premise that advances in human connectivity are so pervasive that consumers everywhere will know about and demand the best products for the best prices regardless of their origins. Those who hold this view also argue that because MNEs have built so many international production and distribution networks, they'll pressure their governments to place fewer restrictions on international movements of goods and means to produce them.

Even if we accept this view, we must still meet at least one challenge to riding the wave of the future: Because the future is what we make of it, we must figure out how to spread the benefits of globalization equitably while minimizing the hardships placed on those parties—both people and companies—who suffer from increased international competition.

The *Wall Street Journal* posed a question to all living Nobel Prize winners in economics: "What is the greatest economic challenge for the future?" Several responses addressed globalization and international business. Robert Fogel said it's the problem of getting available technology and food to people who are needlessly dying. Both Vernon Smith and Harry Markowitz specified the need to bring down global trade barriers. Lawrence Klein called for "the reduction of poverty and disease in a peaceful political environment." John Nash felt we must address the problem of increasing the worldwide standard of living while the amount of the earth's surface per person is shrinking.[47] Clearly, each of these responses projects both managerial challenges and opportunities.

More Regional Than Global Growth

The second view—that growth will be largely regional rather than global—is based on studies showing that almost all of the companies we think of as "global" conduct most of their business in home and neighboring countries.[48] Most world trade is regional, and many treaties to remove trade barriers are regional. Transport costs favor regional over global business. For example, largely because of rising and uncertain oil prices that raise transport costs, Mexico is on track to displace China as the largest exporter to the United States.[49] And regional sales may be sufficient for companies to gain scale economies to cover their fixed costs adequately. Nevertheless, regionalization of business may be merely a transition stage. In other words, companies may first promote international business in nearby countries and then expand their activities once they've reached certain regional goals.

Globalization and International Business Will Slow

The third view argues that the pace of globalization will slow, or may already have begun collapsing.[50] In light of the antiglobalization sentiments mentioned earlier, it's easy to see that some people are adamant and earnest in voicing their reservations. The crux of the antiglobalization movement is the perceived growing schism between parties (including MNEs) who are thriving in a globalized environment and those who aren't. For example, in the 2010-2012 period, about 870 million people, or about 12 percent of the world's population, were chronically undernourished.[51]

Antiglobalists pressure governments to promote nationalism by raising trade barriers and rejecting international organizations and treaties. Historically, they have often succeeded (at least temporarily) in obstructing either technological or commercial advances that threatened their well-being. Recently, antiglobalization sentiments have grown in many countries, such as law changes in some U.S. states that hinder activities of undocumented aliens, the deportation by France of ethnic Roma (gypsies), the evacuation in Italy of immigrants to protect them against local residents, and gains by Sweden's anti-immigration Democrat's Party.[52] In Brazil and South Africa, the governments have authorized domestic companies to copy pharmaceuticals under global patent protection. Bolivia and Venezuela have nationalized some foreign investments, and Canada prevented the Malaysian state energy firm, Petronas, from buying Progress Energy, a natural gas producer. The sparring between pro- and anti-globalists is one reason why the globalization process has progressed in fits and starts.

Other uncertainties may hamper globalization. First is the question of oil prices, which affect international transportation because they can constitute more than 75 percent of operating costs on large ships.[53] In early 2008 global oil prices rose 44 percent, fell 74 percent by the end of the year, more than doubled by the end of 2010, and rose another 7.9 percent in 2011. Many U.S. companies, such as furniture manufacturers, have responded by reshoring rather than facing transport cost uncertainty.[54] Second, the economic recession and lingering unemployment since 2008 have led countries to enact measures to protect their work forces.[55] Third, safety concerns—property confiscation, terrorism, piracy of ships, and outright lawlessness—may inhibit companies from venturing abroad as much.

Finally, one view holds that for globalization to succeed, efficient institutions with clear-cut mandates are necessary; however, there is concern that neither the institutions nor the people working in them can adequately handle the complexities of an interconnected world.[56]

Going Forward

Only time will tell, but one thing seems certain: If a company wants to capitalize on international opportunities, it can't wait too long to see what happens on political and economic fronts. Investments in research, equipment, plants, and personnel training can take years to pan out. Forecasting foreign opportunities and risks is always challenging. Yet, by examining different ways in which the future may evolve, a company's management has a better chance of avoiding unpleasant surprises. That's why each chapter of this book includes a feature that shows how certain chapter topics can become subjects for looking into the future of international business. ■

CASE Transportation and Logistics: The Case for Dubai Ports World[57]

The world economy and global trade has been gradually growing since the recession of 2008–2009. Growth is coming from Europe and Japan where trade is stronger than expected, from China and India where high growth rates continue to be recorded, and from less developed countries where trade is primarily based on petroleum and basic commodities. The global transportation and logistics industry is one of the most important factors that contributes to the expansion of trade and logistics. Thus, it is important to understand how business is done in this industry and know more about the trends in the transportation and logistics industry.

Several factors have led to the growth in the transportation and logistics industry: the separation of raw materials, labor and production, decline in tariffs, import restrictions, and exchange rate controls are some of the main factors that led to this growth. These factors have resulted in an increased demand for transporting raw materials, unfinished goods, and finished goods in the global economy. These trends have increased the demand for global transportation and logistics services. For the year 2010, it was estimated that there was a total of 545 million TEU (twenty-foot equivalent unit) that was handled globally, an increase of 113 percent over the year 2000.

The Transportation and Logistics Industry

Ports play an important role in the transportation and logistics industry. They provide quality services, advanced technologies, and skilled labor that lead to increased productivity. The World Bank has developed a logistics performance indicator (LPI) for around 150 countries. The LPI measures the different dimensions of supply-chain performance in the different countries such as customs clearance procedures, quality of trade-related infrastructure, quality of transport services, timeliness of delivery, and ability to track and trace consignments. The World Bank has also highlighted the influence that government policies have on logistics performance. Countries that attempt to develop policies to improve supply-chain activities find themselves scoring higher on the LPI than countries that do not pay attention to such policies.

Logistics has in the past focused on reducing barriers to trade, and on governmental procedures implemented regarding getting clearance for goods at customs. While the laws and regulations are important, they are not enough to advance the industry that includes various stakeholders working and interacting together. It is also necessary to develop policies that integrate all elements of the supply chain so that various players can easily manage different steps of their business. This aspect has been lacking lately and arguably should be given more attention. An approach that centers on all the policies will have a major impact on the productivity and efficiency of the logistics business. This requires bringing all the integrators together in the

MAP 1.2 Where Dubai Ports World Operates

Dubai Ports World operates in more than 65 terminals across 6 continents. On the map below, some of these major locations have been indicated.

Source: Data from "Dubai Ports World" at http://web.dpworld.com/images/DP_World_Brochure_2013_Eng.pdf (accessed January 2013).

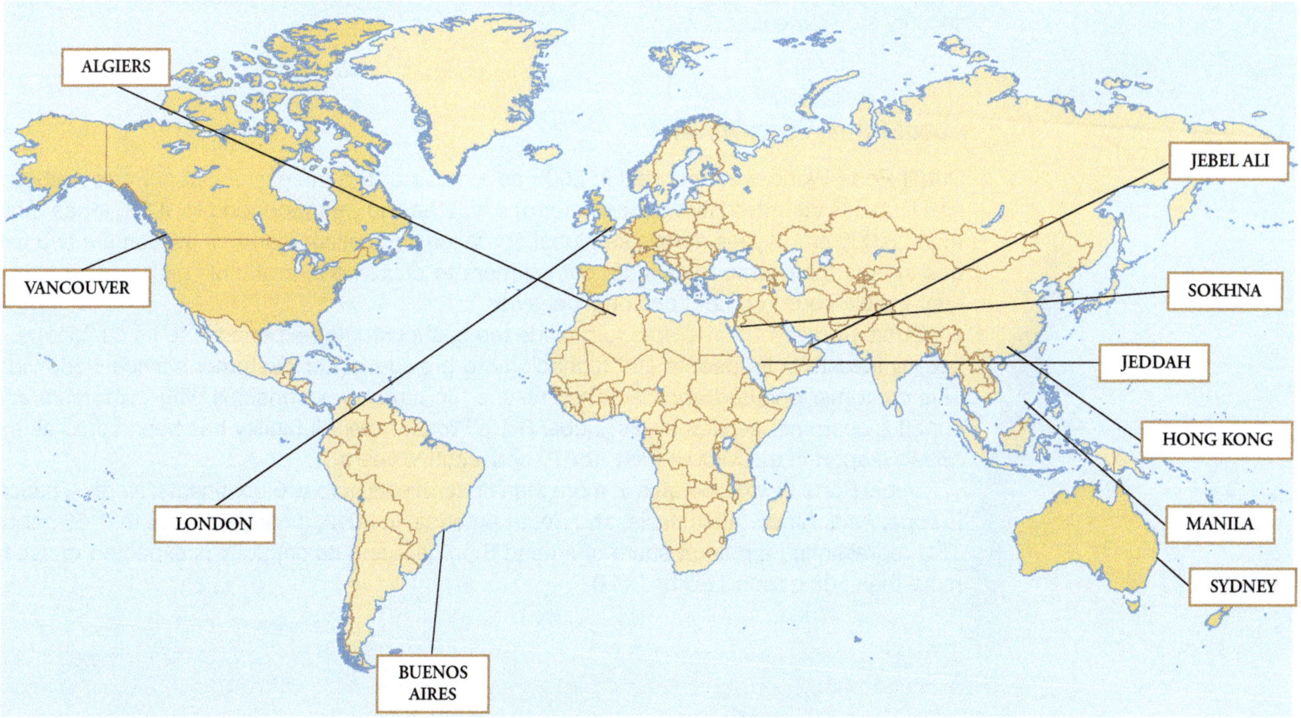

logistics chain: cargo handling, storage, warehousing, freight services, air road, and courier. This should result in an improvement in the global supply chain business.

Developing Logistics Clusters

Logistics clusters are geographically concentrated sets of logistics-related activities. They are known to have high transportation services, low transportation costs, and an efficient flow of goods. According to the *World Financial Review,* governments around the world are investing significant resources in developing logistics clusters.

The advantages of such clusters are economies of scope, economies of scale, economies of density, better service, and price stability. They also bring value by generating other business activities and bring in new jobs. These benefits create a positive feedback loop attracting more companies to them, resulting in further cost reduction and better efficiency.

Developing logistics clusters requires investment in seaports, airports, railways, and highways. This helps in improving the overall infrastructure of a nation. Examples of leading logistics clusters include Singapore, the Netherlands, Los Angeles, Dubai, Sao Paulo, and Aragon. These clusters are also referred to as logistics parks, transport centers, logistics platform, and logistics centers.

Doing Business in Different Countries

Local or domestic policies may affect the logistics operations in various markets. Some of these policies may raise costs, reduce efficiency, give preferential treatment for local or public owned corporations, and put limitations on investment in certain activities. These policies can significantly impact the supply chain, which may add costs to a firm and also affect the business activity.

Foreign countries may introduce restrictive policies such as importing raw material as opposed to processed products where the processing might be more efficient. Other restrictions include bilateral agreements that distort competition, embargoes, business visa restrictions, and security requirements.

About Dubai Ports World

Dubai Ports World was founded in 2005 as a result of the merger of Dubai Ports Authority and Dubai Ports International, the latter of which having been founded in 1999. It has more than 28,000 employees across its global operations. Excellence and innovation are two values the company embodies in its commitment to customers, profitable global growth, and responsible corporate and personal behavior.

Dubai Ports World attempts to provide the best customer experience to its customers. It heavily invests in its people and technology to provide better customer service worldwide. This customer-oriented approach has resulted in strong relationships with customers and superior customer service levels. Dubai Ports World Jebel Ali facility has been voted as the "Best Seaport in the Middle East" for 19 consecutive years.

Dubai Ports World operates in more than 65 terminals across 6 continents: North America, Europe, Asia, Africa, Australasia, and South America. In 2012, it handled more than 56 million TEU representing a market share of around 8 percent and its capacity is expected to rise to more than 100 million TEU by 2020.

Dubai Ports World is among the top three global terminal operators. It is one of the new players in the global market, with an aggressive growth and acquisition strategy. The majority of its business comes from emerging markets in South America and Africa. Their global expansion initially started in the Middle East, then extended into major ports in India. One of the major expansions for Dubai Ports World took place in 2006 when it acquired Peninsular and Oriental Steam Navigation Company (P&O) of the United Kingdom in 2006, for US$ 7 billion.

This was considered highly controversial by many in the United States, because it included a number of ports in the U.S. as well. These ports were sold shortly after they were purchased.

The Overseas Environment

Operating in various markets offers opportunities as well as challenges. The opportunities include access to new markets, access to natural resources, and innovative technology. The industry remains dynamic and profitable where emerging markets experience a significant growth in business. Governments are constantly aspiring to open their ports to logistics companies to facilitate economic growth and jobs. Logistics companies offer blue-collar, white-collar, and no-collar jobs while also providing opportunities to open new businesses.

Dubai Ports World faces challenges with regard to the complexity of operating in certain countries such as Africa, where the supply chain is an expensive and time-consuming activity. Transportation costs comprise up to 75 percent of the retail price in markets such as Malawi, Rwanda, and Uganda. For example, transporting a car from China to Tanzania could cost around $5,000 while transporting the same car from China to Uganda would cost $9,000.

Dubai Ports World's mission is to use a global approach in local business environments, and of course to offer good value and service to their customers.

Source: © ewlyn - Fotolia.com

Finding the Right Skills

The logistics industry is primarily a people's business. Around 25 percent of the costs of logistics are labor costs. Thus, it becomes essential to attract, train, and motivate qualified people at all levels. One of the first issues that Dubai Ports World faces when it operates in a foreign country is finding qualified and skilled labor. There is usually a low supply of qualified candidates, low wages, low industry profile, and poor working conditions.

Risk Issues

Addressing risk in the supply chain is becoming a priority for businesses. Supply-chain risk can be caused by various disruptions: environmental risk such as natural disasters; geopolitical risk such as threat of attacks and terrorism; economic risk such as currency fluctuations, demand shocks and supplier failings; technological risk such as outage in IT and telecommunication systems, etc. Risk can be controlled by conducting scenario analyses, collaborating with the different players by sharing information, identifying vulnerabilities and synchronizing back-up plans.

Technology in Business

Dubai Ports World has been keen to use advanced information technology tools to facilitate its business. It has been using mobile technology to make life easier for customers by saving time and money. They also use mobile technology for their employees. Issues such as labor deployment, vessel arrival and gate appointments are communicated via mobile devices. This is linked to the human resource department which assigns labor to points of work, which results in more efficient work. Recently, this technology enabled container shipping lines to access bay and stowage, which helped reduce port call time.

Environmental Considerations

The presence of logistics companies may result in air pollution. This increases the health hazards around those clusters. Thus, there is always a tradeoff between the economic benefits of logistics operations and the hazards of their effects on the environment and health of the surrounding community. There are "green innovations" in logistics operations and processes that are ultimately minimizing the negative effects of logistics operations on the environment.

The Future

The logistics industry has high prospects for growth as the global economy grows. There are several matters that need attention to support this growth. There is a need for more comprehensive logistics policies that bring the various components of logistics together: land transportation, railway, shipping, commerce, and finance. More coordination is needed between these institutions. Additionally, more investment in logistics infrastructure such as roads, rail, and shipping is needed to ease traffic congestion, reduce costs and air pollution. Thirdly, people issues are becoming increasingly prominent and need to be addressed by those with the right skills in order to ensure high quality services throughout the industry.

The future of Dubai Ports World looks promising. It continues to sustain its growth by penetrating new markets while offering a unique customer experience. Its people remain the key stakeholder responsible for delivering the best service. Dubai Ports World is a global leader in logistics and transportation.

QUESTIONS

1-3. What global factors have contributed to the growth of the transportation and logistics industry? How have they contributed to this growth?

1-4. What steps has Dubai Ports World taken to benefit from global economic changes?

1-5. What economic factors influence the success of the international transportation and logistics industry?

1-6. How can logistics companies increase business with countries in Europe, Asia, or Africa?

1-7. What threats exist for Dubai Ports World? How would you overcome these threats?

1-8. Discuss some of the legal issues that have faced Dubai Ports World? How has this affected their operations in the United States and other places?

SUMMARY

- Globalization is the ongoing process that deepens and broadens interdependence among countries. International business is a mechanism to bring about globalization.
- International business has grown rapidly in recent decades because of technological expansion, liberalized government policies on cross-border movements (goods, services, and the resources to produce them), the development of services to facilitate international transactions, consumer desires to buy foreign products and services, increased global competition, changing political situations, and cooperation in dealing with transnational problems and issues. Because of these factors, companies use foreign countries increasingly as a source of both production and sales.
- Many critics feel that globalization weakens national sovereignty, promotes growth that is detrimental to the earth's environment, and skews income distributions.
- Offshoring—transferring production abroad—is controversial in terms of who benefits when costs are reduced and whether the process exchanges good jobs for bad ones.
- Companies engage in international business to expand sales, acquire resources, and diversify or reduce their risks.
- A company can engage in international business through various operating modes, including exporting and importing merchandise and services, making direct and portfolio investments, and entering into collaborative arrangements with other companies.
- Multinational enterprises (MNEs) are companies with foreign direct investments. Sometimes they are referred to as multinational corporations or companies (MNCs) or transnational companies (TNCs).
- When operating abroad, companies may have to adjust their usual methods of carrying out business. This is because (a) foreign conditions often dictate a more suitable method and (b) some international operating modes differ from those used domestically.
- Because country environments differ from each other, international managers must have a working knowledge of the basic physical and social sciences that impact operations: geography, political science, law, anthropology, sociology, psychology, and economics.
- A company's competitive strategy and resources influence how and where it can best operate. Likewise, from one country to another, its competitive situation may differ in terms of its relative strength and which competitors it faces.
- There is disagreement about the future of international business—that globalization is inevitable, that it will be primarily regional, and that its growth will slow.

KEY TERMS

agglomeration
born-global company
clustering
collaborative arrangement
foreign direct investment (FDI)
franchising
globalization
international business
joint venture
licensing agreement
management contract
merchandise export
merchandise import
multinational corporation or company (MNC)

multinational enterprise (MNE)
offshoring
portfolio investment
reshoring
royalty
service export
service import
sovereignty
strategic alliance
transnational company (TNC)
turnkey operation

ENDNOTES

1 ***Sources include the following:*** "The Swedish Model," *The Economist* (October 27, 2012): 56; Kim Daekwan, "The Global Impacts of World Event Sponsorships on Firm Market Performance: A Hierarchical Linear Modeling Approach," *Proceedings of the 54th Annual Meeting of the Academy of International Business* (Washington: June 30 – July 3, 2012); "Percentage of Foreign Players Rises," (April 5, 2012) http://espen.go.com/mlb/story (accessed December 7, 2012); Mike Esterl, "Olympics Sponsors Go for the Young," *Wall street Journal* (July 3, 2012): B8; Andrew Zimbalist, "Is It Worth It?" *Finance & Development* 47:1 (March 2010): 6–11; Harald Dolles and Sten Söderman (eds.), *Sport as a Business: International Professional and Commercial Aspects* (Houndsmills, UK: Palgrave Macmillan, 2011); Mark Mulligan, "Football, Funding and MBAs," *Financial Times* (December 13, 2010): 11; Roger Blitz, "Sports Organisers Play High Stakes Games," *Financial Times* (September 29, 2010): 7; Jeremy Kahn, "N.B.A. in India, In Search of Fans and Players," *New York Times* (December 28, 2010): B13; George Vecsey, "When the Game Absorbs the Globe," *New York Times* (April 1, 2007): A+; Simon Kuper, "Lost in Translation," *Financial Times* (February 2–3, 2008): p. life & arts 2; Matthew Graham, "Nike Overtakes Adidas in Football Field," *Financial Times* (August 19, 2004): 19; L. Jon Wertheim, "The Whole World Is Watching," *Sports Illustrated* (June 14, 2004): 73–86; Wertheim Jon, "Hot Prospects in Cold Places," *Sports Illustrated* (June 21, 2004): 63–66; Grant Wahl, "Football vs. Fútbol," *Sports Illustrated* (July 5, 2004): 72; Wahl, "On Safari for 7-Footers," *Sports Illustrated* (June 28, 2004): 70–73; André Richelieu, "Building the Brand Equity of Professional Sports Teams," Paper presented at the annual meeting of the Academy of International Business, Stockholm, Sweden (July 10–13, 2004).

2 For a good discussion of the versatility of the term *globalization,* see Joyce S. Osland, "Broadening the Debate: The Pros and Cons of Globalization," *Journal of Management Inquiry* 10:2 (June 2003): 137–54.

3 Amy M. Thomas, "Brussels: The Chocolate Trail," *New York Times* (December 25, 2011): tr7.

4 Andrew Batson, "Not Really 'Made in China,'" *Wall Street Journal* (December 16, 2010): B1–B2.

5 Günther G. Schulze and Heinrich W. Ursprung, "Globalisation of the Economy and the Nation State," *The World Economy* 22:3 (May 1999): 295–352.

6 "Globalisation Going Backwards," The *Economist* (December 22, 2012): 105 referring to conclusions by the DHL Global Connectiveness Index.

7 "Africa's Economy: Bulging in the Middle," *The Economist* (October 20, 2012): 43.

8 For example, see OECD, *Measuring Globalisation: OECD Economic Globalisation Indicators* (Paris: OECD, 2005); Pim Martens and Daniel Zywietz, "Rethinking Globalization: A Modified Globalization Index," *Journal of International Development* 18:3 (2006): 331–50; "The Globalization Index," *Foreign Policy* (November–December 2007): 68–76; Raab, M., Ruland, M., Schonberger, B., Blossfeld, H.-P., Hofacker, D., Buchholz, S., et al. (2008). "GlobalIndex: A Sociological Approach to Globalization Measurement," International Sociology 23(4): pp. 596-631; "KOF Globalization Index, 2011," http://globalization.kof.ethz.ch/ (accessed November 5, 2012).

9 Gardiner Harris, "Tiny Bean, Crucial to Halliburton, Lifts India Farmers from Mud," *New York Times* (July 17, 2012): A1+.

10 Daniel Henninger, "Capitalism saved the Miners," *Wall Street Journal* (October 14, 2010): A19.

11 Jeffrey A. Trachtenberg, "Book Deal a Tale of Reunions," *Wall Street Journal* (November 5, 2012): B4; and Antonio Regalado and Lauren Etter, "Brazil Food Merger Creates Export Giant," *Wall Street Journal* (May 20, 2009): B2.

12 See Rodney C. Shrader, Benjamin M. Oviatt, and Patricia Phillips McDougall, "How New Ventures Exploit Trade-Offs among International Risk Factors: Lessons for the Accelerated Internationalization of the 21st Century," *Academy of Management Journal* 43:6 (2000): 1227–47.

13 Mark Scott, "Companies Born in Europe, but Based on the Planet," *New York Times* (June 12, 2012): B7.

14 Stephanie A. Fernhaber, Brett Anitra Gilbert, and Patricia P. McDougall, "International Entrepreneurship and Geographic Location: An Empirical Examination of New Venture Internationalization," *Journal of International Business Studies* 39:2 (2008): 267–90.

15 Dan McGraw, "The Foreign Invasion of the American Game," *The Village Voice* (May 28–June 3, 2003) (accessed June 4, 2007).

16 "Charlemagne: Coming off the Rails," *The Economist* (October 20, 2012): 51.

17 Susan Carey, "Calculating Costs in the Clouds," *Wall Street Journal* (March 6, 2007): B1+.

18 His views are discussed in Joellen Perry, "Nobel Laureates Say Globalization's Winners Should Aid Poor," *Wall Street Journal* (August 25, 2008): 2.

19 Lorraine Eden and Stefanie Lenway, "Introduction to the Symposium Multinationals: The Janus Face of Globalization," *Journal of International Business Studies* 32:3 (2001): 383–400.

20 Christopher DeMorro, "One Container Ship Pollutes As Much As 50 Million Cars," (June 3, 2009), accessed September 14, 2012.

21 His views are discussed in Joellen Perry, "Nobel Laureates Say Globalization's Winners Should Aid Poor," *Wall Street Journal* (August 25, 2008): 2.

22 Steve Lohr, "An Elder Challenges Outsourcing's Orthodoxy," *New York Times* (September 9, 2004): C1+; Paul A. Samuelson, "Where Ricardo and Mill Rebut and Confirm Arguments of Mainstream Economists Supporting Globalization," *Journal of Economic Perspectives* 18:3 (Summer 2004): 135–47.

23 An examination of this subject may be found in Arne Kalleberg, "Precarious Work, Insecure Workers: Employment Relations in Transition," *American Sociological Review* 74:1 (2009): 1–22.

24 Bernhard G. Gunter and Rolph van der Hoeven, "The Social Dimension of Globalization: A Review of the Literature," *International Labour Review* 143:1/2 (2004): 7–43.

25 Jagdish Bhagwati, "Anti-Globalization: Why?" *Journal of Policy Modeling* 26:4 (2004): 439–64.

26 Craig Karmin, "Offshoring Can Generate Jobs in the U.S.," *Wall Street Journal* (March 16, 2004): B1.

27 William M. Bulkeley, "IBM Documents Give Rare Look at 'Offshoring,'" *Wall Street Journal* (January 19, 2004): A1+; William M. Bulkeley, "IBM to Cut U.S. Jobs, Expand in India," *Wall Street Journal* (March 26, 2009): B1.

28 Richard Waters, "Big Blueprint for IBM," *Financial Times* (March 3, 2009): 14.

29 N. Gregory Mankiw and Phillip Swagel, "The Politics and Economics of Offshore Outsourcing," NBR Working Paper No. 12398 (July 2006); Kristien Coucke and Leo Sleuwaegen, "Offshoring as a Survival

Strategy: Evidence from Manufacturing Firms in Belgium," *Journal of International Business Studies* 39:8 (2008): 1261–77.

30 Matthew J. Slaughter, "Globalization and Employment by U.S. Multinationals: A Framework and Facts," *Daily Tax Report* (March 26, 2004): 1–12; Olivier Bertrand, "What Goes Around, Comes Around: Effects of Offshore Outsourcing on the Export Performance of Firms," *Journal of International Business Studies* 42:2 (February/ March 2008): 334–44.

31 Robert C. Feenstra and Gordon H. Hanson, "The Impact of Outsourcing and High-Technology Capital on Wages: Estimates for the United States, 1979–1990," *Quarterly Journal of Economics* 114:3 (1999): 907–40.

32 Alan S. Brown, "A Shift in Engineering Offshore," *Mechanical Engineering* 131:3 (2009): 24–29.

33 "An Internet of Airborne Things," *The Economist* (December 1, 2012): Monitor 3.

34 Paul Markille, "Cars on Autopilot," *The Economist* (The World in 2013 special issue): 152.

35 Timothy Aeppel, "Coming Home: Appliance Maker Drops China to Produce in Texas," *Wall Street Journal* (August 24, 2009): B1+; Linda Tucci, "Offshoring Has Long Way to Go," *CIO News Headlines* (June 2, 2005): n.p.; Paulo Prada and Niraj Sheth, "Delta Air Ends Use of India Call Centers," *Wall Street Journal* (April 18–19, 2009): B1+; Adrianna Gardella, "A Company Grows, and Builds a Plant Back in the U.S.A." *New York Times* (October 12, 2011): B9.

36 Tali Kristal, "Good Times, Bad Times: Postwar Labor's Share of National Income in Capitalist Democracies," *American Sociological Review* 75.5 (Oct 2010): 729–63.

37 Deborah Solomon, "Federal Aid Does Little for Free Trade's Losers," *Wall Street Journal* (March 1, 2007): A1+.

38 Paul Windrum, Andreas Reinstaller, and Christopher Bull, "The Outsourcing Productivity Paradox: Total Outsourcing, Organisational Innovation, and Long Run Productivity Growth," *Journal of Evolutionary Economics* 19:2 (2009): 197–232.

39 Carlos Tejada, "Paradise Lost," *Wall Street Journal* (August 14, 2003): A1+.

40 "The Hackett Group; New Hackett Research Forecasts Offshoring of 750,000 More Jobs In Finance, IT, Other Key Business Services Areas by 2016," Investment Weekly News (April 14, 2012): 612.

41 Small Business Export Association, 'New Report: SME Exports Support 4 Million Jobs," (December 6, 2010) www.nsba.biz/content/3647.shtml (accessed December 21, 2011); and "Rep. Sam Graves Holds a Hearing on U.S. Trade strategy and Small Business Exporters," Political Transcript Wire *[Lanham]* 17 (May 2012): n.p.

42 Heather Berry, "Leaders, Laggards, and the Pursuit of Foreign Knowledge," *Strategic Management Journal* 27 (2006): 151–68; and Jaeyong Song and Jongtae Shin, "The Paradox of Technological Capabilities: A Knowledge Sourcing from Host Countries of Overseas R&D Operations," *Journal of International Business Studies* 39:2 (2008): 291–303.

43 Diana Cimilluca and Mike Esterl, "PepsiCo Nears U.S. Yogurt Deal," *Wall Street Journal* (October 14, 2011): B3.

44 Devon Maylie, "Gap Sells Style in South Africa," *Wall Street Journal* (March 20, 2012):B1+.

45 Aaron Chatterji, ""Why Washington Has It Wrong," *Wall Street Journal* (November 12, 2012): R1+.

46 "Ships Take to Arctic Ocean as Sea Ice Melts," www.msnbc.com/id/39394645/ns/world_news-worldenvironment (accessed September 28, 2010).

47 David Wessel and Marcus Walker, "Good News for the Globe," *Wall Street Journal* (September 3, 2004): A7+.

48 Alan M. Rugman and Cecelia Brain, "Multinational Enterprises Are Regional, Not Global," *Multinational Business Review* 11:1 (2004): 3; and Alain Verbeke and Liena Kano, "An Internalization Theory Rationale for MNE Regional Strategy," *Multinational Business Review* 20. 2 (2012): 135–52.

49 "The Rise of Mexico," *The Economist* (November 24, 2012): 14.

50 John Ralston Saul, "The Collapse of Globalism," *Harpers* (March 2004): 33–43; James Harding, "Globalisation's Children Strike Back," *Financial Times* (September 11, 2001): 4; Bob Davis, "Wealth of Nations," *Wall Street Journal* (March 29, 2004): A1; Harold James, *The End of Globalisation: Lessons from the Great Depression* (Cambridge, MA: Harvard University Press, 2001).

51 Food and Agricultural Organization of the United Nations (FAO), *The State of Food Insecurity in the World, 2012* (Rome: FAO, 2012).

52 Peter Mayer, "Yearender: Europe Toughens Attitudes on Immigrants," *McClatchy – Tribune Business News* (December 15, 2010): n.p.

53 D. Ronen, "The Effect of Oil Price on Containership Speed and Fleet Size," *The Journal of the Operational Research Society* 62:1 (January 2011): 211–16.

54 Larry Rohter, "Shipping Costs Start to Crimp Globalization," *New York Times* (August 3, 2009): 1+.

55 Annie Lowrey, "An Increase in Barriers to Trade Is Reported," *New York Times* (June 23, 2012): B1+.

56 On the schism between those who thrive in a globalized environment and those who don't, see Jagdish Bhagwati, "Anti-Globalization: Why?" *Journal of Policy Modeling* 26:4 (2004): 439–64; Roger Sugden and James R. Wilson, "Economic Globalisation: Dialectics, Conceptualisation and Choice," *Contributions to Political Economy* 24:1 (2005): 13–32; J. Ørstrøm Møller, "Wanted: A New Strategy for Globalization," *The Futurist* (January–February 2004): 20–22.

57 ***Sources include the following:*** The public-private infrastructure advisory facility (PPIAF), Port Reform Tool Kit, http://www.ppiaf.org; Le Rossignol, Marie-Helene, 2007, Global Terminal Operators: an overview, Washington DC. http://www.dpworld.com; Outlook on the Logistics and Supply Chain Industry 2012, World Economic Forum, Containerization International Yearbook 2010; "Logistics Clusters: The Feedback Loop Leading to Economic Growth and Jobs," "Logistics Clusters: Delivering Value and Driving Growth," *The World Financial Review*, http://www.worldfinancialreview.com/?p=2265 (October 15, 2013).

Chapter 1

REGIONAL AND GLOBAL STRATEGY

Objectives of the chapter

In this chapter we are going to define the boundaries of the field of international business in an introductory overview of the main themes of this book. We will then examine trade and foreign direct investment, as well as the emergence of the triad economic blocs of North America, the European Union (EU), and Japan. We will then examine some of the worldwide economic and political changes that are taking place and look at how technology is altering the way international business is conducted. We will also study some of the approaches being used by multinational enterprises both to establish and to maintain their competitive advantage. In the last part of the chapter, we will present the framework that we are going to use in our study of international business.

The specific objectives of this chapter are to:

1. *Define* the terms international business and multinational enterprise.
2. *Discuss* the two primary ways in which international business occurs: trade and foreign direct investment.
3. *Examine* the impact of the triad on international trade and investment.
4. *Describe* the current state of world economies and the role of government and trade regulations in the conduct of international business.
5. *Discuss* the importance of technology and the role of small and medium-sized enterprises in the international business arena.
6. *Examine* how multinational enterprises use triad/regional strategies to compete effectively in the international marketplace.
7. *Discuss* the determinants of national competitive advantage.
8. *Present* the model that will be used in this text for studying international business.

…le with a local strategy

…nk in the world, but …mericans consume …annually, in contrast …f this amount, and in …ly, and Portugal, the …s. In the 1990s, Coke …its European sales.

One of these … al franchisors who had become too complacent with … e active, market-driven sellers. In France, for example, Pernod, a Coca-Cola franchisee, was forced to sell some of its operations back to Coke which, in turn, appointed a new marketing manager for the country. In addition, Coke's price was lowered and advertising was sharply increased. As a result, per capita consumption in France went up.

In England, Beecham and Grand Metropolitan used to be Coke's national bottlers but that was turned over to Cadbury Schweppes, most famous for its Schweppes mixers. The latter immediately began a series of marketing programs that resulted in sales tripling within three years.

In Germany the pace has been even faster. Beginning in the early 1990s Coke identified Germany as one of its primary targets and began building a distribution network there to both package and sell Coke locally. Meanwhile, throughout the entire country the company has taken even bolder steps including the replacement of an inefficient bottling network and the institution of a new, well-financed marketing campaign. As a result, Germany became Coke's largest and most profitable market in Europe.

But all of this came at a price. For example, some government agencies and companies expressed concern about Coke's overriding emphasis on cost control and market growth and its willingness to push aside those who are unable to meet these goals. As a result, the European Union's Competition Department was asked to investigate possible anti-competitiveness tactics. Meanwhile, in the UK, the British Monopolies and Mergers Commission investigated Coke regarding its joint venture with Schweppes, and San Pellegrino, the mineral water company, filed a complaint with the Commission of the European Communities, contending that Coca-Cola abused its dominant position by giving discounts to Italian retailers who promised to stock only Coke.

Yet none of these actions stopped Coke's efforts to establish a strong foothold in Europe. As the European Union eliminated all internal tariffs, it became possible for a chain store with operations in France, Germany, Italy,

Source: Getty Images/AFP

and the Netherlands to buy soft drinks from the lowest-cost supplier on the continent and not have to worry about paying import duties for shipping them to the retail stores. Low cost and rapid delivery were going to be key strategic factors for success. Coke believes that its current European strategy puts it in an ideal competitive position against competitors.

Recent developments shed some doubt on whether the company will be as successful as it is forecasting. Worldwide market growth has been flat and there has been a move away from carbonated drinks. In Eastern Europe; it is the market for bottled water that is booming. Between 1998 and 2004, per capita consumption of bottled water in Eastern Europe doubled. Although Coca-Cola Water Division is one of four major players, it is not the market leader and smaller, local competitors account for a large portion of the market. Other efforts to develop innovative, non-carbonated products have not proven very successful. The company knows that its future growth is going to depend heavily on its ability to supplement its current product line with new offerings such as vitamin-enriched drinks, and perhaps coffee and tea offerings. Worst of all perhaps, a few years ago the company began centralizing control and encouraging consolidation among its bottling partners. Coke believed that by making all key operating decisions in Atlanta, it could drive up profitability. Unfortunately, at the same time that it was pushing for this centralized type of operation, regional markets began demanding that the company be more responsive to local needs. In short, Coke was going global while the market wanted it to go local.

Coke is now trying to turn things around. In particular, the firm is implementing three principles that are designed to make it more locally responsive. First, the company is instituting a strategy of "think local, act local" by putting increased decision making in the hands of local managers. Second, the firm is focusing itself as a pure marketing company and pushing its brands on a regional basis and local basis rather than on a worldwide basis. Third, Coke is now working to become a model citizen by reaching out to local communities and getting involved in civic and charitable activities.

Europe remains an important market for Coke, which derives about a quarter of its revenues from the region, about the same as the Asia–Pacific region. North America, though the dominant market, accounts for just under a third of Coke's revenues. Indeed, Coke now attracts both investors and consumers in Europe as it listed on the Paris NYSE Euronext from May 2011. Similar to many secondary listings, this move to Paris is more about raising awareness than cash. John Brock, chairman and chief executive, said the secondary listing "reflects our commitment to Europe and will provide convenient access" for European investors.

In the past, Coke succeeded as a multinational because of its understanding and appeal to global commonalities. Today, it is trying to hold its market share by better understanding and appealing to local differences.

Websites: www.coca-cola.com; www.cokecce.com; www.coca-colahbc.com; www.cadburyschweppes.com.

Sources: Alan Rugman and Richard Hodgetts, "The End of Global Strategy," *European Management Journal*, August 2001, p. 336; "Competition, Coolers, Drive East European Water Sales," *Food and Drink Europe*, February 2, 2004; John C. Gardner and Carl B. McGowan Jr., "A Note on the Regional Triad Model and the Soft Drink Industry," *Multinational Business Review*, Vol. 18, N 1 (2010); Adapted from Louise Lucas, "Coke Seeks Cultural Shift in Paris Listing," *Financial Times*, May 23, 2011.

1. **Why did Coke engage in foreign direct investments in Europe?**
2. **How did Coke improve its factor conditions in Europe?**
3. **How is local rivalry helping to improve Coke's competitive advantage?**
4. **Is the Coca-Cola Company a multinational enterprise? Is it global? Why?**

OVERVIEW OF THE BOOK

International business is a wonderful and exciting field of study. Today it can be said that all business is international business. The days are over when an understanding of domestic business alone was sufficient to prosper. In this book we will examine the basic data on business activities, operations, supply chains, strategies, structures, ethics, etc., and we will find that all of these have strong international elements. In other words, international business is not just the study of international trade, foreign direct investment, international joint ventures, cross-cultural management, international organizations, etc., although these topics will all be covered in the book. Today international business is much more than this: it is the study of the international aspects of business itself. Therefore, in this book, two parallel lines of thinking will be developed.

Country and firm factors

First, the book will help students to review and understand the classic components of an international business course. We will define and discuss country-level issues on international business. These will cover the importance and growth of international trade (imports and exports) and of foreign direct investment (FDI). We will define these terms and provide summary data on them later in this chapter. Next, we will discuss the nature and role of international institutions such as the World Bank, World Trade Organization, United Nations agencies, etc. We will define many of these terms later in this chapter and then explore them in greater detail in Chapter 4 which deals with the role of governments as they affect international business. We also discuss the relevance of the regional economies of the European Union, North American Free Trade Agreement (NAFTA), and the major economies in the Asia–Pacific. We refer to these as the broad "triad" regions, and again we will define these in more detail later in this chapter and, then discuss their importance in Chapter 3.

Second, the major focus of this book is upon the key actor on the stage of international business: the multinational enterprise (MNE). The MNE is defined later in this chapter, and, in Chapter 2, as a firm operating across national borders. The world's largest 500 MNEs dominate international business. It has been shown that they account for 90 percent of the world's stock of FDI and that they also undertake over half the world's trade.[1] In addition to these extremely large MNEs (with sales of $15 billion or more) there are thousands of smaller MNEs. There are also thousands of mainly small domestic firms. These small MNEs and small domestic firms are often parts of clusters (a type of network) affiliated with one or more of the world's large MNEs. The nature of these business clusters is analyzed in Chapter 22 of this book using the "flagship" framework of international business. Other forms of business organization besides the MNE are also studied. These include: international joint ventures, licensing agreements, and franchises. We explore the timing of foreign entry for these types of organizational forms starting in Chapter 2 and then in later parts of the book. We also report new research on the relationship between the degree of multinationality and the performance of MNEs and other types of organizations.

The preceding two paragraphs indicate that the book will have a focus upon country factors and firm factors. In Chapter 2 we develop a framework to integrate these two basic aspects of international business. We look into the advantages and disadvantages of the home-country effect. For example, when countries such as Canada or Sweden are endowed with bountiful natural resources, for example, trees, then this is likely to lead to the growth of pulp and paper and newsprint firms. Similarly, countries with oil deposits will generate energy firms. We call these country-specific advantages (CSAs). Of course some countries, for example, Japan, have no oil, so we can say that Japan has a country disadvantage in energy (a negative CSA). In a similar manner, using modern concepts about the strategic advantages of firms, we can use the concept of firm-specific advantages (FSAs). These are unique assets proprietary to the firm, sometimes called capabilities and/or core competencies in the resourced-based view of the firm.

International competitiveness and firm strategy

In order to examine the country effect in full detail, we will introduce issues in international competitiveness. We will examine the home-country "diamond" model popularized by Michael Porter.[2] This diamond framework is relevant for mainly large countries, but for smaller economies a double-diamond framework will be introduced in Chapter 10.

In a similar vein some of the complexities of international management strategy can be captured through use of an economic integration and national responsiveness framework. This integration responsiveness model of international management strategy is also introduced in Chapter 10 and is then used as a basis for the remaining sections of the book. We also discuss organizational structures which are used by MNEs and other types of businesses.

To summarize, building upon the distinction between country and firm factors in this book we adopt a strategic management focus. This serves to integrate and simplify the many topics relevant in the study of international business. To illustrate the relevance of the strategic management approach to international business we include over a hundred case studies in the book. There are five of these in each chapter. In addition, in the text itself we discuss many other examples of individual firm strategy and country-level institutions.

Globalization

International business is sometimes confused with globalization. We define international business as the study of country-level and firm-level factors, as outlined above. However, globalization needs to be more narrowly defined. In its extreme form, globalization means the existence of a perfectly integrated world economic system. In such a global system there would be perfect mobility of financial capital, goods, and people. There would be a global commonality whereby identical values and tastes would occur. Yet, such a situation of perfect integration (technically called homogenization) does not exist. In fact, the data in this book will demonstrate that there is not even a trend toward globalization; nor do most firms have a global strategy, defined as selling the same product at the same price around the world. Instead, there remain strong barriers to the integration of the world's goods markets and people tend to be highly immobile (only financial markets appear to be global). Government regulation, at the national and regional levels, serves to segment country and regional markets. As a result, international business needs to study the nature of regions and the importance of regional strategy.

Regionalization

This book on international business differs from all other textbooks in this area because of its focus on the reality of regionalization. Most of the world's business activity takes place across countries but within the broad triad regions of Europe, North America, and Asia–Pacific. Indeed, the core triad of the EU, NAFTA, and Japan account for the majority of world trade and FDI. Of the world's 500 largest firms, the vast majority are home-region based. There are only a handful of "global" firms operating at a significant level in all three broad regions of the triad. In fact the world's 500 largest firms average 77 percent of their sales (and assets) in their home region. (We discuss these data in Chapter 3.) This indicates that international business needs to be analyzed more carefully than is the tradition in international business textbooks. We are proud that this book offers students up-to-date data and new insights into the true nature of globalization and the reality of regional business activity. Again, these themes are illustrated in the dozens of cases reported throughout the book. It will be seen that the majority of the world's MNEs have a regional strategy rather than a global strategy.

INTRODUCTION

International business
The study of transactions taking place across national borders for the purpose of satisfying the needs of individuals and organizations

Multinational enterprise (MNE)
A company headquartered in one country but having operations in other countries

International business is the study of transactions taking place across national borders for the purpose of satisfying the needs of individuals and organizations. These economic transactions consist of trade, as in the case of exporting and importing, and foreign direct investment, as in the case of companies funding operations in other countries. Over half of all world trade and approximately 80 percent of all foreign direct investment is made by the 500 largest firms in the world. These companies, called **multinational enterprises (MNEs)**, are firms that are headquartered in one country but have operations in one or more other countries. Who are these firms? Some of them you know by name because you have used their products or seen their advertising. In order of annual revenue, here is a list of the largest 20 MNEs that each grossed more than $125 billion in 2009 (Fortune Global 500, 2010 ranking, data are for 2009):

1 Wal-Mart (US)
2 Royal Dutch/Shell Group (UK/Netherlands)
3 Exxon Mobil (US)
4 BP (UK)
5 Toyota Motor (Japan)
6 Japan Post Holdings (Japan)

7 Sinopec (P.R. China)	14 Total (France)
8 State Grid (P.R. China)	15 Bank of America Corp. (US)
9 AXA S.A (France)	16 Volkswagen (Germany)
10 China National Petroleum (P.R. China)	17 ConocoPhillips (US)
11 Chevron (US)	18 BNP Paribas (France)
12 ING Group (the Netherlands)	19 Assicurazioni Generali (Italy)
13 General Electric (US)	20 Allianz (Germany)

A close look at this list shows that 17 of these 20 companies come from one of three geographic regions: the United States, the EU, or Japan. We call this the core "triad." And of these 17 companies, 6 were from the United States, 9 from the EU, and 2 from Japan. It is noteworthy that 3 of the top 20 companies are from China. The list helps point up an important fact and one that we will continue to emphasize throughout the book: companies from one of these core three geographic regions account for most of the world's international business.

In the next section we will discuss the core triad in more detail. It is important that we include Japan in the core triad as in Asia there are 71 firms from Japan and 46 from China in the top 500. Overall there are 155 firms from Asia, 160 from the EU(15), and 152 from North America. So later, from Table 2.1, we can develop the concept of the "broad" triad of the EU, North America, and Asia. The implications of this statement will be explained in greater detail in this next section where a brief overview of the world of international business is provided. We then elaborate on the triad theme in Chapter 3.

WORLD BUSINESS: A BRIEF OVERVIEW

There are thousands of MNEs that collectively perform a wide range of operations and services.[3] However, if we were to examine what these companies are doing, we would discover that much of their activity could be classified into two major categories: (1) exports and imports and (2) foreign direct investment (FDI). International business operations are discussed in more detail in Chapter 2.

Exports and imports

International trade
The exchange of goods and services across international borders

Exports
Goods and services produced by a firm in one country and then sent to another country

Imports
Goods and services produced in one country and bought in by another country

International trade is the exchange of goods and services across international borders and is also known as exports and imports. **Exports** are goods and services produced by a firm in one country and then sent to another country. For example, many companies in China export clothing and other textile products to the United States. **Imports** are goods and services produced in one country and brought in by another country. Japan, for example, is a major importer of petroleum because it must rely on outside suppliers for all of its energy needs. For the UK, the City of London generates exports of financial services that are "invisibles" in the British balance of payments. (See the Appendix to Chapter 6 for further discussion of the balance of payments.)

In most cases people think of exports and imports as physical goods (clothes, oil, cars), but they also include services such as those provided by international airlines, cruise lines, reservation agencies, and hotels. Indeed, many international business experts now recognize that one of the major US exports is its entertainment and pop culture such as movies, television, and related offerings.

Table 1.1 World Trade, 2008

Country/region	Imports		Exports	
	Billions of US $	% of total	Billions of US $	% of total
North America	2,093.06	12.63	2,682.54	16.70
United States	1,338.51	8.07	2,036.77	12.68
Canada	458.60	2.76	394.86	2.45
Mexico	295.95	1.78	250.91	1.56
European Union (15)	5,801.39	35.00	6,169.56	38.42
Asia including Japan	4,931.92	29.76	4,245.34	26.43
Japan	830.66	5.01	684.06	4.26
Other Asia	4,101.26	24.74	3,561.28	22.17
All others	3,745.63	22.60	2,959.16	18.42
Total	16,572.00	100.00	16,056.60	100.00

Note: Data for European Union include intra-EU trade. Exports are calculated by including freight and insurance while imports do not include freight and insurance. As a result data might not be consistent with other data in this book.

Source: Adapted from International Monetary Fund, *Direction of Trade Statistics Yearbook, 2009* (Washington, DC: IMF, 2009), pp. 2–5.

Table 1.1 provides a breakdown of worldwide trade in a recent year. The data show that the EU is the world's single largest exporter, followed by Asia and North America. These data are for 2008, when there were 15 member countries in the EU (there are now 27). We call them the EU15. The EU is also the largest importer, followed by Asia and North America. If you were to investigate further, you would find that the majority of this export and import activity involves manufactured goods such as industrial machinery, computers, cars, televisions, Consumer electronics, and other electronic goods. However, as will be seen later, an increasing proportion of world trade is in services.

Information on exports and imports is important to the study of international business for a number of reasons. First, trade is the historical basis of international business and trade activities help us understand MNE practices and strategies. In 2008 the world's largest importers were the United States, China, and Germany (see the Appendix, Table 1A). The world's largest exporters were China, Germany, and the United States (see the Appendix, Table 1B). Note that the world's top importers are also the world's largest exporters but in a different order. Some of the major products that are traded by these countries include computers, farm machinery, machine tools, automobiles, and electronic goods.

Second, trade helps us better understand the impact of international business on world economies. For example, Japan imports all of its oil. So when the price of oil in the world market rises sharply, we can readily predict that the cost of manufacturing cars in Japan will rise and Japanese auto exports will decline. Conversely, if oil prices decline, we can predict that world imports of Japanese cars are likely to increase.

A third reason why exports and imports are important in the study of international business is that they are the main drivers of international trade (FDI is another driver, which we discuss below and then in detail in Chapter 3). When worldwide exports and imports begin to slow down, this is a very good sign that world economies are going into a slump.

The US trade ties to Canada and Mexico reflect the triad effect, as these three countries are members of the North American Free Trade Agreement (NAFTA). Indeed, more than 57 percent of the exports of the United States, Canada, and Mexico are intra-regional, that is, to each other.[4] A similar picture of regional trade concentrations appears in the EU, where over 67 percent of all the exports of the EU 15 member states are with each other.[5] Similarly, over 54 percent of Asian exports are to other Asian countries.[6] Table 1.2

Table 1.2 Intra-regional trade in the triad, 1980–2008

Year	Intra-regional exports (%)		
	EU	NAFTA	Asia
2008	67.6	57.0	54.2
2000	67.2	58.1	42.4
1980	53.5	33.6	27.3
Cumulative Average Annual Change			
1980–2008	0.26	0.70	0.90
2000–2008	0.01	−0.02	0.28

Note: Asia data were calculated using information for exports from Japan, China, India, Indonesia, South Korea, Malaysia, Singapore, Thailand, and Australia to the Asian region and the world. Data for EU are for intra-EU exports in 2000 and 2008 and intra-EEC Exports in 1980.

Source: Authors' calculations based on the IMF, *Direction of Trade Statistics Yearbook*, 2009 and 1985.

reports that the majority of exports of these triad areas now occurs within each region and that this intra-regional trade has increased significantly since 1980. The recent decrease in intra-regional trade in the Asian region is partly due to the emergence of China as a manufacturer for the US market.

Foreign direct investment

Foreign direct investment (FDI)
Equity funds invested in other nations

Foreign direct investment (FDI) is equity funds invested in other nations. It is different from portfolio (financial) investment in that FDI is undertaken by MNEs which exercise control of their foreign affiliates. Like exports and imports, FDI is a driver of international business and many companies use FDI to establish footholds in the world marketplace by setting up operations in foreign markets or by acquiring businesses there. Firms engage in FDI for a number of reasons: to increase sales and profits, to enter rapidly growing markets, to reduce costs, to gain a foothold in economic unions, to protect domestic markets, to protect foreign markets, and to acquire technological and managerial know-how. These will be discussed in more detail in Chapter 3.

When examined from an overall perspective, FDI data show that industrialized countries have invested very large amounts of money in other industrialized nations as well as smaller amounts in less developed countries (LDCs) such as those in Eastern Europe or newly industrialized countries (NICs) such as Korea and Singapore. However, most of the world's FDI is invested both by and within the three broad triad groups we identified earlier: NAFTA, EU 15, and Asia. The United States is an excellent example of a country that is a major target of investment as well as a major investor in other countries. Its high GDP per capita and consumer spending make it an attractive market for foreign multinationals. Conversely, US firms have specialized capabilities that can be exploited in other countries.

By 2008 the United States had become such a major investment target that foreign holdings were over $2.3 trillion. (See Table 1.3a on stocks of FDI in the United States.) The largest investors are the UK, Japan, the Netherlands, Canada, Germany, Switzerland, and France. Collectively these countries account for over two-thirds of the stock of all FDI in the United States. Note that the Chinese stock of FDI in the United States is still so small that it does not make the list. At the same time, as seen in Table 1.3b, US companies have substantial FDI in other countries which amounts to more than $3.2 trillion. The major areas for this FDI are the Netherlands, the UK, Canada, Bermuda, and Luxembourg. Note that the US FDI stock in China is now on this list, but still only 1.45 percent of the total. Using FDI flow data the amount of Chinese FDI in the United States is much higher, but

Table 1.3a Foreign direct investment in the United States, 2008 (by US$ size ranking)

Economy/region	Millions of US $	% of total
All economies/ all countries	2,278,892	100.00
Canada	221,870	9.74
Europe	1,622,911	71.21
United Kingdom	454,123	19.94
Netherlands	259,385	11.38
Germany	211,521	9.28
Switzerland	165,697	7.27
France	163,430	7.17
Luxembourg	113,248	4.97
Spain	38,662	1.70
Sweden	35,020	1.54
Ireland	34,094	1.50
Belgium	18,580	0.82
Italy	17,575	0.77
Finland	12,499	0.55
Norway	6,755	0.30
Denmark	4,992	0.22
Austria	2,406	0.11
Latin America and other Western hemisphere	49,233	2.16
UK Islands, Caribbean	21,604	0.95
Bermuda	10,750	0.47
Mexico	7,948	0.35
Africa	2,002	0.09
Middle East	14,676	0.64
Asia and Pacific	368,200	16.15
Japan	259,569	11.39
Australia	64,316	2.82
Korea, South	15,632	0.69
Singapore	12,718	0.56
Hong Kong SAR (P.R. China)	3,973	0.17
Taiwan (Taiwan Province of China)	3,900	0.17

Note: Data are on a historical-cost basis. Numbers might not add up due to rounding.

Sources: Authors' calculations and ranking by US$ size and US Department of Commerce, *Survey of Current Business*, July 2009. Table 1255. Foreign Direct Investment Position in the United States on a Historical-Cost Basis by Selected Country, and by Industry

this is not reflected in the stock FDI data as it is much newer than the US FDI in Europe and Japan, where this grows through retained earnings.

A close look at Tables 1.3a and Table 1.3b shows that the UK and Japan have larger FDI stocks in the United States than the United States has FDI stock in the UK and Japan. The United States has larger FDI stocks in Europe than Europe has FDI stocks in the United States. On the other hand, US businesses have more FDI in Latin America and the Western hemisphere relative to the Europeans or Japanese. US companies have put much more FDI into Australia than Australia has FDI in the United States.

These recent data reveal two important trends. First, the United States is a prime site for FDI by both Japan and countries in Western Europe. Second, US firms have invested most heavily in Canada, Europe, Latin America, and other Western hemisphere areas, and Asia–Pacific. These four areas account for over 97.8 percent of the stock of all US FDI. (For more on FDI see the Appendix, Tables 1C and 1D, at the end of this chapter. We also discuss FDI and the role of MNEs in more detail in Chapter 2.)

Table 1.3b Foreign direct investment by the United States, 2008 (by US$ size ranking)

Economy/region	Millions of US $	% of total
All economies/ all countries	3,162,021	100.00
Canada	227,298	7.18
Europe	1,809,876	57.23
Netherlands	442,926	14.00
UK	420,873	13.31
Luxembourg	163,167	5.16
Ireland	146,194	4.62
Switzerland	123,358	3.90
Germany	110,784	3.50
France	75,040	2.37
Spain	69,649	2.20
Belgium	65,054	2.06
Sweden	43,391	1.37
Italy	28,653	0.91
Austria	17,518	0.55
Poland	15,597	0.49
Latin America and other Western hemisphere	563,809	17.83
Bermuda	165,857	5.24
UK Islands, Caribbean	139,290	4.40
Mexico	95,618	3.02
Brazil	45,500	1.43
Africa	36,640	1.16
Middle East	32,488	1.02
Asia and Pacific	491,910	15.55
Singapore	106,529	3.37
Australia	88,549	2.80
Japan	79,235	2.51
Hong Kong SAR (P.R. China)	51,505	1.63
China	45,695	1.45
Korea, South	27,673	0.88

Note: Data are on a historical-cost basis. Numbers might not add up due to rounding.

Sources: Authors' calculations and ranking by US$ size and US Department of Commerce, *Survey of Current Business*, July 2009. Table 1260. U.S. Direct Investment Position Abroad on a Historical-Cost Basis by Selected Country

✓ Active learning check

Review your answer to Active Learning Case question 1 and make any changes you like. Then compare your answer to the one below.

1 Why did Coke engage in foreign direct investments in Europe?

Coke made these investments in order to improve its market position. This is being done in three ways. First, the construction of new bottling plants is helping the company produce a low-cost product. Second, marketing expenditures are helping the firm gain the product recognition needed for growth. Third, direct investments in facilities closer to the market are reducing delivery time and eliminating associated expenses.

The triad

Triad
The three major trading and investment blocs in the international arena: the United States, the EU, and Japan

North American Free Trade Agreement (NAFTA)
A regional free trade agreement among Canada, the United States, and Mexico

As we noted above, companies in the United States, Western Europe, and Japan conduct most of the world's trade and FDI. Of these companies, those located in Western Europe mainly come from nations that are members of the EU. The core **triad** is a group of three major trading and investment blocs in the international arena: the United States, the EU, and Japan. Before looking more closely at the impact of the triad on international business, it is important to discuss the countries that are members of this group.

The first of these, the *United States*, has the largest economy in the world with a GDP of over $14.14 trillion (2009 estimate)![7] Sometimes when the United States is discussed as a member of the triad, Canada and Mexico are included. This is because these three countries implemented the **North American Free Trade Agreement (NAFTA)** in 1994, an international covenant that has resulted in the elimination of many trade and investment barriers between the three. We further discuss NAFTA in Chapter 19. In our discussions of the triad in the book, we will be talking only about the United States; if we intend to include Canada and Mexico we will indicate so by referring to them as members of NAFTA. The reason that our triad discussions will include only the United States is that the US economy is extremely large when compared to those of Canada and Mexico. As a result, if we were to talk about the 25 largest MNEs in NAFTA we would be discussing US firms only. Canadian or Mexican firms are not big enough to make this list of 25. Simply put, the US economy is so large that this one country constitutes an entire segment of the triad.

The second segment of the triad is the *European Union*. This group of nations, whose history and current developments will be discussed in Chapters 3 and 17, was formed by six countries in the late 1950s. Today there are 27 members of the EU. This includes the EU15—Austria, Belgium, Denmark, Finland, Germany, Greece, France, Ireland, Italy, Luxembourg, the Netherlands, Portugal, Spain, Sweden, and the UK—an additional 8 East European countries that joined on May 1, 2004—Czech Republic, Estonia, Latvia, Lithuania, Hungary, Poland, Slovenia, and Slovakia—as well as Cyprus and Malta. Bulgaria and Romania became members of the EU in 2007 (see map, European Union timeline) while Turkey continues to negotiate its entry into the union. In this book, unless noted otherwise, data are for the EU15. These are the largest countries in the group, accounting for 90 percent of the GDP of the EU. Statistical information on the EU27 is not yet generally available. The collective GDP of the EU is greater than that of the United States or Japan, and a brief look at some of the economic data in this chapter helps show how important the EU is in the international arena. For example, in terms of imports and exports, as seen back in Table 1.1, the EU accounts for more than 35 percent of all imports and over 38.4 percent of all world exports. Again, over 60 percent is intra-EU trade. Quite clearly, the EU is a worldwide economic force.

The third group in the core triad is *Japan*, which like the other two members plays a major role in international business. This is made particularly clear by looking at areas such as importing, exporting, and FDI. As seen in the Appendix, Tables 1A and 1B, at the end of the chapter, Japan is the world's fourth largest importer and fourth largest exporter. At market prices it is the largest economy in Asia and it has by far the highest GDP per capita. Japan accounts for 5 percent of all the world's imports and 4.3 percent of all of the world's exports. Japan also accounts for 4.2 percent of all outward stocks of FDI. (See the Appendix, Table 1D.)

In examining the current state of world business, the core triad merits close attention. Every year companies from these three groups account for more trade and FDI than those of any other economic bloc. As a result, during the twenty-first century the triad will be of central importance in the study of international business. We will discuss the power of the core triad in greater detail in Chapter 3.

Although the triad dominates international business, as discussed in this book, over the past few years a number of emerging economies have become increasingly important for international business. In particular, Brazil, Russia, India, and China (BRIC) are growing players in international trade and FDI. These countries will be explored further in Chapters 20 and 21, which deal with non-triad economies. (Chapter 21 deals entirely with China.)

TODAY'S INTERNATIONAL ENVIRONMENT

Although the triad continues to dominate the international business arena, the international environment has been changing rapidly in recent years. Today the world economy is quite different from what it was just five years ago. Some of the reasons include an overall slowdown in the triad economies, the introduction of more local and international trade regulation, the impact of technology, and the rise of small and medium-sized multinationals. The following briefly examines each of these.

Organization for Economic Cooperation and Development (OECD)
A group of 30 relatively wealthy member countries that facilitates a forum for the discussion of economic, social, and governance issues across the world

Economic developments are detailed by the **Organization for Economic Cooperation and Development (OECD)**, a Paris-based intergovernmental organization of the world's most economically advanced nations that provides its members with a forum for examining their economic problems and discussing solutions.

International trade regulation

Another important international business trend has been the emergence of trade and investment liberalization. Firms in triad countries have prospered in more open markets. Yet, at the same time, triad rivalry has led to some setbacks in trade liberalization. For example, Japan and China have been threatened with trade sanctions by the United States unless they allow US firms to sell products and services in their countries. There are also trade conflicts between the EU and the United States over biotech foods and crops, steel, beef hormones, and export subsidies.[8] Many such trade disputes, however, are handled not by countries but by international organizations set up to regulate international commerce. The main one is the World Trade Organization.

World Trade Organization (WTO)
An international organization that deals with the rules of trade among member countries; one of its most important functions is to act as a dispute-settlement mechanism

General Agreement on Tariffs and Trade (GATT)
A major trade organization that has been established to negotiate trade concessions among member countries

The **World Trade Organization (WTO)** was established on January 1, 1995, and it is now the umbrella organization that governs the international trading system. It is the successor to the **General Agreement on Tariffs and Trade (GATT)**. The GATT was established in 1947. The purpose of the GATT was to liberalize trade and to negotiate trade concessions among member countries. Although the early years saw a great deal of progress in reducing tariffs, by the 1980s there was a trend toward protectionism by many countries. At the GATT's eighth round of negotiations in 1986 (called the Uruguay Round because this is where the group met), negotiations dragged on for years before culminating in a number of agreements including reductions on industrial goods and agricultural subsidies, the increased protection of intellectual property rights under the Agreement on Trade-Related Aspects of Intellectual Property Rights (TRIPS), the creation of the General Agreement on Trade in Services (GATS), and the creation of the WTO to implement the GATT agreement. Today the WTO is enforcing these agreements. Presently, the Doha Round of the WTO has opened the door for further trade negotiations.

When member nations have a dispute they can turn to the WTO to help resolve it. For example, the United States brought a case against the EU charging it with a discriminatory banana import policy and the WTO ruled in its favor. In another case the United States requested that Japan be instructed to reorganize its commercial economy so that Kodak could better compete in that market against Fuji, its major rival, but the WTO rejected the claim and ruled in Japan's favor. In recent years the United States, the EU, and Japan, in particular, have been using the WTO to help resolve trade disputes, and this bodes well for the future of the organization. The important thing to remember about the WTO is that it can enforce its decisions. Countries that refuse to comply can find themselves suffering severe consequences in the form of trade retaliation. Despite minor conflicts, international trade liberalization has arrived and this promises to help stimulate international business transactions.

Technology

Another major development that is changing the way MNEs do business is technology. Two areas, in particular, are having a major impact. One is communication technology that has advanced at such a rapid rate that all businesses now use computers and rely on the World Wide Web to both access and send information. In addition, thanks to cellular technology, individuals can now remain in constant contact with both their customers and their home office. Communication technology has advanced so much that the latest technology

INTERNATIONAL BUSINESS STRATEGY IN ACTION

Amazon.com is not a global business

There are thousands of "global" businesses on the internet. However, the best known of these may well be Amazon.com. Everyday, thousands of people go to the company's website to browse and purchase books. A novel that is reviewed by Sunday in *New York Times Book Review* is likely to get a minimum of 10,000 hits within the next week, as readers read the comments of others, and check for price and availability. For example, the *Times Book Review* gave a good review to *Nickel and Dimed*, a book which had to that date generated lukewarm sales and for which its publisher had little hope, thousands went to Amazon.com to place an order and within a few hours the current inventory was exhausted. The incident shows the impact of not only the *Times Book Review* but also Amazon.com. The first created the demand while the second facilitated the distribution.

Amazon.com was founded in 1995 by Jeff Bezos. In less than 10 years the company became one of the largest 1,000 US corporations according to Fortune. In 2009, sales were $24,509 million. On the other hand, Amazon.com has consistently lost money. In 2000, every dollar sales the company took in, it lost 51 cents. Losses continued through to 2003, when a small profit was first reported.

Amazon was initially created to change the way people buy books. The company wanted to offer buyers a virtual store where they could use their computer to place an order that would then be delivered to them by mail. Going to a bookstore was going to be a thing of the past. In addition to making it easy to buy books, Amazon's prices were lower than those at most bookstores - even when shipping costs were added in, it was often less expensive to shop online with Amazon than it was to visit the local bookstore.

From the beginning, Bezos's strategy was to grow as fast as possible. He began recruiting highly skilled staff to design the e-commerce end of the business, as well as less skilled workers to handle warehouse, distribution, and supply operations. Initially, all of the employees had a common vision regarding what the company wanted to do. However, in a few short years, this rapid growth resulted in both confusion and internal problems. Among other things, some of the personnel filed lawsuits against the company for better compensation. Continued losses and the dot.com crash of 2000 severely reduced the price of its stock.

Today the biggest problem for Amazon.com is that it is not a global company - it is a US firm. The Internet is really only a tool for business and, in Amazon's case, a way to sell products that are produced by others. While the company now sells more than just books, it continues to be a US company. One reason is because books tend to sell most heavily in the market where they are published. A college text published in North America, for example, will not sell very much in Europe or Japan. Quite simply, triad and geographic regions segment the market—and even within this grouping, it can be difficult to sell to other countries. For example, in 2009, Amazon generated 53.3 percent of its sales in North America and 47.7 percent internationally. But even in Canada, the firm continually confronts a number of problems doing business including how to address Canadian sales taxes and how to deal with the threat by Canadian publishers of having the state-run postal service refuse to deliver "foreign" books. In fact, these problems have created such a headache for Canadian buyers that many of them now order their online books from Canadian suppliers such as Chapters and Borders rather than from Amazon. And in Europe, where Amazon operates through foreign subsidiaries, such as Amazon.co.uk, Amazon.fr, and Amazon.de, the company offers a totally different stock of books from those marketed in North America, and it targets a smaller, more affluent group of customers in this niche. The same marketing strategy is used in Asia. On both of these continents, customers are finding that local book suppliers often do a better job of meeting their needs in terms of both the range of their offerings and the price of their products. In short, Amazon.com is finding that if it wants to be a global competitor it is going to have to formulate a strategy that helps it expand out of the US market and become much more competitive throughout the triad. At the present time, Amazon.com is only half of the way there.

Websites: www.amazon.com; www.amazon.co.uk; www.amazon.co.jp; www.amazon.fr; www.amazon.de.

Sources: Amazon.com, *Annual Report*, 2009; Alan M. Rugman, *The End of Globalization* (London: Random House, 2001; New York: Amacom, 2000; Toronto: McGraw-Hill Ryerson, 2001); Robert Spector, *Amazon.com Get Big Fast* (New York: HarperCollins, 2000; London: Random House, 2000); *Fortune*, April 16, 2000, p. F63; *Fortune*, the Fortune 500, May 3, 2010.

reports reveal that there now are more than 499 million mobile (cellular) phone users in the EU15 (2009), or 77 percent of the population. In some EU countries, mobile users account for 90 percent of the population![9] Over 55 percent of the US population has access to the Internet.[10] The case **International Business Strategy in Action: Amazon.com is not a global business** discusses the issues of fast growth of new service businesses.

The other major application of technology is for the production of goods and services. Modern factories can now produce goods in a shorter period of time and with fewer defects thanks to production process programs. One example is the introduction of "Six Sigma"— a statistical term that means 3.4 errors per million—that eliminates performance problems in the production process and encourages worker participation and innovation to create products that meet the needs and wants of consumers.[11] Since Motorola engineers introduced the concept into their production process in the 1980s, hundreds of MNEs, including GE, Coca-Cola, and Boeing, have adopted the process, reducing defects, lowering costs, and improving quality.[12] (See Chapter 12 for a discussion of Six Sigma and other production process programs.)

Small and medium-sized enterprises (SMEs)

SMEs or small-and-medium-sized enterprises (SMEs)
Defined by Governments using different criteria for policy purposes. SMEs are firms with less than 250 employees in Europe, but less than 500 in the United States. Indian manufacturing firms qualify as SMEs if they invest less than US$2 million in plant and equipment.

Whenever MNEs are discussed, it is common to hear about large firms. In fact, the best-known multinationals are companies that have become household words. In the auto industry everyone knows of Honda, General Motors, and Volkswagen. However, there are thousands of **small and medium-sized enterprises (SMEs)**, many of whom are suppliers to these MNEs.[13] Most of these companies have annual sales of less than $5 million, but thanks to innovation, technology, and a well-trained workforce, they are able to compete effectively and perform functions that multinationals cannot do as efficiently. For example, some SMEs are able to provide their customers with two-day deliveries. In this way, their customers can keep a minimum amount of inventory on hand because the suppliers will replenish the stock every other day. And since these SMEs are small operations that focus heavily on cost control and quality, they are critical to the success of their customers. The result is that SMEs are proving to be the backbone of many industries because of their efficiency and flexibility. In addition, a number of SMEs compete effectively against large companies in niche markets. In this book we will be studying a large number of international business concepts that are used not just by MNEs but also by SMEs. In particular, we discuss the strategies of some SMEs in cases like Command Alkon in Chapter 9 and Mountain Equipment Co-op in Chapter 8.

GLOBALIZATION AND STRATEGIC MANAGEMENT

At the end of each chapter in this book we use Real Cases to illustrate some of the ways MNEs use the ideas that have been presented. In this opening chapter we introduced the world of international business and showed the impact of the triad on international trade and investment. We also noted that the major world economies are beginning to slow down and this, of course, is putting increased pressure on MNEs to maintain growth and profitability. In this section we want to address three areas that are important in understanding how companies are coping with this international environment. First, we are going to look at some of the misconceptions that people have about MNEs and how they formulate their international strategies. Second, we are going to look at some of the criteria that are important to MNEs in achieving strategic competitive advantage. Third, we are going to examine some examples of MNEs that are using concepts that we have introduced in this chapter.

Regional triad strategies

There are a number of misconceptions that people have about the world of international business, and it is important to dispel these at the very start of this book. One is the belief that multinationals have far-flung operations and earn most of their revenues overseas.

Nestlé is often cited as an example. This company sells over 8,500 products in more than 100 countries and earns more than 65 percent of its revenues outside of Switzerland.[14] Although this is true, Nestlé is an exception to the rule. Most MNEs earn the bulk of their revenues either within their home country or by selling in nearby locales. In fact, recent research reports that:

> More than 85 percent of all automobiles sold in North America are built in North American factories owned by General Motors, Ford, Daimler, Chrysler, or European or Japanese MNEs; over 90 percent of the cars produced in the EU are sold there; and more than 93 percent of all cars registered in Japan are manufactured domestically.
>
> In the specialty chemicals sector over 90 percent of all paint is made and used regionally by triad based MNEs and the same is true for steel, heavy electrical equipment, energy, and transportation.
>
> In the services sector, which now employs approximately 70 percent of the work force in North America, Western Europe, and Japan, these activities are all essentially local or regional.[15]

To be successful, MNEs need to create strategies that are regional, not worldwide, in focus and they need to be responsive to local consumers as opposed to being global in nature and uniform throughout.

Another misunderstanding about MNEs is the belief that they are globally monolithic and excessively powerful in political terms. Actually, the latest research shows that, of the 500 largest MNEs, well over 400 are headquartered in North America, the EU, and in Japan/Asia. We discuss this further in Chapter 2, Table 2.1. In short, these firms are not spread out around the world but are clustered in the triad. This relatively even distribution across the three regions of the triad implies not a dominant MNE culture but the interaction of different cultures in the international business arena. Recent research has also shown that the vast majority of MNEs have not been able to spread their marketing operations evenly across the world but depend on their own regions of the triad for over half of their revenue.[16] These companies are engaged not in global competition but in triad/regional competition, and this rivalry is so strong that it has effectively eliminated the possibility of their either achieving sustainable long-term profits or building strong, enduring political advantage. In fact, it is now common to find MNEs joining forces with local firms which can help them in their efforts to penetrate local markets. In recent years the **strategic alliance**, a business relationship in which two or more companies work together to achieve a collective advantage, has become extremely popular with MNEs which now realize that they need to develop strategies with a regional or local focus if they hope to succeed.

Strategic alliance
A business relationship in which two or more companies work together to achieve a collective advantage

A third misunderstanding is the belief that MNEs develop homogeneous products for the world market and through their efficient production techniques are able to dominate local markets everywhere. In fact, multinationals have to adapt their products for the local market. For example, there is no worldwide, global car. Rather, there are regionally based auto factories that are supported by local and regional suppliers which provide steel, plastic, paint, seats, tires, radios, and other necessary inputs for producing cars for that geographic region. Additionally, the car designs that are popular in one area of the world are typically rejected by buyers in other geographic areas. The Toyota Camry that dominates the US auto market is a poor seller in Japan and fares even worse in Europe.[17] And the Volkswagen Golf, which does extremely well in Europe, has not made much of an impact in North America. Pharmaceutical firms, which manufacture medicines that are often referred to as "universal products," have to modify their goods to satisfy national and state regulations, thus making centralized production and worldwide distribution economically difficult.[18]

In this book we are going to use examples throughout of what is happening in the international environment and show how an understanding of international business concepts can be useful to companies in addressing these developments. In many cases you will find that things you believed to be true are not. There is a great deal of misinformation about the world of international business. One of these misperceptions is that MNEs are giant corporations that are world dominant. In fact, their success comes most heavily from formulating and implementing strategies on a regional and local basis.

Maintaining economic competitiveness

The United States is one of the most competitive nations in the world.[19] How do US companies manage to achieve and then maintain this international competitive advantage? Another way of asking this question is: why are some firms able to innovate consistently while others cannot? Michael Porter of Harvard University has provided one of the best answers to this question. After conducting a comprehensive study of 100 industries in 10 countries, Porter found that the success of nations in international competition is determined by four broad attributes that individually and interactively determine national competitive advantage: factor conditions, demand conditions, related and supporting industries, and the environment in which firms compete.[20] These four determinants are briefly discussed below. This "diamond" model of Porter can be applied not only to US firms but to firms from any country.

Factor conditions

Factor conditions
Land, labor, and capital

According to basic international trade theory, a nation will export those goods that make most use of the factor conditions with which it is relatively well endowed. These **factor conditions** include land, labor, and capital. As a result, if a country has a large, relatively uneducated workforce, it will seek to export goods that are highly labor intensive. On the other hand, if the workforce is highly educated, the country will seek to produce goods and services that tap the intellectual abilities of these people. However, there is more to international trade theory than merely capitalizing on these basic factors. To maintain a competitive position, a country must continually upgrade or adjust its factor conditions. For example, Denmark has two hospitals that specialize in studying and treating diabetes; Denmark also is a world leader in the export of insulin. By creating specialized factors and then working to upgrade them, the country has maintained its premier position in the health-care field. Similarly, the Netherlands, the world's leading exporter of flowers, has created research institutes in the cultivation, packaging, and shipping of flowers. As a result, no one has been able to dislodge that country's foothold in the international flower industry.

✔ Active learning check

Review your answer to Active Learning Case question 2 and make any changes you like. Then compare your answer to the one below.

2 How did Coke improve its factor conditions in Europe?

Coke's factor conditions include land, labor, and capital. The company is using land and capital to build new bottling plants that are more efficient and better suited to meet market demand. It is working to improve the effectiveness of the labor force by getting the personnel to become more market oriented and to sell the product more vigorously throughout Europe.

Demand conditions

Porter states that a nation's competitive advantage is strengthened if there is strong local demand for its goods and services. This demand provides a number of benefits. First, it helps the seller understand what buyers want. Second, if changes become necessary, such as customer desires for a product that is smaller, lighter, or more fuel efficient, the local seller has early warning and can adjust or innovate for the market before more distant competitors can respond. In fact, the more sophisticated the local buyers, the greater the advantage to the local seller. For example, one reason that Japanese firms pioneered small, quiet air-conditioning units is that many Japanese live in small houses and apartments where loud noise can be a problem. Japanese firms also developed units that were powered by energy-saving rotary compressors because customers complained that the price of energy was very high and they wanted a more fuel-efficient unit. Similarly, Sweden, long concerned with helping the disabled, has spawned a competitive industry that focuses on the special needs of these people, and Denmark's environmental concern has resulted in Danish companies developing highly effective water-pollution control equipment and windmills. In the United States, consumers helped to develop a highly efficient fast-food industry, and as the desire for this cuisine spread worldwide, US franchisors like McDonald's and Pizza Hut have been able to tap international demand for their products.

Related and supporting industries

Porter's third major determinant of national competitive advantage is the presence of related and supporting industries that are internationally competitive. When suppliers are located near the producer, these firms often provide lower-cost inputs that are not available to the producer's distant competitors. In addition, suppliers typically know what is happening in the industry environment and are in a position to both forecast and react to these changes. By sharing this information with the producer, they help the producer maintain its competitive position. The Italian shoe industry is an excellent example. Shoe producers interact on a regular basis with leather manufacturers, exchanging information that is useful to each in remaining competitive. This interaction is mutually beneficial to both parties.[21]

Firm strategy, structure, and rivalry

Porter's fourth broad determinant of national advantage is the context in which the firms are created, organized, and managed, as well as the nature of domestic rivalry. No one managerial system is universally appropriate. Nations tend to do well in industries where the management practices favored by the national environment are suited to their industries' sources of competitive advantage. In Italy, for example, successful firms typically are small or medium sized; operate in fragmented industries such as lighting, furniture, footwear, and packaging machines; are managed like extended families; and employ a focus strategy geared toward meeting the needs of small market niches. Germany, in contrast, tends to have hierarchical organizations that emphasize technical or engineering content (optics, chemicals, complicated machinery) that demand precision manufacturing, a careful development process, after-sale service, and a highly disciplined management structure. In Japan, successful firms are often those that require unusual cooperation across functional lines and that demand management of complex assembly operations. Auto production, television manufacturing, and computer assembly are examples of such industries.

National goals are also important. Some countries want rapid results. Others tend to do best in industries where long-term development is valued more. In the United States, for example, investors like fast financial returns. So US firms are more likely to invest in new industries such as software and biotechnology where success can come quickly. In Germany and Switzerland, investments are held for long-term appreciation and are rarely traded. These countries are more likely to invest in mature industries where ongoing investment in research and development and new facilities are important but return on investment is only moderate.

Another area of importance is domestic rivalry. Researchers have found that vigorous domestic rivalry and competitive advantage are related. Nations with leading world positions often have a number of strong, local rivals. For example, in Switzerland, the pharmaceutical firms Roche and Novartis help the country to maintain its internationally competitive edge. In Germany, BASF and Bayer help the country to keep ahead in chemicals.

✓ Active learning check

Review your answer to Active Learning Case question 3 and make any changes you like. Then compare your answer to the one below.

3 How is local rivalry helping to improve Coke's competitive advantage?

Coke faces strong competition in Europe. Europeans do not drink as much Coke as do Americans; beverages such as coffee and tea are more popular. As a result, Coke has had to modify its strategy to address this market. This includes the building of new bottling plants that can help drive down costs and make the company more price competitive, and new marketing campaigns that are designed to draw customers away from competing products. Coke is also working to develop non-carbonated drinks to address local tastes. Finally, competition from locals who better understand their market is forcing Coke to "think local, act local."

Porter's determinants as a system

As noted earlier, each of Porter's determinants of international competitiveness often depends on the others. For example, even if a country has sophisticated buyers that can provide a company with feedback about how to modify or improve its product (demand conditions), this information will not be useful if the firm lacks personnel with the skills to carry out these functions (factor conditions). Similarly, if suppliers can provide the company with low-cost inputs and fresh ideas for innovation (related and supporting industries) but the firm clearly and easily dominates the industry (firm strategy, structure, and rivalry) and does not feel a need to upgrade the quality of its products and services, it will eventually lose this competitive advantage.

Research shows that of Porter's determinants of competitiveness, domestic rivalry/geographic clustering is particularly important. Domestic rivalry promotes improvements in the other three determinants and geographic concentration magnifies the interaction of the four separate influences.[22]

A firm's international abilities and competitiveness can also be described through a combination of firm-specific advantages (FSAs) and country-specific advantages (CSAs). This theoretical framework is developed in Chapter 2. The Porter country diamond framework, discussed in this section, is an excellent framework to capture the CSAs. In Chapter 2, we will start to discuss the FSAs of the MNE. The CSAs and FSAs can then be combined into the matrix of Chapter 2. This becomes the building block for the book. For example, the CSAs will be explored in more detail in Part Two of the book (Chapters 4, 5, 6, and 7), which deal respectively with political, cultural, trade, and financial issues. These are all issues affecting the environment of international business. Then, Part Three of the book looks into international business strategies. These includes MNE strategy, organizing strategy, corporate strategy and national responsiveness, and innovation, entrepreneurship and born global firms. Part Five provides insights of regional strategies. These includes European Union, Japan, North America, Emerging economies, China and corporate ethics and natural environment.

Multinationals in action

In each chapter of this book we are going to provide examples of how MNEs are using the ideas that we have been presenting. Usually we do this by highlighting a relevant case example, as in the box **International Business Strategy in Action: Tata**. In this first chapter we

INTERNATIONAL BUSINESS STRATEGY IN ACTION

Tata

One of India's largest multinational enterprises is Tata Group. In 2009, the total revenues for Tata Group are US $70.9 billion. The majority of its sales are still in Asia. Tata Group is one of the world's largest emerging economy MNEs. Its financial clout was shown when it purchased Corus in 2007, beating off a competing bid from a Brazilian company, Cia Siderurgica National.

Tata has about 100 different operating companies in all three regions of the triad, but still mainly in Asia. There are no data on its regional sales. Its major enterprises are: Tata Steel; Tata Consulting Services; Tata Motors; and Tata Tea. It employs over 250,000 people.

Its foreign holdings include the UK's largest steel company, Corus Group, which it bought in February 2007 for $12.2 billion. Its first foreign purchase was of the former stalwart of the British Empire, Tetley Tea, which it bought in 2000. Tata Group also own Eight O'Clock Coffee Co. of the United States which it bought in 2006 and Daewoo Commercial Vehicle Co. of South Korea which it bought in 2004. In September 2007 it was announced that Tata Motors Limited (part of the Tata Group) was going to buy up Jaguar and Land Rover from Ford Motor Company at a price of over $2 billion. Why has Tata become so successful?

Source: Getty Images/AFP

Tata's history is tightly intertwined with the history of India. Jamsetji Nusserwanji Tata founded a trading company in 1868, when India was still under British control, and soon entered the textiles market. It then forayed into the hotels business with the construction, in Mumbai, of the Taj Mahal Palace and Tower, the first Indian-owned luxury hotel. The story surrounding this event is that the owner of Tata was not allowed into British hotels because he was Indian and so now the international hotel chain has become a symbol of national pride. Today, Tata's influence can be seen throughout the Indian economy. Near the hotel you can see a Tata Power Plant that generates about 80 percent of the power in India's largest city. The urban landscape is filled with Tata cars, buses, and trucks as well as billboards advertising everything from Tata Tea to Tata credit cards.

The recent growth of this vast conglomerate is the result of two important events, deregulation and the appointment of Ratan Tata as chairman of the company. In 1991, the Indian government began to dismantle many of the bureaucratic impediments that had constrained Indian businesses. The same year, Ratan Tata took control of his family's company and began to rationalize the group by divesting itself of hundreds of companies. He kept about a hundred companies in key sectors and began to implement a series of strategic plans, including internationalization. Since 2000, Tata has purchased Tetley Tea (of the UK), 30 percent of Glaceu (a US manufacturer of bottled water), and Eight O'Clock Coffee (a US firm), all these in the beverages sector alone. Foreign acquisitions have also been part of the strategic plan of Tata Steel and Tata Motors.

Over the past few years, the steel industry has been consolidating through acquisitions. One example of this is Mittal Steel's purchase of Arcelor in 2007. Run by an India-born UK entrepreneur, the new company had shown interest in setting up integrated iron and steel plants in India. Tata Steel is considered the lowest-cost producer in the world but it felt threatened by such industry-wide consolidation. Mittal–Arcelor production capacity is much higher than Tata Steel's and its entry into the Indian market could reduce its costs, thus eroding Tata Steel's competitive advantage. For years, Tata Steel has been growing its capacity through acquisitions. In 2004 it purchased Singapore's NatSteel and the following year Thailand's Millennium Steel. Its biggest acquisition, however, came at the heels of Mittal's acquisition of Arcelor. In 2007 Tata Steel beat a Brazilian company to purchase Corus, an Anglo-Dutch steel maker that was much larger than itself. The price was $12 billion, the largest outward foreign acquisition by an Indian firm. Together, the new company is the world's fifth-largest steel producer, though, notably, it is still smaller than Mittal–Arcelor.

In the automotive sector, Tata chose not to partner up with a foreign company to produce passenger cars. The company's strategy is to create a cheap, functional car for the large untapped markets of developing nations and use that as a stepping stone for markets in developed countries. In 1988, Tata Motors launched the Indica, and in 2005 the car was retailing at $7,000. Not cheap enough. The company then developed the Ace, a small car that turned profitable rather quickly, covering its developing costs within a year of its release. The car cannot be exported to developed countries because of safety and emission regulations. If all goes well Tata Motors will start production of a $3,000 car. However, it is not going at it alone. In 2004 it purchased Daewoo's Commercial Vehicles of South Korea and in 2008 it bought up Jaguar and Rover from Ford Motor for a price of about $2.3 billion. This will infuse the company with the knowledge, technology, and capacity to carve itself a new and more upmarket niche in the automobile world market.

Tata companies might have the highest profile, but they are hardly the only ambitious Indian companies expanding overseas. In the first three quarters for 2006, Indian companies made 115 foreign acquisitions for a total value of $7.4 billion. Almost as many as foreign companies have invested in Indian companies. Over the past few years, Wipro, an IT company, has purchased companies in Portugal, Finland, and California. Ranbaxy, a maker or generic drugs, purchased Etimed of Belgium and Munogen of Spain, the generics arm of GlaxoSmithKline. This foreign expansion is being driven by strong balance sheets due to a domestic boom in India, the availability of credit, and a capable and ambitious group of entrepreneurs with a new-found confidence.

In summary, with total group revenue of $70.9 billion and about 100 companies, the Tata Group is the largest publicly traded company in India. Highly diversified, the conglomerate produces steel, cars, tea, and chemicals, and provides a series of services, including hotels, consulting, and telecommunications. Most of its operations are in its home market of India, where it derives about two-thirds of its total revenues, but it has recently aggressively increased its international presence to access the triad markets of Europe and North America, in addition to its presence in Asia.

Sources: Adapted from *Wall Street Journal*, August 27, 2007, p. A6; BBC News; *Financial Times*, various pages; "Steel Logic," *The Economist*, October 6, 2006; "Circle the Wagons," *The Economist*, October 12, 2006; "What is next for Tata Group?" *Forbes.com*, October 31, 2005; Eric Ellis, "Tata Steels Itself for Change," April 21, 2002; www.thebostonchannel.com/automotive/16456794/detail.htm; Annual Reports of the company, www.tata.com.

have examined the roles of importing, exporting, and FDI in international business, as well as discussing some of the things that MNEs have to do in order to create sustainable competitive advantage. Here are an additional three examples of how multinationals are using some of these ideas in their operations.

Volkswagen

Volkswagen (VW) is well known in the auto market, although like most MNEs it does much better in its regional market (Europe, where it has 71.41 percent of its sales in 2009) than it does in other areas of the triad. North America, VW's second-largest market, accounts for just 10.83 percent of total sales. The company's VW and Audi brand groups collectively hold 18.2 percent of the West European new passenger car market and 4.8 percent of the US market. In the past decade VW's market share in both Europe and America has increased because the company has been doing a number of things well. One is the use of innovative design. The top-selling VW brands in the United States, for example, all have innovative features, such that dashboard instruments such as the speedometer and clock light up in red at night, while those items that the driver touches, such as the radio, are backlit in blue. Commenting on these design features, one auto researcher remarked, "It gives the vehicle some soul, which many of VW's competitors lack horribly."[23] A second factor accounting for VW's success is its commitment to using the most efficient technology in building its cars. Its Wolfsburg plant in Germany is one of the most innovative in the world. It has the largest state-of-the-art paint shop in Europe, which uses eco-friendly, water-based paints. A combination of human skill and automation allows VW to design each car to each customer's specifications. Yet VW is not counting on its present achievements in design and production processes to maintain its competitive advantage. It must continuously update these to keep at the top of its game.

Carrefour

Carrefour is the world's second-largest retailer (behind Wal-Mart) and the largest in terms of number of stores and geographic coverage. In 2009, Carrefour had 69 percent of its sales in Europe but it had almost 15,594 stores spread throughout 29 countries on four continents. What makes the company particularly successful is its ability to create a local strategy for each of its units. Carrefour has a knack for designing its stores to meet local tastes. At least 90 percent of the goods that it sells in a store cater to the local market because the company believes that each unit should reflect the image of that country.[24] "You have to adapt your food and other products to the local culture," notes the company's chairman and chief executive officer; and this is done in a wide variety of ways.[25] For example, in Catholic Poland, the latest Carrefour hypermarket has a special religion section featuring Bibles, candles, and primers for children who are preparing for their first communion. In China, where many shoppers are superstitious, the company takes care to ensure that vegetables are chopped vertically—not laterally—so as not to bring bad luck to shoppers. And to make sure that it does not stumble badly by getting into countries where it truly does not know how to do business effectively, the company never sets up operations until it has researched the local market for at least one year so that it familiarizes itself with the customs of doing business there. As a result, while Wal-Mart has had a wide variety of operating problems in markets such as China, Thailand, and Brazil, Carrefour's efforts in these countries have all worked out well.

Kawasaki and Suzuki

Competition in the international motorcycle marketplace today is greater than ever. Japan is a good example. In this market where Honda and Yamaha are the leaders and Kawasaki and Suzuki are the next largest competitors, the four firms have consistently led the world market with their technologically innovative sports bikes. The problem for all four, however, is that the high cost of R&D has resulted in very high prices for their bikes. And to make matters worse, international rivals such as Harley Davidson of the United States, Triumph of the UK, Ducati of Italy, and BMW of Germany have all been aggressively remodeling their own products, improving the quality and specifications of these machines, setting competitive prices, and stepping up their worldwide marketing efforts. To meet these challenges, Kawasaki and Suzuki have now created a strategic alliance.[26] This alliance, the first ever in the Japanese motorcycle industry, breaks the pattern of each company competing fiercely with the other three. In particular, the two firms are going to jointly develop new models and unify their parts procurement and production activities in order to cut costs. They also plan on developing and building off-road motorcycles and high-powered scooters. The alliance could not have come at a better time. Worldwide market demand for motorcycles is poor, and both companies have seen declining sales in all three of their market regions: Asia, Europe, and the United States. However, the biggest competition is in the large-bike market, and Kawasaki and Suzuki intend to bypass this niche and focus instead on small bikes and scooters. The two believe that, if they can produce quality products at a competitive price, they can make major inroads in China. In the past this market has proved very difficult for Japanese motorcycle makers because Chinese companies have been able to pirate copies of their machines and then produce them in their own factories, without fear of any government intervention to stop such practices.[27] Under WTO rules this is something that China will have to do in the future or run the risk of severe economic retaliation. The decision by Kawasaki and Suzuki to form a strategic alliance and focus on China may prove to be a very profitable strategic move.

✓ Active learning check

Review your answer to Active Learning Case question 4 and make any changes you like. Then compare your answer to the one below.

4 Is the Coca-Cola Company a multinational enterprise? Is it global? Why?

Coke indeed is an MNE. The firm conducts production and distribution activities in nations other than its home country. And in terms of strategy and management orientation, Coke does three things that illustrate its multinational nature. First, the company modifies its operations to meet local needs. The firm markets on a country-by-country basis. Second, Coke has international partners which help to run the operation and do not report directly to the company on day-to-day matters. Third, the multinational relies heavily on teamwork by all involved parties and, to a large degree, serves more as a coordinator and cheerleader for the product than as an on-site manager.

Coke is a global company. Together, the United States and Canada account for just a third of its revenues. European and Asian operations are just as important for the company. No one region absolutely dominates. Unlike MNEs that depend predominantly on their home market, Coke has a global view and a global strategy.

THE STUDY OF INTERNATIONAL BUSINESS

As you have seen from the material in this chapter, the world of international business is undergoing a number of major changes. Quite clearly, international business is both an interesting and a challenging area! In this book we are going to study what international business is all about and what MNEs are now doing in order to compete effectively. In this section we examine the current state of the field of international business and then discuss the approach that will be used in this book in studying this field.

From general to strategic emphasis

The field of modern international business began to develop in the 1950s. At this time there were not a great number of MNEs and most of them were American. World War II had ended less than a decade before and many nations, including Japan and the European countries, were more concerned with rebuilding than with overseas investing. Early international business textbooks were often written by US professors and offered a general, descriptive approach to the field. There were few international research studies to provide substantive information. International companies that served as teaching examples were often those with international divisions, rather than true MNEs. And professors teaching international business were frequently educated in areas such as economics or general business and relied on an interdisciplinary approach to address the varied needs of the course. (Table 1.4 provides additional comparisons.)

During the 1970s and 1980s the field of international business changed greatly. The economic growth of Europe and Japan, coupled with great strides by newly industrialized countries (NICs), resulted in more and more attention being focused on international business. Professors were now becoming much more research oriented and the number of PhD-granting institutions offering at least a minor in international business began to increase. Articles and books by Canadian, European, and Asian professors started to appear and US research sophistication significantly improved. International economics

Table 1.4 Comparative differences in the study of international business, 1950–2010

Topic	1950–1969	1970–1989	1990–2010
Focus of interest	General information	Functional areas of development	Strategic emphasis
Approach to studying international business	Descriptive	Analytical	Integrative
Method of explanation	Heavily historical	Functional	Multidisciplinary
Research emphasis	Interdisciplinary	More quantitative research methods and overseas travel	Quantitative research methods, overseas travel, and international assignment
Enterprise viewpoint	US enterprises	MNEs	Networks
Countries examined	Industrialized	Industrialized, NICs, and LDCs	Industrialized, NICs, and LDCs
Number of journals	Some	Many	Ever increasing
Journal emphasis	General international topics	Functional	Functional and strategic
Amount of joint research	Some	Much more	Ever increasing

and finance now became primary areas of interest and the general research approach of the 1950s and 1960s was supplanted by more rigorous quantitative and methodological designs. More and more research studies were conducted and the number of journals in the field rose sharply. In the latter part of the 1980s we also saw the beginning of efforts to bring together much of what was happening into a meaningful composite. How could we understand what was going on in the world of international business, when so much seemed to be occurring at the same time? It was becoming evident that many of the developments of the 1970s and 1980s were being studied in too micro a fashion and a more macro approach to the field was needed.

The 1990s saw the emergence of a strategic management focus for drawing together the field of international business. The descriptive ideas of the 1950s and 1960s and the analytical ideas of the 1970s and 1980s were now being combined into an integrative approach. Historical and quantitative research was now being incorporated into models for describing, explaining, and helping predict what was happening in the international business arena. The earlier interdisciplinary and functional approaches were being supplemented by a multidisciplinary approach that drew on information from a wide variety of disciplines that affected international business. New journals in the field were also taking a more strategic management view of developments. This theme of **strategic management**, managerial actions that include strategy formulation, strategy implementation, evaluation, and control, encompasses a wide range of activities, including environmental analysis of external and internal conditions and evaluation of organizational strengths and weaknesses. In this text strategic management will serve as the basis for our overall framework.

Strategic management
Managerial actions that include strategy formulation, strategy implementation, evaluation, and control and encompass a wide range of activities, including environmental analysis of external and internal conditions and evaluation of organizational strengths and weaknesses

FRAMEWORK FOR THIS BOOK

This book employs a strategic management approach to the study of international business. In each chapter we will first study international business concepts and then we will examine how MNEs integrate these concepts into their overall strategy.

There are five major parts in this text. Part One is an introduction and encompasses this chapter and Chapters 2 and 3. The focus of attention in this part of the book is on such areas as imports, exports, FDI, the nature of MNEs, and the role and importance of the triad. Part Two examines the environments of international business with particular attention on international politics, culture, trade, and finance. Part Three focuses on overall international business strategies with a new chapter on Entrepreneurship and Innovation (Chapter 11). Part Four focuses on functional area strategies with particular attention to production strategy, marketing strategy, human resource management strategy, political risk, negotiation strategies, and international financial management and accounting. Part Five looks at the ways in which the information presented thus far in the book is being used by organizations to do business internationally. In this part, specific attention is given to strategic alliances, the flagship framework, and ways of doing business in the EU, Asia, North America, and emerging economies, including China.

Figure 1.1 presents an illustration of the model that will be used throughout this book. The current chapter has set the stage for the study of international business. In Chapter 2 we will examine the key actor on this stage: the MNE.

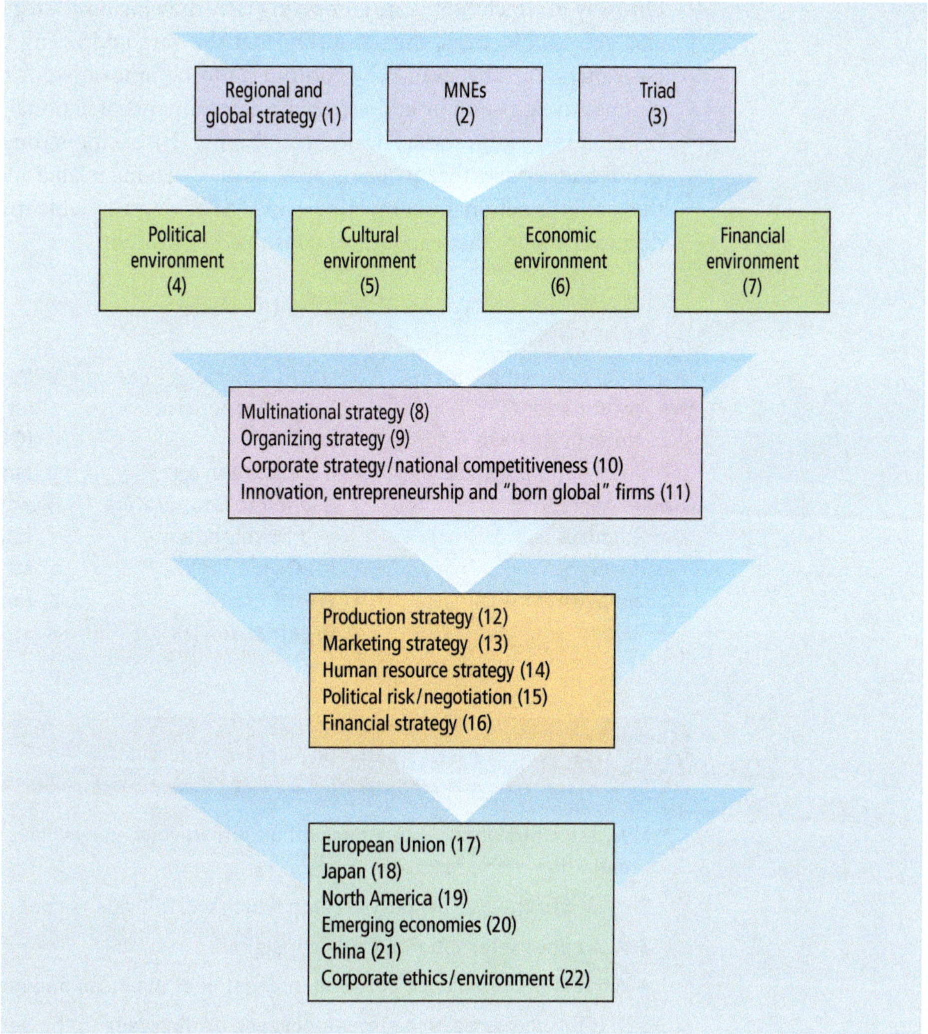

Figure 1.1 Model for this book

KEY POINTS

1 International business is the study of transactions taking place across national borders for the purpose of satisfying the needs of individuals and organizations. Two of the most common types of international business activity are export/import and foreign direct investment (FDI). In recent years both have been on the rise. Much of this is a result of large multinational enterprises (MNEs) that are headquartered in triad countries. In particular, triad members account for most of the worldwide trade and FDI. The majority of trade is intra-regional.

2 Small and medium-sized enterprises (SMEs) often function as the backbone of large MNEs, efficiently providing goods and services that are integrated into the production process of large MNEs. SMEs also compete with MNEs in niche markets.

3 Trade regulation has become an important issue in international business. Today the World Trade Organization is the major group responsible for governing the international trading system.

4 Changes taking place in both communication and production technologies are transforming the way in which MNEs do business.

5 One way in which MNEs are competing is by drawing up strategies that focus on regions and geographic areas, thus ensuring that they are addressing the needs of their local customers. Another way is by continuing to be innovative. A third is by maintaining competitive position by addressing the determinants of national competitive advantage: (a) creating the necessary factor conditions; (b) having strong local demand for the goods and services that are being produced; (c) having related and supporting industries that are internationally competitive; and (d) having a suitable strategy and structure and domestic rivalry that encourages continued innovation.

Key terms

- international business
- multinational enterprise (MNE)
- international trade
- exports
- imports
- foreign direct investment (FDI)
- triad
- North American Free Trade Agreement (NAFTA)
- Organization for Economic Cooperation and Development (OECD)
- World Trade Organization (WTO)
- General Agreement on Tariffs and Trade (GATT)
- small and medium-sized enterprises (SMEs)
- strategic alliance
- factor conditions
- strategic management

REVIEW AND DISCUSSION QUESTIONS

1 What is international business all about? In your answer be sure to include a definition of the term.

2 What are the two primary ways in which world trade is conducted?

3 What does international trade consist of?

4 What is the difference between international business and international trade?

5 Will foreign direct investment increase or decrease in the current decade? Why?

6 How important are the triad areas in promoting international commerce? Explain.

7 What role does the World Trade Organization play in the international business arena? Is the WTO helpful to international trade or is it a hindrance? Why?

8 Multinational enterprises do not formulate worldwide strategies, but rather regional strategies. What does this statement mean and how does it help us better understand international business?

9 How do the four determinants of national competitive advantage help explain how companies can maintain their economic competitiveness? Be complete in your answer.

10 What are two of the advantages associated with using strategic alliances?

REAL CASE

Big oil gets bigger

Between 1998 and 2009 there were a series of mergers in the oil industry that resulted in a handful of private companies emerging as dominant players. In the United States the largest of these was Exxon Mobil, the result of a 1999 merger. In 2009 this company had sales of $284.650 billion (see Table 1).

Table 1 Ranking of oil and gas MNEs, 2010

MNE	Country	Revenue (Millions of US $)
1 Royal Dutch Shell	UK/ the Netherlands	285,129
2 Exxon Mobil	United States	284,650
3 BP	UK	246,138
4 Sinopec	China	187,518
5 China National Petroleum	China	165,496
6 Chevron	United States	163,527
7 Total	France	155,887
8 ConocoPhillips	United States	139,515
9 ENI	Italy	117,235
10 Gazprom	Russia	94,472
11 Petrobras	Brazil	91,869
12 PDVSA	Venezuela	91,182
13 Pemex	Mexico	80,722
14 Statoil	Norway	74,000
15 Valero Energy	United States	70,035

Note: Revenues represent total revenues, including revenues from non-petroleum business.

Sources: Authors' calculations and research and Fortune, *The Fortune Global 500*, July 26, 2010 issue. Data are for 2009.

In Europe mergers and acquisitions had created two dominant firms. Royal Dutch/Shell Group is the largest with $285.129 billion in revenues, overtaking BP. In 2002, Royal Dutch/Shell purchased Pennzoil-Quaker State for $1.8 billion and consistently purchases stakes in other companies. Unlike most of its competitors, however, Royal Dutch has remained clear of any major mergers with competitors and has instead opted to rely on restructuring of its operations to remain competitive.

With $246.138 billion in revenues, the next largest European firm in the oil industry is BP. In 1998 Amoco merged with BP and subsequently the firm acquired a number of other companies, including Arco and Burmah Castrol. However, in 2010, BP had to conduct a massive divestment to raise funds of $30 billion by the end of 2011 to help meet the legal obligations for the environmental clean up arising from the explosion and fire accident on the Deep Horizon Rig in the Gulf of Mexico on April 20, 2010.

The fourth and fifth largest oil firms are Sinopec and China National Petroleum from China.

Texaco and Chevron merged in 2000 creating the world's sixth-largest oil firm. In 2001, Oklahoma-based Phillips Petroleum acquired Tosco, a major oil refiner. Soon after, Phillips merged into Conoco. Conoco Phillips is the world's eighth-largest oil firm, with revenues of $139.515 billion.

The seventh-largest firm in the industry is French-based Total, the result of a merger between Total Fina and Elf in 2000. Today the firm has revenues of $155.887 billion.

This pattern of increasing company size through acquisitions has also been occurring in Asia. In 1999 Nippon Oil bought Mitsubishi Oil, creating Japan's largest oil company. In 2005, Nippon Oil merged with Nippon Petroleum Gas. In 2006 Nippon Oil had revenues of $48.01 billion. In 2008, Nippon Oil conducted a management integration with Kyushu Oil.

Why are these oil companies merging? One of the main reasons is that the maturity of existing oil fields is forcing companies to search for new oil deposits in areas that are not easily accessible. Oil exploration in mountainous ▶

regions, the frigid Arctic, and ocean depths of more than a mile (1.6 km) requires extremely large capital outlays and entails a great deal of risk. In addition, these firms have to invest millions of dollars in research and development and sometimes end up spending years negotiating with governments for the right to drill for oil in the country (or in offshore waters that are controlled by them) and to build refineries and pipelines there. Only large companies with enormous financial resources are able to do this. State-owned oil MNEs are major competitors (see Table 2) and often hold a privileged position when accessing their own country's reserves. Moreover, if a company has a major oil strike, it has to be able to take advantage of economies of scale in order to bring the oil to market at competitive prices. Again, this development favors large firms. This is why experts in the energy business predict that there will be continual mergers and acquisitions in the industry as the large firms jockey for position and acquire smaller rivals and others in complementary businesses such as chemicals and oil-related products.

Table 2 The largest state-owned oil MNEs, 2010

MNE	Country	Revenue (Millions of US $)
1 Sinopec	China	187,518
2 China National Petroleum	China	165,496
3 Petrobras	Brazil	91,869
4 PDVSA	Venezuela	91,182
5 Pemex	Mexico	80,722
6 Statoil	Norway	74,000
7 Petronas	Malaysia	62,577
8 Indian Oil	India	54,288

Sources: Authors' calculations and research and Fortune, *Fortune*, The Global 500, July 26, 2010 issue. Data are for 2009.

Websites: www.shell.com; www.exxon.com; www.bp.com; www.total.com; www.chevron.com; www.eni.it; www.repsol-ypf.com; www.marathon.com; www.conoco.com; www.sk.com; www.nmoc.co.jp; www.phillips66.com; www.saudiaramco.com; www.pdvsa.com; www.sinopec.com.cn; www.petrobras.com.br; www.statoil.com; www.iocl.com.

Sources: Adapted from annual reports; "The Fortune Global 500," *Forbes*, July 26, 2010; "In Praise of Big Oil," *The Economist*, October 19, 2000; "ChevronTexaco Merger Approved by US Regulator," BBC.co.uk, September 7, 2001;" BP To Sell $1.8bn Assets to Help Pay for Oil Spill Bill," BBC.co.uk, October 18, 2010.

1 Are companies such as Exxon Mobil, BP Amoco, and Royal Dutch/Shell MNEs? What criteria do they meet that makes them MNEs?
2 How important is an understanding of governmental regulation to success in this industry?
3 In terms of Porter's determinants of national competitive advantage, which one of these four determinants is most important for these oil companies? Why?

REAL CASE

Wal-Mart

In 2001, Wal-Mart became the world's biggest company in terms of sales revenues, a title it has kept to date, a breathtaking achievement for the company that Sam Walton started in Arkansas as recently as 1962. Indeed, with revenues of $408.214 billion for the year ending in 2009, Wal-Mart is now ahead of General Motors and Exxon Mobil. The second-largest retailer, Carrefour with revenues of $121.452, is only about one-fourth the size of Wal-Mart.

Wal-Mart's success can be attributed to a scale strategy based on reduction of costs to steadily generate its "always low prices" formula and physical growth or market coverage. The United States offers the perfect landscape for Wal-Mart's expansion. Large, wealthy suburbs with vast, inexpensive land allow the firm to set up huge warehouse-style retail centers, reducing overall prices. This is complemented by an entrepreneurial culture in which store managers have a lot of decision-making power. Wal-Mart pushes its suppliers to provide the best product they can at the lowest possible price, making its products of better quality than those of other discount stores.

Presently, Wal-Mart commands an 8 percent share of the retail sales in its home market and its growth shows no signs of slowing down any time soon. The firm's critics accuse it of exploiting its workers, destroying traditional retail stores, and eroding the manufacturing industry by importing from countries with low labor costs, among other things. Even those who sympathize with objectors, however, might not resist saving $100 for an appliance. The criticism can be argued both ways. Some traditional retail stores suffered as a result of Wal-Mart's expansion, but if Wal-Mart sets up shop in a run-down mall, neighboring stores benefit from the increased traffic. This might include dollar-stores, haircutting places, and sportswear outlets, among others. Wal-Mart's bicycle section falls short of offering all the equipment, not to mention the service, of a traditional bicycle store. A mother buying her daughter her first bicycle might go to Wal-Mart, but a young woman looking for quality, accessories, service, and a knowledgeable salesperson might instead visit her local bike store. The same can be said for most product sections within the store. Large competitors have either stopped competing with Wal-Mart or sought to beat it at its own game. Indeed, Wal-Mart may be responsible for a more consumer-oriented retail service sector in the United States.

One main criticism of Wal-Mart is its dependence on imports from low-cost countries such as China. In 2003, the firm purchased approximately $15 billion in Chinese products, a fraction of revenues perhaps, but a sizeable amount just above the total revenues of McDonald's for the same year. Here, Wal-Mart had done nothing more than take advantage of the opportunities, available to all US retailers, that arose from the liberalization of China.

Those things that have helped Wal-Mart grow might be the same things that eventually will halt its growth. Low-cost laborers have a higher turnover. The firm hires approximately 600,000 new employees a year, and if it wants to reduce the costs of searching for personnel and training them, it might find that increased salaries and benefits are its only alternative. The firm has been constantly lowering the prices of its products, but this too will come to a stop when it exploits all available opportunities in low-cost areas and as China begins to see its production costs increase in the face of development. Finally, the entrepreneurial nature of Wal-Mart's decentralized business structure has meant that the organization lacks a coordinated bureaucracy with the power to impose corporate rules on store managers. For that reason, the firm is now being plagued with lawsuits, including a class action suit by its female employees for gender discrimination.

For future long-term growth, Wal-Mart has looked beyond its borders. However, while it has done extremely well in Canada, Mexico, and the UK, it has had a rough time in other markets, including Germany, Japan and Korea.

Wal-Mart's international expansion began in 1992 when it entered into a joint venture with Cifra SA, a successful Mexican retailer, in which it held 50 percent interest in its partner's retail operations. In 1998, Wal-Mart acquired a controlling interest in Cifra and officially changed the company's name to Wal-Mart of Mexico in 2000. Wal-Mart entered Canada in 1994 when it acquired 122 Woolco stores. Since then, the firm has established itself successfully in the markets of its NAFTA partners. One reason for this success is that it can rely on suppliers for its US stores to deliver products for the Canadian and Mexican market. In addition, the landscape, culture, and economic situation in Canada are much like in the United States.

The group entered Europe in the late 1990s, by purchasing the Wertkauf and Interspar supermarkets in Germany. Here, Wal-Mart ran into some trouble. Competitors in Europe had emulated the company's most successful strategies in cost reduction and supply-chain management, reducing Wal-Mart's relative competitive advantage. In Germany, local competitors offer very low prices, and Wal-Mart is not big enough to achieve the local economies of scale required to compete on price alone. There was also a different cost structure. Real estate development, when possible, was more costly and wages were also higher. The scale effect does not work in Europe. When the company must source 90 percent of its goods locally, which bargain or logistics savings can it cash in with so few stores? To top it all, Wal-Mart's US managers had problems adapting to the culture and did not speak German.

Wal-Mart entered the British market by acquiring ASDA and retained the name. ASDA had already adopted a focus on low prices and so it had exactly the type of consumer that Wal-Mart was looking for. Even though it has done relatively well in England, a low-cost strategy was secondary to developing long-term relationships with suppliers of well-known, quality-oriented, differentiated brands.

Wal-Mart launched its first store in South Korea in 1998, but in 2005, it ranked bottom of the nation's five discount store chains. Wal-Mart lost about 9.9 billion won in 2005 from its business in Korea, on sales of 750 billion won. In 2006, Wal-Mart pulled out of South Korea—selling its 16 Korean stores to the country's biggest discount chain. Shinsegae paid 825 billion won ($882 million) for Wal-Mart's South Korean operations.

Time, patient investment, and key expertise in each foreign market may help Wal-Mart to successfully expand its international operations to become a more international player. Until then, however, the firm remains extremely NAFTA focused.

Website: www.walmart.com.

Sources: Adapted from www.walmart.com; Wal-Mart, ***Annual Report 2002 and 2009; Fortune***, The Fortune Global 500, July 2002; Alan M. Rugman and Stephane Girod, "Retail Multinationals and Globalization: The Evidence Is Regional," ***European Management Journal***, 21, no. 1 (2003), pp. 24–37; "How Big Can It Grow?" ***The Economist***, April 15, 2004; 'Wal-Mart to Exit from South Korea," BBC.co.uk, May, 22, 2006; "Fortune Global 500," *Fortune*, July 26, 2010 issue.

1. Is Wal-Mart a multinational enterprise? Why?
2. Why is Wal-Mart making foreign direct investments in Europe?
3. Using the Porter model, what are the determinants of Wal-Mart's competitive advantage?
4. Is Wal-Mart's competitiveness in Europe dependent on the same determinants listed in question 3? Why?

ENDNOTES

1 Alan M. Rugman, *The End of Globalization* (London: Random House, 2000).

2 Michael E. Porter, "The Competitive Advantage of Nations," *Harvard Business Review*, March/April 1990, pp. 80–81.

3 United Nations, *World Investment Report 2007* (Geneva: UNCTAD, 2007) stated that there over 60,000 MNEs in the world. But most of them are small companies. The largest 500 MNEs account for over 80 percent of all the sales of the MNEs. We focus on the 500 MNEs in this book.

4 See Alan M. Rugman, *The End of Globalization* (London: Random House, 2000), Chapter 7, pp. 120–137. These data were for 1999 and have been updated for this book using the same sources.

5 Ibid. Chapter 7, pp. 120–129. These data were for 1999 and have been updated to 2009 for this book using the same sources.

6 Ibid. Chapter 7, pp. 120, 134–136. These data were for 1999 and have been updated to 2009 for this book using the same sources.

7 GDP is at purchasing power parity. CIA, *The World Factbook 2010*. www.cia.gov.

8 Nancy Dunne, "US Sends Top Official to Help Solve Trade Dispute," *FT.com*, November 27, 2001; United States Department of Agriculture, "U.S. and Cooperating Countries File WTO Case Against the EU Moratorium on Biotech Foods and Crops," *USDA News Release*, May 13, 2003; Jagdish Bhagwati, "The Unwinnable War," *FT.com*, January 29, 2002; "EU Hits Back Against US Steel Duties," *BBC News*, March 7, 2002; Andrew Walker, "EU Says Science Backs Its Beef Ban," *BBC News*, October 15, 2003.

9 EUROSTAT, Number of Mobile Phone Subscriptions (1000), http://epp.eurostat.ec.europa.eu "International Roaming," *Press Release*, July 26, 2004.

10 International Telecommunications Union, www.itu.int. The World in 2010: ICT Facts and Figures.

11 Richard M. Hodgetts, *Measures of Quality and High Performance* (New York: American Management Association, 1998).

12 Debby Arkell, "Better, Faster, Cheaper—But Most of All, Better," *Boeing Frontiers*, vol. 2, no. 3, July 2003.

13 Also see Paul Ellis and Anthony Pecotich, "Social Factors Influencing Export Initiation in Small and Medium-Sized Enterprises," *Journal of Marketing Research*, February 2001, pp. 119–130.

14 UNCTAD, *World Investment Report 2003* (New York: United Nations, 2003).

15 Alan Rugman and Richard Hodgetts, "The End of Global Strategy," *European Management Journal*, August 2001, pp. 333–343.

16 Alan M. Rugman, *The Regional Multinationals* (Cambridge: Cambridge University Press, 2005).

17 Dan Lienert, "The Best-Selling Cars," *Forbes*, August 2, 2004.

18 Rugman, op. cit. (2005).

19 IMD, World Competitiveness Yearbook, 2010.

20 The following section is based on Michael Porter, *The Competitive Advantage of Nations* (New York: Free Press, Macmillan, 1990), especially Chapters 3 and 4.

21 Michael E. Porter, "The Competitive Advantage of Nations," *Harvard Business Review*, March/April 1990, pp. 80–81.

22 Porter, ibid., p. 83.

23 Christine Tierney et al., "Volkswagen," *Business Week*, July 23, 2001, p. 64.

24 Sarah Ellison, "Carrefour and Ahold Find Shoppers Like to Think Local," *Wall Street Journal*, August 31, 2001, p. A5.

25 Richard Tomlinson, "Who's Afraid of Wal-Mart?" *Fortune*, June 26, 2000, p. 188.

26 David Ibison and Rpohit Jaggi, "Kawasaki Joins Suzuki in Search of an Easier Ride," *Financial Times*, August 30, 2001, p. 15.

27 "Kawasaki and Suzuki Join Forces," *BBC News*, August 29, 2001.

ADDITIONAL BIBLIOGRAPHY

Boddewyn, Jean J., Toyne, Brian and Martinez, Zaida L. "The Meanings of 'International Management'," *Management International Review*, vol. 44, no. 2 (Second Quarter 2004).

Collinson, Simon and Rugman, Alan, M. "Case Selection Biases in Management Research: Implications for International Business Studies," *European Journal of International Management*, vol. 4, no. 5 (2010).

Dicken, Peter. "*Global Shift*", 6th Edition (London: Sage, 2011).

Dunning, John H. "The Study of International Business: A Plea for a More Interdisciplinary Approach," *Journal of International Business Studies*, vol. 20, no. 3 (Fall 1989).

Forsgren, Mats and Yamin, Mo, "A Commentary on Adam Smith and International Business," *Multinational Business Review*, vol. 18, no. 1 (2010).

Fruin, W. Mark. "Bringing the World (Back) into International Business," *Journal of International Business Studies*, vol. 38, no. 2 (March 2007).

Ghemawat, Pankaj. "Distance Still Matters: The Hard Reality of Global Expansion," *Harvard Business Review*, vol. 79, no. 8 (September 2001).

Ghemawat, Pankaj. *Redefining Global Strategy: Crossing Borders in a World Where Differences Still Matter* (Harvard Business School: Harvard Business School Press, 2007).

Girod, Stéphane J.G. and Rugman, Alan M. "Regional Business Networks and the Multinational Retail Sector," *Long Range Planning*, vol. 38, no. 4 (August 2005).

Jones, Geoffrey and Khanna, Tarun. "Bringing History (Back) into International Business," *Journal of International Business Studies*, vol. 37, no. 4 (July 2006).

Morck, Randall and Yeung, Bernard. "History in Perspective: Comment on Jones and Khanna 'Bringing History (Back) into International Business'," *Journal of International Business Studies*, vol. 38, no. 2 (March 2007).

Porter, Michael E. *The Competitive Advantage of Nations* (New York: Free Press, Macmillan, 1990).

Rugman, Alan M. *Inside the Multinationals: The Economics of Internal Markets* (New York: Columbia University Press, 1981).
Rugman, Alan M. *Rugman Reviews International Business* (Basingstoke: Palgrave Macmillan, 2009).
Rugman, Alan M. "The International Financial Crisis and Multinational Enterprise Strategy," *Transnational Corporation*, forthcoming (2011).
Rugman, Alan M. and Girod, Stéphane. "Retail Multinationals and Globalization: The Evidence is Regional," *European Management Journal*, vol. 21, no. 1 (2003).
Rugman, Alan M. and Verbeke, Alain. "A New Perspective on the Regional and Global Strategies of Multinational Service Firms," *Management International Review*, vol. 48, no. 4 (2008).
Rugman, Alan M., Verbeke, Alain and Nguyen, Quyen T.K. (2011). "Fifty Years of International Business Theory and Beyond," *Management International Review*, vol. 51, no. 6 (November 2011).
Yip, George S. *Total Global Strategy 2* (Upper Saddle River, NJ: Prentice Hall, 2002).

APPENDIX TO CHAPTER 1

Table 1A The top 25 importers in the world, 2008

Rank	Country	Value of world imports (billions of US $)
1	United States	2,166.0
2	China, PR	1,526.3
3	Germany	1,204.8
4	Japan	761.8
5	France	706.7
6	UK	634.8
7	Netherlands	581.6
8	Italy	556.3
9	Belgium	470.2
10	Korea	435.2
11	Canada	408.2
12	Spain	403.0
13	Singapore	319.7
14	India	315.1
15	Mexico	308.6
16	Russia	266.9
17	Brazil	208.9
18	Poland	205.1
19	Turkey	201.9
20	United Arab Emirates	196.6
21	Australia	191.9
22	Austria	184.5
23	Switzerland	183.0
24	Thailand	178.5
25	Sweden	167.6

Note: China includes mainland China, Hong Kong, and Macao.

Source: Adapted from the individual country sections of the International Monetary Fund, *Direction of Trade Statistics Yearbook, 2009* (Washington, DC: IMF, September 2009).

Table 1B The top 25 exporters in the world, 2008

Rank	Country	Value of world exports (billions of US $)
1	China, PR	1,794.0
2	Germany	1,465.1
3	United States	1,300.0
4	Japan	783.1
5	France	606.6
6	Netherlands	638.6
7	UK	461.0
8	Italy	539.9
9	Belgium	477.1
10	Russia	459.7
11	Canada	456.5
12	Korea	426.7
13	Singapore	399.4
14	Saudi Arabia	303.9
15	Mexico	291.3
16	Spain	267.5
17	Brazil	202.5
18	Switzerland	200.0
19	Malaysia	199.5
20	India	198.2
21	Australia	185.6
22	United Arab Emirates	185.0
23	Sweden	184.0
24	Austria	181.7
25	Thailand	173.2

Note: China includes mainland China, Hong Kong, and Macao.

Source: Adapted from the individual country sections of the International Monetary Fund, *Direction of Trade Statistics Yearbook, 2009* (Washington, DC: IMF, September 2009).

Table 1C Inward stocks of world foreign direct investment, 2008 (by US$ size ranking)

Country/region	2000		2008	
	(millions of US $)	% of total	(millions of US $)	% of total
Developed countries	3,960,321	68.79	10,212,893	68.50
Europe	2,281,563	39.63	6,932,525	46.50
EU				
France	259,775	4.51	991,377	6.65
United Kingdom	438,631	7.62	982,877	6.59
Germany	271,611	4.72	700,471	4.70
Netherlands	243,733	4.23	644,598	4.32
Spain	156,348	2.72	634,788	4.26
Belgium	—	—	518,940	3.48
Italy	121,170	2.10	343,215	2.30
Sweden	93,995	1.63	253,502	1.70
Ireland	127,089	2.21	173,420	1.16
Poland	34,227	0.59	161,406	1.08
Denmark	45,916	0.80	150,492	1.01
Austria	31,165	0.54	139,340	0.93
Czech Republic	21,644	0.38	114,369	0.77
Portugal	32,043	0.56	99,820	0.67
Finland	24,273	0.42	87,860	0.59
Luxembourg	23,492	0.41	85,353	0.57
Hungary	22,870	0.40	63,671	0.43
Slovakia	4,746	0.08	45,933	0.31
Greece	14,113	0.25	36,703	0.25
Cyprus	2,910	0.05	20,706	0.14
Estonia	2,645	0.05	15,962	0.11
Slovenia	2,894	0.05	15,782	0.11
Lithuania	2,334	0.04	12,847	0.09
Latvia	2,084	0.04	11,447	0.08
Malta	2263	0.04	9,142	0.06
Belgium/Luxembourg	195,219	3.39	—	—
Other developed Europe	118,209	2.05	500,632	3.36
Switzerland	86,804	1.51	374,054	2.51
Norway	30,265	0.53	121,521	0.82
Others	1,140	0.02	5,057	0.03
North America	1,469,583	25.53	2,691,160	18.05
United States	1,256,867	21.83	2,278,892	15.29
Canada	212,716	3.69	412,268	2.77
Other developed countries	209,175	3.63	589,207	3.95
Australia	111,139	1.93	272,174	1.83
Japan	50,322	0.87	203,372	1.36
Others	47,714	0.83	113,661	0.76
Developing countries	1,736,167	30.16	4,275,982	28.68
Africa	154,244	2.68	510,511	3.42
Asia and Oceania	1,079,436	18.75	2,583,855	17.33
Latin America and the Caribbean	502,487	8.73	1,181,615	7.93
South East Europe and CIS	60,873	1.06	420,414	2.82
South-East Europe				
Total	5,757,360	100.00	14,909,289	100.00
Least developed countries	39,061	0.68	136,167	0.91

Note: Numbers might not add up due to rounding.

Source: Authors' calculations and ranking by US$ size and United Nations, *World Investment Report*, 2009, pp. 251–254.

Table 1D **Outward stocks of world foreign direct investment, 2008 (by US$ size ranking)**

Country/region	2000 (millions of US $)	2000 % of total	2008 (millions of US $)	2008 % of total
Developed countries	5,186,178	85.44	13,623,626	84.06
Europe	3,250,775	53.55	8,997,437	55.52
EU				
United Kingdom	897,845	14.79	1,510,593	9.32
Germany	541,861	8.92	1,450,910	8.95
France	445,091	7.33	1,396,997	8.62
Netherlands	305,461	5.03	843,737	5.20
Spain	129,194	2.12	601,849	3.71
Belgium	—	—	588,269	3.63
Italy	180,275	2.96	517,051	3.19
Sweden	123,256	2.03	319,310	1.97
Denmark	44,981	0.74	192,523	1.18
Ireland	27,925	0.46	159,363	0.98
Austria	24,821	0.40	152,562	0.94
Finland	52,109	0.85	114,526	0.71
Portugal	19,793	0.32	63,642	0.39
Luxembourg	7,927	0.13	62,664	0.38
Greece	6,094	0.10	32,441	0.20
Poland	1,018	0.01	21,814	0.13
Hungary	1,280	0.02	14,179	0.08
Cyprus	560	0.01	10,493	0.06
Czech Republic	738	0.01	9,913	0.06
Slovenia	768	0.01	8,650	0.05
Estonia	259	0.01	6,686	0.04
Lithuania	29	0.00	1,990	0.01
Slovakia	373	0.01	1,901	0.01
Malta	193	0.00	1,517	0.01
Latvia	24	0.00	1,066	0.01
Belgium/Luxembourg	179,773	2.96	—	—
Other developed Europe	266,850	4.39	910,633	5.61
Switzerland	232,161	3.82	724,687	4.47
Norway	34,026	0.56	171,164	1.05
Others	663	0.01	14,782	0.09
North America	1,553,886	25.59	3,682,420	22.72
United States	1,316,247	21.68	3,162,021	19.51
Canada	237,639	3.91	520,399	3.21
Other developed countries	381,518	6.28	943,768	5.82
Japan	278,442	4.58	68,033	4.19
Australia	85,385	1.40	194,721	1.20
Others	17,691	0.29	68,716	0.42
Developing countries	862,358	14.20	2,356,649	14.54
Africa	44,155	0.72	97,958	0.60
Asia and Oceania	613,815	10.11	1,697,259	10.47
Latin America and the Caribbean	204,388	3.36	561,432	3.46
South East Europe and CIS	21,345	0.35	225,387	1.39
South-East Europe				
Total	6,069,882	100.00	16,205,663	100.00
Least developed countries	3,172	0.05	10,284	0.06

Note: Numbers might not add up due to rounding.

Source: Authors' calculations and ranking by US$ size and United Nations, *World Investment Report*, 2009, pp. 251–254.

CHAPTER 5

Trade and Factor Mobility Theory

OBJECTIVES

After studying this chapter, you should be able to

1. Understand how different approaches to international trade theories help policy makers achieve economic objectives
2. Comprehend the historical and current rationale for interventionist trade theories
3. Explain how free trade improves global efficiency
4. Distinguish factors affecting national trade patterns
5. Recognize why a country's export capabilities are dynamic
6. Detect why production factors, especially labor and capital, move internationally
7. Describe the relationship between foreign trade and international factor mobility
8. Grasp scenarios of possible changes in trade patterns

Source: © Edelweiss - Fotolia.com

MyManagementLab®

Improve Your Grade!

When you see this icon, visit **www.mymanagementlab.com** for activities that are applied, personalized, and offer immediate feedback.

A market is not held for the sake of one person.

—African (Fulani) proverb

CASE Costa Rica's Trade Evolution

Costa Rica is a Central American country of about 4.7 million people that borders the Pacific Ocean and the Caribbean arm of the Atlantic.[1] Bearing a name that means "Rich Coast," referring to its fertile soil and bountiful biodiversity, the country possesses attributes of both developed and developing countries. With a per capita GDP of $12,600 (based on purchasing price parity in 2012), Costa Rica depends on agricultural commodities—primarily bananas, pineapples, and coffee—for about 36 percent of its merchandise export earnings. However, its tourism earnings are higher than for those top three agricultural exports combined. (The opening photo is in a bio-diverse area that attracts ecotourism.) Costa Rica has a fairly high level of external debt, a literacy rate of about 95 percent, a life expectancy of 78 years, and a fairly even income distribution (the highest 10 percent of the population earns about 40 percent of its income). It has also enjoyed a long history of democracy and political stability. Map 5.1 shows Costa Rica's location and major export markets.

FOUR ERAS

Like all countries, Costa Rica relies on international trade and factor-mobility policies—strategies related to the movement of goods, services, and production factors across borders—to pursue its economic objectives. In any country, these two sets of policies evolve as domestic and foreign conditions change. They're also politically sensitive, especially when it comes to the economic priorities and judgments of the nation's leaders.

For Costa Rica, it's convenient to trace policy evolution through four historical periods, each characterized by particular strategies of international trade and factor mobility:

- *Late 1800s–1960: Liberal trade*—a policy calling for minimal government interference in trade and investment
- *1960–1982: Import substitution*—a policy calling for the local production of goods and services that would otherwise be imported
- *1983–early 1990s: Liberalization of imports,* export promotion, and incentives for most types of foreign investments
- *Early 1990s–present: Strategic trade policy* (or *industrial policy*) calling for the production of specific types of products and openness to imports

LATE 1800s–1960

In the latter part of the 1800s, most nations permitted goods, capital, and people to move with relative freedom from one country to another. Governments tended to interfere only minimally, and the general result was an economic environment in which individual producers determined what to produce and where to produce it. Trade flourished and countries tended to specialize in selling what they could best produce.

Most Latin American countries, including Costa Rica until the early 1960s, specialized in either a single or a few commodities (raw materials or agricultural products), which they exported in exchange for other commodities and manufactured goods. Costa Rican farmers specialized first in coffee and later, after the development of refrigerated ships, in bananas as well. For most of the period, the country was well served by this policy, primarily because commodity prices, especially coffee prices, remained high.

Eventually, however, three factors convinced Costa Rican leaders to encourage more diversified production and economic self-sufficiency:

- Two world wars disrupted the country's ability to export its commodities and import what it did not produce.
- Coffee and banana prices dropped relative to the prices of manufactured products, particularly as new commodity producers (especially in Africa) entered world markets.
- Latin American countries with less open international markets had insulated themselves more from adverse international conditions.

As a result of these developments, Costa Rica turned to policies centered on the idea of import substitution.

1960–1982

In the early 1960s, Costa Rican authorities reasoned that if they limited imports (say, by taxing them heavily), they'd give both home and foreign investors an incentive to produce and sell more things within the country; this policy is known as **import substitution**. They also realized that, unfortunately, the Costa Rican market was too small to support investments requiring large-scale production.

To address this problem, Costa Rica joined with four other countries—El Salvador, Guatemala, Honduras, and Nicaragua—to form the Central American Common Market

MAP 5.1 Costa Rica

In 2011, a bit more than 50 percent of Costa Rica's exports went to three countries. (Much of the exports shown for the Netherlands are transshipped to other European countries.)

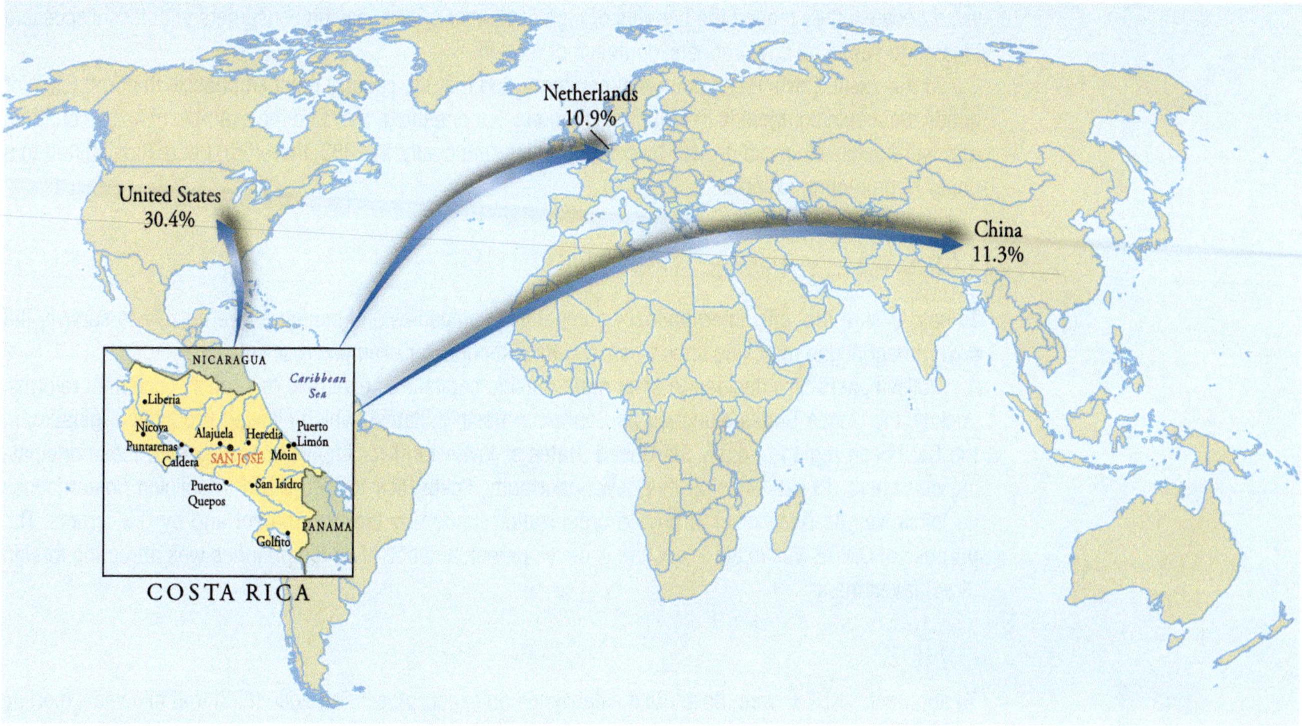

(CACM), which allowed goods produced in any member country to enter freely into the market of any other member. Thus, a company located in a member country could serve a five-country rather than a single-country market.

Miscalculations and Mixed Results

The results were mixed. Costa Rica's economic dependence on agriculture was already declining before the import substitution policy, from 40.9 percent to 25.2 percent of GDP between 1950 and 1960. Thus, the decline to 18 percent by 1980 could not be attributed completely to the policy change.

Likewise, most investors earmarked their new manufacturing to sell domestically and not in the larger CACM market. For example, import substitution helped attract pharmaceutical investment, but the availability of a larger market was not the primary reason; in this case, the strategy worked basically because small-scale packaging and processing are efficient within this industry.

So why was the strategy of import substitution, even coupled with a complementary regional trade agreement, less successful than CACM leaders had hoped? Quite simply, investors were convinced that CACM was destined for disruption—and, as it turned out, they were right. By the late 1970s, civil wars in both El Salvador and Guatemala stifled those economies, and a new regime in Nicaragua was ideologically committed to complete governmental control of all aspects of the economy, including trade.

In some cases, import substitution did lead to increased exports, such as for Costa Rican processed coffee and cottonseeds. Many economists and prospective investors, however, began to worry that policies designed to protect local production—including price controls, import bans, and subsidies—were channeling the country's resources toward inefficient production. For example, Costa Rica became nearly self-sufficient in rice production, but only because government policies kept lower-cost foreign-produced rice out of the market.

Moreover, the government held down consumer rice prices by subsidizing domestic rice producers. The money for these subsidies came largely from higher taxes on efficient industries—industries that, in turn, found expansion hard because they were strapped for cash. Finally, some inefficient producers survived because they reaped the benefits of high consumer prices, leaving consumers with less disposable income to spend on any products, domestic or foreign.

At this point, Costa Rican policymakers concluded that the country must emphasize the production of goods that could compete in international markets. For one thing, they had the example of Asian countries that were achieving rapid growth by competing internationally. In 1983, therefore, Costa Rica shifted to a policy of promoting exports.

1983–EARLY 1990s

To help ensure that only internationally competitive companies and industries were likely to survive, the government began removing import barriers. Rice imports, for example, rose substantially.

Policymakers also decided to seek more outside capital and expertise to support economic reforms. Luckily, the United States launched its Caribbean Basin Initiative, which allowed products originating in the Caribbean region to enter the United States at lower tariff (or import tax) rates than those originating elsewhere. To capitalize on this new opportunity, Costa Rica formed CINDE (Coalición Costarricense de Iniciativas de Desarrollo), a private organization funded by the government and by U.S. grants. The purpose of CINDE was to aid in economic development, and one of its top priorities was attracting foreign direct investment.

CINDE

To augment CINDE's work, Costa Rica established an export processing zone (EPZ) that allowed exporting companies to import all inputs and equipment tax free, exempted them from paying Costa Rican income tax for eight years and taxed them at only 50 percent for the next four. By 1989, 35 companies—mainly textile and footwear producers seeking to take advantage of the country's pool of inexpensive labor—had located in the EPZ.

By this time, however, CINDE's officials were beginning to worry about two potential problems facing its ambitious new initiatives:

1. Costa Rica could not remain cost-competitive in the type of products exported from the EPZ because other countries (mainly Mexico) were benefiting from even lower U.S. tariffs.
2. Costa Rica's highly skilled and educated workforce was being underutilized by the types of industries attracted to the EPZ.

CINDE decided to work with the Costa Rican government to identify and attract investors who matched up better with Costa Rican resources.

EARLY 1990s–PRESENT

Costa Rica targeted industries (a policy known as a **strategic trade policy**) for international competition (including medical instruments and appliances, electronics, and software) that promised high growth potential and could pay higher wages and salaries than most of those that had already invested in the EPZ.

The government also identified characteristics of developing countries that were attracting significant amounts of the type of foreign investment it wanted: a highly educated and largely English-speaking workforce (especially the availability of engineers and technical operators), political and social stability, a relatively high level of economic freedom, and a quality of life that would appeal to the managers and technical personnel that foreign investors would bring in to work in the facilities. The conclusion? In its targeted industries, Costa Rica should be able to compete internationally.

What CINDE Recommended

CINDE also hired the Foreign Investment Advisory Service (FIAS) of the World Banks' International Finance Corporation to study whether and how to attract companies in these industries. FIAS concluded that attracting the right number of the right companies was well within Costa Rica's reach, and suggested areas within this selection of targeted industries, such as power technologies, that best fit with the country's main advantage—a labor force that was well educated in relation to its cost. It also recommended that officials target companies that supported the electronics and computer industries, such as plastics and metalworking. Finally, FIAS noted that Costa Rica needed to improve the English proficiency of its technicians and engineers and the protection of intellectual property rights. In response, Costa Rica put English language skills in a revised curriculum for training mid-level technicians and set up Spanish-language training for the personnel brought in by foreign investors.

Progress Report

Setting out to attract investments in electronics and software, Costa Rica landed such high-tech investors as Reliability, Protek, Colorplast, and Sensortronics. By far, the largest investor was the computer-chip giant Intel. CINDE officials worked to attract Intel. They drew up a list of all the questions and concerns Intel might have and prepared knowledgeable responses to them. They also involved top government and corporate leaders in meetings with Intel executives, even enlisting the country's president, José Figueres, to pilot them on a helicopter survey of plant sites.

Since then, Costa Rica has turned its attention to medical devices, and attracted investments by such companies as Abbott Laboratories, Baxter, and Procter & Gamble. Although exports of coffee and bananas are still important to the nation's economy, about 60 percent of Costa Rica's merchandise exports are now manufactured goods, with high-tech products constituting the backbone of the economy and export earnings. ■

CRN
Case Review Note

QUESTIONS

5-1. Using the framework in Table 5.1, explain which of the theories relate to Costa Rican trade policy during each of the four eras described in the case.

5-2. Map 5.1 shows that a bit over 50 percent of Costa Rican exports go to only three countries. Which trade theories may help to explain this concentration and why?

INTRODUCTION

The preceding case shows how Costa Rica has used trade and factor mobility (movement of capital, technology, and people) to help achieve its economic objectives. Figure 5.1 shows that countries are linked internationally by trade in goods and services and the movement of production factors. Like Costa Rica, other countries wrestle with the questions of what, how much, and with whom to trade. These questions are intertwined with considerations of what they can produce competitively by boosting the quality and quantity of capital, technical competence, and worker skills.

CRN
Case Review Note

Trade theory helps managers and government policymakers focus on these questions:

- What products should we import and export?
- How much should we trade?
- With whom should we trade?

LAISSEZ-FAIRE VERSUS INTERVENTIONIST APPROACHES TO EXPORTS AND IMPORTS

Once countries set economic and political objectives, officials enact policies—including trade policies—to achieve desired results. This influences which countries can produce given products more efficiently and whether countries will permit imports to compete against their

FIGURE 5.1 International Operations and Economic Connections

To meet its international objectives, a company must gear its strategy to trading and transferring its means of operation across borders—say, from (Home) Country A to (Host) Country B. Once this process has taken place, the two countries are connected economically.

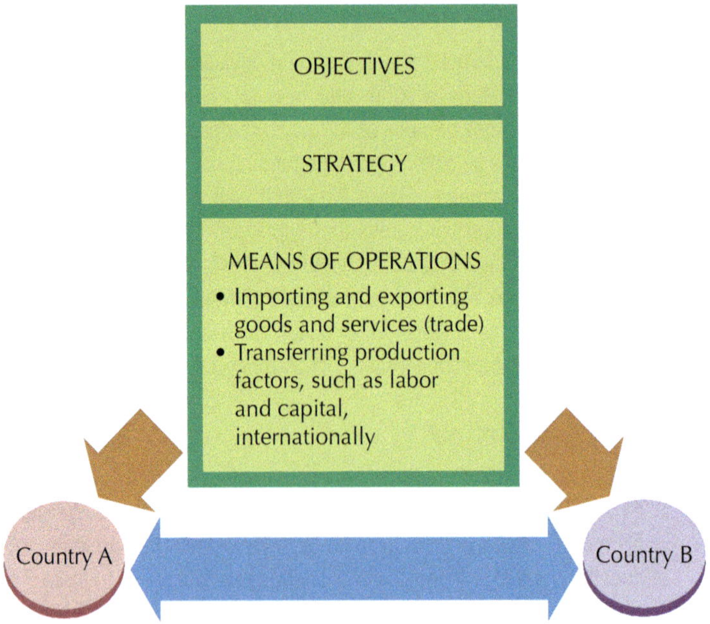

CONCEPT CHECK

Compare Figure 5.1 with Figure 1.1, which outlines certain conditions that may affect a firm's operations when it decides to do business on an international scale. Here the graphic focuses in on operational adjustments that a company faces when it takes specific strategic actions to go international—namely, to trade and transfer means of production.

domestically produced goods and services. Some nations take a more *laissez-faire* approach, one that allows market forces to determine trading relations. *Free-trade theories* (absolute advantage and comparative advantage) take a complete laissez-faire approach because they prescribe that governments should not intervene directly to affect trade. At the other extreme are *mercantilism* and *neomercantilism,* which prescribe a great deal of government intervention in trade. Whether taking a laissez-faire or interventionist approach, countries rely on trade theories to guide policy development.

Some trade theories prescribe that governments should influence trade patterns; others propose a laissez-faire treatment of trade.

THEORIES OF TRADE PATTERNS

After taking a look at theories dealing with trade intervention, we examine those that help explain trade patterns (how much countries depend on trade, in what products, and with whom), including theories of *country size, factor proportions,* and *country similarity.* We then consider theories dealing with the dynamics of countries' trade competitiveness for particular products, which include the *product life cycle theory* and the *diamond of national competitive advantage theory.*

TRADE THEORIES AND BUSINESS

Table 5.1 summarizes the major trade theories and their emphases. These different theories expand our understanding of how government trade policies might affect business competitiveness. For instance, they provide insights on favorable locales and products for exports, thereby helping companies determine where to locate their production facilities when governments do or do not impose trade restrictions.

FACTOR-MOBILITY THEORY

Because the stability and dynamics of countries' competitive positions depend largely on the quantity and quality of their production factors (land, labor, capital, technology), we'll conclude this chapter with a discussion of factor mobility.

TABLE 5.1 What Major Trade Theories Do and Don't Discuss: A Checklist

A check mark indicates that a theory of trade concerns itself with the question asked at the head of the column; if there's a dash, it doesn't. In columns 4–7, you can see how each theory responds to the specific question; again, a dash indicates that the theory does not address the question.

	Description of Natural Trade			Prescription of Trade Relationships			
Theory	**How Much Is Traded**	**What Products Are Traded?**	**With Whom Does Trade Take Place?**	**Should Government Control Trade?**	**How Much Should Be Traded?**	**What Products Should Be Traded?**	**With Whom Should Trade Take Place?**
Mercantilism	—	—	—	yes	✓	✓	✓
Neomercantilism	—	—	—	yes	✓	—	—
Absolute advantage	—	✓	—	no	—	✓	—
Comparative advantage	—	✓	—	no	—	✓	—
Country size	✓	✓	—	—	—	—	—
Factor proportions	—	✓	✓	—	—	—	—
Country similarity	—	✓	✓	—	—	—	—
Product life cycle (PLC)	—	✓	✓	—	—	—	—
Diamond of national competitive advantage	—	✓	—	—	—	—	—

INTERVENTIONIST THEORIES

Let's begin with mercantilism because it is the oldest trade theory, out of which neomercantilism has more recently emerged. These theories are based on some of the reasons for governmental intervention, but there are other reasons as well that we discuss in the next chapter.

MERCANTILISM

According to mercantilism, countries should export more than they import.

Mercantilism holds that a country's wealth is measured by its holdings of "treasure," which usually means its gold. According to this theory, which formed the foundation of economic thought from about 1500 to 1800,[2] countries should export more than they import and, if successful, receive gold from countries that run deficits. Nation-states were emerging during this period, and gold empowered central governments to raise armies and invest in national institutions so as to solidify the people's primary allegiance to the new nations.

Governmental Policies To export more than they imported, governments restricted imports and subsidized production that otherwise could not compete in domestic or export markets. Some countries used their colonies to support this trade objective by having the colonies supply commodities that the colonial powers would otherwise have to purchase from nonassociated countries and by running trade surpluses as an additional way to obtain gold. They did this not only by monopolizing colonial trade but also by forcing their colonies to export less highly valued raw materials to them and import more highly valued manufactured products from them.

As the influence of the mercantilist philosophy weakened after 1800, the governments of colonial powers seldom directly intended to limit the development of industrial capabilities within their colonies. However, their home-based companies had technological leadership, ownership of raw material production abroad, and usually some degree of protection from foreign competition—a combination that continued to make colonies dependent on raw material production and tie their trade to their industrialized mother countries. We still see vestiges of these relationships, which we discuss in the next chapter.

Running a favorable balance of trade is not necessarily beneficial.

The Concept of Balance of Trade Some terminology of the mercantilist era has endured. For example, a **favorable balance of trade** (also called a **trade surplus**) still indicates that a country is exporting more than it imports. An **unfavorable balance of trade** (also known as a **trade deficit**) indicates the opposite. Many of these terms are misnomers. For example, the word *favorable* implies "benefit," and the word *unfavorable* suggests "disadvantage." In fact, it is not necessarily beneficial to run a trade surplus or detrimental to run a trade deficit. A country with a favorable balance of trade is, for the time being, supplying people in foreign countries with more than it receives from them.[3]

In the mercantilist period, the difference was made up by a transfer of gold; today it is made up by granting credit to the deficit country by holding its currency or investments denominated in that currency. If that credit cannot eventually buy sufficient goods and services, the so-called favorable trade balance actually may turn out to be disadvantageous for the country with the surplus.

NEOMERCANTILISM

A country that practices neomercantilism attempts to run an export surplus to achieve a social or political objective.

The term **neomercantilism** describes the approach of countries that try to run favorable balances of trade in an attempt to achieve some social or political objective. A country may aim for increased employment by setting economic policies that encourage its companies to produce in excess of the demand at home and send the surplus abroad. Or it may attempt to maintain political influence in an area by sending more merchandise there than it receives from it, such as a government granting aid or loans to a foreign government to use to purchase the granting country's excess production.

CONCEPT CHECK

In Chapter 1, we observe that nations are currently in the mood to reduce barriers to the movement of trade, capital, technology, and people; we also explain that this policy reflects a couple of key facts—namely, that consumers want a greater variety of goods and services at lower prices and that competition spurs efficiency.

FREE-TRADE THEORIES

Why do countries need to trade at all? Why can't Costa Rica (or any other country) be content with the goods and services it produces? In fact, many countries following mercantilist policy tried to become as self-sufficient as possible. In this section, we discuss two theories supporting free trade: *absolute advantage* and *comparative advantage.*

Both theories hold that nations should neither artificially limit imports nor promote exports.[4] The market will determine which producers survive as consumers buy those products that best serve their needs. Both free trade theories imply *specialization.* Just as individuals and families produce some things that they exchange for things that others produce, national specialization means producing some things for domestic consumption and export while using the export earnings to buy imports of products and services produced abroad.

THEORY OF ABSOLUTE ADVANTAGE

According to Adam Smith, a country's wealth is based on its available goods and services rather than on gold.

In 1776, Adam Smith questioned the mercantilists' assumptions by stating that the real wealth of a country consists of the goods and services available to its citizens rather than its holdings of gold. This theory of **absolute advantage** holds that different countries produce some goods more efficiently than others, and questions why the citizens of any country should have to buy domestically produced goods when they can buy them more cheaply from abroad. Smith reasoned that unrestricted trade would lead a country to specialize in those products that gave it a competitive advantage. Its resources would shift to the efficient industries because it could not compete in the inefficient ones. Through specialization, it could increase its efficiency for three reasons:

1. Labor could become more skilled by repeating the same tasks.
2. Labor would not lose time in switching production from one kind of product to another.
3. Long production runs would provide incentives for developing more effective working methods.

The country could then use its excess specialized production to buy more imports than it otherwise could have produced. But in what products should a country specialize? Although Smith believed the marketplace would make the determination, he thought that a country's advantage would be either *natural* or *acquired.*

Natural advantage considers climate, natural resources, and labor force availability.

CRN
Case Review Note

Natural Advantage A country's **natural advantage** in creating a product or service comes from climatic conditions, access to certain natural resources, or availability of certain labor forces. As we saw in our opening case, Costa Rica's climate and soil support the production of bananas, pineapples, and coffee, while its biodiversity supports a thriving ecotourism industry. Costa Rica imports wheat. If it were to increase its wheat production, for which its climate and terrain are less suited, it would have to use land now devoted to the cultivation of bananas, pineapples, and coffee, or convert some of its biodiverse national park areas to agricultural production, thus reducing those earnings.

Conversely, the United States could produce coffee (perhaps in climate-controlled buildings), but at the cost of diverting resources away from products such as wheat, for which its climate and terrain are naturally suited. Trading coffee for wheat and vice versa is a goal more easily achieved than if these two countries were to try to become self-sufficient in the production of both. The more the two countries' natural advantages differ, the more likely they will favor trade with one another.

Variations among countries in natural advantages also help explain where certain manufactured or processed items might best be produced, particularly if a company can reduce transportation costs by processing an agricultural commodity or natural resource prior to exporting. Processing coffee beans into instant coffee reduces bulk and is likely to reduce transport costs on coffee exports; producing canned latte could add weight, lessening the industry's internationally competitive edge.

Acquired advantage consists of either product or process technology.

Acquired Advantage Most of today's world trade is of manufactured goods rather than agricultural goods and natural resources. Countries that are competitive in manufactured goods have an **acquired advantage**, usually in either product or process technology. An advantage of *product technology* is that it enables a country to produce a unique product or one that is easily distinguished from those of competitors. For example, Denmark exports silver tableware, not because there are rich Danish silver mines but because Danish companies have developed distinctive products.

An advantage in *process technology* is a country's ability to efficiently produce a homogeneous product (one not easily distinguished from that of competitors). Japan has exported steel despite having to import iron and coal to produce it because its steel mills have encompassed new labor- and material-saving processes. Thus, countries that develop distinctive or less expensive products have acquired advantages, at least until producers in another country emulate them successfully.

Acquired advantage through technology has created new products, displaced old ones, and altered trading-partner relationships. The most obvious examples of change are production and export of new products and services, such as software. Products that existed in earlier periods have increased their share of world trade because of technological changes in the production process. For example, early hand-tooled automobiles reached only elite markets, but a succession of manufacturing innovations, from assembly lines to robotics, has enabled automobiles to reach an ever-widening mass market.

In other cases, companies have developed new uses for old products, such as aloe in sunscreen. Other products, such as artificial fibers, have partially displaced traditional ones. Finally, technology may be used to overcome natural advantages. Iceland now exports tomatoes grown near the Arctic Circle, while Brazil exports quality wine produced near the equator—both of which were impossible until the development of fairly recent technology.[5]

Free trade will bring
- Specialization.
- Greater efficiency.
- Higher global output.

How Does Resource Efficiency Work? We can demonstrate absolute trade advantage here by examining two countries and two commodities. Because we are not yet

FIGURE 5.2 Production Possibilities under Conditions of Absolute Advantage

In short, specialization increases potential output.

ASSUMPTIONS
for Costa Rica

1. 100 units of resources available
2. 10 units to produce a ton of wheat
3. 4 units to produce a ton of coffee
4. Uses half of total resources per product when there is no foreign trade

ASSUMPTIONS
for United States

1. 100 units of resources available
2. 5 units to produce a ton of wheat
3. 20 units to produce a ton of coffee
4. Uses half of total resources per product when there is no foreign trade

PRODUCTION	Coffee (tons)	Wheat (tons)
Without Trade:		
Costa Rica (point *A*)	$12\frac{1}{2}$	5
United States (point *B*)	$2\frac{1}{2}$	10
Total	15	15
With Trade:		
Costa Rica (point *C*)	25	0
United States (point *D*)	0	20
Total	25	20

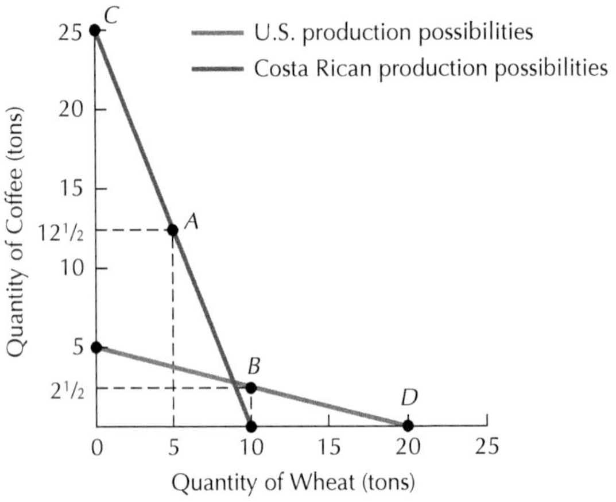

considering the concepts of money and exchange rates, we define the cost of production in terms of the resources needed to produce either commodity. This example is realistic because real income depends on the output of goods compared to the resources used to produce them.

Say that Costa Rica and the United States are the only two countries and each has the same amount of resources (land, labor, and capital) to produce either coffee or wheat. Using Figure 5.2, let's say that 100 units of resources are available in each country. In Costa Rica, assume that it takes four units to produce a ton of coffee and 10 units per ton of wheat. The purple Costa Rican production possibility line shows that Costa Rica can produce 25 tons of coffee and no wheat, 10 tons of wheat and no coffee, or some combination of the two.

In the United States, it takes 20 units per ton of coffee and five units per ton of wheat. The green U.S. production possibility line indicates that the country can produce five tons of coffee and no wheat, 20 tons of wheat and no coffee, or some combination of the two. Costa Rica is more efficient (that is, takes fewer resources to produce coffee), while the United States is more efficient in wheat production.

How can production be increased through specialization and trade? Let's say the two countries have no foreign trade. We could start from any place on each production possibility line; for convenience, let's assume that if each country devotes half of its 100 resources to production of each product, Costa Rica can produce 12.5 tons of coffee (divide 50 by 4) and five tons of wheat (divide 50 by 10), shown as point A in Figure 5.2, while the United States can produce 2.5 tons of coffee (divide 50 by 20) and 10 tons of wheat (divide 50 by 5), shown as point B in Figure 5.2.

Because each country has only 100 units of resources, neither can increase wheat production without decreasing coffee production, or vice versa. Without trade, the combined production is 15 tons of coffee (12.5 + 2.5) and 15 tons of wheat (5 + 10). If each country specialized in the commodity for which it had an absolute advantage, Costa Rica could then produce 25 tons of coffee and the United States 20 tons of wheat (points C and D in the figure).

You can see that specialization increases the production of both products. By trading, global efficiency is optimized, and the two countries can have more coffee and more wheat than they would without trade.

THEORY OF COMPARATIVE ADVANTAGE

Gains from trade will occur even in a country that has absolute advantage in all products, because the country must give up less efficient output to produce more efficient output.

We have just described absolute advantage, which is often confused with *comparative advantage*. In 1817, David Ricardo examined the question, "What happens when one country can produce all products at an absolute advantage?" His resulting theory of **comparative advantage** says that global efficiency gains may still result from trade if a country specializes in what it can produce most efficiently—regardless of other countries' absolute advantage.

Comparative Advantage by Analogy Although this theory may seem initially incongruous, an analogy should clarify its logic. Imagine that the best physician in town also happens to be the best medical administrator. It would not make economic sense for the physician to handle all the administrative duties of the office, because of earning more money by concentrating on medical duties, even though that means having to employ a less-skilled office administrator. In the same manner, a country gains if it concentrates its resources on the commodities it can produce most efficiently. It then trades some of those for commodities produced abroad. The following discussion clarifies this theory.

Production Possibility Assume the United States is more efficient in producing coffee and wheat than Costa Rica is, thus having an absolute advantage in the production of both.[6] Take a look at Figure 5.3. As in our earlier example, it assumes that there are only two countries, each with a total of 100 units of resources available, and half of each used in each product. It takes Costa Rica 10 units of resources to produce either a ton of coffee or a ton of wheat, whereas it takes the United States only five units to produce a ton of coffee and four for a ton of wheat. Costa Rica can produce five tons of coffee and five tons of wheat (point A on the purple line), and the United States can produce 10 tons of coffee and 12.5 tons of wheat (point B on the green line). Without trade, neither country can increase its coffee production without sacrificing some wheat production, or vice versa.

Although the United States has an absolute advantage in producing both commodities, its comparative advantage is only in wheat. This is because its wheat production is 2.5 times that of Costa Rica, whereas its coffee production is only twice as much. Although Costa Rica has an absolute disadvantage in the production of both products, it has a comparative

FIGURE 5.3 Production Possibilities under Conditions of Comparative Advantage

There are advantages to trade even if one country enjoys an absolute advantage in the production of all products.

ASSUMPTIONS
for Costa Rica

1. 100 units of resources available
2. 10 units to produce a ton of wheat
3. 10 units to produce a ton of coffee
4. Uses half of total resources per product when there is no foreign trade

ASSUMPTIONS
for United States

1. 100 units of resources available
2. 4 units to produce a ton of wheat
3. 5 units to produce a ton of coffee
4. Uses half of total resources per product when there is no foreign trade

PRODUCTION	Coffee (tons)	Wheat (tons)
Without Trade:		
Costa Rica (point *A*)	5	5
United States (point *B*)	10	12½
Total	15	17½
With Trade (increasing coffee production):		
Costa Rica (point *C*)	10	0
United States (point *D*)	6	17½
Total	16	17½
With Trade (increasing wheat production):		
Costa Rica (point *C*)	10	0
United States (point *E*)	5	18¾
Total	15	18¾

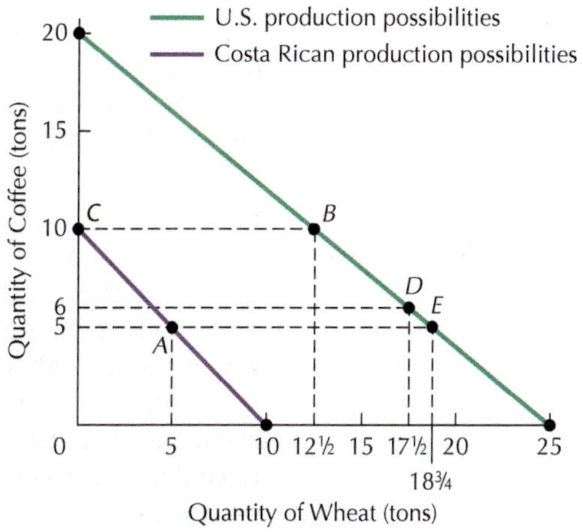

advantage (or less of a comparative disadvantage) in coffee. Why? Because its production is half as efficient in coffee and only 40 percent as efficient in wheat.

Without trade, the combined production is 15 tons of coffee (5 in Costa Rica plus 10 in the United States) and 17.5 tons of wheat (5 plus 12.5). Through trading, the combined production of the commodities within the two countries can be increased. For example, if the combined wheat production is unchanged from when there was no trade, the United States could produce all 17.5 tons by using 70 units of resources (17.5 tons times 4 units per ton). The remaining 30 units could be used for producing six tons of coffee (30 units divided by 5 units per ton), shown by point D in Figure 5.3. Costa Rica would use all its resources to produce 10 tons of coffee (point C). The combined wheat production has stayed at 17.5 tons, but the coffee production has increased from 15 to 16 tons.

If the combined coffee production is unchanged from the time before trade, Costa Rica could use all its resources to produce coffee, yielding 10 tons (point C in Figure 5.3). The United States could produce the remaining five tons of coffee by using 25 units, with its remaining 75 units being used to produce 18.75 tons of wheat (75 divided by 4). This production possibility is point E. Without sacrificing any of the coffee available before trade, wheat production has increased from 17.5 to 18.75 tons.

If the United States were to produce somewhere between points D and E, both coffee and wheat production would increase over what was possible before trade took place. Whether the production target is a rise in coffee or wheat or a combination of the two, both countries can gain by having Costa Rica trade some of its coffee production to the United States for some U.S. wheat output.

Don't Confuse Comparative and Absolute Advantage Most economists accept the comparative advantage theory and its influence in promoting policies for freer trade. Nevertheless, many government policymakers, journalists, managers, and workers confuse comparative advantage with absolute advantage and do not understand how a country can simultaneously have a comparative *advantage* and absolute *disadvantage* in the production of a given product.

THEORIES OF SPECIALIZATION: SOME ASSUMPTIONS AND LIMITATIONS

Both absolute and comparative advantage theories are based on increasing output and trade through specialization. However, these theories make assumptions, some of which are not always valid.

Full employment is not a valid assumption of absolute and comparative advantage.

Full Employment The physician/administrator analogy we used earlier assumed that the physician could stay busy full time practicing medicine. If not, the physician might perform the administrative work without sacrificing earnings from medical duties. The theories of absolute and comparative advantage both assume that resources are fully employed. When countries have many unemployed or unused resources, they may seek to restrict imports to employ or use idle resources.

Countries' goals may not be limited to economic efficiency.

Economic Efficiency Our analogy also assumes that the physician is interested primarily in maximizing income. Yet there are a number of reasons for choosing not to work full time at medical tasks, such as finding administrative work relaxing and self-fulfilling, fearing that a hired administrator would be unreliable, or wishing to maintain administrative skills in the somewhat unlikely event that administrators will command higher wages than physicians in the future. Often, countries also pursue objectives other than output efficiency. They may avoid overspecialization because of the vulnerability created by changes in technology and by price fluctuations or because they do not trust foreign countries to always supply them with essential goods.

CONCEPT CHECK

Recall from Chapter 2 our discussion of "Work Motivation," in which we explain that in cultures ranking high on so-called masculinity, people tend to value economic achievement over certain other values; we also observe, however, that in other cultures "work to live" is valued over economic performance.

Division of Gains Although specialization brings potential economic benefits to all trading countries, the earlier discussion did not indicate how countries will divide increased output. In the case of our wheat and coffee example, if both the United States and Costa Rica receive some share of the higher output, both will be better off economically through specialization and trade. However, many people are concerned with relative as well as absolute economic gains. If they perceive that a trading partner is gaining too large a share of benefits, they may prefer to forgo absolute gains for themselves so as to prevent others from gaining a relative economic advantage.[7]

Transport Costs If it costs more to transport the goods than is saved through specialization, the advantages of trade are negated. In other words, in our two-country scenario, some workers would need to forgo producing coffee or wheat in order to work in transporting the coffee and wheat abroad. However, as long as the diversion reduces output by less than what the two countries gain from specialization, there are still gains from trade.

Statics and Dynamics The theories of absolute and comparative advantage address countries statically—by looking at them at one point in time. However, the relative conditions that give countries production advantages and disadvantages change. For example, the resources needed to produce coffee or wheat in either Costa Rica or the United States could change because of advancements in and acceptance of genetically modified crops. In fact, most trade today is due to acquired advantage; thus, technical dynamics cause countries to gain or lose both absolutely and relatively.[8]

CRN
Case Review Note

As we show in our opening case, when Costa Rica focused on goods that could compete in international markets, it developed and enhanced a competitive advantage in some promising high-tech industries. Thus, we should not assume that future absolute or comparative advantages will remain as they are today. We return to this theme later in the chapter as we examine theories to explain the dynamics of competitive production locations.

Services The theories of absolute and comparative advantage deal with products rather than services. However, with a growing portion of world trade made up of services, the theories apply because resources must also go into service production. For instance, the United States sells an excess of such services as education to foreign countries (many foreign students attend U.S. universities). At the same time, it buys an excess of foreign shipping services. To become more self-sufficient in international shipping, the United States might have to divert resources from its more efficient use in higher education or in the production of competitive products.

CONCEPT CHECK

As we point out in discussing the ramifications of globalization in Chapter 1, although any given product may carry a "made in" label (as in "Made in Taiwan"), such labels may actually obscure rather than clarify the origins of products, which nowadays often include components or ingredients from a surprising variety of countries.

Production Networks Both theories deal with trading one product for another. Increasingly, however, portions of a product may be made in different countries. A company might conduct R&D in Country A, secure components in Countries B and C, assemble final products in Country D, manage finances in Country E, and carry out call-center services in Country F. Although this type of development adds complexity to the analysis, it fits well with the concept of advantages through specialization. In other words, costs are saved by having activities take place in those countries where there is an absolute or comparative advantage for their production.

Mobility These theories assume that resources can move domestically from the production of one good to another—and at no cost. But this assumption is not completely valid. For example, steelworkers might not move easily into software development jobs because of different skill needs. Even if they do, they may be less productive than before.[9] The theories also assume that resources cannot move internationally. Increasingly, however, they do, and the movement affects countries' production capabilities. For instance, over 300 thousand Nicaraguans have moved to Costa Rica, mainly because of better job opportunities there.[10] Further, foreign companies have moved both personnel and capital to support their investments there, which has contributed to changing Costa Rican capabilities. Such movement is clearly an alternative to trade, a topic discussed later in the chapter. However, it is safe to say that resources are more mobile domestically than they are internationally.

CRN
Case Review Note

TRADE PATTERN THEORIES

The free trade theories demonstrate how economic growth occurs through specialization and trade; however, they do not deal with trade patterns such as how much a country trades, what products it trades, or who will be its trading partners when following a free trade policy. In this section, we discuss the theories that help explain these patterns.

HOW MUCH DOES A COUNTRY TRADE?

Free-trade theories of specialization neither propose nor imply that only one country should or will produce a given product or service. **Nontradable goods**—products and services (haircuts, retail grocery distribution, etc.) that are seldom practical to export because of high transportation costs—are produced in every country. However, among tradable goods, some countries depend on imports and exports more than others. We will now examine theories that help explain country differences.

Bigger countries differ in several ways from smaller countries. They

- Tend to export a smaller portion of output and import a smaller part of consumption.
- Have higher transport costs for foreign trade.

Theory of Country Size Land area is an obvious way to measure a country's size and largely explains countries' relative dependence on trade. The **theory of country size** holds that large countries usually depend less on trade than small ones. Countries with large land areas are apt to have varied climates and an assortment of natural resources, making them more self-sufficient than smaller ones. Most large countries (such as Brazil, China, India, the United States, and Russia) import much less of their consumption needs and export much less of their production output than do small nations (such as Uruguay, Belgium, and Taiwan).

Furthermore, distance to foreign markets affects large and small countries differently. Normally, the farther the distance, the higher the transport costs, the longer the inventory carrying time, and the greater the uncertainty and unreliability of timely product delivery. The following example illustrates why distance is more pronounced for a large country than for a small one.

Assume that the normal maximum distance for transporting a given product is 100 miles because prices rise too much at greater distances. Although almost any location in tiny Belgium is within 100 miles of a foreign country, the same isn't true for its two largest neighbors, France and Germany. Thus, Belgium's dependence on trade as a percentage of its production and consumption is greater than the comparable figures in either France or Germany, a fact that can be partially explained by the distance factor due to country size.

Size of the Economy While land area helps explain the *relative* dependence on trade, countries' economic size helps explain differences in the *absolute* amount of trade. Nine of the world's top 10 exporters in 2012 were developed countries, and the only exception was China, which is the world's second largest economy. Similarly, developed countries account for well over half of the world's exports. Simply put, they produce so much that they have more to sell, both domestically and internationally. In addition, because they produce so much, incomes are high and people buy more from both domestic and foreign sources. At the same time, most of developing countries' trade is with developed countries, but there has been a recent upsurge of trade among developing countries mainly because of economic growth in China and India that has increased their demand for raw materials found mainly in developing countries.[11]

The United States offers a good example of the difference between relative and absolute dependence on trade because it is the third largest country in area and the largest economically. Although its dependence on either imports or exports is comparatively low, it is the world's largest trader (imports + exports). Map 5.2 illustrates the large U.S. economic size by showing how each of its states compares economically with countries.

MAP 5.2 U.S. States' Economies Compared to National Economies

The U.S. size, both geographically and economically, results in its being one of the world's largest traders while also depending relatively less than most countries on imports and exports.

Source: GDP figures for U.S. states based on "Gross Domestic Product by State," http://lwd.dol.state.nj.us/labor/lpa/industry/gsp/gsp_index.html (accessed June 26, 2013). Country GDP figures came from Wikipedia, "List of Countries by GDP (Nominal)" http://en.wikipedia.org/wiki/List_of_countries_by_GDP_%28nominal%29 (accessed June 26, 2013).

WHAT TYPES OF PRODUCTS DOES A COUNTRY TRADE?

In our discussion of absolute advantage, we indicated that this advantage might be either natural or acquired. Here, we discuss theories that help explain what types of products result from these natural and acquired advantages. We won't delve again into those factors we've already discussed (climate and natural resources) that give a country a natural advantage; however, we will examine the factor endowment theory of trade. For acquired advantage, we discuss the importance of production and product technology.

According to the factor-proportions theory, factors in relative abundance are cheaper than factors in relative scarcity.

Factor-Proportions Theory Eli Heckscher and Bertil Ohlin developed the **factor-proportions theory**, maintaining that differences in countries' endowments of labor compared to land or capital endowments explain differences in the cost of production factors. For instance, if labor were abundant in comparison to land and capital, labor costs would be low relative to land and capital costs; if scarce, the costs would be high. These relative factor costs would lead countries to excel in the production and export of products that used their abundant—and therefore cheaper—production factors.[12]

People and Land Factor-proportions theory appears logical. In countries that have many people relative to the amount of land, such as Hong Kong and the Netherlands, land price is very high because it's in such demand. Regardless of climate and soil conditions, neither Hong Kong nor the Netherlands excels in the production of goods requiring large amounts of land, such as wool or wheat. Businesses in countries such as Australia and Canada produce these goods because land is abundant compared to the number of people.

Manufacturing Locations Casual observation of manufacturing locations also seems to substantiate the theory. The most successful industries in Hong Kong are those in which technology permits the use of a minimum amount of land relative to the number of people employed. Its clothing production occurs in multistory factories where workers share minimal space, but it does not compete in the production of automobiles, which requires much more space per worker.

Production factors, especially labor, are not homogeneous.

Capital, Labor Rates, and Specialization In countries where little capital is available for investment and the amount of investment per worker is low, managers might expect to find cheap labor rates and export competitiveness in products that need large amounts of labor relative to capital.

However, because the factor-proportions theory assumes production factors to be homogeneous, tests to substantiate the theory have been mixed.[13] Labor skills, in fact, vary within and among countries because of training and education differences. Training and education require capital expenditures that do not show up in traditional capital measurements, which include only plant and equipment values. When the factor-proportions theory accounts for different labor groups and the capital invested to train them, it seems to explain many trade patterns.[14] For example, because developed countries employ a higher proportion of professionals such as scientists and engineers than do developing economies, they depend on their abundant resources (in this case, professionals) in the production that they export. Low-income countries, though, show a high dependence on less-skilled labor in their exports.[15]

This variation in labor skills has led to more international task specialization to produce a given product. For example, a company may locate its R&D and management functions primarily in countries with a highly educated population, while locating its labor-intensive production work in countries where it can employ less educated and less expensive workers.

Companies may substitute capital for labor, depending on the cost of each.

Process Technology Factor-proportions analysis becomes more complicated when the same product can be created by different methods, such as with labor or capital. The photos on the next page show rice harvesting in Indonesia, where many manual laborers are employed, versus Italy, where mechanized methods require few workers. In the final analysis, the optimum location of production depends on comparing the cost in each locale based on the type of production that minimizes costs there.

Bigger countries depend more on products requiring larger production runs.

Not all products lend themselves to such trade-offs in production methods. Some require huge amounts of fixed capital and long production runs to spread the fixed capital costs over more output units, usually resulting in development in large countries with large markets.[16] However, companies may locate long production runs in small countries if they expect to be able to export from them.[17] In industries where long production runs reduce unit costs substantially, companies tend to locate production in only a few countries, using these locations to export. Where long production runs are less important, we find a greater prevalence of multiple production units scattered around the world in different countries so as to minimize transportation costs through exporting.

In addition, high R&D expenditures create high up-front fixed costs. Therefore, a technologically intensive company from a small nation may need to sell more abroad than a

Source: Roberto Caucino/Shutterstock

The rice harvesting is capital intensive in Italy, (top) where labor rates are high. It is labor intensive in Indonesia (bottom), where labor rates are low.
Source: mosista/Shutterstock

company in a large domestic market. It may, in turn, pull resources from other industries and companies within its domestic market, which means the country will have more national specialization than one finds in a larger country.[18]

Most new products originate in developed countries.

Product Technology Figure 5.4 shows the changing composition of world trade. Manufacturing is by far the largest sector, with commercial services the fastest-growing sector. Manufacturing competitiveness depends largely on technology to develop new products and processes. The technology depends, in turn, on a large number of highly educated people

FIGURE 5.4 Worldwide Trade by Major Sectors

As a percentage of total world trade, manufactured products are more important than products in any other category. Services, however, constitute the fastest-growing category.

Source: Based on World Trade Organization, *Annual Report* (Geneva, various years).

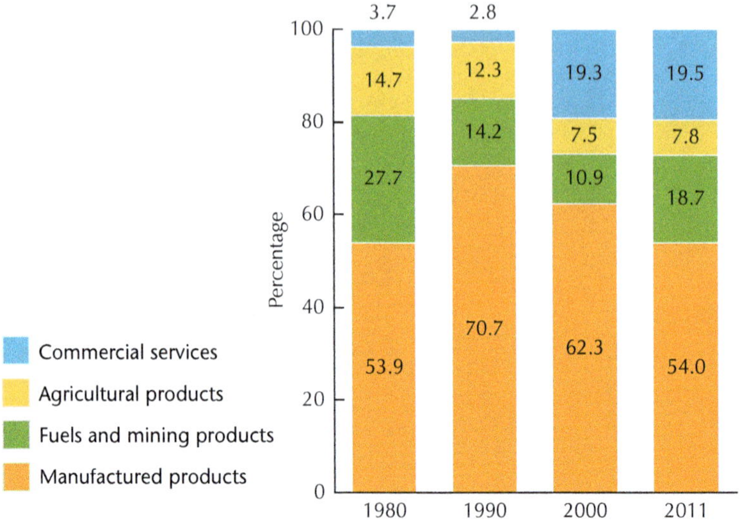

(especially scientists and engineers) and a large amount of capital to invest in R&D. Because developed countries have an abundance of these features, they originate most new products and account for most manufacturing output and trade. Developing countries depend much more on the production of primary products; thus, they depend more on natural advantage.

WITH WHOM DO COUNTRIES TRADE?

We have already noted that developed countries account for the bulk of world trade. They also trade primarily with each other, whereas developing countries mainly export primary and labor-intensive products to developed countries in exchange for new and technologically advanced products. Below, we discuss the roles that country similarity and distance play in determining trading partners.

Developed countries trade primarily with each other because they

- Produce and consume more.
- Emphasize technical breakthroughs in different industrial sectors.
- Produce differentiated products and services.

Country-Similarity Theory The theories explaining why trade takes place have focused so far on the differences among countries in terms of natural conditions and factor endowment proportions. That most trade takes place among developed countries can be further explained by the **country-similarity theory**, which says that companies create new products in response to market conditions in their home market. They then turn to markets and consumer economic levels they see as most similar to what they are accustomed.[19]

Specialization and Acquired Advantage However, in order to export, a company must provide consumers abroad with an advantage over what they could buy from their domestic producers. Trade occurs because countries' producers spend more on R&D in some sectors than in others, thus leading to countries' specialization and acquired advantage. Germany, for instance, is traditionally strong in machinery and equipment, Switzerland in pharmaceutical products, and Denmark in food products.[20] Even developing countries gain advantages through specialization in very narrow product segments. Bangladesh has succeeded in exporting shirts, trousers, and hats, but not bed linens or footballs, which Pakistan has successfully exported.[21]

Product Differentiation Trade also occurs because *companies* differentiate products, thus creating two-way trade in seemingly similar products. The United States is both a major exporter and a major importer of tourist services, vehicles, and passenger aircraft because different firms from different countries have developed product variations with different appeals. For instance, both Boeing from the United States and Airbus from Europe produce large jet passenger aircraft that will fly from point A to point B, but U.S. and European airlines buy both companies' aircraft because their models differ in such features as capacity, flying range, fuel consumption, and perceived reliability.[22] As a result, Boeing and Airbus sell within their own and each other's home markets as well as within countries that produce no aircraft.

Trading partners are affected by

- Cultural similarity.
- Political relations between countries.
- Distance.

The Effects of Cultural Similarity Importers and exporters perceive greater ease in doing business in countries that are culturally similar to home, such as those that speak a common language. Likewise, historic colonial relationships explain much of the trade between specific developed and developing economies. For instance, France's colonial history in Africa has given Air France an edge in serving the continent's international air passenger markets.[23] Importers and exporters find it easier to continue business ties than to develop new distribution arrangements in countries where they are less experienced.

CONCEPT CHECK

In discussing "Cultural Distance" in Chapter 2, we show that "distance" is an index of similarities between countries based primarily on such shared cultural attributes as language, ethnicity, or values. We indicate that, by and large, a company from one country should expect fewer adjustments when moving to a country whose culture is close to that of its home base, but we also caution that even in these cases, executives should be aware of subtle cultural differences.

The Effects of Political Relationships and Economic Agreements Political relationships and economic agreements among countries may discourage or encourage trade between them. Witness the political animosity between the United States and Cuba that has diminished their mutual trade for about five decades. An example of trade encouragement is the agreement among many European countries to remove all trade barriers with each other, thereby causing a greater share of the countries' total trade to be conducted with each other.

The Effects of Distance Although no single factor fully explains specific pairs of trading partners, the geographic distance between two countries is important. In essence, greater distances usually mean higher transportation costs; that's why Intel's cost to ship semiconductors from Costa Rica to the United States is lower than if it had to bring them from, say, Argentina. However, distance is more important for homogeneous products than for differentiated products inasmuch as the former compete more on the basis of price.[24] In addition, analysis of cost differences must take into account the available transportation modes. Wine exports from Australia can reach the United Kingdom (UK) by container ship for about the same cost as wine exports shipped overland to the UK from southern France.[25]

Overcoming Distance Transport cost is not the only factor in trade partner choice. New Zealand competes with Chile, Argentina, and South Africa for out-of-season sales of apples to the Northern Hemisphere—but with a disadvantage in freight costs to the United States and Europe. It has countered this disadvantage by boosting yields, developing new premium varieties, bypassing intermediaries to sell directly to supermarkets abroad, and consolidating efforts through a national marketing board. However, such methods to overcome distance drawbacks are difficult to maintain. For example, rival orchardists have smuggled new strains of apple tree cuttings out of New Zealand.[26]

Does Geography Matter?

Variety Is the Spice of Life

As you study this chapter, you'll see that geography plays a role in many of the theories and questions on trade. We pull them together in this discussion.

Part of a country's trading advantage is explained by its natural advantage—climate, terrain, arable land, and natural resources. Thus, Saudi Arabia trades oil, a natural resource, for U.S. rice, which needs huge wet areas for production. Remember that technology (acquired advantage) may often negate natural advantage, as in the development of substitutes (synthetic nitrate for natural nitrate) and the development of different production methods (Chile not using traditional bogs for growing cranberries). Nevertheless, a country's geography—particularly the ease of moving goods to markets in other countries—may give it an advantage or disadvantage. For instance, landlocked countries have a considerable transport cost disadvantage relative to countries with seacoasts.[27]

Factor-proportions theory helps explain where certain goods may be more efficiently produced, such as labor-intensive goods where labor is plentiful in relation to capital and land. Bangladesh excels in producing clothing that requires lots of labor in relation to either capital or land. However, these factors can change in both quantity and quality. Singapore, with its very high population density, once excelled in the production of labor-intensive goods. But because it has accumulated capital and upgraded the education of its workforce, its competitive production and exports now encompass more capital intensity and skilled labor.

Usually, small countries need to trade more than large countries, primarily because they are apt to have fewer natural advantages. At the same time, small countries that also have low incomes tend to trade little because they produce and consume so little. Distance from foreign markets also plays a role. Geographically isolated countries such as Fiji trade less than would be expected from their size because transportation costs raise the price of traded goods substantially.[28]

Conversely, Canada is a large developed country whose dependence on trade and trade per capita are not only among the world's highest but also much higher than we would expect from the theory of country size. This may be explained largely by Canada's population dispersion. Ninety percent of its population is within 100 miles of the U.S. border, so shipping goods between, say, Vancouver and Seattle or Toronto and Cleveland is often more feasible than between Vancouver and Toronto.

Although we have discussed the effect of economic development on trade, this discussion raises the question of why some countries are developed and others are not—a very complex issue we cannot hope to answer. Nevertheless, some of the factors affecting income levels, and thus trade, are geographic. One study showed that 70 percent of countries' differences in per capita income can be accounted for by four factors: malaria, hydrocarbon endowments, coastal access, and transportation costs—all of which relate to geography.[29] ■

THE STATICS AND DYNAMICS OF TRADE

We've alluded to the fact that trading patterns change due to such factors as political and economic relations among countries and the development of new product capabilities. We now discuss two theories—the product life cycle theory and the diamond of national advantage—that help explain how countries develop, maintain, and lose their competitive advantages.

PRODUCT LIFE CYCLE (PLC) THEORY

According to the PLC theory of trade, the production location for many products moves from one country to another depending on the stage in the product's life cycle.

The international **product life cycle (PLC) theory** of trade states that the production location of certain manufactured products shifts as they go through their life cycle. The cycle consists of four stages: *introduction, growth, maturity,* and *decline.*[30] Table 5.2 highlights these stages.

Changes over the Cycle

Companies develop new products primarily because they observe nearby needs for them; thus a U.S. company is most apt to create a new product for the U.S. market, a French company for the French market, and so on. At the same time, almost all new technology that results in new products and production methods originates in developed countries,[31] which have most of the resources to develop new products and most of the income to buy them.

The introduction stage is marked by

- Innovation in response to observed need.
- Exporting by the innovative country.
- Evolving product characteristics.

Introduction Once a company has created a new product, theoretically it can manufacture it anywhere in the world. In practice, however, the early-production stage, called the *introductory stage,* generally occurs in a domestic location so the company can obtain rapid market feedback and save on transport costs, since most sales are domestic. Any export sales are mainly to other developed countries because of more affluent customers there.

Production is apt to be more labor-intensive than in later stages because more labor-saving machinery may be introduced only when sales begin to expand rapidly and the product becomes highly standardized. Although production is in developed countries with high labor rates, their education and skills usually make this labor efficient in

TABLE 5.2 Life Cycle of the International Product

During the life cycle of a product, focus on its production and market locations often shifts from industrial to developing markets. The process is accompanied by changes in the competitive factors affecting both production and sales, as well as in the technology used to produce the product.

	Life Cycle Stage			
	1: Introduction	**2: Growth**	**3: Maturity**	**4: Decline**
Production location	• In innovating (usually industrial) country	• In innovating and other industrial countries	• Multiple countries	• Mainly in developing countries
Market location	• Mainly in innovating country, with some exports	• Mainly in industrial countries • Shift in export markets as foreign production replaces exports in some markets	• Growth in developing countries • Some decrease in industrial countries	• Mainly in developing countries • Some developing country exports
Competitive factors	• Near-monopoly position • Sales based on uniqueness rather than price • Evolving product characteristics	• Fast-growing demand • Number of competitors increases • Some competitors begin price cutting • Product becoming more standardized	• Overall stabilized demand • Number of competitors decreases • Price is very important, especially in developing countries	• Overall declining demand • Price is key weapon • Number of producers continues to decline
Production technology	• Short production runs • Evolving methods to coincide with product evolution • High labor input and labor skills relative to capital input	• Capital input increases • Methods more standardized	• Long production runs using high capital inputs • Highly standardized • Less labor skill needed	• Unskilled labor on mechanized long production runs

nonstandardized production. Even if production costs are high because of expensive labor, companies can often pass costs on to consumers who are unwilling to wait for possible price reductions later.

Growth is characterized by

- Increases in exports by the innovating country.
- More competition.
- Increased capital intensity.
- Some foreign production.

Growth Sales growth attracts competitors to the market, particularly in other developed countries. Let's say the innovator is in the United States and a competitor puts a manufacturing unit in Japan. The Japanese production is sold mainly in Japan for several reasons:

1. The growing demand there does not allow for much attention to other markets.
2. Producers there stay occupied in developing unique product variations for Japanese consumers.
3. Japanese costs may still be high because of production start-up problems.

Sales growth creates an incentive for companies to develop labor-saving process technology, but this incentive is partly offset because competitors are differentiating their products, especially to fit the needs of different countries. Thus the capital intensity, though growing, is less than will come later. The original producing country will increase its exports, especially to developing countries, but will lose certain key export markets in which local production commences.

Maturity is characterized by

- A decline in exports from the innovating country.
- More product standardization.
- More capital intensity.
- Increased competitiveness of price.
- Production start-ups in emerging economies.

Maturity In the *maturity stage,* worldwide demand begins to level off, although it may be growing in some countries and declining in others. Typically, there is a shakeout of producers, more standardized production, and increased importance of price as a competitive weapon. Capital-intensive production reduces per-unit cost, thus creating even more demand in developing economies. Because markets and technologies are widespread, the innovating country no longer commands a production advantage. Firms have incentives to shift production to developing economies where they can employ less skilled and less expensive labor efficiently for standardized (capital-intensive) production. Exports decrease from the innovating country as foreign production displaces it.

Decline is characterized by

- A concentration of production in developing countries.
- An innovating country becoming a net importer.

Decline As a product moves into the *decline stage,* those factors occurring during the maturity stage continue to evolve. The markets in developed countries decline more rapidly than those in developing economies as affluent customers demand ever newer products. By this time, market and cost factors have dictated that almost all production is in developing economies that export to the declining or small-niche markets in the developed world. In other words, the country in which the innovation first emerged—and was exported from—then becomes the importer.

Verification and Limitations of PLC Theory The PLC theory holds that the location of production facilities that serve world markets shifts as products move through their life cycle. Such items as ballpoint pens and hand calculators have followed this pattern. They were first produced in a single developed country and sold at a high price; then, production shifted to multiple developed country locations to serve those local markets. Today, most production has located in developing countries, and prices have declined.

Not all products conform to the dynamics of the PLC.

Types of products abound for which production locations usually do not shift. Such exceptions include the following:

- Products with high transport costs that may have to be produced close to the market, thus never becoming significant exports.
- Products that, because of very rapid innovation, have extremely short life cycles, making it impossible to reduce costs by moving production from one country to another. Some fashion items fit this category.
- Luxury products for which cost is of little concern to the consumer. In fact, production in a developing country may cause consumers to perceive the product as less luxurious.
- Products for which a company can use a differentiation strategy, perhaps through advertising, to maintain consumer demand without competing on the basis of price.
- Products that require specialized technical personnel to be located near production so as to move the products into their next generation of models. This seems to explain the long-term U.S. dominance of medical equipment production and German dominance in rotary printing presses.

Regardless of product, the trend is for international companies to introduce new products at home and abroad almost simultaneously. In other words, instead of merely observing needs within their domestic markets, companies develop products and services for observable worldwide market segments. In so doing, they eliminate delays as products are diffused internationally, and they choose an initial production location (which may or may not be in the innovating company's home market) that will minimize costs for serving markets in multiple countries.

According to the diamond of national competitive advantage theory, companies' development and maintenance of internationally competitive products depends on favorable

- Demand conditions.
- Factor conditions.
- Related and supporting industries.
- Firm strategy, structure, and rivalry.

THE DIAMOND OF NATIONAL COMPETITIVE ADVANTAGE

Why have countries developed and sustained different competitive advantages? The **diamond of national competitive advantage** is a theory showing four features as important for competitive superiority: demand conditions; factor conditions; related and supporting industries; and firm strategy, structure, and rivalry[32] (see Figure 5.5).

We have largely discussed these conditions in the context of other trade theories, but how they combine affects the development and continued existence of competitive advantages. The framework of the theory, therefore, is a useful tool for understanding how and where globally competitive companies develop and sustain themselves.

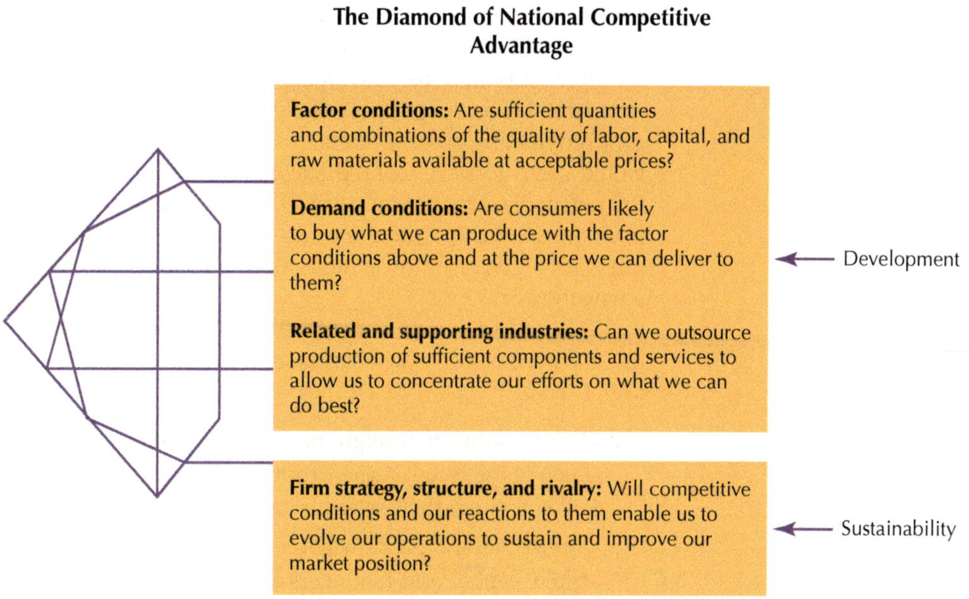

FIGURE 5.5 The Diamond of National Competitive Advantage

The interaction of these conditions must usually be favorable if an industry in a country is to develop and sustain itself. The theory was developed with domestic conditions in mind, but globalization results in favorable conditions that may come from anywhere.

Source: Based on Michael E. Porter, "The Competitive Advantage of Nations," Harvard Business Review, Vol. 68, No. 2, March-April 1990.

CONCEPT CHECK

In discussing the concept of the market economy in Chapter 4, we explain that such a system encourages an open exchange of goods and services among producers and consumers, both of which groups consist of "individuals" who make their own economic decisions; in this respect, then, the interaction among producers and consumers determines what products will be produced and in what quantities.

Facets of the Diamond Usually, all four conditions need to be favorable for an industry within a country to attain and maintain global supremacy.

Demand Conditions *Demand conditions* are the first feature in the theory. Both PLC theory and country-similarity theory show that new products (or industries) usually arise from companies' observation of need or demand, which has traditionally been in their home country, where they start up production. This was the case for the Italian ceramic tile industry after World War II: In a postwar housing boom, consumers wanted cool floors (which tile would provide) because of the hot Italian climate.

Factor Conditions Continuing our example, the second feature—*factor conditions* (recall natural advantage within the absolute advantage and factor-proportions theories)—influenced both the choice of tile to meet consumer demand and the choice of Italy as the production location. Wood was expensive, and most production factors (skilled labor, capital, technology, and equipment) were available within Italy on favorable terms.

Related and Supporting Industries The third feature—the existence of nearby *related and supporting industries* (enamels and glazes)—was also favorable. Recall, for instance, the importance of transport costs in the theory of country size, in assumptions of specialization, and in the limiting factors of the PLC theory.

Firm Strategy, Structure, and Rivalry The combination of three features—demand, factor conditions, and related and supporting industries—influenced companies' decisions to initiate production of ceramic tiles in postwar Italy. The ability of the companies to develop and sustain a competitive advantage required favorable circumstances for the fourth feature: *firm strategy, structure,* and *rivalry.*

Barriers to market entry were low in the tile industry (some companies started up with only three employees), and hundreds of companies initiated production. Rivalry became intense as companies tried to serve increasingly sophisticated Italian consumers. These circumstances forced breakthroughs in both product and process technologies, which gave the Italian producers advantages over foreign firms and enabled them to gain the largest global share of tile exports.

Domestic existence of all conditions

- Does not guarantee an industry will develop.
- Is not necessary with globalization.

Limitations of the Diamond of National Advantage Theory The existence of the four favorable conditions does not guarantee that an industry will develop in a given locale. Entrepreneurs may face favorable conditions for many different lines of business. In fact, comparative advantage theory holds that resource limitations may cause a country's firms to avoid competing in some industries despite an absolute advantage. Conditions in Switzerland would seem to have favored success if companies in that country had become players in the personal computer industry. However, Swiss companies preferred to protect their global positions in such product lines as watches and scientific instruments rather than downsize innovation efforts in those industries by moving their highly skilled people into developing a new industry.

A second limitation concerns the growth of globalization. The industries on which this theory is premised grew when companies' access to competitive capabilities was much more domestically focused. We can see how globalization affects each of the four conditions:

1. Observations of foreign or foreign-plus-domestic demand conditions have spurred much of the recent Asian export growth. In fact, such Japanese companies as Uniden and Fujitech target their sales almost entirely to foreign markets.[33]
2. Companies and countries do not depend entirely on domestic factor conditions. For example, capital and managers are now internationally mobile, and companies may depend on foreign locations for portions of their production.
3. If related and supporting industries are not available locally, materials and components are now more easily brought in from abroad because of transportation advancements and relaxed import restrictions. In fact, many MNEs now assemble products with parts supplied from a variety of countries.
4. Companies react not only to domestic rivals but also to foreign-based rivals they compete with at home and abroad. Thus the prior domestic absence of any of the four conditions from the diamond may not inhibit companies and industries from gaining these conditions and becoming globally competitive.

Using the Diamond for Transformation By expanding the diamond of national advantage theory to include changes brought about by globalization, we can see its validity for countries' economic policies. In our opening case, Costa Rica diversified its economy from agricultural products to modern high-tech products by satisfying the market entry conditions of the diamond. This transformation could not have occurred had Costa Rican authorities looked only at what was available within their own borders. In Costa Rica itself, there was (and still is) very little demand for the high-tech products it now produces, such as microchips and medical devices; good transportation, however, makes efficient export possible. Similarly, the country initially lacked some of the factor conditions necessary for producing high-tech products, especially trained personnel. Eventually, though, it altered its educational system to fit human resource development to production needs and allowed companies to bring in foreign managers and technicians to fill personnel gaps. Finally, it developed local factors, such as additional power and metalworking expertise, and attracted enough high-tech companies to ensure a vibrant competitive environment. Thus, understanding and having the necessary conditions to be globally competitive is important, but these conditions are neither static nor purely domestic.

CRN
Case Review Note

FACTOR-MOBILITY THEORY

As both the quantity and quality of countries' factor conditions change, their relative capabilities change as well, possibly because of internal circumstances. For instance, if savings rates increase, countries have more capital relative to their factors of land and labor. If they spend relatively more on education, they improve the quality of the labor factor.

Point

Should Nations Use Strategic Trade Policies?

Point **Yes** What's so important about acquiring advantage in world trade? For one thing, if you're a country that wants to compete in today's globalized business environment (and you have to), you obviously must develop and maintain some industries that will be internationally competitive. But those industries also must grow and earn sufficient revenues to keep your domestic economy performing. What's the role of your government in the process of going global? It should be central to your whole effort; after all, we're talking about national economies here.

A government's role is rarely neutral. The government may claim that its economic policies don't affect the performance of specific domestic industries on the world stage, but a lot of those policies are bound to have precisely that effect. Who will argue that U.S. efforts to "improve agricultural productivity" and "enhance defense capabilities" have nothing to do with the fact that the United States does a healthy business in the export of farm and aerospace products?

Moreover, just about every government policy designed to help one industry will have a negative effect on another. European airlines complain (with some justification) that government support for high-speed rail traffic in Europe deprives them of the revenue they need to compete with U.S. overseas carriers, which don't have much to worry about from railroad passenger traffic at home. In other words, national policymakers everywhere face trade-offs. So if every government policy will help one party while hurting another, why shouldn't a country's practices call for taking special care of the industries that will likely give it its best competitive advantage?

Executing such a plan can be pretty simple. First, target a growth industry and figure out what factors make it competitive (or potentially competitive). Next, identify your country's likely competitive advantages (and make sure you know why you have them). Finally, develop a little synergy between the strong points you've uncovered during both processes: Target the resources needed to support the industries that fit best with your country's advantages.

This program—which comes under the general heading of strategic trade policy or industrial policy—is particularly effective if you're a developing country. Why? Because you've probably already decided that (1) you need to integrate yourself into the global economy and (2) you need to figure out the best way to excel in the international game. If your competitive countries support high-potential start-ups and you don't, your new industries will be disadvantaged.[34] So far, so good, but you need to remember that simply opening up your borders to foreign competition doesn't necessarily mean that domestic producers will have an easier time competing either abroad or at home.

When you throw open your borders, the first companies to take you up on the invitation will be foreign competitors with considerable advantages over the homegrown companies you're trying to develop. They've had a head start that's allowed them to develop not only certain internal efficiencies but cozy relations with everybody in the international distribution channel.

Moreover, no matter how promising your targeted industries may be, or how carefully you've tried to match up your industries with your competitive advantages, as a developing country your businesses probably lack the technology and marketing skills they'll need to compete. So, why not help them?[35]

This brings us back to why strategic trade policy is your optimal choice if you're a developing country: Your government must protect your local industries—say, by helping them get the skills and technology they'll need. You could also focus your efforts to attract foreign investment on companies that have the marketing and technical skills you need; that's one good way to bring in the kind of production you need. It also wouldn't hurt to extend incentives to the industries you're counting on.

Want some evidence that strategic trade policy is effective in helping developing nations go global? Look at South Korea, which not only managed to attract companies with experience in consumer-electronics production but eventually emerged as a global competitor because it built on imported technologies and targeted technical education to become both a competitive and technical leader.[36] By the same token, we have ample evidence that laissez-faire often doesn't work in developing countries. In sub-Saharan Africa, for example, government institutions are so deeply rooted that it's almost impossible for anyone—either individuals or multinationals—to make a move without getting entangled in the bureaucratic undergrowth.[37]

Moreover, because no single institution in developing countries has much in the way of resources, all are better off focusing their collective efforts on specific industries that have some potential for international competitiveness; otherwise, what you have is a bunch of under-resourced agencies and ministries aiming at markets scattered all over the economic landscape.[38]

Should Nations Use Strategic Trade Policies?

Counterpoint

No Of course, countries should try to become most competitive in the industries that promise the best returns and have the most potential for going global. Obviously, they're the ones most likely to add value (in the form of high profits and good wages) to national production. However, strategic trade policy is not the best way to achieve these goals—about which nearly everybody agrees.

I'll make a concession: Under limited circumstances a targeting program will work, particularly for small countries such as Costa Rica. Because Costa Rica's GDP amounts to less than 10 percent of the value of Walmart's annual sales, parties involved can manageably work together to reach mutually beneficial agreements with minimal frustration. But in a large economy? Impossible.

However, it's debatable just how much Costa Rica's economic success is due to strategic trade policy and how much goes back to conditions that existed before the government started the whole process of targeting industries. Costa Rica already had a well-educated workforce, a relatively high level of economic freedom, a large population of English-speaking workers, a quality of life that had some appeal to foreign personnel, and a high level of political stability. Yes, Costa Rica landed Intel, but it's only fair to point out that Intel had already decided to put a plant somewhere in Latin America. Costa Rica's job, then, was basically convincing Intel it was a better choice than certain countries, such as Brazil and Chile, which were at a distance disadvantage when it came to sending output to the United States.

An alternative is for a country to focus on conditions affecting its attractiveness to profitable companies in general instead of targeted industries in particular. In other words, a government can alter conditions affecting, say, factor proportions, efficiency, and innovation by upgrading production factors—improving human skills, providing an adequate infrastructure, encouraging consumers to demand higher-quality products, and promoting an overall competitive environment—for any industry interested in doing business within its borders.

Let's turn to your comments about sub-Saharan Africa. I'll even make another concession: Institutional inertia is indeed a way of life in much of the area, and there's no reason to expect that it will go away any time soon.[39] But what if we looked at things from another perspective? Rather than trying to focus on a specific industry in, say, the global high-tech universe, wouldn't all these

Counterpoint

bureaucratic agencies and ministries find it easier to review (and enforce) their own laws, take steps to stabilize their populations, rectify their most glaring economic, social, and gender inequities, and support entrepreneurial activity in the informal sectors of their economies? Wouldn't they find it more productive to foster an environment of trust—one in which, say, the government helps cut transaction costs so local firms will be willing to work with other companies, domestic and foreign, to acquire a little of the knowledge and a few of the resources they need to compete?[40]

Again, instead of picking and haggling over special industries, wouldn't they be better advised to improve the investment environment in which, after all, everybody will ultimately have to operate anyway?

At this point, I might as well take the offensive in this debate. Strategic trade policies typically result in no more than small payoffs—primarily because most governments find difficulty in identifying and targeting the right industries.[41] What if a country targets an industry in which global demand never quite lives up to expectations? That's what happened to the United Kingdom and France when they got together to underwrite supersonic passenger planes. Or what if the domestic companies in a targeted industry simply fall short of being competitive? That's what happened when Thailand decided to get into the steel business.[42]

What if too many nations target the same global industries, thereby committing themselves to excessive competition and inadequate returns?[43] What if two countries compete to support the same industry, as happened when both Brazil and Canada decided to produce regional jets in the same hemisphere?[44] Finally, what if a country successfully targets an industry only to find unexpected conditions? Should it stay the course by reacting to various pressures, such as the pressure to support employment in a distressed industry?[45]

Finally, even if a government can identify a future growth industry in which a domestic firm is likely to succeed—a very big if—it doesn't follow that a company deserves public assistance. History recommends that nations permit their entrepreneurs to do what they do best: take risks that don't jeopardize whole sectors of the economy. The upshot will probably be the same as always: Some will fail, but the successful ones will survive and thrive competitively.

Currently, one of the biggest changes underway concerns relative population numbers. At present rates, 33 countries, including Japan and Italy, are projected to have smaller populations in 2050 than today, primarily because of low fertility rates. They are also encountering aging populations along with more people entering the workforce at a later age because of education, leaving fewer people to provide output and needing large immigration increases just to maintain the present ratios of employed people to retirees. Concomitantly, nine countries are expected to account for half of the world's population increase, with India, Pakistan, and Nigeria leading the pack.[46]

These changes, of course, are important in understanding and predicting changes in export production and import market locations. At the same time, the mobility of capital, technology, and people affect trade and relative competitive positions. Here we address the **factor-mobility theory**, which focuses on why production factors move, the effects of that movement on transforming factor endowments, and the impact of international factor mobility (especially people) on world trade.

CONCEPT CHECK

As we explain in Chapter 1, a foreign investment is an interest in a company or ownership of a loan made to another party in a foreign country. Companies typically use some form of portfolio investment for short-term financial gain as they routinely move funds from country to country to earn higher yields.

WHY PRODUCTION FACTORS MOVE

Capital Capital, especially short-term capital, is the most internationally mobile production factor. Companies and private individuals primarily transfer capital because of differences in expected return (accounting for risk). They find information on interest-rate differences readily available, and they can transfer capital by wire instantaneously at a low cost. Short-term capital is more mobile than long-term capital, such as direct investment, because there are more active markets to buy foreign holdings and sell them if investors want to transfer capital back home or to another country.

Political and economic conditions affect investors' perceptions of risk and where they prefer to put their capital. At the same time, companies invest abroad for the long term to tap markets, improve quality, and lower operating costs. However, businesses do not make all the international capital movements. Governments give foreign aid and loans. Not-for-profit organizations donate money abroad to relieve worrisome economic and social conditions. Individuals remit funds to help their families and friends in foreign countries. Regardless of the donor or motive, the result affects factor endowments.

Capital and labor move internationally to

- Gain more income.
- Flee adverse political situations.

People People are less mobile than capital. Some, of course, travel to other countries as tourists, students, and retirees; however, this does not affect factor endowments because these travelers do not work in the destination countries. Unlike funds that can be cheaply transferred by wire, people usually must incur high transportation costs to work abroad. Also, if they move legally they must get immigration papers, which most countries provide sparingly. Finally, they may have to learn another language and adjust to a different culture away from their customary support groups. Despite such barriers, people do endure hardships and risks to move to other countries.

Migration was the major engine of globalization during the late nineteenth and early twentieth centuries, and at present it is important again. About 3 percent of the world's population (over 200 million people) has migrated to another country. Because this 3 percent is spread unevenly, the percentage is much greater in some countries than in others; in Hong Kong and Singapore, it represents over 40 percent, and in Brazil and Mexico less than 1 percent of the population.[47]

Of the people who go abroad to work, some move permanently, some temporarily. Some might immigrate to another country, become citizens, and plan to reside there for the rest of their lives. In contrast, MNEs may assign some to work abroad for periods ranging from a few days to several years (usually to a place where they also transfer capital), while some countries allow workers to enter on temporary work permits, usually for short periods. For instance, most workers in the United Arab Emirates are there on temporary work permits.[48] In many cases, workers leave their families behind in the hopes of returning home after saving enough money working in the foreign country. Some move legally, others illegally

FIGURE 5.6 Some illegal or undocumented immigrants simply overstay their visas. Some sneak into a country.

Source: Alex Matthews/CartoonStock

(undocumented); that is to say they lack government permission to enter or work. Figure 5.6 shows an undocumented movement humorously.

Economic Motives People work in another country largely for economic reasons, such as Indonesian laborers working in Malaysia to earn more than at home. After the economic downturn of 2008, substantial numbers of immigrants worldwide returned to their native countries, such as an estimated 60,000 Indonesians who had been working in wealthier Asian nations.[49]

Political Motives People also move for political reasons—for example, because of persecution or war dangers, in which case they are known as refugees and usually become part of the labor pool where they live. It is not surprising that most refugees emanate from war-torn countries and go to a neighboring country; the largest recent movement has been from Afghanistan to Pakistan.[50] Sometimes it is difficult to distinguish between economic and political motives for international mobility because poor economic conditions often parallel poor political conditions. In the early twenty-first century, hundreds of thousands of Colombians left the country, fleeing both violence and unemployment. Map 5.3 highlights some major recent global migration.

Factor movements alter factor endowments.

EFFECTS OF FACTOR MOVEMENTS

Neither international capital nor population mobility is a new occurrence. For example, had it not been for historical mass immigration, Australia, Canada, and the United States would have greatly reduced populations today. Further, many immigrants brought human capital with them, thus adding to the base of skills that enabled those countries to be newly competitive in an array of products they might otherwise have imported. Finally, these same countries received foreign capital to develop infrastructure and natural resources, which further altered their competitive structures and international trade.

MAP 5.3 Major Net Migration, 2005–2010

The map shows net migration (immigration less emigration) for the 15 countries that had a figure of at least a million during the five-year period. (The figures are in thousands.)

Source: Based on data in United Nations Department of Economic and Social Affairs, Population Division, "World Population Prospects, the 2010 Revision," esa.un.org/wpp/Excel-Data/migration.htm (accessed February 1, 2013).

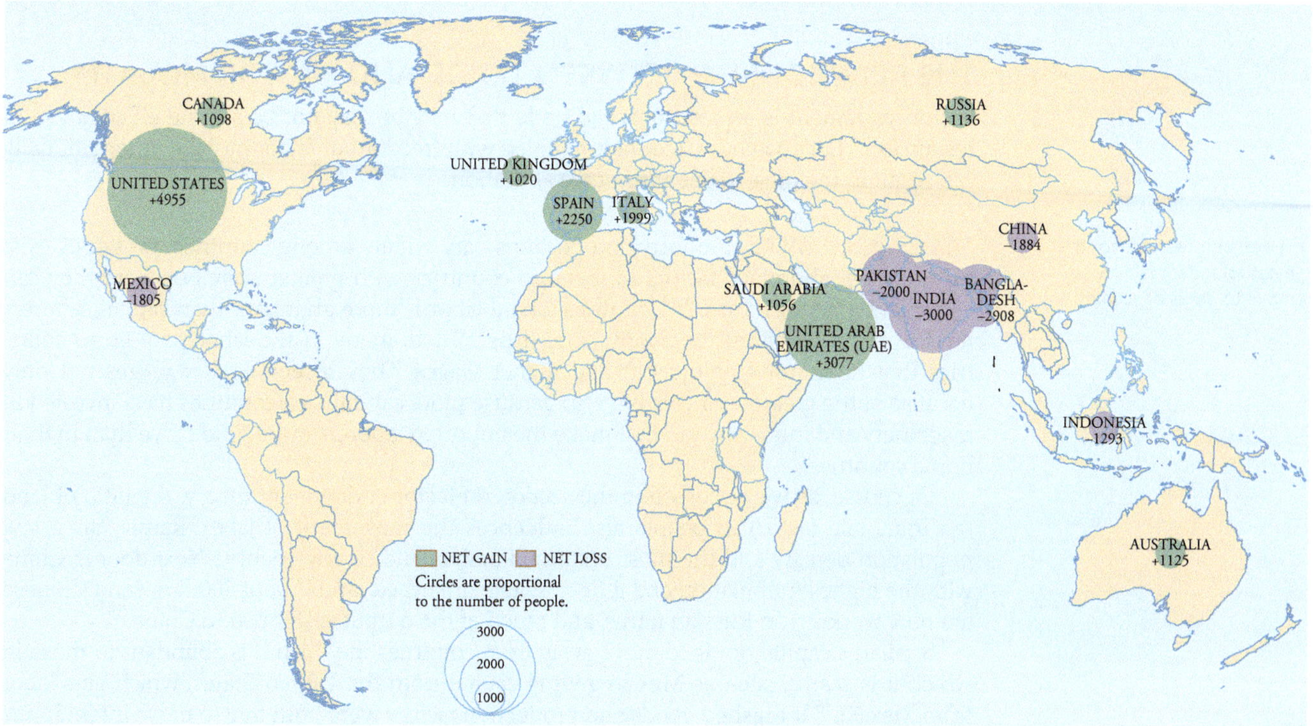

What Happens When People Move? Recent evidence is largely anecdotal. Nevertheless, we have indicated that immigration is substantial for many countries and insignificant for others.[51]

The United States is currently an example of a country whose recent immigration is largely concentrated at the high and low ends of human skills. Over a third of all people with doctoral degrees in the United States are foreign-born. At the other extreme, much recent U.S. immigration has been made up of low-skilled workers. At both extremes, the United States has had shortages of native-born workers, which has been partially alleviated through immigration.

A controversial issue is the effect of outward migration on countries. On the one hand, countries lose potentially productive resources when educated people leave—a situation known as a **brain drain**. On the other hand, they may receive money from those people. Developing countries have lost people with substantial work skills. However, many of these people are now sending remittances back. In fact, remittance flows to developing countries for 2011 were estimated at U.S. $372 billion.[52]

There is also evidence that the outward movement and remittances of people leads to an increase in start-up companies and capital in their home countries. Further, the emigrants learn abroad, transfer ideas back home, use remitted capital to start businesses with family members or on their own, and export to companies with which they had connections abroad.[53]

Finally, countries receiving productive human resources also incur costs by providing social services and acculturating people to a new language and society. Thus, on the one hand there is an employment need for the immigrants; on the other hand, there've been backlashes concerning the costs. The unskilled workers who take jobs that native-born workers don't want—dishwashing, maintaining grounds, picking agricultural produce—often have children who eventually enter the workforce. If these children are also unskilled, the country is perpetuating a long-term class of "have-nots." If the children attain skills, then there is a need to bring in even more unskilled workers from abroad.

THE RELATIONSHIP BETWEEN TRADE AND FACTOR MOBILITY

Factor movement is an alternative to trade that may or may not be a more efficient use of resources.[54] Let's see how free trade coupled with freedom of factor mobility internationally can result in the most efficient resource allocation.

There are pressures for the most abundant factors to move to areas of scarcity.

Substitution When the factor proportions vary widely among countries, pressures exist for the most abundant factors to move to countries with greater scarcity, where they can command a better return. In countries where labor is more abundant than capital, laborers tend to be unemployed or poorly paid. If permitted, many in the labor pool go to countries that have full employment and higher wages. They receive higher wages not only because of the greater scarcity, but also because more capital-rich countries have invested in machinery and infrastructure that make the imported laborers more productive than in their home countries.

Of course, as we discussed in the section on factor endowment theory, the ratio of land (an immobile factor) to people also influences the movement of labor. Russia has a low population density and the most unfarmed arable land of any country. Next door is China with the highest population and little available unfarmed land. About 400 thousand Chinese are now working on Russian farms, and much of the output is shipped to China.[55]

Similarly, capital tends to move away from countries in which it is abundant to those in which it is scarce, such as Mexico getting capital from the United States, which gets labor from Mexico.[56] If finished goods and production factors were both free to move internationally, the comparative costs of transferring goods and factors would determine production location.

However, as is true of trade, there are restrictions on factor movements that make them only partially mobile internationally—such as both U.S. immigration restrictions and Mexican foreign capital ownership restrictions in the petroleum industry.

A hypothetical example, shown in Figure 5.7, should illustrate the substitutability of trade and factor movements under different scenarios. Assume the following:

- The United States and Mexico have equally productive land available at the same cost for growing tomatoes.
- The cost of transporting tomatoes between the United States and Mexico is $0.75 per bushel.
- Workers from either country pick an average of two bushels per hour during a 30-day picking season.

The only differences in price between the two countries are due to variations in labor and capital cost. In the United States the labor rate is $20.00 per day, or $1.25 per bushel; in Mexico it is $4.00 per day, or $0.25 per bushel. The capital needed to buy seeds, fertilizers, and equipment costs the equivalent of $0.30 per bushel in the United States and $0.50 per bushel in Mexico.

If neither tomatoes nor production factors can move between the two countries (see Figure 5.7[a]), the cost of tomatoes produced in Mexico for that market is $0.75 per bushel ($0.25 of labor plus $0.50 of capital), whereas those produced in the United States for the U.S. market cost $1.55 per bushel ($1.25 of labor plus $0.30 of capital). If the two countries eliminate trade restrictions on tomatoes between them (Figure 5.7[b]), the U.S. will import from Mexico because the Mexican cost of $0.75 per bushel plus $0.75 for transporting the tomatoes will be $0.05 less than the $1.55-per-bushel cost of growing them in the United States.

FIGURE 5.7 Unrestricted Trade, Factor Mobility, and the Cost of Tomatoes

Costs are lowest when trade is unrestricted and production factors are mobile.

Assumptions, cost per bushel:

1. U.S. labor = $1.25
2. Mexican labor = $0.25
3. Mexican labor in the United States (including incremental costs) = $1.15
4. U.S. capital = $0.30
5. Mexican capital = $0.50
6. U.S. capital in Mexico = $0.40
7. Transport for exports = $0.75
8. Transport of Mexican workers to the United States = $0.90

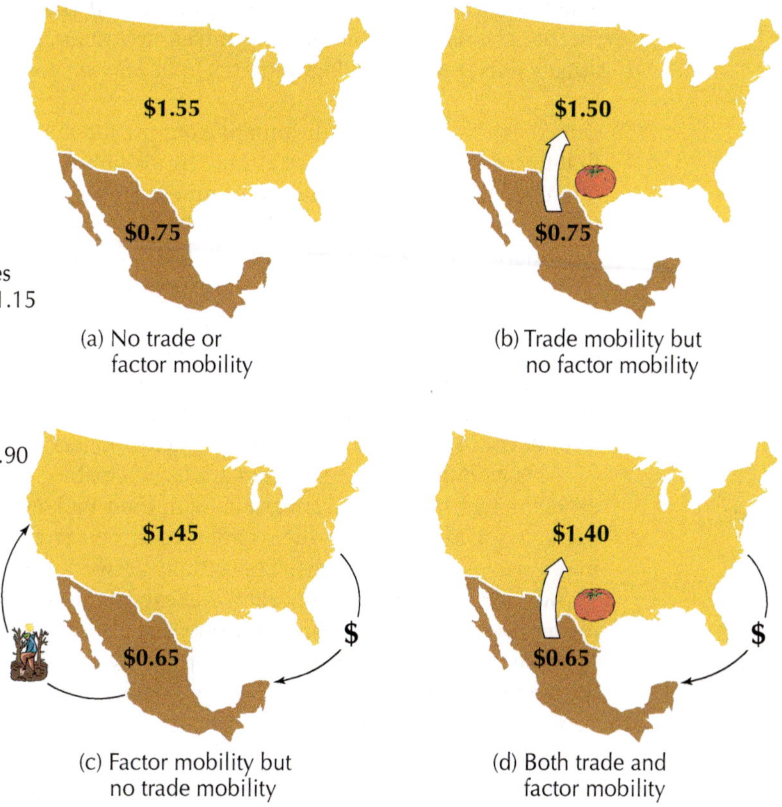

Consider another scenario in which neither country allows the importation of tomatoes but both allow certain movements of labor and capital (Figure 5.7[c]). Mexican workers can enter the United States on temporary work permits for an incremental travel and living expense of $14.40 per day per worker, or $0.90 per bushel. At the same time, U.S. companies will invest capital in Mexican tomato production, provided the capital earns more than it would earn in the United States—say, $0.40 per bushel, which is less than the Mexican going rate.

In this scenario, Mexican production costs per bushel will be $0.65 ($0.25 of Mexican labor plus $0.40 of U.S. capital), and U.S. production costs will be $1.45 ($0.25 of Mexican labor plus $0.90 of travel and incremental costs plus $0.30 of U.S. capital). Each country would reduce its production costs—from $0.75 to $0.65 in Mexico and from $1.55 to $1.45 in the United States—by bringing in abundant production factors from abroad.

The lowest costs occur when trade and production factors are both mobile.

With free trade *and* the free movement of production factors (Figure 5.7[d]), Mexico will produce for both markets by importing capital from the United States. According to the three assumptions just stated, doing this will be cheaper than sending labor to the United States. In reality, because neither production factors nor the finished goods they produce are completely free to move internationally, slight changes in the extent of restrictions can greatly alter how and where goods may be produced most cheaply.

In some cases, however, the inability to gain sufficient access to foreign production factors may stimulate efficient methods of substitution, such as the development of alternatives for traditional production methods.[57] For example, at one time U.S. tomato growers in California depended almost entirely on Mexican temporary workers under what was known as the *bracero program.* Since the termination of this program, the California tomato harvests have quadrupled, while mechanization has replaced 72 percent of the number of workers.

However, not all harvesting jobs can reasonably be mechanized at present. Because cantaloupes ripen at different times, pickers go through a cantaloupe field about 10 times. A robot would have to be able to distinguish colors so as to leave green cantaloupes behind.[58] However, advancement of robots using cameras that distinguish ripeness foretell the diminished need for future agricultural laborers.[59] At the same time, many other jobs that defy mechanization—such as bussing tables at restaurants and changing beds in hotels—are largely filled by unskilled immigrants in developed countries.

Complementarity In our tomato example for the United States and Mexico, we showed that factor movements may substitute for or stimulate trade. Companies' investments abroad often stimulate exports from their home countries. In fact, about a third of world exporting takes place among companies' controlled entities, such as from the firms' parents to their subsidiaries, from their subsidiaries to the parents, and from subsidiary to subsidiary.

Many of the exports would not occur without foreign investments, partly because a company may export equipment as part of its foreign investment. Another reason is that domestic operating units may export materials and components to their foreign facilities for use in a finished product, such as Coca-Cola's exports of concentrate to its bottling facilities abroad. Finally, a company's foreign facility may produce part of the product line while serving as sales agent for exports of its parent's other products.

CONCEPT CHECK

In Chapter 2, we emphasize societal differences in trust along with strength in family ties, especially as it affects trust. We also discussed that higher trust reduces the cost of business transactions.

Finally, immigration enhances trade by creating ethnic enclaves that form one side of ethnic networks linking immigrants with their native countries. The enclaves serve as niche markets for imports from their native countries, such as early U.S. soy sauce imports sold mainly to Asian-Americans. The ethnic networks embody product and country-specific knowledge that aid both importers and exporters. This is more important when a network is from a low-trust culture, especially one that also values family ties strongly. In such a culture most people have higher trust for people they know better, which leads to a first preference for business within the family, next with close friends, etc. Thus, conducting business with people from another country is well down this hierarchy of trust. But the ethnic network offers an alternative, allowing people from low-trust cultures to deal in the foreign country with others whose language and responses are similar to their home country experiences. Without this network, one needs much more time to overcome the perceived risk brought about by lack of knowledge and low trust of potential business partners. Thus potential importers and exporters are more willing to trade when they are part of the ethnic network.[60]

Factor mobility through foreign investment often stimulates trade because of

- The need for components.
- The parent company's ability to sell complementary products.
- The need for equipment for subsidiaries.

Looking to the Future

In What Direction Will Trade Winds Blow?

When countries have few restrictions on foreign trade and factor mobility, companies have greater latitude in reducing operating costs. For example, fewer trade restrictions give them opportunities to gain economies of scale by servicing markets in more than one country from a single base of production. Fewer restrictions on factor movements allow them to combine factors for more efficient production. However, government trade and immigration restrictions vary among countries, over time, and under different circumstances.

Nevertheless, it's probably safe to say that trade restrictions have been diminishing, primarily because of the economic gains that countries foresee through freer trade. Further, restrictions on the movement of capital and technology have become freer, but whether restrictions on the movement of people are freer is questionable.

There are uncertainties as to whether the trend toward the freer movement of trade and production factors will continue. Groups worldwide question whether the economic benefits of more open economies outweigh some of the costs, both economic and noneconomic. Although the next chapter discusses import restrictions (protectionism) in detail, it is useful at this point to understand the overall evolution of protectionist sentiment.

One key issue is the trade between developed and developing economies. As trade barriers are being lowered, some developing economies with very low wage rates are growing economically more rapidly than developed countries. Concomitantly, as companies shift production to developing economies, they displace jobs at home. These displaced workers need to find new jobs. But it is uncertain how fast new jobs will replace old ones and how much developed countries will tolerate employment displacement and job shifts. If they become intolerant, they may enact protectionist measures that would stifle trade.

Another key issue is the future of factor endowments. If present trends continue, relationships among land, labor, and capital will continue to evolve. For example, the population growth rate is expected to be much higher in developing economies than in developed ones. This could result in continued shifts of labor-intensive production to developing economies and pressures on the developed countries to accept more immigrants.

Urbanization will likely grow faster in developing than in developed countries, which are already heavily urbanized. Considerable evidence indicates that productivity rises with urbanization because firms can more likely find people with the exact skills they need, because there are economies in moving supplies and finished products, and because knowledge flows more easily from one company and industry to another. Thus we might expect higher growth in some developing countries due to their pace of urbanization. Such growth should also help them account for a larger share of world trade.

At the same time, on the one hand the finite supply of natural resources may lead to price increases for these resources, even though oversupplies have often depressed prices. The limited supply may work to the advantage of developing economies, because their supplies have been less fully exploited. On the other hand, technology to find and extract natural resources, such as fracking to secure natural gas from shale, may shift supply locations and lessen price rises.

We will probably see the continued trend toward a more finely tuned specialization of production among countries to take advantage of specific conditions. Although part of this will be due to wage and skill differences, other factors are important as well. For instance, country differences in property right protection may influence businesses to locate more of their technologically intensive activities within countries that offer more protection. Or they may disperse portions of production to different countries in order to hinder potential competitors from gaining the full picture needed to pirate their products and processes.

Four interrelated factors are worth monitoring because they could cause product trade to become relatively less significant in the future:

1. As economies grow, efficiencies of multiple production locations also grow because they can all gain sufficient economies of scale. This may allow country-by-country production to replace trade in many cases. For example, most automobile producers have moved into China and Thailand—or plan to do so—as a result of those countries' growing market size.
2. Flexible, small-scale production methods, especially those using robotics and digital technologies, may enable even small countries to produce many goods efficiently for their own consumption, thus eliminating the need to import those goods. For example, before the development of efficient minimills that can produce steel on a small scale, steel production took larger capital outlays that needed enormous markets. Similarly, consumers' demand for evermore differentiated products largely negates the cost advantages of long production runs, thus making smaller scale manufacturing close to markets more advantageous.[61]
3. Output from 3D printers has already reached the point at which 20 percent is of final products (e.g., medical implants, jewelry, lampshades, car parts, mobile phones); some predict that this figure will reach 50 percent by 2020. Basically, this permits a user to choose plans and use software for the printer to produce the product. It involves an additive technology (building a product up from raw materials) rather than a traditional subtractive technology (cutting, drilling, and bashing of raw materials). As this develops, products can be fabricated efficiently where they are used rather than traded from one country to another.[62] However, there will still be a need to trade production-grade metals and plastics as inputs to the computers.
4. Services are growing more rapidly than products as a portion of production and consumption within developed countries. Part of this change involves technology, such as the substitute of digitalized products like music and reading material, for traditionally manufactured products. Thus, one buys the right to copy (a service sale) from anywhere in the world with no need to ship products. Consequently, product trade may become a less important part of countries' total trade. Further, many of the rapid-growth service areas, such as retail gasoline distribution and dining out, are not easily traded, so trade in goods plus services could become a smaller part of total output and consumption. ■

CASE LUKOIL: Foreign Trade and Investment

To keep a lamp burning, we have to keep putting oil in it – Mother Teresa.

To keep an economy growing, we also have to keep putting oil into energy expansion. A major oil and energy player is LUKOIL, which with 2012 sales of $139 billion, produces and distributes a wide range of petroleum and energy products such as gasoline, heating oil, crude petroleum, jet fuel, lubricants, natural gas, and petrochemicals. It is listed in both *Fortune's* and *Forbes'* world's 100 largest companies; in the former by sales, and the latter by valuation. It is not only Russia's second largest company, but also its largest privately-owned company. Many of the world's largest oil companies are government-owned, such as in Saudi Arabia, Iran, and Venezuela. Among privately owned oil firms, LUKOIL is the world's fourth largest, accounting for 17 percent of Russian crude oil production and refining.

The Russian Economy

LUKOIL's position is inexorably tied to conditions in Russia. Before the fall of the Berlin Wall in 1989 and the collapse of the Soviet Union, the Russian oil industry was government-owned within a command economy. In addition, the Soviet Union followed an inward-looking economic policy that depended minimally on foreign trade. In fact, a government monopoly handled all foreign trade and did not always relate prices to production costs. Russia privatized most industries in the 1990s; however, it has only partially privatized the energy sector because of its essentiality to national well-being. Russia faced abundant economic problems during the 1990s when it was transitioning to a market economy. Among other factors, many newly privatized companies lacked sufficient management and marketing skills, especially for selling abroad.

However, during the 10-year period from 1999 to 2008, Russia enjoyed significant GDP growth, led by the export of commodities. During this period, Russia became the world's largest natural gas and second largest oil exporter. The Russian economy was one of the hardest hit by the global economic crisis since 2008. Its GDP fell by 8 percent in 2009, but has since recovered by growing 4 percent, due largely to high oil prices in 2010. Russia's oil and gas sector accounts for about 25 percent of its GDP and a third of all its exports. Russia consumes about 5 percent of its oil and exports the rest.

On the downside, its dependence on petroleum exports makes Russia vulnerable to fluctuations in global petroleum markets, such as that caused by the 2009 economic downturn when global demand and prices for energy plummeted. Further, when the yearly average price per barrel of oil shifts by as much as $1, Russian revenues shift by about $2 billion in the same direction. In recent years, Russia has discovered so much oil that the country now has the world's eighth-highest level of proven reserves. In addition, Russia also controls petroleum exports from the former Central Asian Soviet republics of Azerbaijan and Kazakhstan, both of which, like Russia are oil rich.

Although some oil producing countries, especially members of the Organization of Petroleum Exporting Countries (OPEC), cut back production to maintain higher prices, Russia, which is not an OPEC member, is content to sell all the oil it can produce. This helps to explain the disparity between Russia's rank in exports versus proven reserves. However, its prices depend, of course, on world petroleum prices. Because of fierce competition in the global oil industry, even control of such vast supplies is no guarantee that Russia can sell its output at an acceptable margin. Additionally, Russia depends on oil exports to pay for imports (over half of which include machinery and transportation equipment), a top priority for the Russian government for three primary reasons:

1. At a purchasing price parity of $15,900 in 2010, Russian GDP per capita is still well below that of any other G8 country.

2. The oil sector—which is a capital- rather than labor-intensive industry—employs less than 1 percent of the country's population.
3. Natural disasters, such as the 2010 drought and fires, wreak havoc directly on the agricultural sector and indirectly on other economic sectors.

A Little History of LUKOIL

LUKOIL was formed in 1991 as a government-owned enterprise through a merger of three state-run companies in Siberia. LUK is an acronym for the names of the home cities of the three preexisting companies. At the time, the former Soviet deputy minister of oil production, Vagit Alekperov, believed the only way Russian oil companies could successfully compete against Western companies would be to vertically integrate the three main components of their business—exploration, refining, and distribution. In the old Soviet system, these components were strictly separate.

After its founding, LUKOIL moved quickly to establish this integration. In 1993, the government approved LUKOIL's privatization plan, and a little more than 9 percent of the ownership went private, mainly by giving shares to its employees. The following year LUKOIL sold its first private shares through an auction, which reduced government ownership to 80.59 percent. Government ownership fell to 33 percent in 1996, to 20 percent in 2000, and to 0 in 2004 when ConocoPhillips bought the last 7.59 percent of the company from the government. In the interim, LUKOIL began selling shares over the counter in New York and through several German exchanges. In 2002, LUKOIL became the first Russian company listed on the London Stock Exchange. The decrease in government ownership occurred partially by selling government shares and partially by issuing additional shares that diluted the government's ownership. Subsequent to being fully privatized, ConocoPhillips upped its ownership to 20 percent, but sold its holdings in 2010.

Although the Russian government is no longer a shareholder, it maintains close ties with LUKOIL because of its economic significance—LUKOIL controls about 19 percent of all Russian production and refining—and its political importance as a symbol of Russian prestige in foreign markets. An illustration of the latter was President Vladimir Putin's attendance to open a LUKOIL filling station in New York City. LUKOIL began its first foreign project in 1994, when it took a stake in an Azerbaijan oilfield. It has since expanded so that it now does business in 37 countries through a combination of exploration (10 countries), refining (5 countries), and distribution or transshipment (27 countries).

Map 5.4 identifies LUKOIL's foreign operations. Note that most of these countries are close to Russia. As of 2012, LUKOIL had almost 6000 filling stations worldwide. One of its farthest locations from Russia is the United States, where the company's expansion has occurred mainly through the acquisition of Getty Petroleum in 2000, and a string of gasoline stations owned by ConocoPhillips in 2004. Despite LUKOIL's foray into international business, it depends mainly on the Russian market for its sales and oil reserves.

Why Export?

As we've already seen, Russia and LUKOIL have a lot of oil reserves. When countries or companies have an abundant storable commodity, which is not easily spoiled, a number of factors may influence the quantity they try to sell in the short term, especially to export markets. One is the expectation of future prices compared with present ones (i.e., if future prices are expected to be higher than the net present value of investment earnings from immediate sale), one may be better off by limiting current sales. However, in the case of oil exports, projecting future prices is particularly problematic because they depend so much on derived demand, which in turn depends on uncertainties about industrial output, climatic and natural disaster conditions. Real natural and technical changes lead to hypothetical market changes for the future, (consider the future uncertainty of energy sources brought about by concern after a 2011 tsunami damaged a Japanese nuclear facility), and technological

MAP 5.4 LUKOIL's Global Oil and Gas Production and Sales

LUKOIL has expanded its operations internationally, not only by exporting (notably to the United States) but also by investing in foreign production, exploration, refining operations and marketing efforts. Note that the preponderance of the company's expansion has taken place in nearby countries. In addition to the information shown on the map, LUKOIL has petrochemical operations in Ukraine and Bulgaria and power production in Ukraine, Romania, and Bulgaria.

Source: Information to prepare the map is taken from LUKOIL *Annual Report* (2012).

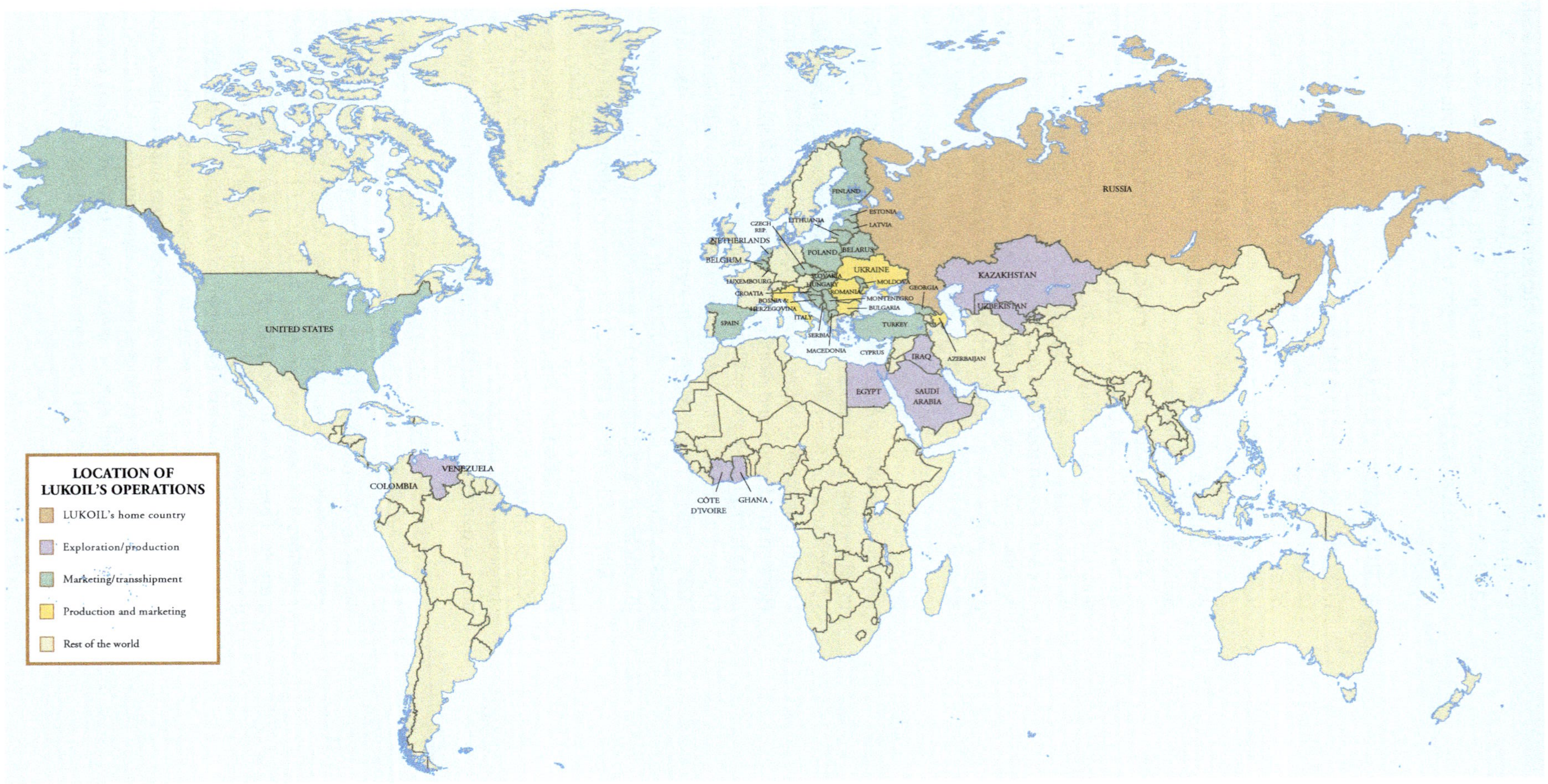

changes (consider, that the United States displaced Russia as the largest oil and gas producer in 2013 because of innovations in fracking technology). Likewise, prices depend on competition, and competitors never know what other producing countries and companies will do. At any rate, we have discussed reasons for the Russian policy of expanding current export oil sales, thus the decision is a "given" from the country's standpoint. We should point out that, since the beginning of the twenty-first century, the global price of oil has fluctuated substantially even though there has been a trend towards higher prices. For instance, the average monthly prices in 2008 were 42 percent higher than in 2007. Then they fell 41.5 percent in 2009. (If the highs and lows within particular years are compared rather than the yearly averages, the fluctuations are even greater.) Some of the factors influencing both price changes and price trends have been the uncertainty following 9/11, Chinese economic expansion, production cutbacks by OPEC, unsettlement in and trade embargoes in various oil-producing countries (e.g., Libya, Venezuela, and Iran), seasonal abnormal temperatures, and the global economic crisis that began in 2008. Nevertheless, Russia's export position has been generally quite good throughout the twenty-first century's first decade, with favorable balances of trade each year that have helped to pay for both imports and a high level of external credit.

But what about LUKOIL's dreams? Despite a growing domestic market, Russian demand is insufficient to absorb all of LUKOIL's capacity. Overall, it has been able to sell more oil at higher prices outside Russia than it could just a few years ago. Further, if LUKOIL were to curtail exporting, it might incur a political backlash of the Russian government as a result of economic policies deemed favorable for the entire economy. In addition to its increase in sales through exporting, the practice has enabled LUKOIL to amass a substantial store of capital that it has been able to channel into foreign investment.

Why LUKOIL Went the Foreign Investment Route

LUKOIL's management has long seen foreign expansion as a means both of earning bigger margins and ensuring more reliable, full, on-time payment than it can get in Russia. The question, however, remains: why doesn't LUKOIL simply export rather than risk foreign investment? The answer lies in a combination of factors.

Fluctuating World Markets

We have discussed how supply and demand changes have influenced prices, but they also affect the ability to sell. In the late 1990s, when a global oil glut impaired foreign sales, LUKOIL decided to emulate its larger Western competitors with a strategy of forward integration into the ownership of foreign distribution outlets. (Nevertheless, its plan for the 2012–2021 period is for over 80 percent of investment to be spent on exploration and production.) LUKOIL made its first foreign distribution investments not far from home in former Soviet satellite countries by buying long time retail customers in Bulgaria and Romania that were state-owned operations being privatized. Since then, LUKOIL has ventured farther afield, almost exclusively by means of purchasing existing operations. It's a sound strategy. When oil producers invest in distribution, they strengthen their ties to markets where they may be better able to sell crude oil in times of global oversupply. Moreover, integrating into distribution can potentially reduce operating costs, primarily because a producer doesn't have to rely on negotiating and enforcing a network of agreements by which it sells oil to intermediaries in other countries. Further, this vertical integration enables LUKOIL to smooth its profits by operating in the ever-changing portion going to production versus distribution. Concomitantly, LUKOIL has rebranded its acquisitions to gain uniformity in its image, which also helps to promote sales better.

Political Uncertainty

LUKOIL has been well aware of the fact that export sales are always subject to political disruptions. What if an importing country decides to reduce its purchases of Russian oil to protest some internal Russian political policy (or simply to diversify its own supply sources)? In turn, this risk has been a factor in LUKOIL's decision to expand into exploration and refining outside Russia. Or consider another problem that's more or less unique to LUKOIL's situation.

An oil rig in the North Sea. Thousands work around the clock to extract energy and natural gas along the coastline.
Source: © Simon Pedersen – Shutterstock

As it turns out, the Russian government owns the pipeline system through which virtually all Russian oil exports must pass, allocating access to the system by means of quotas among domestic oil companies. What if a competitor manages to gain sufficient influence with certain political decisionmakers to siphon off part of LUKOIL's quota? Although LUKOIL will never forget its own complete privatization, the Russian government still owns some of its domestic competitors, and has often bestowed on its firms preferential treatment in various matters. That is just one reason why LUKOIL is trying to increase foreign oil supplies to 20 percent of its total. However, moving internationally creates other political risks, such as ownership of assets in volatile environments such as Egypt and Venezuela. International sanctions caused LUKOIL to cease operating in Iraq when Saddam Hussein was in power. Some U.S. Congressmen have made scathing attacks against LUKOIL because some oil it shipped to China was then shipped to Iran despite a contract clause stating "not for supplies to the territory of Iran."

Efficiency Imperatives

To be a major global competitor, LUKOIL must become as efficient as its major Western competitors. Toward that end, it must not only achieve operating efficiencies but also acquire state-of-the-industry technology and marketing skills. For instance, it must adhere to ever-changing national product requirements concerning gasoline octane and cleanliness. In the past, LUKOIL's administrative expenses and cost of capital were high, compared with those of Western competitors. At home, such inefficiencies resulted in only minor problems because the competition consisted solely of other Russian oil companies hampered by the same operational inefficiencies inherited from the former state-owned oil monopoly. Even in Russia, however, new competitive threats are starting to emerge as Western oil firms have bought interests in Russian oil companies. LUKOIL, however, views foreign oil companies to be a stiffer threat than domestic competition: They are valuable sources of the technology and knowledge that must be competed with at home and abroad. With this strategy in mind, it has placed independent directors from Western oil companies on its board, used ConocoPhillips's management expertise when it owned 20 percent of the company, and has established several partnerships abroad, such as with Norway's Statoil. Meanwhile, foreign acquisitions, such as Getty in the United States, present another source of experienced personnel, technology, and competitive know-how.

QUESTIONS

5-3. What theories of trade help explain Russia's position as an oil exporter? Why? Which ones don't? Why not?

5-4. How do global political and economic conditions affect global oil markets and prices?

5-5. Discuss the following statement as it applies to Russia and LUKOIL: *Regardless of the advantages a country may gain by trading, international trade will begin only if companies within that country have competitive advantages that enable them to be viable traders—and they must foresee profits in exporting and importing.*

5-6. In LUKOIL's situation, what is the relationship between factor mobility and exports?

5-7. Why do you think LUKOIL's first foreign direct investments were in countries nearby to Russia (e.g. former Soviet republics and satellite countries)?

SUMMARY

- Some trade theories examine what will happen to international trade in the absence of government interference. Other theories prescribe how governments should affect trade flows to achieve certain national objectives.
- Trade theory is useful because it helps explain what might be produced competitively in a given locale, where a company might go to produce a given product efficiently, and whether government practices might interfere with the free flow of trade among countries. Other theories address the explanation of trade patterns.
- Mercantilist theory proposes that a country should try to achieve a favorable balance of trade (export more than it imports) to receive an influx of gold. Neomercantilist policy also seeks a favorable balance of trade, but its purpose is to achieve some social or political objective.
- The theory of absolute advantage proposes specialization through free trade because consumers will be better off if they can buy foreign-made products priced more cheaply than domestic ones.
- According to the theory of absolute advantage, a country may produce goods more efficiently because of a natural advantage (e.g., raw materials or climate) or because of an acquired advantage (e.g., technology or skill for a product or process advantage).
- Comparative advantage theory also proposes specialization through free trade because it says that trade can increase total global output even if one country has an absolute advantage in the production of all products.
- Policymakers have questioned some of the assumptions of the absolute and comparative advantage theories: that full employment exists, output efficiency is always a country's major objective, countries are satisfied with their relative gains, there are no transport costs among countries, advantages appear to be static, and resources move freely within countries but are immobile internationally.
- The theory of country size holds that because countries with large land areas are apt to have varied climates and natural resources, they are generally more self-sufficient than smaller countries. A second reason for this greater self-sufficiency is that large countries' production and market centers are more likely to be located at a greater distance from other countries, raising the transport costs of foreign trade.
- The factor-proportions theory holds that a country's relative endowments of land, labor, and capital will determine the relative costs of these factors. These factor costs, in turn, determine which goods the country can produce most efficiently.
- According to the country-similarity theory, most trade today occurs among developed countries because they share similar market characteristics and because they produce and consume so much more than developing economies.
- Much of the pattern of two-way trading partners may be explained by cultural similarity between the countries, political and economic agreements, and the distance between them.
- Manufactured products comprise the bulk of trade among high-income countries. This trade occurs because countries apportion their research and development differently among industrial sectors. It also occurs because consumers from high-income countries want and can afford to buy products with a greater variety of characteristics than are produced in their domestic markets.
- The international product life cycle (PLC) theory states that companies will manufacture products first in the countries in which they were researched and developed, which are almost always developed countries. Over the product's life cycle, production will shift to foreign locations, especially to developing economies, as the product reaches the stages of maturity and decline.
- The diamond of national competitive advantage theory shows that four conditions are important for gaining and maintaining

competitive superiority: demand conditions; factor conditions; related and supporting industries; and firm strategy, structure, and rivalry.

- Production factors and finished goods are only partially mobile internationally. The cost and feasibility of transferring production factors rather than exporting finished goods internationally will determine which alternative is better.
- Although international mobility of production factors may be a substitute for trade, the mobility may stimulate trade through sales of components, equipment, and complementary products.

KEY TERMS

absolute advantage
acquired advantage
brain drain
comparative advantage
country-similarity theory
diamond of national competitive advantage theory
factor-mobility theory
factor-proportions theory
favorable balance of trade
import substitution
mercantilism
natural advantage
neomercantilism
nontradable goods
product life cycle (PLC) theory
strategic trade policy
theory of country size
trade deficit
trade surplus
unfavorable balance of trade

ENDNOTES

1 ***Sources include the following:*** "Costa Rica Exports," www.tradingeconomics.com/costa-rica/exports, accessed January 31, 2013; World Trade Organization, "Trade Profiles: Costa Rica," retrieved January 31, 2013, from stat.wto.org/CountryProfile/WSDBCountryPFView.aspx?Language=E&Country=CR; Debora Spar, *Attracting High Technology Investment: Intel's Costa Rican Plant* (Washington, DC: The World Bank, Foreign Investment Advisory Service Occasional Paper No. 11, 1998); CIA Factbook, retrieved January 31, 2013, from CIA.GOV/CIA/publications/factbook/geos/cs.html; Gail D. Triner, "Recent Latin American History and Its Historiography," *Latin American Research Review* 38:1 (2003): 219–38; John Weeks, "Trade Liberalisation, Market Deregulation and Agricultural Performance in Central America," *The Journal of Development Studies* 35:5 (June 1999): 48–76; Niels W. Ketelhöhn and Michael E. Porter, "Building a Cluster: Electronics and Information Technology in Costa Rica," *Harvard Business School Case 9703422* (November 7, 2002); John Schellhas, "Peasants against Globalization: Rural Social Movements in Costa Rica," *American Anthropologist* 103:3 (2001):862–863; Jose Itzigsohn, *Developing Poverty: The State, Labor Market Deregulation, and the Informal Economy in Costa Rica and the Dominican Republic* (University Park, IL: Pennsylvania University Press, 2000); Roy Nelson, "Intel's Site Selection Decision in Latin America," *Thunderbird International Business Review* 42:2 (2001): 227–49; Andrés Rodríguez-Clare, "Costa Rica's Development Strategy Based on Human Capital and Technology: How It Got There, The Impact of Intel, and Lessons for Other Countries," *United Nations Human Development Report 2001* (New York: United Nations Development Programme, 2001).

2 For a good survey of mercantilism and the mercantilist era, see Gianni Vaggi, *A Concise History of Economic Thought: From Mercantilism to Monetarism* (New York: Palgrave Macmillan, 2002).

3 For reviews of the literature, see Jordan Shan and Fiona Sun, "On the Export-Led Growth Hypothesis for the Little Dragons: An Empirical Reinvestigation," *Atlantic Economic Review* 26:4 (1998): 353–71; George K. Zestos and Xiangnan Tao, "Trade and GDP Growth: Causal Relations in the United States and Canada," *Southern Economic Journal* 68:4 (2002): 859–74.

4 For a good discussion of the history of free trade thought, see Leonard Gomes, *The Economics and Ideology of Free Trade: A Historical Review* (Cheltenham, UK: Edward Elgar, 2003).

5 "Year Round Production of Tomatoes in Iceland," retrieved July 16, 2007, from www.freshplaza.com/news_detail.asp?id=3791; "The History of Wine Production in Brazil," retrieved July 16, 2007, from www.brazilianwines.com/en/brazilie_histoire.asp.

6 For simplicity's sake, both Smith and Ricardo originally assumed a simple world composed of only two countries and two commodities. Our example makes the same assumption. Now, although this simplification is unrealistic, it does not diminish the usefulness of either theory. Economists have applied the same reasoning to demonstrate efficiency advantages in multiproduct and multicountry trade relationships. Smith's seminal treatise remains abundantly in print; for a reliable recent edition, see *An Inquiry into the Nature and Causes of the Wealth of Nations* (Washington, DC: Regnery Publishing, 1998). Like Smith's *Wealth of Nations,* Ricardo's seminal work on comparative advantage, originally published in London in 1817, is continuously reprinted; see, for example, *On the Principles of Political Economy and Taxation* (Amherst, NY: Prometheus Books, 1996).

7 For a good discussion of this paradoxical thinking, see Paul R. Krugman, "What Do Undergraduates Need to Know about Trade?" *American Economic Review Papers and Proceedings* (May 1993):23–26. For a discussion of some developing countries' views that monopolistic conditions keep them from gaining a fair share of gains from international trade, see A. P. Thirwell, *Growth and Development,* 6th ed. (London: Macmillan, 1999).

8 Thomas I. Palley, "Institutionalism and New Trade Theory: Rethinking Comparative Advantage and Trade Theory," *Journal of Economic Issues* 42:1 (2008): 195–08.

9 Murray Kemp, "Non-Competing Factor Groups and the Normative Propositions of Trade Theory," *International Review of Economics and Finance* 17 (2008): 388–90.

10 Andrew Avery Herring, Roger Enrique Bonilla-Carrı́on, Rosilyne Mae Borland, and Kenneth Hailey Hill, "Differential Mortality Patterns Between Nicaraguan Immigrants and Native-born Residents of Costa Rica," *Immigrant Minority Health* 12 (2010): 33–42.

11 Gordon H. Hanson, "The Rise of Middle Kingdoms: Emerging Economies in Global Trade," *The Journal of Economic Perspectives* 26:2 (Spring 2012): 41–64.

12 Eli J. Heckscher, *Heckscher-Ohlin Trade Theory* (Cambridge, MA: MIT Press, 1991).

13 For a discussion of ways in which the theory does not fit the reality of trade, see Antoni Estevadeordal and Alan M. Taylor, "A Century of Missing Trade?" *The American Economic Review* 92:1 (2002): 383–93. For a study supporting the theory, see Yong-Seok Choi and Pravin Krishna, "The Factor Content of Bilateral Trade: An Empirical Test," *The Journal of Political Economy* 112:4 (2004): 887–915.

14 See, for example, Donald R. Davis and David E. Weinstein, "An Account of Global Factor Trade," *The American Economic Review* 91:5 (2001): 1423–53; Oner Guncavdi and Suat Kucukcifi, "Foreign Trade and Factor Intensity in an Open Developing Country: An Input-Output Analysis for Turkey," *Russian & East European Finance and Trade* 37:1 (2001): 75–88.

15 See, for example, P. Krugman and A. J. Venables, "Globalization and the Inequality of Nations," *Quarterly Journal of Economics* 110 (1995): 857–80.

16 See Paul Krugman, "Scale Economies, Product Differentiation, and the Patterns of Trade," *The American Economic Review* 70 (1980): 950–59; James Harrigan, "Estimation of Cross-Country Differences in Industry Production Functions," *Journal of International Economics* 47:2 (1999): 267–93.

17 Drusilla K. Brown and Robert M. Stern, "Measurement and Modeling of the Economic Effect of Trade and Investment Barriers in Services," *Title Review of International Economics* 9:2 (2001): 262–86, discuss the role of economies of scale and trade barriers.

18 See Gianmarco I. P. Ottaviano and Diego Puga, "Agglomeration in the Global Economy: A Survey of the 'New Economic Geography'," *The World Economy* 21:6 (1998): 707–31; Gianmarco I. P. Ottaviano, Takatoshi Tabuchi, and Jacques-François Thisse, "Agglomeration and Trade Revisited," *International Economic Review* 43:2 (2002): 409–35.

19 Stefan B. Linder, *An Essay on Trade Transformation* (New York: Wiley, 1961).

20 Dirk Pilat, "The Economic Impact of Technology," *The OECD Observer* 213 (August–September 1998): 5–8.

21 Anthony J. Venables, "Shifts in Economic Geography and Their Causes," *Economic Review—Federal Reserve Bank of Kansas City* 91:4 (2006): 61–85, referring to work by R. Hausmann and D. Rodrik, "Economic Development as Self Discovery" (2003), Harvard Kennedy School working paper.

22 Two discussions of intra-industry trade are: Don P. Clark, "Determinants of Intra-industry Trade between the United States and Industrial Nations," *The International Trade Journal* 12:3 (Fall 1998): 345–62; H. Peter Gray, "Free International Economic Policy in a World of Schumpeter Goods," *The International Trade Journal* 12:3 (Fall 1998): 323–44.

23 Daniel Michaels, "Landing Rights," *Wall Street Journal* (April 30, 2002): A1+.

24 Lars Håkanson and Douglas Dow, "Markets and Networks in International Trade: On the Role of Distances in Globalization," *Management International Review* 52:6 (2012): 761–90.

25 Christopher A. Bartlett, "Global Wine Wars: New World Challenges Old," Harvard Business School Case 9-303-056 (July 21, 2003).

26 Terry Hall, "NZ Finds Pirated Varieties in Chile," *Financial Times* (January 21, 1999): 24.

27 Anthony J. Venables, "Shifts in Economic Geography and Their Causes."

28 Jeffrey A. Frankel and David Romer, "Does Trade Cause Growth?" *The American Economic Review* 89:3 (June 1999): 379–99.

29 J. L. Gallup and J. Sachs, "Geography and Economic Development," in B. Pleskovic and J. E. Stiglitz, eds., *Annual World Bank Conference on Development Economics* (Washington, DC: The World Bank, 1998).

30 See Raymond Vernon, "International Investment and International Trade in the Product Life Cycle," *Quarterly Journal of Economics* 80 (May 1996): 190–207; David Dollar, "Technological Innovation, Capital Mobility, and the Product Cycle in North–South Trade," *American Economic Review* 76:1 (1986): 177–90.

31 This is true according to various indicators. See, for example, International Bank for Reconstruction and Development, "Science and Technology," *The World Development Indicators* (Washington, DC: International Bank for Reconstruction and Development, 2000): 300.

32 Michael E. Porter, "The Competitive Advantage of Nations," *Harvard Business Review* 68:4 (1990): 73–93.

33 Kiyohiko Ito and Vladimir Pucik, "R&D Spending, Domestic Competition, and Export Performance of Japanese Manufacturing Firms," *Strategic Management Journal* 14 (1993): 61–75.

34 Jeremy Wiesen, "The U.S. Needs Its Own Industrial Policy," *Wall Street Journal* (September 13, 2010): A19.

35 Hubert Schmitz, "Reducing Complexity in the Industrial Policy Debate," *Development Policy Review* 25:4 (2007): 417–28.

36 Liviu-George, Ion Ignat, and Andre Teofil Postolachi, "Theoretical Controversies on Strategic Trade Policy," *Economy Transdisciplinarity Cognition*15:1 (2012): 300–07.

37 Sonny Nwankwo and Darlington Richards, "Institutional Paradigm and the Management of Transitions: A Sub-Saharan African Perspective," *International Journal of Social Economics* 31:1/2 (2004): 111.

38 Jeffrey Sachs, "Institutions Matter, but Not Everything," *Finance and Development* (June 2003): 38–41.

39 Nwankwo and Richards, "Institutional Paradigm and the Management of Transitions," 111.

40 Andrés Rodríguez-Clare, "Clusters and Comparative Advantage: Implications for Industrial Policy," *Journal of Development Economics* 82 (2007): 43–57.

41 Paul Krugman and Alasdair M. Smith, eds., *Empirical Studies of Strategic Trade Policies* (Chicago: University of Chicago Press, 1993); Howard Pack and Kamal Saggi, "Is There a Case for Industrial Policy?" *The World Bank Research Observer* 21:2 (2006): 267.

42 Paul M. Sherer, "Thailand Trips in Reach for New Exports," *Wall Street Journal* (August 27, 1996): A8.

43 Richard Brahm, "National Targeting Policies, High-Technology Industries, and Excessive Competition," *Strategic Management Journal* 16 (1995): 71–91.

44 Andrea E. Goldstein and Steven M. McGuire, "The Political Economy of Strategic Trade Policy and the Brazil-Canada Export Subsidies Saga," *The World Economy* 27:4 (2004): 541.

45 Theresa M. Greaney, "Strategic Trade and Competition Policies to Assist Distressed Industries," *The Canadian Journal of Economics* 32:3 (1999): 767.

46 Department of Economic and Social Affairs, Population Division, *World Population Prospects: The 2008 Revision Highlights* (New York: United Nations, 2009): xi.

47 "List of Countries by Foreign-Born Population," en.wikipedia.org/wiki/List_of_countries_by_foreign-born_population_in_2005 (accessed February 1, 2013).

48 Sevil Sönmez, Yorghos Apostopoulos, Diane Tran, and Shantyana Rentrope, "Human Rights and Health Disparities for Migrant Workers in the UAE," *Health and Human Rights* Vol 13, No 2 (2011).

49 Patrick Barta and Joel Millman, "The Great U-Turn," *Wall Street Journal* (June 6–7, 2009): A1.

50 "Flight to Nowhere," *The Economist* (March 2, 2013): 58–59.

51 *Trends in International Migration,* retrieved March 18, 2005, from oecd.org/dataoecd/7/49/24994376.

52 Miriam Jordan, "Migrants' Cash Keeps Flowing Home," *Wall Street Journal (Online)* [New York, N.Y] 23 Sep 2012: n/a.," *Wall Street Journal (Online)* [New York, N.Y] 23 Sep 2012: n/a.

53 Paul M. Vaaler, "Immigrant Remittances and the Venture Investment Environment of Developing Countries," *Journal of International Business Studies* 42:9 (December 2011): 1121–49.

54 Keith Head and John Ries, "Exporting and FDI as Alternative Strategies," *Oxford Review of Economic Policy* 20:3 (2004): 409–29.

55 Andrew E. Kramer, Russian Farm, Chinese Farmer,"*New York Times* (September 11, 2012): B1+.

56 See Frank D. Bean et al.,"Circular, Invisible, and Ambiguous Migrants: Components of Differences in Estimates of the Number of Unauthorized Mexican Migrants in the United States,"*Demography* 38:3 (2001): 411–22; United Nations Conference on Trade and Development, *World Investment Report 2000: Cross-Border Mergers and Acquisitions and Development* (New York and Geneva: United Nations, 2000): 312.

57 Paul Windrum, Andreas Reinstaller, and Christopher Bull,"The Outsourcing Productivity Paradox: Total Outsourcing, Organisational Innovation, and Long Run Productivity Growth,"*Journal of Evolutionary Economics* 19:2 (2009): 197–229.

58 June Kronholtz,"Immigrant Labor or Machines?"*Wall Street Journal* (December 19, 2006): A4.

59 "March of the Lettuce Bot,"*The Economist* (December 1, 2012): monitor 5.

60 ***Sources include the following:*** *LUKOIL Annual Report* 2012, retrieved October 14, 2013 from http://www.lukoil.com/materials/doc/Annual_Report_2012/Lukoil_GO_2012_eng.pdf; "Alliances, Acquisitions Key to LUKOIL Ambitions," International Petroleum Finance (June 8, 2007): 1; "World; LUKOIL to Boost Investment in 2011," Interfax: Ukraine Business Daily [Kiev], December 13, 2010; "Iran Claims Denied as LUKOIL Looks East," NEFT Compass, September 16, 2010; Sabrina Tavernise and Peter S. Green, "Oil Concerns in Russia Branch Out," *New York Times* (April 2, 2002): W1; Bhushan Bahree, "Western Oil Flirts with Russia Firms, Insider Says," Wall Street Journal (April 29, 2002): A13; Reuters, "Mobius and Chevron Exec Nominated for LUKOIL Board," (January 17, 2002), www.highbeam.com/doc/1G1-81866356.html; Paul Starobin, "LUKOIL Is Lonesome," Business Week Online, retrieved October 2, 2009, http://www.businessweek.com/stories/2000-04-23/lukoil-is-lonesome-intl-edition; www.lukoil.com; Vidya Ram, "A More Refined Lukoil," Forbes.com, retrieved October 2, 2009, www.forbes.com/2008/06/24/erg-lukoil-refining-markets-equity-cx_vr_0624markets11.html; "Focus, the Russians Are Coming," Petroleum Economist (December 31, 2000); Andrew Jack and Arkady Ostrovsky, "LUKOIL in U.S. Petro Deal," Financial Times (November 4, 2000): 8; David Ignatius, "The Russians Are Pumping," Pittsburgh Post-Gazette (December 28, 2001): A-21; Tina Obut, "Perspective on Russia's Oil Sector," Oil & Gas Journal (February 1, 1999): 20; LUKOIL Annual Report, various years; "Event Brief of September 30: ConocoPhillips and LUKOil," CCBN Wire Service (September 30, 2004); "LUKOIL Leading Peers in Adding to Production outside Russia," Platts Oilgram News (April 13, 2004): 1; "Russia," retrieved October 14, 2013, www.cia.gov/library/publications/the-world-factbook/geos/rs.html.

61 Paul Markillie,"Manufacturing the Future,"*The Economist* (special issue, the world in 2013, no date): 128.

62 "Print Me a Stradivarius,"*The Economist* (February 10, 2011), retrieved February 17, 2011, from www.economist.com/node/18114327?story_id=18114327&fsrc=nwl; J. M. Pearce, C. Morris Blair, K. J. Laciak, R. Andrews, R. Nosrat, and I. Zelenika-Zovko,"3-D Printing of Open Source Appropriate Technologies for Self-Directed Sustainable Development," *Journal of Sustainable Development* 3:4 (December 2010): 17–29.

CHAPTER 9

Formulation of National Trade Policies

Tyrone Siu/Reuters/Newscom

AFTER STUDYING THIS CHAPTER, YOU SHOULD BE ABLE TO:

1. Present the major arguments in favor of and against governmental intervention in international trade.
2. Identify the advantages and disadvantages of adopting an industrial policy.
3. Analyze the role of domestic politics in formulating a country's international trade policies.
4. Describe the major tools countries use to restrict trade.
5. Specify the techniques countries use to promote international trade.
6. Explain how countries protect themselves against unfair trade practices.

HUAWEI LEADS THE WAY

Huawei (pronounced hwah-way) can lay claim to being China's most successful multinational corporation. Headquartered in Shenzhen, the company employs 140,000 workers in 140 countries. In 2012, Huawei's sales reached $35 billion, and it captured the title of being the world's largest telecommunications equipment manufacturer, displacing Sweden's Ericsson from that perch. It is a major supplier of mobile and fixed broadband networking equipment. It is the third-largest seller of smartphones, although its presence in this market in the United States is relatively small. It, along with Haier, the world's largest white goods manufacturer, and Lenovo, a leading PC manufacturer, is at the vanguard of Chinese companies that have enjoyed multinational success.

Huawei was founded in 1987 by Ren Zhengfei, who began his career as an engineer in the People's Liberation Army (PLA). After leaving the army, he sold private branch switching equipment for a Hong Kong manufacturer. He soon turned to manufacturing such equipment under the Huawei name. Ren built his company by producing high-quality products that sell for low prices. Huawei initially focused on serving smaller cities and rural areas in inland China, where competition was less intense. It then expanded into larger Chinese cities. By 1992, Huawei had developed its own digital telephone switch for the mainstream telecommunications market. Two years later Huawei branched into long-distance transmission equipment. Ten years after its founding, Huawei went international, marketing landline networking equipment to Hong Kong's Hutchinson Whampoa. Huawei built a research and development (R&D) center in India in 1999, in Sweden in 2000, and four in the United States shortly thereafter. In the 2000s it established R&D joint ventures with 3Com Communications, Siemens, Motorola, and Symantec. To maintain its position in the fiercely competitive and highly innovative telecom equipment market, Huawei ploughed $4.8 billion of its revenues into R&D in 2012. Huawei's strategies seem to be working: executives forecast revenue growth of 10 percent a year for the next five years, driven in part by the LTE mobile phone networks that China Mobile, China Telecom, and China Unicom, the three largest Chinese mobile operators, will be rolling out. With a billion customers, their LTE upgrades will provide a lucrative new stream of revenues for Huawei.

Although triumphant in its domestic market, Huawei has also successfully competed in international markets, with 70 percent of the company's revenues generated outside of China. However, Huawei's efforts to enter additional new market niches have been increasingly hindered by trade and investment barriers erected by governments in host countries. Australia stymied Huawei's proposed collaboration in the construction of a nationwide high-speed broadband network. India has limited Huawei's expansion there as well. Canada's government excluded Huawei's participation in the building of a secure government communications network. Huawei has been effectively banned from many U.S. markets on national security grounds as well.

Some of these governments are suspicious of Ren's links to the PLA. Huawei's growing presence in providing critical elements of the information infrastructure has generated concerns about cybersecurity. Critics have raised fears that Huawei could embed computer code in its telecommunications equipment that would facilitate industrial espionage and cyberattacks. In 2012 the U.S. House Permanent Select Committee on Intelligence released a report suggesting that hackers with ties to the PLA were responsible for systematic cyberattacks on numerous U.S. military, commercial, and journalistic organizations. The congressional report argued that Huawei should be banned from doing business in the United States because of these security issues. A UK parliamentary committee examining Huawei raised similar cybersecurity concerns.

Huawei is fighting other battles as well. In 2003 Cisco sued Huawei, claiming that the Chinese rival had infringed its patents and stolen the source code that controlled its switchers and routers. Motorola filed similar complaints in 2010. Both lawsuits were settled out of court, and confidentiality agreements have cloaked the settlements. The European Commission (see Chapter 10) has launched an investigation into whether Huawei has unfairly benefitted from subsidies—low-interest loans and favorable export credits—granted by the Chinese government. Huawei denies these charges, arguing that it is not a state-owned enterprise (SOE). But Huawei's secretive nature and its opaque ownership structure make it vulnerable to such attacks. Company spokespersons report that Ren owns 1.4 percent of Huawei's shares, with most of the rest owned by company employees. However, Huawei has disclosed little information about key corporate governance issues, such as selection procedures for its board of directors, share ownership by the board, or the transferability of its shares. Huawei has rejected these criticisms, dismissing them as protectionist arguments. Cathy Meng, Ren's daughter and the company's chief financial officer, notes "Whenever trade protectionism intervenes with competition in the market, it is the consumer who suffers in the end."

Huawei is not the only Chinese company facing difficulties in its international expansion strategy. President Barack Obama rejected the application of a Chinese firm attempting to purchase an Oregon wind farm, deeming it too close to a military base. The re-emergence of SOEs as key drivers of China's economic growth and their often opaque ties to the Chinese Communist Party and the PLA raises concerns that diplomatic, political, and economic agendas may drive their decisions as much as commercial opportunities. Critics claim that the SOEs have benefitted from favorable governmental treatment, including access to cheap loans and land and protection from domestic and foreign competitors. The SOEs allegedly contribute to corruption and create an aura of favoritism. Often they pay small or nonexistent dividends to the state; profits are allegedly siphoned off by company leadership and shared with their political patrons in the party. Their power hinders the ability of smaller Chinese firms to develop and market new products that threaten the market power of the SOEs.[1]

In today's global economy, many firms benefit from international trade, finding foreign markets a rich source of additional customers. Exports generate domestic jobs, so many national governments promote the success of their countries' domestic firms in international markets. But at times, firms believe that their foreign competitors have gained an unfair advantage because of policies adopted by their governments. As a result, as is the case in the telecommunications market, a firm may ask its national government for protection against the foreigners. In this chapter, we discuss the development of national trade policies that protect domestic firms from foreign competition and help promote the country's exports. We also explore the rationale for these policies and the means by which governments implement them.

Rationales for Trade Intervention

Politicians, economists, and businesspeople have been arguing for centuries over government policy toward international trade. Two principal issues have shaped the debate on appropriate trade policies:

1. Whether a national government should intervene to protect the country's domestic firms by taxing foreign goods entering the domestic market or constructing other barriers against imports
2. Whether a national government should directly help the country's domestic firms increase their foreign sales through export subsidies, government-to-government negotiations, and guaranteed loan programs

In North America, the trade policy debate has recently focused on the issue of whether the government should promote "free" trade or "fair" trade. **Free trade** implies that the national government exerts minimal influence on the exporting and importing decisions of private firms and individuals. **Fair trade**, sometimes called **managed trade**, suggests that the national government should actively intervene to ensure that domestic firms' exports receive an equitable share of foreign markets and that imports are controlled to minimize losses of domestic jobs and market share in specific industries. Some fair traders also argue that the government should ensure a "level playing field" on which foreign and domestic firms can compete on equal terms. Although sounding reasonable, the level playing field argument is often used to justify policies that restrict foreign competition.

The outcome of the debate is critical to international managers. The policies individual countries adopt affect the size and profitability of foreign markets and investments, as well as the degree to which firms are threatened by foreign imports in their domestic markets. Governments worldwide are continually pressured by successful and efficient firms that produce goods for export, as well as by the firms' labor forces and the communities in which their factories are located, to adopt policies supporting freer trade. Companies such as Huawei, Samsung, Volkswagen, and Caterpillar gain increased sales and investment opportunities in foreign markets when international trade barriers are lowered. At the same time, governments are petitioned by firms beleaguered by foreign competitors, as well as by these firms' labor forces and the communities in which their factories are located, to raise barriers to imported goods by adopting fair-trade policies because they gain increased sales opportunities in their domestic markets when international trade barriers exist.

The debate also affects consumers in every country, influencing the prices they pay for automobiles, clothing, televisions, and thousands of other goods. Barriers erected by the U.S. government against free trade in textiles and sugar, for example, raise the prices that parents must pay to clothe and feed their children.

Industry-Level Arguments

The argument for free trade follows Adam Smith's analysis outlined in Chapter 6: Voluntary exchange makes both parties to the transaction better off and allocates resources to their highest valued use. In Smith's view the welfare of a country and its citizens is best promoted by allowing self-interested individuals, regardless of where they reside, to exchange goods, services, and assets as they see fit. However, many businesspeople, politicians, and policymakers believe that, under certain circumstances, deviations from free trade are appropriate. In this section, we review the primary arguments against free trade and for government intervention, and we discuss trade policies that focus on the needs of individual industries. In the next section, we explore broader, national-level policies.

THE NATIONAL DEFENSE ARGUMENT National defense has often been used as a reason to support governmental protection of specific industries. Because world events can suddenly turn hostile to a country's interests, the **national defense argument** holds that a country must be self-sufficient in critical raw materials, machinery, and technology or else be vulnerable to foreign threats. For instance, the vulnerability of Japan's supply lines was demonstrated by the extensive damage done to its merchant marine fleet by Allied submarines during World War II. After the war, Japan banned the importation of rice as a means of promoting domestic self-sufficiency in the country's dietary staple. Similarly, the United States, to retain shipbuilding skills and expertise within the country in case of war, has developed numerous programs to support its domestic shipbuilding industry. For example, all U.S. naval vessels must be built in U.S. shipyards, and ocean transportation between U.S. ports must be conducted by U.S.-built ships. Many of the jobs in the U.S. shipbuilding industry would be lost without these federal protections because U.S. shipyards are not competitive with those of Korea, Norway, China, or Vietnam. And, as noted in the chapter's opening case, Huawei's ability to expand its presence globally has been limited by government officials concerned about cybersecurity and cyberattacks.

The national defense argument appeals to the general public, which is concerned that its country will be pushed around by other countries that control critical resources. Many special-interest groups have used this politically appealing argument to protect their industries from foreign competition. The U.S. mohair industry, for example, produces wool that was once used in military uniforms. It benefited from federal subsidies after passage of the 1954 National Wool Act, which protected the industry purportedly in the country's strategic interest. Even though the military had long since replaced mohair with synthetic fabrics, the subsidy remained in effect for more than 40 years. Other U.S. industries receiving favorable treatment for national defense reasons include steel, electronics, machine tools, and the merchant marine.[2]

Reuters/Corbis

To ensure that critical technology and skills remain in the country, the United States government requires that all American naval vessels be built in American shipyards, such as this guided missile destroyer constructed at the Bath Iron Works in Maine.

THE INFANT INDUSTRY ARGUMENT Alexander Hamilton, the first U.S. secretary of the treasury, articulated the **infant industry argument** in 1791. Hamilton believed that the newly independent country's infant manufacturing sector possessed a comparative advantage that would ultimately allow it to thrive in international markets. He feared, however, that the young nation's manufacturers would not survive their infancy and adolescence because of fierce competition from more mature European firms. Hamilton thus fought for the imposition of tariffs on numerous imported manufactured goods to give U.S. firms *temporary* protection from foreign competition until they could fully establish themselves. His philosophy has been adopted by countries worldwide. Japan has been particularly effective in nurturing its domestic industries. Since the end of World War II, Japan has developed thriving metal fabrication industries (iron and steel, aluminum, copper, and zinc) despite its lack of significant natural resources. Japan has done this by eliminating tariffs on imports of raw ores and ore concentrates while imposing high tariffs on processed and fabricated metals. For instance, in 1970 no tariff was imposed on copper ore imported in Japan, but fabricated copper products bore tariffs as high as 22 percent. As its metal fabrication industry matured, Japan reduced the level of import protection. Today its tariffs on copper products are negligible.[3]

Governmental nurturing of domestic industries that will ultimately have a comparative advantage can be a powerful economic development strategy, as Japan's postwar economic success indicates. However, determination of which industries deserve infant industry protection is often done on a political rather than an economic basis. Firms, workers, and shareholders are not shy about using the infant industry argument to bolster support for import protection or export subsidies for their industries. Moreover, once an industry is granted protection, it may be reluctant to give it up. Many infant industries end up being protected well into their old age.

MAINTENANCE OF EXISTING JOBS Well-established firms and their workers, particularly in high-wage countries, are often threatened by imports from low-wage countries. To maintain existing employment levels, firms and workers often petition their governments for relief from foreign competition. Government officials, eager to avoid the human and economic misery inflicted on workers and communities when factories are shut down, tend to lend a sympathetic ear to such pleas. Assistance may come in the form of tariffs, quotas, or other barriers, which we discuss in more detail in the next section. The assistance may be temporary, as was the case when Harley-Davidson received tariff protection from Japanese imports for five years in the mid-1980s to allow the firm to revamp its operations and restore its image in the marketplace. Conversely, the assistance may be long lived, as in the case of governmental protection of the U.S. commercial shipbuilding industry, which has extended that industry's life by more than 40 years.

STRATEGIC TRADE THEORY When firms and labor union officials plead for government intervention to help them compete internationally, their efforts are usually criticized by economists, who claim that such intervention ultimately harms the economy. The economists base this claim on the theoretical predictions of the classical trade theories—absolute advantage and comparative advantage—discussed in Chapter 6. These trade theories, however, assume that firms operate in perfectly competitive markets of the sort that exist only in economics textbooks. The theories also assume that each country's consumers are able to buy goods and services at the lowest possible prices from the world's most efficient producers. According to the classical theories, any governmental intervention that denies consumers these buying opportunities will make the country as a whole worse off, although it could make certain groups within the society better off.

In the early 1980s, however, new models of international trade—known collectively as **strategic trade theory**—were developed. These models provide a new theoretical justification for government trade intervention, thereby supporting firms' requests for protection. Strategic trade theory makes different assumptions about the industry environment in which firms operate than do the classical theories. Strategic trade theory applies to those industries capable of supporting only a few firms worldwide, perhaps because of high product development costs or strong experience curve effects. A firm can earn monopoly profits if it can succeed in becoming one of the few firms in such a highly concentrated industry. Strategic trade theory suggests that a national government can make its country better off if it adopts trade policies that improve the competitiveness of its domestic firms in such oligopolistic industries.

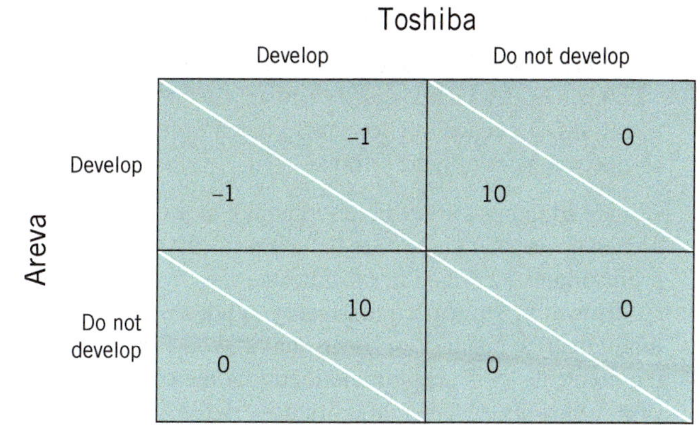

FIGURE 9.1
Payoff Matrix: Profits from Developing a Nuclear Power Plant Design (in billions of dollars)

Consider the potential market for a new nuclear power plant design, one that could safely and cheaply supply electrical energy. Assume that because of economies of scale, the market will be extremely profitable if one—and only one—firm decides to enter it. Further assume that only two firms, France's Areva and Japan's Toshiba, have the engineering talent and financial resources to develop the new plant design and that both are equally capable of successfully completing the project. Figure 9.1 shows the payoff matrix for the two firms. If Toshiba decides to develop the plant design and Areva decides not to (see the lower left-hand corner of the figure), Toshiba profits by \$10 billion, whereas Areva makes nothing. If Areva decides to develop the plant design and Toshiba does not, Areva profits by \$10 billion, and Toshiba makes nothing (see the upper right-hand corner of the figure). If neither firm chooses to develop the design, they both make nothing (see the lower right-hand corner of the figure). If both decide to develop the design, both will lose \$1 billion because the market is too small to be profitable for both of them. Neither firm has a strategy that it should follow regardless of what its rival does.

Now suppose the French government learns of the large profits that one of its country's firms could earn if that firm were the sole developer of the new plant design. If France were to offer Areva a subsidy of \$2 billion to develop the new nuclear technology, the payoff matrix would change to that shown in Figure 9.2. Because of the subsidy, Areva's payoff is increased by \$2 billion if and only if it develops the technology (see the first row of the figure). With the subsidy, Areva will develop the technology regardless of what Toshiba does because Areva makes more money by developing than by not developing. If Toshiba chooses to develop, Areva makes nothing if it does not develop and \$1 billion if it does develop. If Toshiba does not develop, Areva makes nothing if it does not develop and \$12 billion if it does develop. Thus, Areva will always choose to develop. But if Toshiba knows that Areva will always choose to develop, then the best strategy for Toshiba is not to develop.

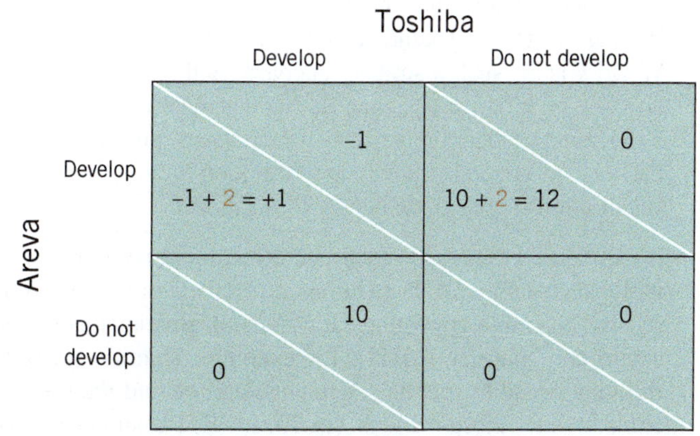

FIGURE 9.2
Payoff Matrix: Profits Resulting from a \$2 Billion Subsidy to Areva (in billions of dollars)

What has the French government accomplished with its $2 billion subsidy?

1. It has induced Areva to develop the new nuclear power plant technology.
2. It has induced the Japanese firm to stay out of the market.
3. It has succeeded in allowing a French firm to make a $12 billion profit at a cost to French taxpayers of only $2 billion.

By adopting a strategic trade policy in a market where monopoly profits are available, the French government has made French residents as a group better off by $10 billion ($12 billion in profits minus $2 billion in subsidies).

However, strategic trade theory applies only to markets that are incapable of supporting more than a handful of firms on a worldwide basis. (One industry that may meet the requirements of strategic trade theory is the commercial aircraft industry; see the part-closing case following Chapter 10, "Jumbo Battle over Jumbo Jets.") Most global industries are more competitive than this. A country's wholesale adoption of strategic trade policies to cover a broad group of industries may actually reduce the country's overall international competitiveness because favoring certain industries inevitably hurts others. For example, if the French government chooses to subsidize the nuclear power industry, the demand for and the salaries paid to the mechanical engineers, computer programmers, and systems analysts needed by the nuclear power industry will rise, thereby reducing the international competitiveness of other French industries requiring such skilled personnel. Further, the benefit of the subsidy could be neutralized if another country adopts a similar strategy. If Japan responded to France's $2 billion subsidy by giving a $3 billion subsidy to Toshiba, the payoff matrix would change: Toshiba would be encouraged to develop the power plant as well. Any anticipated monopoly profits might be dissipated if the two countries engaged in an all-out subsidy war.

National Trade Policies

The policies just discussed address the needs of individual industries. A national government may also develop trade policies that begin by taking an economy-wide perspective. After assessing the needs of the national economy, the government then adopts industry-by-industry policies to promote the country's overall economic agenda.

ECONOMIC DEVELOPMENT PROGRAMS An important policy goal of many governments, particularly those of developing countries, is economic development. International commerce can play a major role in economic development programs. Countries that depend on a single export often choose to diversify their economies to reduce the impact of, say, a bad harvest or falling prices for the dominant export. For example, the West African country of Ghana, which once depended heavily on cocoa, began an industrialization program to protect itself from fluctuations in cocoa prices. Dubai chose to diversify away from its heavy dependency on oil sales, electing to do so by making the emirate a business center and aviation hub. Dubai's international airport, already the world's third largest, is on track to handle 160 million passengers a year once its expansion program, worth $8 billion, is completed.[4]

As discussed in Chapter 2, some countries, such as Singapore, South Korea, and Taiwan, based their post–World War II economic development on heavy reliance on exports. According to this **export promotion strategy**, a country encourages firms to compete in foreign markets by harnessing some advantage the country possesses, such as low labor costs. Other countries, such as Australia, Argentina, India, and Brazil, adopted an **import substitution strategy** after World War II; such a strategy encourages the growth of domestic manufacturing industries by erecting high barriers to imported goods. Many multinational corporations (MNCs) responded by locating production facilities within these countries to avoid the costs resulting from the high barriers. In general, the export promotion strategy has been more successful than the import substitution strategy, as Chapter 2 indicated.

INDUSTRIAL POLICY In many countries, the government plays an active role in managing the national economy. Often an important element of this task is determining which industries should receive favorable governmental treatment. Bureaucrats within Japan's Ministry of International Trade and Industry (MITI), for example, identify emerging technologies and products and through subsidies, public statements, and behind-the-scenes maneuvering encourage Japanese firms to enter those markets. (In 2001, MITI's name was changed to the Ministry of Economy,

Trade, and Industry.) During the 1950s and 1960s, MITI actively diverted scarce credit and foreign exchange from low-value-added, labor-intensive industries such as textiles into high-value-added, capital-intensive heavy industries such as steel and automobiles. During the 1970s and 1980s, MITI targeted industries with high growth potential, such as semiconductors, aerospace, biotechnology, and ceramics. The South Korean government patterned its economic development strategies after the successful Japanese model.

Because of the post–World War II economic successes of Japan and South Korea, the governments of many countries have debated whether to adopt **industrial policy**, by which the national government identifies key domestic industries critical to the country's future economic growth and then formulates programs that promote their competitiveness. Ideally, industrial policy assists a country's firms in capturing large shares of important, growing global markets, as MITI has done for Japanese MNCs.

Many experts, however, do not view industrial policy as a panacea for improving the global competitiveness of a country's firms. They argue that government bureaucrats cannot perfectly identify the right industries to favor under such a policy. As an example, they cite France, in which postwar industrial policies targeting automobiles, computers, military and commercial aircraft, and telecommunications created some spectacularly unprofitable enterprises that required large government subsidies. These industries became a drag on the French economy rather than a generator of new wealth. Similarly, Argentina created a vibrant electronic goods manufacturing center in Tierra del Fuego by doubling its value-added tax and tightening import-licensing controls on imported electronic goods, as well as slashing taxes on assemblers of such goods in that remote province—but Argentina's consumers often pay twice as much for electronics goods as their counterparts in neighboring Chile (see Map 9.1).[5] Even Japan has not been infallible. During the early 1980s, MITI bureaucrats encouraged domestic consumer electronics firms to develop high-definition television (HDTV), which relied on Japan's lead in analog-based TV technology. Unfortunately, the technical transmission standards for HDTV adopted by U.S. and European regulators relied on more sophisticated digital technology being developed by Western firms rather than the dated analog technology imposed on Japanese firms by MITI. Consequently, the multibillion-dollar investment of the leading Japanese consumer electronics firms in analog-based HDTV turned out to be a total loss.

Opponents of industrial policy also fear that the choice of industries to receive governmental largesse will depend on the domestic political clout of those industries, rather than on their potential international competitiveness. Instead of selecting future winners in the international marketplace, opponents say, industrial policy will become a more sophisticated-sounding version of pork-barrel politics.

At the heart of the industrial policy debate is the question of what is the proper role of government in a market economy. Not surprisingly, in the United States recent Republican administrations have rejected formally adopting an industrial policy, on the grounds that the government should limit its role in the economy. Conversely, Democratic administrations believe that improving the global competitiveness of the country's firms was too important to be left to the private sector. To further this belief, the Clinton administration designated five emerging technologies that would receive increased federal research and development (R&D) support: genetics, health care information systems, electronics, automobiles and highway systems, and computer software. Similarly, the Obama administration has promoted the development of renewable energy and electric cars through tax credits, R&D support, and accommodative regulatory policies.

PUBLIC CHOICE ANALYSIS Although many arguments favoring governmental trade intervention are couched in terms of national interest, such intervention typically helps some special-interest groups but invariably hurts other domestic interests and the general public. For example, President George W. Bush's decision to impose tariffs on imported steel during his first term in office helped U.S. steel producers but jeopardized the more numerous steel-using domestic firms. It also reduced the work available to dockworkers who unload foreign steel in Baltimore, New York, Houston, Long Beach, and other port cities and raised the prices that U.S. consumers pay for automobiles, refrigerators, and other goods made of steel. Similarly, Argentina's industrial policy helps manufacturers and workers in Tierra del Fuego's electronic goods sector but harms domestic consumers.

MAP 9.1
Argentina

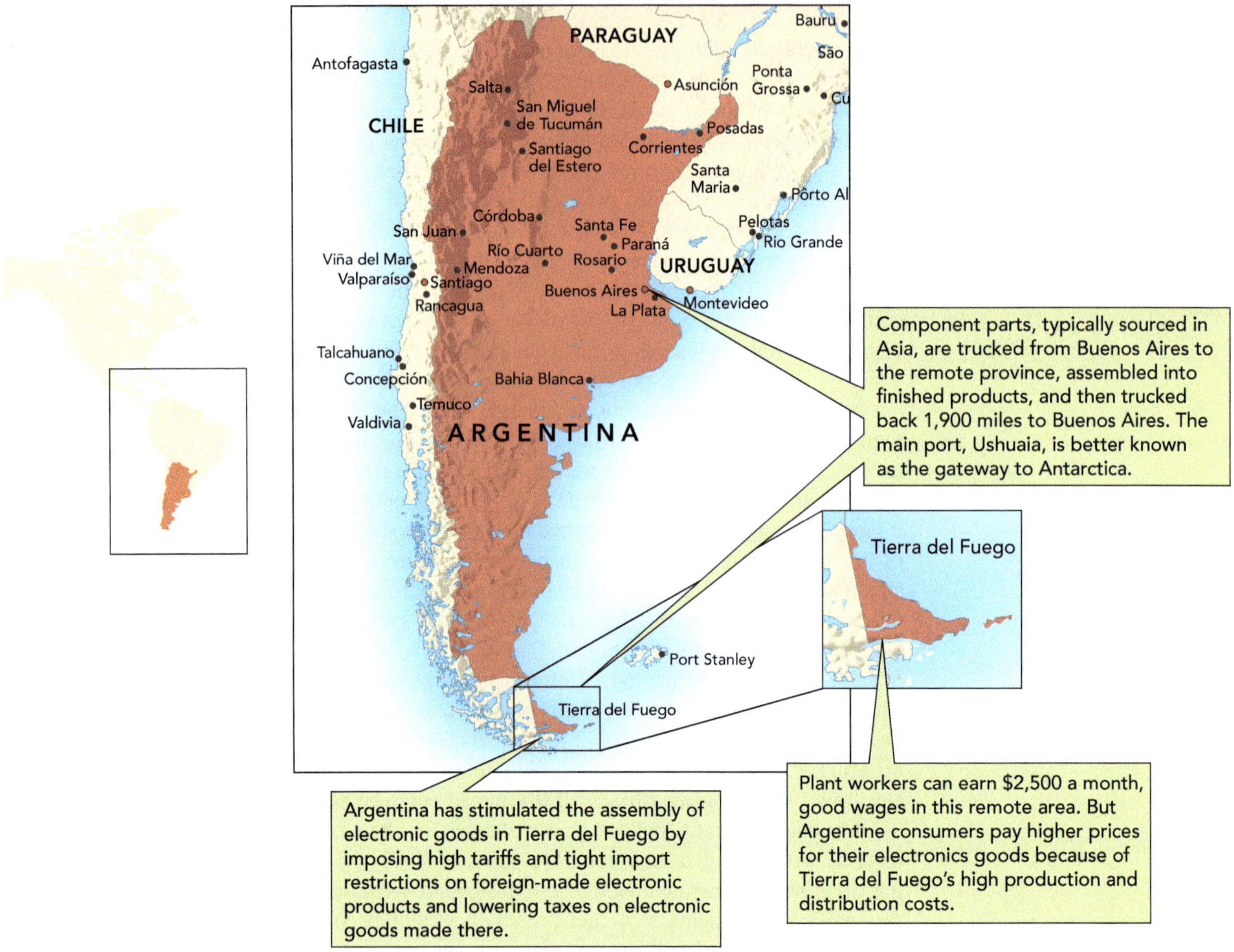

Why do national governments adopt public policies that hinder international business and hurt their own citizenry overall, even though the policies may benefit small groups within their societies? According to **public choice analysis**, a branch of economics that analyzes public decision making, the special interest will often dominate the general interest on any given issue for a simple reason: Special-interest groups are willing to work harder for the passage of laws favorable to their interests than the general public is willing to work for the defeat of laws unfavorable to its interests. For example, under the 1920 Jones Act, the United States restricts foreign ships from providing transportation services between U.S. ports. This restriction is supported by owners of U.S. oceangoing vessels, who gain increased profits estimated at $630 million per year. However, the Jones Act is also estimated to increase the transportation costs that consumers pay by $10.5 billion annually, or $35 per person. Further, like other restrictions on free trade, the Jones Act has had unintended consequences, as Map 9.2 suggests.

Public choice analysis suggests that few consumers will be motivated to learn how the Jones Act impacts them or to write or call their elected officials to save a trivial sum like $35. The special interests, however, such as ship owners and members of U.S. maritime unions, are motivated to know all the ins and outs of the Jones Act and to protect it from repeal because what they gain makes it worth their while to do so. As a result, members of Congress constantly hear from special-interest groups about the importance of preserving the Jones Act, whereas the average consumer is silent on the issue.[6] Knowing that they will be harmed by the

MAP 9.2

An Effect of the Jones Act

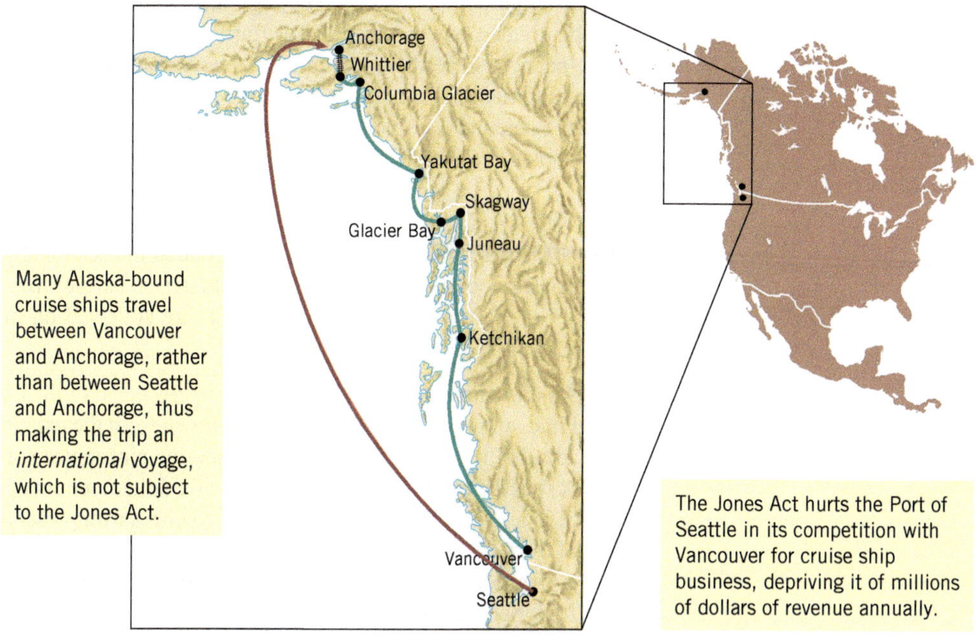

special-interest groups and will not be rewarded by the general public if they repeal the Jones Act, members of Congress will rationally vote with the special interests on this issue.

According to public choice analysis, domestic trade policies that affect international business stem not from some grandiose vision of a country's international responsibilities but rather from the mundane interaction of politicians trying to get elected. And who elects the politicians? The people in their legislative districts. Hence, former Speaker of the House of Representatives Tip O'Neill's brilliant insight: "All politics is local." A good example is Japan's unwillingness to open its markets to imported rice because of the need of Japan's ruling party in the Diet (Japan's parliament) to retain the votes of local farmers. The impact of this policy on Texas rice farmers, the port of Houston, or the world economy is of little concern to the domestic politicians.

Savvy international businesspeople recognize these political realities. Often a foreign firm needs to find domestic political allies to run interference for it. For example, Nissan and Toyota received much criticism for the size of their exports to the U.S. market, so in the 1980s they began building new factories in the United States. The congressional delegations of the states where factories are located can now be expected to support the firms legislatively to protect the jobs of their constituents working for the Japanese firms. Clearly, Toyota and Nissan understand that "all politics is local."

In Practice

- The trade policy debate centers on whether governments should promote "free" trade or "fair" trade.
- The infant industry argument, the national defense argument, maintenance of existing jobs, and strategic trade theory are among the primary arguments offered for government intervention in international trade.

For further consideration: Characterize the firms that are likely to be in favor of free trade.

Barriers to International Trade

We have seen that domestic politics often causes countries to try to protect their domestic firms from foreign competitors by erecting barriers to trade. Such forms of government intervention can be divided into two categories: tariffs and nontariff barriers. Countries have been erecting trade barriers since the creation of the modern nation-state in the sixteenth century in hopes of increasing national income, promoting economic growth, or raising their citizens' standard of living. Sometimes, as you just read, national trade policies that benefit special-interest groups are adopted at the expense of the general public or society at large.

Tariffs

A **tariff** is a tax placed on a good that is traded internationally. Some tariffs are levied on goods as they leave the country (an **export tariff**) or as they pass through one country bound for another (a **transit tariff**). Most, however, are collected on imported goods (an **import tariff**). Three forms of import tariffs exist:

1. An **ad valorem tariff** is assessed as a percentage of the market value of the imported good. For example, in Table 9.1 (which is drawn from the existing U.S. tariff code) a 2.1 percent ad valorem tariff is levied against imported pineapples preserved by sugar.
2. A **specific tariff** is assessed as a specific dollar amount per unit of weight or other standard measure. As Table 9.1 shows, imported citrus fruit preserved by sugar bears a specific tariff of 6 cents per kilogram.
3. A **compound tariff** has both an ad valorem component and a specific component. Imported cherries preserved in sugar are levied a 6.4 percent ad valorem tariff and a 9.9 cents per kilogram specific tariff.

In practice, most tariffs imposed by developed countries are ad valorem. The tariff applies to the product's value, which is typically the sales price at which the product enters the country. Suppose Target buys a large shipment of canned pineapples preserved by sugar from a Philippine food processor at $400 a ton. When the pineapples are delivered to the Port of Los Angeles,

VENTURING ABROAD

EMIRATES AIRLINE EXPANSION – THE CASE OF THE CANADIAN MARKET

Dubai's flagship carrier, Emirates Airline represents one of the fastest-growing corporations in the United Arab Emirates (UAE) and has received more than 400 global awards for service excellence in linking Asia to Europe and the Americas. In its effort to further expand internationally and cater to the increasing demand of its Asian customers, Emirates requested that the Canadian government enable it to increase its current quota of three flights per week to Pearson International Airport in Toronto to daily service from Dubai to Toronto, Calgary, and Vancouver airports.

Negotiations between the two lasted a few years. In the fourth quarter of 2010, the Canadian government decided to retain the non-tariff barrier (NTB) on Emirates' flights to Canada, claiming that more landing rights will result in an unfair "capacity dumping" into its airline market.

Unlike Emirates Airline, Canada's leading airline (Air Canada) does not offer services to most key cities in Southeast Asia, Africa, and the Middle East and relies on its European partners to transport passengers onto these routes. Therefore, by protecting a prime national firm against a foreign competitor, the Canadian government has deprived travelers (mostly Canadian) from shorter journey times and more choice in prices and services. Furthermore, in retaliation to Canada's action, the UAE government placed restrictions on several Canadian firms dealing with the UAE (which is ranked the seventeenth largest export market for Canada) and removed it from the Visa Waiver Program, thus forcing all its citizens to obtain an entry visa to the UAE prior to traveling.

Emirates argued that increasing the current frequency and adding more cities to its network would create 2,800 jobs in Canada, while keeping its share to just under 2 percent of the country's international airline services. On the other hand, Air Canada is facing increasing criticism from customers relating to bad service, despite it being supported with millions of dollars provided by the Canadian government.

Currently, Emirates Airline's expansion efforts into the Canadian market seem to rely on a change in Canada's airline protection policies. As a result, Emirates has launched multiple campaigns that portray the benefits that Canada could obtain from such an endeavor and focused its energy on further expansion within other North and South American countries. To that end, starting in January 2012, Emirates has been flying to six U.S. cities, some of them at the rate of two and three flights per day. Thus, it remains to be seen if Asian customers would start using Emirates routes to the United States as connection to Canadian cities.

TABLE 9.1 A Section of the Harmonized Tariff Schedule of the United States

Heading/ Subheading	Statistical Suffix	Article Description	Units of Quantity	Rates of Duty
2006.00		Fruit, nuts, fruit peel, and other parts of plants, preserved by sugar (drained, glacé, or crystallized):		
2006.00.20	00	Cherries	kg	9.9¢/kg + 6.4%
2006.00.30	00	Ginger root	kg	2.4%
2006.00.40	00	Pineapples	kg	2.1%
		Other, including mixtures:		
2006.00.50	00	Mixtures	kg	16%
2006.00.60	00	Citrus fruit; peel of citrus or other fruit	kg	6¢/kg
2006.00.70	00	Other fruit and nuts	kg	8%
2006.00.90	00	Other	kg	16%

Source: U.S. International Trade Commission, *Harmonized Tariff Schedule of the United States* (Washington, DC: ITC Trade Data Base as of July 14, 2013).

Target will have to pay the U.S. Customs Service a duty of 2.1 percent of $400, or $8.40, for each ton it imports, a cost Target will pass on to its customers.

Most countries have adopted a detailed classification scheme for imported goods called the **harmonized tariff schedule (HTS)**. Because of its complexity, the HTS can sometimes be difficult to use. The first problem facing an importer is anticipating what customs officials will decide is the appropriate tariff classification for an imported good. For example, leather ski gloves imported into the United States are assessed a 5.5 percent ad valorem tariff, but if the gloves are specifically designed for cross-country skiing, then the ad valorem tariff is only 3.5 percent.

The tariff code is complex, and an importer's expected profit margin on a transaction can shrink or disappear if a customs official subjects the imported good to a higher tariff rate than the importer expected. To reduce this risk, U.S. importers can request an advance tariff classification on prospective importations by writing the U.S. Customs Service. Importers who ignore this advice often find themselves embroiled in costly litigation.

Tariffs historically have been imposed for two reasons:

1. Tariffs raise revenue for the national government. Tariff revenues account for a significant portion of government revenues of developing countries such as Ghana, Togo, Benin, and Ethiopia. Such countries often depend heavily on subsistence agriculture and so find it difficult to collect significant tax revenues from domestic sources. Customs duties, however, are reasonably easy to collect. Further, imported goods tend to be purchased by the wealthier members of society, so heavy reliance on import tariffs adds progressivity to the domestic tax system. Conversely, taxes on international trade form a relatively small percentage of government revenues in more developed countries that have broader tax bases such as Thailand, Egypt, and Mexico.
2. A tariff acts as a trade barrier. Because tariffs raise the prices paid by domestic consumers for foreign goods, they increase the demand for domestically produced substitute goods.

Tariffs affect both domestic and foreign special-interest groups. For example, suppose the U.S. government imposes a $2,000 specific tariff on imported SUVs. Foreign producers of SUVs will be forced to raise their U.S. prices, thereby reducing their U.S. sales. However, foreign-made SUVs and U.S.-made SUVs are substitute goods. Thus, the higher prices of foreign SUVs will increase the demand for U.S.-made SUVs. This is shown in Figure 9.3 by the shift in the demand for U.S.-made SUVs from D to D_1, resulting in more domestic vehicles being sold at higher prices. The $2,000 specific tariff creates both gainers and losers.

FIGURE 9.3

Impact of an Import Tariff on Demand for U.S.-Made SUVs

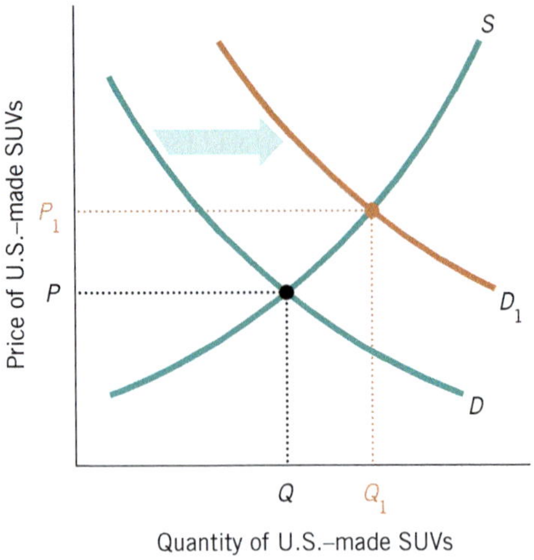

Gainers include GM, Ford, and Chrysler dealerships selling domestic SUVs; suppliers to domestic producers; workers at domestic GM, Ford, and Chrysler SUV assembly plants; and the communities in which domestic SUV factories are located. Domestic consumers are losers because they pay higher prices for both domestic and foreign SUVs. Foreign producers also lose, as do people and firms that depend on them, including Toyota and Mazda dealerships in the United States, workers and suppliers in Japan, and communities in Japan in which the SUVs are manufactured.

Nontariff Barriers

Nontariff barriers are the second category of governmental controls on international trade. Any government regulation, policy, or procedure other than a tariff that has the effect of impeding international trade may be labeled a **nontariff barrier (NTB)**. In this section we discuss three kinds of NTBs: quotas, numerical export controls, and other NTBs.

QUOTAS Countries may restrain international trade by imposing quotas. A **quota** is a numerical limit on the quantity of a good that may be imported into a country during some time period, such as a year. Quotas have traditionally been used to protect politically powerful industries, such as agriculture, automobiles, and textiles, from the threat of competition, as in the use of quotas to limit imports of rice by Japan, Korea, Taiwan, and the Philippines. However, as a result of trade agreements such as the Uruguay Round (see Chapter 10), many countries have replaced quotas with tariff rate quotas. A **tariff rate quota (TRQ)** imposes a low tariff rate on a limited amount of imports of a specific good; above that threshold, a TRQ imposes a prohibitively high tariff rate on the good. This situation is depicted in Figure 9.4, where the first 100,000 widgets imported into a country are subjected to a low tariff rate, T_L; all widgets after the first 100,000 are subjected to the high tariff rate, T_H. Canada, for example, has substituted a TRQ for its previous quotas on imports of eggs, dairy products, and poultry. Imports of these goods above the threshold may carry tariffs as high as 350 percent. Japan imposes a 341-yen tariff on imported rice in excess of the quota, the equivalent of a 400-percent tariff.[7] Korea imposes tariffs of 243 percent on over-quota honey and 304 percent on over-quota potatoes.[8] In the short run, such high tariffs have the same effect as a quota: They normally limit imports of a good to the threshold level. However, at least in concept, exporters are allowed to increase their sales to the country as long as they are willing to pay the high tariff. And because tariffs are more visible than quotas, most experts believe that converting quotas to TRQs makes it easier to eliminate this type of trade barrier over time through trade negotiations.

A quota or TRQ helps domestic producers of the good in question but invariably hurts domestic consumers. Consider the impact on the U.S. market of the TRQ on sugar. The U.S. government normally restricts the amount of foreign sugar that can be imported to less than 2 million tons annually by slapping a 17-cent specific tariff on each pound of sugar imported into the United States above that amount. (Domestic producers normally produce about

FIGURE 9.4

Tariff Rate Quota on Widgets

A tariff rate quota imposes high tariff rates on imports above the threshold level

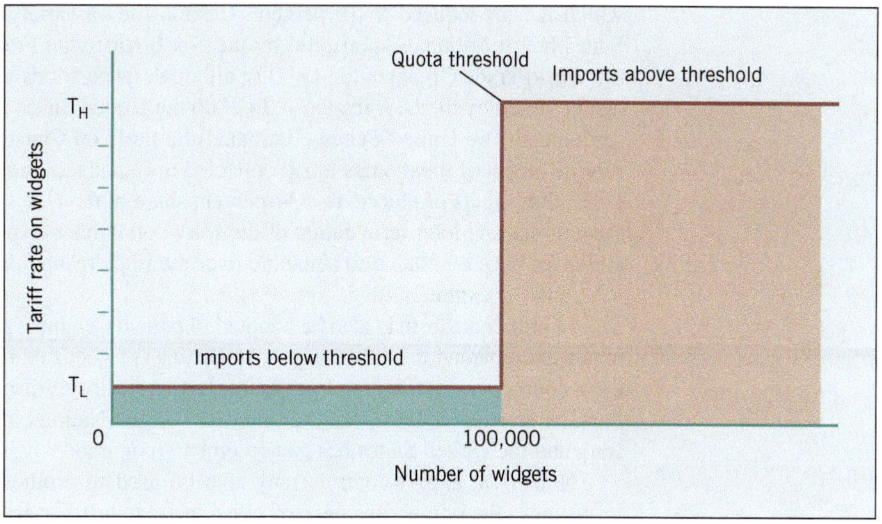

8 to 9 million tons per year.)[9] The price of sugar is higher in the United States than elsewhere in the world because the TRQ prevents more imports from flowing into the U.S. market to equalize the prices. In September 2013, for instance, the U.S. price for sugar was 21¢ per pound, whereas the world price was only 16¢ per pound.

Who gains from the TRQ? Domestic sugar producers, such as sugarcane growers in Louisiana and sugar beet growers in North Dakota, benefit because domestic production is increased and the price that domestic suppliers receive rises. Producers of sugar substitutes, such as Archer Daniels Midland, the largest domestic producer of corn-based fructose sweeteners, and Corn Belt farmers who supply the corn for the fructose sweeteners also gain as manufacturers of sweetened products substitute lower-cost fructose sweeteners for sugar. Losers from the policy include domestic candy manufacturers and soft-drink makers, which must pay higher prices for sugar, as well as U.S. consumers, who pay a higher price—an estimated $1.5 billion in a typical year—for all goods containing sugar. U.S. firms, such as San Francisco's Ghirardelli Chocolate Company (premium chocolates) or Corsicana, Texas' Collin Street Bakery (fruitcakes), which export goods with high sugar content, become less competitive in world markets because the sugar quota increases the cost of their ingredients.[10] A Department of Commerce study in 2006 suggests that more than 10,000 Americans working for confectionary companies lost their jobs between 1997 and 2002 because of the sugar quota.[11]

Anyone with the right to import sugar into the United States within the 2-million-ton threshold also gains because the holder of such a right can buy sugar at the lower world price and resell it in the United States at the higher U.S. price. For this reason, the U.S. government uses such rights as instruments of foreign policy and foreign aid. Countries that are politically sympathetic to the United States or that the United States is trying to woo often receive generous rights, whereas countries hostile to the United States find their rights reduced or eliminated.

NUMERICAL EXPORT CONTROLS A country also may impose quantitative barriers to trade in the form of numerical limits on the amount of a good it will export. A **voluntary export restraint (VER)** is a promise by a country to limit its exports of a good to another country to a prespecified amount or percentage of the affected market. Often this is done to resolve or avoid trade conflicts with an otherwise friendly trade partner. For example, since 1982 the United States and Canada have been squabbling over whether Canada has been subsidizing its lumber industry by charging low stumpage fees (rights to harvest timber) in government-owned forests. To bring a truce to the conflict, in 1996 Canada agreed to adopt a VER for five years, limiting its annual exports to the United States of softwood lumber from Alberta, British Columbia, Ontario, and Quebec to 14.7 billion board feet. Canada also pledged to levy a substantial tax on any exports above that level bound for the United States. After the five-year window expired, however, the United States imposed a 27-percent duty on Canadian softwood lumber imports, which it later reduced to 10 percent. Canada filed a variety of complaints against the United States before tribunals sponsored by the North American Free Trade Agreement (NAFTA) and the World Trade Organization (WTO); although its positions were generally upheld, Canada was disappointed by the U.S. response. In 2006 the United States and Canada negotiated yet another settlement. The United States eliminated the tariff on Canadian softwood lumber exports and returned most of the monies it had collected to Canada. In return, Canada once again agreed to a VER, limiting its producers to a 34-percent share of the U.S. softwood lumber market. Given the contentious and long-term nature of the softwood lumber dispute, it is not surprising that the two countries have continued to squabble over the implementation of the 2006 agreement, which is scheduled to expire in 2015.[12]

Export controls may also be adopted to punish a country's political enemies. An **embargo**—an absolute ban on the exporting (or importing) of goods to a particular destination—is adopted by a country or international governmental authority to discipline another country. After Iraq invaded Kuwait in 1990, for example, the United Nations imposed an embargo on trade with Iraq, and the United States has had an embargo on trade with Cuba since the 1960s.

Numerical export controls may also be used to promote a country's industrial policy or to promote the competitiveness of other of its industries. Russia limits the export of logs and round wood to stimulate its wood-processing industry: The export controls lower the price paid by Russian wood processors but raise the input costs of their foreign competitors.[13] For similar reasons, China restricts exports of many minerals, such as antimony, bauxite, and fluorspar. For many of these minerals, China is one of the world's largest suppliers.[14] "Bringing the World into Focus" discusses the impact of China's export controls on the market for rare earths.

OTHER NONTARIFF BARRIERS Countries also use various other NTBs to protect themselves from foreign competition. Some NTBs are adopted for legitimate domestic public policy reasons but have the effect of restricting trade. Most NTBs, however, are blatantly protectionist. As we discuss in Chapter 10, international negotiations in the post–World War II era have reduced the use of tariffs and quotas. For this reason, nonquantitative NTBs have now become major impediments to the growth of international trade. These NTBs are more difficult to eliminate than tariffs and quotas because they often are embedded in bureaucratic procedures and are not quickly changeable. Among the most common forms of nonquantitative NTBs are the following:

- Product and testing standards
- Restricted access to distribution networks
- Public-sector procurement policies
- Local-purchase requirements
- Regulatory controls
- Currency controls
- Investment controls

We discuss these in the following sections.

PRODUCT AND TESTING STANDARDS A common form of NTB is a requirement that foreign goods meet a country's product standards or testing standards before the goods can be offered for sale in that country. Foreign firms often claim that these standards discriminate against their products. Brazil, for instance, requires that new pharmaceutical products undergo clinical testing in Brazil, even though they may have already undergone similar trials elsewhere and received approval from foreign regulators, such as the U.S. Food and Drug Administration.[15] Korea requires that its National Intelligence Service certify any telecommunications network equipment incorporating encryption technology,[16] while Russia similarly limits the importation of any product using encryption technology.[17]

RESTRICTED ACCESS TO DISTRIBUTION NETWORKS Restricting foreign suppliers' access to the normal channels of distribution may also function as an NTB. China requires that imported sugar and petroleum be distributed only by state-owned trading enterprises, while Indonesia granted exclusive rights to import rice to a state agency.[18] Foreign films may occupy only one-third of the screen time in Chinese movie theaters, a restriction that reduces the revenues of foreign

© Richard Ellis/Alamy

China restricts the number of foreign films that can be shown in its movie theaters, limiting them to no more than one-third of total screening time. It also regulates the share of the box office revenues allocated to the foreign films' owners. Hollywood movie studios complain that such practices facilitate piracy of their products and restrict their ability to compete in the large and growing Chinese market.

movie studios and stimulates the widespread counterfeiting of DVDs. Indonesia similarly limits the screen time of foreign films to 60 percent in its movie theaters.[19]

India has historically limited foreign participation in its retailing sector, fearing that competition from Western chains such as Carrefour, Marks & Spencer, and Walmart would devastate the country's army of small mom-and-pop retailers. India has been pressured to eliminate these restrictions by its trading partners. The government has responded cautiously: In 2006, it relaxed the restrictions against single-brand stores, allowing foreign investors to own

BRINGING THE WORLD INTO FOCUS

THE FIGHT OVER RARE EARTHS

Most trade conflicts arise from a country's erecting barriers against the importation of goods. In 2010, China decided to tighten its export controls on rare earths, announcing a 35-percent reduction in exports in 2011 from their 2010 levels. The intensity of the ensuing battle triggered over these obscure minerals reflects the globalization of supply chains and China's desire to transition its economy from manufacturing low-value-added goods to producing higher-value-added ones.

Rare earths is a term used to denote 17 different minerals that are critical for the production of many high-tech products, such as smartphones, computer chips, and batteries for hybrid cars. For example, cerium oxide is used to polish hard drives, while less than a penny's worth of neodymium allows cell phones to vibrate. Despite their name, rare earths are not that rare. However, they are expensive to produce, and environmental damage can ensue if the toxic chemicals used in their refining are not carefully handled. Moreover, bringing a new mine into production can take years.

China currently accounts for more than 90 percent of the world's rare-earth production, although it possesses only one-third of global reserves. It exported almost $1 billion of these minerals in 2010. China's dominance in the market is attributed to the low prices its mines charged starting in the 1990s. As prices fell, foreign producers closed their mines, unable to compete with the "China price."

China has claimed its export controls are motivated by its desire to protect the environment, save energy, and protect national resources. Critics in Europe, North America, and Japan see less benign reasons. They fear that the export controls are designed to boost Chinese production of high-tech goods by driving up the costs of key inputs to foreign users and encouraging foreign high-tech firms to relocate production facilities to China. They note that a 2009 policy paper issued by the country's Resource Ministry stressed that the quotas would enable the ministry to promote the government's industrial policy and influence the demand-supply relationships in the market, allowing China to boost the prices it receives for its exports of rare earths. Moreover, it has announced plans to stockpile these minerals and has assured foreigners that any factories located in China will continue to have access to the rare earths they need.

China's policies have caused firms to seek to diversify their sourcing of rare earths. Japan is the largest importer of them, accounting for about 20 percent of annual usage. Its government is promoting recycling and funding R&D efforts in such areas as robotic deep-sea mining to lessen its dependence on Beijing. In late 2010,

(*Continued*)

Japan's Toyota Tsusho Corporation signed an agreement with Indian Rare Earths Ltd. to construct a new rare-earths processing plant in India. Several companies, such as U.S.-based Molycorp, Australia's Lynas Corp., and Brazil's Vale, have announced plans to open or reopen rare-earth mines that had been closed as a result of low prices charged by Chinese competitors in the 1990s.

Free trade advocates fear that this overt manipulation of the rare-earths market by the Chinese government will cause other countries to retaliate, imposing their own quotas on critical resources or subsidizing new rare-earth mines and then raising trade barriers to rare-earth imports to reduce their dependence on Chinese mines. In their worst case scenario, they fear protectionists around the world will seize on China's rare-earths quotas as a justification for raising barriers to trade in goods they view as vital for their nations' economic security.

Sources: "China April Rare-Earth Exports 2,196 Tons, up 28% on Month," *Wall Street Journal*, May 21, 2013; "Postcards from the Rare-Earth Front," *Wall Street Journal*, March 27, 2013; "Miners ready to call on rare earth 'heavies'," *Financial Times*, December 31, 2012, p. 13; "Rare earths," *The Economist*, March 17, 2012; "Brazil's Vale gears up for rare earths," *Financial Times*, May 31, 2011, p. 13; "China rare earth metals soar as Beijing cuts sales," *Financial Times*, May 27, 2011, p. 21; "Rare-earth metals add heat," *Wall Street Journal*, March 23, 2011, p. B4; Office of the U.S. Trade Representative, *National Trade Estimate Report on Foreign Trade Barriers 2013*, p. 78; "Trade judges see flaw in China policies," *Wall Street Journal*, February 18, 2011; "India and Japan look to expand rare-earth alliance," *Wall Street Journal*, February 16, 2011; "China moves to strengthen grip over supply of rare-earth metals," *Wall Street Journal*, February 7, 2011, p. B1; "Rare action," *The Economist*, January 22, 2011; "Rare earth quotas: Big bark, less bite," *Wall Street Journal*, January 19, 2011; "Rare earths and China," *The Economist*, October 2, 2010.

51 percent of such establishments. In 2012, it delegated discretion to India's states to determine if foreigners could own up to 51 percent of multibrand stores.[20]

PUBLIC-SECTOR PROCUREMENT POLICIES Public-sector procurement policies that give preferential treatment to domestic firms are another form of NTB. In the United States, "Buy American" restrictions are common at the federal, state, and local levels. The American Recovery and Reinvestment Act of 2009, for instance, requires that any iron, steel, and manufactured goods purchased using funds provided by the act to build or repair a public building or public work must be produced in the United States. The federal government generally requires that international air travel purchased with U.S. government funds occur on U.S. airlines; China imposes similar restrictions on many employees of SOEs.

Public-sector procurement policies are particularly important in countries that have extensive state ownership of industry and in industries in which state ownership is common. If a national government adopts procurement policies that favor local firms, then foreigners are locked out of much of the market. Egypt gives SOEs a 15-percent bidding preference on public contracts, and Argentina grants domestically owned firms a 5- to 7-percent preference; Turkey, a 15-percent preference; Thailand, 7 percent; and Paraguay, 20 percent.[21] Russia grants local firms a 15-percent preference on pharmaceutical contracts, and Kenya's Public Procurement and Disposal Act requires that certain government contracts be given only to Kenyan citizens.[22]

LOCAL-PURCHASE REQUIREMENTS Host governments may hinder foreign firms from exporting to or operating in the host countries by requiring the firms to purchase goods or services from local suppliers. Indonesia encourages pharmaceutical companies to manufacture locally if they wish their drugs to be approved for sale.[23] China requires that all travel agents and Chinese airlines use China's state-owned reservation service when booking flights.[24] Kazakhstan mandates that oil companies purchase any necessary services from Kazakh-owned companies.[25] The Philippines charges lower excise taxes on distilled spirits made from local raw materials.[26] Egypt requires that 60 percent of the managers of new computer-related companies be Egyptian nationals within three years of the firms' entry into the Egyptian market.[27]

The Canadian government requires that at least 50 percent of the programs broadcast by over-the-air TV stations be Canadian in origin; for cable stations, a majority of the programs must qualify as Canadian, as must 35 percent of the music played by radio stations.[28] No more than 20 percent of the shows broadcast by Korean TV stations can be of foreign origin.[29] The French government requires local TV services, such as TF1 or Canal Plus, to show French-made films at least 40 percent of the time and European-made films at least 60 percent of the time, thus restricting the market available to non-European films. Such quotas exist in radio broadcasting as well. During prime time, at least 40 percent of the songs played on France's 1,700 AM and FM stations must be written or sung by French or Francophone artists.[30] The European Union (EU), Malaysia, and Australia have similar requirements for broadcasters.[31] The U.S. government has strongly protested such requirements, arguing that they are designed to restrict competition from U.S. music, movie, and television producers.

REGULATORY CONTROLS Governments can create NTBs by adopting regulatory controls, such as conducting health and safety inspections, enforcing environmental regulations, requiring firms to obtain licenses before beginning operations or constructing new plants, and charging taxes and fees for public services that affect the ability of international businesses to compete in host markets. For instance, Singapore uses a tiered tax system based on engine deplacement, which hurts the sales of large motorcycles. Taiwan's transportation ministry has been slow to issue regulations that would allow motorcycles with engines larger than 500cc to travel on its highways throughout the day, whereas Thailand has an outright ban of motorcycles on its highways.[32] To enforce its consumer privacy rules, Korea mandates that financial services firms locate their computer servers in Korea, thereby foreclosing the market to cloud-computing companies operating elsewhere.[33] Brazil requires that producers of health and fitness equipment, processed food, and cosmetics register their products with the Ministry of Health; approvals routinely take three to six months.[34] China's requirement that goods in numerous product categories—accounting for about one-fifth of U.S. exports to China—receive the China Compulsory Certification mark prior to their sale discourages importers. Typically such certifications may only be done in Chinese facilities, which are often backlogged. The additional expense and time delays reduce the competitiveness of imported goods in the Chinese market.[35]

CURRENCY CONTROLS Many countries, particularly developing countries and those with centrally planned economies, raise barriers to international trade through currency controls. Exporters of goods are allowed to exchange foreign currency at favorable rates so as to make foreign markets attractive sales outlets for domestic producers. Importers are forced to purchase foreign exchange from the central bank at unfavorable exchange rates, thus raising the domestic prices of foreign goods. Tourists may be offered a separate exchange rate that is designed to extract as much foreign exchange as possible from free-spending foreigners.

For example, Venezuela imposed currency controls to protect its currency reserves in 2003. It currently uses a dual-exchange rate system, whereby certain favored transactions can obtain foreign exchange at the official exchange rate; the remaining transactions receive a less favorable rate. The controls make it more expensive for importers of nonessential goods to acquire foreign exchange.[36] Similarly, the National Bank of Ethiopia often makes it difficult for importers to obtain scarce foreign exchange, although SOEs or firms controlled by the ruling party normally have no such problems.[37]

INVESTMENT CONTROLS Controls on foreign investment and ownership are common, particularly in key industries such as broadcasting, utilities, air transportation, defense contracting, and financial services. Such controls often make it difficult for foreign firms to develop an effective presence in such markets. The Philippines restricts foreign ownership in advertising to 30 percent and in telecommunications to 40 percent, while foreigners can own no more than 49 percent of local accounting firms in Thailand and 50 percent of Korean power generators.[38] Thailand and Kazakhstan cap foreign ownership of telecommunication companies at 49 percent,[39] while foreigners may own no more than 49 percent of Peruvian broadcasters and 20 percent of South African broadcasters.[40] Indonesia limits foreign ownership in its telecommunications, film and video distribution, and construction industries. The United States similarly constrains foreign ownership of airlines and broadcast stations.

These NTBs are now more important impediments to international trade than tariffs are. And because they are sometimes imposed for sound domestic policy reasons but affect the competitiveness of foreign firms, NTBs can quickly cause intense international conflicts.

FIGURE 9.5

Types of Barriers to International Trade: A Summary

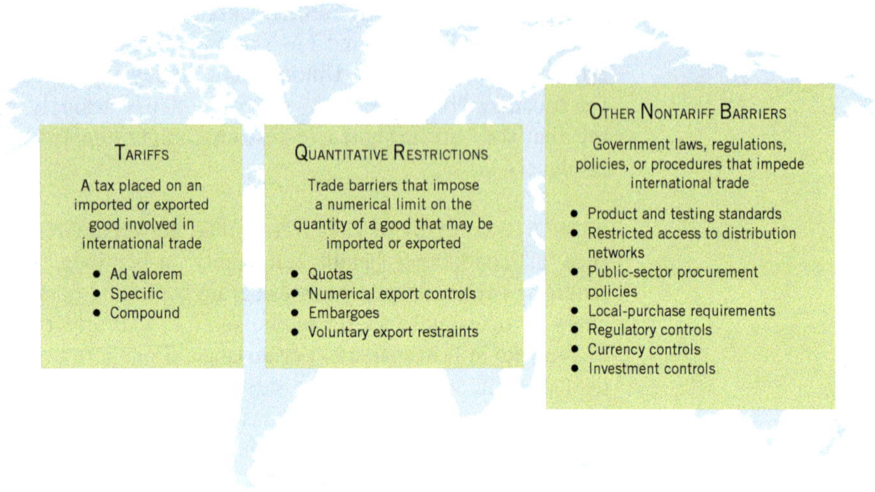

International businesses whose operations are affected by NTBs often need the support of their home governments to help resolve these problems. Figure 9.5 summarizes the various forms that trade barriers can take.

In Practice

- The major barriers to international trade include tariffs, quotas, and other trade barriers.
- Government regulations controlling access to distribution networks, public-sector procurement policies, and access to foreign exchange can serve as trade barriers.

For further consideration: Consider France's policy limiting non-French music on its radio stations. Is this a trade barrier or a legitimate attempt by the French government to protect French culture?

Promotion of International Trade

We have just explored some techniques that governments use to restrict foreign business activity. In this section, we discuss government policies that promote international business, including subsidies, establishment of foreign trade zones, and export financing programs. Typically, these programs are designed to create jobs in the export sector or to attract investment to economically depressed areas.

Subsidies

Countries often seek to stimulate exports by offering subsidies designed to reduce firms' costs of doing business. Brazil, for example, provides a variety of tax, tariff, and financing incentives to spur exports, while Jordan exempts profits generated by exporting from income taxation in many industries.[41] The Turkish Grain Board lowers the cost of wheat to Turkish exporters of pasta and flour.[42] Our opening case detailed the concerns expressed by U.S. and European politicians that Huawei has benefited from subsidies granted by the Chinese government.

National, state, and local governments often provide economic development incentives—another type of subsidy—to entice firms to locate or expand facilities in their communities to provide jobs and increase local tax bases. These incentives may be in the form of property tax abatements, free land, training of workforces, reduced utility rates, new highway construction, and so on. Competition among different localities can be fierce. For instance, Georgia agreed to provide Kia Motors with $400 million in incentives to capture that firm's first U.S. plant and the 2,500 jobs it was estimated to produce.[43] Similarly, the U.S. Virgin Islands pledged to spend $100 million to help expand Fortune Brand's rum distillery on St. Croix and to build a new wastewater treatment facility for it.[44]

Because subsidies reduce the cost of doing business, they may affect international trade by artificially improving a firm's competitiveness in export markets or by helping domestic firms fight off foreign imports. Subsidies, however, can grow so large as to disrupt the normal pattern of international trade. The shipbuilding, wheat, and butter industries are notorious examples of markets in which trade is distorted because of the high level of subsidies. The big losers in the subsidy wars are efficient producers in countries that lack large-scale subsidies, such as Australia's wheat industry or New Zealand's dairy industry. "People, Planet, and Profits" discusses the impact of subsidies on the market for cotton.

Foreign Trade Zones

A **foreign trade zone (FTZ)** is a geographic area in which imported or exported goods receive preferential tariff treatment. An FTZ may be as small as a warehouse or a factory site (such as Caterpillar's diesel engine facility in Mossville, Illinois) or as large as the entire city of Shenzhen, China (which neighbors Hong Kong).[45] FTZs are used by governments worldwide to spur regional economic development. For example, an FTZ has played a key role in the economic development of the small African island nation of Mauritius (see Map 9.3). Through the use of an FTZ, a firm typically can reduce, delay, or sometimes totally eliminate customs duties. Generally, a firm can import a component into an FTZ, process it further, and then export the processed good abroad and avoid paying customs duties on the value of the imported component.

The *maquiladora* system represents another example of the use of FTZs. A **maquiladora** is a factory located in an FTZ in Mexico; most are situated near the U.S. border. These factories import unfinished goods or component parts, further process the goods or parts, and re-export them. The goods produced by maquiladoras enjoy preferential customs and tax treatment. Mexico levies no customs duties on unfinished goods imported by a maquiladora, provided the goods are re-exported after having been further processed in Mexico. Machinery imported into Mexico and used by a maquiladora is also exempt from customs duties. U.S. customs duties on maquiladoras' exports are applied only to the value of the processing performed in Mexico. Today the maquiladora industry is the second-largest sector of the Mexican economy (after oil production) and the second-largest source of Mexico's foreign-exchange earnings. However, as a result of NAFTA, many tariff advantages once enjoyed only by the maquiladoras are now available to factories throughout Mexico. Thus, interior cities such as Monterrey and Saltillo have been put on a more even footing with border communities such as Nuevo Laredo and Matamoros in terms of attracting new plants to serve the North American market.

MAP 9.3

Foreign Trade Zone on Mauritius

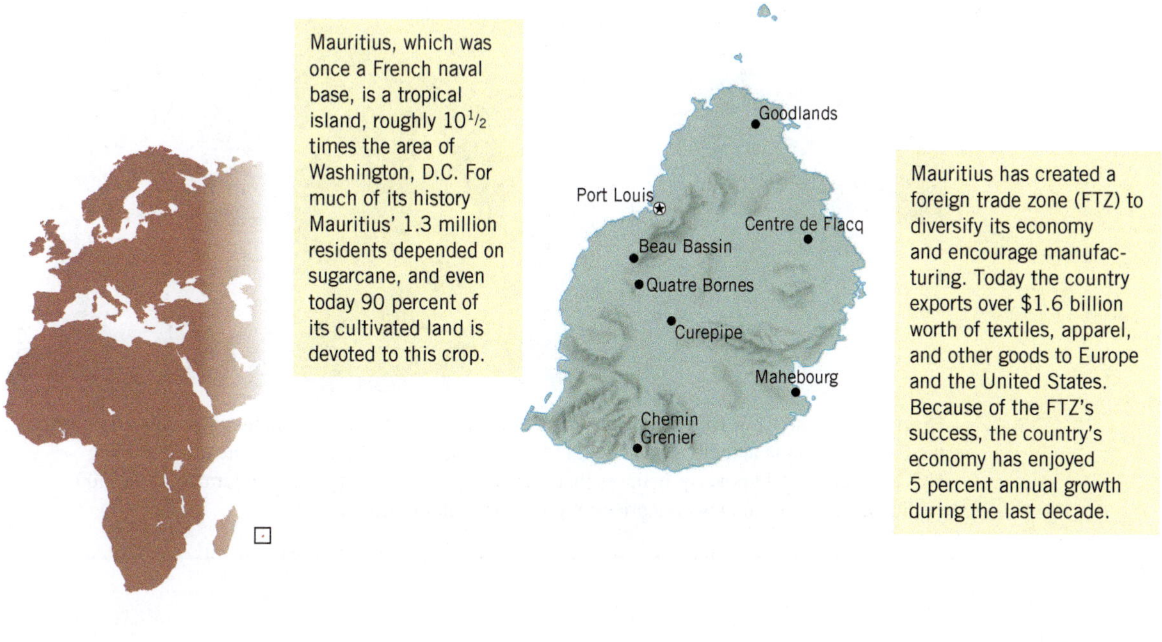

PEOPLE, PLANET, AND PROFITS

COTTON SUBSIDIES AND WORLD POVERTY

For years the United States and the European Union (EU) have poured money into subsidizing their agricultural sectors. These subsidies have been criticized by the Cairns Group, an organization of efficient agricultural producers who believe the U.S. and EU subsidies are distorting trade in agricultural goods. These critics have recently been joined by advocates concerned about alleviating poverty in developing countries; these advocates include nongovernmental organizations (NGOs) such as Oxfam and U2's lead singer, Bono, who believe these subsidies contribute to the impoverishment of farmers in less-developed countries. Oxfam estimates that EU subsidies depress world butter prices by 20 percent, while its sugar subsidies cost Thailand $150 million and Brazil $500 million a year.

Cotton provides another example of this phenomenon. In a complaint filed with the WTO, Brazil argued that the $3 billion-a-year subsidies paid to U.S. farmers increase U.S. cotton production by 29 percent, thereby depressing world cotton prices by 12.6 percent. Brazilian officials estimate these U.S. subsidies cost Brazilian farmers $600 million in lost sales. After the WTO found in Brazil's favor, the two countries negotiated a settlement requiring the U.S. government to provide $147 million in annual subsidies to Brazilian cotton farmers.

This settlement did not alleviate the impact of the U.S. cotton subsidies on parts of Central and Western Africa that are heavily dependent on cotton production. Thousands of farmers in Benin, Burkina Faso, Chad, and Mali, many living below the poverty line, make their living farming cotton. Oxfam estimates that the subsidies paid to U.S. cotton farmers cost these countries $300 million a year and reduce their exports by a tenth. And the subsidies often neutralize whatever aid Western countries provide them. In a typical year Oxfam estimates that U.S. cotton subsidies cost Mali $43 million, offsetting the $38 million in foreign aid the United States provided that country.

The United States is not the only country that subsidizes its cotton farmers. China provides an estimated $1.2 billion in subsidies to its farmers, and the EU subsidizes its cotton growers, primarily in Spain and Greece, to the tune of $700 million a year. China and the United States produce about 45 percent of the world's supply.

Sources: "Why the U.S. is also giving Brazilians farm subsidies," *Time*, April 9, 2010; "U.S. and Brazil reach agreement on cotton dispute," *New York Times*, April 6, 2010; "WTO allows Brazil to fine U.S.," *Wall Street Journal*, August 1, 2009; "In fight against farm subsidies, even farmers are joining foes," *Wall Street Journal*, March 14, 2006, p. A7; "Unpicking cotton subsidies," *The Economist*, April 30, 2004 (online); "Cultivating poverty," Oxfam Briefing Paper 30, Oxfam International; "A great yarn," *The Economist*, December 20, 2003, pp. 43ff.; "WTO chief leads cotton review," BBC News online, September 12, 2003.

ISSOUF SANOGO/AFP/Getty Images/Newscom

Brazil filed a complaint with the World Trade Organization, urging it to end the large subsidies that the European Union and the United States offer their cotton farmers. Oxfam, one of the leading NGOs fighting world poverty, believes that such subsidies cost African cotton farmers over $300 million in lost sales and lowered prices, monies they can ill-afford to lose.

Export Financing Programs

For many big-ticket items such as aircraft, offshore drilling rigs, and large construction projects, success or failure in exporting depends on a firm's producing a high-quality product, providing reliable repair service after the sale, and—often the deciding factor—offering an attractive financing package. For example, Boeing competes with Airbus to sell Air Canada 200-seat short-range aircraft. When Air Canada is deciding which firm's aircraft to buy, it carefully weighs price, after-sale technical support, aircraft operating costs, and financing expenses. All other things being equal, the financing terms offered to Air Canada may be critical in its decision of which firm wins the contract.

Because of the importance of the financing package, most major trading countries have created government-owned agencies to assist their domestic firms in arranging financing of export sales, both large and small. The **Export-Import Bank of the United States (Eximbank)** provides financing for U.S. exports through direct loans and loan guarantees; in 2012 it supplied financing for almost 3,800 export transactions worth $35.8 billion. Large firms such as Boeing are important clients, but the Eximbank also services small U.S. exporters. For example, it guaranteed $9.4 million in bank loans that helped three Midwestern companies, including two small businesses, to export equipment needed to construct a hydroelectric dam in Turkey.[46] Another U.S. government–sponsored organization, the **Overseas Private Investment Corporation (OPIC)**, provides a different type of insurance—political-risk insurance, a subject covered in Chapter 3. If a foreign country confiscates an insured firm's goods or assets, OPIC will compensate the firm for its losses. Most major trading countries have similar organizations that provide export financing, commercial insurance, and political-risk insurance. In China, state-owned banks play a key role in supporting the growth of China's exports by offering such services.[47] Other countries, such as Malaysia, rely on their central bank to provide low-cost export financing.

In Practice

- Governments often promulgate policies that expand the role of domestic firms in international commerce to create jobs or to attract investment to economically depressed regions.
- These policies can include subsidies, establishment of foreign trade zones, and export financing programs.

For further consideration: Although these government policies benefit some firms, are they unfair to other firms who do not benefit from the policies?

Controlling Unfair Trade Practices

With governments around the world adopting programs designed to protect domestic industries from imports and other programs to promote their exports, it should not be surprising that competitors often cry foul. In response to these complaints, many countries have implemented laws protecting their domestic firms from unfair trade practices.

In the United States, complaints from firms affected by alleged unfair trade practices are first investigated by the International Trade Administration (ITA), a division of the U.S. Department of Commerce, which determines whether an unfair trade practice has occurred. The Department of Commerce transfers confirmed cases of unfair trading to the U.S. International Trade Commission (ITC), an independent government agency. If a majority of the six ITC commissioners decide that U.S. producers have suffered "material injury," the ITC will impose duties on the offending imports to counteract the unfair trade practice. The ITC, like the Canadian International Trade Tribunal and other similar government agencies worldwide, focuses on two types of unfair trade practices: government subsidies that distort trade and unfair pricing practices.

Countervailing Duties

Most countries protect local firms from foreign competitors that benefit from subsidies granted by their home governments. A **countervailing duty (CVD)** is an ad valorem tariff on an imported good that is imposed by the importing country to counter the impact of foreign subsidies. The CVD is calculated to just offset the advantage the exporter obtains from the subsidy. In this way, trade can still be driven by the competitive strengths of individual firms and the laws of comparative advantage, rather than by the level of subsidies that governments offer their firms. For instance, the EU and the United States each imposed CVDs on high-end glossy paper imported from China, in the belief that Chinese producers had benefited from cheap governmental financing and land sales.[48]

Not all government subsidies give a foreign firm an unfair advantage in the domestic market. Most countries impose CVDs only when foreign subsidization of a product leads to a distortion of international trade. For example, the U.S. government, in administering its CVD rules, tries to determine whether a particular subsidy is generally available to all industries in a country, in which case CVDs will not be applied, or whether the subsidy is restricted to a specific industry, in which case CVDs may be imposed. If a foreign government grants a tax credit to all employers for training handicapped workers, a CVD will not be applied because the tax credit is available to all the country's firms. If the tax credit is restricted to the footwear industry, however, a CVD may be imposed on imported footwear equal to the value of the tax credit.

CVD complaints are often triggered by some governmental action designed to overcome some other governmental action. For example, the EU's common agricultural policy has had the effect of raising the prices paid to European grain farmers. Unfortunately, the high cost of feed grains raised the costs of European swine producers and made their meat products uncompetitive in world markets. To undo the damage caused to swine producers by high grain prices, the EU agreed to provide an export subsidy for canned hams and other processed meat products. With the aid of this subsidy Danish and Dutch pork processors were able to capture 25 percent of the Canadian canned ham and canned luncheon meat market. As a result, Canadian pork-packing houses successfully petitioned the Canadian International Trade Tribunal to impose a CVD on Danish and Dutch canned pork products.

Antidumping Regulations

Many countries are also concerned about their domestic firms being victimized by discriminatory or predatory pricing practices of foreign firms, such as dumping. There are two types of dumping. **Dumping** can occur when a firm sells its goods in a foreign market at a price below what it charges in its home market. This type of dumping is a form of international price discrimination. The second type of dumping involves the firm's selling its goods below cost in the foreign market, in which case the dumping is a form of predatory pricing. The concern with predatory pricing is that a foreign company may lower its prices in the host country, drive host country firms out of the market, and then charge monopoly prices to host country consumers once competitors have been eliminated. Antidumping laws protect local industries from dumping by foreign firms.

Determining whether the first type of dumping—price discrimination—has actually occurred is not always easy. For example, many Western politicians incorrectly accuse Japanese companies of dumping, noting that Japanese goods often retail for higher prices in Tokyo than in New York City. Retail prices, however, are irrelevant in determining whether dumping has occurred. The comparison should be made between the prices charged foreign customers and domestic customers at the factory gate; these prices are often difficult to obtain. The high retail prices in Tokyo might reflect the inefficient Japanese distribution system or high costs of retailing there rather than dumping by the manufacturer.

In the second type of dumping—predatory pricing—defining costs is complicated, particularly when dealing with a large, multidivisional MNC such as Toyota or Nissan. For example, when the ITA is determining the "cost" of a Toyota Sienna minivan, should it measure cost as the marginal cost of producing one more Sienna? Should it include some of

Toyota's minivan-related R&D expenses, or should it simply recognize that these R&D costs would have been incurred whether or not the U.S. market existed? Should it include charges for Toyota's corporate overhead? Foreigners' guilt or innocence in dumping cases often turns on the answers to such accounting questions.

Should Countries Enforce Their Unfair Trade Practice Laws?

It may be surprising to learn that many economists argue for abolishing unfair trade practice laws. Who, after all, would support promoting unfair trade? Advocates of abolishing unfair trade practice laws generally agree with the objectives of these laws:

- Promote global efficiency by encouraging production in those countries that can produce a good most efficiently.
- Ensure that trade occurs on the basis of comparative advantage, not the size of government subsidies.
- Protect consumers from predatory behavior.

However, abolition advocates assert that in practice these laws do more harm than good. Much of their concern rests on how the laws are enforced. Foreign firms alleged to have dumped goods in the United States must provide comprehensive documentation of their pricing and cost-accounting procedures, in English, using U.S. generally accepted accounting principles (GAAP). Firms failing to comply with the short deadlines for supplying these documents find themselves at a disadvantage in defending themselves before the ITC. Moreover, critics of unfair trade practice laws argue that the ITC's costing methodology is flawed and biased toward finding dumping when none exists. New Zealand kiwi fruit was subjected to high dumping duties in the U.S. market for nearly a decade, for example, on what many experts consider to be flimsy evidence. Indeed, most major trading countries believe that U.S. enforcement of its unfair trade practice laws is based on politics, not the law, and thus the laws serve as a protectionist trade barrier.

Some economists go even further in their disdain for unfair trade practice laws. They believe the laws make no sense, either in theory or in practice, because of the harm they cause consumers. These economists are skeptical of the predatory pricing argument, contending that decades of economic research have failed to find many real-world examples of such behavior. With regard to international price discrimination or government subsidization, the economists argue that if foreigners are kind enough (or dumb enough) to sell their goods to our country below cost, why should we complain?

Safeguards

The previous sections refer to unfair trade practices. International trade law also allows countries to protect themselves from sudden surges in imported goods, even if the goods were traded fairly, to allow them time to adjust to the changed economic environment. Such actions use "safeguard clauses" or "escape clauses." In U.S. trade law, Section 201 of the Trade Act of 1974 permits the imposition of temporary tariffs, quotas, or other trade barriers by the federal government if the ITC finds that U.S. firms have been seriously harmed by increased imports and if the president approves the ITC's findings.

For instance, in 2009, President Obama imposed temporary tariffs for three years on tires imported from China after the ITC ruled that U.S. tire producers were harmed by rapid increases in imports, causing them to trim their workforces by 5,000 employees. Between 2004 and 2008, the ITC found that the U.S. market share of Chinese tires rose from 4.7 percent to 16.7 percent, and that four U.S. tire factories had shuttered their gates as a result. Obama chose to levy a 35-percent tariff on Chinese tires for one year. The president determined that the tariff should decline to 30 percent in the second year and to 25 percent in the final year. While the United Steelworkers, who filed the original complaint, were delighted by the president's decision, many U.S. tire wholesalers, who rely on imports to keep their costs down, were not.[49]

In Practice

- Many countries have implemented laws protecting their domestic firms from unfair trade practices.
- The two primary unfair trade practices result from government policies that distort international trade and from dumping.

For further consideration: Should governments enforce their unfair trade practices law?

MyManagementLab®

Go to **mymanagementlab.com** to complete the problems marked with this icon ✪.

CHAPTER REVIEW

Summary

Formulating trade policies that advance the economic interests of their citizens is an important task facing most national governments. Although some policymakers suggest that free trade is the most appropriate policy, numerous firms, government bureaucrats, and other interested parties argue for active governmental intervention in international trade.

Some rationales for governmental intervention focus on the specific needs of an industry (national defense, infant industry, maintenance of existing jobs, and strategic trade arguments), whereas others focus on the country's overall needs (economic development and industrial policy).

Over the centuries, governments have developed a variety of trade barriers. Import tariffs raise revenues for the government as well as help domestically produced goods compete with imported goods. Quotas and VERs place a numerical limitation on the amount of a good that can be imported or exported. Other NTBs may also disadvantage foreign products in the market. These barriers include product and testing standards, restricted access to distribution systems, public-sector procurement policies that favor local firms, local-purchase requirements, regulatory powers, and currency and investment controls.

National governments also seek to promote the interests of domestic firms in international trade through other programs. The governments may subsidize local production of goods and services to make them more competitive in international markets. They also may authorize the establishment of FTZs to help domestic firms export goods. Export financing programs have been developed to assist exporters in marketing their goods.

National governments protect local producers from unfair foreign competition by enacting unfair trade laws. CVDs are imposed on foreign products that benefit from government subsidies that distort international trade. Antidumping laws protect domestic producers from being victimized by predatory pricing or price discrimination policies of foreign firms.

Review Questions

9-1. How does free trade benefit the consumer?
9-2. What is the national defense argument?
9-3. What are the different types of tariffs?
9-4. Why is it useful for an importer to seek out an advance tariff classification from the U.S. Customs Service?
9-5. Why might a country adopt a VER?
9-6. What are the major forms of NTBs?
9-7. What are subsidies?
9-8. What is the role of OPIC?
9-9. What is the purpose of a CVD?
9-10. What are the two definitions of *dumping*?

Questions for Discussion

✪ 9-11. What are the advantages and disadvantages of an industrial policy?
9-12. Because of Japan's success in competing in international markets, it has been the target of numerous complaints that it restricts foreign access to its local markets. As Japan reduces its barriers to imported goods, who is likely to gain from lowered barriers? Who is likely to lose from them?

9-13. In your opinion, what are the main disadvantages of adopting the strategic trade theory? In your answer, list and briefly explain at least three disadvantages.

9-14. Refer back to Figure 9.2 on page 265. What would happen if Japan offered Toshiba a subsidy of $1.5 billion after it learns that France granted Areva a subsidy of $2 billion?

9-15. Canada places a non-tariff barrier (NTB) on Emirates Airline (Dubai flagship carrier) flights by limiting the landing rights of this foreign carrier within Canadian airports. If the Canadian government removes this NTB what would be the implications of this decision on Canadian firms (including Air Canada, the national airline) and the Canadian economy?

9-16. Should we worry if foreigners sell us goods cheaply?

Building Global Skills

Assessing Trade Barriers

The ability of firms to market their products in foreign countries is often affected by trade barriers imposed by individual countries. Your assignment is to pick an industry or product and report on the barriers to trade or investment that five countries impose on it. Because the members of the EU have common trade policies, only one of the five countries can be an EU member.

Fortunately, there are numerous sources of useful information available in published form and on the Internet. The Office of the U.S. Trade Representative publishes annually an analysis of trade barriers imposed by other nations titled the *National Trade Estimate Report on Foreign Trade Barriers.* This study also provides a detailed description of the evolution of current trade conflicts between the United States and its trading partners. The European Commission provides similar information for the EU in the Trade section of its website (see http://ec.europa.eu/trade/). The U.S. Customs Service's website provides information on tariffs imposed by the United States. Other groups, such as the WTO and industry trade associations, also publish useful information.

CLOSING CASE Green Energy and Free Trade

The trauma of the Global Recession of 2008–2009 motivated politicians around the world to seek new ways of rejuvenating their struggling economies. Many of them focused on the promotion of green energy as a critical element of their economic recovery programs. (Green energy encompasses power generated by sustainable, renewable sources, such as solar, wind, waves and tide, geothermal deposits, biomass, and low-impact hydroelectric power.) In 2008, then presidential candidate Barack Obama proposed a "New Energy for America" initiative, which sought to invest $150 billion over 10 years to promote clean energy, reduce dependence on foreign oil, lower greenhouse gas emissions, and create five million new jobs. By stimulating new green energy technologies, candidate Obama believed that the United States would become a dominant exporter in the green energy markets of the future. During his 2010 election campaign, British Prime Minister David Cameron pledged to create a £20 billion green homes program. German Chancellor Angela Merkel announced her Nine-Point Program designed to increase over a 40-year period the role of renewable sources in generating Germany's electricity. For 2020, Merkel established a goal of having renewable sources provide 35 percent of Germany's electricity needs. The Canadian province of Ontario's Green Energy and Green Economy Act of 2009 promised to stimulate green energy production and to increase energy efficiency. Similar green energy programs were announced by the governments of China (with a price tag of $220 billion), South Korea ($60 billion), and Japan ($35 billion).

These green energy initiatives typically had dual goals: rejuvenate stagnating economies and address the global climate change problem. The Kyoto Protocol, the result of a 1997 enclave, and the Copenhagen Accord, the product of the 2009 United Nations Climate Change Conference, highlighted the need to reduce greenhouse gas emissions. Although these two international meetings were less successful than many climate experts wished—the United States did not ratify the Kyoto Protocol and the Copenhagen Accord was not framed as a legally binding treaty—national leaders recognized the magnitude of the global climate change threat.

The dual goals of these well-intentioned and politically appealing green energy initiatives have created numerous problems for the world's trade officials, however. As we will discuss in detail in the next chapter, most countries are members of the WTO and have pledged to reduce barriers to international trade. Yet many of these green energy initiatives contain provisions that are contrary to countries' obligations to the WTO. For example, to reduce its reliance on coal-fired electricity generation, Ontario's Green Energy and Green Economy Act mandates increased power generated by solar and wind. Unfortunately, the cost of producing electricity using solar panels or wind turbines is more expensive than by burning coal. To overcome this obstacle, Ontario requires electrical utilities to buy power produced by renewable providers at an above-market price.

Such "feed-in tariffs" are a common feature in laws promoting green energy use. Essentially they guarantee green energy producers a market for their expensive energy. The level of the feed-in tariff can be manipulated to promote other policy objectives. Spain's system, for example, offers higher tariffs for electricity generated by small suppliers than by large ones. Of course, by raising the average cost of producing electricity, they raise the price paid by users, both industrial and home, of electricity. Supporters of feed-in tariffs argue that in the short-run higher prices are necessary to induce investors to build green energy production facilities; in the long-run, they hope that by expanding the size of the green energy market, producers of green energy goods will capture economies of scale, thereby making green energy more cost competitive with coal-fired generators.

Feed-in tariffs do create political problems, however. They raise the cost of electricity to voters. They also raise the cost of electricity to local manufacturers, who may have to shut down if they no longer can compete with goods produced by distant rivals unaffected by the feed-in tariff. To address these concerns, Ontario mandated that 25 to 50 percent of the cost of the green energy facilities benefiting from the feed-in tariffs be locally sourced. In that way, although electricity costs might rise, local jobs would also be created. Indeed, Samsung, Siemens, SunEdison, and Celestica announced that they would build plants in Ontario to take advantage of the 2009 law.

Other countries have adopted local content rules in their green energy programs as well. China's wind energy program used a 70-percent local content rule. (It withdrew this requirement in 2009 under diplomatic pressure from U.S. trade officials.) India's Jawaharlal Nehru National Solar Mission envisions the country will add 20,000 megawatts of solar power by 2022. The government's $20 billion in subsidies include a 30-percent local content requirement. Unfortunately, such local content provisions may be contrary to the rules of the WTO.

Many of the national programs promoting green energy provide subsidies for suppliers or consumers. The Indian government subsidizes homeowners 30 percent of the cost of installing rooftop solar panels. The American Recovery and Reinvestment Act of 2009 provided tax breaks for Americans who made their homes more energy efficient or purchased electric vehicles. The Chinese government subsidized local companies who entered the solar panel supply business by providing cheap credit from state-owned banks, as well as subsidizing solar-equipment purchases and generation of solar power. Total subsidies by China to its solar panel manufacturers are an estimated $30 billion. One Massachusetts solar panel factory, which had received $43 million in state subsidies, moved its production to China because China's subsidies were too attractive to ignore, costing 800 U.S. jobs.

Such subsidies raise concerns for the WTO and advocates of free trade. Direct subsidies to the manufacturers of goods embodying green technologies give recipients a competitive advantage in export markets and make it more difficult for manufacturers in countries who offer no subsidies to compete both domestically and internationally. For example, China has become the world's largest producer of solar panels, due in part to the subsidies offered producers by the Chinese government.

Indeed, the first round of trade disputes is winding its way through the legal processes of countries and the WTO. In 2012, the U.S. International Trade Commission found that U.S. solar panel manufacturers were victimized by dumping by Chinese producers and imposed antidumping duties exceeding 30 percent on Chinese solar panels. In 2013, the European Commission came to the same conclusion, slapping a 47 percent antidumping duty on Chinese-fabricated panels. The United States petitioned the WTO to declare India's local content rules in violation of WTO rules, and Japan filed a complaint with the WTO against Canada's. China has asked the WTO to investigate solar power rules adopted by Greece and Italy, while the U.S. and the EU have launched similar proceedings against China.

Another concern of free trade advocates involves proposed border tax adjustments (BTAs), or tariffs, on imported goods that have benefited from the regulatory "race to the bottom." Suppose country A requires its domestic manufacturers to adopt expensive technologies to reduce their greenhouse gas emissions and country B does not. Country A's manufacturers might argue that production and firms will move to country B where costs are cheaper. Country B then benefits from the "race to the bottom." To deter countries from lowering their environmental regulations to attract new investment and industries, some countries, including the United States and the EU, are proposing to impose BTAs on goods imported from countries whose environmental standards are lower than theirs. One study commissioned by the World Bank suggested that a $50 a ton tax on carbon dioxide would be equivalent to a 10-percent tariff on a typical Chinese import. Development specialists fear that BTAs of this magnitude could cripple the ability of small manufacturers, which form the backbone of China's manufacturing sector, to compete in developed markets. Environmental specialists conversely fear that attempts to control greenhouse gas emissions will come to naught unless such small manufacturers also comply with higher environmental standards.

Case Questions

9-17. Why have so many governments chosen to subsidize green energy initiatives? Can all of these programs be successful?

9-18. China has passed the United States as the largest emitter of greenhouse gases, which displeases environmentalists concerned about global climate change. China has subsidized its green energy manufacturers, allowing them to dominate key industries, such as solar panels, which displeases advocates of free trade. What would you recommend China do? Should it accommodate its critics? Should it ignore them?

9-19. What is the rationale for BTAs? Under what conditions, if any, should countries be allowed to impose BTAs?

9-20. What is the appropriate trade-off between promoting free trade and promoting green energy? Should the WTO rules be suspended when dealing with green energy?

Source: "EU hands China solar reprieve," *Financial Times*, June 5, 2013, p. 2; "China solar panel makers negotiate with U.S. and EU," *Financial Times*, May 24, 2013, p. 2; "The Cloudy Logic of Europe's Solar Tariffs," *Wall Street Journal*, May 13, 2013, p. C8; "EU Plans Tariffs Up to 67.9% on Chinese Solar Panels," *Wall Street Journal*, May 9, 2013, p. B3; "Europe's Green Central Planning," *Wall Street Journal*, May 9, 2013; "Chinese sun panels face EU levies," *Financial Times*, May 6, 2013, p. 2; "India Plans Subsidies to Boost Solar-Power Sector," *Wall Street Journal*, April 21, 2013; "Wind-Power Subsidies? No Thanks.," *Wall Street Journal*, April 2, 2013, p. A13; "Suntech Rattles Investors in U.S.," *Wall Street Journal*, March 21, 2013, p. B5; "Suntech's China solar panel venture declares bankruptcy," *Financial Times*, March 21, 2013, p. 11; "U.S. fuels global energy battle with solar trade case against India," *Financial Times*, February 7, 2013, p. 1; "Washington to Hit Beijing With Solar-Panel Tariffs," *Wall Street Journal*, November 8, 2012, A15; "China Files WTO Complaint on EU Solar Subsidies," *Wall Street Journal*, November 5, 2012; "The way the world turns," *Financial Times*, November 29, 2011, p. 10; "Overrun by Chinese Rivals, U.S. Solar Company Falters," *Wall Street Journal*, August 17, 2011, p. B1; Office of the U.S. Trade Representative, *National Trade Estimate Report on Foreign Trade Barriers 2011*, pp. 54, 181; "Wind power hits a trough," *Wall Street Journal*, April 4, 2011; "Indian solar rules burn U.S.," *Wall Street Journal*, February 8, 2011; "U.S. seals energy deals as Hu arrives for visit," *Wall Street Journal*, January 19, 2011; "U.S. pushes India to lift solar import restrictions," *Wall Street Journal*, December 15, 2010; "Asia's green tech rivals," *The Economist*, November 13, 2009; "Obama lays out clean-energy plans," *Washington Post*, March 24, 2009; "Barrack Obama and Joe Biden: New energy for America," www.barackobama.com; G. Atkinson, Hamilton G. Ruta, and D. van der Mensbrugghe, 2009, "Trade in 'Virtual Carbon': Empirical Results and Implications for Policy," Background paper for the World Development Report 2010; German government press release at http://www.germany.info/Vertretung/usa/en/_pr/P_Wash/2010/09/07_EnergyPlan_PR,archiveCtx=1992696.html.

MyManagementLab®

Go to **mymanagementlab.com** for the following Assisted-graded writing questions:

9-21. Discuss the primary barriers that countries erect to protect domestic firms from foreign competition. Who benefits from the erection of these barriers? Who loses?

9-22. The enforcement of antidumping laws in controversial. Discuss why this is so. Should nations enforce their antidumping laws? Defend your answer.

9-23. Mymanagementlab Only—comprehensive writing assignment for this chapter.

Endnotes

1. "U.K. Raises Cybersecurity Concerns Over Huawei," *Wall Street Journal*, June 7, 2013, p. A8; "Huawei shifts focus after U.S. U-turn," *Financial Times*, April 30, 2013, p. 15; "Huawei predicts 10% annual rise in revenues," *Financial Times*, April 9, 2013, p. 17; "China's Huawei Sees Wireless Growth Despite U.S. Shutout," *Wall Street Journal*, April 4, 2013, p. B4; "Huawei dismisses claims over Beijing ties," *Financial Times*, March 1, 2013, p. 13; "Huawei builds clout through R&D," *Wall Street Journal*, February 25, 2013, page B1; "Clear as mud," *The Economist*, February 2, 2013; "China Eyes Electronics Clout," *Wall Street Journal*, January 23, 2013, p. B10; "ZTE Girds for Loss, While Huawei Forecasts 33% Rise in Net," *Wall Street Journal*, January 22, 2013, p. B3; "Huawei in pledge to disclose more information," *Financial Times*, January 22, 2013, p. 15; "Huawei pins hope on fresh face," *Financial Times*, January 22, 2013, p. 17; "Not just tilting at windmills," *The Economist*, October 6, 2012; "Who's afraid of Huawei?," *The Economist*, August 4, 2012.

2. "The trough," *The Economist*, June 27, 1992, p. 22.

3. Edward J. Lincoln, *Japan's Unequal Trade* (Washington, DC: The Brookings Institution, 1990), p. 112.
4. "Climbing through the clouds," *The Economist*, July 9, 2011 (online).
5. "Taxes put Chill on Electronics," *Wall Street Journal*, February 27, 2012, p. B1.
6. "Torpedo shipping protectionism," *Wall Street Journal*, November 26, 1991, p. A14.
7. Office of the U.S. Trade Representative, *National Trade Estimate Report on Foreign Trade Barriers 2011*, p. 195; Office of the U.S. Trade Representative, *National Trade Estimate Report on Foreign Trade Barriers 2006*, p. 352. Current tariff found at http://www.customs.go.jp/english/tariff/2011_4/data/i201104e_10.htm.
8. Office of the U.S. Trade Representative, *National Trade Estimate Report on Foreign Trade Barriers 2011*, p. 226.
9. "U.S. faces sugar squeeze," *Wall Street Journal*, May 2, 2011, p. C8.
10. "A Sugar Showdown," *Wall Street Journal*, June 13, 2012, p. A14; "Bitter about sugar prices," *Houston Chronicle*, April 27, 2006, p. D3.
11. "Shielding sugar industry 'costs thousands of jobs'," *Financial Times*, February 15, 2006, p. 6.
12. Office of the U.S. Trade Representative, *National Trade Estimate Report on Foreign Trade Barriers 2013*, p. 55; Office of the U.S. Trade Representative, *National Trade Estimate Report on Foreign Trade Barriers 2011*, pp. 52, 53; "U.S., Canada have tentative deal in dispute over softwood lumber," *Wall Street Journal*, April 28, 2006, p. A4; "U.S. will lift a lumber duty in a trade deal with Canada," *New York Times* (online), April 28, 2006.
13. Office of the U.S. Trade Representative, *National Trade Estimate Report on Foreign Trade Barriers 2013*, p. 317; Office of the U.S. Trade Representative, *National Trade Estimate Report on Foreign Trade Barriers 2011*, p. 309.
14. Office of the U.S. Trade Representative, *National Trade Estimate Report on Foreign Trade Barriers 2013*, p. 77.
15. Office of the U.S. Trade Representative, *National Trade Estimate Report on Foreign Trade Barriers 2013*, p. 41.
16. Office of the U.S. Trade Representative, *2013 Report on Technical Barriers to Trade*, p. 237.
17. Office of the U.S. Trade Representative, *National Trade Estimate Report on Foreign Trade Barriers 2013*, p. 315.
18. Office of the U.S. Trade Representative, *National Trade Estimate Report on Foreign Trade Barriers 2013*, pp. 71 and 194.
19. Office of the U.S. Trade Representative, *National Trade Estimate Report on Foreign Trade Barriers 2013*, pp. 88 and 197.
20. Office of the U.S. Trade Representative, *National Trade Estimate Report on Foreign Trade Barriers 2013*, p. 185.
21. Office of the U.S. Trade Representative, *National Trade Estimate Report on Foreign Trade Barriers 2013*, pp. 24, 127, 265, 294, and 355.
22. Office of the U.S. Trade Representative, *National Trade Estimate Report on Foreign Trade Barriers 2013*, pp. 230 and 316.
23. Office of the U.S. Trade Representative, *National Trade Estimate Report on Foreign Trade Barriers 2011*, p. 184.
24. Office of the U.S. Trade Representative, *National Trade Estimate Report on Foreign Trade Barriers 2013*, p. 89; Office of the U.S. Trade Representative, *National Trade Estimate Report on Foreign Trade Barriers 2008*, pp. 126ff.
25. Office of the U.S. Trade Representative, *National Trade Estimate Report on Foreign Trade Barriers 2011*, p. 219.
26. Office of the U.S. Trade Representative, *National Trade Estimate Report on Foreign Trade Barriers 2011*, p. 296.
27. Office of the U.S. Trade Representative, *National Trade Estimate Report on Foreign Trade Barriers 2013*, p. 129.
28. Office of the U.S. Trade Representative, *National Trade Estimate Report on Foreign Trade Barriers 2013*, p. 59.
29. Office of the U.S. Trade Representative, *National Trade Estimate Report on Foreign Trade Barriers 2013*, pp. 238 and 253.
30. Office of the U.S. Trade Representative, *National Trade Estimate Report on Foreign Trade Barriers 2013*, p. 150.
31. Office of the U.S. Trade Representative, *National Trade Estimate Report on Foreign Trade Barriers 2013*, pp. 30, 149, 229, and 246.
32. Office of the U.S. Trade Representative, *National Trade Estimate Report on Foreign Trade Barriers 2013*, pp. 327, 346, and 354.
33. Office of the U.S. Trade Representative, *National Trade Estimate Report on Foreign Trade Barriers 2013*, p. 239.
34. Office of the U.S. Trade Representative, *National Trade Estimate Report on Foreign Trade Barriers 2011*, p. 40.
35. Office of the U.S. Trade Representative, *2011 Report on Technical Barriers to Trade*, p. 64.
36. Office of the U.S. Trade Representative, *National Trade Estimate Report on Foreign Trade Barriers 2013*, p. 376; "Venezuela Takes Aim At Dollar Shortage," *Wall Street Journal*, March 20, 2013, p. C3.
37. Office of the U.S. Trade Representative, *National Trade Estimate Report on Foreign Trade Barriers 2013*, p. 135.
38. Office of the U.S. Trade Representative, *National Trade Estimate Report on Foreign Trade Barriers 2013*, pp. 240 and 258; Office of the U.S. Trade Representative, *National Trade Estimate Report on Foreign Trade Barriers 2011*, pp. 298, 299.
39. Office of the U.S. Trade Representative, *National Trade Estimate Report on Foreign Trade Barriers 2013*, p. 226 and 356.
40. Office of the U.S. Trade Representative, *National Trade Estimate Report on Foreign Trade Barriers 2013*, p. 299 and 333.
41. Office of the U.S. Trade Representative, *National Trade Estimate Report on Foreign Trade Barriers 2013*, pp. 40 and 221.
42. Office of the U.S. Trade Representative, *National Trade Estimate Report on Foreign Trade Barriers 2013*, p 362.

43. "U.S. States Become Addicted to Use of Economic Sweeteners," *Financial Times*, March 23, 2006, p. 19.
44. "Rum Maker Wins Incentives," *Wall Street Journal*, October 7, 2009, p. B6.
45. Committee on Ways and Means, *Operation of the Foreign Trade Zones Program of the United States and Its Implications for the U.S. Economy and U.S. International Trade*, October 1989, Serial 101–56, pp. 281 and 326.
46. Export-Import Bank of the United States, *2012 Annual Report* (Washington, DC: Eximbank, 2013); Export-Import Bank of the United States, *2010 Annual Report* (Washington, DC: Eximbank, 2011).
47. "U.S. export terms pose test for Beijing," *Wall Street Journal*, January 12, 2011, p. A11.
48. "Stakes raised in EU bid to curb China exports," *Financial Times*, May 16, 2011, p. 2; "Glossy paper from China, Indonesia to face U.S. anti-subsidy import duties," *Bloomberg News*, October 22, 2010.
49. "Get-Tough Policy on Chinese Tires Falls Flat," *Wall Street Journal*, January 20, 2012, p. B1; "WTO backs U.S. in tire dispute with China," *Wall Street Journal*, December 13, 2010; "U.S. to impose tariff on tires from China," *Washington Post*, September 12, 2009; "U.S. adds tariffs on Chinese tires," *New York Times*, September 11, 2009.

Source: © mkmakingphotos/Fotolia

Culture and Management: Google in China

Google has enjoyed spectacular success since its founding in 1998. The search engine firm operates in more than 50 countries and established operations in China in 2006. Google brought its laid-back Silicon Valley culture to sprawling headquarters in Beijing, which was outfitted with a fully equipped gym, foosball tables, videogames, and other frills.

Google clashed with the Chinese government, which closely monitors business in China, especially firms from abroad. As a condition for entering China, Google agreed to censor certain types of search results, especially those that criticize the Chinese government. Google pushed the limits by complying as little as possible with government orders to block search engine content.

Google's Chinese employees experienced difficulties adjusting to the firm's freewheeling style. Many were uncomfortable with company policy that requires employees to devote 20 percent of their work time to developing independent projects. Google blocked its Chinese engineers from accessing the firm's software code. The policy emerged in response to China's loose approach to private property rights, which encourages access to foreign technology and know-how.

CHAPTER 4

The Cultural Environment of International Business

LEARNING OBJECTIVES *In this chapter, you will learn about the following:*

1. The nature of cross-cultural risk
2. Characteristics of culture
3. Lenses to understand culture
4. Subjective and objective dimensions of culture
5. Language: A key dimension of culture
6. Cultural change
7. Context of international business
8. Overcoming cross-cultural risk: Managerial guidelines

Google hired a Chinese executive to manage the firm's government relations. However, communication gaps arose partly because she could not speak English. She criticized Google corporate management for not working hard enough to understand Chinese customs. Later, she was fired after giving free iPods to government officials. Giving expensive gifts to public officials is often viewed as a form of bribery in Western cultures, but is more accepted in parts of Asia.

Management grew alarmed when Chinese hackers accessed sensitive information in Google's private files. In some cases, Chinese government officials hacked the Gmail accounts of Chinese dissidents and human rights activists. A government official launched a personal campaign against the firm when he Googled himself and found an abundance of critical material. Eventually, Google senior management grew weary of China and decided to stop complying with government censorship rules.

In 2010, Google withdrew from mainland China. Google's China personnel were shocked by this decision, which was reached without gaining their input or support. Many had begun to think of themselves as members of the "Google family."

Google's experience in China demonstrates the importance of culture in international business. China has a *collectivist* mind-set, which emphasizes conformity, duty, prescribed roles, and sacrifice for the greater good. Family-style management emphasizes personal relations and leaders concerned for employee happiness. Families are at the center of Chinese culture. In society, family members "know their place" and maintain the family name. Younger generations respect and obey their elders. At one time, a father could legally kill his children if they displeased him. Such is the cultural context in which Google confronted the Chinese government.

The Chinese are *long-term oriented* and invest much time in planning business ventures. They emphasize patience, respect for tradition, and hard work. They avoid conflict and favor societal harmony. The focus on harmony derives from teachings of the ancient philosopher Confucius, who urged a nonassertive approach to resolving differences. China is a *high-context, relationship-oriented* culture. Maintaining strong, long-term relationships is essential to developing trust. Major decisions are rarely taken without informing employees first.

Guanxi refers to informal personal relationships that emphasize reciprocal obligations and the exchange of favors. In China, guanxi profoundly influences commercial activities and organizational behaviors. An individual or firm that receives favors from another has a moral obligation to reciprocate and maintain the relationship. In China, government officials did many favors for Google, starting with allowing it to launch its business there. Skillful guanxi can open dialogue, build trust, and facilitate the exchange of favors that augment business performance.

In 2012, Google renewed efforts to enter China, acknowledging that it cannot afford to miss out on the world's biggest Internet market. Top management has softened its position, and is seeking to introduce new services in China, especially those not subject to censorship.

SOURCES: H. Chen, A. Ellinger, and Y. Tian, "Manufacturer–Supplier Guanxi Strategy," *Industrial Marketing Management* 40, no. 4 (2011): 550–560; W. Chunxia, "The Influence of Confucian Culture on Business Management," *International Journal of Business Anthropology* 1, no. 2 (2010): 117–134; A. Efrati, L. Chao, and K. Zhang, "Google Softens China Stance," *Wall Street Journal*, January 12, 2012, pp. B1–B2; E. Fyrwald, "Five Keys to Profiting in China," *Bloomberg BusinessWeek*, March 16, 2011, accessed from www.Businessweek.com; P. Gwynne, "Google's Experience Raises Doubts about High-Tech Business in China," *Research Technology Management*, May/June, 2010, pp. 2–3; S. Levy, "Google and Its Ordeal in Ordeal in China," *Fortune*, May 2, 2011, accessed at http://money.cnn.com/magazines/fortune; S. Levy, *In the Plex: How Google Thinks, Works, and Shapes Our Lives* (New York: Simon & Schuster, 2011); *New York Times*, "China and Intellectual Property," Dec. 23, 2010, accessed at www.nytimes.com; A. Rabkin, "The Social(ist) Networks," *Fast Company*, February 2011, pp. 68–75.

The opening story on Google's entry into China highlights the challenges of operating in diverse national cultures. In international business, success requires sensitivity to national interests and cultural expectations. By contrast, Google corporate management displayed an ethnocentric orientation, viewing China through the lens of American values and business customs. As reflected in the story, **culture** refers to the learned, shared, and lasting orientation patterns in a society. In China and around the world, people demonstrate their culture through values, ideas, attitudes, behaviors, and symbols. In international business, firms such as Google step into cultural environments characterized by unfamiliar languages and unique value systems, beliefs, behaviors, and norms. These differences influence all dimensions of international business.

Culture
The learned, shared, and enduring orientation patterns in a society. People demonstrate their culture through values, ideas, attitudes, behaviors, and symbols.

Exhibit 4.1 summarizes the culture-related essentials addressed in this chapter. Scholars have offered various models and explanations on culture. Culture influences the various social environments that managers encounter. Religion and language are particularly relevant expressions of culture. Culture is difficult to identify and analyze, but its effects on international business are profound. Culture is evolving constantly and is affected by globalization and numerous other contemporary trends. In this chapter, we focus on the business dimensions of culture and implications for managers.[1]

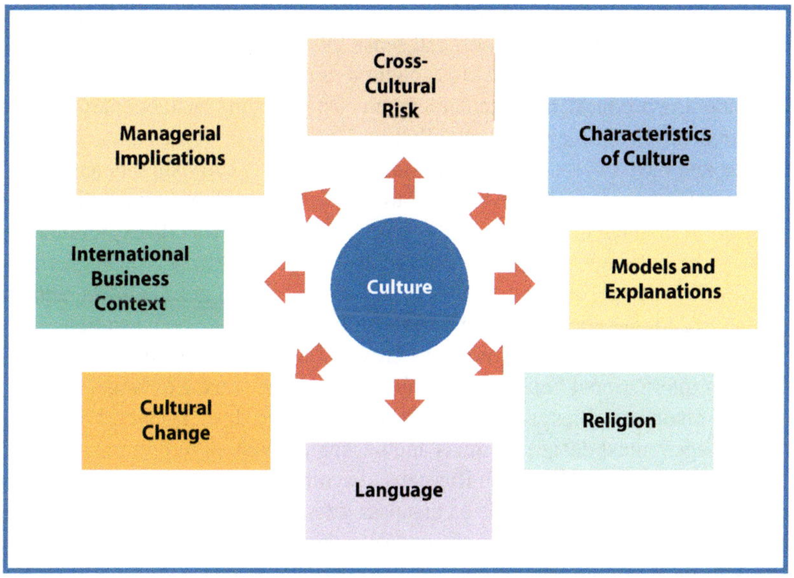

EXHIBIT 4.1

Essentials for Understanding Culture in International Business

The Nature of Cross-Cultural Risk

Culture represents one of the four risks of international business that we introduced in Chapter 1. We highlight these risks in Exhibit 4.2. **Cross-cultural risk** is a situation or event in which a cultural misunderstanding puts some human value at stake. Misunderstanding and miscommunication arise because people have differing values and expectations. They do not always communicate (verbally or nonverbally) what the other party is anticipating, or may have different ways of communicating. For example, a head nod has different meanings in India and the United Kingdom.

Cross-cultural risk
A situation or event in which a cultural misunderstanding puts some human value at stake.

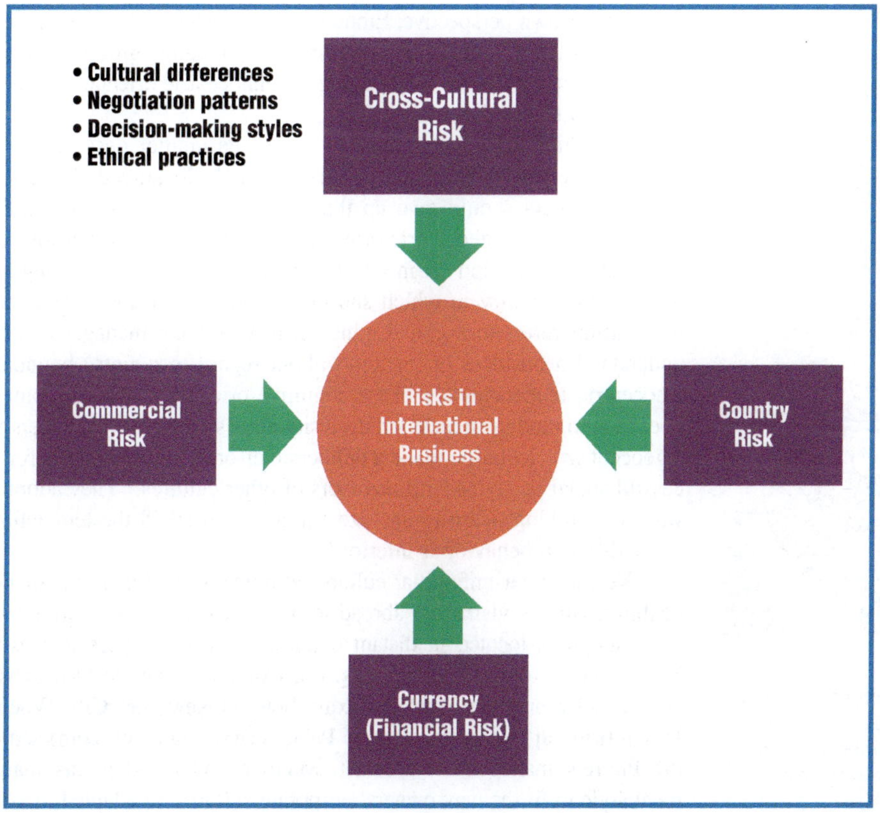

EXHIBIT 4.2

The Four Major Risks in International Business

Cross-cultural misunderstandings can ruin business deals, hurt sales, or harm the corporate image. Today, developing an appreciation of, and sensitivity for, cultural differences has become an imperative for any manager. Those with cross-cultural savvy hold various advantages in managing employees, marketing products, and interacting with customers and business partners.

Culture affects even simple rituals of daily life. Greeting ceremonies are a deeply embedded cultural marker and have evolved over many centuries. They specify such behaviors as whether to shake hands, what to say, and how far apart to stand. These cultural conventions may vary as a function of the age, gender, or status of the greeters. In China, friends express thoughtfulness by asking each other whether they have had their meal yet. In Turkey, a typical greeting is "What is new with you?" In Japan, elaborate greeting and parting rituals are the norm, and individuals routinely apologize to the other party just before ending a telephone conversation.

Ethnocentric orientation
Using our own culture as the standard for judging other cultures.

Polycentric orientation
A host-country mind-set in which the manager develops a strong affinity with the country in which she or he conducts business.

Geocentric orientation
A global mind-set in which the manager is able to understand a business or market without regard to country boundaries.

Unlike political, legal, and economic systems, culture is difficult to identify and analyze, but its effects on international business, as well as on interpersonal exchange, are profound. Its effects on value-chain activities, such as product and service design, marketing, and sales, are substantial. Managers must design products and packaging with culture in mind, even regarding color. While red may be beautiful to the Russians, it symbolizes mourning in South Africa. Items such as pens are universally acceptable as business gifts, but chrysanthemums are often associated with funerals and handkerchiefs may suggest sadness. In some cultures, knives or scissors imply cutting off the relationship or other negative sentiments.

Some firms train their employees about foreign cultures, helping them become cross-culturally proficient. In California's Silicon Valley, Intel offers a seminar called "Working with India" to enhance work effectiveness with the estimated 400,000 Indian nationals in the valley. Computer firm AMD flies IT workers from India to its facilities in Texas for a month of cultural training with U.S. managers. Workers role-play and study subjects such as Indian movies, political history, and Hinduism. Training includes lessons on assigning work (Indian workers may agree to unattainable deadlines), preparing food (many Indians eat vegetarian food), and socializing (since it is polite to initially decline an invitation to a colleague's home, managers should offer more than once).[2]

Source: iStock

Limited interaction among societies, such as between Kenyans, Mexicans, and Russians, tends to magnify differences in values, behaviors, and symbols. Such differences decrease, however, with growing cross-cultural interaction.

Cross-cultural risk can be triggered by an **ethnocentric orientation**—using our own culture as the standard for judging other cultures. Most of us are raised in a single culture; we have a tendency to view the world primarily from our own perspective. Ethnocentric tendencies are widespread and entail the belief that one's own race, religion, or ethnic group is somehow superior to others. In this way, having an ethnocentric orientation is an obstacle to cultural understanding.[3]

International business scholar Howard Perlmutter described ethnocentric views as "home-country orientation."[4] He argued that international managers should give up their ethnocentric orientations in favor of a polycentric or geocentric orientation. **Polycentric orientation** refers to a host-country mind-set in which the manager develops a strong affinity with the country in which she or he conducts business. **Geocentric orientation** refers to a global mind-set in which the manager is able to understand a business or market without regard to country boundaries. Geocentric tendencies are like a cognitive orientation that combines an openness to, and awareness of, diversity across cultures.[5] Managers with a geocentric orientation make a deliberate effort to develop skills for successful social behavior with members of other cultures.[6] They adopt new ways of thinking, learn to analyze cultures, and avoid the temptation to judge different behavior as inferior.[7]

We encounter unfamiliar cultures at home as well as in international dealings. Buyers visit from abroad to make deals, domestic firms source from suppliers located in distant countries, and employees increasingly have diverse cultural backgrounds. For example, Maurice Dancer is the head concierge at The Pierre, a luxury hotel in New York City. When the Indian firm Taj Hotels Resorts and Palaces (www.tajhotels.com) acquired the Pierre's management contract, Maurice had to adapt his management style to fit the new owners' corporate culture. He adapted to aspects of Indian culture, demonstrated in Taj's administrative style. Maurice also manages employees from Asia, Europe, and Latin America who bring cultural traits to their jobs typical of their home countries. For example, Asians may be reserved when dealing with customers. In the past, Maurice had to encourage Asian subordinates to be more outgoing. Finally, much of The Pierre's clientele is foreign-born. Without even leaving the United States, Maurice interacts with a wide variety of foreign cultures every day.

The cross-cultural integration of firms like The Pierre is yet another manifestation of globalization. Globalization is leading to convergence of cultural values as well. While people worldwide maintain traditional cultural values, common norms and expectations of behavior are gradually emerging, and many universal values apply to cross-cultural encounters.

Cross-cultural encounters are increasingly common. Maurice Dancer (far right), head concierge at The Pierre hotel in New York, interacts with a wide variety of international cultures every day, without even leaving the United States.

Characteristics of Culture

Anthropologists study culture perhaps more than any other scholars. Anthropologists view culture as people's shared experiences and the schemas they acquire on the basis of those experiences.[8] Gary Ferraro sees culture as all the things that people have, think, and do as members of their society.[9] Ann Jordan views culture as an integrated system of shared thoughts, actions, and material artifacts that characterize a group or society.[10] In a typical greeting scenario, for example, an executive holds the *thought* that he wants to meet a prospective client. Upon meeting, the executive performs the appropriate *action*, a handshake in some societies and a bow in others. The executive may then exchange business cards or gifts, which constitute *artifacts*. Anthropologists view culture as an umbrella concept, within which various *systems* are incorporated, such as economic, political, technological, and educational systems.

Geert Hofstede, a well-known Dutch organizational anthropologist, views culture as a "collective mental programming" of people.[11] The "software of the mind," or how we think and reason, differentiates us from other groups. Such intangible orientations shape our behavior. Another scholar, Harry Triandis, views culture as an interplay of sameness and differences; all cultures are simultaneously very similar and very different.[12] While as human beings we share many commonalities and universals, as groups of people or societies we exhibit many differences. For example, some cultures are more complex than others. Some are more individualistic, while others are more collectivist. Some impose many norms, rules, and constraints on social behavior, while others impose very few.

Culture captures how the members of the society live—for instance, how they feed, clothe, and shelter themselves. It also explains how they behave toward each other and with other groups. Finally, it defines their beliefs and values and the way they perceive the meaning of life.

What Culture Is *Not*

Now that you have an idea of what culture is, let's also define what it is not.

Culture is:

- **Not right or wrong.** Culture is relative; there is no cultural absolute. People of different nationalities simply perceive the world differently. Each culture has its own notions of acceptable and unacceptable behavior. In some Islamic cultures, for example, a wife cannot divorce her husband. In many countries, nudity is acceptable on TV. In Japan and Turkey, wearing shoes in the home is taboo.

- **Not about individual behavior.** Culture is about groups. It refers to a collective phenomenon of shared values and meanings. Thus, while culture defines the collective behavior of each society, individuals often behave differently. In most countries, for example, men wear their hair short. But a few mavericks have very long hair and stand out among their peers. In other countries, men may wear makeup. But such behavior does not represent the cultural values of the larger population.
- **Not inherited.** Culture is derived from the social environment. People are not born with a shared set of values and attitudes. Children gradually acquire specific ways of thinking and behaving as they are raised in a society. In the United States, for example, children usually acquire values of individualism and Christianity. But in China, children learn to depend on family members and acquire values based on Confucianism. Culture is passed from generation to generation by parents, teachers, mentors, peers, and leaders. Transnational media, such as movies and the Internet, play a large role in transmitting culture.

Socialization and Acculturation

Socialization
The process of learning the rules and behavioral patterns appropriate to one's given society.

This process of learning the rules and behavioral patterns appropriate to one's society is called **socialization**. Each society has rules—do's, don'ts, expectations, and preferences that guide behavior, particularly of children as they mature.[13] Such rules may be explicitly stated—for example, "we don't do things that way around here." Or they may be implicit, that is, everyone is expected to know how to function at work, at school, with friends, and so forth. Breaking a rule amounts to a failure to conform. As each of us matures, failing to follow society's rules provides opportunities for learning what the rules are. Socialization is cultural learning and provides the means to acquire cultural understandings and orientations shared by a particular society. It is a subtle process; we often adapt our behavior unconsciously and unwittingly.

Acculturation
The process of adjusting and adapting to a culture other than one's own.

Acculturation is the process of adjusting and adapting to a culture other than one's own. It is commonly experienced by people who live in other countries for extended periods, such as expatriate workers. In many ways, acculturation is challenging because adults are often less flexible than children.

The Many Dimensions of Culture

More than any other feature of human civilization, culture signals the differences among societies on the basis of language, habits, customs, and modes of thought. Yet most of us are not completely aware of how culture affects our behavior until we come into contact with people from other cultures.

Exhibit 4.3 illustrates the iceberg concept of culture using three layers of awareness: high culture, folk culture, and deep culture. Anthropologists use the iceberg metaphor to understand culture's many dimensions, some subtle and some not so subtle. Above the surface certain characteristics are visible, but below, unseen to the observer, is a massive base of assumptions, attitudes, and values that strongly influence decision making, relationships, conflict, and other dimensions of international business. While conditioned by our own cultural traits, we are usually unaware of the nine-tenths of our cultural makeup that exists below the surface. Often we are not aware of our own culture unless we encounter another one.

Lenses to Understand Culture

When they study culture, anthropologists distinguish between "emic" and "etic" perspectives. An "emic" analysis of culture describes behavior in terms meaningful to a person functioning within the culture. Scholars examine the culture from the perspective of those who dwell there, gaining their viewpoints and seeing the world as they do.[14] By contrast, an "etic" analysis is from the perspective of an outside observer. It aims to be scientific and "culturally neutral."[15] An etic observer compares the culture to others and explains it in unbiased, objective terms.

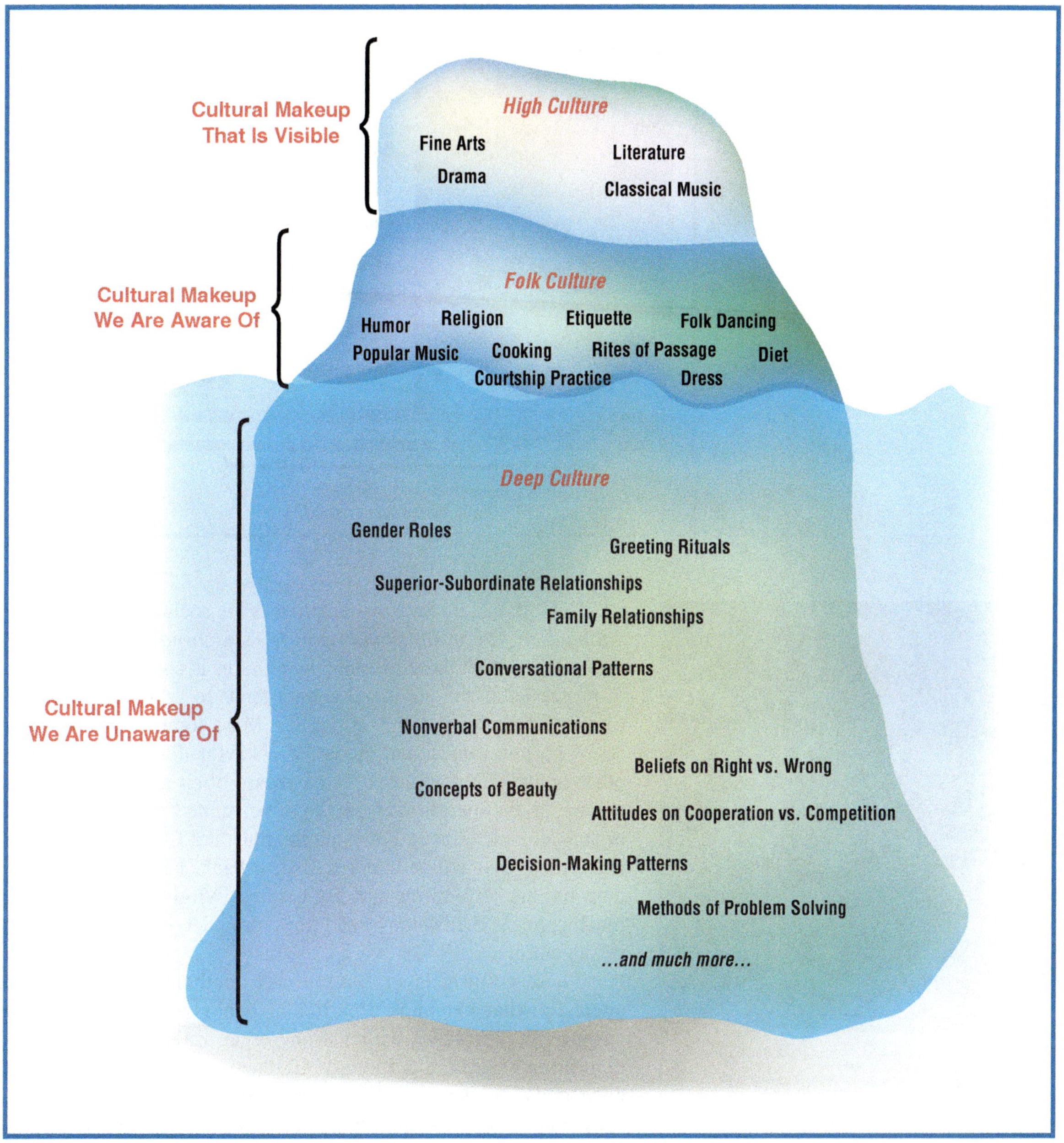

EXHIBIT 4.3
Culture as an Iceberg

Culture is linked with particular groups based on various factors, including:

- **Geography.** Unique cultural perspectives arise within distinct analytical levels—the world, the nation, the region, individual cities, and the neighborhoods where we live.
- **Ethnicity.** Nations consist of distinct ethnic groups. In England, for example, people of African, Indian, and Middle Eastern heritage tend to perceive reality in their own way.
- **Gender.** Men and women often experience the world differently.
- **Age.** Imagine how each of seniors, baby boomers, teenagers, and children perceive their communities and the world.
- **Language.** As we will see later in this chapter, language is a vital dimension that both reflects, and is reflected by, cultural differences.
- **Occupation.** Depending on your field, you may view matters uniquely, whether from the perspective of a blue-collar worker, a day laborer, a licensed professional, or an artist.[16]

EXHIBIT 4.4

National, Professional, and Corporate Culture

Source: Based on V. Terpstra and K. David, *Cultural Environment of International Business*, 3rd ed. (Cincinnati, OH: South-Western, 1991).

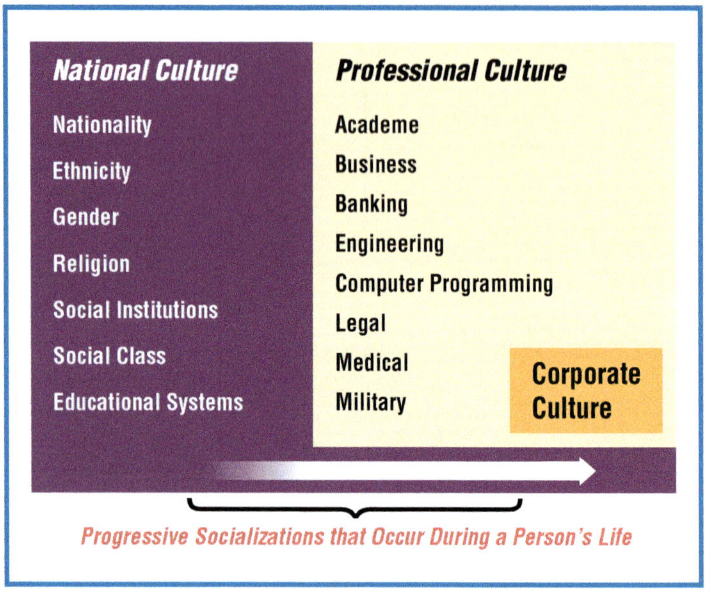

Source: © Daily Mail/Rex/Alamy

The edgy, risk-taking culture of companies under the Virgin brand owes much to the independent and flamboyant spirit of company founder Richard Branson and contrasts sharply with the conservative cultures of other British firms, despite sharing the same national culture.

Exhibit 4.4 suggests that employees are socialized into three cultures: *national culture, professional culture*, and *corporate culture.*[17] Working effectively within these overlapping cultures is challenging. The influence of professional and corporate culture tends to grow as people are socialized into a profession and workplace. Most companies have a distinctive set of norms, values, and modes of behavior that distinguish them from other organizations. Such differences are often as distinctive as national culture, so that two firms from the same country can have vastly different organizational cultures. For example, Standard Chartered (www.standardchartered.com), a time-honored British bank, has a conservative culture that may be slow to change. By contrast, Virgin (www.virgin.com), the much younger British music and travel provider, has an experimental, risk-taking culture.

These cultural layers present yet another challenge for the manager: To what extent is a particular behavior attributable to national culture? In companies with a strong organizational culture, it is hard to determine where the corporate influence begins and the national influence ends. In the French cosmetics firm L'Oreal (www.loreal.com), for example, the distinction between national and corporate cultures is not always clear. The French have much experience in the cosmetics and fashion industries, but L'Oreal is a global firm staffed by managers from around the world. Their influence has shaped L'Oreal into a unique organization distinctive within French culture. Thus, in international business, the tendency to attribute all differences to national culture is simplistic.

High- and Low-Context Cultures

Context, or "the information surrounding an event," strongly influences culture, especially communication behavior. Anthropologist Edward T. Hall made a distinction between cultures he characterized as "low context" and "high context."[18] **Low-context cultures** rely on elaborate verbal explanations, putting great emphasis on spoken words. As Exhibit 4.5 shows, the low-context countries tend to be in northern Europe and North America, which have long traditions of rhetoric, placing central importance on delivering verbal messages. The primary function of speech in such cultures is to express ideas and thoughts clearly, logically, and convincingly. Communication is direct and explicit, and meaning is

Low-context culture
A culture that relies on elaborate verbal explanations, putting much emphasis on spoken words.

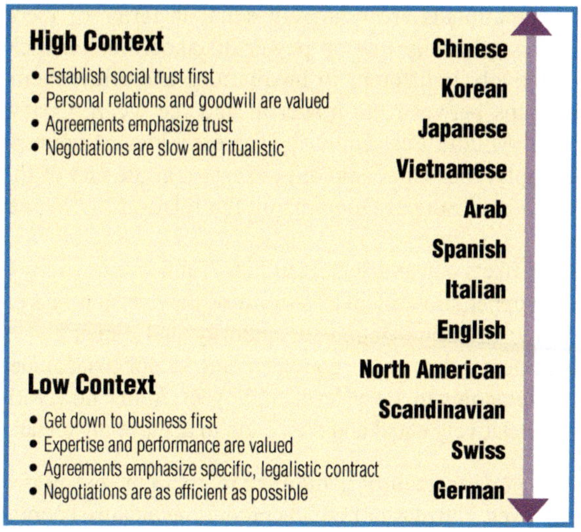

EXHIBIT 4.5

Hall's High- and Low-Context Typology of Cultures

Source: Based on *Beyond Culture* by Edward T. Hall, copyright © 1976, 1981 by Edward T. Hall. Used by permission of Doubleday, a division of Random House, Inc. For online information about other Random House, Inc. books and authors, see the Internet Web Site at http://www.randomhouse.com.

straightforward. For example, in negotiations Americans typically come to the point and do not beat around the bush. Low-context cultures tend to value expertise and performance and conduct negotiations as efficiently as possible. These cultures use specific, legalistic contracts to conclude agreements.

By contrast, **high-context cultures** such as Japan and China emphasize nonverbal messages and view communication as a means to promote smooth, harmonious relationships. They prefer an indirect and polite face-saving style that emphasizes a mutual sense of care and respect for others. They are on guard not to embarrass or offend others. This helps explain why Japanese people hesitate to say "no" when expressing disagreement. They are more likely to say "it is different," an ambiguous response. In East Asian cultures, showing impatience, frustration, irritation, or anger disrupts harmony and is considered rude and offensive. Asians tend to be soft-spoken, and people typically are sensitive to context and nonverbal cues (body language). At a business luncheon in Tokyo, for example, the boss is almost always the senior-looking individual seated farthest from the entrance to the room. This arises because reverence for superiors is the norm in Japan. To succeed in Asian cultures, it is critical to have a keen eye for nonverbal signs and body language. Negotiations tend to be slow and ritualistic, and agreement is founded on trust.

High-context culture
A culture that emphasizes nonverbal messages and views communication as a means to promote smooth, harmonious relationships.

Hofstede's Research on National Culture

Dutch anthropologist Geert Hofstede conducted one of the early empirical studies of national cultural traits. He collected data on the values and attitudes of 116,000 employees at IBM Corporation representing diverse nationality, age, and gender. Hofstede identified four independent dimensions of national culture, which we describe next.[19]

INDIVIDUALISM VERSUS COLLECTIVISM **Individualism versus collectivism** refers to whether a person functions primarily as an individual or as part of a group. In individualistic societies, ties among people are relatively loose, and each person tends to focus on his or her own self-interest. These societies prefer individualism over group conformity. Competition for resources is the norm, and those who compete best are rewarded financially. Australia, Canada, the United Kingdom, and the United States tend to be strongly individualistic societies. In collectivist societies, by contrast, ties among individuals are more important than individualism. Business is conducted in the context of a group in which others' views are strongly considered. The group is all-important, as life is fundamentally a cooperative experience. Conformity and compromise help maintain group harmony. China, Panama, and South Korea are examples of strongly collectivist societies.

Individualism versus collectivism
Describes whether a person functions primarily as an individual or as part of a group.

POWER DISTANCE **Power distance** describes how a society deals with the inequalities in power that exist among people. In societies with low power distance, the gaps between the powerful and weak are minimal. In Denmark and Sweden, for example, tax and social

Power distance
Describes how a society deals with the inequalities in power that exist among people.

welfare systems ensure nationals are relatively equal in terms of income and power. The United States also scores relatively low on power distance. Societies characterized by high power distance are relatively indifferent to inequalities and allow them to grow over time. There are substantial gaps between the powerful and the weak. Guatemala, Malaysia, the Philippines, and several Middle East countries are examples of countries that exhibit high power distance. The Apply Your Understanding exercise at the end of this chapter illustrates high power distance using an Ethical Dilemma on the relationship between an executive and a maid in Colombia.

Social stratification affects power distance. In Japan, almost everybody belongs to the middle class, while in India the upper stratum controls most of the decision making and buying power. In companies, the degree of centralization of authority and autocratic leadership determines power distance. In high power-distance firms, autocratic senior managements focuses power at the top and grants little autonomy to lower-level employees. In low power-distance firms, managers and subordinates are relatively equal and cooperate to achieve organizational goals.

Uncertainty avoidance The extent to which people can tolerate risk and uncertainty in their lives.

UNCERTAINTY AVOIDANCE **Uncertainty avoidance** refers to the extent people can tolerate risk and uncertainty in their lives. Citizens of high uncertainty-avoidance countries create institutions that minimize risk and ensure financial security. Companies emphasize stable careers and produce many rules to regulate worker actions and minimize ambiguity. Managers may be slow to make decisions as they investigate the nature and potential outcomes of several options. Belgium, France, and Japan are countries that score high on uncertainty avoidance.

Societies that score low on uncertainty avoidance socialize their members to accept and become accustomed to uncertainty. Managers are entrepreneurial and relatively comfortable taking risks, and they make decisions relatively quickly. People accept each day as it comes and take their jobs in stride because they are less concerned about ensuring their future. They tend to tolerate behavior and opinions different from their own because they do not feel threatened by them. India, Ireland, Jamaica, and the United States are leading examples of countries with low uncertainty avoidance.

Masculinity versus femininity Refers to a society's orientation based on traditional male and female values. Masculine cultures tend to value competitiveness, assertiveness, ambition, and the accumulation of wealth. Feminine cultures emphasize nurturing roles, interdependence among people, and taking care of less fortunate people.

MASCULINITY VERSUS FEMININITY **Masculinity versus femininity** refers to a society's orientation based on traditional male and female values. Masculine cultures tend to value competitiveness, assertiveness, ambition, and the accumulation of wealth. They are characterized by men and women who are assertive and focused on career and earning money, and may care little for others. Typical examples include Australia and Japan. The United States is a moderately masculine society. Hispanic cultures are relatively masculine and display a zest for action, daring, and competitiveness. In business, the masculinity dimension manifests as self-confidence, proactiveness, and leadership. Conversely, in feminine cultures, such as the Scandinavian countries, both men and women emphasize nurturing roles, interdependence among people, and caring for less fortunate people. Welfare systems are highly developed and education is subsidized.

Source: SVLuma/Shutterstock

Mexico emphasizes collectivism and loyalty to the group. Business is characterized by long-term, easy-going relationships. Substantial power distance is the norm in larger companies, where the dress code is typically conservative.

THE FIFTH DIMENSION: LONG-TERM VERSUS SHORT-TERM ORIENTATION Hofstede's four dimensions of cultural orientation are widely accepted. They provide a tool to interpret cultural differences and a foundation for classifying countries. Yet, the Hofstede framework suffers from some limitations. First, his study was based on data collected from 1968 to 1972. Much has changed since then, including successive phases of globalization, widespread exposure to transnational media, technological advances, and changes in the role of women in the workforce. The framework fails to account for convergence of cultural values that has occurred during the last several decades. Second, Hofstede's findings are based on the employees of a single firm—IBM—in a single industry, making it difficult to generalize. Third, the data were collected using questionnaires, which are inferior for probing deep cultural issues. Finally, Hofstede did not capture all potential dimensions of culture.

Later, Hofstede added a fifth dimension to his framework: **long-term versus short-term orientation.**[20] It refers to the degree to which people and organizations defer gratification to achieve long-term success. Firms and people in cultures with a long-term orientation tend to take the long view to planning and living. They focus on years and decades. The long-term dimension is best illustrated by the so-called Asian values—cultural orientations of several Asian societies, including China, Japan, and Singapore. These values are partly based on the teachings of the Chinese philosopher Confucius (K'ung-fu-tzu), who lived about 2,500 years ago. In addition to long-term orientation, Confucius advocated other values that are still the basis for much of Asian culture today. These include discipline, loyalty, hard work, regard for education, esteem for family, focus on group harmony, and control over one's desires. Scholars credit these values for the *East Asian miracle*, the remarkable economic growth and modernization of East Asian nations during the last several decades.[21] By contrast, the United States and most other Western countries emphasize a short-term orientation.

Long-term versus short-term orientation
Refers to the degree to which people and organizations defer gratification to achieve long-term success.

The Hofstede framework should be viewed as only a general guide, useful for a deeper understanding in cross-national interactions with business partners, customers, and value-chain members.

Cultural Metaphors

A metaphor is a figure of speech that uses the attributes of one thing to describe a different thing. Metaphors are useful because they provide models that help simplify explanations of complex phenomena, such as culture.[22] Martin Gannon offered a particularly insightful analysis of cultural orientations.[23] In his view, a **cultural metaphor** refers to a distinctive tradition or institution strongly associated with a particular society. It is a guide to deciphering people's attitudes, values, and behavior.

Cultural metaphor
A distinctive tradition or institution strongly associated with a particular society.

For example, American football is a cultural metaphor for traditions in the United States, such as being a team player and having a strong leader who moves an organization aggressively toward a desired goal. The Swedish *stuga* (cottage or summer home) is a cultural metaphor for Swedes' love of nature and desire for individualism through self-development. Other examples of cultural metaphors include the Japanese garden (tranquility), the Turkish coffeehouse (social interaction), the Israeli kibbutz (community), and the Spanish bullfight (ritual). The Brazilian concept of *jeito* or *jeitinho Brasileiro* refers to an ability to cope with the challenges of daily life through creative problem solving or manipulating the arduous bureaucracy of the country. In the Brazilian context, manipulation, smooth talking, and patronage are not necessarily viewed negatively, because individuals often use these methods to conduct business.

Country Realities

China is home to Mandarin Chinese, the language with the world's largest number of speakers. Although Hindi and English are widely spoken in India, the country is home to roughly 440 separate languages. Italy is home to the largest number of major languages in Europe, including Italian, Catalan, French, German, Greek, and English. In Latin America, Spanish and Portuguese are the most common languages. On the African continent, English and French are widely spoken.

Idioms

An **idiom** is an expression whose symbolic meaning is different from its literal meaning. It is a phrase you cannot understand by knowing only what the individual words in the phrase mean. For example, "to roll out the red carpet" is to extravagantly welcome a guest—no red carpet is actually used. The phrase is misunderstood when interpreted in a literal way. In Spanish, the idiom "*no está el horno para bolos*" literally means "the oven isn't ready for bread rolls." But the phrase is understood as "the time isn't right." In Japanese, the phrase *"uma ga au"* literally means "our horses meet," but the everyday meaning is "we get along with each other." Idioms exist in virtually every culture, and people often use them as a short way to express a larger concept. Managers can study national idioms to gain a better understanding of cultural values. Exhibit 4.6 offers several expressions that reveal cultural traits of different societies.

Idiom
An expression whose symbolic meaning is different from its literal meaning.

Subjective and Objective Dimensions of Culture

We saw in Exhibit 4.3 that there are numerous dimensions of national culture. We can group them into two broad dimensions: subjective and objective. The *subjective dimension* includes values and attitudes, deal versus relationship orientation, manners and customs, perceptions of

EXHIBIT 4.6 Idioms that Symbolize Cultural Values

Country	Expression	Underlying Value
Japan	"The nail that sticks out gets hammered down."	Group conformity
Australia and New Zealand	"The tall poppy gets cut down." (Criticism of a person who is perceived as presumptuous, attention-seeking, or without merit.)	Egalitarianism
Sweden and other Scandinavian countries	"*Janteloven*" or "Jante Law." "Don't think you're anyone special or that you're better than us."	Modesty
Korea	"A tiger dies leaving its leather, a man dies leaving his name."	Honor
Turkey	"Steel that works, does not rust."	Hard work
United States	"Necessity is the mother of invention."	Resourcefulness
Thailand	"If you follow older people, dogs won't bite you."	Wisdom

time, perceptions of space, and religion. The *objective dimension* includes symbolic, material, and creative productions, such as the tools, architecture, and infrastructure unique to a society. In this section, we examine key examples of each dimension.

Values and Attitudes

Values represent a person's judgments about what is good or bad, acceptable or unacceptable, important or unimportant, and normal or abnormal.[24] Our values guide the development of our attitudes and preferences. *Attitudes* are similar to opinions but are often unconsciously held and may not have a rational basis. *Prejudices* are rigidly held attitudes, usually unfavorable and usually aimed at particular groups of people.[25] For example, typical values in North America, northern Europe, and Japan include hard work, punctuality, and the acquisition of wealth. People from such countries may misjudge those from developing economies who may not embrace such values.

Deal versus Relationship Orientation

In deal-oriented cultures, managers focus on the task at hand and prefer getting down to business. At the extreme, such managers may even avoid small talk and other preliminaries. They prefer to seal agreements with a legalistic contract, and take an impersonal approach to settling disputes. Australia, northern Europe, and North America are deal-oriented cultures. By contrast, relationship-oriented cultures emphasize affiliations with people. Managers seek to build trust and rapport and get to know the other party in business interactions. For example, it took nine years for Volkswagen to negotiate the opening of a car factory in China, a strongly relationship-oriented society. For the Chinese, Japanese, and many in Latin America, relationships are often more important than the deal.[26] Trust is valued in business agreements.

Source: Erico Sugita/Reuters/Corbis

In Japan and South Korea, bowing is common in business and personal settings.

Example: Contrasting Mexico and the United States

Culture can differ sharply, even between neighboring countries. Exhibit 4.7 examines cultural differences between Mexico and the United States.

Manners and Customs

Manners and customs are ways of behaving and conducting oneself in public and business situations. Some countries are characterized by egalitarian, informal cultures,

EXHIBIT 4.7 Perceived Cultural Attributes of Mexico and the United States

Dimension	Mexico	United States
Role of context	High-context culture that values social trust, personal goodwill, and ritualized business	Low-context culture that emphasizes efficiency, explicit communications, and "getting down to business"
Individualism versus collectivism	Relatively group oriented. Extended families, teamwork, and group loyalty are valued.	Relatively individualistic. Emphasis on personal freedom and working alone. Group loyalty is less valued.
Time orientation	Fluid and polychronic. Long-term relationships are valued. Mexicans emphasize the past and believe they have little control over the future.	Rigid and monochronic. Business is short-term oriented and values profit above all else. Americans believe they can control the future.
Space perceptions	Conversational distance is close. Personal space is less valued.	Conversational distance is ample. Personal space is highly valued.
Religion	Christianity is very influential in daily life, and often in business.	Americans' religious orientation is diverse and declining.
Language	Spanish dominates, with little linguistic diversity.	While English dominates, there is much linguistic diversity.
Negotiations	Tend to progress slowly. Decisions take time. Legalism is avoided in agreements.	Emphasis on efficiency and quick decision making. Agreements are often legalistic.
Business relations	Relationship-oriented. Mexicans are easy-going, valuing personal bonds.	Deal-oriented. Business performance takes precedence over relationships.
Business meetings	Arriving late is acceptable. Meetings are informal and usually don't follow a strict agenda.	Americans are time-oriented, arriving promptly to meetings, which often follow a formal agenda.
Superior-subordinate relations	Firms are hierarchical, with much power distance. Senior managers are relatively authoritarian.	Lower power distance. Firms are "flatter," with less hierarchy. Relations with superiors are informal and easy-going.
Style of dress in business	Conservative, emphasizing dark suits. High-status personnel are expected to dress the part.	Business casual is widely accepted. "Dressing the part" is less important.

Sources: Based on Geert Hofstede, *Culture's Consequences* (Beverly Hills, CA: Sage, 1980); Boye De Mente, *The Mexican Mind* (Beverly Hills, CA: Phoenix Books, 2011); Lucila Ortiz, *A Primer for Spanish Language, Culture and Economics* (Bloomington, IN: Xlibris, 2011).

in which people are equal and work together cooperatively. In other countries, people are more formal, and status, hierarchy, power, and respect are important. Customs that vary most worldwide are those related to eating habits and mealtimes, work hours and holidays, drinking and toasting, appropriate behavior at social gatherings, gift giving, and the role of women. Handshaking varies across the world: limp handshakes, firm handshakes, elbow-grasping handshakes, and no handshake at all. In much of the world, people greet by kissing each other on both cheeks. In some countries it is appropriate to kiss the other's hand. In Southeast Asia, greeting involves placing the palms together in front of the chest, as in praying. In Japan, bowing is the norm.[27] Gift giving is a complex ritual in much of the world. It is ingrained in Japanese culture, where it is usually a blunder to not offer a gift in initial meetings. The Middle East is characterized by generous gift giving.

Perceptions of Time

In business, time dictates expectations about planning, scheduling, profit streams, and promptness, or what constitutes lateness in arriving for work and meetings. Japanese managers tend to prepare strategic plans for extended periods, such as a decade. The planning horizon for Western companies is much shorter, typically a few years. Some societies are more oriented to the past, others to the present, and still others to the future. People in past-oriented cultures believe plans should be evaluated in terms of their fit with established traditions, customs, and wisdom. Innovation and change are infrequent and are justified to the extent they fit with past experience. Europeans are relatively past-oriented, aiming to conserve traditions and historical precedents.

By contrast, young countries like Australia, Canada, and the United States are relatively focused on the present. They have a **monochronic** view of time—a rigid orientation in which the individual is focused on schedules, punctuality, and time as a resource. People in these cultures view time as *linear*, like a river flowing into the future, carrying workers from one activity to the

Monochronic
A rigid orientation to time, in which the individual is focused on schedules, punctuality, and time as a resource.

next. In such cultures, managers make commitments, set deadlines, and adhere to a strict schedule of meetings and activities. Punctuality is a virtue and time is money. Throughout the day, workers glance at their watches, their computer's clock, or the clock on the wall. Managers and investors are impatient and want quick returns. Company performance is measured quarterly. In this way, people in the United States have acquired a reputation for being hurried and impatient. Indeed, the word *business* was originally spelled *busyness*.

Polychronic
A flexible, nonlinear orientation to time, whereby the individual takes a long-term perspective and emphasizes human relationships.

Some cultures have a **polychronic** perspective on time. In such societies, instead of performing single tasks serially, people are inclined to do many things at once. In this way, members of polychronic cultures are easily distracted. They can change plans often and easily, and long delays are sometimes needed before taking action. Punctuality per se is relatively unimportant, and managers consider time commitments flexible. They do not adhere strictly to the clock and schedules. They put more value on relationships and spending time with people.

Chinese and Japanese firms are future-oriented, focusing not on how the firm will perform next quarter, but on how it will perform a decade from now. Large Japanese firms offer lifetime employment and invest heavily in employee training, expecting workers to remain with the firm for 30 or 40 years. Latin Americans similarly have a flexible perception of time and are more inclined to arrive late for appointments than people from other cultures. In the Middle East, strict Muslims view destiny as the will of God ("Inshallah" or "God willing" is a frequently used phrase) and downplay the importance of future planning. They perceive appointments as relatively vague future obligations.

Perceptions of Space

Cultures also differ in their perceptions of physical space; we have our own sense of personal space and feel uncomfortable if others violate it. Conversational distance is closer in Latin America than in northern Europe or the United States. When a North American national interacts with a Latin American, he or she may unconsciously back up to maintain personal space. Those who live in crowded Japan or Belgium have smaller personal space requirements than those who live in land-rich Russia or the United States. In Japan, it is common for employee workspaces to be crowded together in the same room, desks pushed against each other. One large office space might accommodate fifty employees. North American firms partition individual workspaces and provide private offices for more important employees. In Islamic countries, close proximity may be discouraged between a man and a woman who are not married.

Religion

Religion is a system of common beliefs or attitudes concerning a higher being or a system of thought that people consider to be sacred, divine, or the highest truth. Religion includes the moral codes, values, institutions, traditions, and rituals associated with this system. Religious conceptions of right and wrong have played a major role in the development of ethics and social responsibility. Almost every culture is underpinned by religious beliefs. Because religion influences culture, it also affects managerial and customer behavior in various ways. Exhibit 4.8 shows the dominant religions worldwide.

Although this exhibit displays the most common religion in each location, most countries are home to people of various beliefs. Religion appears to have a positive effect on economic activity.[28] Religious affiliations help create bonds of trust and shared commitment, which facilitate lending and trade. Religion can boost GDP in a country by reducing corruption, and by increasing respect for law and order. Conversely, a lack of ethical values tends to coincide with economic decay.

Christianity substantially affects culture and business. For example, Sunday is still regarded a day of rest when most people do not work. Scholars suggest a relationship between Protestantism and capitalism.[29] Protestantism emphasizes the necessity of hard work to achieve worldly success and as a duty that benefits both the individual and society. Protestantism has long emphasized religious freedom and independent thinking. Such views are consistent with the political and economic freedoms that encouraged the rise of capitalism, especially in Europe and North America.

Islam is based on the *Qur'an*, the religion's holy book. In most Middle East countries, Islam is the basis for government and legal systems. Islam strongly influences culture and society. Most Muslims adhere to Islamic law, known as *Sharia*, which covers aspects of daily life, economic activity, and public governance. Islam disapproves of economic activity that might harm others or that is not in the public interest. Islam encourages free trade by prohibiting restraints such as monopolies and price fixing. The *Qur'an* condemns charging interest for money loaned. Thus, banks in Islamic countries have devised methods for financing debt without violating Sharia law. Many multinational firms are reaching out to Muslim communities. Nokia launched a mobile phone that shows Muslims the direction toward Mecca, Islam's holiest site, when they pray. Heineken, the Dutch brewing giant, rolled out the nonalcoholic malt drink *Fayrouz* for the Islamic market. Experienced MNEs operating in Islamic countries respect Sharia law and avoid business activities that exploit people.[30]

Hinduism is the dominant indigenous religion of South Asia, especially India. Hindus believe in reincarnation, a cycle of birth, life, death, and rebirth. The nature of actions taken during one's lifetime, *karma*, determines future destiny. *Karma* implies that people are born into a social level, or *caste*, because of their good or bad deeds in earlier lives.[31] Such thinking can influence superior-subordinate relations in organizations. Some scholars view Hinduism's quest for spiritual enlightenment as potentially at odds with the profit orientation of business and entrepreneurship.[32] However, others argue that business management can be enhanced by embracing Hinduism's teachings in areas such as self-control, discipline, and devotion to duty.[33]

Ethical Connections

Ethical values vary by culture. Consider two scenarios given to students. In scenario one, a car salesman failed to inform his superiors about a serious engine problem of a car he had received as trade-in on a new car sale. In scenario two, a dealership neglected to fully repair a car transmission under warranty in the hope of securing lucrative repair work after the warranty expired. Students from China and Russia felt relatively little harm had been done in these scenarios, while students from Finland and South Korea judged the scenarios to be unethical.

Source: M. Ahmed, Y. Kung; J. Eichenseher, "Business Students' Perception of Ethics and Moral Judgment," *Journal of Business Ethics*, 43 (2003): 89–102.

Buddhism is both a religion and philosophy that encompasses various traditions and practices. It is common to Asia, especially China and Japan. Buddhism promotes harmony and peaceful relations with others. In this way, it supports harmony and stability in commercial relations. Buddhism also encourages tolerance for others and mutual cooperation, which are good for business. Followers are comfortable with acquiring wealth, as long as it is done with harmony and patience. Buddhism promotes a life centered on spiritual rather than worldly matters. Accordingly, it is seen to support ethical and responsible behavior in business. However, Buddhism's focus on spirituality and moderation can restrain entrepreneurial action.

Now that we have reviewed the subjective dimensions of culture, we turn to its objective dimensions—symbolic and material productions.

Symbolic Productions

A *symbol* can be letters, figures, colors, or other characters that communicate a meaning. For example, the cross is the main symbol of Christianity. The red star was the symbol of the former Soviet Union. National symbols include flags, anthems, seals, monuments, and historical myths. These symbols represent nations and national values and help to unite people. Mathematicians and scientists use symbols as types of language. Businesses have many types of symbols, in the form of trademarks, logos, and brands. Can you easily identify popular company logos such as Apple's apple, Cadbury's unique lettering, and the three diamonds of Mitsubishi?

Material Productions and Creative Expressions of Culture

Material productions are artifacts, objects, and technological systems that people construct to cope with their environments. They are integral to human life and provide the means to accomplish objectives, as well as to communicate and conduct exchanges within and between societies. The most important technology-based material productions are the infrastructures that supply energy, transportation, and communications. Others include social infrastructure (systems that provide housing, education, and health care), financial infrastructure (systems for managing means of exchange in

EXHIBIT 4.8
World Religions

Sources: Based on http://www.godweb.org/religionsofworld.htm and http://www.mapsofworld.com/religion-map.htm.

ARCTIC OCEAN
PACIFIC OCEAN
INDIAN OCEAN
SOUTH ATLANTIC OCEAN
RUSSIA
CHINA
INDIA
KAZAKHSTAN
MONGOLIA
JAPAN
AUSTRALIA
INDONESIA
IRAN
ALGERIA
LIBYA
EGYPT
SUDAN
SAUDI ARABIA
Christianity
Judaism
Hinduism
Islam
Buddhism
Nature religion
Chinese religion
Other groups

banks and other financial institutions), and marketing infrastructure (systems that support marketing-related activities, such as ad agencies).

Creative expressions of culture include arts, folklore, music, dance, theater, and high cuisine. Food is among the most interesting cultural markers. In Japan, pizza is often topped with fish and seaweed. In the United States, pizza can be piled high with meat. In France, it often comes with various cheeses. McDonald's aims for a standardized menu worldwide, but often must vary offerings to suit individual countries. In India, for example, McDonald's offers items such as "paneer salsa wrap," and various chicken and vegetarian burgers, to comply with Indians distaste for red meat, which is rooted in religious beliefs. McDonald's experienced much difficulty adapting its menu to the tastes of consumers in Bolivia.[34]

Language: A Key Dimension of Culture

Often described as the expression or mirror of culture, language is not only essential for communications, it also provides insights into culture. The world has nearly 7,000 active languages, including more than 2,000 each in Africa and Asia. But most of these languages have only a few thousand speakers.[35] Exhibit 4.9 highlights the world's major languages. Arabic comprises fifteen major and often highly distinct language variants across forty-six countries. In much of the world, English tends to dominate cross-national commerce. MNEs whose first language is English typically perform better in international business.[36] However, buyers always prefer appeals offered in their native tongue. Subordinates usually respond more eagerly when they receive instructions in their mother language. Linguistic proficiency is a great asset in international business because it facilitates cross-cultural communications and understanding. Learning one or more common languages can greatly enhance an international business career.

EXHIBIT 4.9

The Most Common Primary Languages in the World

Sources: Based on R. Gordon (ed.), *Ethnologue: Languages of the World*, 16th ed. (Dallas, TX: SIL International, 2009 at http://www.ethnologue.com), and CIA World Factbook, 2011, at http://www.cia.gov.

World Rank	Language	Approximate Number of Native Speakers (Millions)	Countries with Substantial Number of Native Speakers
1	Chinese	1,213	China, Singapore
2	Spanish	329	Argentina, Mexico, Spain
3	English	328	Australia, Canada, United States
4	Arabic	221	Algeria, Egypt, Saudi Arabia
5	Hindi	182	India
6	Bengali	181	Bangladesh, India
7	Portuguese	178	Brazil, Portugal
8	Russian	144	Russia, Kazakhstan, Ukraine
9	Japanese	122	Japan
10	German	90	Austria, Germany
11	Javanese	85	Indonesia, Malaysia
16	French	68	Canada, France, Mali
17	Korean	66	South Korea, North Korea
18	Tamil	66	India, Sri Lanka
19	Italian	62	Italy, Malta, San Marino
20	Turkish	51	Turkey, Turkmenistan

Company and Location	Intended Ad Slogan	Literal Translation
Parker Pen Company in Latin America	"Use Parker Pen, avoid embarrassment!"	"Use Parker Pen, avoid pregnancy!"
Pepsi in Germany	"Come Alive with Pepsi"	"Come out of the grave with Pepsi."
Pepsi in Taiwan	"Come Alive with Pepsi"	"Pepsi brings your ancestors back from the dead."
Fisher Body (car exteriors) in Belgium	"Body by Fisher"	"Corpse by Fisher"
Salem cigarettes in Japan	"Salem—Feeling Free"	"Smoking Salem makes your mind feel free and empty."

EXHIBIT 4.10

Blunders in International Advertising

Language has both verbal and nonverbal characteristics. Much language is unspoken and entails facial expressions and gestures.[37] In fact, most verbal messages are accompanied by nonverbal ones. In this and other ways, language is extremely subtle.

Sometimes it is difficult to find words to convey the same meaning in a different language. For example, a one-word equivalent to "aftertaste" does not exist in many languages. Even when a word can be translated well into other languages, its concept and meaning may not be universal. The Japanese word *muzukashii* can be variously translated as "difficult," "delicate," or "I don't want to discuss it," but in business negotiations it usually means "out of the question."

National languages, dialects, and translation have a tendency to complicate straightforward communication. Ignorance can be embarrassing. Advertising themes often lose their original meaning in translation or convey unfavorable interpretations. Even people from different countries who speak the same language may experience communication problems because of unique colloquial words. The same word can convey different meanings in the two countries. Exhibit 4.10 shows how the popular slogans of some languages translate into offensive phrases in other languages. Exhibit 4.11 shows how two English-speaking countries interpret the same word in very different ways. These exhibits demonstrate how easy it is for misinterpretations to get in the way of intended meaning.

Business jargon unique to a culture can also impede communication. For example, many expressions in United States English are based on sports or military terms and pose problems for non-U.S. businesspeople. Examples of English jargon that puzzle nonnative speakers include: "the bottom line," "to beat around the bush," "shooting from the hip," and "feather in your cap." Imagine the difficulty professional interpreters encounter in translating such phrases!

Word	Meaning in U.S. English	Meaning in British English
Scheme	A somewhat devious plan	A plan
Redundant	Repetitive	Fired or laid off
Sharp	Smart	Conniving, unethical
To table	To put as issue on hold	To take up an issue
To bomb	To fail miserably	To succeed grandly
Windscreen	A screen that protects against wind	Automobile windshield

EXHIBIT 4.11

Examples of Differences in Meaning between the United Kingdom and the United States

Cultural Change

We have seen that culture is relatively stable. However, the globalization of markets, transnational media, technological advances, and government regulations substantially influence culture, and culture is so powerful and pervasive that it influences these factors in turn. In this section, we explore the link between culture and factors that can transform it over time.

Technology, the Internet, and Culture

Technological advances are a key determinant of culture and cultural change. They have freed up leisure time and led to the proliferation of computers, multimedia, and communications systems that bring geographically separated cultures in closer contact than ever before. Communications, information, and transportation technologies have increased people's ability to learn about and connect with unfamiliar cultures. Just as distinctive societies developed in the distant past because regions had limited contact with each other, today cultures are homogenizing due to increased contact among peoples of the world.

The Internet and other technologies help promote foreign cultures. Artistic traditions from Africa, Asia, and Latin America have received a big boost from the rise of world cinema and television. We can also choose our information sources. People usually prefer information in their native language that represents familiar culture. Thus, Spanish speakers in the United States prefer Spanish mass media, limiting the culturally homogenizing effect of English-speaking media. Global communications allow widely dispersed ethnic groups to remain in touch with each other.[38] The number of Internet users is growing rapidly worldwide, and the potential for cultural blunders arising from international e-mail use is higher than ever. To help reduce such problems, managers can use software that instantly converts messages into any of dozens of languages.[39]

Globalization's Effect on Culture: Are Cultures Converging?

There is little consensus about globalization's effects on culture. On the one hand, critics charge that globalization harms local cultures and their artistic expressions and sensibilities, replacing them with a homogeneous, often "Americanized" culture. Others argue that increased global communications is positive because it permits the free flow of cultural ideas, beliefs, and values. Clearly, globalization is a major factor in the emergence of a common worldwide culture.

People in many parts of the world consume the same Big Macs and Coca-Colas, watch the same movies, listen to the same music, drive the same cars, and stay in the same hotels. Although food often represents a distinct culture, hamburgers, tacos, and pizza are increasingly popular worldwide.[40] Movies and TV shows promote the convergence of customs, fashions, and other manifestations of culture. Today, college students listen to much the same music and wear similar clothing worldwide. In Trinidad, the U.S. television series *The Young and the Restless* is so popular that in many places work effectively stops when it airs, and it has inspired calypso songs of the same name. *CSI Miami* and *Desperate Housewives* have ranked among the most popular TV series worldwide. The iconic Barbie doll has become a global phenomenon, even as the values it represents do not fit conservative cultures.[41]

In reality, however, the larger trend is more complex than these examples imply. As international business integrates the world's economies, it also increases the choices available to local people by making their countries culturally richer. Cultural homogeneity and heterogeneity are not mutually exclusive alternatives or substitutes; they may exist simultaneously. Cross-cultural exchange promotes innovation and creativity. Globalization brings a wider menu of choices to consumers and increases diversity within society.[42] Cultural flows originate in many places. Just as McDonald's hamburgers are popular in Japan, so is Vietnamese food in the United States and Japanese sushi in Europe. Integration and the spread of ideas and images tend to provoke reactions and resistance to cultural homogenization, thereby spurring individual peoples to insist on their differences. While some past customs will disappear due to globalization, the process is also liberating people culturally by undermining the ideological conformity of nationalism.

Context of International Business

Effective handling of the cross-cultural interface is a critical source of firms' competitive advantage. Managers not only need to develop empathy and tolerance toward cultural differences but also must acquire a sufficient degree of factual knowledge about the beliefs and values of foreign counterparts. Cross-cultural proficiency is paramount in many managerial tasks, including:

- Developing products and services
- Preparing advertising and promotional materials
- Preparing for international trade fairs and exhibitions
- Screening and selecting foreign distributors and other partners
- Communicating and interacting with foreign business partners
- Negotiating and structuring international business ventures
- Interacting with current and potential customers from abroad[43]

Let's consider specific examples of how cross-cultural differences may complicate company activities.[44]

Developing products and services Cultural differences necessitate adapting marketing activities to suit the specific needs of target markets. In China, Burger King (www.burgerking.com/bkglobal) had to introduce the concept of all-beef hamburgers to local consumers. The Chinese prefer chicken, so the firm also added several chicken dishes to its menu. In addition, KFC offers "pumpkin porridge" and "Beijing chicken rolls" to accommodate local tastes.

Organizational structure Some companies prefer to delegate authority to country managers, which results in a *decentralized* organizational structure. Other firms have *centralized* structures, in which power is concentrated at regional or corporate headquarters. Firms may be bureaucratic or entrepreneurial. How do you deal with a bureaucratic partner or manage distantly located, decentralized subsidiaries?

Teamwork Cooperating with partners and host-country nationals to achieve common organizational goals is critical to business success. But what should managers do if foreign and domestic nationals don't get along? The Chinese home appliance manufacturer Haier (www.haier.com) delayed acquiring overseas firms because management felt it lacked the ability to manage foreign nationals and integrate differing cultural systems.

Pay-for-performance system In some countries, merit is not the main basis for promoting employees. In China and Japan, a person's age is the most important determinant. But how do such workers perform when Western firms evaluate them using performance-based measures?

Lifetime employment In some Asian countries, firms are very protective of their employees who may work for the same company all their lives. The expectations that arise from such devoted relationships can complicate dealings with outside firms. Western managers may struggle to motivate employees who expect they will always have the same job.

Union–management relationships In Germany, union bosses hold the same status as top-level managers and are allowed to sit on corporate boards. Many European firms have a business culture in which workers are relatively equal to managers. This approach can reduce the flexibility of company operations because it makes it harder to lay off workers.

Attitudes toward ambiguity In some countries, people have a hard time tolerating *ambiguity*, which refers to situations in which information can be understood in more than one way. For example, some bosses give exact and detailed instructions, while others give vague and incomplete instructions. If you're not comfortable working with minimum guidance or taking independent action, then you may not fit well into some cultures.

Negotiations Negotiations arise in virtually all aspects of business, as when the firm takes on a partner or a supplier–buyer relationship. Goals, interests, ethics, and cultural assumptions vary cross-culturally, which may complicate forming and maintaining business relationships. In most of Northern Europe, negotiations are relatively efficient, impersonal, and unsociable; negotiators "get down to business" quickly.

Culture and the Services Sector

In the advanced economies, firms that engage in services such as lodging and retailing account for a greater share of FDI than firms that manufacture products.[45] Contact-based services such as architecture, consulting, and legal services bring providers into direct contact with foreign customers. Asset-based services include banks, restaurants, and retail stores.[46]

Cultural differences can create problems for service firms and lead to mishaps in the exchange process. The greater the cultural distance between the service provider and its customers, the more likely there will be cognitive and communication gaps. Imagine a Western lawyer who tries to establish a law office in China. Without a thorough knowledge of Chinese culture and language, the lawyer's efforts can be futile. Imagine how much success a Western restaurant chain would have in Russia if it knew nothing of Russian food culture or the work habits of Russian workers!

Differences in language and national character have the same effect as trade barriers. Service firms that internationalize through FDI are vulnerable because each firm is shaped by both a national and an organizational culture.[47] A Chinese bank that establishes a branch in New York or London remains distinctly Chinese because its business approach is based on Chinese culture.[48]

To overcome these challenges, service firms seek to understand the cultures and languages of the countries where they do business. For example, at the global express company FedEx, management constantly seeks to hire, train, and motivate hundreds of sales representatives who speak different languages, represent different cultures, and serve different markets.[49] Without such efforts, service firms would not likely succeed at international business.

The *Recent Grad in IB* feature highlights the cross-cultural experiences of Chinese-born Lawrence Yu, who lived, studied, and worked in the United States. Having an inquiring mind and being open to new experiences helped Lawrence bridge cultural gaps.

Overcoming Cross-Cultural Risk: Managerial Guidelines

Seasoned managers attest to the importance of a deep knowledge of culture and language in international business. Managers can achieve effective cross-cultural interaction by keeping an open mind, being inquisitive, and not rushing to conclusions about others' behaviors.

Even experienced managers undergo cultural training that emphasizes observational skills and human relations techniques. Skills are more important than pure information because skills can be transferred across countries, while information is often country-specific. Planning that combines informal mentoring from experienced managers and formal training through seminars, courses, and simulations abroad and at home can go far in helping managers meet cross-cultural challenges.

Although every culture is unique, certain basic guidelines are appropriate for consistent cross-cultural success. Let's review three guidelines managers can follow in preparing for successful cross-cultural encounters.

Source: Getty Images-Photodisc

Cross-cultural proficiency increases the effectiveness of meetings and other encounters in international business.

Guideline 1: *Acquire factual and interpretive knowledge about the other culture, and try to speak the language.* Successful managers acquire a base of knowledge about the values, attitudes, and lifestyles of the cultures with which they interact. Managers study the political and economic background of target countries—their history, current national affairs, and perceptions about other cultures. Such knowledge facilitates understanding the partner's mind-set, organization, and objectives. Decisions and events become substantially easier to interpret. Sincere interest in the target culture helps establish trust and respect, laying the foundation for open and productive relationships. Even modest

You Can Do It | RECENT GRAD IN IB

ZHIBO (LAWRENCE) YU

Lawrence's major: Supply-Chain Management
Objectives: Make a difference in the world. Exciting career in international business.
Jobs held since graduating:

- Global Supply Manager, Logistics Program Manager, Dell Inc., Austin, Texas
- Senior Manager, Lenovo, Beijing, China

Since opening to foreign investors, China's economy has grown rapidly. Lawrence Yu lived in China and witnessed amazing changes there as a teenager in the 1990s. He ate at McDonald's, wore Nike shoes, and watched NBA games. At 16, Lawrence came to the United States and eventually earned a bachelor's degree in supply-chain management.

While in college, Lawrence went on a study-abroad program in Mexico where he studied Spanish, lived with a Mexican family, and toured manufacturing firms. He got an internship at Whirlpool Corporation, where he created an asset-tracking system for the global procurement group and conducted market research in China. After Whirlpool, he completed another internship with Unilever North America.

After graduation, Lawrence worked at Dell Inc. as a master scheduler for notebook computers. He was primarily responsible for forecasting, planning, lead-time setting, and product transition management. One of Dell's key suppliers is located in Malaysia. Since Chinese was the first language of most of the Malaysian team members, Lawrence helped to increase communication quality and work efficiency. Management next sent Lawrence to Dell China to work with the procurement group in Shanghai.

After working as a master scheduler, Lawrence was recruited to Dell Global Logistics as a program manager, where his responsibilities included business reviews, financial analysis, contract negotiations, and process-improvement projects. With responsibility for overseeing eight U.S. logistics centers and a 100-truck fleet, Lawrence learned people-management skills and the ability to make decisions under pressure.

Lawrence was then promoted to Global Supply Manager, helping administer Dell's annual spending in semiconductor products. In this role, he negotiated prices with suppliers such as Samsung, Siemens, and Kingston. Most recently, Lawrence accepted a position as a senior manager at Lenovo headquarters in Beijing.

Lawrence's Advice for an International Business Career

"While it was risky, I'm glad I did it. Language barriers, cultural differences, and being apart from family were all difficult. Language can be improved over time, and culture can be learned while you live in that culture. I got used to living alone pretty fast. In addition to going to class, by living, studying, and working in another country, I was naturally learning every day. The knowledge you gain from being in another country cannot be learned any other way. I now have greater confidence in whatever I pursue than I ever had before, thanks to my international experience!"

attempts to speak the local language are welcome. Higher levels of language proficiency pave the way for acquiring competitive advantages. In the long run, managers who can converse in multiple languages are more likely to negotiate successfully and have positive business interactions.

***Guideline 2:** Avoid cultural bias.* Problems arise when managers make ethnocentric assumptions that foreigners think and behave just like the folks back home. Ethnocentric assumptions lead to poor business strategies in both planning and execution. Managers new to international business can find the behavior of a foreigner odd and perhaps improper. For example, it is easy to be offended when a foreign counterpart does not appreciate our food, history, entertainment, or everyday traditions. In this way, cultural bias can be a significant barrier to successful interpersonal communication.

A person's own culture conditions how he or she reacts to different values, behavior, or systems. Most people unconsciously assume those in other countries experience the world as they do. They view their own culture as the norm; everything else may seem strange. This

GLOBAL TREND

Minimizing Cross-Cultural Bias with Critical Incident Analysis

To compete effectively, companies must continually improve ways to communicate with and manage customers and partners around the world. Global teams with members from various cultural backgrounds enable firms to profit from knowledge amassed across the organization's worldwide operations. Such teams function best when the members engage in high-quality communications, minimizing miscommunications caused by differences in language and culture.

Nevertheless, inexperienced managers often misunderstand the behavior of foreign counterparts, which hinders the effectiveness of cross-cultural meetings. One way to minimize such problems is *critical incident analysis (CIA)*.

Consider the following scenario: Working on a joint product design, engineers from Ford (United States) and Mazda (Japan) interact intensively with each other. Ford wants to share its engineering studies and critical materials with its Japanese counterpart. After a week of interaction, the Ford team has grown uncomfortable because the Japanese appear strangely indifferent and do not exhibit much reaction. When the teams meet, the Japanese appear to keep conversation among themselves and offer little feedback. Eventually, the Ford team's surprise turns to frustration and anger. They now believe the Japanese are arrogant, indifferent about Ford's designs, and uninterested in collaboration.

In reality, the Ford team has jumped to conclusions and judged the Japanese with its own culturally bound expectations. An expert on Japanese business culture could have provided alternative explanations. For one, the Japanese engineers may not be proficient in English. They are unable to explain themselves easily or to understand the Ford team's briefings, which all occur in English. Japanese are generally thoughtful and typically show respect for counterparts by listening intently while remaining quiet. Furthermore, before their team meets in private and reaches consensus, Japanese usually refrain from speaking out. These and other explanations are all plausible in the context of Japanese culture.

What should you do when confronted with an awkward or uncomfortable situation in a cross-cultural interaction? CIA involves the following steps:

1. Identify the situations where you need to be culturally aware to interact effectively with people from another culture. These may include socializing, working in groups, negotiating, and reaching agreement.
2. When confronted with seemingly strange behavior, discipline yourself to avoid making hasty judgments. Instead, try to view the situation or the problem in terms of the unfamiliar culture. Make observations and gather objective information from native citizens or secondary sources. In this way, you can isolate the self-reference criterion that led to your possibly inaccurate conclusion.
3. Learn to make a variety of interpretations of others' behavior, to select the most likely one in the cultural context, and only then to formulate your own response. In this way, you can avoid the self-reference criterion and likely make a better decision.
4. Learn from this process and continuously improve.

Sources: Elizabeth K. Briody, Robert T. Trotter, and Tracy L. Meerwarth, *Transforming Culture: Creating and Sustaining a Better Manufacturing Organization* (New York: Palgrave Macmillan, 2010); Robert Keller, Christoph Senn, and Axel Thoma, "Worldly Wise: Attracting and Managing Customers Isn't the Same When Business Goes Global," *Wall Street Journal*, March 3, 2007, p. R5; "Cross-Functional Project Groups in Research and New Product Development," *Academy of Management Journal* 44, no. 3 (2001): 547–555; David Armstrong, "Building Teams Across Borders," *Executive Excellence* 17, no. 3 (2000): 10.

Self-reference criterion
The tendency to view other cultures through the lens of your own culture.

Critical incident analysis (CIA)
A method for analyzing awkward situations in cross-cultural encounters by developing objectivity and empathy for other points of view.

is known as the **self-reference criterion**—the tendency to view other cultures through the lens of your own culture. Understanding the self-reference criterion is a critical first step to avoiding cultural bias and ethnocentric reactions.

Critical incident analysis (CIA) is a method that managers use to analyze awkward situations in cross-cultural encounters. CIA encourages a more effective approach to cultural differences by helping managers develop objectivity and empathy for other points of view. The *Global Trend* feature details how managers can avoid the self-reference criterion by using CIA.

Guideline 3: Develop cross-cultural skills. Working effectively with counterparts from other cultures requires you to make an investment in your professional development. Each culture has its own ways of conducting business transactions, negotiations, and dispute resolution. You are exposed to high levels of *ambiguity* regarding concepts and relationships that can be understood in a variety of ways.[50] Success in international business requires you to strive for cross-cultural proficiency. It is can be obtained from various sources, including reading books, cross-cultural training, learning from expatriates, and befriending natives in one's own country. Direct experience with the culture is generally best. There is no substitute for direct experience with cross-cultural groups and situations.[51]

Ultimately, cross-cultural proficiency is characterized by four key personality traits:

1. **Tolerance for ambiguity:** The ability to tolerate uncertainty and apparent of clarity in the thinking and actions of others.
2. **Perceptiveness:** The ability to closely observe and appreciate hard-to-see information in the speech and behavior of others.
3. **Valuing personal relationships:** The ability to recognize the importance of interpersonal relationships, which is often much more important than achieving one-time goals or winning arguments.
4. **Flexibility and adaptability:** The ability to be creative in finding innovative solutions, to be open-minded about outcomes, and to show grace and kindness under pressure.

Managers with a geocentric view of the world are generally better at understanding and accommodating similarities and differences among cultures. Successful multinational firms seek to instill a geocentric cultural mind-set in their employees and use a geocentric staffing policy to hire the best people for each position, regardless of national origin. Over time, such firms develop a core group of managers who are comfortable in any cultural context.

One way for managers to determine the skills they need to approach cultural issues is to measure their cultural intelligence.[52] *Cultural intelligence (CQ)* is a person's ability to function effectively in situations characterized by cultural diversity. It focuses on specific capabilities important for high-quality personal relationships and effectiveness in culturally diverse settings and work groups.

CLOSING CASE Hollywood's Influence on Global Culture

The most commercially successful filmmaker of all time, Steven Spielberg, is synonymous with U.S. cinema. He has directed and produced international blockbusters like *Jurassic Park, War of the Worlds,* and the Indiana Jones movies. As U.S. dominance of the international film industry grows, Spielberg also has been the target of complaints about how Hollywood is changing world cultures. The values represented in his films are often viewed as part of the larger trend of the homogenization or, worse, Americanization of global values and beliefs.

Jurassic Park ignited a storm of protest. Film critics and cultural ministries around the globe found it to be a brainless film, lacking plot and succeeding wholly through special effects and big-budget bells and whistles. French officials labeled the film a threat to their national identity. Three leading filmmakers—Pedro Almodóvar, Bernardo Bertolucci, and Wim Wenders—wrote Spielberg to reprimand him for the poor quality of the film, calling him personally responsible for undermining their efforts to keep culturally rich European cinema afloat.

Another popular U.S. movie, *Lost in Translation*, came under fire from Los Angeles to Tokyo. Set in Japan's capital and starring Bill Murray, the film was nominated for four Academy Awards and won for best screenplay. It also won three Golden Globes. But it was criticized for its portrayal of Japanese people as robotic caricatures who mix up their Ls and Rs. The image-conscious Japanese were disappointed by their depiction as comic relief. In a scene where Bill Murray's character is taking a shower in what is meant to be a five-star hotel, he has to bend and contort to get his head under the shower head. In reality, there isn't a five-star hotel in Tokyo that hasn't accounted for the varying heights of its potential guests. Another scene, in which Murray is shown towering at least a foot above an elevator full of local businessmen, mocks the smaller physique of the Japanese. The film was seen to reinforce negative stereotypes about the Japanese.

Is the U.S. film industry overwhelming the cultures of the world? And if so, can the world really blame Hollywood? American studios produce two-thirds or more of the films viewed internationally. The European film industry is now about one-ninth the size it was in 1945. After aerospace, Hollywood is often the United States' largest net export. The copyright-based industries, which also include software, books, music, and TV, contributed more to the U.S. economy in the 2000s than any single manufacturing sector. While the United States imports few foreign films, Hollywood's output remains in high demand worldwide. Today, foreign films hold less than 1 percent of the U.S. market.

Distorting History and Religious Values

Under attack since their origin, Hollywood war films are widely accused of presenting biased accounts of history. War movies portray U.S. soldiers as patriotic heroes, protecting all that is good from all that is evil. *Apocalypse Now* painted an ethnocentric view of the Vietnam War, focusing on the U.S. tragedy while ignoring that of the Vietnamese.

Mel Gibson's controversial film *The Passion of the Christ* enraged religious groups and governments in various countries. The government of Malaysia found it inappropriate for its largely Muslim population and banned its initial release in the country. (Christians were later allowed to view it.) International organizations and individuals also attacked *The*

Passion of the Christ as anti-Semitic. Other nations with deep religious values were offended by *Brokeback Mountain*, which portrayed a homosexual relationship between two cowboys in the United States.

Crucial to U.S. dominance of world cinema is widespread acceptance of the cultural associations inherent in Hollywood films, an obstacle competitors must overcome. U.S. stars and Hollywood directors are well established in the international movie scene, and their drawing power transcends national boundaries. Hollywood's global success is partly based on the association of the American lifestyle, seen as attractive to many around the world.

Movies and Comparative Advantage

According to the theory of comparative advantage, countries should specialize in producing what they do best and import the rest. Economists argue this theory applies to films as much as to any industry. Movies are like any other commodity, they say, and the United States has advantages in producing entertainment and exporting it to the rest of the world. However, critics suggest such an assertion ignores the fact that movies influence national culture and social development. The motion picture industry is a venue for enhancing cultural identity. As a former Canadian Prime Minister noted, the culture inherent in movies is not a commodity; it is usually intrinsic to the nations that create them.

This view highlights why governments often engage in *cultural protectionism*—a systematic effort to prevent local film industries from being swamped by U.S. imports. This effort includes erecting legal and bureaucratic trade barriers to prevent the import of foreign films, especially from the United States. Governments may also subsidize domestic filmmakers to ensure the survival and growth of the home-country film industry. *Quotas* restrict the number of foreign films that can be imported or require that a minimum number of movies be produced domestically.

However, subsidies can weaken film industries by insulating them from competitive pressures and reducing their ability to create globally viable films. Quotas may prevent movie-goers from seeing the films they want to see. Cultural protectionism can result in the local production of films simply to fulfill government mandates. At one time France had its own booming film industry. But a complex system of quotas and subsidies has done little to slow its gradual demise. Meanwhile, the proportion of Hollywood revenues generated from abroad continues to grow.

A Cultural Dilemma

Despite plenty of arguments on both sides of this ongoing debate, many big-budget Hollywood movies these days are in fact multinational creations. The James Bond thriller *Quantum of Solace*, with its German-Swiss director and stars hailing from Ukraine, France, and the United Kingdom, was filmed in Austria, Chile, Italy, Panama, and the United Kingdom. Russell Crowe, Charlize Theron, Penelope Cruz, Nicole Kidman, and Daniel Craig are just a few of the many global stars not from the United States. Two of the seven major film companies collectively known as Hollywood aren't even U.S. firms. Hollywood is not as "American" as it once was.

In recent years, movies from various regions—Africa, Eastern Europe, Southeast Asia, and Latin America—are enjoying increasing popularity. This has resulted thanks to the Internet, more movie channels on TV, innovative distribution systems, and technologies that help expose audiences to a far greater range of films.

As the lines connecting Hollywood with the United States are increasingly blurred, protectionists should not abandon their quest to salvage the intellectual and artistic quality of films. In an interview with *The New York Times*, French director Eric Rohmer stated that his countrymen should fight back with high-quality movies, not protectionism.

AACSB: Reflective Thinking Skills

Case Questions

1. Most aspects of foreign culture, like language, religion, gender roles, and problem-solving strategies, are hard for the casual observer to understand. In what ways do Hollywood movies affect national culture outside the United States? What aspects of U.S. culture do Hollywood films promote around the world? Can you observe any positive effects of Hollywood movies on world cultures?
2. Culture plays a key role in business. In what ways have movies influenced managerial tasks, company activities, and other ways of doing business around the world? Can watching foreign films be an effective way of learning how to do business abroad? Justify your answer.
3. Hollywood movies are very popular abroad, but foreign films are little viewed in the United States. What factors determine the high demand for Hollywood films? Why are they so popular in Europe, Japan, Latin America, and elsewhere? Why are foreign films so little demanded in the United States? What can foreign filmmakers do to increase demand for their movies in the United States?
4. Worldwide, protectionism of most goods is declining. Do movies constitute a separate category, or should they be treated like any other good? Given the nature of movies, should a country shield and support its own film industry via protectionism? Are there better ways to maintain and enhance a home-grown film industry? Justify your answer.

Sources: K. Lee, "'The Little State Department': Hollywood and the MPAA's Influence." *Northwestern Journal of International Law & Business* 28, no. 2 (2008): 371–383; K. Day, "Totally Lost in Translation," *The Guardian*, January 24, 2004; J. Delacroix and J. Bornon, "Can Protectionism Ever Be Respectable?" *The Independent Review* 9, no. 3 (2005): 353–365; A. Marvasti and E. Canterbery, "Cultural and Other Barriers to Motion Picture Trade," *Economic Inquiry*, January 2005, pp. 39–55; A. Scott, "A Golden Age of Foreign Films, Mostly Unseen," *New York Times*, January 26, 2011, at www.nytimes.com; T. Teachout, "Cultural Protectionism," *Wall Street Journal*, July 10, 1998, p. W11.

Note: This case was written by Sonia Prusaitis, under the supervision of Dr. Gary Knight.

CHAPTER ESSENTIALS

MyManagementLab

Go to **www.mymanagementlab.com** to complete the problems marked with this icon ✪.

Key Terms

acculturation
critical incident analysis (CIA)
cross-cultural risk
cultural metaphor
culture
ethnocentric orientation
geocentric orientation
high-context culture
idiom
individualism versus collectivism
long-term versus short-term orientation
low-context culture
masculinity versus femininity
monochronic
polycentric orientation
polychronic
power distance
self-reference criterion
socialization
uncertainty avoidance

Summary

In this chapter, you learned about:

1. The nature of cross-cultural risk

In international business, we step into different cultural environments characterized by unfamiliar languages, distinctive motivations, and different values. **Culture** is the learned, shared, and enduring orientations of a society, expressed in values, ideas, attitudes, behaviors, and other meaningful symbols and artifacts. **Cross-cultural** risk arises from a situation or event in which a cultural misunderstanding puts some human value at stake. **Ethnocentric orientation** refers to using our own culture as the standard for judging other cultures. **Polycentric orientation** refers to a host country mind-set that gives the manager greater affinity with the country in which she or he conducts business. **Geocentric orientation** refers to a global mind-set with which the manager is able to understand a business or market without regard to country boundaries.

2. Characteristics of culture

National culture influences consumer behavior, managerial effectiveness, and the range of value-chain operations, such as product and service design, marketing, and sales. The influence of professional and corporate cultures grows as people are socialized into a profession and their workplace. Most corporations exhibit a distinctive set of norms, values, and beliefs that distinguish them from other organizations. Managers can misinterpret the extent to which a counterpart's behavior is attributable to national, professional, or corporate culture.

3. Lenses to understand culture

Low-context cultures rely on elaborated verbal explanations, putting much emphasis on spoken words. **High-context cultures** emphasize nonverbal communications and a more holistic approach to communication that promotes harmonious relationships. Hofstede's typology of cultural dimensions consists of **individualism versus collectivism**, **power distance**, **uncertainty avoidance**, **masculinity versus femininity**, and **long-term versus short-term orientation**. Culture can be interpreted through **cultural metaphors**, distinctive traditions or institutions that serve as a guide or map for deciphering attitudes, values, and behavior. An **idiom** is an expression whose symbolic meaning is different from its literal meaning.

4. Subjective and objective dimensions of culture

Values and attitudes are shared beliefs or norms that individuals have internalized. **Monochronic** cultures exhibit a rigid orientation to time in which the individual is focused on schedules, punctuality, and time as a resource. **Polychronic** cultures have a flexible, nonlinear orientation to time in which the individual takes a long-term perspective. Religion provides meaning and motivation that define people's ideals and values. Symbolic and material productions refer to the intangible and tangible meanings, institutions, and structures that cultures construct for themselves.

5. **Language: A key dimension of culture**

   There are nearly 7,000 active languages in the world, but most have only a few thousand speakers. The major languages include Mandarin Chinese, Hindi, English, Spanish, and Arabic. Language has both verbal and nonverbal characteristics and is conditioned by our environment. Sometimes it is hard to find words to convey the same meaning in two different languages.

6. **Cultural change**

   While culture is relatively stable, it is influenced by contemporary issues. In contact-based services, providers interact directly with foreign nationals in culture-laden transactions. Cultural differences may lead to mishaps in the exchange process. Technological advances are a key determinant of culture and cultural change. Improved transportation and communications technologies have removed the boundaries that once separated nations. Technology also promotes culture. The Internet emphasizes the role of language in communications. Globalization promotes common culture and the consumption of similar products and services worldwide.

7. **Context of international business**

   Culture matters in international business in areas such as developing products and services, interacting with foreign business partners, selecting foreign distributors, negotiating, dealing with customers, preparing for trade fairs, and preparing promotional materials. Cross-cultural differences complicate workplace issues such as teamwork, employment, pay-for-performance systems, organizational structures, union–management relationships, and attitudes toward ambiguity. Managers need to develop understanding and skills in dealing with other cultures.

8. **Overcoming cross-cultural risk: Managerial guidelines**

   Managerial guidelines include the need to acquire factual and interpretive knowledge about the other culture, and to try to speak the language. Managers should avoid cultural bias and engage in **critical incident analysis** to avoid the **self-reference criterion**. Critical incident analysis requires being culturally aware, not making value judgments, and selecting the most likely interpretation of foreign behaviors. Experienced managers develop cross-cultural skills, including tolerating ambiguity, developing perceptiveness, valuing personal relationships, and being flexible and adaptable. Cultural intelligence is the ability to function effectively in culturally diverse situations.

Test Your Comprehension

1. Describe culture and cross-cultural risk.
2. Distinguish between socialization and acculturation.
3. Distinguish the three layers of culture. What are the major elements of country-level and professional culture?
4. How does a manager with a deal orientation differ from a manager with a relationship orientation?
5. What are the two major perceptions of time, and how does each affect international business?
6. What are the five dimensions that make up Hofstede's model of culture?
7. Distinguish between cultural metaphors and idioms.

Apply Your Understanding AACSB: Communication Abilities, Reflective Thinking Skills, Ethical Understanding and Reasoning Abilities, Multicultural and Diversity Understanding

1. Suppose you get a job at Kismet Indemnity, a life insurance company. In its 45-year history, Kismet has never done any international business. Now its president, Randall Fraser, wants to expand abroad. You have noted in meetings that he seems to lack much awareness of the role of culture. Write a memo to him in which you explain why culture matters in international business. Be sure to speculate on the effects of various dimensions of culture on sales of life insurance.
2. People tend to see other cultures from their own point of view. They accept their own culture and its ways as the norm—everything else seems foreign, or even mysterious. This chapter described a technique called critical incident analysis (CIA) that encourages an objective reaction to cultural differences by helping managers develop empathy for other points of view. Using the CIA approach, define a situation that you or someone else has experienced that led to a cross-cultural misunderstanding—perhaps an interaction with a fellow student, a visit to a store in your town, or an experience you had while traveling abroad. Explain what actually happened and how a more culturally sensitive

response might have been possible if you or your fellow student had used CIA.

3. *Ethical Dilemma*: Suppose you work for a multinational firm and are posted to Bogota, Colombia. After renting a house in a posh neighborhood, you hire a full-time maid to perform household chores, a common practice among wealthy Colombians. A colleague at work tells you local maids are typically poor women who live in Bogota's slums and earn about $200 a month. As an executive, you feel guilty about paying such a cheap wage when you can afford much more. But for cultural and socioeconomic reasons, your colleague insists you cannot pay more than the going rate. Doing so might embarrass your maid and risk upsetting the economic balance in her community. Analyze this dilemma. Do you pay your maid the customary local rate or a higher wage? Justify your decision. Can you think of any creative solutions to this dilemma?

globalEDGE INTERNET EXERCISES

(http://www.globalEDGE.msu.edu)

AACSB: Reflective Thinking Skills

Refer to Chapter 1, page 58, for instructions on how to access and use globalEDGE™.

1. Ethnologue (www.ethnologue.com/web.asp) is a site that lists the world's known languages. It is an excellent resource for scholars and others with language interests and contains statistical summaries of the number of language speakers by language size, family, and country. Using Ethnologue, try the following:
   a. Visit the "Languages of China" site by clicking on the Country link, and then China. What is the population of China? Of the country's more than 200 languages, which has the largest number of speakers? Which has the second-most speakers? How do these figures compare to the total number of English speakers in the English-speaking countries of Australia, Canada, New Zealand, the United Kingdom, and the United States?
   b. Visit the "Languages of Spain" site. How many people live in Spain? How many native Spanish speakers are in Spain? How many languages altogether are spoken in Spain? If you decided to learn Spanish in Spain, what part of Spain would you stay in?
   c. Switzerland is one of the smallest European countries. What are the major languages of Switzerland, and how many speakers does each have?
   d. Find the table "Linguistic Diversity of Countries," which shows the population for each language as a proportion of the total population for most countries. What are the most linguistically diversified countries in the world? What are the least diversified countries?
2. Cultural intelligence is a person's ability to function effectively in situations characterized by cultural diversity. Various online resources feature cultural intelligence scales, which you can find by entering "cultural intelligence" using Google or some other search engine. What are the components of cultural intelligence? Answer the questions on the scale and calculate your score on cultural intelligence. Compare your score to those of your classmates.
3. Various Web sites list cultural blunders or *faux pas* (false steps) that people make in their international interactions. Neglecting to develop relationships (as in "Just sign the contract, I'm in a hurry!") and making too-casual use of first names (as in "Just call me Bill!") are examples of such blunders. Research online sources such as International Education Systems (www.marybosrock.com), or simply by entering "cultural blunders" in an Internet search engine, to identify examples of improper cultural behaviors. How can managers avoid these errors?

CHAPTER 2
Culture

OBJECTIVES

After studying this chapter, you should be able to

1. Understand methods for learning about cultural environments
2. Grasp the major causes of cultural difference and change
3. Discuss behavioral factors influencing countries' business practices
4. Recognize the complexities of cross-cultural information differences, especially communications
5. Analyze guidelines for cultural adjustment
6. Grasp the diverse ways that national cultures may evolve

© loiren - Fotolia.com

If you see men stroking their beards, stroke yours.

—Arab proverb

CASE Saudi Arabia's Dynamic Culture

Saudi Arabia (see Map 2.1), a land of contrasts and paradoxes, can be perplexing to foreign managers as they try to exercise acceptable personal and business behavior.[1] Its mixture of strict religious convictions, ancient social traditions, and governmental economic policies results in laws and customs that sometimes shift with little advance notice and vary by industry and region as dominant forces evolve. Many of these laws and customs contrast markedly with those in the home countries of the companies doing business there. Thus, foreign companies and the employees they send there must determine what these differences are and how to adjust to them. A brief discussion of the roots of Saudi traditions and a sample of both cultural norms and foreign operating adjustments should help you understand the importance of culture in international business.

A LITTLE HISTORY AND BACKGROUND

Although the land encompassing the Kingdom of Saudi Arabia has a long history, until recently most inhabitants' loyalty was primarily tribal rather than national. In most times past, invaders controlled a divided land. Nevertheless, the inhabitants have shared a common language (Arabic) and religion (Islam). In fact, Saudi Arabia is the birthplace of Islam and the location of its two holiest cities, Mecca and Medina. (The opening photo shows the Grand Mosque at Mecca.) Beginning in 1745, the Wahabi movement swept across and united most of the peninsula by calling for the purification of Islam through a literal view of the Koran. King Ibn Saud (1882–1953), a descendant of Wahabi leaders, took power in 1901, merged independent areas, created an entity that was both political and religious, and legitimized his monarchy and succession by being the defender of Islamic holy areas, beliefs, and values.

The growing importance of oil for Saudi Arabia, particularly since the 1970s, has led to rapid urbanization and given the government the means to offer social services such as free education. These changes have furthered its citizens' sense of a national identity, while diminishing their traditional ways of living. Since 1950, the rural population has decreased from more than 80 percent (about half nomadic) to less than 20 percent. Cities have also modernized physically. However, below the physical surface, Saudis hold attitudes and values that are neither like the norm elsewhere nor easily discerned.

Modernization has been controversial within Saudi Arabia. The liberal group, supported by an elite segment that has traveled abroad, wants such trappings from economic growth as greater choices in products and lifestyles. At the same time, the conservative group is supported by religious leaders and people who fear that modernization will upset traditional values and adherence to strict Koranic teachings. The government (the Royal Family) must balance these viewpoints while taking care not to overstep the acceptable boundaries of conservatism lest it become vulnerable to being replaced. For instance, it is well aware that Iran's Islamic Revolution was spearheaded in part by dissenters who viewed the Shah's modernization movements as corrupt and too secular. In 1979, a group largely marginalized by modernization seized the Grand Mosque of Mecca, which brought questions about the Royal Family's ability to protect Islam's holiest site. Meanwhile, liberals have been largely pacified by taking well-paid government jobs and slowly gaining the transformation they wish. The government has sometimes made tradeoffs to appease conflicting groups, such as requiring women to wear longer robes (women must wear *abayas* and men customarily wear *thobes*) in exchange for advancing women's education.

THE RELIGIOUS FACTOR

If your country maintains more or less strict separation between religion and the state, you will probably find the pervasiveness of religious culture in Saudi Arabia daunting. Religious proscriptions prohibit the sale or use of pork products and alcohol. During the holy period of Ramadan, when people fast during the day, restaurants serve customers only in the evening. Because Muslim men are called to prayer five times a day, restaurants such as McDonald's dim their lights and close their doors during those periods. Many companies convert revenue-generating space to prayer areas; Saudi Arabian Airlines does this in the rear of its planes, the British retailer Harvey Nichols in its department store.

However, there are regional differences. In the capital, Riyadh, women traditionally wear *niqabs* that cover their faces. But in the port city of Jeddah, which has more contact with foreigners and is less conservative, dress codes are more relaxed and fewer women wear them. Nevertheless, merchants routinely remove mannequins' heads and hands and keep them properly clad to prevent public objections. Starbucks franchises even altered the company logo and Coty Beauty its point-of-purchase exhibits in order not to display women's faces.

Rules of behavior may also be hard to comprehend because of the ways in which religious and legal rules have

MAP 2.1 Saudi Arabia and the Arabian Peninsula

The kingdom of Saudi Arabia comprises most of the Arabian Peninsula in Southwest Asia. The capital is Riyadh. Mecca and Medina are Islam's holiest cities. Jeddah is the most important port. All of the country's adjacent neighbors are also Arabic—that is, the people speak Arabic as a first language. All the nations on the peninsula are predominantly Islamic.

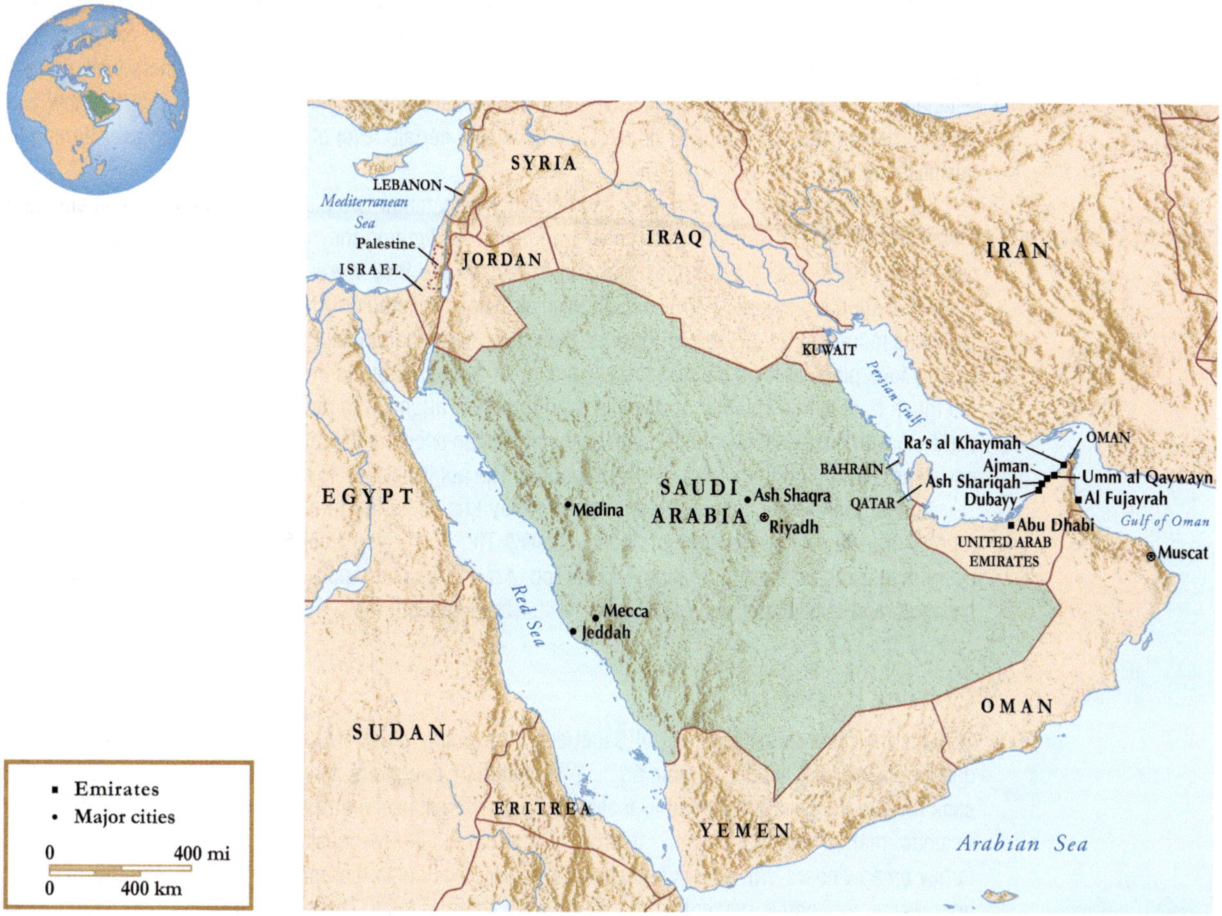

been adapted to contemporary situations. Islamic law, for instance, forbids charging interest and selling accident insurance (strict doctrine holds there are no accidents, only preordained acts of God). In the case of mortgages, the Saudi government gets around this proscription by offering interest-free loans. The government has simply eliminated the prohibition against accident insurance because Saudi businesses, like businesses elsewhere, need the coverage.

Nor are expected behaviors necessarily the same for locals and foreigners. Non-Muslim foreign women are not required to wear head scarves, although religious patrols may admonish them for not doing so. Saudi Arabian Airlines does not hire Saudi women as flight attendants (being in direct contact with men might tempt promiscuous behavior), but it hires women from other Arab nations. In addition, some compounds are inhabited largely by Americans and Europeans, who work in specialized positions and for foreign companies. To attract these needed specialists and investors, Saudi Arabia allows compound residents to dress and behave within the compounds much the way they do back home (alcohol, pornography, and drugs are still prohibited). However, in an example of a reverse dress code, some compounds prohibit residents and their visitors from wearing *abayas* and *thobes* in public areas.

TRADITIONAL FACTORS

Some Saudi Arabian traditions are probably the outgrowth of a tribal and nomadic past. For instance, the oft-quoted saying "Me against my brother, my brothers and me against my cousins, then my cousins and me against strangers" illustrates a family-centered society where trust of others is highly correlated with the degree of familiarity with them.

Given the trust factor, most Saudi businesses have historically been family owned and operated, preferring to hire family members or people they know well even though others might be better qualified. However, these companies have seen the need to partner with foreign firms to gain expertise. The process of partnering is usually lengthy because Saudis take time to know the foreigners well and are reluctant to make full financial disclosures outside the family. They generally prefer to get to know you well, perhaps invite you into their homes, and develop a certain level of friendship before ever turning to business details.

Not understanding this norm, a British publisher dispatched two salesmen to Saudi Arabia and paid them on commission. The salesmen moved aggressively, figuring they could make the same number of calls—and sales—per day as they made in Britain, where they were used to punctual schedules, the undivided attention of potential clients, and conversations devoted only to business transactions. To them, time was money. In Saudi Arabia, however, they soon found that appointments seldom began on time and usually took place at local cafés over casual cups of coffee. As far as they were concerned, Saudis spent too much time in idle chitchat and would even turn their attention to personal acquaintances rather than continue with business. Eventually, both salesmen began showing their irritation, and their Saudi counterparts came to regard them as rude and impatient. The publisher had to recall them.

Saudis' preference for dealing with people they know has led to a system known as *wasta*, which roughly translates into English as "connections." Thus, who you know helps a great deal in almost everything, such as moving a résumé to the top of a pile, gaining approval of a zoning request, getting a passport, and obtaining a visa to bring in a visitor from headquarters.

Gender Roles

Perhaps the most baffling aspect of Saudi culture to many outsiders is the expected role of people by gender. Based largely on a Koranic prescription whereby daughters receive only half the inheritance that sons receive, females are placed in a separate and often subservient position. Their role has been to be virtuous, marry young, and have offspring, while males take responsibility as their protectors and the family breadwinners. Not only is female virtue required, but also the appearance of it. Because of family importance, a negative perception of one member reflects on all. These beliefs have led to a number of proscriptions for women, such as no traveling abroad without permission of a male relative and no studying abroad without a male relative escort. Basically, non-kin males and females may interact personally only in "open areas," or in "closed areas" when the females are accompanied by a male relative. However, applying this restriction may seem a bit confusing to outsiders. For instance, restaurants are considered closed areas, and proprietors must maintain separate dining rooms and entrances for men without female companions. However, the food malls at most shopping centers are considered open areas where members of both sexes intermingle.

Nevertheless, several happenings since 2011 foretell possibly fewer future differences in gender requirements: women received future rights to vote and hold political offices, there was little intimidation when a group of women drove autos to protest their prohibition against driving, a Saudi prince spoke out in favor of women's driving as a means of limiting the number of foreign workers, a two-member women's team participated in the Olympics for the first time (but critics labeled them prostitutes for doing so), and prohibitions were lifted on female physical education classes in schools.

A 2008 royal decree lifted a ban on mixing men and women in the workplace, but the situation is complex. Male and female employees within the public sector work in separate buildings. When they must meet together, they do so within meeting rooms in the Governor's office, where they must use separate entrances. Men and women may work together within the private sector, but there are other limitations.

Although there are now more female than male university graduates in Saudi Arabia, only about 15 percent of the workforce is female. Why? The answer is partly cultural. Some women prefer traditional family roles. Some find driving restrictions to be too much of a hassle. And some families prohibit female members from working because of family honor ("What will people think?"). Economic factors blend with cultural ones as well, such as companies incurring the cost of providing separate entrances and toilet facilities. However, the genders do interact at work, especially in multinational companies. For example, Unilever's female brand managers, as long they adhere to dress codes, interact with male colleagues and meet with men from other companies. However, they are limited in traveling abroad on company business because they need permission from their male relatives. Some multinationals ease this problem by paying the travel costs for a male relative to accompany a woman abroad.

At one time, visas for single women to enter Saudi Arabia were nearly unobtainable. However, the Saudi Arabian General Investment Authority (SAGIA) has successfully attracted investments by MNEs that need visas to send female executives there for short- and long-term assignments. While these visas are not given automatically, they can be obtained—more easily for women over 40, but also possibly for younger women, especially with the use of *wasta.* The U.S. consulting company Monitor Group brought in American women in their twenties, and L'Oreal has sent its female human resources manager there.

Restrictions on gender interactions also lead to other adjustments. For instance, four young Saudis who had lived and studied abroad wanted to test the market potential for opening an upscale restaurant—the Java Lounge—in Jeddah. Ordinarily, it can be difficult to conduct such research in Saudi Arabia because limitations on male-female interactions restrain family-focused interviews. In this case, however, consultants interviewed apparently affluent families by approaching them in restaurants after noting how they comported themselves, whether they wore custom-made versus off-the-rack robes, what quality of wristwatches showed beneath long sleeves, and how well the men kept their beards—all indicators that researchers from outside the society would probably overlook.

At upscale U.S.- and U.K.-based department stores like Saks Fifth Avenue and Harvey Nichols, mixed shopping is allowed only on the lower floors. There, all salespeople are men (even those specializing in such products as cosmetics and lingerie), and there are no changing rooms or places to try cosmetics. Meanwhile, the upper floors are for women only, and female shoppers can check their *abayas* and shop in jeans or whatever they choose. (Meanwhile, the men who drove the women there can relax in a space the stores have set aside for them.) One problem: Because male managers can visit these upper floors only when a store is closed, they are limited in their ability to observe operations.

CULTURAL DYNAMICS

Almost all aspects of culture evolve, and Saudi Arabia is no exception. Take the case of women in the workplace. In terms of preparation, the first public school for girls did not open until 1960, and the government had to provide troops in one city because of protests that the schooling would negatively affect girls' religious and social values. Since then, the country has seen a gradual increase in years of study and curriculum offered for females. Economic need has spurred both changes in education and the use of education within the workforce. At the same time, critics have had to be persuaded that changes are compatible with women's roles. One of the first acceptances of working women (alongside men) was in the medical field because of the shortage of doctors, the high cost of separate male and female specialists, and the compatibility of healing with women's role as nurturers.

In addition, Saudi opinion and policy has been to reduce the heavy dependence on and cost of foreign workers. Thus, the government pays for foreign university education of its citizens while recognizing the disregard of much female talent.

The Saudi business world has seen much change. Consider that women own about 20 percent of all Saudi businesses, or that a woman is CEO of one of the country's largest concerns, the Olayan Financing Company. Three things will likely boost Saudi female workforce participation: (1) an increase in inward foreign investment, (2) more women studying abroad, and (3) women's psychological drive to prove themselves. Bear in mind, however, that changes tend to be uneven, particularly among geographic areas of the country and people of certain income and educational levels. ■

CRN
Case Review Note

QUESTIONS

2-1. Assume you are a manager in a multinational company that needs to send a team of three to five people to Saudi Arabia for about two weeks to investigate the feasibility of selling your products there. What advice should you give them to help assure that cultural problems do not impede their success in this task?

2-2. Assume your company is from North America or Europe and considering the establishment of an office in Saudi Arabia. What additional operating costs might it have to assume because of the Saudi culture?

INTRODUCTION

CONCEPT CHECK

In Chapter 1, we explained that behavioral factors, values, attitudes, and beliefs can be studied as keys both to cultural conditions and to ways of developing suitable business practices.

Our opening case illustrates companies' need to understand and be sensitive to ever-changing operating environments. Figure 2.1 shows how **culture**—learned norms based on the values, attitudes, and beliefs of a group of people—is an integral part of a nation's operating environment. Culture is sometimes an elusive topic to study. Why? Because people belong to different groups based on nationality, ethnicity, religion, gender, work organization, profession, age, political party membership, and income level, and each group comprises a culture. In this chapter, we emphasize *national cultures,* but also discuss how major cultural memberships differ among countries.

CONCEPT CHECK

Keep in mind our definition of *international business* in Chapter 1, where we stress that it involves "all commercial transactions"—sales, investments, transportation, and so forth—involving more than one country.

THE PEOPLE FACTOR

Business involves *people.* Every business employs, sells to, buys from, and is owned and regulated by people. International business, of course, involves people from different national cultures, which affects every business function—managing a workforce, marketing and transporting output, purchasing supplies, dealing with regulators, securing funds.

Cultural diversity can be a competitive advantage, but managing it can be difficult.

Cultural Diversity Chapter 1 explained how international business creates values and helps firms gain competitive advantages for themselves, such as acquiring knowledge-based resources abroad. But a company may also gain by nurturing the cultural diversity that international operations foster. As different nationalities come together through projects and teams, their diverse backgrounds, perspectives, and experiences often enable businesses to gain a deeper knowledge of products and services and how to create and deliver them. To keep team members from feeling threatened when expressing divergent viewpoints,

FIGURE 2.1 Cultural Factors Affecting International Business Operations

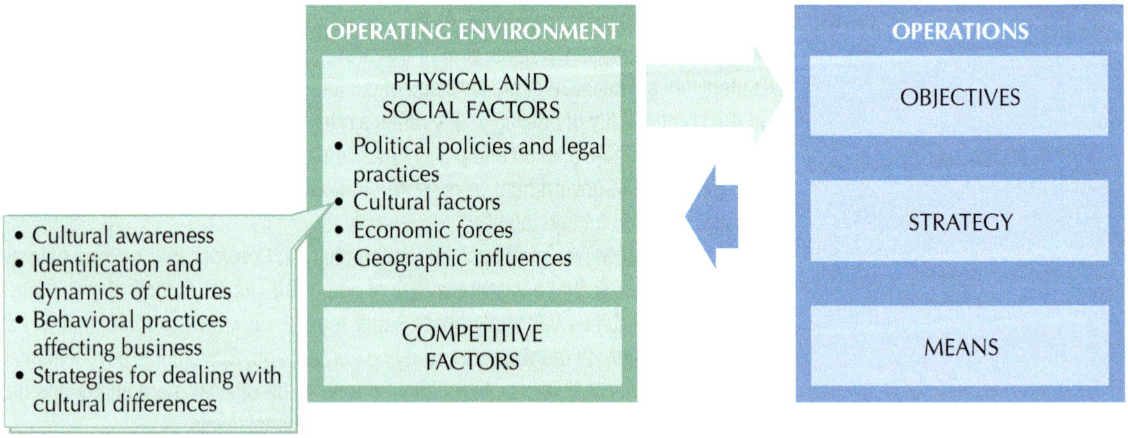

especially those from a minority nationality, leaders must strive to develop an open and non-threatening atmosphere.[2]

Successfully cultivating such diversity is difficult because individuals may interact with others as they do within their own cultures. A study of nationally diverse company teams found that some nationalities competed with other team members while others cooperated, some awaited precise directions while others took self-initiative, and some expected to divide tasks while others sought a team solution to each task. Another study found that language differences inhibited a common understanding of team roles, priorities, and sentiments.[3] The more successful teams worked to understand each other's cultures before dealing with the tasks at hand.[4] Yet a third study found that an expectation of high diversity among the teams led members to prepare more to deal with differences and keep open minds.[5]

Cultural Collision When divergent cultures come in contact, **cultural collision** occurs. In international business, the major problems of *cultural collision* arise under two conditions:

- When a company implements practices that are less effective than intended
- When a company's employees encounter distress because of difficulty in accepting or adjusting to foreign behaviors

Sensitivity and Adjustment A firm doing business in another country must determine which of that nation's business practices differ from its own and then decide what adjustments, if any, are needed to operate efficiently. This chapter first examines *cultural awareness,* especially the need for building it, and discusses the causes of cultural differences, rigidities, and changes. Next, it describes the major behavioral factors that affect the conduct of international business. Finally, it takes a look at the reasons why some businesses—and some individuals—do or don't adjust to other cultures.

CULTURAL AWARENESS

Almost everyone agrees that national cultures differ, but they disagree on what the differences are.

Most cultural variables—daily routines and rules, codes of social relations, language, emotive expression, concepts of luck—are universal. The forms of these variables, however, differ among cultures, and not everyone responds to them in the same way. Every national culture, for instance, features dancing, but types of and participation in dancing vary among and even within cultures.[6]

Problem areas that can hinder managers' cultural awareness are

- Subconscious reactions to circumstances.
- The assumption that all societal subgroups are similar.

No foolproof method exists for building cultural awareness.[7] Travelers remark on cultural differences, experts write about them, and international businesspeople note how they affect operations. Even so, people disagree on what they are, whether they're widespread or limited, and whether they're deep-seated or superficial. Nor is it easy to isolate culture from such factors as economic and political conditions. A survey measuring people's entrepreneurial attitudes, for example, could be influenced not only by respondents' risk-taking values but also by their economic conditions.[8] China's changing preference for male versus female offspring offers an example of cultural and economic interaction. Under the country's one-child policy, millions of families aborted female fetuses and put girls up for adoption. Why? Because males could carry on a family name (cultural), help work fields in rural areas (economic), and care for parents in old age (cultural and economic). Recently, however, China has seen a shift toward preference for female offspring. Why? Urbanization requires fewer male workers on farms (economic), while rising property values (economic) have taken a toll on families' tradition (cultural) of buying living quarters for sons before they can marry.[9]

CRN
Case Review Note

Some cultural differences, such as acceptable attire, are fairly obvious; others aren't. And people in every culture often react to given situations by expecting the same responses they would likely get in their own. In our opening case, PRI's British sales reps expected their potential Saudi customers to be punctual and give them their undivided attention; in fact, the reps' compensation system discouraged them from spending much time on each business transaction. Their response was typical of countries with a **deal-focus (DF) culture,** where people are primarily task-oriented. The Saudis, meanwhile, had less compulsion to wrap things up; they regarded time spent in small talk at a café as a means to identify good business partners. They also put dealings with friends ahead of business dealings, a situation typical in a **relationship-focus (RF) culture**.[10] DF people may view RF people as time-wasters, whereas RF people may view DF people as offensively blunt.

A LITTLE LEARNING GOES A LONG WAY

CONCEPT CHECK

We stress in Chapter 1 that understanding cultural values, attitudes, and beliefs is often crucial in deciding when and how to alter operations in foreign countries.

Some people seem to have an innate ability to say and do the right thing at the right time, while others offend unintentionally or seem ignorant. Experts note, however, that businesspeople can improve their awareness and sensitivity and, by educating themselves, enhance the likelihood of succeeding abroad. Gathering research on another culture can be instructive. However, managers must assess information to determine if it perpetuates unwarranted stereotypes, covers only limited aspects of a country and its culture, or is obsolete. They should also observe the behavior of those people who have garnered the kind of respect and confidence they themselves will need.

Of course, cultural variations are too numerous to memorize completely. Just consider the many different ways to address people. Should you use a given name or a surname? Does a surname come before or after a given name? Do people take a parent's name as a surname? If so, is it taken from a parent's first or last name? If so, is it from one or both parents? Does a wife take her husband's name? What titles are appropriate for different professions? Note also that many languages have pronouns and verb forms (familiar and polite) that reflect status and familiarity. These can vary even among countries using the same language. Mistakes that may seem minor can nevertheless be perceived as ignorance or rudeness, thus jeopardizing a business deal. Fortunately, you can find country guidebooks based on people's experiences, including those by international managers. You can also consult with knowledgeable people at home and abroad.

Look at the other side of the cultural coin: Too often when we can't explain some difference—say, why the Irish consume more cold cereal than the Spanish do—we attribute it to culture without trying to understand it. (Perhaps the difference is simply that cereal companies have marketed more in Ireland.) Fortunately, we now have access to many recent studies on cross-cultural attitudes and practices that concern businesspeople.[11] Nevertheless, many attitudes, practices, and cultures remain unstudied.

Before reporting major research findings, we should emphasize a few common shortcomings:

1. Comparing countries by what people say can be risky. For one thing, responses may be colored by the very culture you're trying to understand. Some groups may be happiest when they're complaining; some respond with what they think you want to hear. In responding to degrees of agreement, say on a scale of one to five, some cultures are more apt to select the middle point, others the extremes.[12]
2. Researchers who focus on national differences in terms of *averages* may overlook specific variations within countries and believe in unrealistic stereotypes. For instance, the *average* Scandinavian may be uncomfortable with bargaining, but assuming that an IKEA buyer from Sweden doesn't expect to bargain on prices could be a grave mistake.[13] And of course, personality differences make some people outliers in their own cultures, with no certainty that they'll eventually integrate and conform to cultural norms.[14] Try scoring yourself on some common cultural comparison tests—ethnocentrism, individualism/collectivism, and power distance—to see how you compare with your national norm.[15]
3. Because cultures evolve, research may be outdated. Our opening case, for instance, details some changing Saudi attitudes toward women.

THE IDEA OF A "NATION": DELINEATING CULTURES

Let's examine why national culture is a useful but imperfect cultural reference for international business. Afterward, we'll take a look at why cultures evolve and discuss the influence of language and religion.

THE NATION AS A POINT OF REFERENCE

The nation is a useful definition of society because

- Similarity among people is a cause and an effect of national boundaries.
- Many laws affecting business are along national lines.

Nation provides a workable definition of *culture* because similarity among people is both a cause and effect of national boundaries. Laws governing business operations are largely along national lines. Within its borders, a nation's people chiefly share such essential attributes as values and language. The feeling of "we" casts foreigners as "they." National identity is perpetuated through rites and symbols—flags, parades, rallies—while the preservation of national sites, documents, monuments, and museums promotes a common perception of "we."

Managers find country-by-country analysis difficult because

- Subcultures exist within nations.
- Similarities link groups from different countries.

The Nation as Cultural Mediator Obviously, the existence of shared attributes doesn't mean everyone in a country shares all the same values and attitudes, or that each country is unique in all respects. Nations include various subcultures, ethnic groups, races, and classes, and a national culture must be flexible enough to accommodate such a mixture. In fact, a nation legitimizes itself by mediating its diversity;[16] those that fail to do so often dissolve, as happened with Yugoslavia. Yet a nation's shared and mediated characteristics constitute its national identity and affect the practices of any company that does business there. At the same time, some people (probably a growing number) are **bicultural** or **multicultural**, meaning that they have internalized more than one national culture. This occurs because they hold dual or multiple nationalities, have parents from another country, or have lived abroad at an impressionable age.

Cultural value systems are set early in life but may change through

- Choice or imposition
- Contact with other cultures

Certain cultural attributes can link groups from different nations more closely than groups in a given nation. People in urban areas differ in certain attitudes from people in rural areas; managers have different work attitudes than do production workers. Thus, Country A managers may hold work values closer to those of Country B managers than to those of Country A production workers. As a consequence, when international businesspeople compare nations, they must be careful to examine *relevant groups*—differentiating between, say, the typical attitudes of rural and urban dwellers, or between young and old people.

HOW CULTURES FORM AND CHANGE

Culture is transmitted in various ways—from parent to child, teacher to pupil, social leader to follower, peer to peer. Developmental psychologists believe that most people acquire their basic value systems as children, including such concepts as evil versus good, dirty versus clean, ugly versus beautiful, unnatural versus natural, abnormal versus normal, paradoxical versus logical, and irrational versus rational. These values are not easily changed later on.[17]

SOURCES OF CHANGE

Both individual and collective values and customs may evolve, however. Examining this evolution explains how a culture comes to accept (or reject) certain business practices—knowledge that is useful to companies attempting to introduce changes there. The important thing here is *change,* which may result from either *choice* or *imposition.*

FIGURE 2.2 Some aspects of a foreign culture are accepted easily; others not.

Source: Roy Delgado/CartoonStock

Change by Choice Change by choice may occur as a reaction to social and economic situations that present people with new alternatives. When rural people choose to accept factory jobs, for example, they change some basic customs—notably, working regular hours doesn't allow them the sort of work-time social interactions that farm work allowed.

Change by Imposition Change by imposition—sometimes called **cultural imperialism**—involves imposing certain elements from an alien culture, such as a forced change in laws by an occupying country that, over time, becomes part of the subject culture.

As a rule, contact among countries brings change; this is known as *cultural diffusion.* When the change results in mixing cultural elements, we have *creolization.* In many Asian countries, ethnic Chinese embody a mixture of Chinese and local cultures.[18] In the United States, the popularity of Mexican tortillas led to U.S. innovations in their use, such as tortilla chips and burritos. (Figure 2.2 offers a humorous example of creolization.)

Some groups and governments have tried to protect national cultures but have not succeeded entirely because people travel and access foreign information through a variety of sources. Further, protecting a culture may result in the disadvantage of limiting foreign contact, thus restraining the adoption of foreign technical advancements. Thus, most countries seek to preserve traditions that help maintain national cohesiveness while being open to changes that grow their economies. South Korea, for example, has recently become more multi-ethnic because it needs the influx of foreigners to work in globally competitive factories that bring domestic modernization and growth. To help maintain traditions, the government now sponsors programs and language centers to "Koreanize" the foreigners.[19] The photo on the next page illustrates another Korean means of bringing tradition to modern life.

LANGUAGE AS BOTH A DIFFUSER AND STABILIZER OF CULTURE

A common language within countries is a unifying force.

Like national boundaries and geographic obstacles, language limits people's contact with other cultures. Map 2.2 shows the distribution of the world's major language groups. Not surprisingly, when people from different areas speak the same language, culture spreads

Although the buildings in the photo illustrate South Korean economic modernization, the members of the Royal Guard dress traditionally.

Source: © sandro lacarbona / Alamy

MAP 2.2 Distribution of the World's Major Languages

The people of the world speak thousands of different languages, but only a few of them remain important in the dissemination of culture. A significant portion of countries, for example, speaks English, French, or Spanish. But take a look at China: It's the only place where people speak Mandarin, but it's important in international business because the population of China comprises a lot of people. The classification "Regional" actually takes in two categories: (1) countries in which the dominant language is not dominant anywhere else (e.g., Japan) and (2) countries in which several different languages are spoken (e.g., India).

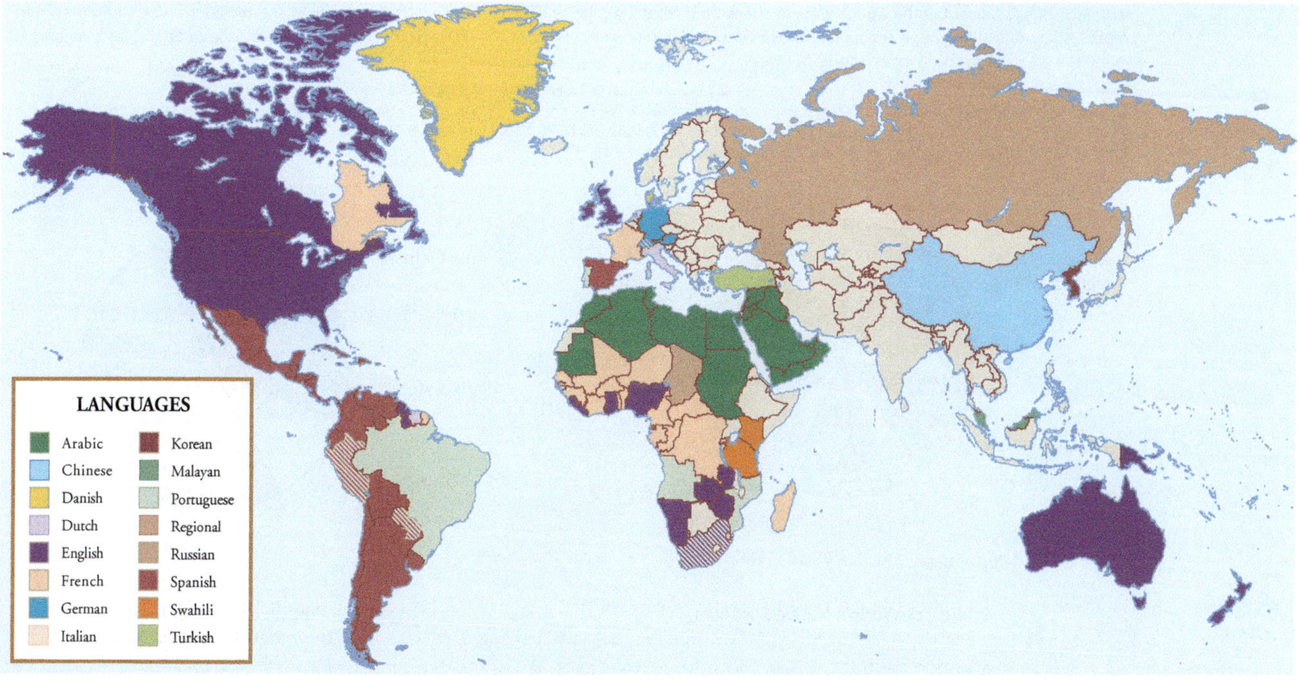

more easily. This helps explain the greater cultural homogeneity among English-speaking countries and among Spanish-speaking countries than *between* English-speaking and Spanish-speaking countries.

The map omits most of the world's approximately 6,000 languages because they are spoken by proportionately few people. Further, 50 to 90 percent of languages are expected to be extinct by the end of the 21st century.[20] When people understand only one language that has relatively few users—especially concentrated in a small geographic area—they tend to cling to their culture because they have little meaningful contact with others.

CONCEPT CHECK

As we observe in Chapter 1, improved communications and transportation are key factors in the increased international interactions that we know as **international business**.

Languages like English, French, and Spanish have such widespread acceptance (they're the most prevalent in 52, 21, and 21 countries and territories, respectively) that, as a rule, the native speakers don't feel the same need to learn other languages as do speakers of languages that, like Armenian or Bulgarian, are found only in limited geographic areas. Commerce is easier among nations that share the same language because there is no need to translate everything. Thus, when people study second languages, they usually choose those most useful in interacting with other countries, especially in the realm of commerce.

WHY ENGLISH TRAVELS SO WELL

In Figure 2.3, the pie chart on the right shows portions of worldwide output by language. As you can see, native English-speaking countries account for a third of the world's production, much more than any other language group—a fact that goes a long way toward explaining why English is the world's most important *second* language. Remember, too, that MNEs—which are largely headquartered in English-speaking countries—decide on the common language to use for communicating among their employees in different countries. Not surprisingly, it's usually English, because many of their managers either speak only English or have English as a second language. In addition, many MNEs from non-English-speaking countries have adopted English—the "international language of business"—as their operating language.

FIGURE 2.3 Major Language Groups: Population and Output

Native speakers for just a few languages—notably English—account for much more of the world's economic output than their population would indicate. Only 8 percent of the world's people speak English as their native (first) language, but the countries and territories where English is the most spoken native language account for 33 percent of global economic output, which helps to explain the prevalence of English as a second language when conducting international business.

Sources: The data for constructing the pie chart on the left came from by List of Languages by Number of Native Speakers,"http://en.wikipedia.org/wiki/List_of_languages_by_number_of_native_speakers (accessed February 26, 2011); For constructing the pie chart on the right, the primary language by country came from "Languages Spoken in Each Country of the World,"www.infoplease.com/ipa/A0855611.html (accessed February 26, 2011). The output per country and territory came from Central Intelligence Agency, The World Factbook, at www.cia.gov.

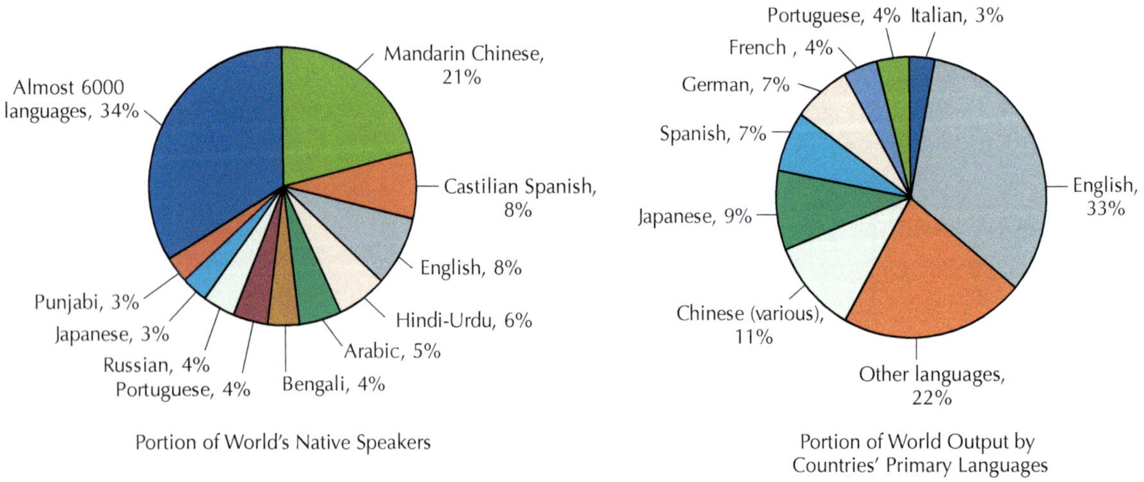

However, downsides of this are that hiring decisions may overemphasize English language capability at the expense of task competence and that people with higher English language proficiency may dominate meetings even though their ideas are not as good.[21] Further, our ending case demonstrates that there are sometimes backlashes about accepting English as an operating language.

CRN
Case Review Note

One prominent linguist has predicted that monolingual English speakers will eventually experience more difficulty in communicating worldwide. Why? Because the percentage of them will decrease, while the languages of such countries as China and India will grow rapidly along with their economies.[22] As is so often the case, history may teach us about this matter: Latin and French were once the languages of scholarship and diplomacy, respectively. Aramaic was once so dominant in the Middle East that conquering groups adopted the language rather than imposing their own.[23] But the use of these languages has long since been supplanted.

Nevertheless, for some time now, English words—especially American English—have been entering other languages. An estimated 20,000 can be found in Japanese. English travels so well partly because the U.S. media are so influential and because the United States originates a healthy percentage of new products and technology. When, say, a U.S. product enters a foreign market, its vocabulary often enters the language as well—sometimes in a strange form. In a Spanish-speaking country, for instance, you might see a sign announcing *Vendemos blue jeans de varios colores* ("We sell various colors of blue jeans"). At other times, the local language provides an Anglicized twist; thus, the French call a self-service restaurant *le self.* Finally, the intrusion of English into another language may result in the development of a hybrid tongue, such as "Spanglish" (Spanish and English) or "Chinglish" (Mandarin Chinese and English), which may ultimately become a distinct language.[24]

Note that some countries, such as Finland, prefer to coin their own new words rather than accept Anglicized items into their vocabularies. Because many countries see language as an integral part of culture, they regulate linguistic changes, such as requiring that all public signs be in the local language.

RELIGION AS A CULTURAL STABILIZER

Many strong values are the result of a dominant religion.

Map 2.3 shows the approximate distribution of the world's major religions. In many countries, the practice of religion has declined significantly; indeed, a few nations in northern Europe are sometimes called "post-Christian" societies. At the same time, religion has been a cultural stabilizer because centuries of religious influence continue to shape cultural values even in these societies.[25] Among people with strong religious convictions, the role of religion in shaping behavior is even stronger.

Many of these religions—Buddhism, Christianity, Hinduism, Islam, and Judaism—influence specific beliefs that may affect business, such as inhibiting the sale of certain products or the performance of work at certain times. McDonald's serves neither beef nor pork in India to keep from offending its Hindu or Muslim populations. El Al, the Israeli national airline, does not fly on Saturday, the Jewish Sabbath. In fact, religion has an impact on almost every business function. To be viewed legitimately, companies must take religious beliefs into account.[26]

Of course, not all nations with the same dominant religion impose the same constraints on business. In predominantly Muslim countries, for example, Friday is a day of worship, whereas in Turkey (a secular Muslim country that adheres to the Christian work calendar to keep in step with European business activity) it is a workday. In places where rival religions vie for political control, the resulting strife can cause so much upheaval that business activity suffers from property damage, broken supply chains, breaches in customer connections, and so on. Unfortunately, the problem is substantial. In recent years, religious violence has erupted in such countries as India, Iraq, Sudan, and Sri Lanka.

MAP 2.3 Distribution of the World's Major Religions

Most countries are home to people of various religious beliefs, but a nation's culture is typically influenced most heavily by a dominant religion. The practices of the dominant religion, for instance, often shape customary practices in legal and business affairs.

Source: The numbers for adherents are taken from "List of Religious Populations," http://en.wikipedia.org/wiki/list_of_religious_populations **

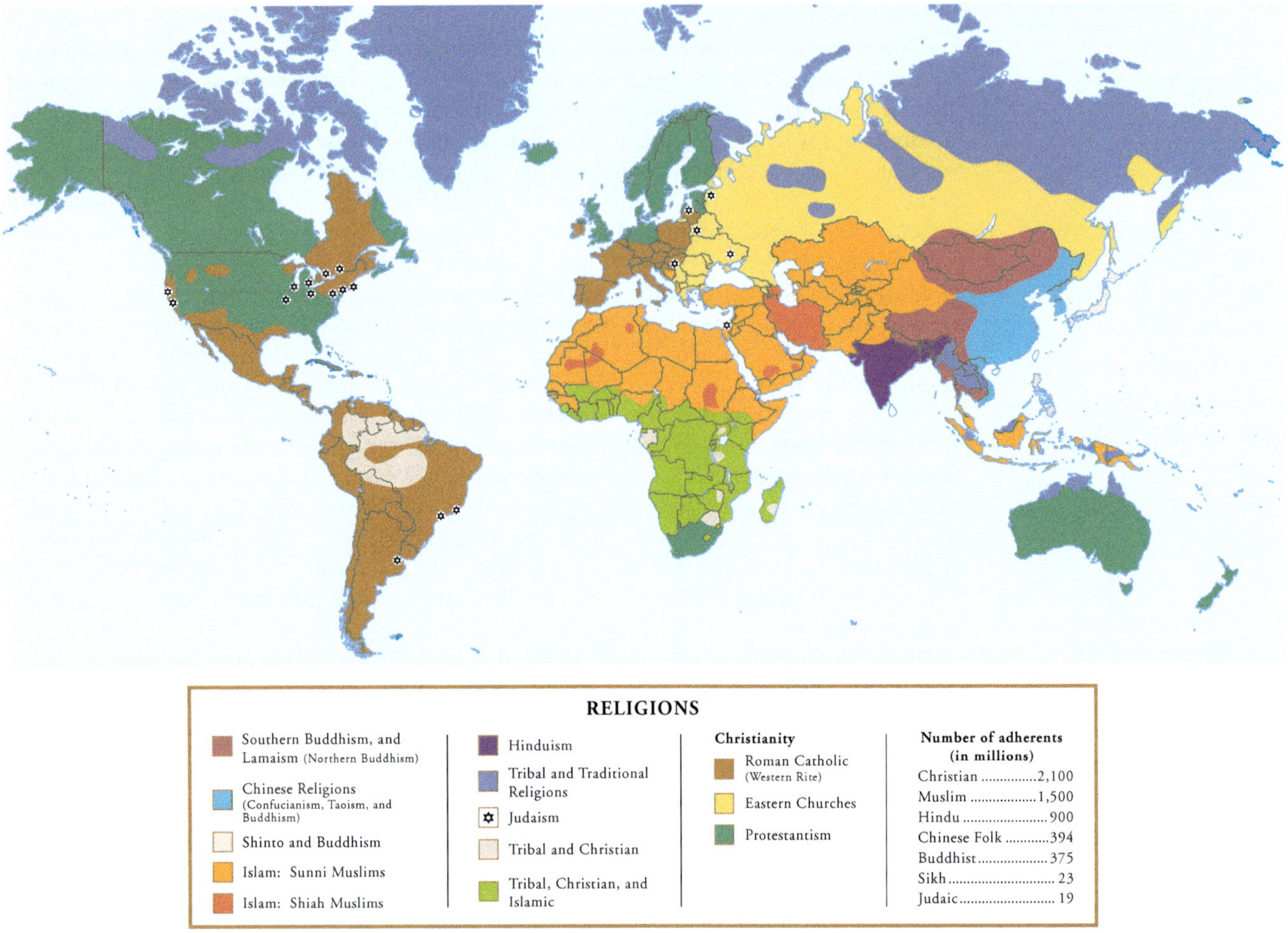

BEHAVIORAL PRACTICES AFFECTING BUSINESS

CONCEPT CHECK

In Chapter 1, we emphasize the importance of studying the behavioral factors that affect business conditions to help managers decide why and how they may need to alter operations in different countries.

Attitudes and values are composed of many *cultural variables,* which both researchers and businesspeople define differently, attaching various names to slightly different and sometimes overlapping concepts. Because of all these nuances in terms and concepts, there are thousands of possible ways to relate culture to business—far too many to cover in one chapter. We'll settle for hitting the highlights.

ISSUES IN SOCIAL STRATIFICATION

Every culture ranks some people higher than others. Such *social stratification* dictates a person's class, status, and financial rewards within that culture. In business, this practice may entail ranking members of managerial groups more highly than production group members. Social stratification is determined by (1) individuals' achievements and qualifications and (2) their affiliation with or membership in certain groups. These two factors interact, but the importance of one versus the other varies among cultures. Further, although this social stratification creates hierarchies, more formal cultures expect more status-oriented

Does Geography Matter?

Birds of a Feather Flock Together

Some groups of people are more isolated from the rest of the world, sometimes by natural barriers (rugged terrain, geographic remoteness), sometimes by others (unique languages, outmoded transportation and communications, xenophobia). Historically, natural conditions have been quite important in determining where people do and don't live. Take a quick look at any map and you'll see that a large portion of big cities are situated where waterways facilitate the interaction of people and interchange of goods.

Although many natural barriers are now less formidable because of airplanes and communication systems, they still play a role in determining which people are harder to get to know than others. In Papua New Guinea, the mutual isolation of tribal groups has resulted in about 800 different languages and has permitted little cultural diffusion. Similarly, natural conditions continue to affect physical cultures, such as clothing for native Inuits of the Arctic differing from the attire typically worn on Brazil's beaches. There is also evidence that these natural conditions, particularly temperature, have affected work values.[27] Then again, some places have traditionally enjoyed more-than-average outside contact. As we saw in our opening case, the Saudi port of Jeddah, having long experienced more external contact than the rest of Saudi Arabia, has a more liberal attitude toward dress than the interior.

CRN
Case Review Note

Consider also the effect of proximity on cultural diffusion. Understandably, people generally have more contact with nearby groups than with remote ones. Take a look at Map 2.2. As you can see, most German-, Arabic-, and Spanish-speaking countries are more or less adjacent to each other. Likewise, Map 2.3 reveals that virtually all the world's major religions are geographically clustered. The notable exceptions to this have resulted from colonization and immigration. Both English and Spanish, for instance, spread to distant parts of the world during eras of European colonization.

Finally, cultural (and subcultural) clusters tend to confirm the old adage that "Birds of a feather flock together." Immigration patterns, for example, often reflect the tendency of people to go where they can find a subcultural support group. That's why there's a heavy concentration of Central American immigrants in the Los Angeles area; even if friends and family aren't already waiting there, they'll find affinities in language, diet, and general customs. Globally, we find many such patterns—Hong Kong Chinese in Vancouver, Canada, Algerians in Marseilles, France, and so on. ■

communications between the hierarchical levels. Higher-status individuals, for example, may be offended if people from a lower status address them by a first name or without using a title.

Businesses reward competence highly in some societies.

CONCEPT CHECK

In the opening case of Chapter 1, we discussed that many top sports players are effectively global brands as companies pay them to use and endorse their products.

Individual Qualifications and Their Limitations In most societies, individual achievement is important, such as in choosing a successful athlete as a spokesperson to advertise sportswear. Similarly, in some nations, such as the United States, companies tend to base a person's eligibility for employment and promotion largely on individual achievements and qualifications. However, we shall see that this is not always the case even in the United States.

Just as companies look for individual qualifications for choosing spokespersons for advertising, they also match spokespersons with the audience (group membership) they wish to reach, such as using older models for products aimed at older consumers. Societies look at these group affiliations differently, thus causing certain business functions to be carried out differently. Because Japan stresses cooperation over competition in the workplace more than the United States does, companies in Japan generally place more weight on seniority for employee promotion, thus favoring older employees.[28] Similarly, a study comparing banks' hiring, promotion, compensation, and staff-reduction practices showed that they differed by nationality on all four functions. When needing to reduce staff, for example, British banks were most prone to save costs by discharging on a performance-to-salary basis (targeting, say, a middle-aged manager with a high salary and average performance), whereas German banks were more concerned with minimizing personal hardship (targeting younger managers, regardless of performance, because they could find new jobs more easily).[29]

Group affiliations can be
- Ascribed or acquired
- A reflection of class and status

The above examples dealt with group memberships based largely on age, but there are many other ways to define memberships. Those determined by birth are **ascribed group memberships**, including gender, family, age, caste, and ethnic, racial, or national origin. **Acquired group memberships** include those based on religion, political affiliation, educational place and achievement, and profession.

Egalitarian societies place more importance on acquired group memberships.

The more egalitarian, or"open,"a society, the less group memberships determine rewards. However, laws may be designed to reinforce or undermine group differences, such as moves in Europe to require large companies to include women in at least 40 percent of their board membership.[30] In other cases, group memberships deny many people equal access to the preparation they need to qualify for jobs; an example is the lack of education for women that results in a lower literacy rate for them than for men in much of sub-Saharan Africa. The Nobel economist Amartya Sen referred to this exclusion of people from the workforce as *unfreedom* and pointed out its negative effect on economic advancement.[31]

Even when individuals qualify for given positions and no legal barriers exist to hold them back, opposition to certain groups—by other workers, customers, shareholders, or government officials—may limit their equal access to employment.

The following sections focus on some of the group memberships that influence how a person is viewed from country to country. An additional factor that is often important is a person's *social connections,*[32] which corresponds to the old adage, "It's *who* you know, not *what* you know."

Country-by-country attitudes vary toward
- Race and ethnicity
- Male and female roles
- Rules and expectations based on age
- Family ties

Ethnic and Racial Groups Laws may reinforce or undermine rigid stratification. Malaysia, for example, has political parties defined explicitly by three ethnic groups. It has also long maintained employment quotas for these ethnic groups—Malays, Chinese, and Indians—primarily to upgrade the economic position of Malays because, at the time of the country's independence, the Chinese and Indian minorities dominated business ownership and the professions, respectively.[33] The Malaysian system requires companies to maintain expensive record-keeping systems of their hiring practices; in fact, it has recently come under increasing criticism from within the country.[34] Likewise, Brazil, which has five official racial classifications in its census and many more terms to designate skin color, has racial quotas in universities and has been pressured to enact quotas for employment as well.[35] (But there has been no pressure for national football team racial quotas, where only competence counts.)

CRN
Case Review Note

Gender-Based Groups Country-specific differences in gender equality and attitudes toward gender are sometimes quite pronounced. [36] As you'll recall from our opening case, there are almost seven employed men for every employed woman in Saudi Arabia, and women are excluded from driving and from certain professions. Compare that employment figure with Norway, where only 1.1 men are employed for every woman. In Lithuania, more than 50 percent of both males and females agreed with the following statement:"When jobs are scarce, men have a better right to a job than women"; in Sweden and Iceland, the number was under 10 percent.[37]

In many parts of the world, however, barriers to gender-based employment practices are coming down, due to changes in both attitudes and work requirements. In the United States, one noticeable change is reflected in the number of people of one gender employed in occupations previously dominated by the other, such as more male nurses and more female physicians. But some of this change may be economic as males have gravitated to where there are jobs; few boys still say they want to grow up to be nurses.[38] Other economic factors matter as well. The decrease in production jobs requiring brawn and increase in jobs for people with specialized education, such as X-ray technicians and psychiatric caseworkers, has caused shifts in the relative demand for female employees and type of job for both genders.

Age-Based Groups Countries treat age groups differently, and each country expresses its attitudes toward age in different ways. All enforce age-related laws such as statutes applying to employment, driving privileges, rights to obtain products and services (alcohol, cigarettes, certain pharmaceuticals, bank accounts), and civic duty (voting, serving in the military or on juries). Sometimes the logic of these laws seems contradictory. In the United States, for example, people can vote, marry, drive, and die for their country before they can legally buy alcohol at age 21, whereas in parts of Switzerland one can legally buy alcohol at age 14.[39] U.S. firms bombard children with TV advertising, but Sweden prohibits ads targeted to children.

National differences toward employment age are substantial. Both Finland and the Netherlands enforce mandatory retirement ages, but with few exceptions (e.g., airline pilots) U.S. law specifically prohibits the practice. In Britain, age discrimination laws apply to everyone, regardless of age, whereas U.S. law is designed to protect only people over age 40.[40] When the proposition "When jobs are scarce, people should be forced to retire early" was put to people in different countries, almost three-quarters of Bulgarians agreed, but only 10 percent of Japanese.[41] Why this latter difference? For one thing, Japanese hold strongly to the assumption that there's a significant correlation between age and wisdom.

Family-Based Groups In some cultures, such as in much of Latin America, the most important group membership is the family. A person's position in society depends heavily on the family's social status or "respectability" rather than on individual achievement. Because family ties are so strong, there may also be a tendency to cooperate more closely within the family unit than in other relationships. In such cultures, not surprisingly, small family-run companies are quite successful; conversely, however, they often encounter difficulties in growing because owners are reluctant to share responsibility with professional managers hired from outside the family who may run the operation more efficiently. When its business culture is hampered by this state of affairs, a country (or region) may lack sufficient numbers of indigenously owned *large-scale* operations that are usually necessary for long-term economic development.[42]

WORK MOTIVATION

Not surprisingly, motivated employees are normally more productive than those who aren't. On an aggregate basis, of course, this influences companies' efficiency and countries' economic development. The following discussion summarizes studies showing major differences in how and why people in different nations are motivated to work.

The desire for material wealth is
- A prime motivation to work
- Positive for economic development

Materialism and Motivation When developing his *Protestant ethic* theory, Max Weber observed that predominantly Protestant countries were the most economically developed. He attributed this "ethic" to an outgrowth of the Protestant Reformation in sixteenth-century Europe, which reflects the belief that work is a pathway to salvation and that material success does not impede redemption. Although we no longer accept a strict distinction between Protestant and non-Protestant attitudes toward work and material gain, we do tend to adhere to the underlying values of Weber's concept: namely, that self-discipline, hard work, honesty, and a belief in a just world foster work motivation and, thus, economic growth.[43] As a matter of fact, on one hand there is evidence indicating a positive correlation between the intensity of religious beliefs per se (regardless of specific belief systems) and adherence to some attributes that lead to economic growth (say, confidence in the rule of law and belief in the virtue of thrift).[44] Moreover, strong evidence indicates that the desire for material wealth motivates individuals to perform the kind of work that leads to community-wide economic development.[45] On the other hand, values held by people with strong religious beliefs, such as maintenance of the status quo and predetermination, retard self-motivation to work for economic advancement.[46] Further, in societies such as Myanmar (shown in the adjacent photo) and Bhutan, a large portion of the population vanishes from the economic work force temporarily or permanently while living with few possessions in monasteries and nunneries and being supported by others.

Buddhist monks in Myanmar (Burma) line up to await lunches that are donated to them.
Source: Peter Zurek/Shutterstock

The Productivity/Leisure Trade-Off Some cultures place more value on leisure time than others. They push for working shorter hours, take more holidays and vacations, and generally spend more time and money on leisure activities. In a study of OECD (fairly high-income) countries, France and the United States offered an example of contrast. The French had 30 days mandated vacation; Americans had none. The French also spent more time per day eating and sleeping than Americans.[47] In the United States, there is still some disdain for people who work very little: people of privilege who appear to contribute too little to society and people who appear to be satisfied with a lifestyle maintained by social benefits. Americans who give up work (primarily retirees) often complain that they're no longer allowed to contribute anything useful to society—one reason for laws prohibiting mandatory retirement.

People are more eager to work if

- Rewards for success are high
- There is some uncertainty of success

Expectation of Success and Reward Motivation toward work is influenced by the perceived likelihood of success and its rewards versus failure. Generally, people have little enthusiasm for effort when the likelihood of success seems too easy or too difficult. Few would care to run a race against either a snail or a racehorse; in either case, the outcome is too predictable. Our enthusiasm peaks when uncertainty of success is high, such as the challenge of racing another human of roughly equal ability. Likewise, the reward for a successfully completed task—say, winning a fair footrace—may be high or low, and most of us usually work harder the more we expect success to lead to a higher reward.

Success and Reward Across Borders Performed in different countries, the same tasks come with different probabilities of success, different rewards for success, and different consequences for failure. In cultures in which the probability of economic failure is almost certain and the perceived rewards of success are low, people tend—not surprisingly—to view work as necessary but unsatisfying, mainly because they foresee little benefit to themselves. This attitude may prevail in harsh climates, in very poor areas, or in subcultures subject to discrimination. Likewise, if there is little difference in reward between working hard or not, there is less motivation to work hard. In Cuba, for instance, where public policy allocates output from productive to unproductive workers, there is not much enthusiasm for work. When high uncertainty of outcome is combined with the likelihood of a positive reward for success and little or no reward for failure, we find the greatest work enthusiasm.[48]

Performance and Achievement

The Masculinity–Femininity Index A study using the **masculinity–femininity index** found significant differences in attitudes toward achievement among employees in 50 countries. Those with a high-masculinity score admired successful work achievers, harbored little sympathy for the unfortunate, and preferred to be better than others rather than on a par with them. They shared a money-and-things orientation rather than a people orientation, a belief that it's better "to live to work" than "to work to live," and a preference for performance and growth over quality of life and the environment.[49]

Such attitudes help explain why an international company may encounter managers abroad who behave differently than expected or preferred. Let's say a firm in a high-masculinity country such as Austria sets up operations in a high-femininity country such as Sweden. Typical purchasing managers in Sweden probably prefer smooth social relationships and amiable, ongoing dealings with suppliers to, say, immediate lower costs or faster delivery. They may also place such organizational goals as employee and social welfare ahead of the Austrian firm's goals of minimizing workers' compensation.

The hierarchy of needs

- May differ among countries
- Is useful in deciding how to motivate differently among countries

Hierarchies of Needs According to the **hierarchy-of-needs theory** of motivation, people try to fulfill lower-level needs before moving on to higher-level ones.[50] As you can see from Figure 2.4, the most basic needs are *physiological*: food, water, and sex. We have to satisfy (or nearly satisfy) those before our *security* needs—safe physical and emotional environments—which must be satisfied before triggering social needs, or the motivational effect of *affiliation,* such as peer acceptance. Then we're motivated to satisfy our *esteem* needs—bolstering our self-image through recognition, attention, and appreciation. The highest-order need calls for *self-actualization*—self-fulfillment, or (to quote Robert Lewis Stevenson) "becom[ing] all that we are capable of becoming." Finally, the theory also implies that we'll typically work to satisfy a need, which, once satisfied, diminishes in value as a motivator.

What can the hierarchy-of-needs theory tell us about doing business in foreign countries? For one thing, research has shown that different cultures not only attach different degrees of importance to various needs, they also rank higher-order needs differently. Thus, the theory can help in distinguishing among the reward preferences of employees in different parts of the world. This is important because of differences in workforce composition.[51] In very poor countries, for example, a larger portion of workers are likely engaged in manual jobs; thus, a company can motivate a larger portion of them simply by providing enough compensation to satisfy their needs for food and shelter. Elsewhere, a larger portion of workers are motivated by other needs.

Compensation (even at low levels of income) cannot fully explain differences in work motivation. A long-term ethnographic study among a U.S. airline's back-office employees in

FIGURE 2.4 The Hierarchy of Needs and Need-Hierarchy Comparisons

The pyramid on the left represents the five-level hierarchy of needs formulated by Maslow. The two block pyramids on the right (a, b) represent two different groups of people—say, the populations of two different countries. Note that the block representing affiliation needs (level 3) is wider in (b) than in (a); conversely, the block representing self-actualization needs (level 5) is wider in (a) than in (b). In other words, even if we rank various needs in the same order (or hierarchy), the people in one country may regard a given higher-order need as more important (wider) than do people in another country.

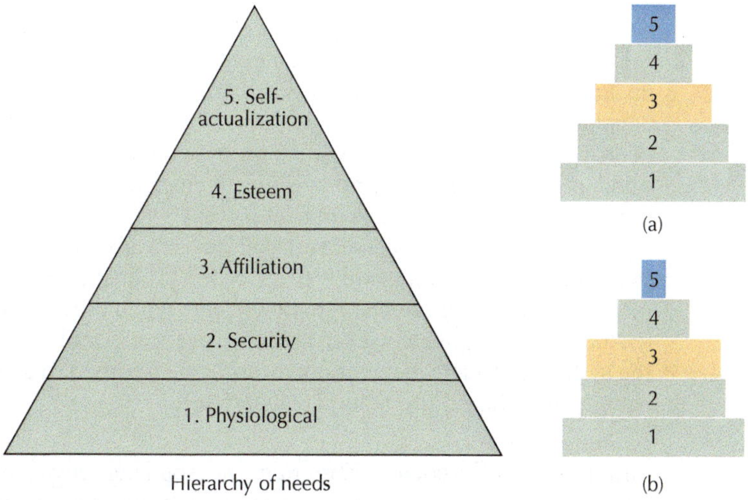

three countries found that those in the United States and the Dominican Republic saw the job as a stepping-stone to higher-level positions. However, few in Barbados wanted a promotion because it would change their relationships with friends. U.S. workers usually dressed very casually because outsiders would not see them in the back office, but Barbadians dressed up to be seen going to what was considered a prestige job. In fact, the company offered Barbadian employees free company-owned bus transport, but the employees preferred to pay for slower public transportation where others could see them. The largely female staff in Barbados had low absenteeism and turnover rates because Barbados has a history of women working long-term. In the Dominican Republic, however, most female employees stayed on only until they married.[52]

RELATIONSHIP PREFERENCES

So far, we've discussed two categories of behavioral practices affecting business: social stratification systems and work motivation. Next, we examine some of the values underlying interpersonal differences in behavior.

There are national variations in the preference for autocratic or consultative management.

Power Distance

From country to country, employee preferences tend to differ in terms of interacting with bosses, subordinates, and peers. Considerable evidence suggests that people perform better when the nature of their interactions fits their preferences. That's why companies are well advised to align management styles with superior-subordinate interaction preferences, which are known in general as **power distance**.

With *high* power distance, people prefer little consultation between the two tiers and one of two management styles: *autocratic* (ruling with unlimited authority) or *paternalistic* (regulating conduct by supplying needs). With *low* power distance, they prefer "consultative" styles.[53] What might happen, therefore, if a Dutch company assigned domestic managers, who typically prefer low power distance, to work in Morocco, where workers typically prefer high power distance? The Dutch managers might consult with Moroccan subordinates in an attempt to improve employee productivity. Unfortunately, subordinates may lose confidence in their superiors ("Why don't they know what to do?"), so that performance deteriorates rather than improves.

Interestingly, managers who prefer an autocratic style of superior–subordinate relationship are also quite willing to delegate and accept decision-making by a majority of subordinates. What they don't accept well is consultative interaction between the two tiers, which implies a more equal relationship between them. Clearly, worker-participation methods may need to be adjusted to fit different countries.

"Safe" work environments motivate collectivists. Challenges motivate individualists.

Individualism Versus Collectivism

High **individualism** describes an employee's preference to fulfill leisure time and improve skills outside the organization, receive direct monetary compensation as opposed to fringe benefits, and engage in personal decision making and on-the-job challenges. *High* **collectivism**, in contrast, typifies an employee's penchant for dependence on the organization through training, satisfactory workplace conditions, and good benefits. In countries with high individualism, a self-actualization opportunity is a prime motivator because employees want challenges. In those with high collectivism, fulfilling security needs is a prime motivator.[54]

Degrees of individualism and collectivism also influence employee interactions. Levi Strauss attempted to introduce team-based production into several U.S. plants because its management had observed high productivity when the system was used in the highly collectivist culture of Japan. However, U.S. employees, especially the most skilled workers, detested the system; productivity went down, and Levi returned to a more individualistic system that better suited the culture of its U.S. workforce.

Situational Differences: The Family

Applying any measure of *individualism versus collectivism* is complex because preferences may vary by situation.[55] Although Japan and

Mexico are both characterized as collectivist cultures, Mexico's collectivist preference is based more on kinship relations that do not carry over easily into the workplace.[56] Moreover, the Mexican concept of family sometimes includes not only the *nuclear family* (husband, wife, and minor children) but also the *vertically extended family* (members of several generations) and the *horizontally extended family* (aunts, uncles, and cousins).

Such differences can affect business in a variety of ways:

- Individualists in a family-oriented collectivists country may be less motivated to receive material rewards from their work because of dividing the rewards among more family members.
- Because relocation means that family members must also find new jobs, a worker's geographic mobility is limited. Even when extended families don't live together, mobility may be reduced because people prefer to remain near relatives.
- Interrelated familial roles may complicate purchasing decisions.
- Security and social needs may be met more effectively at home than in the workplace.

RISK-TAKING BEHAVIOR

Nationalities differ in

- Ease of handling uncertainties
- Degree of trust among people
- Future orientation
- Attitudes of self-determination and fatalism

Cultures differ in people's willingness to accept the status quo and control over destiny. The following discussion examines four types of *risk-taking behavior* that reflect these attitudes: *uncertainty avoidance, trust, future orientation,* and *fatalism.*

Uncertainty Avoidance

In countries where **uncertainty avoidance** is high, most employees prefer to follow set rules even if they believe that breaking them may be in the company's best interests. They also tend to stay with current employers for a long time, preferring the certainty of present positions over the uncertainty of their future elsewhere.[57] When uncertainty avoidance is high, superiors may need to be more precise in their directions to subordinates, who typically don't want to be responsible for actions that counter what their superiors want.

Moreover, fewer consumers are prepared to risk being early product adopters. Gillette, for example, depends heavily on introducing new products, so it is likely better off to enter markets like Denmark and the United Kingdom, which rate low on uncertainty avoidance, before venturing into Belgium and Portugal, which rate high.

Trust

Surveys measuring *trust* have found country differences in evaluations of such statements as "Most people can be trusted" and "You can't be too careful in dealing with people." Many more Norwegians than Brazilians, for example, regard most people as trustworthy.[58] Where trust is high, business costs tend to be lower because managers spend less time fussing over every possible contingency and monitoring every action for compliance and more time producing, selling, and innovating.[59] At the same time, the degree of trust may differ between what people consider their in-group and their out-group.[60] For instance, we discussed that in some family oriented societies, people have high trust of other family members, but low trust to people they do not know.

Future Orientation

Cultures differ in their perceptions of the risks from delaying gratification. A **future orientation** (living for the future) is more pronounced in Switzerland, the Netherlands, and Canada than in Russia, Poland, and Italy.[61] In the former cultures, it may be easier for companies to motivate workers through such delayed-compensation programs as retirement plans.

Fatalism

If people believe strongly in self-determination, they may be willing to work hard to achieve goals and take responsibility for performance. But if they're *fatalistic*—if they believe every event in life is inevitable—they're less likely to accept the basic cause-and-effect relationship between work and reward. In countries that rate high on fatalism, people plan less for contingencies, such as not buying insurance. Religious differences play a significant role in this regard. Conservative or fundamentalist groups, for instance, are more likely to view occurrences as "the will of God." Thus, managers are less apt to sway them with cause-and-effect logic than by making personal appeals or offering them rewards for complying with requests.[62]

INFORMATION AND TASK PROCESSING

"Beauty," we're often told, "is in the eye of the beholder." So, apparently, are perceptions and judgments, both of which are based on what people consider accurate *information*. Because different cultures handle information differently, the following discussion examines some of the ways in which people perceive, obtain, and process information.

Perception of Cues As a rule, we're selective in perceiving *cues*—features that inform us about the nature of something. We may identify things through any of our senses, and each sense can provide information in various ways, such as seeing color, depth, and shape through vision. People rely on cues that are partly physiological, and growing evidence suggests that evolution and genetics play a role in how different groups perceive.[63] Genetic differences in eye pigmentation, for instance, allow some people to differentiate colors more precisely than others.

Cultural differences, especially language, also reflect differences in perception of cues. The richness of a language's descriptive vocabulary allows its speakers to note and express very subtle nuances that speakers of a different language may not discern, or to perceive certain subjects more precisely than others. The Arabic language has many more words for camels, their body parts, and the equipment associated with them than other languages,[64] and Arabic speakers who work around camels can express nuances about them that most other people overlook.

It helps managers to know whether cultures favor

- Focused or broad information
- Sequential or simultaneous handling of situations
- Handling principles or small issues first

Obtaining Information: Low-Context Versus High-Context Cultures Researchers classify some countries (including the United States and most of northern Europe) as **low-context cultures**, in which people generally regard as relevant only firsthand information that bears directly on the subject at hand. Businesspeople will spend little time on small talk and tend to get to the point. In **high-context cultures**, people tend to regard seemingly peripheral information as pertinent and infer meanings from things said either indirectly or casually. They tend to follow these patterns in written communications as well, even in emails, and take them into account in international litigation.[65] Miscommunication can result as well. For example, because Japan is a high-context culture in which subordinates understand superiors' indirect instructions, Japanese managers have been challenged in conveying work expectations to their low-context United Kingdom subordinates, who expect more explicit explanations.[66] Even seemingly minor contextual differences may be misconstrued. For instance, on teams involving both Germans and Austrians, the low-context Germans were prone to say, "This is completely wrong" whereas the high-context Austrians would say, "This is a very interesting and important issue, but maybe we should also concentrate on this fact." The Austrians viewed the Germans as assertive and arrogant; the Germans viewed the Austrians as disorganized and less reliable.[67]

Information Processing Insofar as all cultures categorize, plan, and quantify, information processing is a universal activity. However, every culture has its own systems for ordering and classifying information. In U.S. directories, people's names appear in alphabetical order by last (family) name; in Iceland, they're organized by first (given) names (Icelandic last names are derived from the father's first name: Jon, son of Thor, is Jon *Thorsson*, and his sister's last name is *Thorsdottir*, "daughter of Thor"). To perform efficiently and work amicably in a foreign environment, you need to understand such differences in processing systems. Perhaps more important, different processing systems create challenges in sharing global data. Even the use of global personnel directories is problematic because of different alphabets and alphabetizing systems.

Monochronic Versus Polychronic Cultures Cultural differences also affect people's comfort with different degrees of multitasking. In **monochronic** cultures people may prefer to work sequentially, such as finishing transactions with one customer before dealing with another. Conversely, **polychronic** people are more comfortable when working simultaneously on a variety of tasks, such as dealing immediately with multiple customers who need service. Imagine the potential misconceptions when monochronic businesspeople see their polychronic counterparts as uninterested in doing business with them because they don't bother to give them their undivided attention. Further, when teams combine people from both types of cultures, the former sometimes feel that the latter delay results by wasting time.[68]

Idealism Versus Pragmatism Some cultures tend to focus first on the whole and then on the parts; others do the opposite. When asked to describe an underwater scene in which one large fish was swimming among some smaller fish and other aquatic life, most Japanese first described the overall picture, whereas most Americans first described the large fish.[69] Similarly, some cultures prefer to establish overall principles before they try to resolve small issues—an approach sometimes labeled **idealism**. Cultures in which people focus more on details than on abstract principles are said to be **pragmatic**.

These different approaches can affect business in a number of ways. In a culture of pragmatists (as in the United States), labor negotiations tend to focus on well-defined issues—say, hourly pay increases for a specific bargaining unit. In an idealist culture (as in Argentina), labor disputes tend to blur the focus on specific demands as workers tend to rely first on mass action, such as general strikes or political activities, to publicize basic principles.

COMMUNICATIONS

Cross-border communications do not always translate as intended.

We now look at problems in *communications*—especially translating spoken and written language. Problems occur not only when you shift from one language to another, but also when you communicate with someone from another country with the same official language. Finally, we discuss communication that occurs by means other than spoken and written language—a so-called "silent language."

SPOKEN AND WRITTEN LANGUAGE

Translating one language directly into another is not as straightforward as it may seem. Some words simply don't have direct translations. In English, for example, *children* may mean either "young people" or "offspring." In Spanish, *niños* and *hijos* distinguish between the two, and there is no word that encompasses both meanings that exist in English. Thus, despite recent great strides in the use of machines to translate, many errors still occur. Moreover, many translations—say, Galician into Welsh—go through an intermediate language, usually English.[70]

Language, including common word meanings, is constantly evolving. When Microsoft purchased a thesaurus code for its Spanish version of Word, the connotations of many synonyms had shifted by the time it implemented the software; some, in fact, were transformed into outright insults that alienated potential customers.[71] Of course, in any language words mean different things in different contexts. For example, the English word "old" can mean "former" or "long-standing."

Finally, remember that grammar is complex and the seemingly slight misuse (or even placement) of a word can substantially change the meaning. All of the following, each originally composed to assist English-speaking guests, have appeared on signs in hotels around the world:

FRANCE: "Please leave your values at the desk."

MEXICO (to assure guests about the safety of drinking water): "The manager has personally passed all the water served here."

JAPAN: "You are invited to take advantage of the chambermaid."

NORWAY: "Ladies are requested not to have children in the bar."

SWITZERLAND: "Because of the impropriety of entertaining guests of the opposite sex in the bedroom, it is suggested that the lobby be used for this purpose."

GREECE (at check-in line): "We will execute customers in strict rotation."

These examples offer a comical look at language barriers that usually result in only a little embarrassment. Poor translations, however, can cause commercial disputes; in 2011 the Shanghai Maritime Court dealt with almost 2000 such disputes between Chinese and foreign companies.[72] So choose your words carefully. Although there's no foolproof way of ensuring translations, experienced international businesspeople rely on such following suggestions:

- Get references for the people who will do your translating.
- Make sure your translator knows the technical vocabulary of your business.
- For written work, do *back translations:* Have one person go from, say, English to French and a second from French back to English. If your final message says what you said originally, it's probably satisfactory.
- Make sure that the tone, not just the words, fit both your own intentions and the expectations of recipients.
- Use simple words whenever possible (such as *ban* instead of *interdiction*).
- Avoid slang. American slang, especially words or phrases originating from sports—*off base, out in left field, threw me a curve, ballpark figure*—are probably meaningless to most businesspeople outside the United States.[73]
- When either you or your counterpart is dealing in a language other than your first language, clarify communications in several ways (repeat things in different words and ask questions) to ensure that all parties have the same interpretation.
- Recognize the need and budget from the start for the extra time needed for translation and clarification.

Be careful with humor because some lacks universal appeal. A Microsoft executive quipped to Indian executives that he really didn't have the qualifications to speak because he did not complete his MBA. The comment was badly received because Indians place high importance on education and on persevering rather than dropping out.[74]

Finally, even when all parties to a communication come from countries that share an official language, don't assume that understanding will go smoothly. Table 2.1, for instance, lists just some of the approximately 4,000 words that have different meanings in British and American English. What could go wrong? When Hershey's launched its Elegancita candy bar in Latin America, its expensive advertising campaign boasted about the *cajeta* in the product.

TABLE 2.1 Dangers of Misspeaking the Language(s) of Business

Below are a couple of short lists containing words used in business whose meanings are different in the United States and the United Kingdom—"two countries separated by a common language," as the British playwright G.B. Shaw once quipped. There are approximately 4,000 words with the potential to cause problems for people who—in theory—speak the same language.

United States	United Kingdom
turnover	redundancy
sales	turnover
inventory	stock
stock	shares
president	managing director

Unfortunately, although *cajeta* means "goat's-milk caramel" in Mexico, in much of South America it's vulgar slang for a part of the female anatomy.[75]

SILENT LANGUAGE

CRN Case Review Note

Of course, spoken and written language are not our only means of communicating. We constantly exchange messages through a host of nonverbal cues that form a **silent language**.[76] Recall from our opening case that in the process of conducting market research for the Java Lounge, researchers depended on several non-verbal cues to deduce who was affluent.

Silent language includes color associations, sense of appropriate distance, time and status cues, body language, and prestige.

Colors Colors are an interesting aspect of a culture's silent language. For a product to succeed, its colors obviously must be consistent with the consumer's frame of reference. Colors invoke distinct connotations in different countries, such as being lucky or unlucky or being associated with a specific business (e.g., yellow cabs in the United States and black ones in the United Kingdom). In most Western countries, black is a color for mourning death; in parts of Africa, it's white; in Thailand, it's purple. In the United States pink is used to denote femininity, while in Japan it denotes masculinity. United Airlines' promotion of a new passenger service in Hong Kong is an example of an effort that backfired because of color. Why? It handed out white carnations to its best customers, but Hong Kong residents give white carnations in sympathy for a death in the family.

Distance Another aspect of silent language is the accustomed distance people maintain during conversations or when conducting business. In the United States people customarily maintain a higher distance between each other than is typical in Mexico or elsewhere in Latin America. And except for handshakes, there is little or no touching in the United States, whereas touching one another in Mexico is quite common.[77] Thus, U.S. managers conducting business in Mexico may find themselves constantly moving backward to avoid the closeness their Mexican counterparts maintain. At the end of the discussion, both parties may well feel uneasy about each other without realizing why.

Time and Punctuality Different perceptions of time and punctuality also may create confusion. U.S. businesspeople usually arrive early for business appointments, a few minutes late for dinner at someone's home, and a bit later still for large social gatherings. In another country, the concept of punctuality in any or all of these situations may be different. A Latin American host may find it surprising and perhaps discourteous if a U.S. guest arrives only a few minutes later than the stated time for dinner.

Culturally, there are different ways of looking at time. People in English-speaking, Germanic, and Scandinavian countries tend to value time as a scarce commodity; if it's lost, it can't be recouped.[78] They tend to stick to schedules, even if taking longer would yield better results. In contrast, people who view time as an event prefer to take as long as necessary to complete a task to their satisfaction. In one case, the managers of a U.S. company competing for a contract were so confident of winning on the basis of better technology that they scheduled a tight, one-day meeting in Mexico City, thinking this was plenty of time for their presentation and questions. Unfortunately, the Mexican team arrived one hour after the scheduled start. Then, when one member of the Mexican team was called out of the room for an urgent phone call, the whole group got upset when the U.S. team tried to proceed without him. The competing French team, in contrast, allocated two weeks for discussions and won the contract with less sophisticated technology.[79]

Body Language Body language, or *kinesics*—the way people walk, touch, and move their bodies—also differs among cultures. Indeed, very few gestures have universal meanings. A Greek, Turk, or Bulgarian may indicate "yes" with a sideways movement of the head that could be construed as "no" in the United States and much of Europe. As Figure 2.5 shows, certain gestures may have several, even contradictory meanings.

FIGURE 2.5 Body Language Is Not a Universal Language

The fine line between approval and put-down: Very few gestures have universal meanings. In the United States, you'd probably be safe in approving of another person's statement by forming an O with your thumb and index finger (the so-called high sign). In Germany, Greece, and France, however, you'd be expressing a very different opinion.

Source: The meanings are based on descriptions in Roger E. Axtell, *Gestures* (New York: John Wiley, 1998). Reprinted by permission of John Wiley & Sons, Inc.

Prestige Another factor in silent language relates to a person's status, particularly in an organizational setting. A U.S. manager who places great faith in physical things as cues to prestige may underestimate the status of foreign counterparts who don't have large, plush corner offices on high floors. Foreigners may underestimate U.S. counterparts who perform their own services, such as opening doors, fetching coffee, and answering unscreened phone calls.

DEALING WITH CULTURAL DIFFERENCES

After managers identify key cultural differences abroad, must they alter their customary practices to succeed there? Can people overcome culturally related adjustment problems when working abroad? There are no easy answers to these questions, but the following discussion highlights four issues that affect *degrees* of successful adjustment:

1. The extent to which a culture is willing to accept the introduction of anything foreign
2. Whether key cultural differences are small or great
3. The ability of individuals to adjust to what they find in foreign cultures
4. The general management orientation of the company involved

The following sections address each of these issues in some depth.

HOST SOCIETY ACCEPTANCE

Host cultures do not always expect foreigners to adjust to them.

Although our opening case illustrates the advantages of *adjusting* to a host country's culture, international companies sometimes succeed in introducing new products, technologies, and operating procedures with relatively little alteration. They pull it off either because what they're introducing does not run counter to deep-seated attitudes or because the host culture is willing to accept the foreign product or practice as an agreeable trade-off. Bahrain needs non-Muslim workers, so it permits the sale of pork products (ordinarily prohibited by religious law) as long as transactions are limited to special grocery store departments in which Muslims can neither work nor shop.

Sometimes the local society regards foreigners and domestic citizens differently. When staying overnight in Jeddah, Western female flight attendants can wear types of clothing publicly that local women cannot.[80] In other instances, local citizens may actually feel their cultures are being mocked when foreigners bend over backward to make adjustments, such as dressing in local traditional garb.[81]

DEGREE OF CULTURAL DIFFERENCES

When doing business in a similar culture, companies
- Usually have to make fewer adjustments
- May overlook subtle differences

Obviously, some countries are much like others, usually because they share many characteristics such as language, religion, geographic location, ethnicity, and level of economic development.

Cultural Distance A human values study comparing 43 societies on 405 cultural dimensions[82] could determine their *cultural proximity* by averaging the **cultural distance** separating them (number of countries apart) on each dimension. For instance, the United Kingdom is culturally close to the United States while China is culturally distant. When a company moves into a culturally similar foreign country, it should encounter fewer cultural adjustments than when entering a dissimilar country. An Ecuadorian company doing business in Colombia should expect to adjust more easily than if it were to do business in Thailand.

Even among similar countries, however, significant cultural differences could still affect business dealings. Moreover, managers may assume that such similar countries are more alike than they really are, and perhaps overlook important subtleties. Women's roles and behavior, for example, differ substantially from one Arab country to another even though the countries overall are culturally similar.

Hidden Cultural Attitudes Even if the home and host countries have seemingly similar cultures, people in the host country may reject the influx of foreign practices because they see them as additional steps that threaten their self-identities.[83] And with thousands of *minute* cultural dimensions, it may not be easy to discern operating impediments by comparing countries on the *broad* ones that are both obvious and studied. Disney had much more success in opening a theme park in Japan than in France, even though France is culturally closer to the United States. Why? First, France was very concerned about its separate identity, especially vis-à-vis the United States—encroachment of American English words into the French language, fast-food restaurants' threat to customary long lunches with traditional cuisine, U.S. companies' acquisition of French firms considered focal to French distinctiveness. Next, subtle differences separated the Japanese from the French. The Japanese were more receptive to Disney because (1) both Japanese children and adults perceived Mickey Mouse as a wholesome, nonthreatening figure, (2) the Japanese had a tradition of buying souvenirs on family excursions, and (3) Disney's reputation for super-cleanliness and smiling faces fit well with Japanese preferences for harmony and order. The French, in contrast, knew Mickey Mouse only as a comic-book conniver who'd been reformulated for the French market. They regarded Disney souvenirs as tacky and policies requiring personnel to dress uniformly and smile mindlessly as violations of personal dignity.[84]

ABILITY TO ADJUST: CULTURE SHOCK

International companies send personnel abroad for both short and long periods, subjecting them to potentially traumatic foreign practices. In fact, cultural practices all over the world are considered by many outsiders as downright wrong, such as polygamy, child marriage, the punishment of people (sometimes severe) for activities not considered crimes at home, and the public display of executed bodies. Both companies and individuals must decide if they're ready to work in places that countenance such practices.

CRN
Case Review Note

Even in countries whose practices aren't necessarily traumatic to them, workers who go abroad often encounter **culture shock**—the frustration that results from having to absorb a vast array of new cultural cues and expectations. Even such seemingly simple tasks as using a different type of toilet or telephone, getting a driver's license, or finding where to buy specific merchandise can be taxing experiences at first. Our ending case shows that help from your fellow citizens who have already learned the different tasks can speed your understanding of them.

Some people get frustrated when entering a different culture.

Some people working in a culture significantly different from their own may pass through certain adjustment stages. At first, much like tourists, they're delighted with quaint differences. Later, however, they grow depressed and confused (the *culture shock* phase), so their effectiveness in the foreign environment suffers. Fortunately for most people, culture shock begins to ebb after a month or two as they grow more comfortable. In fact, some people experience **reverse culture shock** when they go back home, having become partial to aspects of life abroad that are not options back home.

COMPANY AND MANAGEMENT ORIENTATIONS

Whether and how a company and its managers adapt abroad depends not only on the host-country culture but also on their own attitudes. The following sections discuss three such attitudes or orientations: polycentrism, ethnocentrism, and geocentrism.

Polycentrist management may be so overwhelmed by national differences that it won't introduce workable changes.

Polycentrism A *polycentric* organization tends to believe that its business units abroad should act like local companies. Given the unique problems (and publicity about them) often inherent in foreign ventures, it's not surprising that many companies develop polycentric perspectives. However, polycentrism may be an overly cautious response to cultural variety, causing a firm to shy away from certain countries or avoid transferring home-country practices or resources that will actually work well abroad.

Look at it this way. To compete effectively, an international company—and its foreign units—must usually perform some functions differently from the competitors it encounters abroad in order to have an advantage over them. They may, for instance, need to sell and market new products or produce old ones differently. Thus, the overly polycentric firm may rely too heavily on imitating proven host-country practices and, in the process, lose the innovative edge it has honed at home.

Ethnocentrist management overlooks national differences and

- Ignores important factors
- Believes home-country objectives should prevail
- Thinks acceptance by other cultures is easy

Ethnocentrism *Ethnocentrism* reflects the conviction that one's own culture is superior to that of other countries. In international business, the term is usually applied to a company (or individual) so strongly committed to the principle of "What works at home will work abroad" that its foreign practices tend to ignore differences in cultures and markets. In turn, it underestimates the complexity of introducing new management methods, products, or marketing means, which likely leads to poor performance.

Before we go any further, we should point out that ethnocentrism isn't entirely an inappropriate way of looking at things. Obviously, much of what works at home will in fact work abroad. Further, concentrating on national differences in terms of *averages* overlooks specific variations within countries. A company may be able to deal with outliers even though the *average* person in the country has a strong cultural bias against what the company does in its home country. For example, although the average person in India has a strong cultural bias against eating meat, a company could sell meat products to the many Indians who do eat meat regularly or on occasion. Likewise, a company may identify partners, suppliers, and employees among a population minority whose attitudes don't fit the cultural average (there are always individualists in even the most collectivist societies).

Geocentric management often uses business practices that are hybrids of home and foreign norms.

Geocentrism Between the extremes of polycentrism and ethnocentrism, there is an approach to international business practices called *geocentrism,* which integrates company and host-country practices as well as some entirely new ones.[85] In our opening case, both Saks Fifth Avenue and Harvey Nichols have adjusted to Saudi customs (such as by setting aside women-only floors). At the same time, they've introduced home-country merchandising practices (what they sell) along with entirely new practices (providing lounges for the drivers of female customers).

CRN
Case Review Note

Geocentrism requires companies to balance informed knowledge of their own organizational cultures with home- and host-country needs, capabilities, and constraints. Because it encourages innovation and improves the likelihood of success, geocentrism is the preferred approach for companies to succeed in foreign cultures and markets.

STRATEGIES FOR INSTITUTING CHANGE

Because people do not necessarily accept change readily, the management of change is important.

As we've seen, companies wanting to establish competitive advantages in foreign markets may need to operate in some ways differently from other companies in those markets, i.e., they introduce some degree of change into foreign markets. Thus, they need to bear in mind that people don't always accept change very readily, in either the home- or host-country market. The methods they choose for managing such changes are important for ensuring success.

Fortunately, we can gain a lot of insight by examining the international experiences of both for-profit and not-for-profit organizations. Moreover, a great deal of material is available on potential methods and so-called *change agents* (people or processes that intentionally cause or accelerate social, cultural, or behavioral change). The following sections discuss both experiences with and approaches to successful change, focusing on strategies in nine different areas:

- Value systems
- Cost-benefit analysis of change
- Resistance to too much change
- Participation
- Reward sharing
- Opinion leadership
- Cultural bridges
- Timing
- Learning abroad

We conclude with a discussion on the importance of learning as a two-way process—one in which companies transfer knowledge to and from both domestic and foreign markets.

Value Systems The more something contradicts our value system, the harder it is to accept. In Eritrea, for example, people eat less seafood than those in many other countries, despite having suffered several periods of agricultural famine while boasting a long coastline rich in seafood. One reason is economic. Because much of the population has traditionally not been able to afford the ice and refrigeration to prevent seafood spoilage, many adults have never developed a taste for seafood, worry about its safety, and believe it has a foul taste. Another reason is cultural: Eritrea's Cushitic speakers have religious taboos against eating fish without scales and insect-like sea creatures (including shrimp and crayfish). Thus, in trying to persuade these adults to eat more seafood, the Eritrean government and the United Nations World Food Program have faced formidable opposition. Among schoolchildren, however, whose value systems and habits are still flexible, officials have faced little opposition.[86]

Point

Does International Business Lead to Cultural Imperialism?

Point **Yes** The idea is pretty well accepted: International business influences globalization and globalization influences culture. Now, I have nothing against international business or globalization—at least part of it. What I don't like is *modern cultural imperialism*, which is what happens when the West, especially the United States, imposes its technical, political, military, and economic supremacy on developing countries.[87]

For years now, U.S. firms have been in the business of exporting U.S. culture—mostly through tactics that are rarely in the best interests of the national cultures it targets for economic domination. Because these firms nearly monopolize the international entertainment media, people all over the world are bombarded with U.S. movies, CNN, MTV, and the Disney Channel, not to mention the barrage of accompanying ads.

And what about the hordes of U.S. tourists who pay more for a night's lodging in a developing country than the hotel maid makes in a year? They'll tell you they're just taking a look at how the other half lives, but the fact is they're selling the U.S. lifestyle to a market that can't afford it and that's probably better off without it. Thanks to canned entertainment, nonstop advertising, and a sales force posing as tourists, culture shoppers in developing countries can sample U.S. possessions and practices to their hearts' content. Never mind that they come from a place (at least according to TV and the movies) populated mostly by the super-wealthy and by cops and psychotic malcontents whose daily lives are taken up with bullet-spattered body parts, round-the-clock sex, and inane family relationships. The lifestyle is seductive and promotes everything that's "Made in the U.S.A." That's why people everywhere are starting to behave and even talk like fictional Americans—after all, every speech from Manila to Managua is now peppered with U.S. slang. Along the way, people are letting their own cultural identities slip away.

Once they have a foot in the door, Western companies barge in to exploit the demand they've created, further destabilizing local cultures. In Mexico, Walmart thought nothing of putting up a superstore virtually next door to ancient ruins—eradicating the nearby street market—and bribing officials to alter zoning laws and sidestep required archaeological surveys, thereby destroying ancient artifacts with bulldozers and backhoes.[88] What's more, MNEs tend to cluster in urban markets, dragging workers away from rural areas to work under managers who speak only English and don't even allow time to go home for lunch.

I admit, if a country is rich enough, it can afford to resist cultural exploitation. Canada says no to foreign investment in culturally sensitive industries and makes sure there's Canadian content in local entertainment media. Finland discourages architecture that runs counter to tradition. France shuns outside languages and subsidizes a national motion picture industry. But even rich countries are affected. Some French TV programs and films are now being produced in English to cater to international audiences and more university courses are being taught in English, while some MNEs are contributing to the undermining of the French language in French-speaking Quebec.[89] In the developing world, where there's precious little cash for fighting off cultural extinction, people are at the mercy of foreign culture brokers.

Does International Business Lead to Cultural Imperialism?

Counterpoint

No You imply that people in poor countries passively accept everything they see in movie theaters and on TV. But they've turned their backs on a lot of products that international companies have promoted. Like most of us, they pick and choose.[90] You also imply that cultures in developing countries are the same. They aren't. They interpret what they see and hear—and what they buy—quite differently.

Like cultural purists everywhere, you've overlooked how cultural diffusion works. Through contact, culture heads in both directions and evolves. Way back between 100 BCE (BC) and 400 CE (AD), about 50 Mediterranean languages disappeared when people took up reading and writing in Latin and Greek.[91] Today, of course, very few of us converse in Latin, but that doesn't mean it's completely disappeared; it's evolved—namely, into the "Romance" languages.

I agree that many languages are in trouble today, and it's important to study them while they're still around. But the thing to remember is this: Most of them are giving way to dominant languages in the countries where they're spoken, such as Spanish, Mandarin, or Arabic. Of course, American English is seeping into other languages, but Americans have recently added a lot of foreign words as well. If you're a macho (Spanish) guy in charge of the

Counterpoint

whole enchilada (Spanish), for example, you're probably called the "head honcho" (Japanese).

Similarly, although U.S.-style fast food is almost everywhere, it has not entirely displaced local foods anywhere. When it comes to food, the result of international business is greater diversity for everybody. What we're witnessing is not "cultural imperialism" but cultural hybridization. In most countries, U.S. hamburgers, Japanese sushi, Italian pizza, Mexican tacos, and Middle Eastern pita bread coexist with the local cuisine. Mexico's Grupo Bimbo (owner of Sara Lee from the United States) sells tortillas in the United States and U.S.-style bagels in Mexico.[92]

Also, just because people in developing countries have taken a liking to soft drinks and fast food doesn't mean they've scrapped their traditional values. Moreover, some evidence suggests that, although young people are most likely to adopt elements from a foreign culture, they tend to revert to traditional values and habits as they get older. If that's the case, it's hard to argue that they're spearheading any permanent changes in their local cultures.[93]

As people seek to fulfill different wants, they must make trade-offs. But are people (and societies) worse off because they give up, say, lunch with the family to be able to afford certain consumer goods that will satisfy the whole family's needs? Globalization simply gives people more options. And tourism is also a two-edged sword. Rather than having a primarily negative effect, quite often it has helped maintain certain features of a traditional culture, such as the revival of traditional Balinese dancing because tourists want to see it.

A successful business, whether local or foreign-owned, must accommodate itself sufficiently to the culture in which it operates. This may mean revising plans to respond to local demands. Before Walmart finalized its construction plans in Mexico, executives consulted with anthropologists, reduced the store's height, and decided on a stone facade in a subdued color. Now it can be seen only from atop the pyramids. And while we're on the subject, you also failed to mention that the so-called traditional street market in question was peddling imported plastic goods rather than indigenous Mexican handicrafts. Many local residents had long complained about the lack of parking, stores that did not list prices, and rigged scales to inflate prices.

Cost-Benefit Analysis of Change Introducing products and practices abroad is sometimes costly, sometimes not. It can result in greatly improved performance, or only marginal change. Thus, a company must consider the expected *cost-benefit relationship* of what it does abroad. When U.S.-based Cummins Engine wanted to improve employee commitment in its Mexican plant, it succeeded by shutting down one day a year so workers could observe a religious holiday. On that day, Cummins hosts a celebration for employees and families at a cost that is much less than the benefits it has gained from improved performance.

Resistance to Too Much Change When the German magazine publisher Gruner + Jahr (G+J) bought U.S.-based *McCall's,* it immediately overhauled the magazine's format: changed editors, eliminated long stories and certain features, increased celebrity coverage, made layouts more robust, supplemented articles with sidebars, and refused discounts for big advertisers. Before long, morale declines led to greater employee turnover. More important, revenues fell because advertisers saw the change in format as too radical.[94] According to most observers, G+J might have obtained more employee and advertiser acceptance had it phased in its plans for change a little more gradually.

Participation One way to avoid problems like those encountered by G+J is to discuss proposed changes with stakeholders (employees, suppliers, customers, and the like) in advance. The discussion might help management assess the strength of the resistance, stimulate stakeholders to recognize the need for change, and ease fears about the consequences of changes. People might be satisfied that management has at least listened to them, regardless of the decisions it ultimately makes.[95]

Companies sometimes make the mistake of thinking that stakeholder participation in decision making is effective only with sufficiently educated people who are willing to speak up to make substantial contributions. Anyone who has had to deal with foreign aid programs can tell you that participation can be extremely important even in countries where education levels are low and power distance and uncertainty avoidance high.

Reward Sharing Sometimes a proposed change may have no foreseeable benefit for those whose support is needed. Production workers, for example, may have little incentive to try new work practices unless they see some imminent benefit for themselves. What can an employer do? It might develop the means of sharing gains with stakeholders both within and outside the company. For example, China National Petroleum has faced property damage from angry Iraqi farmers who have perceived problems without gains from living near drilling operations.[96] In contrast, a U.S.-Peruvian gold-mining venture won the support of skeptical Andean villagers simply by donating sheep to them.[97]

Opinion Leadership By making use of local channels of influence, or *opinion leaders,* a firm may be able to facilitate the acceptance of change. Opinion leaders may emerge in unexpected places. When Ford wanted to instill U.S. production methods in a Mexican plant, management relied on Mexican production workers rather than either Mexican or U.S. supervisors to observe operations at U.S. plants. What was the advantage of this approach? The production workers had more credibility with the Mexican workforce who would have to implement the new methods.[98]

Cultural Bridges Closely linked to opinion leadership are the attributes of people deciding about and then implementing changes abroad. People in the host country are persuaded not only by the details of a proposal, but also by their confidence in the presenters' technical qualifications, understanding of host-country constraints, and flexible attitudes toward reaching solutions. Bicultural and multicultural individuals may serve as bridges, especially if their cultures are from both the company's home and host countries. Even if the cultures are from other countries, these individuals may discern the new culture more quickly than unicultural individuals in much the same way that young bilingual children have an easier time than unilingual children in learning another language later on. Further, they have demonstrated empathy for divergent viewpoints and may be more positively perceived in the host country because of assumptions that they are not pushing an ethnocentric agenda.[99]

Timing Many well-conceived changes fail simply because they're ill-timed. A proposed labor-saving production method, say, might make employees nervous about losing their jobs no matter how much management tries to reassure them. If, however, the proposal is made during a period of labor shortage, the firm will likely encounter less fear and resistance.

In certain cases, of course, crisis precipitates the acceptance of change. In Turkey, for example, where family members have traditionally dominated business organizations, poor performance has stimulated a rapid change in this practice: rather than "running" the business, many families now serve in "advisory capacities" instead (often on the board of directors).

Learning Abroad Remember, as companies gain more experience in foreign operations, they may learn as well as impart valuable knowledge—knowledge that proves just as useful at home as in the host country. Such learning may concern any business function; however, access to R&D personnel is a particularly potent advantage in operating abroad. Nevertheless, if one goes abroad with the belief of already knowing everything, there is little chance to learn. But there are many examples of being open-minded with good results. For example, the merger between Renault and Nissan brought complementary strengths together. Renault brought its better financial management (typical of French firms) to Nissan. Meanwhile, Renault is learning more about Nissan's (and Japanese companies') ability to have functional groups work together to meet a common company objective.[100]

Finally, companies should examine economies and businesses abroad that are performing well in order to determine practices they can emulate. In India, for example, some large companies have performed extremely well recently, not in spite of but because of placing social missions and heavy investments in their employees.[101]

Looking to the Future

What Will Happen to National Cultures?

Scenario I: New Hybrid Cultures Will Develop and Personal Horizons Will Broaden

International contact is growing at a rate perhaps unimaginable a few decades ago—a process that should lead to a certain mixing and greater similarity among national cultures. At first glance, that's exactly what's happening. The mixing seems evident when one sees, say, a group of Japanese tourists listening to a Philippine band perform an American pop song in a British hotel in Indonesia. Likewise, combination languages such as "Spanglish" have emerged. The growing mix seems evident when people in every corner of the world wear similar clothing and listen to international recording stars alongside other people wearing local styles and listening to local recording artists. Competitors headquartered in far-flung areas of the globe are increasingly copying each other's operating practices, thus creating a competitive work environment that's more global than national. As companies and people get used to operating internationally, they should continue to gain confidence in applying the benefits of cultural diversity and globally inspired operating procedures to explore new areas in both workplace productivity and consumer behavior.

We'll also likely see people taking advantage of greater mobility and broadening their concepts of what it means to enjoy global or flexible citizenship.[102] Historically, most people who immigrated to foreign countries were able to return to their homelands perhaps once in their lives. They were thus compelled to accept the cultures of their adopted countries, sacrificing much of their native cultural identity in the process. Today, however, many who come to high-income countries to find work often obtain dual citizenship and maintain contact with their native cultures through travel, direct-dial phone calls, and Internet communications. On the one hand, these immigrants may tend to transfer culture in both directions, bringing greater diversity to both host and home countries. Further, as people travel more abroad, marriage among different nationalities increases; the number of Americans with foreign born spouses doubled between 1960 and 2010.[103] Evidence suggests that children in these circumstances are becoming bi- or multicultural, resulting in a class of international managers whose traditional ties to specific cultures are much looser than those of most people (witness CEO Carlos Ghosn of Japan's Nissan and France's Renault, a Brazilian of Lebanese extraction educated in France).[104] On the other hand, multiculturalism appears to be failing because immigrants no longer have to assimilate into the culture of their new residency, which could lead to more cultural strife within nations.[105]

Scenario 2: Although the Outward Expressions of National Culture Will Continue to Become More Homogeneous, Distinct Values Will Tend to Remain Stable

Beneath the surface of the visual aspects of culture (including most of the elements touched on in the previous section), people continue to hold fast to some of the basics that distinguish national cultures. In other words, although certain material and even behavioral facets of cultures will become more universal, certain fundamental values and attitudes will vary. Religious differences are as strong as ever; language differences still bolster ethnic identities. What's important is that such differences are still powerful enough to fragment the world culturally and stymie the global standardization of products and operating methods.

Scenario 3: Nationalism Will Continue to Reinforce Cultural Identity

If people didn't perceive the *cultural* differences among themselves and others, they'd be less likely to regard themselves as distinct *national* entities. That's why appeals to cultural identity are so effective in mobilizing people to defend national identity. Typically, such efforts promote the "national culture" by reinforcing language and religion, subsidizing nationalistic programs and activities, and propagandizing against foreign influences on the national culture. Further, even though people will be more internationally mobile, peer pressure will force them to adapt to their national cultures.

Scenario 4: Existing National Borders Will Shift to Accommodate Ethnic Differences

Several countries are showing more evidence of subcultural power and influence. Why? Basic factors include immigration and the rise of religious fundamentalism. Equally important seems to be the growing desire among ethnic groups for independence from dominant groups where they reside. Both Yugoslavia and Czechoslovakia have broken up for this reason, while ethnic groups in Britain and Spain (Scots, Catalons, and Basques) are currently pushing for independence. Meanwhile, some subcultures—such as the Inuits in the Arctic and the Kurds in the Middle East—transcend national boundaries and simply resist being "nationalized." Because they have less in common with their "countrymen" than with ethnic brethren in other countries, it's hard to assign them an identity on the basis of geographic circumstances.

Regardless of the scenario that unfolds in any given arena, international businesspeople must learn to examine specific cultural differences if they hope to operate effectively in a foreign environment. In the future, analysis based only on national characteristics won't be sufficient; business will have to pay attention to all the other myriad factors that contribute to distinctions in values, attitudes, and behavior. ■

CASE Tesco PLC: Leveraging Global Knowledge

—Mary Yoko Brannen and Terence Mughan

David Potts stared out the window of the 747 as it taxied for take-off.[106] His first visit to China as CEO of Tesco Asia had been exciting but had posed a number of big questions. The United Kingdom-based retailing giant had been in Asia for a little over a decade and sales and profits were already comfortably outstripping the UK and other Tesco areas, including Central Europe and the United States. Yet it was also clear that every Asian market was unique. Thailand, Malaysia, and South Korea had been great successes (the adjacent photo shows a Tesco store in Malaysia), Japan and Taiwan less so. The sheer size of China and India put them in a category of their own. How, then, was this venture going to develop across such a huge continent? And how could he capture and direct the energy and growth of Tesco Asia so as to continue to strengthen its core operations in the UK? Maybe Tesco could find an innovative answer to this challenge. It had done so supremely in other circumstances since its great transformation in the mid-1980s.

Company Background

Jack Cohen, who died in 1979, founded Tesco in the aftermath of World War I by purchasing surplus military supplies and selling them to a working-class population. Headquartered since 1973 outside London, his company became a readily identifiable feature of the UK retail scene. Known as a "Pile it high, sell it cheap" retailer with outlets in almost every town and city, Tesco knew its place in the class-based pecking order of the UK market, in which chains such as Sainsburys and Marks & Spencer met the needs of consumers with more disposable income and more refined tastes.

In the midst of the recession of the mid-1980s, Managing Director Ian McLaurin became chairman and ushered in a new management team that changed Tesco and its market

The photo shows a Tesco hypermarket in Ampang, Malaysia.
Source: © Beaconstox / Alamy

position radically. Relying on a cohort of young, talented executives with a Tesco background and an innate understanding of the UK consumer market (Potts and the current and past CEOs Phillip Clarke and Terry Leahy), McLaurin made Tesco into a store to meet all shoppers' needs. In fact, Tesco crushed the competition, including the Walmart-backed Asda, in the UK market.

Tesco's approach to the challenge of becoming market leader was to improve in every aspect of its operations, including distribution, marketing, land acquisition, and product innovation. The key driver of this approach was a change in corporate culture to emphasize attention to people. The new management prized loyalty and commitment from staff and was determined to make Tesco the employer of choice in the retailing sector. Such an attitude manifested itself in a company language that was simple and clear: "Treat people how we like to be treated" for customers, "Listen, support and say thank you" among employees.

David Potts took this belief in language a step further by compiling a "Jargonbuster"—a corporate dictionary that banished obscure terms and acronyms and laid down exactly how simple words make for clear communication. Such simple, clear language was increasingly important in Tesco's UK home base as immigrants and people with multicultural backgrounds permeated both the workforce and customer demographics. In the course of the 1990s this desire for clear communication extended further to the customer interface as the company increased the size range of stores: the *Super* stores, the smaller *Express* stores in urban centers, and the large *Extra* stores carrying the widest range of merchandise. Tesco bolstered its own branded food product range by adding the "Value" line at the lower end and the "Finest" line at the top end. With the help of an aggressive marketing campaign dubbed "The Tesco Way," which was led by the "Every Little Helps" slogan and the Clubcard incentive scheme, Tesco gained invaluable customer data and overtook its local competition. During a six-year period with Terry Leahy at the helm, its sales and profits grew by over 300 percent, making it the largest internet retailer and private sector employer in the UK. Thus, it began actively looking to international markets for the next phase of expansion.

Internationalization

In 1995 Tesco entered the Hungarian market by acquiring the S-Market chain. In 1998 it ventured further to find a local partner in Thailand and established Tesco-Lotus. An innovative partnership in 1999 with Samsung in South Korea formed HomePlus, thereby creating the bedrock for a sustained Asian presence—despite a disastrous £11 billion failure in Taiwan when Tesco sought to sell all of its Taiwan sites but had to settle on swapping them for stores owned by Carrefour (a major competitor from France) in the Czech Republic and Slovakia.

Tesco initially entered most of its foreign markets with an ethnocentric approach that sought to replicate its home success and culture in foreign locations. In the smaller and less distant cultures of central Europe this had worked well: then came France. The fact that the first international setback happened across the Channel was no great surprise; UK competitors such as Marks & Spencer had also found the British-French cultural gap too wide to cross, even though France was Britain's nearest neighbor. In fact, making English Tesco's operating language was harder in France than in any other country in which it operated.

Another problem occurred when Tesco launched Taiwanese operations by parading its Britishness—complete with Union flags and Beefeaters—in front of the store, and hence learned a strong lesson about foreign market entry strategy. Determined to banish any signs of imperialism and restore the qualities of hard work, humility, and customer dedication in future ventures, the company resolved to move toward a more locally responsive stance in foreign markets.

This desire to grow internationally in a bottom-up, locally inclusive fashion characterizes Tesco PLC. Of the young executives who came through the ranks in the 1990s, almost all were "lifers": people who started on the bottom rung of the corporate ladder, stayed with the company, and worked their way up. None, however, was more of a lifer than David Potts, who left school at the age of sixteen to work in his local Tesco supermarket. Gaining experience by stacking shelves on the shop floor and gradually moving into management gave him a deep understanding of the store, its customers, and the challenges involved in meeting their daily needs. Tesco even institutionalized this philosophy in the practice of TWIST—Tesco Week In Stores—whereby all management level employees must work one week a year in a Tesco store so as to always stay close to the customer and the stores' basic operations. All other activities of the company, whether supplier management, executive meetings, or government relations, are built around this key process. Extending this philosophy to include a policy of growing local talent from the bottom up in its international subsidiaries was a natural next step. Now, as CEO Asia, Potts was facing the challenges of operating in 14 countries across Asia, Europe, and North America. (Map 2.4 shows the countries with Tesco operations as of 2013.)

The main challenge for Tesco lay both in identifying the global advantages of its foreign subsidiaries as part of the Tesco group and learning from them in ways that would reinvigorate its home country competitive advantage. As a member of the Board for several years, Potts had accumulated a vast working knowledge of international business as Tesco rapidly became the world's third largest food retailer. How could he go about managing flourishing growth in Asia while maintaining and even enhancing the competitive position of Tesco's UK home market? Was there a way to transfer Tesco's leading-edge data, purchasing, and distribution resources across its global operations while also learning from the best practices evolving from operations in its foreign subsidiaries? And would it be possible to do all this and still maintain a globally integrated corporate culture? Was this a job for a consulting company? Could outsiders help solve this puzzle?

As he pondered over his challenge, Potts's thoughts kept coming back to the fact that in 2010, for the first time in over two decades, Tesco was losing its competitiveness in its home market: UK sales figures were down .5% for the year. Still, worldwide profits had risen by 12.9%, a growth led by the performance in Tesco's Asian regional markets. Clearly there was a lot that Tesco might learn from its Asian subsidiaries. But how?

MAP 2.4 Tesco Locations and Its Cross-Cultural Project

The orange-colored countries on the map show Tesco's operations by country as of 2013. The arrows indicate the countries sending personnel to the United Kingdom to participate in the project. Note that Japan participated, but Tesco has since closed operations there.

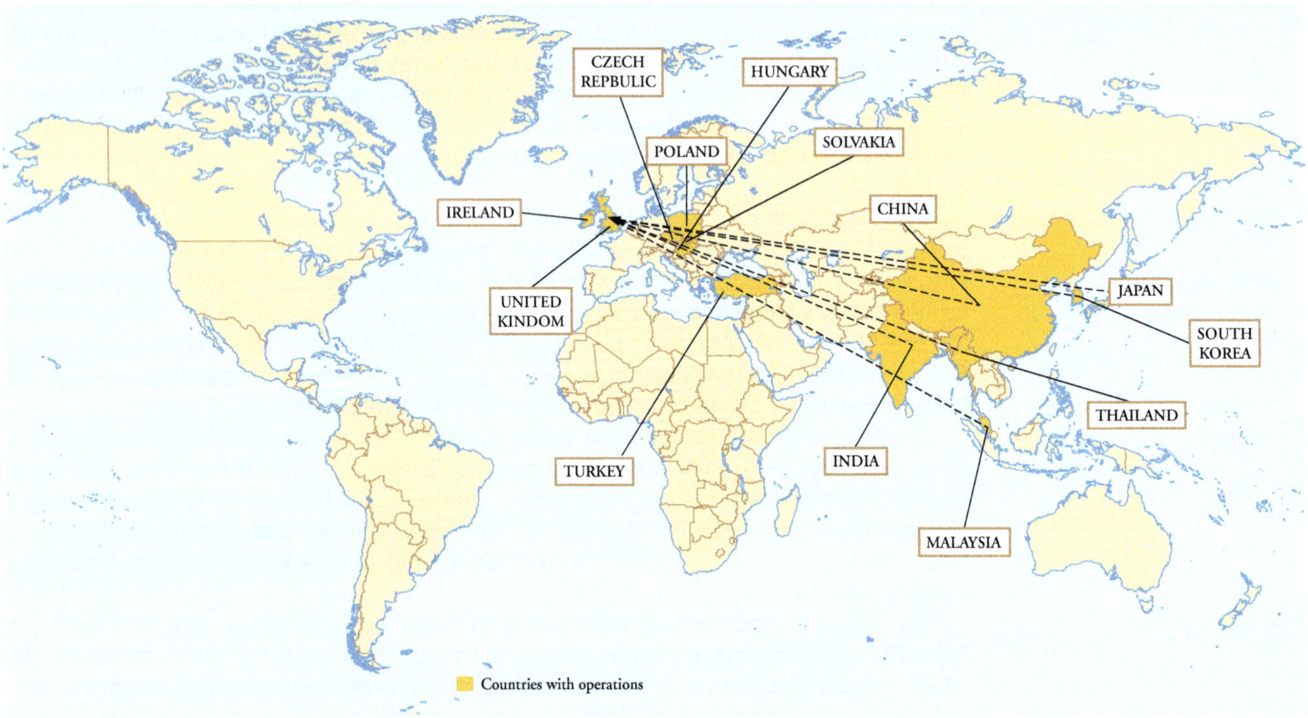

The Essence of the Tesco Project

Potts finally came up with a novel solution that was more consistent with Tesco's philosophy of building on its internal resources. Aware that declining growth at home is often a signal of complacency that can go unnoticed by people close to the situation, he decided to bring together a team of Asian managers who would visit Tesco in the UK to examine the home operations. As Tesco insiders they would be familiar with the company's mission, values, processes, and procedures and thus would be able to feel at home in the store context; as outsiders in the UK, they would be able to see things differently from the British managers, thereby bringing valuable insights from their home country perspective and sharing best practices that had evolved in their local markets. Potts called the project "The Essence of Tesco" and gave it a two-pronged strategic purpose: (1) to conduct a health-check of Tesco UK's current corporate state and determine what was and wasn't working; and (2) to compare and contrast that state with the processes and practices that had evolved in Tesco's Asian subsidiaries so as to learn from and leverage them globally for Tesco.

Nine managers were chosen from Tesco's six Asian subsidiaries: two each from Thailand, South Korea, and China—its largest Asian markets—and one each from Malaysia, Japan, and India. This Asian project team was then brought to the UK, trained in skills needed to observe and make sense of organizational behavior, values, and assumptions (a kind of corporate ethnography), and deployed for a three-month period to observe and work in 52 stores across the UK and Ireland. The task of helping Tesco reinvigorate home operations was not easy; nor had it been easy to find nine managers who could leave their job for an extended three-month period. In the end, the main criteria stipulated that team members had to have worked for Tesco for at least three years, had a working knowledge of English, and were store-level employees rather than country-level managers. The team was also assessed on various cultural adaptability skills needed to get by in a foreign environment, such as flexibility and openness, emotional resilience, and personal autonomy.

Three of the project team members were completely bilingual, having lived extensively in English-speaking environments; in fact, one had actually studied in England and thus had a deep cultural knowledge of the UK. These three proved very helpful to the team, especially with such practical things as opening bank accounts, navigating the public transportation system, setting up mobile phone contacts, shopping, and the like. The others had varying degrees of cross-cultural exposure and competencies in the English language. All were from group-oriented, high-context cultures, a fact that allowed teamwork to emerge quite naturally and ensured that the team would pay attention to unarticulated details—factors that proved invaluable for being able to see things in the stores that others from low-context countries might not notice. Team members' natural perceptual ability helped ensure that they would be able to act as organizational bridges between their home subsidiaries and Tesco UK.

This journey of nine Asian Tesco managers across the United Kingdom took place at a time when many British cities were shaken by riots and store looting. Still, the team compiled many pages of observances to use in creating their analysis of Tesco operations. Their exposure to British culture was intense on many levels. Two of them were actually locked in a Liverpool store during a riot and, though frightened, were impressed by the calm manner in which store managers handled the situation. The day-to-day experiences, though less exciting, were also very informative and gave rise to many comparisons and contrasts in implementing such core company values as customer focus in the UK and the home countries.

Brief anecdotes the team exchanged at the end of each working day can provide some insight into their findings. For instance, while watching a Tesco UK produce handler throw a bunch of bananas onto a display, Thai managers felt that UK standards were below what they were accustomed to. A Japanese project team member was shocked to learn that a UK fishmonger had only a couple of days' training before taking on the new role of learning to cut and prepare fresh fish, which was almost an art form in Japan and required several months of intensive training. Was Tesco still a place where everybody could develop a career? It certainly didn't seem so when the team exchanged stories of how one shop floor worker had never been enrolled in the career advancement program, or how another had been working at the same job-grade level for quite a few years. What were the reasons for this? By engaging with store staff, the project team found out that, although there was a clearly developed "Opportunity to Get On" program, an employee had to be willing to move geographically and/or take up a new job role in order to benefit from the program. The team uncovered many discrepancies between Tesco's espoused corporate culture and its everyday practices in the UK. Noting these discrepancies and asking follow-up questions, the project team members brought new perspectives to the company culture and were able to offer solutions from their own home practices.

In noting that Tesco UK does not take every opportunity to make the customer's experience as good as it can be, the Asian team offered suggestions about product promotions, family and community engagement, and customer service that would make UK stores more competitive. They provided great insights into taking advantage of the stock of market knowledge stemming from innovations that arose from the diverse partnerships forged in Asia. For example, by leveraging Samsung's technological strengths at Tesco Home-Plus Korea, Tesco-UK was able to come up with a smart phone app that could read bar codes off a panel shopping screen in the subway station and allow customers to easily shop online while waiting for their train. These and many other observations were absorbed by senior management in the form of a project report and in ongoing face-to-face meetings with the Asian team.

After almost two years, Tesco UK showed definite signs of reinvigoration at home. It employed 8000 new store personnel. It provided customer training to 250,000 staff members. Overall UK sales rose 1.8 percent. It has refreshed more than 300 of the UK stores, improved the bakeries in 850 stores, and increased online grocery sales by 12.8%. It has launched a club card and a T.V. channel, and the Tesco bank has 6.6 million account holders.

Tesco also continues to make great progress in Asia, which delivers twice the trading profits of continental Europe from only 33 percent more stores. The international strategy of the company has clearly moved beyond its ethnocentric past to become not only locally responsive but also capable of learning from its global operations. This is illustrated by the following statement on Tesco's web site:

> We will **win locally by applying our skills globally**. The key word here is "locally"—all retailing is local. But increasingly we are utilising the skill and scale of the Group to benefit the performance and competitiveness of each of our businesses around the world.

QUESTIONS

2-3. The United States and France are more culturally similar to the UK than are Thailand and South Korea, yet Tesco failed in the former two and has been highly successful in the latter two. How might you explain the difference?

2-4. In the context of global retailing, describe what you think is meant by "utilising the skill and scale of the Group."

2-5. What is the role of global teams in sharing best practices across a firm's global operations? What advice would you give to make the teams more effective?

2-6. What cultural skill sets are needed for individuals from multiple cultures to share best practices across the global group?

2-7. What are some things an MNE can do to facilitate knowledge sharing and global integration across its global businesses?

2-8. Look at the Tesco website. What exactly are its businesses and what do you think this tells us about its internationalization trajectory?

2-9. How would this business model translate into policies of recruitment, training and development, and career management across the Group?

SUMMARY

- *Culture* includes norms based on learned attitudes, values, and beliefs. Almost everyone agrees there are cross-country differences in culture, but most experts disagree as to exactly what they are.
- International companies and individuals must evaluate their business and personal practices to ensure that their behavior may fit with national norms.
- In addition to being part of a *national* culture, people are simultaneously part of other cultures, such as professional or organizational ones. Further, they may have more than one national culture.
- While studying other cultures is useful, there are problems in depending on self-reports to describe attitudes and values, assuming that everyone within a culture more or less fits the average, and depending on outdated information in dynamic situations.
- Distinct societies are often found within a given country. People also may have more in common with similar groups in foreign countries than with groups in their own countries.
- Cultural change may take place as a result of choice or imposition. Isolation from other groups, especially because of language, tends to stabilize cultures.
- People fall into social-stratification systems according to their *ascribed* and *acquired group memberships*, which influence their level of access to economic resources, prestige, social relations, and power. Individuals' affiliations may influence their qualifications and access to certain jobs.
- People work far more than they must to satisfy their basic needs for food, clothing, and shelter. They're motivated to work for various reasons, including the preference for material possessions over leisure time, the belief that work will bring success and reward, and the desire for achievement.
- There are national differences in norms that influence people's workforce preferences, such as whether they prefer autocratic or consultative working relationships, whether they prefer their activities to follow set rules, and how much they prefer to compete or cooperate with fellow workers.
- National differences in norms determine such behavioral factors as trust, belief in fate, and confidence in planning for the future.
- Failure to perceive subtle distinctions in culturally determined behavior can result in misunderstandings in international dealings.
- People communicate through spoken, written, and silent language—all governed by culturally determined cues. Cultural background also plays a major role in how people process information.
- Host cultures don't always expect foreign companies or individuals to conform to their norms. Sometimes they accommodate them because of trade-offs, sometimes they apply different standards to their behavior.
- A company usually needs to make fewer adjustments when entering a culture similar to its own, but it must be quite careful to heed subtleties both in host-country behaviors and in host-country perceptions of foreigners' behaviors.
- People living and working in foreign environments should be sensitive to the dangers of excessive *polycentrism* and excessive *ethnocentrism*. Usually, *geocentrism* is a safer approach.
- In deciding whether to make changes in either home- or host-country operations, a company should consider several factors: the importance of the proposed changes to every party involved, the cost and benefit to the company of each proposed change, the value of opinion leaders in implementing the changes, whether one can use people as cultural bridges, and timing.
- The future of national cultures may involve the emergence of new hybrid cultures, an adoption of similar visual aspects of culture while maintaining distinct values, the continuance of differences because of nationalism, and new nations based on prevailing cultural identities.

KEY TERMS

acquired group membership
ascribed group membership
bicultural
collectivism
cultural collision
cultural distance
cultural imperialism
culture
culture shock
deal-focus (DF) culture
future orientation
hierarchy-of-needs theory
high-context culture
idealism
individualism
low-context culture
masculinity–femininity index
monochronic (approach to multitasking)
multicultural
polychronic (approach to multitasking)
power distance
pragmatic
relationship-focus (RF) culture
reverse culture shock
silent language
uncertainty avoidance

ENDNOTES

1 We are particularly appreciative of personal insights given us by the following people in Saudi Arabia: Nora al Jundi, lecturer at Effat University; Omar Aljindi, consultant at Saudi Diyar Consultants; and Talah Tamimi, former executive at Saudi Investment General Authority. Additional Sources include the following: Sue Tibballa, *"Saudi Women Make History," New Statesman* 141:5118 (August 13, 2012): 17; "Saudi Prince Backs Letting Women Drive," *Miami Herald* (April 15, 2013): 11A; "Saudi Arabia: The Western Compound," americanbedu.com/2011/03/07/saudi-arabia-the-western-compound/ (Accessed March 15, 2011); Summer Said, "Saudi Activism Accelerates As Women Dare to Drive," *Wall Street Journal* (June 18-19, 2011): A9; Abeer Allam, "Saudi Women Bridle at Business Rules," *Financial Times* (May 22, 2009): 4; Karen Elliott House, "Pressure Points," *Wall Street Journal* (April 10, 2007): A1+; Karen Elliot House, "For Saudi Women, a Whiff of Change," *Wall Street Journal* (April 7, 2007): A1+; Roula Khalaf, "Saudi Women Carve a Place in the Future of Their Country," *Financial Times* (January 25, 2002): 3; Steve Jarvis, "Western-Style Research in the Middle East," *Marketing News* (April 29, 2002): International section, 37; Barbara Slavin, "U.S. Firms' Saudi Offices Face Manpower Issues," *USA Today* (May 13, 2002): 5A; Colbert I. King, "When in Saudi Arabia…Do as Americans Do," *Washington Post* (February 2, 2002): A25; Donna Abu-Nasr, "Saudis Begin to Show Wear and Tear of Life under Feared Religious Police," *AP Worldstream* (April 28, 2002): n.p.; Cecile Rohwedder, "The Chic of Arabia," *Wall Street Journal* (January 23, 2004): A11+.

2 Christian Tröster and Daan van Knippenberg, "Leader Openness, Nationality Dissimilarity, and Voice in Multinational Management Teams," *Journal of International Business Studies* 43:6 (2012): 591–613.

3 Helene Tenzer and Markus Pudelko, "Language Differences as Impediments to Shared Mental Model Formation in Multinational Teams," paper presented at the 54th Annual Meeting of the Academy of International Business (Washington: June 30-July 3, 2012).

4 Jeanne Brett, Kristin Behfar, and Mary C. Kern, "Managing Multicultural Teams," *Harvard Business Review* 84 (November 2006): 84–91; Yaping Gong, "The Impact of Subsidiary Top Management Team National Diversity on Subsidiary Performance: Knowledge and Legitimacy Perspectives," *Management International Review* 46:6 (2006): 771–98; and Aida Hajro, Markus Pudelko, and Christina Gibson, "Multinational Teams: Cultural Differences, Interactions, Organizational Context, and Performance," paper presented at the 54th Annual Meeting of the Academy of International Business (Washington: June 30–July 3, 2012).

5 Vas Taras, Pawel Bryla, Dan V. Caprar, Alfredo Jimenez, Peter Magnusson, and Riikka Sarala, "A Comparative Analysis of the Effects of Different Forms of Team Diversity on Global Virtual Team Performance," paper presented at the 54th Annual Meeting of the Academy of International Business (Washington: June 30–July 3, 2012).

6 David E. Brown, "Human Universals, Human Nature and Human Culture," *Daedalus* 133:4 (Fall 2004): 47–54.

7 Tomasz Lenartowicz and Kendall Roth, "The Selection of Key Informants in IB Cross-Cultural Studies," *Management International Review* 44:1 (2004): 23–51.

8 Ben Casselman, "Risk-Averse Culture Infects U.S. Workers, Entrpreneurs," *Wall Street Journal* (June 3, 2013): A1+ shows how a variety of entrepreneurial indicators changed with the economy.

9 Patti Waldmeir, "Property Bubble Erodes China's Traditional Preference for Sons," *Financial Times* (November 2, 2010): 1.

10 Richard Gesteland, *Cross-Cultural Business Behavior* (Copenhagen: Copenhagen Business School Press, 2012).

11 Four of the most significant are Geert Hofstede, *Cultures and Organizations: Software of the Mind* (New York: McGraw-Hill, 1997), which explores attitudes in 50 countries, primarily those concerning workplace relationships; Ronald Inglehart, Miguel Basañez, and Alejandro Moreno, *Human Values and Beliefs: A Cross-Cultural Sourcebook* (Ann Arbor: University of Michigan Press, 1998) analyzes political, religious, sexual, and economic norms in 43 countries; Robert J. House, Paul J. Hanges, Mansour Javidan, Peter W. Dorfman, and Vipin Gupta, eds., *Culture, Leadership, and Organizations* (Thousand Oaks, CA: Sage, 2004) examines leadership preferences in 59 countries. S, Schwartz, " A Theory of Cultural Value Orientations: Explication and Applications," *Comparative Sociology* 5:2–3:(2006): 137–82.

12 Anne-Wil Harzing, Michelle Brown, Katherin Köster, and Shuming Zhao, "Response Style Differences in Cross-National Research," *Management International Review* 52:3 (2012): 341–63.

13 Mary Lou Egan and Marc Bendick, Jr., "Combining Multicultural Management and Diversity into One Course on Cultural Competence," *Academy of Management Learning & Education* 7:3 (2008): 387–93; and Paul Brewer and Sunil Venaik, "National Culture versus Individual Culture: The Importance of the Ecological Fallacy," paper presented at the 54th annual meeting of the Academy of International Business (Washington, DC, June 30–July 3, 2012).

14 Geert Hofstede and Robert R. McCrae, "Personality and Culture Revisited: Linking Traits and Dimensions of Culture," *Cross-Cultural Research* 38:1 (February 2004): 52–88.

15 James W. Neuliep, *International Communication: A Contextual Approach*, 4th edition (Thousand Oaks, CA: Sage Publishing, 2009).

16 Robert J. Foster, "Making National Cultures in the National Acumen," *Annual Review of Anthropology* 20 (1991): 235–60, discusses the concept and ingredients of a national culture.

17 Harry C. Triandis, "Dimensions of Cultural Variation as Parameters of Organizational Theories," *International Studies of Management and Organization* 12:4 (Winter 1982–1983): 143–44.

18 See Aihwa Ong, *Flexible Citizenship: The Cultural Logics of the Transnationality* (Durham, NC: Duke University Press, 1999); Leo Paul Dana, *Entrepreneurship in Pacific Asia* (Singapore: World Scientific, 1999).

19 Choe Sang-Hun, "In Changing South Korea, Who Counts as 'Korean'?" *New York Times* (December 7, 2012): A10.

20 Ariel Sabar, "Last Words," *Smithsonian* (February 2013): 31–34.

21 Yadong Luo and Oded Shenkar, "The Multinational Corporation as a Multilingual Community: Language and Organization in a Global Context," *Journal of International Business Studies* 37 (2006): 321–39; and Vesa Peltokorpi and Eero Vaara, "Language Policies and Practices in Wholly Owned Foreign Subsidiaries: A Recontextualization Perspective," *Journal of International Business Studies* 43 (2012): 808–33.

22 David Crystal, *English as a Global Language* (Cambridge: Cambridge University Press, 1997): 1–23; Jon Boone, "Native English Speakers Face Being Crowded Out of Market," *Financial Times* (February 15, 2006): 8.

23 Sabar, loc. cit.

24 Evelyn Nien-Ming Ch'ien, *Weird English* (Boston: Harvard University, 2004).

25 Inglehart et al., *Human Values and Beliefs*, 21.

26 Matthew Coy Mitchell, "Corporate Legitimacy across Cultural Contexts: Mapping the Cultural Schemata of Religio-Institutional Actors," (Columbia, SC: unpublished PhD dissertation, Moore School of Business Administration, 2010).

27 Jong-Wook Kwon and Chuanxuan Shan, "Climate and Work Values: A Comparison of Cold, Warm, and Hot Regions in China," *Management International Review* 52 (2012): 541–64.

28 "When Culture Masks Communication: Japanese Corporate Practice," *Financial Times* (October 23, 2000): 10; Robert House et al., "Understanding Cultures and Implicit Leadership Theories across the Globe: An Introduction to Project GLOBE," *Journal of World Business* 37 (2002): 3–10.

29 Michael Segalla, "National Cultures, International Business," *Financial Times* (March 6, 1998): mastering global business section, 8–10.

30 James Kanter, "Renewed Push in Europe to Seat Women on Boards," *New York Times* (November 14, 2012): B3.

31 Amartya Sen, *Development As Freedom,* (Oxford: Oxford University Press, 1999): 192.

32 Fons Trompenaars, *Riding the Waves of Culture* (Burr Ridge, IL: Richard D. Irwin, 1994): 100–16.

33 "Putting the Malaise into Malaysia," *Asia Times Readers Forum,* at forum.atimes.com/topic.asp?topic_ID=9002& whichpage=10 (accessed May 27, 2007); Thomas Fuller, "Malaysia Vote May Rule on Racial Divide," *New York Times* (April 4, 2013): A10.

34 Clara Chooi, "Poor English Skills, Race Quotas in Way of Malaysian Prosperity, says ST," *The Malaysian Insider* (December 11, 2011): n.p.

35 "Black Women of Brazil," (November 20, 2011) www.blackwomen ofbrazil.com/2011/11 /(accessed November 23, 2012); "Affirming a Divide," *The Economist* (January 28, 2012).

36 Information on a number of gender-related indices can be found in UN Human Development Report (2011). *Gender Inequality Index,* pp. 139–42. Available at hdr.undp.org/en/statistics/gii/ (accessed 19 November 2012). For a discussion of the relationship between gender gaps and a number of cultural values, see Andy Bertsch and Gillian Warner-Soderholm, "Updating Cross Cultural Management: Exploring the Relationships between Cultural Values and Gender Inequality Practices," paper presented at the 54th annual meeting of the Academy of International Business (Washington, DC, June 30–July 3, 2012).

37 Inglehart et al., *Human Values and Beliefs,* question V128.

38 Shaila Dewan and Robert Gebeloff, "More Men Enter Fields Dominated by Women." *New York Times* (May 21, 2012): A1+; Josh Mitchell, "Women Notch Progress," *Wall Street Journal* (December 5, 2012): A3 citing Census Bureau data that showed women comprised about 10 percent of U.S. doctors in 1970, but 32 percent in 2010.

39 "Minimum Legal Ages for Alcohol Purchase or Consumption around the World," at www.geocities.jp/m_kato_clinic/mini-age-alcohol-eng-l.html (accessed May 28, 2007).

40 "The Employers Forum on Age," *Legal: Europe,* at www.efa.org.uk/legal/europe.asp (accessed May 27, 2007); Cindy Wu, John J. Lawler, and Xiang Xi, "Overt Employment Discrimination in MNC Affiliates: Home-Country Cultural and Institutional Effects," *Journal of International Business Studies* 39:5 (2008): 772–94.

41 Inglehart et al., *Human Values and Beliefs,* questions V129.

42 Francis Fukuyama, *Trust: The Social Virtues and the Creation of Prosperity* (New York: Free Press, 1995); Ana Paula Matias Gama, Jorge Manuel Mendes Galvão, "Performance, Valuation and Capital Structure: Survey of Family Firms, *Corporate Governance*12. 2 (2012): 199–214.

43 For a good overview of the literature on the Protestant ethic, see Harold B. Jones Jr., "The Protestant Ethic: Weber's Model and the Empirical Literature," *Human Relations* 50:7 (1997): 757–86. For evidence that other religions have equal or higher work ethics, see Yavuz Fahir Zulfikar, "Do Muslims Believe More in Protestant Work Ethic than Christians? Comparison of People with Different Religious Background Living in the US," *Journal of Business Ethics*105.4 (Feb 2012): 489–502.

44 Luigi Guiso, Paola Sapienza, and Luigi Zingales, "People's Opium? Religion and Economic Attitudes," *Journal of Monetary Economics* 50:1 (2003): 225–38.

45 See, for example, David S. Landes, *The Wealth and Poverty of Nations* (New York: Norton, 1998).

46 Hamid Yeganeh, "An Investigation into the Cultural and Religious Determination of National Competitiveness," paper presented at the 54th annual meeting of the Academy of International Business (Washington, DC, June 30–July 3, 2012).

47 David Gauthier-Villars, "France Wrests Title of Sleeping Giant," *Wall Street Journal* (May 5, 2009): A8.

48 Triandis, "Dimensions of Cultural Variation as Parameters of Organizational Theories," 159–60.

49 Hofstede, *Cultures and Organizations.*

50 Abraham Maslow, *Motivation and Personality* (New York: Harper & Row, 1954).

51 F. Pichler and C. Wallace, "What Are the Reasons for Differences in Job Satisfaction Across Europe?" *European Sociological Review* 25: (2009): 535–49.

52 Richard Metters, "A Case Study of National Culture and Offshoring Services," *International Journal of Operations & Production Management* 28:8 (2008): 727–47.

53 Hofstede, *Cultures and Organizations* 49–78; House et al., *Culture, Leadership, and Organizations.*

54 Hofstede, *Cultures and Organizations.*

55 Maxim Voronov and Jefferson A. Singer, "The Myth of Individualism-Collectivism: A Critical Review," *The Journal of Social Psychology* 142:4 (August 2002): 461–81.

56 See John J. Lawrence and Reh-song Yeh, "The Influence of Mexican Culture on the Use of Japanese Manufacturing Techniques in Mexico," *Management International Review* 34:1 (1994): 49–66; P. Christopher Earley, "East Meets West Meets Mideast: Further Explorations of Collectivistic and Individualistic Work Groups," *Academy of Management Journal* 36:2 (1993): 319–46.

57 Hofstede, *Cultures and Organizations.*

58 Inglehart et al., *Human Values and Beliefs,* question V94.

59 Srilata Zaheer and Akbar Zaheer, "Trust across Borders," *Journal of International Business Studies,* 37:1 (2006): 21–29.

60 Miriam Muethal and Michael Harris Bond, "National Contextt and Individual Employees' Trust of the Out-Group: The Role of Societal Trust," *Journal of International Business Studies* 44:4 (2013): 312–33.

61 Examples in this section come from the GLOBE (Global Leadership and Organizational Behavior Effectiveness) project. See Bakacsi et al., "The Germanic Europe Cluster: Where Employees Have a Voice," *Journal of World Business* 37 (2002): 55–68; Jorge Correia Jesino, "Latin Europe Cluster: From South to North," *Journal of World Business* 37 (2002): 81–89.

62 Ping Ping Fu, Jeff Kennedy, Jasmine Tata, Gary Yuki, Michael Harris Bond, Tai-Kuang Peng, Ekkirala S. Srinivas, Jon P. Howell, Leonel Prieto, Paul Koopman, Jaap J. Boonstra, Selda Pasa, Marie-François Lacassagne, Hiro Higashide, and Adith Cheosakul, "The Impact of Societal Cultural Values and Individual Social Beliefs on the Perceived Effectiveness of Managerial Influence Strategies: A Meso Approach," *Journal of International Business Studies* 35:4 (2004): 284–304.

63 Shirley Wang, "The Science Behind Why We Love Ice Cream," *Wall Street Journal* (November 9, 2010): D1+; and Nicholas Wade, "Human Culture, an Evolutionary Force," *New York Times* (March 2, 2010): D1+.

64 Benjamin Lee Whorf, *Language, Thought and Reality* (New York: Wiley, 1956): 13 claimed there are more than 6,000 words. "How Many Words Are There for 'Camel' in Arabic?" *Arabglot* (November 11, 2011) www.arabglot.com/2011/02/how-many-words-are-there-for-camel-in.html (accessed November 23, 2012) found many fewer, but nevertheless, many more than one would find in any other language.

65 "Legal Language," *The Economist* (November 10, 2012): 66.

66 Hyun-Jung Lee, Katsuhiko Yoshikawa, and Carol Reade, "Culture Under strain? Leadership Challenges of Japanese Managers in the UK and China," paper presented at the 54th annual meeting of the Academy of International Business (Washington, DC, June 30-July 3, 2012).

67 Hajro, Pudelko, and Gibson, loc cit.
68 Viviane A. Winkler and Ricarda B. Bouncken, "How Does Cultural Diversity in Global Innovation Teams Affect the Innovation Process?" *Engineering Management Journal* 23.4 (December 2011): 24–35.
69 Richard E. Nisbett et al., "Culture and Systems of Thought: Holistic versus Analytic Cognition," *Psychological Review* 108:2 (April 2001): 291–310.
70 "Babel or Babble?: Machine Translation," *The Economist (Online)* (Jun 11, 2012).
71 Don Clark, "Hey, #@*% Amigo, Can You Translate the Word 'Gaffe'?" *Wall Street Journal* (July 8, 1996): B6.
72 Wenting Zhou, "Translation Errors Cause Disputes over Contract Terms," *McClatchy - Tribune Business News* [Washington] (March 23, 2012) accessed November 24, 2012.
73 Terry Mughan, "Culture and Management Crossing the Linguistic Rubicon," *Language and Intercultural Training* 13:1 (Spring 1993).
74 Manjeet Kripalani and Jay Greene, "Culture Clash," *Business Week* (February 14, 2005): 9.
75 Christina Hoag, "Slogan Could Offend Spanish Speakers," *Miami Herald* (March 8, 2005): C1+.
76 Much of the discussion on silent language is based on Edward T. Hall, "The Silent Language in Overseas Business," *Harvard Business Review* (May–June 1960). Hall identified five variables—time, space, things, friendships, and agreements—and was the first to use the term *silent language*.
77 Alberto Rubio Sanchez, Alejandro Pico, Lucette B. Comer, Purdue University, "Salespeople's Communication Competence: A Study of the Mexican Market," *Journal of Business & Economic Studies*, Vol. 16, No. 1, (Spring 2010): 1–18.
78 For an excellent explanation of four ways to view time, see Carol Saunders, Craig Van Slyke, and Douglas Vogel, "My Time or Yours? Managing Time Visions in Global Virtual Teams," *Academy of Management Executive* 18:1 (2004): 19–31. See also Lawrence A. Beer, "The Gas Pedal and the Brake: Toward a Global Balance of Diverging Cultural Determinants in Managerial Mindsets," *Thunderbird International Business Review* 45:3 (May–June 2003): 255–70.
79 Trompenaars, *Riding the Waves of Culture*, 130–31.
80 Daniel Pearl, "Tour Saudi Arabia: Enjoy Sand, Surf, His-and-Her Pools," *Wall Street Journal* (January 22, 1998): A1.
81 June N. P. Francis, "When in Rome? The Effects of Cultural Adaptation on Intercultural Business Negotiations," *Journal of International Business Studies* 22:3 (1991): 321–22.
82 Inglehart, *Human Values and Beliefs*, 16.
83 Amin Maalouf, *In the Name of Identity* (New York: Penguin Group, 2000): 26, asserts that people pinpoint the aspect of their identity that is most under threat.
84 Mary Yoko Brannen, "When Mickey Loses Face: Recontextualization, Semantic Fit, and the Semiotics of Foreignness," *Academy of Management Review* 29:4 (2004): 593–616.
85 Mary Yoko Brannen and Yoko Salk, "Partnering across Borders: Negotiating Organizational Culture in a German-Japanese Joint Venture," *Human Relations* 53:4 (June 2000): 451–87; Baruch Shimoni and Harriet Bergman, "Managing in a Changing World: From Multiculturalism to Hybridization—The Production of Hybrid Management Culture in Israel, Thailand, and Mexico," *Academy of Management Perspectives* (August 2006): 76–89.
86 Geraldine Brooks, "Eritrea's Leaders Angle for Sea Change in Nation's Diet to Prove Fish Isn't Foul," *Wall Street Journal* (June 2, 1994): A10; M.Y. Teweldemedhin, "The Fish Industry in Eritrea: from Comparative to Competitive Advantage," *African Journal of Agricultural Research*, Vol. 3 (5), (May 2008): 327–33; "Taboo Food and Drink," *Wikipedia*, en.wikipedia.org/wiki/Taboo_food_and_drink (accessed November 26, 2012).
87 John Tomlinson, *Globalization and Culture* (Chicago: University of Chicago Press, 1999).
88 David Barstow and Alejandra Xanic von Bertrab, "The Bribery Aisle," *New York Times* (December 18, 2012): A1+.
89 Sam Schechner, "C'est What? French TV in English," *Wall Street Journal* (November 21, 2012): B8; Ian Austen, "Crackdown in Quebec: 'Le Gap' Won't Do," *New York Times* (November 23, 2012): B1+; Maïa de la Baume, "Bid in France to Add Course in English Raises Fear for Language, *New York Times* (May 24, 2013): A10.
90 Nader Asgary and Alf H. Walle, "The Cultural Impact of Globalisation: Economic Activity and Social Change," *Cross Cultural Management* 9:3 (2000): 58–76; Tyler Cowen, *Creative Destruction: How Globalization Is Changing the World's Cultures* (Princeton, NJ: Princeton University Press, 2002): 128–52.
91 Clive Cookson, "Linguists Speak Out for the Dying Languages," *Financial Times* (March 26, 2004): 9.
92 "Schumpeter: The Global Mexican," *The Economist* (October 27, 2012): 70.
93 Adrian Furnham and Stephen Bochner, *Culture Shock* (London: Methuen, 1986): 234.
94 Patrick M. Reilly, "Pitfalls of Exporting Magazine Formulas," *Wall Street Journal* (July 24, 1995): B1; James Bandler and Matthew Karnitschnig, "Lost in Translation," *Wall Street Journal* (August 19, 2004): A1+.
95 Mzamo P. Mangaliso, "Building Competitive Advantage from Ubuntu: Management Lessons from South Africa," *Academy of Management Executive* 15:3 (August 2001): 23–34.
96 Gina Chon, "China Faces Unexpected Problem Drilling for Oil in Iraq—Farmers," *Wall Street Journal* (May 22, 2009): A6.
97 Sally Bowen, "People Power Keeps Peru's Investors in Check," *Financial Times* (February 6, 1998): 6.
98 Roberto P. Garcia, "Learning and Competitiveness in Mexico's Automotive Industry: The Relationship between Traditional and World-Class Plants in Multination Firm Subsidiaries," unpublished Ph.D. dissertation (Ann Arbor, MI: University of Michigan, 1996).
99 Mary Yoko Brannen and David C. Thomas, "Bicultural Individuals in Organizations: Implications and Opportunity," *International Journal of Cross Cultural Management* 10:1 (2010): 5-16; and David C. Thomas, Mary Yoko Brannen, and Dominie Garcia, "Bicultural Individuals and Intercultural Effectiveness," *European Journal of Cross-Cultural Competence and Management* l:4 (2010): 315–33.
100 Mary Yoko Brannen, "Building Cross-Cultural Leadership Competence: An Interview With Carlos Ghosn," *Academy of Management Learning & Education* (Special Issue on Cross-Cultural Management) (forthcoming 2013).
101 Peter Capelli, Harber Singh, Jitendra Singh, and Michael Useem, "The Indian Way, Lessons for the U.S.," *The Academy of Management Perspectives* 24:2 (May 2010): 6–24.
102 Aihwa Ong, *Flexible Citizenship: The Cultural Logics of Transnationality* (Durham, NC: Duke University Press, 1999).
103 Neil Parmar, "A Global Love Affair," *WSJ.Money* (Summer 2013): 12–13.
104 James Mackintosh, "A Superstar Leader in an Industry of Icons," *Financial Times* (December 16, 2004): 10.
105 James Wilson and Quentin Peel, "Multicultural attempts 'Failed,' Claims Merkel," *Financial Times* (October 18, 2010): 3.
106 Mary Yoko Brannen is Professor of International Business/Jarislowsky CAPI East Asia (Japan) Chair, and Terrence Mughan is Associate Professor of International Business. Both are at the Gustavson School of Business, University of Victoria, British Columbia, Canada.

CHAPTER 4

Economic Systems and Market Methods

OBJECTIVES

After studying this chapter, you should be able to

1. Communicate the importance of economic analysis
2. Discuss the idea of economic freedom
3. Profile the characteristics of the types of economic systems
4. Introduce the notion of state capitalism
5. Profile leading indicators of economic development, performance, and potential
6. Profile the benefits and drawbacks of economic growth
7. Profile leading global indices of economic performance

Source: © picadillu - Fotolia.com

MyManagementLab®

Improve Your Grade!

When you see this icon, visit **www.mymanagementlab.com** for activities that are applied, personalized, and offer immediate feedback.

A man is rich who owes nothing.

—French proverb

CASE The Comeback Accelerates[1]

In the world of globalization, one often struggles to separate the rhetoric from reality. Optimists view it as an unstoppable wave transforming everything. Realists see it as just the latest stage in the evolution of the market, improving transactional efficiencies and expanding market frontiers. Cynics see it as the final stage before forces of deglobalization usher in the inevitable return to local enterprise. Despite wide-ranging opinions, few doubt that the ongoing integration of national economies resets the scale and scope of the global market.

Discussions have taken a far more dramatic tone the past few years. Some commentators see the flattening of the world whereby advances in institutions, communications, and technology fundamentally change the economics of globalization. "Flatliners" speak of "distributed tools of innovation and connectivity empowering individuals from anywhere to connect, collaborate, and compete."[2] Powered by hardware and software innovations, anyone, anywhere, can trade anything, anytime.

Others emphasize the effect of the entry of billions of people into the global marketplace. Some reason that qualitative change in the magnitude of the market drives a two-part transformation. Notes a leading analysis, "Three billion new people—a billion and a half Chinese, a billion Indians, half a billion people from former Soviet bloc—have suddenly come into the global economy all at one time. Within these three billion people is a population as big as the United States, bigger than anybody in Europe or Japan, who are every bit as skilled and can do anything that could be done in the U.S. or Japan or any of the developed countries for ten cents on the dollar."[3] Perhaps once or twice a millennium do these sorts of revolutions occur. Inevitably, the supply shock of billions of low-wage skilled workers radically resets how we interpret capital and labor in the production of goods and services. Forecasts of an end state of "globality" see a world where everyone from everywhere competes for everything.[4]

Finally, the ongoing fallout of the global financial meltdown raises the specter of slowing markets triggering deglobalization. Growing debt burdens, deflationary dynamics, risk-averse companies, and nationalistic consumers slow the cross-national movement of information, people, products, capital, and jobs. Governments constrain the animal spirits of capitalism, regulating what had become hazardously free markets. Economic freedom, as we saw with political freedom in Chapter 3, is under siege from surging state intervention.

WHAT'S NEXT?

Provocative in their own right, these interpretations suggest that in the opening decades of the twenty-first century, globalization has reinforced long-running developments and initiated powerful trends. The combined effects challenge one's lifestyle, job, company, country, and future. The possibility that globalization has reached an inflection point—namely, a time when old strategic patterns give way to the new—signals the need for managers to rethink economic principles and practices.

Understanding where we are heading calls for highlighting where we have come from. Initially, attention turns to how the world economy evolved from 1950 through 2000. During this time, the diffusion of democracy and free market principles powered growing trade among the richer developed nations. It also spilled over to many poorer developing countries. Institutions such as the IMF, WTO, and World Bank stabilized the playing field. Companies from the United States, Western Europe, and Japan—the so-called "Triad"—ruled international business and globalized the world in their image.

The precedents from this era, however, increasingly fall short in helping managers interpret today's puzzles. Indeed, focusing on the tried-and-true indicators of the past distorts one's interpretation of the contemporary global economy. Unquestionably, measures of the performance and potential in developed countries matter. However, they no longer matter decisively. Unfolding trends direct attention toward an epochal shift in the center of gravity of the global economy.

THE EMERGENCE

By 2050, four of the six largest economies in the world—Japan, China, India, and Russia—will be in greater Asia. Their growth will create a second tier of robust economies among their Asian neighbors, such as Singapore, Philippines, South Korea, Indonesia, Taiwan, Kyrgyzstan, Vietnam, Thailand, and Australia. Countries in other, once sluggish, parts of the world—Brazil in South America, South Africa in Africa, and Israel and Saudi Arabia in the Middle East—will develop along with their Asian counterparts (see Map 4.1). All are inexorably moving from the periphery to the center of the global economy, though each at a different pace.

Extrapolating from 2013 out to 2050 is, unquestionably, more speculation than estimation. Still, these countries are implementing powerful pro-growth policies. Hard data

MAP 4.1 Leading Emerging Economies

There are various types of market designations, including advanced, industrial, postindustrial, and developing. Here, we highlight those markets that are commonly referred to as emerging economies. These countries earn this designation given the status of their market development and high rate of economic growth.

Source: Based on Morgan Stanley Emerging Market Index and the *Economist*.

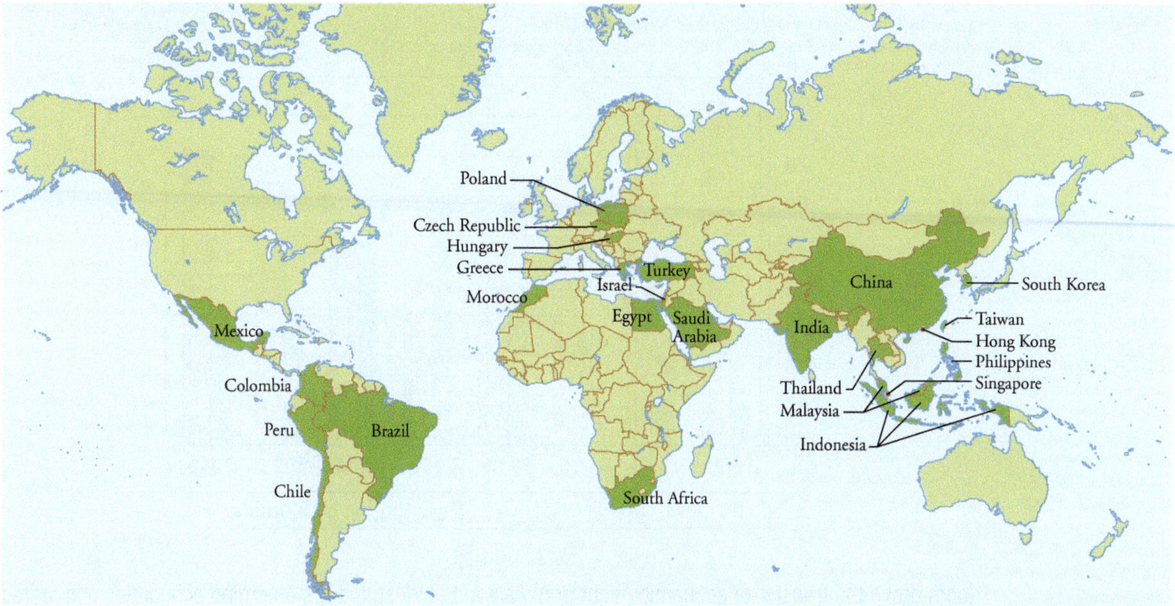

confirm their success so far. In 1980, the combined output of emerging economies accounted for 36 percent of global GDP. They crossed a milestone in 2009, accounting for more than half of total world GDP.[5] Similarly, emerging economies' share of world exports is nearly 50 percent (up from 20 percent in 1970). Their share of the world's foreign-exchange reserves is 70 percent (up from net deficits in the mid-1990s). China alone holds more than 28 percent of total reserves in the world. Elsewhere, the IMF reports that the ten fastest-growing economies during the years ahead will all be in emerging markets. Others suggest that 400 midsize emerging-market cities, many unfamiliar in the West (e.g., Sanaa, Ouagadougou, Chittagong, Kinshasa), will produce about 40 percent of global growth over the next 15 years.[6] Institutionally, the G-7, long a developed market stronghold, expanded into the G-20, thereby giving new members like China, India, Brazil, Mexico, and South Korea greater say in global governance. These new stakeholders advocate different views of trade promotion and investment regulation. Collectively, the accelerating rise of emerging economies signaled that the wealthy countries of the twentieth century would not dominate the global economy in the twenty-first century.[7]

The budding economics in emerging markets suggests the revolution has only begun. Ambition to improve infrastructure, increase productivity, create jobs, and alleviate poverty has put into motion what will likely be the biggest economic stimulus in history. The last transformation of similar magnitude—the Industrial Revolution—involved far fewer people in far fewer nations but still produced a century-and-a-half economic expansion that altered lives everywhere. Today's revolution spans the globe, includes far more people in far more countries, and represents the biggest opportunity in the history of capitalism. We are currently experiencing roughly ten times the economic acceleration of the Industrial Revolution, on more than 100 times the scale, resulting in an economic transformation that carries over 1,300 times the force of change. The transfer of the leadership baton from wealthy countries to emerging markets, for better and for worse, revolutionizes our interpretation of economic environments.

PRECEDENTS AND PREDICTIONS

Making sense of the situation moves some to review a broader span of history. Tracking the past millennium, they say, puts the current economic drama into perspective. Before the steam engine and the power

FIGURE 4.1 Emerging Markets Make a Comeback

Throughout most of the past millennium, today's emerging economies, most notably China and India, accounted for about 70 percent of global economic output. By the twentieth century, today's developed economies, such as the United States, Germany, and Japan, generated more than half of global economic output. Trends suggest that, by 2050, if not sooner, emerging economies will again account for more than 70 percent of global economic output, thereby culminating their comeback.

Source: Based on Development Centre Studies, *The World Economy:* A Millennial Perspective, OECD Publishing, 2006. Looking to 2060: *A Global Vision of Long-Term Growth,* OECD Economic Policy Papers, November 2012.

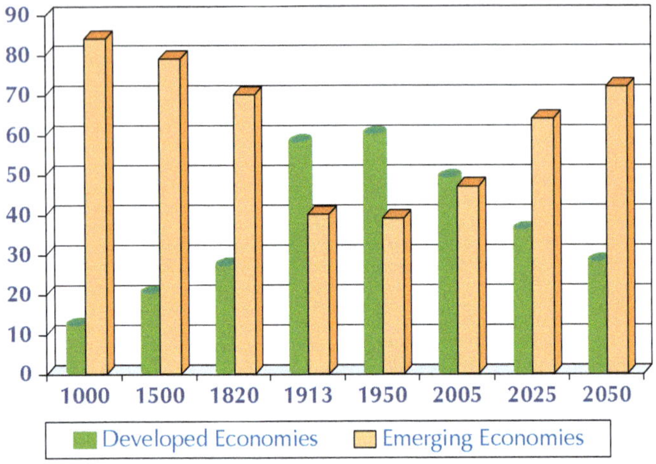

loom drove the transfer of economic might from Asia to the West, today's emerging economies dominated world output. From 1000 to the mid-1880s, they produced, on average, 70 to 80 percent of world output (see Figure 4.1). Over this span, China and India were the world's two biggest economies; China alone generated one-third of the world's gross domestic product in 1820. In 1850, China produced the highest percent of all the goods consumed in the world. Britain, riding the Industrial Revolution, soon claimed this title before ceding the top spot to the United States around the beginning of the 20th century. By 1950, emerging economies' share of global output had fallen to 40 percent, China's to 5 percent. They lost their lead (temporarily, trends now suggest) as internal political failure, aggravated by colonial exploitation and unfair trade agreements, spurred isolationism and xenophobia. Consequently, the Industrial Revolution benefited the West while bypassing today's emerging markets.

Today, their ambition is straightforward: Restore their historic stature as the engine of the global economy. Since 2001, annual growth in emerging markets has averaged 6.4 percent. While they expand, the global financial crisis slows and shrinks many developed economies, which on average have shown 1.6 percent annual average growth. Over the next decade, emerging economies will grow at an average of 6.8 percent a year. In addition, nearly 70 percent of the world growth over the next few years will come from emerging markets, with 40 percent coming from China and India and another 15 percent from Brazil, Indonesia, Russia, and South Korea.[8] In contrast, most developed economies will be fortunate just to grow. If these trends persist, in a couple of decades today's emerging economies will complete their comeback, again accounting for more than 70 percent of global output.[9] Symbolizing this process, China reclaimed the top spot it last held in 1850—producing 19.8 percent of all the goods consumed in the world in 2009; the United States, leader for the previous 110 years, produced 19.4 percent and fell to second.[10] Likewise, the IMF reported that by 2012 China had become the most "central" trading power in the world—the biggest or second-biggest trading partner for 78 countries.[11]

The diminishing role of today's rich economies, coupled with the accelerating scope of emerging ones, changes investment, trade, consumption, wealth, poverty, fiscal, and monetary patterns. For some, these shifts pose threats. For others, they create opportunities. Figure 4.2 suggests who sees which. Noted one observer, "No visitor to the emerging world can fail to be struck by its prevailing optimism, particularly if his starting point is the recession-wracked West. . . . [Emerging markets] see opportunities in every difficulty rather than difficulties in every opportunity."[12] In other words, strategic inflection points do not necessarily lead to disaster, as computers did to typewriters or the Internet to print-centric media.

FIGURE 4.2 Taking Stock of the Situation

Surveys regularly tap citizens' sense of their nation's economic situation. These results, the latest in a long-running series, suggest folks in emerging economies have greater confidence in their current economic situation than do their counterparts in developed markets.

Source: Based on Pew Global Attitudes Project: Country's Economic Situation, 2012, Retrieved April 15, 2013 from www.pewglobal.org/database/?indicator=5.

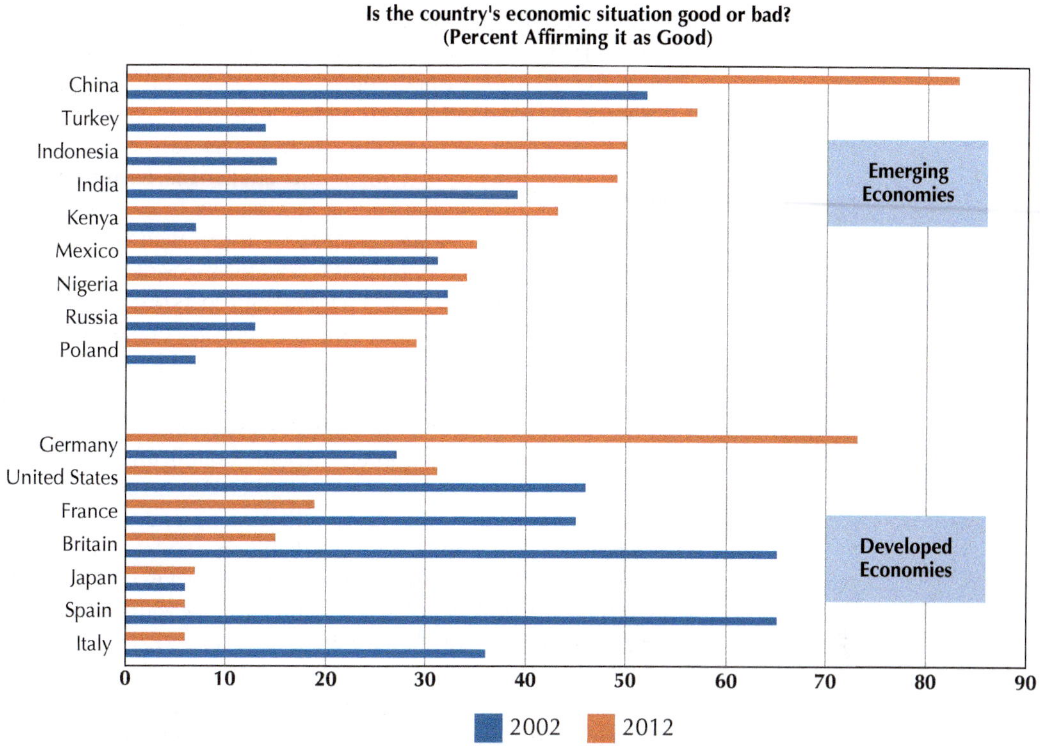

Change creates prospects for players, whether newcomers or incumbents, who are adept at operating in the new economy.

HERE AND NOW

Megatrends such as "The Comeback" are millennial events. And, unquestionably, trends often go awry. Still, at this point the odds are that policymakers, executives, workers, and investors will wrestle with the consequences of the Comeback. Against such a backdrop, this chapter profiles the frameworks they use to interpret the brave new world. Economic change, particularly the sort we have seen during the global financial crisis, seems unpredictable. Nevertheless, as this chapter shows, there is rhyme and reason that helps managers interpret the development, evaluate the performance, and assess the potential of economic environments. ■

CRN
Case Review Note

QUESTIONS

4-1. Transformations such as the Comeback happen quite rarely. Their infrequency, however, only amplifies their revolutionary impact on our lives. Identify from the case how your life has changed, or will likely change, given the Comeback of the emerging economies. For a point of comparison, think about what you've learned through your studies about how the transition from the Agrarian to the Industrial Revolution changed the way people lived their lives.

4-2. Identify from the case the three most important factors that you believe drive the Comeback of emerging economies. Explain why you think they would have the greatest impact on the development, performance, and potential of the economic environment in a developed country such as Germany, Japan, or the United States.

INTRODUCTION

As our first three chapters have shown, cultural, political, and legal systems influence a company's decisions on where, when, and how to do business. Completing our profile of the key dimensions of the macro-business environment, this chapter presents the general perspectives and specific tools managers use to analyze economic systems. All along, it identifies frameworks to integrate otherwise complicated and confusing interpretations.[13] Also, in the spirit of our opening case, throughout the chapter we compare and contrast the economics of developed and emerging markets.

Although easily overdramatized, these tasks are perhaps more decisive than ever in our lifetimes given the opportunities and challenges currently facing individuals, companies, and countries. Consider the following situation: In 2007, shortage of polycrystalline silicon—the main raw material for solar panels—threatened China's nascent solar-energy industry. Polysilicon prices soared tenfold in a year, hitting $450 a kilogram in 2008. Foreign companies then dominated production and passed high costs onto Chinese producers. Beijing's response was swift: The development of domestic polysilicon supplies was declared a national priority. State-owned banks, along with China's sovereign-wealth fund, poured money into local manufacturers. Local governments expedited approvals for new plants. In the West, polysilicon factories require lengthy reviews that add years to building plans. In China, entrepreneur Zhu Gongshan raised $1 billion for a plant, built it, and started production within 15 months. Since then, he has created one of the world's biggest polysilicon makers, GCL-Poly Energy—which counts China's sovereign wealth fund as a key owner. By 2013, the 10 largest Chinese solar manufacturers had borrowed $18 billion, almost entirely from state-controlled banks, to expand capacity and production in excess of worldwide demand. Today, China makes about a quarter of the world's polysilicon and supplies roughly half the global market for finished solar-power equipment.[14] To top it off, wholesale prices have declined by nearly 75 percent since 2008 as Chinese companies have flooded the market.

Managers study a country's economic environment to assess its development, explain its performance, and estimate its potential.

Rather than an isolated situation, the tale of GCL-Poly Energy is becoming the norm. Emerging economies are reinventing systems of production and distribution and experimenting with entirely new business models. From mobile money in Kenya to frugal innovation in India, innovations change the business environment. As a result, Western MNEs increasingly rethink strategies and reposition assets. IBM India's headcount, for example, has grown from a few hundred in 1999 to more than 150,000 today. Likewise, Cisco combined all of its emerging-markets activities into a single unit: "Cisco East" in Bengaluru. To spearhead change, one of its highest-ranking executives moved to Cisco East with the title of chief globalization officer. All the while, policymakers worldwide watch the game, adding this or taking away that in order to boost performance.

NEW MARKETS, NEW PERSPECTIVES

Studying an economic environment helps managers make better investment choices and operating decisions.

Managers track changes, evaluating events and trends to spot opportunities and preempt difficulties. The scale and scope of new markets easily thwart analysis. Therefore, managers commensurately stress-test their interpretations by qualifying analysis with new perspectives. Key viewpoints include:

Countries Differ in Various Ways Countries have different levels of economic development, performance, and potential. For instance, in absolute terms, gross world output more than quintupled between 1970 and 2012, growing from $12 to $69 trillion. Thus, globalization seemingly expanded the economy for all. In relative terms, though, many countries prospered, some more than others, and a few not at all. Why? Different reasons explained different performances in different countries. Hence, dissimilar economic processes require anticipating new situations. Forecasting, say, China's response to polycrystalline silicon shortages would have encouraged some options while rejecting others. Estimating the attractiveness of a country as a place to do business and, once there, making prudent investment and operational decisions depends on how well managers understand, anticipate, and adapt to the peculiarities of its economic environment.

Economic and Political Changes Alter Market Circumstances Although the pace varies from country to country, economic environments continually change. Since the 1980s, companies came to enjoy opportunities as nations adopted the principles of capitalism and practices of free markets. China's fast-tracking its polysilicon factories, impossible in 1980, moved it from the periphery to the center of the solar power industry in 2013.[15] Indeed, Chinese businesses' eagerness to rush into attractive industries, such as wind turbines, solar power, and robotics, and swamp it with state-backed investment disrupts normal economic practices. In the West, the global financial crisis has reset the game, triggering market reforms and tighter regulation. In the East, it has endorsed growing government manipulation of market activities to achieve political goals.

In both worlds, changing economic policies reveal government ambitions and spotlight implications for economic freedom. Executives worldwide must determine if events are isolated or signal the start of a trend.[16] Consequently, managers study changes, both big and small, both here and there, that shape economic environments. And, in the back of their minds, managers realize that steps taken in Ireland, Thailand, Australia, or Mexico differ from those taken in China, Brazil, Estonia, or South Africa. Moving from good to great performance hinges on distinguishing common trends from unique events.

CONCEPT CHECK

"The Forces Driving Globalization" explained how an economic environment responds to technology, trade, competition, consumer attitudes, and cross-border relationships. The scope of the connections among these conditions spurs MNEs to examine them as both independent and interdependent factors.

Connections, Change, and Consequences Globalization connects countries. Choice in one has consequence in others. So companies monitor changes in countries where improving macro trends or revised policies open markets or strengthen competitors. For instance, the United Nations estimates there are approximately 22,000 multinationals based in the emerging world. Few of these existed 10 years ago. Many more will exist 10 years from now.[17] The number of companies from Brazil, India, China, or Russia on the *Financial Times 500* moved from 15 in 2006 to 55 in 2012. Going forward, 400 midsize emerging-market cities will generate about 40 percent of global growth over the next 15 years.[18] Figure 4.3 highlights this process, showing the changing center of economic gravity in our world. It has shifted over the past centuries, but, since the mid-1980s, the pace of change—from the West toward the East-has been increasing. Since this trend shows strong signs of continuing, executives and policy makers must respond.

Consider, for example, the consequence of this shift to Evergreen Solar. Aided by $43 million in public assistance, it became one of the largest makers of solar panels in the United States by 2009. In 2011, it shut its Massachusetts factory, fired 800 workers, and shifted production to a joint venture with a company in Wuhan, China, citing the superior location economics and higher government support.[19] Others fared far worse; more than a dozen solar panel makers in the United States, as well as in Europe, have shut factories or gone bankrupt since 2012.[20]

CONCEPT CHECK

A principle of the globalization doctrine is the broadening network of relationships among people, companies, countries, and institutions. Philosophically, the same principle applies to the emergence and evolution of economies.

Challenges of the Comeback The rise of emerging economies distort traditional economic indicators. Greater competition for scarce resources raises the prices of commodities but lowers the costs of manufactured goods; more people are working worldwide but poverty is increasing; growing political control of economic processes improves efficiencies in the East but lessens them in the West; and recycling massive foreign exchange reserves means capital is too cheap here, too expensive there.[21] More than 70 percent of the world's growth over the next few years will be in emerging markets. Managers' macroeconomic instincts, tried and tested for the past decades in the West, must adapt to the changing, sometimes contradictory, circumstances in emerging markets.

CRN
Case Review Note

Choices of Citizens, Policymakers, and Institutions Economics is vital to citizens, policymakers, and institutions. By 2000, the apparent triumph of free markets over state-controlled economies had led many countries to launch bold liberalization programs.

FIGURE 4.3 Evolution of the Earth's Economic Center of Gravity: 1 CE to 2025

The world's center of economic gravity has changed over the past centuries. One sees here the big jump from Asia to Europe in the 1800s, due to the Industrial Revolution, and then onward to the United States in the 19th century. Since the mid-1980s, however, the direction and pace of shift has changed. Now, for a host of reasons, the center of economic gravity increasingly moves toward Asia.

Source: Based on Richard Dobbs, Jaana Remes, James Manyika, Charles Roxburgh, Sven Smit and Fabian Schaer, *Urban World: Cities and the Rise of the Consuming Class*, McKinsey Global Institute, June 2012.

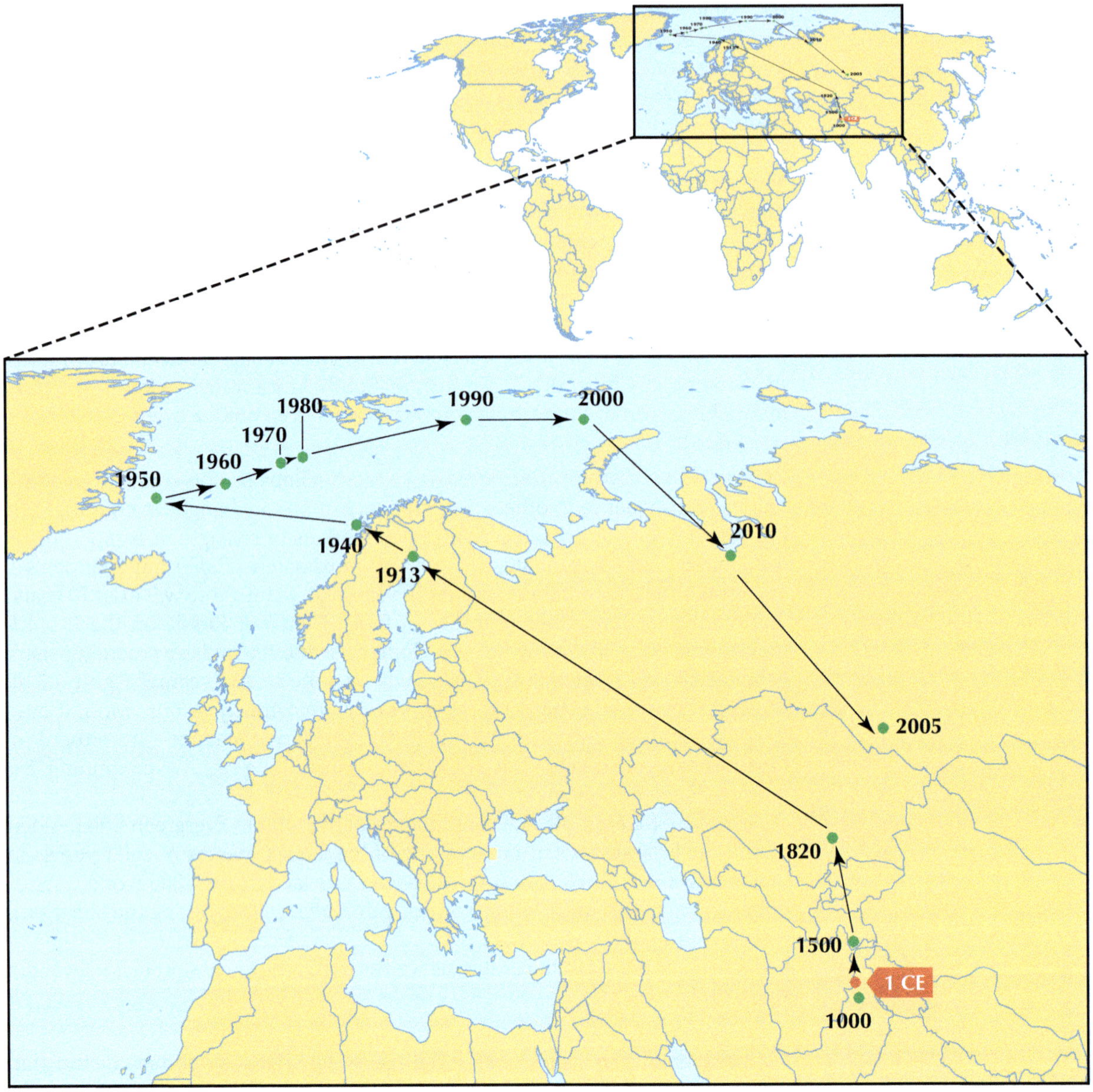

Pro-market reforms increased investment, consumption, employment, and wealth. The global financial crisis, however, contested the legitimacy and sustainability of market-led change. Free markets, the crisis showed, can also misallocate capital and fan opportunism. Governments, particularly those in the West, increasingly constrain the animal spirits of unbridled capitalism through stricter regulations. New market standards reset asset valuation and resource allocation, reshape trade and investment, and reconfigure industries. This perfect storm, as we saw unfold in the global solar power industry, changes efficiency frontiers, pricing patterns, competitive relationships, and government regulations. Hence, a fuller understanding of economic transitions and market evolution helps citizens, policymakers, and institutions make better decisions.

INTERNATIONAL ECONOMIC ANALYSIS

The World Bank identifies 214 discrete economic environments in the world today—188 countries and 26 economies with populations of more than 30,000.[22] Few MNEs can fund and run operations in all 214 markets. Resource constraints mean managers must prioritize their options, operating in countries that offer the greatest return with the least risk. Improving the odds of success depends on assessing the development, performance, and potential of an economy.

Given ever-present resource constraints, managers inevitably ask which countries in the world warrant investment as well as those they must avoid.

The study of economics has identified a host of objective measures that help systematize evaluation. However, although economics champions many scientific principles, it still relies on various behavioral assumptions to interpret activity.[23]As a result, the assessment of economic environments is often more conditional than universal because:

- *System Complexity* The complexity of even the simplest economic system defies straightforward classification. Stipulating indicators that definitively represent a country's economic performance and potential is difficult. Certainly, managers consult an ever-expanding set of indicators. The challenge is identifying those that matter, mapping them onto a market, and monitoring their performance.
- *Market Dynamism* Often, market changes make today's valid measures invalid tomorrow. In the wake of the global financial crisis, some indicators that worked in 2007 were flawed by 2009 and remained dubious in 2013. On a larger scale, analysis anchored in the market fundamentalism of the West poorly fits the state-sponsored capitalism at play in the East. Challenges arise in determining how to adjust trusted market analytics for new circumstances.
- *Market Interdependence* Just as no one is an island, no country is isolated. The consequence of connections is an integrated system in which actions in one market influence outcomes in others. Interdependencies complicate interpretations. Adjusting analysis for actions and reactions across a broad scope of markets is difficult.
- *Data Overload* Managers are flooded with more information, raw knowledge, and clever insights than ever before. Rather than improving market analysis, increasing data streams from workplace chats, mail, email, websites, voicemails, instant messaging, telephone and cellphone calls, memos, and onward complicates interpretation. If unchecked, analysis paralysis confounds decision-making.

Figure 4.4 shows how managers approach these issues. It identifies the macro-economic conditions that shape a country's development, performance, and potential. It also highlights

FIGURE 4.4 Economic Factors Affecting International Business Operations

Although economic environments vary from country to country, they share telltale principles. Managers often focus on universal characteristics, tors, notably the matters of economic freedom, type of economic system, and leading economic indicators, to organize analysis.

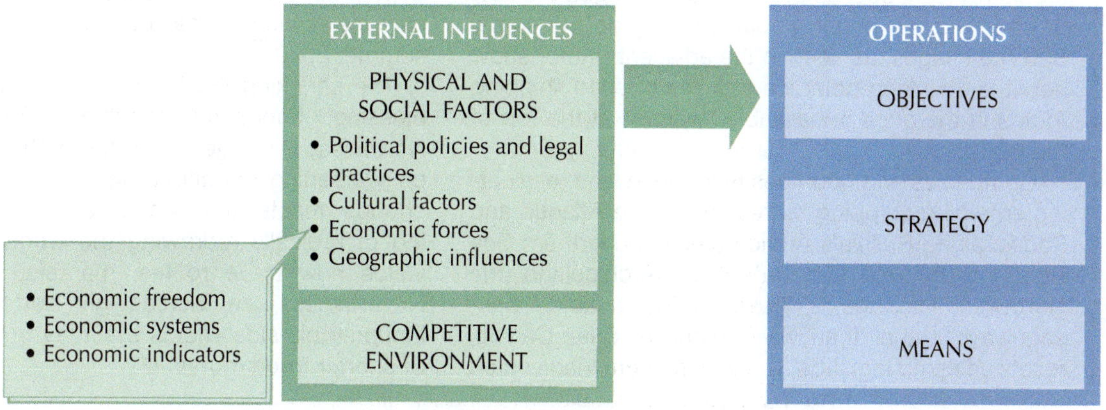

CONCEPT CHECK

Chapter 1 notes changing environmental conditions promote and constrain globalization, Chapter 2 notes changing cultural identities, and Chapter 3 notes changing political philosophies and legal outlooks. The same perspective applies here as well—namely, the changing economic environments of international business create opportunities and impose constraints.

the elements that guide assessment—namely, economic freedom and type of economic system—and suggests that linkages among them signify that a change in one causes change in others. Clarifying interactions among elements of an economy helps estimate its development path and performance potential. Therefore, managers typically integrate insights from company activities, analysts' reports, and news articles in developing a mosaic profile that represents an economy's features and estimates its interactions.

Figure 4.4 confirms the usefulness of applying a systems perspective.[24] It helps managers qualify their interpretation of economic conditions in terms of three criteria: (1) how much economic freedom they will have to make investments and run operations as they see fit; (2) the country's type of economic system and how current macro policies shape its development and performance; and (3) the drivers of economic change, particularly the micro-conditions that moderate economic freedom and the country's shifts in economic systems. Collectively, these insights pinpoint where investments should go and, more importantly, where they should not.

Does Geography Matter?

Consequence of Change in Arctic Sea Ice

Understanding economic environments moves managers to mind the world's changing dimensions, both physical as well as virtual. For example, economic geography is the study of the location, distribution, and spatial organization of economic activities across the earth. One would think, given the relentless expansion of trade and investment, that the terrain of our planet had been thoroughly mapped over the past millennium. However, for both good and bad reasons, we see intriguing developments in the geography of globalization.

Logistic Options: Canals and Passages Before the Panama and Suez Canals were built, shipping lanes circumnavigated the far reaches of the continents. Today, the bulk of goods moving between eastern United States, northern Europe, and Asia navigate the Panama Canal. Others, moving between Asia and southern Europe travel through the South China Sea, cut past Singapore, round the bottom of India, and pass through the Suez Canal to access the Mediterranean. Just as these canals changed the flow of trade, so too might global warming do the same. Satellite images, as seen in the adjacent photo, show how the shrinking polar ice cap has opened shipping routes in the once impassable "waters" at the top of the world.

Companies and countries respond in kind, evaluating emerging shipping routes linking the Atlantic and Pacific along Russia's Arctic coast (the Northern Sea Route) or through Canada's Arctic Archipelago (the Northwest Passage).[25] Traveling these fabled passageways, rather than via Panama or Suez Canals, resets shipping logistics. The voyage from Vladivostok in far east Russia to Rotterdam, Germany via the Northern Sea Route takes less than a month, compared to six to eight weeks through the Panama Canal. Shipping goods from Shanghai to Hamburg via the Northwest Passage shaves around 6,400 nautical miles (4,000 miles) and two to three weeks off the traditional journey through the Suez Canal.[26]

Ice Melts: Consequences and Choices Presently, ships can feasibly ply the northern routes at the end of the summer melt season.[27] Accelerating ice loss may largely free the Arctic Ocean of summer ice before 2050. Scientists tracking the annual maximum extent of the ice reported that 2011 was among the lowest ever measured. "For the first 20 years of the satellite record, the average annual maximum was basically uniform," reported NASA. "Then, in 2011, we see an abrupt decline."[28] Conditions continued deteriorating in 2012, with the total ice melt demolishing records. Satellite scans found that half of the ice went missing in September 2012, compared to the average September during 1979-2000. Current melt rates indicate the Arctic Sea may be largely ice-free as early as summer 2020.[29]

The shrinking Arctic ice cap is, at best, a mixed blessing. Improving conditions for traveling the Northwest Passage or Northern Sea Route depend on worsening conditions for the planet. As climate change resets the Arctic ice cap, to say nothing of radically redrawing the world's coastlines, it yields new trade routes, markets, and resources. Nevertheless, an increasingly hotter world poses innumerable side effects that may trump the benefits of shorter trade routes. ■

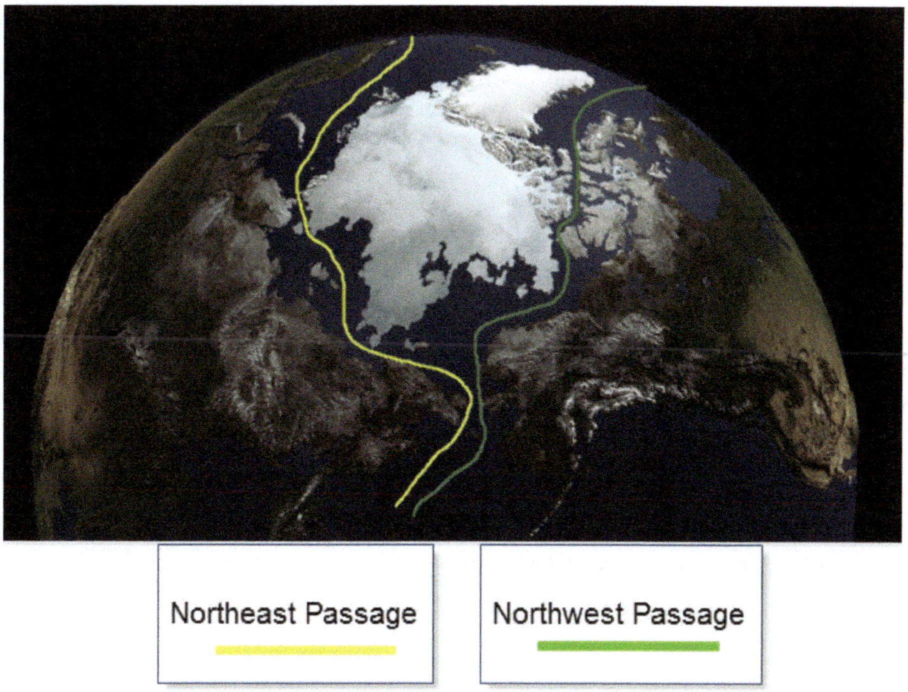

Passages through the Arctic Sea Ice

The shrinking Arctic ice cap is, at best, a very mixed blessing. If ice melt rates continue, they threaten to destabilize the environment. But, as less ice steadily opens the Northern Sea Route and Northwest Passage, it creates significant trade and logistic options.

Source: Based on NASA satellite image taken September 2010

ECONOMIC FREEDOM

Chapter 3 discussed political freedom for a simple reason: Any dialogue on politics, no matter the terminology, dimensions, or dynamics, ultimately addresses the issue of what one is free to do. We reapply the same logic here. Although managers monitor a range of economic issues, analysis ultimately centers on what they are free to do as economic agents: What investments can they make? How can they allocate resources? What property rights can they claim? How can they compete? Whom can they hire and fire? What forms of operations can they engage? In many countries, these sorts of freedoms are so taken for granted that they rarely cross one's mind. In many others, however, the freedoms are so repressed that they serve as ongoing points of fascination and recurring points of controversy.

Economic freedom holds that one has the right to work, produce, consume, save, and invest in the way that one prefers.

Against this backdrop, **economic freedom** is the "absolute right of property ownership, fully realized freedoms of movement for labor, capital, and goods, and an absolute absence of coercion or constraint of economic liberty beyond the extent necessary for citizens to protect and maintain liberty itself."[30] Put simply, the greater the degree of economic freedom, the greater freedom individuals have to decide how they wish to work, produce, consume, save, and invest. Economic freedom does not exist independent of the state. Rather, it is both protected and regulated by the state.

The **Economic Freedom Index** estimates the extent to which a government constrains free choice and free enterprise for reasons that go beyond the need to protect property, liberty, safety, and efficiency. The index rests on Adam Smith's notion that "basic institutions that protect the liberty of individuals to pursue their own economic interests result in greater prosperity for the larger society."[31] The Index of Economic Freedom analyzes 50 indicators that comprise 10 components organized into four categories (see Table 4.1). The Heritage Foundation annually applies this index to 177 countries, grading the performance of each. The higher the score on a factor, within the range of 0 to 100 percent, the higher the degree of economic freedom (or, conversely, the lower the level of government interference).

TABLE 4.1 Dimensions of the Index of Economic Freedom

The Index of Economic Freedom is constructed of 10 specific components of economic freedom. They are grouped into four broad categories.

Category	Component	Measure
Rule of Law	Property Rights	Ability of individuals to accumulate private property, secured by clear laws that are fully enforced by the state.
	Freedom From Corruption	Degree that corruption introduces insecurity and uncertainty into economic relationships
Limited Government	Fiscal Freedom	Tax burden imposed by government on its citizens.
	Government Spending	Government expenditures as a percentage of GDP.
Regulatory Efficiency	Labor Freedom	Aspects of the legal and policy framework that regulates the country's labor market.
	Business Freedom	The ability to start, operate, and close a business that represents the overall burden of regulation as well as the efficiency of government in the regulatory process.
	Monetary Freedom	The degree of price stability and the extent of price controls.
Open Markets	Trade Freedom	The absence of tariff and non-tariff barriers that affect imports and exports of goods and services.
	Investment Freedom	Ability of individuals and firms to move resources, without restriction, into and out of activities both internally and across the country's borders.
	Financial Freedom	Efficiency of banking as well as the independence of the financial sector from government control and interference.

Source: Based on information reported in "Methodology, 2013 Index of Economic Freedom Book," *The Heritage Foundation*, in partnership with the *Wall Street Journal*, retrieved February 6, 2013. www.heritage.org/index/book/methodology.

ECONOMIC FREEDOM TODAY

The aftermath of the great financial crisis and ensuing global recession has seen a decrease in economic freedom among countries worldwide. In 2011, economic freedom regained momentum, but by 2013 the global advance had ground to a halt.[32] Certainly, governments reiterated the importance of sound finances, open markets, regulatory reform, and property rights. And, among the 177 countries ranked in the 2013 Index, economic freedom scores improved for 91 of them while declining for 78. Nonetheless, the worldwide average freedom score was 59.6 percent in 2013, down from the pre-crisis high of 60.2 percent set in 2007.[33]

Asia-Pacific countries set the standard for both the best and the worst: Hong Kong, Singapore, Australia, and New Zealand are the world's freedom flagships, while North Korea, Uzbekistan, Turkmenistan, and Timor-Leste rank among the least economically free. Despite the United States' registering its fifth consecutive year of declining economic freedom, progress in Canada and Mexico supported North America as the world's freest region. Elsewhere, countries in South and Central America/Caribbean showed the sharpest drop in economic freedom; a continued decline held throughout the Middle East/North Africa; and the "mostly unfree" or "repressed" countries of sub-Saharan Africa struggled to gain traction. Europe shows progress with improvement in 32 countries and decline in just nine.

Worldwide, the expansion of economic freedom slowed in 2013; it remains below its pre-crisis high set in 2007.

Map 4.2 indicates that five countries have free economies, 30 are rated mostly free, 50 moderately free, 59 mostly unfree, and 33 repressed. The freest economies are Hong Kong, Singapore, Australia, New Zealand, and Switzerland; the least free include North Korea, Cuba, Zimbabwe, Eritrea, and Venezuela. The United States dropped to ninth place in 2013 largely due to increased government spending, debt, and regulations. Its score of 77.8

MAP 4.2 Global Distribution of Economic Freedom

The Index of Economic Freedom classifies a country as either: *free, mostly free, moderately free, mostly unfree,* and *repressed* given the degree to which its government regulates individual's economic choices. The greater the regulation, as indicated by a lower score, the less choice an individual commands.

Source: Terry Miller and Kim Holmes, 2013 Index of Economic Freedom, Washington, DC: The Heritage Foundation and Dow Jones & Co., Inc. 2013 (www.heritage.org/index/images/book/2013/region-web-map-WORLD-large.jpg, retrieved January 31, 2013).

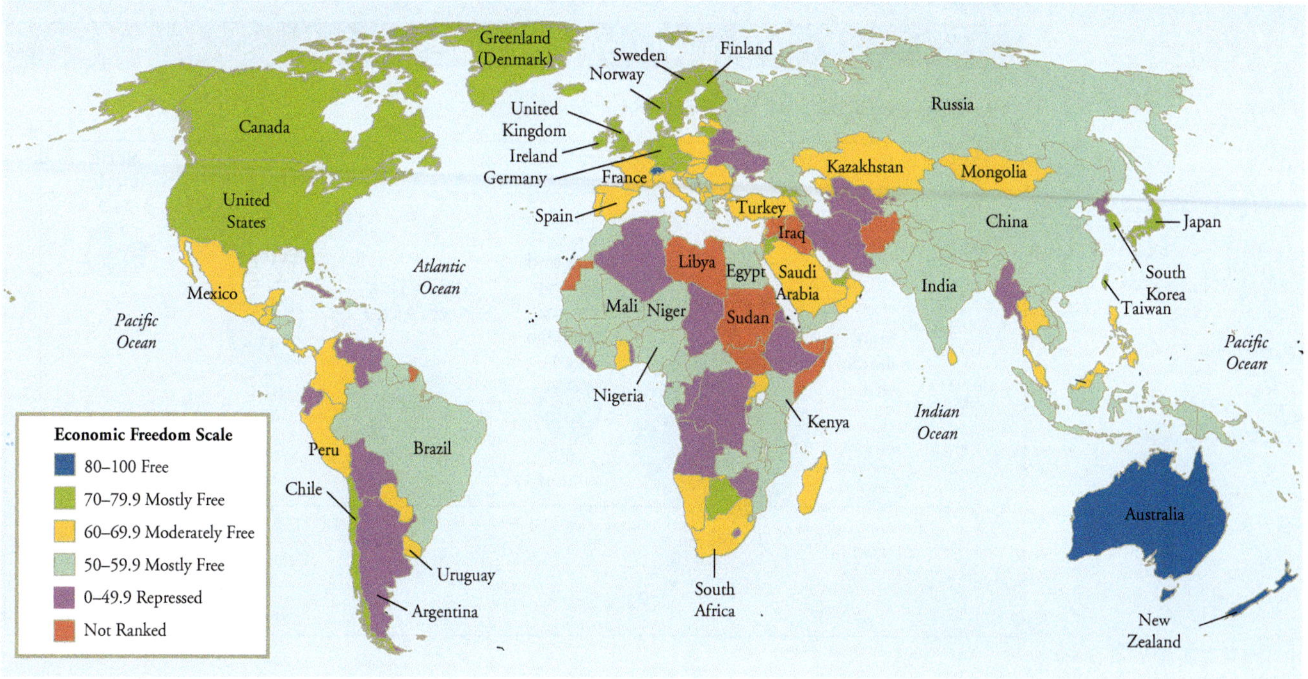

placed it in the "mostly free" category. In 2007, its score of 81.2 ranked it fifth worldwide and earned it a slot in the "Free" category. Lastly, qualifying the rankings by demographics refines analysis. Roughly 5.5 billion people reside in countries with somewhat to low degrees of economic freedom (see Figure 4.5), whereas approximately 1.3 billion live with moderate to high degrees.

THE VALUE OF ECONOMIC FREEDOM

Economic freedom helps explain a country's development, performance, and potential. Higher-rated countries generally outperform laggards on a variety of measures. They have higher rates of growth and productivity, and their average income is more than double the worldwide average and seven times higher than in mostly unfree and repressed economies (see Figure 4.6). Furthermore, inflation and employment rate better in economically free countries, as do life expectancy, literacy, poverty reduction, and environmental sustainability.[34] The message of economic freedom is unequivocal: liberating resources from government control improves financial performance, economic stability, and standards of living.

The track record of free markets around the world indicates that economic freedom is positively related to financial prosperity, economic stability, and standards of living.

TRENDS IN ECONOMIC FREEDOM

For the past few decades, managers had reasonably presumed that countries would reform their markets to increase economic freedom. Driving change was the fact that nations with free markets consistently outperformed unfree countries. The fall of the Berlin Wall in 1989, in punctuating the triumph of capitalism over communism, symbolized the supremacy of

FIGURE 4.5 Economic Freedom by Region, with Population

The relationship between economic freedom and population indicates that the vast majority of the world, approximately 5.5 billion people, lives in countries whose governments constrain their choices on how they wish to work, produce, consume, save, and invest.

Source: Terry Miller and Kim Holmes, 2013 Index of Economic Freedom, Washington, DC: The Heritage Foundation and Dow Jones & Co., Inc. 2013, retrieved January 31, 2013 from www.heritage.org/index/book/chapter-1, Chart 7.

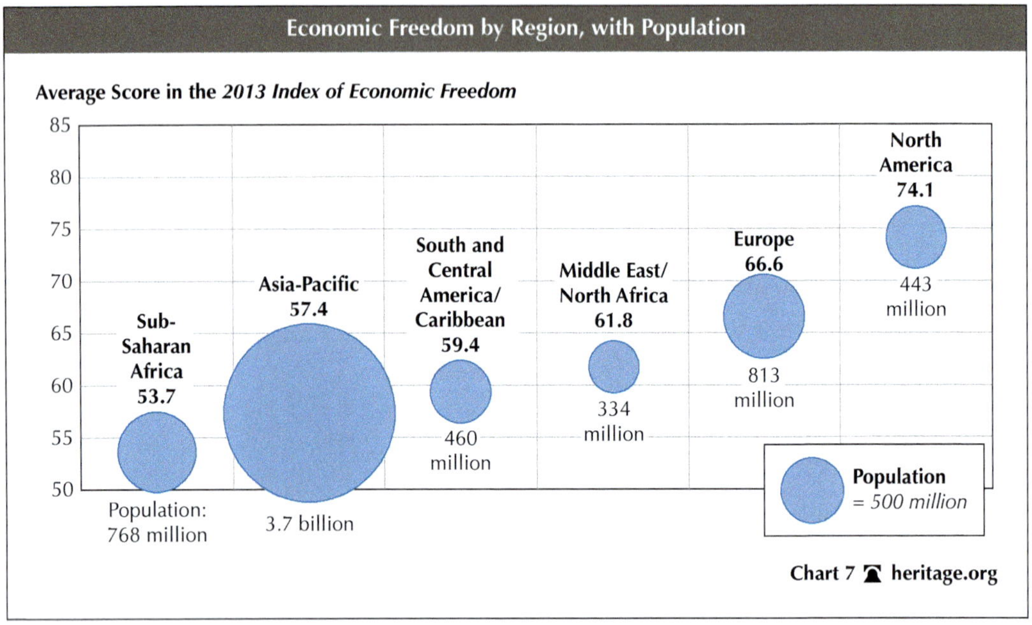

FIGURE 4.6 Economic Freedom and the Standard of Living

Economic freedom has powerful relationships with a variety of market, social, and political measures. Here, we see a strong positive correlation between economic freedom and a broad indicator of the standard of living.

Source: Terry Miller and Kim Holmes, 2013 Index of Economic Freedom, Washington, DC: The Heritage Foundation and Dow Jones & Co., Inc. 2013, retrieved January 31 from www.heritage.org/index/book/chapter-1, Chart 3, 2013.

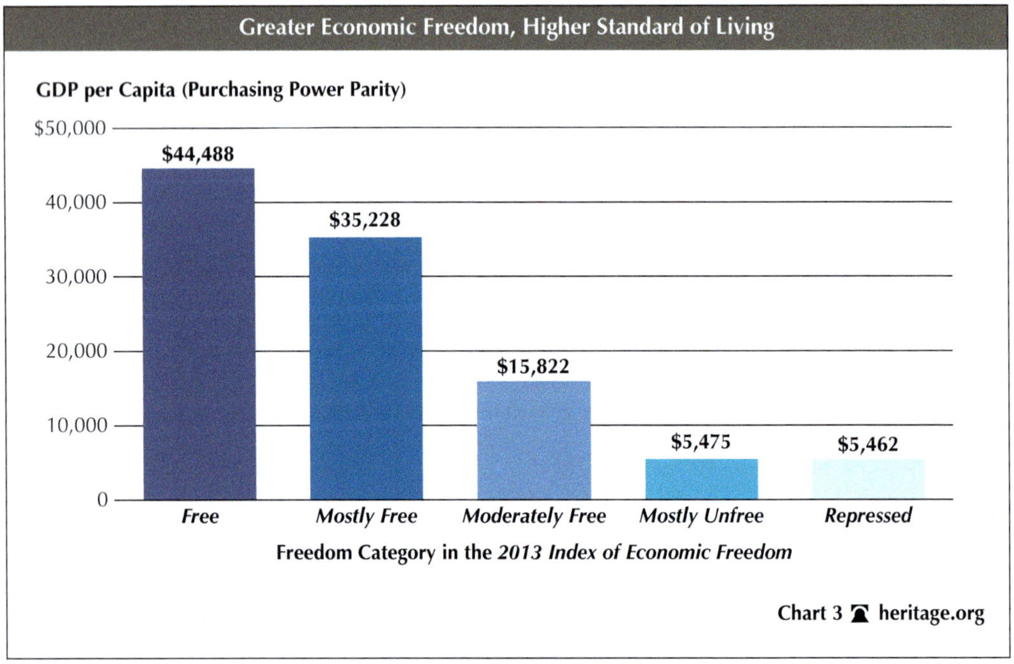

economic freedom over state tyranny. Large and growing majorities believed that people's lives benefit more, not less, with greater personal choice. Increasingly, countries abandoned the policies of state control and adopted the principles of economic freedom and practices of capitalism. Throughout the world, governments deferred to the laws of supply and demand—the invisible hand of the marketplace rather than the visible hand of politicians—to anchor the philosophy and regulate the practices of their economic environments.

The global financial crisis, by spurring a resurgence of state intervention, has interrupted the decades-long expansion of economic freedom.

Today, changing marketplace conditions and unfolding political trends threaten MNEs with increasingly uncertain economic circumstances. The global financial crisis has disrupted the expansion of economic freedoms. In the United States and elsewhere, the immediate aftermath of the crisis saw measures of consumption, investment, industrial production, exports, and equity valuations tracking or doing worse than trends seen during the Great Depression.[35] Stubborn downturns in many economies signaled the biggest global economic contraction since World War II.

The scale, scope, and swiftness of the global financial crisis highlighted the limits of a market economy, contested the usefulness of market fundamentalism, and spurred rethinking of government's role in the economy. To that end, declared former U.S. President George W. Bush during the height of the crisis, "I've abandoned free-market principles to save the free-market system."[36] States' neoliberal policies tightened controls in a rush to regulate the animal spirits of free markets. Stabilizing panics, safeguarding citizens, redistributing wealth, and sustaining demand took precedence; each objective inevitably diminished economic freedom.

Today, some seven years down the road from the start of the crisis, many economies have stabilized and begun recovering. Still, sovereign debt crises, deflationary dynamics, sluggish growth, and rising unemployment complicate projections. As the world regroups, managers struggle to pinpoint the implication of these trends.

Fear of Freer Markets The causes and consequences of the crisis challenge the legitimacy of the quest to maximize economic freedom. Many countries, especially those hit hardest and still experiencing anemic growth—such as Spain, Italy, Ireland, Portugal, Cyprus, Greece, France, and Japan—show weakening support for free markets. Rather than regarding economic freedom as an unconditional ideal, many fortify safeguards to prevent market disruptions. Consequently, state control of economic affairs escalates. Concurrently, dissatisfaction with neoliberal capitalism prevails across the globe. An average of 11 percent of respondents across 27 countries held the opinion that capitalism works well.[37] Some 23 percent saw it as fatally flawed. Many called for a new economic system—including 43 percent in France, 38 percent in Mexico, 35 percent in Brazil, and 31 percent in Ukraine. Only in two countries—United States (25 percent) and Pakistan (21 percent)—did more than one in five feel that capitalism works well as it stands.[38]

CRN
Case Review Note

Our opening case cautions against qualifying attitudes in developed versus emerging economies. In 2002, 80 percent of Americans regarded the free market as the best economic system for the future—then the bellwether of support. By 2010, support had fallen to 59 percent. Conversely, emerging economies' enthusiasm for free markets exceed that now found in the United States. Nominally Communist China is one of the world's strongest supporters of free markets at 68 percent, up from 66 percent in 2002. Some 67 percent of Brazilians and 59 percent of Indians see free markets as the best option for the future, though they concede that its endemic flaws require reform and regulation.[39] Overall, about half of the "world" reasons that the free market is still the best option. However, as we will see below, standards of economic freedom differ between developed and emerging markets.

Managers watch key events to gauge the contest between economic freedom and state control. These include how the government

- regulates the economy
- protects property rights
- sets fiscal and monetary policies
- enforces antitrust regulation

The Market Test A first-order goal of an economic system is straightforward: apply sound macroeconomic policies that sustain productive enterprise. Low inflation, high employment, prudent public finances, and openness to trade and FDI are telltale signs. Meeting these standards powers performance and boosts potential. In situations like those we see today, the legitimacy of the prevailing economic outlook is ultimately tied to how people feel about their particular situation. Those whose lives improve support it; those whose lives deteriorate clamor for change. Dire circumstances spur calls for government intervention as citizens appeal to politicians to impose stability. Presently, if the legacies of the global financial crisis persist or worsen, we will see more people contest the legitimacy of free markets. Continuing skepticism will push for greater state control and, consequently, less economic freedom.

In summary, the question of whether free markets and their endorsement of maximum economic freedom create the superior economic system is no longer a straw man. The global financial crisis, besides disrupting markets, disrupts interpretations.[40] In many countries, notably those in the developed block, praise for the virtues of economic freedom has turned to criticism of its deficiencies. In others, notably emerging economies, we see the opposite. The evolution and interplay of these quite dissimilar perspectives alters the relationship between markets and governments. Managers watch trends evolve, resetting interpretations as needed.

TYPES OF ECONOMIC SYSTEMS

An economic system organizes the production, distribution, and consumption of goods and services.

Wherever they go, managers question how the host government might regulate the economy, authorize property rights, implement fiscal and monetary policies, and ultimately interpret economic freedom. Managers frame analysis by evaluating the particular type of **economic system** in a country. Despite variation here and there, throughout the world we see three types of economic systems: the *market*, *mixed*, and *command* economies (see Figure 4.7).

CONCEPT CHECK

Chapter 3 notes that the individual voter is the cornerstone of a democracy. Here we add that the individual, as a consumer, is the key factor in a free market. Whereas democracy recognizes the supremacy of voter sovereignty, the market economy recognizes the supremacy of consumer sovereignty.

MARKET ECONOMY

An economic system whereby individuals, rather than the government, make most decisions is a **market economy**. It is anchored in the doctrine of **capitalism** and the principle that private ownership confers inalienable property rights that legitimize the profits earned by one's initiative, investment, and risk. Optimal resource allocation follows from consumers exercising their freedom of choice and producers responding accordingly. A market economy of the sort seen in Hong Kong, Singapore, Australia, Switzerland, Canada, and the United States, for instance, grants people the economic freedom to decide where to work, what to do and for how long, how to spend or save money, and whether to consume now or later.[41]

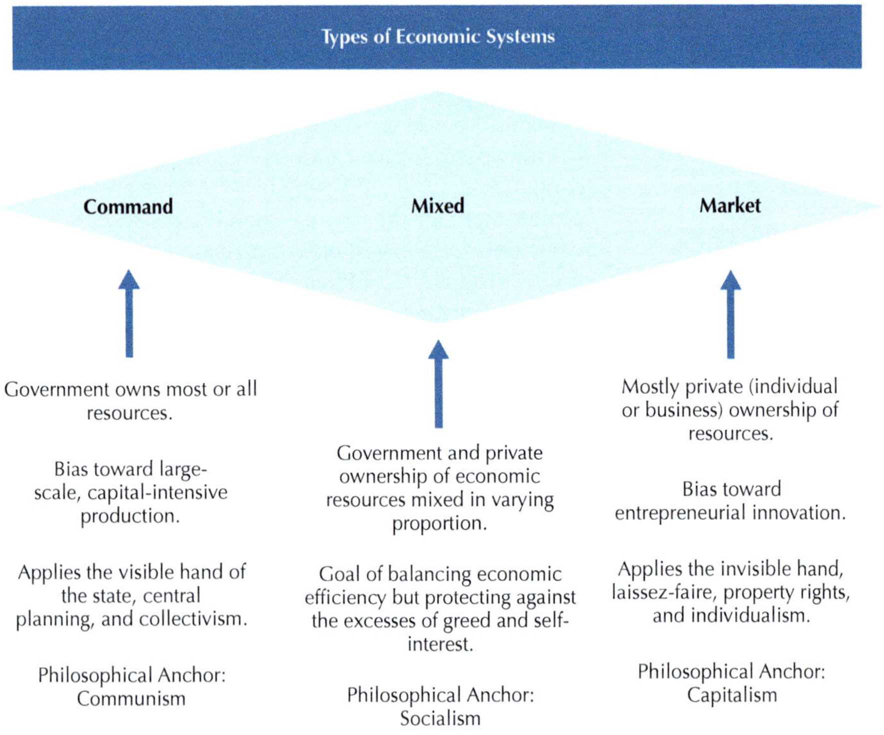

FIGURE 4.7 Types of Economic Systems

The three predominant types of economic systems endorse different philosophies, advocate different principles, and apply different approaches.

TABLE 4.2 Means and Methods of a Market Economy

Telltale signs of a market economy endorse themes of individualism and principles of economic freedom. Here, we profile key means and methods of developing and sustaining a market economy.

Privatization	A necessary condition of a market economy is the state's sale and legal transfer of government-owned resources to private interests. Privatization, by letting the private sector regulate supply and demand, improves production and consumption decisions.
Deregulation	Government regulations reduce individual choice—i.e., "Government is not a solution to our problem. Government is the problem."[42] Deregulation helps markets optimize productivity.
Property Rights	Property rights give entrepreneurs ownership of their idea, effort, and risk. Protection boosts economic freedom by assuring individuals, not the government, will prosper from their ingenuity.
Antitrust Legislation	Antitrust laws encourage the formation of industries with as many competing businesses as the market can sustain. They prevent monopolies from exploiting consumers and restraining market growth.

Ultimately, individuals' free choice in a market economy powers a country's progress toward prosperity.

Capitalism is based on the principle of private ownership of capital.

The market economy champions the doctrine of **laissez-faire**, which can be literally translated as "Let do," and more broadly advises "Let it be" or "Leave it alone." Whatever the translation, it opposes governmental interference in economic affairs beyond the minimum necessary for the maintenance of peace, safety, and property rights. It sees the "invisible hand" of self-interested consumers as the foundation of efficient markets. Consumers, through their interactions with producers, optimally determine relationships among price, quantity, supply, and demand. As Adam Smith observed, a market economy pushes producers, spurred by the profit motive, to make products that consumers, spurred by their quest to maximize purchasing power, buy. Consequently, by virtue of what they buy—and, for that matter, do not buy—consumers direct the efficient allocation of resources and the optimal valuation of assets.

The doctrine of laissez-faire endorses governmental noninterference in economic affairs.

Less Is More An enduring bias toward minimal government intervention anchors market economies. The less visible the "hand" becomes due to government intervention, the more efficient the market. Still, the invisible hand is fallible. The need for public goods (e.g., traffic lights, flood control, national defense) and regulatory protections (e.g., minimum wage, product safeguards, environmental standards) requires some governmental involvement. Therefore, a market economy calls upon the state to enforce contracts, protect property rights, ensure fair and free competition, regulate certain activities, and provide general safety and security (see Table 4.2). Nevertheless, the anchor of the market economy remains the invisible hand of economically free agents driving growth and prosperity.

COMMAND ECONOMY

The invisible hand of a market economy, due to the need to provide public goods and protect society, is made visible by government involvement.

In theory, **communism** champions state ownership of resources and control of all economic activity. Nominally a political ideology, communism calls for an egalitarian, classless, and ultimately stateless society based on the government's command of the economy.[43] Implementing this socioeconomic structure imposes a **command economy** in which the government owns and controls resources, taking on the authority to decide what products to make, in what quantity, at what price, and in what way. For example, in a market economy, if the government wants computers, it collects taxes and buys computers at market prices from privately held companies. In a command economy, the visible hand of the government, with little if any regard for price, orders state-owned companies to make computers.[44]

In a command economy, the visible hand of the state supersedes the invisible hand of the market.

Making the invisible hand visible means that government officials—not consumers—determine the prices of goods and services. Often, product quality is erratic and typically deteriorates. Products are usually in short supply and there are few substitutes. State-owned companies, typically large-scale, capital-intensive, inefficient, and unprofitable, have few resources to upgrade or incentives to innovate. Indisputably, command economies can outperform for short periods. Controlling everything and everybody lets the state mobilize idle resources, usually labor, to generate high-growth spurts. High productivity continues as long as the state competently manages slack, low-cost resources. Improving performance often moves state officials to proclaim that a command economy is a productive alternative to capitalism. History, however, shows otherwise. Central planning often proves counterproductive, given that officials, no matter how clever, cannot consistently predict consumers' preferences. Far more typically, command economies crash in the face of growing inefficiency, inequality, cronyism, corruption, and, ultimately, disgruntlement.

CONCEPT CHECK

Totalitarianism subordinates people's day-today lives—including their market behavior and economic outlook—to the state. Government command of the economy supports this policy, enabling it to determine asset valuation and resource allocation.

Command economies have included the Soviet Union (which, at its height, was the world's second-largest economy), China during its Great Leap Forward era beginning in 1958, India prior to its economic reforms in 1991, and Afghanistan during the rule by Soviet occupation and the Taliban. Today, we see few pure examples, most notably North Korea and, to a lessening degree, Myanmar and Cuba. More often, managers operate in economies that exhibit many but not all methods of state control. These sorts of states, such as Iran, Venezuela, Turkmenistan, Belarus, Zimbabwe, Ethiopia, Vietnam, Saudi Arabia, Russia, and China, fall in the "mostly unfree" and "repressed" categories of the Economic Freedom Index. Their predominant bias toward political stability spurs the state to regulate individual choice extensively.

MIXED ECONOMY

A mixed economic system combines elements of the market and command economic systems; both government and private enterprise influence production, consumption, investment, and savings.

Most economies, broadly labeled **mixed economies**, fall between the market and command types. A mixed economy is a system in which economic decisions are principally market-driven and ownership is largely private, but the government intervenes, from a little to a lot, in allocating resources. For example, U.S. President Obama reasoned that it is the government's responsibility to make "strategic decisions about strategic industries."[45]

The mixed economy integrates elements of the command and market systems. On one hand, the state intermingles ownership of some resources, centralizes certain planning functions, and regulates the market. On the other hand, the interaction of supply and demand, signaled to producers through the price system, rather than public dictate, optimizes production.[46] For example, in a mixed economy the government may have partial ownership stakes in computer manufacturers. Rather than instructing these firms on the type, quantity, style, and price of computers to make, the government permits firms to decide given prevailing market conditions.

A market economy is anchored in capitalism, a command economy is anchored in communism, and a mixed economy is anchored in socialism.

Democracy, we saw, calls for a market economy. Communism calls for a command economy. Likewise, socialism calls for a mixed economy. Specifically, **socialism** advocates regulating economic activity with an eye toward social equality and fair distribution of wealth. It utilizes the market to allocate resources, as does capitalism, but it subjects investment to social controls that are directed by the government, as does communism. Socialism holds that a fair and just economy, besides optimizing efficiencies, defends the weak by supporting low unemployment, prevents the consolidation of wealth and privilege, helps the impoverished by fairly redistributing income, stabilizes the system by intervening in market failures, and protects society by limiting abuses of market power. Proponents argue that governments far more conscientiously promote an egalitarian ethos that deters opportunistic individualism than does a free market.

The aftermath of the global financial crisis supported many of these views. Countries that favored a strong state presence, higher taxes, heavier regulation, tougher job-protection laws, and generous social safety programs better navigated the economic upheaval than had their free market counterparts.[47] As the economically free United States regrouped and wondered "What next?" the socialism of Denmark supported its steady economic performance and citizens' status as the happiest people in the world.[48] As Britain's free market struggled, Sweden's mixed economy persevered, given its government's ownership of national companies.[49]

Advocates of the mixed economy do not unconditionally endorse state intervention as a panacea. Unchecked, the entanglement between politics and economics often makes it impossible to tell where the government ends and the corporation begins. Political agendas, the particular slate of officials, and social circumstances shape how the government balances economic freedom and state control.[50] Hence, the extent and nature of government intervention differs, depending on local circumstances, from country to country. At present, countries commonly classified as mixed economies include South Africa, Japan, South Korea, Sweden, Austria, France, Brazil, Germany, and India. They typically fall in the "mostly" and "moderately" free categories of the Economic Freedom Index.

Looking to the Future

State Capitalism: Detour or Destination?

Managers wonder: Will free markets prevail, protecting hard-won economic freedoms? Or will governments reclaim the commanding heights of the economy, taking control of development, regulating performance, and determining potential? For decades, economies had steadily adopted the free market model given the success of countries that had migrated from command and mixed to market economies. However, the financial crisis hurled markets into disarray. Now, buffeted by the choices and consequences, we see countries resorting to greater state economic control.

So, managers watch and wait as the contest between the siren call of free markets and the surge of state power determine the sort of economy that works best in the modern world. As they do, many reflect on a perplexing riddle: Notwithstanding its documented dividends, why do so few countries maximize economic freedom? Map 4.2 shows that five of 177 countries have "free economies" while another 30 are "mostly free." Put differently, 35 of 177 countries—just over 19 percent—grant their residents significant economic freedom. Worse still, just five of 177 countries—about 3 percent and home to less than one percent of the world's population—rank as "free."[51] The rest do not. Instead, many of these countries, such as China, Russia, United Arab Emirates, Mexico, Venezuela, and Saudi Arabia, practice forms of state capitalism.

State Capitalism

State capitalism is an economic system whereby political officials decide how assets are valued and when and where they are used.[52] The state nurtures national champions, manages trade relations and exchange rates to promote exports and discourage imports, leverages control of the financial system to provide low-cost capital to domestic industries, and runs nationalist legal and regulatory systems. Recall our earlier profile of GCL-Poly Energy of China. Zhu Gongshan, the owner, relied on quick approvals, cheap government loans, and state support to build a global-scale company in 15 months. China's ensuing disruption of the solar power industry prompted many firms to shut down; some, such as Evergreen Solar of the U.S., relocated to China.

Some may contend that state capitalism sounds a lot like a mixed or command economy. In some ways it is. But in important other ways, it is not. Foremost, state capitalism is a system whereby the government explicitly manipulates market outcomes for political purposes. Politics has a profound and pervasive impact on the performance of markets. The government uses markets to promote stability and growth, thereby creating the prosperity and wealth that maximize state power and legitimate its ongoing rule. State capitalism, unlike capitalism or communism, does not stipulate an ideological component; the government manages markets for long-term political survival and power projection, not to enforce an abstract ideal or promote the cult of personality. Instead of politicized revolutionaries promising a brave, new future, state capitalism relies on pragmatic technocrats who, applying sophisticated management ideas, develop a prosperous, productive economy. The payoff is plain: subverting political freedom with economic prosperity fortifies the authority of the state.

Visible Only as Needed

Absent an ideological agenda, the state prefers relative market anonymity. As long as a growing economy supports stability, it stays in the shadows, influencing activities and shaping outcomes. In the event plans go awry, the invisible hand quickly turns visible. The state steps in, revises policies, resets funding, and redirects activities. National, provincial, and local officials, by controlling resources, can direct operations and markets as needed.

State capitalism promotes the growth of particular industrial sectors and companies in order to speed economic development. Typically, the state attracts innovative foreign companies, using state-owned banks to provide cheap loans, favorable regulations, and stable industry settings. The state uses the tax code, for example, as a tool for economic, not social, engineering. Bolstering its solar power industry, for example, led China to recruit Evergreen Solar, a technology-rich U.S. company, by providing financial incentives and tax breaks.

Who Owns Whom

The state typically owns its national champions, using them to influence market activity as well as consolidate its authority. For instance, China is the majority owner of 99 of the 100 largest publicly listed Chinese companies, including all major banks, its three major oil companies, its three telecom carriers, and its major media firms. Collectively, 129 huge conglomerates in finance, media, mining, metals, transportation, communication, and so on answer directly to the Chinese central government.[53] Furthermore, China's provinces and cities own and run thousands of medium-sized and smaller ones. State officials, while discrete, are not shy. At all levels, "the tentacles of state-owned enterprises extend into every nook where profits can be made."[54] Similar situations in Saudi Arabia, Russia, and Brazil, for instance, spotlight the state's expanding economic clout.

Telltale Marks

State capitalist economies, whether in the Middle East, Asia, Eastern Europe, or South America, have telltale marks. Public investment, public wealth, and public enterprise prevail. Officials fan economic nationalism. The state promotes domestic markets as sanctuaries for national champions. The state favors local companies at the expense of their foreign rivals in order to nurture national companies into global leaders. State capitalism has little need for an independent judiciary; the state typically treats the legal system as an apparatus that legitimates its policies as needed. It games the system, capturing competitive advantages through whatever means necessary. Officials install barriers to trade and investment in order to generate local development and prosperity. Regulations require foreign investors to form joint ventures with local companies when entering strategic industries. Moreover, foreign companies receive scant protection and even weaker legal defense.

Gaining Momentum

The global financial crisis has expanded the scale and scope of state capitalism. On one hand, countries that favored a larger state presence, higher taxes, heavier regulation, tougher job-protection laws, and more generous social safety programs dealt more successfully with market disruptions than did their free-market counterparts. On the other, state capitalism professes to better protect social values, equalize income distribution, and prevent the accumulation of vast wealth and powerful self-interests that threaten social harmony. Allowed to run free, market economies encourage the psychology that greed is good. Only a strong state, goes the reasoning, stops it from devolving into psychosis.[55]

Presently, some 70 strategically important countries worldwide are at a critical crossroads in determining their political and economic futures.[56] Whether they advocate free markets or state capitalism remains to be seen. Many see China as the bellwether; where it goes, both good and bad, many will follow. China has used state capitalism to develop and direct the world's fastest growing economy, which has, in turn, powered the swiftest, most extensive rise out of poverty any nation has ever seen. Its success—not just surviving but also prospering during the crisis—convinced "Chinese leadership that state control of much of the country's economic development is the steadiest path toward prosperity—and, therefore, domestic tranquility."[57] Likewise, Brazil reasoned that the state succeeded where the private sector failed during the crisis; said its current president, state capitalism "prevented the economy from being shipwrecked."[58] Economic renaissance in these and many other countries suggests that Western-style economics is no longer the only viable route to modernization.[59] A generation ago, the state-controlled economy was seen as a way station on the path to a capitalism market. Now, many see state capitalism as a sustainable economic model.

Given economic circumstances in the world today, one should not be surprised if others, particularly authoritarian one-party political systems, find state capitalism attractive. Arcing through Asia, the Middle East, Africa, and Latin America, authoritarian governments emulate China's model.[60] Through this arc, state-backed companies grow and expand, having accounted for more than a third of the emerging world's FDI over the past decade. Democracy's retreat, covered in Chapter 3, along with the surging success of state capitalism, helps explain why, out of 177 countries, 147 significantly regulate, restrict, or repress economic freedom. ■

ASSESSING ECONOMIC DEVELOPMENT, PERFORMANCE, AND POTENTIAL

Given an understanding of the general types of economic systems, managers turn to evaluate their critical components. They tap a rich portfolio of macro and micro measures to assess a country's economic development, performance, and potential. Some measures may be informal or idiosyncratic, such as number of wireless subscriptions, amount of electrical power generated, internet searches for telltale terms, or military officers running companies.[61] Typically, convention dominates practice. Matters of income and wealth often anchor analysis. Managers elaborate their analyses with indicators of sustainability and stability.

Broad classes of countries include

- Developing countries
- Emerging economies
- Developed countries

CONCEPT CHECK

In discussing "Growing Consumer Pressures" among the drivers of globalization, Chapter 1 notes that worldwide consumption grew six-fold in the second half of the twentieth century. Such information improves managers' investment choices and operating decisions.

CRN Case Review Note

Before reviewing each class, a brief note on how we classify countries is in order. We follow the lead of the United Nations and World Bank in labeling low- and middle-income nations as *developing countries.* Less commonly, some refer to them as "underdeveloped" or Third World Countries; the latter was in vogue during the Cold War Era when the First World referred to the Democratic West and the Second World designated the Communist East. The 150 or so developing countries, as a rule, have low per capita income—an average of $3,813 in 2012. The vast majority of their residents have low living standards, marked by limited access to few goods and services.[62] Virtually all future population growth will occur in today's developing countries.

The faster-growing, relatively prosperous developing countries such as China, Brazil, and India are increasingly referred to as *emerging markets* or *emerging economies.* Currently, there are approximately 30 or so **emerging economies** in the world (see Map 4.1). Table 4.3 lists some of the acronyms used to sort them. When one speaks of the emerging economies, one usually speaks principally of Brazil, Russia, India, and China (**BRICs**). Although much larger in scale and scope than other emerging economies, the BRICs are the vanguard of the Comeback. Many presume that where the BRICs go, both good and bad, others will follow. Our closing case highlights trends afoot in the BRICs.

Developed countries are those with high per capita income—an average of $37,545 in 2012. Their citizens enjoy a high standard of living with access to a variety of goods

TABLE 4.3 The Alphabet of Emerging Economies

Commonly, one comes across acronyms that classify various sets of emerging economies. As different countries develop, observers have coined a variety of shorthand codes.

Acronym	Members
BRIC	B for Brazil, R for Russia, I for India, C for China
BIC	Remove R for Russia
BRICS	Add S for South Africa
BRICK	Add K for South Korea
BASIC	Add AS for South Africa, Removes R for Russia
BRIIC	Add I for Indonesia
BRICIT	Add I for Indonesia, T for Turkey
BRIMC	Add M for Mexico
BRICET	Add E for Eastern Europe, T for Turkey
BRICA	Add A for Arab countries—Saudi Arabia, Qatar, Kuwait, Bahrain, Oman, and the United Arab Emirates
MIST	Mexico, Indonesia, South Korea, Turkey
N-11 (The Next 11)	Bangladesh, Egypt, Indonesia, Iran, Mexico, Nigeria, Pakistan, Philippines, South Korea, Turkey, and Vietnam
CIVETS	C for Colombia, I for Indonesia, V for Vietnam, E for Egypt, T for Turkey, S for South Africa

FIGURE 4.8 If Only It Was All In the Name

Source: Lee Lorenz/New Yorker Cartoon Bank/www.cartoonbank.com

"No, no—we used to be an undeveloped country, but now we're a developing country."

and services. Developed countries include Japan, Australia, New Zealand, Canada, the United States, and most European nations. Less commonly, some refer to them as high-income countries, advanced markets, or industrial countries. In the future, we may see the developed countries relabeled Established Market Economies, given their high per capita income, high standard of living, and sophisticated institutional framework but comparatively slower growth.

MEASURES OF ECONOMIC PERFORMANCE

The expanding barrage of data spurs managers to streamline market evaluation. Many anchor analysis in comprehensive single-item measures that provide a quick indicator of whether an economy (1) is expanding or contracting, (2) needs a boost or should be constrained, and (3) is threatened by recession or inflation. Akin to taking the temperature of a patient, measures such as **gross national income (GNI)** or **gross national product (GNP)** efficiently summarize the economic activity of households, business, and government in terms of their consumption, investment, spending, and trading. Indeed, Paul Samuelson, a Nobel Laureate in economics, described the measure of gross domestic product as "truly among the great inventions of the 20th century, a beacon that helps policymakers steer the economy toward key economic objectives."[63]

GNI is the broadest measure of economic activity for a country.

Gross National Income (GNI) is the broadest measure of a country's economy. It measures the value of all production in the domestic economy together with the income that the country receives from other countries (mainly interest and dividends), less similar payments it has made to other countries. Thus, the value of a Samsung TV built in South Korea as well as the portion of the value of a Samsung TV made in Japan using Samsung's resources is

TABLE 4.4 The 10 Largest Economies by GNI, 2011[a]

Rank	Country	GNI ($, billions)[i]	% of World Total
1	United States	15,148	22.75
2	China	6,643	9.98
3	Japan	5,739	8.62
4	Germany	3,617	5.43
5	France	2,755	4.14
6	United Kingdom	2,370	3.56
7	Italy	2,114	3.18
8	Brazil	2,107	3.16
9	India	1,746	2.62
10	Canada	1,570	2.36
**	World	$66,577	

[i] Data calculated by the Atlas Method, which smoothes exchange rate fluctuations by applying a three-year moving average, price-adjusted conversion.

Source: Based on World Bank Development Indicators 2011. Copyright 2013 by the World Bank. Reproduced with permission of the World Bank.

counted in South Korea's GNI. Similarly, the portion of the value of a Sony TV built in South Korea using Sony's resources counts in the GNI of Japan. Last, if Samsung's Japanese subsidiary repatriates profits to headquarters in Seoul, it increases South Korea's GNI. Table 4.4 identifies the 10 largest economies in the world in terms of GNI. Recall that the World Bank identifies 214 discrete economic environments in the world today; the 10 countries listed in Table 4.4 account for 65.8 percent of world GNI.

GNP is the total value of all final goods and services produced within a nation in a particular year.

Gross National Product (GNP) is the value of all final goods and services produced within a nation in a given year, plus the income earned by its citizens abroad, minus the income earned by foreigners from domestic production. Conceptually, world GNP and world GNI are equal. However, their slightly different calculation can result in a small discrepancy at the country level.[64] Consequently, managers crosscheck their analyses, noting the assumptions of the measure and characteristics of a particular country.

GDP is the total market value of goods and services produced by workers and capital within a nation's borders; it provides the truest measure of national economic activity.

Gross Domestic Product (GDP) The total market value of all output produced within a nation's borders, no matter whether generated by a domestic or foreign-owned company, is reported as a nation's GDP.[65] It the most commonly used estimator of the true performance of an economy given that it measures income, not wealth. That is, GDP estimates the flow of economic activity within a country, not simply its stock of productive assets. It also assesses economic environments in which the output of the multinational sector is a significant share of total activity. For example, about 90 percent of Irish exports are made by foreign-owned firms; GDP, not GNI, more accurately measures Ireland's economic performance. Technically, GDP plus the income generated from exports, imports, and the international operations of a nation's companies equal GNI. Therefore, both Samsung and Sony TVs made in South Korea contribute to South Korea's GDP, but TVs made in Japan by Samsung do not.

ADJUSTING ANALYTICS

GNI and its offshoots estimate an economy's absolute performance. Despite their strengths, they can mislead managers when comparing countries. For example, economic powers like the United States, Japan, and Germany consistently claim the top rankings when sorted by GNI. Some may mistakenly presume that they are also more productive and faster growing than lower-ranked countries. Often, the opposite is true. Therefore, managers improve the usefulness of GNI, GNP, and GDP by adjusting each for the (1) rate of economic growth, (2) size of the population, and (3) purchasing power of the local currency.

Managers improve the usefulness of GNI by adjusting it for the

- Growth rate of the economy
- Number of people in a country
- Local cost of living

CRN Case Review Note

Rate of Economic Growth Gross aggregates give a static snapshot. They do not measure the rate of change in an indicator. Interpreting present and forecasting future performance require pinpointing an economy's growth rate. The growth rate of GNI indicates a country's economic potential: If it grows faster (or *slower*) than its population, the country's standards of living are rising (or *falling*).[66] Figure 4.9 reports the forecast for real GDP growth rates of various developed and emerging economies.

The growth rate of GNI also indicates business opportunities. Looking at countries in terms of their growth rate finds a wide range. For instance, GDP in approximately 80 developing economies is rising at twice the rate of per capita growth in the world's richest countries, thereby powering their "Comeback." More specifically, China has been one of the fastest growing economies over the past three decades; it has expanded by 9.8 percent

FIGURE 4.9 A Divided World

Nominal GDP increases from year to year partly because a country produces more goods and services and partly because prices increase. Real GDP strips out price effects in order to estimate the annual growth in the actual production of goods and services. This conversion shows that many emerging markets are forecast to grow faster than developed markets between now and 2030.

Source: Based on *Looking to 2060: A Global Vision of Long-Term Growth*, OECD Economic Policy Papers, November 2012.

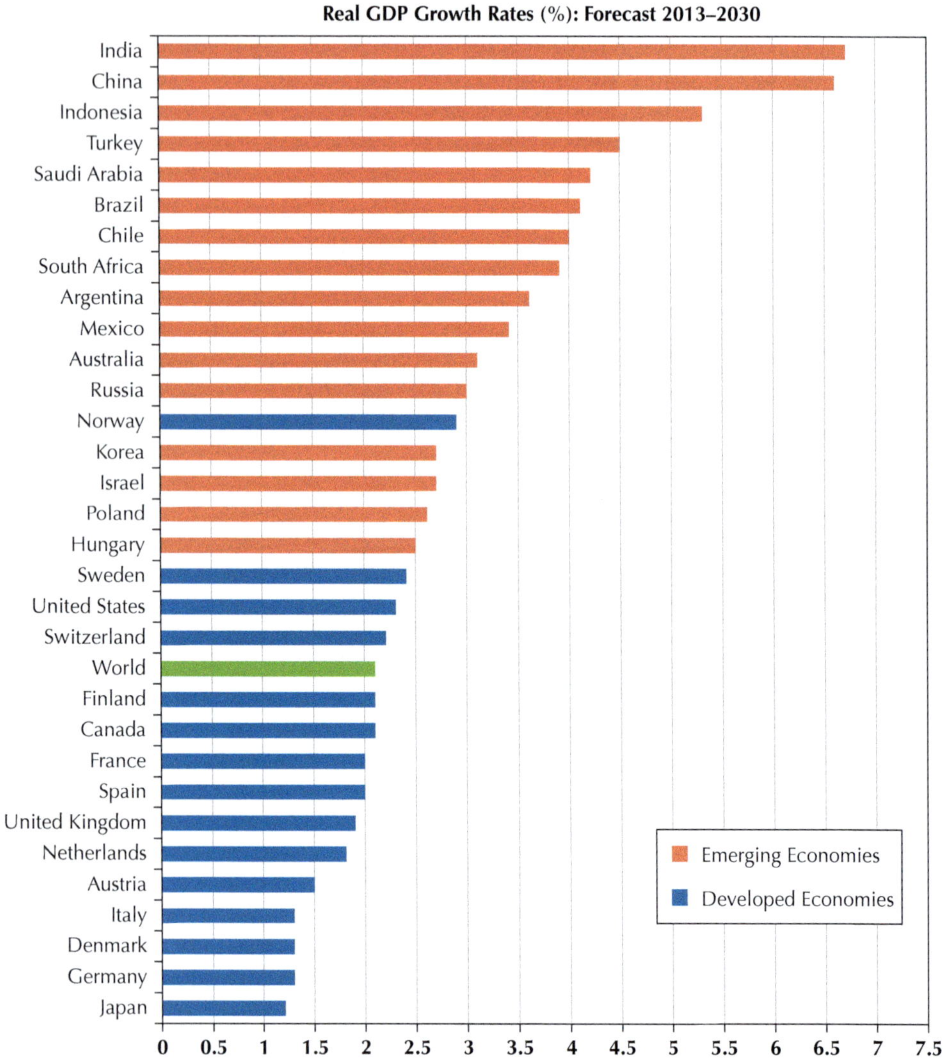

on average since 1995. Commensurately, its GDP has gone from about $600 billion then to $7.2 trillion in 2012. Rising income has fueled consumer demand, thereby attracting foreign investment.

Population Size Managers adjust GNI, like many other economic indicators, by the number of people who live in a country.[67] This conversion is common sense, given how unevenly the world's population of 7,174,530,636 (as of August 2013) is distributed—e.g., from a high of 1.34 billion in China to the low of 54 in the Pitcairn Islands.[68] Adjusting GNI by population, therefore, lets managers remove the effects of demography in assessing a country's relative performance.

For example, GNI may be low in absolute terms, such as is the case for Norway. However, Norway, with its 4.7 million residents, ranked first in the world by GNI per capita in 2012 at $98,860.[69] In comparison, the United States ranked 18th ($50,120), Japan 22nd ($47,870), Brazil 79th ($11,630), China 114th ($5,740), and India 164th ($1,530).

Map 4.3 shows that high-income countries are clustered in a few regions of the world. These countries account for about 15 percent of the world population but more than 70 percent of global GNI. On average, they report an average GNI per capita in the mid-tens of thousands ($). Lower-income countries are spread throughout the world and comprise a large share of the world population but a far smaller share of the world's GNI. They report GNI per capita from the mid-hundreds to low thousands ($).

Purchasing power parity provides a method of measuring the relative purchasing power of different countries' currencies for the same basket of goods and services.

Purchasing Power Parity GNI per capita does not account for the cost of living from one country to another. Instead, it presumes that a dollar of income in Minneapolis has the same purchasing power as a dollar of income in Mumbai, even though the cost of living differs between the United States and India. To state the obvious, costs of goods and services vary from country to country. Consequently, GNI per capita is unable to tell us much about

MAP 4.3 GNI Per Capita, 2011

A country's economic performance can change significantly when controlling for its demography. *GNI per capita* qualifies a country's economic performance in terms of the size of its population. For instance, China is the world's second largest economy when ranked by aggregate GNI. Adjusting its performance for its population of 1.344 billion people, however, moves it to the lower-middle income tier.

Source: Based on World Bank Indicators, The World Bank, http://data.worldbank.org/indicator/NY.GNP.PCAP.CD/countries?display=map

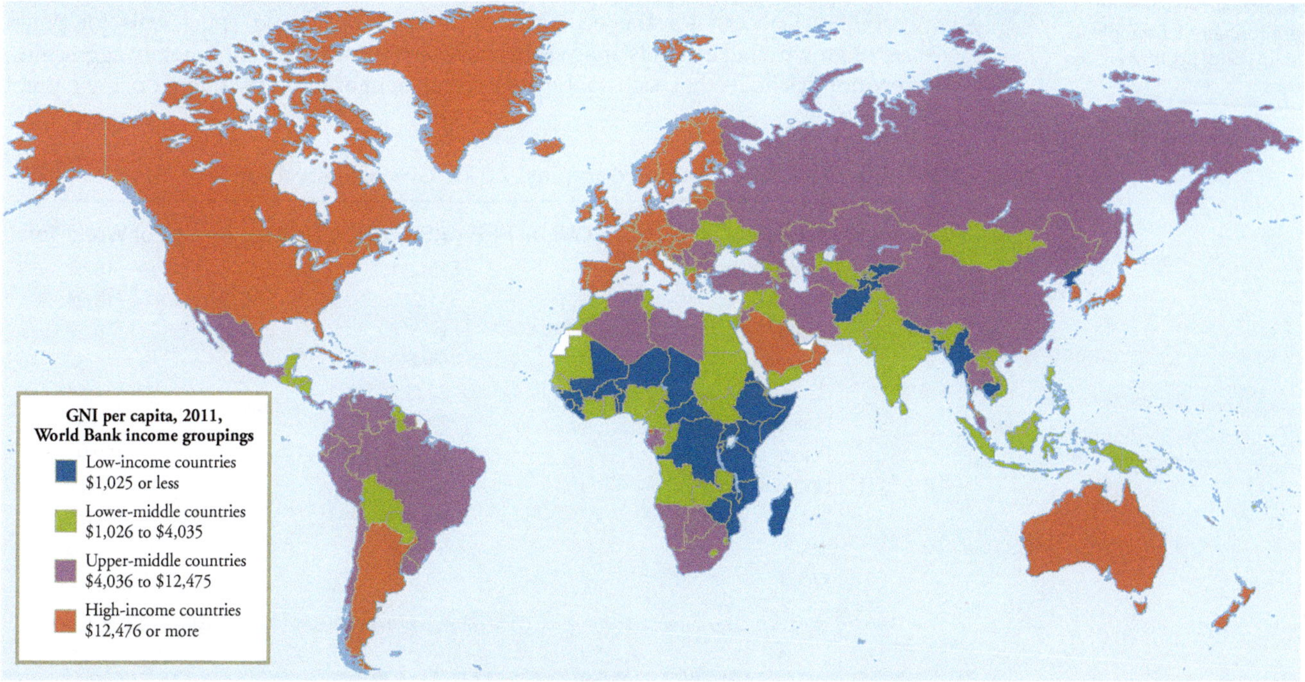

how many goods and services one can buy with a unit of income in one country relative to how much one can buy with a unit of income in another. Therefore, managers adjust GNI in terms of *purchasing power parity (PPP)*—namely, determining how much money is needed to purchase the same goods and services in two countries and using that information to calculate an implicit foreign exchange rate that reflects the same purchasing power, per unit of currency, in the different countries.[70] Adjusting income data for PPP essentially creates an international dollar that has the same purchasing power as a dollar has in the United States.

Table 4.5 shows the impact of adjusting national economic performance by PPP. Notably, the raw country rankings by GNI reported in Table 4.4 change. For instance, China, India, Russia, and Mexico move up while Japan, the United Kingdom, France, Italy, and Canada drop down or out. Second, PPP reduces some of the otherwise extreme variability in many country-to-country comparisons. Revisiting our comparison of the United States and India finds that India's GNI per capita in 2012 is $1,530 but rises to $3,840 when adjusted for local purchasing power.[71] The opposite occurs in the case of countries with expensive standards of living, such as Norway. Its GNI per capita falls from $98,860 to $64,030 when adjusted for the reduced purchasing power a unit of currency commands in that high-priced country. Map 4.4 profiles the countries of the world in terms of GNI per capita adjusted for PPP.[72]

PERFORMANCE AND POTENTIAL: ALTERNATIVE INTERPRETATIONS

Green measures gauge economic performance in terms of the effect of current choices on long-term sustainability.

Sustainability and stability perspectives hold that the objective of economic activity is to create an enabling environment for people to enjoy long, healthy, and happy lives.

Measures of gross national income emphasize monetary aggregates. As a result, GNI, GNP, and GDP, even after adjusting for growth rates, population size, and cost of living, only partially profile a country's performance and potential. Further complicating matters is the so-called "black" or "shadow" economy, namely legal and illegal business activities that fall beyond official measurement. In India, for example, the World Bank estimates the shadow economy was equivalent to a fifth of official GDP in 2010. Likewise, Europe's various shadow economies represent 22 percent of regional market activity—about $3.55 trillion and as large as Germany's entire economy.[73] In recourse, managers can improve analysis by estimating an economy's sustainability and stability.

Sustainability

Concern for the ecological welfare of the world spurs calls for green measures of growth that expands analysis beyond narrow measures of monetary aggregates. **Green economics** holds that each country is a component of, and dependent on, the natural

TABLE 4.5 The 10 Largest Economies, 2011: GNI Adjusted for PPP

Rank	Country	GNI by PPP (U.S. $, 000 trillions)	% of World Total
1	United States	$15,211	18.82
2	China	$11,270	13.94
3	Japan	$4,516	5.59
4	India	$4,460	5.52
5	Germany	$3,287	4.07
6	Russian Federation	$2,917	3.61
7	France	$2,349	2.91
8	United Kingdom	$2,255	2.79
9	Brazil	$2,245	2.78
10	Italy	$1,968	2.43
**	World	$80,843	

Source: Based on World Bank Development Indicators 2011. Copyright 2013 by the World Bank. Reproduced with permission of the World Bank.

MAP 4.4 GNI Per Capita, 2011, Adjusted for Purchasing Parity

Adjusting raw income data in terms of purchasing power parity helps control for the relative costs of living and currency effects among countries. Doing so helps managers clarify a country's absolute economic performance in terms that reflect its particular living standards and market conditions.

Source: Based on World Bank Indicators, http://data.worldbank.org/indicator/NY.GNP.PCAP.PP.CD/countries?display=map

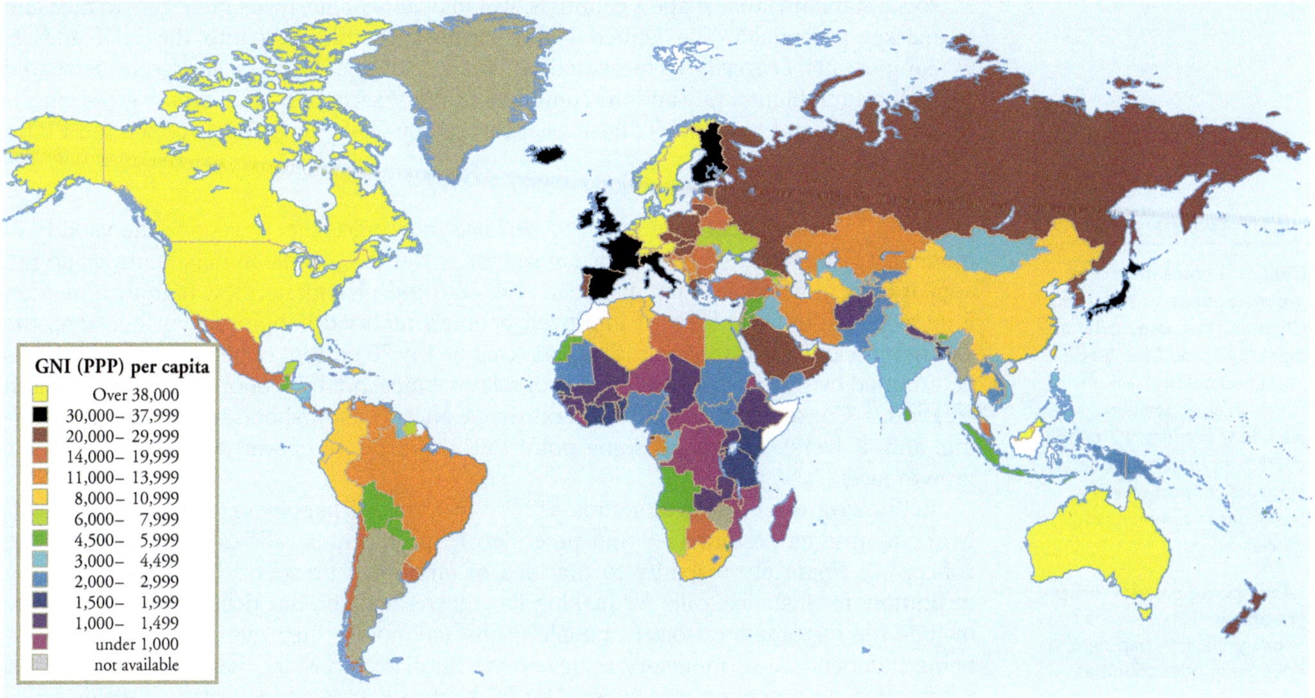

world. Measuring the monetary quantity of market activity through GNI, GNP, and GDP—without accounting for the associated social and ecological costs that result from the activity that generated economic growth—misrepresents performance and misinterprets potential. Instead, **sustainable development** proponents encourage interpreting economic activity in terms of its capacity to "meet the needs of the present without compromising the ability of future generations to meet their own needs."[74] As such, it endorses a broader accounting of the gains and costs of growth to better gauge an economy.

Presently, there is no consensus on how to greenify GNI, GNP, or GDP. Current candidates include:

- *Net National Product (NNP):* Measures the depletion of natural resources and degradation of the environment that result from generating GNI. As a company must depreciate its tangible and intangible assets when making a product, goes this reasoning, so too should countries. NNP does so by depreciating the country's assets commensurate with their use to generate growth.[75]

Fully understanding growth, progress, and prosperity calls for assessing the consequences of economic choice on sustainability and stability.

- *Genuine Progress Indicator (GPI):* Starts with the same accounting framework used to calculate GDP but then adjusts for values assigned to environmental quality, population health, livelihood security, equity, free time, and educational attainment. For example, unlike GDP, GPI values voluntary and unpaid household work as paid labor and subtracts the costs of crime, pollution, and family breakdown. Effectively, GDP versus GPI is analogous to the difference between the gross profits versus net profits—net is gross less the costs incurred. Accordingly, GPI will equal zero if the costs of pollution, crime, and family breakdown, holding all other factors constant, equal the monetary gains from the production of goods and services.

- *Human Development Index (HDI)* Matters of human development do not show up immediately in income or growth figures. Ultimately, the reasoning goes, they will, given that improving the human condition improves economic performance. So, estimating a country's degree of human development, in terms of the physical, intellectual, and social standards that shape a country's overall quality of life, helps managers to measure market potential.[76] The United Nations translates this view into the HDI and its components: *Longevity*, as measured by life expectancy at birth; *Knowledge*, as measured by the adult literacy rate and the combined primary, secondary, and tertiary gross enrollment ratio; and *Standard of Living*, as measured by GNI per capita expressed in PPP for U.S. dollars.

CONCEPT CHECK

Chapter 1 notes that some groups oppose globalization, Chapter 2 discussed cultural objections, and Chapter 3 identified political reasons that inspire opposition. Here, we add that critics charge that overly emphasizing monetary measures misrepresents the economic benefits of globalization.

An ongoing paradox is that people in rich countries are not significantly happier than people in poor countries.

Stability Policymakers have long puzzled over a paradox that questions the validity of monetary aggregates as performance measures.[77] Namely, people in rich countries do not appear to be any happier than people in poor countries. No matter how high income rose, little evidence indicated that it improved people's reported happiness. Furthermore, the emerging science of Happynomics reports that nearly 70 percent of personal satisfaction is determined by the quantity and quality of relationships, not by economic output or wealth creation.[78] Consequently, some contend that GNI and its offshoots are at best misleading, and at worst, flawed (as some point out, the expense of war boosts the economic growth rate).[79]

Rethinking the goal of economic activity in terms of happiness, the argument goes, better represents performance and potential. **Happynomics** calls for moving "from the concept of financial prosperity to the idea of emotional prosperity."[80] The constitution of Bhutan, for instance, calls for making its citizens happier, not richer, every year; goals include the happiness of society, people's satisfaction with their lives, and national well-being independent of monetary achievement. Similarly, consider that the United States, when rated on monetary measures, is far in front of France and Germany. Qualifying its performance in terms of life expectancy, leisure time, and income equality, however, moves living standards in France and Germany ahead of those in the United States.[81] Some may contend that mapping happiness unnecessarily confuses economic analysis. However, an unhappy citizenry may be a leading indicator of change in government policy that alters the economic environment.

Presently, estimation is difficult. Defining happiness, like beauty, is often in the eye of the beholder. Potential indicators, such as love, friendship, family relations, and actualization, are tough to pin down. In addition, how does one value goals, like safe streets and clean air, which can be measured? The intricacies of happiness capture increasing attention; insight should clarify measures. In the meantime, managers consider the following indices:

Estimators of economic progress toward improving happiness include

- Your Better Life Index
- Gross National Happiness
- Happy Planet Index

- *Your Better Life Index (YBLI)* This index measures well-being and perceptions of living conditions. Developed by the Organization for Economic Cooperation and Development (OECD), the YBLI advocates evaluating economic performance in terms of matters that people worldwide believe are important, such as housing, jobs, social relationships, health, security, work-family balance, and education, but that fall beyond the narrow scope of monetary measures. Explained the OECD, YBLI pushes the "boundaries of knowledge and understanding in a pioneering and innovative manner…It has extraordinary potential to help us deliver better policies for better lives."[82] The top ten countries, in terms of the YBLI and beginning with the leader, are Denmark, Canada, Norway, Australia, the Netherlands, Sweden, Switzerland, Finland, Israel, and Austria.[83]
- *Gross National Happiness (GNH):* Progressive society presumes that material and spiritual development occur side by side; one reinforces the other or both suffer. GNH measures a country's ability to promote equitable and sustainable socioeconomic development, preserving and promoting cultural values, conserving the natural environment, and establishing good governance.
- *Happy Planet Index (HPI):* Utilitarian views hold that people aspire to live long, healthy, happy lives. Therefore, a country's economic performance and potential is represented

by how well it helps its citizens do so while not infringing on the opportunity of future generations, and people in other countries, to do the same. HPI advocates measuring the environmental costs of growth while emphasizing that maximizing happiness and health, not monetary wealth, is the objective.

Point

Growth: Positive and Productive?

Point **Yes** Growth is not only good, it is a fundamental necessity. Growth is life, actualizing the productive potential of individuals, communities, institutions, and society. Growth provides long-term benefits to everyone in every country. It morally stabilizes society. It liberates those trapped in poverty. It reduces violent conflict. It raises living standards. It funds safety nets and government backstops. It creates material improvements that comfort life. It creates jobs, income, wealth, and prosperity for individuals and society. Let's take a closer look at each.

Moral Stability Growth affects social attitudes and political institutions, the keystone to the moral stability of society. People experiencing rising incomes and improving economies are commensurately tolerant of and benevolent toward each other. In a word, wealth engenders humanity. Growth creates the resources that promote transparency of authority, openness of opportunity, tolerance of diversity, pathways of social mobility, fair and just laws, and virtues of democracy.

Poverty Reduction Notwithstanding the kindness of strangers, growth is the only means to alleviate poverty for the billions struggling to sustain life. Growth in many impoverished countries has reduced the number of people living in abject poverty. Some 1.94 billion people, or 43 percent of the world population, lived below the extreme poverty line of $1.25 a day in 1981. Today, as freer markets fuel growth, it has dropped to 19 percent of the world—about 1.3 billion people.[84] Without growth, humanity loses the war against poverty. Billions, presuming they survive, suffer physically and psychologically.

Business Dividend Growth stimulates higher employment, capital investment, and profits. Rising asset valuations, stabilizing wealth effects, and resolute confidence in surviving tough times supports the prosperity of individuals and companies. Moreover, amidst the panic of the recent global crisis, people endorsed the virtue of growth. Some 76 percent of Americans agreed that U.S. strength is "mostly based on the success of American business" and that 90 percent admired people who "get rich by working hard."[85]

Fiscal Dividend Government finances are ultimately at the mercy of growth. A thriving economy boosts tax revenues, thereby providing local, state, regional, and national governments the monies to finance spending projects that support, enrich, and sustain society. Although appealing, history shows cheap government does not translate into good government.

Peace Dividend Growth creates more opportunities for more people in more places. People who see the potential for prosperity behave peacefully. Moving poor people into the middle class, for example, enables them to think and behave differently. Free from the tyranny of ceaselessly seeking sustenance and shelter, they become more open-minded, more concerned about their children's future, more influenced by abstract values than traditional norms, more inclined to settle conflicts peacefully, more supportive of free markets and democracy, and more inclined to have faith in the future.

Environmental Benefits Growth encourages innovations. People specialize in what they do best and, courtesy of pro-growth policies, outsource the rest. Together, these drive the efficient allocation of resources. The falling ratio of energy consumption per unit of GDP over the past 40 years, in the face of the growing abundance of goods and services, testifies to the benefits of growth. By making resources valuable, growth spurs us to consume them wisely.

Quest to Excel Growth incents people to bring to bear their ingenuity, their imagination, and their industriousness to find a better way, every day, to make a difference. Pushing back the frontier of human experience—whether it involves the trivial (e.g., forms of entertainment) or the substantive (e.g., alternative energy)—is powered by the quest to grow. Eliminating the pursuit of progress saps society's vibrancy.

Life Growth supports longer lives. In 1900, life expectancy at birth was 47 years in the United States; by 2013, after a century marked by an epic burst in economic growth, it was 78.2 years. Moreover, people now need to work just half the time they once had to, relying on new tools to boost productivity, finding comfort in rising quality-of-life standards, and taking solace in improving health care.

Progress or Decline Unquestionably, as the Counterpoint argues, growth imposes costs on individuals, humanity, and the planet. Moreover, we fully agree that these costs are striking. Still, our position is crystal clear: No matter the costs of growth, they pale in comparison to the unacceptable price of not growing. Put bluntly, when growth stops, decay starts.

Growth: Positive and Productive?

Counterpoint

No We accept the premise that growth supports life, fostering morality, transparency, tolerance, mobility, justice, and liberty. However, ignoring or, worse, denying the costs of these benefits—costs that seem to grow faster than growth itself—imperils civil society and, ultimately, the survival of humanity and the planet. Once you untangle the strands of half-truths, falsehoods, and self-interests that lace insidious pro-growth arguments, the promise of endless milk and honey for all devolves into a bitter delusion. The problems of growth span the immediate and the future; where one stops and the other starts is tough to pinpoint. Still, as this list shows, each hits society hard.

Growth Privileges Few The quintessential promise of growth is "a rising tide lifts all boats." In theory, as an economy grows, it generates higher wages, income, and wealth for all. In reality, the benefits of growth are unevenly distributed, creating extreme inequalities of income, wealth, and power. We agree that over the long run, increasing growth has lifted the tide for millions around the world. However, a share of the global population has seen their patchwork-rafts capsize, many struggle to keep their leaky boats afloat, and a tiny fraction upgraded to nicer yachts.

Growth Is Misleading Despite the hype and hoopla, growth does not deliver the benefits it promises. It rewards the financially strong but punishes the economically weak. It liberates people from old routines but enslaves them to new habits. It creates free time to spend with family and community but then demands mobility and migration that disrupt connections. It promises newer, cooler products to enable self-fulfillment but then restarts a never-ending cycle of hope and deception. In a phrase, economic growth oversells and under delivers, condemning people to "spiritual despair scarcely concealed by the frantic pace of life."[86] People, trapped on hedonic treadmills in the quest for newer, shinier, better, bigger, faster, or fancier, confuse consumption of the latest and greatest as the path toward actualization. Instead, the destination is alienation.

Growth Threatens Life Polluted air, poisoned water, and toxic land—let alone global warming, biodiversity collapse, and resource depletion—are the by-products of growth. Granted, we need some production and consumption. Overproduction and overconsumption, however, destabilize the basis of life. Ironically, when we measure the value created by an economy—say, in GNI—no costs are tallied. Rather, they are mysteriously called "externalities," understood to affect society but conveniently excluded while we praise the wondrous "benefits" of growth. Effectively,

Counterpoint

since "nobody" is responsible for the costs of externalities, "nobody" pays for them, and the growth engine chugs merrily along. Ultimately, "everybody" pays with a despoiled environment, warped society, and financial servitude.

Growth Destroys Individuality Growth's mandate to optimize efficiency requires massification—mass production, mass consumption, mass distribution, mass markets, mass media, and so on. Massification delivers great benefits, but at high cost. One observer noted that "a part of the price that people in the West pay for this unending procession of shiny assembly-line products is the concomitant loss of those now rarer things that once imparted zest and gratification—the loss of individuality, uniqueness and flavor; the loss of craftsmanship, local variety and richness; the loss of intimacy and atmosphere, of eccentricity and character."[87]

Current Growth Is Unsustainable Humanity plunders the earth at an unprecedented rate. Presently, human consumption is 30 percent larger than nature's capacity to regenerate. By 2050, at current trends, humanity will require three to five planets of natural resources just to keep the game going. "For more than 20 years we have exceeded the Earth's ability to support a consumptive lifestyle that is unsustainable and we cannot afford to continue down this path," warned the Worldwatch Institute.[88] Barring black-swan innovations in mining, agriculture, and manufacturing, no matter how hard we wish otherwise, Mother Earth is going to stop current growth patterns sooner than later.

Change the Game In summary, our position is straightforward. Epic poverty for billions, slow-motion death spiral of the ecosystem, false hope of actualization by consumption, binge-buying alienation, and the deterioration of nominal democracies into functional plutocracies puts the world at the proverbial fork in the road. We can remain blissfully ignorant of the price of growth, lost in the endless rush of apparent gains but continually surprised by inevitable and underestimated externalities. Alternatively, we can face the issue full on and radically reset the equation so that growth "meets the needs of the present without compromising the ability of future generations to meet their own needs."[89]

1. Put yourself in the following scenario: Tomorrow, while having lunch with your friends, the issue of economic growth pops up as a topic of discussion. Given your read of the information in the Point-Counterpoint, what three points of perspective would you use to communicate your understanding of economic growth?

ECONOMIC ANALYSIS

Narrow (e.g., GNI, GDP, and GNP) and broad (e.g., HDI, HPI, NPP) estimators profile absolute and relative economic conditions. They meaningfully indicate a country's performance and potential. Managers study other features to refine analyses and elaborate interpretation. Popular indicators include inflation, unemployment, debt, income distribution, poverty, and the balance of payments. Let's take a closer look at each.

INFLATION

Inflation measures the increase in the cost of living.

Inflation is the sustained rise in prices measured against a standard level of purchasing power. We estimate it by comparing two sets of products at two points in time and then computing the increase in cost that is not due to quality improvement. Mainstream economics holds that inflation results when aggregate demand grows faster than aggregate supply—essentially, too many people try to buy too few goods, thereby creating demand that exceeds supply that makes prices rise faster than incomes. Other theories, such as the Austrian School of Economics, hold that inflation results from an increasing supply of money by Central Banks.[90] Last, some define inflation as the continuous fall in the value of the currency.[91] No matter the explanation, managers watch inflation for its influence on interest rates, living costs, consumer confidence, political stability, and other factors.[92]

Inflation and the Cost of Living Consider how inflation affects the cost of living.[93] Unless incomes rise at the same pace or faster, consumers struggle to buy groceries, gas, and so forth. Sometimes just buying stuff is practically impossible. For example, during periods of rapid inflation, or "hyperinflation" as seen in Brazil, Yugoslavia, Turkmenistan, and Iran, consumers spent their money as fast as they got it or else watched it turn worthless.[94] More pointedly, in Zimbabwe over the past few years, prices rose up to 95 percent per day; by 2009, the annual inflation rate hit an astounding 79,600,000,000 percent, prices doubled every 25 hours and people used a hundred-trillion-dollar note to trade.[95] Noted one Zimbabwean, "There's a surrealism here that's hard to get across to people. If you need something and have cash, you buy it. If you have cash, you spend it today, because tomorrow it's going to be worth 5 percent less. Normal horizons don't exist here."[96] Even in normal circumstances, inflation significantly influences price. For example, in the United States, an item that cost $10.00 in 1950 would go for $95.27 in 2013.[97]

A country experiencing rising prices for a prolonged period suffers chronic inflation.

History shows that chronic inflation—high inflation over a prolonged period—erodes confidence in a country's currency and spurs people to seek other ways to store value. Chronic inflation has bleak implications for companies; neither they nor their customers can plan long-term investments. There is a disincentive to save. Ordinary investment instruments such as insurance policies and long-term bonds turn speculative. Inflation compels government response, often by raising interest rates, regulating wages and prices, or escalating protectionism. These measures slow performance and erode potential.

Measuring Inflation The measurement of inflation highlights a common difficulty: what a country measures when estimating an economic variable. Price indices are sensitive to decisions about their scope and the calculations applied.[98] For instance, the United States uses the Consumer Price Index (CPI). In the European Union, it is the Harmonized Index of Consumer Prices (HICP). Unlike the CPI, the HICP surveys the rural population and excludes owner-occupied housing. Consequently, managers mind the estimation process.[99]

Deflation, a decrease in the general price level of goods and services, is often caused by a reduction in the supply of money or credit.

If Not Inflation, Then Deflation A nagging consequence of the global financial crisis has been the movement of deflation from academic conjecture to practical concern. For the first time in generations, deflation, not just inflation, menaces economic performance and potential. Overcapacity, systematic deleveraging, shrinking credit, reduced corporate spending, declining real estate values, and falling consumer demand fan deflationary dynamics.

Deflation is the opposite of inflation—prices for products go down, not up. Technically, it occurs when the annual inflation rate is less than zero.

Deflation's rather ordinary circumstances create extraordinary pressures. Reduction in the supply of money or credit means a contraction in personal and investment spending. Declining demand and growing supply trigger increasing quantity and falling prices. Unchecked, economies fall into deflationary spirals wherein companies increasingly struggle to sell products. In recourse, they discount prices to appeal to consumers who delay purchases in order to exploit tomorrow's cheaper price. Japan, for example, has lost two decades of growth due to deflationary dynamics. Explained a Japanese analyst, "Profits fall, then wages come down, then consumers stop shopping. And because people aren't shopping, companies lower prices.... It isn't easy to break out of."[100]

Deflation and unemployment are intricately linked. Lower demand slows the activity of a company, which then fires workers, who then scale back consumption, which then lowers demand, which leads companies to slow production further, and so on. At present, Central Banks and governments rely on **reflation**—increasing the money supply and reducing taxes to accelerate economic activity—to combat deflation. For example, the OECD urged the Bank of Japan to keep pumping cash into the economy until inflation turned positive.[101] This task is far easier said than done; from 1998 through mid-2013, Japan experienced falling prices and wages. Similarly, dealing with the consequences of the credit crisis has pushed the Federal Reserve of the United States to "quantitatively ease," essentially printing money to stimulate demand in order to preempt deflation.

UNEMPLOYMENT

Unemployment measures the number of workers who want to work but do not have paid jobs.

The **unemployment rate** is the share of out-of-work citizens seeking employment for pay relative to the total civilian labor force. Countries that cannot create jobs suffer sluggish growth, social pressures, and political instability. The proportion of employed workers in a country shows how well it productively uses its human resources. People gainfully employed testify to the competency of policymakers to sustain a productive economy. Persistent unemployment harshly spotlights government ineptitude.

Some economists advise tracking the **misery index** which is the sum of a country's inflation and unemployment rates. The higher the sum, the greater the economic misery, and the more likely consumers curtail spending, companies curb investment, and society confronts austerity. In addition, misery loves company; as the misery index increases, so do social costs, such as crime, despondency, and family stress.[102] In early 2013, Spain had the world's highest misery index score, at just under 30 percent; it was followed by South Africa, Croatia, Greece, Venezuela, Argentina, Egypt, Portugal, Slovakia, and Ireland. Recent work has expanded this idea in the form of the *Economic Security Index*; it assesses household economic instability in terms of the population that experiences at least a 25 percent decline in household wealth.[103]

Measuring Unemployment Change in unemployment over time may reflect change in the demand for and supply of labor; it may also reflect changes in reporting practices. Different assumptions (i.e., survey timing and seasonality effects) and exclusions (i.e., women tend to be undercounted) means that the unemployment rate often underestimates the scale and scope of the jobless. Technically, it measures how many people are not working for pay but seek paid employment. However, it excludes people who do not work at all, work without pay, or have stopped looking for work. Hence, unemployment measures often underestimate the true degree of joblessness.

Underemployment occurs when individuals work fewer hours a day than they would prefer or when individuals work below the level for which they have been trained.

Also, unemployment checks often underreport worker productivity. Countries in Asia, Africa, and South America commonly face economic, political, and social problems due to underemployment. That is, even though officially employed, people work only part time, thereby reducing productivity, lowering incomes, and decreasing social stability. Some propose an alternative measure to minimize these distortions, namely, the simple-to-calculate

Payroll to Population. This tracks the number of people employed full-time for an employer as a percentage of the nation's population, thereby eliminating the volatility of various adjustments.[104] Besides measurement issues, the unemployment rate means different things in different countries due to different social policies.[105] Some countries, such as France and Germany, provide generous unemployment protection, whereas countries like China, Kenya, or Jordan offer little to none.

DEBT

Internal debt: Portion of the government debt that is denominated in the country's own currency and held by domestic residents.

Debt, the total of a government's financial obligations, measures what the state borrows from its citizens, foreign organizations, foreign governments, and international institutions. The larger the total debt, the more uncertain an economy's performance and potential are. Interest expenses divert resources from more productive uses. More insidiously, future worries about the ability of coming generations to repay the debt saps consumer confidence and constrains government flexibility.

The national debt for many countries had been steadily, albeit slowly, increasing prior to 2007. This changed dramatically as governments responded to the global financial crisis. Company bailouts, unemployment benefits, fiscal resets, and macroeconomic stimulus led to unprecedented debt creation. The IMF estimates that the debt of the 10 wealthiest countries will have risen from 78 percent of their GDP in 2007 to nearly 115 percent by 2014; these governments, on average, will then owe approximately $50,000 for each citizen.[106]

External debt: Debt owed to foreign creditors and denominated in foreign currency.

A country's debt has two parts: internal and external. *Internal debt* results when the government spends more than it collects in revenues. Deficits occur for several reasons, such as when an imperfect tax system under-collects revenue, security and social programs exceed tax revenues, or state-owned enterprises run deficits.[107] Consequently, governments struggle with spending priorities, budget management, and tax policy. Growing internal debt, an early indicator of growing austerity and rising taxes, creates uncertainties for consumers, investors, and companies.

Growing public debt is a leading indicator of

- Tax increases
- Reduced growth
- Rising inflation
- Increasing austerity

External debt results when a government borrows money from lenders outside the country, such as private commercial banks, other governments, or international financial institutions (e.g., the IMF or World Bank). Interest on the debt, and eventually the debt itself, must be repaid in the currency in which the loan was made. Hence, the borrowing country may have to export its goods to the lender's country to earn that currency or to convert its currency into that of its creditor. Dreaded debt crises often occur when a weak economy can do so only at high political, economic, and social cost. In this situation, economic activity grinds to a halt. Stress and loss usually precede its reboot to an efficient, smaller-scale version.

INCOME DISTRIBUTION

Income distribution estimates the proportion of the population that earns various levels of income.

Income distribution often defines a market's performance and potential. GNI, even when adjusted for population size or purchasing power, can misestimate the relative wealth of a nation's citizens. That is, GNI per capita reports how much income the average person earns. However, because not everyone is average, we cannot determine what share of income goes to what segments of the population. For example, the GNI of the United States exceeds $15 trillion, a performance that ranks first among nations. Similarly, its GNI per capita was an impressive $50,120 in 2012.[108] However, its performance looks less awe-inspiring when qualified by its distribution of income among 314 million citizens. Presently, the richest 1 percent of Americans receive more income than the bottom 40 percent—the widest gap in 70 years. The top 1 percent own 37 percent of all privately held stock, 65 percent of financial securities, and 62 percent of business equity.[109] The top 10 percent own 85 to 90 percent of stocks, bonds, trust funds, and business equity, and over 75 percent of non-home real estate. Essentially, approximately 10 percent of U.S. citizens "own" the country.[110] The United States is not the exception; dozens of countries exhibit similar income distributions.

Across the world, inequality grows. In 1960, the richest 20 percent of the world's population had 30 times the income of the poorest 20 percent; by 2010 the number had grown to 85 times. Correspondingly, the richest 20 percent spent more than 75 percent of the world total, while the poorest 20 percent spent less than 2 percent.[111] The richest 1 percent claim as much income as the bottom 57 percent—in other words, the 70 million richest people in the world receive as much income as do the 4 billion poorest people. On average, the income of the richest 10 percent of the population is about nine times that of the poorest 10 percent in most countries; we see bigger multiples in Israel, Turkey, South Africa, the United States, Chile, and Mexico.[112]

There is a growing gap between the rich and poor in virtually every country in the world

Benefits and Costs Some income inequality is useful in rewarding effort, talent, and innovation. However, widening inequality threatens the stability that supports growth as it fuels conflicts that tear the social fabric.[113] Countries that are more unequal perform poorly on social indicators, have lower human-development records, and higher economic insecurity. Rising income disparities between booming cities and impoverished countrysides threaten social stability and economic performance.[114] China's steadfast commitment to a "harmonious society," for instance, reflects the CCP's fear of growing income inequality between the 800 million people living on its coastal plain and the 500 million who populate its interior.[115] Whereas Lexus, Lamborghini, and Bentley dealerships operate in Shanghai, many people in rural China rely on bicycles and animals for transportation.

Widening inequality eventually triggers destructive outcomes, including shrinking opportunity, resource inefficiencies, and excessive individualism.[116] Ultimately, income inequality erodes a country's sense of identity, in which unfair play and inequality of opportunity weaken performance and erode potential. For example, people with incomes below $20,000 in the United States have increasingly lost confidence in the free market; support dropped from 76 percent to 44 percent between 2009 and 2010.[117]

The Gini coefficient, the most commonly used measure of inequality, indicates the extent to which income shares deviate from a perfectly equal distribution.

Gini Coefficient Managers use the **Gini coefficient** to estimate the degree of inequality in a country's distribution of income. A score of zero implies perfect equality (everybody has the same income); a score of one implies perfect inequality (one person has all the income). Most countries range between 25 and 60 percent. Countries with lower inequality include Sweden (.23), Hungary (.24), Denmark (.24), and Austria (.26); those with higher inequality include South Africa (.65), Bolivia (.58), Guatemala (.55) China (.47), and the United States (.47).[118]

The Gini coefficient presumes that there is a reasonable degree of income within a country.[119] If not, then it partially represents income distribution. One controls for this error by assessing the scale and scope of poverty. Consider India. Although it reports a Gini coefficient of 33 percent, its performance does not reflect enlightened ideals of equality. Rather, it represents the cheerless reality that many Indians are poor: 80 percent of its population lives on less than $2 per day.[120] So income may be distributed evenly on a relative basis, but there is very little to distribute in absolute terms. India, although extreme, is not the exception.

CONCEPT CHECK

As we suggest in Chapters 1 and 3, both income inequality and poverty should diminish as international business improves the efficiency of resource allocation. The historic record of globalization, Chapter 1 suggested, showed that the productive use of liberated capital creates jobs and fosters income growth.

POVERTY

Poverty is the state of having little or no money, few or no material possessions, and limited access to education, health, and community.

Poverty prevails throughout the world. Managers fine-tune their study of income and wealth by considering its conditions and consequences. **Poverty** is a multidimensional condition whereby a person or community lacks the essentials for a minimum standard of well-being and life (See Table 4.6).[121] These essentials can be life-sustaining resources such as food, clean water, and shelter; they may be social resources such as access to information, education, and healthcare; they may be the opportunity to sustain extended families or connect with people to build communities.

Extreme poverty, according to the World Bank, is rated as living on less than $1.25 per day (PPP); moderate poverty is less than $2 per day (PPP). Approximately 1.3 billion people live

TABLE 4.6 The Multidimensional Poverty Index

Lack of income certainly indicates a state of poverty. Research increasingly assesses the broad mix of conditions that deprive people of sustenance, shelter, stability, and security. Technically, the index below rates a household poor if its sum deprivations exceed 33 percent.

Dimension of Poverty	Indicator	Deprived if...	Relative weight in index (%)
Education	Years of Schooling	No one has completed five years of schooling.	16.6
	Child School Attendance	A child is not attending school up to grade eight.	16.6
Health	Child Mortality	A child has died in the family.	16.6
	Nutrition	Anyone is malnourished.	16.6
	Electricity	The household had no electricity.	5.5
	Sanitation	No decent toilet or facilities are available but shared with other families.	5.5
	Drinking Water	No access to safe drinking water or it is more than a 30-minute roundtrip walk from home.	5.5
Living Standards	Flooring	Has a dirt, sand, or dung floor.	5.5
	Cooking fuel	Cooks with dung, wood, or charcoal.	5.5
	Asset ownership	The household does not own more than one radio, TV, telephone, bike, motorbike or refrigerator and does not own a car or truck.	5.5

Source: Based on *The Multidimensional Poverty Index*, The Oxford Poverty & Human Development Initiative, retrieved March 26, 2013 from www.ophi.org.uk/policy/multidimensional-poverty-index/.

in extreme poverty while some 2.5 billion live in modest poverty.[122] Today, the world population is roughly 80 percent poor, 10 percent middle income, and 10 percent rich. The historical record adds an important perspective. While dramatic income inequality is a recent phenomenon, widespread poverty is not.[123]

Prevalence of Poverty Poverty grows worldwide. Granted, estimates of the number of people in extreme poverty have fallen by approximately 300 million since 1990. However, this reduction has been concentrated in essentially one country. Removing China from the tally reveals that the number of the extreme poor in the developing world has changed little. The global financial crisis and resulting fiscal austerity has threatened many more; in 2013, global unemployment topped 200 million for the first time, pushing tens of millions more into poverty.[124] Presently, rising healthcare, education, and food costs imperil millions more.[125]

Consequences Poverty shapes economic environments. People struggle for food, shelter, clothing, clean water, and health services, to say nothing of safety, security, and education. Failure to find these results in malnutrition, mental illness, death, epidemics, famine, and war. For example, 100 percent of Canadians have access to clean water, compared to 13 percent of Afghans; the per capita dietary protein supply in the United States is 121 grams but 32 grams in Mozambique; the average life expectancy is 83 years in Japan yet 46 in the Central African Republic.[126]

The worldwide growth of business activity and economic progress ultimately depends on alleviating poverty.

The growth of business activity and economic progress ultimately depends on alleviating poverty. Markets experiencing extreme poverty mean MNEs must reassess many taken-for-granted aspects of an economy. Market systems may not exist, national infrastructures may not work, crime may be pervasive, and governments may struggle to regulate society consistently or adopt prudent economic policies.

The Potential of the Poor Managers monitor the buying potential of today's poor. For example, the number of mobile phone subscribers in India in 2002 was under 15 million; by 2006 it was 136 million; and in late 2012 it hit 930 million—even though more than 80 percent of Indians are poor, scraping by on less than $2 a day. Today, however, Indian companies offer the cheapest mobile services in the world while still earning profits. India and China (its mobile carriers report nearly 950 million subscribers) account for more than half the world's increase in wireless subscriptions over the past five years. Similar developments with computers (e.g., the XO-1 programs of low-cost systems for children), automobiles (the development of cheap, functional cars such as Tata's Nano), and housing (Idealab's program to provide functional homes for about $2,500) highlight finding opportunities in the face of dire circumstances. More dramatically, one manager noted, "A billion customers in the world are waiting for a $2 pair of eyeglasses, a $10 solar lantern, and a $100 house."[127]

The Base of the Pyramid is the largest, but poorest, socioeconomic group in the world.

This perspective alerts managers to the **Base of the Pyramid** phenomenon—the nearly four billion people that earn less than US$4 per day who live primarily in Asia, Africa, and South America. Largely excluded from formal markets, the Base represents a tremendous volume of consumption. Though long seen as inaccessible and unprofitable, the poor for some represent the next market frontier of the global economy.[128] Accelerating income growth in emerging economies will move many of today's poor into their expanding middle class.[129] Presently, the middle class includes about two billion people in a dozen emerging economies who collectively spend $6.9 trillion a year. During the next decade, their annual spending will rise to $20 trillion—twice current U.S. consumption.[130] The global middle class—or as some call them, "consumer class"—will include 4 billion people by 2025, up from a billion in 1990. They will inject almost $25 trillion into the global economy, thereby powering a surge unlike any we have ever seen.[131]

Frugal engineering takes the needs of poor consumers as a starting point in developing functional, cost-conscious products.

Success Standards As the world moves from being mostly poor to mostly middle class, the contours of the Pyramid will change. This multi-year process creates immense opportunities. Serving the Base has two preconditions. First, "seeing" opportunity calls for market pioneers that have a particular mindset. More pointedly, "When you look behind the success stories of leading globalizers, you find companies that have learned how to think differently from the herd. They seek out different information, process it in a different way, come to different conclusions, and make different decisions. Where others see threats and complexity, they see opportunity. Where others see a barren landscape, they see a cornucopia of choices."[132]

Second, the task at hand is developing affordable, easily used, eco-sensitive products that work in harsh environments. For example, Nokia, Samsung, and Motorola offer phones with sealed faceplates (for water and dirt resistance), 400 hours of standby time on one battery charge, and larger screens that work in reflected light, use no internal lamp, and are specially enabled for text messaging. Kenya's Safaricom takes these technologies to the next level, pioneering mobile money services in markets lacking efficient means of transaction. At the grassroots level, similar initiatives have built a refrigerator from clay (which uses no electricity yet keeps vegetables fresh for several days), a cheap crop duster (a sprayer mounted on a motorcycle), and smart phones with two SIM card slots (useful in countries with unreliable wireless services).[133]

CONCEPT CHECK

Although the Base of the Pyramid is attractive in terms of economic potential, managers heed the discussions of Chapters 2 and 3 concerning the different cultural, political, and legal environments found in developing countries. Still, Chapter 1 notes the drivers of globalization steadily narrow the gap between developed and developing countries.

Increasingly, these changes also benefit the rich. MNEs translate frugal innovations into new products that serve Western consumers. Chinese firms have introduced reusable sutures (versus the old approach of higher-cost disposable ones) as well as heart stents that run 40 percent cheaper than those in the West.[134] GE developed a low-cost electrocardiograph machine for rural India. Its efficiency and performance soon led to marketing these units in Germany and the United States.[135] A string of similar successes led GE to set India as its global center of "low-cost innovation."

The standards of the Base of the Pyramid—low-cost, high-performance, resource-minimizing, lifestyle-sensitive innovations—increasingly appeal to price-conscious consumers in Western markets. Declining affluence and slowing upward mobility in many rich countries results in a growing number of *nouveaux pauvres:* former middle-class folks who face tightening budgets. The dawning age of austerity in the United States, Ireland, Spain,

TABLE 4.7 Components of a Country's Balance of Payments

Current Account

- Value of exports and imports of physical goods, such as oil, grain, or computers (also referred to as *visible trade*)
- Receipts and payments for services, such as banking or advertising, and other intangible goods, such as copyrights and cross-border dividend and interest payments (also referred to as *invisible trade*)
- Private transfers, such as money sent home by expatriate workers
- Official transfers, such as international aid, on which the government expects no returns

Capital Account

- Long-term capital flows (i.e., money invested in foreign firms as well as profits made by selling those investments and returning the money home)
- Short-term capital flows (i.e., money invested in foreign currencies by international traders as well as funds moved around the world for business purposes by companies with international operations)

England, Greece, and fellow rich countries creates opportunities for frugal shops (notably Wal-Mart and Aldi), pre-paid service providers (Leap Wireless, TracFone), and new business designs such as "collaborative consumption" that lets people share or rent rather than own (as seen in Zipcar and Airbnb). In sum, the Base of the Pyramid is far wider and far more diffused than most realize. Frugal innovators like Tata and Haier see natural markets spanning Dresden, Delhi, Dongguan, and Detroit.[136]

THE BALANCE OF PAYMENTS

The BOP is a system of recording all of a country's economic transactions with the rest of the world.

A country's **balance of payments (BOP)** officially known as the *Statement of International Transactions,* reports its trade and financial transactions (as conducted by individuals, businesses, and government agencies) with the rest of the world.[137] The BOP tracks two different kinds of transactions: the *current account***,** which tracks cross-border payments for goods and services (i.e., exports and imports) and the *capital account,* which tracks loans for cross-border payments for assets.

Table 4.7 lists the components of each account. Technically, exports generate positive sales abroad while imports generate negative sales domestically. Positive net sales, resulting when exports exceed imports, create a *current account surplus*. Conversely, importing more than exporting creates a *current account deficit*. Table 4.8 lists the five countries with the largest current account surpluses and those with the largest current account deficits.[138]

ELABORATING ECONOMIC ANALYSIS WITH GLOBAL INDICES

The study of individual dimensions of a nation's economic environment, much in the spirit of partial equilibrium analysis, is a productive approach. The complexity of modern market

TABLE 4.8 Current Account Balances: The Top and the Bottom Five

Top 5	Country	Current Account Surplus (in millions of US$)	Bottom 5	Country	Current Account Deficit (in millions of US$)
1	Germany	$208,100	159	Turkey	–$59,740
2	China	$170,800	160	Canada	–$59,920
3	Saudi Arabia	$150,000	161	Brazil	–$65,130
4	Russia	$85,060	162	India	–$80,150
5	Japan	$84,700	163	United States	–$487,200

Source: Based on Central Intelligence Agency, "Country Comparison—Current Account Balance," The World Factbook (2013), retrieved March 13, 2013 from www.cia.gov/library/publications/the-world-factbook/rankorder/2187rank.html

systems, however, both absolute and relative, means that the properties of a given system cannot be fully explained by evaluating a snapshot of disaggregated components. Studying the connections that link the parts of the systems improves analysis of its performance and potential. Let's take a look at various meta-models that guide managers.

Managers often consider meta-models to improve their understanding of the absolute and relative potential of an economic environment. Popular indices include:

- Global Competitiveness Index
- Global Innovation Index
- Where-To-Be-Born Index
- World Competitiveness Index

Global Competitiveness Index (GCI) The World Economic Forum assesses the basis of competitiveness in 144 economies.[139] Its analytics assume that providing prosperity to citizens hinges on how effectively a country develops institutions, applies policies, and employs resources to improve productivity. A country's skill in managing these responsibilities translates directly to its competitiveness among the world of nations. Operationally, the GCI summarizes the performance and relationship among 110 variables that comprise 12 so-called "pillars of competitiveness" within a nation. These pillars tap key dimensions, such as financial market development, macroeconomic environment, technological readiness, market efficiency, and innovation. The GCI links a broad set of economic indicators, effectively integrating macroeconomic and micro/business aspects of competitiveness into a single index. Continuing a long-running pattern, today's top 10 competitive economies are dominated by European countries. Switzerland sets the standard; Finland, Sweden, the Netherlands, Germany, and the United Kingdom also make the cut. The United States, along with three Asian economies—Singapore, Hong Kong, and Japan—complete the set. The United States, now ranked seventh, has dropped in the rankings for four consecutive years. Of the big emerging economies, China sets the pace, with Brazil moving up.

World Competitiveness Index (WCI) The World Competitiveness Project assesses a nation's ability to create and maintain an environment in which enterprises, private or state-owned, can compete, prosper, and create wealth. Four primary factors determine a nation's competitiveness index: economic performance, government efficiency, business efficiency, and infrastructure. These categories consist of various subfactors such as international trade, employment, prices, business legislation, productivity, and management practices. Ultimately, the WCI evaluates more than 300 criteria in developing its summary judgment about a nation's performance.

In 2012, Hong Kong topped the WCI scoreboard, followed by the United States, Switzerland, Singapore, Sweden, Canada, Taiwan, Norway, Germany, and Qatar. Again, U.S. performance has slipped over the past few years, forgoing the country's role as global pacesetter. Still, as the 2012 Report concludes, "despite all its setbacks, the U.S. remains at the center of world competitiveness because of its unique economic power, the dynamism of its enterprises and its capacity for innovation."[140]

Global Innovation Index (GII) Countries, as we noted in Chapter 3, increasingly look to their brainpower to create innovations that confer competitive advantage. The growing power of ideas and insights in the global market makes a country's ability to support innovation a critical facet of its economic environment. The GII measures a country's success in doing so, assessing its competency in promoting technologies, expanding human capacities, streamlining organizational capabilities, and improving institutional responsiveness that best leverages knowledge into market-changing innovation.[141] The GII anchors analysis in terms of five input pillars (Institutions and Policies, Human Capacity, Infrastructure, Technological Sophistication, Business Markets and Capital) and three output pillars (Knowledge, Competitiveness, Wealth). Combined, these measures estimate a nation's capacity to generate ideas, leverage them into innovative products, and improve knowledge, competitiveness, and wealth.

Presently, wealthy, developed countries claim the top spots in the GII standings: Switzerland is the global leader, followed by Sweden, Singapore, Finland, the United Kingdom, the Netherlands, Denmark, Hong Kong, Ireland, and the United States. Accelerating innovation in Asia sees India, Turkey, and China rising in rank. Collectively, Asia appears to be shifting from practices that optimized efficiency to policies that improve the environment for innovation.

Schoolchildren with their newly arrived laptops at a previously off-the-grid school in Ulaanbaatar, capital and largest city of Mongolia. The government is providing a laptop to every schoolchild with the goal of equipping the next generation of value creators with the tools to engage globalization. Similar programs are unfolding in countries throughout the world. The implications of this program to the division of labor, the trade of products, and the performance of markets will shape MNEs' strategies.
Source: VAN CAKENBERGHE TO/SIPA/Newscom

In general, smaller economies score higher in the lottery of life.

Where-To-Be-Born Index (WTBBI) Finally, looking a bit further into the future, the WTBBI holds that how well a country provides opportunities for a healthy, safe, and prosperous life helps explain both its current and future economic environment.[142] The WTBBI evaluates 11 indicators, such as geography, demography, quality of life, per capita income, and life expectancy. Today, the "lucky baby" league table, comprising 80 countries, is topped by Switzerland, followed by Australia, Norway, Sweden, and Denmark. Smaller nations dominate the top performers, accounting for the top 15 countries in the lottery of life. Large, wealthy countries—notably, United States (16), Japan (25), France (26), and Great Britain (27)—do not rank particularly well. Developing economies fall from the middle down to the bottom of the ranking—e.g., Brazil (37), China (49), India (66), and Russia (72).

CASE The BRICs: Vanguard of the Revolution[143]

Improving performance showcases the accelerating success of emerging economies. The focus of attention is now squarely on the vanguard of emerging economies, the so-called BRICs: Brazil, Russia, India, and China. Together, they are home to nearly 2.8 billion people (40 percent of the planet's population) and cover a quarter of the area of the world, spanning three continents. Combined, they presently account for about 18 percent of global GDP. That share will head to 25 percent over the next 10 years and about one-third by 2030. Adjusting for PPP turbocharges this performance: the BRICs currently generate about 30 percent of the world's GDP, with a projected 38 percent by 2020 and nearly 45 percent by 2030.

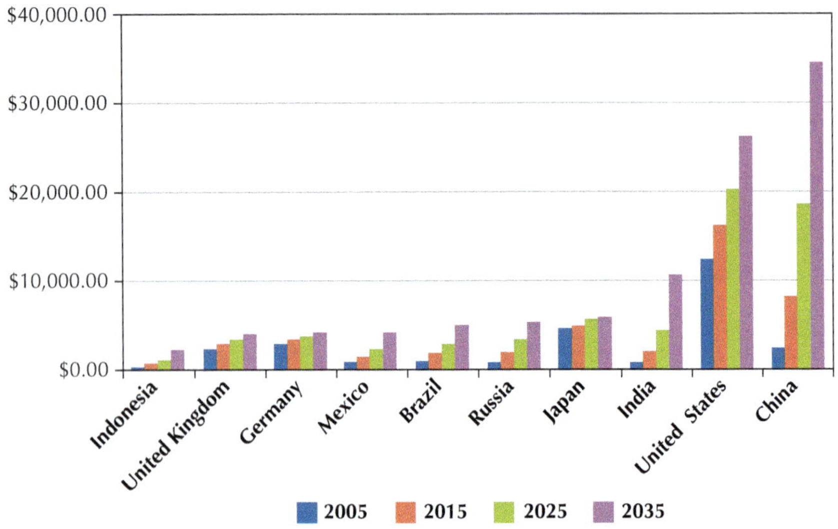

FIGURE 4.10 GDP of Top Ten Economies: 2005, 2015, 2025, 2035 ($ billions)

Here we see the trend in nominal GDP among the ten largest economies in the world, projected as of 2035. The baseline is set in terms of 2006 $ billions.

Source: Based on data in *Looking to 2060: A Global Vision of Long-Term Growth*, OECD Economic Policy Papers, November 2012; as well as assorted reports by the IMF World Bank, and McKinsey Global Institute."

Unquestionably, the BRICs are much larger in scale and scope than other emerging markets. Still, they are leading indicators of consumption patterns, investment policies, and social trends that are gaining momentum worldwide. Many see the BRICs as vanguards of the revolution: where they go, both good and bad, others will follow. We now profile their emergence, highlighting implications to the global marketplace and closing by identifying looming threats.

Changing of the Guard

First off, remind yourself where the BRICs were just 30 or so years ago. Brazil was an economic basket case suffering hyperinflation, Russia was in lockdown behind the Iron Curtain, India's aggressive socialism had led it to expel IBM and Coca-Cola, and China was recovering from the bedlam of the Cultural Revolution and struggling with the legacies of Mao Zedong. Today, conditions and circumstances have radically changed. At current trends and with reasonable projections, over the next few decades the four of them will become premier, powerful economies (see Figure 4.10).

Originally, some thought it would take until 2050 or so before the BRICs bypassed today's rich countries. The global financial crisis, however, has accelerated the schedule. Whereas the BRICs are growing, Germany, Japan, England, Italy, France, and the United States, among others in the West, struggle mightily. Wealthy countries also face a raft of other constraints: their aging workforces, overwhelming debt, and slowing productivity suggest growth will be hard-fought. Moreover, as shown in Figure 4.10, it will fall short of the growth in emerging markets. In the meantime, the speed of the BRICs' recovery paints the global financial crisis as a pivot point in the redistribution of economic power.

So, again, thinking of where the BRICs were 30 or so years ago, mapping their accomplishments, and projecting trend lines out 30 years from today makes for, depending on your perspective, an astonishing or worrisome outcome. Current circumstances make any timeline for the changing of the guard speculative. It does not, however, change secular trends that will culminate in the BRICs' converting demographic dividends, rising productivity, improving innovation, and increasing capital efficiency into the comeback of the emerging economies.

Changing Markets

The BRICs, like many fellow emerging markets, report rapidly growing economies. Historically, consumer demand takes off when GNI per capita is between US$3,000 and $10,000. Russia hit those levels first; China, India, and Brazil are steadily heading there. When adjusted for purchasing power, all have crossed the threshold.

The BRICs, save Russia, have growing middle classes. Forecasts see them expanding from 50 million to almost 600 million by 2025. More immediately, between 2005 and 2015, over 800 million people in the BRICs will cross the annual income threshold of US$3,000. By 2025, approximately 200 million people in the BRICs will have annual incomes above $15,000. Escape from poverty is a game changer; besides permitting more consumption, it often allows people to move from consuming generic necessities to preferring branded goods.

As income grows, so does demand for what once were unreachable luxuries. For example, there are roughly two cars for every 100 people in India and nine per 100 in China. In contrast, there are 63 and 82 cars per 100 people, respectively, in Germany and the United States. By 2030, India and China's car ownership will likely increase 5- to 25-fold. The total number of cars in the two countries combined could rise from around 150 million today to north of a billion by 2030, thereby accounting for more than half of all cars on the world's roads. Other countries show similar vehicle per capita rates: the Philippines' is 3.3 percent, Indonesia's 7 percent, and Turkey's 14 percent. Introduction of low-price autos like Tata's Nano—a frugally engineered rear-engine, four-passenger car targeting poorer folks—expand the global auto market. Similar trends in virtually every product class, many anchored in frugal innovation programs targeting the Base of the Pyramid, indicate market potentials last seen at the start of the Industrial Revolution.

Big Plans but Big Problems

Notwithstanding the spectacular performance and potential of the BRICs, there are skeptics. First, there is the problem of recency bias, which is the delusion that current trends will continue indefinitely and uninterrupted. History shows great mistakes made by many who extrapolated the present into the future. Invariably, economic growth rates slow as the base of activity expands. Moreover, advantages such as cheap labor or low-cost capital wane as growing demand increases marginal price pressures. And always on the horizon is a black-swan event—a large-impact, hard-to-predict, but rare event beyond the realm of normal expectations that resets the game, such as the collapse of the Soviet Union, the emergence of the Internet, or the global financial crisis.

Despite perils, people on the go need to move. Here we see Indian passengers catching a ride in ways that defy reason. The hazard of traveling this way, apparently, falls short of missing India's economic surge.

Source: © Terje Lillehaug / Alamy

Despite high-octane growth, the BRICs face futures of persistent poverty and distorted income distributions. By 2025, the income per capita in today's richer countries will exceed $35,000 for more than a billion people. In contrast, only 10 to 20 percent of the nearly 3 billion folks in the BRIC economies will hit that threshold. For the longer term, income per capita in the United States is projected to reach $80,000 by 2050, while China will likely be just over $31,000, Brazil about $26,600, and India just $17,400. With the possible exception of Russia, hundreds of millions of people in the BRICs will be far poorer on average than individuals in Germany, France, Japan, Italy, Canada, and the United States. Consequently, for the first time in history, the largest economies in the world will no longer be the richest when measured by GNI per capita.

National Challenges

Each of the BRICs struggles with its particular problems. Russia is particularly vulnerable. It depends on various energy and mineral exports for revenue. Erratic swings in commodity prices complicate setting budgets and planning programs. Additionally, Russia is considered riskier because of long-simmering tensions with the West and a legal and political infrastructure that imposes the rule of man. Going forward, besides its aging and declining population, Russia's oligarchic government and crumbling infrastructure confound growth projections. Hence, some advise replacing the BRIC notion with that of "BICs."

Brazil's economic potential has been anticipated for decades, but it has struggled to achieve expectations. Difficulties in income equality, productivity, and education have often snatched defeat from the jaws of victory. India, in addition to pressing economic and political challenges, has immense infrastructure shortfalls and hundreds of millions of poor people. Meeting current demands while building for the future poses immense resource demands. China's particular interpretation of the rule of law, rights of citizens, environmental sustainability, and principles of governance poses problems. China also faces a steadily closing window of opportunity; by 2020, it will have the largest number of old and very old people on earth. The IMF forecasted in 2013 that China's demographic dividend would end by 2020; its working age population would then go into precipitous decline. By 2030, China will face a labor shortage of almost 140 million workers, arguably the greatest jobs crunch in history.

Green Constraints

Wish as we might, the sad fact that there are only so many resources to go around shadows the bright futures of all. The emergence of the BRICs sorely challenges the sustainability of the global environment. Global warming, diminishing raw materials, and escalating pollution suggest that there is a limit to how much the BRICs, to say nothing of the 150 or so countries who seem intent on following in their footsteps, can develop before exceeding the capacity of the global economy to supply the necessary resources and of the environment to support them. More worrisomely, notes the *Worldwatch Institute*, if China and India were to consume resources and produce pollution at the current U.S. per capita level, we would need the resources of two additional Earths. Throwing everyone else into the mix ratchets up the pressure—estimates are that we are short approximately five planets of resources if the living standards found in today's wealthy countries prevailed worldwide.

Adding Mortar

BRIC leaders have not been idly sitting by, watching these threats thwart their future. Overlapping ambitions and agendas have led them to develop bilateral and multilateral agreements. India and China, the world's two most populous countries, formed a strategic partnership to end border disputes and boost trade. The agreement eased decades of mutual distrust between the two following a 1962 border war. "India and China can together reshape the world order," Indian Prime Minister Manmohan Singh proclaimed at a ceremony for then Chinese Premier, Wen Jiabao, at India's presidential palace.[144]

Similarly, indications show strengthening ties between Russia and China. Bilateral China-Russia trade was $84 billion in 2011, up from $20 billion in 2005, and is targeting $200 billion by

2020. In many people's eyes, Russia, by rolling back democracy and reviving its imperialist past, is now more politically aligned with the one-party state of China than the multiparty democracies in the West. Spearheading these efforts was then-President, now Prime Minister, Putin of Russia, with his goal to build "a new world economic architecture" that would reflect the rising power of emerging economies and the decline of the old heavyweights like the United States, Japan, and European countries.[145]

Dethroning the Dollar

The global financial crisis has accelerated these trends. Besides trade and economic relationships, the BRICs amplify their political, legal, and strategic influence in other ways. Attention often centers on the unit of exchange used to settle trade transactions. Since the Bretton Woods Agreement of 1944, the U.S. dollar has functioned as the world's reserve currency; as such, it is widely held by governments and institutions around the world and is used to finance every sort of international transaction. The BRICs increasingly try to erode the hegemony of the dollar. In 2009, China and Brazil agreed to no longer use it in doing business, instead adopting a yen-cruzeiro currency-swap agreement. China and Russia stopped using the dollar to settle bilateral trade in 2010, switching instead to the ruble or the yuan. By 2013, China had negotiated currency swaps with some 20 countries, including Australia, United Arab Emirates, Japan, France, and Turkey, to bypass the dollar in settling bilateral trade. We see similar moves elsewhere; notably, Turkey arranged with Russia and Iran to sidestep U.S. dollars and use their own currencies in bilateral transactions.

Stronger Ties

To cap matters, the BRIC leaders have begun holding BRIC-only summits to discuss ways to reset the global trade structure and champion a new supranational currency. In the backdrop is a sense, explained Prime Minister Putin, that the world "is changing before our very eyes. Countries that seemed hopelessly backward only yesterday are becoming the world's fastest-growing economies today." The BRICS, backed by fellow emerging economies, no longer merely want to be part of the world's outdated architecture—instead, they aim to go forward into a brave new world largely unencumbered by the past. Seeing their performance improve while that in the West stagnate has moved the BRICs to push farther ahead. Their 2011 summit increased the pressure on the West for a revamped global monetary system that relies less on the dollar as well as a louder voice in international financial institutions.

The Road Ahead

Inevitably, some speculate that the BRICs might turn into bricks in their march to miracle economies. Granted, their governments have developed economically sensible policies, opened trade and domestic markets, and begun building institutions that support economic freedom. The global financial crisis, however, brutally illustrated that economics can quickly move out of sync.

Despite ever-present gloom, reasonable optimism prevails. Research identifies four preconditions of consistent macro growth: sound macroeconomic policies; political institutions committed to transparency, fairness, and the rule of law; openness to trade and capital; and strong education systems. By and large, the BRICs, along with other emerging markets, steadily meet the general spirit of some of these standards. None, however, presently meets all. That said, the success of the BRICS questions whether, in fact, one needs to meet all. Their improving performance as their rich-country counterparts struggle suggests that conventional understanding of markets possibly mismaps the dynamics of economic environments. If so, perhaps Western markets, not the BRICs, must reform.

No matter what the future holds, few question that the ride will be captivating. The emergence of the BRICs signals that the next phase of the global economy has begun. And even if the BRICs fall short of their potential, their successes will redefine the structure of economic environments, patterns of growth, and dynamics of economic activity.

QUESTIONS

4-3. Estimate the likely market evolution of the BRICs over the next decade. What economic indicators might companies monitor to best guide their investments and actions?

4-4. Identify three implications of the emergence of the BRICs for careers and companies in your country.

4-5. Do you think recency bias has led to overestimating the potential of the BRICs? How would you, as a manager for a company assessing these markets, try to control this bias?

4-6. How might managers interpret the potential for their product in a market that is, in absolute economic terms, large but, on a per capita basis, characterized by a majority of poor consumers?

4-7. In the event that the BRICs fail to meet projected performance, what would be some of the implications for the international business environment?

4-8. Compare and contrast the merits of GNI, Net National Product, and Your Better Life Index as indicators of economic performance in Brazil, Russia, China, and India.

SUMMARY

- Economic freedom measures the absence of government coercion or constraint on the production, distribution, or consumption of goods and services beyond the extent necessary for citizens to protect and maintain liberty.
- Economically free countries tend to have higher per capita income, standards of living, and social stability than do less-free or repressed countries.
- The global financial crisis challenges the legitimacy of free markets. Governments in many countries have expanded their regulation of the economy to manage the consequences.
- In a market economy, private interests own resources while price and quantity, conveyed via the invisible hand, determine supply and demand.
- In a command economy, the government plans what goods and services a country produces, the quantity in which they are produced, and the price at which they are sold.
- A mixed economy includes some elements of market and command economies. Both influence investment activities and consumption behavior.
- A market economy endorses the doctrine of capitalism, its principles of the invisible hand and laissez-faire, and the goal of maximizing economic freedom.
- A command economy endorses the doctrine of communism, its principle of an activist government that commands and controls most if not all factors of production, and the goal of constraining economic freedom.
- A mixed economy endorses the doctrine of socialism, its principle of the partly visible hand of an activist government that commands and controls some factors of production, and the goal of regulating economic freedom.
- State capitalism is a system whereby the government manipulates market outcomes for political purposes.
- Managers assess markets in terms of size (GNI, GNP, GDP), income (GNI, GNP, or GDP per capita), stability (HDI, HPI), and sustainability (NNP, GPI, YBLI).
- Green measures of economic performance call for considering ecological aspects that support sustainable development.
- Concern that monetary measures misestimate economic performance leads to calls to expand the concept of prosperity to include aspects of happiness.
- Managers use several indicators to assess the performance and potential of an economy, including inflation, unemployment, debt, income distribution, poverty, and the balance of payments.
- The Base of the Pyramid is the largest but poorest socioeconomic group in the world. Although poor in terms of individual wealth, the aggregate income of the Base arguably makes it the next market frontier.
- Various global indices help managers develop a holistic profile of particular markets in terms of competitiveness, innovation, and the quality of life.

KEY TERMS

balance of payments
Base of the Pyramid
BRICs
capitalism
command economy
communism
debt
deflation
economic freedom
Economic Freedom Index
economic system

emerging economies
Gini coefficient
green economics
gross national income (GNI)
gross national product (GNP)
happynomics
income distribution
inflation
laissez-faire
market economy
mixed economy
misery index
poverty
reflation
socialism
state capitalism
sustainable development
unemployment rate

ENDNOTES

1 ***Sources include the following:*** Thomas Friedman, *The World Is Flat: A Brief History of the Twenty-first Century"* (Farrar, Straus and Giroux, 2005); Clyde V. Prestowitz, *Three Billion New Capitalists: The Great Shift of Wealth and Power to the East* (New York: Basic Books, 2006); Clyde Prestowitz,"Three Billion New Capitalists,"video transcript, *News Hour* (August 15, 2005), www.pbs.org/newshour/bb/economy/july-dec05/prestowitz_8-15.html; Kenneth Rogoff,"Betting with the House's Money,"*Project Syndicate*, retrieved May 7, 2007 from www.project-syndicate.org/commentary/rogoff27; Anne O. Krueger,"Stability, Growth, and Prosperity: The Global Economy and the IMF,"retrieved June 7, 2006 from www.imf.org/external/np/speeches/2006/060706.htm; Angus Maddison, *The World Economy, 1–2030 AD* (London: Oxford University Press, 2007); *The World Economy: Volume 1: A Millennial Perspective* (Paris: Development Centre, 2001); *Volume 2: Historical Statistics* (Paris: Development Centre, 2003);"BRICs, Emerging Markets and the World Economy: Not Just Straw Men,"*The Economist* (June 18, 2009): 45;"Government v. Market in America: The Visible Hand,"*The Economist* (May 28, 2009): 25–28, retrieved August 12, 2009 from www.economist.com/displaystory.cfm?story_id=13743310;"The Next Billions: Unleashing Business Potential in Untapped Markets,"*World Economic Forum* (January 2009): 44;"A Special Report on Innovation in Emerging Markets: The World Turned Upside Down,"*The Economist*, retrieved April 21, 2011 from www.economist.com/node/15879369;"China Claims #9 Rank In United States Patents!"retrieved April 23, 2011 from www.defence.pk/forums/china-defence/55892-china-claims-9-rank-united-states-patents.html; Ian Morris, *Why the West Rules... For Now* (New York, Farrar, Straus and Giroux, 2010).

2 Thomas Friedman, *The World Is Flat: A Brief History of the Twenty-first Century* (Farrar, Straus and Giroux, 2005).

3 Clyde V. Prestowitz, *Three Billion New Capitalists: The Great Shift of Wealth and Power to the East,* (New York: Basic Books, 2006).

4 Hal Sirkin, James W. Hemerling, Arindam Bhattacharya, *Globality: Competing with Everyone from Everywhere for Everything,* Grand Central Publishing, 2008.

5 "Global Economic Outlook,"The Conference Board,"retrieved April 11, 2011 from www.conference-board.org/data/globalout look.cfm. They moved to 50.4 percent in 2010. "Global Development Horizons 2011—Multipolarity: The New Global Economy,"*The World Bank* (retrieved May 19, 2011).

6 Martin Dewhurst, Jonathan Harris, and Suzanne Heywood, "The Global Company's Challenge,"*McKinsey Quarterly*, December 31, 2012, from www.mckinseyquarterly.com/The_global_companys_challenge_2979.

7 So, for example, in May 2011, Chinese Central Bank governor Zhou Xiaochuan noted that"The new IMF leadership needs to reflect changes in the world economic order and be more representative of emerging market economies."

8 "A Special Report on Innovation in Emerging Markets: The World Turned Upside Down,"*The Economist*, retrieved April 21, 2011 from www.economist.com/node/15879369; James Politi,"World Bank Sees End to Dollar's Hegemony,"*Financial Times* (May 17, 2011).

9 Ibid.

10 Dustin Ensinger,"China Takes the Crown, Economy in Crisis," retrieved April 13, 2011 from www.economyincrisis.org/content/china-takes-crown.

11 People's Republic of China: Spillover Report."International Monetary Fund, retrieved January, 26, 2013 from www.imf.org/external/pubs/ft/scr/2011/cr11193.pdf.

12 Dustin Ensinger,"China Takes the Crown, Economy in Crisis,"5.

13 Clyde Prestowitz,"Three Billion New Capitalists,"video transcript, *News Hour* (August 15, 2005), retrieved July 18, 2007 from www.pbs.org/newshour/bb/economy/july-dec05/prestowitz_815.html.

14 Jason Dean, Andrew Browne, and Shai Oster,"China's'State Capitalism' Sparks a Global Backlash - WSJ.com" (November 16, 2010); Keith Bradsher,"In Trade Cases, Solar Panel Industry Follows Lead of Steel Industry,"*New York Times* (October 12, 2012): B2.

15 Bradsher, Keith."Strategy of Solar Dominance Now Poses a Threat to China,"*New York Times* (October 5 2012): B1.

16 For example, in mid-2011, Bolivia dismantled its privatization model that governed the mining industry and expropriated all assets owned by private, largely foreign-owned mining companies. The fear was this action signaled rising resource nationalism worldwide.

17 "A Special Report On Innovation In Emerging Markets: The World Turned Upside Down."

18 Martin Dewhurst, Jonathan Harris, and Suzanne Heywood, "The Global Company's Challenge,"*McKinsey Quarterly*, retrieved December 31, 2012 from www.mckinseyquarterly.com/The_global_companys_challenge_2979.

19 Jason Dean, Andrew Browne, and Shai Oster,"China's'State Capitalism' Sparks a Global Backlash,"WSJ.com, retrieved January 30, 2013 from online.wsj.com/article/SB10001424052748703514904575602731006315198.html.

20 Cardwell, Diane, and Keith Bradsher,"U.S. Will Place Tariffs on Chinese Solar Panels."*New York Times,* (October 11, 2012): B3.

21 Stephen King, *Losing Control: The Emerging Threats to Western Prosperity,* (New Haven, CT: Yale University Press, 2010).

22 "How We Classify Countries | Data,"*The World Bank,* retrieved February 6, 2013 from data.worldbank.org/about/country-classifications.

23 See, for example, www.econlib.org/library/Enc/BehavioralEconomics.html.

24 Consider, for example, the consequences of a reduction in interest rates; a cut spurs more borrowing that fans greater demand that boosts inflation that erodes purchasing power that creates wage pressure that reduces profits that lowers savings and so on.

25 Kim Murphy,"Melting Ice Caps Open Up Shipping Routes,"*Los Angeles Times* (October 13, 2009).

26 Simon Wilson,"Global Trade: The Opening of the Northeast Passage," *MoneyWeek* (September 25, 2009):45.

27 Ships attempting the Northern Sea Route or Northwest Passages face hundred-mile long swathes of shifting pack ice, even during the two months or so of each summer when safe passage is feasible.

28 "NASA—Arctic Ice Gets a Check Up," retrieved April 18, 2011 from www.nasa.gov/mission_pages/icebridge/multimedia/arcticseaice-max2011.html.

29 Arctic Sea Ice Volume Now One-fifth Its 1979 Level," *Weather Underground*, retrieved February 20, 2013 from www.wunderground.com/blog/JeffMasters/show.html; Justin Gillis, "Arctic Sea Ice Stops Melting, but Record Low Is Set," *New York Times*, (January 23, 2013): C4.

30 William W. Beach and Marc A. Miles, "Explaining the Factors of the Index of Economic Freedom," *2005 Index of Economic Freedom*, retrieved August 14, 2006 from www.heritage.org/research/features/index:33.

31 Quotation extracted from *The Wealth of Nations*. Reported in "Executive Summary," Index of Economic Freedom , retrieved February 4, 2008 from www.heritage.org/research/features/index/chapters/pdf/index2008_execsum.pdf.

32 "March Toward Economic Freedom Stalls With Only Two Regions Improving," The Heritage Foundation, retrieved January 23, 2013 from www.heritage.org/index/press-release-overview.

33 *The 2013 Index of Economic Freedom*, retrieved January 24, 2013 from www.heritage.org/Index.

34 E.g., Robert Lawson "Measuring Economic Freedom," Cato Institute, retrieved April 13, 2011 from www.cato.org/pub_display.php?pub_id=6101.

35 Barry Eichengreen and Kevin H. O'Rourke, "A Tale of Two Depressions," retrieved June 5, 2009 from www.voxeu.org/index.php?q=node/3421.

36 "Bush Says Sacrificed Free-market Principles to Save Economy," *Agence France-Presse*, retrieved January 28, 2013 from www.google.com/hostednews/afp/article/ALeqM5jyyKrPjYt7VhpS8G8DrRkr18B0hA.

37 Data drawn from 12,884 interviews across 25 countries. "Sharp Drop in American Enthusiasm for Free Market," *Globescan*, retrieved April 19, 2011 from www.globescan.com/news_archives/radar10w2_free_market; "Capitalism's waning popularity," *The Economist*, (April 7, 2011): 45.

38 Ibid.

39 Ibid.

40 Anatole Kaletsky, "*Capitalism 4.0: The Birth of a New Economy in the Aftermath of Crisis*, (New York: Public Affairs, 2010).

41 Strictly speaking, none of them is a "pure" market economy because their governments intervene in the marketplace. Still, their historic advocacy of economic freedom endorses the philosophy of capitalism and the principle of laissez-faire.

42 "Quote by Ronald Reagan: Government Is Not the Solution...." retrieved February 24, 2013 from www.goodreads.com/quotes/179719-in-this-present-crisis-government-is-not-the-solution-to.

43 Only then, the thinking goes, are the proletariat (the social class that does manual labor or work for wages) protected from exploitation by the bourgeois (the social class that owns the factors of production).

44 Companies in centrally planned economies exhibited a particular quirk. The absence of competition and bankruptcy in this sort of economic system meant that once an enterprise was up and running, it survived indefinitely, irrespective of performance.

45 "The Global Revival Of Industrial Policy: Picking Winners, Saving Losers," *The Economist*, (April 27, 2011):55.

46 Michael Todaro, *Economic Development*, 6th edition (Reading, MA: Addison Wesley, 1996):705.

47 "The French Model: Vive la Différence!" *The Economist*, (May 7, 2009):37.

48 "Denmark 'happiest place on earth,'" BBC News, 28 July 2006. retrieved April 18, 2011 fromnews.bbc.co.uk/2/hi/health/5224306.stm; see also Russell Shorto, "Going Dutch: How I learned to love the welfare state," *New York Times*, retrieved April 17, 2011 from www.nytimes.com/2009/05/03/magazine/03european-.html.

49 For instance, the French government holds significance ownership stakes in several large companies, including Areva (15.88 percent stake), Renault (15 percent stake), Safran (30.2 percent stake), EDF (84.44 percent stake), and GDF Suez (36.36 percent stake).

50 Most worrisome to free market proponents is that, once a crisis passes, government control sometimes shrinks, but it never returns to its original size. Indeed, some argue that a mixed economy is essentially a move toward a socialist state.

51 Specifically, according to 2013 rankings, Hong Kong, Singapore, Australia, New Zealand, and Switzerland.

52 "Q&A with Ian Bremmer on State Capitalism," *Foreign Affairs*, retrieved April 13 2011 from www.foreignaffairs.com/discussions/interviews/qa-with-ian-bremmer-on-state-capitalism?page=show.

53 Michael Wines, "Make No Mistake: In China, State-run Firms Rule," *The New York Times* (August 31, 2010): B-4.

54 "China's Future: Rising Power, Anxious State," *The Economist*, Special Report: China (June 25, 2011): 14.

55 The state essentially prevents systemic distortions threatening the stability of the system and promoting societal welfare—or, as Marx prophesied, capitalism eventually is destroyed by its own contradictions.

56 "Countries at the Crossroads," retrieved April 18, 2011 from www.freedomhouse.org/template.cfm?page=139&edition=9.

57 Ian Bremmer, "State Capitalism and the Crisis," *McKinsey Quarterly*, (July, 2009): 4.

58 "Brazil's Presidential Campaign: Falling in Love Again with the State," *The Economist*, (August 18, 2012): 57.

59 Eric Li, "How China Broke The West's Monopoly On Modernization," CSMonitor.com, retrieved April 28, 2011 from www.csmonitor.com/Commentary/Global-Viewpoint/2011/0428/How-China-broke-the-West-s-monopoly-on-modernization.

60 Ian Bremmer, *The End of the Free Market: Who Wins the War Between States and Corporations?* (New York: Portfolio, 2010); Stefan Halper, *The Beijing Consensus: How China's Authoritarian Model Will Dominate the Twenty-First Century* (New York: Basic Books, 2010).

61 Regarding the informal, the *Economist* reported that "When Alan Greenspan was chairman of the Federal Reserve, he monitored several unusual measures. One favorite, supposedly, was sales of men's underwear, which are usually pretty constant, but drop in recessions when men replace them less often." See "Fast Food for Thought," *The Economist* (July 30, 2011): 12.

62 "Fact Sheet: World Population Trends 2012," *Population Reference Bureau*," retrieved January 24, 2013 from www.prb.org/Publications/Datasheets/2012/world-population-data-sheet/fact-sheet-world-population.aspx.

63 "GDP: One of the Great Inventions of the 20th Century," *Bureau of Economic Analysis*, retrieved from January 24, 2013 from www.bea.gov/scb/account_articles/general/0100od/maintext.htm.

64 For example, Indonesia's GNP is larger than its GNI—the former was $706 billion in 2010, while the latter was $599 billion. The same held for its neighbor, Thailand, with a GNI of $286 billion versus GNP of $318 billion the same year. In contrast, the GNI of the United States in 2010 was $14.60 trillion, while its GNP was $14.66 trillion. This discrepancy results from the fact that the net foreign factor income was negative for Indonesia and Thailand (i.e., a net outflow), but roughly balanced for the United States. Since GNI takes net flows into account, we have the resulting variance between GNI and GNP. As a rule, many developing countries produce more value than they receive as income, thereby leading to a higher GNP than GNI.

65 Historically, GNI was referred to as gross national product. The definition and measurement of GNI and GNP are analogous, but

institutions such as the World Bank and International Monetary Fund now use the term GNI.

66 For example, Latin America has seen income per capita drop five times since the 1980s. The current global credit crisis has triggered a sixth occurrence—population in the region is growing 1.3 percent a year but the economy "grew" –2.2 percent in 2009. As expected, consumer demand, public finances, financial reserves, and currency valuations tumbled. This calamity is not unique to Latin America; at least 60 developing markets suffered income drops in 2009, with especially hard times for Central and Eastern Europe and sub-Saharan Africa.

67 Technically, we compute per capita GNI by taking the GNI of a country and converting it into a standard currency—say, the U.S. dollar at prevailing exchange rates—and then dividing this sum by population size.

68 U.S. and World Population Clocks—POPClocks, retrieved January 30, 2013. Check www.census.gov/main/www/popclock.html for current statistic.

69 Technically, the World Bank estimates a higher per capita income level for Monaco. However, the 2011 report is an approximation and, moreover, there is no estimate for its purchasing power parity conversion. Hence, we use Norway given its complete data file for 2011.

70 We calculate PPP between countries by estimating the value of a universal "basket" of goods (e.g., soap and bread) and services (e.g., telephone and electricity) that can be purchased with one unit of a country's currency. For example, a loaf of bread that sells for 53.70 rupees in India should cost U.S. $1.00 in the United States given an exchange rate between India and the United States of 53.70 INR to U.S. $1. Exchange rates as of January 24, 2013.

71 World Bank, 2013 Survey (Atlas methodology for GNI per capita). Typically, the prices of many goods are considered and weighted according to their importance in the economy of the particular country.

72 The most common PPP exchange rate comes from comparing a basket of goods and services in a country with an equivalent basket in the United States.

73 "Europe's Shadow Economy: As Big As Germany," *Zero Hedge.*" Retrieved May 13, 2013 from www.zerohedge.com/news/2013-05-06/europes-shadow-economy-big-germany.

74 "Process of Preparation of the Environmental Perspective to the Year 2000 and Beyond," General Assembly Resolution 38/161," retrieved May 27, 2007 from www.un.org/documents/ga/res/38/a38r161htm.

75 Joseph Stiglitz, "Good Numbers Gone Bad: Why Relying on GDP as a Leading Economic Gauge Can Lead to Poor Decision-Making," *Fortune* (September 25, 2006):45-49.

76 Some maintain that the purpose of development is to enlarge people's choices. In principle, these choices can be infinite and can change over time. People often value achievements that do not show up at all, or not immediately, in income or growth figures: greater access to knowledge, better nutrition and health services, more secure livelihoods, security against crime and physical violence, satisfying leisure hours, political and cultural freedoms, and sense of participation in community activities. The objective of development is to create an enabling environment for people to enjoy long, healthy, and creative lives. Statement by Dr. Mahbub ul Haq, co-conceiver, with Amartya Sen of HDI.

77 Richard Easterlin, "Does Economic Growth Improve the Human Lot?" in Paul A. David and Melvin W. Reder, eds., *Nations and Households in Economic Growth: Essays in Honor of Moses Abramovitz* (New York: Academic Press, 1974); Richard Easterlin, "Income and Happiness: Towards a Unified Theory," *The Economic Journal* (2001): 465–84.

78 Eric Weiner, "The Happiest Places in the World," *Forbes* (April 23, 2008):55.

79 Mark Whitehouse, "GDP Can Be a Poor Measure of Success," WSJ.com, retrieved January 17, 2011 from online.wsj.com/article/SB10001424052748704064504576070343252409876.html; "Noreena Hertz: Even War Is Good for Economic Growth," *Spiegel Online*, retrieved January 28, 2013 from www.spiegel.de/international/world/globalization-critic-noreena-hertz-even-war-is-good-for-economic-growth-a-685491.html.

80 Roger Cohen, "The Happynomics of Life," NYTimes.com, retrieved April 27, 2011 from nytimes.com/2011/03/13/opinion/13cohen.html?_r=1.

81 Charles Jones and Peter Klenow, *Beyond GDP? Welfare across Countries and Time*, NBER Working Papers 16352, National Bureau of Economic Research (2010).

82 "OECD Launches Happiness Index, *AFP*, retrieved May 26, 2011 from www.google.com/hostednews/afp/article/ALeqM5jj15a9ZCL9ETVD9UAn18y7MlrG_g?docId=CNG.b86506f095cbf61164e88f98b0d5d21c.2a1.

83 The Happiest Countries in the World," *24/7 Wall St*, retrieved June 4, 2011 from 247wallst.com/2011/06/01/the-happiest-countries-in-the-world/2.

84 *World Bank Indicators, 2013*, The World Bank, data.worldbank.org/data-catalog/world-development-indicators.

85 "Government v. Market in America: The Visible Hand," *The Economist* (May 28, 2009): 25–28.

86 E. Mishan, *The Costs of Economic Growth* (New York: Praeger, 1967).

87 Ibid.

88 Jerome Glenn, Theodore Gordon, and Elizabeth Florescu, *2009 State of the Future, The Millennium Project*, retrieved May 15, 2011 from www.millenniumproject.org/millennium/sof2009.html; "Humans using Earth's Resources at Unsustainable Rate, Conservation Group Claims," retrieved June 2, 2011 from www.naturalnews.com/020873.html.

89 *Process of Preparation of the Environmental Perspective to the Year 2000 and Beyond*, General Assembly Resolution 38/161, retrieved May 27, 2007 from www.un.org/documents/ga/res/38/a38r161htm.

90 Murray Rothbard, "Ludwig von Mises (1881–1973)," retrieved May 27, 2009 from www.mises.org/content/mises.asp.

91 See www.usinflationcalculator.com/frequently-asked-questions-faqs.

92 For example, discontent with rising prices sparked China's Tiananmen Square protests of 1989. "China's Future: Rising Power, Anxious State," *The Economist*, Special Report: China (June 25, 2011): 9.

93 Economists use different types of indexes to measure inflation, but the one they use the most is the *Consumer Price Index (CPI)*. The CPI measures a fixed basket of goods and compares its price from one period to the next. A rise in the index indicates inflation.

94 The Hanke-Krus hyperinflation table documents every known case of hyperinflation of the 20th century.

95 Steve H. Hanke and Alex K. F. Kwok, "On the Measurement of Zimbabwe's Hyperinflation," *Cato Journal*, (Spring/Summer 2009).

96 Steve H. Hanke and Alex K. F. Kwok, "On the Measurement of Zimbabwe's Hyperinflation," *Cato Journal*, (Spring/Summer 2009).

97 Analytics performed at www.usinflationcalculator.com/.

98 Kevin Phillips, "Numbers Racket: Why the Economy Is Worse than We Know," *Harper's*, retrieved April 26, 2001 from www.harpers.org/archive/2008/05/0082023; "Economics focus: Botox and bean counting," *The Economist* (April 30, 2011):84.

99 For instance, as of 2003, only three countries had annual inflation rates in excess of 40 percent, the level above which it is generally considered to be acutely damaging to an economy. All major industrial countries had inflation under 3 percent (and in Japan, deflation persisted). Moreover, inflation in many middle- and lower-income countries, once stuck with extreme inflation pressure, had fallen well into single digits in the early twenty-first century. Many credited the fall in inflation to a combination of the price pressures of globalization along with more vigilant central bankers and economic policymakers. See Ken Rogoff, "The IMF Strikes Back," *Foreign Policy* (January/February 2003): 39–48.

100 View of Junko Nishioka, Chief Japan economist at RBS Securities Japan Ltd. in Tokyo. From "Japan Succumbs to Deflation as Consumer

Prices Fall Record 1.1 percent," Bloomberg.com, retrieved June 29, 2009 from www.bloomberg.com/apps/news?pid=newsarchive&sid=aaQyqjERBorM.

101 Ibid.

102 Presently, the wealthier countries of the world are watching their working-age population shrink from approximately 740 to 690 million people between 2000 and 2025. However, over the same time, the working-age population will increase across poorer countries from about 3 to 4 billion people. In China alone, the population above the age of 16 will grow by 5.5 million annually on average in the next 20 years. The total population of working-age Chinese will reach 940 million by 2020. Presently, the youth of the world suffer the highest rates of unemployment in most countries, with rates twice that of adult (ages 25–65) unemployment. China, for example, sees the age structure of its population creating severe employment pressure within the next two decades.

103 "Economic Security Index: Putting a Face on American Economic Security," retrieved January 24, 2013, from economicsecurityindex.org/.

104 "In U.S., Employment Situation Deteriorates in January," *Gallup Economy*, retrieved January 28, 2013 from www.gallup.com/poll/159866/employment-situation-deteriorates-january.aspx.

105 See Constance Sorrentino, "International Unemployment Rates: How Comparable Are They?" *Monthly Labor Review* (June 2000): 3–20.

106 See U.S. National Debt Clock, www.brillig.com/debt_clock.

107 For example, arguably the U.S. fiscal system is plugged with many tax loopholes that cause inefficiencies, misallocation of resources, and lost revenues. Hence, eliminating the deficit requires eliminating these distortions.

108 GNI per capita data is adjusted by purchasing power parity (data as of February 2013).

109 Bob Herbert, "Losing Our Way," NYTimes.com, retrieved April 12, 2011 from www.nytimes.com/2011/03/26/opinion/26herbert.html?_r=1.

110 William Domhoff, "Wealth, Income, and Power," retrieved May 5, 2009 from sociology.ucsc.edu/whorulesamerica/power/wealth.html; see "Gap between Rich and Poor: World Income Inequality," retrieved July 4, 2009 from www.infoplease.com/ipa/A0908770.html.

111 *World Development Indicators 2012*, The World Bank.

112 "Growing Income Inequality in OECD Countries: What Drives It and How Can Policy Tackle It?" www.oecd.org/els/social/inequality (May 2010). Finally, income inequality is accelerating between top executives and the average employee. In 2010, the average CEO in the United States made 343 times more money than the average American did last year. In 2007, for example, CEOs of the 15 largest companies earned 520 times more than the average worker. This is up from 360 times more in 2003. We see similar patterns Australia, Germany, Hong Kong (China), the Netherlands, and South Africa.

113 "Inequality: Unbottled Gini," *The Economist*," (January 20, 2011):45.

114 "Chinese Scholars Warn Growing Wealth Gap Likely to Trigger Social Instability," *Sina*, retrieved July 8, 2006 from english.sina.com/china/1/2005/0822/43237.html.

115 "China's Urban, Rural Income Gap Widens Despite Economic Recovery," *People's Daily Online*, retrieved April 19, 2011 from english.people.com.cn/90001/90778/90862/6875693.html

116 Joseph Stiglitz, "Of the 1 Percent, by the 1 Percent, for the 1 Percent," *Vanity Fair* (May 2011).

117 Ibid: 26.

118 Some controversy surrounds the Gini estimate with regards to China. China officially reported its Gini coefficient, for the first time in 12 years, in 2012 as .474. Skeptics argue otherwise. For example, a study based on the China Household Finance Survey reports a Gini coefficient of .58.

119 Others advocate refining analysis by calculating a "Global Gini" that measures the scale of income distribution among everyone in the world. Global inequality increased in the 19th and 20th centuries as richer countries, on average, consistently grew faster than poorer countries. Recently, the accelerating comeback of developing countries shows up in declining global inequality, indicating that the planet as a whole is increasingly fair.

120 "80 Percent of Indians Live on Less than $2 a day—World Bank," livemint.com, retrieved April 17, 2011 from www.livemint.com/articles/2007/10/16235421/80-of-Indians-live-on-less-th.htm.

121 "A Wealth of Data: A Useful New Way to Capture the Many Aspects of Poverty," *The Economist*, retrieved April 18, 2011 from www.economist.com/node/16693283.

122 "Impossible Architecture," *Social Watch Report 2006*, retrieved May 27, 2007 from www.socialwatch.org/en/portada.htm.

123 Noted Jeffery Sachs, "The world is more unequal than at any time in world history. There's a basic reason for that which is that 200 years ago everybody was poor. A relatively small part of the world achieved what the economists call a modern economic growth. Those countries represent only about one-sixth of humanity, and five-sixths of humanity is what we call the developing world. It's the vast majority of the world. The gap can be 100 to 1, maybe a gap of $30,000 per person and $300 per person. And that's absolutely astounding to be on the same planet and to have that extreme variation in material well-being." Transcript, Chapter 18, "Episode Three: The New Rules of the Game," *Commanding Heights: The Battle for the World Economy*, retrieved June 28, 2007 from www.pbs.org/wgbh/commanding-heights/lo/index.htm.

124 "Global Unemployment Expected to Surpass 200 Million," *Zero Hedge*, retrieved January 29, 2013 www.zerohedge.com/news/2013-01-22/global-unemployment-expected-surpass-200-million).

125 Sandrine Rastello and Wendy Pugh, "Food Surge Is Exacerbating Poverty, World Bank Says," Bloomberg.com, retrieved May 10, 2011 from www.bloomberg.com/news/2011-02-15/food-price-jump-pushes-44-million-into-extreme-poverty-world-bank-says.html.

126 The Food and Agriculture Organization of the United Nations translates the food commodities available for human consumption in a country into their protein equivalent. This measure compensates for differences in protein supplied by different foods across countries (go to www.fao.org).

127 Donald McNeil Jr., "Design That Solves Problems for the World's Poor," *New York Times* (May 29, 2007): B-2.

128 "The Next Billions: Unleashing Business Potential in Untapped Markets," *World Economic Forum* (January 2009): 44; C. K. Prahalad and S. L. Hart, "The Fortune at the Bottom of the Pyramid," *Strategy+Business* (2002) 26: 54–67.

129 Christa Case Bryant, "Surging BRIC Middle Classes Are Eclipsing Global Poverty," CSMonitor.com, retrieved May 25, 2011 from www.csmonitor.com/World/2011/0517/Surging-BRIC-middle-classes-are-eclipsing-global-poverty.

130 David Court and Laxman Narasimhan, "Capturing the World's Emerging Middle Class," *McKinsey Quarterly* (July 2010): 67.

131 "Chart Focus: The World's Economic Center of Gravity Shifts," *McKinsey Quarterly*, retrieved February 25, 2013 from www.mckinseyquarterly.com/newsletters/chartfocus/2013_02.html.

132 Jane Fraser and Jeremy Oppenheim, "What's New about Globalization," *The McKinsey Quarterly* (May 1997): 178. Erik Simanis, "When selling to poor consumers, companies first need to create the market," WSJ.com," retrieved January 29, 2013 from online.wsj.com/article/SB10001424052970203946904574301802684947732.html.

133 See, for example, www.nextbillion.net.

134 "Medical Technology: Frugal Healing," *The Economist*," (January 11, 2011):45.

135 "Innovations to Create New Streams of Profitable Growth," *Accenture Outlook*, retrieved June 9, 2009 from www.accenture.com/in-en/outlook/Pages/outlook-journal-2010-less-is-new-more-innovation.aspx.

136 "The Tata Group: Out of India," *The Economist* (March 5, 2011):76–78; "The Bottom of the Pyramid," *The Economist* (June 25, 2011): 80.
137 The notion of *balance* means that all BOP transactions have an offsetting receipt. For instance, a country might have a surplus in merchandise trade (indicating that it is exporting more than it is importing) but may then report a deficit in another area, such as its investment income. In other words, because the current account and the capital account add up to the total account—which is necessarily balanced—a deficit in the current account is accompanied by an equal surplus in the capital account and vice versa. A deficit or surplus in the current account cannot be explained or evaluated without simultaneous explanation and evaluation of an equal surplus or deficit in the capital account.
138 Retrieved October 2, 2009 from www.cia.gov/library/publications/the-world-factbook/rankorder/2187rank.html.
139 "Global Competitiveness Index," *World Economic Forum,"* retrieved January 25, 2013 from www.weforum.org/issues/global-competitiveness.
140 "IMD Announces Its 2012 World Competitiveness Rankings," IMD, retrieved January 25, 2013 from www.imd.org/news/IMD-announces-its-2012-World-Competitiveness-Rankings.cfm.
141 "The Global Innovation Index 2012," retrieved January 25, 2013 from www.globalinnovationindex.org/gii/.
142 "The Lottery of Life," *The Economist: The World in 2013,* (November 21, 2012):91.
143 ***Sources include the following:*** Dominic Wilson and Roopa Purushothaman, "Global Economics Paper No. 99: Dreaming with BRICs: The Path to 2050," Goldman Sachs, at www.gs.com/insight/research/reports/report6.html; "The BRICs Are Coming—Fast," *Business Week* (October 27, 2003): 33; Daniel Gross, "The U.S. Is Losing Market Share. So What?" *New York Times* (January 28, 2007): A-2; Andrew Kramer, "Putin Wants New Economic 'Architecture,' " *International Herald Tribune* (June 10, 2007): 1; "Chilling Time," *The Economist* (June 14, 2007): 24; State of the World 2006: China and India Hold World in Balance, Worldwatch Institute; see www.worldwatch.org; N. Taleb, *The Black Swan: The Impact of the Highly Improbable* (New York: Random House, 2007); "Emerging Markets and the World Economy: Not Just Straw Men," *The Economist,* (June 18, 2009): 53. "What the West Doesn't Get About China - *Harvard Business Review,"* retrieved August 29, 2011 from hbr.org/2011/06/what-the-west-doesnt-get-about-china/ar/pr; *The World Economic Forum,* retrieved September 7, 2011 from www.reports.weforum.org/global-competitiveness-2011-2012/; Abhijit Neogy and Alexei Anishchuk, "BRICS demand global monetary shake-up, greater influence," *Reuters,* retrieved October 26, 2011 from www.reuters.com/article/2011/04/14/us-brics-idUSTRE73D18H20110414; Ambrose Evans-Pritchard, "IMF Sees 140m Jobs Shortage in Ageing China as 'Lewis Point' Hits," *Telegraph,* retrieved February 4, 2013 from www.telegraph.co.uk/finance/comment/9845959/IMF-sees-140m-jobs-shortage-in-ageing-China-as-Lewis-Point-hits.html; Arvind Subramanian, "BRICs Share of Global GDP Will Go up from 18% to 26% over the Next Decade," *Economic Times,* retrieved February 4, 2013, from articles.economictimes.indiatimes.com/2012-09-06/news/33650208_1_bric-countries-brics-share-punita-kumar-sinha; "Russia and China to Strengthen Trade Ties," FT.com, retrieved February 4, 2013 from www.ft.com/cms/s/0/d8999462-af27-11e1-a8a7-00144feabdc0.html.; "China Busy Signing Currency Deals," *Forbes,* retrieved February 4, 2013 from www.forbes.com/sites/jackperkowski/2012/06/26/china-busy-signing-currency-deals/.
144 India, China Hoping to 'Reshape the World Order' Together," Washingtonpost.com, retrieved February 24, 2013 from www.washingtonpost.com/wp-dyn/articles/A43053-2005Apr11.html.
145 Andrew E. Kramer, "Putin Wants New Economic 'Architecture'" *The New York Times,* (June 10, 2007): B-1.

Chapter 7

INTERNATIONAL FINANCIAL MARKETS AND INSTITUTIONS

Objectives of the chapter

This chapter considers financial markets that allow firms to find sources and uses of funds outside their home countries and to deal in currencies other than the domestic one. It also considers the risks involved in operating in these markets and the tools available to deal with those risks. The main risk has to do with dealing in foreign currencies, so **exchange risk** and the functioning of the **foreign exchange** market are key elements of the discussion. For example, when a German firm borrows from a bank in dollars, because of the low interest rate, the firm faces a problem of exchange risk. The firm has to decide what to do in case the dollar rises in value relative to the euro and makes loan repayment more expensive.

The main goals of the chapter are to:

1 *Review* the basic characteristics of all the financial markets that may be available to a firm in international business.

2 *Examine* the foreign exchange market, its operation, and the main participants.

3 *Explain* the fundamental economic factors that determine the exchange rates in the absence of government intervention in the foreign exchange markets.

4 *Show* how firms can operate successfully in more than one currency without facing unacceptable levels of exchange risk.

5 *Give* insights into domestic money and capital markets that exist around the world.

6 *Describe* the functioning of the euromarkets, both short term and long term.

7 *Explain* how the international monetary system functions and how it relates to both private-sector firms and governments.

8 *Look* at a country's balance of payments and show what lessons can be drawn from it.

9 *Show* how firms can take advantage of the opportunities available in all of these markets.

ACTIVE LEARNING CASE

Barclays Bank international financial dealings

Barclays Bank, one of the largest banks in the world (measured by capital), had a worldwide spread of branches, representative offices, and other affiliates in the early 2000s. As at 2009, Barclays is the world's ninth largest banking and financial services group and the UK's second largest bank (Global Fortune 500, 2010 ranking). The bank was actively involved in businesses such as corporate finance for major firms around the world, retail banking in the UK and a few other countries in Europe, and in foreign exchange dealing in London, New York, Tokyo, and other financial capitals of the world. At the end of 2009 Barclays' business was divided among the currencies shown in Table 1. Growth in income and costs was constrained by foreign exchange translation movements. These are not necessarily major concerns for a multinational bank, since Barclays has lengthy experience in using these currencies, and the bank regularly deals with foreign exchange risk. Still, some banks had encountered huge crises due to foreign exchange losses. For example, National Australia Bank lost US $360 million in 2003–2004 due to currency trading, and Allied Irish Banks lost more than US $770 million in 2002 from similar trading. Back in 1974 the entire world financial system was shaken by a pair of foreign exchange losses that caused two banks to fail (Franklin National Bank in the United States and Bankhaus Herstatt in Germany) and the entire **eurocurrency** system to briefly come to a halt. (In 2008 the British government nationalized Northern Rock to prevent its failure, while banks in the United States also faced failure due to losses on the subprime mortgage market leading to the world financial crisis)

Barclays is heavily involved in financial activities in more than 30 countries worldwide. This is an overstatement of the firm's global activity. Instead, Barclays is a home region bank, with 60 percent of its revenues in Europe. A geographical analysis of revenues from external customers for continuing operations for the year ended December 31, 2009 shows that 44.06 percent of Barclays' revenues are in the UK, the bank's country of origin. Another 15.11 percent of the bank's business is in other European Union countries, about 19.06 percent in the United States, 10.24 percent in South Africa. This leaves 11.53 percent of Barclays' business in the remaining countries where it operates. With this exposure to risks in other countries, as Table 1 shows, Barclays has a large exposure in US dollars.

From another perspective, Barclays had an international financial exposure through its lending activities in various countries. Table 2 shows this distribution of activity.

Table 1 The Barclays Group's structural currency exposures as at December 31, 2009

Functional currency of the operation involved	Foreign currency net investment £m	Borrowings which hedge the investment £m	Derivatives which hedge the investment £m	Structural currency exposures pre economic hedges £m	Economic hedges £m	Remaining structural economic exposures £m
At 31/12/2009						
US dollar	16,677	3,205		13,472	6,056	7,416
Euro	6,772	3,418		3,354	2,902	452
South Africa Rand	4,055		1,542	2,513	189	2,324
Japanese Yen	4,436	3,484	940	12		12
Swiss Franc	2,840	2,734	92	14		14
Other	2,983		677	2,306		2,306
Total	37,763	12,841	3,251	21,671	9,147	12,524
At 31/12/2008						
US dollar	14,577	6,019		8,558	6,720	1,838
Euro	6,336	2,922		3,414	3,125	289
South Africa Rand	3,725		1,306	2,419	164	2,255
Japanese Yen	5,009	801	4,212	−4		−4
Swiss Franc	3,042	2,936	101	5		5
Other	2,940		880	2,060		2,060
Total	35,629	12,678	6,499	16,452	10,009	6,443

Table 2 Analysis of loans and advances to customers as at December 31, 2009

	The Group		The Bank	
Credit risk concentrations by geographical sector (£m)	**2009**	**2008**	**2009**	**2008**
United Kingdom	203,582	213,079	375,761	392,153
Other European Union	84,343	91,109	61,909	66,326
United States	58,355	75,826	47,520	59,971
Africa	47,495	44,373	3,654	2,987
Rest of world (ROW)	26,449	37,428	23,284	32,452
Total	**420,224**	**461,815**	**512,128**	**553,889**
Credit risk concentrations by maturity (£m)				
On demand	44,826	51,155	39,694	71,170
Not more than 3 months	68,876	87,624	226,426	216,131
Over three months but not more than six months	8,987	12,447	6,472	9,237
Over six months but not more than one year	17,848	21,976	10,977	15,692
Over one year but not more than three years	51,886	60,927	44,604	52,651
Over three years but not more than five years	38,357	44,982	35,637	38,584
Over five years but not more than ten years	63,180	57,409	57,177	55,631
Over ten years	126,264	125,295	91,141	94,793
Total	**420,224**	**461,815**	**512,128**	**553,889**

A key concern of Barclays is how to manage these overseas and foreign currency activities, especially with respect to the risk of currency losses. As an international bank, Barclays wants to operate in major financial centres, but as a prudently managed firm it doesn't want to take undue risk in foreign currencies or put significant amounts of assets in high-risk environments.

Website: www.barclays.com.

Source: Barclays, *Annual Report*, 2009.

1. **What exchange risk does Barclays have as at December 31, 2009?**
2. **What should Barclays' expectation be about the value of the pound relative to the euro or the dollar?**
3. **How should Barclays deal with the risk involved in its foreign currency positions?**
4. **How can Barclays use the eurocurrency market in its international business, and will this help in dealing with the exchange rate problem?**

Exchange risk
The risk of financial loss or gain due to an unexpected change in a currency's value

Foreign exchange
Foreign currency-denominated financial instruments, ranging from cash to bank deposits to other financial contracts payable or receivable in foreign currency

Eurocurrency
A bank deposit in any country that is denominated in a foreign currency. A yen-denominated bank deposit in Germany is a euro-yen deposit, a form of eurocurrency

INTRODUCTION

International financial markets are relevant to companies, whether or not they become directly involved in international business through exports, direct investment, and the like. Purchases of imported products or services may require payment in foreign exchange, thus involving exchange risk. A company may choose to invest in a foreign business or security, and face both different interest rates and different risks from those at home. Often companies find that borrowing funds abroad is less expensive than borrowing domestically, in the United States or in any other home country. The relatively unrestricted "euromarkets" generally offer better terms to borrowers (*and* lenders) than do domestic financial markets in any country. Likewise, in the 2000s, investors are discovering more and more opportunities to diversify their portfolios into holdings of foreign securities. This chapter explores the various foreign and international financial markets, including the foreign exchange market, and examines ways to utilize them for domestic and international business.

FOREIGN EXCHANGE MARKETS

Currencies, like any other products, services, or claims, can be traded for one another. The foreign exchange market is simply a mechanism through which transactions can be made between one country's currency and another's. Or, more broadly, a foreign exchange market is a market for the exchange of financial instruments denominated in different currencies. The most common location for foreign exchange transactions is a commercial bank, which agrees to "make a market" for the purchase and sale of currencies other than the local one. In the United States, hundreds of banks offer foreign exchange markets in dozens of cities. However, over 40 percent of all foreign exchange business is done through the 10 largest banks in New York.

Foreign exchange is not simply currency printed by a foreign country's central bank; rather, it includes such items as cash, checks (or drafts), wire transfers, telephone transfers, and even contracts to sell or buy currency in the future. Foreign exchange is really any financial instrument that carries out payment from one currency to another. The most common form of foreign exchange in transactions between companies is the draft (denominated in a foreign currency). The most common form of foreign exchange in transactions between banks is the telephone or Internet transfer, generally for transactions of $1 million or more. Far down the list of instruments, in terms of the value exchanged, is actual currency, which is often exchanged by tourists and other travelers.

Exchange rate
The value of one currency in terms of another; for example, US $1.2378 / €1

Since no currency is necessarily fixed in value relative to others, there must be some means of determining an acceptable price, or **exchange rate**. How many British pounds (£) should one dollar buy? How many Brazilian reals should be paid to buy a dollar? Since 1973, most of the industrialized countries have allowed their currency values to fluctuate more or less freely (depending on the time and the country), so that simple economics of supply and demand largely determines exchange rates. In graphic form, Figure 7.1 shows that the intersection of the supply curve and the demand curve for European euros (c) sets the price, or exchange rate, of euros in terms of dollars. Some of the participants in the foreign exchange market are listed below the graph; their specific activities are discussed in the following section.

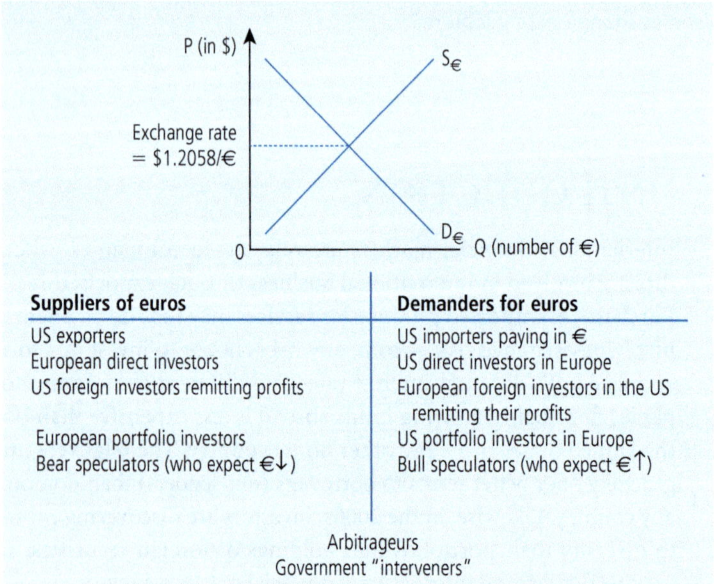

Figure 7.1 Foreign exchange market for euros in New York

The exchange rate of $1.2378 per euro is offered by one specific bank. This was the closing exchange rate quoted by Bankers Trust Company of New York for purchases of at least $1 million worth of euros on June 26, 2010. Another bank in New York may have quoted a slightly higher or slightly lower rate at the same time, and banks in San Francisco, London, or Tokyo probably quoted rates that differed even more. The rates quoted depend on each bank's interest in being involved in foreign exchange transactions and on the varying strategic positions and risks taken by the banks. Thus, the foreign exchange market among banks may be viewed as one large market or as many small markets with extensive (potential and actual) interrelations. Generally, the interbank market within any country is viewed as one market, and intercountry dealings are somewhat segmented by different rules and risks (though in the United States, the San Francisco market often offers quotations from various banks that differ noticeably from rate quotations in New York, due partly to the difference in time zones).

The differences in rate quotations may appear very small to an outsider. For example, Euros may be quoted at $1.23236 at Citibank in New York and at $1.23386 at Bank of America in San Francisco. This difference seems small, but for every 1 million euros sold, the buyer of dollars in San Francisco receives an extra $1,500. Since the transactions are generally rapid, for values of $5 million to $10 million such differences may add up to a substantial gain (or cost) to the participant in the foreign exchange market.[1]

The various foreign exchange transactions just mentioned involve large commercial banks and large amounts of money. Most of the companies that do international business also utilize foreign exchange markets, but far less frequently than banks and for transactions that involve less money. Consequently, these companies' access to foreign currencies differs from that of the banks. (Specifically, banks make the market and companies pay for the use of this service.) The next section describes the various participants in the US foreign exchange market.

Foreign exchange markets in the United States

Figure 7.2 presents an overview of the foreign exchange markets operating today in the United States. This section discusses each of these markets in some detail.

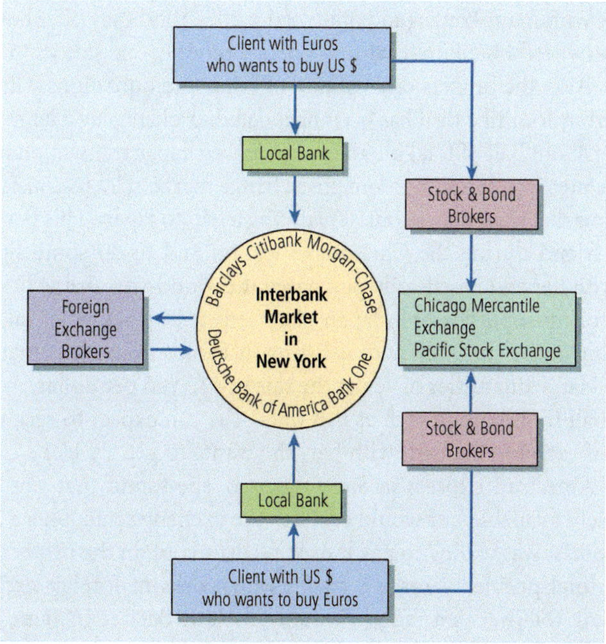

Figure 7.2 US foreign exchange markets

Source: Adapted from K. Alec Chrystal, *St. Louis Fed Review*, March 1984, Figure 1, p. 8.

The interbank market

Although the foreign exchange dealings of most managers involve a company buying from, or selling to, a bank, managers must understand the foreign exchange market among banks. This is because, as noted above, the vast majority of large-scale foreign exchange transactions are interbank, and these transactions tend to determine exchange rates, with which occasional market participants such as companies must deal.

Local and regional commercial banks may offer clients a foreign exchange service, which such banks provide on request by dealing through a larger bank, typically in a large city (such as New York, Los Angeles, or Chicago). If a local bank receives a request to buy Swiss francs (SF) for an importer in New Jersey, it will call its correspondent bank in New York (say, JP Morgan-Chase Bank) and arrange to buy the SF for, say, \$0.6753/SF. Then the local bank will add on its service charge so that the importer pays \$0.6853/SF. Thus, the local bank earns \$0.01 per SF, or about 1.5 percent on the transaction.

JP Morgan-Chase Bank, in turn, will either take the requested Swiss francs from its own holdings of that currency or enter the interbank market to buy them. Assuming that Chase does *not* have the SF on hand, one of its **foreign exchange traders** will call several other major banks (or brokerage houses, which are discussed below) and contract to buy Swiss francs from the lowest bidder.

Foreign exchange traders
Bankers who deal in foreign exchange, buying and selling foreign currencies on behalf of clients and/or for the bank itself; typically they deal in foreign currency-denominated bank deposits

The interbank market generally operates with large transactions only of about \$1 million to \$10 million exchanged for the equivalent foreign currency. On a typical day in 2010, the more than 45 members of the main association of commercial banks in foreign exchange dealings (called the Clearinghouse Interbank Payments System, or CHIPS) transacted roughly \$2 trillion in currency trades.[2]

The brokers' market

Another facet of large-scale foreign exchange dealing in the United States is the brokers' market. About six **foreign exchange brokers** make markets for foreign currencies in New York (as well as in London and elsewhere), creating trading in many currencies similar to that in the interbank market. In this case, the key differences are that the brokers seek to match buyers and sellers on any given transaction, without taking a position[3] themselves; they deal simultaneously with many banks (and other companies); and they offer both buy and sell positions to clients (where a bank may wish to operate on only one side of the market at any particular time). Also, the brokers deal "blind," offering rate quotations without naming the potential seller/buyer until a deal has been negotiated. Brokers play a large role in the total market, arranging about half of total interbank foreign exchange transaction in the early 2000s.

Foreign exchange brokers
A company that provides specialized services to commercial banks in the interbank foreign exchange market, essentially functioning to unite interested buyers and sellers of foreign currency-denominated bank deposits; brokers intermediate about half of all wholesale foreign exchange transactions in New York and London

Before moving on to other foreign exchange markets, let us consider an example in which the spot market is used by a tourist planning a trip to Japan. This person wants to visit Tokyo to see a friend during the Christmas vacation and to do some sightseeing. She is taking \$1,000 with her and has already purchased the round-trip airline ticket. Since dollars cannot be used for most purchases in Japan, she needs to buy Japanese yen. How should she do it?

Looking at the currency trading listing in Table 7.1, she sees that Bankers Trust is offering to sell large quantities of yen at the rate of 112 yen per dollar. At the "retail" level—that is, for small transactions such as this one—she can expect to receive fewer yen per dollar. Instead of carrying the cash with her, she wants to get traveler's checks. Upon calling the office of American Express in San Francisco, she found that yen-denominated traveler's checks were available but would cost her the exchange rate, plus a \$5 service charge.

The tourist was willing to pay the extra cost to obtain the protection of traveler's checks, but one final problem arose. A friend who works in foreign exchange dealing at Wells Fargo Bank told her that the yen would probably decline in value relative to the dollar in the next few days. Since she would not leave for Tokyo for another week, she wondered whether it was worth waiting for the expected devaluation. The answer to this question is that no one knows! She can hope for a devaluation and delay purchase of the yen for

Spot rate
The exchange rate offered on the same day as the request to buy or sell foreign currency; actual settlement (payment) may occur one or two days later

Forward rate
An exchange rate contracted today for some future date of actual currency exchange; banks offer forward rates to clients to buy or sell foreign currency in the future, guaranteeing the rate at the time of the agreement

Table 7.1 Exchange rates in the inter-bank market, June 26, 2010

Foreign currency exchange rates (mid)	UK sterling (£)	Europe euro (€)	Japan yen (¥)
Spot rate—closing (foreign currency units per US dollar)	1.5072	1.2378	0.0112
Forward rate—closing			
1 month outright	1.4750	1.2200	0.0110
3 months outright	1.5000	1.2500	0.0109
12 months outright	1.5500	1.3000	0.0110

Source: *Financial Times*, June 26, 2010

a week, or ignore the potential gain or loss and buy the yen today. In such a short time period, it is probably better to ignore the few days' variability in the exchange rate—since it could be favorable or unfavorable—and just buy the yen at the most convenient time before departing for Tokyo. (One more point to confuse the matter: she could buy traveler's checks in US dollars and exchange them for yen in Japan when needed. Again, no one can be sure what the yen's value will be during her vacation time in Tokyo.)

Although this example does not offer a guaranteed way to make money from foreign exchange dealings, it does illustrate the kinds of problems that beset individuals and companies as they work with foreign currencies. Fortunately, there are some methods to help avoid the uncertainty involved in foreign exchange; they are discussed in the section below on "Protecting against exchange risk."

So far, our discussion has focused only on the *spot market*; that is, the market for immediate exchange of one currency for another. An additional, very large part of the US foreign exchange market is the set of instruments that allow contracting today for delivery of currency in the future. The main instruments of this type are forward contracts, foreign exchange futures contracts, and foreign currency options.

The forward foreign exchange market

The forward foreign exchange market at commercial banks in the United States offers banks, companies, and individuals the opportunity to contract *today* for a specific foreign exchange transaction in the *future*, at a fixed price (that is, exchange rate). Forward contracts are negotiated between the offering bank and the client as to size, maturity, and price. Referring to Table 7.1, we see that Bankers Trust was offering to sell British pounds for \$1.5500/£ in 360 days on June 26, 2010 (for quantities of at least \$1 million).

The rationale for forward contracts in currencies is analogous to that for futures contracts in commodities: the firm can lock in a price today to eliminate uncertainty about the value of a future receipt or a payment of foreign currency. A firm may undertake such a transaction because it has made a previous contract, for example, to pay €1 million to a supplier in three months for some needed inputs to its operations. If the firm wants to eliminate the risk that its payment in three months will change in dollar terms (that is, the c1 million may cost more dollars then), it can contract with a bank to buy €1 million three months forward, at a price established today. (From Table 7.1, we see that the price was \$1.2500/EUR for a contract with Bankers Trust on June 26, 2010.) Thus, firms can use forward contracts to eliminate the risk of variability in future dollar costs or revenues due to exchange rate changes. This concept, called *hedging*, and other motives for using the forward market are discussed later.

Notice that in the above example, the forward contract used for hedging is not the same thing as an insurance contract. The forward contract does fix a minimum "loss" for the firm by setting the guaranteed price of exchange in the future. Even if the dollar devalues to \$1.30 per € in three months, the forward contract holder is still able to buy €1 million for \$1.3710/€. However, if the euro devalues over the next three months to, say, \$1.2400/€, the forward contract holder will have an opportunity cost of the difference between the forward rate and the (eventual) future spot rate. Thus, the forward contract insures against potential losses *and* against potential gains in foreign currency value.

Forward markets exist in any currencies and for any maturities that banks are willing to offer. Most of the forward contracts used in the United States involve exchanges of US dollars for euros, Japanese yen, British pounds, Swiss francs, and Canadian dollars. Maturities tend to be six months or less, though single-year and multiyear forward contracts are sometimes available.

The futures market in currencies

A very similar type of instrument is available on several securities exchanges in the United States and abroad. The foreign exchange futures contract is an agreement to buy or sell a fixed amount of foreign currency for delivery at a fixed future date at a fixed dollar price. The main difference between futures and forward contracts in the United States is that futures contracts have fixed sizes (about $50,000 to $100,000, depending on the currency) and pre-established maturity dates. (All are 3-, 6-, 9-, or 12-month contracts maturing on the third Wednesday of March, June, September, or December.) Also, futures contracts are available for only a few currencies (Canadian dollars, euros, Swiss francs, British pounds, Japanese yen, Mexican pesos, Australian dollars, and a few others), and only if a buyer and a seller can be found at the time.

The futures market at the Chicago Mercantile Exchange is currently very thin (that is, few contracts are traded) except for the three-month contracts denominated in Canadian dollars, euros, Swiss francs, British pounds, and Japanese yen.

Futures contracts are more widely accessible to firms and individuals than forward contracts because of their smaller value and the margin requirements that enable brokers to obtain collateral from market participants. (However, the currently thin nature of this market does not allow participants the wide range of currencies and maturities that are available for large-scale transactions in the forward market.) The standard contracts available at the Chicago Mercantile Exchange (CME) are described in Table 7.2. Trading hours have been extended via the GLOBEX system, which permits worldwide access to CME contracts. In 2010, GLOBEX trading was available for about 19 hours per day around the world.

Foreign currency *options* are an additional instrument of the foreign exchange market in the United States; they offer participants the *right* to buy or sell foreign currency in the future rather than the obligation to do so. Foreign currency options are similar to foreign

Table 7.2 Currency futures contract specifications at the Chicago Mercantile Exchange

	British pound (£)	Eurozone euro (€)	Japanese yen (¥)
Trading Unit	£62,500	€125,000	¥12,500,000
Quotations	US $ per £	US $ per €	US $ per ¥
Minimum price fluctuation	0.0001	0.0001	0.000001
Value of 1 point	$6.25	$12.50	$12.50
Months traded	Six months in the March quarterly cycle (Mar, Jun, Sep, Dec)		
Trading hours	*GLOBEX (ETH): Sundays: 5:00 p.m. – 4:00 p.m. Central Time (CT) next day* *Monday – Friday: 5:00 p.m. – 4:00 p.m.* CT the next day, except on Friday – closes at 4:00 p.m. and reopens Sunday at 5:00 p.m. CT. CME ClearPort: Sunday – Friday 6:00 p.m. – 5:15 p.m. (5:00 p.m. – 4:15 p.m. Chicago Time/CT) with a 45-minute break each day beginning at 5:15 p.m. (4:15 p.m. CT) *OPEN OUTCRY (RTH): 7:20 a.m. – 2:00 p.m.*		
Last day hours	9:16 a.m. Central Time (CT) on the second business day immediately preceding the third Wednesday of the contract month (usually Monday).		

Source: Adapted from Chicago Mercantile Exchange, June 26, 2010.

E-resources: http://www.cmegroup.com/trading/fx/.

currency futures in the Unites States in that the contracts are for fixed quantities of currency to be exchanged at a fixed price in the future. The key difference is that the option may be *exercised*, that is, presented for currency exchange, at *any* time between its issuance and the maturity date, or not at all.[4]

Foreign exchange arbitrage involves simultaneous contracting in two or more foreign exchange markets to buy and sell foreign currency, profiting from exchange rate differences *without* incurring exchange rate risk. Foreign exchange arbitrage may be two-way, three-way, or intertemporal and is generally undertaken by large commercial banks that can exchange large quantities of money to exploit small rate differentials.

The simplest form of exchange arbitrage is two-way arbitrage, between any two currencies and between two places. Assume quotations for Swiss francs in the spot market on June 26, 2010, were:

At Bankers Trust in New York:	\$0.91038/SF
At Bank of America in San Francisco:	\$0.91158/SF
At Lloyds Bank in London:	\$0.91398/SF

Arbitrageur
A person or firm that deals in foreign exchange, buying or selling foreign currency with simultaneous contracting to exchange back to the original currency; arbitrageurs thus do not undertake exchange risk

An **arbitrageur** can buy SF in New York and simultaneously sell them in London, making a profit of \$0.0036/SF, or 0.37 percent per transaction. While the percentage gain is small, it translates to \$3,600 for every SF 1 million traded, and it involves no exchange risk. By repeatedly arbitraging this price (exchange rate) differential, the arbitrageur will make a profit until the exchange rate differential drops below the transactions cost (that is, the telephone bill, plus the arbitrageur's salary, plus other relevant costs).

The same two-way arbitrage may also occur in the forward market or between forward and futures markets. From the quotations here, we see that profitable arbitrage opportunities exist between the New York forward market and the Chicago futures market, as well as between the New York and San Francisco forward markets:

At Bankers Trust in New York: ¥109.00/\$ for delivery in 90 days.

At Bank of America in San Francisco: ¥109.90/\$ for delivery in 90 days.

At the Chicago Mercantile Exchange: ¥107.38/\$ for delivery on June 26, 2010.

An arbitrageur can buy yen in New York and sell them in San Francisco, both for exchange in 90 days, and earn ¥0.9/\$, or 0.77 percent per transaction. Similarly, an arbitrageur can buy yen in Chicago and sell them in San Francisco, to make ¥1.62/\$, or 1.4 percent per transaction. The difficulties with the latter transaction are that contracts may not be available for the desired amount or maturity date and transaction costs are higher for the intermarket exchanges. Nonetheless, both transactions may be feasible and profitable, even after costs are considered.[5]

✓ Active learning check

Review your answer to Active Learning Case question 1 and make any changes you like. Then compare your answer to the one below.

1 What exchange risk does Barclays have as at December 31, 2009?

Barclays has exchange risk on the various assets and liabilities that were on its books at year-end 2009. These include exposures of £6,056 million in US dollars and £2,902 million in euros, among others. From the second table in the case, it appears that these exposures may be from lending to corporations in the European Union and the United States (though this is not certain, since some other activities are missing from the table). These are net asset exposures, or long positions, since Barclays will receive future cash flows in these currencies, and their values may change in terms of British pounds.

DETERMINATION OF THE EXCHANGE RATE

Exchange rates are determined by the activities of the various actors described earlier. If one could calculate the supply and demand curves for each exchange market participant and anticipate government constraints on the exchange market, exchange rate determination would be fairly simple. The composite supply and demand for foreign exchange would be as depicted in Figure 7.1.

Lacking this information, the analyst can still rely on two fundamental economic relationships that underlie exchange rate determination. Note that this section considers only economic factors; government restrictions on the exchange market are ignored.

The two fundamental economic relationships are **purchasing power parity** and the **international Fisher effect**. The former posits that shifts in exchange rates will occur to offset different rates of inflation in pairs of countries, and the latter proposes that exchange rates will shift to offset interest rate differentials between countries.

Purchasing power parity
The theory of exchange rate determination that states that differences in prices of the same goods between countries will be eliminated by exchange rate changes

International Fisher effect
Theory of exchange rate determination that states that differences in nominal interest rates on similar-risk deposits will be eliminated by changes in the exchange rate

Purchasing power parity[6]

The purchasing power parity (PPP) theory is based on the law of one price and explains the long-run exchange rates. If two countries produce an identical product and transportation costs are extremely low, the price of the product should be the same in two countries. Under the law of one price, the price of the product is the same not only in two countries but also around the world. If a standard ton of polyurethane plastic costs $200 in the United States and €190 in Germany, PPP requires an exchange rate of $1.05/€. The same reasoning could be used for all products whose production processes are equivalent in two countries and that are traded between these countries. The exchange rate that comes closest to simultaneously satisfying all of these equilibrium conditions is the PPP rate—a rate that equates the internal purchasing power of the two currencies in both countries.

Assuming we begin from that exchange rate, what will happen if Germany' inflation is 5 percent and the US inflation is 10 percent in the following year? PPP requires that the exchange rate adjust to eliminate this differential. Specifically, it requires that:

$$\frac{1 + \text{Infl}_{\text{US}}}{1 + \text{Infl}_{\text{Ger}}} = \frac{\text{XR}_{t+1}}{\text{XR}_t}$$

where:

Infl = inflation rate

t = time period

This means that inflation in the United States relative to inflation in Germany should be the same as the future exchange rate compared to the spot exchange rate. The relationship can also be written in a form similar to the interest parity equation by rearranging terms:

$$(1 + \text{Infl}_{\text{us}}) = (1 + \text{Infl}_{\text{Ger}})\frac{\text{XR}_{t+1}}{\text{XR}_t}$$

Purchasing power in each currency will be retained if:

$$\text{XR}_{t+1} = \frac{1.10}{1.05}(\$1.05/€) = \$1.10/€\text{ , or }€0.909/\$$$

International Fisher effect

The international Fisher effect (IFE) translates Irving Fisher's reasoning about domestic interest rates to the transnational level. Fisher showed that inflation-adjusted (that

Nominal interest rate The actual rate of interest offered by a bank, typically given as an annual percentage rate

Real interest rate The nominal interest rate adjusted for price changes. Domestically, this means adjusting for inflation; internationally, this means adjusting for exchange rate (currency price) changes

is, "real") interest rates tend to stay the same over time; as inflation rises or falls, so do **nominal** (unadjusted) **interest rates**, such that **real interest rates** remain unchanged. At the transnational level, nominal national interest rates are expected to differ only by the expected change in the national currency's price (that is, the exchange rate). The international Fisher effect thus concludes that interest differentials between national markets will be eliminated by adjustments in the exchange rate. In terms similar to PPP, we see that:

$$\frac{1 + i_{US}}{1 + i_{foreign}} = \frac{XR_{t+1}}{XR_t}, \text{ or } (1 + i_{US}) = (1 + i_{foreign})\frac{XR_{t+1}}{XR_t}$$

where i = the interest rate, usually on a eurocurrency deposit denominated in the given country's currency.

If the eurodollar deposit rate is 3 percent/year and the euro–euro rate is 6 percent/year, the euro will be expected to devalue in the coming year by:

$$\frac{1.06}{1.03} = 1.029, \text{ or } 2.9 \text{ percent}$$

Notice that the international Fisher effect *will* operate in a free market, because investors will receive a higher return in euros otherwise. As more and more investors put their money in euros, the spot price of the euro will rise. Similarly, as US investors return their euro earnings to dollars at the end of the period (year), this increased demand for dollars will cause the euro to devalue (in the future). Thus, dollar and euro earnings will tend to be equalized.

Combined equilibrium relationships

The future exchange rate, XR_{t+1}, will be partially determined by both of the above factors (PPP and IFE), which can be viewed in a general equilibrium context as shown in Figure 7.3. This figure also demonstrates the interest parity relationship, which provides another link between current and future currency values. Remember that these relationships are *equilibrium* economic conditions, which hold only approximately since substantial uncertainty exists about future conditions. Also, if a government intervenes to prohibit the market from determining exchange rates, the relationships may diverge substantially from the equilibrium conditions. Figure 7.3 shows the main economic influences that, along with government policies and other factors, combine to determine exchange rates. Note that the expected exchange rate is in the top box, and the determinants of that rate (interest difference and inflation difference) are presented as fractions, so that they show the precise relationship between the spot exchange rate, XRT, and the expected future rate, E[XRT].

A final caveat is in order. Despite the strong relationships among interest differentials, inflation differentials, and exchange rates, other important *economic* influences operate in international finance. Pure speculation can cause shifts in exchange rates, despite the fundamental economic conditions that have been described above. A country' balance of payments position may affect the exchange rate, even though that position also affects interest and inflation rates as well. Since the abandonment of the Bretton Woods system of fixed exchange rates, exchange rate determination has been extremely uncertain—perhaps similar to the determination of future values of stock exchange indexes.

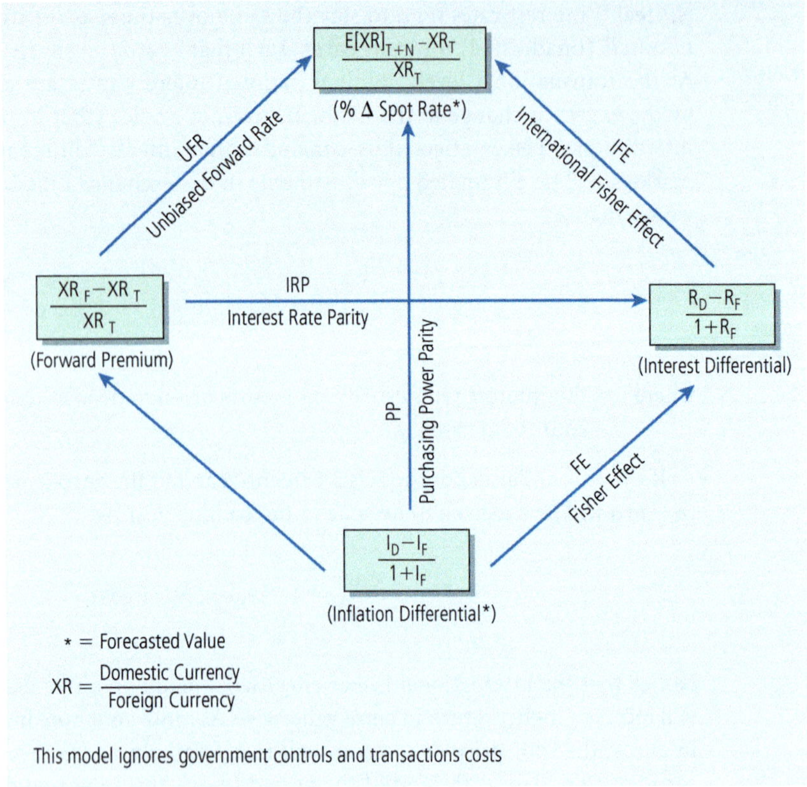

Figure 7.3 Exchange rate determination

Other factors determining exchange rates

PPP and IFEs explain overall exchange rate well, but other factors also determine exchange rates. In general factors affecting the demand and supply of domestic products over foreign products determine exchange rates because these factors affect the demand and supply of local and foreign currencies in exchange rate markets. First, changes in demand affect the exchange rate. For example, the changes in trade barriers, such as tariffs and quotas, can affect the exchange rate. If the United States raises the tariff rates over Chinese products due to antidumping or countervailing regulation, the demand for domestic products will be increased over Chinese products and the US dollar tends to appreciate. Second, the changes in supply will affect the exchange rate. For example, China becomes more productive than before. Chinese auto manufacturers recently developed their own models and produced them with great productivity, and the Chinese auto manufacturers can lower the price over foreign auto manufacturers. This affects the demand for Chinese automobiles, and the Chinese currency tends to appreciate. Third, national governments reserve foreign currencies and actively control foreign exchange rates to lower the price of exporting goods, to stabilize exchange rate volatility, and to protect the national economy from a currency crisis. According to the Central Intelligence Agency (CIA) and International Monetary Fund, China and Japan are the No.1 and No.2 country in terms of reserves of foreign exchange and gold. China's reserves for foreign exchanges and gold are \$2.426 trillion (31 December 2009 est.) \$1.953 trillion (31 December 2008 est.). Japan's reserves of foreign exchange and gold amounts of \$1.024 trillion (31 December 2009 est.) and \$1.011 trillion (31 December 2008 est.).

✓ Active learning check

Review your answer to Active Learning Case question 2 and make any changes you like. Then compare your answer to the one below.

2 What should Barclays' expectation be about the value of the pound relative to the euro or the dollar?

Barclays can forecast the value of the euro or the dollar based on PPP, the IFE, or a chartist method, in addition to simply using the forward exchange rate. Since Barclays' business includes currency trading, the bank probably should use one or more methods for the minute-by-minute activity in the foreign exchange market, and another method or methods for its longer-term concerns such as future maturities of loans and accounting reporting periods. In sum, Barclays should forecast using market-based tools such as IFE and PPP, as well as using additional methods such as technical forecasting or leading indicators for short periods of time such as hours or a few days.

PROTECTING AGAINST EXCHANGE RISK

Exchange risk is a very real concern for financial managers, whether or not their firms are directly involved in international business. The fact that the prices of imported products and services often vary with the exchange rate means that a local firm's costs may depend on the exchange rate. Similarly, if any of the firm's sales are exported, its earnings may vary as foreign sales change due to exchange rate changes. Even a purely domestic firm faces these problems, since suppliers and competitors that *are* doing international business will adjust to exchange rate changes, and this will affect the domestic firm.

From this perspective, exchange risk is *not* the risk that a local currency will decrease in value (devalue) relative to the home currency. *Exchange risk is the possibility that a firm will be unable to adjust its prices and costs to exactly offset exchange rate changes.* Thus, a US importer which faces 10 percent higher costs because of a dollar devaluation from €0.80/$ to €0.72/$ still has no exchange risk as long as the importer can raise its own prices by 10 percent without lowering total sales. (This result is the microeconomic version of PPP.) The problem may be viewed as one of "passing through" cost increases to the firm' customers via higher sales prices.

Similarly, the appropriate measure of exchange risk for financial instruments is the firm's possible loss or gain in purchasing power from exchange rate-adjusted interest rates. Investing in a US dollar account that pays 5 percent per year is better than investing in a Swiss franc account that pays 10 percent per year if, during the year, the franc devalues by 6 percent.

Alternatives to minimize exchange risk

Exchange risk exists whenever the firm's prices and costs cannot be exactly adjusted to offset changes in the exchange rate. Let us now consider a group of alternatives that will allow a firm to minimize (or at least reduce) its exchange risk. These alternatives fall into four categories:

1. Risk avoidance
2. Risk adaptation
3. Risk transfer
4. Diversification

INTERNATIONAL BUSINESS STRATEGY IN ACTION

Wall Street and world financial markets

International finance affects virtually every business. Companies with overseas operations, for example, are continually concerned with the rise and fall of the currencies in the countries where they operate. Indonesia is a good example as seen by the country's currency crisis of the late 1990s that sent shock waves through the Asian business market. As a result, thousands of firms went bankrupt, the country's currency lost 80 percent of its value, and the stock market plummeted by 60 percent. In the aftermath, Indonesia was hit with soaring unemployment and inflation led to riots that forced the resignation of the government. (See the Real Case "World Financial Crises" at the end of this chapter.)

Yet the international financial markets have never suffered anything like the initial effect from the terrorist attacks on the twin towers of New York City's World Trade Center (WTC) on September 11, 2001. In addition to totally demolishing the two buildings as well as several large surrounding structures, the terrorists killed nearly 3,000 people, many of them Wall Street employees, and rocked the major international financial markets from London to Tokyo. One of the hardest-hit groups was the insurers who had losses of more than $15 billion. In addition, while the important financial records of businesses in the WTC were located in safe havens such as central computer banks miles away from Ground Zero, the effect of the terrorist actions began to quickly surface.

This was reflected on Wall Street where the stock market began a sharp downturn. Within two weeks of the terrorist act, the New York Stock Exchange's (NYSE's) Dow Index had lost 14 percent of its value. Only during the Great Depression had the United States seen a downturn this sharp. And for the rest of the world, the financial shock was shared very quickly. The NYSE and other major international stock exchanges saw massive sell-offs as investors headed for the sidelines, and companies seeking to raise capital in the international market put their plans on hold. Simply put, as the US economy began to slow down and focus its investment efforts on rebuilding and regenerating its own hard-hit industries, there were going to be less funds available for other things. The international finance lesson is clear: today's money markets are linked very, very closely. And a catastrophe in one geographic area can have major implications in all of the others. New York City remains a financial hub of the business world, and the effects of the September 2001 crisis have passed. Yet the financial risks that international business firms must assume will not diminish because of the large interdependency that now exists between the major centers of worldwide commerce.

In 2007–2008 another international financial crisis occurred and until 2010, the world economy has not yet recovered. Following defaults by borrowers in the US subprime mortgage markets many banks found that their balance sheets were in a mess as their housing assets had been overvalued. Not only US banks suffered—in early 2008 the British bank, Northern Rock, was nationalized by Prime Minister Brown's government in order to stop its default. The US financial crisis became a worldwide problem for all financial institutions due to the close interconnections in the international money markets. International capital markets are highly integrated (indeed globalized), unlike goods markets (which are regional) and factor markets (where labor is localized).

Website: www.nyse.com.

Sources: *Financial Times*, September 12-30, 2001; October 1-13, 2001 and other supplemental news sources in 2007–2008.

Risk avoidance

Exchange risk avoidance
An exchange risk management technique through which the firm tries to avoid operating in more than one currency

Exchange risk avoidance is the strategy of trying to avoid foreign currency transactions. A purely domestic firm can try to make all of its purchases from local suppliers of locally produced goods and make all of its sales to local buyers in competition only with other domestic firms. Obviously, this strategy is impractical, if only because all firms are affected by goods priced in foreign currency—automobiles, chemicals, steel, and so on. Also, there are very few industries that do not use imported materials, export some of their output, or compete with imported products.

Risk adaptation

Exchange risk adaptation
An exchange risk management technique through which a company adjusts its business activities to try to balance foreign currency assets and liabilities, and inflows and outflows

Exchange risk adaptation offers a more realistic alternative for protecting the firm against exchange risk. This strategy includes all methods of "hedging" against exchange rate changes. In the extreme, exchange risk calls for protecting all liabilities denominated in foreign currency with equal-value, equal-maturity assets denominated in that foreign currency. An illustration can best clarify this point.

Assume a French firm has contracted to buy $100,000 of machinery from a foreign supplier for use in its manufacturing operations. The purchase is payable in six months in US dollars. To eliminate foreign exchange risk completely, the firm may do two things. First, it may raise its own prices to customers once the six months pass to equate euro devaluation to price increase. (Note that this does *not* involve a foreign currency hedge.) If this option is not available, which is often the case, the firm may look to its other option: obtain some equal-value *dollar asset* maturing in 180 days. This may be as simple as depositing funds in a dollar-denominated bank account for six months or as arcane as arranging a swap of the dollar liability for some other firm's euro liability. Fairly standard methods of hedging an exposed dollar liability include:

1. Obtaining a dollar-denominated financial asset (for example, a time deposit or a Certificate of Deposit (CD)) that matures when the liability comes due.
2. Finding a buyer for your firm's products and agreeing to receive payment in US dollars for the same value and time as the liability.
3. Finding a bank that will contract to buy euros from you and sell you dollars at a price fixed today for exchange when the liability comes due. (This is called a *forward contract.*)
4. Agreeing with another (for example, North American) firm to exchange your dollar liability for that firm's (that is, its French subsidiary's) euro liability.
5. Contracting for any other equal-value, equal-maturity dollar-denominated asset that will offset the exposed liability.

The firm's goal in choosing among these methods is to minimize the cost of protection against exchange rate risk.

Risk transfer

Exchange risk transfer
An exchange risk management technique through which the firm contracts with a third party to pass exchange risk on to that party, via such instruments as forward contracts, futures, and options

The third strategy for reducing exchange risk is **exchange risk transfer**. This strategy involves the use of an insurance contract or guarantee that transfers the exchange risk to the insurer or guarantor. In many countries, the central bank offers exchange risk guarantees to importers and exporters of some products according to the bank's policies. Technically, though perhaps not realistically, any firm or government agency could issue a guarantee covering exchange rate changes to a local importer, at a price that would presumably reflect the risk.

Diversification

Currency diversification
An exchange risk management technique through which the firm places activities or assets and liabilities into multiple currencies, thus reducing the impact of exchange rate change for any one of them

The final strategy for reducing exchange risk is **currency diversification**. Here a firm can reduce the risk of unexpected local currency devaluations by spreading its assets and liabilities across several currencies (for example, euros, Swiss francs, and pounds in addition to US dollars). This strategy simply means, "Don't put all of your eggs in one basket." Domestically, a firm should deal with several suppliers and a variety of customers to reduce risk through diversification. Internationally, a firm should hold assets (and liabilities) in several currencies to reduce the impact of unexpected exchange rate changes.

The strategy that is probably most useful to the majority of firms is risk adaptation, or hedging. A key point of this section is to recognize that other alternatives may be used in many instances when hedging would be more expensive or otherwise less desirable. Nonetheless, the central problem in exchange risk management is hedging, and corporate treasurers should always be on the lookout for new instruments and techniques.

✔ Active learning check

Review your answer to Active Learning Case question 3 and make any changes you like. Then compare your answer to the one below.

3 How should Barclays deal with the risk involved in its foreign currency positions?

As an international bank, Barclays is constantly becoming involved in foreign exchange transactions. The bank needs to have a policy for its traders and its other bankers as to how much exchange risk the bank is willing to tolerate before looking for protection. The bank presumably knows more than most people about what to expect in the foreign exchange market, and it is very likely that Barclays will choose to run exchange risk without hedging because of this knowledge. Still, the bank must limit its exposure, and the usual hedging techniques for banks are forward contracts and matching loans with deposits in the same currency.

FOREIGN MONEY AND CAPITAL MARKETS

In each country an MNE enters, it will be able to obtain some degree of access to local financial markets. The MNE will generally utilize such markets to perform necessary local financial transactions and often to hedge its local asset exposure through local borrowing (or its local liability exposure through local deposits or investments). But the MNE can also utilize local financial markets to obtain additional funding (or place additional funds) for its non-local activities. A Mexican firm, for example, may choose to borrow funds through its Houston affiliate to finance its local needs in Texas *and* finance some of its needs in Mexico.

Usually national financial markets are not fully accessible to foreign firms; they are largely reserved for domestic borrowers and lenders. In these cases, use of local financial markets must be supplemented by use of the financial markets in the country of the parent company or elsewhere. Typically, such problems arise in countries that impose exchange controls, which limit the MNE's ability to put needed funds in the affiliate.

MNEs and national money markets

The advantages MNEs obtain from entering national money markets as *borrowers* of funds stem from the portfolio effect of holding liabilities in more than one (fluctuating) currency and from the local risk hedging that occurs as the MNE moves to balance local assets such as plant and equipment with local liabilities, such as local-currency borrowing. Additional benefits may occur if the local government subsidizes such loans through interest rate reduction, through tax breaks, or otherwise; a policy of this kind may be offered to attract the MNE's investment. This may lower the whole MNE's cost of capital if the subsidy does not disappear and if the interest rate remains below the comparable home-currency rate during the borrowing period.

The advantages MNEs obtain from entering national money markets as *lenders* of funds stem from the portfolio effect of holding financial instruments in more than one currency. There may also be a gain from balancing local-currency assets and liabilities if an excess of local liabilities was held previously. In addition, local financial investments may be a necessary strategy when exchange controls or profit remittance limits exist; such investments offer the firm an outlet for retained earnings that yield interest. Sometimes an exchange control policy may make the local-currency interest rates higher than those available in other currencies (after adjusting for expected exchange rate changes). In these cases, higher-than-normal profits can be earned by investing funds in local instruments, although exchange controls may limit conversion of the profits into the home-country currency, or a government-imposed exchange rate change may wipe out the advantage.

MNEs and national capital markets

The advantages MNEs obtain from entering national capital markets as *borrowers* are similar to those obtained from entering national money markets. However, the opportunities are generally much more limited. Very few countries have substantially developed stock markets, and those that do usually restrict the issuance of shares by foreigners. A few exceptions exist, such as the United States, the UK, Germany, and France, but even they serve only the largest and most creditworthy MNEs. National bond markets, when they exist, are also very restrictive. Thus far, virtually all of the **foreign bond** issues have taken place in New York (called "Yankee bonds"), London, Switzerland, Germany, and Japan (called "Samurai bonds").

Foreign bond
A bond issued by a foreign company in another country's financial market

Eurobond
A bond denominated in foreign currency issued in any country's financial market; most eurobonds are issued in London or in Luxembourg (for tax reasons)

The **eurobond** market, which functions mostly outside the United States, is dominated by dollar issues, which constitute about 40 percent of that total. In all, dollar-denominated issues account for about 36 percent of the two types of international bonds.

The advantages MNEs obtain from entering national capital markets as *lenders* come mainly from diversification and from higher returns that may be protected by exchange controls, just as in the short-term market. Since the national capital markets are generally small, opportunities to use them are quite limited for foreign as well as domestic investors. Of course, since the main currencies of interest to MNEs and other international investors *are* those of the few large industrial countries, opportunities in those national capital markets do exist.

REGIONAL MONEY AND CAPITAL MARKETS

Until recently, the scope of financial markets and instruments was predominantly domestic or fully international, but not regional. In the past two decades, however, the European Union has designed both a regional monetary system (the **European Monetary Union**, or EMU) and a regional currency unit (the euro) for intergovernmental financial transactions in the European Union.

European Monetary Union (EMU)
The agreement among, initially, 11 of the European Union countries to eliminate their currencies and create the euro; European Union countries do not necessarily have to join the EMU

The eurocurrency market

A **eurodollar** is a dollar-denominated bank deposit located outside the United States. This simple statement defines the basic instrument called the eurodollar. (Eurodollars are *not* dollars in the pockets of people who live in Europe! They are deposit liabilities of banks.) The widely discussed eurocurrency market is simply a set of bank deposits located outside the countries whose currencies are used in the deposits. Since over half of the deposits are denominated in US dollars, it is reasonably accurate to call this the eurodollar market. Notice that the eurodollar market is not limited to Europe; very large eurodollar markets exist in Tokyo, Hong Kong, Bahrain, Panama, and other cities throughout the world. For this reason, the eurodollar market is sometimes called the *international money market.*

Eurodollar
A dollar-denominated bank deposit outside the United States

What is the significance of the international money market? Since the eurocurrency market rivals domestic financial markets as a funding source for corporate borrowing, it plays a key role in the capital investment decisions of many firms. In addition, since this market also rivals domestic financial markets as a deposit alternative, it absorbs large amounts of savings from lenders (that is, depositors) in many countries. In fact, the eurocurrency market complements the domestic financial markets, giving greater access to borrowing and lending to financial market participants in each country where it is permitted to function. Overall, the eurocurrency market is now the world's single most important market for international financial intermediation.

This market is completely a creation of the regulatory structures placed by national governments on banking or, more precisely, on financial intermediation. If national governments allowed banks to function without reserve requirements, interest rate restrictions, capital controls, and taxes, the eurocurrency market would involve only the transnational deposits and loans made in each country's banking system. Instead, national governments heavily regulate national financial markets in efforts to achieve various monetary policy goals. Thus, the eurocurrency market provides a very important outlet for funds flows that circumvent many of the limitations placed on domestic financial markets. Many national governments have found the impact of the eurocurrency market on their firms and banks to be favorable, so they have allowed this market to operate.[7]

Since the eurocurrency market is a creation of the regulatory structure, it may be helpful to think about the key underpinnings of the system that allow eurodollars. Essentially three conditions must be met for a eurocurrency market to exist. First, some national government must allow foreign currency deposits to be made so that, for example, depositors in London can obtain dollar-denominated time deposits there. Second, the country whose currency is being used—in this example, the United States—must allow foreign entities to own and exchange deposits in that currency. Third, there must be some reason, such as low cost or ease of use, that prompts people to use this market rather than other financial markets, such as the domestic ones. The eurocurrency market has met these conditions for the past three decades, and its phenomenal growth testifies that the demand for such a market has been very large.

A wide range of countries allow foreign currency deposits to be held in their banking systems. Many of them impose restrictions (interest rate limits, capital controls, and so on) on these as well as on local-currency deposits, so that a free market does not exist. Other countries, including most of the developed countries and many of the newly industrializing countries, allow foreign currency deposits that are not subject to the regulations placed on domestic deposits. In such countries, participants find more favorable interest rates, greater availability of funds, and greater ease of moving funds internationally. These countries tend to be the euromarket centers.

Only a few currencies have become popular as eurocurrencies. Generally, these are the ones used widely in international trade—the US dollar, the euro, the British pound, and the Japanese yen. The governments of all the nations whose currencies are being used have consented (or, more accurately, have not objected) to allowing foreign banks, companies, and individuals to hold and use deposits denominated in those currencies. This may appear to be a trivial point, but any limitation on non-residents' use of dollar (or other eurocurrency) deposits would quickly eliminate that currency from the euromarket. The US government's temporary freeze on Iranian assets held in US banks in 1979 caused a tremendous crisis in the eurodollar market, because other participants saw the possibility of losing use of their eurodollars at the whim of the US government. The potential problem will continue to exist, but on the whole participants in the euromarket expect that full freedom to use the (dollar-denominated) deposits will continue indefinitely.

The third condition fundamental to the success of the euromarket is that it must possess advantages that will attract participants to the market. Those advantages include the ability to carry out dollar-denominated transactions outside the United States and the availability of favorable interest rates relative to rates in the domestic market. The first advantage clearly exists, because eurodollar account owners can sell their accounts to pay for other transactions, with no need to deal directly in the United States. The second advantage also exists, primarily because lack of regulation of the euromarket allows banks to reduce their costs and pass on the savings to clients in the form of lower loan rates and higher deposit rates. (The difference in lending rates to prime borrowers essentially disappeared during the 1980s.)

Eurocurrency interest rates

London interbank offered rate (LIBOR) The interest rate on large-scale foreign currency-denominated deposits offered from one bank to another in London

The base interest rate paid on deposits among banks in the eurocurrency market is called **LIBOR**. (Outside London, which is the center of the entire euromarket, the base rate on deposits is generally slightly higher.) LIBOR is determined by the supply and demand for funds in the euromarket for each currency. Because participating banks could default (and, infrequently, do default) on their obligations, the rate paid for eurodollar deposits is always somewhat above the domestic Treasury bill rate. Also, because domestic banks must comply with Federal Reserve requirements, they offer slightly lower deposit rates than unregulated eurobanks. The history of the LIBOR rates is shown in Figure 7.4.

The lending rate has no name comparable to the prime rate, but it is determined as LIBOR plus some margin, or spread, charged to the borrower. Banks generally do not require compensating balances or other implicit charges in addition to the spread over LIBOR in the euromarket. This also helps reduce the cost of using the euromarket for borrowers. The total cost of borrowing in the euromarket for a prime US corporation historically was marginally below the domestic US prime rate. Because of competition among lenders in both markets, prime borrowers have been able to obtain the same rate in both markets since the early 1980s.

Interest rates on other eurocurrencies generally follow the same pattern, though when capital controls exist in a particular country (say, France), borrowing rates may be higher in the euromarket (which is not restricted) than in the domestic market. Figure 7.5 traces three-month eurocurrency deposit rates during the past two decades. Notice that the countries whose currencies have tended to decline relative to other currencies during this period (such as France and the UK) show generally higher eurocurrency deposit rates than the "strong-currency" countries (such as Germany and Japan).

Other market characteristics

Transactions in the eurodollar market generally involve $1 million or more, although in the past several years many deposits of $50,000 to $100,000 have been given at LIBOR, and loans of similar amounts have been offered at the analogous lending rates. The market is directly accessible to banks, which carry out about three-fourths of the total volume of transactions among themselves. Companies and individuals participate through their banks, generally at interest rates slightly less favorable than those offered among banks. (Investors may also participate in the euromarket indirectly by purchasing money market

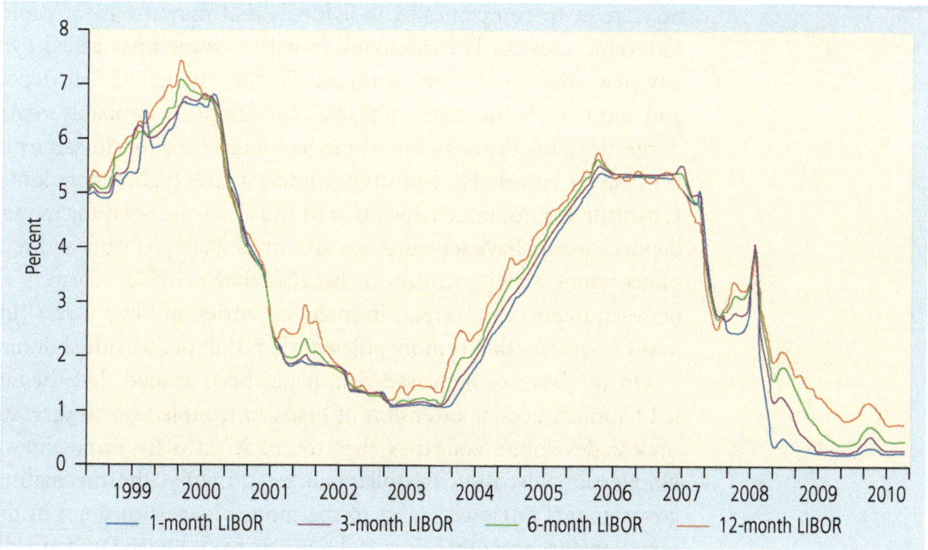

Figure 7.4 History of the LIBOR rates, January 1, 1999–December 31, 2010

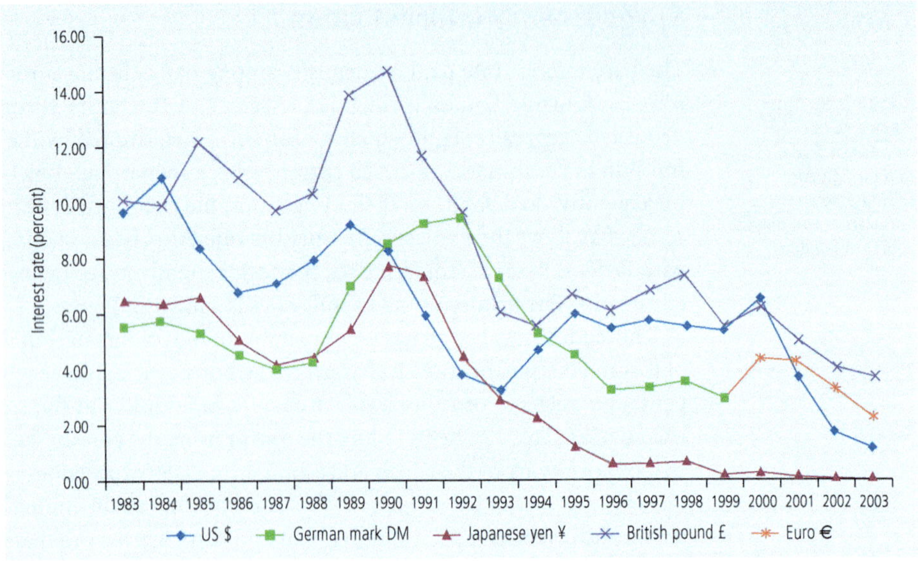

Figure 7.5 Three-month eurocurrency deposit rates (year-end)

funds in the United States, when the funds themselves place large portions of their pooled investments in eurodollar accounts.)

Criticisms of the euromarkets

Over the years, the eurodollar market has been criticized as contributing to worldwide inflation and creating major new risks in the international banking system. While neither claim has been proved (or disproved) conclusively, each is worth considering here.

Because the eurodollar market adds to the worldwide volume of dollar-denominated assets, it has been accused of increasing the global money supply beyond the control of the US authorities. This may be true to some extent, but a number of factors mitigate the total impact of eurodollars. First, eurodollars exist only as time deposits and certificates of deposit, never as demand deposits or cash. Hence, in the narrow definition of money that includes only cash and demand deposits, eurodollars do not even appear at all. Second, as already noted, about three-fourths of all eurodollars are interbank deposits rather than new credit to companies or individuals that may use it for capital investment and thus economic growth. The interbank transfers (sometimes called *pyramiding*) do not create any new credit, however measured. Finally, the eurodollar deposits used by companies and individuals for investment and consumption probably replace other (for example, domestic) bank deposits that would have been used for the same purposes anyhow. That is, because the eurodollar deposits pay interest rates higher than domestic deposits, they often substitute for domestic deposits, and thus they are used for the same purposes that those deposits would have served. All in all, eurodollars probably add slightly to the total volume of economic activity worldwide because they provide a form of financial intermediation between depositors (savers) in many countries and borrowers (investors or spenders) in many countries that is more efficient than that of individual domestic financial markets.

On the issue of increased risk, it has been argued that the eurocurrency market has led to much greater extension of loans to troubled borrowers, such as the governments of less developed countries that found it virtually impossible to repay in the 1980s. Unquestionably, the eurodollar market provided the mechanism through which these governments borrowed most of the money loaned to them in the 1970s. It is not clear, however, that any other financial markets would have fared any differently in the absence of eurodollars. Essentially, participation in the euromarket has opened one more type of business to international banks, and these banks must manage this business as prudently as they manage the other businesses in which they participate.

✓ Active learning check

Review your answer to Active Learning Case question 4 and make any changes you like. Then compare your answer to the one below.

4 How can Barclays use the eurocurrency market in its international business, and will this help in dealing with the exchange rate problem?

Barclays can and does use the eurocurrency market for much of its international lending, since conditions in this market favor the large clients and banks with which Barclays deals extensively. Barclays can offer eurodeposits for various maturities in various currencies to its clients, and the bank can use this market to find offsetting exposures such as loans or investments in those same currencies and maturities.

Eurobonds and euroequities

Eurobonds are the long-term analogue of eurocurrencies. They are issued in countries of convenience and denominated in currencies other than the local one. With eurobonds, *taxation* of the interest income that investors receive is a key concern, so most of them are issued in tax jurisdictions that do not impose taxes on such interest payments (for example, Luxembourg). Eurobonds, like domestic US bonds, are issued by corporations and government agencies. They may be convertible into equity, and they may have fixed or floating interest rates.

Borrowers (namely, issuers of eurobonds) utilize this market for three main reasons. First, no regulatory agency establishes rules for disclosure by issuers, so substantial red tape is avoided; however, this generally limits participation to blue-chip corporations and governments. Second, the interest rates can be marginally lower than those on domestic issues, because investors can usually avoid taxes on their interest income. Third, the issuer gains access to potential investors in many countries simultaneously because the investment banks that place the issue offer it internationally. From time to time, eurobond issue is stimulated by additional reasons, such as domestic bond market restrictions that lead issuers to seek overseas funding. In 1964, for example, the United States established capital controls that made foreign bonds less attractive to US investors (the interest equalization tax was effectively a tax on interest received by US citizens from foreign bond investments) and limited lending by US parent companies to their foreign subsidiaries. As a result, both US and foreign issuers that were trying to place dollar-denominated bonds turned to the fledgling eurobond market for their funding.

For the investor, the eurobond market offers these advantages: (1) all issues are structured to allow exemption from interest withholding tax on the income earned; and (2) the terms of eurobond issues are more varied than those of domestic bond issues. For example, eurobonds usually have shorter maturities than domestic bonds (five to eight years) and often have floating-rate interest payments.

Euroequities

Euroequities have emerged in the past decade in the London Stock Exchange as another long-term euromarket, analogous to domestic stock markets. As the name implies, euroequities are shares of publicly traded stocks traded on an exchange outside the issuing firm's home country. They are bought and sold in shares denominated in the firm's home currency, so both company performance and exchange rate performance affect the returns on investments in euroequities.

In the United States, a market for such issues has operated for many years through an instrument called the American Depositary Receipt (ADR), which is essentially a claim on a share of stock in the foreign stock exchange intermediated by a securities broker who issues the ADR. Euroequities rival ADRs and offer the flexibility of being direct share issues by the non-local firms. The market exists primarily in London, and thus it encompasses non-British company shares. In fact, even the ADRs of British companies are now traded on the London Stock Exchange, so full global trading is possible through the exchange.

The London Stock Exchange euroequity market grew rapidly in the late 1980s. By 1989, 52 brokerage firms were making a market for euroequities issued by 707 firms. The monthly turnover during January 1989 was 278 million shares. The growing demand for these instruments (based on the firms available for investment and the tax-avoiding structure of the issues), as well as the growing supply (by firms that are blue chip and want to gain access to investors from many countries through the London Stock Exchange), make it likely that this market will increase in importance in global equities trading.

INTERNATIONAL BUSINESS STRATEGY IN ACTION

AngloGold Ashanti

When it comes to international finance, one of the primary concerns of MNEs is the ability to raise capital through new stock offerings and bank loans. For many years this was a major problem for the Anglo American Corporation of South Africa (AAC), which operated gold mines in that country. During South Africa's apartheid period, trade sanctions, controls on exchange currency, and protectionism all combined to isolate AAC from outside financial markets. Unable to do business in the international arena, AAC focused on expanding its domestic operations by acquiring holdings in a variety of industries including automobiles, newspapers, and vineyards.

As apartheid came to an end, however, there was a gradual liberalization of both trade and investment. And as its opportunity to move into the international arena began to increase, the firm put its gold mining activities into a new subsidiary, AngloGold, and began restructuring its operations. Non-core businesses were sold off and the company began focusing heavily on development of its gold and uranium mines. However, its profitability and performance were handicapped by the small size of the South African economy and the fact that the Johannesburg stock market was not very influential in the worldwide financial markets. In addition, the local currency, the rand, was weak and the company needed to tie its operations to a stronger currency.

In response, AngloGold determined that it needed to link itself to the triad and expand its mining operations

Source: Corbis/Reuters.

worldwide. As a result, in 1998 the company was listed on the New York Stock Exchange, and today it is also listed on the Ghana and Australian Stock Exchanges. The firm now has access to equity capital in the EU and North America, as well as Australia. In 2003 AngloGold merged with Ashanti Goldfields, so that the combined firm had mines in eight countries and a total market capitalization of about $3.5 billion in 2004. AngloGold Ashanti has 21 operations and a number of exploration programs in gold-producing regions of the world. As of December 31, 2009, AngloGold Ashanti's ore reserve totalled 71.4 million ounces. During the year ended December 31, 2009, the Company produced 4.6 million ounces of gold from its operations. AngloGold Ashanti's main product is gold. Revenue is also derived from the sales of silver, uranium oxide and sulphuric acid. The Company sells its products on international markets. By the end of 2009, AngloGold Ashanti has a workforce of 62,895 and mining operations in North America, South America, Australia, and Africa. As a result of its recent expansion efforts, the company now accounts for 10 percent of the world' annual gold production, and it is able to raise money for expansion operations in a number of worldwide locations.

Websites: www.anglogold.com; www.nyse.com.

Sources: AngloGold, *Annual Report*, 2009 and company web page.

Sometimes an MNE will lend money in the international money market. For example, if Bank of America finds that it can get a higher interest rate in Singapore than in the United States, it may deposit some money there. Similarly, if General Motors finds that there are limitations on the amount of profit that it can transfer out of a country, the company may invest in local financial instruments and thus gain interest on funds that would otherwise sit idle.

THE IMF SYSTEM

International monetary system
The arrangement between national governments/central banks that oversees the operation of official foreign exchange dealings between countries

International Monetary Fund (IMF)
The international organization founded at Bretton Woods, New Hampshire, in 1944 that includes most countries of the world and offers balance of payments support to countries in crisis along with financial advising to central banks

The last international financial market we will examine here may be viewed as either a very important framework for international financial dealings or a market that is generally irrelevant to private business managers. The **international monetary system** is a financial market in which only central banks and the **International Monetary Fund** (IMF, or "the Fund") operate, so private business plays no active role in it. On the other hand, rules for international financial dealings among countries are often set at the IMF, and substantial international loan decisions are made between governments and the IMF. Thus, the rules of the game in the other international financial markets are sometimes influenced by IMF activities.

The international monetary system oversees the exchange rate regime that prevails among the major developed countries, whose currencies are used for the vast majority of international payments. The IMF negotiates with governments of debtor nations (usually less developed countries) for loans directly from the Fund and for loan conditions that are used, subsequently, as a basis for lending by private banks to these same borrowers. In addition, the IMF serves as an intermediary for emergency loans between member governments to cope with the capital flow or exchange rate crises that occur from time to time due to speculation in foreign exchange markets or other causes. All in all, the international monetary system plays an important role in determining the rules of the game for private companies and banks in some spheres of international business, so managers need to understand its functioning.

The IMF was designed in 1944 at a conference of the Allied nations held at Bretton Woods, New Hampshire. Its general purpose was to provide a multilateral framework for avoiding international financial crises by establishing rules for national exchange rate policies and for adjustment to balance of payments disequilibria (discussed in the Appendix to Chapter 6). It was specifically intended to avoid the disastrous financial contraction that occurred during the 1930s. As originally negotiated, and as implemented in 1946 when the Articles of Agreement were signed by the initial 46 member countries, the IMF system required *fixed* exchange rates among member countries, with gold as the basis for currency valuation. The US dollar was initially fixed at a value of $35 per ounce of gold, and all other currencies were fixed at values expressed in both dollars and gold.

Fixed exchange rates were a fundamental base of the Bretton Woods system. Under the Articles of Agreement, each country was obligated to maintain its currency value at the initially set value (the "par" value), with a band of ±1 percent of flexibility around the par value. If a foreign central bank demanded to sell a country's currency back to the issuer, that country was required to pay the equivalent amount of gold, US dollars, or some other acceptable currency.

To join the IMF, a country was required to make a deposit of gold (25 percent), plus its own currency (75 percent), such that each member country's total deposit relative to the total of IMF deposits was roughly in proportion with its share of world trade. Then each member country received the right to borrow up to 200 percent of its initial deposit at the Fund, in any currency, to help pay for imbalances such as the one mentioned above. If a country borrowed more than its original deposit, the IMF would stipulate economic policies that the borrower had to follow to receive more financial support. (This imposition of policy demands by the IMF is called *conditionality*.)

While the IMF sought to provide assistance for nations facing balance of payments problems, its only resources were the contributions of its member countries: quotas based on each country's part in world trade, which initially constituted about $9 billion. This relatively small amount of liquidity was not sufficient to support the post-World War II economic recovery, or specifically the payments imbalances, of even the European countries.[8] Ultimately, the US Marshall Plan injected the needed funding into the international financial system, and specifically into Europe, during 1948–1952.

Speculator
A person or firm that takes a position in foreign exchange with no hedging or protection mechanism to try to gain from expected exchange rate changes

In fact, the IMF provided very little funding to its member countries in its early years. During the Suez crisis in 1956, it loaned $1.7 billion to the UK, France, and India. Later, during speculative runs on the British pound (that is, periods when **speculators** sold large quantities of pounds for other currencies in expectation of a devaluation of the pound) in 1961 and 1964, it extended loans to the UK. By the end of the 1960s, the IMF was regularly providing credit to member countries, though still not at the levels that many analysts believed necessary to stabilize the system. (The alternative view is that the IMF should not provide credit to the member countries at all; rather, these countries should be forced to adjust their economies to escape balance of payments problems.)

At the end of the 1960s, the US dollar began to be the object of speculative pressure. The problem was severe, since the dollar constituted the base for the entire system of value (through its formal link to gold at $35 per ounce). The United States was unable to devalue to stop the speculation, and later it was unwilling to continue selling its gold holdings to foreign central banks that wanted to redeem their dollars. In August 1971, President Nixon announced that the United States would no longer sell gold to foreign central banks in exchange for dollars. In December 1971, he announced a devaluation of the dollar to $38 per ounce of gold; in February 1972 it was devalued to $42 per ounce, and later that year the United States declared that it would not support the dollar value at any price in gold.

These events essentially destroyed the Bretton Woods system of fixed exchange rates. Many initiatives to repair the system were presented during the following two years, but the United States would no longer accept the responsibility of providing the dollar as a fixed base for other currencies. In subsequent months, the IMF system was changed de facto to a floating exchange rate system that allowed each country to leave the value of its currency free to change with market forces or to fix that value to some other currency. Since that time, the United States has allowed the dollar to float in value relative to all other currencies, with occasional efforts by the Fed (the Federal Reserve System) to influence the dollar's relationship to particular currencies, such as the former German mark and the Japanese yen.

Under the current IMF system, no limitations are set on each member country's decision either to fix its currency value relative to some other currency or to allow it to fluctuate as supply and demand dictate. (Note that it is impossible for one country to keep its currency fixed relative to all others if the others are not fixed relative to one another.) In 1976, an accord called the Jamaica Agreement altered the IMF charter to formally allow for floating exchange rates. Today, the exchange rate regimes used by each nation are substantially unrestricted, and government strategies to influence exchange rates are altered as desired.[9]

Special drawing right (SDR)
The currency of the IMF; accounts at the IMF are denominated in SDRs, and the IMF has issued about $204 billion of SDRs as currency since its inception in 1969

At about the same time that the link between the dollar and gold was broken, the IMF's members agreed to create a new currency that the Fund would issue when authorized to do so by a vote of the members. This currency, called the **special drawing right** (SDR), allows its holder to obtain (or draw) other currencies from the IMF (or from other members) when desired. SDRs have been created and issued on seven occasions to date. A total SDR of 21.4 billion existed in 2004; the total value was about $30 billion. In each instance, the SDRs were allocated to Fund members according to their quotas. This new "international money" has served to support a number of countries that encountered financial crises since 1971, allowing them to finance their imbalances, but it has not been a solution to imbalances in international financial flows. During the international debt crisis of the early 1980s, SDR use was wholly inadequate to deal with the more than $350 billion of dollar debt owed by Latin American countries to foreign lenders. Total IMF resources include member country quotas, which totaled over $300 billion at the end of 2004. With a general SDR allocation that took effect on August 28 and a special allocation on September 9, 2009, the amount of SDRs increased from SDR 21.4 billion to SDR 204 billion (equivalent to about $308 billion, converted using the rate of August 31, 2010). So the Fund actually has quite substantial lending power today.

During the late twentieth century, SDRs became fairly widely used as a currency of denomination for private-sector financial instruments such as bonds and long-term bank loans. Because the SDR has a value based on four currencies (see Figure 7.6), it is more stable as a borrowing or lending tool than any individual currency. As of 2006 an SDR consists of US dollars, euros, Japanese yen, and British pounds, and their relative contributions are 44, 34, 11, and 11 percent respectively.

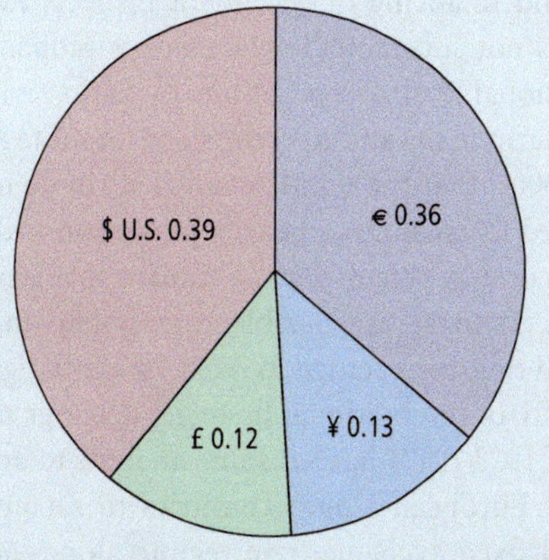

Distribution of value of the SDR, the basic monetary unit of the International Monetary Fund

For example, in dollars: $1\ \text{SDR} = \frac{\$(0.426)}{€} + \frac{\$(21)}{¥} + \frac{\$(0.0984)}{£} + \frac{(0.577)}{\$} = \$1.47$

Figure 7.6 Special drawing right (October 15, 2004)

When the dollar devalues relative to other widely traded currencies, so does the SDR—but only 39 percent of the SDR's value is affected negatively. The other 61 percent of the SDR's value is based on pounds, yen, and euros, and these currencies may rise or fall relative to the dollar in such a situation. Overall, the changes must net out over all currencies, and an instrument such as the SDR changes relatively little in value compared to any single currency. The SDR is really a "basket" of currencies whose value is generally more stable than that of any one of its components.

Just as the euro has gained wide acceptance as an instrument for denominating international financial transactions, so the SDR promises to maintain its acceptance as a risk-reducing instrument. (The SDR has the advantage of including the US dollar in the group of currencies that determine its value, whereas the euro is based only on European currencies.) At present private-sector investors and borrowers are using a much greater volume and value of euro-denominated instruments than SDR-denominated instruments.

Unresolved problems with the IMF system

The IMF system today differs dramatically from the model established at Bretton Woods in 1944. Flexible exchange rates have been substituted for fixed ones; gold has been greatly reduced as an international monetary asset,[10] and its link to the dollar has been severed; a new reserve currency, the SDR, has been created to increase world liquidity; and, perhaps most important, the US dollar is no longer the single base for the IMF system of value. These major changes have come in response to problems and crises that have occurred during the past 60 years—yet the IMF system itself survives. While few people would argue that the IMF has led directly to greater international financial stability over its history, at least the system has been flexible enough to accommodate the various crises that have threatened it.

Several problems that remain in the system deserve note. First, there has always been an uncomfortable tension between the countries that want to utilize the IMF simply as a bank for reducing the negative impacts of balance of payments difficulties and the countries that want to utilize it to subsidize economic development. The "link" between the IMF and development finance was originally delegated to the **World Bank** (the IMF' sister institution). Traditionally, the IMF has loaned funds only for short-term uses, sometimes extending to two or three years. Many borrowing countries, especially the less developed ones, have repeatedly called for greater use of IMF resources to finance development projects. While there are often no clear differences between financing payments imbalances and financing development projects that may later reduce those imbalances, the IMF has not substantially widened its scope. In the 1980s, under the cloud of multiple international loan renegotiations by Latin American countries, the Fund began to extend longer-term loans and to reconsider its strategy. The ultimate result of this crisis is, in the early 2000s, that the Fund retained its basic form, and the resources of the World Bank expanded to assist more heavily in economic development.

World Bank
The world's largest development bank, formed along with the IMF at Bretton Woods in 1944. Its original name was the International Bank for Reconstruction and Development (IBRD). The World Bank assists developing countries with loans and economic advising for economic development

A second problem that continues to plague the Fund is the issue of exchange rate regimes. Even as the flexible rate system moves through its fourth decade, there are repeated calls for a return to fixed, or more tightly constrained, currency values. The great instability of international financial dealings during the period since the initial OPEC oil crisis of 1973–1974 has led some analysts to argue for a return to fixed rates. The decision of most European Union countries to set up a single currency, the euro, has placed a regional fixed exchange rate regime alongside of the floating rate system globally. The evidence during the entire twentieth century tends to suggest that no matter what exchange rate regime prevails, if international trade relations are unstable and payments imbalances are substantial, no exchange rate regime will be able to solve the problem. Thus, this problem most likely cannot be eliminated.

On the whole, the international monetary system plays an important role in all international financial dealings by being the focal point for establishing rules on exchange rates, exchange controls, intergovernmental loans, and other official transactions. On a day-to-day basis, most international business people, especially in the triad countries, do not feel the international monetary system's impact.

MNEs AND INTERNATIONAL FINANCIAL MARKETS AND INSTITUTIONS

Whether or not a company or bank is involved in international trade, investment, or other international business, it is important that its managers understand some of the key aspects of international financial markets. The eurocurrency market may offer a low-cost borrowing opportunity, or the eurobond market may provide an outlet for selling new debt to a wider group of investors. The international monetary system establishes a framework within which governments set international financial policies that may affect many firms. The money and capital markets in foreign countries may offer opportunities to multinational firms that operate in those countries. The foreign exchange market determines the cost and availability of foreign currencies, used in business by many firms. Finally, all of these markets influence the functioning of the markets for real goods and services, the ultimate use for all financial claims.

KEY POINTS

1 Foreign exchange is any financial instrument that can be used to carry out payment from one currency to another. There are two major foreign exchange markets in the United States and the UK: interbank (including brokers) and futures/options (at stock and commodities exchanges). The most important participants in foreign exchange markets are banks—acting as traders, speculators, hedgers, and arbitrageurs. Exchange rates are determined by the activities of these five groups. The rates are also influenced by purchasing power parity, interest rates, and technical factors such as national economic statistics and seasonal demands.

2 There are a number of international finance strategies that can be of value to firms doing business overseas. Two of the most important are strategies for managing currency exchange rate risk and strategies for financing international operations.

3 The international monetary system is a market among central banks of the countries that belong to the International Monetary Fund (IMF). The IMF's objectives include the facilitation of balanced growth of international trade, promotion of exchange stability, and the making of financial resources available to the members of the Fund. In recent years the fixed monetary system created by the IMF members in 1944 has been replaced by a managed float system. Currently the IMF faces a number of major problems, including helping Third World countries to deal with their international debt crises and increasing international liquidity.

Key terms

- exchange risk
- foreign exchange
- eurocurrency
- exchange rate
- foreign exchange traders
- foreign exchange brokers
- spot rate

- forward rate
- arbitrageur
- purchasing power parity
- international Fisher effect
- nominal interest rate
- real interest rate
- exchange risk avoidance
- exchange risk adaptation
- exchange risk transfer
- currency diversification
- foreign bond
- eurobond
- European Monetary Union (EMU)
- eurodollar
- London interbank offered rate (LIBOR)
- international monetary system
- International Monetary Fund (IMF)
- speculator
- special drawing right (SDR)
- World Bank

REVIEW AND DISCUSSION QUESTIONS

1 If your firm had a subsidiary in Japan and about 100 million yen in exposed assets (that is, plant and equipment), how would you protect it against exchange risk?

2 If you managed the European operations of a large US-based MNE, in what market(s) would you seek long-term funding? Why?

3 Given that the euro area's inflation is about 3 percent per year at present, while US inflation is about 2 percent per year, what do you expect to happen to the euro/dollar exchange rate in the next few months? Why?

4 What is the difference between a eurobond and a domestic bond in the United States? Which one would you prefer to issue as a company manager? Which one would you prefer to buy as an investor? Why?

5 How can a firm such as Ajax Steel in Peoria, Illinois, utilize the eurodollar market to minimize its financing costs? This firm is a medium-size manufacturer with no foreign sales.

6 Assume that the interest rate on 12-month US dollar deposits in London is currently 2.6875 percent per year and the rate on British pound deposits there is 4.1875 percent per year. The spot exchange rate is US $1.93/£. What do you expect the exchange rate to be in one year?

7 If you were offered the opportunity to establish a deposit in London-denominated euros, would you choose that rather than a deposit in British pounds or dollars? Why or why not?

8 What are the important differences between the Bretton Woods fixed exchange rate system and the current IMF system? How do these differences affect the MNE manager?

9 How may the International Monetary Fund affect companies' activities in international business?

10 How would you hedge the value of your export sale of €10 million of computers to a French customer? You will be paid in 180 days in euros. On what basis would you choose among hedging methods?

REAL CASE

HSBC

What is the world's largest bank? Prior to the merger of Citicorp and Travelers in 1998, it was the Hong Kong and Shanghai Banking Corporation (HSBC). As at December 31, 2009, HSBC is the world's eighth largest banking and financial services group and the UK's No.1 largest banking group (Fortune Global 500, 2010 ranking). Formed in 1865 by a Scotsman in the then British Colony of Hong Kong, HSBC grew to over 10,000 bank offices in 76 countries by 2009. In the process it became the world's first truly global bank, offering a full range of financial services from retail to corporate banking to insurance and financial management. HSBC built this global business based on its strong Hong Kong base. The bank owns the Hong Kong Bank and most of the Hang Seng Bank, giving it over 40 percent of the market in the Hong Kong Special Administrative Region of China that was created on July 1, 1997.

Perhaps less well known is that HSBC is also the owner of the former Midland Bank chain in the UK, the Marine Midland and Republic New York Banks and Household Finance in the United States, and the Hong Kong Bank of Canada. It has also acquired large banks in Latin America including Banco Bamerindus in Brazil and Bital in Mexico. In all these cases HSBC greatly improved the efficiency of the underperforming local banks through better systems and processes. Over recent years, HSBC has implemented a rebranding strategy of all its subsidiaries under the HSBC title and logo "the world's local bank". This is meant to build HSBC into a global brand.

Today HSBC is well developed across the triad regions of Asia, Europe, and the Americas. It is a global bank in terms of assets, but not revenues. Its diversification strategy has helped to insulate it from the Asian financial crisis 1997–1998.

There is an old saying that the best test of a business is how well it does in a downturn. Again in the world financial crisis starting in 2007, HSBC looked pretty good. HSBC reported revenue of $142.069 billion and profits after tax of $5.728 billion for 2008. Although revenue was down 3 percent on a year earlier, but that looked very healthy compared to sickly peers such as Citigroup, UBS, and Royal Bank of Scotland (RBS). RBS required a British government bailout.

HSBC was thriving because of its strong presence in emerging markets including India, China, the Middle East, and Brazil to cushion the big losses it took in the US market due to subprime mortgage crisis. Since 2007, HSBC expanded into Japan, Korea, Vietnam, and India by launching new branches and services. Profits in some of HSBC's Middle East businesses, such as capital markets and private banking, were growing at a near 100 percent. HSBC reported revenue of $103.736 billion and profits after tax of $5.834 billion for 2009.

Significant events in 2009 included its decision to sell landmark buildings in New York, London and Paris to raise cash. HSBC agreed to sell its London base at Canary Wharf to the National Pension Service of Korea for $1.25 billion in cash and its New York headquarters to Israeli investment holding IDB Group for $330 million. HSBC sold its Paris building to private investors represented by French Properties Management for $573 million. HSBC would lease back these buildings. Importantly, HSBC announced in 2009 that it relocated the principal office of the Group Chief Executive to Hong Kong. This underscores HSBC commitments to emerging markets' businesses and reflects the historic shifts now taking place in the world economy. HSBC's corporate headquarters remain in the UK where it continues to benefit from being at the heart of the world's financial centers.

And its first-mover advantage as a truly global bank may prove hard to match by its competitors. There is constant pressure in banking to reduce costs through greater scale economies and improved information technology. HSBC is well positioned to continue as an industry leader because of its successful strategy.

In retrospect, one of the world's largest banks came from one of the world's smallest economies. And it did this despite the regulatory barriers to entry for foreign-owned firms in Europe and North America. As a result HSBC is an example of a bank using modern management systems and market forces to win out over old-fashioned protectionism in a highly regulated worldwide industry.

Perhaps the biggest influence of HSBC and its new efficient banking methods has been on British banking. A further restructuring occurred in British banking in November 1999 when one of the country's four major banks (Lloyds, Barclays, Natwest, and HSBC) was taken over by a much smaller bank. Natwest was acquired by the Royal Bank of Scotland, only one-third the asset size of Natwest, in a drawn-out and controversial takeover. Another bank, the Bank of Scotland, first bid for Natwest and the takeover efforts of both the Royal Bank of Scotland and the Bank of Scotland were defended by Natwest Chairman, Sir David Rowland, who was also President of Templeton College, University of Oxford. The takeover was successful because investors were critical of Natwest's old-style management and were supportive of the cost-cutting and new information technology methods of the Royal Bank of Scotland. After the acquisition, many Natwest branches were closed; bank buildings were turned into coffee bars, restaurants, and hotels; and a leaner, more efficient bank emerged to reclaim its place in British retail banking.

The Bank of Scotland and Halifax, the largest mortgage lender in the country, finalized a merger. This has fast-forwarded Halifax into mainstream banking and greatly increased the Bank of Scotland's scope of operations. Halifax then became a trading name of Bank of Scotland. The merger would also allow both banks to streamline their businesses and increase their market focus. These efforts toward restructuring operations and eliminating waste are not going unnoticed by rival banks. Barclays, for example, closed some of its branches in the early 2000s and introduced a wide array of tools and techniques that are designed to cut costs and increase operational efficiency. It realizes that, to be a successful international operation, it must not only have wide geographic coverage but also be able to offer efficient services. A takeover of Bank of Scotland by Lloyds TSB was approved by the Court of Session on January 12, 2009. On January 19, 2009, Bank of Scotland formally became part of Lloyds Banking Group.

In looking at these recent developments, it is clear that the steps taken by HSBC to modernize its own operations are proving to be a wake-up call for British banks as well.

Sources: www.hsbc.com; www.citigroup.com; www.bankofscotland.co.uk; www.royalbankscot.co.uk; www.natwest.co.uk; www.barclays.com; "HSBC: World's Strongest Bank," *Bloomberg Business Week*, www.businessweek.com, August 4, 2008; "HSBC to Sell New York Building for $330 Million," www.bloomberg.com, October 10, 2009; "HSBC to Sell Paris Building for $573 Million," in.reuters.com, December 21, 2009; HSBC, *Annual Report*, 2008–2009; Lloyds, *Annual Report*, 2009; "Fortune Global 500," *Fortune*, 2008, 2009, 2010 issues.

1. Since HSBC does business with the People's Republic of China and has substantial holdings of Chinese yuan (renminbi) on hand, what risk does this pose for the bank?
2. How could HSBC manage its currency exchange rate risk?
3. As the British retail banks are merged to achieve cost savings and economies, does this increase or decrease the barriers to entry for foreign banks wishing to do business in the EU?

REAL CASE

World financial crises

Throughout the 1990s, a series of financial crises rocked the world' economy. The first of these was the 1994 Mexico peso crisis. This was followed by the Asian crisis of 1997. Since then there have been the Russian crisis of 1998, the 1999 Brazilian financial crisis, the 2001 Argentine crisis, and the 2007 world financial crisis. The following examines the first two of these.

Source: Corbis/Reuters.

The Mexican peso crisis

In late 1994 Mexico suffered one of the worst financial crises in its history. In less than one month the Mexican peso devalued from 3.45 to the US dollar to 5.57 to the dollar, and by the end of 1995 it was trading at 6.5 to the dollar. This was accompanied by heavy inflation, unemployment, and a severe stock market crash. Some critics claimed that all of this was a result of NAFTA, but this was not so. The crisis was caused by the Mexican government itself, which had liberalized trade and financial flows but had not allowed the peso to float. Moreover, previous governments had kept the peso overvalued. As a result, in less than one year Mexico's foreign reserves were depleted by 75 percent and the country's current account deficit was equal to 8 percent of GDP.

Other factors also contributed to the low price of the peso. For instance, as a result of the Zapatista armed rebellion of 1996 in Chiapas, in southern Mexico, both foreign and Mexican investors took tens of millions of dollars out of the country. These developments had far-reaching consequences throughout the region. For example, many investors in other Latin American countries, fearing a similar crash, withdrew their funds from these economies and deposited them in the United States for safe keeping.

One unexpected development of the Mexican peso crisis was the devaluation of the Canadian dollar, which was sideswiped by the Latin American currency crisis. Thanks to NAFTA, Canada and Mexico had become linked in the international currency markets. At the same time international investors began showing a preference for the US dollar against both the Mexican peso and the Canadian dollar.

Perhaps the most surprising thing about the peso crisis was how quickly the country bounded back. With the help of a $50 billion loan from the United States and other countries, a tough economic reform that saw cuts in government spending, and increases in deregulation and privatization, the Mexican economy began to revive. Hardly a year had passed when investors who were running from the region were quickly lured back by short-term interest rates of up to 40 percent. Additionally, the stock market crash had led to underpriced shares, and investors began buying these issues and driving the prices back up. Today the financial crisis of 1995 in Mexico is a thing of the past. The country' economy is healthy and investors are back.

The Asian financial crisis

In the early 1990s, the Asian economies of South Korea, Indonesia, Thailand, Malaysia, and Japan were being praised as economic miracles. In 1997, these countries faced one of the worst blows to their economies. The Asian crisis began in July 1997, when Thailand stopped pegging its currency to the US dollar. In two months the Thai bath had devaluated by nearly 40 percent. The effect was twofold. First, Asian exporters to Thailand faced decreased demand for their product. Second, there was the decrease of investor confidence in the region.

Individual countries in the region faced their own sets of problems. In Malaysia, it was excessive lending to the property sector. Once foreign investment was cut short, overlending, overinvestment, and overproduction led to a downward spiral in the economy. In South Korea, the *chaebols* (large manufacturing conglomerates) that dominated the economy had invested recklessly without regard to profit. In Indonesia, President Suharto's corruption and lack of accountability led investors to flee the country. In addition, the banking system that the government there had fostered was plagued with bad loans for many unreliable projects. These loans benefited and created wealth for well-positioned individuals—in particular, members of the Suharto family—but they did nothing for the rest of the country.

Some financial observers believe that Western speculators were a major reason for the financial troubles in the region. The trend toward deregulation of the world capital markets and the free flow of capital, it was argued, contributed to the currency panic. Additionally, the relatively good health of these nations prior to 1997 made them attractive to foreign investors and lenders. Unfortunately, many of these loans were short term and were in foreign currency. So while the economy grew, the loans presented no problem. But when trouble looked likely the foreign lenders began calling in their loans. When this happened, the value of the local currencies plummeted and the loans payable in foreign currencies created a debt crisis.

It was initially believed that the Asian economic problem would be contained in that geographic region. However, by mid-1998 the crisis was having an effect on the world economy. The cross-border interconnections of global industries and the resulting interdependence pushed the problem to other regions. Among other things, the crisis led to decreases in the prices of many commodities including oil, metals, grain, pulp, and paper.

Industrial nations came to the aid of these Asian governments. The IMF negotiated billions of dollars in bailouts. Initially, the IMF wanted these governments to decrease their budget deficit and to maintain stable interest rates. By July 1998, however, the IMF was allowing increases in deficits and lower interest rates. This helped ease some of the problems, although there was still a great deal of disagreement regarding what else needed to be done. For example, some observers argued that the government needed to continue to deregulate the country's capital markets, while others blamed the economic disaster on this deregulation.

Sources: "Crisis-ridden Indonesia to Overhaul Ailing Banking Sector," *Boston Globe on Line*, January 27, 1998, www.boston.com/dailynews/; Richard Gwyn, "Asian Flu Shows No Sign of Letting Up," *Toronto Star*, July 10, 1998; "A Crisis of Dictatorship," *Washington Post*, January 11, 1998; Raffi Anderian, "Everybody Is Going Down," *Sunday Star*, July 12, 1998; "The Downward Spiral of the Asian Tigers," *BBC News*, January 8, 1998.

1 How does a decrease in the value of the Mexican peso affect foreign direct investment?

2 How is trade affected by currency devaluations as a result of a financial crisis?

3 How are customers in countries undergoing a financial crisis affected by the devaluation of the peso?

ENDNOTES

1 Exchange rate quotations come as two-digit numbers, bid/asked, with the preceding numbers assumed. A British pound quote of 50/70 on October 14, 2004, meant an actual price of:

$1.7950 bid to buy one British pound.

£1.7970 asked for selling one British pound.

The bank is offering (bidding) to buy pounds for 1.795 dollars per pound and also offering (asking) to sell pounds for 1.797 dollars per pound. Of course, the actual transaction will involve $1 million or more, to be exchanged at those prices.

Rates are typically quoted on the **Continental basis**, as units of foreign exchange per dollar, everywhere. US banks have traditionally used the **American basis**, quoting $US per unit of foreign exchange. Clearly, whether the quote is SF2.0/$ or $0.50/SF, the value is the same. The *Wall Street Journal* offers both types of quotations, as shown in Table 7.2.

Another means used to distinguish the two ways of presenting an exchange rate is to call a quotation of domestic currency/foreign exchange an **indirect quote**. Conversely, a quotation of units of foreign exchange/domestic currency is called a **direct quote**. This system has more general applicability to any pair of currencies, whereas the American/ Continental system relates only to rates involving the US dollar.

2 See http://www.chips.org.

3 "Taking a position" means purchasing an asset (or a liability) denominated in a foreign currency without simultaneously matching it with a liability (asset) of the same value and maturity in the same currency. Realistically, if any one government disallows the euromarkets, they can still function almost as effectively in other countries and currencies. At present, the US government has the most important role, since about 80 percent of eurodeposits are denominated in US dollars. If a US bank buys Swiss francs, it takes a position in Swiss francs. When the bank sells those Swiss francs to a client, it eliminates the position.

4 A **foreign currency option** is a contract offering the holder the right to buy (namely, a **call option**) or sell (namely, a **put option**) a fixed amount of foreign currency for a fixed price during a fixed time period. The buyer of a call option on British pounds obtains the right to buy £31,500 at a fixed dollar price (that is, the **exercise price**) at any time during the (typically) three-month life of the option. The seller of the same option faces a **contingent liability** in that the seller will have to deliver the British pounds at any time if the buyer chooses to exercise the option.

The market value (that is, the price on "premium" that the buyer must pay to purchase the option) of an option depends on its exercise price, the remaining time to its expiration, the exchange rate in the spot market, and expectations about the future exchange rate. An option may sell for a price near zero, for thousands of dollars, or for anywhere in between. Notice that the buyer of a call option on British pounds may pay a small price to obtain the option but does *not* have to exercise the option if the actual exchange rate moves favorably. Thus, an option is superior to a forward contract having the same maturity and exercise price because it need *not* be used, and the cost is just its purchase price. However, the price of the option is generally higher than the expected cost of the forward contract, so the user of the option pays for the flexibility of the instrument.

5 Yet another kind of foreign exchange arbitrage involves comparing interest rates on similar investments between two currencies. Interest arbitrage is the choice of investing, say, $1 million in a eurodollar bank deposit, versus investing the same money in pounds, depositing in a europound deposit, and contracting a forward contract to convert back to dollars. This comparison can be used for whatever currencies that may be available, and the investor benefits from taking the highest return available, with the exchange rates guaranteed through forward contracts (that is, with no exchange risk).

6 This entire discussion refers to *relative* purchasing power parity (PPP). The stronger, absolute version refers to parity in the values of factor inputs used in the production of products whose prices reflect relative factor productivities. Relative PPP considers only *changes* in the relative price levels between countries, not the initial (absolute) levels.

7 Realistically, if any one government disallows the euromarkets, they can still function almost as effectively in other countries and currencies. At present, the US government has the most important role, since about 80 percent of eurodeposits are denominated in US dollars.

8 See the Economic Cooperation Act of 1948 (Public Law 472, 80th Congress), US Code Congressional Service, 1948.

9 Exchange rate policies *are* constrained by the IMF if a country seeks to borrow more than its quota from the Fund. Also, a country does operate in violation of IMF rules if it imposes new exchange controls on current transactions without obtaining IMF approval; however, sanctions are seldom applied unless the country seeks to borrow as above.

10 Almost one-third of the world's monetary reserves were still being held in the form of gold at year-end 1991. See IMF *Survey*, November 8, 1993, p. 345.

ADDITIONAL BIBLIOGRAPHY

Agmon, Tamir. "Bringing Financial Economics into International Business Research: Taking Advantage of Paradigm Change," *Journal of International Business Studies*, vol. 37, no. 5 (September 2006).

Banalieva, Elitsa R. and Robertson Christopher J. "Performance, Diversity, and Multiplicity of Foreign Cross-Listing Portfolios," *International Business Review*, vol. 19, no. 6, (December 2010).

Beaulieu, Marie-Claude, Cosset, Jean-Claude and Essadam, Naceur. "The Impact of Political Risk on the Volatility of Stock Returns: The Case of Canada," *Journal of International Business Studies*, vol. 36, no. 6 (November 2005).

Berg, David M. and Guisinger, Stephen E. "Capital Flows, Capital Controls, and International Business Risk," in Alan M. Rugman and Thomas Brewer (eds.), *The Oxford Handbook of International Business* (Oxford: Oxford University Press, 2001).

Boulton, Thomas J, Smart, Scott B. and Zutter, Chad J. "IPO Underpricing and International Corporate Governance," *Journal of International Business Studies*, vol. 41 (2010).

Bowe, Michael, Filatotchev, Igor and Marshall, Andrew. "Integrating Contemporary Finance and International Business Research," *International Business Review*, vol. 19, no. 5 (October 2010).

Bowe, Michael "International Financial Management and Multinational Enterprises," in Alan M. Rugman (ed.), *Oxford Handbook of International Business*, 2nd ed. (Oxford: Oxford University Press, 2009).

Bowe, Michael and Saltvedt, Thina M. "Currency Invoicing Practices, Exchange Rate Volatility and Pricing-To-Market: Evidence from Product Level Data," *International Business Review*, vol. 13, no. 3 (June 2004).

Carrieri, Francesca and Majerbi, Basma. "The Pricing of Exchange Risk in Emerging Stock Markets," *Journal of International Business Studies*, vol. 37, no. 3 (May 2006).

Cheng, Louis T. W., Chan, Kam C. and Mak, Billy S. C. "Strategic Share Allocation and Underpricings of IPOs in Hong Kong," *International Management Review*, vol. 14, no. 1 (February 2005).

Connelly, Brian L., Hoskisson, Robert E., Tihanyi, Laszlo and Certo, S. Trevis. "Ownership as a Form of Corporate Governance," *Journal of Management Studies*, vol. 47, no. 8, (December 2010).

Covrig, Vincentiu Lau, Sie, Ting and Ng, Lilian. "Do Domestic and Foreign Fund Managers Have Similar Preferences for Stock Characteristics? A Cross-Country Analysis," *Journal of International Business Studies*, vol. 37, no. 3 (March 2007).

Cumming, Douglas– and Walz, Uwe. "Private Equity Returns and Disclosure Around the World," *Journal of International Business Studies*, vol. 41 (2010).

Bergh, Donald D. and Gibbons, Patrick. "The Stock Market Reaction to the Hiring of Management Consultants: A Signalling Theory Approach," *Journal of Management Studies*, vol. 48, no. 3 (May 2011).

Doidge, Craig, Carolyi, Andrew and Stulz, Rene M. "Why Do Foreign Firms Leave US Equity Market?", *Journal of Finance*, vol. 65, no. 4 (2010).

Eckert, Stefan, Dittfeld, Marcus, Muche, Thomas and Rässler, Susanne. "Does Multinationality Lead to Value Enhancement? An Empirical Examination of Publicly Listed Corporations from Germany," *International Business Review*, vol. 19, no. 6, (December 2010).

Eden, Lorraine and Rodriguez, Peter. "How Weak Are the Signals? International Price Indices and Multinational Enterprises," *Journal of International Business Studies*, vol. 35, no. 1 (January 2004).

Eiteman, David K., Stonehill, Arthur I. and Moffett, Michael H. *Multinational Business Finance*, 12th ed. (Boston, MA: Pearson Addison Wesley, 2009).

Faff, Robert W. and Marshall, Andrew. "International Evidence on the Determinants of Foreign Exchange Rate Exposure of Multinational Corporations," *Journal of International Business Studies*, vol. 36, no. 5 (September 2005).

Giddy, Ian and Dufey, Gunter. "Uses and Abuses of Currency Options," *Bank of America Journal of Applied Corporate Finance*, vol. 8 (1995).

Grosse, Robert. *The Future of Global Financial Services* (Oxford: Blackwell, 2004).

Hejazi, Walid and Pauly, Peter H. "Motivation for FDI and Domestic Capital Formation," *Journal of International Business Studies*, vol. 34, no. 3 (May 2003).

Hejazi, Walid and Santor, Eric. "Foreign Asset Risk Exposure, DOI, and Performance: An Analysis of Canadian Banks," *Journal of International Business Studies*, vol. 41 (2010).

Hearn, Bruce, Piesse, Jenifer and Strange, Roger. "Market Liquidity and Stock Size Premia in Emerging Financial Markets: The Implications for Foreign Investment," *International Business Review*, vol. 19, no. 5 (October 2010).

Hutson, Elaine and Stevenson, Simon. "Openness, Hedging Incentives and Foreign Exchange Exposure: A Firm-Level Multi-Country Study," *Journal of International Business Studies*, vol. 41 (2010).

Hutson, Elaine and O'Driscoll, Anthony. "Firm-Level Exchange Rate Exposure in the Eurozone," *International Business Review*, vol. 19, no. 5 (October 2010).

Ito, Kiyohiko and Rose, Elizabeth L. "The Implicit Return on Domestic and International Sales: An Empirical Analysis of US and Japanese Firms," *Journal of International Business Studies*, vol. 41 (2010).

Johnson, Robert and Soenen, Luc. "European Economic Integration and Stock Market Co-Movement with Germany," *Multinational Business Review*, vol. 17, no. 3 (2009).

Lessard, Donald R. "Finance and International Business," in B. Toyne and D. Nigh (eds.), *International Business: An Emerging Vision* (Columbia: University of South Carolina Press, 1997).

Leung, Kwok, Chahat, Rabi S., Buchan, Nancy R., Erez, Miriam and Gibson, Cristina B. "Culture and International Business: Recent Advances and Their Implications for Future Research," *Journal of International Business Studies*, vol. 36, no. 4 (July 2005).

Ling-yee, Li. "Effect of Export Financing Resources and Supply-Chain Skills on Export Competitive Advantages: Implications for Superior Export Performance," *Journal of World Business*, vol. 36, no. 3 (Fall 2001).

Lopez-Duerte, Cristina and Garcia-Canal, Esteban. "Stock Market Reaction to Foreign Direct Investments: Interaction between Entry Mode and FDI Attributes," *Management International Review*, vol. 47, no. 3 (2007).

Miller, Kent D. and Reuer, Jeffrey J. "Firm Strategy and Economic Exposure to Foreign Exchange Rate Movements," *Journal of International Business Studies*, vol. 29, no. 3 (Fall 1998).

Oxelheim, Lars and Randøy, Trond. "The Anglo-American Financial Influence on CEO Compensation in Non-Anglo-American Firms," *Journal of International Business Studies*, vol. 36, no. 4 (July 2005).

Radebaugh, Lee H., Gray, Sidney J. and Black, Ervin L. *International Accounting and Multinational Enterprises* 6th ed. (Hoboken, NJ: Wiley, 2006).

Remmers, Lee. "International Financial Management: 35 Years Later–What Has Changed?" *International Business Review*, vol. 13, no. 2 (April 2004), pp. 155–180.

Rugman, Alan M. *International Diversification and the Multinational Enterprise* (Lexington, MA: D.C. Heath, 1979).

Rugman, Alan M. "International Diversification and Multinational Banking," in Sarkis J. Khoury and Alo Gosh (eds.), *Recent Developments in International Banking and Finance* (Lexington, MA: D.C. Heath, 1987).

Rugman, Alan M. and Brain, Cecilia. "The Regional Nature of the World's Banking Sector," *The Multinational Business Review*, vol. 12, no. 3 (Winter 2004).

Rugman, Alan M. and Li, Jing (eds.). *Real Options and International Investment* (Cheltenham: Edward Elgar, 2005).

Purda, Lynnette D. "Risk Perception and the Financial System," *Journal of International Business Studies*, vol. 39 (2008).

Shapiro, Alan C. *Multinational Financial Management*, 9th ed. (New York: Wiley, 2009).

Strange, Susan. *Mad Money* (Manchester: Manchester University Press, 1998).

Strange, Roger, Filatotchev, Igor, Buck, Trevor and Wright, Mike. "Corporate Governance and International Business," *Management International Review*, vol. 49, no. 4 (2009).

Tang, Gordon Y. N. and Shum, Wai Cheong. "The Conditional Relationship between Beta And Returns: Recent Evidence from International Stock Markets," *International Business Review*, vol. 12, no. 1 (February 2003).

Tang, Gordon Y. N. and Shum, Wai Cheong. "The Relationships between Unsystematic Risk, Shrewdness and Stock Returns during Up and Down Markets," *International Business Review*, vol. 12, no. 5 (October 2003).

Tong, Tony W. and Reuer, Jeffrey J. "Real Options in Multinational Corporations: Organizational Challenges and Risk Implications," *Journal of International Business Studies*, vol. 38, no. 2 (March 2007).

APPENDIX TO CHAPTER 7: REGIONAL ASPECTS OF MULTINATIONALITY AND PERFORMANCE

In order to link Parts One and Two, this Appendix reports on recent research on the topic of multinationality and performance. A basic premise of international business is that foreign operations are profitable—otherwise, they would not take place! Thus it is hypothesized that the performance of the firm (usually an MNE) improves as its degree of foreign operations increases.

In Part One we have explored the reasons for MNEs and some ideas about why and how their degree of multinationality might increase across the home region, rather than globally. In Part Two we have examined country factors which (often indirectly) may affect firm performance. Thus, in this Appendix we bring these themes together by examining the regional aspects of multinationality and performance.

Introduction

Rugman (2005) has shown that the world's largest firms operate mainly on an intra-regional basis, in terms of both sales and assets. We relate traditional literature on multinationality and performance to the new metrics available, which includes new data on regional sales and on the return on foreign assets. Several recent papers examine regionalization and performance across industries, others over time and for various regions of the triad. This recent empirical work provides a very useful starting point in bringing the regional nature of MNEs into the literature on multinationality and performance.

In the field of international business one of the most basic issues is the relationship between multinationality and performance. Several hundred studies have examined the nature of this relationship, with somewhat inconclusive results. Here this literature is reviewed and extended and then related to the regional dimension of multinationality and performance. The regional aspects of multinational activity are explored in Rugman and Verbeke (2004) and Rugman (2005). The traditional empirical work on multinationality and performance can be extended by including this regional dimension.

Recent research on the S curve

Contractor (2007) presents a theoretical justification for the three-stage *S* curve, see Figure 7.7. The horizontal axis represents the degree of multinationality, here proxied by

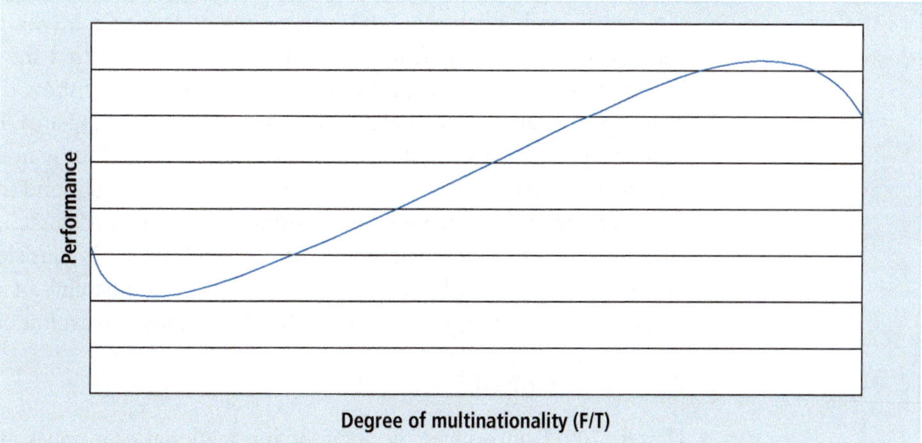

Figure 7.7 Multinationality and performance

the ratio of foreign (F) to total (T) sales, (F/T). The vertical axis represents a performance measure, here the return on total assets (ROTA). There is generally a positive relationship between these two variables. In an interesting twist Contractor argues that the middle stage is consistent with the observations on the regional nature of multinational activity. He also suggests that the final stage, where performance suffers due to excessive multinationality, is typically populated by relatively few firms. This fall-off in performance beyond a certain threshold of multinationality may correspond to an attempt by some companies to reach a "global" stage. While these propositions remain to be tested, Contractor provides strong new insights into the possible relationship between the regional dimension of multinationality activity and the emerging literature on the *S* curve. He also reviews seven generic reasons why studies of multinationality and performance yield different results, and he provides an agenda for research to further test the viability of the three-stage *S* curve concept.

Regional versus total sales

Oh and Rugman (2007) provide new data examining the trends of regional sales between 2001 and 2005. They start with the 2001 benchmark year used in the pathbreaking paper by Rugman and Verbeke (2004) as further developed in the databank reported in the book by Rugman (2005). They find a remarkable degree of stability over time where the ratio of regional to total sales averages 75.7 percent. They also provide data for the first time on the regional nature of assets of the world's largest 500 firms. This averages 76.7 percent again with less than a 1 percent variation over the five-year period.

Osegowitsch and Sammartino (2007) conduct an analysis by taking the set of 380 firms reported in Rugman and Verbeke (2004) and going back to 1991 to find trends in regionalization over the period 1991–2001. One problem is that this yields a greatly reduced sample of 159 firms biased towards US firms. Indeed, most of their results exclude the Asian firms completely, and represent only 90 North American firms and 36 from Europe. Osegowitsch and Sammartino (2007) find that there is a reduction in intra-regional sales for this small set of US and European firms from 84 percent to 76 percent. Over this period they also find that some firms increase their sales outside their home region. They also find that a somewhat larger percentage of firms can be classified as biregional in contrast to those found in the Rugman and Verbeke (2004) chapter. However, in contrast to their own conclusions their own data actually confirm the main two insights of Rugman and Verbeke (2004). First, the vast majority of firms remain home region oriented over the 1991–2001 period. Second, there are very few global firms. Their chapter is useful in provoking a debate about trends in regionalization and hopefully a more extensive dataset can be constructed to help reconcile their findings with those of Oh and Rugman (2007).

Goerzen and Asmussen (2007) use a set of Japanese MNEs to test the relationship between regional and global firms. They argue correctly that the performance of a firm is determined by its firm-specific advantages (FSAs). They show that regional firms build more upon location-bound FSAs, especially in the marketing area. In contrast, global firms have technological (R&D) FSAs, and these are presumed to be non-location bound. They find evidence that the FSAs of global firms are less location bound than the FSAs of regional firms. This work needs to be extended beyond the Japanese dataset in order to test the generalization of these findings. However, their theoretical logic is consistent with that of Rugman and Verbeke (2007), where it is argued that there is a liability of regional foreignness. In other words, the FSAs of MNEs are difficult to deploy and exploit outside the home region.

Gravity model

Hejazi (2007) introduces the logic of international economics and transaction costs to analyze the regional dimension of the activities of MNEs. He uses the well-known gravity model of international economics which has been used to analyze the importance of geography on the determination of international trade flows. He adapts the gravity model to measure foreign direct investment (FDI) instead of trade flows. The gravity model measures the country-level frictions affecting trade and can only be applied to FDI with some difficulty as FDI is partly a method to overcome such frictions. Thus the gravity model yields a new type of test of the activities of MNEs, although it is not a direct test of their strategies. Hejazi finds that there is a strong regional bias in the activities of MNEs from the EU, but he does not find this effect for North American MNEs, which is not surprising given the asymmetrical large size of the US market. (The size bias of the US market may also affect the results by Osegowitsch and Sammartino (2007).) While Hejazi does not test performance directly, his work offers new conceptual lenses on the nature of the regional dimension of multinationality. Such work using econometric techniques based on the gravity model needs to be taken up and related to the empirical literature on multinationality and performance.

Multinationality and performance

Bowen (2007) provides a theoretical critique of the extant empirical work in the multinationality and performance literature. He points out that basic statistical issues have not been resolved, including the issues of endogeneity and non-linearities in the tests. He argues that the multinationality and performance literature does not take into account the heterogeneous nature of firms, industries, or countries. He argues further that the multinationality and performance literature needs to be much better integrated into basic international business theory and that the various "modes of multinationality" (exporting, FDI, outsourcing) can affect measurement. Such variations in types of multinationality are consistent with the observations of Rugman (2005) on the regional nature of multinational activity. A related criticism of the lack of theoretical underpinnings in the multinationality and performance literature has been advanced by Verbeke, Li, and Goerzen (2009). It is clear that much more effort needs to be put into the development of appropriate theoretical frameworks to model the observed empirical relationship between multinationality and performance.

Bausch et al. (2007) conduct a meta-analysis of a large set of previously published studies in the literature on multinationality and performance. They confirm a positive relationship between multinationality and performance. They have a broad definition of multinationality and include the traditional type of merger and acquisition (leading to wholly owned subsidiaries through the process of FDI) along with the non-traditional type of alliance formation. This leads them to invent yet another term for multinationality, namely international business combinations. It is unusual to include alliances in this type of work since it is difficult to assess the impact of alliances on firm performance in a direct manner, as can be done with the merger and acquisition mode of multinationality. Some challenging ideas are presented in this paper which attempts to extend the field of study by adding the alliance as an additional unit of analysis. It is particularly important to extend these tests to fully address the regional significance of different types of international business combinations.

Fortanier et al. (2007) offer a cautionary tale for researchers on multinationality and performance. They find that the empirical results testing this relationship are strongly affected by moderating variables. In particular the so-called "strategic fit" affects performance in a significant and positive manner. Strategic fit moderates the basic aspects of multinationality and performance including the shape, size, and direction of the relationship. Strategic fit is based upon the integration and national responsiveness framework, which is also used by Li and Li (2007). Fortanier and her coauthors (2007) collect archival data on the chain of ownership of multiple subsidiaries that allow them to conduct more robust econometric analysis on aspects of integration and responsiveness. They have data for 336 of the world's largest 500 firms for the year 2002. These variables enter as moderators when testing the basic relationship between multinationality and performance. The results indicate a significant positive relationship between multinationality and return on sales, but this relationship is not a stable one since the strategic fit varies by firm. In other words, firms with an integration strategy perform well internationally in industries which are integrated. In contrast, in multidomestic industries only firms with a national responsiveness strategy do well internationally, so industry effects matter, as also found by Li and Li (2007). While the paper is interesting because it attempts to introduce organizational structure and strategy issues more explicitly into the literature on multinationality and performance, the regional dimension is not explored.

Kumar and Gaur (2007) examine the relationship between multinationality and performance within the context of 240 of India's MNEs, many of which are smaller firms than the world's largest 500 for which the regional effect has been tested. They find strong evidence of a positive J-shaped exponentially increasing relationship between the internationalization of Indian firms and their performance. They also find that India's outward FDI differs between developing and developed economies and between manufacturing and service sectors. A key contribution is that their data include relatively small and medium-sized firms, not just the world's largest 500 firms. This helps us better understand the country context in studies of multinationality and performance, as India has many small multinational firms. Usually size of firms is a moderating or control variable, but Kumar and Gaur link it to a country factor for India.

Nachum and Wymbs (2007) offer an interesting contrast to the literature as their geographic unit of analysis is the city. This is a subnational unit of analysis, and it can be contrasted with the triad regions developed in Rugman (2005). A very good reason is given for choosing cities—namely, that the data tested relate to the financial and professional service industries. These are clustered in the world's major cities. The authors analyze 673 MNEs in these service sectors that entered New York and London through mergers and acquisitions. They find an interaction between geographic location and the FSAs of these MNEs. It is a useful idea to apply the location decision for an industry and firm at the appropriate geographic level. These findings can be usefully contrasted with other papers where regions cross national borders, rather than being subnational.

Regional aspects of multinationality and performance

Li and Li (2007) provide an innovative test of the regional aspects of multinationality and performance. The authors use the well-known integration and responsiveness matrix to distinguish between a "global" industry, which has a high degree of economic integration, and a "multidomestic" industry, which is nationally responsive. They choose the computer and office equipment industry as an example of a global industry, and the soap, cleanser, and toilet goods industry as an example of a multidomestic industry. They find significant differences between the two industries in terms of international strategies, which lead to confirmation of the regional dimension in multinational operations. They also test the impact of FSAs in the two industries in terms of both R&D and marketing intensity. Their results indicate that FSAs are largely non-location bound in the global industry, but much home-region bound in the multidomestic industry. In addition, they show that internationalization pace has a direct positive impact on firm performance in the global industry but not in the multidomestic industry.

Rugman et al. (2007) introduce a new dependent variable called return on foreign assets (ROFA). They contrast it with the traditional variable, return on total assets (ROTA). They also introduce a regional variable representing regional sales. They test the explanatory power of the regional sales variable with linear, quadratic, and cubic fits. They find that the regional variable explains ROTA in terms of the cubic fit, but not ROFA. These data are focused upon a set of 27 UK multinationals of which 8 are in manufacturing and 19 are in service sectors; the regional variable represents sales in the EU. The results indicate that the 27 large UK MNEs experience strong intra-regional sales and that the regional sales variable is a significant variable affecting firm performance in a positive but non-linear manner allowing for standard control variables.

In a related chapter Sukpanich (2007) also includes an independent variable representing intra-regional sales, this time across MNEs in the triad regions of North America and the EU. She has data on 91 firms of which 67 are from North America and 24 from Europe. Of the 91 firms, 66 are in manufacturing and 25 in services. She uses the COMPUSTAT database to access data on the FSAs of MNEs. These FSAs include R&D and marketing variables. She finds a strong positive linear relationship between the measure of intra-regional sales and performance. Performance is higher for firms based in their home region. This result contrasts with that of Chen as discussed next.

Chen (2007) conducts a test of the multinationality and performance relationship across some service sector firms in an Asian context. He distinguishes between intra-regional sales and extra-regional sales for this set of service sector firms. He uses the same Osiris database as in Rugman et al. (2007). He does not find support for the hypothesis that intra-regional sales are a significant determinant of performance where performance is measured by return on total assets. Instead, he finds that extra-regional sales are significant, in contrast to Sukpanich (2007). To some extent this may support some findings by Osegowitsch and Sammartino (2007). Further research is required, but it is encouraging to see this focus on the Asian firms missing from Osegowitsch and Sammartino (2007).

Richter (2007) tests the importance of a regional sales variable across the UNCTAD set of the world's 100 largest firms as ranked by foreign assets. This is a somewhat unrepresentative sample as it consists of the world's most internationalized firms and is thus biased toward finding internationalization (and therefore regionalization). Richter uses the *S* curve and finds a significant cubic fit between performance and multinationality where the latter is measured by the UNCTAD transnationality index. When testing the foreign intra-regional sales variable, her results are ambiguous with either an S curve or inverted U curve being supported. However, as with other recent papers, she finds that this regional sales variable is a significant determinant of performance.

It would be useful to extend this type of research beyond the largest 100 firms (or the 500 largest in Rugman (2005)) to include many more MNEs that are small to medium sized. Indeed, it would be useful to test the regional dimension in the emerging literature on international entrepreneurship, some of which is focused upon the internationalization process of small and medium-sized firms. This will require some theoretical adjustments to the assumption that many of these firms are "born global." This literature seems to find relatively fast internationalization of small firms in the information technology and computer sector, but there has not been careful testing of the regional aspects of such internationalization, and other sectors need to be added. Furthermore, the normal metric used is a scope variable dealing with the opening of foreign subsidiaries, whereas a better metric is to use the ratio of foreign to total sales (in this case, regional to total sales).

While this work on international entrepreneurship remains to be undertaken, this recent empirical work provides a very useful starting point in bringing the regional nature of MNEs into the literature on multinationality and performance. There is uniformity in showing that the basic relationship between multinationality and performance is beset by issues of heterogeneity across countries, industries, and firms. Yet many of them also show that the regional nature of multinationality can be included in this work in a useful manner. Therefore, the regional dimension of strategy needs to be considered in future work analyzing the relationship between multinationality and performance.

References

Bausch, A., Fritz, T. and Bösecke, K. "Performance Effects of Internationalization Strategies: A Meta-analysis," in A. M. Rugman (ed.), *Regional Aspects of Multinationality and Performance* (Oxford: Elsevier, 2007).

Bowen, H. P. "The Empirics of Multinationality and Performance," in A. M. Rugman (ed.), *Regional Aspects of Multinationality and Performance* (Oxford: Elsevier, 2007).

Chen, S. "Testing Regional Effects in the International-Performance Relationship in Asia Service Firms," in A. M. Rugman (ed.), *Regional Aspects of Multinationality and Performance* (Oxford: Elsevier, 2007).

Contractor, F. J. "The Evolutionary or Multi-stage Theory of Internationalization and the Regionalization of Firms," in A. M. Rugman (ed.), *Regional Aspects of Multinationality and Performance* (Oxford: Elsevier, 2007).

Fortanier, F., Muller, A. and Tulder, R. van. "Internationalization and Performance: The Moderating Role of Strategic Fit," in A. M. Rugman (ed.), *Regional Aspects of Multinationality and Performance* (Oxford: Elsevier, 2007).

Goerzen, A. and Asmussen, C. G. "The Geographic Orientation of Multinational Enterprises and its Implications for Performance," in A. M. Rugman (ed.), *Regional Aspects of Multinationality and Performance* (Oxford: Elsevier, 2007).

Hejazi, W. "The Regional Nature of MNE Activities and the Gravity Model," in A. M. Rugman (ed.), *Regional Aspects of Multinationality and Performance* (Oxford: Elsevier, 2007).

Kumar, V. and Gaur, A. S. "Internationalization and Performance of Indian Firms," in A. M. Rugman (ed.), *Regional Aspects of Multinationality and Performance* (Oxford: Elsevier, 2007).

Li, L. and Li, D. "Testing the Global and Regional Strategies of Multinational Enterprises," in A. M. Rugman (ed.), *Regional Aspects of Multinationality and Performance* (Oxford: Elsevier, 2007).

Nachum, L. and Wymbs, C. "The Location and Performance of Foreign Affiliates in Global Cities," in A. M. Rugman (ed.), *Regional Aspects of Multinationality and Performance* (Oxford: Elsevier, 2007).

Oh, C.-H. and Rugman, A. M. "Multinationality and Regional Performance, 2001–2005," in A. M. Rugman (ed.), *Regional Aspects of Multinationality and Performance* (Oxford: Elsevier, 2007).

Osegowitsch, T. and Sammartino, A. "Exploring Trends in Regionalization," in A. M. Rugman (ed.), *Regional Aspects of Multinationality and Performance* (Oxford: Elsevier, 2007).

Richter, N. "Intra-regional Sales and the Internationalization and Performance Relationship," in A. M. Rugman (ed.), *Regional Aspects of Multinationality and Performance* (Oxford: Elsevier, 2007).

Rugman, A. M. *The Regional Multinationals: MNEs and 'Global' Strategic Management* (Cambridge: Cambridge University Press, 2005).

Rugman, Alan M. and Verbeke, Alain. "A Perspective on Regional and Global Strategies of Multinational Enterprises," *Journal of International Business Studies*, vol. 35, no. 1 (January 2004), pp. 3–18.

Rugman, A. M. and Verbeke, Alain "Liabilities of Regional Foreignness and the Use of Firm-level versus Country-level Data: A Response to Dunning *et al.* (2007)," *Journal of International Business Studies*, vol. 38, no. 1 (January 2007), pp. 200–205.

Rugman, A. M., Yip, G. S. and Kudina, A. "The Regional Dimension of UK Multinationals," in A. M. Rugman (ed.), *Regional Aspects of Multinationality and Performance* (Oxford: Elsevier, 2007).

Sukpanich, N. "Intra-regional Sales and Performance," in A. M. Rugman (ed.), *Regional Aspects of Multinationality and Performance* (Oxford: Elsevier, 2007).

Verbeke, A., Li, L. and Goerzen, A. "Towards More Effective Research on the Multinationality–Performance Relationship," *Management International Review*, vol. 49, no. 2 (2009), pp. 1–13.

Additional bibliography

Banalieva, E., Santoro, M. "Local, Regional, or Global? Geographic Orientation and Relative Financial Performance of Emerging Market Multinational Enterprises," *European Management* Journal, vol. 27, no. 5 (2009).

Beleska-Spasova, E. and Glaister, K. W. (2010). "Geographic Orientation and Performance," *Management International Review*, vol. 50, no. 5 (October 2010).

Chen, S. and Tan, H. "Region Effects in the Internationalization-Performance Relationship in Chinese Firms," *Journal of World Business* (2010). doi:10.1016/j.jwb.2010.10.022.

Oh, C. H. "The International Scale and Scope of European Multinationals," *European Management Journal*, vol. 27, no. 5 (2009).

Oh, C. H. "Value Creation and Home Region Internationalization of U.S. MNEs," *Multinational Business Review*, vol. 18, no. 4 (2010).

Qian, G., Khoury, T., Peng, M. W. and Qian, Z. "The Performance Implication of Intra- and Inter-regional Geographic Diversification," *Strategic Management Journal*, 31 (2010).

Rugman, A. M. and Oh, C. H. "Does the Regional Nature of Multinationals Affect the Multinationality and Performance Relationship?" *International Business Review*, vol. 19, no. 5 (2010).

Rugman, A. M. and Oh, C. H. "Methodological Issues in the Measurement of Multinationality of U.S. Firms," *Multinational Business Review* vol. 19, no. 3 (2011).

Rugman, A. M. and Oh, C. H. "Regional Integration and the International Strategies of Large European Firms," *International Business Review*, vol. 20 (2011), forthcoming.

Rugman, A. M. and Verbeke, A. "Internalization Theory and Its Impact on the Field of International Business," in J. J. Boddewyn (ed.) *International Business Scholarship: AIB Fellows on the First 50 Years and Beyond*, Research in Global Strategic Management, vol. 14 (Bradford: Emerald Group, 2008).

Rugman, A. M., Yip, G. S. and Kudina, A. "Testing the Link Between Multinationality and the Return on Foreign Assets," *Multinational Business Review*, vol. 17, no. 3 (2009).

Sullivan, Daniel. "Measuring the Degree of Internationalization of a Firm," *Journal of International Business Studies*, vol. 25, no. 2 (1994).

Verbeke, A. and Brugman, P. "Triple-Testing the Quality of Multinationality–Performance Research: An Internalization Theory Perspective," *International Business Review*, vol. 18, no. 3 (June 2009).

Verbeke, A., Li, L. and Goerzen, A. "Toward More Effective Research on the Multinationality–Performance Relationship," *Management International Review*, vol. 49, no. 5 (2009).

Source: © kalafoto - Fotolia.com

The Legal and Political Framework of Doing Business in China

In 1979, the Chinese supreme leader Deng Xiaoping declared the opening of China to Western companies and set up the now-famous four SEZs (Special Economic Zones)—Shenzhen, Zhuhai, and, Shantou in Guangdong Province, and Xiamen in Fujian Province.

The first corporations entering the market were as aliens in a brave new world. China offered incredibly favorable conditions, including tax rebates, exemptions from corporate tax, and cut rates for land occupancy and energy, and the promise of having a stronghold in a potential market of 1.3 billion consumers when domestic consumption began to pick up.

However, the challenges to Western companies were as serious as the prospective advantages, including the Chinese legal system.

China had only recently started implementing a rule-of-law system comparable to Western standards, and most of the commercial and company laws had been enacted as recently as the 1990s or later. This meant that courts, while existing, often didn't function in the way corporations expected in other countries, and mediation was still the preferred method of settlement.

This had an immediate effect on sensitive issues such as intellectual property. There was no real international

CHAPTER 7

Political and Legal Systems in National Environments

LEARNING OBJECTIVES *In this chapter, you will learn about the following:*

1. The nature of country risk
2. Political and legal environments in international business
3. Political systems
4. Legal systems
5. Participants in political and legal systems
6. Types of country risk produced by political systems
7. Types of country risk produced by legal systems
8. Managing country risk

protection until China became member of the Trade Related Aspects of Intellectual Property Rights (TRIPS) agreement in 2001, and some companies immediately found out the hard way that even having a patent would not mean automatically being protected. A lot of companies ended up having their products copied, often by the same local companies that manufactured them on their behalf. Another problem was the brand recognition, still low among the so-called two-tier cities (i.e., all cities other than Shanghai, Beijing, and Guangzhou).

Dealing with party officials was another issue, especially when authorizations were involved. Of course, China had distinctive advantages over other emerging economies, including the so-called BRICs (Brazil, Russia, India, and China) from Goldman Sachs' now-famous definition. Compared to Russia, for instance, there was no organized crime to worry about in China. Century-old Chinese Triads, particularly active in the South and even in Hong Kong, avoid Western business and only deal with Chinese companies and interests.

Thirty years from the start of the "Open Door Policy," the business environment has certainly improved, and doing business in China, while more expensive than it used to be, is less problematic.

However, some important challenges remain, including the legal system that still does not offer protection to business comparable to Western standards. Counterfeiting also continues to present a problem. While it has been curbed in Hong Kong, for example, it is still present in China, where in the open markets of main cities it is still possible to buy various types of pirated goods.

And finally, according to some economists, the system driven from an export-led growth has started showing its limits, especially in a global business environment of limited growth and stagnant imports. How China will address these issues and the way this will affect Western companies relocated in its territory is unclear.

SOURCES: "Intellectual property in China. Still murky," *The Economist*, April 21, 2012, http://www.economist.com/node/21553040; "The Legal System in China," *World Savvy Monitor*, Issue 2, June 2008, http://worldsavvy.org/monitor/index.php?option=com_content&view=article&id=113&Itemid=176.

Most of us expect a familiar business landscape when we conduct business at home. But foreign markets differ in terms of political and legal systems, as well as business norms. As illustrated by the opening story, foreign markets often pose major challenges and create vulnerabilities for the firm. Managers must be able to navigate difficult regulations and practices and avoid unethical or questionable conduct.

At the same time, the political and legal context may also present opportunities for companies. Preferential subsidies, government incentives, and protection from competition reduce business costs and influence strategic decision making. Many governments encourage domestic investment from foreign MNEs by offering tax holidays and cash incentives to employ local workers.

The Nature of Country Risk

Country risk
Exposure to potential loss or adverse effects on company operations and profitability caused by developments in a country's political and/or legal environments.

Country risk is defined as exposure to potential loss or adverse effects on company operations and profitability caused by developments in a country's political and/or legal environments. Sometimes termed *political risk,* it is one of four major types of international business risks introduced in Chapter 1. While the immediate cause of country risk is a political or legal factor, underlying such factors may be economic, social, or technological developments. Exhibit 7.1 identifies dimensions of country risk prevalent in international business. We address them in this chapter. Government intervention, protectionism, and barriers to trade and investment are particularly notable in international business. Mismanagement or failure of the national economy can lead to financial crises, recessions, market downturns, currency crises, and inflation. Such events usually arise from business cycles, poor monetary or fiscal policies, a defective regulatory environment, or imbalances in the underlying economic fundamentals of the host country.

Political or legislative actions can harm business interests, such as laws that are unexpectedly strict or result in unintended consequences. Many laws favor host-country interests—that is, interests in foreign countries where the firm has direct operations. For example, Coca-Cola's business suffered in Germany after the German government enacted a recycling plan that required consumers to return nonreusable soda containers to stores for a refund of 0.25 euros. Rather than coping with unwanted returns, big supermarket chains responded by yanking Coke from their shelves and pushing their own store brands instead.[1] In China, the government censors material that is critical of its actions and policies. Yahoo must monitor the information that appears on its Web sites to prevent the Chinese government from closing its China operations. In 2010, Google took a censorship stand against the Chinese government when it moved its search engine business to Hong Kong.

How Prevalent Is Country Risk?

Exhibit 7.2 presents the level of country risk in selected countries, measured as political stability, legal environment, economic indicators, and tax policy. Iraq is risky in the wake of war and efforts to establish political stability. Venezuela is dominated by an unpredictable, dictatorial government. Libya has experienced popular unrest. Such countries suffer from unstable governments,

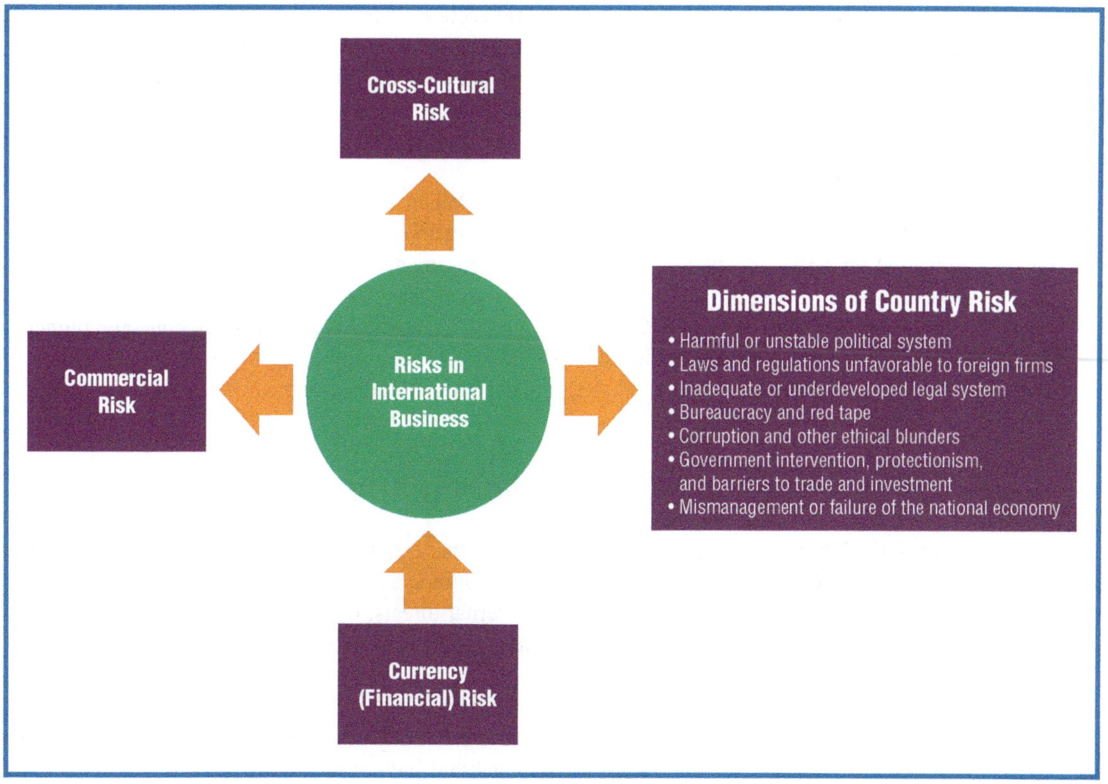

EXHIBIT 7.1

Country Risk as One of Four Major Risks in International Business

underdeveloped legal systems, or biased law enforcement. Conversely, countries such as Canada, Japan, and Singapore are characterized by stable, transparent, and well-founded political and legal systems. Exhibit 7.2 implies that risk tends to be lower in countries with a favorable legal climate and political stability and higher in countries with political instability and substantial government intervention. Many of the riskiest states are poor countries that would benefit enormously from

EXHIBIT 7.2

Country Risk in Selected Countries, 2011 (ranked 0 to 10; a high number indicates greater risk)

Source: Based on Economist Intelligence Unit (2011), "Risk Briefing," www.viewswire.eiu.com, accessed January 28, 2012.

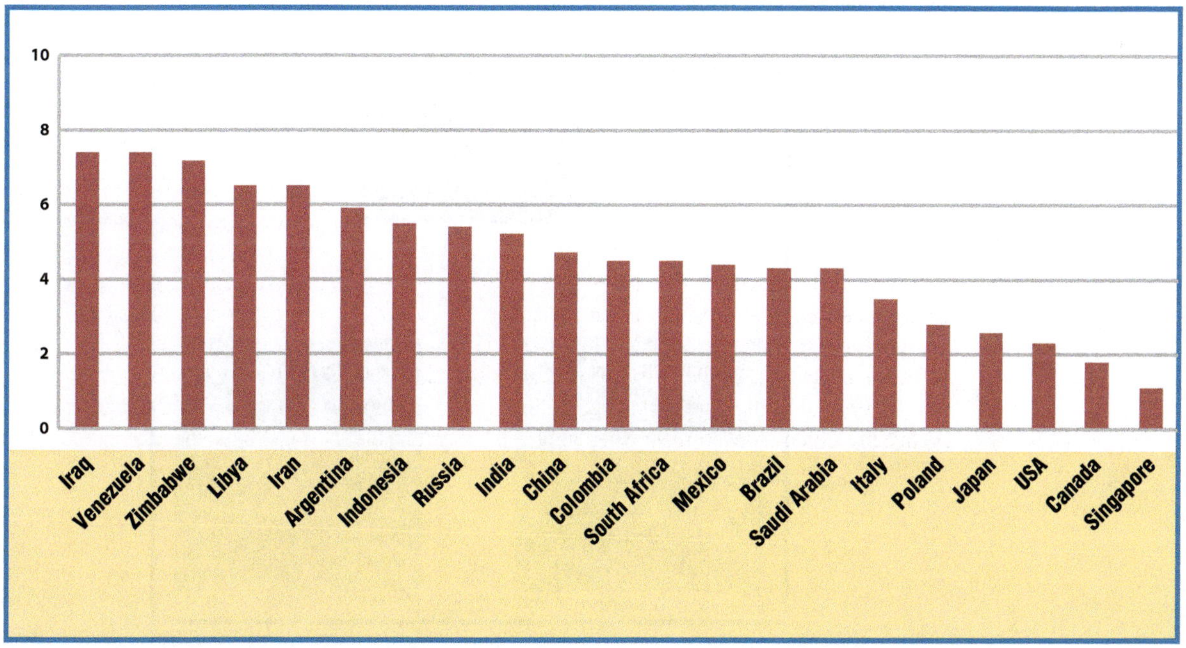

direct investment and integration into the world economy.[2] For the complete list of countries ranked by risk, visit the Risk Briefing site at the Economist Intelligence Unit (www.viewswire.eiu.com).

Country risk may affect all firms in a country equally or only a subset. Unrest in Egypt in 2011 tended to affect all firms. By contrast, the Russian government targeted only Yukos with politically motivated persecution, despite the presence of several competitors in Russia like ConocoPhillips and Royal Dutch Shell.[3]

Country risk occasionally occurs in India. When they held power in India's government, Hindu nationalists openly opposed foreign investment and influence on Indian society and enacted laws that targeted foreign firms for harassment. The KFC restaurant chain stepped up security after local political groups threatened to destroy the firm's fast-food outlets. About one hundred farmers ransacked a KFC restaurant in Bangalore. ArcelorMittal, Nissan, and numerous other firms have faced delays in establishing operations in India due to government bureaucracy and Indian activist groups, which often oppose industrial development.[4]

Political and Legal Environments in International Business

Political system
A set of formal institutions that constitute a government.

A **political system** is a set of formal institutions that constitute a government. It includes legislative bodies, political parties, lobbying groups, and trade unions. The principal functions of a political system are to provide protection from external threats, establish stability based on laws, and govern the allocation of valued resources among the members of a society. A political system also defines how these groups interact with each other.

Each country's political system is unique, having evolved within a particular historical, economic, and cultural context. Political systems are also constantly evolving in response to constituent demands and the evolution of the national and international environment. *Constituents* are the people and organizations that support the political system and receive government resources.

Legal system
A system for interpreting and enforcing laws.

A **legal system** is a system for interpreting and enforcing laws. Laws, regulations, and rules establish norms for conduct. A legal system incorporates institutions and procedures for ensuring order and resolving disputes in commercial activities, as well as taxing economic output and protecting intellectual property and other company assets.

Exhibit 7.3 identifies the aspects of political and legal systems that contribute to country risk. Political and legal systems are dynamic and constantly changing. The two systems are interdependent—changes in one affect the other. Adverse developments in political and legal systems give rise to country risk. They can result from installation of a new government, shifting values or priorities in political parties, initiatives developed by special interest groups, and the creation of new laws or regulations. Gradual change is easier for the firm to accommodate, while sudden change is harder to deal with and poses greater risk to the firm.

EXHIBIT 7.3
Sources of Country Risk

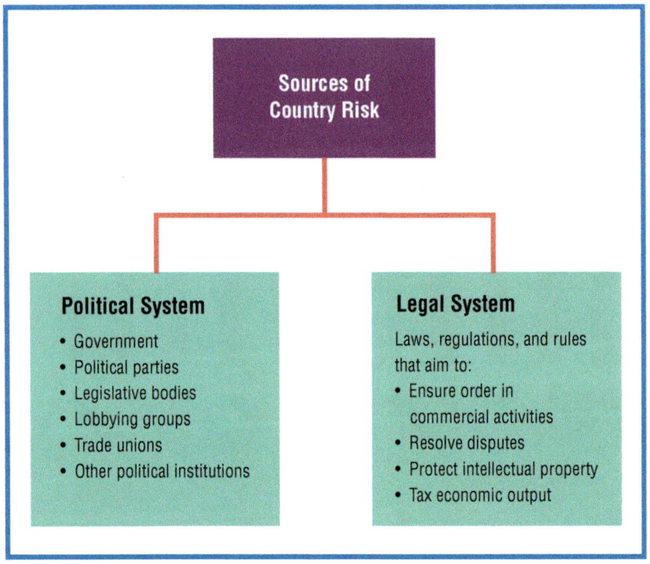

Unfavorable developments give rise to new conditions that may threaten the firm's products, services, or business activities. For example, a new import tariff may increase the cost of a key component used to manufacture a product. A modification in labor law may alter the hours the firm's employees are allowed to work. The installation of a new political leader may lead to government takeover of corporate assets.

Country risk is *always* present, but its nature and intensity vary over time and from country to country. In China, for example, the government is currently overhauling the national legal system, making it more consistent with Western systems. Some new regulations have been poorly formulated or are confusing or contradictory. For example, at one point, the Beijing government announced that foreign investments in China's Internet industry were illegal. By this time Western firms had already invested millions in the Chinese dot.com sector, without notice that the investments were inappropriate. In disputes between local and foreign firms, governments are often inclined to protect local interests. Even where Western firms obtain favorable judgments in the courts, they may not be enforced. Let's delve into political and legal systems in more detail.

Political Systems

The world is characterized by three major types of political systems: totalitarianism, socialism, and democracy. Exhibit 7.4 highlights countries that exemplify these systems. These categories are not mutually exclusive. Most democracies also include some elements of socialism. Most former totalitarian regimes now embrace a mix of socialism and democracy. To resolve the recent global financial crisis, governments in Europe and the United States implemented relatively socialistic policies, such as nationalizing firms in the banking and automotive industries. China applied some democratic approaches, such as land reforms and open markets, to stimulate commercial activity.

Totalitarianism

Well-known totalitarian states from the past include Nazi Germany (1933–1945), Spain (1939–1975), China (1949–1980s), and the Soviet Union (1918–1991). Under totalitarianism, the state attempts to regulate most aspects of public and private behavior. A totalitarian government seeks to control not only all economic and political matters but also the attitudes, values, and beliefs of the citizenry. Often, the entire population is mobilized in support of the state and a political or religious ideology. Totalitarian states are generally either theocratic (religion-based) or secular (non-religion-based). Usually there is a state party led by a dictator, such as Kim Jong-un in North Korea. Party membership is mandatory for those seeking to advance within the social and economic hierarchy. Power is maintained by means of secret police, propaganda disseminated through state-controlled mass media, regulation of free discussion and criticism, and the use of terror tactics. Totalitarian states usually do not tolerate activities by individuals or groups such as churches, labor unions, or political parties that are not directed toward the state's goals.[5]

Over time, many of the world's totalitarian states have either disappeared or evolved toward democracy and capitalism. China initiated major reforms in the 1980s, and the Soviet Union collapsed in 1991. Agricultural land and state enterprises were sold to private interests and entrepreneurs gained the right to establish their own businesses. The transition has

EXHIBIT 7.4

Examples of Countries under Various Political Systems

Elements of Totalitarianism Found in	Elements of Socialism Found in	Largely Democratic
Cuba	Bolivia	Australia
North Korea	China	Canada
Several countries in Africa (such as Eritrea, Sudan, Equatorial Guinea, Zimbabwe)	Egypt	Japan
	India	New Zealand
	Romania	United States
	Russia	Most European countries
	Venezuela	Most Latin American countries

not been easy, and former totalitarian states continue to maintain political control. Former Soviet Union states and China are still characterized by substantial red tape and bureaucracy that hinder economic activity (for examples, see the World Bank's www.doingbusiness.org). Today, numerous states exhibit elements of totalitarianism, particularly in Africa, Asia, and the Middle East. Several countries are controlled by individuals with substantial dictatorial powers.

Socialism

Socialism's fundamental tenet is that capital and wealth should be vested in the state and used primarily as a means of production rather than for profit. Socialism is based on a collectivist ideology in which the collective welfare of people is seen to outweigh the welfare of the individual. Socialists argue that capitalists receive a disproportionate amount of society's wealth relative to workers. They believe that in a capitalist society, the pay of workers does not represent the full value of their labor, and thus government should control the basic means of production, distribution, and commercial activity.

Socialism has manifested itself in much of the world as *social democracy* and has been most successful in Western Europe. It has also played a major role in the political systems of large countries such as Brazil and India, and today it remains a viable system in much of the world. In social democratic regimes, such as Italy and Norway, government frequently intervenes in the private sector and in business activities. Corporate income tax rates are often relatively high, as in France and Sweden. Even robust economies like Germany have experienced net outflows of FDI as businesses seek to escape extensive regulation.

Source: Dhoxax/Shutterstock

By protecting private property rights, democracies promote entrepreneurship. The proprietors of these shops in Denmark enjoy the profits of their ownership.

Democracy

Democracy is characterized by two major features:

- *Private property rights*, or the ability to own property and assets and to increase one's asset base by accumulating private wealth. Property includes tangibles, such as land and buildings, as well as intangibles, such as stocks, contracts, patent rights, and intellectual assets. Democratic governments devise laws that protect property rights. People and firms can acquire property, use it, buy or sell it, and bequeath it to whomever they want. These rights are important because they encourage individual initiative, ambition, and innovation, as well as thrift and the desire to accumulate wealth. People are less likely to have these qualities if there is uncertainty about whether they can control their property or profit from it.
- *Limited government*. The government performs only essential functions that serve all citizens, such as conducting national defense, maintaining law and order and diplomatic relations, and constructing and maintaining infrastructure such as roads, schools, and public works. State control and intervention in the economic activities of private individuals or firms is minimal. By allowing market forces to determine economic activity, the government ensures resources are allocated with maximal efficiency.[6]

Under democracy, the individual pursuits of people and firms are sometimes at odds with equality and justice. Because people have differing levels of personal and financial resources, each performs with varying degrees of success, leading to inequalities. Critics of pure democracy argue that when these inequalities become excessive, government should step in to correct them. Each society balances individual freedom with broader social goals. In democracies such as Japan and Sweden, the democracy's rights and freedoms are construed in larger societal terms rather than on behalf of individuals.

Most democracies include elements of socialism, such as government intervention in the affairs of individuals and firms. Socialism emerges because of abuses or negative externalities that occur in purely democratic or capitalistic systems. Japan has been striving to achieve the right balance between democracy and socialism. Poor management practices and an economic recession led to the bankruptcy of thousands of Japanese firms. To maintain jobs and economic stability, the Japanese government intervened to support numerous large firms and banks that, under pure capitalism, would have failed. But such policies have led to inflexibility in the Japanese economy and a delay of needed structural improvements.

Many countries, including Australia, Canada, the United States, and those in Europe, are best described as having a mixed political system—characterized by a strong private sector and a strong public sector, with considerable government regulation and control.

Democracy's Link to Economic Freedom and Openness

Compared to totalitarianism and socialism, democracy is associated with greater economic freedom and higher living standards. Economic freedom flourishes when governments support the institutions necessary for that freedom, such as freely operating markets and the rule of law.[7] Exhibit 7.5 reveals that the greater the political freedom in a nation, the more economic freedom its citizens enjoy. As countries develop economic ties with foreign trading partners and integrate themselves with the global economy, they tend to liberalize their markets and reduce restrictions on foreign business. This happened, for example, with the introduction of economic reforms and open markets in India in the 1990s.

Political freedom is characterized by free and fair elections; the right to form political parties; fair electoral laws; existence of a parliament or other legislative body; freedom from

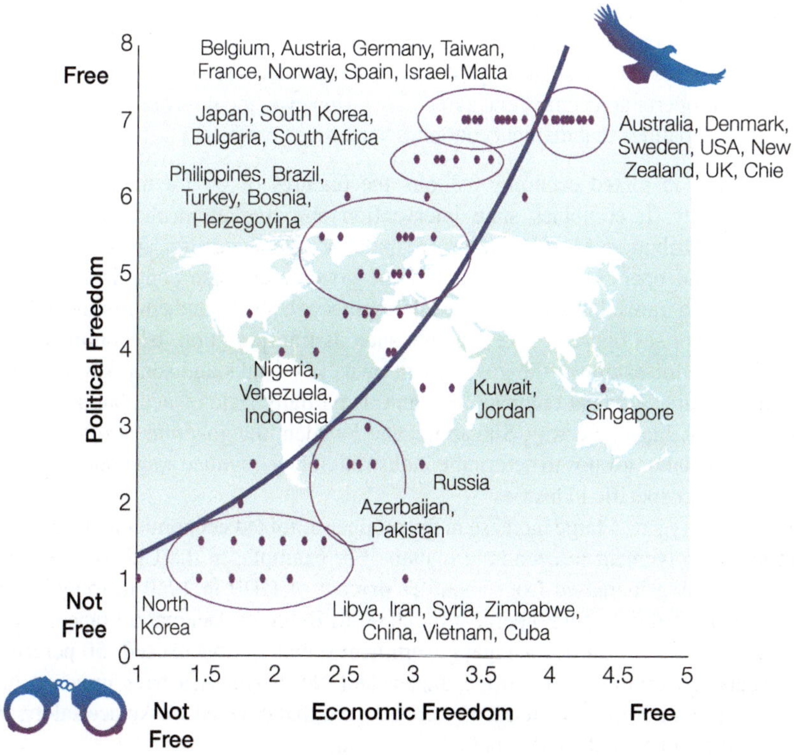

EXHIBIT 7.5

Relationship between Political Freedom and Economic Freedom for a Sample of Countries

Source: Based on data at Freedom House, 2012. Accessed at http://www.freedomhouse.org.

domination by the military, foreign powers, or religious hierarchies; and self-determination for cultural, ethnic, and religious minorities. Economic freedom is related to the extent of government interference in business, the strictness of the regulatory environment, and the ease with which commercial activity is carried out according to market forces. Visit Freedom House (www.freedomhouse.org) to view the latest information on political and economic freedom around the world.

Democracy is closely associated with *openness*, or lack of regulation or barriers to the entry of firms in foreign markets. The greater the openness, the fewer the constraints placed on foreign firms. Absence of excessive regulations also benefits buyers because openness increases the quantity and variety of products available. Competition pressures firms to continuously improve product quality. Increased efficiency and lower prices may follow. After India's government lowered entry barriers in the Indian automobile market, foreign automakers steadily entered the market. Their presence increased the number of models available for sale, raised the quality of available cars, and lowered prices. A similar phenomenon occurred in the mobile telephone market in China.[8]

The Relationship between Political Systems and Economic Systems

Each political system tends to be associated with a particular type of economic system. Generally speaking, totalitarianism is associated with command economies, democracy with market economies, and socialism with mixed economies. Let's review these economic systems.

COMMAND ECONOMY Also known as a centrally planned economy, a command economy makes the state a dominant force in the production and distribution of goods and services. Central planners make resource allocation decisions, and the state owns major sectors of the economy. In command economies, sizable bureaucracy thrives, and central planning tends to be less efficient than market forces in synchronizing supply and demand. For example, goods shortages were so common in the Soviet Union that people often waited in lines for hours to buy basic necessities like sugar and bread. Today, countries such as China and Russia still exhibit some characteristics of command economies. However, the system is gradually dying out in favor of market economies and mixed economies.

MARKET ECONOMY In a market economy, market forces—the interaction of supply and demand—determine prices. Government intervention in the marketplace is limited, and economic decisions are left to individuals and firms. Market economies are closely associated with capitalism, in which the means of production are privately owned and operated. Participants typically exhibit a market-oriented mentality and entrepreneurial spirit. The task of the state is to establish a legal system that protects private property and contractual agreements. However, the government may also intervene to address the inequalities that market economies sometimes produce.

MIXED ECONOMY A mixed economy exhibits the features of both a market economy and a command economy. It combines state intervention and market mechanisms for organizing production and distribution. Most industries are under private ownership, and entrepreneurs freely establish, own, and operate corporations. But the government also controls certain functions, such as pension programs, labor regulation, minimum wage levels, and environmental regulation. State-owned enterprises operate in key sectors such as transportation, telecommunications, and energy. In France, for example, the government owns key banks and some key industries, such as aluminum refining. One car company, Renault, is partially state owned, but another, Peugeot, is not. In Germany, Japan, Norway, Singapore, and Sweden, the government often works closely with business and labor groups to determine industrial policy, regulate wage rates, and/or provide subsidies to support specific industries.

The last century saw a large increase in the number of mixed economies and a concurrent rise in government involvement in economic matters. For example, in the United States, combined government spending increased from about 27 percent of GDP in 1960 to roughly 40 percent today, and is expected to attain 50 percent by 2038. In Belgium, Denmark, France, Sweden, and several other countries in Europe, annual government spending now exceeds 50 percent of GDP. In recent years, governments in Europe, Japan, and North America have imposed many new regulations on private firms.[9] Regulations were adopted that covered workplace safety, minimum wages, pension benefits, and environmental protection.

Country Realities

Home to a huge base of oil reserves, Libya is one of Africa's wealthiest countries. But Libya's economy is state-dominated, which hinders investment from abroad. Recent political unrest and civil war interrupted the country's huge oil output, which may remain volatile for some time. Fortunately, Libya has an educated workforce and little government debt. The country has much potential to prosper by leveraging the oil and tourism industries. Progress can come through wise public policies that foster investment and economic development.

Legal Systems

Legal systems provide a framework of rules and norms of conduct that mandate, limit, or permit specified relationships among people and organizations and provide punishments for those who violate these rules and norms. Laws require or limit specific actions while empowering citizens to engage in others, such as entering into contracts and seeking remedies for contract violations. Legal systems are dynamic—they evolve over time to represent each nation's changing social values and the evolution of their social, political, economic, and technological environments.

Prevailing political systems—totalitarianism, socialism, and democracy—tend to influence their respective legal systems. Democracies tend to encourage market forces and free trade. In countries with well-developed legal systems, such as Australia, Canada, Japan, the United States, and most European countries, laws are widely known and understood. They are effective and legitimate because they are applied to all citizens equally, issued by means of formal procedures by recognized government authorities, and enforced systematically and fairly by police forces and formally organized judicial bodies.

In these countries, a culture of law exists in which citizens consistently respect and follow the rule of law. **Rule of law** refers to a legal system in which rules are clear, publicly disclosed, fairly enforced, and widely respected by individuals, organizations, and the government. International business flourishes in societies where the rule of law prevails. In the United States, for example, the Securities and Exchange Act encourages confidence in business transactions by requiring public companies to frequently disclose their financial indicators to investors. Legal systems can be eroded by declining respect for the law, weak government authority, or burdensome restrictions that attempt to forbid behavior prevalent in the society. In the absence of the rule of law, firms must contend with great uncertainty and economic activity may be impeded.

Rule of law
A legal system in which rules are clear, publicly disclosed, fairly enforced, and widely respected by individuals, organizations, and the government.

Nations are primarily governed by one of four basic legal systems: common law, civil law, religious law, or mixed. These legal systems are the foundation for laws and regulations. Exhibit 7.6 provides examples of countries where these legal systems are dominant.

Common Law

Also known as case law, common law is a legal system that originated in England and spread to Australia, Canada, the United States, and former members of the British Commonwealth. The basis of common law is tradition, previous cases, and legal precedents set by the nation's courts through interpretation of statutes, legislation, and past rulings. The national legislature in common-law countries (such as Parliament in Britain and Congress in the United States) holds ultimate power to pass or amend laws. In the United States, because the constitution is difficult to amend, the Supreme Court and even lower courts have much flexibility to interpret the law. Because common law is more open to interpretation by courts, it is more flexible than other legal systems. Judges in a common-law system have substantial power to interpret laws based on the unique circumstances of individual cases, including commercial disputes and other business situations.

EXHIBIT 7.6
Dominant Legal Systems in Selected Countries

Source: Based on World Legal Systems at www.juriglobe.ca.

Primarily Common Law	*Primarily Civil Law*	*Primarily Religious Law*	*Mixed Systems*
Australia Canada Ireland New Zealand United Kingdom United States	Much of western Europe and Latin America Japan Russia South Korea	Much of the Middle East and North Africa Afghanistan Mauritania Pakistan Sudan	Bangladesh India Indonesia Israel Kenya Malaysia Philippines

Civil Law

Also known as code law, civil law is found in France, Germany, Italy, Japan, Turkey, and Latin America. Its origins go back to Roman law and the Napoleonic Code. Civil law is based on an all-inclusive system of laws that have been "codified"; the laws are clearly written and accessible. It is divided into three separate codes: commercial, civil, and criminal. Civil law is considered complete as a result of catchall provisions found within the law. Rules and principles form the starting point for legal reasoning and administering justice. The codified rules emerge as specific laws and codes of conduct produced by a legislative body or some other supreme authority.

Both common law and civil law systems originated in western Europe and represent the common values of western Europeans. A key difference between the two systems is that common law is primarily judicial in origin and based on court decisions, whereas civil law is primarily legislative in origin and based on laws passed by national and local legislatures. Differences in common and civil law give rise to differing business approaches in different countries. These are highlighted in Exhibit 7.7. In reality, common-law systems generally contain elements of civil law and vice versa. The two systems complement each other, and countries that employ one also tend to employ some elements of the other.

Religious Law

This legal system is strongly influenced by religious beliefs, ethical codes, and moral values viewed as mandated by a supreme being. The most important religious legal systems are based on Hindu, Jewish, and Islamic law. Among these, the most widespread is Islamic law, found mainly in the Middle East and North Africa. In addition to these areas, other countries with substantial populations of Muslims (followers of Islam) include India (about 175 million Muslims), Indonesia (205 million), Nigeria (75 million), and Pakistan (178 million). Islamic law, also known as the *shariah*, is based on the Qur'an, the holy book of Muslims, and the teachings of the Prophet Mohammed. Adherents generally do not differentiate between religious and secular life. Islamic law governs relationships among people, between people and the state, and between people and a supreme being. It spells out norms of behavior regarding politics, economics, banking, contracts, marriage, and many other social issues. Thus, Islamic law might be said to encompass all possible human relationships. Because it is seen as divinely ordained, it is relatively static and absolute. Unlike other legal systems, it evolves very little over time.

Most Muslim countries currently maintain a dual system, in which both religious and secular courts coexist. Other countries with large Muslim populations, such as Indonesia, Bangladesh, and Pakistan, have secular constitutions and laws. Turkey, another country with a majority Muslim population, has a strongly secular constitution. Saudi Arabia and Iran are unusual in that religious courts have authority over all aspects of jurisprudence.

EXHIBIT 7.7

Examples of Differences between Common Law and Civil Law

Legal Issues	*Civil Law*	*Common Law*
Ownership of intellectual property	Determined by registration.	Determined by prior use.
Enforcing agreements	Commercial agreements become enforceable only if properly notarized or registered.	Proof of agreement is sufficient for enforcing contracts.
Specificity of contracts	Contracts tend to be brief because many potential problems are already covered in the civil code.	Contracts tend to be very detailed, with all possible contingencies spelled out. Usually more costly to draft a contract.
Compliance with contracts	Noncompliance is extended to include unforeseeable human acts such as labor strikes and riots.	Acts of God (floods, lightning, hurricanes, etc.) are the only justifiable excuses for noncompliance with the provisions of contracts.

Modern liberal movements within Islam oppose traditional views of religious law. For example, strict interpretation of Islamic law prohibits the giving and receiving of interest on loans or investments. To comply with Islamic law, financial institutions employ a variant of international banking known as "Islamic finance," based on the principles of shariah law. Many Western banks—for example, JP Morgan and Deutsche Bank—have subsidiaries in Muslim countries that comply with shariah laws. Instead of requiring interest payments, they charge administrative fees or take equity positions in the projects they finance. Many issue *sukuks*, Islamic-compliant bonds that offer revenue from an asset, such as a rental property, rather than interest. The global market for shariah-compliant financial instruments now exceeds $1 trillion.[10]

Source: Mark Shenley/Alamy

Iranian women with Iran's flag attend a football match in Tehran after the Iranian government rescinded a quarter-century ban that had prohibited women from going to stadiums for sports events.

Mixed Systems

Mixed systems consist of two or more legal systems operating together. In most countries, legal systems evolve over time, adopting elements of one system or another that reflect their unique needs. The contrast between civil law and common law has become blurred as many countries combine them. For example, legal systems in South Africa and the Philippines mix elements of civil law and common law. Legal systems in Indonesia and most Middle Eastern countries share elements of civil law and Islamic law.

Historically, socialist law was a legal system found in the former Soviet Union, China, and a few states in Africa. It was based on civil law, with elements of socialist principles that emphasized state ownership of property. The rights of the state dominated those of the individual. When the Soviet Union collapsed and China began transitioning to capitalism, socialist law gave way to other legal systems, especially civil law.

Participants in Political and Legal Systems

Political and legal systems evolve from the interplay among various societal institutions, at both the national and international levels. Five types of participants are active in transforming political and legal systems.

Government

The government, or the public sector, is the most important participant, operating at national, state, and local levels. Governments have the power to enact and enforce laws. They strongly influence how firms enter host countries and how they conduct business there. Governments regulate international business activity through a complex system of institutions, agencies, and public officials. Agencies that possess such powers in the United States include the U.S. Trade Representative and the International Trade Administration (www.ita.doc.gov). In Canada, such functions are handled by the Ministry of Foreign Affairs (www.international.gc.ca), the Ministry of Finance, and the Export and Import Controls Bureau. Similar agencies operate in Australia, Britain, and virtually all other countries.

International Organizations

Supranational agencies such as the World Trade Organization (www.wto.org), the United Nations (www.un.org), and the World Bank (www.worldbank.org) strongly influence international business. For example, the United Nations Conference on Trade and Development (UNCTAD, www.unctad.org) helps oversee international trade and development in the areas of investment, finance, technology, and enterprise development. Such organizations facilitate free and fair trade by providing administrative guidance, governing frameworks, and, occasionally, financial support.

Regional Economic Blocs

Regional trade organizations, such as the European Union (EU), the North American Free Trade Agreement (NAFTA), and the Association of Southeast Asian Nations (ASEAN), aim to advance the economic and political interests of their members. The EU is especially well developed, with its own executive, legislative, and bureaucratic bodies. It enacts and enforces laws and regulations that directly affect business. For example, following new regulations forced by Lithuania's entry into the EU, the supermarket chain IKI had to spend millions to build separate entrances for fresh meat delivery in each of its 136 stores.[11]

Special Interest Groups

Special interest groups serve the interests of particular countries, industries, or causes. For example, the Organisation for Economic Co-operation and Development (OECD, www.oecd.org) supports the economic developmental and business goals of advanced economies. The Organization of Petroleum Exporting Countries (OPEC, www.opec.org) is a powerful cartel that controls global oil prices, which, in turn, affect consumer prices and everyone's cost of doing business. OPEC emerged as a powerful voice for oil-producing countries, including Saudi Arabia, Iran, Venezuela, Nigeria, and Indonesia. Other groups exercise similar control over the production and allocation of commodities such as sugar, coffee, and iron ore.

Special interest groups engage in political activity to advance specific causes, ranging from labor rights to environmental protection. They often influence national political processes and produce outcomes with far-reaching consequences for business. Many target particular industries and affect individual firms accordingly. Special interest groups operate not only in host countries but also in the home country. For example, well-orchestrated U.S. interest groups forced U.S.-owned firms to reduce their investments in South Africa when its apartheid policies were in force.[12] Greenpeace, Friends of the Earth, and other environmentalist groups opposed construction of the Keystone pipeline system, intended to transport synthetic crude oil from Canada to the United States. Protesters argued the pipeline would produce oil spills, polluting ground water and killing wildlife. Environmentalist groups were instrumental in halting construction of the pipeline in 2012.[13] Greenpeace also has been successful in pressuring appliance manufacturers to produce environmentally friendly refrigerators in Germany and the United States.[14] Exhibit 7.8 provides a sample of interest groups and their likely stance toward various business issues.

Competing Firms

Rival domestic firms with a strong presence in the host country naturally have an interest in opposing the entry of foreign firms into the local market and may lobby their government for protection. For example, host-country competitors often complain when foreign firms receive financial support from the parent or host-country governments. Asterix, a French theme park, opposed French government support for the U.S.-based Disney when the latter established Disneyland Paris. Similarly, U.S. automakers in Detroit opposed BMW's construction of a factory in South Carolina. However, the state government of South Carolina supported the BMW facility on the grounds that it would generate jobs and increase tax revenues.

EXHIBIT 7.8 Issues of Concern to Special Interest Groups

Group	Typical Issue	Example
Labor unions	Oppose imported goods and global sourcing	U.S. united steelworkers union opposed imports of steel from China
Competing businesses	Dislike competition from foreign firms	Japanese rice producers opposed imports of rice from the United States
Customers	May avoid foreign-made products. Dislike improper marketing practices.	Motorists in Australia accused BP of unfair pricing of petroleum products
Conservationists	Fight against wildlife loss and destruction of the natural environment	Environmentalists oppose lumber imports from countries with tropical rain forests

Types of Country Risk Produced by Political Systems

How do political systems create challenges for firms engaged in international business? Let's examine the specific risks produced by political systems.

Government Takeover of Corporate Assets

Governments occasionally seize the assets of corporations. The industry sectors most often targeted by government seizure are natural resources (for example, mining and petroleum), utilities, and manufacturing. Fortunately, aggressive seizure is less common these days as governments in many developing countries have adopted institutional reforms that aim to attract FDI from abroad and foster economic growth.

Government seizure takes on various forms:

- *Confiscation* is the seizure of corporate assets without compensation. Beginning in the 1980s, for example, Zimbabwe's dictator Robert Mugabe systematically seized more than 5,000 farms owned by farmers of mostly European descent, and redistributed the land to native Zimbabweans. Recently, Mugabe announced plans to confiscate mines owned by foreign mining companies.[15]
- *Expropriation* is seizure with compensation. In Venezuela, ExxonMobil and ConocoPhillips were forced to abandon multi-billion-dollar investments in the local oil industry. Recently, Venezuela President Hugo Chavez ordered troops to seize two plants owned by Mexico's Cemex, the country's largest cement producer. In 2008, gradual yet persistent pressure from the Russian government led TNK-BP, a Russian subsidiary of British energy giant BP, to sell a major stake in its oil business to the national gas monopoly Gazprom.[16]
- *Nationalization* describes government seizure of an entire industry, with or without compensation. For example, the government of Bolivia nationalized much of the oil and gas industry in that country. In 2008, President Hugo Chavez nationalized the cement industry in Venezuela.[17] Nationalization occurs in advanced economies as well. Following the global financial crisis, the federal government of Iceland nationalized most of the country's banking industry.[18]

"Creeping expropriation" is a subtle form of country risk in which governments modify laws and regulations after foreign MNEs have made substantial local investments in property and plants.[19] Examples include abrupt termination of contracts and the creation of new laws that favor local firms. As reported in the opening story, corporate raiders and government officials in Russia occasionally raid the offices of competitors and subject them to questionable criminal investigations. Such tactics occasionally force foreign MNEs to cede control of their operations to local interests.[20] Governments in Bolivia, Kazakhstan, Russia, and Venezuela have modified tax regimes to extract revenues from foreign coal, oil, and gas companies. Troops stormed the Kazakhstan offices of U.S. mining company AES to enforce an alleged tax fine amounting to some $200 million. One of the country's largest providers of electricity, AES reduced its operations in Kazakhstan in the wake of persistent abuse by the Kazakh government.[21] Subtle or devious approaches to government takeover make country risk harder to predict.

Embargoes and Sanctions

Most countries are signatories to international treaties and agreements that specify rules, principles, and standards of behavior in international business. Nevertheless, governments may unilaterally resort to sanctions and embargoes to respond to offensive activities of foreign countries. A *sanction* is a type of trade penalty imposed on one or more countries by one or more other countries. Sanctions typically take the form of tariffs, trade barriers, import duties, and import or export quotas. They generally arise in the context of an unresolved trade or policy dispute, such as a disagreement about the fairness of some international trade practice. There is

Source: javarman/Shutterstock

Exports of natural gas and other commodities were threatened in the wake of revolution in Egypt in 2011. Shown here is the harbor at Alexandria, Egypt's chief port.

much evidence suggesting that sanctions often do not achieve desired outcomes. For example, the United States has imposed trade sanctions on Iran and Syria. However, goods continue to flow in and out of both countries from China, Germany, Japan, and numerous other trading partners.[22]

An *embargo* is an official ban on exports to or imports from a particular country, in order to isolate it and punish its government. It is generally more serious than a sanction and is used as a political punishment for some disapproved policies or acts. For example, the United States has enforced embargoes against Iran and North Korea, at times labeled as state sponsors of terrorism. The European Union has enacted embargoes against Belarus, Sudan, and China in certain areas, such as foreign travel, to protest human rights and weapon-trading violations.

Boycotts against Firms or Nations

Consumers and special interest groups occasionally target particular firms perceived to have harmed local interests. Consumers may refuse to patronize firms that behave inappropriately. A *boycott* is a voluntary refusal to engage in commercial dealings with a nation or a company. Boycotts and public protests result in lost sales and increased costs (for public relations activities needed to restore the firm's image). Disneyland Paris and McDonald's have been the targets of boycotts by French farmers, who believe these firms represent U.S. agricultural policies and globalization, which many French citizens despise. Activists in numerous countries organized a boycott of petroleum company BP following its oil spill in the Gulf of Mexico in 2010.[23]

Terrorism

Terrorism is the threat or actual use of force or violence to attain a political goal through fear, coercion, or intimidation.[24] It is sometimes sponsored by national governments. Terrorism has escalated in much of the world, as exemplified by the September 11, 2001, attacks in the United States and the 2011 terrorist bombing of Moscow's Domodedovo Airport. In India, more than 30,000 people have died in terrorist attacks since 1993.[25] In addition to causing loss of life, terrorism can severely damage commercial infrastructure and disrupt business activities. It induces fear in consumers, who reduce their purchasing, potentially leading to economic recession. The hospitality, aviation, entertainment, and retailing industries can be particularly affected. Terrorism also affects financial markets. In the days following the 9/11 attacks, the value of the U.S. stock market dropped some 14 percent.[26]

War, Insurrection, and Violence

War, insurrection, and other forms of violence pose significant problems for business operations. While such events usually do not affect companies directly, their indirect effects can be disastrous. Violent conflict among drug cartels and security services along the U.S.-Mexico border has led some firms and financiers to withdraw investments from Mexico because of perceived heightened risks and political instability. In India, Tata Motors (www.tatamotors.com) shifted the location of a major new factory due to violent protests by local farmers who feared the loss of their livelihood.[27] To minimize losses from violent acts, firms can purchase risk insurance.

Example: Country Risk in the Middle East

Arab countries of the Middle East experience various risks, which can hinder entrepreneurial activity and inward investment. In 2011 and 2012, Egypt, Libya, Syria, and other Arab states were affected by citizen revolts protesting authoritarian regimes and political corruption.[28]

The 2011 uprising in Egypt overthrew the country's long-standing ruler. The rebellion halted industrial production, closed banks, and triggered capital flight. Tourism, a key source of revenue for Egypt, declined by one-third. Consumer and investor confidence fell and affected the value-chain activities of countless firms.[29] Many worried the crisis would disrupt cargo transportation through the Suez Canal, a key world shipping route.[30] A sharp decline in Egypt's currency added to the nation's already substantial price inflation.[31]

A survey of business leaders by the World Economic Forum ranked Middle Eastern countries on factors that hinder business. In the Middle East, the survey found that restrictive labor regulations and poorly educated workers hinder labor-intensive ventures, such as factories. Bureaucracy and corruption deter launching new firms and running existing ones. By contrast, crime and theft are relatively minor concerns in the Middle East. The World Economic Forum advocates policies in the region that spur job creation via private sector development of high value-adding businesses.[32]

Types of Country Risk Produced by Legal Systems

In addition to political concerns, country risk also arises due to peculiarities of national legal systems. Especially relevant to international business are *commercial law*, which specifically covers business transactions, and *private law*, which regulates relationships between persons and organizations, including contracts, and liabilities that may arise due to negligent behavior. In many countries, the legal system favors home-country nationals. Laws are designed to promote the interests of local businesses and the local economy.

Legal systems in both the host country and the home country pose various challenges to firms, which we review next.

Country Risk Arising from the Host-Country Legal Environment

Governments in host countries impose various laws and regulations on foreign companies doing business there.

FOREIGN INVESTMENT LAWS These laws affect the type of entry strategy firms choose, as well as their operations and performance. Many nations impose restrictions on inward FDI. For example, Japan's *daitenhoo* (large retail store law) restricted foreigners from opening warehouse-style stores such as Walmart or Toys "R" Us. The law protected smaller shops by requiring large-scale retailers to obtain the approval of local retailers, a painstaking and time-consuming process. In Malaysia, firms seeking to invest in local businesses must obtain permission from the Malaysian Industrial Development Authority. The United States restricts foreign investments that might affect national security. Proposed investments can be reviewed by the U.S. Committee on Investments. In 2006, the U.S. Congress opposed a management contract that would have granted control of several U.S. ports to Dubai Ports World, a firm based in the United Arab Emirates. Under opposition from the U.S. public and Congress, the firm abandoned its investment plans.

Source: Peter Wilson © Dorling Kindersley

In Japan, foreign-owned large stores such as Carrefour and Walmart have faced restrictive laws designed to protect local retailers.

CONTROLS ON OPERATING FORMS AND PRACTICES Governments impose laws and regulations on how firms can conduct production, marketing, and distribution activities within their borders. Such restrictions can hinder company performance abroad. For example, host countries may require companies to obtain permits to import or export. They may devise complex regulations that complicate transportation and logistical activities or limit the options for entry strategies. In China's huge telecommunications market, the government requires foreign investors to seek joint ventures with local firms; local operations cannot be wholly owned by foreigners. The government's goal is to ensure that China maintains control of its telecommunications industry and obtains inward transfer of technology, knowledge, and capital.[33]

MARKETING AND DISTRIBUTION LAWS These laws determine which practices are allowed in advertising, promotion, and distribution. For example, Finland, France, and Norway prohibit cigarette advertising on television. Germany largely prohibits comparative advertising, in which a product is promoted as superior to a competing brand. Many countries cap the prices of critical goods and services, such as food and health care. Such constraints affect firms' marketing and profitability. Product safety and liability laws hold manufacturers and sellers responsible for damage, injury, or death caused by defective products. In the case of violations, firms and company executives are subject to legal penalties such as fines or imprisonment, as well as civil lawsuits. Product liability laws in developing countries are generally weak. Some firms take advantage of these weaknesses. For example, as litigants pursued tobacco companies in Europe and the United States, these companies shifted much of their marketing of cigarettes to developing countries.

LAWS ON INCOME REPATRIATION MNEs earn profits in various countries and typically seek ways to transfer these funds back to their home country. However, in some countries, governments devise laws that restrict such transfers. The action is often taken to preserve hard currencies, such as euros, U.S. dollars, or Japanese yen. Repatriation restrictions limit the amount of net income or dividends that firms can remit to their home-country headquarters. While such constraints often discourage inward FDI, they are common in countries experiencing a shortage of hard currencies.

ENVIRONMENTAL LAWS Governments enact laws to preserve natural resources; to combat pollution and the abuse of air, earth, and water resources; and to ensure health and safety. In Germany, for example, companies must follow strict recycling regulations. Manufacturers and distributors bear the burden of recycling product packaging. Governments usually try to balance environmental laws against the impact such regulations may have on employment, entrepreneurship, and economic development. For example, environmental standards in Mexico are looser or less well enforced than in some other countries, but the Mexican government is reluctant to strengthen them for fear that foreign MNEs may reduce their investments there.

CONTRACT LAWS International contracts attach rights, duties, and obligations to the contracting parties. Contracts are used in five main types of business transactions: (1) sale of goods or services, especially large sales; (2) distribution of the firm's products through foreign distributors; (3) licensing and franchising—that is, a contractual relationship that allows a firm to use another company's intellectual property, marketing tools, or other assets for a fee; (4) FDI, especially in collaboration with a foreign entity, in order to create and operate a foreign subsidiary; and (5) joint ventures and other types of cross-border collaborations.

Numerous countries are attempting to develop an international standard for international sales contracts. The United Nations Convention on Contracts for the International Sale of Goods (CISG) is a uniform text of law for international sales contracts. More than 75 countries are now party to the CISG, covering about three-quarters of all world trade. Unless excluded by the express terms of a contract, the CISG is deemed to supersede any otherwise applicable domestic law(s) regarding an international sales transaction.

INTERNET AND E-COMMERCE REGULATIONS Internet and e-commerce regulations are the new frontier in legal systems. As highlighted in the *Global Trend*, these laws are still evolving. Firms that undertake e-commerce in countries with weak laws face considerable risk. In China, for example, the government has developed legislation to ensure security and privacy due to the rapid spread of the Internet and e-commerce. Many consumer-privacy laws have yet to be enacted, and progress has been delayed on the development of methods to protect private data from criminal or competitive eyes. Protections for online contracting methods have been implemented with the recent adoption of e-signature laws. Emergent e-signature laws offer protections for online contracting.

INADEQUATE OR UNDERDEVELOPED LEGAL SYSTEMS Just as laws and regulations can lead to country risk, an underdeveloped regulatory environment or poor enforcement of existing laws can also pose challenges for the firm. Worldwide, safeguards for intellectual property are often inadequate. Regulations to protect intellectual property may exist on paper but not be adequately enforced. When an innovator invents a new product, develops new computer software, or produces some other type of intellectual property, another party may copy and sell the innovation without paying the inventor. As reported in the opening story, Russia's legal framework is relatively weak and inconsistent. Russian courts lack substantial experience ruling on business matters. Due to the unpredictable and potentially harmful legal environment, Western firms frequently abandon joint ventures and other business initiatives in Russia.[34]

Source: Demetrio Carrasco © Dorling Kindersley

Governments around the world are contemplating ways to tax and regulate e-commerce and the Internet. Pictured is an Internet café in Budapest, Hungary.

Inadequate legal protection is most common in developing economies, but can be a factor in developed economies as well. The most recent global financial crisis was precipitated, in part, by insufficient regulation in the financial and banking sectors of the United States, Europe, and other regions. Government authorities have been considering how regulatory structures can be revamped to provide a sounder footing for connecting global savers and investors, as well as reliable methods for managing financial instability. Governments seek to expand regulation, provide new means to increase transparency and information flows, and find ways to harmonize regulatory policies and legal frameworks across national borders. Banks and other financial institutions are revising disclosure rules to make information more specific and consistent. Some experts believe the financial crisis does not imply that more regulation is needed. Rather, they argue for more intelligent regulation, better enforcement of existing regulation, and better supervision of financial institutions.[35]

Country Risk Arising from the Home-Country Legal Environment

Does country risk arise only due to the host country's legal environment? Home-country legal systems are just as relevant. **Extraterritoriality** refers to the application of home-country laws to persons or conduct outside national borders. In most cases, such laws are intended to prosecute individuals or firms located abroad for some type of wrongdoing.

Extraterritoriality
Application of home-country laws to persons or conduct outside national borders.

Examples of extraterritoriality in international business abound. A French court ordered Yahoo! to bar access to Nazi-related items on its Web site in France and to remove related messages and images from its sites accessible in the United States.[36] In 2001, the United States enacted the Patriot Act, authorizing the U.S. government to seize funds held by non-U.S. banks in the United States. The European Union pursued the U.S. firm Microsoft for perceived monopolistic practices in the marketing of its operating system software. Monopolies are considered harmful because they can unfairly restrain trade. Businesses generally oppose extraterritoriality because it tends to increase the costs and uncertainty of operating abroad.

THE FOREIGN CORRUPT PRACTICES ACT (FCPA) Passed by the U.S. government in 1977, the Foreign Corrupt Practices Act (FCPA) banned firms from offering bribes to foreign parties in order to secure or retain business. The FCPA was enacted after more than 400 U.S. companies admitted paying bribes to foreign government officials and politicians. The Act was strengthened in 1998 to cover foreign firms and managers who act in furtherance of corrupt payments while in the United States. The FCPA also requires companies with securities listed in the United States to meet U.S. accounting provisions. Such firms must devise and maintain accounting systems that control and record all company expenditures.[37] One problem with the FCPA is that a "bribe" is not clearly defined. For example, the Act draws a distinction between bribery and "facilitation" payments; the latter may be permissible if making such payments does not violate local laws.[38]

Some U.S. managers argue the FCPA harms their interests because foreign competitors often are not constrained by such laws. FCPA criminal and civil penalties are increasingly harsh. Firms can be fined up to $2 million, while individuals can be fined up to $100,000 and face imprisonment. Recently, the U.S. Justice Department stepped up FCPA prosecutions against smaller companies and non-U.S. firms that do business in the United States. In 2010, the United States settled allegations against Panalpina, a Switzerland-based logistics company, regarding claims it had violated the FCPA in Nigeria to secure energy contracts.[39]

ANTIBOYCOTT REGULATIONS Such rules prevent companies from participating in restrictive trade practices or boycotts imposed by foreign countries against other countries. Firms are not allowed to participate in boycotts to the extent they discriminate against others on the basis of race, religion, gender, or national origin. For example, some Arab nations have long boycotted Israel because of political disagreements and made it a requirement for any foreign company that wishes to do business with the Arab countries to also observe this boycott. The antiboycott regulations passed by the U.S. Congress in 1977 effectively prohibit U.S. firms from participating in the boycott of Israel when operating in these Arab nations.

ACCOUNTING AND REPORTING LAWS Accounting practices and standards differ greatly around the world, posing difficulties for firms. For example, when assigning value to stocks and other securities, most countries use the lower of cost or market value. Brazil, however, encourages firms to adjust portfolio valuations because of historically high inflation. When valuing physical assets such as plant and equipment, Canada uses historical costs. Some Latin American countries use inflation-adjusted market value. While firms can write off uncollectible accounts in the United States, the allowance is not permitted in France, Spain, and South Africa. Research and development costs are expensed as incurred in most of the world but capitalized in South Korea and Spain. Belgium, Malaysia, and Italy use both conventions.

Transparency
The degree to which companies regularly reveal substantial information about their financial condition and accounting practices.

TRANSPARENCY IN FINANCIAL REPORTING The timing and transparency of financial reporting vary widely around the world. **Transparency** is the degree to which firms regularly reveal substantial information about their financial condition and accounting practices. In the United States, public firms are required to report financial results to stockholders and to the Securities and Exchange Commission each quarter. In much of the world, however, financial statements are prepared annually or less often, and they often lack transparency. Transparency improves business decision making and the ability of citizens to hold companies accountable.

GLOBAL TREND

Evolving Legal Aspects of E-Commerce

While still a fraction of world trade, international e-commerce is growing fast. E-commerce reduces traditional barriers of distance from markets.

However, most countries lack adequate legal protections, leaving e-commerce fraught with thorny issues. For example, individuals or firms that place information, photographs, or music online may be violating the intellectual property laws of some countries but not others. Although electronic contracts are in digital format, existing contract law typically covers only paper documents. Consumers who use the Internet to make purchases with credit cards may risk identity theft and fraud.

Taxation of international e-commerce is complex because of the difficulty of defining merchandise sold online. Do software, books, and music constitute products—or services? For tax purposes, the two categories are usually treated differently. E-commerce can also circumvent tariffs and other trade barriers. Most e-commerce is free of customs duties because it is too difficult to apply them. A related problem is identifying the location of a sale. When a customer in Japan buys software from Microsoft's Web site, which is based in the United States, does the sale originate in Japan or the United States? Such questions affect not only taxation but also legal jurisdiction in the event of disputes between buyers and sellers.

E-commerce laws are evolving differently in different countries and represent the distinct values, culture, and approaches of each locale. The resulting inconsistency can create conflicts between national jurisdictions. When creating e-commerce law, some governments favor strong control and regulation. Others opt for a liberal, hands-off approach. The European Union aims to accelerate integration of the EU single market through increased e-commerce in Europe, to create a "single digital market."

Strong legal frameworks are needed to ensure trust between buyers and sellers. Experts argue that evolving regulatory frameworks should be governed by consistent principles that lead to predictable results, regardless of where buyers and sellers reside. Law enforcement authorities need to cooperate cross-nationally to reduce online crime. Governments must devise frameworks that ensure the security of electronic payment systems and the privacy of online data but are not so restrictive as to hinder the promise of international e-commerce.

Several international organizations are driving efforts to devise internationally appropriate laws. For example, the *United Nations Commission on International Trade Law (UNCITRAL)* developed the Model Law on Electronic Commerce to ensure that online transactions and legal documents are legally recognized and that a course of action is available to enforce them. The UNCITRAL model is only a guide, and national governments are not bound by it.

Sources: C. Primo Braga, "E-Commerce Regulation: New Game, New Rules?," *Quarterly Review of Economics and Finance* 45, no. 2/3 (2005): 541–558; *Economist*, "The Coming Retail Boom," February 4, 2012, p. 72; George Takach, "E-Procurement E-Performance," *Summit*, May/June 2008, pp. 16–17; UNCITRAL Model Law on Electronic Commerce Guide to Enactment, retrieved from United Nations Web site at http://www.un.org; Ling Zhu and Sherry Thatcher, "National Information Ecology: A New Institutional Economics Perspective on Global E-Commerce Adoption," *Journal of Electronic Commerce Research* 11, no. 1 (2010): 53–72.

In 2010, the U.S. Congress passed the Dodd–Frank Wall Street Reform and Consumer Protection Act, which aims to increase transparency in the United States financial sector. Passed in response to the late-2000s recession, the Act created an oversight board that monitors banking activities. It aims to reduce financial risk-taking by restricting certain banking activities and requiring bank executives to be responsible for compliance. Running to more than 2,000 pages of new regulations, banks have condemned the Act for imposing too many regulatory costs. U.S. affiliates of foreign multinational banks must comply with the Act's provisions. In an effort to avoid rigid financial requirements, some European banks are reducing their banking activities in the United States. In 2011, the European Union introduced the Basel III global regulatory standard, which aims to increase the quality and transparency of the capital base of European banks. U.S. banks will be required to comply with the new Basel III rules.[40]

Ethical Connections

Many countries lack antibribery laws for international transactions. The *Organisation for Economic Cooperation and Development* recently called for a ban on "grease payments," small-scale bribes intended to speed up telephone hookups, government paperwork, and other everyday matters in international commerce. A culture of grease payments and other corruption is corrosive, harming the rule of law and sustainable economic development.

Managing Country Risk

How should managers respond to country risk? In the discussion that follows, we highlight several specific strategies managers can employ to manage country risk.

Proactive Environmental Scanning

Anticipating country risk requires advance research. Initially, managers develop a comprehensive understanding of the political and legal environment in target countries. They then engage in *scanning* to assess potential risks and threats to the firm. Scanning allows the firm to improve practices in ways that conform with local laws and political realities and to create a positive environment for business success.[41]

One of the best sources of intelligence in the scanning process is employees working in the host country. They are knowledgeable about evolving events and can evaluate them in the context of local history, culture, and politics. Embassy and trade association officials regularly develop and analyze intelligence on the local political scene. Some consulting firms, such as PRS Group (www.prsgroup.com) and Business Entrepreneurial Risk Intelligence (www.beri.com), specialize in country-risk assessment and provide guidelines for appropriate strategic responses. Once the firm has researched the political climate and contingencies of the target environment, it develops and implements strategies to facilitate effective management of relations with policymakers and other helpful contacts in the host country. The firm then takes steps to minimize its exposure to country risks that threaten its performance.

Strict Adherence to Ethical Standards

Ethical behavior is important not only for its own sake but also because it helps insulate the firm from some country risks that less-conscientious firms encounter. Those companies that engage in questionable practices or operate outside the law naturally invite redress from the governments of the host countries where they do business.

Alliances with Qualified Local Partners

A practical approach to reducing country risk is to enter target markets in collaboration with a knowledgeable and reliable local partner. Qualified local partners are better informed about local conditions and better situated to establish stable relations with the local government. Western firms often enter China and Russia by partnering with local firms that assist in navigating complex legal and political landscapes.

Protection through Legal Contracts

A legal contract spells out the rights and obligations of each party. Contract law varies widely from country to country, and firms must adhere to local standards. For example, a Canadian firm doing business in Belgium generally must comply with the laws of both Belgium and Canada, as well as with the evolving laws of the European Union.

Firms generally employ any of three approaches for resolving international disputes:

1. *Conciliation* is the least adversarial method. It is a formal process of negotiation with the objective to resolve differences in a friendly manner. The parties in a dispute employ a conciliator, who meets separately with each in an attempt to resolve their differences. Parties can also employ mediation committees—groups of informed citizens—to resolve civil disputes.
2. *Arbitration* is a process in which a neutral third party hears both sides of a case and decides in favor of one party or the other, based on an objective assessment of the facts. Compared to litigation, arbitration saves time and expense, while maintaining the confidentiality of proceedings. Arbitration is often handled by supranational organizations, such as the International Chamber of Commerce in Paris or the Stockholm Chamber of Commerce.
3. *Litigation* is the most adversarial approach and occurs when one party files a lawsuit against another in order to achieve desired ends. Litigation is most common in the United States; most other countries favor arbitration or conciliation.

CLOSING CASE Political, Legal, and Ethical Dilemmas in the Global Pharmaceutical Industry

The $900 billion global pharmaceutical industry is dominated by about ten firms; five are headquartered in the United States, two in the United Kingdom, two in Switzerland, and one in Israel. Examples include GlaxoSmithKline (United Kingdom, www.gsk.com), Novartis AG (Switzerland, www.novartis.com), Teva (Israel, www.tevapharm.com), Merck (United States, www.merck.com), and Pfizer (United States, www.pfizer.com). Europe and the United States account for roughly 25 percent and 50 percent of worldwide pharmaceutical sales, respectively. The industry is confronted with several challenges.

High Cost of Research and Development

Pharmaceutical firms engage in large-scale, intensive R&D to create and market drugs meant to treat everything from cancer to hair loss. Thousands of pharmaceutical drugs allow people to live longer and healthier lives. Europe and the United States are home to the major pharmaceutical firms and to industry R&D. They benefit from strong patent protection laws and abundant investment capital. According to industry statistics, it takes 12 to 15 years, and more than $800 million in R&D expense, to successfully bring a new pharmaceutical compound to market. Only 1 in 10,000 investigated and tested compounds is approved for patient use. Only three out of every ten new, approved compounds are successful enough to recover their R&D costs. For their successful products, pharmaceutical firms must charge prices high enough to recover not only the high costs of product development, but also to recover the cost of products that never achieve profitability.

Limited Protection for Intellectual Property

Governments grant patents and provide other types of protections for intellectual property. In practice, such protection is frequently inadequate, especially in developing countries. India has a history of weak intellectual property protection, which has discouraged R&D and innovation. It is one of the world's poorest countries, and very few of its citizens can afford health care or medications. In 1972, a major revision to the Indian Patent Act revoked all patents for medicines. Following this dramatic shift, foreign-branded pharmaceutical manufacturers abandoned India, and numerous pharmaceutical "chop shops" emerged. The new firms freely infringed on drug patents and engaged in a selling "free-for-all" in the huge Indian pharmaceutical market. They reverse-engineered patented compounds developed by European and U.S. companies and began selling the pirated generics at drastically lower prices. The foreign pharmaceuticals launched legal actions against these violations but, in the absence of strict patent protection and with little local competition, India's generic drug manufacturers flourished.

The Challenge from Generic Brands

Under World Trade Organization (WTO) rules, a patent protects a drug inventor from competition for up to 20 years. In reality, when the lengthy testing and approval phase is factored in, the effective life of a drug patent is often less than 12 years. The manufacturer typically has only 5 to 8 years of patent protection in which to recover its investment before generic manufacturers can legally enter the market. Once a patent expires, generic manufacturers have the right to produce medications originally invented by major pharmaceuticals. Generic manufacturers typically sell the medications that they produce at very low prices. Patent protections are important because they encourage innovation by allowing inventors a limited opportunity to recover their R&D investments. However, patent protection laws governing pharmaceuticals differ substantially around the world.

A *branded compound* is produced under patent protection by a pharmaceutical manufacturer that has undertaken expensive R&D to invent the drug. Each year, pharmaceutical firms typically invest some 20 percent of revenues into R&D to invent new compounds. "Approved generic compounds," manufactured in countries with strict bio-equivalency regulations, are comparable to branded compounds in safety, efficacy, and intended use. The main reason that generic manufacturers can charge lower prices is that they do not incur the high costs of R&D to develop new drugs. Because the medications are already established in the marketplace, generic manufacturers also incur substantially lower marketing and sales expenses.

In the world of generic drugs, Israel-based Teva is the largest manufacturer with global sales of more than $16 billion. Teva and other generic producers have greatly increased their world market share in recent years due to the patent expiration of leading medications and rising demand for medications in developing economies and countries with weak patent protection. In the United States alone, generic medications now account for over half of all dispensed prescriptions. Once a branded compound's patent expires, generic manufacturers, after receiving government approval, begin producing generic versions almost immediately. Retail prices for the compound can fall by as much as 90 percent within 12 to 18 months.

Counterfeit Drugs

Many governments fail to ensure the quality of imported medicines. As a result, a growing industry of counterfeit and bio-inequivalent medications has emerged worldwide. A counterfeit ring from China supplied 1 million fake OneTouch Test Strips (used to treat diabetes) to hundreds of pharmacies in Canada, India, the United States, and numerous other countries. A healthy 22-year-old woman in Argentina died from liver failure after receiving iron injections to treat mild anemia. The medicine she received was a highly toxic counterfeit. In Niger, some 2,500 people died after receiving fake vaccines for meningitis. Recently, European Union officials seized more than 35 million fake pills at ports around Europe, including drugs intended to treat malaria, cancer, cholesterol, and pain.

The United Nations estimates that sales of counterfeit pharmaceuticals exceeds $500 billion annually. Counterfeiting is greatest in countries where regulatory oversight is weakest. The WHO estimates that up to 30 percent of medicines sold in developing countries may be counterfeit. It is estimated that between 200,000 and 300,000 people die each year in China due to counterfeit or substandard medicine.

Internet-based pharmacies are especially dubious. A woman in Canada died of metal poisoning after taking a tainted prescription medicine obtained from an Internet pharmacy. MarkMonitor, an industry watchdog, found that only a fraction of several thousand online pharmacies it examined were legitimate. Many of the pharmacies claiming to be based in Canada and the United States were in fact traced to China, Russia, and India. It is estimated that over 50 percent of medicines sold through the Internet are fake—often containing no or too little of the active ingredient.

Because of the threats posed by counterfeit manufacturers, branded pharmaceutical firms spend significant resources to protect their patents and intellectual property around the world. Branded pharmaceutical manufacturers have pursued legal actions at the WTO and against individual nations. In 1995, the WTO's agreement on Trade-Related Aspects of Intellectual Property Rights (TRIPS) was approved by approximately 150 WTO member countries.

Neglected Therapeutic Areas

A large portion of pharmaceutical research is focused on developing treatments for diseases that can return the cost of capital and generate profits. For these reasons, pharmaceutical firms tend to target the most attractive markets. For example, these firms are much more likely to develop a drug for cancer and central nervous system diseases (such as psychiatric ailments) than for ailments common to poor countries (such as tuberculosis). Some in the pharmaceutical industry believe that R&D is too costly and risky to invest in diseases common to poor countries.

At the same time, governmental and private initiatives have begun to address these market realities by providing incentive packages and public-private partnerships. For example, the Bill and Melinda Gates Foundation (www.gatesfoundation.org) is investing billions of dollars to fight AIDS, tuberculosis, and various infectious diseases that affect developing countries.

Public Scrutiny

The pharmaceutical industry's actions are often subject to public scrutiny. For example, the government of South Africa got into a tussle with several manufacturers of branded AIDS drugs. Because of high prices, the government sanctioned the importation of nonapproved generics. The reaction from branded pharmaceutical manufacturers was to sue South Africa, which created an international backlash against the firms. Not only did the episode generate much negative publicity for the branded pharmaceutical firms, it made people more aware of the generic drug industry and its potential for helping those affected by the AIDS pandemic. In the wake of the South African debacle, Brazil and several other countries threatened to break patents if pharmaceutical firms did not make their drugs more affordable. In the interest of good public relations, several branded pharmaceutical firms began to offer their AIDS drugs at lower prices in Africa. In all, the pharmaceutical firms have developed at least eighty-eight medicines to treat AIDS and related conditions. The United States and various European governments have provided billions of dollars in subsidies to support AIDS treatment in Africa.

The Future

Without adequate intellectual property protection, the pharmaceutical industry has fewer incentives to invent new drugs. At the same time, consumers in poor countries need access to drugs but can't afford them. Lax intellectual property laws facilitate the production of cheap generic drugs, but without these protections, major pharmaceutical firms have fewer incentives to fund the R&D that results in new treatments for the diseases that plague the world.

Case Questions

1. Specify the types of country risks that pharmaceutical firms face in international business. How do the political and legal systems of countries affect the global pharmaceutical industry?
2. People need medications, but the poor often cannot afford them. Governments may not provide subsidies for health care and medications. Meanwhile, pharmaceutical firms focus their R&D on compounds likely to provide the best returns. What is the proper role of the following groups in addressing these dilemmas: national governments, branded pharmaceutical firms, and generic manufacturers?
3. Consult www.phrma.org, The Pharmaceutical Research and Manufacturers of America. What steps is the branded industry taking to address the various ethical issues it faces, such as providing affordable drugs to poor countries?
4. Consult the TRIPS agreement at the WTO portal (www.wto.org). What are the latest developments regarding this treaty? What types of protection does this treaty provide to pharmaceutical firms? What enforcement mechanisms does TRIPS provide for ensuring that these protections will be carried out?
5. Recommend a strategy that management at a large pharmaceutical firm should employ to reduce the likelihood of political and legal risks that such firms face. What steps should management take to minimize its exposure to such risks?

Sources: "Competitive Landscape," *U.S. Pharma & Healthcare Report*, no. 4 (2011): 63–69; Robert Coopman, "The Road Ahead for Research-Based Drug Companies," *Chain Drug Review*, January 2, 2012, p. 71; Chris Enyinda, Chris Mbah, and Alphonso Ogbuehi, "An Empirical Analysis of Risk Mitigation in the Pharmaceutical Industry Supply Chain: A Developing-Country Perspective," *Thunderbird International Business Review* 52, no. 1 (2010): 54–69; Sarah Houlton, "Cracking Down on Counterfeit Drugs," *Pharmaceutical Executive*, February 2009, p. 18; Nancy Shute, "Fake Medications Are a Growing Threat," *US News and World Report*, August 21, 2007, retrieved from http://www.health.usnews.com; P. Trouiller et al., "Drug Development for Neglected Diseases," *Lancet* 359 (June 2002): 2188–2194; G. Glass, "Patent Attack," *Pharmaceutical Executive* 25, no. 4 (2005): 76–81; "Survey: Prescription for Change," *Economist*, June 18, 2005; "Business: Big Generic Pharma; Pharmaceuticals," *Economist*, July 30, 2005; "Business: Corrupted; Medications and Intellectual Property," *Economist*, July 23, 2005; IMAP, *Pharmaceuticals & Biotech Industry Global Report—2011*, retrieved from http://www.imap.com; Pharmaceutical Research and Manufacturers Association of America, "What Goes Into the Cost of Prescription Drugs?," June 2005, retrieved from http://www.phrma.org; World Health Organization, "Counterfeit Medicines," Fact Sheet No. 275, November 14, 2006, retrieved from http://www.wto.int; Peter Pitts, "Counterfeit Drugs and China," 2009, retrieved from the Center for Medicine in the Public Interest Web site http://www.cmpi.org; U.S. Food and Drug Administration, "Counterfeit Drugs," 2009, retrieved from http://www.fda.gov/counterfeit/.

Note: Kevin McGarry assisted in the development of this case.

CHAPTER ESSENTIALS

MyManagementLab

Go to **www.mymanagementlab.com** to complete the problems marked with this icon ✪.

Key Terms

country risk
extraterritoriality
legal system
political system
rule of law
transparency

Summary

In this chapter, you learned about:

1. **The nature of country risk**

   International business is influenced by political and legal systems. **Country risk** refers to exposure to potential loss or to adverse effects on company operations and profitability caused by developments in national political and legal environments.

2. **Political and legal environments in international business**

   A **political system** is a set of formal institutions that constitute a government. A **legal system** is a system for interpreting and enforcing laws. Adverse developments in political and legal systems increase country risk. These can result from events such as a change in government or the creation of new laws or regulations.

3. **Political systems**

   The three major political systems are totalitarianism, socialism, and democracy. They provide frameworks within which laws are established and nations are governed. Democracy is characterized by private property rights and limited government. Socialism occurs mainly as social democracy. Today, most governments combine elements of socialism and democracy. Totalitarianism is associated with command economies, socialism with mixed economies, and democracy with market economies.

4. **Legal systems**

   There are four major legal systems: common law, civil law, religious law, and mixed systems. The **rule of law** implies a legal system in which laws are clear, understood, respected, and fairly enforced.

5. **Participants in political and legal systems**

   Actors include government, which exists at the national, state, and municipal levels. The World Trade Organization and the United Nations are typical of international organizations that influence international business. Special interest groups serve specific industries or country groupings and include labor unions, environmental organizations, and consumers that promote particular viewpoints. Companies deal with competing firms in foreign markets, which may undertake political activities aimed at influencing market entry and firm performance.

6. **Types of country risk produced by political systems**

   Governments impose constraints on corporate operating methods in areas such as production, marketing, and distribution. Governments may expropriate or confiscate the assets of foreign firms. Governments or groups of countries also impose embargoes and sanctions that restrict trade with certain countries. Boycotts are an attempt to halt trade or prevent business activities and are usually pursued for political reasons. War and revolution have serious consequences for international firms. Terrorism has become more salient recently.

7. **Types of country risk produced by legal systems**

   Foreign investment laws restrict FDI in various ways. Such laws include controls on operating forms and practices, regulations affecting marketing and distribution, restrictions on income repatriation, environmental laws, and Internet and e-commerce regulations. **Extraterritoriality** is the application of home-country laws to conduct outside of national borders. Antiboycott regulations prevent companies from participating in restrictive trade practices. Accounting and reporting laws vary around the world. **Transparency** is the degree to which firms reveal substantial and regular information about their financial condition and accounting practices.

8. Managing country risk

Successful management requires developing an understanding of the political and legal context abroad. The firm should scan the environment proactively. It should strictly adhere to ethical standards. Country risk is also managed by allying with qualified local partners abroad. The firm should seek protection through legal contracts.

Test Your Comprehension **AACSB: Reflective Thinking Skills**

1. What are the components of political systems? What are the components of legal systems? How do these systems lead to country risk?

2. Distinguish between totalitarianism, socialism, and democracy. What are the implications of each for internationalizing firms?

3. What are the specific characteristics of democracy? How do these characteristics facilitate international business?

4. Describe the major types of legal systems. Which systems are most widely encountered?

5. Who are the major actors in political and legal systems? Which participant do you believe is most influential in international business?

6. Describe proactive actions that firms can take to minimize country risk.

Apply Your Understanding **AACSB: Reflective Thinking Skills, Communication Abilities, Ethical Understanding and Reasoning Abilities**

1. Country risk refers to the ways governments restrict, or fail to restrict, business activities. The nature of such restrictions varies around the world. In each country, national economic success substantially depends on the quality of laws and regulations. Government must strike the right balance—too little regulation promotes uncertainty; too much causes hardship. Country risk is revealed in various ways:

   - Foreign investment laws
   - Controls on operating forms and practices
   - Environmental laws
   - Contract laws
   - E-commerce laws
   - Underdeveloped legal systems
   - Accounting and reporting laws

   Conduct research online and give specific examples of each type of country risk. Describe how each might help or hinder company activities.

2. Suppose you get a job at Aoki Corporation, a firm that manufactures glass for industrial and consumer markets. Aoki is a large firm but has little international experience. Senior managers are considering a plan to move Aoki's manufacturing to China, Mexico, or Eastern Europe, and to begin selling its glass in Latin America and Europe. However, they know little about the country risks that Aoki may encounter. Describe how each of the following factors might contribute to country risk as Aoki ventures abroad: foreign investment laws, controls on operating forms and practices, and laws regarding repatriation of income, environment, and contracts.

3. *Ethical Dilemma*: The United States imposed a trade and investment embargo on Iran. U.S. citizens were barred from doing business with Iran. Proponents argue the embargo is justified because Iran has supported terrorism and is developing nuclear weapons. However, critics condemn the trade sanctions for several reasons. First, they argue the sanctions represent a "double standard," as the United States supports other countries that have engaged in terrorism and other bad behaviors. Second, the best way to nurture healthy dissent and civil society in Iran may be to engage the country, rather than restrict economic relationships. Third, the sanctions harm the Iranian people, who are deprived of the benefits of trade with the United States. Fourth, the sanctions are largely ineffective since other countries supply Iran with products it needs. Finally, the sanctions harm U.S. companies, especially oil and gas firms, which cannot do business with Iran. What is your view? Using the Ethical Framework in Chapter 5, analyze the arguments for and against trade with Iran. Can the United States, acting alone, compel desired changes in Iran by imposing sanctions? Justify your answer.

globalEDGE INTERNET EXERCISES

(http://www.globalEDGE.msu.edu)

AACSB: Reflective Thinking Skills, Communication Abilities, Use of Information Technology, Ethical Understanding and Reasoning Abilities

Refer to Chapter 1, page 58, for instructions on how to access and use globalEDGE™.

1. Supranational organizations such as the World Bank (www.worldbank.org) and the World Trade Organization (www.wto.org) oversee much of the legal framework within which the world trading system operates. Political frameworks for industries or country groupings are influenced by organizations such as the Organization of Petroleum Exporting Countries (www.opec.org) and the Organisation for Economic Co-operation and Development (www.oecd.org). Using globalEDGE™ and the online portals cited here, address the following question: What is the goal of each organization, and how does it go about achieving its goal? By viewing the news and press releases at each Web site, summarize the latest initiatives of each organization.
2. When companies venture abroad, managers seek information on the legal and political environments in each country. This information is available from various Web sources, as illustrated in the following exercises. (I) Suppose you want to sign up distributors in the European Union and want to learn about EU contract law. What should you do? Consult the globalEDGE™ portal to learn about EU trade and contract laws. Try the following: At globalEDGE™, click Reference Desk, then Global Resource Directory, then Trade Law. Describe the resources there for learning about contract law in Europe. (II) The Central Intelligence Agency's portal provides up-to-date information about national governments and political environments. Go to www.cia.gov, click on World Factbook, and summarize the political environment in each of China, Colombia, France, and Russia.
3. Freedom House is a nonprofit organization that monitors the state of freedom worldwide. It conducts an annual "Freedom in the World Survey," which you can view at www.freedomhouse.org. The survey compares the state of political rights and civil liberties in nearly 200 countries over time. Visit the site and answer the following questions: (a) What is the role of political rights and civil liberties in the Freedom House rankings? (b) What can governments in these countries do to facilitate more rapid social and political development? (c) What are the implications of the rankings for companies doing international business?

Source: © Paul Cowan/Shutterstock.com

Qatar Welcomes New Foreign Investment

Qatar, looking forward to speeding up its economic growth and improving its external competitiveness, has identified the importance of trade and investment liberalization in economic growth. It has been implementing development strategy to reduce the high dependence on crude oil since the mid-1990s by increasing the production of natural gas and promoting gas-intensive industries. Policies to boost tourism, reduce unemployment, raise levels of education, and improve infrastructure have addressed some deep-rooted problems. The gradual structural reforms in the transport, energy, and telecommunications industries helped create an environmentally friendly business environment and aim to increase the role of the private sector in the economy.

Authorities have been implementing these strategies to improve the investment environment in the country. New laws have been issued or replaced to help attract foreign investment inflows. Incentive opportunities for investors have been enhanced after the 2000 investment law simplified Qatari law for foreign investors—speeding up approval processes and reducing red tape. Under the new laws, the

CHAPTER 8

Government Intervention in International Business

LEARNING OBJECTIVES *In this chapter, you will learn about the following:*

1. The nature of government intervention
2. Rationale for government intervention
3. Instruments of government intervention
4. Consequences of government intervention
5. Evolution of government intervention
6. How firms can respond to government intervention

majority of foreign firms operating in Qatar are required to import certain products through local agents. Only firms granted 100 percent foreign ownership are excluded from the local agent requirement with distributor rights. Foreign Direct Investment helps advance Qatar's technology infrastructure, R&D, programmers, technical or marketing assistance, and education or training of the local labor force. Qatar's membership in the World Trade Organization (WTO) indicates to potential foreign investors that it is committed to trade liberalization through a multilateral framework. Qatar's economy is somewhat open and tariffs on imports are applied on a non-discriminatory basis except for the Gulf Cooperation Council (GCC), Qatar's trading partners, which has six members since January 2003. Qatar purses regional agreements such as the GCC because it believes regionalization would help rather than hinder the globalization of the world economy, and it is open to negotiating bilateral agreements.

A remarkable economic performance in the past few years took place following the development strategy spurred by the rapid rise of crude petroleum and natural gas output and prices, as well as the boost in non-hydrocarbon production as a result of increased energy-intensive industrial and government investments. Qatar's real GDP rate grew from an annual average of 1.3 percent during 1986–1995 to around 9 percent during 1996–2003. Qatar's annual inflows of foreign direct investment have been fluctuating over the years, growing from $113 million in 1999 to a peak of $8.1 billion in 2009 before declining to $5.5 billion in 2010. However, as percentage of GDP, the stock of FDI has been increasing rapidly, starting with 2.66% in 2003, and reaching from 8.26% in 2009. According to UNCTAD's Inward FDI Potential Index, Qatar was ranked 21st during the period 1993–1995 and 11th during the period 2005-2007. Qatar has especially attracted a great deal of foreign investments since it won the bid to host the 2022 FIFA World Cup.

SOURCES: "Further reforms would help sustain already impressive economic growth." *World Trade Organization*, February 21, 23, 2005, http://www.wto.org/english/tratop_e/tpr_e/tp244_e.htm; Wallace, Douglas. "Consider Qatar." http://export.gov/middleeast/country_information/qatar/ConsiderQatarGuide.pdf, Accessed October 22, 2012.

Governments intervene in trade and investment to achieve political, social, or economic objectives. They often create trade barriers that benefit specific interest groups, such as domestic firms, industries, and labor unions. A key rationale is to create jobs by protecting industries from foreign competition. Governments also intervene to support home-grown industries or firms.

Government intervention is at odds with *free trade*, the unrestricted flow of products, services, and capital across national borders. Market liberalization and free trade are best for supporting economic growth and national living standards.[1] One study of more than one hundred countries in the 50 years after 1945 found a strong association between market openness—that is, unimpeded free trade—and economic growth. Countries with an open economy enjoyed average annual per-capita GDP growth of 4.49 percent, while relatively closed countries—those with less free trade—grew at only 0.69 percent per year.[2]

Exhibit 8.1 shows how increasing free trade translates into an expanded production possibilities frontier, moving from PPF1 to PPF2. Let's use Poland as an example. Over time, Poland lowered trade barriers and participated more freely in international trade, adopting the principle of comparative advantage.[3] As Poland expanded its free trade, the country focused on producing and exporting goods it was best suited to produce, and importing those goods that other nations produce more efficiently. The end result was that Poland's production possibilities frontier for products and services shifted outward (Exhibit 8.1). Due to growing free trade, Poland began

EXHIBIT 8.1

Benefits of Free Trade: Outward Shift of Production Possibilities Frontier for Products and Services

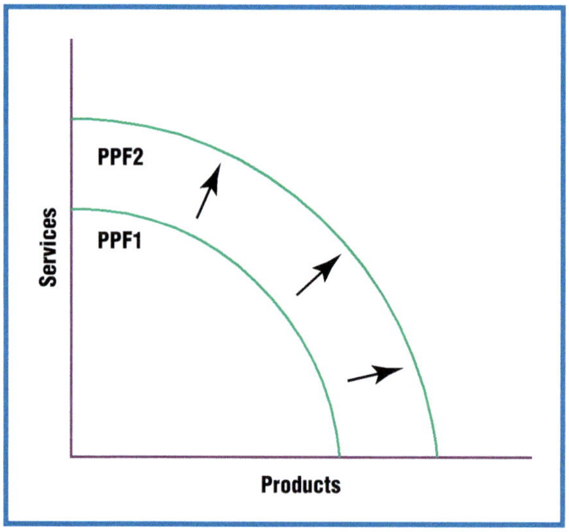

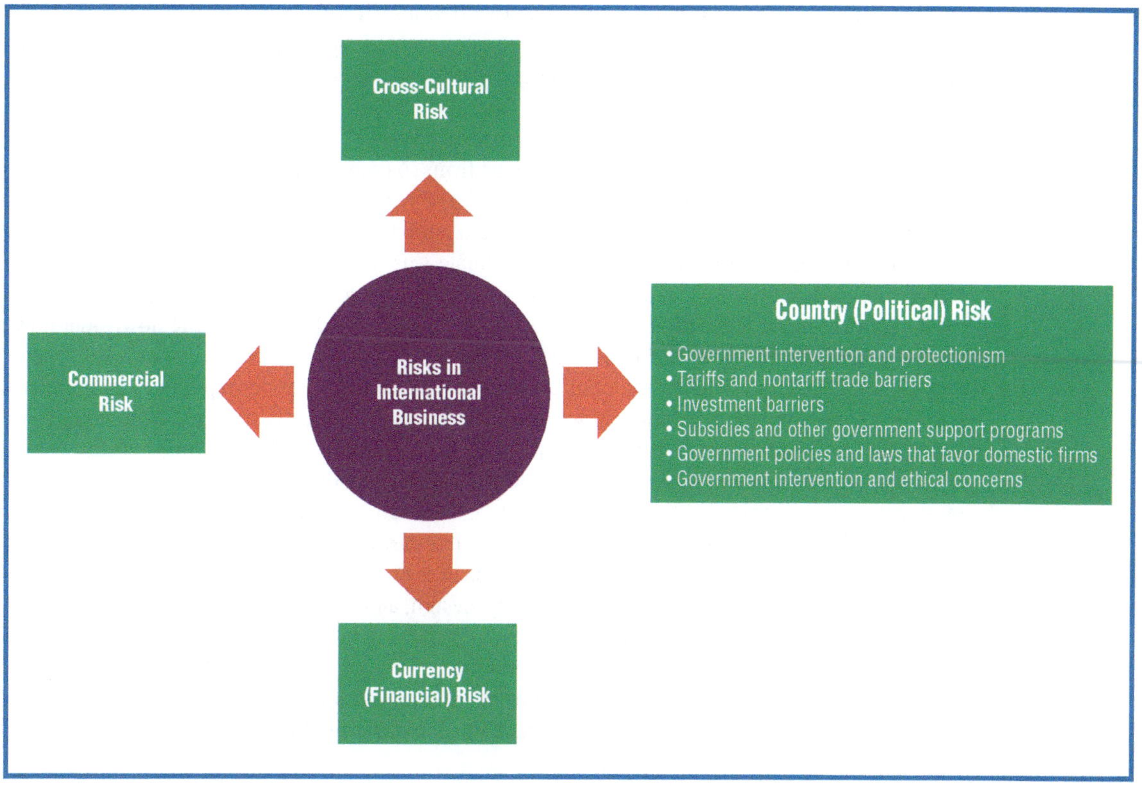

EXHIBIT 8.2

Government Intervention as a Component of Country Risk

to use its resources more efficiently, generating more overall profits for firms and workers, and, in turn, acquiring more resources with which to import the goods that Polish consumers desire.

As it gradually embraced free trade, Poland's average annual income rose, from about $1,625 in 1990 to more than $14,000 in 2012. These gains did not occur without some turmoil—unemployment in Poland increased in some industries as jobs producing certain goods shifted to other countries better suited to make those goods. However, free trade's positive effects substantially outweighed the negative ones.[4] Free trade provides enormous benefits for economic growth and the welfare of nations worldwide.

In reality, however, governments intervene in business and the international marketplace in ways that obstruct the free flow of trade and investment. Intervention alters the competitive position of companies and industries and the status of citizens. As highlighted in Exhibit 8.2, intervention is an important dimension of country risk. In this chapter, we examine the nature, rationale, and consequences of government intervention. We also describe what companies can do to enhance international performance in the face of government intervention worldwide.

The Nature of Government Intervention

Government intervention is often motivated by **protectionism**, which refers to national economic policies designed to restrict free trade and protect domestic industries from foreign competition. Protectionism is typically manifested by tariffs, nontariff barriers such as quotas, and arbitrary administrative rules designed to discourage imports. A **tariff** (also known as a *duty*) is a tax imposed by a government on imported products, effectively increasing the cost of acquisition for the customer. A **nontariff trade barrier** is a government policy, regulation, or procedure that impedes trade through means other than explicit tariffs. Trade barriers are enforced as products pass through **customs**, the checkpoints at the ports of entry in each country where government officials

Protectionism
National economic policies designed to restrict free trade and protect domestic industries from foreign competition.

Tariff
A tax imposed on imported products, effectively increasing the cost of acquisition for the customer.

Nontariff trade barrier
A government policy, regulation, or procedure that impedes trade through means other than explicit tariffs.

Customs
Checkpoints at the ports of entry in each country where government officials inspect imported products and levy tariffs.

Quota
A quantitative restriction placed on imports of a specific product over a specified period of time.

inspect imported products and levy tariffs. An often-used form of nontariff trade barrier is a **quota**, a quantitative restriction placed on imports of a specific product over a specified period of time. Government intervention may also target FDI flows via investment barriers that restrict the operations of foreign firms.

Government intervention affects the normal operation of economic activity in a nation by hindering or helping the ability of its indigenous firms to compete internationally. Often companies, labor unions, and other special interest groups convince governments to adopt policies that benefit them. For example, in the 2000s, the Bush administration imposed tariffs on the import of foreign steel into the United States. The rationale was to give the U.S. steel industry time to restructure and revive itself following years of decline due to tough competition from foreign steel manufacturers. The action may have saved hundreds of U.S. jobs. On the downside, however, the tariffs also increased production costs for firms that use steel, such as Ford, Whirlpool, and General Electric. Higher material costs made these firms less competitive and reduced prospects for selling their products in world markets.[5] The steel tariffs were removed within two years, but in the process of attempting to do good, the government also did some harm.

Another example of intervention was the U.S. government's response to the growing threat of Japanese car imports in the 1980s, when it established "voluntary export restraints" on the number of Japanese vehicles that could be imported into the United States. This move helped insulate the U.S. auto industry for several years. In a protected environment, however, Detroit automakers had less incentive to improve quality, design, and overall product appeal. Government intervention motivated by protectionism has been one of several factors that, over time, weakened Detroit's ability to compete in the global auto industry.

Protectionist policies may also lead to price inflation because tariffs can restrict the supply of a particular product. Tariffs may also reduce the choices available to buyers by restricting the variety of products available for sale.

These examples illustrate that government intervention may lead to adverse *unintended consequences*—unfavorable outcomes of policies or laws. In a complex world, legislators and policymakers cannot foresee all possible outcomes. The problem of unintended consequences suggests that government intervention should be planned and implemented with great care.

Rationale for Government Intervention

Why does a government intervene in trade and investment activities? There are four main motives.

Tariffs and other forms of intervention allow governments to:

1. **Generate revenue.** For example, the "Hamilton Tariff," enacted July 4, 1789, was the second statute passed by the newly founded United States, providing revenue for the federal government. Today, Ghana and Sierra Leone generate more than 25 percent of their total government revenue from tariffs.
2. **Ensure citizen safety, security, and welfare.** For example, governments pass laws to prevent importation of harmful products such as contaminated food.
3. **Pursue economic, political, or social objectives.** In most cases, tariffs and similar forms of intervention are intended to promote job growth and economic development.
4. **Serve company and industrial interests.** Governments may devise regulations to stimulate development of home-grown industries.

Special interest groups often advocate *trade and investment barriers* that protect their interests. Consider the recent trade dispute between Mexico and the United States over Mexican cement. The U.S. government imposed duties of about $50 per ton on the import of Mexican cement after U.S. cement makers lobbied Congress. The stakes were huge, as Mexican imports can reach 10 percent of U.S. domestic cement consumption. Mexico proposed substituting import quotas in place of the tariffs. The two governments have negotiated for years to resolve the dispute.[6]

Trade and investment barriers can be considered either defensive or offensive. Governments impose defensive barriers to safeguard industries, workers, and special interest groups and to promote national security. Governments impose offensive barriers to pursue strategic or public policy objectives, such as increasing employment or generating tax revenues. Let's review the specific rationale for government intervention.

Defensive Rationale

Four major defensive motives are particularly relevant: protection of the nation's economy, protection of an infant industry, national security, and national culture and identity.

PROTECTION OF THE NATIONAL ECONOMY Proponents argue that firms in advanced economies cannot compete with those in developing countries that employ low-cost labor. In the opening story, labor activists called for government intervention to prevent the outsourcing of jobs from Europe and North America to India. Protectionists demand trade barriers to curtail the import of low-priced products, fearing that advanced-economy manufacturers will be undersold, wages will fall, and home-country jobs will be lost.

In response, critics counter that protectionism is at odds with the theory of comparative advantage, according to which nations should engage in more international trade, not less. Trade barriers interfere with country-specific specialization of labor. When countries specialize in the products they can produce best and then trade for the rest, they perform better in the long run, delivering superior living standards to their citizens. Critics also charge that blocking imports reduces the availability and increases the cost of products sold in the home market. Industries cannot access all the input products they need. Finally, protectionism can trigger retaliation, resulting in foreign governments imposing their own trade barriers, which reduces sales prospects for exporters.

PROTECTION OF AN INFANT INDUSTRY In an emerging industry, companies are often inexperienced and lack the latest technologies and know-how. They may also lack the scale typical of larger competitors in established industries abroad. An infant industry may need temporary protection from foreign competitors. Governments can impose temporary trade barriers on foreign imports to ensure that young firms gain a large share of the domestic market. Protecting infant industries has allowed some countries to develop a modern industrial sector. For example, government intervention allowed Japan and South Korea to become dominant players in the global automobile and consumer electronics industries.

Once in place, such protection may be hard to remove. Industry owners and workers tend to lobby to preserve government protection. Infant industries in many countries (especially in Latin America, South Asia, and Eastern Europe) have shown a tendency to remain dependent on government protection for many years. Protected companies may become inefficient, costing the nation's citizens higher taxes and higher prices for the products produced by the protected industry.[7]

NATIONAL SECURITY Countries impose trade restrictions on products viewed as critical to national defense and security, such as military technology and computers that help maintain domestic production in security-related products. For example, Russia blocked a bid by German engineering giant Siemens to purchase the Russian turbine manufacturer OAO Power Machines, on grounds of national security. The Russian government has strict legislation that limits foreign investment in sectors considered vital to Russia's national interests.[8] Countries may also impose **export controls**, government measures intended to manage or prevent the export of certain products or trade with certain countries. For example, many countries prohibit exports of plutonium to North Korea because it can be used to make nuclear weapons. The United States generally blocks exports of nuclear and military technology to countries it deems state sponsors of terrorism, such as Iran, Libya, and Syria.

Export control
A government measure intended to manage or prevent the export of certain products or trade with certain countries.

Ethical Connections

North Korea is a dictatorship with a poor record of human rights and one of the world's lowest living standards. Australia, Canada, the European Union, and the United States have long imposed trade embargos against North Korea, due to national security concerns. International trade is known to improve economic conditions in poor countries, and foreign government sanctions are making North Korea's terrible poverty even worse.

Source: © Guillaume Tunzini/Fotolia

To safeguard its national culture, the French government prevents foreign companies from owning television and movie companies in France. Shown here is Cannes, the site of France's popular film festival.

NATIONAL CULTURE AND IDENTITY Should foreign entities, say the Japanese or the Saudis, be allowed to purchase national landmarks such as the Eiffel Tower or Rockefeller Center? In most countries, certain occupations, industries, and public assets are seen as central to national culture and identity. Governments may impose trade barriers to restrict imports of products or services seen to threaten such national assets. Switzerland has imposed trade barriers to preserve its long-established tradition in watchmaking. In the United States, authorities opposed Japanese investors' purchase of the Seattle Mariners baseball team, because it is viewed as part of the national heritage. France does not allow significant foreign ownership of its TV stations because of concerns about foreign influence on French culture.

Offensive Rationale

Offensive rationales for government intervention fall into two categories: national strategic priorities and increasing employment.

NATIONAL STRATEGIC PRIORITIES Government intervention sometimes aims to encourage the development of industries that bolster the nation's economy. It is a *proactive* variation of the infant industry rationale and related to national industrial policy. Countries with many high-tech or high value-adding industries, such as information technology, pharmaceuticals, car manufacturing, or financial services, create better jobs and higher tax revenues than economies based on low value-adding industries, such as agriculture, textile manufacturing, or discount retailing. Accordingly, governments in Germany, South Korea, and numerous other countries have devised policies that promote the development of relatively desirable industries. The government may provide financing for investment in high-tech or high value-adding industries, encourage citizens to save money to ensure a steady supply of loanable funds for industrial investment, and fund public education to provide citizens the skills and flexibility they need to perform in key industries.[9]

INCREASING EMPLOYMENT Governments often impose import barriers to protect employment in designated industries. Insulating domestic firms from foreign competition stimulates national output, leading to more jobs in the protected industries. The effect is usually strongest in import-intensive industries that employ much labor. For example, the Chinese government has traditionally required foreign companies to enter its huge markets through joint ventures with local Chinese firms. This policy creates jobs for Chinese workers. A joint venture between Shanghai Automotive Industry Corporation (SAIC) and Volkswagen created jobs in China.

Instruments of Government Intervention

Principal instruments of trade intervention and the traditional forms of protectionism are tariffs and nontariff trade barriers. Individual countries or groups of countries, such as the European Union (http://www.europa.eu), can impose these barriers. In aggregate, barriers constitute a serious impediment to cross-border business. The United Nations estimated that trade barriers alone cost developing countries more than $500 billion in lost trading opportunities with developed countries every year.[10] Exhibit 8.3 highlights the most common forms of government intervention and their effects.

Tariffs

Some countries impose *export tariffs*, taxes on products exported by their own companies. For example, Russia charges a duty on its oil exports with the intention of generating government revenue and maintaining high oil stocks within Russia. The most common type of tariff, however, is the *import tariff*, a tax levied on imported products.

EXHIBIT 8.3 Types and Effects of Government Intervention

Intervention Type	Definition	Practical Effect on Customers, Firms, or Government	Contemporary Examples
Tariff	Tax imposed on imported products.	Increases cost to the importer, exporter, and usually the buyer of the product. Discourages product imports. Generates government revenue.	Switzerland charges a 37% tariff on imported agricultural products. Bolivia charges a 35% tariff on most apparel and textiles.
Quota	Quantitative restriction on imports of a product during a specified period of time.	Gives early importers monopoly power and the ability to charge higher prices. Harms late importers. Usually results in higher prices to the buyer.	Japan maintains strict quotas on the import of leather shoes and various types of seafood.
Local content requirements	Requirement that firms include a minimum percentage of locally-sourced inputs in the production of given products or services.	Discourages imports of raw materials, parts, and supplies, which harms manufacturers' sourcing options. May result in higher costs and lower product quality for buyers.	At least 50% of the value of all cars assembled in Venezuela must be from parts or other inputs produced in Venezuela.
Regulations and technical standards	Safety, health, or technical regulations; labeling requirements.	May hinder the entry of imported products; and reduce the quantity of available products, resulting in higher costs to importers and buyers.	Saudi Arabia bans imports of firearms and used clothing. The EU requires extensive testing on thousands of imported chemicals.
Administrative and bureaucratic procedures	Complex procedures or requirements imposed on importers or foreign investors that hinder trade and investment.	Slows the import of products or services. Hinders or delays firms' investment activities.	Russia imposes extensive inspections and bureaucratic procedures on the import of alcoholic beverages.
FDI and ownership restrictions	Rules that limit the ability of foreign firms to invest in certain industries or acquire local firms.	Limits how much foreigners can invest in a country, and/or the proportion of ownership that foreigners can hold in firms in the country.	In Switzerland, foreign-owned insurance companies must by managed by a Swiss national, and most board members must be European citizens.
Subsidy	Financing or other resources that a government grants to a firm or group of firms, to ensure their survival or success.	Increases the competitive advantage of the grantee, while diminishing the competitive advantages of those that do not receive the subsidy.	Turkey gives export subsidies of up to 20% to local, Turkish producers of wheat and sugar.
Countervailing duty	Duties imposed on products imported into a country to offset subsidies given to producers in the exporting country.	Reduces or eliminates the competitive advantages provided by subsidies.	India imposes countervailing duties on the import of numerous products.
Anti-dumping duty	Tax charged on an imported product whose price is below usual prices in the local market or below the cost to manufacture the product.	Reduces or eliminates the competitive advantage of imported products priced at abnormally low levels.	The United States has imposed anti-dumping duties on imports of low-cost steel, to support U.S.-based steel manufacturers.

Source: Based on the Office of the United States Trade Representative, retrieved from http://www.ustr.gov.

Import tariffs are usually *ad valorem*—that is, they are assessed as a percentage of the value of the imported product. Or a government may impose a *specific tariff*—a flat fee or fixed amount per unit of the imported product—based on weight, volume, or surface area, such as barrels of oil or square meters of fabric. A *revenue tariff* is intended to raise money for the government. A tariff on cigarette imports, for example, produces a steady flow of revenue. A *protective tariff* aims to protect domestic industries from foreign competition. A *prohibitive tariff* is one so high that no one can import any of the items.

The amount of a tariff is determined by examining a product's harmonized code. Products are classified under about 8,000 different unique codes in the *harmonized tariff* or *harmonized code* schedule, a standardized system used worldwide. Without this system, firms and governments might have differing opinions on product definitions and the tariffs charged.

EXHIBIT 8.4 A Sampling of Import Tariffs, Percentages

Country	Average Import Tariff	
	Agricultural Products	Non-agricultural Products
Australia	1.3%	3.0%
Canada	11.3	2.6
China	15.6	8.7
European Union	12.8	4.0
India	31.8	10.1
Japan	17.3	2.5
Mexico	21.5	7.1
United States	4.9	3.3

Note: Exhibit shows the average, most favored nation applied tariff.

Source: Based on *World Tariff Profiles 2011*, World Trade Organization, retrieved from www.wto.org.

Import tariffs can generate substantial revenue for national governments. This helps explain why they are common in developing economies. Even in advanced economies, tariffs provide a significant source of revenue for the government. The United States charges tariffs on many consumer, agricultural, and labor-intensive products. The U.S. typically collects high tariffs (often 48 percent) on imports of basic, low-quality shoes, and low tariffs (just 9 percent) on luxury shoes. Low-income shoe buyers end up paying the highest tariffs. The European Union applies tariffs of up to 191 percent on meat, 118 percent on cereals, and 106 percent on sugar and confectionary products.[11]

Exhibit 8.4 provides a sample of import tariffs in selected countries. Despite its reputation as a challenging market to enter, Japan maintains average tariffs for nonagricultural products at low levels. Under the North American Free Trade Agreement (NAFTA), Canada, Mexico, and the United States have eliminated nearly all tariffs on product imports from each other. However, Mexico maintains significant tariffs with the rest of the world—21.5 percent for agricultural products and 7.1 percent for nonagricultural goods. India's tariffs are relatively high, especially in agriculture, where the average rate is 31.8 percent. India's tariff system lacks transparency, and officially published tariff information is sometimes hard to find. China has reduced its tariffs since joining the World Trade Organization (WTO, www.wto.org) in 2001, but trade barriers remain high in some areas.

In Africa, over half of all workers are employed in agriculture. Significant tariffs and other trade barriers in the advanced economies hinder imports of agricultural goods from Africa, which worsens already-severe poverty in many African countries.

Because high tariffs inhibit free trade and economic growth, governments have tended to reduce them over time. This was the primary goal of the General Agreement on Tariffs and Trade (GATT; now the WTO). Countries as diverse as Chile, Hungary, Turkey, and South Korea have liberalized their previously protected markets, lowering trade barriers and subjecting themselves to greater competition from abroad. Exhibit 8.5 illustrates trends in average world tariff rates over time. Notice that developing economies have been lowering their tariff rates since the early 1980s. Continued reductions represent a major driver of market globalization.

Nontariff Trade Barriers

Nontariff trade barriers are government policies or measures that restrict trade without imposing a direct tax or duty. They include quotas, import licenses, local content requirements, government regulations, and administrative or bureaucratic procedures. The use of nontariff barriers has grown substantially in recent decades. Governments sometimes prefer them because they are easier to conceal from the WTO and other organizations that monitor international trade.

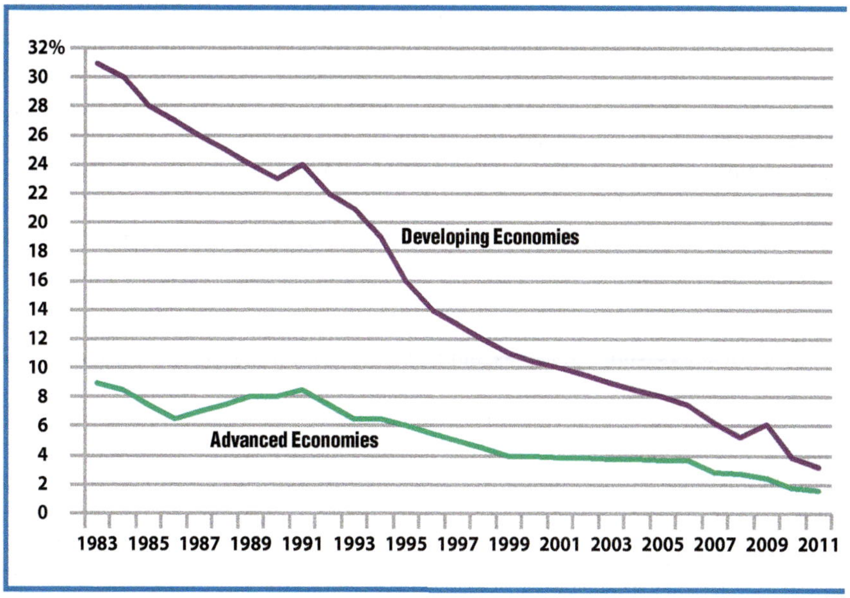

EXHIBIT 8.5

Trends in Average Tariff Rates, Percentages

Source: Based on The World Bank, http://www.data.worldbank.org.

Quotas restrict the physical volume or value of products that firms can import into a country. In a classic type of quota, the U.S. government imposed an upper limit of roughly 2 million pounds on the total amount of sugar that can be imported into the United States each year. Sugar imports that exceed this level face a tariff of several cents per pound. The upside is that U.S. sugar producers are protected from cheaper imports, giving them a competitive edge over foreign sugar producers. The downside is that U.S. consumers and producers of certain types of products, such as Hershey's and Coca-Cola, pay more for sugar. It also means companies that manufacture products containing sugar may save money by moving production to countries that do not impose quotas or tariffs on sugar.

Governments can impose voluntary quotas, under which firms agree to limit exports of certain products. These are also known as *voluntary export restraints*, or VERs. For example, import quotas in the European Union led to an impasse in which millions of Chinese-made garments piled up at ports and borders in Europe. The EU impounded the clothing because China had exceeded the voluntary import quotas it had negotiated with the EU. The action created hardship for European retailers, who had ordered their clothing stocks several months in advance.[12]

Import license
Government authorization granted to a firm for importing a product.

Governments occasionally require importing firms to obtain an **import license**, a formal permission to import, which restricts imports in a way that is similar to quotas. (Do not confuse import licenses with "licensing," a strategy for entering foreign markets in which one firm allows another the right to use its intellectual property in return for a fee.) Governments sell import licenses to companies on a competitive basis or grant the licenses on a first-come, first-served basis. This tends to discriminate against smaller firms, which typically lack the resources to purchase them. Obtaining a license can be costly and complicated. In some countries, importers must pay hefty fees to government authorities. In other countries, they must deal with bureaucratic red tape. In Russia a complex web of licensing requirements limits imports of alcoholic beverages. Until the 1990s, the government of India imposed the "license raj," an especially elaborate system of licenses that regulated establishing and running businesses in the country.

Local content requirements require manufacturers to include a minimum of local value added—that is, production that takes place locally. Local content requirements are usually imposed in countries that are members of an economic bloc, such as the EU and NAFTA. The so-called *rules of origin requirement* specifies that a certain proportion of products and supplies, or of intermediate goods used in local manufacturing, must be produced within the bloc. For a car manufacturer, the tires or windshields it purchases from another firm are intermediate goods. When the firm does not meet this requirement, the products become subject to trade barriers that member governments normally impose on nonmember countries. Thus, producers within the NAFTA zone of Canada, Mexico, and the United States pay no tariffs on the products and supplies they obtain from each other, unlike countries such as China or the United Kingdom that are not part of NAFTA. Roughly 60 percent of the value of a car manufactured within NAFTA must originate within the NAFTA member countries. If this condition were not met, the product became subject to the tariffs charged to non-NAFTA countries.

Government regulations and technical standards are another type of nontariff trade barrier. Examples include safety regulations for motor vehicles and electrical equipment, health regulations for hygienic food preparation, labeling requirements that indicate a product's country of origin, technical standards for computers, and bureaucratic procedures for customs clearance, including excessive red tape and slow approval processes. The European Union strictly regulates food that has been genetically modified (GM), a policy that blocks some food imports into Europe from the United States. In China, the government requires foreign firms to obtain special permits to import GM foods. Chinese government censorship of material it considers subversive has hindered Google's attempts to enter China's huge Internet market.[13]

Country Realities

Construction and zoning rules vary from country to country. In the United Kingdom, a law restricts new buildings from blocking sunlight received by neighboring structures. The law was passed in the twelfth century, when everything was lit with candles. Developers must negotiate with neighbors and pay steep compensation when new buildings block their sunlight. The law deters foreign FDI in Britain's construction industry.

Source: Bloomberg Businessweek, "The Trouble with London's Right to Light," April 23–29, 2012, pp. 25–26.

Governments may impose *administrative or bureaucratic procedures* that hinder the activities of importers or foreign firms. India's business sector is burdened by countless regulations, standards, and administrative hurdles at the state and federal levels. In Mexico, government-imposed bureaucratic procedures led United Parcel Service to temporarily suspend its ground delivery service across the U.S.-Mexican border. Similarly, the United States barred Mexican trucks from entering the United States on the grounds that they were unsafe. Business regulations vary worldwide. Many countries in Africa and Latin America impose countless bureaucratic procedures that hinder commercial activities and business start-ups. By contrast, Australia, Canada, Ireland, New Zealand, Singapore, and the United Kingdom impose relatively few such procedures.[14]

Saudi Arabia is home to various restrictive practices that hinder international trade. Every foreign business traveler to the Arab kingdom must hold an entry visa that can be obtained only by securing the support of a sponsor—a Saudi citizen or organization who vouches for the visitor's actions. Because few Saudis are willing to assume such responsibility, foreigners who want to do business in Saudi Arabia face great difficulty.[15]

Convoluted administrative procedures are widespread in national customs agencies. The revenue generated by tariffs depends on how customs authorities classify imported products. Products often appear to fit two or more tariff categories. For example, a sport utility vehicle could be classified as a truck, a car, or a van. Each of these categories can entail a different tariff. Depending on the judgment of the customs agent, the applicable tariff might end up being high or low. Because thousands of categories exist for customs classification, a product and its corresponding tariff can be easily misclassified, by accident or intent.

Investment Barriers

Countries also impose restrictions on FDI and ownership that restrict the ability of foreign firms to invest in some industry sectors or acquire local firms. Excessive restrictions in India prevent the approval of countless investment proposals that could produce billions of dollars in revenue to the local economy and government. Worldwide, FDI and ownership restrictions are particularly common in such industries as broadcasting, utilities, air transportation, military technology, and financial services, as well as industries in which the government has major holdings, such as oil and key minerals. The Mexican government restricts FDI by foreign investors to protect its oil industry, which is deemed critical to the nation's security. The Canadian government restricts foreign ownership of local movie studios and TV networks to protect its indigenous film and TV industries from excessive foreign influence. FDI and ownership restrictions are particularly burdensome in the services sector because services usually cannot be exported and providers must establish a physical presence in target markets to conduct business there. Occasionally, governments impose investment barriers aimed at protecting home-country industries and jobs.

Currency control
Restrictions on the outflow of hard currency from a country or on the inflow of foreign currencies.

Currency controls restrict the outflow of widely used currencies, such as the dollar, euro, and yen, and occasionally the inflow of foreign currencies. Controls can help conserve especially valuable currency or reduce the risk of capital flight. They are particularly common in developing economies. Some countries employ a system of dual official exchange rates, offering exporters a relatively favorable rate to encourage exports, while importers receive a relatively unfavorable rate to discourage imports.

Currency controls both help and harm firms that establish foreign subsidiaries through FDI. They favor companies when they export their products from the host country but harm those that rely heavily on imported parts and components. Controls also restrict the ability of MNEs to *repatriate* their profits—that is, transfer revenues from profitable operations back to the home country.

As an example, in Venezuela, currency controls have led to a shortage of dollars and other hard currencies. Multinational firms avoid doing business in Venezuela because strict currency rules limit the amount of profits they can take out of the country or limit their ability to receive payment for imports at reasonable prices. Venezuela imposed the controls to keep imports inexpensive and maintain a base of hard currencies in the country.[16]

Source: © Keith Dannemiller/Alamy

State-owned oil company PEMEX (Petroleos de Mexico) benefits from investment barriers in Mexico that prevent foreign firms from gaining control of Mexican oil companies.

Subsidies and Other Government Support Programs

Subsidies are monetary or other resources that a government grants to a firm or group of firms, intended either to encourage exports or simply to facilitate the production and marketing of products at reduced prices, to help ensure the involved companies prosper. Subsidies come in the form of outright cash disbursements, material inputs, services, tax breaks, the construction of infrastructure, and government contracts at inflated prices. For example, the French government has provided large subsidies to Air France, the national airline.

Subsidy
Monetary or other resources that a government grants to a firm or group of firms, usually intended to encourage exports or to facilitate the production and marketing of products at reduced prices, to ensure the favored firms prosper.

The *Closing Case* focuses on European government support of Airbus, the leading European manufacturer of commercial aircraft. Perhaps the ultimate examples of subsidized firms are in China. Several leading corporations, such as China Minmetals ($39 billion annual sales) and Shanghai Automotive ($34 billion annual sales), are in fact state enterprises wholly or partly owned by the Chinese government, which provides them with huge financial resources. Indeed, state-owned enterprises account for more than 40 percent of China's economic output.[17]

Critics argue that subsidies confer unfair advantages on recipients by reducing their cost of doing business. In India, the government provides massive subsidies to state-owned oil companies, which allow them to offer gasoline at very low prices. Foreign MNEs such as Royal Dutch Shell cannot compete profitably against rivals that offer such prices and consequently avoid doing business in the market.[18] The WTO prohibits subsidies when it can be proven that they hinder free trade. Subsidies, however, are hard to define. For example, when a government provides land, infrastructure, telecommunications systems, or utilities to the firms in a corporate park, this is technically a subsidy. Yet many view this type of support as an appropriate public function.

In Europe and the United States, governments frequently provide agricultural subsidies to supplement the income of farmers and help manage the supply of agricultural commodities. The U.S. government grants subsidies for more than two dozen commodities, including corn, soybeans, wheat, cotton, and rice.[19] In Europe, the Common Agricultural Policy (CAP) is a system of subsidies that represents about 40 percent of the EU's budget, amounting to tens of billions of euros annually. The CAP and U.S. subsidies have been criticized for promoting unfair competition and high prices because they tend to prevent developing economies from exporting their agricultural goods to Europe and the United States. Subsidies encourage overproduction and therefore lower food prices at home, making agricultural imports from developing countries less competitive.[20]

Countervailing duty
Tariff imposed on products imported into a country to offset subsidies given to producers or exporters in the exporting country.

Governments sometimes retaliate against subsidies by imposing **countervailing duties**, tariffs on products imported into a country to offset subsidies given to producers or exporters in the exporting country. In this way, the duty serves to cancel out the effect of the subsidy, eliminating the price advantage the exporters would otherwise obtain.

Dumping
Pricing exported products at less than their normal value, generally less than their price in the domestic or third-country markets, or at less than production cost.

Subsidies may allow a manufacturer to practice **dumping**—that is, to charge an unusually low price for exported products, typically lower than that for domestic or third-country customers,

Source: SeanPavonePhoto/Shutterstock

The Ministry of Economy, Trade, and Industry in Japan is typical of national federal agencies that promote international trade and investment.

or even lower than the cost to manufacture the good.[21] The European Union has provided billions of euros in subsidies every year to EU sugar producers, which allowed Europe to become one of the world's largest sugar exporters at artificially low prices. Without the subsidies Europe would be one of the world's biggest sugar importers.

Dumping violates WTO rules because it amounts to unfair competition. But dumping is hard to prove because firms usually do not reveal data on their cost structures. A large MNE that charges very low prices could conceivably drive competitors out of a foreign market, achieve a monopoly, and then raise prices later. Governments in the importing country often respond to dumping by imposing an **antidumping duty**—a tax imposed on products deemed to be dumped and thereby causing injury to producers of competing products in the importing country. The WTO allows this practice.[22] The duties are generally equal to the difference between the product's export price and their normal value.

Antidumping duty
A tax imposed on products deemed to be dumped and causing injury to producers of competing products in the importing country.

Government subsidies are not always direct or overt. For example, governments may support home-country businesses by funding R&D, granting tax exemptions, and offering business development services such as market information, trade missions, and privileged access to key foreign contacts. Most countries have agencies and ministries that provide such services to facilitate the international activities of their own firms. Examples include the Department of Foreign Affairs and International Trade in Canada (www.dfait-maeci.gc.ca), U.K. Trade & Investment in the United Kingdom (www.uktradeinvest.gov.uk), and the International Trade Administration of the U.S. Department of Commerce (www.doc.gov).

Investment incentive
Transfer payment or tax concession made directly to foreign firms to entice them to invest in the country.

Related to subsidies are governmental **investment incentives**, transfer payments or tax concessions made directly to individual foreign firms to entice them to invest in the country. Hong Kong's government put up most of the cash to build the Hong Kong Disney park (www.park.hongkongdisneyland.com). While the park and facilities cost about $1.81 billion, the government provided Disney an investment of $1.74 billion to develop the site.

Recently, Austin, Texas, and Albany, New York, competed for the chance to have the Korean manufacturer Samsung Electronics (www.samsung.com) build a semiconductor plant in their regions. Austin offered $225 million worth of tax relief and other concessions in its successful bid to attract Samsung's $300 million plant, estimated to create nearly 1,000 new jobs locally. To entice MNEs to establish local production facilities, the country of Macedonia offers such incentives as low corporate taxes, immediate access to utilities and transportation, and financial support for training workers (see www.investinmacedonia.com).

Such incentives often help the economic development in a particular region or community. In the 1990s, Germany encouraged foreign companies to invest in the economically disadvantaged East German states by providing tax and investment incentives. The government of Ireland has undertaken various initiatives aimed at promoting Ireland as a place to do business. It targeted foreign companies in the high-tech sector—including medical instruments, pharmaceuticals, and computer software—and offered preferential corporate tax rates of 12 percent. These targeted efforts paid dividends by creating substantial new employment and helping diversify the Irish economy away from agricultural activities.

Governments also support domestic industries by adopting *procurement policies* that restrict purchases to home-country suppliers. Several governments require that air travel purchased with government funds be booked with home-country carriers. Such policies are especially common in countries with large public sectors, such as China and Russia. In the United States, government agencies favor domestic suppliers unless their prices are high compared to foreign suppliers. In Japan, government agencies often do not even consider foreign bids, regardless of pricing. Public procurement agencies often impose requirements that effectively exclude foreign suppliers.

Consequences of Government Intervention

As illustrated in Exhibit 8.5, average tariffs have declined over time. Simultaneously, as shown in Exhibit 8.6, world trade and GDP have flourished. Decreasing trade barriers are a major factor in the growth of global commerce and consequently in rising incomes around the world. Firms that participate actively in international trade and investment not only improve their performance but also contribute to reducing global poverty.[23]

One way of evaluating the effects of government intervention is to examine each nation's level of *economic freedom*, defined as the "absence of government coercion or constraint on the production, distribution, or consumption of goods and services beyond the extent necessary for citizens to protect and maintain liberty itself. In other words, people are free to work, produce, consume, and invest in the ways they feel are most productive."[24] The *Index of Economic Freedom* measures economic freedom in 179 countries.

Exhibit 8.7 shows the degree of economic freedom for each country in the Index for 2012, based on criteria such as the level of trade barriers, rule of law, level of business regulation, and protection of intellectual property rights.[25] The Index classifies virtually all the advanced economies as "free," all the emerging markets as either "free" or "mostly free," and all the developing economies as "mostly unfree" or "repressed," underscoring the close relationship between limited government intervention and economic freedom.

Economic freedom flourishes when government supports the institutions necessary for that freedom and provides an appropriate level of intervention and regulation. In 2010 for the first time, the United States fell into the second highest category, due to increased U.S. federal government intervention in that nation's economy, following the recent global financial crisis. The United Kingdom scores especially well on business freedom and property rights. Canada has been a strong proponent of the Anti-Counterfeiting Trade Agreement (ACTA), which established an international framework for combating infringement of intellectual property rights.[26]

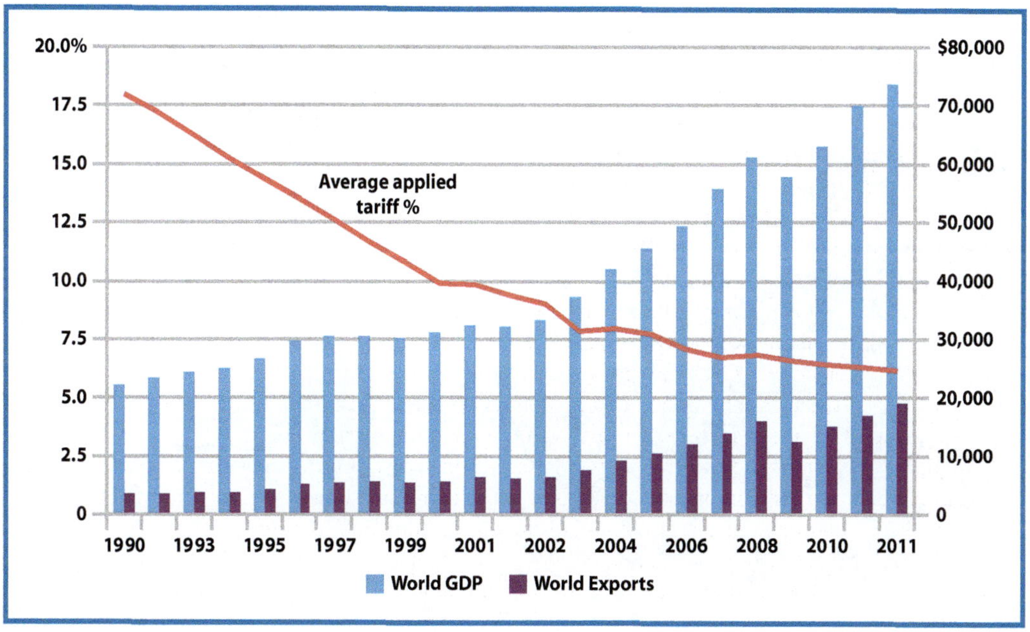

EXHIBIT 8.6

Relationship between Tariffs, World GDP, and the Volume of World Trade

Note: Tariffs given as average percent (red line), World GDP given in billions of U.S.$ (blue column), and Volume of World Trade given in billions of U.S.$ (purple column). Left axis measures Tariffs. Right axis measures World GDP and Volume of World Trade.

Sources: Based on International Monetary Fund World Economic Outlook Database, at www.imf.org; UNCTAD, at http://www.unctadstat.unctad.org; World Bank, http://www.data.worldbank.org.

EXHIBIT 8.7

Countries Ranked by Level of Economic Freedom, 2012

Sources: Based on *2012 Index of Economic Freedom*, The Heritage Foundation, Washington, DC, and the *Wall Street Journal*, New York, accessed at http://www.heritage.org.

ARCTIC OCEAN
Norway
Sweden
Finland
Estonia
Latvia
Lithuania
Russia
Denmark
United Kingdom
Ireland
Netherlands
Belgium
Luxembourg
Germany
Poland
Belarus
Czech Rep.
Slovakia
Ukraine
France
Switz.
Liech.
Austria
Hungary
Moldova
Slovenia
Croatia
Romania
Bosnia-Herzegovina
Serbia
Montenegro
Bulgaria
Macedonia
Albania
Monaco
Andorra
Italy
Greece
Turkey
Georgia
Armenia
Azerbaijan
Portugal
Spain
Malta
Tunisia
Cyprus
Syria
Lebanon
Israel
Jordan
Iraq
Iran
Kuwait
Bahrain
Qatar
United Arab Emirates
Saudi Arabia
Oman
Yemen
Morocco
Algeria
Libya
Egypt
Mauritania
Mali
Niger
Chad
Sudan
Eritrea
Djibouti
Somalia
Ethiopia
Burkina Faso
Guinea
Ivory Coast
Ghana
Togo
Benin
Nigeria
Liberia
Central African Republic
Cameroon
Equatorial Guinea
Gabon
Congo Republic
Congo Democratic Republic (Zaire)
Uganda
Kenya
Rwanda
Burundi
Tanzania
Angola
Zambia
Malawi
Mozambique
Zimbabwe
Namibia
Botswana
Madagascar
Swaziland
South Africa
Lesotho
Comoros
Seychelles
Mauritius
Réunion
SOUTH ATLANTIC OCEAN
Russia
Kazakhstan
Mongolia
Uzbekistan
Kyrgyzstan
Turkmenistan
Tajikistan
Afghanistan
Pakistan
China
Nepal
Bhutan
India
Bangladesh
Sri Lanka
Maldives
INDIAN OCEAN
North Korea
South Korea
Japan
Macau
Hong Kong
Taiwan
Myanmar (Burma)
Laos
Thailand
Vietnam
Cambodia
Philippines
Brunei
Malaysia
Singapore
Indonesia
Timor-leste
Papua New Guinea
Solomon Islands
Micronesia
PACIFIC OCEAN
Samoa
Vanuatu
Fiji
New Caledonia
Tonga
Australia
New Zealand
Level of economic freedom
80-100% free
70-79.9% free
60-69.9% free
50-59.9% free
0-49.9% free
Not ranked
Others

Government intervention and trade barriers raise ethical concerns for developing economies. For example, United States import tariffs on clothing and shoes often exceed 20 percent. The tariffs hurt poor countries like Bangladesh, Pakistan, India, and several nations in Africa, where clothing and shoe exporters are concentrated. United States' tariffs on imports from Cambodia are far higher than on imports from the United Kingdom. The tariffs that confront less-developed economies are often several times those faced by the richest countries.[27]

Government intervention can also offset harmful effects. For example, trade barriers can create or protect jobs. Subsidies can help counterbalance harmful consequences that disproportionately affect the poor. In Denmark, for example, globalization has affected thousands of workers whose jobs have been shifted to other countries with lower labor costs. The Danish government provides generous subsidies to the unemployed, aimed at retraining workers to upgrade their job skills or find work in other fields.[28]

Evolution of Government Intervention

A century ago, trade barriers worldwide were relatively high. The trading environment worsened through two world wars and the Great Depression. In 1938, the United States passed the Smoot-Hawley Tariff Act, which raised U.S. tariffs to near-record highs of more than 50 percent, compared to only about 4 percent today. Tariffs that other countries imposed to retaliate against Smoot-Hawley choked off foreign markets for U.S. agricultural products, leading to plummeting farm prices and many bank failures. In an effort to revive trade, governments began to reduce restrictive tariffs. By the late 1940s, prudent policymaking had begun to substantially reduce tariffs worldwide.

In the 1950s, Latin America and other developing nations adopted protectionist policies aimed at industrialization and economic development. Governments imposed high tariffs and quotas on imports from the developed world, established government-supported enterprises to make the products they formerly imported, and sought to substitute local production for imports. Known as *import substitution*, the approach did not succeed. Companies enjoyed big government subsidies and the protection of high tariffs and quotas. However, these enterprises never became competitive in world markets or raised living standards to the levels of free-trading countries. Meanwhile, the protected industries required ongoing subsidies. Most countries that experimented with import substitution eventually rejected it.

By contrast, from the 1970s onward, Singapore, Hong Kong, Taiwan, and South Korea achieved rapid economic growth by encouraging the development of export-intensive industries. Their model, known as *export-led development*, proved much more successful than import substitution. These countries, along with others in East Asia, such as Malaysia, Thailand, and Indonesia, substantially increased living standards and gained strong international trading links. A rising middle class helped transform these countries into competitive economies.

Elsewhere in Asia, Japan had launched an ambitious program of industrialization and export-led development. The country's rise from poverty in the 1940s to one of the world's wealthiest countries by the 1980s has been called the *Japanese miracle*. The feat was achieved with the help of national strategic policies, including tariffs that fostered and protected Japan's infant industries such as automobiles, shipbuilding, and consumer electronics.

India once embraced a model of high trade and investment barriers, state intervention in labor and financial markets, a large public sector, heavy business regulation, and central planning. The model contributed to the nation's poor economic performance over several decades. Beginning in the early 1990s, however, India began to open its markets to foreign trade and investment. Trade liberalization and privatization of state enterprises have progressed slowly, but reforms have fueled much progress. Between 1992 and 2012, India's average annual income rose from about $330 in real terms to more than $1,400 in 2012, an impressive achievement.

After adopting communism in 1949, China relied on centralized economic planning, in which agriculture and manufacturing were controlled by state-run industries. The country remained relatively closed to international trade until the 1980s, when it began to liberalize its economy. In 2001, China joined the WTO and committed to reducing trade barriers. Trade has stimulated the Chinese economy. By 2012, its GDP was more than ten times the 1995 level, and the value of exports had reached nearly $1.9 trillion. China has become a leading exporter of manufactured products and home to numerous large MNEs that compete with Western firms.

General Agreement on Tariffs and Trade

In 1947, twenty-three nations signed the General Agreement on Tariffs and Trade (GATT), the first major effort to systematically reduce trade barriers worldwide. The GATT created: (1) a process to reduce tariffs through continuous negotiations among member nations; (2) an agency to serve as watchdog over world trade; and (3) a forum for resolving trade disputes.

The GATT introduced the concept of *most favored nation* (renamed *normal trade relations* in 1998), according to which each signatory nation agreed to extend the tariff reductions covered in a trade agreement with a trading partner to all other countries. Thus, a concession to one country became a concession to all. Eventually, the GATT was superseded by the WTO in 1995 and grew to include about 150 member nations. The organization proved extremely effective and resulted in the greatest global decline in trade barriers in history. The *Global Trend* feature highlights the founding and current progress of the WTO.

Source: Liba Taylor/Alamy

Bangladesh is a major clothing exporter that faces high tariffs. Here, women work at Dhaka, the Bangladesh capital and a center of garment manufacturing.

GLOBAL TREND

The World Trade Organization and Collapse of the Doha Round

Based in Geneva, Switzerland, the World Trade Organization (www.wto.org) is the main watchdog for world trade and counts some 150 countries as its members. The WTO works to ensure world trade operates smoothly, fairly, and with as few restrictions as possible. Since joining the WTO in 2001, for example, China has gradually reduced import tariffs and quotas. Most recently, the WTO has been working to reduce trade barriers in the agricultural and services sectors.

Services like the expertise of a lawyer or an accountant are intangible. Consequently, as they do not pass through ports or customs stations, governments usually cannot impose tariffs on them. Thus, services are subject to various *nontariff* trade barriers. For example, some countries in Europe refuse to license foreign insurance companies. In transportation, the United States and numerous other nations require their own merchandise fleets to carry their country's cargo, creating a barrier to foreign-based cargo handlers.

Governments also restrict services by setting licensing and professional standards that may be difficult for foreigners to meet. Regulations usually ensure that law, medicine, accounting, and other professions are undertaken by people who are educated locally, speak the national language, and are socialized according to local standards and norms. Standards in one country are usually not recognized by other countries. Thus, lawyers, doctors, accountants, and many other professionals face restrictions when attempting to do business abroad.

The Doha Development Agenda was a round of WTO negotiations launched in Qatar in 2001 that sought to reduce barriers in the services sector. The WTO wants to ensure that banks, hotel chains, insurance firms, tour operators, transport companies, and other service firms enjoy the same trade and investment freedoms that apply to goods producers. The Doha Agenda also sought freer trade in agricultural goods, where restraints are particularly burdensome to developing countries. Free global trade in agricultural products is the best way to ensure widespread access and lower prices for food. Doha was the first round of WTO negotiations in which big emerging markets, especially Brazil, China, and India, played a strong role. The unique circumstances of such countries have increased the complexity of negotiations.

Unfortunately, the talks collapsed in 2008 when trade negotiators were unable to reach agreement. The main reason was that, under WTO rules, all nations were required to agree to all parts of the final deal. This proved impossible for various reasons. For example, China and India insisted on protecting the agricultural sectors in their countries. India alone has more than 200 million farmers, and the Indian government is reluctant to expose them to international competition. In the wake of Doha's collapse, many nations are choosing to concentrate on negotiating bilateral (two-country) and regional trade deals instead. As of mid-2012, the Doha round of talks had not yet restarted.

Sources: P. Coy, "Free Trade: After the Impasse," *BusinessWeek*, August 11, 2008, p. 29; "Beyond Doha," *Economist*, October 11, 2008, pp. 30–33; Carolyn Evans, "Bilateralism, Multilateralism, and Trade Rules," *FRBSF Economic Letter*, January 9, 2012, pp. 1–5; Oxford Analytica Daily Brief Service, "International: Stalled Doha Spurs Trade Discrimination," February 12, 2010, p. 1; United States Trade Representative, "National Trade Estimate Report," 2011, retrieved from http://www.ustr.gov; World Trade Organization, 2007, retrieved from http://www.wto.org.

Intervention and the Global Financial Crisis

The recent global recession and financial crisis have raised new questions about government's role in business and the world economy. The crisis arose largely from inadequate regulation and insufficient enforcement of current regulations in the banking and finance sectors. In response, governments worldwide increased regulation and examined ways to improve enforcement. For example, the U.S. government has increased the power of its Treasury Department, Federal Reserve System, and Federal Deposit Insurance Corporation (FDIC). The European Central Bank is creating a new agency that aims to take aggressive action in needed areas. The European Union has increased oversight of multinational banks and supervision of financial institutions. The United Nations has called for greater transparency in financial activities and closure of loopholes that allow excessive speculation in global finance.[29]

Some governments increased protectionism in an effort to safeguard jobs and wage levels. Argentina and Brazil, for example, increased import tariffs on numerous products. Russia raised tariffs on dozens of goods, including cars and combine harvesters.[30] Hoping to jump-start economic growth, governments also increased subsidies to their own industries. The EU granted more than $50 billion in aid to Daimler (Germany), Skoda (Czech Republic), and other struggling carmakers in Europe. The government of the United Kingdom provided substantial subsidies to U.K. banks and financial institutions. China has pumped hundreds of billions of dollars into its own economy.[31]

In addition to the harmful fallout of the recession and financial crisis, rising protectionism impacted international commerce. Ripple effects of government reforms are extending beyond the banking and financial areas.[32]

How Firms Can Respond to Government Intervention

Although managers' initial tendency might be to avoid markets with high trade and investment barriers or excessive government intervention, this course is not usually practical. Depending on the industry and country, firms generally must cope with protectionism and other forms of intervention. In extractive industries such as aluminum and petroleum, for example, companies may have little choice but to operate in nations that impose formidable barriers. The food-processing, biotechnology, and pharmaceutical industries also encounter countless laws and regulations abroad.

Strategies for Managers

We've seen that China, India, and numerous other countries in Africa, Asia, Latin America, and Eastern and Central Europe feature extensive trade barriers and government involvement. Yet many firms seek to target emerging markets and developing economies because of the huge long-term potential they offer.[33] Firms devise various strategies to manage harmful government intervention.

RESEARCH TO GATHER KNOWLEDGE AND INTELLIGENCE Experienced managers continually scan the business environment to identify the nature of government intervention and to plan market-entry strategies and host-country operations. They review their return-on-investment criteria to account for the increased cost and risk of trade and investment barriers. For example, the EU is devising new guidelines that affect company operations in areas ranging from product liability laws to standards for investment in European industries.

CHOOSE THE MOST APPROPRIATE ENTRY STRATEGIES Tariffs and most nontariff trade barriers apply to exporting, whereas investment barriers apply to FDI. Most firms choose exporting as their initial entry strategy. However, if high tariffs are present, managers should consider other strategies, such as FDI, licensing, and joint ventures that allow the firm to operate directly in the target market, avoiding import barriers. For example, Taiwan's Foxconn, a contract manufacturer for Apple and other electronics firms, built a factory in Brazil partly to avoid the country's high tariffs on imported goods.

However, even investment-based entry is affected by tariffs if it requires importing raw materials and parts to manufacture finished products in the host country. Tariffs usually vary with the *form* of an imported product. To minimize tariff costs, many companies ship manufactured products "knocked-down" and assemble them in the target market. In countries with relatively high tariffs on imported personal computers, importers often bring in the parts and assemble the computers locally. Eastman Kodak (www.kodak.com) imports parts and components into the United States, which it then uses to manufacture photographic equipment. Kodak could produce the finished equipment abroad, but the tariff on parts and components is lower. By manufacturing in the United States, Kodak avoids paying higher tariffs.[34]

Source: © Bernd Kröger/Fotolia

Many firms lobby national governments, such as Germany's parliament in Berlin, for lower barriers to trade and investment.

TAKE ADVANTAGE OF FOREIGN TRADE ZONES In an effort to create jobs and stimulate local economic development, governments establish foreign trade zones (also known as *free trade zones* or *free ports*). A **foreign trade zone (FTZ)** is an area within a country that receives imported goods for assembly or other processing and subsequent re-export.[35] Products brought into an FTZ are not subject to duties, taxes, or quotas until they, or the products made from them, enter into the non-FTZ commercial territory of the country where the FTZ is located. Firms use FTZs to assemble foreign dutiable materials and components into finished products, which are then re-exported. Alternatively, firms may use FTZs to manage inventory of parts, components, or finished products that the firm will eventually need at some other location. In the United States, for example, Japanese carmakers store vehicles at the port of Jacksonville, Florida, without having to pay duties until the cars are shipped to U.S. dealerships.

Foreign trade zone (FTZ)
An area within a country that receives imported goods for assembly or other processing and re-export. For customs purposes the FTZ is treated as if it is outside the country's borders.

FTZs exist in more than seventy-five countries, usually near seaports or airports. They can be as small as a factory or as large as an entire country. The United States is home to several hundred FTZs used by thousands of firms. The Colon Free Zone (www.colonfreezone.com), located on the Atlantic side of the Panama Canal, is an enormous FTZ where products are imported, stored, modified, repacked, and re-exported without being subject to tariffs or customs regulations. The many private firms and wholesalers that set up shop inside the huge zone transship their merchandise from Panama to other parts of the Western Hemisphere and Europe. Some firms obtain FTZ status within their own physical facilities.

A successful experiment with FTZs has been **maquiladoras**—export-assembly plants in northern Mexico along the U.S. border that produce components and finished products, usually destined for the United States. Since the 1960s, "maquilas" have imported materials and equipment on a tariff-free basis for assembly or manufacturing and then re-exported the assembled products. Today under NAFTA, maquiladoras employ millions of Mexicans who assemble clothing, furniture, car parts, electronics, and other goods. The arrangement enables firms from the United States, Asia, and Europe to tap low-cost labor, favorable duties, and government incentives while serving the U.S. market. Maquilas account for about half of Mexico's exports.

Maquiladoras
Export-assembly plants in northern Mexico along the U.S. border that produce components and typically finished products destined for the United States on a tariff-free basis.

SEEK FAVORABLE CUSTOMS CLASSIFICATIONS FOR EXPORTED PRODUCTS One approach for reducing exposure to trade barriers is to have exported products classified in the appropriate harmonized product code. As noted earlier in this chapter, many products can be classified within two or more categories, each of which may imply a different tariff. For example, some telecommunications equipment can be classified as electric machinery, electronics, or measuring devices. The manufacturer should analyze the trade barriers on differing categories to ensure exported products are classified under the lowest tariff code. Or the manufacturer may be able to modify the exported product in a way that helps minimize trade barriers. South Korea faced a quota on the export of nonrubber footwear to the United States. By shifting manufacturing to rubber-soled shoes, Korean firms greatly increased their footwear exports.

TAKE ADVANTAGE OF INVESTMENT INCENTIVES AND OTHER GOVERNMENT SUPPORT PROGRAMS Obtaining economic development incentives from host- or home-country governments is another strategy to reduce the cost of trade and investment barriers. When Mercedes built a factory in Alabama, it benefitted from reduced taxes and direct subsidies provided by the Alabama state government. When Siemens built a semiconductor plant in Portugal, it received subsidies from the Portuguese government and the EU. Incentives cover nearly 40 percent of Siemens's investment and training costs. In Europe, Japan, and the United States, governments increasingly provide incentives to entice firms to set up shop within their borders. In addition to cash outlays, incentives also include reduced utility rates, employee training programs, tax holidays, and construction of new roads and other infrastructure.

LOBBY FOR FREER TRADE AND INVESTMENT More nations are liberalizing markets to create jobs and increase tax revenues. The trend results partly from the efforts of firms to lobby domestic and foreign governments to lower their trade and investment barriers. The Japanese have achieved much success in reducing trade barriers by lobbying U.S. and European governments. In China, domestic and foreign firms lobby the government to relax protectionist policies and regulations that make China a difficult place to do business. Foreign firms often hire former Chinese government officials to help lobby their former colleagues.[36] European automakers have obtained various concessions by lobbying individual state governments in the United States. BMW leased its 1,039-acre factory site in South Carolina at an annual rent of one dollar. The private sector lobbies federal authorities to undertake government-to-government trade negotiations, aimed at lowering barriers. Private firms bring complaints to world bodies, especially the WTO, to address unfair trading practices of key international markets.

CLOSING CASE Government Intervention at Airbus and Boeing

In the 1960s, United States companies such as Boeing (www.boeing.com) and McDonnell Douglas were the dominant players in global aircraft manufacturing. Boeing was founded in 1916 in Seattle, and had many years to develop the critical mass necessary to become the world's leading aerospace manufacturer. During World War II and the subsequent Cold War years, Boeing was the recipient of many lucrative contracts from the U.S. Department of Defense.

In Europe, no single country possessed the means to launch an aerospace company capable of challenging Boeing. Manufacturing commercial aircraft is complex and capital-intensive and requires a highly skilled workforce. In the 1970s, the governments of France, Germany, Spain, and the United Kingdom formed an alliance, supported with massive government subsidies, to create Airbus S.A.S. (www.airbus.com). By 1981, the four-country alliance succeeded in becoming the world's number-two civil aircraft manufacturer. Airbus launched the A300, among the best-selling commercial aircraft of all time. Airbus also created the A320, receiving more than 400 orders before its first flight and becoming the fastest-selling large passenger jet in aviation history. By 1992, Airbus had captured roughly one-third of the global commercial aircraft market.

Government Support for Airbus

Since the 1940s, European governments have pursued public policies based on democratic socialism. Under this system, the government plays a strong role in the national economy and provides key services such as health care, mass transit, and sometimes banking and housing. Most Europeans are accustomed to government playing a significant role in guiding the national economy.

In this context, Airbus has benefitted enormously from government support. The firm has received tens of billions of euros of subsidies and soft loans from the four founding country governments and the EU. Airbus must repay the loans only if it achieves profitability. Government aid has financed, in whole or part, every major Airbus aircraft model. European governments have forgiven Airbus's debt, provided huge equity infusions, dedicated infrastructure support, and financed R&D for civil aircraft projects.

Airbus is currently a stock-held company jointly owned by the British, Germans, French, and Spanish. It is based in Toulouse, France, but has R&D and production operations scattered throughout Europe. European governments justify their financial aid to Airbus on several grounds. First, Airbus R&D activities result in the development of valuable new technologies. Second, Airbus provides jobs to some 53,000 skilled and semiskilled Europeans. Third, its value-chain activities attract massive amounts of capital into Europe. Finally, Airbus generates enormous tax revenues.

Complaints about Unfair Government Intervention

Boeing and the U.S. government have long complained about the massive subsidies and soft loans that were responsible not only for Airbus's birth, but also for its ongoing success. The outcry became louder in the 2000s, when Airbus surpassed Boeing in annual sales, becoming the world's leading commercial aircraft manufacturer. Boeing has argued that Airbus never would have gotten this far without government support.

In 2005, the U.S. Trade Representative brought its case to the WTO. The case arose because EU member states approved $3.7 billion in new subsidies and soft loans to Airbus. The case alleged that financial aid for the A350, A380, and earlier Airbus aircraft qualified as subsidies under the WTO's Agreement on Subsidies and Countervailing Measures (ASCM) and that the subsidies were actionable because they adversely affected international trade. Under the ASCM, subsidies to specific firms or industries from a government or other public bodies are prohibited. Airbus had applied to the governments of France, Germany, Spain, and the United Kingdom for aid to launch its model A350.

In 2011, the WTO ruled that EU aid to Airbus had caused Boeing to lose market share in Asia and other markets. EU officials argued that government subsidies to Airbus were permissible and that it was up to individual EU countries to decide whether to provide them. However, the WTO also ruled that Boeing received more than $5 billion in U.S. government subsidies in the development of the 787 Dreamliner.

Government Support for Boeing

The EU argues the United States government has indirectly subsidized Boeing through massive defense contracts paid via tax dollars. The U.S. government gave Boeing more than $23 billion in indirect government subsidies by means of R&D funding and other indirect support from the Pentagon and NASA, the nation's space agency. Boeing is at liberty to use the knowledge acquired from such projects to produce civilian aircraft. The state of Washington, Boeing's primary manufacturing and assembly location, has provided the firm with tax breaks, infrastructure support, and other incentives totaling billions of dollars.

The EU also has a case at the WTO regarding Boeing's relations with Japanese business partners. Boeing entered an alliance with Japan's Mitsubishi, Kawasaki, and Fuji to build the 787 Dreamliner. The Japanese firms provided billions in soft loans, repayable only if the aircraft is commercially successful.

New Aircraft from Airbus and Boeing

In 2007, Airbus launched the A380, an innovative airplane with an upper deck extending the entire length of the fuselage and a cabin that provides 50 percent more floor space than Boeing's largest aircraft. The A380 can seat between 555 and 853 passengers, depending on the seating configuration. It has a maximum range of 15,000 kilometers (8,000 nautical miles). The total cost to develop and launch the A380 reached 15 billion euros (U.S. $21 billion), partly supported by funding from European governments.

Boeing successfully launched the 787 Dreamliner in 2007 and is ahead of Airbus in launching innovative and fuel-efficient aircraft. Airbus is developing a mid-sized A350 model to compete with Boeing's 787.

In 2008, the government of China established a company to make passenger jumbo jets, part of its quest to challenge Boeing and Airbus in the global aircraft industry. China Commercial Aircraft Co. was established in Shanghai amid forecasts that China's domestic market for commercial aircraft will increase fivefold by 2026.

Global Financial Crisis

The recent global financial crisis adversely impacted Airbus and Boeing. Both companies had to reduce output and lay off thousands of workers. Following sharp drops in passenger traffic, airlines grounded planes and cut routes. Longer term, Airbus aims to reorganize its global operations, outsource more manufacturing, and sell all or part of six factories. It has begun to produce aircraft in the United States. Airbus and Boeing are generating much new business from emerging markets, and ramped up production substantially to meet anticipated demand. In 2012, however, an industry expert warned that both Airbus and Boeing were producing too many commercial aircraft, risking a potential global glut.

AACSB: Reflective Thinking Skills, Ethical Understanding and Reasoning Abilities

Case Questions

1. Where do you stand? Do you think EU subsidies and soft loans to Airbus are fair? Why or why not? What advantages does Airbus gain from free financial support from the EU governments? Are complaints about EU subsidies fair in light of Europe's history of democratic socialism?
2. Do you believe U.S. military contracts with Boeing amount to subsidies? Have these types of payments provided Boeing with unfair advantages? Justify your answer.
3. Assuming that Airbus cannot compete without subsidies and loans, is it likely that the EU will discontinue its financial support of Airbus? Is it in the EU's interests to continue supporting Airbus? Justify your answer.
4. In the event the WTO rules against Airbus and tells it to stop accepting subsidies and soft loans, how should Airbus management respond? What new approaches can management pursue to maintain Airbus's lead in the global commercial aircraft industry?

Sources: Doug Cameron and David Kesmodel, "Warning is Issued about Plane Glut," *Wall Street Journal*, February 23, 2012, pp. B6–B6; Corporate profiles of Airbus and Boeing at http://www.hoovers.com; K. Epstein & J. Crown, "Globalization Bites Boeing," *BusinessWeek*, March 24, 2008, p. 32; D. Gauthier-Villars & D. Michaels, "Airbus Buyers Get French Aid," *Wall Street Journal*, January 27, 2009, p. B4; Max Kingsley-Jones, "Throwing Down the Gauntlet," *Airline Business*, October 2011, pp. 28–30; N. Luthra, "Boeing to Sell India $2.1 Billion in Planes," *Wall Street Journal*, January 6, 2009, p. B4; D. Michaels, "Airbus Trims Jumbo Output as Carriers Defer Orders," *Wall Street Journal*, May 7, 2009, p. B1; Pilita Clark, Joshua Chaffin, and James Politi, "WTO Rules that Boeing Received $5.3bn in Aid," *Financial Times*, April 1, 2011, p. 19; "China to Make Jumbo Jetliners, Trim Roles of Boeing, Airbus," *Wall Street Journal*, May 12, 2008, p. B4; "How Airbus Flew Past Its American Rival," *Financial Times*, March 17, 2005, p. 6; J. Lunsford and D. Michaels, "Bet on Huge Plane Trips Up Airbus," *Wall Street Journal*, June 15, 2006, p. A1; Stephan Wittig, "The WTO Panel Report on Boeing subsidies: A Critical Assessment," *Intereconomics*, May 2011, pp. 148–153.

Note: The authors acknowledge the assistance of Stephanie Regales with this case.

CHAPTER ESSENTIALS

MyManagementLab

Go to **www.mymanagementlab.com** to complete the problems marked with this icon ✪.

Key Terms

antidumping duty
countervailing duty
currency control
customs
dumping
export control
foreign trade zone (FTZ)
import license
investment incentive
maquiladoras
nontariff trade barrier
protectionism
quota
subsidy
tariff

Summary

In this chapter, you learned about:

1. **The nature of government intervention**

   Despite the value of free trade, governments often intervene in international business. **Protectionism** refers to national economic policies designed to restrict free trade and protect domestic industries from foreign competition. Government intervention arises typically in the form of tariffs, nontariff trade barriers, and investment barriers. **Tariffs** are taxes on imported products, imposed mainly to collect government revenue and protect domestic industries from foreign competition. **Nontariff trade barriers** consist of policies that restrict trade without directly imposing a tax. An example of a nontariff trade barrier is a quota, a quantitative restriction on imports. Managers find out what tariffs apply to their products by consulting harmonized code schedules, available from government agencies.

2. **Rationale for government intervention**

   Governments impose trade and investment barriers to achieve political, social, or economic objectives. Such barriers are either defensive or offensive. A key rationale is the protection of the nation's economy, its industries, and its workers. **Export controls** limit trade in sensitive products deemed critical to national security. Governments also impose barriers to protect infant industries.

3. **Instruments of government intervention**

   Governments also impose regulations and technical standards, as well as administrative and bureaucratic procedures. Countries may also impose **currency controls** to minimize international withdrawal of national currency. FDI and ownership restrictions ensure that the nation maintains partial or full ownership of firms within its national borders. Governments also provide **subsidies**, a form of payment or other material support. Foreign governments may offset foreign subsidies by imposing **countervailing duties**. With **dumping**, a firm charges abnormally low prices abroad. A government may respond to dumping by imposing an **antidumping duty**. Governments support home-grown firms by providing investment incentives and biased government procurement policies.

4. **Consequences of government intervention**

   Economic freedom refers to the extent of government intervention in the national economy. Government intervention and trade barriers can raise ethical concerns that affect developing economies and low-income consumers. However, government intervention also can be used to offset such harmful effects.

5. **Evolution of government intervention**

   Intervention has a long history. In the late 1800s, many countries imposed substantial protectionism. From the 1930s onward, countries reduced trade barriers worldwide. The nature and outcomes of government intervention have varied across Latin America, Japan, India, and China. The most important development for reducing trade barriers was the General Agreement on Tariffs and Trade (GATT), replaced by the World Trade Organization (WTO). The 150 members of the WTO account for nearly all world trade.

The recent global financial crisis arose from inadequate regulation in the banking and finance sectors. In response, governments implemented new regulations and some protectionism. Government reforms have had ripple effects extending beyond the financial sector.

6. How firms can respond to government intervention

Firms should conduct research to understand the extent and nature of trade and investment barriers abroad. When trade barriers are substantial, FDI or joint ventures are often the most appropriate entry strategies. Where importing is essential, the firm can take advantage of **foreign trade zones**, areas where imports receive preferential tariff treatment. Government assistance in the form of subsidies and incentives helps reduce the impact of protectionism. Firms sometimes lobby the home and foreign governments for freer trade and investment.

Test Your Comprehension AACSB: Reflective Thinking Skills

1. Distinguish among tariffs, nontariff trade barriers, investment barriers, and government subsidies.
2. What are the major types of nontariff trade barriers? Suggest business strategies for minimizing the effect of nontariff trade barriers.
3. Distinguish between countervailing duties and antidumping duties.
4. In what ways do government subsidies and procurement policies amount to protectionism?
5. What is the rationale for intervention? Why do governments engage in protectionism?
6. How has government intervention evolved during the global financial crisis?
7. Describe various company strategies to manage government intervention.
8. What is the role of FDI, licensing, and joint ventures in reducing the impact of import tariffs?

Apply Your Understanding AACSB: Ethical Understanding and Reasoning Abilities, Reflective Thinking Skills, Communication Abilities

1. TelComm Corporation is a manufacturer of components for the cell phone industry. TelComm founder Alex Bell heard that China has the world's largest number of cell phone users and wants to begin exporting the firm's products there. But TelComm has little international experience. Mr. Bell is unaware of the various types of nontariff trade barriers that TelComm might face in China and other foreign markets. Please summarize major nontariff trade barriers to Mr. Bell. What types of investment barriers might TelComm face in the event management decides to establish a factory in China to manufacture cell phone components? What can TelComm management do to minimize the threat of these nontariff trade and investment barriers?

2. *Ethical Dilemma*: The United States steel industry, once the world leader, now produces less steel than China, Japan, or the European Union. American steel producers are threatened by price-competitive suppliers in India, Russia, and other emerging markets. The U.S. steel industry dealt with this threat by launching a lobbying campaign to persuade the U.S. government to impose barriers on the import of foreign steel. The following advertisement is an example of this effort:

   > In recent years, the United States has lost millions of manufacturing jobs because domestic factories have shifted their operations to low-wage countries. Manufacturing assures our national defense, our global leadership, and the living standards of more than 17 million workers. Other nations subsidize their domestic steel industries. Longer-term, subsidized imports will destroy a vital American industry and U.S. jobs. In an uncertain and dangerous world, does America really want to become dependent on China, India, Russia, and developing countries for something so basic as steel?

   Evaluate this statement. How valid is the argument? Using the Ethical Framework in Chapter 5, analyze the arguments for and against imposing trade barriers on the import of steel from abroad. Should the U.S. government impose trade barriers? What is the effect of barriers on (a) U.S. steel producers, (b) U.S. firms that use a lot of steel to manufacture finished products, and (c) consumers of products made with U.S. steel. Recall that China, India, and Russia are emerging markets with substantial poverty. What is the effect of the barriers on these countries?

3. *Ethical Dilemma*: You are Vice President for International Sales at FoodTrade, a large trading company that exports processed foods to Africa. You are often frustrated that African countries impose high tariffs (typically 75 percent) on processed food imports. These barriers raise FoodTrade's cost of doing business and make your prices less competitive in African markets. But Africa suffers from widespread poverty and African governments use tariffs to raise needed revenues and achieve policy objectives. Using the concepts in this chapter and the Ethical Framework in Chapter 5, analyze the arguments for and against high agricultural tariffs in Africa. How do the tariffs harm or benefit Africa? Do you perceive any ethical concerns in Africa's use of high tariffs on agricultural goods? What ethical concerns do you perceive in FoodTrade's efforts to avoid the tariffs? How should FoodTrade respond to the tariffs?

globalEDGE INTERNET EXERCISES

(http://www.globalEDGE.msu.edu)

AACSB: Reflective Thinking Skills, Analytic Skills, Ethical Understanding and Reasoning Abilities

Refer to Chapter 1, page 58, for instructions on how to access and use globalEDGE™.

1. Your firm is considering exporting to two countries: Kenya and Vietnam. However, management's knowledge about the trade policies of these countries is limited. Conduct a search at globalEDGE™ to identify the current import policies, tariffs, and restrictions in these countries. Prepare a brief report on your findings. In addition to globalEDGE™, other useful sites include the World Trade Organization (www.wto.org; enter country name in the search engine) and the U.S. Commercial Service (www.buyusa.gov).
2. The United States Trade Representative (USTR) develops international trade and investment policies for the U.S. government. Visit the USTR Web site from globalEDGE™ or directly (www.ustr.gov). Search for "National Trade Estimate Report" for the latest year. This document summarizes trade barriers around the world. See the reports for the country of your choice. What are the country's import policies and practices? What are its nontariff trade barriers? What about barriers in the services sector? Are there any sectors that seem to be particularly protected (for example, energy, telecommunications)? What is the nature of government restrictions on e-commerce? If you worked at a firm that exported its products to the country, how would you use the USTR report to develop international business strategies?
3. Visit the following Web portals and review their perspectives on the debate about free trade and government policies on trade barriers. Given the inherent conflict between national interests, special interests, asymmetries in world wage rates, and other economic conditions, what is the best path forward for national governments? That is, should governments generally favor free trade, or should they intervene to protect national interests? Justify your answer.

   http://www.aflcio.org/globaleconomy

   http://www.citizen.org/trade

   http://www.heritage.org/issues

   http://www.sierraclub.org/trade

   http://www.wto.org.

CHAPTER 13

Evaluation of Countries for Operations

OBJECTIVES

After studying this chapter, you should be able to

1. Grasp company strategies for sequencing the penetration of countries
2. See how scanning techniques can help managers limit geographic alternatives and consider otherwise overlooked areas
3. Discern the major opportunity and risk variables to consider in deciding whether and where to expand abroad
4. Know the methods and problems of collecting and comparing international information
5. Understand some simplifying tools for helping decide where to operate
6. Consider how companies allocate emphasis among the countries where they operate
7. Comprehend why location decisions do not necessarily compare different countries' possibilities
8. Fathom the conditions that may cause prime business locations to change in the future

Source: © Nitr - Fotolia.com

The place to get top speed out of a horse is not the place where you can get top speed out of a canoe.

—African (Hausa) proverb

CASE Burger King®

As of 2013, Burger King was the world's largest flame-broiled fast food hamburger chain, with 12,997 restaurants in 84 countries and two U.S. territories (Guam and Puerto Rico).[1] Only Yum Brands, Subway, McDonald's, and Starbucks had more. Its regional distribution of restaurants was North America (Canada and the United States), 57 percent; Europe, Middle East, and Africa, 24 percent; Latin America and Caribbean, 11 percent; and Asia-Pacific, 8 percent. It plans to have 17,000 restaurants by 2016, with most growth occurring internationally. Despite such a widespread global presence, 60 percent of its foreign restaurants were in only eight countries. Map 13.1 shows the countries with the largest number of restaurants.

Two major ways Burger King differentiates itself from competitors are the way it cooks hamburgers—flame-broiling rather than grilling or frying—and the options it offers customers as to how they want their burgers prepared. The company began in 1954 by offering a menu of beef burgers, fries, milk shakes, and sodas; that menu now includes breakfast as well as turkey burgers, wraps, smoothies, desserts, a variety of coffees, and various chicken, fish, and salad offerings. Many of these additions have come since 2011 as the company has sought to fill menu gaps and broaden its target market. Nevertheless, hamburgers remain the company's mainstay, and 2007 marked the 50th anniversary of the Whopper® sandwich, its signature product.

Burger King has also differentiated itself with some inventive advertising campaigns, such as its use of *HAVE IT YOUR WAY*® ads and the figure of a man who was the Burger "King" for a long time. The company logo has changed slightly through the years, yet it has always been displayed and recognizable globally, as illustrated in the chapter opener photo of a sign advertising a restaurant in Thailand.

A BIT OF HISTORY

Starting out as Insta-Burger King in 1954, the corporation opened five restaurants during its first five years—all in the Miami, Florida area. In 1959, with its name shortened to Burger King, it began domestic franchising and grew to 274 restaurants. Pillsbury, owner of several other retail food groups, purchased the corporation in 1967 and franchising increased substantially over the next few years. When Pillsbury shed its restaurant business in 1989, it sold Burger King to the British company Grand Metropolitan, which then converted most of its Wimpy restaurants in the United Kingdom to Burger King restaurants. Grand Metropolitan merged with Guinness in 1997 to form Diageo, and when Diageo divested itself of restaurant operations in 2002, it sold Burger King to a consortium of private equity firms controlled by TPG Capital, Bain Capital Partners, and the Goldman Sachs Funds. In May 2006, Burger King consummated its initial public offering, becoming a publicly traded company on the New York Stock Exchange. In 2010, however, 3G Capital, backed by Brazilian investors, took the company private again with the prospect that management could concentrate on medium- and long-term operations rather than being subject to shareholder responses to short-term performance. Two years later, the company once again went public and changed its name to Burger King Worldwide, Inc. to convey its interest in future global expansion. The years of transformed ownership have caused changes in emphasis for Burger King, and its interests have sometimes been secondary to those of its parent company.

Despite the evolving ownership, Burger King did expand internationally: to the Bahamas and Puerto Rico in the early 1960s, and Europe, Asia, and Latin America in the 1970s. Some of these moves turned out to be highly successful, a few did not. It entered and then retreated from operations in such countries as Colombia, France, Israel, Japan, and Oman. (It has reentered some of these markets.) Much of Burger King's early international forays came about either because someone in another country approached someone in the corporation or because someone in the corporation was familiar with a particular country and thought it would offer opportunities. Two reasons have been prevalent in the company's decisions to leave markets: (1) the franchisee not performing adequately, such as not making royalty payments or investing sufficiently in the business; and (2) the market being too small to support the necessary infrastructure, such as slaughterhouse and beef-grinding facilities.

Over time, Burger King has taken a more systematic approach toward restaurant expansion. It still sees substantial growth opportunities within the United States but considers that a more mature market for fast food, especially hamburgers, than other countries. In seeking new places to enter, Burger King looks most favorably at countries with large populations (especially young people), high consumption of beef, availability of capital to franchisees for growth, a safe pro-business environment, growth in shopping centers, and availability of a potential franchisee with experience and resources. Recently its model has been to grant exclusive franchisee rights for a

MAP 13.1 Burger King's Major Restaurant Locations by Country

Although Burger King had restaurants in 84 countries plus two U.S. territories at the start of 2013, 85 percent of those restaurants were located in only nine countries. These nine countries, along with the number of restaurants, are shown on the map. (In Australia, the restaurants use the Jack in the Box name rather than the Burger King name.)

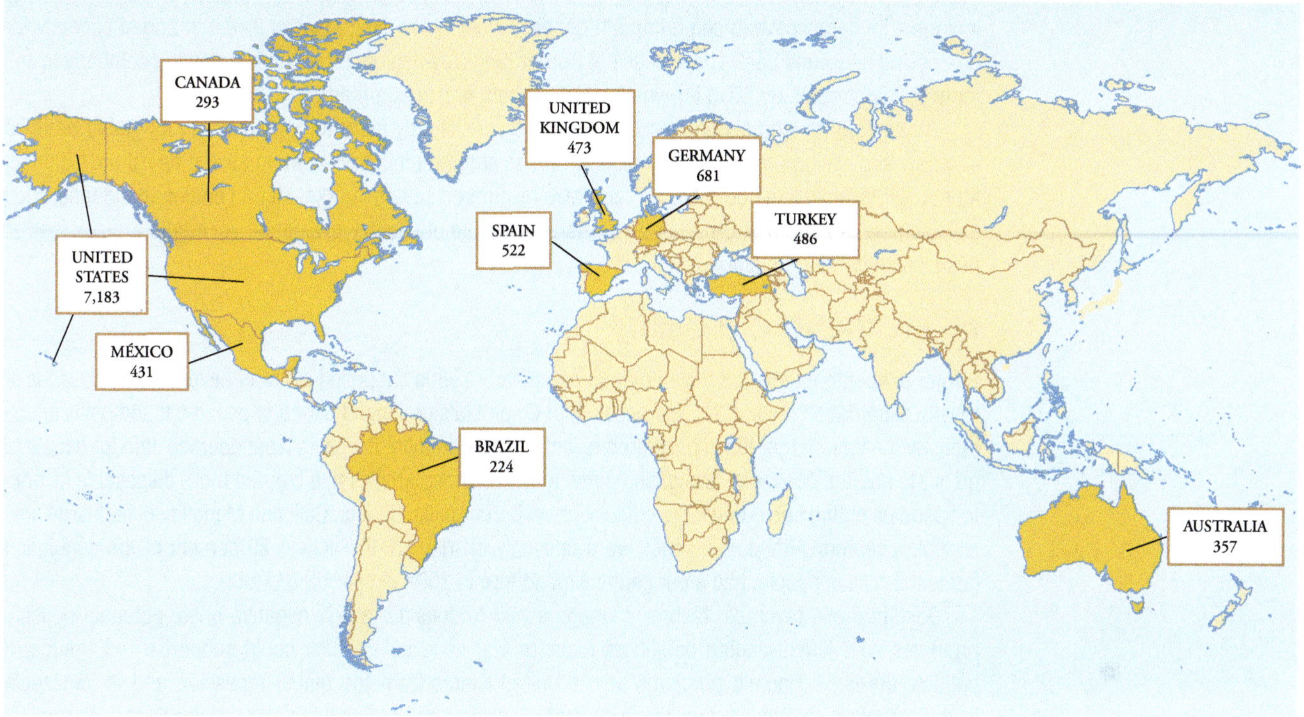

country or group of countries by pairing a private equity firm with an experienced restaurant operator in a joint venture (JV). In some cases, Burger King has become the third party in the JV without committing capital to it.

Overall, Burger King has expanded abroad later than its primary rival, McDonald's, resulting in both advantages and disadvantages. On the one hand, later entry is a drawback in very small markets due to an inadequate number of suppliers, such as only one slaughterhouse whose owners may be unwilling to work with more than one customer. On the other hand, a late entry in larger markets may benefit from the product demand and supply infrastructure created by earlier entrants. In some later-entry markets, Burger King has been able to concentrate almost entirely on emphasizing its product (*HAVE IT YOUR WAY®*, good taste of flame-broiled burgers) without incurring early development costs. For instance, in Latin America and the Caribbean, McDonald's and Burger King compete in almost all countries and territories, with Burger King currently leading in the number of restaurants in about half of those markets.

Keep in mind that local firms also learn from the successes of foreign fast-food companies, sometimes altering their menus and flavorings to appeal to local tastes. Some notable examples are Bembos in Peru, Mr. Bigg's in Nigeria, Pollo Campero in Guatemala, and Quick in Belgium.

The Latin America and Caribbean group has many countries with very small populations, such as the Cayman Islands, Aruba, and Saint Lucia. So why did Burger King develop a presence in these markets long before entering places with much bigger populations, such as China, Russia, and South Africa? The answer is largely due to location—it remains headquartered in Miami, which is often called "the capital of Latin America." Because so many people from that region come to or through Miami, the Burger King reputation spilled over there early on, which simplified gaining brand recognition and acceptance. Further, the nearness of the Latin American and Caribbean countries to Miami enhances the ability of Burger King managers to visit these countries and for franchisees to visit headquarters.

Although Burger King prefers to operate in markets through franchising, doing so has sometimes been initially difficult because suppliers and prospective franchisees did not know the company well enough. When such a market looked attractive enough, Burger King would enter with the operations it owned, thereby displaying market commitment and demonstrating its expectations of franchisees. For instance, its demonstrated commitment entices a meat-processing plant to invest in added capacity for processing of ground beef. The success of Burger King's owned operating units helps the company to sell them to franchisees. By 2013 it owned only 3 percent of its restaurants.

Throughout its long history, the company has consistently focused on expanding its global portfolio into new and existing markets. Very recently, it has entered a number of them for the first time, including Morocco, Slovenia, and South Africa. It has also re-entered several markets it had earlier abandoned, such as Colombia in 2008 and Oman in 2010. As an example of country evaluation, let's take a quick look at decisions regarding Colombia.

RE-ENTERING COLOMBIA

Burger King entered the Colombian market in the early 1980s but pulled out after several years because of royalty expatriation restrictions and because of Colombia's prolonged period of economic and political turmoil. By the time Burger King considered re-entering the country, the cities were deemed safe for people to go out to eat, the peso was strong, and a rise in two-income families had created more disposable income to spend on eating out. Some large cities such as Barranquilla, Bogotá, Cali, and Medellin all had large new shopping centers. Although incomes were unevenly distributed, the richest 20 percent of the population (almost 9 million people) had a per capita expenditure in 2007 of over US $17,000.

Despite these favorable factors, managers had to consider a few negative ones: potential political problems with leftist-leaning neighbors Ecuador and Venezuela, which could support a resurgence of political unrest; economic problems in the United States from the global recession and in Venezuela from fluctuating oil prices—two countries that comprised half of Colombia's export earnings; and roughly 2 percent of Colombian GDP in 2007 coming from remittances of expatriates working abroad, mainly in Spain, which was hard hit by the global recession. In effect, economic downturns could ravage fast-food sales—a lesson Burger King learned in Mexico and Germany that caused it to tactically develop a more relevant value proposition, including value meals.

Overall, the Colombian situation has been bright. Burger King signed an agreement with KINCO, a well-established Colombian company with restaurant experience, for franchise rights to Medellin, Cali, and northern Colombia, then signed a second franchise agreement with Alsea, a Mexican firm, for rights to Bogotá. Alsea owned 75 percent of the Colombian operation of Domino's Pizza and operated Burger King restaurants in Mexico.

THE BRICS

In Chapter 4 we explored why so many companies have been emphasizing the BRIC countries: Brazil, Russia, India, and China. Burger King is no exception. The possibilities are simply too great to ignore.

Burger King opened its first Brazilian and Chinese restaurants in 2004. By then, many foreign fast-food franchisors had entered the markets, some successfully, some not. For the most part, failure occurred because of underestimating what it would take to succeed there. While Burger King has had success in both these countries, it was able to expand much faster in Brazil than in China. By 2013, it had 221 restaurants in the former and 86 in the latter.

Two factors largely explain the rapid Brazilian expansion. First, the company has had much more of a recognition advantage there than in China because a half million Brazilians fly into Florida each year, where Burger King restaurants abound. In addition, about 300,000 Brazilians live in the South Florida area, most of whom have relatives back home. Second, Burger King forged a location strategy that emphasized development in major cities and adjacent geographies with established shopping mall locations. By focusing initially on São Paulo, Brazil's largest city, Burger King developed economies in its marketing and distribution, with subsequent expansion focusing on nearby cities and states.

In China, Burger King encountered laws requiring that it either form a joint venture with a Chinese firm or own and operate two or more stores for at least a year before starting franchise operations. The company chose the latter alternative, which delayed its start of franchising. Later, finding potential franchisees with sufficient financial and restaurant capabilities was difficult, particularly since the franchise concept was rather new to China. (Some of its competitors, mainly Yum Brands and McDonald's, made joint venture investments and expanded with owned stores.) In 2012 Burger King announced the formation of a three-partner JV to serve the Chinese market. One partner, the Carpesian Capital Group, is a global private equity company specializing in developing country investments. The other is the Korduglu family from Turkey, which is Burger King's largest franchisee outside the United States. Its plan is to open 1,000 restaurants in China within five to seven years.

In 2010 Burger King opened its first restaurants in Russia, a country it has found attractive not only because of the population and growth factors affecting all BRICs but also because it can serve as a contiguous area for further expansion into Eastern Europe. Indeed, Burger King's 2011 entry into Slovenia has benefitted from supply integration with the Russian operation. In addition, concluding that finding the right franchisee was essential for the Russian market, Burger King's managers spent over a year getting to know the eventual franchisee, Alex Kolobov, who owns Shokolanitsa, a chain of about 200 Russian coffee shops. Although the formation of the franchise known as Burger Rus has resulted in growth in Moscow and St. Petersburg, more capital has been necessary to expand outside those cities. In 2013 Burger King announced the formation of a joint venture between Burger Rus and Russia's VTB Capital in order to open several hundred new restaurants in the country within the next few years.

India is the one BRIC country Burger King has not yet entered. However, 2013 reports indicate the company is in discussions with Everstone Capital, which is both a private equity firm and the holder of controlling interest in India's largest restaurant group.

THE FUTURE

Recent experience indicates that Burger King's locational emphasis can affect its performance considerably. For the first quarter of 2011, same-store sales fell 6 percent in North America. However, the drop was largely offset by gains in the rest of the world, so the global decline was only 3.6 percent. During 2012, Wendy's overtook Burger King as the second largest burger chain in the United States. To counter this loss of position, Burger King has been augmenting its menu with new items, changing its advertising focus, and getting franchisees to modernize their stores. At the same time, as the case indicates, the company is planning unprecedented international expansion. In fact, some of its competitors have expanded abroad much more than Burger King, which may indicate that it has untapped potential. This raises a number of questions for management regarding location priorities: Should primary emphasis be on bolstering its domestic presence or on expanding internationally? If the former, should the company concentrate on adding more restaurants or on boosting sales within existing ones? If the latter, should it concentrate on entering new markets? (It is presently in only about 40 percent of countries.) If so, which look most promising? Or should it concentrate on sales within existing markets? Are there markets in which Burger King is under-performing? Should it work on bolstering that performance? Or should it pull out of those markets to use its resources more effectively elsewhere? These are all location questions that dog managers in any company with international operations. ■

CRN
Case Review Note

QUESTIONS

13-1. Discuss the risks that an international restaurant company such as Burger King would have by operating abroad rather than just domestically.

13-2. How has the Burger King headquarters location influenced its international expansion? Has this location strengthened or weakened its global competitive position?

INTRODUCTION

Companies lack resources to take advantage of all international opportunities.

The old adage that "location, location, and location" are the three most important factors for business success rings quite true for international business. The world offers different locales, opportunities, and risks as companies try to create value from increasing sales or acquiring competitively useful assets. Because all companies have limited resources, they must be careful in making the following decisions:

1. The location of sales, production, and administrative and auxiliary services
2. The sequence for entering different countries
3. The portion of resources and efforts to allocate to each country where they operate

Companies need to

- Determine the order of country entry.
- Set the rates of resource allocation among countries.

Committing human, technical, and financial resources to one locale may mean forgoing or delaying projects elsewhere. In actuality, a company may first set a strategy of domestic versus international emphasis. For instance, General Electric set an objective of having international operations account for 60 percent of its total sales.[2] Afterward, a company sequences entry by country or region and then chooses where to operate within a country of choice. However, our emphasis in this chapter is in the selection of countries. Even after a firm is well established in most countries, it still needs to allocate resources by emphasizing some locations more than others. Further, when companies add new products they must decide the sequence of countries to sell them and how fast to spread the introduction into different countries.[3] Thus, taking time to pick the right place affects a firm's ability to gain and sustain competitive advantage.[4]

Figure 13.1 highlights the importance of MNEs' location decisions. By examining the external environment and comparing it with a company's objectives and capabilities, managers might ask: Where can we best leverage our existing competencies? And where can we go to best sustain, improve, or extend our competencies?

FIGURE 13.1 Location Decisions Affecting International Operations

In choosing locations for international operations, a company should begin by analyzing three factors: its *objectives*, its *strategies*, and its comparative *environmental fit* with conditions in the countries under consideration.

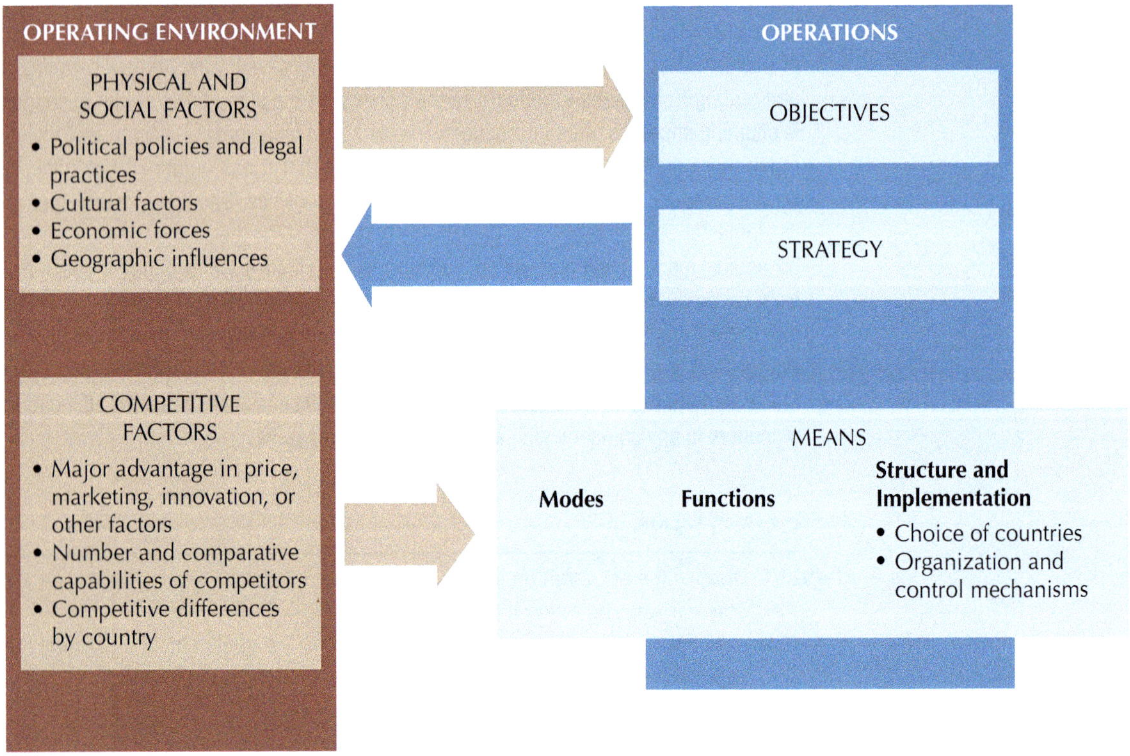

In choosing geographic sites, a company must decide

- Where to sell.
- Where to produce.

To answer those questions, managers need to answer two more: Which markets should we serve? And where should we place production to serve them? On one hand, the answers can be the same, particularly if transport costs or government regulations mean producing in the countries where you sell. Many service industries, such as restaurants, construction, and retailing (like Burger King), must locate facilities near their foreign customers.

On the other hand, large-scale production technology may favor producing in only a few countries and exporting to others, such as with companies in the capital-intensive automobile and steel industries. Finally, location decisions may be more complex, such as using multiple countries for sourcing raw materials and components that go into one finished product. Or a company may divide operating functions—locate headquarters in the United States, a call center for handling service in the Philippines, an R&D facility in Switzerland, and so on.

CRN
Case Review Note

Flexibility in locations is important because country and competitive conditions change. A company needs to respond to new opportunities and withdraw from less profitable ones. Recall in the opening case that Burger King withdrew from Colombia because of prolonged economic and political problems along with difficulty in remitting earnings from royalties. There is no one-size-fits-all theory for picking operating locations because product lines, competitive positions, resources, and strategies make each company unique—a situation that, in turn, will be better realized in some countries than in others.[5] Moreover, hiring the right people to analyze country differences and implement company operations is critical. Highly skilled managers can sometimes compensate for location deficiencies, and poor managers can sometimes cause poor performance in the best locations. However, having skilled managers in the most appropriate locations is the best possible combination. Figure 13.2 shows the major steps international business managers should take in making location decisions. The following discussion examines those steps in depth.

FIGURE 13.2 The Location Decision Process

Location, location, location: Committing resources to a foreign location may entail risky trade-offs—say, forgoing or abandoning projects elsewhere. The decision-making process is essentially twofold: examining the external environments of proposed locations and comparing each of them with the company's objectives and capabilities.

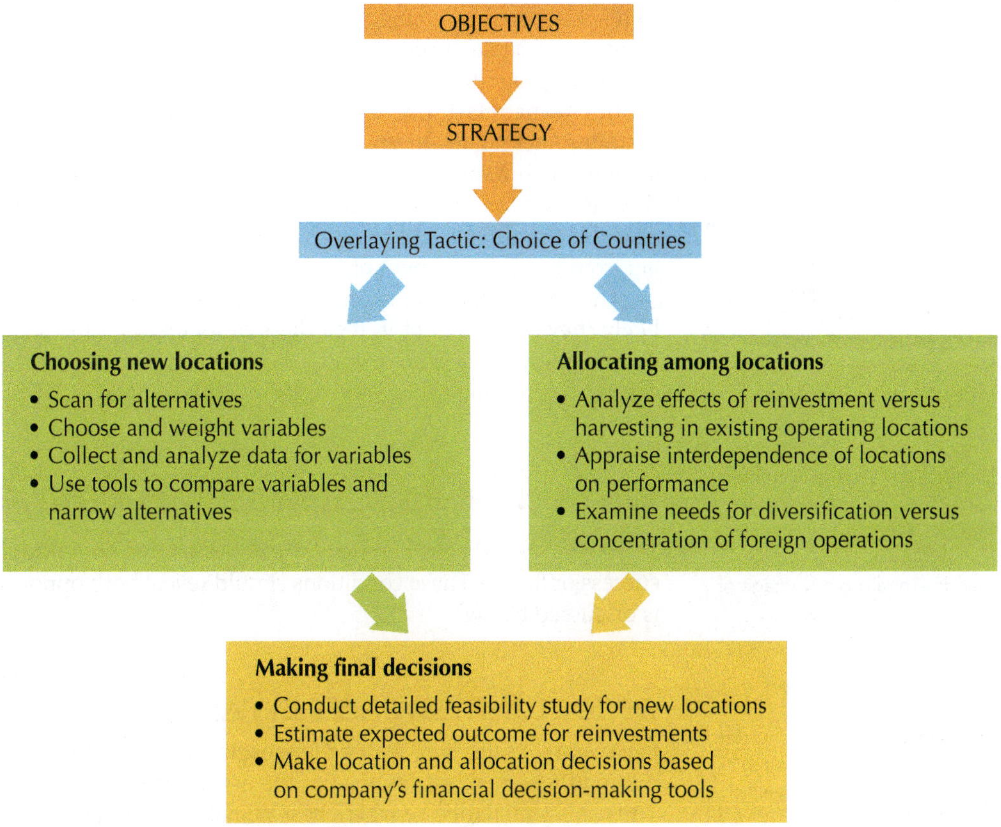

HOW DOES SCANNING WORK?

Without scanning, a company may
- Overlook opportunities and risks.
- Examine too many or too few possibilities.

Managers use scanning techniques to examine and compare countries on broad indicators of opportunities and risks.[6] Scanning is like seeding widely and then weeding out; it is useful insofar as a company might otherwise consider too few or too many possibilities. Given that there are approximately 200 countries, managers might easily overlook some good opportunities without first looking very broadly. Instead, they might zero in on those that come to mind first.

SCANNING VERSUS DETAILED ANALYSIS

Step 1: Scanning **Scanning** is the process by which managers examine many countries broadly and then narrow them down to the most promising ones. That is, they compare country information that is readily available, inexpensive, and fairly comparable—usually without having to incur traveling expenses. They analyze publicly available information, such as from the Internet, and communicate with experienced people. They compare countries on a few conditions that could significantly affect the success or failure of their business and that fit with its resources and objectives. Because of using fairly easy-to-find information, they may consider a large group of countries at this point, such as all those within a global region.

On-site visits follow scanning and are part of the final location decision process.

Step 2: Detailed Analysis Once managers narrow their consideration to the most promising countries, they need to compare the feasibility and desirability of each. At this point, unless they are satisfied enough to outsource all their production and sales, they almost always need to go on location to analyze and collect more specific information.

Take a situation in which managers need to decide where to place their sales efforts. They will likely need to visit the countries shortlisted through scanning in order to conduct market research and visit with distributors before making a final decision. Or let's say managers need to decide where to locate production. If they plan to outsource the production, they may want to inspect potential contractors' facilities. If they plan to own facilities themselves, they will need to collect such specific on-site information as availability of land and suppliers before committing significant resources.

Intel's manufacturing expansion into Latin America illustrates an example. Intel used scanning techniques to limit visits to a few Latin American countries. The follow-up visits sought much more detailed information—even the availability of suitable housing, medical services, and food products for the personnel Intel would need to transfer. The visitors were also able to gain qualitative information, such as their impressions of the welcome they might get from local government officials and business leaders.

The more time and money companies invest in examining an alternative, the more likely they are to accept it, regardless of its merits—a situation known as an **escalation of commitment.** A feasibility study should have clear-cut decision points, whereby managers can cut the commitment before they invest too much.

CONCEPT CHECK

In Chapter 12, we focus on the importance of value—the measure of a company's ability to sell products for more than it costs to make them—in a firm's strategy, adding that "creating value" is primarily a matter of meeting (indeed, exceeding) customer expectations. Here we point out the importance of both factors—cost and customer needs—in taking advantage of foreign opportunities.

WHAT INFORMATION IS IMPORTANT IN SCANNING?

Managers should consider country conditions that could significantly affect their company's success or failure. These conditions should reveal both opportunities and risks, each of which is discussed below.

OPPORTUNITIES: SALES EXPANSION

Expectation of a large market and sales growth is probably a potential location's major attraction.

Expansion of sales is probably the most important factor motivating companies to engage in international business because of the assumption that more sales will lead to more profits. Thus, it is vital to decide where best to make those sales.

Of course, managers would like to have sales figures for the type of product they want to sell, but such information may not be available, especially if the product is a new one. In such instances, they could make rough estimates of sales potential by basing projections on what has happened to sales for a similar or complementary product. For instance, they might project the potential sales of flat-screen televisions based on figures for DVD equipment sales. If complementary figures are unavailable, management can use economic and demographic data to project sales potential.

Of course, you should examine indicators related directly to your products. If you're trying to sell, say, luxury products, GDP per capita may tell you very little. Instead, you need to know how many people have income above a certain level. Take India: Its GDP per capita is low, but it has enough millionaires to support the sale of high-end luxury products.

Moreover, although your product or service may not appeal to the average customer, you may seek out niches within that market. Pollo Campero, a Guatemalan-based fast-food chain, and Gigante, a Mexican supermarket chain, have both entered the United States by going to cities with large Central American and Mexican populations.[7]

Companies must consider variables other than income and population when estimating potential demand for their products in different countries.

Examining Economic and Demographic Variables Primary considerations when examining economic and demographic variables are listed below, with some examples:

- *Obsolescence and leapfrogging of products.* Consumers in developing economies do not necessarily follow the same patterns as those in higher-income countries. In China, consumers have leapfrogged the use of landline telephones by going from having no phones to using cell phones almost exclusively.[8]
- *Prices.* If prices of essential products are high, consumers may spend more on them than what would be expected based on per capita GDP and thus have less to spend on discretionary purchases. The expenditures on food in Japan are higher than would be predicted by either population or income level because food is expensive and work habits promote eating out.
- *Income elasticity.* A common tool for predicting total market potential is to divide the percentage of change in product demand by the percentage of change in income in a given country. The more demand shifts in relation to income changes, the more elastic it is. Demand for necessities such as food is usually less elastic than for discretionary products such as flat-screen TVs.
- *Substitution.* Consumers in a given country may more conveniently substitute certain products or services than those in other countries. There are fewer automobiles in Hong Kong than one would expect based on income and population because the crowded conditions make the efficient mass transit system a desirable substitute for automobiles. Gasoline- and diesel-powered cars are also substitutes. Indian demand for the former fell and the latter increased when government regulations led to high fuel-cost disparities, thus forcing companies such as Suzuki, Toyota, and General Motors to alter their mix of vehicle production.[9]
- *Income inequality.* Where income inequality is high, the per capita GDP figures are less meaningful. Many people have little to spend, while many others have substantial spending money, as noted by Mercedes-Benz sales in India.[10]
- *Cultural factors and taste.* Countries with similar per capita GDPs may have different preferences for products and services because of values or tastes. The same is true for consumer sub-segments within countries. The existence of a large Hindu population in India reduces per capita meat consumption there as compared with some countries with similar per capita GDPs, yet there is a large niche market of Indians who are neither Hindu nor vegetarian.

CONCEPT CHECK

Recall our discussion of "Regional Economic Integration" in Chapter 7, where we explain the dynamic effects of integration. As we point out, when trade barriers come down within a regional bloc, the size of the market available to small member nations typically increases quite dramatically.

- *Existence of trading blocs.* Although a country may have a small population and GDP, its presence in a regional trading bloc gives its output access to a much larger market. Uruguay has a small domestic market, but its production has duty-free access to other countries in MERCOSUR.

Given all these factors, managers cannot project potential demand perfectly. However, by considering factors that may influence the sale of their products, they can make workable estimates that help them narrow detailed studies to a reasonable number.

OPPORTUNITIES: RESOURCE ACQUISITION

Companies undertake international business to secure resources that are either too expensive or not readily available in their home countries. They may purchase them from another organization, or they may establish foreign investments to exploit them. In either case, they must prioritize where they can best secure what they're after.

If they want to acquire a scarce resource, they are obviously limited to those locales that have it, such as securing petroleum only in those countries that have reserves. When resources are very limited, such as prime areas for building beach resorts, land owners and governments are likely in a strong bargaining position when ceding rights to a foreign firm.[11] However, even when the resource is limited to a few countries, some offer better opportunities than others. In the case of petroleum reserves, there are cost differences in extraction, transportation, and taxes. When considering cost differences, a particular resource may be overriding for specific industries or companies, such as sugar for candy companies or low-cost water power for aluminum companies.

Costs—especially labor costs—are an important factor in companies' production-location decisions.

Cost Considerations

A company's total cost is made up of numerous subcosts, many of which are industry- or company-specific. Nevertheless, several of the factors affecting these subcosts—*labor, infrastructure, ease of transportation and communications,* and *government incentives*—apply to a large-cross section of companies.

Labor Although capital intensity is growing in most industries, labor compensation remains an important cost for most companies. The scanning process allows examination of such factors as labor market size, labor compensation, minimum wages, customary and required fringe benefits, education levels, and unemployment rates in order to compare labor cost, skills, and availability. The process should also examine trends and likely changes. For example, many companies have recently been shifting production dependence away from China and toward such countries as Myanmar and Mexico because of rising Chinese costs.[12]

Labor, however, is not homogeneous. Neither are companies' labor needs. The desire to establish a low-cost call center has led many U.S. companies to locate in the Philippines, with its many English speakers, but not in Senegal, where many French companies locate call centers to serve French-language markets. South Africa has been a favorite location for MNEs' African regional offices because of available skilled office personnel there.[13] Or you may wish to establish an R&D facility where figures on the number of science and engineering graduates give you a rough idea that needed skills are available. In fact, many companies have set up R&D facilities in China, Hungary, India, and Israel because of the availability of technical talent at low cost.[14]

If a country's labor force lacks the specific skill levels required, an MNE might have to train, redesign production, or add supervision—all of which are expensive. Keep in mind also that there may be sector and geographic differences in wage rates within countries. In Mexico, tire wages are much higher than the average industrial wage, while wages in the capital and other large cities are higher than elsewhere.[15] In addition, you should look for conditions that can cause changes in labor availability and cost. For example, the HIV rate is very high in southern African countries, a problem that may drastically reduce their future labor forces.

When companies move into developing countries because of labor-cost differences, their advantages may be short-lived for one or more of three reasons:

- Competitors follow leaders into low-wage areas.
- There is little first-mover advantage for this type of production migration.
- The costs rise quickly as a result of pressure on wage or exchange rates.

Infrastructure problems add to operating costs.

Infrastructure Poor internal infrastructure may easily negate cost differences in labor rates. In many developing countries, infrastructure is both substandard and unreliable, which adds to companies' costs of operating. Consider Cadbury in Nigeria. Its workers spend extra hours getting to and from work on congested roads, which decreases their productivity. It uses its own power generators at two and a half times the cost of the unreliable publicly provided power to prevent assembly line stoppages that could cause food products to spoil. Because phone reception is often unreliable, Cadbury must send people out to visit customers and suppliers. When goods are ready for delivery, they must again face the slow roads and congestion.[16] (The adjacent photo shows a congested street in Mexico.)

The need to coordinate product, process, production, and sales influences location decisions.

Ease of Transportation and Communications Related to infrastructure is the advantage of locating near customers and suppliers. However, firms with rapidly evolving technologies need to tightly coordinate product and production technologies to speed new products' introduction and diminish competitors' opportunity to copy them.[17] This tends to push more production into developed countries, where such firms conduct most of their R&D.

Other factors also affect the efficient flow of goods. One is distance, which roughly correlates with time and cost of shipments; thus, a geographically isolated country like New

Although Mexico City has an extensive metro system along with some double-decker expressways, it remains one of the world's most congested cities, as the photo shows. Such congestion delays shipments and raises the cost of distribution.
Source: Paul Franklin/dkimages

Zealand does not fit as easily into a company's global integration strategy because supplies to and production from there may be untimely and costly.[18] Second, countries with few trade restrictions and efficient customs operations offer advantages such as reduced tariff costs and shorter clearance times, leading to a more continuous flow of components when and where they are needed.[19]

When entrepreneurs set up firms, they generally headquarter them where the founders reside to take advantage of personal networks that ease their operations; however, as companies become international, they may also find advantages in being near specialized private and public institutions handling international functions, such as banks, financing firms, insurance groups, public accountants, freight forwarders, customs brokers, and consular offices. Once they shift the geographic center of their sales and operations, they may even move their headquarters to another country.[20] Halliburton relocated its CEO and corporate headquarters from the United States to Dubai to be closer to customers and employees. If a company is looking for a production location that will serve sales in more than one country, the ease of moving goods into and out of the country is very important, so managers should consider the efficiency of port facilities along with the country's trade liberalization agreements.[21]

Government practices may increase or decrease companies' costs.

Governmental Incentives and Disincentives Most countries seek foreign investment because of the jobs it will create, the competitiveness it will enhance, and the impact it will have on their trade balance. It is common to see ads in business newspapers enticing foreign firms to consider a particular country as an investment location.

Because countries compete to attract investors, many offer incentives through regulations or negotiations that cut operating costs. These include such things as lower taxes, employee training, loan guarantees, low-interest loans, exemption of import duties, and subsidized energy and transportation. For example, the European structural funds program aimed at preventing European deindustrialization has helped fund projects for such companies as Coca-Cola, Fiat, and GlaxoSmithKline.[22] Differences in tax rates are particularly important when deciding where to produce within a regional trading bloc, inasmuch as companies can serve the entire region from any country within the bloc.[23]

At the same time, World Bank studies show that companies may begin operating more quickly and with fewer steps in some countries than in others because of differences in the ease or difficulty of starting a business, entering and enforcing contracts, hiring and firing workers, getting credit, and closing a business.[24] Government actions may delay or prevent companies from bringing in expatriate personnel and from getting needed imports cleared through customs in good time.

Countries also differ in corruption and in both legal transparency and enforcement. Too often managers must spend excessive time in satisfying government agencies on taxes, labor conditions, environmental compliance, and other matters when they are unsure of the legal consequences of their actions and competitive consequences of government corruption.[25] A particular thorny question concerns the poor protection of intellectual property rights; some firms prefer to avoid these locations and some others feel they can best protect their rights by operating in those markets. At the same time, poor protection is a double-edged sword. Although companies may relinquish technology to other companies, they may more easily gain access to other companies' technologies as well.[26] Nevertheless, companies appear to prefer operating in countries where both corporate social responsibility and environmental regulation are high, as long as rules and expectations are transparent.[27]

CONCEPT CHECK

We show in Chapter 5 that, in applying factor-proportions theory to determine the best place to locate a manufacturing facility, a company may compare the amount (and cost) of machinery that it will need in one place to the number (and cost) of people that it will need in another. We also show that new technologies, such as 3D printing, can change optimal production locations.

A Caveat The continuous development of new production technologies makes cost comparisons among countries more difficult. With more and more ways to make a product, a company might have to compare the cost of labor-intensive production in a low-wage country with that of capital-intensive production in a high-wage country. A company should also compare the cost from large-scale production that reduces fixed costs per unit by serving multi-country markets with the cost from multiple smaller-scale production units that reduce transport and inventory costs.

RISKS

Any company decision involves weighing opportunity against risk. For example, a sales-seeking company may not necessarily go to the country showing the highest sales potential. Nor will an asset-seeking company necessarily go where the assets are cheapest. In both cases, this is because decision makers may perceive that the risks in those locales are too high.

Factors to Consider in Analyzing Risk Keep in mind several factors as we discuss specific types of risk:

1. *Companies and their managers differ in their perceptions of what is risky,* how tolerant they are of taking risk, the returns they expect, and the portion of their assets they are willing to put at risk.[28]
2. *One company's risk may be another's opportunity.* For example, companies offering security solutions (e.g., alarm systems, guard services, insurance, weapons) may find their biggest sales opportunities where other companies find only operating risks. (This is shown humorously in Figure 13.3.)
3. *Companies may reduce their risks by means other than avoiding locations,* such as by insuring. But all these options incur costs that decision makers should take into account.
4. *There are trade-offs among risks.* Avoiding a country where, say, political risk is high may leave a company more vulnerable to competitive risk if another one earns good profits there. And returns are usually higher where risk is higher.

Besides considering the individual nature of risk assessment, companies should consider several important factors, grouped into three categories: political, foreign exchange, and competitive. It is important to examine risks throughout complex supply chains because your suppliers, although located in low-risk countries, may depend, in turn, on suppliers in high-risk countries, who in turn depend on suppliers elsewhere.[29]

FIGURE 13.3 One company's risk may be an opportunity for another.

Source: Mick Stevens/New Yorker Cartoon Bank/www.cartoonbank.com

"Don't think of them as terrorist states. Think of them as terrorist markets."

CONCEPT CHECK

Recall from Chapter 3 our definition of political risk as the possibility that political decisions, events, or conditions will affect a country's business environment in ways that will cost investors some or all of the value of their investment or force them to accept lower-than-projected rates of return.

Political Risk Changes in political leaders' opinions and policies, civil disorder, and animosity between the host and other countries, particularly the firm's home country, may be politically risky for a company due to lost or damaged property, disrupted operations, and the need to adjust to changes in the rules governing business. Unilever encountered difficulty in attracting foreign executives to work in Pakistan because of security concerns; Chiquita Brands paid money to terrorists in Colombia to protect its employees there; Holcim had its cement investments nationalized in Venezuela; Marriott had a hotel bombed in Indonesia; and Coca-Cola had interrupted services requiring police protection of its trucks and telephone connections in Angola.

Managers use three approaches to predict political risk: *analyzing past patterns, analyzing opinions,* and *examining potentially risky social and economic conditions.*

Analyzing Past Patterns Predicting risk on the basis of past political occurrences is problematic because situations may change for better or worse. Moreover, examining a country's overall situation masks political risk differences within countries and among MNEs. For example, unrest that leads to property damage and disruption of supplies or sales may be limited geographically, such as when companies in Slovenia escaped the damage that others incurred elsewhere during the civil war that led to the breakup of Yugoslavia. With few exceptions, government takeovers of companies have been highly selective, primarily affecting operations that have a visible widespread effect on the country because of their size or monopoly position.

When a company does incur property damage or asset takeover, it is not necessarily a full loss to investors. First, damage may be covered by insurance. Second, governments have preceded most takeovers with formal declarations of intent and have followed with legal processes to determine the foreign investor's compensation, such as the settlement between Venezuela and Holcim.[30] In addition to the investment's book value, other factors may determine the adequacy (or not) of compensation. It may earn a lower return elsewhere, or other agreements (such as purchase and management contracts) may create additional benefits for the former investor. Past settlements may serve as indicators in predicting the likely loss if political problems occur.

Companies should

- Examine views of government decision makers.
- Get a cross-section of opinions.
- Use expert analysts.

Analyzing Opinions Because influential people may sway future political events affecting business, managers should access statements by political leaders both in and out of office to determine their private business philosophies, foreign business relations, the means of effecting economic changes, and their feelings toward given foreign countries. They should also access polls showing different leaders' likelihood of gaining political office. Modern technology has improved access to global media so that reports can be retrieved quickly. When considering a country for the first time, managers should visit to listen to a cross section of opinions from, say, embassy officials, foreign and local businesspeople, journalists, academicians, middle-level local government authorities, and labor leaders. These people usually reveal their own attitudes, which often reflect political conditions that may change and affect the business sector. If already operating within a country, the managers working therein can offer evaluations of changing situations.

Companies have been relying more on commercial-risk assessment services rather than generating their own risk analyses because the services offer concise reports they view as credible. Nevertheless, determining what type of information goes into these reports, how it is collected, and what the track record has been for predictions is certainly useful.

Examining Social and Economic Conditions Countries' social and economic conditions may lead to unrest if population segments have unmet aspirations. Frustrated groups may disrupt business by calling general strikes and destroying property and supply lines, such as in the Niger Delta region of Nigeria, where groups have attacked foreign oil companies' property and kidnapped their employees. Frustrated groups might also replace government leaders, such as in response to the violent 2010–2013 demonstrations in Egypt and Tunisia. And political leaders sometimes harness support by blaming problems on foreigners and foreign companies, which could lead to boycotts or rule changes for MNEs or even expropriation of their properties. However, there is no general consensus as to what constitutes dangerous conditions or how such instability can be predicted. The lack of consensus is illustrated by the diverse reactions of companies to the same political situations.

Rather than political stability itself, the direction of governmental change seems to be very important. But even if a company accurately predicts changes that will affect business, how long the government will take to enact new practices is still uncertain.

CONCEPT CHECK

As we explain in Chapter 8, an exchange rate is the price of a currency; in Chapter 9, we discuss some of the causes of exchange-rate changes (including interest rates and those in floating rate regimes) and explain various methods of forecasting exchange-rate movements (such as focusing on trends in economic variables or trends in the rates themselves).

Foreign Exchange Risk Changes in exchange rates or the ability to move funds out of a country may also affect an MNE. Let's examine these two types of risks.

Exchange-Rate Changes The change in foreign currency value is a two-edged sword, depending on whether you are going abroad to seek sales or resources. Let's say a U.S. company is doing business in India. If it is exporting to India, then a deterioration in the value of the Indian rupee will make it less competitive because it will cost more rupees to buy the U.S. products or services. If it is producing within India to serve the Indian market, its competitiveness in India will not change, but its rupee profits will buy fewer U.S. dollars to bring back to the United States. If, however, it is seeking assets from India, such as Indian personnel to staff a call center, a fall in the rupee value lowers the dollar cost of the personnel.

Companies may accept a lower return in order to move their financial resources more easily.

Mobility of Funds If a company is to invest abroad, then the ability to get funds out of the country is a factor in country comparison. A theory that helps explain this is **liquidity preference,** which is much like option theory in that it relates to investors' desire for some of their holdings to be in highly liquid assets on which they are willing to take a lower return. They need liquidity to make near-term payments, such as paying out dividends; to cover unexpected contingencies, such as stockpiling materials if a strike threatens supply; and to be able to shift funds to even more profitable opportunities, such as purchasing materials at a discount during a temporary price depression.[31]

The comparative liquidity among countries varies because of capital market activity and government exchange control. An active capital market, particularly a stock market, helps a company sell its assets, especially if it wishes to sell shares on a local exchange or sell the entire operation. In the opening case, Burger King moved from being privately held to being publicly held, which was facilitated by its U.S. location with a huge capital market. Thus, when comparing countries you may wish to include the existence of an active stock market as a favorable variable.

CRN
Case Review Note

If the government restricts the conversion of funds (several countries have various degrees of exchange control), the foreign investor will be forced to spend some profits or proceeds from share sale in the host country. Thus, it's not surprising that, if other things are equal, investors prefer projects in strong-currency countries with little likelihood of exchange controls.

Competitive Risk The comparison of likely success among countries is largely contingent on competitors' actions. We now examine four competitive factors to be considered in choice of location: *making operations compatible, spreading risk, following competitors or customers,* and *heading off competitors.*

Companies are highly attracted to countries that

- Are located nearby.
- Share the same language.
- Have conditions similar to those in their home countries.

Making Operations Compatible Because companies operating abroad encounter less-familiar environments, they have more or different operating risks than local firms. Thus, managers initially prefer to operate where they perceive conditions to be more similar to their home country—provided, of course, that the location also offers sufficient opportunities in terms of sales or resource acquisition.[32] (The major types of attributes of similarity versus dissimilarity are shown in Table 13.1.) As they gain experience, they improve their assessments of consumer, competitor, and government actions, thereby reducing their uncertainty. In fact, MNEs have a lower survival rate than local companies for many years after they begin operations—a situation known as the **liability of foreignness.** However, those that learn about their new environments and manage to overcome their early problems eventually have survival rates comparable to those of local firms.[33]

Does Geography Matter?

Don't Fool with Mother Nature

In the past few years, major earthquakes hit Chile, Haiti, and New Zealand, torrential floods inundated parts of northeast Australia, and a deadly flu pandemic spread from Mexico. These events have publicized global vulnerability to natural disasters and communicable diseases. Each year, about 130 million people are exposed to earthquake risk, 119 million to tropical cyclone hazards, 196 million to catastrophic flooding, and 220 million to drought. Natural disasters, on average, claim 184 deaths per day and cause physical damage to factories, crops, inventories, and infrastructure.

These natural disasters are spread unevenly around the world. Parts of Asia are heavily exposed to earthquakes; some African countries are most vulnerable to drought. The United Nations Development Programme has used 450 variables to analyze and publish a disaster risk index (DRI) that compares physical exposure to hazards by country.[34]

Although only 11 percent of those exposed to such disasters are in the world's poorest nations, those nations account for 55 percent of the deaths because so many of their people live in poor housing and lack adequate medical assistance. Likewise, the rural-to-urban migration in developing countries is largely to dangerous mountainsides, ravines, and low-elevation areas ill-equipped to deal with earthquakes and cyclones.

Catastrophic events upset markets, infrastructure, and production while damaging companies' property and injuring their personnel. Who can forget the heartbreaking 2011 telecasts of Japanese houses, cars, and trains being tossed around like toys in a toddler's bath? The earthquake-induced tsunami played havoc with global supplies as well, such as upsetting the world's auto industry production by creating auto parts shortages.[35] Four months later, heavy rains in Thailand hit first-tier auto parts suppliers as well as second- and third-tier suppliers of small parts for bigger suppliers of components abroad.[36]

Thus, natural events create additional operating risks and insurance costs. In turn, insurance companies are challenged to estimate the likelihood and cost of these events. The World Health Organization has, for instance, developed global atlases of infectious diseases,[37] many of which occur where medical facilities are weakest because of the diseases' association with poverty. They are also associated with natural disaster, such as cholera and malaria outbreaks after flooding, and tend to follow geographic patterns. For example, malaria kills about 2 million people a year, mainly in Africa.

The debilitating effects of disease have an impact on labor force participation and life expectancy and are costly to companies, such as Sasol Petroleum's need to set up a clinic in Mozambique to treat its workers for malaria.[38] Companies also hesitate to send their personnel to epidemic areas. During the Asian severe acute respiratory syndrome (SARS) outbreak, Walmart, Gap, Liz Claiborne, and other companies banned employee travel to affected countries, thus hindering their buying and quality-assurance programs.[39] ■

CONCEPT CHECK

In discussing "Cultural Distance" in Chapter 2, we observe that when two countries are culturally close, a company usually expects fewer differences—and must make fewer adjustments— when moving operations from one to the other. Here we point out that economic similarity often fosters the same conditions of compatibility.

CRN Case Review Note

This concept helps explain why, for instance, U.S. companies put earlier and greater emphasis on Canada and the United Kingdom than would be indicated by the opportunity and risk variables discussed so far. In short, managers feel more comfortable doing business in a similar language, culture, and legal system.[40] These similarities may also keep operating costs and risks low because of easier communications. Following early entries, companies also find it useful to create an expansion pattern that will allow management within a portfolio of countries to work interdependently with each other.[41] The opening case shows that Burger King had a strong early emphasis on Latin America and the Caribbean, largely because of distance and communications advantages between that area and the Miami headquarters.

Economic similarity is an important consideration. Both Canada and the United Kingdom have high per capita GDPs, similar to those in the United States, which indicate a likely demand for products first created for the U.S. market. If you first develop products for your domestic market, you might consider other countries' similarity to yours in terms of economic level.

TABLE 13.1 The Distance Sensitivity of Industries: Indicators

Cultural Distance	Administrative Distance	Geographic Distance	Economic Distance
High linguistic content	Government involved in funding, procurement, regulating standard-setting, before international bodies, etc.	Low value-to-weight or bulk	High intensity of labor, other factors prone to absolute cost differences
Strong country of origin effects (vertical distance)	Strategic industry status (votes, money, staples, state control, national champions)	Hazards in transportation	Potential for international scale/scope/experience economies
Significant differences in preferences/standards (horizontal distance)	Specialized, durable sunk capital (and holdup potential)	Perishability/ time-sensitivity	High income-related increases in willingness-to-pay
Entrenched tastes/ traditions	Restraints on trade/FDI (e.g., agriculture)	Need to perform key activities locally (favors FDI over trade)	Differences in customers/channels/ business systems

Source: Based on Pankaj Ghemawat, *World 3.0: World Prosperity and How to Achieve It*, (Boston: Harvard Business Review Press, 2011): 299, which is based on his earlier framework in "Distance Still Matters: The Hard Reality of Global Expansion," *Harvard Business Review*, 79:8 (September 2001): 140.

CONCEPT CHECK

Recall from Chapter 5 that a factor helping to explain trade patterns—why a country trades more with certain countries than with others—is the historical relationship between them, especially continued trade between a former colonizer with its former colonies.

In addition, historical ties between pairs of countries help explain companies' geographic preferences for foreign operations.[42] While many of these ties relate to common culture and ethnicity, others have a history of positive exchanges that reduce the perception of operating risk for companies in home countries and for stakeholders in host countries.

You should also try to ensure that a country's policies and norms are compatible with your company's competitive advantages. Blockbuster failed in Germany because the laws prevented it from operating on evenings, Sundays, and holidays—popular times in the United States and for last-minute impulse decisions to rent videos anywhere.[43]

Companies may also prefer locales that will permit them to operate with product types, plant sizes, and operating practices familiar to their managers. When examining locales, teams that include personnel with backgrounds in each functional area—marketing, finance, human resources, engineering, and production—will more likely uncover the best fits with their companies' resources and objectives.

Finally, companies should consider local availability of resources in relation to their needs. Many foreign operations require local resources, which may severely restrict the feasibility of given locales. A company may need to find local personnel or a viable local partner with an understanding of its type of business and technology. Or it may need to add local capital to what it is willing to bring in.

Geographic Diversification By operating in diverse localities, companies may be able to smooth their sales and profits, which, in turn, gains them a competitive advantage in raising funds.[44] They may further guard against the effects of currency value changes by locating in countries whose exchange rates are not closely correlated with each other.[45] Such a strategy is in many ways opposite to what we just discussed about preferring countries similar to the home country. This is because the best smoothing of sales and profits will likely occur from operating in economies that are the least correlated; however, the downside is that operating in these dissimilar economies may give rise to greater competitive risk because management is less familiar with operating conditions.

Given growing product complexity, companies cannot easily find all needed resources within a single country, especially those based on knowledge. At the same time, such resources are very country-specific because of long-term specialization. Although knowledge flows internationally and from one organization to another, MNEs enhance their access to it by having foreign subsidiaries in source countries. Because pieces of the knowledge emanate from different places, companies need multiple access points to gain a speedy

In terms of competition, some different strategies are to go

- First where other firms are most apt to enter the market as competitors.
- Into markets that competitors have not entered.
- Where there are clusters of competitors.

and comprehensive picture. In fact, evidence indicates that in industries where technology changes rapidly, MNEs with a high breadth of foreign subsidiaries improve their performance more than those concentrating their foreign operations in only a few countries.[46]

Following Competitors or Customers Managers may purposely crowd a market to prevent competitors from gaining advantages there that they can use to improve their competitive positions elsewhere—a situation known as **oligopolistic reaction.**[47] This helps explain why China now has over 170 automobile producers, which is more than any other country and far more than market analysts believe it can sustain.[48]

CRN
Case Review Note

At the same time, companies may gain advantages by locating where competitors are. To begin with, the competitors may have performed the costly task of evaluating locations and building market acceptance for a particular type of product, so followers may get a so-called free ride. Recall that Burger King profited in some markets from McDonald's development of meat suppliers and demand for hamburgers. Moreover, there are clusters of competitors (sometimes called agglomeration) in various locations—think of all the computer firms in California's Silicon Valley. The adjacent photo shows Europe's largest technology park. These clusters attract multiple suppliers and personnel with specialized skills, as well as buyers who want to compare product and service options but don't want to travel great distances among suppliers. A company also gains better access to information about new developments by coming in frequent contact with personnel from the other firms.[49]

There are also advantages of following customers into a market. Bridgestone Tires was a major supplier to Japanese auto companies in Japan, and it followed them when they established U.S. manufacturing facilities. First, Bridgestone's track record with Japanese auto companies, such as Toyota, gave it an advantage over other tire manufacturers in the United States. Second, if another tire manufacturer were to develop a strong relationship with Toyota in the United States, it might use this experience as a successful springboard to undermine Bridgestone's position elsewhere.

Heading Off Competition A company may try to reduce competitive risk by getting a strong foothold in markets before competitors do, by avoiding strong competitors altogether, or, when its innovative advantage may be short-lived, by moving quickly into markets before competitors can copy the innovation. Of course, this strategy implies ample market where one locates.

The aerial photo shows Sophia Antipolis in the south of France, which is Europe's largest technology park. As of January 2011, there were 1,260 companies with facilities there.
Source: Marcel Jolibos/Getty Images

By being first into a market, a firm may more easily gain the best partners, best locations, and best suppliers—a strategy to gain **first-mover advantage.** Another first-mover advantage is the potential of gaining strong relations with the government, such as Volkswagen in China and Lockheed with Russia.[50]

Companies may also develop location strategies to avoid significant competition. PriceSmart, a discount operator, has all its warehouse stores outside its home country (the United States) and has succeeded by targeting locations in Central America, the Caribbean, and Asia that are considered too small to attract early entry of warehouse stores from competitors like Walmart and Carrefour.[51]

COLLECTING AND ANALYZING DATA

Information is needed at all levels of control.

- Companies should compare the cost of information with its value.

Companies undertake business research to reduce outcome uncertainties from their decisions and to assess their operating performance. The research includes finding answers to questions such as: Can we hire qualified personnel? Will the economic and political climate allow us to reasonably foresee our future? Are our distributors servicing sufficient accounts? What is our market share?

Clearly, information helps managers improve corporate performance. However, they can seldom get all the information they want, due to time and cost constraints. So managers should compare the estimated costs of information with the probable payoff it will generate in revenue gains or cost savings.

SOME PROBLEMS WITH RESEARCH RESULTS AND DATA

Because of the lack, obsolescence, and inaccuracy of data on many countries, research can be difficult and expensive to undertake. Such problems are most acute in developing countries. Let's discuss the two basic problems: inaccuracy and non-comparability.

Information inaccuracies result from

- Difficulty in collecting and analyzing data.
- Purposefully misleading data.
- Exclusion of nonmarket and illegal activity.

Inaccuracy For the most part, we can list five basic reasons why reported information may be inaccurate:

1. *Governmental resources may limit accurate data collection.* Countries may have such limited resources that other projects necessarily receive budget priority, such as spending to improve health and literacy rather than to measure them. Even if governments emphasize data collection, funds may be short for buying the latest computer hardware, software, and training programs. The result may be gaps in reliable and timely information.
2. *Governments may purposely publish misleading information.* Of equal concern to researchers is the publication of false or purposely deceptive information designed to mislead government superiors, the country's rank and file, or companies and institutions abroad. For instance, the European Commission rebuked Greece in 2010 for falsifying public finance data.[52]
3. *Respondents may give false information to data collectors.* Mistrust of how the data will be used may lead respondents to answer questions incorrectly, particularly if they probe financial details or anything else that respondents may consider private. For example, many government figures are collected through questionnaires, such as those in the United States to estimate international travel and tourism expenditures. People may misstate their actual expenditures, particularly if they did not report the true value of foreign purchases on incoming customs forms.
4. *Official data may include only legal and reported market activities.* Further distortions may occur because nationally reported income figures don't include illegal income from such activities as the drug trade, theft, bribery, and prostitution. Such income may appear in other economic sectors because of money laundering. Contraband figures do not appear

in official trade statistics and may be substantial, such as an estimated $7 billion per year of Nigerian oil exports.[53] Finally, many economic activities are unreported and substantial, such as payments in cash to avoid tax payments on income.

5. *Poor methodology may be used.* Inaccuracies are also due to questionable collection and analysis by researchers both within and outside the government. Many statistics are based on estimates and sampling. By using two different means for estimating Chinese consumption in 2012, there was a difference of $1.6 trillion, which was more than the entire GDP of Australia.[54]

In addition, too often broad generalizations are drawn from too few observations on non-representative samples and poorly designed questionnaires.

Problems in information comparability arise from

- Differences in definitions and base years.
- Distortions in currency conversions.

Non-Comparability Countries do not necessarily publish reports such as censuses, output figures, and trade statistics for the same time periods or at the same time as each other. So a company must extrapolate in order to estimate how countries compare. Countries also differ in how they define items, such as family income, literacy, and FDI. Activities taking place outside the market economy, such as within the home, do not show up in income figures. Thus, the different extent among countries in terms of people producing for their own consumption (growing vegetables, preparing meals at home, sewing clothes, cutting hair, and so on) distorts country comparisons.

Accounting rules such as depreciation also differ, resulting in non-comparable net national product figures. Another problem concerns exchange rates, which must be used to convert countries' financial data to some common currency. A 10 percent appreciation of the Japanese yen in relation to the U.S. dollar results in a 10 percent increase in the per capita GDP of Japanese residents when figures are reported in dollars. Does this mean the Japanese are suddenly 10 percent richer? Obviously not, because they use about 85 percent of their yen income to make purchases in yen in their economy; thus, they have little additional purchasing power for 85 percent of what they buy.

EXTERNAL SOURCES OF INFORMATION

Although information is needed for making good location decisions, there are simply too many sources for us to include a comprehensive list. Chances are, at least for scanning purposes, that you will use the Internet to collect most of your information. Some searches will lead you to free information, others to services for which you must pay. The following discussion highlights the major types of information sources in terms of their completeness, reliability, and cost.

Individualized Reports Market research and business consulting companies conduct studies for a fee. They generally are the most costly information source because their individualized nature restricts prorating among a number of companies. However, the fact that a company can specify what information it wants often makes the expense worthwhile.

Specialized Studies Research organizations prepare and sell fairly specific studies at costs much lower than those for individualized reports. These specialized studies are sometimes directories of companies that operate in a given locale, perhaps containing financial or other information about the companies. They may also be about business in certain locales, forms of business, or specific products.

Service Companies Most companies providing services to international clients—such as banks, transportation agencies, and accounting firms—publish reports that are usually geared toward either the conduct of business in a given area or some specific subject of general interest, such as tax or trademark legislation. Because the service firms intend to reach a wide market of companies, their reports tend to be fairly general. Some also offer informal opinions about such things as the reputations of possible business associates and the names of people to contact in a company.

Government Agencies When a government wants to stimulate foreign business activity, the amount and type of information it makes available may be substantial. The U.S. Department of Commerce compiles news and regulations about individual foreign countries, disseminates specific information on product sales locations in the National Trade Data Bank, and can also help set up appointments with businesspeople abroad.

International Organizations and Agencies Numerous organizations and agencies are supported by more than one country, including the UN, the WTO, the IMF, the OECD, and the EU. All of them have large research staffs that compile basic statistics and prepare reports and recommendations concerning common trends and problems. Many international development banks even help finance investment-feasibility studies.

Trade Associations Trade associations connected to various product lines collect, evaluate, and disseminate a wide variety of data dealing with technical and competitive factors in their industries. Many of these data are available in the trade journals published by such associations; others may or may not be available to nonmembers.

INTERNALLY GENERATED DATA

MNEs may have to collect much information themselves, sometimes simply by observing keenly and asking many questions. Investigators can see what kind of merchandise is available, determine who is buying and where, and uncover the hidden distribution points and competition. Hidden competition for ready-made clothing may be seamstresses working in private homes; for vacuum cleaners, it may be servants who clean with mops. Surreptitiously sold contraband may compete with locally produced goods. Traditional analysis methods would not reveal such facts.

Companies already operating within a market offer another source of information. Limited Brands has used this source, such as meeting with Apple's management in China, to ascertain experiences encountered during entry.[55]

COUNTRY COMPARISON TOOLS

Once companies scan for information, they need to analyze it. Two common tools for this are *grids* and *matrices.* In preparing either, it is useful to have a team made up of people from different functions so that various perspectives are considered. However, once companies commit to locations, they need continuous updates.

Point

Should Companies Operate in and Send Employees to Violent Areas?

Point **Yes** Where there's risk, there are usually rewards. Companies should not shun areas with violence. Businesspeople have always taken risks, and employees have always gone to dangerous areas. As far back as the seventeenth century, immigrants to what are now the United States, India, and Australia encountered disease and hostile native populations. Had companies and immigrants not taken chances, the world would be far less developed today.

You can't look at the risk from violence apart from others. Although we don't have historical data, most situations are probably safer today. Disease is still a bigger danger than violence, but medical advances against a number of historical killers (polio, measles, smallpox, tuberculosis, etc.)

have reduced that risk, while evacuation in case of a *real* emergency situation is much faster.

But let's assume for a moment that we decide to avoid countries with the potential for violence against our facilities and employees. Is there any such place? To answer this question, you need to consider an array of indicators that include overall crime rate, murder rate, terrorism, kidnapping, and political violence. Because so many occurrences go unreported, the statistics are unreliable. Further, situations can change quickly, as witnessed by the sudden outbreak of violence in Syria. The opinions from so-called risk experts are certainly conflicting. Finally, countries that we think of as safe—Norway, United Kingdom, United States—have had such recent violence as mass shootings, bombings, and street riots. In fact, the deputy assistant director of the FBI said, "We are dealing every single day with a variety of domestic terrorism threats that are alive and well and in this country [United States]."[56] Now about the only place that everyone agrees is low-risk is Greenland.

Some industries don't have the luxury of avoiding violent countries. Take the petroleum industry. Oil companies have to go where there is a high likelihood of finding oil. It would be great to find it all in places like Switzerland, but this is not the reality. Most of the credible alternatives are in areas that have had recent bombings, kidnappings, or organized crime—the Middle East, West Africa, the Central Asian former Soviet republics, and Venezuela. If companies didn't go to these places, they'd be out of business.

In effect, we'll keep operating anywhere there are opportunities. If a place seems physically risky, we'll take whatever precautions we can. We'll share intelligence reports, put people through safety training courses (there are plenty of these available now), and take security actions abroad. And perhaps we won't transfer spouses and children to the "risky" areas so we don't have to be on top of what is happening with as many people.

Should Companies Operate in and Send Employees to Violent Areas?

Counterpoint

No We're no longer concerned simply with being caught in the crossfire between opposing military factions. Antiglobalization groups want to harm our personnel and facilities so that we'll leave, or so that they gain international publicity. Groups see us as easy marks for extortion by threatening harm or kidnapping our personnel. Still others are against foreigners, regardless of their aims. Such a group in Afghanistan killed staff members from Médecins sans Frontières and the Red Cross who were there to treat sick and injured people.[57]

At the same time, getting caught in the crossfire has become a bigger risk. Arms trafficking has risen and has lowered prices not only to revolutionaries but also to drug and alien smugglers and money launderers.[58] As MNEs, we can't help being visible, and thus vulnerable.

In essence, if we operate where risk of violence is great, we put our personnel in danger. Even if no violence comes to them, they endure stress that negatively affects their performance.[59] Although local personnel may be at a lesser risk of, say, kidnapping, experience shows that they too are not immune. Furthermore, we have to send foreign personnel there. Some go as managers or technicians on long assignments; others must go on business trips to do such things as audit books, ensure quality control, and offer staff advice through on-site visits. The dangers are not inconsequential.

Counterpoint

There are thousands of reported kidnappings per year, many targeting foreign workers and their families. Nigeria has been the site of recent kidnappings of foreign oil workers, ship crew members, and even a visiting priest.[60]

It's simply unethical to put our employees in such situations. Of course, we don't force them to go to dangerous places, and we can get enough people to work there, especially during a global recession. However, our experience is that there are three types of people who want or are willing to work in such areas, and none are ideal. First are those who simply want the high compensation and big insurance policies, some of whom are experienced in military or undercover activities. They tend to be highly independent and hard to control. Second are the naïve who don't understand the danger and are difficult to safeguard through training and security activities. Third are the thrill seekers, who find that adrenaline is like an addictive drug; they are most at risk because of the thrill of danger and their reluctance to leave when situations worsen.[61]

High risk to individuals is indicative of a political situation out of control—a harbinger of additional risks that may occur through governmental changes, falls in consumer confidence, and a general malaise that damages revenues and operating regulations. This is not the kind of country in which to conduct operations.

GRIDS

Grids are tools that
- May depict acceptable or unacceptable conditions.
- Rank countries by important variables.

Managers may use a grid to compare countries on whatever factors they deem important. Table 13.2 is an example of a grid with information placed into three categories. The managers may immediately eliminate certain countries from consideration because of characteristics they find unacceptable (companies vary in this). These factors are in the first category of variables, by which Country I is eliminated. The managers assign values and weights to other variables so that they rank each country according to attributes of relative importance to the company. In this hypothetical example, we've attached more weight to the size of investment needed than to the tax rate. For instance, the table graphically pinpoints Country II as high return–low risk, Country III as low return–low risk, Country IV as high return–high risk, and Country V as low return–high risk.

Both the variables and the weights differ by product and company depending on the company's internal situation and its objectives. For instance, managers in a company selling a low-priced consumer product might weigh population size heavily as an indicator of market opportunity, whereas those in a company selling tires might weigh heavily the number of vehicles registered. The grid technique is useful even when a company does not compare countries because it can set the minimum score needed for either investing additional resources or committing more funds to a more detailed feasibility study.

Grids do tend to get cumbersome, however, as the number of variables increases. Although they are useful in ranking countries, they often obscure interrelationships among them.

TABLE 13.2 Simplified Market-Penetration Grid

This table is simply an example: In the real world, a company chooses the variables that it regards as most important and may weight some as more important than others. Here managers rate Country II the most attractive because it's regarded as high return–low risk. Country IV also promises a high return and Country III low risk. Note that Country I is eliminated immediately because the company will go only where 100 percent ownership is permitted.

		Country				
Variable	**Weight**	**I**	**II**	**III**	**IV**	**V**
1. Acceptable (A), Unacceptable (U) factors						
a. Allows 100 percent ownership	—	U	A	A	A	A
b. Allows licensing to majority-owned subsidiary	—	A	A	A	A	A
2. Return (higher number = preferred rating)						
a. Size of investment needed	0–5	—	4	3	3	3
b. Direct costs	0–3	—	3	1	2	2
c. Tax rate	0–2	—	2	1	2	2
d. Market size, present	0–4	—	3	2	4	1
e. Market size, 3–10 years	0–3	—	2	1	3	1
f. Market share, immediate potential, 0–2 years	0–2	—	2	1	2	1
g. Market share, 3–10 years	0–2	—	2	1	2	0
Total			18	10	18	10
3. Risk (lower number = preferred rating)						
a. Market loss, 3–10 years (if no present penetration)	0–4	—	2	1	3	2
b. Exchange problems	0–3	—	0	0	3	3
c. Political-unrest potential	0–3	—	0	1	2	3
d. Business laws, present	0–4	—	1	0	4	3
e. Business laws, 3–10 years	0–2	—	0	1	2	2
Total			3	3	14	13

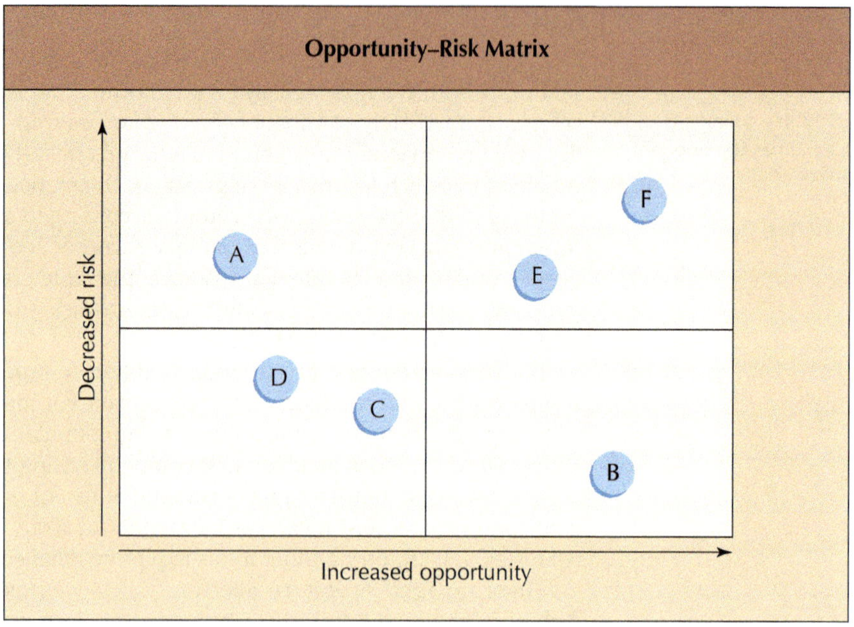

FIGURE 13.4 Opportunity–Risk Matrix

Countries E and F are the most desirable because they boast a combination of a high level of opportunity and a low level of risk. But what if the decision came down to Countries A and B? The level of opportunity in Country A may not be as high as a company would like, but the low level of risk may be attractive. Country B, however, promises a high level of opportunities but also threatens a high level of risk. A decision between Countries A and B will probably take the firm's risk tolerance into consideration.

With an opportunity-risk matrix, a company can

- Decide on indicators and weigh them.
- Evaluate each country on the weighted indicators.

MATRICES

To more clearly show the opportunity/risk relationship, managers can plot values on a matrix such as the one shown in Figure 13.4. In this particular example, Countries E and F are high-opportunity and low-risk countries compared to Countries A, B, C, and D, making them better candidates for detailed analysis.

In reality, however, managers may sometimes have to choose between a country with high risk and high opportunity and another with low risk and low opportunity, thus making a decision based on their tolerance for risk and on the portfolio of countries where the company is already operating. Further, although A, B, C, and D are less appealing than E and F, the company may nevertheless find opportunities in A, B, C, and D—perhaps licensing or shared-ownership arrangements—without necessarily making a large commitment.

But how can managers plot values on such a matrix? They must determine which factors are good indicators of their companies' risk and opportunity and weight them to reflect their importance. For instance, on the risk axis they might give 20 percent (0.2) of the weight to expropriation risk, 25 percent (0.25) to foreign-exchange controls, 20 percent (0.2) to civil disturbances and terrorism, 20 percent (0.2) to natural disasters, and 15 percent (0.15) to exchange-rate change, for a total allocation of 100 percent. They would then rate each country on a scale, such as from 1 to 10 for each variable (with 10 indicating the best score), and multiply each variable by the weight they allocate to it. If they give Country A a rating of 8 on the expropriation-risk variable, they would multiply 8 by 0.2 (the weight they assign to expropriation) for a score of 1.6. They would then sum all of Country A's risk-variable scores to place it on the risk axis, and similarly plot the location of Country A on the opportunity axis.

A key element of this kind of matrix, and one that managers do not always include in practice, is the projection of where countries will be in the future, or at least the direction in which they *should* move. Such a projection is obviously useful, but the farther one forecasts into the future, the less certain the projection.

ALLOCATING AMONG LOCATIONS

The scanning tools just described are useful for narrowing country alternatives and allocating operational emphasis among countries. We now examine three complementary strategies for international expansion: alternative gradual commitments, geographic diversification versus concentration, and reinvestment versus harvesting.

ALTERNATIVE GRADUAL COMMITMENTS

Companies may reduce risks from the liability of foreignness by

- Going first to countries with characteristics similar to those of their home countries.
- Having experienced intermediaries handle operations for them.
- Operating in formats requiring commitment of fewer resources abroad.
- Moving initially to one or a few, rather than many, foreign countries.

As we've discussed, because of liability of foreignness, companies favor operations in areas similar to their home countries. Nevertheless, there are alternative means of risk-minimization expansion patterns they can undertake, as shown in Figure 13.5. As you examine this figure, note that the farther a company moves from the center on any axis, the deeper its international commitment becomes.

However, a company does not necessarily move at the same speed along each axis. In fact, it may jump over some of the steps. A slow movement along one axis may free up resources that allow faster expansion along another.

Let's examine Figure 13.5 more closely. Axis A shows that companies tend to move gradually from a purely domestic focus to one that encompasses operations in countries similar and then dissimilar to one's own country. However, an alternative when moving quickly along the A axis (and even jumping the intermediate step) is to move slowly along the B axis. The B axis shows that a company may use intermediaries to handle foreign operations during early stages of international expansion because this minimizes the resources it puts at risk and its liability of foreignness. It can then commit fewer resources to both international endeavors, relying instead on the intermediaries that already know how to operate in the foreign market. A related example is the foreign expansion of some high-tech companies from developing countries. Rather than first targeting nearby countries with characteristics similar

FIGURE 13.5 The Usual Pattern of Internationalization

The farther a company moves outward along any of the axes (A, B, C, D), the deeper its international commitment. Most companies move at different speeds along different axes.

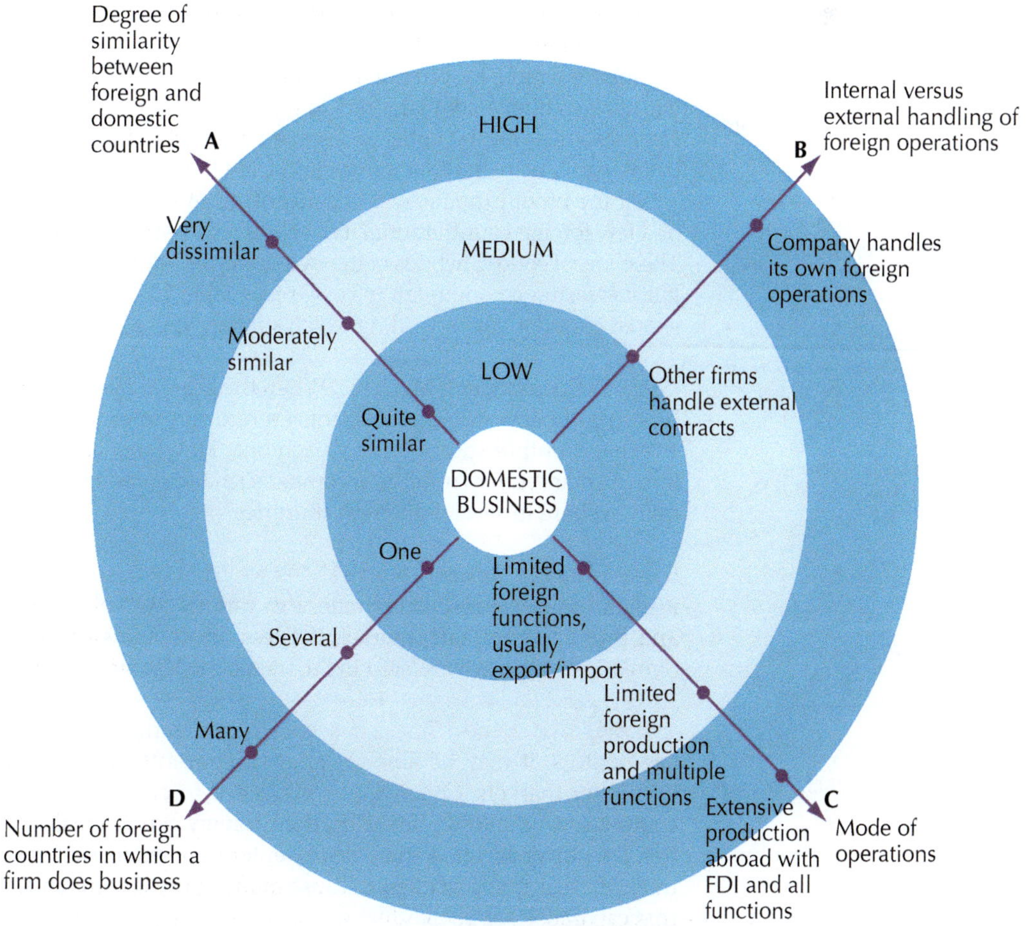

to their home markets, they have gone to high-income countries where short-term market potentials are higher. However, they have relied heavily on intermediaries and have made foreign acquisitions that include the personnel who know the markets they are targeting.

However, if the business grows successfully, the company may want to handle the operations with its own staff. This is because by learning more about foreign operations it perceives them less risky than at the onset, and it realizes that the volume of business may justify the development of internal capabilities such as hiring trained personnel to maintain a department for foreign sales or purchases.

Axis C shows that importing or exporting is usually the first international mode a company undertakes. At an early stage of international involvement, importing and exporting require the placement of few company resources abroad. In fact, it may involve investing few additional resources if the company can use excess production capacity to produce more goods, which it would then export. Thus, moving along the C axis is a means to minimize the risk of the liability of foreignness because of first forgoing such functions as managing a foreign workforce for production.

Later, the company might, in addition to exporting, make an even higher commitment through FDI to produce abroad. Its infusion of capital, personnel, and technology is highest for these operations. Axis D shows that companies can move internationally one country at a time, which keeps them from being overwhelmed by learning about many countries all at once. However, as we discuss in the next section, there may be a competitive drive to move to a number of countries almost simultaneously.

GEOGRAPHIC DIVERSIFICATION VERSUS CONCENTRATION

Strategies for ultimately reaching a high level of commitment in many countries are

- Diversification—go to many fast and then build up slowly in each.
- Concentration—go to one or a few and build up fast before going to others.
- A hybrid of the two.

Ultimately, a company may gain a sizable presence and commitment in most countries; however, there are different paths to that position. Although any move abroad means some geographic diversification, the term **diversification strategy** in the context of location decisions describes a company's rapid movement into many foreign markets, gradually increasing its commitment within each one. A company can do this, say, through a liberal licensing policy to ensure sufficient resources for the initial widespread expansion. It will eventually increase its involvement by taking on activities that it first contracted to other companies.

At the other extreme, with a **concentration strategy,** the company will move to only one or a few foreign countries until it develops a very strong involvement and competitive position. There are, of course, hybrids of the two strategies—for example, moving rapidly to most markets but increasing commitment in only a few. Table 13.3 sums up the major variables a company should consider when deciding which strategy to use.[62] We now discuss each of these.

Growth Rate in Each Market

When the growth rate in each market is high or needs to be high, a company should usually concentrate on a few markets because it will cost a great deal to expand output sufficiently for each one. However, slower growth or the need for growth in each market may result in a company's having enough resources to build and maintain a market share in several different countries.[63]

Sales Stability in Each Market

As we have discussed, a company may smooth its earnings and sales because of operations in various parts of the world. The more stable the sales and profits within each market, the less advantage gained from a diversification strategy. Similarly, the more correlated the markets, the less smoothing is achieved by selling in each.

Competitive Lead Time

If a company determines that it has a long lead time over competitors, it may be able to follow a concentration strategy and still beat competitors into other markets. Otherwise, it may need to either cede leadership in some countries to competitors or follow a diversification strategy. Born global companies are particularly prone to follow diversification strategies by entering markets that are both similar and dissimilar to those in their home markets because many of these companies depend on new technologies that can obsolesce quickly.[64]

TABLE 13.3 To Diversify or to Concentrate: The Role of Product and Market Factors

If a company determines that "Product or Market Factors" satisfy the conditions in the column headed "Prefer Diversification," it may benefit from moving quickly into several markets simultaneously. If the same factors satisfy the conditions under "Prefer Concentration," it may decide to enter and work initially to develop a substantial presence in just one or a few markets.

Product or Market Factor	Prefer Diversification If:	Prefer Concentration If:
1. Growth rate of each market	Low	High
2. Sales stability in each market	Low	High
3. Competitive lead time	Short	Long
4. Spillover effects	High	Low
5. Need for product, communication, and distribution adaptation	Low	High
6. Program control requirements	Low	High

Source: "Marketing Expansion Strategies in Multinational Marketing," *Journal of Marketing* 43 (Spring 1979): 89. Reprinted by permission of the American Marketing Association © 1979.

Spillover Effects Situations in which the marketing program in one country results in awareness of the product in other countries are known as **spillover effects.** These are advantageous because additional customers may be reached with little additional cost, which can happen if the product is advertised through media sent cross-nationally, such as U.S. television ads that reach Canadians. When marketing programs reach many countries, such as by satellite television or the Internet, a diversification strategy has advantages.

Need for Product, Communication, and Distribution Adaptation Companies may have to alter products and methods of operating abroad—a process that, because of cost, favors a concentration strategy. The adaptation cost may limit the resources the company has for expanding in many different markets. Further, if the adaptations are unique to each country, the company cannot easily spread the costs over sales in more than one country to reduce total unit costs.

Program Control Requirements The more a company needs to control its operations in a foreign country, the more favorable a concentration strategy is. This is because the company will need to use more of its resources to maintain that control, such as by taking a larger percentage of ownership in the operation. Its need for more control could be for various reasons, including the fear that collaboration with a partner will create a competitor.

Subsequent Product Diversification The above discussion centers on initial movements into different countries. In addition, companies add new products to their portfolios and must decide where and how quickly to introduce them abroad. The more related the new products are to their existing products, especially those they are already selling abroad, the quicker they can move them into other markets. This is because the companies have experience that is more applicable to their products' introduction.[65]

REINVESTMENT AND HARVESTING

So far, we've discussed the sequencing of country entry. Then, once a company is operating abroad, it must evaluate how much effort to allocate to each location. With FDI, the company transfers financial capital and has physical and human capital in place. If the investment is successful, the company will earn money that it may remit back to headquarters or reinvest to increase the investment value. Over time, most of the value of a company's foreign investment, if successful, comes from reinvesting. If the investment is unsuccessful, the company may consider transferring capital elsewhere.

A company may have to make new commitments to maintain competitiveness abroad.

Reinvestment Decisions Companies treat decisions to replace depreciated assets or to add to the existing stock of capital from retained earnings abroad somewhat differently from original investment decisions. Once committed to a given locale, a company may find no option to move a substantial portion of the earnings elsewhere; to do so would endanger the continued successful operation of the given foreign facility. The failure to expand might result in a falling market share and a higher unit cost than that of competitors.

Aside from competitive factors, a company may need several years of almost total reinvestment and allocation of new funds in one area to attain its objectives, such as meeting target growth. Moreover, a company may treat reinvestment decisions differently because experienced personnel in a given country may be the best judges of what is needed there, so headquarters may delegate certain investment decisions to them.

Companies must decide how to get out of operations if

- They no longer fit the overall strategy.
- There are better alternative opportunities.

CRN
Case Review Note

Harvesting Companies commonly reduce commitments in some countries because those countries have poorer performance prospects than do others—a process known as **harvesting (or divesting).** Burger King, for example, sold off underperforming operations in Korea and Slovakia so as to have funds for more promising ventures in the Chinese and Russian markets. There are other reasons as well. J. Sainsbury withdrew from the Egyptian market because its management did not expect a turnaround in its poorly performing operation there.[66] Dana sold its U.K. facility to use funds to concentrate on developing different automotive technologies.[67] Goodyear sold its Indonesian rubber plantation because of its decision to stop producing rubber.[68]

Some indications suggest that companies might benefit by planning divestments better and by developing divestment specialists. Companies have tended to wait too long before divesting, instead trying expensive means of improving performance, such as those proposed by local managers who fear losing their positions if the company abandons the operation Ideas for investment projects typically originate with middle managers or managers in foreign subsidiaries who are enthusiastic about collecting information to accompany a proposal as it moves upward in the organization. After all, the evaluation and employment of these people depend on growth. They have no such incentive to propose divestments. These proposals typically originate at the top of the organization after upper management has tried most remedies for improving operational performance.[69]

Companies may divest by a sale or closure of facilities, usually preferring a sale because they receive some compensation. A company that considers divesting because of a country's well-publicized political or economic situation may find few potential buyers except at very low prices. In such situations, it may try to delay divestment, hoping that the situation will improve. If it does, the firm that waits out the situation generally is in a better position to regain markets and profits than one that forsakes its operation.

A company cannot always simply abandon an investment either. Governments frequently require performance contracts, such as substantial severance packages to employees that make a loss from divestment greater than the direct investment's net value. Further, the length of time to go through insolvency (up to 10 years in some countries) alters the percentage of value recovered from a divestment. In Japan, investors recover an average of 93 percent of the value, whereas in Madagascar they typically recover only 13 percent.[70] Finally, many MNEs fear adverse international publicity and difficulty in reentering a market if they do not sever relations with a foreign government on amicable terms.

NONCOMPARATIVE DECISION MAKING

Most companies examine proposals one at a time and accept them if they meet minimum-threshold criteria.

Because companies have limited resources at their disposal, it might seem that they maintain a storehouse of foreign operating proposals that they can rank by some predetermined criteria. If this were so, managers could simply start allocating resources to the top-ranked proposal and continue down the list until they could make no further commitments. This is often not the case, however. They make **go-no-go decisions** by examining one opportunity at a time and pursuing it if it meets some threshold criteria.

To begin with, companies sometimes need to respond quickly to prospects they had not anticipated. Many might need to respond to unsolicited proposals to sell abroad or sign joint venture or licensing contracts. Many might initiate export activity passively—that is, foreign companies or export intermediaries approach them to be suppliers. Similarly, undertakings may be onetime possibilities because a government or another company solicits requests. For example, Tasmanian development offices (Australia) proposed that Malaysia's Ta Ann Holdings use its veneer peeling technology by investing in Tasmania. For Ta Ann, it was a one-time opportunity to say "yes" or "no."[71] Or a government may change rules to allow foreign acquisitions, such as Nigeria did for banking.[72] Further, there may be a chance to buy properties that another company divests. When Enron faced bankruptcy, it needed to sell many of its foreign facilities, so companies such as Tractebel from Belgium and Royal Dutch/Shell bid on its Korean facilities.[73] Having discussed the competitive advantages of following customers' and competitors' moves into foreign markets, we know we cannot always foresee when the customers and competitors will move.

Another factor inhibiting the comparison of country operations is that their interdependence can keep them from being meaningfully evaluated separately. Profit figures from individual operations may obscure the real impact on overall company profits. If a U.S. company were to establish an assembly operation in Australia, the operation could either increase or reduce exports from the United States, thus affecting U.S. profit figures. Moreover, headquarters may have to incur additional costs to oversee the Australian operation and coordinate the movement of components into Australia. These costs are difficult to estimate and will likely not show up in the Australian income figures.

Or perhaps by building a plant in Brazil to supply components to Volkswagen of Brazil, the company may increase the possibility of selling to Volkswagen in other countries. As a result of the Australian or Brazilian projects, management would have to make assumptions about the changed profits for the company's total global operations. Finally, interdependence occurs because much of the sales and purchases of foreign subsidiaries are among units of the same parent company. The prices the company charges on these transactions will affect the relative profitability of one unit compared to another.

Clearly, companies cannot afford to conduct very many feasibility studies simultaneously. Even if they can, the studies are apt to be in various stages of completion at any given time. Suppose a company completes its study for an Australian project while continuing studies on New Zealand, Japan, and Indonesia. Can the company afford to hold off on making a decision about Australia? Probably not. Waiting would likely invalidate much of the Australian study, thus necessitating added expense and further delays to update it. In sum, three factors inhibit companies from comparing investment opportunities: cost, time, and the interrelation of operations on global performance.

Looking to the Future

Will Prime Locations Change?

Future sales- and resource-seeking opportunities and risks may shift among countries because of a variety of demographic, sociocultural, political-legal, technological, and economic conditions. We will concentrate here on population changes and where populations can and will prefer to work. In Chapter 5, we discussed how demographers expect a slowing in the growth of global population through 2050, with some countries experiencing declining populations. At the same time, growth should remain robust in many developing economies, particularly those in sub-Saharan Africa. The projection is that the percentage of people living in currently developed countries is expected to fall to 13.7 percent from a 2000 figure of 19.7 percent. The least developed countries will have the biggest population increase.

Further, because the world's population will continue to age, the share of what we now consider the working-age population should fall for developed countries and increase in many developing ones.

Because there is a positive relationship between the proportional size of the working-age population and per capita GDP, the growth in per capita GDP should be higher in today's developing economies than in today's developed countries unless we redefine working age.[74] These demographic changes, if they materialize, will have implications for the location of both markets and labor forces.

An intriguing possibility is the near-officeless headquarters for international companies. Technology may permit more people to work from anywhere as they email and teleconference with their colleagues, customers, and suppliers. In fact, they can live anywhere in the world and work from their homes, as is already occurring at least part-time within some professions. However, if people can work from home, they may move those homes where they want to live rather than living where their employers are now located. Highly creative, innovative, self-motivated people can usually get permission to live in almost any country of the world.

A leading researcher on urbanization and planning has shown that beginning at least as early as the Roman Empire these types of people have been drawn to certain cities that were the centers of innovation. He maintains that this attraction is due to people's improvement through interchange with others like themselves—like "a very bright class in a school or a college. They all try to score off each other and do better." Thus, if he's correct, the brightest minds may work more at home but still need the face-to-face interaction with their colleagues.[75] The continued attraction of young technical people to places like Silicon Valley seems to confirm this viewpoint.[76]

These arguments are provocative, particularly because we now have technology to allow people to communicate without traveling as much. Yet the continued increase in business travel shows that there is still a need for face-to-face interaction. The researcher further suggests that these people will be drawn to the same places that attract tourists.

Concomitantly, another view is that in leading Western societies, the elite made up of intellectuals and highly educated people is increasingly using its capability to delay and block new technologies. If successful, their efforts will result in the emergence of different countries at the forefront of technological development and acceptance.[77] ■

CASE The LEGO® Group[78]

The LEGO® Group is a family business founded in 1932, making wooden toys in the city of Billund, Denmark. In 1958, Godtfred Kirk Christiansen, son of the company founder Ole Kirk Christiansen, created the LEGO© brick, widely praised and acclaimed as the "Toy of the Century," by both *Fortune* magazine and the British Association of Toy Retailers (LEGO, Annual Report, 2011). Today, LEGO is Europe's largest and the world's second-largest toy manufacturer in terms of sales volume. It had a turnover of €2,511 million in 2012, and employed more than 9,000 worldwide. LEGO's sales during the first half of 2013 increased by 13 percent with its strongest growth in Asia. The company has been a pioneer in breaking convention at the cost of failing and almost going bankrupt by 2003, with its adventurous forays and building what it believed was a diverse portfolio that boasted of video and other games, apparel, and theme parks. Riding high on the success of its *Harry Potter* and *Star Wars* themed series, LEGO's road to self-realization was in understanding that the brick was at its core.

The diversification was a direct response to developments and challenges in the industry. In the 1990s, the segment for construction toys was shrinking. The competition for kids' time and their parents' money was getting sharper. LEGO is part of the market called "edutainment," including products with the ability to entertain and educate at the same time. First of all, computer games "stole" a lot of potential LEGO users. Little virtual playgrounds and computer games like SimCity or Civilization soon presented themselves as a threat to

A girl plays with LEGO toys in Thailand
Source: © panitanjohn - Fotolia.com

traditional toymakers like LEGO. Who needed toy bricks, with the deluge of computer and other simulation games flooding the market!

Simultaneously, the power of retailers grew. Especially in the United States, the buyers of LEGO products were reduced to only a few companies like Toys"R"Us, Walmart, and Kmart. LEGO's business model was very dependent on retailers, who now started demanding larger discounts and specially adjusted products. LEGO was caught in a dilemma, between the decision to adopt a flexible price strategy that would cater to lower budgets or to continue with its existing price structures that promised standardized products across the board. To protect its brand in the market, LEGO wanted customers to be able to buy the same products at almost the same price everywhere. If these customers knew that there was only one price and quality level for a certain LEGO product, they would see the company as a lot more trustworthy, as opposed to a situation where all LEGO products were available at a low cost and, possibly, low-quality at some retailers. The company's CEO reached out to LEGO's fanbase who responded with threats to leave their favorite brand if it steered from quality in an attempt to offer their toys for cheaper prices. It was decided that LEGO's overall reputation for reliability was best left untouched with its promise of upholding a single high standard for its corresponding quality and price; conversely LEGO's consumer image would have suffered had it compromised over price.

To become more independent, the company slowly began to look for different platforms and new ways of selling its existing products and building on innovation from within. The internet provided that opportunity. In the early 2000s, LEGO launched LEGO Direct, which was the successor of the not-so-successful LEGO World Shop. With LEGO Direct, it became possible for customers to invent or assemble their own LEGO (virtual) constructions on their personal computers like in video games. When finished, they could order the specific LEGO products required for their dream constructions. This option gave the company some valuable advantages: They became more independent of the retailers and enjoyed a direct communication channel with their customers on their Web site, where they could quickly realize new demands from their consumers. LEGO.com has been very successful and has had over a million visitors per month, with the average visitor staying for 8–9 minutes.

Moreover, LEGO is the only major traditional toy maker that targeted the adult market, and has a strong following in the Adult Fans of Legos or AFOL communities worldwide. LEGO's Architecture Series directly targets this market of adult Lego fans, a solid example of LEGO's attempts to return to its core strength. Seoul's Sungnyemun gate and Tokyo's Imperial Hotel featured in LEGO's Architecture series, further establish the company's hunger for new markets across not just age segments but also different geographies. More recently, LEGO adapted an existing dinosaur set and repackaged it as a commemorative Year of the Snake special edition, sold only in China.

Meanwhile, the global toy industry has been growing at a Compound Annual Growth Rate (CAGR) of 2.9 percent from 2008 to 2012, while the global economy has grown by only 2.6 percent. The industry growth is not equally divided; neither by region, nor by country. While some countries, especially emerging markets, are experiencing relevant growth such as France, Germany, Australia, Brazil, and China, others like USA and Canada are experiencing negative growth in their market shares. To reach its global customer base, LEGO currently has offices in 29 countries. Because its products don't need local adaptation, the company has reduced its office base over time. The company only needs to accommodate the products to local laws, which can be done initially for each product line in a centralized setting. Initially, LEGO moved many production sites to international locations, to lower its costs as with the Czech Republic and Mexico plants, and also the outsourcing of production of Flextronics to Poland.[79]

Over the past two decades, LEGO has made several production location decisions, with its underlying purpose being the accumulation of cost savings. However, this time a growing demand and an effort to reduce lead time between order and delivery are the main drivers behind the company's decision to invest hundreds of millions of euros in the new in-region manufacturing facilities in China. According to the global research firm Companies and Markets, by 2016, the Asia-Pacific region is expected to become the world's largest toy market. In the words of LEGO's spokesperson Roar Rude Trangbaek, the strategy was to shift production closer to its core markets. Factories in the Asia-Pacific region would thus, not supply to Europe or North America. The stated goal is for the LEGO factory in China to be able to supply 70 to 80 percent of the LEGO bricks sold in Asia in 2017.

Although Asia is LEGO's smallest market, contributing less than 10 percent of its revenue, annual sales in the region have peaked by more than 50 percent as millions of Asian consumers are buying educational toys amidst improved wage scenarios and better living standards. In the first half of 2013, the company experienced their strongest performance in Asia with consumer sales growing by about 35 percent. In fact, LEGO's CEO Jørgen Vig Knudstorp, expects higher growth rates in Asia. LEGO's revenue of nearly two billion dollars in the first half of 2013—compared with $1.43 billion for Hasbro, its close competitor—was boosted heavily by its growth of seventy per cent in China. China has become the world's second-largest toy market. It is predicted that the Asia-Pacific region will overtake North America as the largest regional toy market in 2014. The LEGO group also aims for the European, African and the Middle Eastern region, Asian, and American markets to contribute equally to sales and fuel further expansions.

The decision to choose China as the destination for setting up their production facility might have raised eyebrows within the industry. Previously, toy makers faced continuous struggles in China, where parents would rather see their children reading books than playing. In fact, playing has often been considered a dirty word in a culture where formal education is prioritized. However, many toy companies are already discovering that they can influence Chinese parents by positioning their toys as 'educational items.' In this regard, LEGO has already struck a chord with affluent Chinese parents, with toys that are being branded as educational tools to help children with developing dexterity and creativity. In an initiative to make itself known to the Chinese public, LEGO is spearheading several projects including mobilizing a group of students from Tsinghua University to build a low-cost atomic force microscope with LEGO's 3D parts and electronics.

A challenging issue for LEGO in China is consumers get lured by similar products by other manufacturers who build identical looking LEGO bricks, commonly known as "LEGO clones." Already swamped in a history of court battles over its copyright, LEGO is presently also locked in a legal spat with Hong Kong's Best-Lock Construction Toys, accused of ripping off LEGO's signature mini-figures. Although LEGO has been relatively successful in its copyright battles so far, several copies and clones abound in the market either claiming to be LEGO products or stating compatibility/association with the world's leading toy bricks. Blocks marketed by Chinese companies Ligao and Banbao are often direct copies of LEGO designs.

One potential strategy to keep these pirates at bay is to increase LEGO's already high manufacturing standards as most Chinese toy factories are focused on producing and exporting low-cost inferior products rather than high-quality ones for domestic consumption. LEGO has invested in creating customized products for Chinese or Asian markets. Judging by precedent, this is a risky strategy to adopt, with products destined to share the fate of the highly local but now defunct 'Orient Expedition' set which did not sustain the popularity or subscription it was pegged to capture.

LEGO painstakingly researched comparatively new markets in the Asia-Pacific that it wants to turn into a stronghold and came up with two brand new ranges of toys. LEGO Legends of China, with plenty of models and buildable figures of warriors and beasts; and the more controversial LEGO friends, targeted at young girls. LEGO has achieved a complete turnaround in the span of a few years and stands to gain from a host of company decisions that include maintaining its focus on the brick, creatively building on its own patents and storywriters to bolster its theme of unlimited play, and more crucially, shifting part of its production facility to China.

QUESTIONS

13-3. LEGO has placed an emerging country such as China ahead of developed economies of Japan and South Korea in its location decision. Discuss the pros and cons of this strategy.

13-4. LEGO's product portfolio is quite large. Discuss the advantages and disadvantages of product concentration versus diversification in such a context.

13-5. LEGO is a latecomer in the Chinese market. Discuss how it may overcome this barrier to achieve the expected rates of sales growth.

13-6. LEGO is heavily investing in the Chinese consumer first. Discuss the pros and cons of this strategy.

13-7. China is considered the land of knock-offs and imitation products. What are the measures major multinationals could take to stem the spread of clones or pirated products, in their decision to locate to China?

SUMMARY

- Because companies seldom have sufficient resources to exploit all opportunities, two major considerations facing managers are which markets to serve and where to locate the production to serve those markets.
- Companies' decisions on market and production location are highly interdependent because they often need to serve markets from local production and want to use existing production capacity.
- Scanning techniques aid managers in considering alternatives that might otherwise be overlooked. They also help limit the final detailed feasibility studies to a manageable number of those that appear most promising.
- Because each company has unique competitive capabilities and objectives, the factors affecting the choice of operating location will be different for each. Nevertheless, many consider similar-country comparative indicators when seeking advantages from foreign sales or foreign assets.
- Four broad categories of risk that companies may consider are political, foreign exchange, natural disaster, and competitive.

- The amount, accuracy, and timeliness of published data vary substantially among countries. Managers should be particularly aware of different definitions of terms, different collection methods, and different base years for reports, as well as misleading responses.
- Companies frequently use several tools to compare opportunities and risk in various countries, such as grids that rate country projects by a number of separate dimensions and matrices on which companies plot opportunity on one axis and risk on another.
- When allocating resources among countries, companies need to consider how to treat reinvestments and divestments, the interdependence of operations in different countries, and whether they should follow diversification versus concentration strategies.
- Companies may reduce the risk of liability of foreignness by moving first to countries more like their home countries. Alternatively, they may contract with experienced firms to handle operations for them, limit the resources they commit to foreign operations, and delay entry to many countries until they are operating successfully in one or a few.
- Companies must develop location strategies for new investments and devise means of deemphasizing certain areas and divesting if necessary.
- Companies often evaluate entry to a country without comparing it with other countries. This is because they may need to react quickly to proposals or respond to competitive threats, and because multiple feasibility studies seldom are finished simultaneously.
- Optimal future locations are most apt to change because of relative population growth and changes in types of technology.

KEY TERMS

concentration strategy
diversification strategy
escalation of commitment
first-mover advantage
go-no-go decision
harvesting (or divesting)
liability of foreignness
liquidity preference
oligopolistic reaction
scanning
spillover effects

ENDNOTES

1 ***Sources include the following:*** We'd like to acknowledge the invaluable assistance of Jonathan Fitzpatrick, former Executive V.P. and Chief Brand Operations Officer; Julio A. Ramirez, former Executive Vice President Global Operations; Arianne Cento, Senior Analyst, Global Communications; and Ana Miranda, Senior Manager Investor Relations, all with Burger King Corporation. Additional information came from *Form 10-K: Burger King, 2012* (Filed February 22, 2012); Elaine Walker, "BK Plans 1,000 Restaurants in China," *Miami Herald* (June 16, 2012): H1; "Burger King Worldwide Inc at ICR XChange Conference," *Fair Disclosure Wire* (January 16, 2013): n.p.; "Burger King Scouting for Locations in Major Siberian Cities," *Interfax: Russia & CIS Business and Financial Newswire* (January 22, 2013): n.p.; Samidha Sharma and Boby Kurian, "Burger King in Talks to Revive India Plans," *The Economic Times (Online)* [New Delhi] (February 1, 2013): n.p.; Elaine Walker, "Burger King Goes for New Look," *Miami Herald* (May 31, 2011): 1A–2A; Rebecca Ordish, "Testing the Franchising Waters in China," *The China Business Review* 33:6 (November–December 2006): 30–33; "Burger King Plans to Double Restaurant Count in Russia in 2011," *Interfax, Ukraine Business Daily* (Kiev) (November 17, 2010); "Negocio de Resturantes Aumenta 8% en Colombia," *Noticieras Financieras* (December 22, 2010); Business Monitor International, *Colombia Food & Drink Report Q1 2009* (London: Business Monitor International, 2009); Gemma Charles, "Burger King Adds First 'Value Meal' to Menu," *Marketing* (February 11, 2009): 3; "The Burger King's Brand Enters Colombia," *Business Wire* (December 13, 2007): n.p.

2 Paul Glader, "GE Is Reassigning Veteran Rice to Job Focusing on Overseas Sales," *Wall Street Journal* (November 9, 2010): B2.

3 Thomas Hutzschenreuter and Martin Hommes, "What Determines the Speed of New Product Area International Rollout?" Proceedings of the 54th Annual Meeting of the Academy of International Business (June 30–July 3, 2012).

4 Shige Makino, Takehiko Isobe, and Christine M. Chan, "Does Country Matter?" *Strategic Management Journal* 25 (2004): 1027–43.

5 Tony W. Tong, Todd M. Alessandri, Jeffrey J. Reuer, and Asda Chintakananda, "How Much Does Country Matter? An Analysis of Firms' Growth Options," *Journal of International Business Studies* 39:3 (2008): 387–405.

6 Peter Enderwick, "The Imperative of Global Environmental Scanning," *AIB Insights* 11:1 (2011): 12–15.

7 David Gonzalez, "Fried Chicken Takes Flight, Happily Nesting in U.S.," *New York Times* (September 20, 2002): A4; Joel Millman, "California City Fends Off Arrival of Mexican Supermarket," *Wall Street Journal* (August 7, 2002): B1+.

8 Don E. Schultz, "China May Leapfrog the West in Marketing," *Marketing News* (August 19, 2002): 8–9.

9 Amol Sharma, "In India, Subsidies Upend Car Sales," *Wall Street Journal* (July 1, 2012): B1+.

10 Anjli Raval, "Mercedes-Benz Turns to India," *Financial Times* (July 19, 2010): 20.

11 Nicholas James Bailey, "MNE Bargaining Power Under Constrained Location Choices: Evidence from the Tourism Industry," Proceedings of the 54th Annual Meeting of the Academy of International Business (June 30–July 3, 2012).

12 Nicholas Casey, "In Mexico, Auto Plants Hit the Gas," *Wall Street Journal* (November 20, 2012): A1+; "The Rise of Mexico," *The Economist* (November 24, 2012): 14; Keith Bradsher, "Hello, Cambodia," *New York Times* (April 9, 2013): Business 1+.

13 John Manuel Luiz and Busi Radebe, "The Strategic Location of Regional Headquarters for Multinationals in Africa," Proceedings of the 54th Annual Meeting of the Academy of International Business (June 30–July 3, 2012).

14 Anil Khurana, "Strategies for Global R&D," *Research Technology Management* (March/April 2006): 48–59.

15 David Luchnow, "Missing Piece of the Mexican Success Story," *Wall Street Journal* (March 4, 2002): A11+.

16 Michael Peel, "Bitter-Sweet Confections of Business in Nigeria," *Financial Times* (November 20, 2002): 10.

17 Andrew Bartmess and Keith Cerny, "Building Competitive Advantage through a Global Network of Capabilities," *California Management Review* 35: 2 (Winter 1993): 78–103; Emanuela Delbufalo and Corrado Cerruti, "Configuration and the Capability of Firms to Innovate: A Theoretical Framework," *International Journal of Management* 29: 3 Part 1 (September 2012): 16–28.

18 G. Bruce Knecht, "Going the Wrong Way down a One-Way Street," *Wall Street Journal* (March 18, 2002): A1.

19 Alfredo J. Mauri and Arvind V. Phatak, "Global Integration as Inter-Area Product Flows: The Internationalization of Ownership and Location Factors Influencing Product Flows across MNC Units," *Management International Review* 41 (2001): 233–49.

20 Julian Birkinshaw, Pontus Braunerhjelm, and Ulf Holm, "Why Do Some Multinational Corporations Relocate Their Headquarters Overseas?" *Strategic Management Journal* 27 (2006): 681–700; Erik Stam, "Why Butterflies Don't Leave: Locational Behavior of Entrepreneurial Firms," 83: 1 *Economic Geography* (January 2007): 27–50.

21 Nagesh Kumar, "Multinational Enterprises, Regional Economic Integration, and Export-Platform Production in the Host Countries: An Empirical Analysis for the U.S. and Japanese Corporations," *Weltwirtschaftliches Archive* 134:3 (1998): 450–83.

22 Cynthia O'Murchu and Jan Cienski, "Multinationals Reap the Rewards," *Financial Times* (December 2, 2010): 9.

23 C. Denbour, "Competition for Business Location: A Survey," *Journal of Industry, Competition and Trade,"* 8:2 (June 2008): 89–111.

24 World Bank, International Finance Corporation, *Doing Business in 2013, 10th edition* (Washington, DC: The International Bank for Reconstruction and Development, 2013).

25 Hoon Park, "Determinants of Corruption: A Cross-National Analysis," *Multinational Business Review* 11:2 (2003): 29–48.

26 Mario I. Kafouros, Peter J. Buckley, and Jeremy Clegg, "The Effects of Global Knowledge Reservoirs on the Productivity of Multinational Enterprises: The Role of International Depth and Breadth," *Research Policy* 41:5 (June 2012): 848–61.

27 Colin Kirkpatrick and Kenichi Shimamoto, "The Effect of Environmental Regulation on the Locational Choice of Japanese Direct Investment," 40:11 *Applied Economics* (June 2008): 1399; and George Z. Peng and Paul W. Beamish, "The Effect of National Corporate Responsibility Environment on Japanese Foreign Direct Investment," 80:4 (July 2008): 677–95.

28 John D. Daniels and James A. Schweikart, "Political Risk, Assessment and Management of," in Rosalie L. Tung (ed.), *IEBM Handbook of International Business* (London: International Thomson Business Press, 1999): 502–14.

29 Robert Wright, "Continuity Planning is Strengthened," *Financial Times* (March 20, 2012): Risk Management/Supply Chain 1.

30 Haig Simonian, "Venezuela to Pay Holcim $650M Compensation for Seized Assets," *Financial Times* (September 14, 2010): 17.

31 Much like options theory, theory of liquidity preference is associated with the work of Robert C. Merton, Myron S. Scholes, and Fisher Black. For good, succinct coverage, see John Krainer, "The 1997 Nobel Prize in Economics," FRBSF Economic Letter No. 98–05 (February 13, 1998).

32 Paul D. Ellis, "Does Psychic Distance Moderate the Market Size-Entry Sequence Relationship?" *Journal of International Business Studies* 39:3 (2008): 351–69.

33 See Srilata Zaheer and Elaine Mosakowski, "The Dynamics of the Liability of Foreignness: A Global Study of Survival in Financial Services," *Strategic Management Journal* 18 (1997): 439–64; Stewart R. Miller and Arvind Parkhe, "Is There a Liability of Foreignness in Global Banking? An Empirical Test of Banks' X-Efficiency," *Strategic Management Journal* 23 (2002): 55–75.

34 United Nations Environment Programme, *Reducing Disaster Risk: A Challenge for Development* (New York: United Nations, 2004).

35 Sharon Terlep and Mike Ramsey, "Disaster in Japan: Supply Shortages Stall Auto Makers," *Wall Street Journal* (March 19, 2011): 9.

36 Alistair Gray, "Disasters Expose Flaws in Assumptions," *Financial Times* (March 20, 2012): Risk Management/Supply Chain 1.

37 WHO, Public Health Mapping and GIS, Map Library, retrieved June 11, 2007, from gamapserver.who.int/mapLibrary/default.aspx. Also see World Health Organization, *World Health Statistics 2012* (Geneva: World Health Organization, 2012) for statistics on communicable and non-communicable diseases by country.

38 "A Threat Deadlier than a Landmine," *Financial Times* (December 2, 2002): 10.

39 Amy Merrick and Ann Zimmerman, "Wal-Mart Bans Some Work Travel Due to SARS," *Wall Street Journal* (April 10, 2003): 36.

40 Mikhail V. Gratchev, "Making the Most of Cultural Differences," *Harvard Business Review* (October 2001): 28–30.

41 John Cantwell, "Location and the Multinational Company," *Journal of International Business Studies* 40:1 (January 2009): 35–41; Nandini Lahiri, "Geographic Distribution of R&D Activity: How Does It Affect Innovation Quality?" *Academy of Management Journal* 53:5 (2010): 1194–1209; and Lilach Nachum and Sangyoung Song, "The MNE as a Portfolio: Interdependencies in MNE Growth Trajectory," *Journal of International Business Studies* 42:3 (April 2011): 381–405.

42 Shige Makino and Eric W.K. Tsang, "Historical Ties and Foreign Direct Investment: An Exploratory Study," *Journal of International Business Studies* 42:4 (May 2011): 545–57.

43 Khanh T. L. Tran, "Blockbuster Finds Success in Japan," *Wall Street Journal* (August 19, 1998): A14; Cecile Rohwedder, "Blockbuster Hits Eject Button as Stores in Germany See Video-Rental Sales Sag," *Wall Street Journal* (January 16, 1998): B9A.

44 Jon A. Doukas and Ozgur B. Kan, "Does Global Diversification Destroy Firm Values?" *Journal of International Business Studies* 37 (2006): 352–71.

45 B. Kazaz, M. Dada, and H. Moskowitz, "Global Production Planning under Exchange-Rate Uncertainty," *Management Science* 51 (2005): 1101–09.

46 Mario I. Kafouros, Peter J. Buckley, and Jeremy Clegg, loc.cit.

47 Edward B. Flowers, "Oligopolistic Reactions in European and Canadian Direct Investment in the United States," *Journal of International Business Studies* 7:2 (Fall–Winter 1976): 43–55; Frederick Knickerbocker, *Oligopolistic Reaction and Multinational Enterprise* (Cambridge, MA: Harvard University, Graduate School of Business, Division of Research, 1973).

48 Rose Yu, "Chinese Dilemma: 170 Auto Makers," *Wall Street Journal* (April 10, 2013): B10.

49 See J. Myles Shaver and Fredrick Flyer, "Agglomeration Economies, Firm Heterogeneity, and Foreign Direct Investment in the United States," *Strategic Management Journal* 21 (2000): 1175–93; Philippe Martin and Gianmarco I. P. Ottaviano, "Growth and Agglomeration," *International Economic Review* 42 (2001): 947–68; Edward E. Leamer and Michael Storper, "The Economic Geography of the Internet Age," *Journal of International Business Studies* 32 (2001): 641–65.

50 Jedrzej George Frynas, Kamel Mellah, and Geoffrey Allen Pigman, "First Mover Advantages in International Business and Firm-Specific Political Resources," *Strategic Management Journal* 27 (2006): 321–45; Makino, Isobe, and Chan, "Does Country Matter?"

51 Joel Millman, "PriceSmart to Restate Results Due to an Accounting Error," *Wall Street Journal* (November 11, 2003): B9.

52 Tony Barber and Kerin Hope, "Brussels Attacks Greece over False Data," *Financial Times* (January 13, 2010): 8.

53 Benoît Faucon, "Oil Thefts Plague Nigeria," *Wall Street Journal* (April 12, 2013): B1–2.

54 "China: Bottoms Up," *The Economist* (March 30, 2013): 43–44.

55 Andrea Cheng,"Limited Brands Defends Its International Plan," *Market Watch* (October 19, 2011): n.p.

56 Andrew Ward,"Terror Threat from Within Keeps America on High Alert,"*Financial Times* (April 19, 2005): 3, quoting John Lewis.

57 Azam Ahmed,"Suicide Bombers Attack a Red Cross Compound in Eastern Afghanistan,"*New York Times* (May 30, 2014): A6.

58 Moisés Naím,"The Five Wars of Globalization,"*Foreign Policy* (January–February 2003): 29–36.

59 Benjamin Bader and Nicola Berg,"An Empirical Investigation of Terrorism-Induced Stress on Expatriate Performance," Proceedings of the 54th Annual Meeting of the Academy of International Business (June 30–July 3, 2012).

60 A good history of violence and kidnapping in Nigeria appears in Soye Peniel Asawo,"Corporate Integrity and Company-Community Conflict Management in the Niger Delta Region of Nigeria,"*Journal of Leadership, Accountability and Ethics* 8:3 (March 2011): 77–88.

61 "Doing Business in Dangerous Places,"*The Economist* (August 14, 2004): 11.

62 Igal Ayal and Jehiel Zif,"Marketing Expansion Strategies in Multinational Marketing,"*Journal of Marketing* (Spring 1979): 84–94.

63 Makino, Isobe, and Chan,"Does Country Matter?"

64 Susan Freeman, Kate Hutchings, and Sylvie Chetty,"Born-Global and Culturally Proximate Markets,"*Management International Review* 52 (2012): 425–60.

65 Hutzschenreuter and Hommes, op. cit.

66 Susanna Voyle and James Drummond,"J. Sainsbury to Withdraw from Egypt,"*Financial Times* (April 10, 2001): 23.

67 Nikki Tait,"Dana Set to Sell UK-Based Components Arm,"*Financial Times* (November 29, 2000): 22.

68 Makino, Isobe, and Chan,"Does Country Matter?"; Bernard Simon, "Goodyear Sells Its Last Plantation,"*Financial Times* (December 1, 2004): 18.

69 See Jean J. Boddewyn,"Foreign and Domestic Divestment and Investment Decisions: Like or Unlike?"*Journal of International Business Studies* 14:3 (Winter 1983): 28; Michelle Haynes, Steve Thompson, and Mike Wright, "The Determinants of Corporate Divestment in the U.K.,"*Journal of Industrial Organization* 18 (2000): 1201–22; Jose Mata and Pedro Portugal, "Closure and Divestiture by Foreign Entrants: The Impact of Entry and Post-Entry Strategies,"*Strategic Management Journal* 21 (2000): 549–62.

70 World Bank and International Finance Corporation, *Doing Business 2013* (Washington, DC: The International Bank for Reconstruction and Development, 2013).

71 Ricardo Gabriel Flores and Victoria Jordan-Jones,"Inexperienced Firms and Foreign Operation Success," Proceedings of the 54th Annua Meeting of the Academy of International Business (June 30–July 3, 2012).

72 Matthew Green,"Nigeria Set to Lift Decades-Old Ban on Foreign Takeovers of Its Banks,"*Financial Times* (June 22, 2009): 1.

73 "Enron Assets Outside U.S. Go Up for Sale; Activity Seen in South Korea and India," *Wall Street Journal* (January 22, 2002): A6.

74 International Monetary Fund, *World Economic Outlook, September 2004* (Washington, DC: International Monetary Fund, 2004): 143–49.

75 Peter Hall, *Cities in Civilization: Culture, Technology, and Urban Order* (London: Weidenfeld & Nicholson, 1998).

76 "A Sense of Place,"*The Economist* (October 27, 2012): Special Report on Technology and Geography, 6.

77 David Aviel,"The Causes and Consequences of Public Attitudes to Technology: A United States Analysis,"*International Journal of Management* 18 (2001): 166.

78 ***Sources include the following:*** *"The Year of the Lego"*, retrieved November 12, 2013, from www.newyorker.com/online/blogs; Pooja Thakur,"Lego to Boost China Sales With Local Factories Supplying to Asia,"*Bloomberg* (October 2, 2013): n.p.; JENS HANSEGARD and LAURIE BURKITT,"Lego Ramps Up Production for Asia,"*Wall Street Journal Online* (March 18, 2013): n.p.; Fugazi,"LEGO Group to build factory in China,"*Eurobricks Online* (March 18, 2013): n.p.; Lego Annual Report, retrieved November 12, 2013, from http://aboutus.lego.com/en-gb/lego-group/annual-report, n.p; Christian Wienberg, "Lego Beats Hasbro as World's No. 2 Toymaker Amid Asia Sales Jump," <www.bloomberg.com/news/2013-09-05/lego-beats-hasbro-as-world-s-no-2-toymaker-amid-asia-sales-jump.html> *Bloomberg* (September 5, 2013): n.p.; <www.bbc.co.uk/news/business-23968860> "Lego becomes world's second-biggest toy maker" (September 5, 2013): n.p. LEGO Annual Report <http://aboutus.lego.com/en-us/lego-group/annual-report> LEGO website (September 2013):n.p.; Jens Hansegard and Laurie Burkitt,"Lego to Build Plant in China With Eye on Asia Sales,"*Wall Street Journal Online* (March 19, 2013): n.p.; (retrieved September2013); online.wsj.com

79 www.bloomberg.com/news/2013-10-02/lego-to-boost-chinasales-with-local-factories-supplying-to-asia.html; LEGO: Lythke-Jørgensen, Skjøtt-Larsen and Svendsen (2001):"SCM: Supply Chain Management i et ledelsesperspektiv". Børsen

CHAPTER 14

Modes of Trading Internationally

OBJECTIVES

After studying this chapter, you should be able to

1. Explain the idea of exporting and profile its elements
2. Explain the idea of importing and profile its elements
3. Evaluate the relative benefits and drawbacks of the export and import of e-waste
4. Describe the problems and pitfalls that challenge international traders
5. Describe the resources and assistance for international traders
6. Define the idea of an export plan
7. Discuss the practice of countertrade
8. Describe the resources and assistance for international traders
9. Identify and discuss the platforms that support expanding international trade

Source: © RealPhotoItaly - Fotolia.com

When one is prepared, difficulties do not come.

—Ethiopian proverb

CASE SpinCent: The Decision to Export[1]

Big exporters such as General Electric, Caterpillar, and Boeing generate about 60 percent of total exports from the United States. Their smaller shipments are usually much larger than the largest shipments of smaller companies. Still, small and medium-size enterprises (SMEs)—specifically, companies with fewer than 500 workers—account for nearly 98 percent of all U.S. exporters. One such SME is SpinCent of Pennsylvania.

SpinCent manufactures laboratory and industrial centrifuges—machines that spin a substance into high-speed rotation around a fixed axis—that provide separation solutions for firms in the chemical, pharmaceutical, food, environmental, and mining industries. Centripetal acceleration causes the substance to separate, moving heavy elements to the bottom, lighter objects toward the top, and liquid in between. SpinCent's 54 employees—45 workers, four product engineers, and five managers—operate out of its 60,000-square-foot facility in suburban Philadelphia.

SpinCent began operations in 2000 with one goal in mind: to create a line of centrifuges in which customers would have absolute confidence. Its patented technology anchors a full line of automatic and manual centrifuges recognized for quality, high performance, and value. It also offers custom-engineering design and tools that serve the most demanding industries. To this day, management believes it builds "centrifuges for which there simply are no equals."

TO EXPORT OR NOT TO EXPORT: THAT IS THE QUESTION

From its start, SpinCent approached export passively. Its international sales often resulted from other U.S. firms' orders destined for export, occasional sale leads received at trade shows, or an unsolicited order through the Web or the mail. Results were mixed, with exports generating reasonable returns; they would have been higher but for unexpected problems and pitfalls. Consequently, SpinCent's net margins for its export sales were about 20 percent less than for its domestic sales.

Paul Knepper, CEO and founder, explained that recurring problems had deterred his interest in exporting. First, he and his colleagues were skeptical about the likelihood of international success. Previous efforts, they felt, had spent more time on unfocused searching than on purposefully growing export sales. Moreover, serving customers in the domestic market kept them busy. Developing international operations always seemed to overstretch their thin management structure. Going international, they knew, would not be a cakewalk, especially heading into direct competition with seasoned exporters from Germany and Japan.

Finally, Knepper knew the day of reckoning was at hand: SpinCent had to make its decision. Concerns about productivity, profitability, and diversification had bubbled for years. The struggling U.S. economy had slowed SpinCent's growth and pushed some of its customers to import cheaper, lower-end centrifuges from foreign suppliers. Increasing price competition from both domestic and international rivals seemed inevitable. Adding it all up, management realized it could either focus fully on the domestic market and exploit every possible efficiency, or expand aggressively into export. Ultimately, Knepper conceded, market trends forced his hand. The slow-moving deindustrialization of the United States, forecast to continue for years, would systematically reduce domestic demand for centrifuges. Meanwhile, quickly industrializing emerging economies, particularly in Asia, signaled rich opportunities. Hence, Knepper grudgingly accepted that SpinCent had to export to find more promising markets.

ASIA CALLS

Key market trends signaled potential selling opportunities in Asia. "Industries were coming online everywhere and seemingly overnight," Knepper said. Pro-market reform, economic development, and globalization were industrializing activities in several countries. Moreover, the volume of goods moving through Asia's seaports indicated something big was happening. Increasingly, building industries in emerging markets required the sophisticated sorts of centrifuges that SpinCent made. And unlike the United States, which was in the mature part of the product lifecycle, these emerging economies looked set to grow for years.

GETTING STARTED

New to the idea of the Asian market, SpinCent sought help on how best to access the large, diverse region. Knepper feared wasting resources going solo. Moreover, he was not looking to generate a burst of export sales but to develop relationships that would drive long-term growth. Hence, the primary challenge was finding competent and trustworthy distributors who would take responsibility for local sales. "We were looking for a long-term partner and not a quick export sale," said Knepper. "The right partner for SpinCent needed to be as confident and competent about the product as we are, and able to promote, educate, and serve consumers in the respective territories." The key, he added, was partnering with a respected firm in the target country. On the flip side, SpinCent had to assure potential partners that it was a good long-term fit for them.

To that end, Knepper sought background information on potential distributors, making sure possible agents were who they said they were. A few of the company's earlier export transactions, for instance, had run into problems with buyers who wouldn't pay or couldn't arrange letters of credit. As Knepper warned, "Getting paid is a huge part of running a business, and unless a company has the right payment policies in place, it will get scammed."

Mindful of these issues, Knepper attended a trade seminar sponsored by the U.S. Commercial Service's Export Assistance Center of Philadelphia that featured market analysis and trade reports on the fast-growing, emerging economies of Asia. Taking his seat, he couldn't help but wonder about the opportunities. Sure, they sounded great. However, he had seen hype like this come back to bite, not to mention the horror stories he'd heard at trade shows about the inevitable problems and evolving pitfalls of exports. Indeed, he reflected, a key reason for attending the seminar was to reconcile his vague sense of the opportunities and threats.

GETTING HELP

Since exports promote economic growth, policymakers and government agencies offer extensive assistance, such as trade seminars, market research, training programs, financial planning, and many other services. Trade officials especially encourage SMEs like SpinCent, seeing them as the primary beneficiaries of initiatives to improve and accelerate international trade activity. U.S. trade officials, for instance, reason that since 60 percent or so of all SME exporters posted sales to only one foreign market, many could boost performance by entering just one or two new markets. Expanding SMEs' market horizons through trade seminars and such could bolster their confidence.

After a full morning of profiles and presentations, Knepper increasingly believed the Asian markets held more opportunities than risk. He learned quite a bit about Asia, as well as some technicalities of exporting. Still, his unfamiliarity with the region, compounded by the company's lack of local sales representatives, bothered him. He believed that grassroots research was necessary before committing SpinCent. Before leaving that day, he spoke to Commercial Service agents and arranged to tag along on a 12-day trade mission that was heading to Hong Kong, Philippines, Vietnam, and Taiwan the following month.

GOAL SETTING

The goals of his trip were straightforward: assess market potential, identify competitors, get a sense of reasonable price points, and recruit local sales representatives. Although he had never traveled to Asia before, he believed he had prepared well. His time with the trade experts in Philadelphia had educated him on the general characteristics and industry conditions in Asian markets. Also, SpinCent had at some time past received inquiries from Asian distributors asking to represent the company; depending on how busy the company was with its domestic customers, SpinCent had tried to respond. These contacts had been saved, thereby giving Knepper a start on potential distributors and likely customers. In addition, he tapped the Commercial Services' Gold Key program to prescreen potential distributors. This program helps SMEs enlist Commercial Services agents overseas to scan local markets for qualified agents, distributors, and representatives. Exporters report that it ensures that when a firm adds a partner to its network, it is a respected company in the target country.

Thinking back to his days as a Boy Scout, Knepper took comfort in the fact that he believed he had met the sacred command: "Be prepared." With a briefcase full of brochures, a laptop loaded with profiles of his product line, and the sense of doing something potentially great, he headed to Asia. Over the next two weeks, he interviewed potential agents, chatted with likely customers, scouted competitors' offerings, test called their service support, spoke to freight forwarders and logistics companies, and visited local government officials and customs agencies.

ASIA CALLS, SPINCENT ANSWERS

On the flight home, tired but charged, Knepper realized that his misgivings about exporting had been unfounded. There were indeed risks, but they were outweighed by the numerous opportunities he had come across. Exporting was no longer an option for SpinCent; it was an imperative. Perhaps more important, Knepper had a new sense of commitment. He also had a bit more confidence, given the newly signed distributors in the Philippines and Taiwan as well as sales leads there and in Hong Kong.

Back in the office, Knepper tested the Asian market a bit more, sampling potential interest by advertising in trade publications as well as running banner ads on relevant trade sites in tandem with his newly signed distributors (he handled the English ads, they the Mandarin versions). In addition, he began working with an agent from Commercial Services on an export plan. This work helped SpinCent secure its largest overseas partner to date, a distributor in Hong Kong who served the booming Chinese market. Commercial Services also arranged meetings with others, eventually signing a distributor in Singapore and generating leads in Australia.

Having found strong partners, SpinCent continues tapping the counseling and market intelligence provided by various government agencies. Indeed, the more he has dealt with them, the more Knepper appreciates a friend's advice: "Let the government do it for you. This is their niche and they're the best at it." Now, with the export plan in hand, Knepper has begun working with the Export-Import Bank to secure financing options for overseas distributors and customers.[2]

GOING FORWARD

Steadily, as SpinCent gains experience in Taiwan, Philippines, Hong Kong, and Singapore, it looks onward. Although exporting has created challenges, it has helped SpinCent improve its performance. Indeed, overseas sales provided the firm with a growing stream of business during the economic downturn in the United States, while rivals who had not diversified via exports struggled. More important, exporting has given SpinCent a low-cost, high-return opportunity to leverage its core competency in centrifuge technology.

This experience, reflects Knepper, has had straightforward lessons: If you are thinking about exporting internationally, do it. Get going, do your homework, utilize low-cost resources, participate in trade missions, learn about cultures, and build international relationships. Always check on your potential business partners. Gather as much information as you can. Don't assume; the wrong choice costs your business time and money. Above all, no matter the problems you run into, stay committed to the goal. All of these seem tough, but they only cost pennies on the dollar and the returns can be substantial. ■

CRN
Case Review Note

QUESTIONS

14-1. List the three challenges that SpinCent overcame in developing its export activity. Describe and evaluate the processes it followed to overcome each challenge.

INTRODUCTION

Exporting and importing are among the fastest-growing economic activities in the world.

Exports and imports have always been an important facet of the global economy. As globalization, free trade agreements, and institutional development open the economies of more and more countries, the importance of international trade increases. Figure 14.1 shows that the value of trade as a share of world GDP has steadily risen over the past 50 years. This trend, while hitting air pockets now and then, has been relentless. Even the most recent drop in world trade, the consequence of the global financial crisis and sharp fall in consumer confidence in 2008 and 2009, has begun fading. World merchandise exports increased 5 percent in volume in 2011, while exports of commercial services grew by 11 percent in value.[3]

FIGURE 14.1 World Trade, 1960–2010

Despite periodic ups and downs, for the past 50 years the dominant trend in international trade, as a share of global business activity, has been strong, steady expansion. By the way, these trade data combine imports and exports—i.e., a bit of double counting. Still, the upward trend continues.

Source: Based on Assembled from data reported in the WorldBank's World Development Indicators, in particular *Trade* (% of *GDP*) (Series NE_TRD_GNFS_ZS), retrieved February 13, 2013, from data.worldbank.org/data-catalog/world-development-indicators.

Besides general trends, the composition and direction of trade flows continue changing. Export and import flows reflect the ongoing transformation of developing economies into industrializing versions, emerging markets tapping developed countries for tools to continue doing so, and developed countries looking to their developing counterparts for competitively priced goods and services. For instance, emerging markets increasingly drive the growth of Irish food and drink exports: during 2011, Ireland's exports to China rose by 47 percent, South Africa by 43 percent, Nigeria by 38 percent, and Russia by 30 percent.[4] Likewise, U.S. companies continued expanding markets and now trade with 233 countries and territories.[5] Also, as Ireland has experienced, the United States saw increasing trade involving companies in Brazil, Chile, Australia, Columbia, Saudi Arabia, and Nigeria.[6]

Companies worldwide respond accordingly, using exporting and importing to go international. Granted, earlier chapters report that companies engage in international business through a variety of modes. The choice a company makes, say, in choosing exporting rather than licensing, joint ventures, or FDI, follows its analysis of external factors as well as its core competencies (see Figure 14.2).

Exporting sends products to another country; importing brings products in from another country.

Export and import are the most common modes of international business. The number of firms that engage in both have seen steady and substantial growth. Indeed, the United States saw the value of its total exports grow 21 percent and total imports 22.7 percent in 2010. The headcount for identified exporters rose 6 percent that year compared to 2009, climbing to 293,000. The roll of importers also expanded, from 179,800 to 181,600.

CONCEPT CHECK

"Why Companies Engage in International Business" emphasized three operating objectives: expanding sales, acquiring resources, and minimizing risk. To achieve one or more of these objectives, companies choose from various "Modes of International Business." Among these modes, **exporting** and **importing** are the most prevalent, especially among small and medium-sized enterprises (SMEs).

These statistics underestimate the number of exporters and importers; the complexity of trade means that we cannot link all international shipments to specific firms. Many products, for example, are indirectly exported—embedded in other products that are exported via other firms—and tracking them is tough. The key takeaway, though, is straightforward: Exports and imports are a major part of the global economy, a critical feature of the nations' economic performance, and a big strategic choice for companies of all sizes in countries worldwide.

The popularity of export and import follows their key advantages. Both are relatively easy, low cost, and quick means to engage foreign markets; they impose minimum business risk, require relatively low resource commitment, and improve marketplace flexibility. Moreover, whether large or small, international trade helps companies increase sales and profits, tap points of innovation, and stabilize seasonal fluctuations. Then there is the seemingly minor

FIGURE 14.2 Factors Influencing Export and Import Operations

Our interpretation of export and import highlight the environmental and operational factors that influence its practice and performance. This means of international business is a key functional operation in small, medium, and large-sized MNEs.

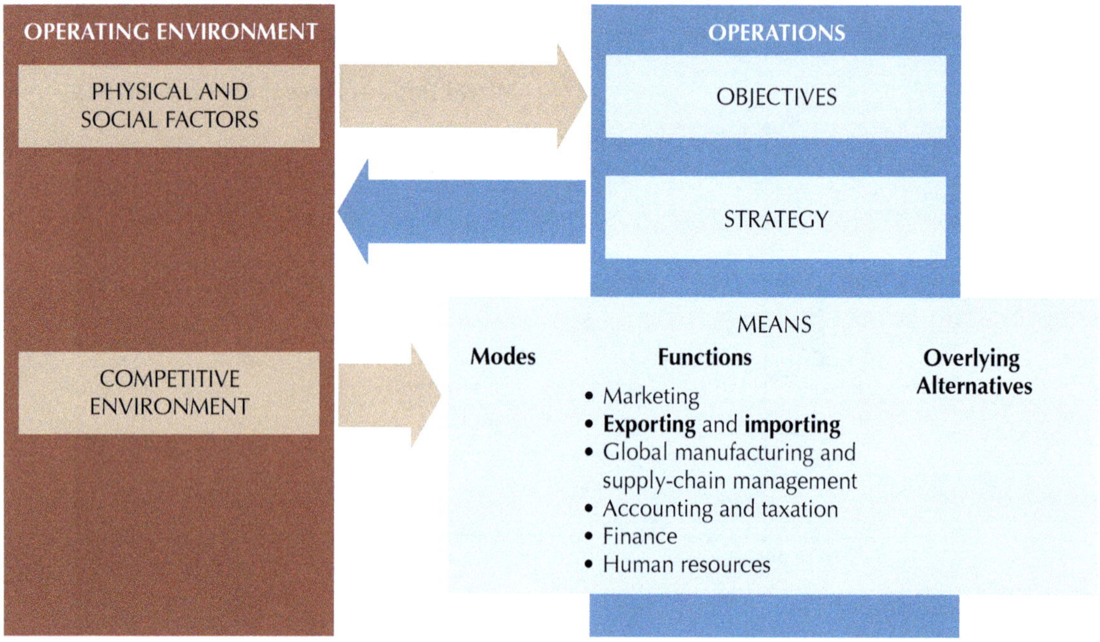

detail that most people live elsewhere in the world than in any one country. In the case of Germany, for example, nearly 99 percent of consumers live outside it and command more than 95 percent of the world's purchasing power. Therefore, a German company selling domestically can reach a maximum of some 81 million consumers. Conversely, a local competitor selling internationally can potentially reach nearly 7 billion more.

Consequently, international trade presents many opportunities to enterprising companies. Perhaps as expected, it also exposes them to a range of problems and pitfalls. Still, as this chapter shows, there are powerful approaches and proven solutions to help them.

EXPORTING

Exporting is the sale of goods or services produced by a firm based in one country to customers that reside in another country. The idea of exporting manufactured goods presents a clear situation, as in the case of Indian carmaker Tata Motors shipping (exporting) automobiles made in Pune to customers (importers) in Bangladesh. Hence, exports involve any good or service that is traded from sellers in one country to buyers in another country.

Technically, a product need not physically leave a country to qualify as an export. Rather, it need only earn foreign currency. For example, you may not normally think of the foreign national students sitting alongside you in class as part of your country's export strategy. However, higher education ranks among the top 10 service exports for several Western nations. In fact, tuition, fees, and living expenses paid by some 765,000 international students and their families contributed more than $22 billion to the U.S. economy during the 2011–2012 academic year.[7] In Canada, the total amount spent by international students—more than $8 billion in 2010—exceeded the country's export of helicopters, airplanes, and spacecraft.[8] Besides education, leading types of service exports include financial, information, professional, scientific, and technical services, travel and tourism, transportation, insurance, and entertainment.

The trade of services, such as we see with higher education, makes it a bit tougher to define what qualifies as an export. Still, service exports occur across a range of industry sectors. Engineering contractors—such as Bechtel, Skanska AB, or Kajima—export services when they construct buildings, roads, utilities, airports, or seaports in a foreign country. Management consultants such as McKinsey & Company export when they perform advisory services for foreign clients. Investment banks, such as Goldman Sachs and UBS, export when they help a foreign client arrange financing or navigate capital markets. Similarly, services are exported indirectly when the Japanese advertising firm Dentsu, the world's largest single-brand agency, creates a marketing campaign for Sony that then uses that campaign outside Japan. Hydraulx Visual Effects, designers of digital monsters and such, exports its services when it helps overseas clients add visual effects to feature films, commercials, and music videos. In these examples, the seller is the exporter while the buyer is the importer.

Conversely, it clarifies matters to define what some mistakenly classify as a service export. Opening a Starbucks in Argentina, which we commonly regard as a service enterprise, does not qualify as a service export. Rather, the foreign ownership of some or all of the productive assets of the local operation qualifies it as a foreign direct investment. Furthermore, a royalty fee paid to Starbucks in the face of no foreign ownership would qualify the Argentina activity as a licensing agreement.

WHO ARE EXPORTERS?

Many companies claim the intention to export, anticipating it will accelerate growth and boost profits. In reality, not all companies export, and among those that do, some do far more than others. Company practices identify three types of exporters.

Types of exporters include

- Non-exporter
- Occasional exporter
- Regular exporter

Non-Exporters Such a company commands little to no knowledge about exporting and often professes no intention to engage in international trade at any time. Although this may sound like a deficiency, many firms grow in their domestic market without exporting simply because they make goods or provide services that do not travel well to foreign markets. Still, many firms whose products appeal to customers elsewhere prefer disregarding exporting. This latter population is a primary target of export promotion programs.

CRN Case Review Note

Occasional Exporters This type of company fills unsolicited orders from foreign buyers but investigates international trade options passively, if at all. Think of SpinCent's international activities prior to Knepper's realization of the need to export. It would try to fill export orders as they arrived, depending on activity in the domestic market. Generally, though, it regarded them as anomalies. Occasional exporters understand the basics of the export process, but, for any number of reasons, they assign it low priority.

CRN Case Review Note

Regular Exporters A company that aggressively pursues export sales as a productive, profitable, strategic activity is regarded as a regular exporter. It has experience along with an improving understanding of the routines and technicalities of international trade. Again, think of SpinCent's activities following Knepper's realization, corroborated by his chats with Commercial Service agents and travels to Asia, of the importance of exporting. Each step demystified aspects of the experience, thereby fortifying Knepper's commitment. And just as success feeds upon success, so it is with exporting.

THE MATTER OF ADVANTAGES

The question of who is likely to start and sustain exporting directs us toward a broader conception of a company's choice of how best to go international. Earlier materials identified several options that firms consider, most notably export, licensing, joint venture, alliance, or FDI. They also profiled the influence of ownership, location, and internalization advantages on a firm's preferred entry mode into foreign markets.[9] Here, we apply these discussions to the export decision.

Ownership advantages of the company, location advantages of the market, and internalization advantages from controlling transactions shape how firms enter foreign markets.

CRN Case Review Note

Ownership Advantages A firm's core competencies—the special outlook, skills, capabilities, or technologies that run through its operations—are the basis of its competitive advantage. These proprietary advantages anchor how a firm enters foreign markets. For instance, SpinCent capitalized on its ownership advantages by leveraging its core competency in designing, manufacturing, and servicing centrifugal equipment. These advantages, "owned" by SpinCent due to its proprietary technology and expertise, support its international expansion. Companies that command weak ownership advantages, anticipating fierce struggles with foreign rivals, typically disregard export.

Resource-constrained or risk-averse companies that have strong ownership advantages often enter foreign markets through export.

Location Advantages The combination of sales opportunity and investment risk in foreign markets creates favorable locations. In other words, stable markets with many consumers increase the odds that someone will demand your product. As expected, favorable business environments such as Canada, Japan, or Germany attract exporters, though high-potential markets in far corners of the world increasingly attract aspiring and experienced traders. Again, SpinCent saw trends in Asia creating favorable locations marked by strong industrial demand, supportive business policies, and attractive industry structures. Because the industrialization of emerging economies spurs local firms to make the sorts of products that require high-performance centrifuges, targeting these fast-developing markets taps location advantages that support SpinCent's international expansion.

CRN Case Review Note

Internalization Advantages Companies often respond to market imperfections—namely, the sorts of circumstances that create uncertainties—by internalizing market processes. Directly controlling and managing market activities inside the company reduces the risks and exploits gaps resulting from market imperfections. Internalizing activities enables executives to retain their core competency within the company rather than licensing or selling it. Again, SpinCent could have opted to license its technology to Asian manufacturers. This likely proves cheap in the short term but costly over the long haul as it helps local licensees evolve into local competitors. Indeed, our earlier discussion of the rule of man as the basis of law, such as that found in several Asian markets, highlighted its poor record of protecting intellectual property. This sort of market imperfection leads companies, such as we see with SpinCent, to retain control of their core competencies through internalization. Granted, SpinCent could have served its Asian customers by directly investing in a local manufacturing facility rather than exporting to local distributors. However, management reasoned that its resource situation and risk tolerance better fit an export strategy than FDI.

CRN Case Review Note

CONCEPT CHECK

The complexity posed by differing cultural, political, legal, and economic environments, many of which we covered in the first half of the text, imposes a so-called "liability of foreignness." This idea holds that foreign companies, by virtue of their spotty familiarity, incur additional economic and social costs of doing business when operating overseas. Companies offset this liability by capitalizing on advantages as well as selecting the mode of international business that best reflects their resource profile and risk tolerance.

CHARACTERISTICS OF EXPORTERS

The effort to promote international trade spurs identifying the characteristics of successful exporters. Pinpointing important attributes, the reasoning goes, will help companies develop the necessary competencies and governments to design better forms of assistance. Analysis often starts with firm size, comparing and contrasting the trading activities of big and small companies.

In exporting, company size matters in interesting ways. Naturally, large MNEs like Samsung, Boeing, and Hon Hai are big exporters. Their ownership, location, and internalization advantages help them identify markets, leverage organizational capabilities, and manage international risks. Thus, many presume that export is an option best left to large companies. In fact, there is some truth to this inference. The largest companies routinely account for the lion's share of exporting throughout countries worldwide. In the United States, the 500 biggest firms accounted for nearly 60 percent of total export value, the 250 biggest accounted for more than half, and the 100 biggest contributed just under one-third.[10] We see the same shares for big importers in the United States.

The largest companies are the biggest exporters. SMEs, however, are steadily expanding export activity.

Nevertheless, many see great potential in **small and medium-sized enterprises (SMEs)**—those firms that, by definition, have fewer than 500 employees. In the United States, SMEs account for 97.8 of all identified exporters and 97.2 percent of all identified importers, while claiming 33.7 percent and 31.6 percent of total export and import value, respectively.[11] This situation is not unique to the United States. Worldwide, more than two-thirds of exporters have fewer than 20 employees. More than 98 percent of companies in the Asia-Pacific region are SMEs. China has more than 42 million SMEs, defined as enterprises with annual revenues of less than $250 million. They account for about 99 percent of all companies and contribute approximately 60 percent of China's GDP, more than 70 percent of the country's employment, and more than 80 percent of its exports.[12]

CRN
Case Review Note

Unquestionably, firm size helps explain who exports. It does not, however, determine who exports. SpinCent, a typical SME, marshaled the resources and made export an important part of its strategy. Its size moderated its decision to seek assistance from federal and state agencies, but did not determine its decision to export. Instead, research directs our attention to the importance of other factors. Specific characteristics, such as core competencies, competitive prices, efficient production, executive leadership, and effective marketing techniques better predict export activity than does the size of the firm.[13] Production efficiency, rather than size, was a better predictor of Swedish companies' export activity; those firms with higher productivity targeted foreign markets while those with lower productivity focused on domestic customers.[14] Chinese SMEs' labor costs, R&D advantages, and state ownership better predicted their export activity than did their size.[15] Likewise, higher-performing Taiwanese firms, no matter how large or small, were more likely to become exporters than lower-performing firms.[16] Similarly, firm competencies, not size, had more to do with Canadian companies' propensity to export, the number of countries they exported to, and their export intensity (the ratio of a firm's revenue from its export sales to its total revenue). Finally, top management's favorable perception of exports, based on their anticipated contribution to growth and profits, fueled the commitment that powered exporting in British companies.[17]

A firm's characteristics moderate its export activity. Size matters, but often management commitment, efficiency, and cost structure matter more.

In summary, firm size can influence a company's inclination to initiate or escalate exporting, but other features matter more. More pointedly, Texas-based Coffee & More, a small company selling premium coffees and related products, looked to boost growth through export. Its CEO's reasoning captures many common themes: "People thought we were cutting our throats by exporting, and I admit we had our own doubts. However, we knew the customer base for our product outside the United States was large, and so was the potential for success. Perseverance and commitment paid off. Now international exporting has become an integral part of the company. Our international exports went from 2 percent of annual income in 2005 to 60 percent of annual income in 2009."[18]

WHY EXPORT?

Several factors motivate export. Companies that are capital- and research-intensive, such as those making pharmaceuticals or avionics equipment, export products to amortize the steep costs of development and production. Many, such as advertisers, lawyers, and consultants, export their services to meet the needs of clients working abroad; they either follow their clients there or risk losing them to the rival that does. Smaller firms in their domestic markets may export as an indirect way to counter the production volume advantage commanded by the industry leader. Finally, some companies export rather than invest abroad because alternate modes such as licensing, joint ventures, and FDI carry higher risks. Serving foreign markets from the home office imposes far fewer operational requirements than other modes.

Exporting helps companies
- Increase profitability,
- Improve productivity,
- Diversify activities

From this diverse set of scenarios, we can derive the three dimensions that drive export: profitability, productivity, and diversification.

PROFITABILITY

Point blank, the key advantage of exporting is the potential to become more profitable. Companies often sell their products for higher prices abroad than at home. Foreign markets may lack competitive alternatives, or they may be in different stages of the product's life cycle. Mature products at home may trigger price competition, whereas growth stages in foreign markets allow premium prices. Also, exports enable a firm to expand its sales frontier. Though not quite decisive for firms in large markets, such as the United States, accessing bigger markets is a make-or-break factor for firms in small markets, such as Switzerland. "By not exporting, we were not tapping our full sales potential—sort of like leaving money on the table," said the Director of Business Development for Certified Worldwide.[19] And, given the link between profitability and sustainability, evidence indicates that exporters have significantly lower bankruptcy rates than nonexporters with similar characteristics.[20]

CONCEPT CHECK

The attractiveness of **trade** as a means of internationalization has been enhanced by the improving efficiencies of import and export. The liberalization of the cross-border movement of resources and the development of services that support trade make these modes more attractive to a broader range of companies.

PRODUCTIVITY

Exporting helps companies improve productivity, which is often tied to increasing economies of scale. Exploiting unused capacity or spreading research costs over more customers, helps companies improve their operational efficiency. Hence, selling more products in more markets drives productivity gains, while the knowledge flows between international buyers and foreign competitors spurs exporters to innovate. Participating in export markets promotes a firm's learning, thereby enhancing the potential for innovation. Research reports a "dynamic virtuous cycle" between export and innovation in which each positively reinforces the other.[21] More precisely, exporters often have access to knowledge that is absent in their domestic market. Exposure prepares them to use this knowledge to generate higher-quality innovations, which in turn powers their entry into new geographic markets with higher-quality products, thereby boosting the benefits of exporting.

When Mississippi-based Domes International, maker of inexpensive housing, decided to expand internationally, it headed to India. Early experiences, though difficult, spurred innovations that improved its productivity and fortified its competitiveness. Its CEO explained, "There's no doubt that Domes International is a better company as a result of our experience in India. We are much more flexible and innovative. The client wanted a less expensive structure, so we went back to our labs and came up with an insulation solution that met their needs. Now we use these discoveries to improve core products and to offer more variations. We are much more confident going into new situations—listening, adapting, and finding the best solution."[22]

The U.S. International Trade Commission reports that despite facing trade barriers and other impediments, SMEs that export outperform those that do not.[23] Beside more than doubling the total revenue of their nonexporting counterparts, their revenue per employee, a rough measure of labor productivity, was over 70 percent greater than that of the nonexporters.

DIVERSIFICATION

CRN
Case Review Note

Exporting enables companies to diversify their activities, thereby fortifying their adaptability to market trends and disruptive innovations. In the least, developing customers in different markets reduces a firm's vulnerability to the loss of a local buyer while improving its bargaining power with existing suppliers. Moreover, different growth rates in different markets enables it to use strong sales in one country to offset weak sales in another. SpinCent, for example, looked to develop export markets in faster growing Asia to reduce its overdependence on the slowing U.S. economy.

In the aftermath of the recent global financial crisis, national unemployment hit a high of 10.6 percent in the United States. In Greene County, Tennessee, it soared to 17.9 percent. Jarden Zinc Products, headquartered there, makes solid zinc strips and zinc-based products used in coinage, automotive and electronic applications, building materials, rain goods, plumbing hardware, and cathodic protection products. Anxiety about sustaining sales moved managers to look to exporting. Scanning global markets identified an opportunity in a call for bids by the Bangko Sentral ng Pilipinas (BSP), the central bank of the Philippines. After several months of effort, BSP awarded the coinage contract to Jarden Zinc, which enabled the SME to retain jobs that had been at risk, recall over twenty employees from earlier layoffs, and create fifteen new jobs. Explained its Vice President of Coinage Sales, "Having a global presence has been essential in Jarden's growth. The diversity of the opportunities abroad has provided us with the ability to prosper even during challenging economic times in the U.S. domestic market."[24]

Keeping the global trade game going requires accurately storing, stacking, sorting, and shipping cargo. The logistic flow of the game is astounding–from 1990 through 2011, the global stock of 20-foot equivalent units (TEUs) containers, the most common means of transporting goods, grew from 28.7 million to more than 200 million. In 2011, port container traffic saw those TEUs make nearly 600 million "trips" among trading partners. Here, we see TEUs in transit at a Hong Kong terminal.

Source: Lee Yiu Tung/Shutterstock

The shift in economic power from the West to the East is often portrayed as a threat to developed countries. Alternatively, it likely signals that companies will increasingly look to diversify through export. The industrial and infrastructure ambitions of emerging economies push them to import machinery from rich countries. In fact, imports into emerging markets have grown twice as fast as those into richer nations over the past decade.[25] The U.S., for instance, saw 30 percent of its export go to emerging markets in 1990; by 2012, almost 60 percent did. As SpinCent and Jarden Zinc show, it represents an opportunity for companies in such Western markets as the United States, Italy, and the United Kingdom to diversify sales by exporting to faster-growing, increasingly wealthy emerging countries.[26]

EXPORT: INITIATION AND DEVELOPMENT

Two views of export shape interpretation: the deliberate, sequential dynamic of incremental internationalization and the instant internationalization of the born global.

Research assesses how, when, and why companies initiate and develop exporting. Reports cover a lot of territory, evaluating the influence of managerial attitudes, product features, organizational resources, firm strategy, market trends, technology tools, disruptive innovations, public policy, and so on. Although there is some consensus, divergence persists. Indeed, as far back as 1991, research compiled more than 700 explanatory variables as plausible drivers of export initiation and expansion.[27] Today, two perspectives anchor interpretation: the incremental internationalization and the born global.

SEQUENCES AND INCREMENTS

Incremental internationalization sees physical distance, cultural ties, and market similarities fundamentally shaping how companies approach export. Specifically, exporting follows a sequential process that leads a company to sell initially from its home market to the most geographically and psychologically proximate countries. From there, it deliberately expands exports to more and more dissimilar and distant countries.

Initially, companies find it easier and less risky to trade with customers in countries that share geographic, cultural, linguistic, political, and legal commonalities. As one would expect, trading with folks in similar markets who speak the same or similar languages and share historical legacies puts less stress on managers' competencies. Trade data indicate strong effects: countries will engage in 42 percent more trade if they share a common language than if they do not, 47 percent more if both countries belong to a trading bloc such as the European Union or NAFTA, 114 percent more if they share a common currency, and 188 percent more if they have a common colonial past.[28]

Progressively gaining experience in successfully dealing with dissimilarity encourages managers to expand their international horizon to include increasingly different markets.

The dynamic of incremental internationalization is straightforward: Initial success trading with similar foreign customers, by developing managers' outlook and competencies, moderates ensuing export activity. That is, the firm's country-by-country export expansion follows a learning process through which managers' growing experience with and knowledge of increasingly dissimilar foreign markets creates the confidence to export to countries that share even fewer commonalities and are farther afield. Essentially, as the company exports more, managers' perception of the severity of problems and pitfalls declines. At the same time, their courage and confidence to expand further abroad increases.

Consider the experiences of Analytical Graphics of Pennsylvania, a manufacturer of software applications that support cost-effective development and deployment of space, defense, and intelligence missions. It began exporting in the late 1990s, targeting opportunities in Europe. Gradually, success there encouraged management to pursue export opportunities in Japan and South Korea. Its growing experience with the various business cultures in the Asian region, particularly regarding language customization and local training requirements, led it to open an office in Singapore to coordinate its increasing Asian sales.[29]

The interaction of managers' experiential learning and the market features of various countries often results in common export expansion scenarios. SMEs in the United States, for example, typically export first to Canada or the United Kingdom, then move on to Mexico, Europe, and eventually countries in South America, Asia, Africa, and the Middle East.[30] Conversely, an SME in Vietnam, Thailand, or Malaysia would typically follow a different path, exporting first to countries in Southeast Asia, moving on to greater Asia, and then, as business practices improved based on lessons learned, head to the United States, Europe, and Africa.

BORN GLOBALS

Born globals, owing to their executives' international orientation and improving technological options, begin trading internationally at inception.

The second perspective, derived from the international entrepreneurship literature, holds that some firms initiate exporting as a **born global** (also known as an "instant international" or "international new venture"). Rather than methodically engaging a sequence of increasingly dissimilar foreign markets, born globals step onto the world stage immediately upon their founding or soon after. The born global does not regard international markets as a refuge when sales slow in the home market. Rather, it begins with the belief that the domestic market is one of many opportunities in the world.[31] Granted, Figure 14.3 overly dramatizes the appeal of international business. Still, going global is an increasingly common scenario for an increasing number of companies worldwide.

We find born globals worldwide. In big markets, the choice to go global initially is still a choice, since the scale of the domestic market provides many business opportunities. But startups in smaller countries, such as Israel, Estonia, Djibouti, or Macau, must look beyond their borders from the get-go. No matter the scale of the local market, a key characteristic of born globals is that their executives have an international focus from the outset and pursue rapid globalization. Logitech, the Swiss-based maker of such computer devices as mice, keyboards, and speakers, was founded by a Swiss and an Italian who met while studying at Stanford University in the United States and was exporting products worldwide soon after startup.[32] Similar examples indicate that folks who establish born globals have a strong international orientation due to the insights gained from living or studying abroad. Often, too, we see a seasoned executive who leaves an MNE and launches a firm that goes global at the outset.[33]

Perhaps most critically, managers of born globals can do so because environmental circumstances enable it. Technological advances and the growing openness of countries to international trade enable them to implement their global visions quickly and cheaply. The born global phenomenon largely follows the ongoing globalization of markets, falling

FIGURE 14.3

Source: Robert Weber/New Yorker Cartoon Bank/www.cartoonbank.com

"Grab some lederhosen, Sutfin. We're about to climb aboard the globalization bandwagon."

trade barriers, growing demand for specialized products, and improving communication technologies. The enterprising firm exploits these circumstances, building a powerful business platform to develop and deliver innovations in niche markets that, although specialized, span the world.

Take the case of Evertek Computer, a U.S. SME, which started up in 1990 and quickly began to export. By 2009, it was exporting to customers in 105 countries, 30 percent of which were in South America, 20 percent in Europe, and 20 percent in the Middle East and North Africa. Its success comes from selling refurbished computers and parts, for which worldwide demand is booming because buyers, particularly poorer ones, don't need the latest and most expensive equipment. "They want cheap," says Evertek's international sales manager, John Ortley. "The firm's business model," he adds, "matches these folks with those who want to sell their used personal computer equipment."[34]

At first glance, liquidating obsolete pieces and parts seems an unlikely basis for successful exporting. And Evertek does not command the intimidating ownership advantage that usually supports exporting. However, the international orientation of its top management creates a powerful driver. Mr. Oxley's enthusiasm for international business, for example, fortifies the firm's belief that a big part of its business is found abroad: "For me," he says, "it started with being curious about the world. I enjoy learning about other cultures and respecting people who have a different background than mine."[35] Then, speaking like a true born global, he adds, "We're thriving. The world is shrinking, and it's getting easier and less expensive to do business on a global basis."[36]

CONCEPT CHECK

Change in the structure and dynamics of world business has taken a significant turn to new and novel standards. A flat world, billions of new capitalists, emerging economies, the global financial crisis, and so on, challenge many of our conventional theories. Consequently, scholars study trends, such as those dealing with incremental internationalization and the born-global phenomenon, to assess the direction and momentum of change.

INTERACTION: TIME AND PLACE

Neither the incremental nor the born global perspective definitively represents how companies initiate and escalate exporting. Research as well as company practices confirm that each credibly interprets the export process. For instance, recall that U.S. exports travel to 233 countries and territories. Many reflect long-running trade relationships, such as that between the United States and Canada. Others reflect more recent relationships, such as the United States and Kyrgyzstan. The scale and scope of this export universe supports scenarios in which companies have developed the competencies to service more markets (the incremental internationalization perspective) and can reach faraway markets with greater ease and immediacy (the born global view).

Table 14.1, by indicating an interaction between the two perspectives, proposes a useful way to interpret the export process. Among the top 15 countries that the United States both exports to and imports from, nine overlap. Its top four international trade partners—Canada, China, Mexico, and Japan—account for 45 percent of its total exports and 52 percent of its total imports. Most notably, the past two decades have seen trade with China and Mexico grow significantly. In 1992, for example, about 12 percent of total U.S. imports came from China and Mexico; by 2011, their combined share was 31 percent. Regarding trends, Mexico's import share rose from 4.3 percent in 1992 to 12.3 percent in 2011. Likewise, China's share of total U.S. imports grew from 4.8 to 18.5 percent over the same span.[37] Hence, on one hand we have the steady rise of Mexico while on the other we see the accelerating emergence of China.

Mexico's performance fits well with the incremental expansion thesis. Its geographic proximity, cultural overlap, similar institutional set-up, and membership in NAFTA present few problems and pitfalls to the occasional or regular exporter in the United States. China, as we saw in Chapters 2, 3, and 4, is culturally, politically, legally, and economically dissimilar to the United States. Still, Table 14.1 highlights its consequence to U.S. trade activity.

Firm-level data elaborate the trade relationship between China and the United States.[38] In 1992, 4,092 U.S. firms exported to China; by 2010, this number had increased more than 700 percent to 32,213 firms. This trend is particularly dramatic for SMEs in absolute terms

TABLE 14.1 Top Trade Partners of the United States: Exports and Imports

While the United States trades with 233 different countries and territories, its top 15 trade partners dominate total volume. On the export side, its top trade partner is Canada. On the import side, its leading supplier of goods and services is China.

Rank	Country	Exports	%, Total Exports	Rank	Country	Imports	%, Total Imports
1	Canada	245.2	19.1	1	China	351.3	18.5
2	Mexico	181.1	14.1	2	Canada	270.8	14.2
3	China	89.6	7.0	3	Mexico	233.7	12.3
4	Japan	58.4	4.5	4	Japan	122.8	6.4
5	United Kingdom	46.4	3.6	5	Germany	89.2	4.7
6	Germany	41.1	3.2	6	South Korea	49.4	2.6
7	Brazil	36.3	2.8	7	Saudi Arabia	47.7	2.5
8	South Korea	35.8	2.8	8	United Kingdom	45.9	2.4
9	The Netherlands	33.5	2.6	9	France	34.5	1.8
10	Hong Kong	29.7	2.3	10	India	34.5	1.8
11	Australia	26.1	2.0	11	Taiwan	32.6	1.7
12	France	25.8	2.0	12	Venezuela	32.1	1.7
13	Singapore	25.1	2.0	13	Italy	30.7	1.6
14	Belgium	24.6	1.9	14	Ireland	28.3	1.5
15	Switzerland	22.6	1.8	15	Brazil	27.6	1.5
-	Total, Top 15 Countries	921.2	71.6	-	Total, Top 15 Countries	1431	75.2
-	Total, All Countries	1286	100	-	Total, All Countries	1903.6	100

Source: U.S. Census Bureau, Foreign Trade, U.S. International Trade Data, 2012. Data: Year-to-Date October 2012.

as well as relative to large exporters. From 1992 to 2009, the number of SMEs exporting to China surged 776 percent versus 167 percent for large-company exporters. This effect is far more pronounced on the import side; SMEs accounted for 96 percent of the 87,910 U.S. firms that imported merchandise from China in 2009. The scale and scope of U.S.-China trade by a growing variety of SMEs speaks to the born global phenomenon.

Trade data suggest increasing interaction between the incremental international and born global perspectives.

Going forward, we anticipate stronger interaction effects between the incremental internationalization and born global perspectives. First, e-commerce continues turbo charging the latter. A generation ago, going global involved slow-acting trade officials directing slow-moving flows between tough-to-understand markets that differed on countless regulations and routines. Hence, incremental, market-by-market export expansion was not only feasible, it was arguably the only practical option.[39] Now e-commerce, fortified by social media, immediately gives small startups global reach, providing a platform that efficiently overcomes historic barriers to internationalization. Our closing case profiles a leading intermediary, Alibaba.com, which facilitates this process. Second, for those exporters more inclined toward incremental expansion, the Internet provides cheap, easy, and effective means to analyze and access dissimilar markets. Hence, their expansion to far more such markets fits the incremental view, whereas the acceleration of this process fits the born global perspective.

CRN
Case Review Note

THE WILDCARD ROLE OF SERENDIPITY

Exporters are often proactive decision makers. Sometimes, however, serendipity—making fortunate discoveries by accident—initiates exports.

It is appealing to depict export initiation and development, whether done incrementally or immediately, as a purposeful strategy designed and delivered by proactive executives. However, research tells of accidental exporters who, responding to happenstance or odd circumstances, successfully enter foreign markets. Essentially, some companies start exporting because of fortuitous events rather than purposeful intent. Perhaps the most common trigger is the arrival of an unsolicited order in the mail, either postal or electronic. Others include a new hire that has connections to foreign buyers, an international contact made at an industry conference, personal travel abroad that alerts one to new options, and so on. Thus, **serendipity**—making fortunate discoveries by accident—is not an uncommon export trigger.

Edward Cutler is such a case. He is the owner and founder of Pennsylvania-based Squigle, a unique brand of toothpaste for people who cannot tolerate mass-produced varieties.[40] Upon launching Squigle, Mr. Cutler exclusively focused on the U.S. market. Internet posters spread the news of his product, and Squigle soon received inquiries from Taiwan, Turkey, and elsewhere. One customer, a canker-sore sufferer in Britain, was so enthusiastic about it that he began importing Squigle into England for local sale. That was good news for Mr. Cutler because it let him expand abroad at little cost and low risk. Now he is eager to export more, explaining, "We're looking to sell overseas for the same reason the big companies do: Most of the world's population lies outside the United States."[41]

Similarly, Vellus, a small Ohio-based company that makes a line of high-end pet grooming products, began its export odyssey when a Taiwanese businessperson, after trying its customized shampoos, bought $25,000 worth of the company's products to sell in Taiwan. Soon, word spread from show to show on the global canine circuit. Recounted Vellus's CEO, "I started receiving calls from people around the world who would hear of our products at dog shows and ask organizers how they could get in touch with me to buy our products."[42] Today, Vellus exports its products to about 30 countries.

CONCEPT CHECK

The Internet influences political change, improves the operations of **foreign-exchange markets,** and changes the location economies that drive **value chain** configurations. Similarly, the Internet reshapes export and import activity by opening new markets, supporting new strategies, and providing new tools.

APPROACHES TO EXPORTING

Granted, export sounds straightforward—make it, sell it, pack it, and ship it.[43] To some degree, this holds true for many trades. Generally, the ease of exporting reflects how a company chooses to do so. As we explain below, there are several options.

Exporting directly involves independent representatives, distributors, or retailers outside of the exporter's home country.

Direct Exporting In this scenario, the company directly sells its products to an independent intermediary, such as an agent, distributor, or retailer outside its home country, who then sells the product to the local consumer. **Direct exporting** is an ambitious approach. It requires that the company manage the export process, minding the many aspects of making and marketing the product for foreign buyers. *Ceteris paribus*, most direct exporters are larger-scale enterprises. They are efficient, low-cost suppliers leveraging economies of scale, able to spread high fixed costs of storage, processing, marketing, and transportation over large sales volumes.

CRN
Case Review Note

Still, SMEs can develop successful approaches to direct exporting. Recall that as of 2010 SMEs comprised 97.8 percent of all identified exporters and accounted for 33.7 percent of the known exports of the United States. SpinCent highlights this situation. Its CEO analyzed markets, assessed industries, prepped his company, traveled overseas, and sought, screened, and hired trustworthy distributors to supervise sales in Asian markets. As needed, he called upon federal and local agencies for assistance in developing his export strategy. Consequently, direct exporting requires executive commitment and company resources to get the show started and then to sustain activity. Once up and running, exporting directly through trustworthy distributors is often administered efficiently.

Indirect exports are products sold to an intermediary in the home market, which then exports those products to other countries.

Indirect Exporting A company can use distributors, agents, or export management companies to export its products. Alternatively, it can supply inputs to other companies for incorporation into their products that are then exported. In the former scenario, the company sells its products to an independent intermediary in the domestic market, which then exports the product to its foreign agents, who then sell it to the end consumer. In this case, **indirect exporting** results because the exporter makes its product but relies on an intermediary—say, a global retailer—to supervise marketing, terms of sale, packaging, distribution, and credit and collection procedures. The approach is often relatively stress-free. Edward Cutler, maker of Squigle toothpaste, explained, "It is just easier to deal with distributors. We prefer to deal in master shippers of 144 tubes. We don't have to do anything then but slap a label on it."[44] In the other scenario—the firm selling inputs into other products that are then exported—the fact that the ultimate destination may be several transactions beyond its final sale, often leaves the SME unaware if its product was exported.

The intersection of retail and globalization trends makes indirect selling increasingly practical. Global retail chains such as Walmart, Carrefour, and Ahold facilitate the movement of products from exporters to storefronts. Think of, for example, a DVD manufacturer in China who supplies Walmart International with a product that Walmart then sells in its retail locations worldwide. Though not as lucrative as direct exporting, indirect exporting makes far fewer demands. Too, it is often a transition phase whereby the neophyte can gain familiarity with foreign consumers and competitors.

Many service companies export their product indirectly rather than directly. An indirect service export results when a nonexporting firm provides services to another company that ultimately exports its products abroad. We commonly associate indirect services exports with professional and business services such as accounting, advertising, consulting, and legal services. An indirect service export on the part of, say, a Swedish accounting firm occurs when it prepares the books of a Swedish company that exports to foreign markets. Indirect services exports occur across many industries, including audiovisual providers to film and television studios whose media are viewed overseas, or a hedge fund that sells shares to foreign investors through a wealth management advisory firm.

Passively Filling Orders from Domestic Buyers Who Then Export the Product From the perspective of the seller, these sorts of international sales are indistinguishable from domestic sales. Essentially, a buyer contacts the company, submits an order, takes delivery, and exports the product. Again, the company may be unaware that its product has been shipped abroad.

Oddly suggestive of a Potemkin village, this exhibition hall hosts the International Business Intelligence and Information Technology trade fair. The meeting and greeting that goes on here creates connections that often sparks export and import activity.

Source: © Robert Harding Picture Library Ltd/Alamy

Selling to Domestic Buyers Who Represent Foreign End Users or Customers MNEs, general contractors, foreign trading companies, foreign governments, and foreign distributors and retailers purchase goods for export. These buyers either need a product or see demand for it in foreign markets, so they buy it here and ship it there. Again, the company that makes the product may not know of its export.

WHICH APPROACH WHEN?

No one approach is intrinsically superior. At the broadest level, the company's particular ownership, location, and internalization advantages moderate its optimal approach. Considering firm size, large MNEs generally serve foreign customers through their foreign affiliates, while SMEs typically export directly or indirectly.[45] There is no hard and fast rule that one option is superior—approximately half of SMEs' exports are direct (i.e., produced by the exporting SME immediately before export) while the other half are indirect (i.e., supplied by the SME to other companies that then ultimately export it).[46]

CRN
Case Review Note

Several factors shape an SME's preferred approach. Protecting ownership advantages endorses exporting directly. SpinCent, for example, saw direct selling as the best means to retain control of its core competency. Similarly, top management's outlook and company resources endorse some choices while discouraging others. A regular exporter is more likely to export directly. Firms new to exporting or those who are unable to commit staff and funds will likely prefer indirect methods.

Internet marketing helps companies—large and small—engage in international trade quickly, easily, and cheaply.

Technology's Role Technology influences the relative merits of the different approaches. The Internet makes direct exporting increasingly efficient and effective by providing immediate, low-cost access that lets regular exporters, particularly born globals, more easily access more markets.[47] In addition, e-commerce helps companies, both big and small, overcome capital and infrastructure limitations.[48] For example, exporters in Chile use extranets to

CRN
Case Review Note

communicate with importers around the world, while exporters in Costa Rica have used online shops to export directly.[49] Our closing case looks at how a little electronic magic at Alibaba.com, the world's largest business-to-business online marketplace, helps SMEs engage buyers and sellers worldwide. Twenty years ago, firm resources, communication channels, and trade logistics mattered immensely if you were a SME in Patagonia trying to reach markets in Europe. Today, due to Alibaba.com and like-minded Internet platforms, they matter far less.

The four approaches to exporting are not mutually exclusive; company and market circumstances moderate whether managers opt to apply one or a mix.

Mix-and-Match The four approaches to exporting are not mutually exclusive. A firm can engage different methods to trade different products to serve different markets. A Canadian company may export directly to similar markets such as the United States, Australia, and Britain while using indirect methods to handle exports to dissimilar markets in Asia or Africa. Recall that Analytical Graphics, which began exporting in the late 1990s, had expanded sales into 13 countries by 2011, serving them through a mix of methods: a direct selling strategy in Canada and United Kingdom, reseller partners in dissimilar countries such as Japan, South Korea, India, Russia, and Brazil.[50] So while there are general rules about which approach when, the ideal choice fits the firm's competencies, its executives' commitment, and the market features of the targeted countries.

IMPORTING

Importing is the purchase of a good or service by a buyer in one country—the importer—from a seller in another—the exporter. Samsung's shipment of a smart phone made in Seoul to a buyer in Belgium registers as an import for Belgium and an export for South Korea. Service imports, given their intangibility, take various forms. Foreign banks, like Royal Bank of Canada, that provide financial services to U.S. customers qualify as service imports. Similarly, when Lloyd's of London writes an insurance policy for a client in Brazil, trade authorities in Brazil record an import.

A service import is a service transaction that does not result in ownership and is rendered by non-residents to local residents.

The import of services has subtle characteristics. For example, the installation of nuclear power equipment in Sweden by French firm Areva, even though it is a hard good, qualifies as a service import for Sweden. The standard to keep in mind is that the import of a service consists of any transaction that (1) does not result in ownership and (2) is rendered by nonresidents to residents.

WHO ARE IMPORTERS?

Our earlier classification of exporters—non-, occasional, and regular—has broad analogues in the import sector. Although terminology can differ, we commonly see three types:

There are three general types of importers:

- Input optimizers
- Opportunistic
- Arbitrageurs

INPUT OPTIMIZERS

This type uses foreign sourcing to optimize, in terms of price or quality, the inputs fed into its supply chain. Essentially, a company scours the globe for optimal inputs, then directs them to its various production points that it has configured worldwide. Its various factories assemble them into finished goods that are then imported by markets worldwide. Logically, the flow of inputs and finished goods from country to country, besides representing imports, also qualifies as exports.

OPPORTUNISTIC

These importers looks for products around the world that they can import and profitably sell to local citizens. They see a gap in the local marketplace, whether real (customers cannot find what they want) or perceived (the presumption that products from some countries are intrinsically superior to local substitutes). They then opportunistically exploit it by finding, buying, transporting, and distributing products available only from foreign suppliers to local customers. The product is secondary; rather, the game is using import channels to fill gaps in the local marketplace profitably. For example, the release of the latest, greatest iPad typically triggers consumer frenzy, including scalpers aiming to exploit a temporary market gap given that it is only available in the United States for the first several weeks. Demand in other countries creates compelling opportunities. Buyers in China, for instance, hired shoppers in New York to buy whatever quantity they could and overnight it to Shanghai, where it is then marked up twice or thrice more.[51] Eventually, as Apple stores begin selling the iPad in China, the gap closed.

ARBITRAGEURS

Arbitrageurs look to foreign sourcing to get the highest-quality product at the lowest possible price. This motivation is timeless—an agent takes advantage of a price or quality difference between two or more markets, transacting deals that exploit the imbalance, and profiting from the difference. For instance, after Utah-based SME ForEveryBody began making bath and body products locally, it became an importer once it discovered low-cost home decorations available from Asian manufacturers that were competitive with premium products in the United States.

CHARACTERISTICS OF IMPORTERS

Extensive research has investigated the characteristics of exporters; for any number of reasons, however, importers have received far less investigation. Data do indicate that importers are also likely to be exporters, and that these firms account for the bulk of the world's exports and imports.[52] In the United States, for instance, 2010 data indicated that 212,491 companies only exported goods, and 101,008 companies only imported goods, while 80,640 companies handled both. Moreover, the latter companies accounted for 94.1 percent of total export value and 85.1 percent of the total import value.[53] In fundamental ways, then, our discussion of the characteristics of exporters applies to importers. For instance, importers tailor international activity to reflect their ownership, localization, and internalization advantages, exhibit incremental and born global characteristics, and indicate that firm size, along with efficiency, innovation, and commitment, explain their activity.

Several points qualify the degree of overlap. Historically, importers traded relatively few products with a relatively few developing countries.[54] Essentially, the bulk of imports tended toward opportunism or arbitrage—i.e., cheap oil in Saudi Arabia became expensive oil in the United States. The emergence of fast-growing economies accelerates and alters this relationship. These countries increasingly produce more goods and services that outperform, in price and function, local choices in advanced markets. They also increasingly provide higher-end products that once were the province of advanced markets—recall U.S. companies importing business process services from India-based firms. Finally, globalization supports far more differentiated supply chains that are longer, have more links, and cross more markets. Their growth has commensurately increased the import of inputs.

Several reasons motivate importing:

- Specialization of labor
- Global rivalry
- Local unavailability
- Diversification
- Top management's outlook

WHY IMPORT?

Various factors spur a firm to begin importing and motivate that firm's ongoing activity. Research emphasizes high product quality, satisfactory order processing, reliable delivery, lower prices, and domestic shortages. These factors, singly and collectively, push importers to scan world markets in search of lower-priced, better-quality, or locally unavailable products. This supposition raises the question: Why do these market anomalies exist? Absent these gaps, there is little need for import or, for that matter, export. Other parts of our text, particularly Chapters 6 and 12, speak to this issue. For our purposes, we highlight the following import drivers.

SPECIALIZATION OF LABOR

Managers commonly divide a production process into a sequence of stages and assign workers to particular stages so that one worker does one task, another does another task, and so on. This specialization of labor enables the organization of production to exploit location economics, especially different wage rates and factor costs, across countries. Improved efficiencies reduce costs that encourage companies to import cheaper products. For instance, Nike buys shoes manufactured by companies in several Asian countries, where local companies make higher quality shoes for lower cost. Nike finds it impossible to manufacture the same products in its home market, sell them at a reasonable price, and still make a profit; as a result, it imports shoes made in Asian factories into markets worldwide.

The same logic applies to the production of the iPad. Specifically, Apple contracts with Foxconn to make the iPad in China, which is then imported into the United States and other markets. Foxconn reportedly pays employees 1,200 yuan per month, or about $185.[55] Generously assuming an average 8-hour-per-day, 250-day-per-year schedule, that works out to about $1.11 per hour.[56] In contrast, the average U.S. manufacturing/mining/construction hourly compensation was officially $32.53 as of December 2010.[57] Reportedly, making the iPad requires about nine hours of direct labor. So, in this admittedly simple scenario, making the 32 GB Wi-Fi 3g iPad in China results in a retail price of $729 in the United States. Making it in the United States would have resulted in a retail price of $1,144.[58] Consequently, Apple imports iPads.

GLOBAL RIVALRY

Industries with a high degree of global competitive rivalry, such as we see in telecommunications, automobiles, and business services, impose relentless cost pressures. Many products, such as aircraft or cars, rely on thousands of parts produced in factories around the world. Companies use foreign suppliers in order to lower input costs or boost the quality of finished products.

LOCAL UNAVAILABILITY

Companies import products they cannot obtain locally for geographic, regulatory, or developmental reasons. Canada imports bananas from tropical climates because of its unsuitable climate; absent imports, Canadians would not enjoy fresh bananas. The same goes for eating seasonal fruits and vegetables out-of-season: e.g., grapes from Chile grace Christmas dinner in Denmark. Food is a rather obvious sector, but the same logic applies to an endless range of products, including tablet computers, medical technology, and financial services.

DIVERSIFICATION

Importers, like exporters, diversify operating risks by tapping international markets. Developing alternative suppliers makes a company less vulnerable to the dictates of a local supplier. For example, customers of U.S. steelmakers, such as automobile companies, have diversified their purchases to include European, Indian, and South Korean suppliers. This strategy reduces the risk of supply shortages or unilateral price hikes by U.S. steelmakers.

Point

Exporting E-waste: A Useful Solution?

Point **Yes** Exporting is a win-win situation: The more companies and countries export, the more they improve their performance. Exporting enables companies to increase sales, improve productivity, and diversify activities. Likewise, exporting helps countries generate jobs, accelerate innovation, and improve living standards. In broader terms, it promotes connections among countries that improve foreign relations and stabilize international affairs.

Despite these virtues, some contend there is a dark side of exporting, namely the trade of hazardous waste in the form of obsolete computer equipment. E-waste—trash composed of computers, monitors, electronics, game consoles, smartphones, and other items—inexorably increases as the Information Era rolls on. In 2006, nearly 66 million used electronic components were collected for reuse or recycling in the United States; most were exported.[59] By 2011, e-waste was pushing several hundred million pieces, with the U.S generating about 400 million and China 160 million units. Ongoing trends crank out newer, cooler, faster, smaller, fancier devices that, in replacing their predecessors and then eventually being replaced themselves, will increase e-waste nearly 500 percent over the next decade.

Where Should E-waste Go? Where to put all this e-trash is a tough question. Many counties and municipalities in the United States, for example, ban outright dumping of e-waste in local landfills. This legislation means that disposing of e-waste products, when possible, in any given industrialized country costs from $2,500 to $4,000 a ton. In contrast, selling untreated waste to countries in Africa and Asia, where it will be recycled, reused, or dumped, reportedly goes as low as $50 a ton.[60] Low costs follow from cheap labor, different environmental regulations, and growing processing capacity. Plus, the absence of public opposition reduces processing expenses and desperate folks seeking work dampens public objections. As might be expected, major e-waste shipping routes show that the industrial nations export the bulk of their e-waste to developing countries, notably China, Malaysia, India, Nigeria, and Bangladesh (see Map 14.1).[61]

Benefits for All Exporting e-waste to recycling centers throughout the world is an efficient solution to an escalating problem. First and foremost, recycling sustains our resources and helps us protect the environment. In developing countries, industries have sprung up to recycle old computers, monitors, circuit boards, scanners, printers, routers, cell phones, and

MAP 14.1 The Patterns of Trade of Electronic Waste

When computers, cell phones, and other electronic equipment become obsolete, they are no longer worth much in rich countries. E-waste, however, has some value in developing countries. That is exactly where, as exports, it usually ends up. Proponents note it promotes productive recycling as well as local economic development. Critics charge it is viciously hazardous and callously exploits cheap labor and lax regulations.

Source: Basel on Action Network; Silicon Valley Toxics Condition, www.ban.org/about/.

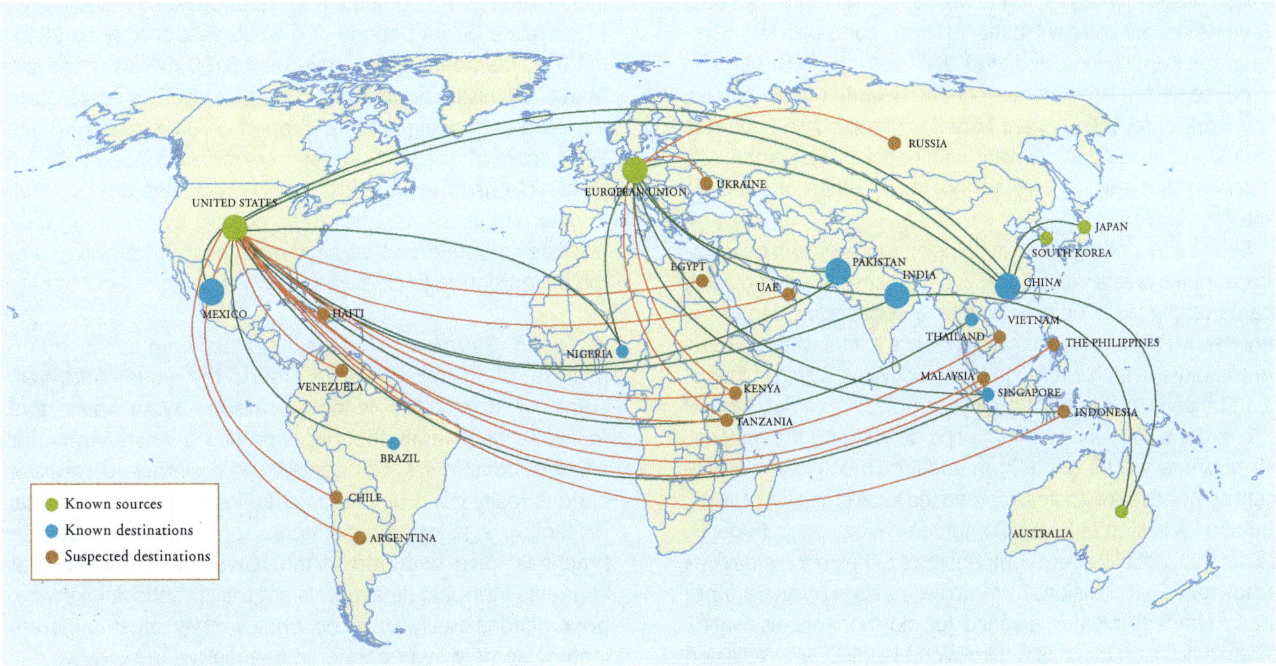

Here we see an enterprising Nigerian child running a grassroots e-recycling facility. Although junk to many, scavenging and selling useful parts creates value for him, his community, and the world.

Source: Enrique Soriano-Silverlens/ ZUMA Press/Newscom

network cards. While rudimentary, these industries create jobs in places where jobs are hard to find and difficult to sustain. To their credit, developing countries have converted their superior location economics into vital jobs, income, and markets. There are more than 5,500 businesses employing 100,000 workers at ground zero of the e-waste trade: Guiyu, China. Previously subsistence farmers and fishermen, they now process more than 100 truckloads of e-waste that arrive daily.[62] Mexico has similar spots, many waiting for the more than sixty 18-wheelers full of spent batteries from cars, phones, computer, solar appliances, and tools that cross the U.S.-Mexican border each day. Again, locals benefit. Despite the dangerous, dirty work of recycling spent batteries, people living near the Acumuladores de Jalisco plant find opportunity. As the wife of one worker said, "There are not many other jobs around here."[63]

Similarly, exporting e-waste helps entrepreneurs in developing countries create value by recovering, recycling, and reusing scarce resources. Copper, a valuable commodity, can represent nearly 20 percent of a mobile phone's total weight. Rising commodity prices have made these activities quite profitable. Atul Maheshwar, owner of a recycling depot in India, says of U.S. exports, "If your country keeps sending us the material, our business will be good."[64] In addition, much of the equipment shipped to Asia helps improve the local standard of living. Graham Wollaston of Scrap Computers, a recycler in Phoenix, claims that virtually every component of old electronic devices is reusable. Old televisions turn into fish tanks in Malaysia, while silicon shortage creates demand for old monitors elsewhere. "There's no such thing as a third-world landfill," Mr. Wollaston explains. "If you were to put an old computer on the street, it would be taken apart for the parts."[65] Similarly, Luc Lateille of the Canadian firm BMP Recycling says, "We don't send junk—we only send the materials that they are looking for."[66]

Exporting hazardous waste also helps MNEs improve their social responsibility. Samsung, Mitsubishi, and Nokia, among others, increasingly assume cradle-to-grave responsibility for their products. The eCycling Leadership Initiative, launched in 2010, commits makers of consumer electronics to recycle a billion pounds of e-waste responsibly by 2016; in 2011, members spent more than $100 million to recycle about 500 million pounds of old electronics. Elsewhere, state regulation spurs laggards to support green recycling. Since 2004, more than 20 U.S. states have required manufacturers to recycle used electronics. Likeminded laws are on deck in other states. Companies often comply by exporting their e-waste to countries that have an interest in recycling and the infrastructure to do it.

A Tough Solution Certainly, callous companies dump useless, often toxic e-waste around the world. And, yes, some of it pollutes landfills, poisons waterways, and fouls the air. Overall, though, exporting e-waste works for citizens, consumers, companies, and countries. Ultimately, nations really don't have a choice. The U.S. Environmental Protection Agency, for example, concedes inappropriate practices have occurred in the recycling of e-waste but suggests stopping its export is not truly practical. Likewise, poor nations really have no choice; they must generate income some way or condemn themselves to poverty.

Exporting E-waste: A Useful Solution?

Counterpoint

No In theory, recycling is beneficial. Recycling your e-waste, however, does not always mean you're doing the right thing. Explained the director of the Basel Action Network, "The dirty little secret is that when you take [your electronic waste] to a recycler, instead of throwing it in a trashcan, about 80 percent of that material, very quickly, finds itself on a container ship going to a country like China, Nigeria, India, Vietnam, Pakistan—where very dirty things happen to it."[67] Added the chief executive of RSR, a Dallas-based lead recycler that operates solely in the United States, "We're shipping hazardous waste to a neighbor ill-equipped to process it, and we're doing it legally, turning our heads, and pretending it's not a problem."[68] Growing exports of hazardous waste have created dangerous recycling industries in many developing countries. Going forward, exports will accelerate as e-waste increases far faster than other sorts of rubbish. Collectively, the tsunami of e-trash imposes far more costs than the pittance recycling it generates.

A Witch's Brew Most developing countries lack the regulatory codes or disposal infrastructure to safeguard against such dangers. Locals often use crude methods that, besides being illegal in the United States, expose workers and residents to a witch's brew of toxins. For example, some e-waste contains trace amounts of precious metals like copper and silver. Extracting them encourages cash-strapped, loosely regulated recyclers to use unsafe, antiquated open-air incineration methods. Burning electronic parts to separate copper, solder, or other metals from plastic coatings releases

Counterpoint

dioxins and other hazardous chemicals. Indeed, snagging that sliver of silver unleashes a mixture of more than a thousand chemicals, including toxic metals (e.g., lead, barium, and mercury), flame-retardants, cadmium, acids, plastics, and chlorinated and brominated compounds. Local air quality suffers as "circuit boards are burned after acid washing, spewing deadly smoke and exposing workers and people living around these facilities."[69] Once local scrap shops finish disassembling equipment, the trash goes into public landfills, the acid runoff flows into groundwater, and the noxious fumes follow air currents—all mercilessly contaminating the environment.

Casual Inhumanity Madhumita Dutta of Toxics-Link Delhi argues that these problems are less disturbing than the "appalling" working conditions in recycling facilities: "Everything from dismantling the computer to pulling out parts of the circuit boards to acid-washing boards to recover copper is done with bare hands without any protective gear or face protection." Rare is the worksite that uses proper disposal practices. Workers and society, to say nothing of environmental sustainability, suffer.

What, then, of the premise of charity—that is, sending computer equipment from countries where it has little use to countries where it can make a difference? Critics shred this straw man, asserting that wealthier countries and powerful companies conveniently donate obsolete equipment to dodge high recycling expenses. "Too often, justifications of 'building bridges over the digital divide' are used as excuses to obscure and ignore the fact that these

Here we see a frightful wasteland near Lagos, Nigeria. Notwithstanding the toxic threats of this witches' brew, desperation spurs people to scavenge for anything of value.
Source: n86/ZUMA Press/Newscom

bridges double as toxic waste pipelines," said one critic.[70] Moreover, most of the computer equipment sent is worthless trash—waste that can be neither repaired nor resold.[71]

Institutional Gaps Some argue that manufacturers need to step up and take full responsibility for the hazardous materials they used to build products that had earned them profits.[72] Companies have moved in this direction, sponsoring green campaigns to recycle e-waste. Substantive progress has been slow, however. Environmentalists recommend that countries set tougher standards to monitor, control, and certify cross-border shipments of e-waste. That has proven disappointing. Inspections of e-waste cargo at 18 European seaports awaiting export, for example, found that nearly half was illegal.[73]

Then again, presumed solutions can lead to unintended problems. The fact that many U.S. states require companies to take responsibility for recycling electronic equipment has curtailed the export of e-waste to developing countries—but only of the more valuable components. Processors cherry-pick parts that can be refurbished for reuse. The remainder is disassembled, with urban miners targeting silver, gold, and palladium. The final patch of trash, the worst of the worst, has no reuse market and is shipped to developing countries for disposal.[74]

Who to Turn To? Others endorse stronger enforcement of the Basel Convention on the Transboundary Movement of Hazardous Wastes and their Disposal, a United Nations treaty that regulates the generation, management, movements, and disposal of hazardous waste. It proposes aggressive measures, including an international ban on the export of all toxic waste, no matter whether for recovery, recycling, reuse, or final disposal. As of 2013, 172 countries had ratified the Basel Convention. The United States, which generates more than half of the world's e-waste, has signed the treaty but not ratified it.[75]

1. The export of e-waste to recycling facilities worldwide seems like a win for the world given that recycling is always considered a beneficial activity. However, there are serious costs. Identify three benefits as well as three costs of recycling the U.S.'s e-waste in other countries. Then state whether you believe the benefits exceed the costs or vice versa.

IMPORTING AND EXPORTING: PROBLEMS AND PITFALLS

CONCEPT CHECK

As straightforward as the concept of **exporting** may seem on the surface, whether you are a born-global entrepreneur or an established **MNE**, it is fraught with challenges. *Behavioral barriers* complicate international operations. Political and legal codes pose pitfalls, *government regulation* impacts trade relationships, and *foreign-exchange instruments* necessitate financial sophistication.

Companies, both big and small, identify problems and pitfalls that complicate international trade. Moreover, trade veterans explain that exporting and importing are fraught with ongoing complexities and evolving barriers. Presently, there is considerable variation regarding the type, characteristics, and impact of obstacles. The United States International Trade Commission polled the managers of a stratified random sample of more than 8,400 U.S. firms—both big companies and SMEs from the manufacturing and service sectors—about the influence of 19 potential barriers to trade.[76] Table 14.2 shows the range of opinions. The ratings confirm that international traders deal with a battery of problems and pitfalls. Data indicate that different types of firms differently interpreted different impediments.

Related survey data indicate that as SMEs export more, their perception of the severity of impediments declines—much as we would expect, given our earlier discussion of the internationalization process.[77] Indeed, international experience matters greatly; newer SMEs, particularly those in services versus manufacturing who export less intensively and to fewer regions, regarded barriers as disproportionately more severe than did their experienced counterparts. However, practice was not a panacea. Experienced companies exporting to multiple regions of the world still struggle with impediments to trade. So, as in the past, we anticipate exporters and importers will face recurring difficulties that test the resolve of the most committed internationalist. Let's take a closer look at key areas of concern.

FINANCIAL RISKS

SMEs regularly rate financial constraints as the most daunting barrier to international trade.

Financial constraints are arguably the greatest impediment to international traders. In a survey of 978 SMEs that asked their perceptions of trade barriers, the top-ranked factor was the shortage of working capital to finance export.[78] Likewise, financial concerns consistently rank high in Table 14.2. Traders often reason that export or import offers low profitability given unexpected costs and unknown financial constraints, both of which are aggravated

TABLE 14.2 The Relative Influence of Leading Barriers to Export

International trade presents a range of difficulties. Here we see how managers of both SMEs and large companies, operating in either making a good or providing a service, rate the challenge of leading types of trade impediments.

Note: The higher the percentage, the greater the perceived severity of the particular impediment to trade.

Barrier to Export	SME Manufacturer	Large Manufacturer	SME Services	Large Services Firm
Transportation/shipping costs	88.5	93.6	53.6	35.1
Language/cultural barriers	82.2	86.8	53.4	42.2
Difficulty locating sales prospects	79.1	83.2	55.8	45.2
Foreign regulations	78.0	90.0	51.1	48.3
U.S. regulations	73.4	86.8	45.4	37.8
Foreign sales not sufficiently profitable	72.5	84.4	58.7	46.2
Customs procedures	71.9	87.4	44.6	35.5
Difficulty receiving or processing payments	67.9	87.9	39.3	41.1
U.S. taxation issues	62.8	80.7	37.4	39.2
Lack of trained staff	62.6	85.7	36.7	46.5
Insufficient intellectual property protection	61.8	71.6	43.6	27.3
Foreign taxation issues	60.4	80.5	36.1	40.6
Preference for local goods/services in foreign market	57.4	81.7	37.8	35.8
Difficulty establishing affiliates in foreign markets	57.2	76.9	29.8	33.8
High tariffs	56.6	81.6	36.8	28.8
Lack of government support programs	56.4	70.3	29.2	29.4
Obtaining financing	51.6	63.8	38.5	31.9
Unable to find foreign partners	50.5	66.6	33.0	36.0
Visa issues	30.1	67.8	34.9	33.5

Source: The *United States International Trade Commission* asked 3,500 U.S. big and SME in manufacturing and service industries firms if they had ever exported or considered exporting (the latter point was included to account for the possibility that firms had faced perceived insurmountable barriers). These firms were then asked to report whether they had encountered the various impediments and, if yes, assess the impediment's severity on a scale of 1 to 5, with 1 representing no impediment, 3 a moderate impediment, and 5 a major impediment. See "Small and Medium-Sized Enterprises: Characteristics and Performance," United States International Trade Commission, Investigation No. 332-510, USITC Publication 4189, November 2010.

by fluctuating exchange rates. Managing these risks involves currency and credit processes that call for sophisticated financial expertise. Moreover, completing international sales often requires helping foreign customers obtain credit, whether in the form of trade credits, government-financed support, or bank guarantees.[79] Firms accustomed to offering financing in terms of the traditional 30- or 60-day trade-credit cycle at home regard the need for different arrangements denominated in different currencies as excessively escalating risk.

CUSTOMER MANAGEMENT

An enduring barrier to exporting is misunderstanding the difficulty of profitably serving consumers in foreign markets.

Historically, exports and imports were arm's-length, ship-it-and-forget-it transactions. Contact with customers relied on documents either faxed or posted overnight. This situation created useful time lags with which to deal with questions and complaints. Now, contacting vendors via email or voice-over-Internet-protocol (VoIP) gives customers, no matter how far away, real-time access. The resulting boost of customers' service expectations reduces the appeal of international trade. "The new notch in the bar for us is the requests from our customers for additional services beyond the port of delivery," said the materials manager of Seco/Warwick, a manufacturer of heat-treating equipment. "In previous years, I would be responsible for cost, insurance, and freight (CIF) to the port of import, but now I'm often tasked with all aspects of delivery to the customer's plant location. Now we're often involved in the installation and startup of the equipment, so we have service engineers and cranes waiting for the on-time delivery."[80]

Customer management concerns particularly challenge SMEs. Their orientation toward specialized opportunities and narrow gaps in the market often prompt them to apply niche strategies. Doing so pushes them to customize services and marketing support to fit overseas segments in ways that often exceed those offered in the home market. Recurring resource constraints as well as the preference to avoid head-on competition with larger companies reinforce these tendencies.[81]

INTERNATIONAL BUSINESS EXPERTISE

The problems and pitfalls of international trade consistently frustrate the occasional and regular exporter.

CRN
Case Review Note

International traders note the difficulties of understanding foreign business practices. Ordinary as well as idiosyncratic problems include limited knowledge of foreign competitors, unfamiliarity with local customs regulations, uncertainty about the prevailing price-to-quality standards, difficulty optimizing transportation and insurance options, and confusion about market channels and consumer behavior. Certainly, there are solutions, as we saw with our opening profile of SpinCent. Fear of misunderstanding local markets led it to hire local distributors. Firms that struggle with interpreting export markets typically exit international trade.

MARKETING CHALLENGES

Traders regularly complain of high shipment costs and logistic demands; difficulties in matching foreign rivals' prices, effectively promoting products, and establishing distribution networks; and weak foreign market connections. In addition, providing after-sales service imposes the aggravation of translating warranties as well as navigating ambiguous cultural differences. Non-exporters express greater anxiety about these marketing uncertainties, particularly when they benchmark them against the comparatively lower demands in their home markets. In addition, the decidedly more complex demands of market structures and consumer behaviors in emerging markets amplify problems. Going from the United States to Canada is one thing; going from the United States to Turkmenistan is entirely another.

TOP MANAGEMENT COMMITMENT

Persevering in the face of problems and pitfalls requires executives committed to internationalization.

Management characteristics, especially senior executives' international outlook and risk orientation, influence import activity. Most companies, particularly SMEs, focus on domestic rather than foreign markets. In the United States, for instance, SMEs comprise 97 percent of all exporters, yet less than 1 percent of all SMEs export. Of those that do export, nearly two-thirds export to just one foreign market.[82] Asked about their export-shyness, managers cite familiarity with the home market along with equivocal top management commitment. Even when top management acknowledges the benefit of trade, its riskiness and resource demands dissuade most from internationalizing operations.

CRN
Case Review Note

Exporting and importing put tough demands on management. Rare is the firm that eagerly adjusts its customary practices for foreign business standards. As a result, top management often emphasizes the domestic market and duly notes the intention to export down the road. Recall Knepper's original export outlook at SpinCent; at best, he was an occasional exporter who felt the risks outweighed rewards. Eventually, profitability and diversification concerns forced him to reconsider. From then on, his company's core competency, support from public agencies, and trustworthy distributors fortified his export commitment.

GOVERNMENT REGULATION

Export and import inefficiencies persist due to delays, documents, and administrative fees. The rules and regulations governing trade, notwithstanding the success of the WTO, endure. New Jersey–based Spectra Colors, manufacturer and distributor of high-quality customized dyes and colorants, runs into problems because import regulations differ from one country to the next. "In Europe, REACH regulations (Registration, Evaluation, and Authorization of Chemicals) have caused us lengthy delays and expense," said Spectra's business manager.[83]

Occasionally, shipments to various markets require government clearance. Refusals come easily to officials facing product constraints at home or political tension abroad. REACH disproportionately affects SME exporters, given staff and resource constraints to ensure compliance. Worse still, Canada, China, Japan, Switzerland, Taiwan, and Turkey are developing regulations like those of REACH. [84]

CONCEPT CHECK

"Legal Issues in International Business," profiled in Chapter 3, note how a country's legal system influences operating decisions. Chapter 7 shows how governments influence import flows with instruments of trade control. Here, we add revenue collection and homeland security to the list of moderators.

Similar regulatory situations are emerging in other industries. Exporters of medical devices face complex regulations and lengthy approval times that require extensive test data. Many countries, including Australia, Canada, China, certain EU member states, Japan, and the United States (and the list is growing), impose approval procedures that require firms to implement an ISO-certified production quality management system. Firms intent on complying must pay various fees and related charges to gain and maintain certification. Many exporters, particularly SMEs, struggle to fund such efforts.

Table 14.2 shows that service exporters also run into other problems. Professional service providers, such as the sort found in engineering, legal, finance, and entertainment services, regularly send employees abroad to perform contracted services. In Malaysia, for example, foreign engineers cannot work on building projects unless the hiring company demonstrates to the Malaysian Board of Engineers that a Malaysian engineer cannot do the job.[85] It's harsher in Thailand—its Alien Occupation Act reserves architecture and engineering services jobs for Thai nationals.[86] Morocco likewise prohibits foreign architects registering with its National Association of Architects, then mandates that only members of this Association can legally practice architecture. The Philippines goes even farther, reserving the practice of most licensed professions to Philippine citizens.[87] Finally, India restricts the right to practice law to natural persons who are both Indian citizens and on the advocates' roll in the particular Indian state where legal services will be provided. Furthermore, to qualify as an advocate, candidates must be either an Indian citizen or a citizen of a country that allows Indian nationals to practice law on a reciprocal basis, hold a degree from a university recognized by the Bar Council of India, and be at least 21 years of age.[88] Similar situations in Brazil, Bahrain, and Hong Kong, to name just a few, challenge the legal firm with international ambitions.

E-commerce, while a powerful export platform, does not let companies circumvent barriers. Government regulations may lag company actions, given the speed by which e-commerce occurs, but they eventually regain their authority. For example, Chinese law holds that an enterprise seeking to operate in the digital publishing field of China must obtain at least one of the four licenses for publishing, copying, distributing, or importing e-books in order to operate legally. Within a day of Amazon announcing its Kindle store launch in China, for instance, the Chinese authorities began investigating its legality, claiming its licensing agreement with its Chinese partner, Chineseall.com, was insufficient.[89]

In the United States, homeland security issues constrain trade. The logistics manager at Schott North America notes that the real danger to international trade these days is not tariffs; rather, it's "that your containers are stuck down at the terminal in New York [harbor] waiting for inspection" by radiation detection instruments before being allowed to enter the United States.[90] Likewise, moving goods across borders takes far longer today than it did a dozen years ago given security procedures: processing a truckload of goods across the Canadian–American border takes three times as long as it did pre-September 11, 2001.[91] The United Kingdom, likewise, replaced its "account consignor scheme" that had allowed logistics groups to accept goods for cargo planes from self-certified businesses in order to improve its air cargo safety. As a result, importers and exporters must have all shipments scanned by the freight firms, such as FedEx, TNT, and UPS, or establish high-security sites.[92] Governments work toward common standards, adopting similar screening methods, and harmonizing security measures. The sensitivity of these issues, particularly security, slows progress.[93] Consequently, national, regional, and global trade regulations impose persistent barriers.

TRADE DOCUMENTATION

Governments require international traders to thoroughly document transactions.

A battery of documents regulates international trade. Duty rates, customs clearance, and entry processes, though overlapping, invariably differ across countries. Tariff classifications, value declarations, and duty management spawn confusion and boost costs. Customs and

TABLE 14.3 Types of Export Documents

Many concerns motivate the government to monitor export activities, ranging from tracking transactions to defending national security. Here we see a subset of the forms that exporters commonly complete.

Type	Specification
Pro Forma Invoice	A document from the exporter to the importer that outlines the selling terms, price, and delivery as if the goods had actually shipped. If the importer accepts the terms and conditions, it sends a purchase order and arranges for payment, at which point the exporter issues a commercial invoice.
Shipper's Export Declaration	The most common of all export documents, used by the exporter's government to monitor exports and compile trade statistics.
Bill of Lading	A receipt for goods delivered to the common carrier for transportation, a contract for services rendered by the carrier, and a document of title. The customer usually needs an original as proof of ownership before assuming title.
Consular Invoice	Sometimes required by countries to monitor imports, it is used by governments to track import prices and generate revenue.
Certificate of Origin	Indicates the product's origination and is usually validated by an external source, such as the Chamber of Commerce. It helps countries determine the tariff schedule for imports.
Export-Packing List	Itemizes the material in each individual package, indicates the type of package, and is attached to the outside of the package. Used by the shipper and sometimes customs officials to verify the cargo.
Commercial Invoice	A bill for the goods from buyer to seller listing a description of the goods, buyer/seller addresses, and delivery and payment terms. Governments use it to determine the value of goods when assessing customs duties. Figure 14.4 shows a sample of this form, identifying the various data an exporter must report to comply with current U.S. trade policy.

security initiatives impose various regulations. Navigating these obstacles requires that traders manage the paper trail that documents, certifies, and legalizes transactions. Table 14.3 profiles key customs documents. For many companies, completing these and many others is unacceptably burdensome. A look at Figure 14.4 gives one a sense of this task—and, keep in mind that this is just one of the many required forms.

Mistakes can arise in any number of slots. For example, many loss-and-damage challenges stem in part from the sizable percentage of exporters that use incorrect International Commercial Terms, or Incoterms.[94] Sometimes, exporters fail to classify their products accurately in terms of the tariff schedule of the country of destination. Goods that arrive with commercial invoice descriptions not matching those of the importing country's tariff classification are registered under a catchall description, such as "machinery, other." Besides slowing the transaction, imprecise descriptions often incur higher duty charges.

Importers typically receive products without purchasing them. That is, they take the title of ownership without laying out any money. The arrival of the shipment in-country requires filing documents with various offices and agencies in order to pay up, take title, settle duty charges, and arrange delivery. Required documents vary by country. Typically, customs agencies require an entry manifest, commercial invoice, and packing list.[95]

IMPORTING AND EXPORTING: RESOURCES AND ASSISTANCE

The problems and pitfalls of international trade, besides discouraging potential exporters and importers, complicate the activities of committed internationalists and born globals. SMEs are particularly vulnerable. Many could boost profits and improve productivity by entering new markets.[96] In 2010, 60 percent of U.S. SME exporters sold to customers in only one foreign market, whereas more than half of big exporters recorded sales to five or more foreign

FIGURE 14.4 Sample Commercial Invoice

Here we see a sample of the sorts of forms that U.S. exporters routinely face. In this case, the form is a commercial invoice, a bill for the goods from the foreign buyer to the U.S. seller. Completing this form correctly makes for efficient transfers. Completing it incorrectly results in costly delays and often higher duty charges.

Source: Based on data reported in the WorldBank's World Development Indicators, in particular *Trade* (percent of *GDP*) (Series NE_TRD_GNFS_ZS), retrieved June 15, 2013, from data.worldbank.org/data-catalog/world-development-indicators.

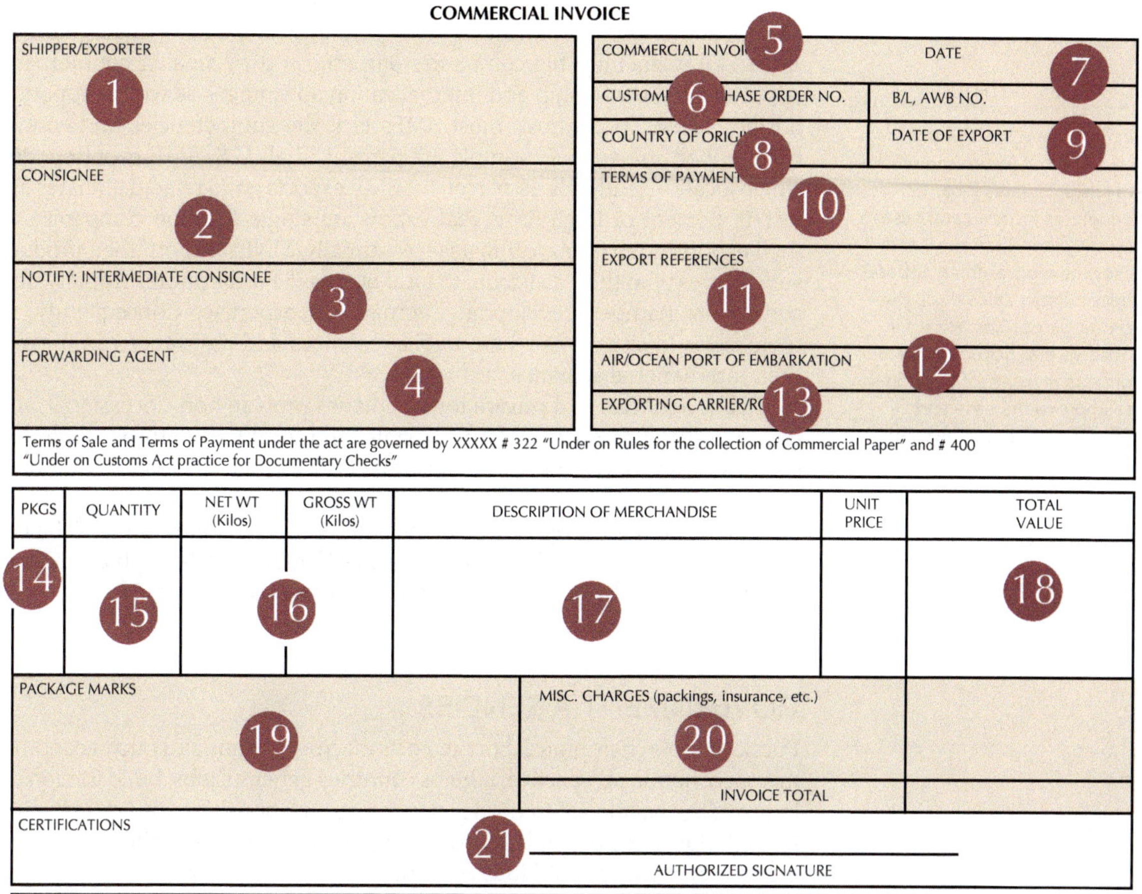

1.	EXPORTER	The name and address of the principal party responsible for effecting export from the United States. The exporter as named on the Export License.
2.	CONSIGNEE	The name and address of the person/company to whom the goods are shipped for the designated end use, or the party so designated on the Export License
3.	INTERMEDIATE CONSIGNEE	The name and address of the party who effects delivery of the merchandise to the ultimate consignee, or the party so named on the Export License.
4.	FORWARDING AGENT	The name and address of the duly authorized forwarder acting as agent for the exporter.
5.	COMMERCIAL INVOICE NO.	Commercial Invoice number assigned by the exporter
6.	CUSTOMER PURCHASE ORDER NO	Overseas customer's reference of order number
7.	B/L, AWB NO.	Bill of Lading, or Air Waybill number, if known
8.	COUNTRY OF ORIGIN	Country of origin of shipment
9.	DATE OF EXPORT	Actual date of export of merchandise
10.	TERMS OF PAYMENT	Describe the terms, conditions, and currency of settlement as agreed upon by the vendor and purchaser per the Pro Forma Invoice, customer Purchase Order, and/or Letter of Credit
11.	EXPORT REFERENCES	May be used to record other useful information, e.g. - other reference numbers, special handling requirements, routing requirements, etc.
12.	AIR/OCEAN PORT OF EMBARKATION	Ocean port/pier, or airport to be used for embarkation of merchandise
13.	EXPORTING CARRIER/ROUTE	Record airline carrier/flight number or vessel name/shipping line to be used for the shipment of merchandise
14.	PACKAGES	Record number of packages, cartons, or containers per description line
15.	QUANTITY	Record total number of units per description line.
16.	NET WEIGHT/GROSS WEIGHT	Record total net weight and total gross weight (includes weight of container) in kilograms per description line.
17.	DESCRIPTION OF MERCHANDISE	Provide a full description of items shipped, the type of container (carton, box, pack, etc.), the gross weight per container, and the quantity and unit of measure of the merchandise.
18.	UNIT PRICE/TOTAL VALUE	Record the unit price of the merchandise per the unit of measure, compute the extended total value of the line.
19.	PACKAGE MARKS	Record in this Field, as well as on each package, the package number (e.g. - 1 of 7, 3 of 7, etc.), shippers company name, country of origin (e.g. - made in USA), destination port of entry, package weight in kilograms, package size (length x width x height), and shipper's control number (e.g. - C/I number; optional).
20.	MISC. CHARGES	Record any miscellaneous charges which are to be paid for by the customer - export transportation, insurance, export packaging, inland freight to pier, etc.
21.	CERTIFICATIONS	Any certifications or declarations required of the shipper regarding any information recorded on the commercial invoice.

Source: www.unzco.com/basicguide/figure2.html Accessed March 19, 2009.

markets. A tiny share of exporters, just 0.4 percent, shipped goods to 50 or more countries. We see similar characteristics on the import side. Sixty-one percent of U.S. SMEs imported from one foreign market, while 57 percent of large firms imported from five or more foreign markets.[97] Likewise, fewer than 0.1 percent of importing companies brought in goods from 50 or more countries.

CONCEPT CHECK

In Parts I and II of the text, we note that **international business** creates jobs, generates income, and raises living standards. Parts II and III show how governments shape trade relationships through pro-trade policies. Here, we observe that governments provide a variety of programs to improve the ease and efficiency of **exporting and importing.**

Globalization spurs companies to expand their market frontiers. Liberalizing markets and opening borders increases the potential for trade—again, take a quick look at Table 14.1. Generally, big companies outperform their smaller counterparts pursuing these opportunities; ownership and internalization advantages as well as superior resources better position them. In contrast, most SMEs lack the competencies and connections to pursue trade opportunities. For example, 92 percent of all U.S. SME exporters do business from a single location, and only 15 percent of SME exports go to related affiliates abroad. In contrast, just 11 percent of large firms that export are single-location companies and 38 percent of their exports go to foreign affiliates—essentially, MNEs "export" their products to their foreign subsidiaries who then distribute to local buyers.[98] Furthermore, SMEs' typically tight resource constraints hamper developing international expertise. Consequently, many SMEs find themselves in situations where public resources and assistance can meaningfully influence their international activities.

Public agencies and private intermediaries provide non-, occasional, and regular exporters a wealth of resources. National, state, and local trade offices along with private parties such as freight forwarders, custom brokers, trade intermediaries, international banks, and consultants are a few of the many resources that help companies navigate international trade (see Table 14.4). Our opening look at SpinCent highlighted the assistance provided by the U.S. Commercial Service's Export Assistance Center of Philadelphia. It helped Knepper assess the Asian markets, supported his tag-along on the Asia trade mission, helped prescreen distributors, and arranged visits with local officials.

CRN
Case Review Note

GOVERNMENT AGENCIES

Public officials champion export given its macroeconomic and microeconomic benefits. From a macroeconomic perspective, it helps countries generate jobs, build foreign exchange reserves, improve the balance of trade, develop foreign relationships, and raise living standards. In the United States, for example, exports support more than 10 million jobs. In the manufacturing sector, export-related jobs accounted for 22 percent or more of total employment in ten U.S. manufacturing industries.[99] Overall, manufacturing exports support more than one of every five jobs in the United States. From a microeconomic perspective, exporting helps firms leverage core competencies, improve financial performance, fortify competitive positioning, and sustain the enterprise. New markets open paths to higher productivity and profitability. Consequently, governments in virtually every country assist potential and active exporters. To a lesser degree, they also protect the interests of their struggling importers.

In the United States, as in most countries, public agencies help firms initiate and develop exports and imports.

In the United States, SMEs often start at the nearest Commercial Service office, the trade promotion arm of the U.S. Department of Commerce's International Trade Administration. Its representatives in more than 100 U.S. cities and 75 countries help U.S. companies to start exporting or to seek sales in new markets. Its global network helps SMEs target markets, organize operations, and overcome barriers. For Analytical Graphics, Commercial Service supports its Asian market expansion, setting up meetings with potential resellers in Japan and South Korea.[100] Other units of the International Trade Administration resolve related trade complications, such as helping Garmine Marine clear its navigational GPS through Turkish customs by informing Turkish government officials that the units can be self-certified by an accredited independent lab, in compliance with the relevant EU standard.[101]

The U.S. government, through these and other resources, provides information and advice on the practicalities and technicalities of exporting. Its official gateway, www.export.gov, offers a variety of support services. Personal help is also available at export centers run by various branches of the Commerce Department, International Trade Administration, and the Small Business Administration. These and related agencies strengthen the competitiveness of U.S.

TABLE 14.4 Trade Assistance by Type and Source

If your company is thinking about initiating or escalating international trade activity, the following organizations and agencies offer assistance on a host of issues.

Source	Nature of Assistance
Government Agencies	Market demographics, product demand, and competition
	Complying with domestic and foreign trade regulations
	Customs, regulatory, and tax issues
	Sales financing, credit, and insurance
	Trade data analysis
	Licenses and regulations
	International financing
	International sales and marketing
	Trade events, partners, and trade leads
	Shipping documentation and requirements
	Pricing, quotes, and negotiations
Trade Associations	Market demographics, product demand, and competition
	Export training seminars online and on-site
	Advertising and sales promotion alternatives
	Profile distribution channels and logistics networks
	Customs regulations and tax issues; compliance with global trade laws
	Navigating homeland security programs
	Standardizing and streamlining trade processes
Trade Intermediaries	Customs management system and tariff classification
	Online trade infrastructures and virtual trade shows
	Legal, accounting, security, and tax compliance
	Secure electronic procurement and automated supply chain processes
	Trade finance, credit-scoring, and insurance
	Exporting training and trade strategies
	Transport and logistics management

industry, promote trade and investment, help U.S. companies compete at home and abroad, and ensure fair trade through the rigorous enforcement of trade laws and agreements.[102]

Similarly, most states and many cities run export financing programs, including pre- and post-shipment working-capital loans and guarantees, accounts receivable financing, and export insurance. The limited reserves of some agencies requires proof of adequate safeguards from the exporter. For instance, authorities usually require a letter of credit or sufficient credit insurance. Often, states and cities stipulate that exporters transact part of the funded activity within their jurisdiction.

CONCEPT CHECK

In Chapter 1, we suggest that **international business** is challenging for people who like to operate solo. Collecting information about foreign markets, navigating export regulations, mastering foreign-exchange procedures, or complying with homeland security policies can prove overwhelming. Consequently, some companies prefer to get help in finding information about potential markers. International trade intermediaries often command sophisticated knowledge of international trade.

EXPORT INTERMEDIARIES

Third-party firms that market products and services abroad on behalf of domestic companies qualify as **export intermediaries.** For many companies, particularly SMEs, they offer an operationally easier and relatively risk-free approach to managing export intricacies.[103] Their expertise and experience provide management skills and economies of scale that are beyond the reach of the typical SME, while their experience with regulations, taxes, duties, insurance, and transportation makes them productive resources. The export management company and the export trading company are prominent types.

Export Management Company (EMC) An EMC, by acting as the international trade arm of a company, helps firms establish overseas markets. An EMC can significantly simplify SMEs' efforts to identify and penetrate foreign markets, thereby reducing key impediments of

Export.gov is the official gateway to a range of resources for international traders in the United States. Here, both the aspiring and experienced exporter finds information, opportunities, and solutions on a host of international trade topics.

Source: export.gov

exporting. Maintaining a close relationship with its clients, it can act as an unofficial marketing department: generating orders, organizing distribution channels, developing promotions, verifying credit information, advising on foreign accounts and payment terms, and even using the firm's letterhead in communicating with foreign sales representatives and distributors. It can also oversee trade documents, schedule transportation, and arrange patent and trademark protection.[104] Finally, it can expedite resolutions and, as needed, represent the client at customs investigations.

Trade intermediaries are third parties that provide exporters a variety of services.

EMCs operate on a contractual basis, providing exclusive representation in a formally defined market. Their contract with a company specifies pricing, credit, and financial policies, promotional services, and method of payment. An EMC might operate on a commission basis (unless it takes title to the merchandise) and charge fees for other services. It usually concentrates on complementary and noncompetitive products from various companies in order to market a full product line.

Many EMCs are entrepreneurial ventures that specialize by product, function, or market area.

In the United States, most EMCs are entrepreneurial firms that specialize by product, function, or market area. Some are large concerns, handling lines from many manufacturers that cut across several industries. Others are smaller and work with fewer clients. Some specialize in certain products or focus on particular places, while others are generalists. The Federation of International Trade Associations (FITA) estimates that more than 1,000 EMCs operate in the United States, each representing, on average, about 10 suppliers. Although few U.S. companies use them, FITA reasons that many would benefit.[105] Still, though versatile, EMCs are not a panacea. Typically small, stand-alone firms with limited resources, some EMCs may struggle to warehouse a company's product or offer extended in-house financing. In addition, they focus on products that bring them the most profit, avoiding those with sketchy prospects.

The United States exempts ETCs from antitrust provisions, thereby permitting competitors to combine forces in foreign markets.

Export Trading Company (ETC) In 1982, the U.S. enacted the Export Trading Company Act, which relaxed some antitrust regulations that had restricted some foreign market behaviors. Groups of direct competitors, once prohibited, were now allowed to form ETCs to develop exports jointly without fear of antitrust action. Dutch, Japanese, and British competitors had long done so profitably.[106] Free of legal barriers that had prevented joining forces with rivals, ETCs boost the export competitiveness of U.S. companies.

ETCs operate based on demand rather than supply. They identify suppliers who can fill orders in overseas markets.

ETCs differ from EMCs in that they operate based on demand rather than supply. An ETC brings buyers and sellers together, functioning as a trade matchmaker. It creates value by determining foreign customers' preferences, identifying domestic suppliers, and expediting transactions between the two parties. Rather than representing a single manufacturer, an ETC works with many. Operating as independent distributors, they avoid carrying inventory in their own name or performing post-sales service.

Fees Trade intermediaries charge for their expertise and services. Commonly, they operate on (1) a commission rate ranging from 10 percent for consumer goods to 15 percent or more for industrial products, (2) a buy-sell basis that asks for a firm's best home country discount plus an extra discount for a product that is marked up when sold abroad, and/or (3) contributions for special events such as exhibiting products in a foreign trade show or an advance payment for advertising and promotion.

Besides payments, hiring a trade intermediary requires that an exporter relinquish some to considerable business control in the matters of buyer segments, price policies, quality of promotion materials, flexibility of delivery schedules, or standards of customer service; these matters are determined by the intermediary. Some companies discover that if an intermediary promotes their products feebly they struggle to generate international sales. To retain control, a company can employ intermediaries less comprehensively. As in any make-vs.-buy situation, companies trade off their preference for control versus the cost of directly managing export activity.[107]

Finally, some feel the fees imposed by EMCs and ETCs reduces their appeal, particularly as language barriers lessen, international communication improves, and trade finance practices harmonize. In response, more intermediaries focus on exporting high-value products within the context of a single industry to select markets, rather than exporting bulk and commodity products. Improving industry expertise boosts effectiveness, whereas offering multiple product lines through foreign distributors improves efficiency. These innovations reduce the time it takes to move SMEs into enter foreign markets, a benefit some see as justifying the corresponding fees.

CUSTOMS BROKERS

Customs agents enforce the rules of trade for a particular country by controlling the flow of goods moving in and out of it. In the United States, for example, the Bureau of Customs and Border Protection (CBP, formerly the U.S. Customs Service) of the Department of Homeland Security monitors imports and exports. The CBP assesses and collects duties, taxes, and fees on imported merchandise, enforces customs and related laws, and administers certain navigation laws and treaties. It also polices smuggling threats and protects the United States from threatening imports.[108]

Countries vary to the degree to which their customs agencies help or hinder international traders (see Table 14.5). Several of the top ten countries on the ease-of-trading list are European. In fact, trading across Europe has become increasingly seamless due to the ongoing market integration efforts of the European Union. Free trade pacts in other parts of the world have similar effects, such as NAFTA expediting trade among Canada, Mexico, and the United States.

In contrast, irregular customs practices in African and South Asian markets routinely hamper exports and imports. Moving from port to port in these markets finds a hodgepodge of arbitrary and often contradictory regulations that can veer toward illegality. One Zambian trader noted, "My cargo of copper wire was held up in Durban, South Africa, for a week. The port authorities required proof that the wooden pallets on which the wire was loaded were free of pests. After a few days, the Ministry of Agriculture's inspector checked that the wood was fumigated—for a $100 fee.[109] No matter the locale, importing requires understanding relevant customs regulations and policies, knowing how to clear goods through customs, assigning the appropriate customs duties, and complying with special procedures.

TABLE 14.5 Where the Trading Is Easy—and Where It's Not

There is wide variability in the ease of exporting and importing among countries. Here, we see those countries that lead and lag the world in increasing the ease of export and import. These rankings reflect the average of a country's performance in terms of the time and cost (excluding tariffs) involved in exporting and importing a standardized cargo of goods by sea transport. Key indicators include the number of documents customs requires traders to complete and the length of time and overall cost required to complete an import or export transaction.

Easiest	Rank	Hardest	Rank
Singapore	1	Burundi	177
Hong Kong, China	2	Afghanistan	178
South Korea	3	Iraq	179
Denmark	4	Chad	180
United Arab Emirates	5	Congo, Republic	181
Finland	6	Tajikistan	182
Estonia	7	Kazakhstan	182
Sweden	8	Central African Republic	183
Panama	9	Tajikistan	184
Israel	10	Uzbekistan	185

Source: Based on The International Bank for Reconstruction and Development/The World Bank, "Doing Business in 2012: Doing Business in a More Transparent World."

A customs broker helps an importer navigate the regulations imposed by customs agencies.

Finding Help In terms of procedures, when merchandise reaches its port of entry, the importer files documents with customs officials, who then assign a provisional value and tariff classification. The United States has nearly 10,000 classifications in its Harmonized Tariff Schedule, approximately 60 percent of which are open to interpretation—that is, a particular product fits more than one classification. Often, it is an art form to determine the tariff classification that minimizes duty assessment. Importing requires considerable expertise to manage this and other processes. Trade paperwork is extensive, involving document preparation and/or electronic submissions, calculating and paying taxes, duties and excises, and overseeing communications between government authorities and traders. Not every company commands these proficiencies, especially SMEs. Consequently, some hire a **customs broker** to clear products through customs agencies. The broker helps through many means, including:

- *Qualifying for duty refunds through drawback provisions.* Some exporters use imported inputs, for which they paid a custom duty, in their manufacturing process. In the United States, drawback provisions allow domestic exporters to apply for a 99 percent refund of the duty paid on the imported goods as long as the goods become inputs into the firm's exports.
- *Deferring duties by using bonded warehouses and foreign trade zones.* Companies need not pay duties on imports stored in bonded warehouses and foreign trade zones until the goods are removed for sale or used in a manufacturing process. A broker oversees compliance with pertinent provisions.
- *Valuing products so they qualify for favorable duty treatment.* Different products incur different duties, or assessed taxes, when crossing borders, such as finished goods typically having a higher duty than components. Customs brokers' expertise helps determine the optimal classification.
- *Managing trade documentation.* Paperwork goes hand in hand with international trade, particularly that which falls under the auspices of homeland security. A customs broker obtains government permissions before forwarding paperwork to the carrier-overseen delivery.

Container ships are the sure-sailing movers of imports and exports. Pound for pound, they are the most efficient means of transporting goods between countries. Here, we see two container ships being unloaded at the Rotterdam Harbor; 24/7/365 activities like this take place in seaports worldwide.
Source: keller/Fotolia

- *Limiting liability by properly marking an import's country of origin.* Governments assess duties on imports based in part on the country of origin. A mistake in marking the country may increase the import duty. In the United States, if a product or its container is improperly marked when it enters the country, the product may be assigned a marking duty equal to 10 percent of the declared customs value. This charge is tacked onto the normal tariff.[110]

A customs broker helps importers in terms of
- Valuation
- Qualification
- Deferment
- Liability

FREIGHT FORWARDERS

A freight forwarder specializes in moving goods from sellers to buyers.

Freight forwarders, popularly known as the "travel agent of cargo," are the largest export/import intermediary in terms of value and weight of products shipped internationally.[111] Operationally, upon finalizing a foreign sale, an exporter hires a freight forwarder to arrange the fastest, cheapest transportation method. Balancing the constraints of space, speed, and cost, it identifies the optimal path to move the shipment from the manufacturer to an air, land, or ocean terminal, supervises clearing customs, and schedules delivery to the foreign buyer.

In the same process, the freight forwarder arranges storage prior to shipment, verifies letters of credit, obtains export licenses, pays consular fees, processes special documentation, and prepares shipping manifests. It may also advise on packing and labeling, transportation insurance, repacking of shipments damaged en route, and warehousing products. It does not take ownership title or act as a sales representative—that falls in the realm of an EMC or ETC. As a rule, freight forwarders offer fewer services than those agents.

Freight forwarders are particularly important when the cost or timing of freight can make or break a deal. One straightforward solution, advises the director of business development of Certified Worldwide, is "seek out your local Commercial Service office and find a freight forwarder, interview different freight forwarders, and remember that the company chosen will be responsible for shipping your product."[112]

The freight forwarder usually charges the exporter a percentage of the shipment value, plus a minimum charge depending on the number of services provided. It also receives a brokerage fee from the carrier. Most companies, especially SMEs, find it costly to deal with logistics. Freight forwarders' expertise enables them to secure shipping space at better rates and provides the flexibility to consolidate shipments.

THIRD-PARTY LOGISTICS

A 3PL is a trade intermediary that applies sophisticated technologies and systems to supervise trade logistics.

Third-party logistics (3PLs) are a growing force in international trade. Like freight forwarders, they move cargo and provide logistic options across virtually every market in the world. Unlike freight forwarders, they collaborate with manufacturers, shippers, and retailers to relieve them of logistics responsibilities. FedEx, for example, represents a one-stop shop that helps traders deal with transportation, warehousing, cross-docking, inventory management, packaging, and freight forwarding. Think of, on a very small scale, your last UPS experience; just as you did, an SME relies on UPS to track and transport the product, all the while providing access to real-time information to chart its progress. 3PLs also consolidate billing inclusive of all transportation, customs brokerage, duties, taxes, and package delivery services. Finally, they handle product returns, warranty claims, parts exchanges, and reverse logistics.

Expanding globalization and trade liberalization are accelerating the growth of 3PLs. Their U.S. gross revenues steadily grow at double-digit rates.[113] They are particularly helpful to the born global company; rather than building its own logistics operation, the born global need only tap the state-of-the-art sophistication of a 3PL. Big companies also benefit: nearly 80 percent of Fortune 500 companies use 3PLs to manage logistics and supply chains. Procter & Gamble, Walmart, PepsiCo, and Ford, for example, use the services of 30 or more of them. Overall, 3PLs have been growing their business at the expense of freight forwarders. In response, the latter are expanding their historic role as the travel agents of cargo to offer some of the services provided by 3PLs.

RECONCILING OPPORTUNITY AND CHALLENGE: AN EXPORT PLAN

From negotiating an international sale to shipping and receiving products, the exporter/importer manages an array of financial, logistic, and legal responsibilities. Each activity represents a link in the international transaction chain (see Figure 14.5). At times, some activities press more than others, such as finance concerns prior to shipment, delivery concerns post-shipment, and so on. Ultimately, all influence the process.

An export plan defines a company's intent to leverage resources and manage constraints in initiating and developing export activity.

The decision to engage or escalate international trade is one that few companies take lightly. It is one thing to consider exporting and quite another to take the first steps in doing so. Going international, as depicted in the transaction chain, imposes many demands that, collectively, influence resource allocation, executive effectiveness, operational flexibility, and financial stability. Successful exporters report that developing an **export plan** manages these demands—think of the notion, for example, that "companies don't plan to fail, they fail to plan."

An export plan prioritizes export markets, formalizes top management export buy-in, organizes international activities, and forecasts future resource needs as foreign sales increase. The process of defining objectives, sequencing tactics, and setting timelines pushes the firm to assess resources, assign responsibilities, and stipulate controls. A rigorous plan helps executives track the performance of an export strategy in the face of the ongoing, if not seemingly endless, decisions along the many steps of the transaction chain. Table 14.6 outlines an export-planning framework. At first glance, it may appear daunting. Remember, though, an export plan need only be just a few pages to start. It will steadily expand as it evolves.

Importantly, managers report that developing an export plan in an open process improves its effectiveness. By no means does that guarantee success. Strategic planning in any context is challenging, especially when one must abandon the familiarity of domestic routines for the anomalies of international trade. External validation goes a long way toward preempting blind spots as well as potential delusions about the likely success of export ventures. More practically, a well-specified plan is a precondition for export financing assistance from public agencies.

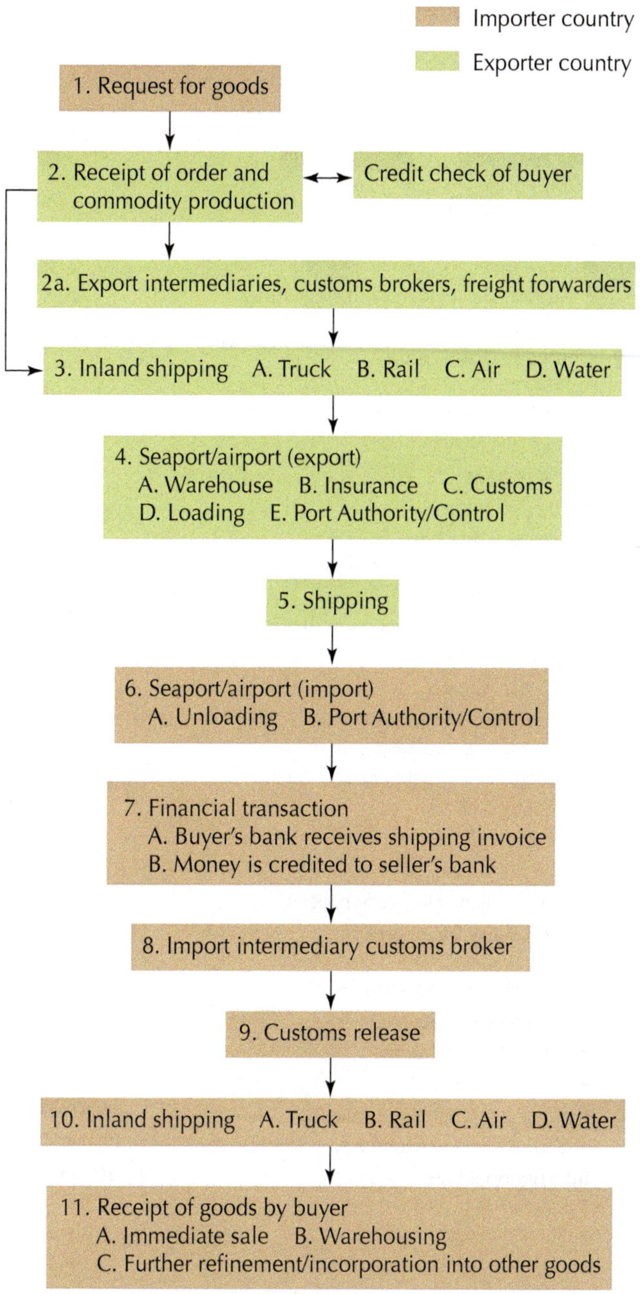

FIGURE 14.5 The International Transaction Chain

Between the point at which they negotiate an international sale and the point at which products have been delivered, both the exporter and the importer manage a complex array of financial, logistics, and legal tasks. Each of these tasks defines a link in the transaction chain that reflects the particular elements of each firm's strategy.

Source: Export America 1 (November 1999): 17. Magazine published by the International Trade Administration of the U.S. Dept. of Commerce.

Managers stress test an export plan by consulting trade specialists and public agencies.

Successful exporters note that consulting government agencies and third-party intermediates helps clarify opportunities and preempt problems. Noted the CEO of Coffee & More, "My advice to other companies considering exporting is to go for it, but be smart and do your homework first. Educate yourself and use your local U.S. Commercial Service office."[114] Added the Manager of International Operations at Analytical Graphics, "Don't just strike out on your own; take advantage of the U.S. Commercial Service. They are familiar with the ways of doing business in your market destination and know how U.S. companies can succeed there. It's saved us valuable time and resources."[115]

The element of an export plan that routinely stymies companies, particularly SMEs, is selecting the "right" foreign market. SMEs are often discouraged when their first foray fails. Instead of applying the standards of sound strategy that made them successful in the first

TABLE 14.6 An Export Planning Framework

An export plan organizes analysis of issues that influence the initiation and escalation of export. Management's assessment of the changing marketplace and the company competencies and culture develops a road map that shows where it is going and how to get there. Companies evaluating international frontiers commonly study the following issues:

1. **Executive Summary**
   - Key elements of the export plan
   - Description of business and target markets
   - Specification of management team
   - Summary of projections
2. **Company Description**
   - History
   - Goals and objectives
   - Core competency
   - Management
   - The export team
   - Company finances
3. **Product/Service Description**
   - Export opportunity
   - Fit of company's products in export market
   - Growth potential
   - Product strategy
4. **Foreign Marketplace Analysis**
   - Rationale for exporting
   - Rationale for targeted foreign market
   - Country profile
   - Industry profile
   - Competitor analysis
   - Specification of key assumptions
5. **Market Entry Strategies**
   - Form of operation
   - Indirect/direct exporting
   - E-commerce options
   - Target customer profile
   - Pricing strategies
   - Sales and promotion strategies
   - Logistics and transportation
6. **International Law**
   - Dispute resolution
   - Language consideration
   - Contract terms and conditions
   - Product liability considerations
   - Intellectual property protection
   - Sales agent and/or distributor agreements
   - Export/import regulations
7. **Financial Analysis**
   - Facility and equipment requirements
   - Sales forecast
   - Cost of goods sold
   - Projected international income statement
   - Projected international cash flow
   - Breakdown analysis
   - Financing requirements
   - Current financing sources
   - Tax consequences
8. **Risk Management**
   - Country risk
   - Commercial risk
   - Credit risk
   - Currency risk
   - Market risk
   - Political risk
9. **External Assistance**
   - Export America
   - U.S. Commerce Department
   - Census Bureau
   - Customs and Border Protection
   - www.export.gov
   - International Trade Administration
   - U.S. Export-Import Bank
   - National, regional, and local organizations
   - Cross-border trade consultancies
10. **Implementation Schedule**
    - Operational time line
    - Performance milestones
    - Contingency plans

place, many follow hunches about foreign markets—i.e.,"China is growing so fast that there must be many people there who want my product." Likewise, it is tough to try to conquer customers from Bonn to Beijing to Benares in a day. A useful rule is to look at a few markets where the odds favor success rather than trying to sell to the world.[116] Useful questions to debate during the development of an export plan include:

- Am I committed to exporting?
- Would our resources be better utilized developing our domestic businesses?
- What do we want to gain from exporting?

- Is exporting consistent with our long-term goals?
- What need does my product or service fill in the targeted foreign market?
- Are there competitive products?
- How much will it cost to get the product to the foreign market?
- Will exporting put undue demands on management, production, finance, and marketing?
- Does exporting leverage our core competency?
- Does exporting fit our value chain configuration?
- Do our coordination and control systems support exporting?
- Do the financial and strategic benefits of exporting exceed its direct and indirect costs?

Last, like yin and yang, import and export are complementary opposites within the greater whole of international trade. Strategic and practical aspects of the import process mirror those of the export process. So, just as the international transaction chain includes a sensitivity to those export and import issues, so too with the export plan. Changing the terminology from "export" to "import" does not require changing the contents of the plan. Rather, companies adjust their analytics, interpreting events from the analogous perspective of importing.

Looking to the Future

Technology and International Trade

The transaction costs of international trade steadily decrease. Advances in transportation and communications systems, by making it easier and cheaper to trade, accelerate export and import activity. The Internet helps individuals throughout the world engage each other easily and quickly. Online filing of cargo manifests, customs documents, and transit forms expedites shipments. Customs software that works in Hamburg or Sydney is also used in Hong Kong and Long Beach. Also, more parties track the shipment than not; the originating shipper, transit depots, and other suppliers and customs agents, along with the buyer and seller, monitor the flow. All in all, greater flexibility and improving efficiency let companies engage an expanding range of export and import options.

Synchronizing import or export activities redefines the way companies, both big and small, connect with foreign buyers and sellers. Historically, big companies reaped the biggest rewards. Their superior resources and organizational competencies positioned them to capture advances in moving goods, funds, and information. Now, the technology of trade seems to offer bigger benefits to smaller companies. Improving technologies create online, software, and logistics platforms that blur the distinction between the big, global giant and the small, neighborhood startup. In fact, it has become harder to tell the difference between an SME operating on a shoestring budget and its larger counterpart.

Online Platforms

Increasingly, companies look to online technologies to start or expand exporting. They rely on the Internet as their primary channel for getting information, sourcing products, finding suppliers, marketing products, and tapping new markets. In many cases, companies build a virtual value chain online, running export transactions from start to finish without ever leaving their hometowns. The inexorable expansion of the Internet gives potential and practicing international traders nearly infinite resources. They can browse through catalog archives, business-to-business exchanges, electronic trade boards, consumer surveys, online trade journals, and virtual trade shows to find a product to import or a market for their export.

Increasingly, as SMEs throughout the world gain Internet access for the first time, they use online platforms to build their export businesses. Besides introducing mom-and-pop shops from around the world to each other, websites open a vast and largely uncharted small-business hinterland in markets from Tibet to Patagonia. Long the unseen production sites for many pieces of the global economy, these small companies had to trade within the context of global supply chains directed by large MNEs. Now, going online lets them go straight to buyers or sellers.

Software Platforms

A burst of business software in the past few years has "created a total revolution in what small businesses are able to accomplish overseas."[117] Collaborative software lets entrepreneurial exporters with single-digit head counts track foreign vendors without traveling the world. For example, U.S.-based Edgar Blazona used to log 100,000 miles of travel annually, visiting factories in the Far East. Now he uses two factories—one in Thailand and one in India—to manufacture his furniture designs that he then imports into the United States. A meeting and document-sharing program lets him work in real time with his overseas factories. Costing less than $100 per month, this software coordinates workflows, expedites exchanges, and eases communications.

Similarly, Evertek Computer Corporation, a U.S. SME, has capitalized on software innovations to build e-commerce Web sites and portals that expand its market frontier. In 1990, Evertek began selling new and refurbished computers and parts; by 2008, it had become the world's largest closeout computer wholesaler, clearance computer supplier, and closeout electronics wholesaler. Within a year of purchasing BuyUSA.com, an Internet-based program from the U.S. Commerce Department that identifies buyers around the world, Evertek began selling in 10 new countries, with single purchases reaching up to $75,000. In 2010, international sales zoomed to $34 million, an increase of 84 percent from the previous year, on exports to 105 countries.

Other companies use similarly innovative programs to manage overseas factories with tools that once were reserved for big MNEs. China Manufacturing Network, for instance, relies on its 10-person staff in California to coordinate production of industrial devices among more than 90 independent factories in China, Malaysia, and Singapore. It uses on-demand, scalable enterprise software to track activity orders, monitor build rates, and manage inventory across its manufacturing network.

Logistics Platforms

Improving logistics helps SMEs move products more cheaply and easily to more places. High-tech, low-cost shipping services rob big firms of a long-running competitive advantage. Now, the no-name, one-person exporter down the street from you, because of its big-name shipping partners spanning the globe, has many of the same logistics capabilities commanded by a large MNE but at a fraction of the cost. In fact, SMEs increasingly have as much, if not a bit more, logistic flexibility. Unlike big companies that rely on their in-house systems, SMEs pick and choose solutions from freight forwarders and 3PLs—think of the ease of using FedEx, for example. The small international trader can hire any of these sorts of intermediaries to warehouse, truck, sail, fly, and deliver goods from factories in Asia to customers in Europe—all the while never taking physical possession of the goods.

South West Trading in Arizona, a family-owned startup, imports yarns made from bamboo, corn, and soy fibers by fabric plants in China. When South West Trading suffered recurring logistics problems as it imported products from China, UPS provided an efficient solution. Its Shanghai facility consolidated orders from various Chinese factories into one transport container, supervised customs paperwork, shipped it, and trucked the goods to South West Trading's warehouse in Phoenix. The company's bottom line immediately benefited. Where it once paid $9,400 to run four China-to-Arizona shipments per month, its once-a-month UPS shipment costs about $3,600 and reliably takes 21 days to travel.

The Great Leveling

Improving online, software, and logistics platforms, by improving the technology of trade, levels the playing field of international trade.[118] The combination of ubiquitous, fast Internet connections and cheap, plentiful, cloud-based computing power make it easier to export and import. Big and small companies respond to these trends, confident that technology will create tools that let them jump hurdles and capture opportunities. SMEs, in particular, stand to prosper from the improving technology of trade. Perhaps most significantly, technology decouples the issues of size and capability. Observed the CEO of China Manufacturing, "Our customers can't really tell how big we are. In a way, it's irrelevant. What matters is that we can get the job done."[119] ■

CONCEPT CHECK

Recall our discussions of poverty in Chapters 4 and 5. Here, we point out that shortages of resources impoverish nations as well as individuals. Some countries struggle to acquire the foreign reserves they need to purchase goods from other nations. If unsuccessful, they may resort to countertrade.

COUNTERTRADE

Currency or credit—easy, fast, and straightforward—are the preferred payment options for export or import transactions. Sometimes, though, companies face the harsh reality that buyers cannot pay in cash because the home country's currency is nonconvertible or the nation holds scant reserves or has insufficient credit. Consequently, if they wish to trade, they must resort to other means.

Consider the following transactions. Coca-Cola has traded its syrup for cheese from the Soviet Union, oranges from Egypt, tomato paste from Turkey, Polish beer, and soft drink bottles from Hungary. Malaysia swapped palm oil for fertilizer and machinery with North Korea, Cuba, and Russia and was negotiating deals with Morocco, Jordan, Syria, and Iran. Thailand, the world's largest exporter of rice, has been negotiating rice-for-oil deals with Middle Eastern countries, whereas the Philippines, the world's largest importer of rice, secured rice supplies through an agreement with Vietnam.[120] Boeing exchanged ten 747s for 34 million barrels of Saudi Arabian oil. Argentina awarded a fertilizer factory to Czechoslovakian firms with the stipulation that suppliers buy vegetables and other agricultural goods produced with fertilizer.[121]

These sorts of trades fall under the umbrella term **countertrade.** Any one of several different arrangements that parties use to trade products via transactions that use limited or no currency or credit qualify as a countertrade. Table 14.7 identifies its principal forms.[122]

Countertrade is an umbrella term for several sorts of trade, such as barter or offset, in which the seller accepts goods or services, rather than currency or credit, as payment.

Inconsistent disclosure hinders estimating the volume of countertrade. Secretive government-to-government deals and disguised transactions are not unusual. Roughly, more than 80 countries nowadays use or require countertrade. These transactions comprise anywhere between 5 to 15 percent of the world trade.[123] Countertrade generally increases in economies that are experiencing economic problems. Since the latter is a seeming inevitability, given the boom-bust market dynamics in many countries, countertrade is likely an enduring feature of international trade.

Countertrade has several disadvantages:

- Inefficiency
- Risk
- Complicated

COSTS

Countertrade, put simply, is an inefficient way of doing business. Companies prefer the efficiency of cash or credit to settle a transaction—all it requires is consulting foreign-exchange tables to set exchange rates. Countertrade, instead, requires buyers and sellers to rely on

TABLE 14.7 Common Forms of Countertrade

The unusual circumstances that surround countertrade transactions leads agents to use different forms in different situations. Here, we see commonly used forms.

Barter	Products are exchanged directly for products of equal value without the use of money as a means of purchase or payment.
Buyback	A supplier of capital or equipment agrees to accept future output generated by the investment as payment. For example: The exporter of equipment to a chemical plant may be repaid with output from the factory to whose owner it "sold" the equipment.
Offset	An exporter sells products for cash and then helps the importer find opportunities to earn hard currency for payment. Offsets are most common when big-ticket products (e.g., military equipment) are involved.
Switch or Swap Trading	One company sells to another its obligation to purchase something in a foreign country. They carry this label because the arrangement often involves switching the documentation and destination of merchandise while it's in transit.
Counter purchase	A company that sells products to a foreign country promises to make a future purchase of a specific product made in that country. A supplier agrees to purchase products from a foreign buyer as a condition of getting the buyer's order.

nonmarket forces to set the value of the trade, negotiating some standards such as how many tons of rice for how many farm tractors. Agreeing to "payment" is not the only hurdle. The traded goods may be of poor quality, packaged unattractively, or difficult to sell and service. Consequently, countertrade deals are prone to price, financial, and quality distortion. Ultimately, countertrade and its variations threaten free market forces with protectionism and price-fixing. Unchecked, trade relations tend toward inefficiency.

BENEFITS

Companies and countries often use countertrade to build mutually beneficial relationships.

The reality of international trade means that countertrade is often unavoidable for companies that want to do business with buyers who have limited or no access to cash or credit. Although some dislike it, companies and countries in tough binds use it to generate jobs, preserve foreign exchange holdings, and develop trade relationships. Countertrade helps countries reduce their need to borrow working capital and gives them access to companies' technological skills and marketing expertise. Companies also benefit; they can resolve bad debts, repatriate blocked funds, or build customer relationships. In addition, accepting countertrade signals a seller's good faith and flexibility. Such sensitivities can position a firm to gain preferential market access in the future.

CASE A Little Electronic Magic at Alibaba.com

E-commerce, by changing the way companies around the world do business, makes trade easier and cheaper.[124] Before the Internet, tracking down a product to import, or finding foreign customers to export to, was daunting for the typical SME. Most relied on occasional trade shows and expensive, time-consuming foreign travel to identify possible products or assess potential suppliers. Certainly, traders could tap local embassies or consulates to support export promotion or provide import assistance. Although sounding straightforward, in practice they typically proved cumbersome. Consequently, international trade was largely limited to big companies that could afford to attend trade shows, translate brochures, travel internationally, hire intermediaries, and supervise the many activities that comprise the export transaction chain (see Figure 14.5).

Today, the Internet gives SMEs cost-effective means to manage these demands. It makes information on any conceivable product from virtually any market readily and inexpensively accessible. Falling trade barriers, courtesy of the WTO, and more efficient logistics from 3PLs like FedEx, DHL, and UPS offer an array of trade possibilities.[125] The Internet, simply put, transforms whatever it touches. It is already the most powerful force for globalization, democratization, economic growth, and education in history. The same, we see, applies to the game of international trade.

The emergence of country-specific portals and Web exchanges accelerates this trend. Replicating what eBay has done for consumer-to-consumer e-commerce, several sites offer online bazaars for international traders. Here, exporters can lay out their wares on the digital carpet and haggle with potential buyers from the far corners of the world. For instance, potential importers looking for products from South Korea can access www.koreatradeworld.

com; those targeting India can check out www.trade-india.com; those focusing on Europe need only visit www.bizeurope.com to tap into high-quality trade boards. One can also shop the world at www.tradekey.com.

These and similar sites promote the commercial potential of a country or region. They provide direct services to large and small international traders, such as export training, cyber trade infrastructures, international special exhibitions, virtual trade shows, and trade strategies. Conceptually, their mission is direct: connect sellers in one place to buyers in another. Operationally, they provide powerful business-to-business tools that improve the mechanics of trade, creating flexible and dynamic platforms that let buyers and sellers of everything from bamboo toothpicks to industrial equipment find each other, negotiate the terms of trade, and seal the deal.

Alibaba: Opening Global Markets

Spearheading these changes is Alibaba, a Chinese Internet company that specializes in introducing Chinese manufacturers to buyers worldwide. Founded in 1999 by Jack Ma, who has been dubbed "the Father of the Chinese Internet," Alibaba makes international trade cheaper, faster, and easier. Based in Hangzhou, about a two-hour drive south of Shanghai, it began operations with the goal of getting big by staying small. Jack Ma believes that his target customers are SMEs, not MNEs—or, in his words, "shrimps," not "whales."

The Framework

Making this happen is the call of www.alibaba.com, an English-language global trade website that connects international buyers with Chinese sellers. Today, it is the world's largest online business-to-business marketplace, reaching Internet users in more than 240 countries and territories. The site supports an interactive community of millions of buyers and sellers who meet, greet, chat, and trade online. Running an online global trade fair, Alibaba enables "shrimps" with import and export ambition but tight budgets to reach the global market. Alibaba also provides an array of business management software, Internet infrastructure services, payment processing, and export-related services.

Many Alibaba users are SMEs in developing countries around the world, from rural areas to large cities, in countries such as Kyrgyzstan, Sierra Leone, and Peru. Few are glamorous and high-tech; most are low-tech firms making labor-intensive, scale-insensitive products. However, Alibaba provides tools to expand their market reach and grow their businesses. An SME, working from the smallest apartment anywhere in the world, yet on the grid, can conceivably create a global business.

Operations

The mechanics of Alibaba are straightforward: Importers around the world shop the site, looking for potential products from a mind-boggling array of goods—as hinted by the adjacent image of Alibaba's home page. Alibaba has organized more than a thousand product categories, each with many subcategories, and offers new channels to trade services. The classic garage inventor in Caracas or Chicago has the option to design a product and then use Alibaba to find Chinese factories that will make, package, and ship it to customers worldwide.

Operationally, buyers use Alibaba to find potential suppliers, thereby eliminating the need to hire a local representative to negotiate with Chinese manufacturers. For example, an enterprising company in Argentina looking to buy 500 DVD players can visit Alibaba.com, search among the dozens of potential suppliers, learn their terms of trade, contact the preferred vendor, negotiate the specifics, and set the deal in motion. Said the cofounder of www.meetchina.com, a similar e-commerce site, "We want to make buying 1,000 bicycles from China as easy as buying a book from Amazon.com."[126]

Trust and Transparency

As a rule, importers worry about being defrauded by unknown suppliers. More practically, how does an importer in Buenos Aires find a trustworthy supplier in Guangzhou? As sites like Alibaba inject more transparency into trade, buyers worry less about fraud. Alibaba users, like those on similar e-commerce sites, post information about their companies and review information about a vendor's reliability from other users. Buyers access Alibaba's profiles of its registered users, as well as the seller's posted references, to verify their status. These data let the importer in Argentina crosscheck the credibility of potential trade partners.

This system of checks and balances is how Alibaba makes money. It offers a basic service of listing a company and its products on its site free of charge, then generates revenue from more than 100,000 members who pay a few hundred to several thousand dollars annually for services such as personalized Web pages, high-quality online introduction, and priority listing of products. It has also increasingly generates revenue from online advertising.

Crisis and Change

The global financial crisis, Jack Ma reasoned, created an opportunity to transform Alibaba from a China-focused e-commerce provider into a global Web marketplace. "Before this financial crisis, we were helping China's products abroad," Ma says. "Now we are thinking about helping small and medium-sized enterprises in other parts of the world." Ma also saw the chance to expand China's historic outward flow of products to the world to include flows throughout the world. "We want to help them sell across the nations, help them sell to China," he explains. "I believe in the next three years, China will be one of the world's largest buying markets. China needs to buy these things."[127]

As the crisis diminished, Alibaba set its sights higher. It now plans to build a network of warehouses across China to transform the country's logistics business. Ma explains, "Hopefully within 10 years' time, anyone placing an order online from anywhere in China will receive their goods within eight hours, allowing for the virtual urbanization of every village across China.... In order to achieve this, we will need to establish a modern, 21st-century logistics network." In addition, Alibaba expanded AliExpress to offer traders warehousing, shipping, and logistics options. Essentially, noted an analyst, Alibaba "wants to be Amazon."[128] Steadily, it has done so; in late 2012, Jack Ma suggested, "It's very likely that next year, our transaction volume will be bigger than all the American e-commerce companies combined."[129]

QUESTIONS

14-2. Do you think most international trade might eventually take place through websites like Alibaba.com? How might that influence your interest in importing and exporting?

14-3. Identify a product you would like to import. Visit www.alibaba.com, go to the advanced search field, and enter it. Select required criteria and click on "Search." Review the list of companies that qualify. Find a suitable seller. Analyze this process for ease, usefulness, and potential value.

14-4. Identify and describe three benefits and three costs of using websites like Alibaba to export and import.

14-5. Visit www.alibaba.com, www.trade-india.com, and www.europages.com. Compare and contrast these Web sites from the view of the seller to the buyer.

14-6. Provide three recommendations that you would offer a SME, based on the opportunities and constraints of electronic websites like Alibaba, as it considers engaging exporting or importing.

14-7. How transparent do sites like Alibaba.com make import-export transactions? To what degree would you worry about fraud? What safeguards would you seek?

SUMMARY

- Exporting refers to the sale of goods or services produced by a company based in one country to customers that reside in another. Importing is the opposite: the purchase of a product by a buyer in one country from a seller in another.
- A company's export activity is (1) related to but not determined by its size and (2) related to and often determined by a range of firm-specific characteristics, such as management interest, production efficiency, labor costs, and R&D advantages that are independent of its size.
- The incremental internationalization view holds that exporting begins as a sequential process of deliberate trial and reasonable error that leads a company to expand from its home market to the most geographically and psychologically proximate markets. It then progressively expands to customers in more distant and dissimilar countries.
- The born-global perspective holds that companies step straight onto the world stage, engaging international trade from inception.
- The idea of serendipity refers to so-called accidental traders who, responding to happenstance or odd circumstances, successfully begin exporting or importing.
- A service import does not result in ownership and is rendered by nonresidents to the local residents in a country.
- The macro and micro benefits of international trade spur governments to help potential and active exporters.
- Exporters may deal directly with agents or distributors in a foreign country or indirectly through third-party intermediaries, such as export management firms or other types of trading companies.
- Trading companies perform many functions that regularly pose problems for clients that lack export and import expertise.
- Freight forwarders act as agents for international traders in supervising the movement of goods to foreign buyers.
- Third-party logistics (3PLs) help traders understand their current practices, identify opportunities and risks, and improve the efficiency of logistics.
- Countertrade is any one of several different arrangements by which products are traded in transactions that do not involve cash or credit.

KEY TERMS

born global
countertrade
customs broker
direct exporting
exporting
export intermediaries
export plan
freight forwarder
importing
incremental internationalization
indirect exporting
serendipity
small and medium-sized enterprise (SME)
third-party logistics

ENDNOTES

1 ***Sources include the following:*** Case developed based on profiles of company management, company activities, and country profiles reported at www.export.gov; United States International Trade Administration; United States Census Bureau, *Profile of U.S. Exporting Companies,* at www.census.gov/foreign-trade/aip/edbrel-0203.pdf; *Small & Medium-Sized Exporting Companies: Statistical Overview,* tse.export.gov/EDB/SelectReports.aspx?DATA=ExporterDB. SpinCent represents the reported experiences of active exporters as well as the observations expressed by their management. In particular, please visit www.export.gov/articles/successstories/eg_success_story_021417.asp for an overview of the source documents.

2 The Ex-Im Bank is the official export-credit agency of the United States. It help create and maintain U.S. jobs by financing the sales of U.S. exports, primarily to emerging markets, providing loan guarantees, export-credit insurance, and direct loans.

3 "WTO Releases 2011 Trade and Tariff Data," retrieved December 18, 2012 from www.wto.org/english/news_e/news12_e/stat_23oct12_e.htm.

4 Joe Dermody, "Emerging Markets Play Growing Role in Exports Growth," *Irish Examiner,* December 4, 2012.

5 "A Profile of U.S. Importing and Exporting Companies, 2009 – 2010," U.S. Department of Commerce, retrieved April 24, 2013, from www.census.gov/foreign-trade/Press-Release/edb/2010/edbrel.pdf.

6 Ibid.

7 Francisco Sánchez, "No Better Export: Higher Education - Commentary - The Chronicle of Higher Education," retrieved May 3, 2011, from chronicle.com/article/No-Better-Export-Higher/126989; John Siegmund, "Higher Education Shows a Big Trade Surplus for the United States, International Trade Administration," retrieved May 15, 2013, from trade.gov/press/publications/newsletters/ita_0909/higher_0909.asp.

8 Tamara Baluja, "Canada Must Attract Foreign Students to Fuel Innovation, Drive Economy," *The Globe and Mail,* August 14, 2012.

9 John H. Dunning, "The Eclectic Paradigm of International Production: Some Empirical Tests," *Journal of International Business Studies* (Spring 1988): 1–31.

10 "A Profile of U.S. Importing and Exporting Companies, 2009–2010."

11 "A Profile of U.S. Importing and Exporting Companies, 2009–2010"; USITC, "Small and Medium-Sized Enterprises: Overview of Participation in U.S. Exports," January 2010; USITC, "Small and

Medium-Sized Enterprises: U.S. and EU Export Activities, and Barriers and Opportunities Experienced by U.S. Firms," July 2010.

12 Hernan Roxas, Vai Lindsay, Nicholas Ashill, and Antong Victorio, "Institutional Analysis of Strategic Choice of Micro, Small, and Medium Enterprises: Development of a Conceptual Framework," *Singapore Management Review* 30.2 (July–Dec 2008): 47; Nancy Ku, "SMEs Look to Non-traditional Lenders," *China Brief*, American Chamber of Commerce in China (March 2009).

13 S. Cavusgil and S. Zou, "Marketing Strategic Performance Relationship," *Journal of Marketing* (1994); J. Meran and A. Moini, "Firm's Export Behavior," *American Business Review* (1999): 86.

14 D. Greenway, J. Gullstrand, and R. Kneller, "Exporting May Not Always Boost Firm Productivity," *Review of World Economics*, 4 (December 1, 2005): 561–82.

15 L. Yun, "Determinants of Export Intensity and FDI Presence: Case of Manufacturing Industries of Guangdong Province, the People's Republic of China," *International Journal of Logistics Systems and Management* (2006): 230–54.

16 B. Aw, M. Roberts, D. Xu, "R&D Investment, Exporting, and Productivity Dynamics," retrieved December 18, 2012, from www.econ.psu.edu/~mroberts/arxmarch2010.pdf.

17 D. Crick, "UK SMEs' Motives for Internationalizing: Differences between Firms Employing Particular Overseas Market Servicing Strategies," *Journal of International Entrepreneurship* (2007): 11–23, retrieved May 15, 2011.

18 Coffee & More, LLC, retrieved May 15, 2011, from www.export.gov/articles/successstories/eg_success_story_022775.asp.

19 Certified Worldwide LLC, retrieved May 15, 2011, from www.export.gov/articles/successstories/eg_success_story_020902.asp.

20 A. Bernard and B. Jensen, "Exceptional Exporter Performance: Cause, Effect, or Both?" retrieved December 18, 2012, from www.nber.org/papers/w6272.

21 Elena Golovko and Giovanni Valentini, "Exploring the Complementarity Between Innovation and Export for SME's Growth," *Journal of International Business Studies*, 42: 362–80, 2011.

22 Domes International, retrieved May 15, 2011, from www.export.gov/articles/successstories/eg_success_story_021027.asp.

23 USITC, "Small and Medium-Sized Enterprises: Overview of Participation in U.S. Exports," January 2010; USITC, "Small and Medium-Sized Enterprises: U.S. and EU Export Activities, and Barriers and Opportunities Experienced by U.S. Firms," July 2010.

24 "Jarden Zinc Products of Tennessee," retrieved December 17, 2012, from export.gov/articles/successstories/eg_main_035140.asp.

25 "Hey Big Spenders," *The World in 2012, The Economist*, retrieved December 22, 2012 from www.economist.com/theworldin/2012.

26 "Global Development Horizons 2011—Multipolarity: The New Global Economy," *The World Bank*, retrieved May 30, 2011, from web.worldbank.org/wbsite/external/extdec/extdecprospects/extgdh/0,,menupk:7933477~pagepk:64167702~pipk:64167676~thesitepk:7933464,00.html.

27 Hans Gemunden, "Success Factors of Export Marketing: A Meta-Analytic Critique of the Empirical Studies," in *New Perspectives on International Marketing*, (Ed.) S. Paliwoda (London: Routledge, 1991): 33–62; Julia Armario, David Ruiz, and Enrique Armario, "Market Orientation and Internationalization in Small and Medium-Sized Enterprises," *Journal of Small Business Management* (October 2008): 485.

28 "Schumpeter: The Case against Globaloney," *The Economist* (April 23, 2011): 72.

29 Analytical Graphics, Inc., Profile at export.gov, retrieved December 15, 2012, from export.gov/articles/successstories/eg_main_033668.asp.

30 Paul Westhead, Mike Wright, and Deniz Ucbasaran, "International Market Selection Strategies Selected by 'Micro' and 'Small' Firms," *Omega* (February 2002): 51.

31 McKinsey & Co. (1993), "Emerging Exporters: Australia's High Value-added Manufacturing Exporters," Melbourne: Australian Manufacturing Council, retrieved May 17, 2011, from catalogue.nla.gov.au/Record/2621131.

32 Examples cited in T. Koed Madsen and P. Servais, "The Internationalization of Born Globals: An Evolutionary Process?" *International Business Review* (1997): 561–83.

33 O. Moen, R. Sorbeim, and T. Erikson. "Born Global Firms and Informal Investors: Examining Investor Characteristics," *Journal of Small Business Management* (October 2008): 536.

34 Evertek Computer Corp., retrieved May 15, 2011, from www.export.gov/articles/successstories/eg_success_story_021490.asp.

35 Ibid.

36 Ibid.

37 Country percentages calculated from data reported at: U.S. International Trade In Goods and Services (www.census.gov/foreign-trade/statistics/historical/), 1992: U.S. trade in goods with China, (www.census.gov/foreign-trade/balance/c5700.html#1992), and 1992: U.S. trade in goods with Mexico (www.census.gov/foreign-trade/balance/c2010.html).

38 Small & Medium-Sized Exporting Companies: Statistical Overview, 2010, International Trade Administration, retrieved December 15, 2012, from www.trade.gov/mas/ian/smeoutlook/index.asp#P44_5045; USITC, "Small and Medium-Sized Enterprises: Overview of Participation in U.S. Exports," January 2010; USITC, "Small and Medium-Sized Enterprises: U.S. and EU Export Activities, and Barriers and Opportunities Experienced by U.S. Firms," July 2010.

39 Daniel Sullivan and Alan Bauerschmidt, "Incremental Internationalization: A Test of Johanson and Vahlne's Thesis," *Management International Review* (1990): 19–30.

40 Some folks object to the abrasives, flavors, tartar-control agents, and bleaches found in mass-market toothpaste.

41 Mark Stein, "Export Opportunities Aren't Just for the Big Guys," *New York Times* (March 24, 2005): C1.

42 Vellus Products, retrieved May 15, 2011, from www.export.gov/articles/successstories/eg_main_020763.asp.

43 Adapted from *A Basic Guide to Exporting*, 10th edition (Washington, D.C.: Commerce Dept., International Trade Administration, 2011).

44 Mark Stein, "Export Opportunities Aren't Just for the Big Guys," *New York Times* (March 24, 2005): C1.

45 In 2007, for example, an estimated 85 percent of foreign sales by large firms were conducted through foreign affiliates of U.S. firms, versus approximately 16 percent of foreign sales conducted via direct exports; Source: "Small and Medium-Sized Enterprises: Overview of Participation in U.S. Exports."

46 "Small and Medium-Sized Enterprises: Characteristics and Performance," United States International Trade Commission, Investigation No. 332-510, USITC Publication 4189, November 2010.

47 Jiang Jingjing, "Walmart's China Inventory to Hit US $18B this Year," *China Business Weekly*, retrieved November 29, 2004, from www.chinadaily.com.cn/english/doc/2004–11/29/content_395728.htm.

48 Anna Thomas and Susan Bridgewater, "Internet and Exporting: Determinants of Success in Virtual Export Channels," *International Marketing Review* 21:4 (2004): 393.

49 Merlin Bettina, "Internet Marketing in Exports—A Useful Tool for Small Businesses," *Small Enterprise Development* (December 2004): 38.

50 Analytical Graphics, Inc., Profile at export.gov, retrieved Saturday, December 15, 2012 from export.gov/articles/successstories/eg_main_033668.asp.

51 Pascal-Emmanuel Gobry, "Asian Scalpers Are Wiping Out Apple's Supply Of iPad 2s In New York," retrieved May 31, 2011, from www.businessinsider.com/ipad-scalpers-new-york-2011-3.

52 Andrew Bernard, Bradford Jensen, and Peter Schott,"Importers, Exporters, and Multinationals: A Portrait of Firms in the U.S. that Trade Goods," NBER Working Paper No. 11404, June 2005.

53 "A Profile of U.S. Importing and Exporting Companies, 2009–2010," U.S. Department of Commerce, retrieved April 24, 2013, from www.census.gov/foreign-trade/Press-Release/edb/2010/edbrel.pdf; Statistical Overview, 2009, U.S. International Trade Administration, retrieved May 12, 2011 from www.trade.gov/mas/ian/smeoutlook/tg_ian_001925.asp.

54 Andrew Bernard, Bradford Jensen, and Peter Schott,"Importers, Exporters, and Multinationals: A Portrait of Firms in the U.S. that Trade Goods," NBER Working Paper No. 11404, June 2005.

55 Based on exchange rates of yuan to dollar of 0.154/$1 as of May 6, 2011.

56 Arguably, an unrealistic assumption but one that we make for the sake of convenience.

57 "Table 1: Civilian workers, by Major Occupational and Industry Group," *U.S. Bureau of Labor Statistics,* retrieved May 9, 2011, from www.bls.gov/news.release/ecec.t01.htm.

58 "How much would the iPad 2 Cost if it was made in the U.S.A?" Stone Street Advisors, retrieved May 9, 2011, from stonestreetadvisors.com/2011/05/06/how-much-would-the-ipad-2-cost-if-it-was-made-in-the-u-s-a; Andrew Rassweiler,"iPad 2 Carries Bill of Materials of $326.60, IHS iSuppli Teardown Analysis Shows," retrieved May 9, 2011, from www.isuppli.com/teardowns/news/pages/ipad-2-carries-bill-of-materials-of-$326-60-ihs-isuppli-teardown-analysis-shows.aspx.

59 J. Laurie Flynn,"Poor Nations Are Littered with Old PC's, Report Says," *New York Times* (October 24, 2005): C2.

60 "Africa Waste Trade," retrieved May 4, 2011, from www1.american.edu/TED/oauwaste.htm; Estimates for developed economies taken from Hazardous Waste Disposal, www.uos.harvard.edu/ehs/environmental/hw_faq_answers.shtml; Leslie Kaufman,"A Green Way to Dump Low-Tech Electronics," *New York Times* (June 30, 2009).

61 Helen Baulch,"Error: Dumping Does Not Compute," *Alternatives Journal* (Summer 2002): 2.

62 "Electronic Waste in Guiyu" *Wikipedia*, retrieved December 22, 2012 from en.wikipedia.org/wiki/Electronic_waste_in_Guiyu.

63 Elisabeth Rosenthal,"Recycled Battery Lead Puts Mexicans in Danger," NYTimes.com, retrieved December 23, 2012 from www.nytimes.com/2011/12/09/science/earth/recycled-battery-lead-puts-mexicans-in-danger.html?pagewanted=all&_r=0.

64 Reported by Karl Schoenberger,"E-Waste Ignored in India," *Mercury News,* retrieved May 4, 2011, from www.ban.org/ban_news/ ewaste_ignored_031228.html.

65 Matthew Khan,"Environmental and Urban Economics: October 2005," retrieved February 25, 2013, from greeneconomics.blogspot.com/2005_10_01_archive.html.

66 "After Dump, What Happens to Electronic Waste?" *NPR,* retrieved April 19, 2011, from www.npr.org/2010/12/21/132204954/after-dump-what-happens-to-electronic-waste.

67 Michelle Castillo,"Electronic Waste: Where Does It Go and What Happens To It?" TIME.com, retrieved February 25, 2013, from techland.time.com/2011/01/14/electronic-waste-where-does-it-go-and-what-happens-to-it/.

68 Elisabeth Rosenthal,"Recycled Battery Lead Puts Mexicans in Danger," *NYTimes.com,* retrieved February 25, 2013 from www.nytimes.com/2011/12/09/science/earth/recycled-battery-lead-puts-mexicans-in-danger.html?pagewanted=all&_r=0.

69 Helen Baulch,"Error: Dumping Does Not Compute," *Alternatives Journal* (Summer 2002): 2.

70 "The Digital Dump: Exporting Reuse and Abuse to Africa," *Basel Action Network,* retrieved May 4, 2011, from www.ban.org/banreports/10-24-05/index.htm.

71 Basel Action Network, retrieved May 5, 2007, from www.ban.org/index.html; Flynn,"Poor Nations Littered with Old PCs."

72 "E-Waste Importers," *Hazardous Waste Superfund Week* (December 23, 2002).

73 "Where Does E-Waste End Up?" retrieved May 4, 2011, from www.greenpeace.org/international/campaigns/toxics/electronics/where-does-e-waste-end-up.

74 Kaufman,"A Green Way to Dump Low-Tech Electronics"; "The Politics of E-waste: A Cadmium Lining," *The Economist,* (January 26, 2013): 56.

75 See "Secretariat of the Basel Convention, Competent Authorities," retrieved March 26, 2009, from www.basel.int. By definition, a "Competent Authority" means one governmental authority designated by a Party to be responsible within such geographic areas as the Party may think fit, for receiving the notification of a transboundary movement of hazardous wastes or other wastes, and any information related to it, and for responding to such a notification. Also, see en.wikipedia.org/wiki/Basel_Convention.

76 *Small & Medium-Sized Exporting Companies: Statistical Overview,* tse.export.gov/EDB/SelectReports.aspx?DATA=ExporterDB.

77 L. Leonidou,"An Analysis of the Export Barriers Hindering Small Business Export Development," *Journal of Small Business Management* (2004): 279–302; Martina Battisti and Martin Perry,"Creating Opportunity for Small-firm Exporters through Regional Free Trade Agreements: A Strategic Perspective from New Zealand," *Australasian Journal of Regional Studies* (2008): 275–86.

78 OECD, OECD-APEC paper on removing barriers to SME access to international market (2006). See also Alan Bauerschmidt, Daniel Sullivan, and Kate Gillespie,"Common Factors Underlying Barriers to Export Studies in the U.S. Paper Industry," *Journal of International Business Studies,* 16:3 (1985): 111–23.

79 "Congress Pushes More Export Financing for Small Business," *Associated Press* (September 5, 2006).

80 John Kerr,"Exporters Need to Connect with Customers," *Logistics Management* (March 1, 2006): 41.

81 O'Gorman, C. (2000),"Strategy and the Small Firm," In S. Carter and D. Jones-Evans (Eds.), *Enterprise and Small Business: Principles, Practice, and Policy* (Harlow: Prentice Hall, FT Pearson).

82 "A Profile of U.S. Importing and Exporting Companies, 2009–2010."

83 Spectra Colors of NJ, retrieved May 15, 2011, from www.export.gov/articles/successstories/eg_success_story_023038.asp.

84 Banerjee,"REACH-Like Regulations Enacted Globally: A Regulatory World Tour," ICIS Chemical Business, May 26, 2010 (accessed June 25, 2010). For a more detailed information about REACH, see European Chemicals Agency Helsinki,"About Reach," (accessed June 25, 2010); European Commission, Enterprise and Industry, Chemicals,"REACH: Registration, Evaluation, Authorization and Restriction of Chemicals," (accessed June 25, 2010).

85 U.S. Trade Representative, 2010 National Trade Estimate Report on Foreign Trade Barriers, 2010.

86 U.S. Department of Commerce, International Trade Administration, "Country Commercial Guide: Thailand," February 18, 2008, 64.

87 U.S. Trade Representative, 2010 National Trade Estimate Report on Foreign Trade Barriers, 2010.

88 WTO, Trade Policy Review: India, April 18, 2007, 147.

89 "China to Amazon Re: Kindle Store: Not So Fast," DBW, retrieved December 17, 2012, from www.digitalbookworld.com/2012/china-to-amazon-re-kindle-store-not-so-fast/.

90 Kerr, "Exporters Need to Connect with Customers."

91 "Schumpeter: The Case against Globaloney," *The Economist* (April 20, 2011): 52.

92 "Exporters Hit by Air Freight Restrictions" *Telegraph*, retrieved December 21, 2012 from www.telegraph.co.uk/finance/yourbusiness/8860814/Exporters-hit-by-air-freight-restrictions.html.

93 "A 'Green Zone' for Firms in Ciudad Juárez: Business on the Bloody Border," *The Economist*, retrieved December 22, 2012 from www.economist.com/node/21540262; "Canada and the United States: The Border Two-step," *The Economist*, retrieved December 22, 2012 from www.economist.com/node/21541421.

94 Incoterms are the rules for the division of cost and risk in international sales transactions. They set three-letter standard trade terms that are commonly used in international sales contracts that help exporters avoid disputes with customers by specifying each party's responsibilities.

95 The commercial invoice, for instance, contains information such as the country of origin, the port of entry to which the merchandise is destined, information on the importer and exporter, a detailed description of the merchandise, including its purchase price, and the currency used for the sale.

96 "A Profile of U.S. Importing and Exporting Companies, 2009–2010."

97 Ibid.

98 Ibid.

99 Ibid.

100 Analytical Graphics, retrieved January 15, 2013, from export.gov/articles/successstories/eg_main_033668.asp.

101 "Garmin Marine Navigation GPS Units Navigate Turkish Customs," retrieved January 15, 2013, from export.gov/articles/successstories/eg_main_046466.asp.

102 Japan, for instance, relies on several offices, such as the Small and Medium Enterprise Agency, the Agency of Industrial Science and Technology, and the Ministry of International Trade and Industry. The latter, often referred to as MITI, develops policies and provides assistance to help Japanese companies trade.

103 Lee Li, "Joint Effects of Factors Affecting Exchanges Between Exporters and Their Foreign Intermediaries: An Exploratory Study," *Journal of Business & Industrial Marketing* (February–March 2003): 162–78. Trade intermediaries help navigate complex homeland security concerns. Increasing government regulation regarding what can be shipped where and to whom has prolonged border delays.

104 See U.S. Department of Commerce, *Guide to Exporting, 1998*, p. 20; Philip MacDonald, Practical Exporting and Importing, 2nd edition (New York: Ronald Press, 1959): 30–40.

105 Courtney Fingar, "ABCs of EMCs," The Federation of International Trade Associations (July 2001); Nelson T. Joyner, "How to Find and Use an Export Management Company," retrieved May 9, 2007, from www.fita.org/aotm/0499.html.

106 Geoffrey G Jones, *The Multinational Trader* (Routledge International Studies in Business History, 1998).

107 "Basic Question: To Export Yourself or to Hire Someone to Do It for You?" *Business America* (April 27, 1987): 14–17.

108 Because a practical discussion of importing procedures in every trading country of the world is impossible within this chapter, we focus on the matter of importing to the United States. We note that although U.S. import requirements and procedures provide a sufficient base for judging situations in other countries, a company must assess the importing regulations at play in those countries that it plans to engage. For an organizational chart of the U.S. Customs Bureau, including a roster of specific responsibilities, go to the home page of the U.S. Bureau of Customs and Border Protection, www.customs.ustreas.gov.

109 International Bank/World Bank, "Doing Business in 2007."

110 U.S. Department of the Treasury, U.S. Customs Service, *Importing into the United States* (Washington, DC: U.S. Government Printing Office, September 1991).

111 U.S. Department of Commerce, *Guide to Exporting* (Washington, DC: U.S. Government Printing Office, 1998): 63.

112 Certified Worldwide LLC, retrieved May 4, 2011, from www.export.gov/articles/successstories/eg_success_story_020902.asp.

113 Richard Armstrong, "The Top 40 3PLs 2010," *Logistics Quarterly Magazine* (2011).

114 Quote from CEO Robert Allen, Coffee & More, LLC, retrieved May 15, 2011, from www.export.gov/articles/successstories/eg_success_story_022775.asp.

115 Analytical Graphics, Inc., Profile at export.gov, retrieved December 15, 2012 from export.gov/articles/successstories/eg_main_033668.asp.

116 Benson Smith and Tony Rutigliano, *Discover Your Sales Strengths* (New York: Warner Business Books, 2003).

117 Julie Sloane, Justin Martin, and Alessandra Bianchi, "Small Companies That Play Big," *FSB Magazine* (November 1, 2006), quoting Ram Iyer.

118 Justin Lahart, "For Small Businesses, Big World Beckons," *WSJ.com*, retrieved January 27, 2011, from online.wsj.com/article/SB10001424052748703951704576092010276714424.html?mod=WSJ_hp_MIDDLENexttoWhatsNewsFifth.

119 Gary Hamel, "*What Matters Now: How to Win in a World of Relentless Change, Ferocious Competition, and Unstoppable Innovation* (Wiley, 2012).

120 Javier Blas, "Nations Turn to Barter Deals to Secure Food," *Financial Times*, retrieved March 11, 2009, from www.ft.com/cms/s/0/3e5c633c-ebdc-11dd-8838-0000779fd2ac.html; Dan West, "Countertrade—An Innovative Approach to Marketing," retrieved May 15, 2007, from www.barternews.com/approach_marketing.htm. On a more exotic note, Pepsi-Cola, which has the marketing rights for all Stolichnaya Vodka in the United States, delivers syrup that is paid for with Stolichnaya Vodka. In addition, early on, Pepsi took delivery of 17 submarines, a cruiser, a frigate, and a destroyer from the Russian government in payment for Pepsi products. In turn, Pepsi sold its "fleet" of 20 naval vessels for scrap steel, thereby paying for the Pepsi products sent to the Soviet Union.

121 V. S. Rama Rao, "Counter Trade," retrieved May 23, 2011, from www.citeman.com/2390-counter-trade.

122 One can divide countertrade into two classes: barter, based on clearing arrangements used to avoid money-based exchange; and buybacks, offsets, and counter purchases, which are used to impose reciprocal commitments between the various parties.

123 Dan West, "Countertrade—An Innovative Approach to Marketing," retrieved March 12, 2009, from BarterNews.com; "Counter trade," Wikipedia, retrieved December 20, 2012 from en.wikipedia.org/wiki/Counter_trade.

124 ***Sources include the following:*** Various sources at www.Alibaba.com; Forbes Global (April 25, 2005): 30; TradeStats Express, retrieved July 1, 2009, from tse.export.gov; John Heilemann, "Jack Ma Aims to Unlock the Middle Kingdom," *Business 2.0 Magazine*, (July 31, 2006); Jack Ma, "China Discovers Its Future," *International Herald Tribune* (December 17, 2008); "Alibaba Prepares for Global Expansion," *Financial Times* (January 19, 2009); "News on Alibaba.com, Business, Price Watch, Finance, Industry, Trade," retrieved December 21, 2012 from news.alibaba.com/; "China's Alibaba Group Q2 Net Profit Doubles: SEC Filing, Yahoo!, accessed December 21, 2012, ca.news.yahoo.com/chinas-alibaba-group-q2-net-profit-doubles-sec-043933703--sector.html; "Alibaba reaches 1 trillion RMB ($157B) in sales to become

biggest e-commerce company in the world, VentureBeat, accessed December 24, 2012, venturebeat.com/company/alibaba/.

125 The U.S. Small Business Administration estimates that the number of small companies exporting products tripled from 1994 through 2004. In terms of monetary flows, the value of exports from the United States grew from $731 billion in 2001 to $1.03 trillion in 2006, while imports grew from $1.14 trillion to $1.9 trillion.

126 "Fast as a Rabbit, Patient as a Turtle," *Forbes.com*, retrieved February 25, 2013 from www.forbes.com/forbes/2000/0717/6602074a_print.html.

127 "Alibaba Prepares for Global Expansion," *Financial Times*, retrieved February 25, 2013 from news.alibaba.com/article/detail/alibaba/100057556-1-alibaba-prepares-global-expansion.html.

128 "Alibaba wields its pricing power," *Asia Times Online*, retrieved February 17, 2011, from www.atimes.com/atimes/China_Business/MB18Cb01.html.

129 "Jack Ma," *Times of India*, retrieved December 21, 2012 from timesofindia.indiatimes.com/topic/Jack-Ma/quotes/.

CHAPTER 15

Forms and Ownership of Foreign Production

OBJECTIVES

After studying this chapter, you should be able to

1. Clarify why companies may use modes other than exporting to operate effectively in international business
2. Comprehend why and how companies make foreign direct investments
3. Understand the major motives that guide managers to choose a collaborative arrangement for international business
4. Compare the major types of collaborative arrangements
5. Describe what to consider when entering into international arrangements with other companies
6. Grasp why collaborative arrangements succeed or fail
7. See how companies can manage diverse collaborative arrangements
8. Appreciate how growth in project size and complexity will require more future collaboration

Source: © FM2 - Fotolia.com

MyManagementLab®

Improve Your Grade!

When you see this icon, visit **www.mymanagementlab.com** for activities that are applied, personalized, and offer immediate feedback.

If you can't beat them, join them.

—American proverb

CASE Meliá Hotels International

—Fidel León-Darder and Cristina Villar

"God bless the inventor of sleep."
(Miguel de Cervantes Saavedra, *Don Quijote de la Mancha*)

Li Feng arrived in London after a 13-hour flight from Beijing, her first company trip since completing her MBA and her first time outside China.[1] *Upon entering her room at the Meliá White House, she felt too exhausted to do much more than shower and enjoy the comfort and amenities in her room. (The quote from Don Quijote was certainly applicable.) However, the excitement of being abroad for the first time kept her from sleeping right away. So she perused the attractive hotel directory on her bedside table and was surprised to read that her hotel belonged to a Spanish company with more than 350 hotels all over the world. (The country locations are shown on Map 15.1.) The photos showed an array of attractive hotels, ranging from those in big cities (primarily to serve businesspeople) to others on pristine beaches surrounded by palm trees and large areas of lush vegetation (primarily to serve vacationers). (The chapter's opening photo shows a Meliá hotel in Morocco.)*

She was also intrigued by a small black and white picture of Gabriel Escarré, who founded the chain in 1956. At only 21, he had leased his first hotel in Majorca (Mallorca), Spain with only the savings he had earned and the expertise he had gained from his job at a travel agency. Li Feng was curious to learn how Meliá had reached its position in the global hospitality industry. She fell asleep and dreamt of holidaying in a Meliá beach resort, but she awoke curious as to how Mr. Escarré had built the business. For the next five days, she worked long hours, squeezed in a little sightseeing, and then returned to Beijing. Despite jet-lag, she went to work the next day and began catching up with the pile of papers that had accumulated on her desk. In her spare time she did some research on Meliá. What she learned is described below.

GROWTH IN SPAIN

That Gabriel Escarré's first hotel was in Majorca is not surprising because most entrepreneurs begin in familiar surroundings. His timing was good—European incomes were rising and package tours for sun-loving tourists were gaining popularity. Most important, Escarré exhibited both a knack for hotel management and a motivation to expand. He grew by acquiring other properties in Spain's Balearic and Canary Islands, branding them first as Hoteles Mallorquines and later as Hoteles Sol, then still later to Sol-Meliá, which many people still call it, and finally to Meliá Hotels International in 2011. The early hotels aimed their sales at beach-seeking tourists. In 1982, three years before its first foreign entry, the company began diversifying by adding urban hotels that targeted business travelers.

In 1984, while still known as Hoteles Sol, the company bought 32 hotel properties of Hotasa, a Spanish chain taken over by the government because its holding company was involved in a massive fraud. Sol acquired the properties but neither Hotasa nor its brand name. Thus, the hotels were re-branded as Sol and entered more Spanish cities. Three years later, Sol acquired Meliá from Paretti, an Italian group, which led to further diversification of the client base because most Sol Hotels were three- and four-star beach properties, whereas most Meliá's were four- or five-star urban hotels. In 2000, Meliá merged with another Spanish hotel chain, TRYP, thus adding 45 hotels in Spain. Meliá is now the largest hotel operator in Spain, and Spain is the largest location for Meliá.

INTERNATIONAL EXPANSION

Despite the importance of Spain to Meliá, 80 percent of its current income is from international operations. Some international expansion came from the acquisitions we've discussed, such as Meliá bringing operations in the Americas and Europe into Sol's portfolio. The TRYP agreement included eight leased agreements in Tunisia and three management contracts in Cuba. Meliá has used its 1999 purchase of the White House in London and the 2007 acquisition of the Inside Inns in Germany to bolster its urban presence in Europe.

Having acquired experience and expertise within Spain, the firm's first hotel venture with a start-up abroad was the Meliá Bali in Indonesia. This resulted from a long and complicated process, in which the firm had difficulty finding local suppliers, then encountered logistics and import problems in sending materials from Majorca. Soon after, the company focused on Latin America and eventually on other areas. (Figure 15.1 shows expansion by regions.) Let's examine some major international forays that demonstrate different modes of operations.

MAP 15.1 Location of Meliá Hotels Operations

The identified countries indicate where Mélia operates. It will soon be adding Austria and Denmark to its portfolio.

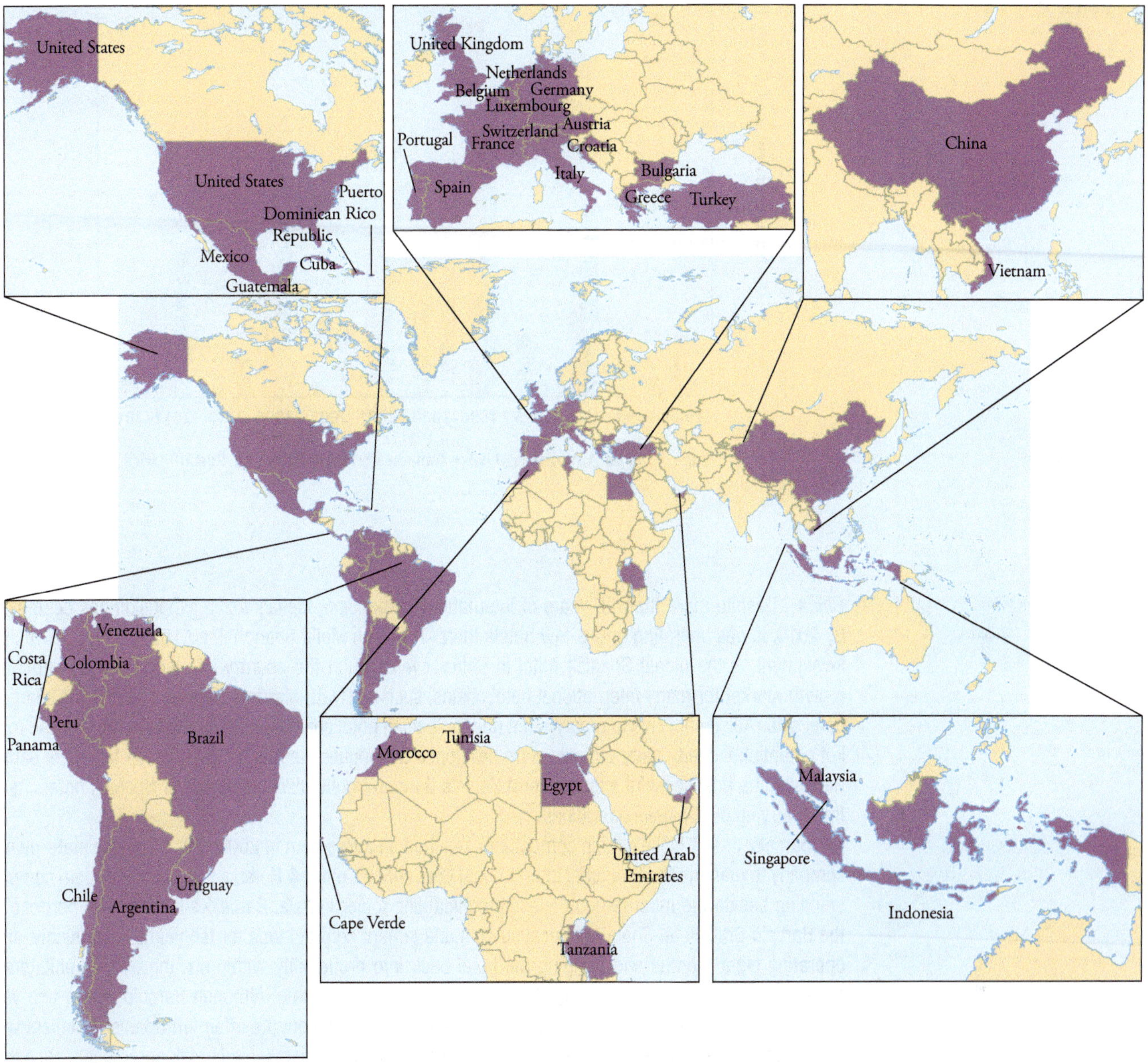

Cuba In terms of the number of hotels, Cuba's 26 make up Meliá's largest foreign presence. Yet the company has no ownership in hotels there because Cuba's centralized economy disallows foreign hotel groups to take full ownership. Thus, Meliá, like other foreign hotel chains, had to establish an agreement with a public agency, which usually owns the properties. Meliá's agreements are to manage those owned by Cubanacán.

Operating in Cuba slowed Meliá's access to the U.S. market because the U.S. government maintains restrictions on companies doing business with Cuba, such as on those managing expropriated assets once owned by U.S. citizens. (Recall the ending case in Chapter 6.) Meliá had to prove that the hotels under its management were not expropriated from U.S. citizens before it could enter the U.S. market, where it currently operates two hotels.

FIGURE 15.1 Meliá's New Foreign Operations by Region and Years

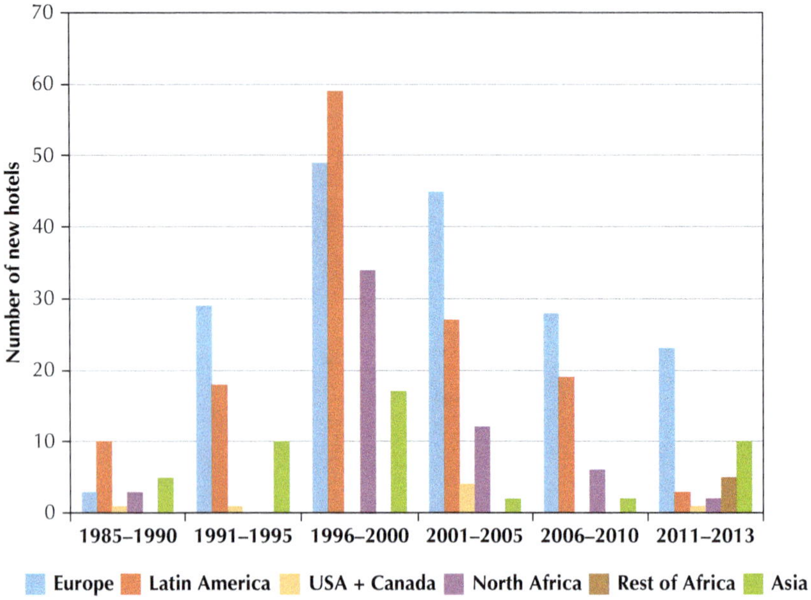

China Despite more than 25 years of international expansion, Meliá's Asian expansion has been slow. By 2010, it was operating only a few hotels there. The Gran Meliá Shanghai, a €180 million construction investment, is the oldest Spanish hotel in China, even though the country has long been an important growth market for many international hotel chains, such as Hyatt, Marriott, Radisson, and China's largest hotel chain, Jin Jiang. This anomaly is not due to Spanish hotel chains' being unaware of the Chinese market potential; indeed, many projects were developed to conquer the market as much as ten years earlier. However, the unsuccessful experience of Spain's Barceló Hotels discouraged other Spanish hotel chains from carrying out Chinese operations.

Barceló, one of Meliá's main competitors, reached an agreement in 2000 with a Chinese state-owned company to manage the Shanghai International Convention Center & Hotel, a five-star, 270-room complex standing beside the most famous telecommunications tower in Asia. Barceló added it to its portfolio as the Barceló Gran Hotel Shanghai because its management contract was for ten years. Surprisingly, after operating eight months and bringing the hotel back into profitability within six, the owners unilaterally terminated the contract by stating that the results were inadequate. Although Barceló won a two-year court battle on breach of contract and received some compensation, the affair left Spanish hoteliers with a bitter aftertaste and the suspicion that Chinese government partners would break agreements once they learned enough from their foreign partners.

Sol Meliá broke the Spanish hotel curse in 2009 by reaching a ten-year management contract agreement, renewable for another ten. Meliá's entry was facilitated by its favorable 20-year relationship with Cubanacán, which shares the Shanghai hotel ownership with the Chinese company Xintian (Suntime). Still, getting the deal was not easy; it took more than five years from the time talks began to the hotel's opening.

Subsequently, Meliá announced co-management plans with Jin Jiang and Greenland, a Chinese real estate company. The plans provide for management sharing in six hotels previously managed separately. This will allow the Chinese partners to extend their operations into three hotels—one each in Germany, Spain, and France—in exchange for Meliá's co-management of hotels in three Chinese cities. The partners will share knowledge and best practices as well as integrate and develop training, information, and booking systems. Meliá expects to learn more about Chinese customers, thus boosting its ability to expand further within China.

Relationship with Wyndham Melía's motivation for an agreement in 2010 with Wyndham was largely to facilitate North American expansion by using Wyndham's knowledge of that market and reputation with developers who are potential hotel investors. (Wyndham is the world's largest hospitality company and hotel franchisor, with 6900 hotels and 15 brands in 50 countries.) Through the agreement, Meliá sold its TRYP brand to Wyndham, but sold no real estate. The hotels in the transaction accounted for about 13,000 rooms and were re-branded as TRYP by Wyndham. Meliá became the franchisee for all the hotels using the TRYP by Wyndham brand for a 20-year period. Wyndham gained by increasing its reservations offerings for a mid-market brand in Europe and Latin America, even though the same hotels are also included in Meliá's reservation system. Of the hotels in the 2010 agreement, Meliá maintains ownership of six, leases 49, has management contracts in 24, and re-franchises twelve to other parties. Subsequently, TRYP by Wyndham has opened hotels in the United States, Canada, Turkey, and Colombia.

INTERNATIONAL HOTEL OPERATING MODES

The hotel industry is included in the so called "soft services" sector because production and consumption cannot be separated. Companies' operations abroad create service rather than product exports and imports, and there is usually a need to adapt the operations to meet local requirements. Further, tourist clientele usually want an ambiance that resembles their perceptions of the foreign country where they're staying. At the same time, they expect a similar threshold level of service and amenities wherever a hotel brand operates.

The industry presents some unique characteristics, such as high investment costs and the possibility of separating ownership and management through contractual operating modes. Thus, firms have a wide range of feasible operating modes, especially management by third parties, for all or a part of necessary hotel services.

To classify hotel operating modes, it is necessary to look at a chain's degree of exercised control over the foreign operation. This control involves four non-mutually-exclusive dimensions:

1. The daily operation of the hotel, e.g., the hiring and scheduling of personnel and the securement of supplies
2. Physical assets (primarily property ownership and the maintenance thereof)
3. Organizational routines and tacit elements of the company, such as the culture and systems to gain both efficiency and effectiveness
4. Codified assets, such as the brand and reservations system

The responsibility for controlling these elements may lie with the international hotel chain or with contractual parties, depending on the operation mode used. The capital contribution for each of the above four dimensions may be categorized as controlling ownership (usually direct investment), shared ownership (usually equity joint ventures), and no ownership (licensing, management contracts, turnkey operations, non equity joint ventures, and franchising).

Operating modes can be combined. For instance, for the TRYP by Wyndham brand, Meliá owns some hotels, pays a franchise fee to Wyndham for using the brand name, and depends both on its own and Wyndham's reservation systems. In some other cases, it has no property ownership, may lease the facility or not, and is paid for managing the operation. The Gran Meliá Shanghai is a joint venture between Chinese and Cuban organizations that, in turn, granted a management contract to Meliá for day-to-day operations and signed a franchise contract with it to use its name and reservations services.

Despite combining international operating modes within the hotel industry, direct investment, particularly if the ownership is 100 percent, normally gives the owner the right to control the four dimensions identified above. In joint ventures, two or more organizations agree on how to divide responsibilities and contribute assets and income between/among them. In management contracts, the hotel chains serving as contractors are responsible for the entire operation of the hotel, so they adopt their systems and procedures while recruiting hotel managers and enacting their human resource and quality policies. In short, the hotel is managed as if it were owned by the chain, and the chain usually agrees, as well, to use its brand name and reservation services. In license agreements the chain gives the rights to its brand name to the owner of the hotel. In franchise agreements, the chain not only gives brand name rights but also assists the hotel on an ongoing basis, most likely by contributing the chain's sales, marketing and quality control systems, and activities. Any of these modes may exist from the start, such as participation in a new hotel (start-ups are known as *greenfield)* or through acquisition of an ongoing operation, either by owning or leasing.

In partnering with other companies, regardless of operating mode, one increases the chance of developing competitors because partners may gain access to critical and core resources, especially knowledge. Thus, companies seek ways to prevent partners' opportunistic behavior. One way, of course, is through contracts. But control of some knowledge-based resources is more difficult. Meliá's main control is over its codified resources, especially brands and reservations system, which are protected legally and which Meliá does not cede to other companies. Meliá has developed the recognition and reputation of its brands over decades, so new ones cannot easily overcome the advantage. The codified resources are tied closely as well to Meliá's tacit resources because the value of the brands is dependent on clients' hotel experience, and both physical resources and human behavior influence their opinions. Competitors can easily copy the former if they have enough money. However, the latter is harder to emulate because learning must take place on a person-to-person basis (tacitly). Such learning in hotel operations is substantial—everything from greeting guests to making beds to assuring the flow of supplies—and affects efficiency and reputation. Over time, the actions become the essence of the company's culture.

MELIÁ'S EVOLVING OPERATING MODES

As we have seen, Meliá has made and continues to make use of various operating modes. (Figure 15.2 shows the evolution of its international entry modes.) However, it has not always had discretion in choosing a mode. When Gabriel Escarré established his first hotels, he had no track record that could entice other hotel owners to pay him to manage their facilities or use his brand name and reservations system. He developed a positive reputation through his successful greenfield and acquisition expansion over nearly

FIGURE 15.2 Meliá's Entry Modes by Time Periods

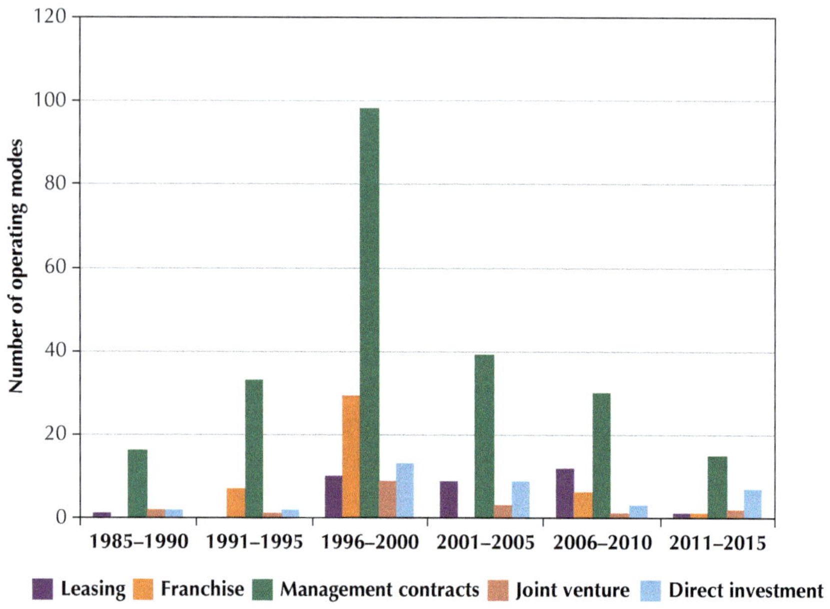

30 years in Spain before moving internationally. During its history, the company has had four names, finally settling on one that includes "Meliá" because the name has long been associated with luxury hotels and thus brings a certain cachet to the company.

Nevertheless, most of Meliá's early international growth resulted from acquisitions, such as its purchase of the Spanish chain TRYP that already had foreign operations and of Inside Inns in Germany. The success of these ventures has built Meliá's reputation as a quality hotel operator, allowing it to keep expanding its hotel portfolio with shared or no capital investment. This expansion has also occurred in China and Cuba, which place restrictions on foreign ownership.

Why grow? There are economies in handling larger hotel portfolios because of the clout and logistics in dealing with suppliers and the spreading of reservation and training system costs over more properties. There are also sales advantages because potential customers are more familiar with the larger chains.

MELIÁ NOW AND IN THE FUTURE

Currently, Meliá Hotels International comprises strong brands such as Meliá, Gran Meliá, ME by Meliá, Paradisus, Innside by Meliá, TRYP by Wyndham, Sol Hotels, and Club Meliá. The maintenance of different brands is important because of brand acquisitions that already had recognition and value. Nevertheless, Meliá is linking that recognition with its name (hence Innside by Meliá and Meliá White House). Additional linkage is due to all the brands being handled through one reservations system. Further, the different brands are aimed at different market niches.

Meliá expects more international growth by entering additional countries and adding hotels in those where it now operates. The latter includes the brands it already uses within those countries as well as the addition of its other brands. It has also indicated an interest in linking with brands held by other companies, such as the Hard Rock Café and Flintstones. Its ambitions seem too great to do everything alone. And it might not want to, even if it has the capital resources. For instance, it has so far been reluctant to make big commitments in countries, such as those in Southeast Asia, where it perceives the operating environment to be too different from its European (especially Spanish) experience. Thus, the use of non-equity operations seems to be the crux of Meliá's future.

As part of its growth strategy in high-potential markets, Meliá has recently entered Africa with operations in Cape Verde, Tanzania, and Egypt, and has indicated an interest in South Africa, Morocco, Kenya, Mauritius, Maldives, Mozambique, Senegal, and Tanzania. As for the Middle East, Meliá has recently entered Dubai by focusing on both the leisure and business traveler. In Latin America, recent growth has been carried out through the TRYP by Wyndham brand in Brazil, which has wide experience in that market.

Fast-forwarding to nearly a year since Li Feng returned to Beijing, we find that she has worked almost non-stop and has taken no more trips. Contractually, physically, and emotionally, she is ready for a vacation. She looks back at the hotel directory she brought from London and focuses on a picture showing a hotel half hidden among the foliage in front of a white sand beach and turquoise waters. "Who knows?" she thought. "Maybe I should forget my laptop and spend some time in such a beautiful place." ■

CRN Case Review Note

QUESTIONS

15-1. After reading the chapter, explain the advantages for Meliá to own its hotels versus managing them for other organizations.

15-2. After reading the chapter, discuss the advantages and risks for Meliá in its non-equity joint venture with Jin Jiang.

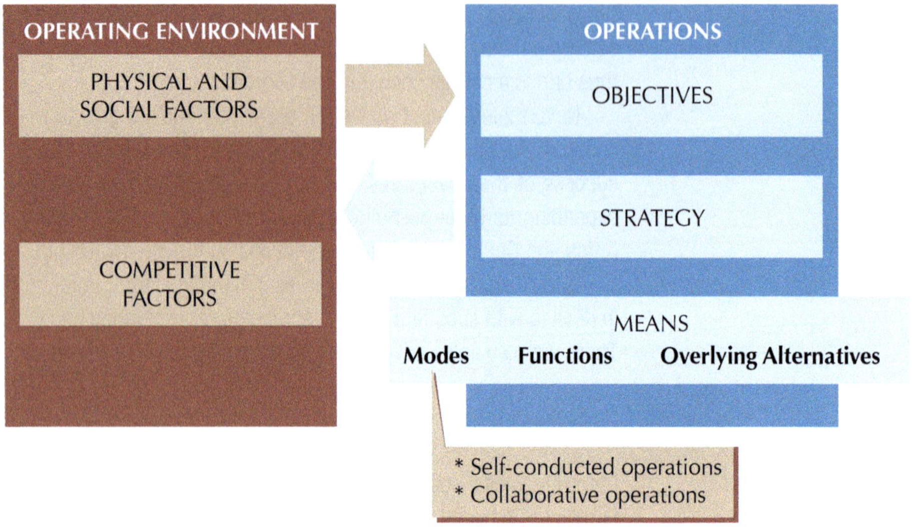

FIGURE 15.3 Factors Affecting Operating Modes in International Business

Companies may conduct international business operations independently or in collaboration with other companies. The choice will be determined both by external factors in the firm's operating environment and by internal factors that include its objectives, strategies, and means of operation (e.g., such modes of international business as exporting, franchising, etc.).

INTRODUCTION

As Figure 15.3 shows, companies must choose an international operating mode to fulfill their objectives and carry out their strategies. The preceding chapter examined exporting and importing—the preferred and most common modes of international business. Nevertheless, compelling factors can make these choices impractical. When companies depend, instead, on foreign production, they may own it in whole or in part, develop or acquire it, and/or use some type of collaborative agreement with another company.

CRN Case Review Note

Figure 15.4 shows the types of operating modes associated with each of these options, categorized by whether the company has foreign ownership, whether collaboration is involved, and whether production is located at home or abroad. The truly experienced MNE with a fully global orientation commonly uses most of the operational modes available, selecting them according to company capabilities, specific product, and foreign operating characteristics. The modes may also be combined, as with the Meliá's contract to manage the Shanghai hotel for a joint venture between Chinese and Cuban organizations. This chapter examines exporting/importing versus other options, the associated operating modes, and the advantages and problems with each, then concludes by discussing the management of these modes, particularly as foreign operations evolve over time.

FIGURE 15.4 Foreign Expansions: Alternative Operating Modes

A firm may choose to operate globally either through equity arrangements (e.g., joint venture) or through non-equity arrangements (e.g., licensing). Exporting operations are conducted in the home country, while all other modes entail production in foreign locations. The modes listed in the shaded area are collaborative arrangements. Note that, in any given location, a firm can conduct operations in multiple modes.

*Joint ventures may also be non-equity, but equity joint ventures are by far the more common.

PRODUCTION OWNERSHIP	PRODUCTION LOCATION Home country	 Foreign country
Equity arrangements	a. Exporting	a. Wholly owned operations b. Partially owned with remainder widely held c. Joint ventures* d. Equity alliances
Non-equity arrangements		a. Licensing b. Franchising c. Management contracts d. Turnkey operations

WHY EXPORTING MAY NOT BE FEASIBLE

Companies may find more advantages by producing in foreign countries than by exporting to them. The advantages occur under six conditions:

1. When production abroad is cheaper than at home
2. When transportation costs to move goods or services internationally are too high
3. When companies lack domestic capacity
4. When products and services need to be altered substantially to gain sufficient consumer demand abroad
5. When governments inhibit the import of foreign products
6. When buyers prefer products originating from a particular country

WHEN IT'S CHEAPER TO PRODUCE ABROAD

Although companies may offer products or services desired by consumers abroad, producing them in their home markets may be too expensive, especially if other companies can make reasonably similar substitutes abroad at a lower cost. For example, Turkey has been a growing market for the sale of automobiles. However, it is generally less expensive to produce the vehicles in Turkey than to export them there because the country's skilled laborers and sophisticated engineers cost less and are willing to work more days per year and longer hours per day than workers in the home countries. Thus, the automakers and many of their parts suppliers have established Turkish production to serve that market.[2]

WHEN TRANSPORTATION COSTS TOO MUCH

Transportation raises costs so much that it becomes impractical to export some products.

The cost of transportation added to production costs makes some products and services impractical to export. Generally, the more distant the market, the higher the transportation costs, and the higher those are relative to production costs, the harder it is for companies to develop viable export markets. For instance, the international transportation cost for a soft drink is a high percentage of the manufacturing cost, so a sales price that includes both would be so high through exporting that soft-drink companies would sell very little of the product. In our opening case, it is obvious that if Meliá wishes to tap the market for visitors to New York, it must provide rooms in New York.

CRN
Case Review Note

However, products such as watches have low transportation costs relative to production costs, so watch manufacturers lose few sales through exporting. The result is that companies such as Universal Genève and Seiko export watches from Switzerland and Japan, respectively, into the markets where they sell them.

Keep in mind that transport costs are dynamic, depending on fuel prices, new infrastructure (e.g., a widened Panama Canal cutting export distances), risk factors (e.g., ship piracy increasing security costs), and climate changes (e.g., warming making the Northwest Passage a viable option).

CONCEPT CHECK

In Chapter 5, we explain the concept of non-tradable goods—products and services that are seldom practical to export because of high transportation costs. Nevertheless, as we showed in Chapter 1, companies provide customers abroad with these non-tradable goods by locating near them.

WHEN DOMESTIC CAPACITY ISN'T ENOUGH

Excess capacity
- usually leads to exporting rather than new direct investment.
- may lead to competitive exports because of variable cost pricing.

As long as a company has excess capacity, it may compete effectively in export markets despite high transport costs. This occurs when domestic sales cover fixed operating expenses, enabling the company to set foreign prices on the basis of variable rather than full (variable + fixed) costs. In fact, its average cost of production per unit usually falls as foreign sales increase, but this decrease continues only as long as there is unused capacity.

Thus, companies typically produce in one location, from which they export before establishing plants in more than one country. Volkswagen, for instance, located its first plant to build the new Beetle at its facilities in Mexico, which served global markets. It wasn't until demand pushed that plant toward capacity that Volkswagen built a second plant in Europe to serve the markets there, thus freeing Mexican capacity to serve nearby markets while reducing transport costs for European sales.[3]

WHEN PRODUCTS AND SERVICES NEED ALTERING

Product alterations for foreign markets may lead to foreign production of the products.

Altering products to gain sufficient sales in a foreign market affects production costs in two ways. First, firms must make an additional investment, such as an automobile company adding an assembly line to put steering wheels on the right as well as on the left. Second, they lose some of the economies from large-scale production. As long as they must run an added assembly line anyway, they may place this line near the market they wish to serve.

The more a product must be altered for foreign markets, the more likely some production will shift abroad. Appliance maker Whirlpool finds that most U.S. demand is for top-loading, large-capacity washing machines using 110 electrical voltage, whereas most European demand is for front-loaders (more efficient in energy and water usage) with less capacity using 220 volts.[4] Given the differences in product preferences, Whirlpool produces in both the United States and Europe.

WHEN TRADE RESTRICTIONS HINDER IMPORTS

CONCEPT CHECK

In Chapter 7, we explain why governments are currently reducing trade restrictions, whether through bilateral integration (in which two countries agree to cooperate), regional integration (in which a group of geographically related countries agrees to cooperate), or agreements reached by the WTO, which serves as a multilateral forum. Here we observe that importers still face certain regulatory restrictions, some of which are designed to encourage forms of direct investment.

Although governments have been reducing import barriers, they still restrict many imports. As a result, companies may find that they must produce in a foreign country if they are to sell there. This has been the case with many auto companies—Volkswagen, Mercedes Benz, BMW, Renault, and Fiat—which decided to manufacture in India because it charged over 100 percent duty on fully built imported cars.[5]

Managers must view import barriers along with other factors, such as the market size of the country imposing the barriers and the scale of technology used in production. For example, import trade restrictions have been highly influential in enticing automobile producers to locate in Brazil because of its large market. Similar restrictions by Central American countries have been ineffective because of their small markets. However, Central American import barriers on products requiring lower amounts of capital investment for production, such as pharmaceuticals, have successfully enticed direct investment because these industries can be efficient with smaller-scale technologies and markets.

Regional or bilateral trade agreements may also attract direct investment, possibly because they create an expanded market that may justify scale economies and an ability to export part of the production.

WHEN COUNTRY OF ORIGIN BECOMES AN ISSUE

Consumers sometimes prefer domestically produced goods because of

- nationalism.
- a belief that these products are better.
- a fear that foreign-made goods may not be delivered on time.

If consumers prefer to buy goods produced in their own country rather than another (perhaps because of nationalism), exporting to them will be difficult.[6] They may push for identification labels showing that goods are domestically produced, such as those for many Australian-made products.[7] They may require labels showing where products originate, as with U.S. labeling of agricultural products.

Consumers may prefer goods from certain countries, believing them to be superior, like German cars and Italian fashion.[8] They may also fear that service and replacement parts for imported products will be more difficult to obtain. Finally, companies using just-in-time manufacturing systems favor nearby suppliers who can deliver quickly and reliably. In any of these cases, companies may find advantages in placing production where their output will best be accepted.

NONCOLLABORATION: FDI

In situations where exporting is not feasible, a company may choose to contract with another company to produce or provide services on its behalf or it may choose to "go it alone." Recall the four types of equity arrangements in Figure 15.2. In this section, we discuss the reasons and methods for making FDI for the two arrangements that do not involve collaboration: wholly owned operations and partially owned with the remainder widely held.

REASONS FOR FOREIGN DIRECT INVESTMENT

CONCEPT CHECK

Recall that in discussing global strategy as a type of international strategy in Chapter 12, we explain why some companies treat the world as a single market, preferring to integrate and measure performance on a global basis rather than on a country-by-country basis. Here we observe that the strategy of having wholly owned subsidiaries supports a global strategy.

Generally, the more ownership a company has, the greater its control over decisions, although if equity shares are widely held a company may be able to effectively control with even a minority interest. However, governments often protect minority owners so that majority owners do not act against their interests; thus, companies may opt for 100 percent ownership if they want control. There are four primary explanations for companies to take a controlling interest: *market failure, internalization theory, appropriability theory,* and *freedom to pursue global objectives.*

Market Failure Collaboration involves a transaction across the market between unrelated entities. Given liability of foreignness and the extra costs of investing abroad (along with other factors to be discussed later), collaboration is appealing, but only if management can find a collaborator at acceptable terms. For instance, they may not be able to find a contractor who is familiar enough with the company's unique technology to deal with it efficiently. In these instances, companies must control foreign activities within their own management structures (internal hierarchies) rather than depending on the external market to do it for them.[9] The extent to which companies take controlling ownership equity (FDI) in foreign operations—such as in warehousing, sales offices, or production facilities—indicates market failure.

Internalization Control through self-handling of operations is known as **internalization.**[10] The concept comes from *transactions cost theory,* which holds that companies should seek the lower cost between conducting operations internally and contracting another party to do so for them. In other cases, self-handling may reduce costs for a number of reasons:

1. *Different operating units within the same company are likely to share a common corporate culture, which expedites communications.* Executives participating in a Thought Leadership Summit on Digital Strategies concluded that a lack of trust, common terminology, and knowledge is a major obstacle to successful collaboration.[11]
2. *The company can use its own managers, who understand and are committed to carrying out its objectives.* When GE acquired a controlling interest in the Hungarian company Tungsram, it was able to expedite control and changes because it put GE managers in key positions.[12]
3. *The company can avoid protracted negotiations with another company on such matters as how each will be compensated for contributions.* The U.S. and Russian automakers GM and AvtoVAZ shut down production in their Russian joint venture while negotiating a higher price for critical components supplied by AvtoVAZ.[13]
4. *The company can avoid possible enforcement problems.* Tommy Hilfiger sued Mountain High Hosiery, manufacturer of its socks, for selling cheaply to unauthorized distributors, who cheapened the brand image.[14]

Companies may want to operate through FDI to lessen the chance of developing competitors.

Appropriability The idea of denying rivals access to resources is called the **appropriability theory.**[15] Companies are reluctant to transfer vital resources—capital, patents, trademarks, and management know-how—to another organization for fear of their competitive position being undermined. In fact, Chinese automakers—such as SAIV, Dongfeng, and Changan—that have collaborative arrangements with major global auto competitors—such as GM, Volkswagen, Nissan, and Ford—make no secret of their desire to learn from their partners so as to become global competitors in their own right.[16] Nevertheless, companies are less concerned about appropriability in countries they perceive as having a strong rule of law.[17] At the same time, they are less concerned about appropriability of non-strategic than of strategic resources. For instance, Coca-Cola, which is committed to a variety of collaborative operating forms with partners all over the world, steadfastly refuses to collaborate in the production of its concentrate. The formula is simply too critical to the company's competitive viability.

Freedom to Pursue a Global Strategy A company that has a wholly owned foreign operation may find it easier to allow the operation to participate in a global strategy. For instance, a U.S. company that owns 100 percent of its Brazilian operation might be able to take actions that, although sub-optimizing Brazilian performance, could deal more effectively with actual or potential competitors and customers globally, such as by decreasing prices to an industrial customer in Brazil to gain that customer's business in Germany. Or it might standardize its product to gain global cost savings even though this might result in some lost sales in Brazil. But if the company shared ownership in Brazil, either action might be detrimental to the Brazilian owners, who would balk at such practices.

ACQUISITION VERSUS GREENFIELD

FDI ownership takes place by transferring abroad financial and/or other tangible or intangible assets. Firms have two ways to use these assets to invest in a foreign country: either acquire an interest in an existing operation or make a greenfield investment. The reasons for each are below.

Acquisition Whether a company makes a direct investment by acquisition or start-up depends, of course, on which companies are available for purchase and at what terms.

The advantages of acquiring an existing operation include

- adding no further capacity to the market,
- avoiding start-up problems,
- making financing easier at times.

There are many reasons for seeking acquisitions. One is to obtain some vital resource that may otherwise be slow or difficult for the investor to secure.[18] Let's say a company has knowledgeable personnel that the investor cannot easily hire at a good price on its own.[19] Or perhaps an investor could hire the personnel, but lacks experience in managing them effectively. For instance, many Russian companies have recently expanded internationally through acquisition. They have had good scientific inventions and innovative products, but many have lacked experience in managing the transformation from R&D to market success.[20] By buying a company, the buyer gets not only labor and management but also an existing organization with experience in coordinating such functions as products' development and subsequent sales.

In addition, a company may gain the goodwill, brand identification, and access to distribution that are important to marketing its products, especially if the cost and risk of breaking in a new brand are high. Recently, much Chinese investment in the United States has been by acquisition, seemingly because of Chinese companies' desire to secure well-known brand names that will help them sell.[21]

There are also financial considerations. A company depending substantially on local financing rather than on transferring capital may find local capital suppliers more willing to put money into a known ongoing operation than to invest in a less familiar foreign enterprise. A foreign firm also may merge with an existing company through an exchange of stock.

In other ways, acquisitions may reduce costs and risks—and save time. A company may be able to buy facilities, particularly those of a poorly performing operation, for less than the cost of new operations. Brazil's José Batista Sobrinho (JBS), the world's largest meat company, bought U.S. companies Swift and Pilgrim's Pride at opportunistically low prices because they were in financial trouble.[22] If an investor fears that a market does not justify added capacity, acquisition enables it to avoid the risk of depressed prices through overcapacity. Finally, by buying a company, an investor avoids start-up inefficiencies and gets an immediate cash flow rather than tying up funds during construction.

Companies may choose greenfield expansion if

- no desired company is available for acquisition,
- acquisition will lead to carryover problems,
- acquisition is harder to finance.

Making Greenfield Investments Although acquisitions offer advantages, foreign companies may opt for greenfield investments if they face local roadblocks. For example, local governments may prevent acquisitions because they want more competitors in the market and fear market dominance by a single foreign enterprise. In addition, a foreign company may find local financing easier to obtain from development banks if it builds facilities because of being able to show that it is creating employment. Finally, companies frequently invest in sectors where there are few, if any, companies operating in their lines of business.

Even if acquisitions are available, they often don't succeed.[23] First, turning around a poorly performing operation is difficult because of potential personnel and labor relations problems, ill will toward its products and brands, and inefficient or poorly located facilities. Second, managers in the acquiring and acquired companies may not work well together because of different management styles and organizational cultures or because of conflicts over decision-making authority.[24] For instance, after acquiring IBM's PC division, Lenova had to overcome cultural differences between its Chinese and U.S. managers; e.g. the former thought the Americans talked without listening even when they had nothing to say, and the latter balked at mandatory exercise breaks and the public shaming of latecomers to meetings.[25] Nevertheless, there is some evidence that acquiring firms' success increases with more international acquisition experience.[26] Intuition tells us that acquisitions in more culturally distant countries would perform less well than those in more culturally similar countries; however, evidence shows the contrary, likely due to a combination of factors: organizational gains from added diversity, greater care in selection in dissimilar countries (particularly to get a better match between organizational cultures), and less of an attempt to integrate these operations into the corporate culture.[27]

CRN Case Review Note

Leasing We saw in our opening case that Meliá began by leasing a hotel in Majorca, and it has since used this operating mode extensively. This mode is much like an acquisition, but one that forgoes the need to invest. While common in the hospitality industry, it is not common in others. Although companies in other industries might lease certain assets abroad—computers, vehicles, buildings—such arrangements are quite different from leasing an entire operating facility.

CRN Case Review Note

WHY COMPANIES COLLABORATE

Companies collaborate (use alliances that are often called *strategic alliances*) abroad for much the same reasons they do domestically. In our opening case, we saw that Melía gains revenue by managing hotels both domestically and internationally. However, there are other reasons for collaborating abroad. For example, Melía's motive to collaborate with Jin Jiang is to learn more about the nuances of the Chinese market. Figure 15.5 shows both the general and internationally specific reasons for collaborative arrangements.

CONCEPT CHECK

We introduce the idea of the value chain in Chapter 12, where we explain how a company configures its global value chain by organizing a series of both primary and secondary activities—activities that naturally include the operations of its overseas partners. Needless to say, its global alliances must accommodate the structure of each firm's value chain.

CRN Case Review Note

ALLIANCE TYPES

Different terms are used to describe alliances based on their objectives and where they fit in a firm's value chain. In terms of objectives, *scale alliances* aim to provide efficiency by pooling similar assets so that partners can carry out business activities in which they already have experience. In our ending case on the oneworld alliance, airlines have gained economies by combining their lounges. *Link alliances* use complementary resources so that participating companies can expand into new business areas.[28] Nokia, once a producer of such products as toilet paper and rubber boots, has used a network of collaborators to develop and market cellular phones.[29] An example of a *vertical alliance* is the link between a food franchiser with

FIGURE 15.5 Collaborative Arrangements and International Objectives

A company may enter into an international collaborative arrangement for the same reasons that it does so domestically (e.g., to spread costs). In other cases, it may enter into a collaborative arrangement to meet objectives that are specific to its foreign-expansion strategies (e.g., to diversify geographically).

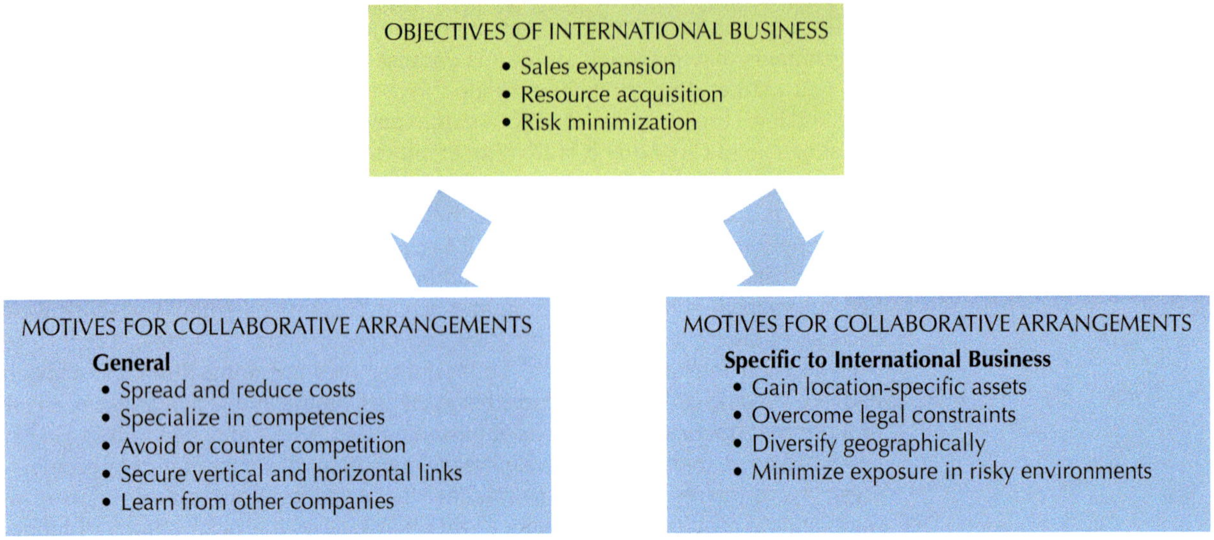

a franchisee because they each operate in a different segment of the value chain. An example of a *horizontal alliance* is the joint venture between GM and Toyota because each partner extends its product offerings on the same level of the value chain.[30] *Coopetition*, such as the GM-Toyota example, refers to collaboration between competing firms.

GENERAL MOTIVES FOR COLLABORATIVE ARRANGEMENTS

Why do companies collaborate in either domestic or foreign operations? As explained in this section, reasons include spreading and reducing costs, the ability to specialize in their competencies, avoiding competition, securing vertical and horizontal links, and gaining knowledge.

Sometimes it's cheaper to get another company to handle work, especially

- at small volume.
- when the other company has excess capacity.

To Spread and Reduce Costs To produce or sell abroad, a company must incur certain fixed costs. At a small volume of business, contracting to a specialist rather than self-handling may be cheaper because a specialist can spread the fixed costs to more than one company. If business increases enough, the contracting company may then be able to handle the business more cheaply itself.

A company with excess production or sales capacity can use that excess to handle the activities for a client company. This may lower its average costs by covering its fixed costs more fully, and can prevent the client from having to incur fixed costs and longer delays for start-up and receipt of cash flows.

Individual companies may lack the resources to"go it alone"—especially small and young ones.[31] By pooling their efforts, they may be able to undertake activities that otherwise would be beyond their means. But large companies may also benefit when the cost of development and/or investment is very high. Disney's theme park in Hong Kong cost so much to develop that Disney and the Hong Kong government share ownership and expenses.[32]

One of the fastest-growth areas for collaborative arrangements has been in industries with projects too large, both in capital and technical-resource needs, for any single firm to handle, such as new aircraft and communication systems. From such an arrangement's inception, different firms (sometimes from different countries) agree to take on the high cost and high risk of development work for different components needed in the final product.

Then a lead company buys the components from the companies that did parts of the development work. A good example of this is the Boeing 787 aircraft, which involves component development and production by companies from around the globe.

Granting another company rights to an asset can yield a return on a product that does not fit the company's strategic priority based on its best competencies.

To Specialize in Competencies The **resource-based view** of the firm holds that each company has a unique combination of competencies. A company may seek to improve its performance by concentrating on those activities that best fit its competencies, depending on other firms to supply it with products, services, or support activities in which it is less competent. This concentration may lead to horizontal or vertical collaboration. However, a collaborative arrangement has a limited time frame, which may allow a company to exploit a particular product, asset, or technology itself at a later date if its core competencies change.

To Avoid or Counter Competition When markets are not large enough to accommodate many competitors, companies may band together so as not to compete. Companies may also combine resources to combat competitors, such as Sony and Samsung did to move faster in the development of LCD technology.[33] Or they may simply collude to raise everyone's profits. For example, Canpotex is made up of a group of Canadian companies that joined together rather than compete with each other to sell potash outside the United States and Canada: the group accounts for more than a quarter of the product's world market.[34] Only a few countries take substantial actions against the collusion of competitors.[35]

To Secure Vertical and Horizontal Links Potential cost savings and supply assurances can be attained through vertical integration. However, companies may lack the competence or resources necessary to own and manage the full value chain of activities. A study of small and medium-sized Argentine furniture manufacturers showed that they gained from both vertical and horizontal alliances. By allying horizontally, they pooled resources to gain manufacturing efficiencies and were able to deal more effectively in vertical alliances to access global markets and gain supplies.[36]

Horizontal links may provide economies of scope in distribution, such as by having a full line of products to sell, thereby increasing the sales per fixed cost of a visit to potential customers. For example, in many parts of the world Avon representatives market such products as books and crayons in addition to the company's usual fare to gain economies of scope.

To Gain Knowledge Many companies pursue collaborative arrangements to learn about a partner's technology, operating methods, or home market so that their own competencies will broaden or deepen, making them more competitive in the future.[37] An example is Chinese authorities allowing foreign companies to tap the Chinese market in exchange for their transference of technology. Sometimes each partner can learn from the other, a motive driving joint ventures between U.S. and European winemakers—such as the Opus One Winery owned by Constellation Brands' Robert Mondavi from the United States and Baron Philippe de Rothschild from France.[38]

INTERNATIONAL MOTIVES FOR COLLABORATIVE ARRANGEMENTS

In this section, we continue discussing why companies enter into collaborative arrangements, covering those reasons that apply only to international operations. Specifically, the reasons are to gain location-specific assets, overcome legal constraints, diversify geographically, and minimize risk exposure.

To Gain Location-Specific Assets Cultural, political, competitive, and economic differences among countries create barriers for firms abroad. Those ill-equipped to handle these differences may seek collaboration with local firms that will help them. When Walmart first tried to enter the Japanese market on its own, it gave up after having disappointing sales. It has since returned with a Japanese partner, Seiyu, which is more familiar with Japanese tastes and rules for opening new stores.[39] In fact, most foreign companies in Japan need to collaborate with Japanese firms that can help in securing distribution and a competent workforce—two assets that are difficult for MNEs to gain on their own there.

In addition to having a local partner advise and handle cross-national differences, a collaboration may facilitate international companies' learning about these differences. However, there is some danger that they assume wrongly that they can apply this learning effectively when entering subsequent countries—even those that appear to be similar to their previous entries.[40]

CRN Case Review Note

Legal factors may be
- direct prohibitions against certain operating forms.
- indirect (e.g., regulations affecting profitability).

CRN Case Review Note

To Overcome Governmental Constraints Recall that in centrally planned economies (e.g., China and Cuba) Meliá cannot own its hotels, so it must collaborate with local organizations. Though centrally planned economies are very restrictive, virtually all countries limit foreign ownership in some sectors. India and Russia exemplify countries that are particularly restrictive in that they set maximum foreign percentage ownership in an array of industries.[41] They also usually require lengthy negotiations with governments to determine the operating terms; a savvy local partner can help in this regard. Our ending case on the airline passenger industry demonstrates that international collaboration has become very important, partly because, with few exceptions, governments allow only domestically owned airlines to carry passengers on domestic routes.

Government procurement is another area that may encourage companies to collaborate because preference is often given to bids that include national companies or foreign firms that provide evidence that they will transfer technology to a local company so that it becomes more internationally competitive in the future. Taiwan does this with purchases by the state enterprise monopoly, Taiwan Power (Tai Power).[42]

Collaboration hinders nonassociated companies from pirating the asset.

Protecting Assets Many countries provide little de facto protection for intellectual property rights such as trademarks, patents, and copyrights unless authorities are prodded consistently. To prevent pirating of these proprietary assets, companies sometimes make collaborative agreements with local companies, which then monitor the market so that no one else uses the asset locally.

CONCEPT CHECK

In discussing a firm's allocation of operational emphasis among countries in Chapter 13, we consider the factors that contribute favorably to a geographic diversification strategy: growth rate, sales stability, and program-control requirements are low in each market; competitive lead time is short; and spillover effects among markets are high.

In addition, some countries provide protection only if the internationally registered asset is exploited locally within a specified period. If not, then whatever entity first does so gains the right to it. Burger King must sell under the Hungry Jack brand in Australia for this reason.[43] Thus, companies may need to follow a geographic diversification strategy to protect assets; doing so may necessitate collaboration to enter multiple markets quickly.

In other cases, local citizens, known as *trademark squatters*, register rights to the unused trademarks, then negotiate sales to the original owners when they do try to enter the market. One Russian company registered over 300 foreign trademarks, including Starbucks's trademark. Foreign companies then had to pay to regain their rights or go through lengthy and potentially expensive court proceedings.[44]

To Diversify Geographically For a company wishing to pursue a geographic diversification strategy, collaborative arrangements offer a faster initial means of entering multiple markets because other companies contribute resources. However, the arrangements will be less appealing for companies whose activities are already widely extended or for those that have ample resources for such extension.

Collaborative arrangements allow for greater spreading of assets among countries.

To Minimize Risk Exposure Companies worry that political or economic changes will affect the safety of assets and earnings in their foreign operations. One way to minimize loss from foreign political occurrences is to minimize the base of assets located abroad—or share them. A government may be less willing to move against a shared operation for fear of encountering opposition from multiple companies, especially if they are from different countries and can potentially elicit support from their home governments. Another way to spread risk is to place operations in a number of different countries, which firms may be unable to afford alone. This strategy reduces the chance that all foreign assets will encounter adversity at the same time.

TYPES OF COLLABORATIVE ARRANGEMENTS

The higher managers' perception of the risk of being in a foreign market, the greater their desire to form collaborative arrangements in that market.

The forms of foreign operations differ in the amount of resources a company commits and the proportion of the resources located abroad. Licensing, for instance, may result in a lower additional capital commitment than a foreign joint venture will. Exporting commits fewer resources abroad than does FDI.

Throughout this discussion, keep in mind that there are *trade-offs*. A decision, let's say, to take no ownership in foreign production, such as by licensing to a foreign company, may reduce exposure to political risk. However, learning about that environment will be slow, delaying (perhaps permanently) the ability to reap the full profits from producing and selling the product abroad.

Companies have a wider choice of operating form when there is less likelihood of competition.

Furthermore, when a company has a desired, unique, difficult-to-duplicate resource, it is in a good position to choose the operating form it would most like to use and to increase its compensation from the arrangement. When it lacks this bargaining strength, competition or governmental actions may force it to settle on a form that is lower on its priority list.

A further constraint is finding a desirable collaboration partner. For example, if the collaboration includes a transfer of technology, it may be impossible to find a local company familiar enough with the technology or having sufficiently similar values and priorities as the company making the transfer.[45] In effect, costs are associated with transferring technology to another entity, which include the time spent in cooperating to ensure that partners are trustworthy and cognizant of technologies and that they agree on objectives and means of implementing practices.[46]

SOME CONSIDERATIONS IN COLLABORATIVE ARRANGEMENTS

Some factors influencing companies' choice of arrangement type are their desire for control over foreign operations, prior foreign expansion, and expected compensation in one versus another.

Control The more a company depends on collaboration, the more likely it is to lose decision-making control, such as on quality, new-product direction, and expansion. This is because each partner favors its own performance and has its own objectives, which necessitates compromises.

Prior Company Expansion When a company already has operations (especially wholly owned ones) in place in a foreign country, some of the advantages of collaboration are no longer as important. It knows how to operate within that country and may have excess plant or human resource capacity it can use for new production or sales.

However, much depends on the compatibility between existing foreign operations and the new ones the company is planning abroad. If there is similarity, as with production of a new type of office equipment already made there, the new production will likely be handled internally. If product, function, or location is dissimilar, collaborating with an experienced company may be more advantageous.

Internal handling of foreign operations usually means more control and no sharing of profits.

Compensation Collaboration also implies sharing revenues and knowledge—an important consideration when profit potentials are high. Although there is a need to share revenue when collaborating, how to divide the revenue is not clear-cut because many variables influence the outcome. Certainly, the bargaining power of the collaborative partners is important in any agreement, but such factors as government mandates, partners' perception of risk, and competitive constraints are all important.[47] Further, the mode of collaboration guides normal practices. As we discuss the different modes, we will introduce some of these practices.

Should Countries Limit Foreign Control of Key Industries?

Point

Point **Yes** I believe they should, because a key industry affects a very large segment of the economy by virtue of its size or influence on other sectors. I'm not talking about either foreign control of small investments or non-controlling interest in large investments. If countries need foreign firms' resources—technology, capital, export markets, branded products, and so on—they can get them through collaborations without ceding control to foreigners. In turn, the foreign companies can still achieve their objectives, such as gaining access to markets.

Of course, each country should—and does—determine for itself what a key industry is. Mexico limits foreign control in its oil industry because it is such a dominant part of the Mexican economy. The United States is primarily concerned about security, so the government can halt any foreign investment that endangers national security.

The United States also prohibits foreign control of television and radio stations because they could be used as foreign propaganda instruments. It protects domestic transportation, a vital sector for national security, by prohibiting foreign control of domestic airlines and by preventing foreign airlines and ships from transporting passengers and cargo directly from one U.S. city to another.

The rationale for protecting key industries is supported by history, which shows that home governments have used powerful companies to influence policies in the foreign countries where they operate. During colonial periods, firms such as Levant and the British East India Company often acted as the political arm of their home governments.

More recently, governments, especially the United States, have pressured their companies to leave certain areas and to prohibit their subsidiaries from doing business with certain countries (Cuba, North Korea), even though the prohibition is counter to the interests of the countries where the subsidiaries were located.[48]

At the same time, some companies are so powerful that they can influence their home-country governments to intercede on their behalf. Probably the most notorious example was United Fruit Company (UFC) in so-called banana republics, which persuaded the United States to overthrow governments to protect its investments. Miguel Angel Asturias, a Nobel laureate in literature, referred to UFC's head as the "Green Pope" who "lifts a finger and a ship starts or stops. He says a word and a republic is bought. He sneezes and a president...falls....He rubs his behind on a chair and a revolution breaks out."[49]

Whenever a company is controlled from abroad, its decisions can be made there. Such control means that corporate management abroad can decide such factors as personnel staffing, export prices, and the retention and payout of profits. These decisions might cause different rates of expansion in different countries as well as possible plant closings, sometimes with subsequent employment disruption.

Finally, by withholding resources or allowing strikes, MNEs may affect other local industries adversely. In essence, the MNE looks after its global interests, which may not coincide with what is best for an operation in a given country.

Should Countries Limit Foreign Control of Key Industries?

Counterpoint

Counterpoint **No** The passionate arguments against foreign control of key industries don't convince me that such control leads to corporate decisions that are any different from those local companies would make. Nor do they convince me that limits on foreign ownership are in the best interests of people in host countries.

Certainly, companies make strategic global decisions at headquarters, but typically they depend on a good deal of local advice beforehand. Further, MNEs staff their foreign subsidiaries mainly with nationals of the countries where they operate, and these nationals make most routine decisions.

Regardless of the decision makers' or companies' nationalities, managers decide based on what they think is best for their firms' business, rather than based on some home-country or local socioeconomic agenda. At the same time, their decisions have to adhere to local laws and consider the views of their local stakeholders. Of course, MNEs sometimes make locally unpopular decisions, but so do local companies. In the meantime, governments can and do enact laws that apply to both local and international companies, and these laws can ensure that companies act in the so-called local interest.

Although preventing foreign control of key industries may be well intentioned, the resultant local control may lead to the protection of inefficient performance. Further, the key-industry argument appeals to emotions rather than reason. That's why arguments in the United States for security make little sense on close examination. Although foreign propaganda through foreign ownership of radio and television stations is the rationale for ownership restrictions, there are no such restrictions on foreign ownership of U.S. newspapers or on material appearing on the Internet. (Is this because people who read the news are presumed to be less swayed by propaganda?) The protection of U.S. domestic transportation for security reasons is a sham, just to protect the shipbuilding industry and maritime employees. For instance, U.S. merchant flagships must employ only U.S. citizens as crews because of the vulnerability to bombs on ships in U.S. waters, but foreign flag carriers regularly use U.S. ports, while foreigners can join the U.S. Navy.

The banana-republic arguments are outdated and go back to ***dependencia* theory**, which holds that emerging economies have practically no power in their dealings with MNEs.[50] More recent ***bargaining school* theory** states that the terms of a foreign investor's operations depend on how much the investor and host country need each other.[51] In effect, companies need countries because of their markets and resources, while countries need MNEs because of their technology, capital, access to foreign markets, and expertise. Through a bargaining process, they come to an agreement or contract that stipulates what the MNE can and cannot do.

I completely disagree that either countries or companies can necessarily gain the same through collaborative agreements as through FDI. Although collaborative agreements are often preferable, there are company and country advantages from foreign-controlled operations. For example, with wholly owned operations, companies are less concerned about developing competitors, so they are more willing to transfer essential and valuable technology abroad.

LICENSING

Licensing agreements may be
- exclusive or nonexclusive.
- used for patents, copyrights, trademarks, and other intangible property.

Under a licensing agreement, a company (the licensor) grants intangible property rights to another company (the licensee) to use in a specified geographic area for a specified period. In exchange, the licensee ordinarily pays a royalty to the licensor. The rights may be for an *exclusive license* (the licensor can give rights to no other company for the specified geographic area for a specified period of time) or a nonexclusive one.

The U.S. Internal Revenue Service classifies intangible property into five categories:

1. Patents, inventions, formulas, processes, designs, patterns
2. Copyrights for literary, musical, or artistic compositions
3. Trademarks, trade names, brand names
4. Franchises, licenses, contracts
5. Methods, programs, procedures, systems

Usually, the licensor is obliged to furnish sufficient information and assistance, and the licensee is obliged to exploit the rights effectively and pay compensation to the licensor.

Licensing often has an economic motive, such as the desire for faster start-up, lower costs, or access to additional resources.

Major Motives for Licensing Frequently, a new product or process may affect only part of a company's total output, and then only for a limited time. In such a situation, the company may foresee insufficient sales volume to warrant establishing its own foreign manufacturing and sales facilities. Meanwhile, it may find a licensee that can produce and sell at a low cost and within a short start-up time. In turn, the licensee's cost may be less than if it developed the new product or process on its own.

For industries in which technological changes are frequent and affect many products, companies in various countries often exchange technology or other intangible property rather than compete with each other on every product in every market—an arrangement known as **cross-licensing**. An example is Kodak (U.S.) and NEC Technology (Japan) entering a cross-licensing agreement for access to each other's patent portfolio.[52]

Payment Considerations The amount and type of payment for licensing arrangements vary, as each contract is negotiated on its own merits. For instance, the value to the licensee will be greater if potential sales are high. Potential sales depend, in turn, on such factors as the geographic scope of the sales territory, the length of time the asset will have market value, and the market experience of using the asset elsewhere.

Putting a Price on Intangible Assets Valuing partners' contributions and rewards is complex and always subject to negotiation. Companies commonly negotiate a "front-end" payment to cover technology transfer costs. Licensors of technology do this because there is usually more involved than simply transferring *explicit* knowledge, such as through publications and reports. The move requires the transfer of *tacit* knowledge, such as through engineering, consultation, and adaptation. The licensee usually bears the incurred transfer costs so that the licensor is motivated to ensure a smooth adaptation. Of course, the license of some other assets, such as copyrights or brand names, has much lower transfer costs.

Intangible assets may be old or new, obsolete or still in use at home when a company licenses it. Many companies transfer rights to assets at an early or even a developmental stage so products hit different markets simultaneously. This is important when selling to the same industrial customers in different countries and when global advertising campaigns can be effective. On one hand, a licensee may be willing to pay more for a new intangible asset because it may have a longer useful life. On the other hand, a licensee may be willing to pay less for a newer one, particularly one in the development phase, because of its uncertain market value.

Selling to Subsidiaries Although we think of licensing agreements as collaborative arrangements among unassociated companies, licensing is also common between parents and their foreign subsidiaries. One reason is that operations in a foreign country, even if 100 percent owned by the parent, are usually subsidiaries, which are legally separate companies. When a company owns less than 100 percent, a separate licensing arrangement may be a means of compensating the licensor for contributions beyond the mere investment in capital and managerial resources.

FRANCHISING

Franchising includes providing an intangible asset (usually a trademark) and continually infusing necessary assets.

Franchising is a specialized form of licensing in which the franchisor not only grants a franchisee the use of the intangible property (usually a trademark), but also operationally assists the business on a continuing basis, such as through sales promotion and training. In many cases, the franchisor provides supplies, such as the concentrate Coca-Cola sells to its bottlers. In a sense, the two parties act almost as a vertically integrated company because they are interdependent and each creates part of the product or service that ultimately reaches the consumer.

Many types of products and many countries participate in franchising.

Today, franchising is mostly associated with U.S. fast-food operations, although many international franchisors are from other countries and in many other sectors, such as Meliá's hotel franchises discussed in the opening case. To illustrate how diverse franchising can be, a Danish company, Cryos International, even franchises sperm banks in about 40 countries. It initially supplied the frozen sperm only from donors in Denmark (In 2012 more than 500 British women were artificially inseminated in Denmark), but it now uses local donors, such as in India.[53]

Franchisors once depended on trade shows and costly visits to foreign countries to promote their expansion. While such trade shows are still important (see the adjacent photo), especially for young franchising operations that are not well-known, the Internet has given companies another channel to send and receive information.

Franchise Organization A franchisor may penetrate a foreign country by dealing directly with individual franchisees or by setting up a *master franchise* and giving that organization the rights to open outlets on its own or to develop subfranchisees in the country or region. In the latter case, subfranchisees pay royalties to the master franchisee, which then remits some

The Franchise Expo in Miami Beach (U.S.) brings franchisors and potential franchisees together.
Source: Jeff Greenberg/Alamy

predetermined percentage to the franchisor. Companies are most apt to use a master franchise system when they are not confident about evaluating potential individual franchisees and when overseeing and controlling them directly would be too expensive.[54]

If the franchisor is not well-known to many local people, or if local people are unsure about its market commitment, convincing them to make investments may be difficult. In effect, people are usually willing to invest only in known franchises because the name is a guarantee of quality that can attract customers. Therefore, if franchisors are not well-known in the foreign market they wish to enter (recall the Burger King case in Chapter 13), they may begin with some company-owned outlets that serve as a showcase to attract franchisees.

Operational Modifications Finding suppliers can add difficulties and expense for food franchisors. McDonald's, for instance, had to build a plant to make hamburger buns in the United Kingdom, while in Thailand it had to help farmers develop potato production.[55]

Franchisors face a dilemma:

- The more global standardization, the less acceptance in the foreign country.
- The more adjustment to the foreign country, the less the franchisor is needed.

Franchisors' success generally depends on three factors: product and service standardization, high identification through promotion, and effective cost controls. A dilemma when operating abroad is that the first of these may be difficult to transfer. In food franchising, for example, standardization is important so that consumers know what to expect. But when a company enters a foreign country, taste preferences may differ—even within regions of large countries. In response to such differences in China, Yum! Brands offers regionally different food in its KFC and Pizza Hut outlets.[56]

At the same time, the more adjustments made for the host consumers' different tastes, the less a franchisor has to offer a potential franchisee. U.S. food franchisors' success in Japan is mostly due to Japan's enthusiastic assimilation of Western products. Even so, food franchisors have had to make adjustments there. Pizza Hut, for instance, offers squid, oysters, and duck breast as pizza toppings.[57]

MANAGEMENT CONTRACTS

Foreign management contracts are used primarily when the foreign company can manage better than the owners.

In a foreign management contract, a company is paid a fee to transfer management personnel and administrative know-how abroad to assist a company. An organization may pay for managerial assistance when it believes another can manage its operation more efficiently than it can. This ability is most apt to occur because of industry-specific capabilities. An illustration is the British Airport Authority (BAA), which has contracts to manage some airports in the United States, Italy, and Australia because of its successful airport management skills.[58]

International management contracts diminish ownership control by foreign companies while allowing host countries to receive foreign expertise. In turn, the management company receives income without having to make a capital investment. This pattern has been important in hotel operations where hotel chains have been shying away from property ownership abroad because of risk and where some host-country property owners know more about real estate than about managing a hotel.[59] Recall the opening case whereby Meliá's demonstrated hotel management skills have attracted property owners to contract its services. At the same time, Meliá is able to expand more rapidly and to more foreign countries than if it had to contribute the capital itself.

CRN
Case Review Note

TURNKEY OPERATIONS

Turnkey operations are

- most commonly performed by industrial-equipment, construction, and consulting companies.
- often performed for a governmental agency.

Turnkey operations are an arrangement in which one company, usually an industrial-equipment manufacturer, a construction company, or a consulting firm, contracts with another to build complete, ready-to-operate facilities. Manufacturers also sometimes provide turnkey services if they believe an investment on their own behalf is infeasible. The customer for a turnkey operation is often a governmental agency. Recently, most large projects have been in those developing countries that are moving rapidly toward infrastructure development and industrialization.

Contracting to Scale One characteristic that sets the turnkey business apart from most other international business operations is the size of many of the contracts, frequently for hundreds of millions into the billions of dollars. This means that a few very large companies—such as Vinci (France), Bechtel (U.S.), and Hochtief (Germany)—account for a significant share of the international market. The most notable change in leadership has been by Chinese firms. In 2003, none were among the world's 10 largest, but by 2012, they had five places there.[60] Often, smaller firms either serve as subcontractors for primary turnkey suppliers or specialize in a particular sector, such as the handling of hazardous waste. The following photos illustrate both the existing Panama Canal and a current large turnkey project to build an additional wider channel in order to accommodate larger ships that now must go around South America for routes between the Atlantic and Pacific Oceans. This project is being handled by a consortium of turnkey operators, led by Spain's Sacyr Vallehermoso.

Making Contacts The nature of these contracts places importance on hiring executives with top-level governmental contacts abroad, as well as on ceremony and building goodwill, such as opening a facility on a country's independence day or getting a head of state to inaugurate a facility. Although public relations is important to gain contracts, other factors—price, export financing, managerial and technological quality, experience, reputation, and so on—are necessary to sell contracts of such magnitude.

Marshaling Resources Many turnkey contracts are for construction in remote areas, necessitating massive housing construction and importation of personnel. Projects may involve building an entire infrastructure under the most adverse conditions, such as Bechtel's complex for Minera Escondida high in the Andes, so turnkey operators must have expertise in hiring people willing to work in remote areas for extended periods and in transporting and using supplies under very adverse conditions.

If a company holds a monopoly on certain assets or resources, such as the latest refining technology, other companies will find difficulty in competing to secure a turnkey contract. As the production process becomes known, however, the number of competitors for such contracts increases. Companies from developed countries have moved largely toward projects involving high technology, whereas those from such countries as China, India, Korea, and

Source: Chris Howey/Shutterstock

Source: Thinkstock

The two photos show a ship passing through the present Panama Canal and construction by a consortium of turnkey operators, led by Spain's Sacyr Vallehermosa SA, that will increase capacity and allow larger ships to pass through instead of having to sail around South America.

Turkey can compete better for conventional projects requiring low labor costs. The Chinese companies China State Construction Engineering and Shanghai Construction Group, in fact, have worked on subway systems in Iran and Saudi Arabia, a railway line in Nigeria, a tourist complex in the Bahamas, an oil pipeline in Sudan, and office buildings in the United States.

Arranging Payment Payment for a turnkey operation usually occurs in stages as a project develops, with final payment made once the facility is operating in accordance with the contract. Because currency fluctuations can occur between conception and completion, contracts commonly include price escalation clauses or cost-plus pricing.

The final payment is usually made only if the facility is operating satisfactorily, so disagreements sometimes arise on what constitutes "satisfactorily." For this reason, many turnkey operators insist on performing a feasibility study as part of the contract so they don't build something that, although desired by a local government, may be too large or inefficient.

JOINT VENTURES

Joint ventures may have various combinations of participants and ownership.

A type of operational sharing popular among MNEs is the joint venture (JV). While they are sometimes non-equity arrangements, JVs usually involve equity ownership by more than one organization. We emphasize this latter type in our discussion. Though usually formed to achieve particular objectives, JVs may continue to operate indefinitely as objectives are redefined. Thought of as 50/50 companies, JVs may nonetheless involve more than two companies, one of which may own more than 50 percent. Global Alumina, a joint venture in Guinea for bauxite extraction and processing, has four partners—two from Dubai and one each from Australia and Canada.[61] When more than two organizations participate, the venture is sometimes called a **consortium**.

Possible Combinations

An international joint venture may contain any combination of partners, as long as at least one partner is foreign. Examples include:

- Two companies from the same country joining together in a foreign market, e.g., NEC and Mitsubishi (Japan) in the United Kingdom
- A foreign company joining with a local company, e.g., Great Lakes Chemical (U.S.) and A. H. Al Zamil in Saudi Arabia
- Companies from two or more countries establishing a joint venture in a third country, e.g., Tata Motors (India) and Fiat (Italy) in Argentina
- A private company and a local government forming a joint venture, or *mixed venture*, e.g., that of Gazprom (Russia) with the Bulgarian government
- A private company joining a government-owned company in a third country, e.g., BP Amoco (private British-U.S.) and Eni (government-owned Italian) in Egypt

The more companies in the joint venture, the more complex its management becomes. Development of the long-delayed Boeing 787 (the Dreamliner) was a joint effort among numerous companies from eight countries.[62] In essence, the project was hard to control, and a delay or performance hitch by any one of the participating companies delayed the others and caused overall project problems. Figure 15.6 shows that as a company increases the number of partners and decreases the amount of equity it owns in a foreign operation, its ability to control that operation decreases.

Certain types of companies favor JVs more than others, such as those new at foreign operations or having decentralized domestic decision making. Because they are accustomed to extending control downward in their organizations, it is easier for them to do the same thing in a JV.

EQUITY ALLIANCES

Equity alliances help solidify collaboration.

An **equity alliance** is a collaborative arrangement in which at least one of the companies takes an ownership position (almost always minority) in the other(s). For instance, the Port of Antwerp (Belgium) took a minority position in Essar Ports (India) when the two signed a long-term alliance to mutually improve quality and productivity.[63] In some cases, each party takes an ownership, such as by buying part of each other's shares or by swapping some shares with each other. Panama-based Copa and Colombia-based AeroRepublic (airlines) took equity in each other.[64]

The purpose of the equity ownership is to solidify a collaborating contract, such as a supplier-buyer contract, so that it is more difficult to break—particularly if the ownership is large enough to secure a board membership for the investing company.

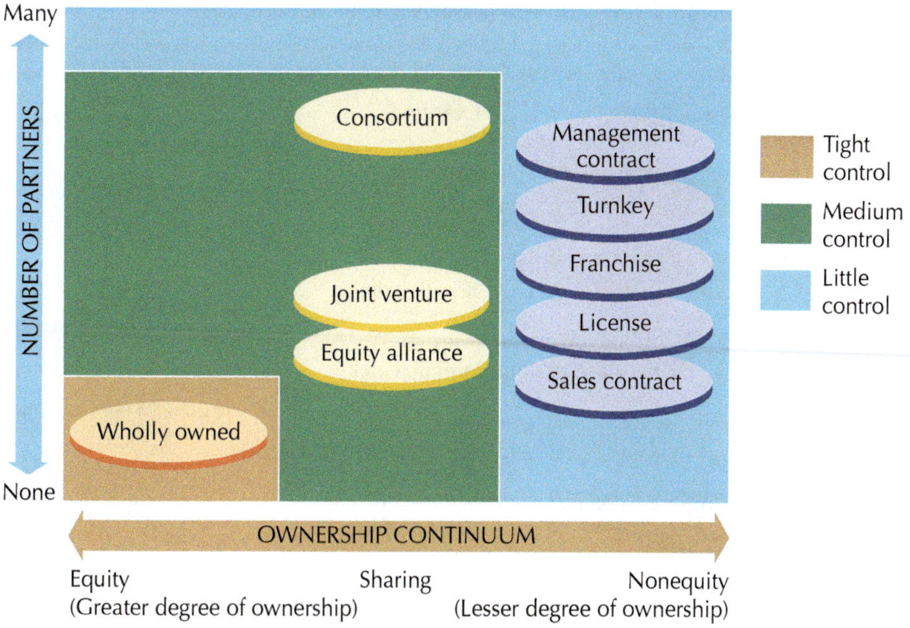

FIGURE 15.6
Collaborative Strategy and Complexity of Control

The more equity a firm puts into a collaborative arrangement, coupled with the fewer partners it takes on, the more control it will have over the foreign operations conducted under the arrangement. Note that non-equity arrangements typically entail at least one and often several partners.

Source: Based on Shaker Zahra and Galal Elhagrasey, "Strategic Management of International Joint Ventures," European Management Journal 12:1 (March 1994): 83–93. Reprinted with permission of Elsevier.

PROBLEMS WITH COLLABORATIVE ARRANGEMENTS

Keep in mind that all parties to a collaborative arrangement must be satisfied with performance. Otherwise, the arrangement may fail. Problems can develop that lead partners to renegotiate in terms of responsibilities, ownership, or management structure. Despite new relationships, many agreements break down or are not renewed at the end of an initial contract period, often because at least one partner becomes dissatisfied with the venture. Frequently, a partner buys out the other's interest and the operation continues as a wholly owned foreign subsidiary. In other breakups, companies agree to dissolve the arrangement or they restructure their alliance.

Figure 15.7 shows that joint venture divorce (and divorce from other collaborative arrangements) can be planned or unplanned, friendly or unfriendly, mutual or non-mutual. The major strains on the arrangements are due to five factors:

- Relative importance to partners
- Divergent objectives
- Control problems
- Comparative contributions and appropriations
- Differences in culture[65]

In spite of our focus on these problems, we do not mean to imply that there are no success stories. There are. The JV between Xerox (U.S.) and Rank (U.K.) is a case in point: not only has it performed well for a long period of time, it even has a JV in Japan with Fuji Photo, which has also performed well.

RELATIVE IMPORTANCE

One partner may give more management attention than the other to a collaborative arrangement. If things go wrong, the active partner blames the less active partner for its lack of attention, while the latter blames the former for making poor decisions. The difference in

FIGURE 15.7 How to Dissolve a Joint Venture

There's more than one way to dissolve a joint venture—and to influence the future of its erstwhile operations.

Source: Based on Manuel G. Serapio Jr. and Wayne F. Cascio, "End Games in International Alliances," *Academy of Management Executive* (May 1996): 67.

DIVORCE SCENARIOS	EXAMPLES
Planned	General Motors (U.S.) and Toyota (Japan)
vs.	
Unplanned	AT&T (U.S.) and Olivetti (Italy)
Friendly	Vitro (Mexico) and Corning (U.S.)
vs.	
Unfriendly	Coors Brewing Co. (U.S.) and Molson Breweries (Canada)
Mutually agreed upon	Ralston Purina (U.S.) and Taiyo Fishery (Japan)
vs.	
Disputed	Sover S.P.A. (Italy) and Suzhou Spectacles No. 1 Factory (China)

OUTCOMES	EXAMPLES
Termination by acquisition	Daewoo Motors (South Korea) and General Motors (U.S.)
Termination by dissolution	Meiji Milk (Japan) and Borden (U.S.)
Termination by reorganization/restructuring of the alliance	Matsushita Electric Industries Co. (Japan) and Solbourne Computer (U.S.)

attention may be due to the partners' different sizes. For example, a JV between a large and a small company uses a larger portion of operations for the small company than for the large one, so the small company may take more interest in the venture.

In addition, if disagreements need to be settled legally, the smaller firm may be at a disadvantage because it lacks the resources to fight its bigger partner. After Igen, a small U.S. firm, licensed its technology to Boehringer Mannheim of Germany, a company with sales of more than 100 times those of Igen, the two companies began to disagree over royalty payments. Igen fought for four years and spent $40 million in legal fees (about the amount of one year of its sales) to win a settlement of over a half billion dollars.[66] This example is unusual, however, because most small firms cannot or will not fight a larger company so effectively.

DIVERGENT OBJECTIVES

Although companies enter into collaborative arrangements because they have complementary goals and capabilities, these may evolve differently over time because one or both change as a result of competitive forces and product dynamics. Thus, a partner may no longer perceive collaboration to be in its best interest. (This is shown humorously in Figure 15.8.) For instance, IBM and Toshiba partnered until IBM's shift in product line required a type of monitor with which Toshiba had little expertise.[67] Further, one partner may want to reinvest earnings for growth while the other wants to receive dividends. Or one partner may want to expand the product line and sales territory while the other may see this as competition with its wholly owned operations (a point of disagreement between BP and its Russian partner, TNK.)[68] If one partner wants to sell or buy from the venture, the other may disagree with the price.

Partners also may differ over performance standards. GM and Fuji Heavy Industries' disagreements in Thailand over quality standards led to both of them performing time-consuming and expensive inspections that even included paint jobs.[69]

"Norman won't collaborate."

FIGURE 15.8 All parties must perceive that their objectives are best met by collaborative arrangements.

Source: Robert Weber/New Yorker Cartoon Bank/www.cartoonbank.com

QUESTIONS OF CONTROL

Sharing assets with another company may generate confusion over control, as happened when the Israeli company Remedia partnered with the German firm Humana Milchunion to make baby formula. Humana Milchunion removed Vitamin B1 from the formula concentrate without notifying its partners, which led to the deaths of three infants.[70] Moreover, when companies license their logos and trademarks for use on products they do not make, they may lack the ability to discern and control quality, with a detrimental effect on sales of all products in various countries using the brand name and logo. Pierre Cardin's licensing of its label for hundreds of products—from clothing to clocks to toilets—led to poor-quality goods that hurt the image of the high-quality ones.[71]

In collaborative arrangements, even though control is ceded to one of the partners, both may be held responsible for problems. Further, the question of control is rife with gray areas and may cause anxiety among employees. In a proposed JV between Merrill Lynch and UFJ, a Japanese senior manager queried, "Who is going to be in charge—a Japanese, an American, or both?"[72] When no single company has control of a collaborative arrangement, the operation may lack direction. At the same time, if one partner dominates, it must still consider the other's interests.

COMPARATIVE CONTRIBUTIONS AND APPROPRIATIONS

Partners' relative capabilities of contributing technology, capital, or some other asset may change over time. Relative contributions may also change when partners alter their strategy. In addition, Partner A may suspect that Partner B is taking more from the operation (particularly knowledge-based assets) than Partner A is, which would enable Partner B to become a competitor. (Recall our discussion of appropriability.) In the face of such suspicions, information may be withheld, eventually weakening the operation. There are many examples of companies "going it alone" after they no longer needed their partner—particularly if the purpose of the collaboration was to gain knowledge.

CULTURE CLASHES

Differences in Country Cultures Managers and companies alike are affected by their national cultures, and collaborative arrangements bring them directly together. For instance, they may vary in preferences in the method, timing, and frequency with which they report on project management progress.[73] Further, there are national differences in whether they evaluate primarily on the operations' effect on shareholders versus stakeholders in general.[74] These differences may mean that one partner is satisfied while the other is not. Such a clash led to the dissolution of a joint venture between Danone and its Chinese government-owned partner because the latter put employment maximization ahead of efficiencies and profits.[75]

Finally, the trust that companies have toward foreign partners is influenced by the general level of trust that exists within their home markets; some companies don't like to collaborate with those of very different cultures.[76] Nevertheless, JVs from culturally distant countries can thrive when partners learn to deal with each other's differences.[77]

Differences in Corporate Cultures Similar corporate cultures aid companies' ability to communicate and transfer knowledge to each other, whereas collaborations can experience problems when these cultures differ.[78] One partner may be accustomed to internal managerial promotions while the other opens its searches to outsiders. One may use a participatory management style and the other an authoritarian style. One may be entrepreneurial, the other risk-averse. This is why many companies delay JV collaboration until they have had long-term positive experiences with each other, such as through distributorship or licensing arrangements. In fact, there is evidence that a gradual increase in commitment, such as developing an alliance with a company before acquiring it, is a means of improving performance.[79] Of course, as with marriage, a good prior relationship between two companies does not guarantee a good match in a joint venture.[80]

MANAGING INTERNATIONAL COLLABORATIONS

The evolution to a different operating mode may

- be the result of experience.
- create organizational tensions.

As collaborative arrangements evolve, partners need to reassess certain decisions. For example, alterations in a company's resource base may render collaborations either more or less advantageous as a mode of operation. Or a country's risk and government ownership requirements may change. Finally, the relationship among partners may evolve positively or negatively. Because of such changes, a company needs to continually reexamine the fit between collaboration and its own strategy.

We now discuss the fit between the attractiveness of countries and the modes of operation, the problem of switching from one mode to another, the importance of learning from experience, and the necessity of dealing with partners.

COUNTRY ATTRACTIVENESS AND OPERATIONAL OPTIONS

Figure 15.9 illustrates a type of matrix that relates country attractiveness with operating forms. A company should ordinarily make a higher level of commitment, such as wholly owned operations, in the countries that appear in the top left corner, which are very attractive and fit best with its capabilities.

Country attractiveness is also high in the top right corner, but a company has weak competitive strength for those markets if, say, it lacks the knowledge of operating therein. If the cost is not too high, the company might attempt to gain greater domination in those markets by partnering with another whose assets are complementary.

A company might divest in countries in the bottom right corner or "harvest" by pulling out all possible cash it can generate while not replacing depreciated facilities. It could also engage in non-equity arrangements, thereby generating some income without investment outlays. In other areas, it must analyze situations individually to decide which approach to take. These are marginal areas that do not fit as neatly in the analysis.

FIGURE 15.9 Country Attractiveness/Company Strength Matrix

In a given scenario, a country in the upper left-hand corner may be the most attractive place for a company to locate operations. Why? Because its market is well suited to the company's greatest competitive strength and thus to its highest level of commitment (e.g., establishing a wholly owned subsidiary). A country in the upper right-hand corner also boasts an attractive market but poses a problem for a company whose competitive strengths don't quite match the opportunity (perhaps it has no experience in this particular market). It needn't forgo the opportunity, but it will probably prefer a joint venture or some other form of collaborative operation. Finally, note that because everything is subject to change—both a company's capabilities and the features of a country's market—firms try to be dynamic in their approach to potential operating modes.

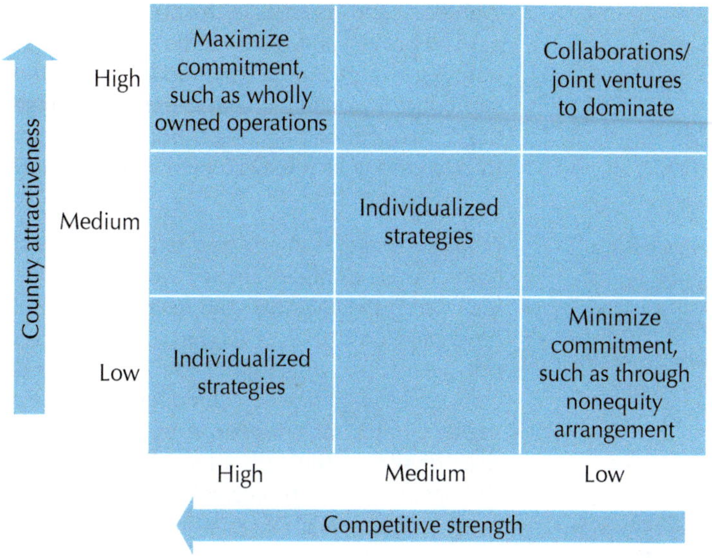

Although such a matrix may serve to guide decision making, managers must use it with caution. First, separating the attractiveness of a country from a company's position is often difficult; the country may seem attractive because it fits with the company. Second, some of the recommended actions take a defeatist attitude toward competitive position. Many companies have built competitive strength in markets previously dominated by competitors or built profitable positions without being the competitive leader.

PROBLEMS OF SWITCHING MODES

As companies switch from one mode of international operations to another, some individuals gain and others lose responsibilities. For example, moving from exporting to foreign production may reduce the size of domestic marketing and manufacturing divisions, thus disadvantaging those people who lost responsibilities if bonuses and promotions are based largely on the size of their sales or profits. Given that lower performance is due to decisions outside their control, companies will need to revise performance evaluations.

LEARNING FROM EXPERIENCE

Some evidence indicates that as companies gain experience by entering more collaborative arrangements, they perform better within them. However, improved performance is most associated with similar types of collaborations, such as JVs, from one place to another and with management approaches that are similar in a series of alliances.[81] In essence, companies may choose partners better and learn how to improve synergies between their partners and themselves. At the same time, effective alliance management has been undergoing significant changes; thus, companies cannot necessarily replicate what has succeeded for them in the past.[82]

DEALING WITH PARTNERS

Finding and Evaluating Potential Partners Whether a company seeks a collaborative partner or reacts to a request for partnership, it must evaluate the potential partner's resources, motivation, and compatibility.

Managers can identify potential partners by monitoring journals, attending technical conferences, developing links with academic institutions—even through social acquaintances.[83] Company visibility and partnership potential can be boosted through trade fairs, brochures, Web sites, and contacts in the potential collaboration locale.

The proven ability to handle similar types of collaboration is a key professional qualification. A good track record may indicate trustworthiness that could negate the need for expensive control mechanisms to carry out interests. Once into a collaboration, partners can also build trust through actions.[84] But every company has to start somewhere. Without a proven track record, a firm may have to negotiate harder and make more concessions.

In technology agreements,

- a seller does not want to give information without assurance of payment.
- a buyer does not want to pay without evaluating information.

Negotiating the Arrangement: The Question of Secrecy The value of many technologies would diminish if they were widely used or understood. Contracts historically have included provisions that the recipient will not divulge such information, while some sellers have held onto the ownership and production of specific components so recipients would not have full knowledge of the product or the capability to produce an exact copy. Often companies want to sell techniques they have not yet used commercially. A buyer is reluctant to buy what it has not seen, but a seller that shows the work in process to the potential buyer risks divulging the technology. For these and other reasons, it is common to set up prearrangements that protect all parties.

A controversial negotiation area is the secrecy surrounding the financial terms of arrangements. In some countries, for example, licensing contracts must be approved by governmental agencies, which consult their counterparts in other countries about similar agreements in order to improve their negotiating position. Many MNEs object to this procedure, believing that contract terms between two companies are proprietary information with competitive importance, and market conditions usually dictate the need for very different terms in different countries.

CONCEPT CHECK

In discussing "Behavioral Factors" with regard to international business in Chapter 2, we observe that there are substantial differences in the degrees of trust that people in different cultures extend to others. We go on to explain that when trust is high, managers tend to spend more time focusing on operational issues and less fussing over every little detail. Not surprisingly, the cost of doing business tends to be lower in this scenario.

Controlling Through Contracts and Trust Contracts with other companies entail some loss of control over the asset or intangible property being transferred. This creates two concerns that are not necessarily analogous—the partner's performance competency and the partner's integrity so as not to act opportunistically.[85] Choice of partner is, of course, important. Additionally, a host of potential problems must be settled as well as possible by setting mutual goals and spelling out all expectations in the contract. Of course, not everything can be included in a contract. The parties need to develop sufficient rapport so that common sense also plays a part in running the collaboration.[86] Partnering with a firm that highly values its reputation is probably a plus as well, inasmuch as it may prefer to settle differences quietly rather than having them exposed in the press. Frank communications may help determine potential partners' underlying expectations, which may otherwise come as a surprise. One study of local firms in China and Russia discovered that they had expected their foreign partners to deal much more with the Chinese and Russian governments (such as to alleviate bribery payments) than the foreign partners actually did.[87]

Although contracts have limits, their provisions should at least address the following issues:

- Will the agreement be terminated if the parties don't adhere to the directives?
- What methods will be used to test for quality?
- What geographic limitations should be placed on an asset's use?
- Which company will manage which parts of the operation outlined in the agreement?
- What will be each company's future commitments?

- How will each company buy from, sell to, or otherwise use intangible assets that result from the collaborative arrangement?
- How will revenues be divided?

In addition to contract terms, trust in the management of another company must be considered in choosing a partner. At the same time, trust is affected by national culture and, in turn, influences how much a partner wants to cover in a contract. Thus, if parties from cultures with similar levels of trust come together, they can more likely agree on what must be incorporated in detailed contractual arrangements and what must be left to trust.[88]

When collaborating with another company, managers must

- Continue to monitor performance,
- Assess whether to change the form of operations,
- Develop competency in managing a portfolio of arrangements.

Improving Performance Contracting with a capable and compatible partner is necessary but insufficient to ensure success. An agreement, once operational, must be run effectively. Management should estimate potential sales and costs, determine whether the arrangement is meeting quality standards, and assess servicing requirements to check whether goals are being met and whether each partner is doing an adequate job.

In addition to continually assessing partners' performance, a company must periodically assess the need for change in the type of collaboration, such as whether to replace a licensing agreement with a joint venture. At the same time, as its number of collaborations grows, it should consider developing competency in managing the portfolio of arrangements so that it applies what it learns in one situation to others.[89]

Looking to the Future

Why Innovation Breeds Collaboration

More than a half century ago, John Kenneth Galbraith wrote that the era of cheap invention was over, noting that "because development is costly, it follows that it can be carried out only by a firm that has the resources associated with considerable size."[90] The statement seems prophetic in terms of the estimated billions of investment dollars needed to bring a new commercial aircraft to market, eliminate death from diseases, develop defenses against unfriendly countries and terrorists, guard against cyberspace intrusions, and commercialize energy substitutes for petroleum. However, it overlooks the ability of companies to pool resources through collaboration—and that such collaboration will likely continue to grow.

Markets must be truly global if high development costs are to be recouped. The sums needed to develop and market solutions to major global problems are out of reach of most companies acting alone. Even if the companies grow ever larger through internal growth or mergers and acquisitions, governments nevertheless place limits because of antitrust concerns.

Moreover, with the realization that the costs of integrating a merged or acquired company can be very high, collaborative arrangements will likely become even more important in the future, involving both horizontal and vertical linkages among firms from many industries in many countries. However, some evidence indicates that collaborations slow the speed of innovation because of internalization and appropriation factors.[91] At the same time, although business strategists have advised companies for some time to specialize on what they do best, there is growing evidence that many customers prefer to deal with one rather than multiple suppliers. The result, especially in emerging economies, may be the return in popularity of conglomerates.[92] Thus, large companies that have the resources to go it alone may have advantages over small companies that do not.

Although some product development requires huge sums, most is much more modest. Nevertheless, companies lack all the product- and market-specific resources to go it alone everywhere in the world, especially if national differences dictate operating changes on a country-to-country basis. Such situations present opportunities for alliances that employ complementary resources from different companies.

Collaborative arrangements will bring both opportunities and problems as MNEs move simultaneously to new countries and to contractual arrangements with new companies. Differences must be overcome in a number of areas:

- Country cultures that may cause partners to obtain and evaluate information differently
- National disparities in governmental policies, institutions, and industry structures that constrain companies from using operating forms they would prefer
- Distinct underlying ideologies and values affecting corporate cultures and practices that strain relationships
- Different strategic directions resulting from partners' interests that cause disagreement over objectives and contributions
- Diverse management styles and organizational structures that cause partners to interact ineffectively[93]

The more partners in an alliance, the more cumbersome the decision-making and control processes. ■

CASE The oneworld Airline Alliance

Following approval by U.S. and Japanese authorities for antitrust immunity, American Airlines (AA) and Japan Airlines (JAL) began sharing routes in 2011 that connect mainland North America with East Asia through a non-equity joint venture.[94] Map 15.2 shows these routes and also illustrates that flights between Honolulu and Japan are not included in the agreement. This JV is similar to one forged among AA, British Airways (BA), and Iberia for trans-Atlantic travel that began operating in 2010. In both cases, the agreements allow representatives from each airline to jointly manage capacity, sell and promote space on flights operated by each other, divide revenues, and schedule connecting flights. The major thrusts for these ventures are to cut operating costs by better controlling capacity, to avoid disruptive price competition, and to improve scheduling so that there are more and better departure times and connections for passengers.

The proposals are merely extensions to a historical series of alliances linking international airlines. In fact, the airline industry is unique in that its need to form collaborative arrangements has been important almost from the start of international air travel because of regulatory, cost, and competitive factors. In recent years, this need has accelerated because of airlines' difficult profit performance.

In effect, the airlines have been squeezed. First, costs have risen, particularly due to oil prices and the need for greater security since 9/11. While pre-departure airport passenger-security checks are well publicized, some other costly airline security processes are not, such as providing governmental agencies with advance passenger information and working with freight forwarders and supply-chain operators to ensure the safety of cargo shipments carried on passenger aircraft. Second, a long-term trend toward greater price competition hinders airlines' ability to pass on increased costs to passengers—a situation exacerbated by the emergence of discount airlines and customers' ability to search the Internet for lower fares. Third, with the global recession curtailing passenger demand the airline industry has added capacity sparingly. Although the growth in international passenger jet travel has largely spurred globalization, no airline has sufficient finances or aircraft to serve the whole world. Yet passengers are traveling the whole world and perceive an advantage in booking on airline connections that will minimize both distances and connecting times at airports while offering reasonable assurance of reaching destinations with checked luggage more or

MAP 15.2 American Airlines and Japan Airlines: Trans-Pacific Routes

Note that the joint activity involves only flights from mainland North America into East Asia.

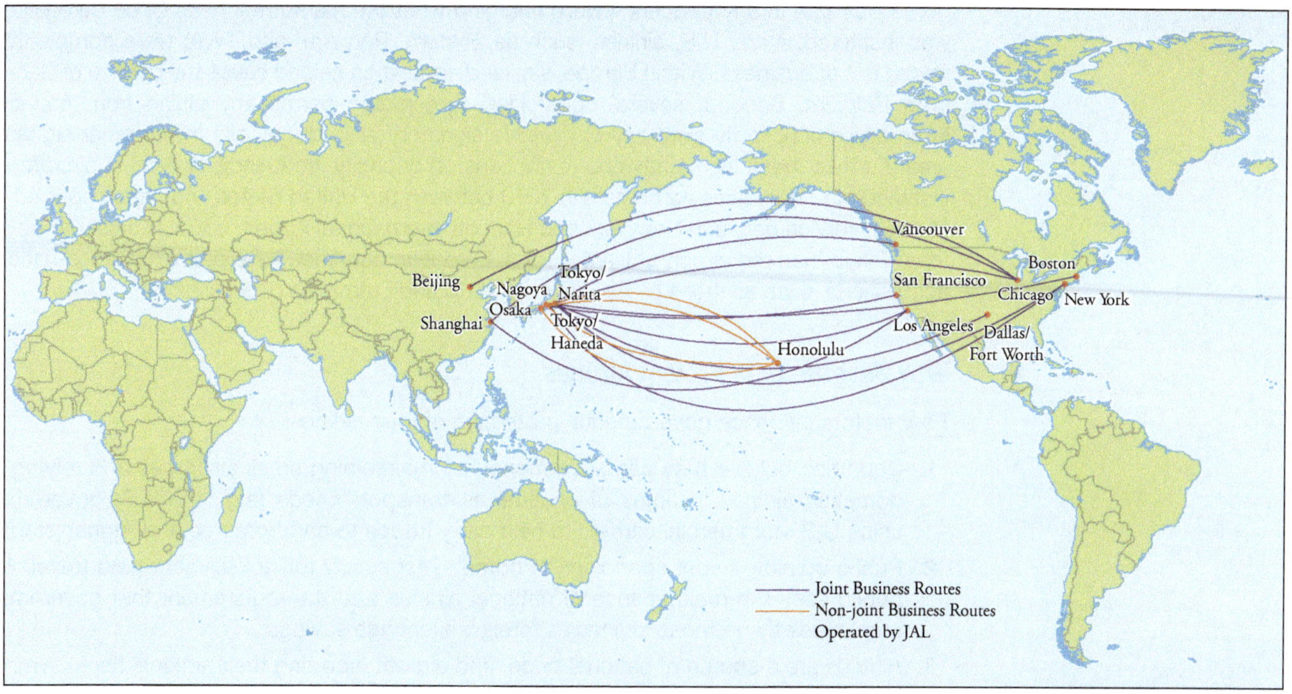

less on schedule. Thus, airlines have increasingly worked together to provide more seamless experiences for passengers and to cut costs.

This discussion, however, should not imply that all cost cuts necessitate collaboration. For example, in recent years, airlines have implemented a number of cost-saving changes that cover the gamut from ticket purchase to arrival at destination. Online purchases of electronic tickets have largely replaced airlines' need to pay hefty commissions to travel agencies and to issue and maintain costly inventories of paper tickets. Self-service check-in at airports reduces the need for agents. On board, especially on short flights, less is included in the price of the ticket, such as food, pillows, and headphones. In fact, the trip may be on one of the airlines' discount subsidiaries.

A Bit of History: Changing Government Regulations

Historically, governments played a major role in airline ownership. Many government-owned airlines were monopolies within their domestic markets, money losers, and recipients of government subsidies. However, there has been a subsequent move toward privatization.

What Governments Can Regulate

Despite the move toward privatization, governments still regulate airlines and agree on restrictions and rights largely through reciprocal agreements. Specifically, they control:

- Which foreign carriers have landing rights
- Which airports and aircraft the carriers can use
- The frequency of flights
- Whether foreign carriers can fly beyond the country (for instance, whether Iberia, after flying from Spain to the United States, can then fly from the United States to Panama)
- Overflight privileges
- Fares airlines can charge

Several notable regulatory changes have occurred in recent years. First, the U.S. domestic market has been deregulated, which means that any approved U.S. carrier can fly any U.S. domestic route in any frequency while charging what the market will bear. Once deregulation was instituted, many U.S. airlines (such as Eastern, Pan Am, and TWA) were competitively forced out of business. Within Europe, similar deregulation helped cause the demise of Sabena from Belgium. Second, several open-skies agreements permit any airline from countries in an agreement to fly from any city in one signatory area to any city in the other signatory area. Further, these flights have no restrictions on capacity, frequency, or type of aircraft. For instance, an open-skies agreement in 2010 between the United States and Japan spurred AA to begin service between New York and Haneda International Airport, which is closer to downtown Tokyo than the airport at Narita. Third, European countries have permitted cross-national acquisitions, such as those by Air France of KLM and Lufthansa of Swissair.

Why Governments Protect Airlines

Four factors influence governments' protection of their airlines:

1. Countries believe they can save money by maintaining small air forces and relying on domestic airlines in times of unusual air transport needs (e.g., the U.S. government using U.S. commercial carriers to help carry troops to and from Iraq and Afghanistan).
2. Public opinion favors spending "at home"—especially for government-paid travel. The public sees the maintenance of national airlines and the requirement that government employees fly on those airlines as foreign-exchange savings.
3. Airlines are a source of national pride, and aircraft (sporting their national flags) symbolize a country's sovereignty and technical competence. This national identification is less important than it used to be, but it is still important in some developing countries.
4. Worries about protecting airspace for security reasons are less of a concern today because foreign carriers routinely overfly a country's territory to reach inland gateways, such as JAL's flights between Tokyo and Chicago. Further, overflight treaties are quite common, even among unfriendly nations (e.g., Cubana overflies the United States en route to Canada, and AA overflies Cuba en route to South America).

Regulatory Obstacles to Expansion

Even if airlines had the financial capacity to expand everywhere in the world, national regulations would limit this expansion. With few exceptions, airlines cannot fly on lucrative domestic routes in foreign countries. For example, JAL cannot compete on the New York to Los Angeles route, nor can AA fly between Tokyo and Nagoya. Further, the U.S. government limits foreign ownership in a U.S. airline to 25 percent of voting stock.

Thus, airlines cannot easily control a flight network abroad that will feed passengers into their international flights. JAL has no U.S. domestic flights to take passengers into Chicago for connections to Tokyo, while AA has scores of such flights. However, JAL does have an advantage within Japan.

Finally, airlines usually cannot service pairs of foreign countries. AA cannot fly between Brazil and South Africa because those governments give landing rights on such routes only to Brazilian and South African airlines. To avoid these restrictions, airlines must ally themselves with carriers from other countries.

Collaboration Examples Related to Motives

Cost Factors

Certain airlines have always dominated certain international airports, thereby amassing critical capabilities in them, such as baggage handlers and aircraft-handling equipment. Sharing these capabilities with other airlines may spread costs. For example, BA has long handled passenger check-in, baggage loading, and maintenance for a number of other airlines at London's Heathrow Airport.

The high cost of maintenance and reservations systems has led to JVs involving multiple airlines from multiple countries, such as ownership in the Apollo and Galileo reservation systems. Actually, the reservations systems are motivated by more than cost savings, inasmuch as the pooling of resources provides customers with better service.

Connecting Flights

Given that governments restrict domestic or regional routes to their own carriers, airlines have long had agreements whereby passengers can transfer from one to another with a through ticket. However, people tend to select from among the first routings that show up on computer screens, and routings from one airline to another often appear on screens after those involving only one airline. Further, when passengers see that they must change airlines, they worry more about making those connections across great distances within ever-larger airports. To help avoid this worry, airlines have agreed to code sharing—a procedure whereby the same flight may have a designation for more than one carrier. For instance, the same flight operated by BA from New York-JFK to London Heathrow is listed as AA 142, BA 1507, and Iberia 4240. Hence, AA passengers originating in, say, Tampa and connecting at JFK to Heathrow may worry less about the JFK connection because they see themselves on the same airline all the way. However, they may still need to go from one terminal to another to make the plane-change. In such a situation, airlines must adhere to a longer minimum connecting time when showing a through/connecting flight.

The oneworld Alliance

The oneworld Alliance comprises 12 airlines: airberlin, American Airlines, British Airways, Cathay Pacific, Finnair, Iberia, Japan Airlines, LAN, Malaysian Airlines, Qantas, Royal Jordanian, and S7 Airlines. (The adjacent photo shows several of these parked alongside each other at Tokyo's Narita Airport.) oneworld competes largely with two other alliances: Star and SkyTeam. Airlines in these alliances cooperate on various programs, such as allowing passengers to earn credits for free or upgraded travel on any one of them. In the case of oneworld, all members flying into Narita Airport in Tokyo have moved into terminal 2, which shortens legal connecting times among them. They also advertise their affiliation; you may have seen aircraft painted with the airline's name and logo along with the oneworld name. These alliances allow for considerable cooperation, such as code-sharing; however, antitrust regulations (unless given immunity) prohibit their members from coordinating routes, schedules, and prices.

The Trans-Atlantic Joint Venture

Three airlines—AA, BA, and Iberia—have a combined network of over 400 destinations in over 100 countries and account for more than 6,000 daily departures. When their JV and antitrust immunity were approved, they collectively had 48 different routes between Europe and North America that included 22 North American and 13 European cities. Of these 48 routes, they competed directly on only nine.

In the short time since the airlines entered this JV, they have been able to coordinate schedules better for the convenience of passengers. For instance, whereas AA and BA used to have flights leaving between New York-JKF and London-Heathrow within minutes of each other, they now operate 16 flights per day between those two airports and have been able to coordinate departure times so that the flights leave approximately one hour apart. This gives passengers more options in finding a departure time convenient to them and allows for more connecting flight alternatives in either direction. Further, the participating airlines can now designate their own flight numbers on domestic connections when they connect

Aircraft from several oneworld alliance members parked at Narita Airport, Tokyo.
Source: Kyodo/AP Images

to trans-Atlantic destinations. For instance, Iberia shows one of its routes as San Diego to Madrid, even though both the San Diego–Chicago and Chicago–Madrid flights are operated by AA.

Because of dual or multiple designations and the sharing of revenue, more than one airline's sales force is trying to fill seats on the same route. The result is boosted sales, which allows the JV members to offer new routes, such as non-stop service between Chicago and Helsinki and between New York and Budapest that have come about since the JV's formation.

The AA–JAL Joint Venture

JAL is also a large airline, serving 85 cities in 20 countries and territories. Its joint venture with AA has the same advantages and objectives as the JV across the Atlantic. Some changes are notable. By altering each company's flight times between Chicago O'Hare and Tokyo Narita and tweaking schedules of connecting flights in both cities, many more passengers can make connections within two hours. For instance, 22 more flights from 20 more departure cities can make such connections for travel from O'Hare to Narita.

JAL has moved its O'Hare flights from the international terminal to be adjacent to AA. Meanwhile, AA has moved its Japanese offices to JAL's headquarters building, a move that eases communications between the two airlines. Both are helping each other with cultural questions, such as JAL aiding AA with public address announcements in Japanese to make them more meaningful to Japanese passengers. Meanwhile, plans are afoot for greatly increasing code sharing between the two airlines, especially to points beyond gateway cities, such as showing a JAL flight as Tokyo–Salt Lake City and as an AA flight beyond Tokyo to JAL-served cities such as Hanoi.

At this writing, JAL and BA are discussing a similar arrangement to connect flights between Japan and the United Kingdom. If this comes to fruition, it will create an effective around-the-world agreement.

Why Not a Merger or an Acquisition?

To begin with, government regulations such as ownership requirements would prevent a merger or acquisition between U.S. and non-U.S. carriers. Even if they didn't, fusing companies together creates daunting problems, even for domestic mergers and acquisitions. At this writing, discussions are underway for a merger between AA and US Airways. Their respective pilots' unions are strong and function under different operating and compensation systems. Although US Airways has no trans-Pacific routes, it does fly trans-Atlantic, and those routes will have to interface with the existing agreement that AA has with BA and Iberia. US Airways is a member of the Star Alliance, thus it will have to sever that relationship and figure out how accrued passenger points will be handled.

In the JVs, each company keeps its own identity and operates independently except for the coordination of the trans-oceanic routes. In addition, each airline in the JVs and within oneworld has developed its own culture and brand to appeal to its own nationality. BA is still strongest with British passengers, JAL with Japanese passengers, etc. By keeping separate identities, despite sharing flights, the member airlines can capitalize on the differences. Nevertheless, natural extensions are possible by strengthening collaboration, such as having check-in counters worldwide that handle all oneworld passengers and combining more airport lounges as a cost-saving measure. It is probably safe to say that future cooperation will strengthen rather than weaken among oneworld members.

QUESTIONS

15-3. Companies within the oneworld, Star, and Sky Team alliances have also engaged in major mergers and acquisitions (M&A): Frontier and US Air (Star), Delta and Northwest (Sky Team), and Continental and United (Star). What are the advantages and disadvantages of M&A versus non-equity alliances in this industry?

15-4. Some airlines, such as Southwest, have survived as niche players without extensive international connections. Can they continue this strategy?

15-5. Why should an airline not be able to establish service anywhere in the world simply by demonstrating that it can and will comply with the local labor and business laws of the host country?

15-6. The U.S. law limiting foreign ownership of U.S. airlines to no more than 25 percent of voting shares was enacted in 1938. Is this law an anachronism, or are there valid reasons for having it today?

15-7. What will be the consequences if a few large airlines or networks dominate global air service?

15-8. Many airlines have recently been no more than marginally profitable. Is this such a vital industry that governments should intervene to guarantee their survival? If so, how?

15-9. What methods could JAL and AA use to divide revenue and expenses on code-shared routes?

SUMMARY

- Selling abroad by exporting home-country production may not be advantageous because of lower production costs abroad, high transport costs, the need to alter products substantially, protectionist barriers, lack of domestic capacity, and consumer preferences to buy from specific countries.
- Companies often operate with FDI, especially wholly owned, because of inability to find an acceptable partner and because such operations may lower operating costs, lessen the possibility of developing competitors, and free them to follow global strategies.
- Some advantages of collaborative arrangements, whether a company is operating domestically or internationally, are to spread and reduce costs, allow a firm to specialize in its primary competencies, avoid certain competition, secure vertical and horizontal links, and learn from other companies.
- Some motivations for collaborative arrangements that are specific to international operations are to gain location-specific assets, overcome legal constraints, diversify among countries, and minimize exposure in risky environments.
- The forms of foreign operations differ in the amount and type of resources a company commits and the proportion of resources committed at home rather than abroad. Collaborative arrangements reduce such commitment.
- Although the type of collaborative arrangement a company chooses should match its strategic objectives, the choice often means a trade-off among objectives.
- Licensing is granting another company the use of some rights (such as patents, copyrights, or trademarks), usually for a fee. It is a means of establishing foreign production and reaching foreign markets that may minimize the licensor's capital outlays, prevent the free use of assets by other companies, allow the receipt of assets from other companies in return, and allow for income in some markets in which exportation or investment is not feasible.
- Franchising differs from licensing in that granting the use of intangible property (usually a trademark) requires the franchisor to assist in operations on a continuing basis.
- An international management contract is a means to secure income by managing a foreign operation while providing little of the capital outlay.
- Turnkey projects are contracts for construction of another company's operating facilities. Historically large and diverse, they necessitate specialized skills and abilities to deal with top-level government authorities.
- Joint ventures are a special type of collaborative arrangement in which two or more organizations share an operation or project, usually with each taking equity in it.
- There are various combinations of joint venture participants, including governments and private companies and two or more participants from the same or different countries.
- Equity alliances occur when a company takes an equity position in the company with which it has a collaborative arrangement so as to solidify the collaborating contract.
- A common motive for collaboration is to take advantage of different companies' complementary resources.
- Problems occur in collaborative arrangements when partners place different levels of importance on them, have different objectives, encounter control problems, worry that their partner is putting in too little or taking out too much from the operation, and misunderstand each other as a result of their different country or company cultures.
- Contracting performance by another company does not negate management's responsibility to develop objectives and assess performance.
- Companies may use different types of collaborative arrangements for their foreign operations in different countries or for different products. As diversity increases, coordinating and managing the foreign operations becomes more complex.

KEY TERMS

appropriability theory
bargaining school theory
consortium
cross-licensing
***dependencia* theory**
equity alliance
internalization
resource-based view (of the firm)

ENDNOTES

1 ***Sources include the following:*** Fidel León-Darder is Associate Professor and Cristina Villar is Assistant Professor, both in the Department of Management, Universitat de València (Spain). They used information from the following sources: J. Pla-Barber, F. León-Darder, and C. Villar, "The Internationalization of Soft-Services: Entry Modes and Main Determinants in the Spanish Hotel Industry." *Service Business* 5:2 (2011): 139–154; M. M. Massot, L.M. Vegas, and M.A. García, (1997): "Sol Meliá: Un Nuevo Paradigma en la Gestión Hotelera". In J. J. Durán (ed.): *Multinacionales Españolas II: Nuevas Experiencias de Internacionalización* (Madrid: Pirámide, 1997): 73–110; www.meliahotelsinternational.com (retrieved April 19, 2013); "Sol Meliá Absorbe la Cadena TRYP en una Operación Valorada en 72,500 Millones," *Cinco Días* (August 22, 2001) at www.cincodías.com (retrieved January 5, 2013); "Sol Meliá Compra una Cadena en Alemania por 16.5 Millones," *Cinco Días* (November 9, 2007) at www.cincodias.com (retrieved February 7, 2013);

"La Cadena Sol Meliá Vende la Marca TRYP al Grupo Hotelero Americano Wyndham: La Operación, Cifrada en unos 32 Millones, No Implica la Transacción de Establecimientos," *Diario de Mallorca* (June 9, 2010) at www.diariodemallorca.es (retrieved March 21, 2013); F. Contractor and S. Kundu, "Modal Choice in a World of Alliances: Analyzing Organizational Forms in International Hotel Sector," *Journal of International Business Studies* 29:2 (1998): 325–57; F. León-Darder, C. Villar , and J. Pla-Barber, "Entry Mode Choice in the Internationalization of the Hotel Industry: A Holistic Approach," *Service Industries Journal* 31:1 (2011): 107–122; "La Primera Aventura Británica de Escarrer – Meliá White House, un Hotel en Londres 'Made in Spain'," *Actualidad Económica* (September 23, 2002) at www.actualidad-economica.com (retrieved February 7, 2013); "Sol Meliá Renueva su Portfolio en el Exterior con Siete Altas y Ocho Bajas," *Alimarket* (March 1, 2008) at www.alimarket.es (retrieved January 19, 2013); "Sol MeliáControla Ya el 32% del Mercado Turístico Cubano," *El País* (May 16, 2005) at www.elpais.com (retrieved March 21, 2013); "Sol Meliá Busca una Alianza para Crecer en EE.UU," *La Vanguardia* (September 18, 1999) at www.lavanguardia.es (retrieved February 7, 2013); "Sol Meliá, Barceló y Blau Hotels Entrarán en China con la Gestión de Hoteles en Shanghai," *Cinco Días* (May 5, 1999) at www.cincodias.com (retrieved January 5, 2013); "Sol Meliá, Barceló y Riu Descartan Nuevas Inversiones en Asia a Corto Plazo por la 'Complejidad' del Mercado," *Europa Press* (February 6, 2006) at www.europapress.es (retrieved January 5, 2013); "Barceló Abandona la Gestión de su Primer Hotel en China," *Cinco Días* (January 5, 2001) at www.cincodias.com (retrieved January 5, 2013); "Sol Meliá Entra en China de la Mano de un Grupo Local y otro de Cuba," *Cinco Días* (July 10, 2010) at www.cincodias.com (retrieved January 5, 2013); "Meliá Apuesta por la Internacionalización en 2013 Para Reforzar su Liderazgo y Hacer Frente al Entorno," at www.meliahotelsinternational.com/es/sala-de-prensa/30012013/melia-apuesta-internacionalizacion-2013-reforzar-su-liderazgo-hacer-frente (retrieved April 19, 2013); "Meliá Hotels International Anuncia en Kenia su Interés de Expansión en África Subsahariana," at www.meliahotelsinternational.com/es/sala-de-prensa/26092012/melia-hotels-international-anuncia-kenia-su-interes-expansion-africa.

2 "Looking to the Future," *Business Europe* 50:18 (October 1, 2010): 7.

3 John Griffiths, "VW May Build Beetle in Europe to Meet Demand," *Financial Times* (November 11, 1998): 17.

4 Peter Marsh, "The World's Wash Day," *Financial Times* (April 29, 2002): 6.

5 "India-EU FTA to Include Tariff Reduction on Import of Vehicles," *Accord Fintech* [Mumbai] (May 20, 2011).

6 Jill Gabrielle Klein, "Us versus Them, or Us versus Everyone? Delineating Consumer Aversion to Foreign Goods," *Journal of International Business Studies* 33:2 (2002): 34563.

7 "'Made in Australia' Label Confuses Shoppers: Choice Survey," *Asia Pulse* (May 18, 2011).

8 John S. Hulland, "The Effects of Country-of-Brand and Brand Name on Product Evaluation and Consideration: A Cross-Country Comparison," *Journal of International Consumer Marketing* 11 (1999): 23–39; Ali Riza Apil and Erdener Kaynak, "Georgian Consumers' Evaluation of Products Sourced from European Union Member Countries," *International Journal of Commerce and Management* 20:2 (2010): 167–87.

9 An excellent overview of the literature is Jean-François Hennart, "Transaction Cost Theory and International Business," *Journal of Retailing* 86:3 (September 2010): 257–69.

10 *Internalization theory,* or holding a monopoly control over certain information or other proprietary assets, builds on earlier market-imperfections work by Ronald H. Coase, "The Nature of the Firm," *Economica* 4 (1937): 386–405. It has been noted by such writers as M. Casson, "The Theory of Foreign Direct Investment," Discussion Paper No. 50 (Reading, UK: University of Reading International Investment and Business Studies, November 1980); Alan M. Rugman, *Inside the Multinationals: The Economics of Internal Markets* (New York: Columbia University Press, 1981); David J. Teece, "Transactions Cost Economics and the Multinational Enterprise," Berkeley Business School International Business Working Paper Series No. IB-3 (1985); B. Kogut and U. Zander, "Knowledge of the Firm and the Evolutionary Theory of the Multinational Corporation," *Journal of International Business Studies* 24:4 (1993): 625–45; Peter W. Liesch and Gary A. Knight, "Information Internalization and Hurdle Rates in Small and Medium Enterprise Internationalization," *Journal of International Business Studies* 30:2 (1999): 383–96.

11 Eric M. Johnson, "Harnessing the Power of Partnerships," *Financial Times* (October 8, 2004): Mastering Innovation, Section 4.

12 Paul Marer and Vincent Mabert, "GE Acquires and Restructures Tungsram: The First Six Years (1990–1995)," *OECD, Trends and Policies in Privatization* III: 1 (Paris: OECD, 1996): 149–85; and their unpublished 1999 revision, "GE's Acquisition of Hungary's Tungsram."

13 James Mackintosh and Arkady Ostrovsky, "Partners Settle Lada Parts Dispute," *Financial Times* (February 21, 2006): 16.

14 Matthew Lynch, "Hilfiger Sues Former Sock Licensee," *WWD* 198:73 (October 7, 2009): 18.

15 Stephen Magee, "Information and the MNC: An Appropriability Theory of Direct Foreign Investment," in Jagdish N. Bhagwati (ed.), *The New International Economic Order* (Cambridge, MA: MIT Press, 1977): 317–40; C. W. Hill, L. P. Hwang, and W. C. Kim, "An Eclectic Theory of the Choice on International Entry Mode," *Strategic Management Journal* 11 (1990): 117–18; Ashish Arora and Andrea Fosfuri, "Wholly Owned Subsidiary versus Technology Licensing in the Worldwide Chemical Industry," *Journal of International Business Studies* 31:4 (2000): 555–72.

16 Peter Wonacott, "Global Aims of China's Car Makers Put Existing Ties at Risk," *Wall Street Journal* (August 24, 2004): B1+; Norihiko Shirouzu and Peter Wonacott, "People's Republic of Autos," *Wall Street Journal* (April 18, 2005): B1+.

17 Jean-Paul Roy and Christine Oliver, "International Joint Venture Partner Selection: The Role of the Host-Country Legal Environment," *Journal of International Business Studies* 40:5 (2009): 779–801.

18 Anne-Wil Harzing, "Acquisitions versus Greenfield Investments: International Strategy and Management of Entry Modes," *Strategic Management Journal* 23:3 (2002): 211–27.

19 Jaideep Anand and Andrew Delios, "Absolute and Relative Resources as Determinants of International Acquisitions," *Strategic Management Journal* 23:2 (2002): 119–34.

20 Sergery Filippov, "Innovation and R&D in Emerging Russian Multiantionals," *Economics, Management and Financial Markets,* 6:1 (March 2011): 182–206.

21 Geoff Dyer, Francesco Guerrera, and Alexandra Harney, "Chinese Companies Make Plans to Join the Multinational Club," *Financial Times* (June 23, 2005): 19.

22 "Beefed Up – The World's Largest Meat Company is Brazilian, But Mostly Operates Abroad," *The Economist* (September 24, 2011): Special Report on the World Economy, 16.

23 Two such indications are from studies by Alan Gregory, which is cited in Kate Burgess, "Acquisitions in U.S. 'Disastrous' for British Companies," *Financial Times* (October 11, 2004): 18; and Ping Deng, "Absorptive Capacity and a Failed Cross Border M&A," *Management Research Review* 33:7 (2010): 673–82.

24 John Child, David Faulkner, and Robert Pitethly, *The Management of International Acquisitions* (Oxford: Oxford University Press, 2001); Peter Martin, "A Clash of Corporate Cultures," *Financial Times* (June 2–3, 2001): Weekend section, xxiv.

25 "From Guard Shack to Global Giant," *The Economist* (January 12, 2013): 55–56.

26 Vlatka Bilas and Vedran Baci, "Utjecaj Akvizicijskog Iskustva Na Uspjesnost Medunarodnih Spajanja I Preuzimanja U Farmaceutskoj Industriji 2001–2009," *Ekonomska Misao* 19:2 (2010): 187–209.

27 Rajesh Chakrabarti, Swasti Gupta-Mukherjee, and Narayanan Jayaraman, "Mars-Venus Marriages: Culture and Cross-Border

M&A,"*Journal of International Business Studies* 40:2 (2009): 216–36; See also Mary Yoki Brannen and Mark F. Peterson,"Merging Without Alienating: Interventions Promoting Cross-Cultural Organization and Their Limitations,"*Journal of International Business Studies* 40:3 (2009): 468–89.

28 Pierre Dussauge, Bernard Garrette, and Will Mitchell,"Asymmetric Performance: The Market Share Impact of Scale and Link Alliances in the Global Auto Industry," *Strategic Management Journal* 25 (2004): 701–11; and Candace E. Ybarra and Thomas A. Turk,"Strategic Alliances with Competing firms and Shareholder Value,"*Journal of Management and Marketing Research* 6 (January 2011): 1–10.

29 Koen Dittrich and Geert Duysters,"Networking as a Means to Strategy Change: The Case of Open Innovation in Mobile Telephony,"*Journal of Product Innovation Management* 24:6 (November 2007): 510–21.

30 Barry J. Dickinson,"Symbiotic Marketing: A Network Perspective," *Journal of Management and Marketing Research* 11 (September 2012): 1-27 offers many examples of horizontal alliances.

31 Gabriel Baffour Awuah, Amal Mohamed,"Impact of Globalization: The Ability of Less Developed Countries' (LDCs') Firms to Cope with Opportunities and Challenges,"*European Business Review* 23:1 (2011): 120–32; Rodney C. Shrader,"Collaboration and Performance in Foreign Markets: The Case of Young High-Technology Manufacturing Firms," *Academy of Management Journal* 44:1 (2001): 45–60.

32 Rahul Jacob,"Hong Kong Banks on New Disney Park for Boost," *Financial Times* (August 31, 2001): 6.

33 Paavo Ritala,"Coopetition Strategy – When Is It Successful? Empirical Evidence on Innovation and Market Performance,"*British Journal of Management* 23:3 (September 2012): 307–24.

34 Phred Dvorak and Scott Kilman,"BHP Roils Potash Cartel,"*Wall Street Journal* (August 25, 2010): 1.

35 John M. Connor,"Global Antitrust Prosecutions of Modern International Cartels,"*Journal of Industry, Competition and Trade* 4:3 (2004): 239.

36 Luiz F. Mesquita and Sergio G. Lazzarini,"Horizontal and Vertical Relationships in Developing Economies: Implications for SMEs' Access to Global Markets,"*Academy of Management Journal* 51:2 (2008): 359–80.

37 Destan Kandemir and G. Tomas Hult,"A Conceptualization of an Organizational Learning Culture in International Joint Ventures," *Industrial Marketing Management* 34:5 (2005): 440.

38 Robert F. Howe,"The Fall of the House of Mondavi,"*Business 2.0* 6:3 (2005): 98.

39 Yumiko Ono and Ann Zimmerman,"Wal-Mart Enters Japan with Seiyu Stake,"*Wall Street Journal* (March 15, 2002): B5.

40 Yuping Zeng, Oded Shenkar, Seung-Hyun Lee, and Sangcheol Song, "Cultural Differences, MNE Learning Abilities, and the Effect of Experience on Subsidiary Mortality in a Dissimilar Culture: Evidence from Korean MNEs,"*Journal of International Business Studies* 44 (2013): 42–65.

41 Peter Wonacott and Eric Bellman,"Foreign Firms Find Rough Passage to India,"*Wall Street Journal* (February 1, 2007): A6; Neil Buckly,"Russia Sets New Rules for Investors in Key Sectors,"*Financial Times* (May 6, 2009): 3; Amy Kazmin,"Ikea Ditches Plans for India after New Delhi Refuses to Change Law,"*Financial Times* (June 12, 2009): 13.

42 Jia-Ruey Ou,"An Analytical Model for Innovating Localization Policy," *International Journal of Electronic Business Management* 8:2 (2010): 110–19.

43 Julie Bennett,"Road to Foreign Franchises Is Paved with New Problems,"*Wall Street Journal* (May 14, 2001): B10.

44 "H&M Wins Back Name in Russia,"*Managing Intellectual Property* (April 2007): 1; and Steven Seidenberg,"Trademark Squatting on the Rise in U.S."*Inside Counsel* (May 2010): n.p.

45 Peter J. Lane, Jane E. Salk, and Marjorie A. Lyles,"Absorptive Capacity, Learning, and Performance in International Joint Ventures,"*Strategic Management Journal* 22 (2001): 1139–61.

46 Steven White and Steven Siu-Yun Lui,"Distinguishing Costs of Cooperation and Control in Alliances,"*Strategic Management Journal* 26 (2005): 913–32.

47 For an extensive discussion of these variables, see Farok J. Contractor and James Woodley, "How Do Alliance Partners Share the Value They Create? Determinants of the Value Split in International Technology Transfer Alliances,"*Proceedings of the 54th Annual Meeting of the Academy of International Business* (Washington: 2012): n.p.

48 Melissa Maleske,"OFAC's Global Reach,"*Inside Counsel* (August 2012): n/a.

49 Miguel Angel Asturias, *Strong Wind,* trans. Gregory Rabassa (New York: Delacorte Press, 1968): 112.

50 For an extensive treatise on the theory, see Robert A. Packenham, *The Dependency Movement: Scholarship and Politics in Development Studies* (Cambridge, MA: Harvard University Press, 1992). For some different national views of its validity, see Ndiva Kofele-Kale,"The Political Economy of Foreign Direct Investment: A Framework for Analyzing Investment Laws and Regulations in Developing Countries,"*Law & Policy in International Business* 23:2/3 (1992): 619–71; and Stanley K. Sheinbaum,"Very Recent History Has Absolved Socialism,"*New Perspectives Quarterly* 13:1 (1996).

51 Ravi Ramamurti,"The Obsolescing 'Bargaining Model'? MNC-Host Developing Country Relations Revisited,"*Journal of International Business Studies* 32 (2001): 23; Yadong Luo,"Toward a Cooperative View of MNC-Host Government Relations: Building Blocks and Performance Implication,"*Journal of International Business Studies* 32 (2001): 401.

52 "Kodak Enters into Technology Cross-Licensing Agreement with NEC,"*Asia Pulse* (December 28, 2010).

53 Lauren Collins,"Danish Postmodern,"*New Yorker* (January 7, 2013): 22; Lizette Alvarez,"Spreading Scandinavian Genes, without Viking Boats," *New York Times* (September 30, 2004): A4; and"Cryos Sets Up Sperm Banks in Mumbai,"*Businessline* (September 25, 2008).

54 Fred Burton, Adam R. Cross, and Mark Rhodes,"Foreign Market Servicing Strategies of UK Franchisors: An Empirical Enquiry from a Transactions Cost Perspective,"*Management International Review* 40:4 (2000): 373–400.

55 John K. Ryans, Jr., Sherry Lotz, and Robert Krampf,"Do Master Franchisors Drive Global Franchising?"*Marketing Management* 8:2 (1999): 33–38.

56 Janet Adamy,"Chinese Food the KFC Way,"*Wall Street Journal Asian Edition* (October 20–22, 2006): 14–15.

57 Julie Bennett,"Product Pitfalls Proliferate in a Global Cultural Maze," *Wall Street Journal* (May 14, 2001): B11; Jane Wooldridge,"Fast Food Universe,"*Miami Herald* (November 28, 2004): J1.

58 British Airport Authority,"International Airports" (2007), retrieved July 6, 2007, from www.baa.com/portal/page/Corporate%5EAbout+BAA%5EWho+does+what%5EInternational+airports/b0ccadc5c5c72010VgnVCM100000147e120a__/448c6a4c7f1b0010VgnVCM200000357e120a__/.

59 "Four Seasons Signs Management Contract with Three C Universal Developers,"*Mint* [New Delhi] (April 21, 2011).

60 "Great Wall Builders,"*The Economist* (October 27, 2012): 66.

61 "Global Alumina Releases Third Quarter 2010 Results,"*PR Newswire* (November 2010).

62 Peter Sanders, Daniel Michaels, and August Cole,"Boeing Delays New Jet Again,"*Wall Street Journal* (June 24, 2009): A1+; Peter Sanders, "Boeing Settles In for a Bumpy Ride,"*Wall Street Journal* (October 7, 2009): B1+.

63 "Essar Ports Announces Strategic Alliance With Port of Antwerp International,"*PR Newswire* (May 31, 2012): n.p.

64 Luis Zalamea,"AeroRepublica, Copa Offer Details of New Alliance," *Aviation Daily* (March 11, 2005): 5.

65 There are many different ways of classifying the problems. Two useful ways are found in Manuel G. Serapio Jr. and Wayne F. Cascio,"End

Games in International Alliances," *Academy of Management Executive* 10:1 (1996): 62–73; and Joel Bleeke and David Ernst, "Is Your Strategic Alliance Really a Sale?" *Harvard Business Review* (January–February 1995): 97–105.

66 Terrence Chea, "No Perfect Partnership," *Washington Post* (June 3, 2002): E1.

67 Anna Shaojie Cui, Roger J. Calantone, and David A. Griffith, "Strategic Change and Termination of Interfirm Partnerships," *Strategic Management Journal* 32:4 (April 2011): 402–23.

68 Mikhail Fridman, "BP Has Been Treating Russians as Subjects," *Financial Times* (July 7, 2008): 9.

69 Gregory L. White, "In Asia, GM Pins Hope on a Delicate Web of Alliances," *Wall Street Journal* (October 23, 2002): A23.

70 Ramit Plushnick-Masti, "German Firm Faulted for Taking Vitamin out of Baby Formula," *Miami Herald* (November 12, 2003): 19A.

71 William H. Meyers, "Maxim's Name Is the Game," *New York Times Magazine* (May 3, 1987): 33–35; Cristina Passariello, "Pierre Cardin Ready to Sell His Overstretched Label," *Wall Street Journal* (May 3, 2011): 1.

72 David Ibison, "Culture Clashes Prove Biggest Hurdle to International Links," *Financial Times* (January 24, 2002): 17.

73 Diana Elena Ranf, "Cultural Differences in Project Management," *Annales Universitatis Apulensis Series Oeconomica* 12:2 (2010): 657–62.

74 Marshall Geiger and Joyce van der Laan Smith, "The Effect of Institutional and Cultural Factors on the Perceptions of Earnings Management," *Journal of International Accounting Research* 9:2 (2010): 21–43.

75 James T. Areddy, "Danone Pulls Out of Disputed China Venture," *Wall Street Journal* (October 1, 2009): B1.

76 Gokhun Ertug, Ilya R. P. Cuypers, Niels G. Noorderhaven, and Ben B. Bensaou, "Trust Between International Joint Venture Partners: Effects of Home Countries," *Journal of International Business Studies* 44 (2013): 263–82.

77 Seung Ho Park and Gerardo R. Ungson, "The Effect of National Culture, Organizational Complementarity, and Economic Motivation on Joint Venture Dissolution," *Academy of Management Journal* 40:2 (April 1997): 279–307; Harry G. Barkema, Oded Shenkar, Freek Vermeulen, and John H. J. Bell, "Working Abroad, Working with Others: How Firms Learn to Operate International Joint Ventures," *Academy of Management Journal* 40:2 (April 1997): 426–42, found survival differences only for differences in uncertainty avoidance.

78 Rikka M. Sarala and Eero Vaara, "Cultural Differences, Convergence, and Crossvergence as Explanations of Knowledge Transfer in International Acquisitions," *Journal of International Business Studies* 41:8 (October-November 2010): 1365–90.

79 Akbar Zaheer, Exequiel Hernandez, and Sanjay Banerjee, "Prior Alliances with Targets and Acquisition Performance in Knowledge-Intensive Industries," *Organization Science* 21:5 (September-October 2010): 1072–91+.

80 Mike W. Peng and Oded Shenkar, "Joint Venture Dissolution as Corporate Divorce," *Academy of Management Executive* 16:2 (May 2002): 92–105.

81 Bharat Anand and Tarun Khanna, "Do Firms Learn to Create Value? The Case of Alliances," *Strategic Management Journal* 21:3 (March 2000): 295–315; Anthony Goerzen and Paul W. Beamish, "The Effect of Alliance Network Diversity on Multinational Enterprise Performance," *Strategic Management Journal* 26 (2005): 333–54; and Maurizio Zollo and Jeffrey J. Reuer, "Experience Spillovers Across Corporate Development Activities," *Organization Science* 21:6 (November-December 2010): 1195–1212.

82 Rachelle C. Sampson, "Experience Effects and Collaborative Returns in R&D Alliances," *Strategic Management Journal* 26 (2005): 1009–31.

83 Doug Cameron, "U.S. Airline Merger to Affect Alliances," *Wall Street Journal (Online)* (February 14, 2013): n.p.; Adrian Schofield, "JAL, British Airways Code-Share Another Step Toward Joint Venture," *Aviation Daily* 389:46 (September 5, 2012): n.p.; Anne Smith and Marie-Claude Reney, "The Mating Dance: A Case Study of Local Partnering Processes in Developing Countries," *European Management Journal* 15:2 (1997): 174–82.

84 Sanjiv Kumar and Anju Seth, "The Design of Coordination and Control Mechanisms for Managing Joint Venture–Parent Relationships," *Strategic Management Journal* 19:6 (June 1998): 579–99; T. K. Das and Bing-Sheng Teng, "Between Trust and Control: Developing Confidence in Partner Cooperation in Alliances," *Academy of Management Journal* 23:3 (July 1998): 491–512; Arvind Parkhe, "Building Trust in International Alliances," *Journal of World Business* 33:4 (1998): 417–37; Prashant Kale, Harbir Singh, and Howard Perlmutter, "Learning and Protection of Proprietary Assets in Strategic Alliances: Building Relational Capital," *Strategic Management Journal* 21:3 (March 2000): 217–37; and Dina Preston-Ortiz, "The Effects of Trust in Virtual Strategic-Alliance Performance Outcomes," unpublished doctoral dissertation (Phoenix: University of Phoenix, 2010).

85 Linda H.Y. Hsieh and Suzana B. Rodrigues, "Partner Trustworthiness and Ex Post Governance Choice in International Joint Ventures: The Role of Performance Satisfaction," AIB 2012 Proceedings of 54th Annual Meeting (Washington: June 30–July 3, 2012).

86 Africa Ariño and Jeffrey J. Reuer, "Designing and Renegotiating Strategic Alliance Contracts," *Academy of Management Executive* 18:3 (2004): 37–48.

87 Gary D. Burton, David Ahlstrom, Michael N. Young, and Yuri Rubanik, "In Emerging Markets, Know What Your Partners Expect," *Wall Street Journal* (December 15, 2008): R5.

88 Srilata Zaheer and Akbar Zaheer, "Trust across Borders," *Journal of International Business Studies* 37:1 (2006): 21.

89 Prashant Kale and Harbir Singh, "Managing Strategic Alliances: What Do We Know Now and Where Do We Go from Here?" *Academy of Management Perspectives* 23:3 (August 2009): 45–62.

90 John Kenneth Galbraith, *American Capitalism* (Boston: Houghton Mifflin, 1952): 91–92.

91 Eric H. Kessler, Paul E. Bierly, and Shanthi Gopalakrishnan, "Internal vs. External Learning in New Product Development: Effects of Speed, Costs and Competitive Advantage," *R & D Management* 30:3 (2000): 213–23.

92 Adrian Wooldridge, "Return of the Giants," *The Economist* (The World in 2013 edition): 25.

93 These are adapted from Arvind Parkhe, "Interfirm Diversity, Organizational Learning, and Longevity in Global Strategic Alliances," *Journal of International Business Studies* 22:4 (1991): 579–601.

94 ***Sources include the following:*** We wish to acknowledge the assistance of several American Airlines and oneworld executives, who, although wishing to remain anonymous, supplied useful information for and feedback on this case. Additional information came from "American Airlines to Operate Only Service between New York and Japan's Tokyo International Airport at Haneda After Historic Open Skies Agreement," *Entertainment Newsweekly* (March 4, 2011): 172; Andrea Ahles, "American Airlines, Japan Airlines Announce Joint Venture," *McClatchy–Tribune Business News* (January 12, 2011): n.p.; Julie Johnsson, "American Airlines Combining Pacific Flights with Japan Airlines," *McClatchy–Tribune Business News* (January 12, 2011): n.p.; "American to Move Its Asia-Pacific Regional Office to the Japan Airlines Building in Tokyo," *Journal of Transportation* (September 18, 2010): 26; "Japan Airlines and American Airlines Announce Joint Business Benefits for Trans-Pacific Consumers," *The Pak Banker* (January 11, 2011): n.p.; "Airline Profits to Tumble in 2011: IATA," *The Pak Banker* (June 8, 2011): n.p.; "Europe: Trans-Atlantic Alliances Are Set to Tighten," *Oxford Analytica Daily Brief Service* (January 3, 2008): 1; Alfred Kahn and Dorothy Robyn, "The Sky Must Be No Limit to Global Competition," *Financial Times* (February 15, 2006): 17; Bruce Bernard, "American Airlines Seeks OK for Trans-Atlantic Tie-up," *Journal of Commerce Online* (August 15, 2008); International Air Transport Association, *Annual Report* (2008).

Chapter 5

Business ethics

The growing awareness of the impact of business decisions on the wider community, the natural environment and the nature of the society has prompted a re-examination of the ethics, standards and values used in business. The rules laid down in the company handbook, the prescriptions of professional societies, even the underlying ethics employed by individuals elsewhere, are seldom adequate guides for executives. In part, this is because the implications of some key decision have consequences that cannot be predicted.

Besides this, the interaction between decisions may mean that the 'right' action is neither obvious nor easy to square with other equally moral outcomes. The predictability issue is perhaps the most widely understood. Firms make decisions about technologies, investments and developments which have consequences which may be impossible to predict.

Firms like ICI developed the use of CFCs for use in refrigeration systems, aerosols, etc., with little knowledge of the long-term environmental impacts. Other developments in chemicals, biotechnology, nanotechnology, etc., may seem beneficial in the predictable future but the long-term consequences cannot be guessed at. The dilemma lies in wedding the need to develop the enterprise and capitalise on new technological opportunities with the imperative to protect the environment or other groups in the community.

A two-legged creature

Two hundred years ago in a famous passage on the nature and source of human values John Locke commented that 'God has not been so sparing to man to make them barely two-legged creatures and left it to Aristotle to make them rational . . . He has given them a mind that can reason without being instructed in methods of syllogising'. Lillie[1] adds that 'a similar remark might be made about man's powers of distinguishing right and wrong . . . (the moralist) lives himself in a social environment where certain moral standards . . . are accepted and these standards serve as the data or material'. The study of ethics is the study of these 'standards' and the criteria used to judge which conduct is right or wrong – good or bad.

Business ethics does not stand outside this study. It is part of the wider field. Implicit in this study is the notion that 'values, moral and non-moral, can be handled systematically, and that business and industrial practices can be objectives evaluated from a moral (ethical) point of view'.

It would be wrong to attempt to summarise this vast field in this book. The roots of the subject are so deep and the evolution of the argument so important that primary sources and their current interpretations call for individual study by the serious student. The aim, here, is merely to provide a perspective and place current thinking on corporate responsibility into context. The contrast between the material success of the mixed or free-market economy and its main rivals, the command or communistic economy calls for an even closer examination of its underlying values and the ways they are translated into action.

The challenge

This is vividly illustrated in the debate about Alfred P. Sloan's decision not to fit safety glass to Chevrolet cars in the 1920s. Mintz and Cohen describe this as 'one of the single most important protections ever devised against avoidable automotive death, disfigurement and injury'. Despite this, and regardless of the apparent success of the introduction of safety glass into Cadillacs, Sloan decided that its use 'would have reduced the return on our capital'. This decision reflects Sloan's wider concern at the time to maximise profits.

His general letter to the General Motors organisation from which this quotation is taken spells out the GM goals for the future. It deals with a range of issues but never mentions safety.

The challenge of the genuine, ethical dilemma is less well understood. Fred Friendly tackles this in the video *Doing Business, Doing Good*. A firm can face a problem with two outcomes, each of which breaks one moral principle but is justifiable on the same grounds. The case of equality of opportunity versus health and safety illustrates this problem. In the example, the firm has a strict policy of non-discrimination on the grounds of gender and produces a product like batteries.

In the product process certain chemicals are used. Research suggests that some of these chemicals can have a harmful effect on the unborn child. The company faces a dilemma. Does it abandon its equal opportunities policy on health and safety grounds or stick with equality of opportunity despite the health risk? Managers will face this type of conundrum with increasing frequency as the implications and interactions of their decisions become more evident. Perhaps the only way to deal with this type of conundrum is to develop value-based standards or criteria that can balance the different peer and corporate pressures on managers, strengthening the 'reinforcing' pressures and weakening the 'undermining' pressures (Figure 5.1).

The role of business in society requires systems which reflect a willingness to internalise that responsibility, not externalise it. The most popular and pragmatic guides to implementing corporate responsibility programmes posit different ways to 'developing' or 'maintaining' an ethical position. Much management thinking acknowledges this responsibility. Current notions of enterprise or corporate and managerial freedom, especially in the development of markets, assume that freedom is not licence. Action by the state or other organisations to liberalise behaviour is part of an implicit contract which assumes a licence to behave responsibly.

Freedom of action and managerial discretion raise important questions for executives and test their knowledge and competence to tackle decisions arising from options which pose ethical dilemmas. Business schools have a special responsibility in this area. In

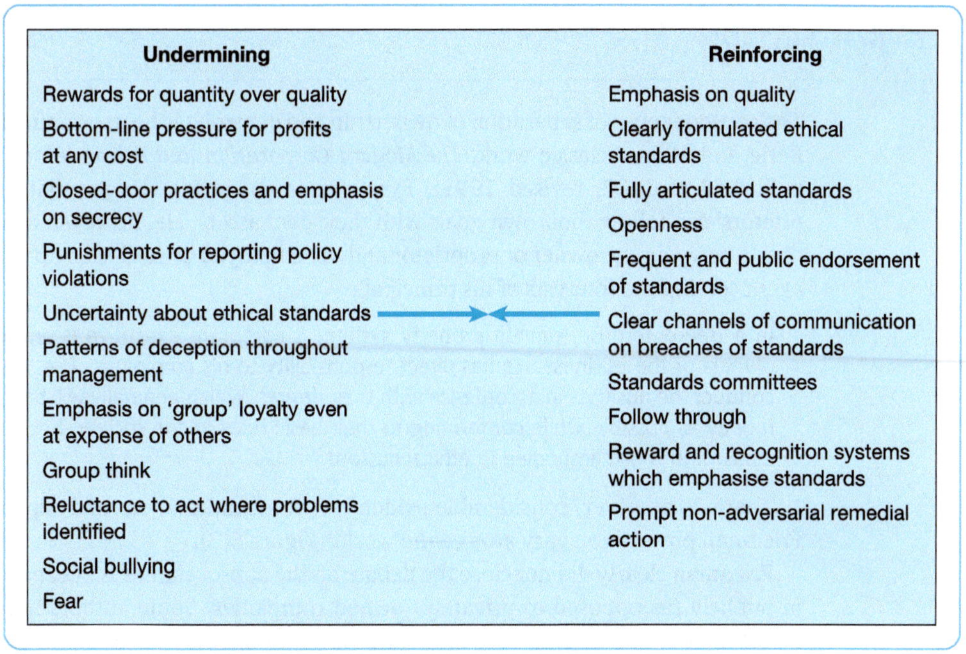

Figure 5.1 Peer and corporate pressures for and against standards

part, this is because they have tended to emphasise short termism, instrumentalism and functionalism. These understate the long-term issues and interdependencies which are highlighted by questions of values and standards. Four substantive areas of discussion have emerged. These go to the heart of the activities of entrepreneurs and managers and the work of their organisations. These are:

1 building systems of corporate ethics and values into the enterprise;
2 tackling questions of compliance and governance;
3 meeting the needs of the economically and socially disadvantaged;
4 satisfying responsibilities to the environment.

These issues can be tackled in several ways. In education, there is a need to explore the individual and corporate strategies which enable firms to acknowledge and meet their responsibilities. In society, opportunities can be created for groups with different experiences, demands and perspectives to gain access to management. This can be through better career opportunities for outgroups, e.g. women, the disabled or minorities and improved lines of communication for those with concerns.

There is an increased coincidence of interest between the call for the individual to behave responsibly, create opportunities and behave morally and the needs of the firm to tap new pools of talent, cope with a changed environment and prosper through freedom. The values and standards that are adopted provide the lubrication for the virtuous circle of opportunity, enterprise and responsibility. Some of the most successful firms are those which acknowledge these responsibilities.

Ownership and control

The consequences of separation of ownership and control has been examined in depth since Berle and Means' classic work, *The Modern Corporation and Private Property*[2] (originally published in 1932, revised 1991). Even Friedman[3] acknowledges that 'individual proprietors' can follow their own goals with their own assets. He, however, articulates a clear divide between the owner or proprietor and the employed or paid executive, who acts as 'an agent serving the interests of his principal':

> In a free-enterprise, private-property system, a corporate executive is an employee of the owners of the business. He has direct responsibility to his employers. That responsibility is to conduct the business in accordance with their desires, which generally will be to make as much money as possible while conforming to their basic rules of the society, both those embodied in law and those embodied in ethical custom.

There is, however, considerable evidence that attitudes about and support for the core Friedman proposition vary around the world (Figure 5.2).

Friedman clearly did not close the debate on the appropriateness of expenditures on CSR in publicly (as opposed to privately) owned companies. Some authors have claimed that investment in CSR can improve the returns to shareholders – in effect, the agents are acting in the owners' best interest. Waddock and Graves[4] found that 'controlling for industries . . . financial performance also depends on good social performance'. Other studies, however, have found either no relationship (McWilliams and Siegel, 2000),[5] or a negative relationship (Wright and Ferris, 1997).[6]

As old as business and trade

This would still raise questions of business ethics and their role in organisational behaviour. Debate about what is and what is not ethical in business behaviour is as old as business and trade. Cicero in his *De Officiis* complains about profiteering by merchants, a theme developed by Thomas Aquinas who developed this theme around the notion of the 'just price' in ways that probably existed before Cicero and have certainly been repeated since.

> If someone would be greatly helped by something belonging to someone else, and the seller not similarly harmed by losing it, the seller must not sell for a higher price: because the usefulness that goes to the buyer comes not from the seller.[7]

The study of business ethics centres on three core propositions that:

1. In business, there is, or ought to be, a morality that shapes behaviour.
2. Executives and owners should not only act in ways consistent with this morality, but equally that they can be held to account for actions inconsistent with this morality.
3. Business ethics is a special applied branch of ethics which focuses general ethical principles and analytical approaches upon a particular field of endeavour – business.

Equally important today is probably the notion that effective corporate governance relies upon an understanding and active implementation of a system of business ethics. This was vividly illustrated in the United Kingdom in 2011 in the 'phone hacking' scandal. Ultimately, this scandal revolved around several of these core principles.

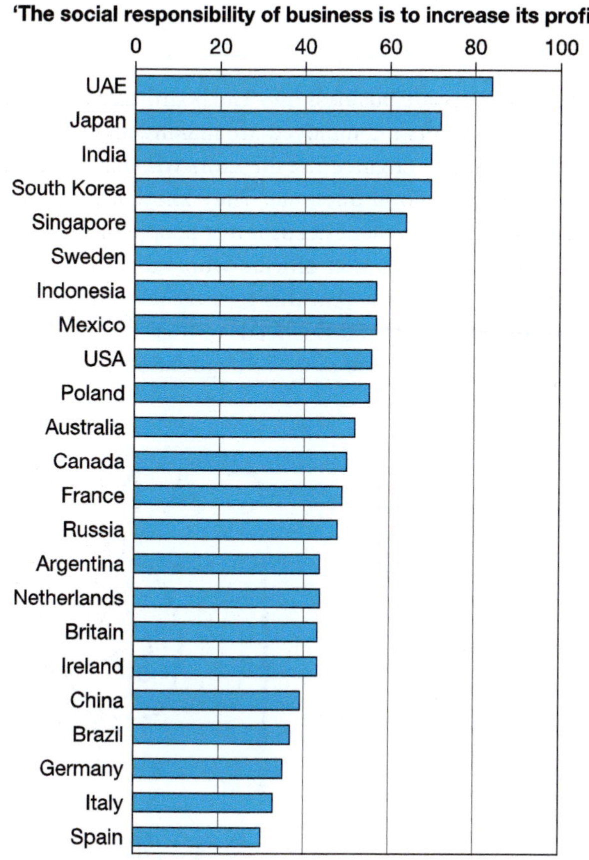

Figure 5.2 Forget CSR, make money: percentage of informed public (ages 25–64) who 'strongly agree' or 'somewhat agree' with this Milton Friedman quote

Source: Edelman (2011) *2011 Edelman Trust Barometer®*, Chicago: Edelman.

First, what were the moral values at News International that were supposed to shape the behaviour of its employees or associates. In effect, was it explicitly or implicitly acceptable for private investigators in the employ of the *News of the World* to gather data from hacked phones or journalists to use this data?

Second, what systems of management, scrutiny and control were in place to ensure that unethical, immoral or (even) illegal behaviours were identified, discouraged, prevented or punished? In organisations it is generally assumed that individual actions are in part at least the responsibility of the organisation and its leaders. Those in charge have a responsibility for the actions of their subordinates.

The term 'willful blindness' has been coined to define the behaviours of these executives who do not exercise this responsibility. Courts, however, around the world have generally rejected this defence, with the US Supreme Court most recently (2010)[8] deciding that 'wilful blindness' will not save a defendant from charges.

The ethical challenges

Ethical issues pervade business life. The board that considers moving production off-shore, leaving local workers unemployed are making an ethical choice between the needs of different stakeholders. Engineering directors who have to decide whether to introduce a new technology face a moral dilemma. They know it might put loyal employees out of work because the new equipment needs fewer people or their skills are redundant.

Likewise, the trade-union officers who want to 'embargo' cheap imports from a poor developing country know that this country desperately needs the foreign exchange. They must decide whether to put the needs of their members before those of Third World peasants. In the Uruguay Round of GATT negotiations, US demands for licence fees for software

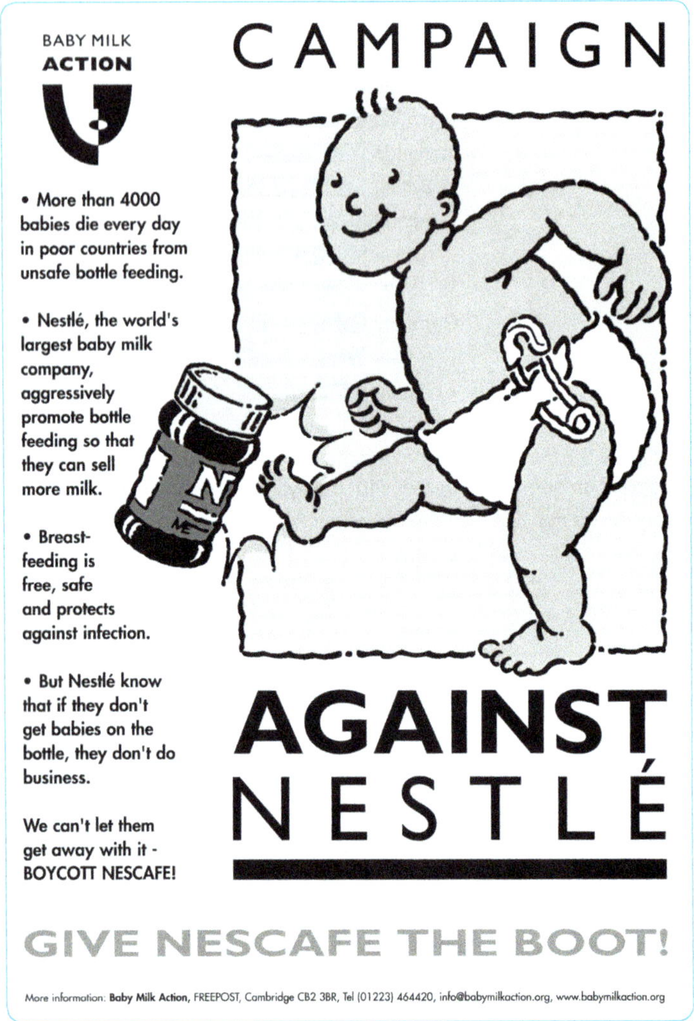

Safe milk action: campaign against Nestlé

Source: Baby Milk Action

products were ranged against the calls for easier access to northern markets for southern agriculture. The current Doha Round is dealing with issues of labour standards, environmental policies, competition rules, investment, transparency and patents, each of which will pose ethical dilemmas for organisations and people.

The marketing policies of firms raise a host of ethical issues. These range from the kinds of images used in advertising, with the exploitation of women in advertising a recurrent theme of many critics of the fashion industry, to the types of products offered to the market. Few products and promotional campaigns have generated more sustained criticism than Nestlé's promotion of its breast milk substitutes to health workers with the claim it 'protects' babies. Nestlé uses a 'protect' logo and the slogans 'Start healthy, Stay healthy' and 'Strengthening the immune defences and reducing the incidence of diarrhea in the crucial first year of life'. The evidence is, however, that babies fed on baby milk are proven to be more likely to suffer diarrhoea and short- and long-term illnesses than breastfed babies.

In recent years, the ethics of a host of firms and industries from banks and utilities to newspapers and retailers have been questioned as seldom before. The most recent (2011) Ipsos MORI Veracity Index showed that only politicians and journalists enjoyed less trust than business leaders.

A matter of trust

To the question, who would 'you generally trust to tell the truth', less than one in three people 'trusted' business leaders to tell the truth (Table 5.1).

The decline in trust for business is especially marked in the USA and northern Europe. The data in Figure 5.3 give some indication of the decline in trust for business. Although there was some recovery between 2009 and 2011, the broad pattern of decline in trust persists.

This decline in trust is especially noticeable in the banking sector. In the USA and UK there was a collapse in trust between 2007 and 2011 (Table 5.2), with banks being transformed from being some of the most trusted organisations to some of the least trusted.

Table 5.1 Who is trusted?

Doctors	89%
Teachers	86%
Professors	77%
Judges	75%
Scientists	67%
Clergyman/priests	75%
The police	61%
Television news readers	68%
Ordinary man/woman in the street	56%
Civil servants	43%
Trade-union officials	36%
Business leaders	28%
Journalists	17%
Government ministers	19%
Politicians generally	14%

Source: IPSOS MORI Trust in Professions 2011.

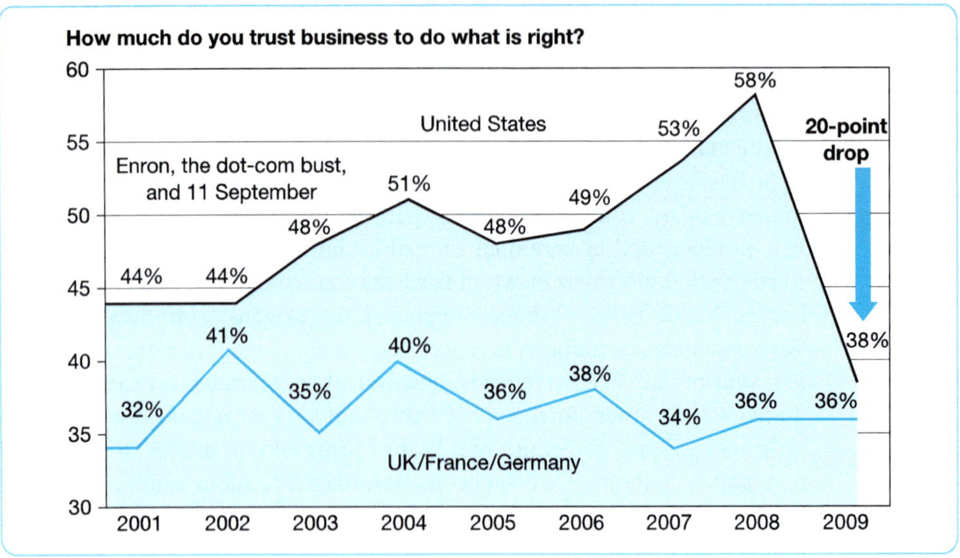

Figure 5.3 Decline in trust in business

Notes: Informed public aged 35 to 64 in the USA, UK, France and Germany; responses 6–9 only on a 1–9 scale; 9 = highest.
Source: Edelman (2009) *2009 Edelman Trust Barometer®*, Chicago, Edelman, Figure 2, p. 3.

Table 5.2 Decline in trust for banks

	Percentage of those who trust banks				
	2011	2010	2009	2008	2007
US	24	29	36	69	68
UK	14	21	31	47	41

Source: Adapted from Edelman (2011) *2011 Edelman Trust Barometer®*, Chicago, Edelman.

The traditional view of ethics and morality in banking was well summarised by Charles Green, one-time deputy group chief executive of National Westminster Bank:

> The financial community has a history of placing moral considerations above legal or opportunistic expedients. But we are often exposed to moral dangers and the dangers of contamination are increasing. Deregulation and the technological revolution are sharpening ethical conflicts. Bankers' role is one of stewardship based on trust. We are trusted by those who ask us to look after their money.

This was not a universally held view of the ethics and values of bankers. Thomas Jefferson claimed that 'banking institutions are more dangerous to our liberties than standing armies'. Until the banking crisis of 2008, however, majorities in most countries trusted the ethics of their bankers.

The building blocks of these moral codes, values and ethics highlight many of the wider issues and analysis of business ethics in general. At the same time, the apparent erosion of these codes, values and ethics illustrates not only other aspects of business ethics but the challenges those seeking to study, understand or implement business ethics face.

Firms and managers try to resolve ethical questions in a host of ways. Traditionally, it was assumed that a general social ethic permeated the society. In the West this was generally seen as a mixture of individualism and Christianity. Smith[9] summarises the first of these with his observation that 'it is not from the benevolence of the butcher, the brewer and the baker, that we expect our dinner, but from their regard to their own best interest'. The Christian tradition was closely linked to the rise of capitalism in the work of Weber. He saw a powerful link between Protestantism and capitalism. The increasingly secular nature of society in the West and the successful industrial development of communities with powerful corporatist or communal traditions has created a more eclectic base for business values and morality.

The shift in economic power and business activity to Asia, the Middle East, Latin America and beyond has reinforced the range of challenges facing those trying to understand and shape business ethics. Domènec Melé[10] notes that 'each of Judaism, Christianity, Islam, Hinduism, Buddhism, Confucianism, Taoism and Shinto has its own organized system of beliefs, ceremonies and worship, and each offers prescriptions for positive endeavour in both life – and in business'.

Sabahuddin Azmi[11] points out, for example, that:

> Islam has its own distinctive value-based ethical system for business dealings. It prescribes certain specific guidelines for governing business ethics. It (i) enumerates the general ethical rules of business conduct, (ii) identifies ethically desirable forms of business, and, (iii) specifies the undesirable modes of transactions . . . (with specific injunctions about) truthfulness, trustworthiness, generosity and leniency, adherence to business commitments and contracts, fair treatment of workers, avoidance of evil practices (such as fraud, cheating, deceit, hoarding of foodstuff, exploitations, giving short measures etc.).

Confucianism with its millennium-long history has developed a foundation for business ethics that 'stresses character formation or personal cultivation of virtues (*de*); first the basic, interdependent virtues of *ren* (love and care for one's fellows), *li* (a set of rules of proper conduct), and *yi* (reasoned judgment concerning the right thing to do); then the dependent virtues of filiality, respectfulness, trustworthiness, and others. It emphasises the Golden Rule of "What I don't want others to do to me, I do not want to do to others"'.[12]

The diverse underpinnings of business ethics help to shape the ways in which both the study and implementation of value or ethical-based behaviour in businesses. Growing awareness of these underpinnings coincides with greater recognition of how economic, social and cultural change influences business ethics. Enderle[13] notes how 'business ethics is an emerging and dynamic field, depending strongly on economic factors, but also on political changes and a growing awareness of value conflicts and ethical and environmental demands'.

Enderle[14] highlights several issues as especially important in shaping the local approach to business ethics around the world. These are that:

1 Ethical issues in business are not merely 'rational problems' but deeply rooted in emotions and cultures.
2 Business environments and some specific issues across national borders play a crucial role in shaping priorities.
3 Corruption, leadership, and corporate responsibility attract particular attention.
4 Among the most common themes in the business ethics/business and society literature especially in North America is about stakeholder obligations and 'stakeholder theory'.

Noland and Philips[15] suggest that 'ethical, that is honest, open and fair engagement of these stakeholders is necessary for a business to function properly'. Noland and Phillips go on to explore the different perspectives that emerge from Habermas's[16] analysis of the moral basis on which businesses engage with stakeholders. They appear to posit two extremes: first that stakeholder engagement should develop 'without considering whether it aligns with my (business) strategy'. At the other extreme is that the core of business ethics lies in 'including honest, open, respectful engagement as *a vital part of a firm's strategy*'.

The challenges managers face and their awareness of the limitations on their ability to predict or control outcomes has made them increasingly aware of the nature of the ethical challenge facing them.

Several key decision areas illustrate the 'rational problems' that raise powerful ethical questions. Among these are:

- innovation and change
- climate change
- taxation.

Innovation and change

No aspect of business raises more questions of ethics and values than innovation and change. This challenge may occur because of the threat that change poses to individuals and communities or because the failure to innovate poses a threat to the enterprise itself.

Communities can be blighted by economic and industrial changes which transform their ability to compete. The changes in the mining and steel industries in Europe and North America demonstrate this. Production in these sectors was typically concentrated in communities with few alternative sources of employment locally. This was as true in industrial communities on the East Coast of the USA like Pittsburgh and Baltimore as in the Wallonia, South Wales and the North-East of England. Closing the mine or steelworks could mean killing the community. The greater the change, the more widespread is the effect. Often, the skills, working methods and environments that underpinned past economic success are inappropriate or unattractive to new industries.

In sharp contrast, firms which are skilful at innovation – the successful exploitation of new ideas – consistently secure a competitive advantage in a rapidly changing world market, while those which are not will be overtaken. In a series of reports the OECD has highlighted the importance of innovation across industries and communities[17] while highlighting the challenges that innovation poses to existing industries, communities, competences and skills.[18]

This is not a new ethical dilemma. The best cultures, systems and plans do not remain static for long. Economic conditions, competitor's behaviour, market dynamic technological advances and the political environment demand changes. Drucker[19] has gone as far as saying that 'innovation' is one of the two basic functions of business. Deane[20] argues that change is the key characteristic in industrial society.

The challenge was recognised from the first by Luddites and other machine wreckers who sought to stop the introduction of the new technology. It is seen every day in the firm that seeks to extend the life of a declining product or resists the pressure to use new technologies and novel techniques. Schumpeter[21] called 'creative destruction' the way innovation and change continually raises questions which affect society, the economy, culture and the environment.

Dock workers in Liverpool
Source: TopFoto

The most common social and, hence ethical, issues around innovation centre on the nature and location of employment. The pressure for change prompts companies to invest in new equipment and plant. It is seldom possible to arrive at an exact fit between the skills available to the current workforce and the skills needed by the new technology.

Sometimes, the innovations require changes that those affected are reluctant to accept. Relatively low-skilled, poorly educated male manual workers have been especially hard hit when an economy moves from 'traditional' heavy industries to high skill, knowledge-based or service industries. Often these workers could learn new skills but the new technologies fundamentally changed the nature of the work they expected or to which they aspired. Elsewhere, those affected were unable to change.

The changed nature of cargo handling on the docks with the advent of containerisation, for example, eliminated many jobs while changing the character of the rest of the work. Ports like Liverpool handle vastly more trade than in the past, but with far fewer workers. Even the type of work changes, and dockers with long service were seldom able to compete with new entrants with more appropriate skills.

A growing and efficient economy must somehow solve the problem of shifting people from declining to growing industries, from low-productivity to high-productivity jobs: it must be able to absorb the consequences of technical change. At a very minimum, this involves overcoming complex problems of education, retraining and relocation.

The ethical challenge to managers and firms exists on two levels:

- Should we make the change?
- What responsibility do we have to minimise the impact?

Seaforth Container Port, Liverpool
Source: Colin McPherson/Corbis

Often, the pressure for change leaves the firm or community with no option. There have been attempts to stand against the pressure of new products and processes. Ghandi's attempt to return to handmade cloth did not reverse the demand for the machine-made product. Clinker-built boats were relegated to a small niche in the market after the introduction of glass reinforced plastic boats. Integrated transport planning has hardly slowed the move from rail to road transport.

Examples abound of firms that tried to resist technological change. It is hard to identify any which have succeeded. The accumulated evidence is a powerful case against resistance. The threat to the enterprise, the industry or community is often a sufficiently strong argument to end any debate about the necessity of change. The UK's Strategy for Sustainable Growth[22] uses a language that is echoed across the world: '(new) skills, science, research and innovation are essential investments for the UK economy, because the introduction of new products, services and processes is the major source of growth in the long term'.

The social cost of change

The social cost of change, however, is seldom paid by the promoters of innovation and novelty. The jobs lost are seldom those held by the advocates nor are the communities destroyed those in which they live. Commerce is a major source of change and has a clear responsibility to address its social consequences. This is especially true when the changes affect the social values which bind communities.

There are several fundamental contradictions in some commonly held propositions. An example is the conflict between:

- Proposition A: that the family is the 'cornerstone' of the community or community care for the elderly or the weak; and
- Proposition B: that in the face of shortages of employment, labour – often heads of families – should get on their bikes and seek work, if necessary away from the family.

There is evidence that geographical mobility in search for work is significantly higher in the USA than in western Europe, but some commentators suggest that this is, also, linked with weaker inter-generational links especially familial support for the aged.

These debates touch upon wider aspects of the debates around business ethics. Implicitly or explicitly, many business leaders embrace the utilitarian notion of 'the greatest good for the greatest number' in justifying changes that have negative impacts on individuals, groups or communities. The work of Jeremy Bentham and John Stuart Mill is seen to justify an approach to business ethics based on the core proposition that 'correct moral conduct is determined solely by a cost-benefit analysis of an action's consequences'.[23]

Hence, if General Motors' factory in Flint is closed with local employment falling from 80,000 in the late 1970s to under 8,000 in 2010, but the company survives, employing over 200,000 in 120 countries and likely to become the world's largest car maker – the greatest good for the greatest number may be achieved.[24] This calculation, however, turns ultimately on more complex questions about whose happiness and the balance of outcomes between the cost of lost jobs in a city like Flint with few alternatives and the (perceived) alternative that, say, executive salaries or dividends are cut to keep jobs in Flint. This challenge, calculating outcomes and balancing interests, poses the greatest difficulty in applying the utilitarian approach to business ethics.

Nowhere was this more vividly illustrated than in the case of the Ford Pinto. It seems that Ford discovered fairly early in its production that there was a significant risk to life from a rear-end collision. Faced with the massive costs and corporate risks of closing production, recalling vehicles and re-tooling, the company appears to have concluded that it was cheaper to accept the cost of compensating for fatalities (at US$200,000 per death).[25]

Innovation and change

Similar issues affect most debate on innovation and change. The imperative for change is now linked with the notion that these changes contain, within them, the benefit of increased choice or wider options. Most of these propositions derive from the positivist view of social and economic change and the resulting emphasis on the tangible, measurable and verifiable benefits. There is, however, greater awareness now of the price of change to the community, the economy and the environment.

Alongside this, the intangible costs are viewed as increasingly relevant to any debate. In sum, the processes which produce economic and business growth without considering the value implications are inevitably unable to recognise the crises and value consequences because the ideologies attached to the techniques forbid it.[26]

The social challenge to the demand for innovation and change comes from many sources. The most basic is the attempt by a society or community to stand outside the process. Japan, between the middle of the sixteenth century and the Meiji Restoration of the 1860s, was a vivid example. The Khmer Rouge terror in Cambodia was an especially vicious attempt to stop certain forms of innovation. In the Islamic world there is widespread concern about the effects of change on values and social systems which are held very strongly.

Havel[27] – with his concern about the automatism of technology and the industrial consumer society, Suggate[28] through his Christianity, Williams[29] and others share this concern about the social and moral case for innovation and change. Williams says:

> If all important problems are technical, they are in principle soluble without risk to our sense of ourselves, our moral self perception. The identification of the technical 'can' with the moral 'should' – or the blotting out by the former of questions about the latter – is endemic in our culture. We are largely incapable of asking ourselves what human purpose technology in such areas serves.

Those businesses and individuals which seek to advocate and introduce change have a responsibility to these communities and their enterprises to acknowledge and address these concerns. Simple advocacy of the benefits of change 'to the greatest number' is unlikely to be sufficient, for those not members of this greatest number.

Corelli Barnett[30] bases much of *The Audit of War* to the thesis that the attempt to create a 'New Jerusalem' in Britain after the end of World War II was partly an attempt to replace the imperatives of change and innovation with social engineering:

> If Britain after the war was to earn the immense resources required to maintain her cherished traditional place as a great power and at the same time pay for New Jerusalem at home, she had to achieve nothing short of an economic miracle. Such a miracle could only be achieved through the transformation, material and human, of her essentially obsolete industrial society into one capable of triumphing in the world markets of the future.
>
> Had all the most powerful groups and institutions in that society been willing to throw themselves behind the process of transformation, it would still have been difficult enough to achieve, given the scale of the inherited problems. But instead of such willingness there existed the massive internal resistance to change which was so manifest in the history of Britain as an industrial society; a resistance that not even the shock of war had proved strong enough to budge more than a little.

Managers in steel, shipbuilding, aerospace and mining were as resistant to new techniques, novel technologies and innovative products as artisans, riveters and miners (Table 5.3).

The extent of this opposition indicates a society in which the pay-offs from economic change are not seen to be sufficient compensation for the risks. Resistance to those changes which affect the vested interests undermines the process of change. Again, there is nothing new in that; 400 years ago Niccolò Machiavelli[31] observed:

> It must be considered that there is nothing more difficult, more dangerous or more apt to miscarry than an endeavour to introduce new institutions. For he that introduces will make enemies of all those who do well out of the old institutions, and will receive only cool support from those who would do well out of the new ones. This coolness is caused partly by fear of their opponents, who have the old laws on their side, and partly from the natural scepticism of mankind, who have no faith in new arrangements until they have been confirmed by experience.

Table 5.3 Resistance to change: the real British disease?

Management	Workers	Policy makers
No to:	**No** to:	**No** to:
Mechanical coal loading and other innovations	End of small pits	Training for mining and other engineers
Specialist technical staff	Productivity agreements	Industrial strategy
Process innovations	Proper apprentice training	Investment allowances
Modular and batch production	End of demarcation disputes	Priority for vocational training
Systematic replacement of obsolete equipment	No to 'dilution' of 'skilled' by trained	Redirection of science to industry
Management education	Training centres	Design education
Re-investment	End of 'slack' time	Concentration
Air conditioned, properly lit plants	Rationalisation of unions	Universal primary education until 1880s
Retooling by choice not necessity	End of restrictive practices	Trade strategy
Agreed delivery and quality standards	Qualifications	Large-scale investment in industrial modernisation

Source: Based on Barnett, C. (2001) *The Audit of War: The Illusion and Reality of Britain as a Great Nation*, new edition, Pan Books.

Climate change and the needs of the natural and built environments

These pose another set of ethical challenges for business. In the face of a global, scientific consensus about the impact of carbon emissions on CO_2 levels in the atmosphere, those firms whose production processes or whose products produce the most carbon face real dilemmas. Oil companies, car makers, chemical companies, utilities and many others can, in theory, cease production and distribution or challenge or ignore the risks. In 2001, Lee Raymond, then CEO of Exxon, summarised the position from its perspective:

> Although the science of climate change is uncertain, there's no doubt about the considerable economic harm to society that would result from reducing fuel availability to consumers by adopting the Kyoto Protocol or other mandatory measures that would significantly increase the cost of energy.

The cost, in Exxon's eyes, of restricting or changing its systems were simply too high for the company and the economy. The taxes that were advocated to reduce US fuel consumption were opposed directly by the company and indirectly through its trade bodies. A utilitarian approach is unlikely to resolve or help to resolve the ethical dilemmas posed by change partly because the evidence (data) can be disputed and partly because of the long-term impacts of climate change.

Caney[32] argues 'that a human rights approach provides an appropriate way in which to evaluate the effects of climate change' and resolve the ethical dilemma faced by business. In his analysis, Caney argues that 'climate change, so I shall argue, jeopardizes three key human rights: the human right to life; the human right to health; and the human right to subsistence'. As such, the human rights approach resolves in many ways the ethical dilemma as actions that violate human rights cannot be counter-balanced by arguments about economic benefits for some in most recognised moral codes.

Taxation

Like death, taxes are 'always with us', the divisions about the who, what, where and why of taxes are equally pervasive. For some, all taxes discourage enterprise and lead to excessive government. For others, taxes, as the minimum, ensure a safe and healthy society and, at the maximum, redistributive taxes ensure a fair society. Taxation raises other issues for business. At one extreme, the core 'economic function' of business requires that taxes are an essential means by which business delivers this economic function, while at the other extreme taxes take resources that might be better employed in dividends, jobs or research.

The vigour of the debate is vividly illustrated in public protest on both sides of the debate. In the USA, for example, Tea Party protests complain about the scale and nature of taxes. In Britain, however, it is tax avoidance by business that stirs emotions and protests.

Advocates of both positions often defend their argument with a version of Kant's categorical imperative. He states that an ethically or morally sustainable position is one 'whereby you can, at the same time, will that it should become a universal law'.[33] Broadly speaking, that means that if you are willing for everyone in the same position to behave in the same way, it is moral.

Tea Party protesters in the USA

Source: Katharine Andriotis Photography, LLC/Editorial/Alamy

UK Uncut protesters picket a shop
Source: Guy Bell/Alamy

It is, therefore, ethical for a firm to seek to reduce the amount of tax that is payable by all means that are within the law, if it accepts that this is universalisable or equally applicable to every relevantly identical situation. A firm, therefore, that avoids taxation cannot complain that other firms adopting the same position means that: new employees are poorly educated, because schools are inadequately funded; crime goes undetected because police resources are limited or roads are poorly maintained when local government is short of finance. Equally, executives who bribe potential customers to win business, should accept that others have the right to do the same, to take business from them.

The central problem with the categorical imperative for business ethics is that two contradictory positions – like too much and too little taxes – can be seen as equally universalisable.

Innovation and change, climate change, taxation are clearly not the only areas that raise issues of business ethics. Some of the greatest dilemmas can be found elsewhere in finance such as insider trading, in marketing around the use of product or service claims, in health and safety around who can do what, where and in human resources around equality and diversity. The complexity and diversity of the challenges and dilemma's faced lends support to Williams's view that the complexity and diversity of the challenges requires complex and diverse responses. He asks[34] 'why should it be conceptually simple, using only one or two ethical concepts . . . rather than many?'

For Arnold, Audi and Zwolinski,[35] 'Moral reality is complex, and any attempt to force that reality into the mold of a single overarching theory will inevitably omit or misinterpret some aspects of it.' They use Ross's notion[36] of intuitionism to appeal to ethical standards that thoughtful educated people find intuitive. Arnold *et al.* identify nine such principles or standards of particular relevance to business:

1 justice: including the positive obligation to prevent and rectify injustice as well as the negative duty not to commit injustice;
2 non-injury: roughly, the obligation to avoid harming others;
3 fidelity: promise-keeping and avoidance of lying (both are cases of fidelity to our word), honesty;
4 reparation: the obligation to make amends for wrong-doing;
5 beneficence: the obligation to do good deeds, in particular, to contribute to virtue, knowledge, or pleasure in others;
6 self-improvement: the obligation to better oneself;
7 gratitude: the obligation to express appreciation for good deeds towards us, where these include good work done under our direction as well as beneficent deeds towards us;
8 liberty: the obligation to preserve and, where possible, enhance freedom and autonomy;
9 obligations of manner (roughly, of respectfulness): these concern how we do what is obligatory as opposed to what we must do in some way or other – our obligations of matter or respect for others such as employees.

This sense of complexity, even powerlessness (in defining absolute principles), is not a basis for denying the ethical and corporate implications of actions. It emphasises the importance of exhaustive attempts to construct 'what if' scenarios and understand the type of social contracts that shape the relationship between the firm, its executives and the society in which they trade.

John Rawls,[37] along with Habermas, is perhaps the most influential recent writer on the 'rules' and 'relationships' which shape behaviour within and between organisations. His theory of justice, deals with 'the way in which the main political and social institutions fit together into one system of social cooperation, and the way they assign basic rights and duties'.

He explores the nature of the social contract that shapes relationships including those in business. He is interested in the consequences of actions rather than their initial purpose or motives but in doing so highlights the importance of fashioning an economic system that generated both wealth and fairness through individual, corporate and regulatory (government) action. These notions of fairness and justice have been developed by a number of writers to define and prescribe ethical behaviour by businesses and their executives in areas as diverse as employment, investment, internationalisation and strategy.[38]

Defining business ethics

One of the most comprehensive attempts to arrive at a definition of business ethics was undertaken by Lewis.[39] After reviewing 158 textbooks and arriving at 38 sub-categories ranging from principles to 'golden rules' he concluded that 'business ethics' is (the) rules, standards, codes, or principles which provide guidelines for morally right behaviour and truthfulness in specific situations.

His analysis went on to conclude that the building blocks include such elements as social responsibility, honesty and fairness, values that are in accord with common behaviour or with one's religious beliefs, obligations, responsibilities, and rights towards conscientious

Table 5.4 Key sources for the study of business ethics

Category	Key work(s)
Primary sources	Hobbes, T. *The Leviathan* (1651) Hume, D. *A Treatise Concerning Human Nature* (1739) Rousseau, J. J. *The Social Contract* (1762) Smith, A. *The Wealth of Nations* (1776) Kant, I. *Groundwork to the Metaphysics of Morals* (1785) Bentham, J. *Introduction to the Principles of Morals and Legislation* (1789) Paine, T. *The Rights of Man* (1791) Mill, J. S. *Utilitarianism* (1861) Spencer, H. *Essays* (1891) Moore, G. *Principia Ethica* (1903)
'Radicals'	Hayek, F. A. *The Road to Serfdom*, London: Routledge (1944) von Mises, L. *Human Action*, London: William Hodge (1949) Galbraith, J. K. *The New Industrial State*, Harmondsworth: Penguin (1967) Medawar, C. *The Social Audit Consumer Handbook*, London: MacMillan (1978) Friedman, M. and Friedman, R. *Free to Choose*, London: Seeker and Warburg (1980)
Modern commentators	Post, J. E. *Research in Corporate Social Performance and Policy*, Annual Series, London: JAI Press Silk, L. and Vogel, D. *Ethics and Profits*, New York: Simon and Schuster (1976) De George, R. *Business Ethics*, New York: Macmillan (1986) Conference Board *Corporate Ethics*, Washington: Research Report No. 900 (1987) Mahony, J. *Business Ethics: Oil and Water*? London: Kings College (1988) Donaldson, J. *Key Issues in Business Ethics*, London: Routledge (1989) Craig Smith, N. *Morality and The Market*, London: Routledge (1990) Freeman, R. E. *Business Ethics*, Oxford: Oxford University Press (1991) Donaldson, T. J. and Freeman, R. E. *Business as Humanity*, Ruffin (1995) Badiou, A. *Infinite Thought. Truth and the Return of Philosophy*, London: Continuum (2005) Crane, A. and Matten, D. *Business Ethics. Managing Corporate Citizenship and Sustainability in the Age of Globalization*, Oxford: Oxford University Press

work or enlightened self-interest. It embraces a philosophy of what is good and bad, the ability to clarify these issues in decision making, a focus on one's individual conscience and/or legal system, and a system or theory of justice questioning the quality of one's relationships. This requires understanding of the relationship of means to ends, concern for integrity, emphasis on virtue, leadership, character, confidentiality, respect for the judgement of others.

The *Blackwell Encyclopedic Dictionary of Business Ethics*[40] offers a more succinct definition but with a hint of circularity, 'Business ethics aims to specify the principles under which (business organizations) must operate to behave ethically'.

Other writers on the study of business ethics are listed in Table 5.4.

QUESTIONS

1. Identify the key features of a meaningful and easy-to-implement code of ethics. How might a firm convert these principles into practice?

2. Describe the corporate social responsibility programmes of a major corporation with which you are familiar. Illustrate how these programmes reflect wider aspirations of the firm.

3 Discuss the proposition that the major determinant of a firm's pattern of corporate philanthropy is the composition of the board.

4 What mechanisms does the community have to shape the attitudes and behaviour of managers and firms? Illustrate with examples of endorsement and censure.

5 Discuss the ethical implications of Friedman's statement that 'capitalism is a – necessary condition for political freedom'.

6 'Scientific management' is fundamentally exploitative and inhumane – outline the arguments for and against this proposition.

7 Using the arguments of a 'school' of philosophy, e.g. utilitarianism, construct an ethically, sustainable case for a developing country refusing to pay its debts to a British or US bank.

8 Define:
(a) Stakeholders
(b) Social endorsement
(c) Peer group pressure
(d) Utilitarianism
(e) Positivism.

CASE STUDY 5

Nurse Margaret Haywood and *Panorama*

Nurse Margaret Haywood was at the centre of one of the UK's most prominent cases of 'whistleblowing' when she helped the *Panorama* BBC TV programme expose serious failings in the care of the elderly at one NHS hospital.

Her concern was that nursing basics were being ignored such as pain control, toileting and even ensuring some terminally ill elderly patients were getting enough to eat and drink.

She failed to get her concerns addressed through normal 'internal means' – she voiced her concerns through her immediate line manager 'but nothing was really taken on board'. After this she agreed to go public, helping the BBC TV programme feature the conditions leading to attempts to have her struck off the nursing register ever since.

She had hoped for some protection from government legislation. A Department of Health spokesperson said:

> Whistle-blowers already have full protection under the Public Interest Disclosure Act passed by this Government.
>
> We expect that any member of staff who reports concerns about the safety or quality of care to be listened to by their managers and action taken to address their concerns.

Despite this, she was struck off by the Nursing and Midwifery Council which said she failed to 'follow her obligations as a nurse'. This initially led to a war of words with a spokesperson for the Nursing and Midwifery Council saying in an email response:

> Margaret Haywood was struck from the register because she failed to gain the consent of the patients prior to secretly filming them and not, as reported by some media, for whistle blowing.
>
> A patient should be able to trust a nurse with his/her physical condition and psychological wellbeing without that confidential information being disclosed to others.
>
> Only in the most exceptional circumstances should the cardinal principle of patient confidentiality be breached. Based upon the evidence it heard, the independent panel did not believe that this was the case and although the conditions on the ward were serious, it was not necessary to breach confidentiality to seek to improve them by the method chosen. The panel believed that the method was unlikely to benefit the

Case study 5 (*cont.*)

patients that were on the ward at the time of filming and under Margaret Haywood's care.

In contrast, her union said:

We can't have a culture where 'whistle blowers' feel intimated into not legitimately reporting wrong doing and bad practice in the NHS. We need a safe environment for 'whistle blowers' who feel that they can complain without losing their livelihood.

There appears to be a number of extenuating circumstances in the case of Margaret Haywood and the NMC could have imposed a lesser punishment than that of being struck off.

The NMC exists as a regulatory body to protect patients and clients first and foremost, and not the alleged failings of members of the nursing profession in caring for the elderly.

After years of debate, the Royal College of Nursing and the Nursing and Midwifery Council settled on a softer punishment for the 59-year-old at the High Court. The striking-off order was replaced with a one-year caution.

Questions

1 Do whistle-blowers act ethically?

2 On what ethical basis can a whistle-blower justify his or her actions?

3 Was Margaret Haywood acting ethically in assisting *Panorama*?

4 Is it possible to say that the Royal College of Nursing and the Nursing and Midwifery Council were acting ethically in striking her off?

References

1 Lillie W. (1961) *An Introduction to Ethics*, London: Methuen.

2 Berle, A. A. and Means, G. C. (1932) with a new introduction (9 pp.) by Weidenbaum, M. and Jensen, M. (1991) *The Modern Corporation and Private Property*, 2nd revised edition, Transaction Publishers.

3 Friedman, M. (1970) 'The Social Responsibility of Business is to Increase Its Profits', *The New York Times Magazine*, 13 September.

4 Waddock, S. A. and Graves, S. B. (1997) 'The Corporate Social Performance–Financial Performance Link', *Strategic Management Journal*, 18: 303–19.

5 McWilliams, A. and Siegel, D. (2000) 'Corporate Social Responsibility and Financial Performance: Correlation or Misspecification?', *Strategic Management Journal*, 21: 603–9.

6 Wright, P. and Ferris, S. (1997) 'Agency Conflict and Corporate Strategy: The Effect of Divestment on Corporate Value', *Strategic Management Journal*, 18: 77–83.

7 Aquinas, T. (2009) *The Summa Theologica*, BiblioLife, LLC.

8 www.supremecourt.gov/opinions/10pdf/10-6.pdf – Global Tech Appliances.

9 Smith, A. and Sinner, A. (2003) *The Wealth of Nations*, new edition, Penguin Classics.

10 Melé, D. (2006) 'Religious Foundations of Business Ethics', in *The Accountable Corporation*, Vol. 2, Epstein, M. E. and Hanson, K. O. (eds), London: Praeger.

11 www.renaissance.com.pk/Mayviewpoint2y5.htm#_ftn1.

12 Enderle, C. (2005) 'Business Ethics in China', in *The Blackwell Encyclopedia of Management* Werhane, P. H. and Feeman, R. E. (eds), second edition, Oxford: Blackwell, 76–80.

13 Enderle, G. (1997) 'A Worldwide Survey of Business Ethics in the 1990s', *Journal of Business Ethics*, 16: 1475–83.

14 Enderle, G. (1997) ibid.

15 Noland, J. and Phillips, R. (2010) 'Stakeholder Engagement, Discourse Ethics and Strategic Management', *International Journal of Management Reviews*: 39–49.

16 Habermas, J. (1990) *The Philosophical Discourse of Modernity*, Cambridge: Polity Press, new edition.

17 OECD (2004) *Understanding Economic Growth*, Paris: OECD Publishing.

18 OECD (2011) *Skills for Innovation and Research*, Paris: OECD Publishing.

19 Drucker, P. (2007) *Innovation and Entrepreneurship*, second revised edition, Butterworth-Heinemann.

20 Deane, P. (1967) *The First Industrial Revolution*, Cambridge: Cambridge University Press.

21 Schumpeter, J. A. (2009) *Can Capitalism Survive?: Creative Destruction and the Future of the Global Economy*, Harper Perennial.

22 Department of Business, Innovation and Skills (2010) *Strategy For Sustainable Growth*, London: HMSO.

23 Pojman, L. P. and Fieser, J. (2009) *Ethics: Discovering Right and Wrong*, 6th edition, Belmont, CA: Wadsworth.

24 Philips, R. (2003) *Stakeholder Theory and Organisational Ethics*, San Francisco, CA: Berrett-Koehler.

25 Fielder, J. and Birsch, D. (1994) *The Ford Pinto Case: A Study In Applied Ethics, Business, and Technology*, New York: State University of New York Press.

26 Donaldson, J. (1989) *Key Issues in Business Ethics*, Academic Press.

27 Havel, V. (1985) *Living in Truth*, Faber and Faber.

28 Suggate, A. M. (1991) 'Personal Responsibility: Hayek and Havel in a Christian Perspective', unpublished mimeo.

29 Williams, R. (1989) 'The Ethics of SDI', in Bauckham, R. and Elford, S. J. (eds), *Nuclear Weapons Debate: Theological and Ethical Issues*, SCM Press.

30 Barnett., C. (2001) *The Audit of War: The Illusion and Reality of Britain as a Great Nation*, new edition, Pan Books.

31 Machiavelli, N. (2003) *The Prince*, new edition, Penguin: Longman.

32 Caney, S. (2009) 'Climate Change, Human Rights and Moral Thresholds', in *Human Rights and Climate Change*, (ed.), Humphrey, S. Cambridge: Cambridge University Press.

33 Kant, I., translated by Ellington J. W. [1785] (1993) *Grounding for the Metaphysics of Morals*, 3rd edition, Hackett: 30.

34 Williams, B. (1985) *Ethics and the Limits of Philosophy*, Cambridge, MA: Harvard University Press.

35 Arnold, D., Audi, R. and Zwolinski, M. (2010) 'Recent Work in Ethical Theory and Its Implications for Business Ethics', *Business Ethics Quarterly*, 20:4, October: 559–81.

36 Ross, W. D. (1930) *The Right and the Good*, Oxford: Oxford University Press.

37 Rawls, J. (2001) *Justice as Fairness: A Restatement*, Cambridge, MA: Harvard University Press.

38 Donaldson, T. and Dunfee, T. (1999) *Ties that Bind: a Social Contracts Approach to Business Ethics* Boston: Harvard Business School Press.

39 Lewis, V. (1985) 'Defining Business Ethics; Like Nailing Jello to a Wall', *Journal of Business Ethics* 4(5): 377–83.

40 Werhane, P. and Freeman, R. E. (1999) *The Blackwell Encyclopedic Dictionary of Business Ethics*, Oxford: Wiley-Blackwell.

Source: © Eye Ubiquitous/Alamy

Corporate Social Responsibility at Coca-Cola

As one of the largest beverage companies, Coca-Cola ("Coke") has a major impact on human and natural environments. Coke has 93,000 employees and more than 900 bottling and manufacturing facilities worldwide. The firm generates about 75 percent of its more than $30 billion in sales from international markets.

In the past, critics have charged that Coke generates pollution, endangers scarce water supplies, markets soft drinks to teenagers, and tolerates inferior workplace conditions in developing economies.

In the meantime, Coca-Cola management has adopted responsible and sustainable approaches in its global operations. Coke has invested millions to develop superior wastewater treatment facilities. In arid areas, it implemented programs to replace all the water it extracts from local aquifers. From China to the Americas, the firm runs water-conservation programs.

Management makes continual efforts to reduce energy consumption throughout its bottling and manufacturing facilities. In Uruguay, Coke uses hybrid electric trucks to deliver product in congested areas to reduce pollution. In North America,

CHAPTER 5

Ethics, Sustainability, and Corporate Social Responsibility in International Business

LEARNING OBJECTIVES *In this chapter, you will learn about the following:*

1. Ethical challenges in international business
2. Key aspects of international ethics
3. Corporate social responsibility
4. The role of sustainability in international operations
5. Corporate governance and its implications for managers
6. A framework for making ethical decisions

Coke operates hundreds of hybrid delivery trucks, which are 30 percent more fuel efficient than diesel counterparts. Coke management is expanding the hybrid program to Europe. The firm switched to 100 percent renewable energy in numerous operating facilities. One plant in Belgium uses 100 percent geothermal energy. Coke is also improving the technology used in vending machines to reduce harmful greenhouse gases.

Coke manages the entire life cycle of product packaging. For example, used bottles are converted into plastic chips, which are then made into new bottles. Many bottles are made from 30 percent plant-based materials, making them more biodegradable. One facility recycles 100 million pounds of plastic bottles annually, equivalent to nearly 2 billion Coca-Cola bottles a year. Management aims to recycle 100 percent of Coke's bottles and cans by 2020. Coke's "Live Positively" pledge is a code of conduct for the firm's sustainability goals. For example, the firm is committed to responsible marketing practices, and avoids advertising aimed at children. Coke established a Workplace Rights Policy that confirms management's commitment to avoiding child labor and discrimination;

offering fair wages and work hours; and ensuring occupational health and safety. Coke's Anti-Bribery Policy provides guidance on how to conduct business in an ethical and legal manner.

The firm's Manual Distribution Center (MDC) program promotes economic development in poor countries. Numerous micro-distribution centers in Africa employ entrepreneurs who distribute product to local retailers in hard-to-reach areas. The MDCs account for over 80 percent of company sales in East Africa while providing small-business ownership and jobs to more than 12,000 people. The MDCs meet customer needs while supporting the sustainability of countless African communities. Coke is seeking to apply similar models in India, China, Indonesia, and Latin America.

SOURCES: "Return To Sender," *BrandPackaging*, Apr/May 2010, pp. 40–42; "The Coca-Cola Company," *Economics Week*, June 5, 2009, p. 7; Andrew Batson, "Coke Aims to Improve Water Recycling," *Wall Street Journal*, June 6, 2007, p. A10; Paul Barrett, "Coke's Got An America Problem," *Bloomberg Businessweek*, October 4–10, 2010, pp. 94–95; Carol Birkland, "Clean Air Initiatives," *Fleet Equipment*, May 2010, p. 2; Coca-Cola Company, *2010/2011 Sustainability Report*, retrieved from http://www.thecoca-colacompany.com; Elizabeth Fuhrman, "Recycling Shows Packaging's Sustainable Value," *Beverage Industry*, November 2009, pp. 42–44; Betsy McKay, "Coke Makes Cleanup Gains," *Wall Street Journal*, January 16, 2008, p. B3A; "The New Face of Africa," *Fortune*, November 21, 2011, Special Advertising Section.

Ethical behavior is an essential component for successful business in today's global environment.[1] Global business leaders define ethical behavior in terms of four key components: (1) ethics, (2) corporate social responsibility, (3) sustainability, and (4) governance. The opening story describes Coca-Cola's ethical approach to international business. **Ethics** are moral principles and values that govern the behavior of people, firms, and governments, regarding right and wrong.[2] By contrast, **corruption** is the abuse of power to achieve illegitimate personal gain. More than 30 percent of MNEs believe corruption is a major concern in their activities worldwide.[3]

Ethics
Moral principles and values that govern the behavior of people, firms, and governments, regarding right and wrong.

Corruption
The abuse of power to achieve illegitimate personal gain.

As examples of unethical behavior, firms may:

- Falsify or misrepresent contracts or financial statements;
- Pay or accept bribes, kickbacks, or inappropriate gifts;
- Tolerate sweatshop conditions or otherwise abuse employees;
- Undertake false advertising and other deceptive marketing practices;
- Engage in pricing that is deceptive, discriminatory, or predatory;
- Deceive or abuse intermediaries in international channels; and
- Engage in activities that harm the natural environment.[4]

Coca-Cola demonstrates social responsibility by ensuring safe working conditions, treating customers and intermediaries fairly, and preventing illicit business activities abroad. **Corporate social responsibility (CSR)** refers to operating a business in a manner that meets or exceeds the ethical, legal, and commercial expectations of customers, shareholders, employees, and the communities where the firm does business. Coke also undertakes programs to conserve energy and water, reduce harmful greenhouse gases, and recycle cans and bottles.

Corporate social responsibility (CSR)
A manner of operating a business that meets or exceeds the ethical, legal, commercial, and public expectations of customers, shareholders, employees, and communities.

Sustainability means meeting humanity's needs without harming future generations. The sustainable firm aims to carry out value chain activities in ways that protect and preserve economic, social, and natural environments. For example, sustainable firms pay fair wages, ensure worker safety, and avoid emitting toxic waste.

Sustainability
Meeting humanity's needs without harming future generations.

Exhibit 5.1 summarizes key managerial approaches addressed in this chapter. Firms operate in a global environment characterized by both ethical and unethical participants and myriad opportunities to engage in corruption. Management can overcome such challenges by developing a system of corporate governance that emphasizes ethics, corporate social responsibility, and sustainability in all value-chain activities.

Corporate governance is the system of procedures and processes by which corporations are managed, directed, and controlled. It provides the means through which firms undertake ethical behaviors, CSR, and sustainability. Ethics and appropriate behavior are essential in international business. Because standards of ethical behavior vary around the world, simply obeying the law is usually insufficient to ensure against violating such standards. Worldwide variance in ethical standards makes ethics a complex issue in international business.

Corporate governance
The system of procedures and processes by which corporations are managed, directed, and controlled.

EXHIBIT 5.1

Organizing Framework for Ethical Behavior in International Business

Ethics and appropriate behavior transcend all international business activities and figure prominently in management decisions about financial performance and competitive advantage. However, corruption is commonplace in many countries, especially those lacking transparent business systems. Most companies seek to ensure ethical practices in their international operations. The most advanced firms proactively emphasize not just ethical behavior, but also corporate social responsibility and sustainability. An integrated, strategic approach to ethical, sustainable, and socially-responsible behavior provides firms with competitive advantages, including stronger relationships with customers, employees, shareholders, suppliers, and the communities where they do business. Let us examine the critical role of ethical conduct in international business.

Ethical Challenges in International Business

Companies around the world now regard ethics as a strategic component in business decisions. Increasingly ethical behavior is seen to play a vital role in determining competitive advantage and long-term company performance. Firms encounter ethical challenges in a range of international activities:

- *Unethical management practices* are especially common in countries that lack appropriate regulation and professional standards. A corporate culture that advocates profit over sustainability and human welfare can lead to employee abuse, harmful procedures, and other unsustainable practices. The global financial crisis that began in 2008 resulted in part because senior managers in banks and financial firms neglected to devise safeguards against making bad loans or offering high-risk securities. Lax management standards also give rise to dishonest accounting practices, in which companies provide deceptive information to investors, customers, and government authorities.
- *Global sourcing* is the procurement of products or services from suppliers located abroad. In a typical scenario, the focal firm buys parts and components from foreign companies that manufacture such goods. In some cases, firms establish their own supply factories abroad. Global sourcing raises concerns about ensuring human rights and protecting the environment. Some companies operate sweatshop factories in which employees are children or work long hours for very low wages, often in harsh conditions.[5] Many factories generate substantial pollution. The use of third-party suppliers is challenging for firms like Nike and Philips, with thousands of partners that operate in a range of cultures and belief systems worldwide.
- *Deceptive marketing, advertising, and selling* to induce people to buy products. Marketers may make false claims about the quality or effectiveness of a product. Advances in communications technologies allow fraudulent marketers to easily target victims in foreign countries. The transnational nature of such scams makes it difficult for law enforcers to catch and prosecute perpetrators. Easy accessibility of the Internet has led shady online

marketers to harm unsuspecting consumers. In developing economies, for example, most online drug stores operate illegally.[6] The drugs offered by such outlets are often fake and may harm users. Phony Viagra made in Thailand was found to contain vodka; bogus Tamiflu has been manufactured with vitamin C and lactose, and some fake medications contain lethal amounts of dangerous chemicals. Although the pharmaceutical industry and governments pursue such firms, violators are often elusive and beyond the reach of authorities.

- *Defective or harmful products or packaging* can lead to disastrous outcomes for public health and safety or for natural environments. For example, millions of electronic products from cell phones to computers are discarded every year. Products that could be recycled end up in landfills. Excessive product packaging generates pollution, and consumes energy and natural resources. Excessive use of plastic packaging is wasteful. Because plastic does not easily decompose, plastic waste is steadily increasing on land and in the oceans.

Intellectual Property Violations

Intellectual property
Ideas or works created by individuals or firms, including discoveries and inventions; artistic, musical, and literary works; and words, phrases, symbols, and designs.

Intellectual property rights
The legal claim through which the proprietary assets of firms and individuals are protected from unauthorized use by other parties.

Illicit use of intellectual property represents yet another ethical violation, especially common in international business. **Intellectual property** refers to ideas or works created by individuals or firms and includes a variety of proprietary, intangible assets: discoveries and inventions; artistic, musical, and literary works; and words, phrases, symbols, and designs. Intellectual property may be stolen or copied illicitly. In Russia, for example, software and movies produced by such firms as Microsoft and Disney often fall prey to *counterfeiting*; the assets are reproduced without compensating those who originally created them. Widely recognized global brands—Rolex, Louis Vuitton, and Tommy Hilfiger, among others—are often counterfeited, eroding firms' brand equity and competitive advantages.

Trademarks, copyrights, and patents are examples of **intellectual property rights**, the legal claim through which proprietary assets are protected from unauthorized use by other parties. *Trademarks* are distinctive signs and indicators that firms use to identify their products and services. *Copyrights* grant protections to the creators of art, music, books, software, movies, and TV shows. *Patents* confer the exclusive right to manufacture, use, and sell products or processes. Intellectual property rights are not guaranteed in much of the world. Laws enacted in one country are enforceable only in that country and confer no protection abroad.[7]

Firms' intellectual property often fall victim to counterfeiting. "Piracy" is equivalent to counterfeiting; it is the unauthorized production and selling of previously copyrighted works. The total value of internationally traded counterfeit and pirated products was expected to reach nearly $1 trillion annually by 2015. The total value of domestically produced and consumed counterfeit and pirated products was expected to reach nearly $600 billion annually by 2015.[8] Counterfeiting and piracy hurt the world economy in various ways, especially regarding trade, foreign investment, employment, innovation, criminal activity, and the environment. Counterfeiting and piracy harm company sales and pricing, and increase business costs. The brand value of heavily counterfeited goods can decline over time. Counterfeiting and piracy also reduce government tax revenues and the moral integrity of nations.

For consumers, counterfeit and pirated products are usually of inferior quality. Counterfeit goods can unknowingly be used in manufacturing, military, critical infrastructure, and consumer products, all of which threaten health and safety.[9] For example, the consumer products company Johnson & Johnson discovered that counterfeiters were selling fake versions of its OneTouch test strips, used by diabetes patients in Canada and the United States. Criminals were promoting bogus versions of OneTouch, which diabetes sufferers use to

Source: © epa european pressphoto agency b.v./Alamy

Workers at a Foxconn factory in China, a leading supplier to Apple. Following charges about poor working conditions at Foxconn plants, Apple and Foxconn took steps to improve the work environment.

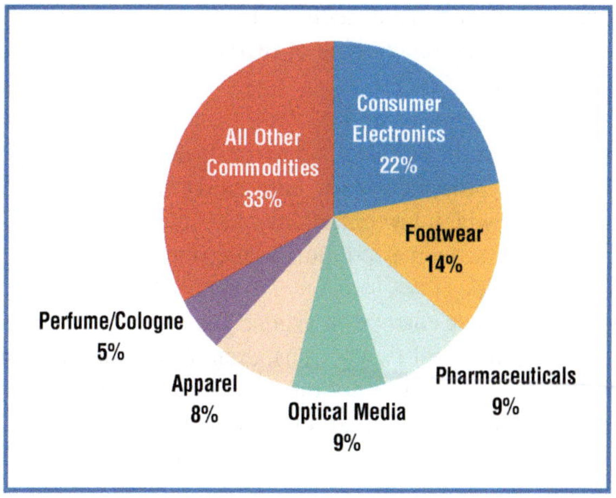

EXHIBIT 5.2

Top Counterfeit Commodities Seized, United States, 2011

Source: Based on CBP Office of International Trade (2012), *Intellectual Property Rights: Fiscal Year 2011 Seizure Statistics*, Washington, DC: U.S. Immigration and Customs Enforcement, at http://www.ice.gov/doclib/iprcenter/pdf/ipr-fy-2011-seizure-report.pdf.

monitor blood-sugar levels. Fake strips give false readings, which can be life-threatening if they cause patients to take too much or too little insulin, the drug used to treat diabetes.[10]

The United States is the top market for counterfeit and pirated goods. In 2011, U.S. Department of Homeland Security agents seized counterfeit and pirated products at U.S. borders with an estimated retail value of more than $1.1 billion. Exhibit 5.2 highlights the categories of illicit commodities seized. Among the most counterfeited goods are consumer electronics, footwear, and pharmaceuticals. In 2011, by far the largest single source of counterfeit products was China, which accounted for 62 percent of Homeland Security seizures. This was followed by Hong Kong, an administrative region of China, amounting to 18 percent of seizures. India represented just 3 percent of seizures, and all other countries accounted for the remaining 17 percent.[11]

MNEs seeking to do business within China may become victims of domestic counterfeiting activities. For example, Disney has struggled to launch its DVD movie business in China, due to rampant local piracy. Legitimate Disney DVDs of films like *Finding Nemo* and *The Lion King* cost up to ten times as much as knockoffs, restricting sales to a trickle.[12]

In Russia, illicit Web sites sell popular music downloads for as little as 5 cents apiece, or less than one U.S. dollar for an entire CD. Russia's laws regarding counterfeiting are often insufficient to thwart such crimes, and enforcement is weak.[13] Suppose you work for a small online retailer that decides to offer pirated music via the company Web site to potential buyers in Russia and other emerging markets with weak intellectual property laws. How should you respond to this dilemma? Later in this chapter, we present a framework that you can use to analyze this and countless other ethical problems that managers encounter in international business.

Bribery

Bribery refers to offering, giving, receiving, or soliciting anything of value to influence the actions of a government official or a corporate manager. Bribery is acceptable in much of the world. It is estimated that more than $1 trillion in bribes are paid worldwide every year to gain access to important markets and achieve other business goals. One study found that 40 percent of business executives have been asked to pay a bribe when dealing with public institutions. Twenty percent claimed to have lost business because of bribes paid by competitors.[14] Bribery often takes the form of *grease payments*, small inducements intended to expedite transactions and gain other favors. In many countries, such facilitating payments are both legal and acceptable.

Bribery is especially common in developing economies, such as Egypt, Indonesia, Nigeria, and Pakistan. In such places, it can be nearly impossible to achieve important business objectives without paying bribes to public officials and other individuals. The problem is especially common in the global energy, mining, and telecommunications industries. Firms from these industries—such as Halliburton and Siemens—have been implicated in major bribery scandals.

Bribery has produced harmful consequences, such as illegal logging in Indonesia, terrible work conditions in China, and poorly constructed buildings that collapsed in Turkey. Paying bribes increases the risks and costs of doing business. It promotes a culture of dishonesty and immorality that opens the door to other types of wrongdoing. It threatens fair competition, merit-based selection, and other equitable business practices. In this way, bribery poses a fundamental threat to confidence in and functioning of market economies.[15]

Corruption

Corruption is an extreme form of unethical behavior. It may appear as political corruption, in which officials abuse public power or profit improperly from government resources. It may arise as police corruption, in which law enforcement officials obtain financial or other benefits in exchange for granting favors, such as not pursuing crimes. In firms, corruption occurs across the range of value chain activities.

Various organizations assess corruption around the world. The most well-known organization is Transparency International (www.transparency.org) and its *Corruption Perceptions Index*, which measures managers' perceptions of bribery, embezzlement, and other illicit behavior worldwide.[16] Exhibit 5.3 lists a sample of countries and their perceived levels of corruption, on a scale of 1 to 100. Countries with the lowest scores have the least corruption, such as Canada and Denmark.

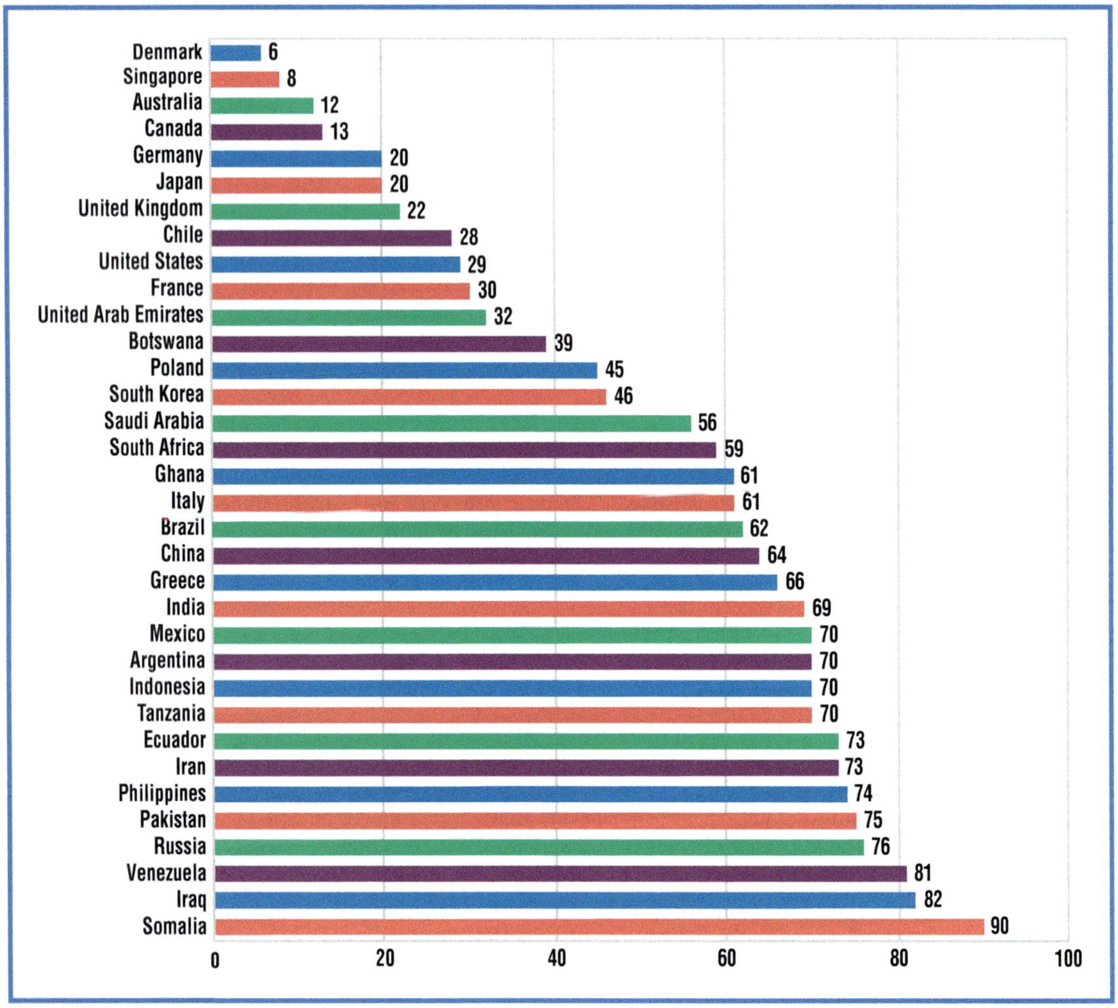

EXHIBIT 5.3

Corruption Perceptions Index 2011

Note: Countries with the highest scores have the most corruption.

Source: Based on *Corruption Perceptions Index*. Copyright © 2011 Transparency International: The Global Coalition Against Corruption, www.transparency.org.

Countries with minimal corruption attract much direct investment because managers know business in such nations is conducted fairly. Commercial laws are fair and adequately enforced. Financial and accounting information is transparent, reliable, and easily accessed. By contrast, foreign firms are reluctant to invest in countries such as Somalia and Venezuela, due to rampant corruption. In Russia, entrepreneurs typically must pay thousands of dollars in bribes to officials to gain the right to launch their businesses and run them efficiently.

Corruption harms the poorest in societies. For example, many are forced to pay bribes to gain access to needed products and services, such as water, electricity, and phone utilities. Widespread corruption hinders economic development. This relationship points to an important dilemma—trade and investment help reduce poverty, but MNEs avoid doing business with corrupt countries.

Various bodies have issued international conventions against corruption. Numerous countries have signed the antibribery convention developed by the Organisation for Economic Co-operation and Development (OECD). The United Nations issued a declaration against corruption in international transactions. The U.S. Foreign Corrupt Practices Act (FCPA) makes it illegal for U.S. firms to offer bribes to foreign parties to secure or retain business. Under the FCPA, firms may be fined $2 million and managers can be imprisoned for up to five years.

Key Aspects of International Ethics

Business plays an enormous role worldwide, affecting people and nations by creating jobs, wealth, and societal value. The goal of business is to make money. But experienced managers understand due consideration also must be given to business ethics. Just as reputation affects the success of individuals, it is critical to companies as well. Failure to protect and nurture the corporate image translates into poor performance and potential ruin. Ethical behavior is critical to business success. Let's examine ethics in terms of value to firms, how ethics vary worldwide, and the role of the MNE.

The Value of Behaving Ethically

Ethical behavior is important for several reasons:

- It is simply the right thing to do.
- It is often prescribed within laws and regulations. Violating laws and regulations has obvious legal consequences.
- It is demanded by customers and governments.
- Firms that commit ethical blunders attract unwanted attention from opinion leaders and the news media.
- Ethical behavior is good business, leading to enhanced corporate image and selling prospects.

The firm with a reputation for high ethical standards gains advantages in hiring, motivating employees, partnering, and dealing with foreign governments. Firms that behave unethically run the risk of criminal or civil prosecution, hurting their own reputations, harming employee morale and recruitment efforts, and exposing themselves to blackmailers or other unscrupulous parties.[17] For all these reasons, companies incorporate ethical considerations in their international activities.

In host countries, firms with iconic global brands, such as Coca-Cola and Volkswagen, are especially conspicuous to consumers and can become targets of public protest. Increasingly, governments insist that firms behave in ways that serve the public interest. For example, the European Union restricts the use of lead, mercury, and other harmful substances in manufacturing, and requires firms to collect and recycle unwanted electronic products. Canada has well-developed complaint procedures for dealing with bribery, including liaison officers in 25 countries and a Web site (www.recol.ca) for filing complaints about possible corruption.[18] However, a major challenge is that ethical standards vary worldwide.

Variation in Ethical Standards among Countries

Appropriate behavior in one culture may be viewed as unethical elsewhere.[19] Let's review some examples:

- In China, counterfeiters frequently publish translated versions of imported books without compensating the original publisher or authors, an illegal practice in most of the world.
- In parts of Africa, accepting expensive gifts from suppliers is acceptable, even if considered improper elsewhere.
- In the United States, CEOs receive compensation often a hundred times greater than that of low-ranking subordinates, a practice considered inappropriate elsewhere.
- Finland and Sweden ban advertising directed at children, but the practice is well accepted in other parts of Europe.

Standards vary by level of economic development. Africa is beset by widespread hunger and some restaurant workers "steal" food on the job to take home to their families. Is this equivalent to restaurant workers stealing food in rich countries? Standards change over time. Although slavery is no longer tolerated, some multinational firms today tolerate working conditions that are akin to it. In China, many MNEs operate factories that pollute local water supplies.

Relativism
Belief that ethical truths are not absolute but differ from group to group.

Normativism
Belief that ethical behavioral standards are universal, and firms and individuals should seek to uphold them around the world.

Scholars and managers examine ethics from two distinct perspectives: relativism and normativism.[20]

Relativism The belief that ethical truths are not absolute but differ from group to group; according to this perspective, a good rule is "When in Rome, do as the Romans do." Thus, a Japanese firm that believes bribery is wrong might nevertheless pay bribes in countries where the practice is customary and culturally acceptable. Relativists opt for passive acceptance of the values, behaviors, and practices that prevail in each of the countries where they do business.

Normativism The belief that ethical behavioral standards are universal, and firms and individuals should seek to uphold them consistently around the world. According to this view, the Japanese firm that believes bribery is wrong will enforce this standard everywhere in the world. The United Nations and other agencies encourage firms to follow a normative approach. Sophisticated firms attempt to correct unethical practices that arise in their ongoing business dealings around the world.[21]

Most firms apply a combination of relativism and normativism abroad. Rightly or wrongly, they strike a balance between corporate values developed in the home country and local standards. However, this approach puts them at risk of violating norms that are increasingly universal. In countries with questionable ethical norms, it is usually best to maintain ethical standards *superior* to what is required by local laws and values. This strategy helps garner goodwill and averts potentially damaging publicity.

An Ethical Dilemma

Deciding what is right and wrong is not always clear. Firms with extensive international operations may face multiple and sometimes conflicting laws and regulations. Requirements may be ambiguous or inconsistent. Occasionally laws in foreign countries conflict with, or fall short of, home-country laws. In the United States, for example, the Occupational Safety and Health Administration (OSHA) specifies numerous regulations regarding labor and employment conditions. However, in most countries, such regulations are relatively underdeveloped, or don't exist at all. National legal systems are often weak and laws are poorly enforced. Many multinational firms struggle to find the right balance between acceptable practices at home and abroad. What should management do? Should it follow weak local laws or follow the laws of the home country? Even when a country has a sound legal system, or even when the firm has a strong code of ethics, managers regularly face the challenge of determining appropriate behavior.

An *ethical dilemma* is a predicament with major conflicts among different interests in which determining the most appropriate course of action is confounded by a set of solutions that are equally justifiable, and often equally imperfect. Possible actions may be mutually exclusive—the choice of one automatically negates the other(s).[22]

Imagine you are a manager and visit a factory owned by an affiliate in Colombia, only to discover the use of child labor in the plant. Upon studying the problem, you learn that child labor is accepted in many developing economies. There are more than 50 million children working in India alone. Girls are vulnerable, and may be abused or exploited. Work prevents children from attending school, which would improve their prospects for a better life. But you also learn that without their children's income, families often go hungry. If the kids are dismissed from the plant, many will turn to other income sources, including prostitution and street crime. The age at which children are deemed adults varies worldwide, sometimes as low as 15 years. What should you do? Do you make a fuss about the immorality of child labor, or do you look the other way?

Source: © B. O'Kane/Alamy

Global companies with well-known brands like McDonald's are especially conspicuous to consumers and need strong ethical values to thrive under public scrutiny. This airport restaurant is in Madrid, Spain.

This example is typical of the type of ethical dilemmas that employees encounter in international business. Managers working internationally may be most exposed because they can be caught between home country ethical norms and those encountered abroad.

Linking Ethics, Corruption, and Responsible Behavior

In a world of seemingly endless ethical challenges, how should managers and companies respond? Consider the framework in Exhibit 5.4. After complying with local law (the bottom of the pyramid), management should ensure that company activities follow high ethical standards (the middle). As they expand abroad, most firms believe it is sufficient to comply with laws, regulations, and basic ethical standards. However, in addition, sophisticated MNEs now emphasize socially responsible behavior (the top of the pyramid). Let's examine this notion in more detail.

Corporate Social Responsibility

Adhering to CSR implies a proactive approach to ethical behavior in which firms not only seek to maximize profits, but also to benefit society and the environment. Typical CSR values include:

- Avoiding human rights abuses,
- Upholding the right to join or form labor unions,

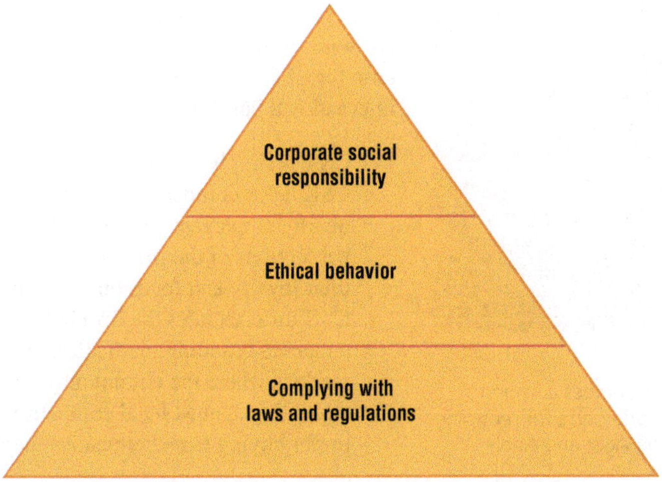

EXHIBIT 5.4

The Pyramid of Ethical Behavior

- Eliminating compulsory and child labor,
- Avoiding workplace discrimination,
- Protecting the natural environment,
- Guarding against corruption, and
- Engaging in philanthropy, such as donating money, products, or volunteer labor to good causes.[23]

CSR is about business giving back to society. However, many firms have been slow to adopt CSR. Failure to adopt CSR behaviors can have adverse, even ruinous, consequences. Efforts by the China National Petroleum Company (CNPC) to raise money on the New York Stock Exchange were harmed by the firm's activities in Sudan, which human rights groups had criticized. The Shell Oil Company has experienced protests and lost revenues due to opposition to its oil-drilling activities in Nigeria, which are seen as harming community interests and generating toxic waste. In India, Walmart experienced lost sales and massive protests because of concerns the firm's market entry would hurt small retailers in the region.[24]

Many companies have improved their performance by adopting CSR. Petrobras (www.petrobras.com) is a Brazilian oil company that developed CSR programs aimed at reducing poverty and child labor, as well as promoting youth education and rights for people with disabilities. In Africa, Petrobras has built hospitals, schools, and day-care centers. In Colombia, it developed a program to train community health agents. In Nigeria, Petrobras cooperates with a local non-governmental organization to provide HIV/AIDS prevention education.[25]

Motorola (www.motorola.com) has delivered more than 16 million low-cost mobile phones to people in fifty developing countries. It developed a mobile phone system for disease management in Africa, through which field health workers file patient reports and check drug supplies. Cellular connectivity helps professionals in poor areas deal more effectively with disease outbreaks, medicine shortages, and health maintenance. Efficient telecommunications promote productivity and raise GDP levels.[26]

Exhibit 5.5 summarizes additional CSR initiatives undertaken by firms worldwide. For example, Africa accounts for most deaths from AIDS. However, few Africans can afford medications used to treat the disease. GlaxoSmithKline (GSK) is a large pharmaceutical firm that offers its AIDS medications to Africans at or below its production costs. In volume terms, GSK sells about 90 percent of its vaccines at not-for-profit prices to customers in developing economies.[27] In Scotland, the large utility firm Scottish and Southern Energy (SSE) emphasizes sustainability in providing energy to its customers. The firm provides electricity through numerous wind farms. Only two of SSE's power plants are fueled by coal, which is more polluting than other energy sources.[28]

Source: © Bob Daemmrich/Alamy

Environmentally friendly policies are an important part of most corporate social responsibility programs. Accepting computers and parts for recycling is an example of CSR initiatives at companies such as Acer and Apple.

The Value of CSR

Customers, partners, shareholders, and the media increasingly believe firms have an obligation to be socially responsible to the societies where they operate. As with ethical behavior, there is a strong business case for CSR.[29] Let's examine the rationale for CSR in international business.

- CSR is simply the right thing to do.
- CSR helps companies recruit and retain high-quality employees. It also improves employee perceptions of the firm, which in turn enhances their loyalty and focus on company goals.
- CSR differentiates the firm in the marketplace and enhances branding, particularly useful in foreign markets where the entrant may be unknown or struggling against local competitors. Consumers prefer buying from companies they trust.

EXHIBIT 5.5 Corporate Social Responsibility: A Sampling of MNE Accomplishments

Company	Industry	Sample Accomplishments
ABN AMRO (Netherlands)	Financial Services	Finances various socially responsible projects, including biomass fuels and micro enterprises.
Dell (United States)	Computers	Accepts old computers from customers for recycling, free of charge.
GlaxoSmithKline (United Kingdom)	Pharmaceuticals	Devotes substantial R&D to poor-country ailments, such as malaria and tuberculosis. Was first to offer AIDS medication at cost.
HSBC (United Kingdom)	Banking	Emphasizes development of financing products for firms in the green energy and battery technology industries.
Nokia (Finland)	Telecommunications	Makes telephones for low-income consumers. Has been a leader in environmental practices, such as phasing out toxic materials.
Norsk Hydro (Norway)	Oil and gas	Cut greenhouse gas emissions by 32 percent. Consistently measures the social and environmental impact of its projects.
Unilever (Netherlands and United Kingdom)	Consumer products	Emphasizes the use of ingredients that minimize the threat of deforestation. Strives to use only energy efficient computers and other information technologies in its global operations.
Duke Energy (United States)	Power utility	Undertakes energy production through various green initiatives, such as wind and solar power. Operates energy efficiency programs for customers.
Toyota (Japan)	Automobiles	The world leader in developing efficient gas-electric vehicles, such as the top-selling Prius.

Sources: Based on Pete Engardio, "Beyond the Green Corporation," *Business Week*, January 29, 2007, pp. 50–64; MIT Sloan Management Review and Boston Consulting Group, *Sustainability: The 'Embracers' Seize Advantage*, research report (Cambridge, MA: Massachusetts Institute of Technology, 2011).

- CSR enhances the quality and effectiveness of intermediary relationships and collaborative ventures. Suppliers, intermediaries, and potential joint venture partners prefer collaborating with reliable firms with strong reputations.
- CSR helps reduce business costs. For example, firms save money when they minimize packaging, recycle materials, trim energy use, and reduce operational waste.
- CSR helps avoid increased taxation, regulation, or legal action by government authorities. In 2009, for example, Denmark enacted laws that require firms to incorporate CSR activities and describe them in their financial reports.

Consumers, other stakeholders, and the media increasingly look to companies to be socially and environmentally responsible. Communications technology allows them to learn quickly about the misdeeds of any firm with which they do business. Over time many consumers prefer products made by firms with strong CSR. The *Global Trend* examines the role of CSR in the multinational firm.

In addition to profit-seeking focal firms, more nongovernmental organizations (NGOs) are undertaking international CSR initiatives, often in conjunction with multinational firms. For example, NGOs such as CARE, Médecins Sans Frontières, and the Bangladesh Rural Advancement Committee work to reduce global poverty and frequently partner with private companies to provide vital products and services.[30]

The Role of Sustainability in International Operations

In a world of increasing population and finite resources, ever-expanding trade and investment have important implications for Earth and the future of humankind. Sustainability is an ideal endorsed by economic development experts, environmentalists, and human rights activists. Companies also increasingly embrace sustainability issues.

GLOBAL TREND

Global Corporate Social Responsibility Rises to the Top of the MNE Agenda

As companies internationalize, they increasingly confront the question of how to be good global citizens. Global corporate social responsibility addresses issues such as workers' rights, workers' pay compared to a reasonable living standard, company activities that disrupt traditional communities and lifestyles, and environmental damage. A study by McKinsey & Co. found executives worldwide overwhelmingly embrace the idea that firms have societal and environmental obligations in addition to ensuring profitability.

IKEA (www.ikea.com) proactively promotes social and environmental responsibility. The firm employs its own specially trained auditors and environmental coordinators. Its products must be manufactured under acceptable working conditions by suppliers who take responsibility for the environment. All must meet the standards of the Forest Stewardship Council. IKEA and its suppliers work closely with UNICEF, Save the Children, and the World Wildlife Fund to prevent child labor and support responsible forestry. All work is in conjunction with the UN Convention on the Rights of the Child. The IKEA Foundation supports various charitable causes through generous contributions.

Governments and stakeholders have expectations of how multinational firms should fulfill their global social responsibilities. Appropriate actions include contributing to a region's employment opportunities, protecting workers and communities from physical harm, providing good working conditions, avoiding discriminatory hiring and work practices, maintaining transparency and avoiding corruption, reducing poverty and injustice, and improving access to quality health care and education.

Accepting social and environmental accountability is increasingly part of how international business gets done. The task is complex, because when companies step onto the global stage, they encounter a wide variety of stakeholders whose expectations often appear overwhelming or even contradictory. Social and environmental problems can appear baffling to headquarters managers, who may lack international experience. Thus, country managers often decide what issues are important and how to address them.

Sources: McKinsey & Co., "From Risk to Opportunity: How Global Executives View Sociopolitical Issues: The McKinsey Quarterly Survey on the Role of Business in Society," 2006, *The McKinsey Quarterly*, retrieved from www.mckinseyquarterly.com; MIT Sloan Management Review and Boston Consulting Group, *Sustainability: The 'Embracers' Seize Advantage*, research report (Cambridge, MA: Massachusetts Institute of Technology, 2011).

A sustainable business simultaneously pursues three types of interests:

1. **Economic interests** refer to the firm's economic impact on the localities where it does business. Management considers the effect of the firm's activities on such local concerns as job creation, wages, tax flows, disadvantaged communities, public works, and other areas where the firm can contribute positively to local economic interests.

2. **Social interests** refer to how the firm performs relative to societies and social justice, often termed *social impact*. The firm with a strong social interest aims to optimize work conditions and diversity in hiring. It avoids using sweatshops, child labor, and other practices that harm workers. Instead, the sustainable firm provides safe work environments, health insurance, retirement benefits, and educational opportunities for employees.

3. **Environmental interests** refer to the extent of the firm's contribution to preserving environmental quality, commonly known as *environmental impact*. This concept refers to reducing the effect of the firm's value-chain activities on the natural environment. The sustainable firm maximizes its use of recycled or renewable raw materials and environmentally friendly energy. It minimizes pollutants, designs production lines to use water and energy efficiently, and constantly seeks ways to reduce waste. Many firms establish a green purchasing policy, through which they source inputs that support environmental interests.[31]

Exhibit 5.6 shows the level of air pollution in selected cities worldwide. Industrialization and other economic activity generate pollutants, which can affect human health, often causing heart and respiratory diseases. In the developing world, air pollution also results from burning dung, wood, and coal, which people use to meet basic energy needs. As indicated in the exhibit, poor industrializing countries tend to produce more air pollution. As nations advance economically, however, they usually develop regulations and technologies that reduce pollutants.

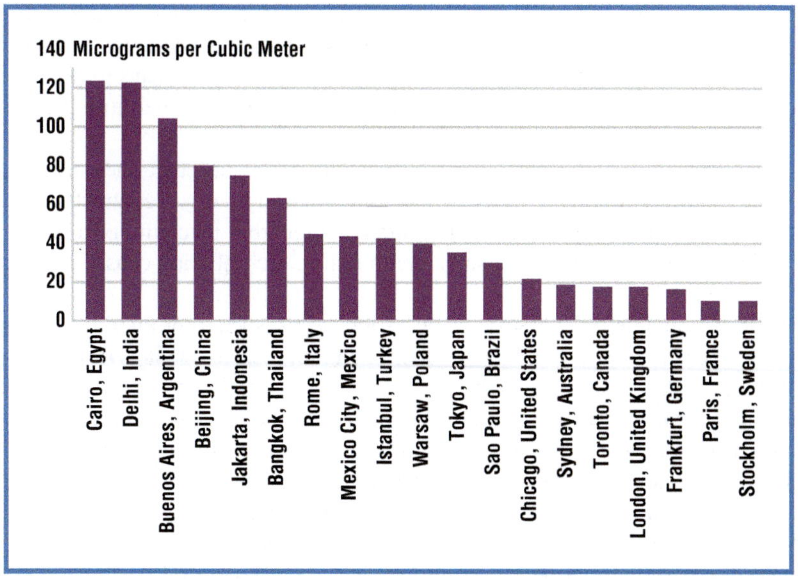

EXHIBIT 5.6

Air Pollution in Selected Cities (particulate matter concentration in micrograms per cubic meter)

Source: Based on World Bank, *World Development Indicators 2011*, Washington DC: World Bank.

Source: © Tim Gainey/Alamy

As water grows scarce in much the world, some multinational firms are conserving their use of this critical resource. Coca-Cola, a major water consumer, conducts a water sustainability program to address shortages in India.

MNEs hold much responsibility to ensure they follow sustainable practices. Businesses function by utilizing resources and raw materials derived from the natural environment. Industrial activities produce smog, acid rain, and other toxins. Many industrial firms use or produce synthetic chemicals and materials that contain hazardous substances. Consumer and industrial products are themselves a major source of toxic waste.[32]

Firms employ vast quantities of water resources, contributing to the creation or expansion of deserts ("desertification"), and loss of important ecosystems around the world. Many countries endure chronic water shortages and industrial activity pollutes clean water supplies. Residential and industrial activity results in land loss and the destruction of ecosystems needed for healthy natural environments. Long-term, successful business performance necessitates healthy ecosystems.

Businesses are major consumers of all the natural environment offers, and hence must take pains to ensure ecological sustainability. Reversing environmental damage requires industrialized countries to substantially reduce their emissions of pollutants. The pace with which resources and raw materials are depleted should not exceed their rate of regeneration. The rate of waste production should not exceed the environment's ability to absorb it. Firms increasingly seek ways to employ renewable resources and to minimize pollutants in their operations.[33] MNEs are among the most important stewards of the environment through skillful use of innovative technologies, improved water productivity, addressing shortages in vulnerable areas, and planning that incorporates sustainability practices.

The Canadian aluminum giant Alcan (www.alcan.com) has invested huge sums to develop clean, fuel-efficient manufacturing technologies. By emphasizing sustainability, Alcan reduced its greenhouse gas output by one-quarter, while increasing production by 40 percent. Alcan is installing additional technology that will further reduce toxic emissions, while increasing energy efficiency in its smelting plants.[34]

The British supermarket chain Tesco (www.tesco.com) uses wind power to provide electricity for many of its U.K. stores and has installed massive solar panels on its U.S. facilities. The firm cut

Country Realities

More than 5 million people die annually from lung cancer and other smoking-related ailments. Smoking also harms national GDP because it incurs billions in tax-funded health care costs. The average price of a pack of cigarettes is high in many countries, relative to local incomes. As cigarette sales have declined in the advanced economies, British American Tobacco, Philip Morris International, and other cigarette companies have targeted emerging markets. In China a pack sells for the equivalent of $2, but smokers earn only a few thousand dollars per year. About 60 percent of Chinese men smoke, making China home to the largest number of smokers. In Ukraine, the average smoker consumes 2,500 cigarettes per year. Russia has the highest density of smokers, where 70 percent of men smoke, and the average lifespan is less than 60 years, partly due to high cigarette consumption.

Sources: N. Byrnes and F. Balfour, "Philip Morris Unbound," *Business Week*, May 4, 2009, pp. 39–42; B. McKay, "Where There's Smoke: Emerging World," *Wall Street Journal*, February 7, 2008, pp. B1–B2.

energy usage in its warehouses and operates low-pollution transportation in its supply chains. It attempts to measure the "carbon costs" of each item it sells to reduce the pollution burden of serving customer needs. Customers are rewarded for bringing reusable shopping bags to stores, instead of using disposable plastic. Senior managers' bonuses are partly based on their meeting energy- and waste-reduction targets.[35]

The most advanced companies monitor suppliers to ensure that they use sustainable practices. For example, following charges that some of its Indian subcontractors were using forced child labor, GAP withdrew a line of children's wear from its clothing stores worldwide. Sustainable firms usually opt for local suppliers to reduce the pollution caused by transporting goods long distances.[36]

Like CSR, sustainable practices pay off in various ways, such as promoting a strong corporate reputation, the ability to hire and retain superior employees, cost savings from more efficient production, better linkages with suppliers, and smoother relations with foreign governments.

Achieving sustainability often requires the firm to be flexible and creative. A good example is Coca-Cola, which had to deal with water sustainability challenges. As water resources dwindled in some countries, Coke began to experience conflicts with communities and other water users, especially in India. To address such challenges, Coke developed a water sustainability program that goes well beyond efficiency and legal compliance needs alone. Management devised global projects that protect water resources and ensure access to clean drinking water. Coke mobilized the international community to anticipate and deal with ever-severe water crises worldwide.[37]

Corporate Governance and Its Implications for Managers

The challenge for management is to increase awareness of ethical, CSR, and sustainability throughout the firm and to view them as opportunities to improve society, the environment, and company performance. Corporate governance provides the means through which firms undertake ethical behaviors, CSR, and sustainability.[38] Employees must learn to recognize and manage the ethical problems that confront the firm. Let's explore this issue in detail. As shown in the box below, scholars have devised five standards that managers can use to examine ethical problems.[39]

Ethical Standards for Corporate Governance

Utilitarian Approach	Rights Approach	Fairness Approach	Common Good Approach	Virtue Approach
The best ethical action is the one that provides the most good or the least harm. It produces the greatest balance of good over harm to customers, employees, shareholders, the community, and the natural environment.	The best action protects and respects the moral rights of everyone involved. It is based on the belief that, regardless of how you deal with an ethical dilemma, human dignity must be preserved.	The best action treats everyone equally and fairly. Workers should be paid a fair wage that provides a decent standard of living, and colleagues and customers should be treated as we would like to be treated.	The best action emphasizes the welfare of the entire community or nation. It asks what action contributes most to the quality of life of all affected people. Respect and compassion for all, especially the vulnerable, is the basis for decision making.	The best action emphasizes virtues that provide for the full development of our humanity. The most important virtues are truth, courage, compassion, generosity, tolerance, love, integrity, and prudence.

Using these five approaches to analyze ethical problems can be challenging because they occasionally conflict with each other, and not everyone agrees on which standard to use in all situations. Different cultures adhere to differing norms of morality and human rights and basic standards of right and wrong. Moreover, ethical dilemmas are complex and proposed approaches may not provide adequate guidance in determining the best course of action. Nevertheless, each standard is useful because it helps guide ethical behavior in almost any predicament. More often than not, they lead to similar solutions.

Code of Conduct

A code of conduct outlines the responsibilities and practices expected of an organization and the individuals who work there. Corporate codes of conduct emphasize standards related to ethics and social responsibilities. A good code of conduct defines the values and principles that are intended to guide the decisions, procedures, and systems of the firm. It aims to ensure respect for the rights of all constituents affected by company operations. The code should serve as a tool to encourage employee discussion on how to deal with the ethical dilemmas that confront the firm. In helping identify ethical problems, the firm's code of conduct should be designed to function like a moral compass for company operations worldwide.[40] Like a mission statement, it should guide employee behavior in all situations, so the firm avoids behaviors that compromise ethical standards wherever it does business.

Deciding What Constitutes Ethical Behavior

When it comes to ensuring ethical behavior, experienced managers follow a systematic process. First, they are sensitive to ethical problems. Before entering a country and throughout operations there, managers remain alert to the various ethical challenges the firm may encounter. They scan operations in each country and potential partners for the possibility of ethical abuses. Such scanning is an ongoing process, because company operations and environments evolve continuously. With enough practice, management creates a systematic approach to scanning and a culture within the firm that supports alertness and ongoing analysis of potential ethical concerns.

Managers should focus not only on specific national environments but also on proposed and existing value-chain activities, which often take place in multiple countries. In each country and venture, areas that merit particular attention encompass commercial environments, labor conditions, partners, customers, accounting practices, and conditions regarding the natural environment, as well as the range of the firm's potential or existing value-chain activities, including sourcing, production, marketing, and distribution.

A study in the *Harvard Business Review* found that improper ethical behavior results when:

- **Top management sets goals and incentives aimed at promoting good outcomes (e.g., profits) that instead encourage bad behaviors.** For example, law and accounting firms often encourage employees to maximize the hours they bill for their services. Under pressure, some employees "pad" their hours or charge clients for work they didn't do.
- **Employees overlook unethical behavior in others because of peer pressure or self-interest.** A manager may fail to complain about toxic waste discharged by a subsidiary because he doesn't want to "rock the boat."
- **Managers tolerate lower ethical standards in value-chain activities performed by suppliers or third-party firms.** Coffee producers sometimes ignore the poor working conditions of supplier farmers in Africa and Latin America.
- **Unethical practices are allowed to accumulate in the firm slowly over time.** When bad behavior is widespread throughout the firm, smaller infractions seem less noticeable. A corrupt environment usually fosters ongoing corruption.
- **Bad means are justified by good ends.** Pharmaceutical firms sometimes use unethical testing procedures in poor countries in order to validate of the effectiveness of new medications for disorders such as cancer and AIDS. The drugs help people, but may be developed through bad practice.[41]

Once managers develop an ongoing awareness of potential ethical abuses, the next step is to systematically explore the ethical aspects of each decision the firm may make regarding its current and potential activities. To further clarify the process of scanning for and analyzing potential ethical problems, we next provide a framework for making ethical decisions.

A Framework for Making Ethical Decisions

Scholars suggest that managers follow a systematic approach to resolving ethical problems. Exhibit 5.7 presents a five-step framework for arriving at ethical decisions. The framework will help you arrive at appropriate solutions.[42] With practice, it can become second nature. The steps in the framework are explained below.

EXHIBIT 5.7

Framework for Arriving at Ethical Decisions

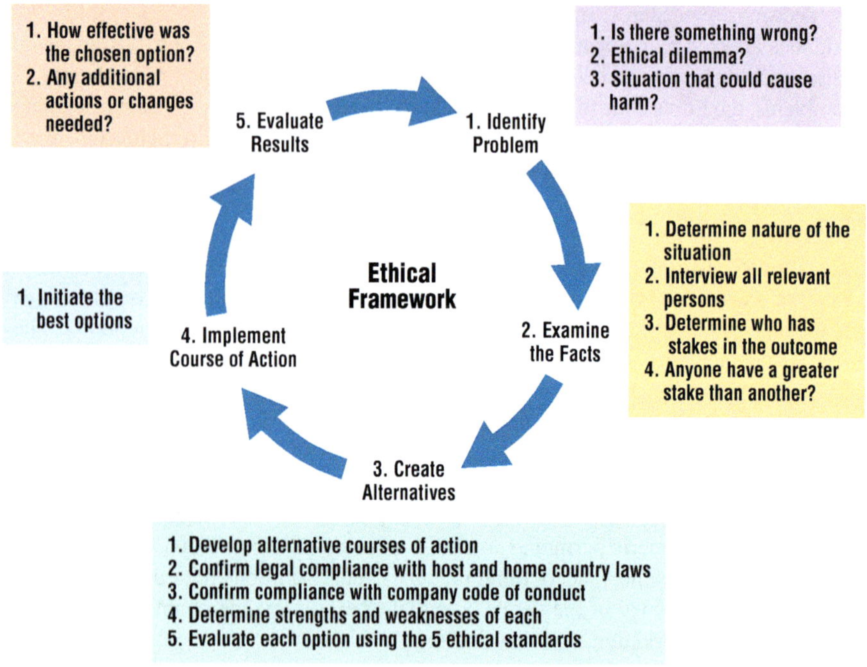

1. Identify the problem. The first step is to acknowledge the presence of an ethical problem. Ask questions such as: Is there something wrong? Is an ethical dilemma present? Is there a situation that might harm personnel, customers, the community, or the nation? In international business, recognizing the issue can be tricky because subtleties of the situation may be outside your knowledge or experience. Often, it is best to rely on your instincts—if some activity or action feels wrong, it probably is.

2. Examine the facts. Determine the nature and dimensions of the situation. Have all the relevant persons and groups been consulted? What individuals or groups have a stake in the outcome? How much weight should be given to the interests of each? Do some parties have a greater stake because they are disadvantaged or have a special need? This stage is often challenging because determining specific details and distinguishing facts from irrelevant information can be tricky. The process often involves interviewing personnel and stakeholders who may offer differing versions or opinions on the issue at hand. The manager's task is to identify and validate the most useful, valid information that makes clear the true nature of the problem.

3. Create alternatives. Identify potential courses of action and evaluate each. Initially, consistent with the pyramid of ethical behavior, review any proposed action to ensure it is legal. If it violates host or home country laws or international treaties, it should be rejected. Next, review any proposed action to ensure it is acceptable according to company policy and the firm's code of conduct. If discrepancies are found, the action should be rejected. Finally, evaluate each proposed action to assess its consistency with accepted ethical standards, using the approaches described earlier:

- Utilitarian—which action results in the most good and least harm?
- Rights—which action respects the rights of everyone involved?
- Fairness—which action treats people most fairly?
- Common good—which action contributes most to the overall quality of life of the people affected?
- Virtue—which action embodies the character strengths you value?

The goal is to arrive at the best decision or most appropriate course of action. Consider consulting local colleagues familiar with the situation, to provide insights and generate options. Assess the consequences of each action from the perspective of all parties it will affect.

Any decision should be tested by asking if you would feel comfortable explaining it to your mother, a colleague you respect, or a valued mentor. If you had to defend the decision on television, would you be comfortable doing so?

4. Implement course of action. Put the chosen plan into action. This implies creating new rules, processes, or procedures, and putting these into effect. Implementation is critical because it determines the success or failure of the chosen action. Managers need to be particularly diligent at this stage, to ensure the action is carried out per plan.

5. Evaluate results. Once the decision is implemented, you will need to assess how effective it was. How did it turn out? If you had it to do again, would you do anything differently? Results evaluation may require collecting, analyzing, and using information to answer questions about the chosen course of action. The goal is to ensure the action achieves its intended effect, and find out if the firm should modify the approach or pursue a different one.

The steps in this framework will help you arrive at appropriate solutions to ethical problems. To briefly illustrate, let's revisit the example of you as a manager visiting a company factory in Colombia, where you discover child labor. Without the children's income, their families may go hungry, or the children may turn to illicit activity, such as street crime. Having identified the problem, you examine facts by consulting colleagues both at the plant and headquarters. You seek information on the status of the employed children, as well as local law and customs on child labor. You then create alternative possible solutions, ensuring they are legal and consistent with company policy. Keeping the five ethical standards in mind, you evaluate each proposed action. Finally, you choose and implement the best course of action, and evaluate its effectiveness.

Embracing CSR and Sustainability

In a world ever sensitive to social and environmental issues, more firms are undertaking the following types of activities:

- Develop closer relations with foreign stakeholders to better understand their needs and work jointly toward solutions
- Build internal and external capabilities to enhance the firm's contribution to the local community and global environment
- Ensure diverse voices are heard by creating organizational structures that employ managers and workers from around the world
- Develop global CSR standards and objectives that are communicated and implemented across the firm worldwide
- Train managers in global CSR principles and integrate these into managerial responsibilities

Managers must make ethical behavior, CSR and sustainability a part of company activities and operations. MNE pursuits generate environmental harm and bring firms into contact with various activities—from R&D to manufacturing to marketing—that can pose various ethical dilemmas. Business executives should balance their obligation to shareholders with explicit contributions to the broader public good. Most executives agree that generating high returns for investors should be accompanied by a focus on providing good jobs, supporting social causes in local communities, and going beyond legal requirements to minimize pollution and other negative effects of business.

A Global Consensus

Incorporating ethics, CSR, and sustainability into global operations is a path to long-term company success. Various resources are available to assist managers. International organizations such as the United Nations, the World Bank, and the International Monetary Fund have launched programs to combat international corruption.

The International Chamber of Commerce has adopted "Rules of Conduct to Combat Extortion and Bribery," and the United Nations issued a "Declaration against Corruption and Bribery in International Commercial Transactions." The Organisation for Economic Co-operation and Development (OECD) has developed an antibribery agreement, which was signed by its thirty member nations (essentially, all the advanced economies) plus several Latin American countries.[43]

The *United Nations Global Compact* (see www.unglobalcompact.org) is a policy platform and practical framework for companies committed to sustainability and responsible business practices. It seeks to align business operations and strategies with universally accepted principles in the areas of human rights, labor, corruption, and the natural environment. It is the world's largest voluntary corporate citizenship initiative, representing thousands of businesses in more than 135 countries.

The *Global Reporting Initiative* (www.globalreporting.org) pioneered the development of the most widely used sustainability reporting framework. The framework sets out the principles and indicators that organizations can use to measure and report their economic, environmental, and social performance. Today, most large MNEs produce sustainability reports, many following the GRI guidelines.

Ultimately, CSR and sustainability require the firm to go "deep, wide, and local." *Going deep* means institutionalizing appropriate behavior into the organization's culture so it becomes part and parcel of strategy. *Going wide* implies a continuous effort to understand how CSR and sustainability affect every aspect of the firm's operations worldwide. *Going local* goes hand-in-hand with globalization. It requires the firm to examine its global operations to identify and improve specific local issues that affect customers, competitive position, reputation, and any other dimension that affects the firm's operations worldwide.[44]

To make ethical practices, CSR, and sustainability succeed in the firm, it is important to undertake a systematic and ongoing process of education for employees, suppliers, and intermediaries alike. As the firm builds a track record of changes and successes, it will begin to build a culture of appropriate behavior in its operations worldwide.

CLOSING CASE Corruption at Siemens

One day in 2004, a senior executive at Siemens Company said he received a disturbing phone call from a Saudi Arabian businessman. The caller said he represented a Saudi consulting firm that had been a business partner of Siemens. He wanted $910 million in U.S. currency in payments and if Siemens didn't pay up, he would forward documents to government authorities detailing bribes paid on Siemens' behalf to win telecommunications contracts in Saudi Arabia. The incident was the beginning of a series of events—police raids, forensic investigations, and arrests of top executives—that became one of the biggest corruption cases in corporate history.

Based in Germany, Siemens is one of the world's largest electronics and industrial engineering firms. It produces industrial controls, lighting products, power generation equipment, and transportation systems. Siemens operates in 190 countries, with recent annual revenues exceeding $100 billion.

A Culture of Corruption?

Since the 1970s, Siemens has been stung by a series of scandals, many of them including accusations of bribery brought by governments in numerous countries, the European Union, and the United Nations. One former executive was accused of handling $77 million in bribes. Another admitted to bribing a labor union. A court found that Siemens had paid millions in 2007 to bribe government officials in Libya, Nigeria, and Russia.

Investigators alleged there was a culture at Siemens, endorsed by senior managers, to use bribes and slush funds to win contracts, especially in its communications and power-generation divisions. Millions of dollars were regularly dispensed, the money carted off to foreign destinations in suitcases by managers who often felt confident they were doing "business as usual."

Reckoning and Deliverance

In the end, bribery caught up with Siemens. In a ruling under the Foreign Corrupt Practices Act, U.S. authorities ordered the company to pay $800 million in fines. The United States found that, in order to win infrastructure contracts, Siemens allegedly spent more than $1 billion bribing government officials around the world, including the former President of Argentina. The U.S. Securities and Exchange Commission (SEC) claimed that Siemens made more than 4,000 bribe payments over seven years. Payments were intended to obtain contracts to supply medical devices in Russia, transmission lines in China, transit systems in Venezuela, medical equipment in Vietnam, power equipment in Iraq, and telecommunications equipment in Bangladesh. In 2006, a U.S. grand jury indicted Siemens and two of its employees in a fraud scheme to pay $500,000 to win a $49 million contract. In 2007, two former Siemens officials were convicted of bribery for their involvement in multimillion-dollar payments to officials of a power utility in Italy.

In response to the scandals, some Siemens customers indicated they would delay ordering telecommunications equipment from the firm, and Nokia Corporation announced it would postpone a planned joint venture. In 2008, Siemens' profits declined, partly due to the creation of a fund for expenses related to bribery investigations. In 2009, the World Bank required Siemens to pay $100 million to help global anticorruption efforts and to forego bidding on World Bank development projects for two years. In the end, Siemens' two top executives, the chairman and the CEO, were forced to resign.

In Germany, Siemens executives indicted in the scandal received only suspended prison sentences. A German court ordered Siemens to pay $284 million, a modest fine for a firm that usually generates billions in annual net profits. Germany is the world's leading exporter, and bribery cases often include efforts to generate foreign business, especially in developing economies. Until 1999, German firms were permitted to write off such bribes as business expenses. Many European countries did not outlaw paying bribes overseas until the late 1990s.

Remedial Actions

In the wake of the scandal, Siemens management took steps to prevent further bribery. The company appointed a law firm to conduct an independent review of its compliance system and uncover possible improprieties. Sixty-five countries were flagged for scrutiny. Siemens' own internal investigation identified more than $1.5 billion in suspicious transactions worldwide between 2000 and 2006. Management remarked on the difficulty of closely monitoring activities of the firm's 430,000 employees in 190 countries and bank accounts that once numbered 5,000 and handled up to 50 million transactions a day. International subsidiaries were free to act with substantial autonomy.

Siemens hired an independent ombudsman, strengthened its business-conduct code, and established a task force to improve internal controls over international funds transfers, reduce the number of bank accounts, and supervise the opening and maintaining of bank accounts. Subsidiaries were required to provide comprehensive details of all transactions. The German government tightened standards for managers, seeking to ensure that those at all large firms report regularly to supervisory boards regarding compliance with ethics codes.

Conclusion

In the United States, the number of companies reporting foreign corruption investigations into their activities abroad is up sharply. Foreign companies that do business in the United States are attracting greater scrutiny as well. In most countries, however, antibribery laws are weak or poorly enforced. Bribery is difficult to detect when funds are channeled through consultants and other intermediaries, or when company operations are widely dispersed and decentralized.

Why should firms care about bribery? For one thing, it is bad business. Bribery distorts legitimate efforts to sustain and enhance company performance. Where corruption becomes a pattern, eventually the firm is caught and its reputation tarnished. Corruption also inhibits development in poor countries and is at the root of persistent poverty in many. It sustains repressive governments and can lead to the failure of societies and national economies.

The best firms create a culture in which ethical conduct is valued as highly as efforts to maximize sales and profits. It is insufficient to merely publicize the need for integrity; managers must lead through ongoing actions that demonstrate adherence to ethical standards. They should establish transparency and compliance processes that ensure senior executives know what is going on throughout the firm.

AACSB: Reflective Thinking Skills, Multicultural and Diversity Understanding, Ethical Understanding and Reasoning Abilities

Case Questions

1. What does the case suggest is the value of ethical behavior? What did Siemens gain by introducing controls to minimize the likelihood of corruption?
2. Most countries lack adequate laws or enforcement to deal with bribery and other forms of corruption. Why is this? How do countries benefit from a strong rule of law that minimizes corruption?
3. Do you think Siemens was penalized enough for its corruption? Why or why not? What can governments or other organizations do to discourage firms and others from engaging in corrupt behavior?
4. Some argue that because ethical standards are lax in many countries, Siemens and other firms must pay bribes to obtain new business. Do you agree with this view? Stated differently, when doing business around the world, is it generally better to emphasize normativism or relativism? Justify your answer.

Sources: C. Bray, J. Palazzolo, S. Romig, and P. Grontzki, "Former Siemens Executives Facing U.S. Bribery Charges," *Wall Street Journal*, December 14, 2011, p. B3; M. Esterl and D. Crawford, "Siemens to Pay Huge Fine in Bribery Inquiry," *Wall Street Journal*, December 15, 2008, p. B1; "Siemens to Tighten Controls on Money," *Financial Times*, April 18, 2007, p. 16; "Action against Bribery Requires Political Will," *Financial Times*, April 10, 2007, p. 14; V. Fuhrmans, "Siemens Settles with World Bank on Bribes," *Wall Street Journal*, July 3, 2009, p. B1; M. Hamblen, "Selloff Plans, Fraud Probe Put Spotlight on Siemens," *Computerworld*, December 18, 2006, p. 12; R. Minder, "Siemens Bows to Pressure for Transparency," *Financial Times*, December 12, 2006, p. 24; A. Preuschat, "Siemens Posts Loss Due to Charges But Says Its Orders Remain Strong," *Wall Street Journal*, November 14, 2008, p. B3; C. Verschoor, "Siemens AG Is Latest Fallen Ethics Idol," *Strategic Finance* 89, no. 5 (2007): 11–13; "Two Siemens Ex-Officials Convicted in Bribery Case," *Wall Street Journal*, May 15, 2007, p. C6; D. Crawford and M. Esterl, "Siemens Fine Ends a Bribery Probe," *Wall Street Journal*, October 5, 2007, p. A2; D. Crawford and M. Esterl, "Siemens Probe Spotlights Murky Role of Consultants," *Wall Street Journal*, April 20, 2007, p. A1; D. Crawford and M. Esterl, "Widening Scandal: At Siemens, Witnesses Cite Pattern of Bribery," *Wall Street Journal*, January 31, 2007, p. A1; M. Esterl, "Ethics Hurdle: Corruption Scandal at Siemens May Derail Restructuring Drive," *Wall Street Journal*, December 18, 2006, p. A1; M. Esterl, "Siemens CEO Hopes New Audit Cuts Scope of Suspected Fraud," *Wall Street Journal*, December 22, 2006, p. B.4; R. Milne, "Siemens 'Had a System for Paying Bribes,'" *Financial Times*, March 14, 2007, p. 27; R. Milne and M. Scheele, "Probe Finds 'General Practice' of Alleged Bribery at Siemens," *Financial Times*, May 7, 2007, p. 1; D. Crawford and M. Esterl, "Siemens Ruling Details Bribery Across the Globe," *Wall Street Journal*, November 16, 2007, p. A1; D. Crawford and M. Esterl, "Inside Bribery Probe of Siemens," *Wall Street Journal*, December 28, 2007, p. A4; M. Esterl and D. Crawford, "Ex-Siemens Manager Sentenced," *Wall Street Journal*, November 25, 2008, p. B2; M. Esterl and D. Crawford, "At Siemens, A Conviction Could Trigger More Cases," *Wall Street Journal*, July 29, 2008, p. B1; "Stopping the Rot; Face Value," *The Economist*, March 8, 2008, p. 89; "Bavarian Baksheesh; The Siemens Scandal," *The Economist*, December 20, 2008, p. 112.

CHAPTER ESSENTIALS

MyManagementLab

Go to **www.mymanagementlab.com** to complete the problems marked with this icon ✪.

Key Terms

corporate governance
corporate social responsibility (CSR)
corruption
ethics
intellectual property
intellectual property rights
normativism
relativism
sustainability

Summary

In this chapter, you learned about:

1. **Ethical challenges in international business**

   Ethics are the moral principles and values that govern the behavior of people, firms, and governments. **Corporate social responsibility (CSR)** refers to operating a business in a manner that meets or exceeds the ethical, legal, and commercial expectations of customers, shareholders, employees, and communities. **Sustainability** means meeting humanity's needs without harming future generations. **Corporate governance** is the system of procedures and processes by which corporations are managed, directed, and controlled. Unethical behavior is revealed in international business in management, global sourcing, and marketing, often as piracy, bribery, and **corruption** Governments aim to protect **intellectual property**. However, protection is not guaranteed in much of the world.

2. **Key aspects of international ethics**

   Behaving ethically adds value to the firm in various ways. But ethical standards vary around the world. **Relativism** is the belief that ethical truths are not absolute but differ from group to group. **Normativism** holds that ethical standards are universal, and firms and individuals should seek to uphold them consistently around the world. An *ethical dilemma* is a predicament with major conflicts among different interests. Determining the best course of action is confounded by several possible solutions that may be equally justifiable.

3. **Corporate social responsibility**

   In addition to complying with laws, regulations, and basic ethical standards, prudent MNEs emphasize corporate social responsibility in their activities. A strong business rationale for CSR includes the firm's ability to motivate employees and develop superior strategy. Failure to develop a CSR has important negative consequences for the firm.

4. **The role of sustainability in international operations**

   Sustainable businesses simultaneously pursue three types of interests: economic, social, and environmental. They maximize the use of recycled or renewable materials and environmentally friendly energy. They reduce waste in manufacturing and minimize harmful air and water pollution. They provide health insurance and training and care for employees in various other ways. They are active in the local community with initiatives in education, health care, and environmental protection. Sustainable firms choose and work with suppliers that adhere to high social and environmental standards.

5. **Corporate governance and its implications for managers**

   A focus on ethics, CSR, and sustainability is in the firm's best interests, in terms of business strategy and organizational performance. Scholars have devised five standards managers can use to examine ethical dilemmas, based on utilitarianism, rights, fairness, common good, and virtue.

Senior managers should develop a *code of ethics* that describes what the firm expects of its employees when facing ethical dilemmas.

6. **A framework for making ethical decisions**

Scholars have devised a five-step framework for making ethical decisions. Initially, the manager should recognize the existence of an ethical problem. The next steps are to get the facts, evaluate alternative courses of action, and then implement and evaluate the decision made. Ethical behavior and CSR must be part of managers' day-to-day pursuits. Various resources are available to assist managers, such as the United Nations and the World Bank.

Test Your Comprehension

1. Distinguish between ethics and corruption in international business.
2. What is the Corruption Perceptions Index, and how can a manager use it to assess international risk?
3. Describe typical ethical problems that firms encounter in international business.
4. What is intellectual property? What industries are most affected by threats to intellectual property?
5. Distinguish relativism and normativism. Which one should the firm apply in its activities?
6. What is an ethical dilemma? Give an example of an ethical dilemma that MNEs encounter abroad.
7. What is corporate social responsibility (CSR)? How does it differ from general ethical behavior?
8. What is sustainability? How might the firm undertake sustainability in its value-chain activities?
9. Describe the five standards managers can use to examine ethical dilemmas.
10. Describe the steps in the framework for ethical conduct.
11. What steps can the firm take to develop its orientation to CSR and sustainability in international operations?

Apply Your Understanding AACSB: Reflective Thinking Skills, Analytic Skills, Communication Abilities, Ethical Understanding and Reasoning Abilities

1. Ethical Dilemma: You were recently hired by ThunderCat Corporation, a major aircraft producer with a manufacturing presence in numerous countries. ThunderCat's sales personnel constantly travel the world, selling fighter jets and commercial aircraft to airlines and foreign governments. You are keenly aware that countries vary enormously in terms of culture, laws, and political systems. Top management has asked you to develop a code of ethics to guide ThunderCat employees in their interactions anywhere in the world. Given the diversity of countries where ThunderCat operates, what sort of code will you develop? What issues should you consider? Given the diversity of countries around the world, is it possible to develop a code that guides ethical behavior everywhere?

2. Ethical Dilemma: Royal Dutch Shell has been doing business in Nigeria since the 1920s and has announced new plans to develop oil and gas projects there. However, over the years Shell has experienced a series of complex issues. Its operations are centered in Nigeria's Ogoni region, where the local citizens have protested Shell's drilling and refining activities, which harm the natural environment and reduce the amount of available farmland. Protestors also accuse Shell of extracting wealth from the region without adequately compensating local residents. Following sabotage of its facilities, the firm suspended some of its Nigerian operations. It then came under pressure to divest its Nigerian operations and pay reparations to the local people. Despite these problems, Shell has persisted in Nigeria. Management instituted various community development programs in the region, budgeted at $50 million per year. Using the ethical framework in this chapter, identify steps Shell can take to be a better corporate citizen in Nigeria.

3. Ethical Dilemma: Suppose you are president of Orwell Corporation, a firm that makes high-tech surveillance equipment. You have received an offer from the government of North Korea to bid on a huge contract to install a network of 4,000 surveillance cameras

throughout the country. The North Koreans say the system will be used to prevent crime and monitor traffic jams. But you know the repressive regime will use the technology to target dissent and repress human rights, resulting in jail time and even torture for citizens who engage in free speech and other legitimate activities. Moreover, your nation's government has laws prohibiting the export of crime-control products to North Korea, although the restrictions don't apply to surveillance cameras. What should you do? Do you bid on the project? Or do you abstain, not wishing to support repression in a tyrannical regime? (Note: This dilemma is similar to real dilemmas faced by Cisco and other firms that have marketed surveillance equipment to repressive governments.)

globalEDGE INTERNET EXERCISES

(http://www.globalEDGE.msu.edu)

AACSB: Analytic Skills, Use of Information Technology, Ethical Understanding and Reasoning Abilities

Refer to Chapter 1, page 58, for instructions on how to access and use globalEDGE™.

1. Various organizations have devised international standards for ethical corporate behavior. These include the United Nations "Universal Declaration for Human Rights" (available at www.un.org), the OECD's "Guidelines for Multinational Enterprise" (www.oecd.org), the International Labour Organization's "Minimum Labor Standards" (www.ilo.org), and the U.S. Department of Commerce's "Model Business Principles" (www.commerce.gov). Visit these online portals and prepare a set of guidelines firms can follow in pursuing acceptable ethical standards in international business.
2. Transparency International (www.transparency.org) publishes information about the nature of corruption around the world. Suppose you worked at a firm that makes computer software and wanted to begin doing business in Brazil and Russia. Your task is to examine reports and indices on these countries at the Transparency International site and write a brief report explaining how your firm should conduct business in these countries, with a view to avoiding problems associated with corruption. Key issues to consider include bribery and threats to intellectual property.
3. The Web sites for Lenovo (China; www.lenovo.com), Nokia (Finland; www.nokia.com), and Banco do Brasil (Brazil; www.bb.com.br, click on "English") contain information about how these firms undertake corporate social responsibility (CSR). Visit each Web site and write a report in which you compare and contrast each firm's CSR. Which firm appears most effective in CSR? How does the CSR of a bank differ from that of manufacturing firms such as Lenovo and Nokia? Lenovo and Banco do Brasil are based in emerging markets, while Nokia is in an advanced economy. What differences in the firms' CSR orientations can you detect based on this distinction? Justify your answer.